THE ART OF COOKING, PIE MAKING, PASTRY MAKING, AND PRESERVING

Arte de cocina, pastelería, vizcochería y conservería

by Francisco Martínez Montiño (1611)

Food for Thought
Food for Pleasure
Food for Change

Series Editors

Jayeeta (Jo) Sharma (Toronto)
H. Rosi Song (Durham)
Robert Davidson (Toronto)

Editorial Advisory Board

Cristiana Bastos (Lisbon)
Shyon Baumann (Toronto)
Daniel Bender (Toronto)
Andrea Borghini (Milan)
Miranda Brown (Michigan)
Sidney Cheung (Hong Kong)
Simone Cinotto (Gastronomic Sciences)
Tracey Deutsch (Minnesota)
Jean Duruz (South Australia)
Rebecca Earle (Warwick)
Beth Forrest (Culinary Institute of America)
Michael Innis-Jiménez (Alabama)
Alice Julier (Chatham)
Lindsay Kelley (New South Wales)
Zeynep Kiliç (Alaska)
Mustafa Koç (Toronto Metropolitan)
Charles Levkoe (Lakehead)
Ken Macdonald (Toronto)
Raúl Matta (Göttingen)
Massimo Montinari (Bologna)
Fabio Parasecoli (New York)
Jeffrey Pilcher (Toronto)
Elaine Power (Queen's)
Signe Rousseau (Cape Town)
Kyla D. Tompkins (Pomona)

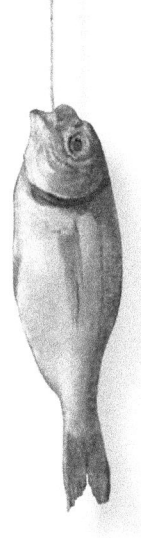

The Art of Cooking, Pie Making, Pastry Making, and Preserving

Arte de cocina, pastelería, vizcochería y conservería

Francisco Martínez Montiño (1611)

A Critical Edition and Translation
by Carolyn A. Nadeau

UNIVERSITY OF TORONTO PRESS
Toronto Buffalo London

© University of Toronto Press 2023
Toronto Buffalo London
utorontopress.com

ISBN 978-1-4875-4937-4 (cloth)   ISBN 978-1-4875-4938-1 (EPUB)
                                    ISBN 978-1-4875-4939-8 (PDF)

Library and Archives Canada Cataloguing in Publication

Title: The art of cooking, pie making, pastry making, and preserving = Arte de cocina, pastelería, vizcochería y conservería / Francisco Martínez Montiño (1611) ; a critical edition and translation by Carolyn A. Nadeau.

Other titles: Arte de cocina, pastelería, vizcochería y conservería. English | Arte de cocina, pastelería, vizcochería y conservería

Names: Martínez Montiño, Francisco, active 16th century, author. | Nadeau, Carolyn A., 1963– translator.

Description: Includes bibliographical references and index.

Identifiers: Canadiana (print) 20230478840 | Canadiana (ebook) 20230478867 | ISBN 9781487549374 (cloth) | ISBN 9781487549381 (EPUB) | ISBN 9781487549398 (PDF)

Subjects: LCSH: Cooking, Spanish – Early works to 1800. | LCGFT: Cookbooks.

Classification: LCC TX723.5.S7 M3713 2023 | DDC 641.594609/032–dc23

Cover design: Alexa Love
Cover image: Kitchen scene of Bodegón / The Picture Art Collection / Alamy Stock Photo

We wish to acknowledge the land on which the University of Toronto Press operates. This land is the traditional territory of the Wendat, the Anishnaabeg, the Haudenosaunee, the Métis, and the Mississaugas of the Credit First Nation.

University of Toronto Press acknowledges the financial support of the Government of Canada, the Canada Council for the Arts, and the Ontario Arts Council, an agency of the Government of Ontario, for its publishing activities.

  Canada Council   Conseil des Arts
                for the Arts   du Canada

*To Chad Sanders, my life-long partner and chef extraordinaire
and to Carmela Ferradáns, with my deepest gratitude*

Contents

Illustrations ix

Acknowledgments xiii

Introduction 3
 I. *The Cookbook as Cultural Artefact* 3
 II. *Spain and the Court in the Late Sixteenth and Early Seventeenth Century* 5
 III. *Martínez Montiño's Biography and the Early Modern Spanish Kitchen* 8
 IV. *Cookbook Organization* 15
 V. *Ingredients* 22
 VI. *Taste at Court and the Emergence of Spanish Cuisine* 51
 VII. *Curiosities of Martínez Montiño's Cookbook* 63
 VIII. *Martínez Montiño's Legacy* 71
 IX. *Previous Editions* 75
 X. *This Edition and Commentary* 92

Arte de cocina, pastelería, vizcochería y conservería 99
 Tasa/Certificate of Price 102
 El Rey (Privilegio)/The King (Privilege) 104
 Prologo al lector/Prologue for the Reader 108
 Advertencia/Notice 112
 Tabla de los banquetes/Table on the Banquets 114
 Capitulo primero/Chapter 1 116
 De la limpieza de la cocina, y del gobierno que ha de tener el Cocinero mayor en ella/On the cleanliness of the kitchen and the governance that the master cook should have in it 116
 Tratado de cómo se ha de servir en los banquetes/Treatise on how to serve at banquets 124
 Cómo se ha de servir la vianda en la cocina/How to serve food in the kitchen 128

BANQUETES por Navidad/Christmas banquet   130
Una comida por el mes de Mayo/A meal for the month of May   132
Una comida por Setiembre/A meal for September   134
Una merienda/Late afternoon supper   136
Capitulo II/Chapter 2   142

Appendix 1. Kitchen Furnishings and Equipment   621

Appendix 2. On Measurements   627

Appendix 3. Images from Recipes Recreated   635

Glossary   663

Works Cited   707

Index   717

Illustrations

Figures

1 Chamberlain's letter of support for Martínez Montiño's request 9
2 Diagram of kitchen equipment and legend. First reproduced in the edition by Juliana Carrasco, Madrid, 1760 14
3 Title page of *Arte de cocina, pastelería, vizcochería y conservería*, 1611 78
4 Detail of title page of *Arte de cocina, pastelería, vizcochería y conservería*, 1637 80
5 Folio 1 of the distinct 1705 BVNP (left) and NYPL (right) editions 85
6 Folio 1 from the Library of Congress, 1763 88
7 Folio 1 from the Lilly Library, Indiana University, 1763 89
8 Folio 1 from the Bibliotequé universitat, Barcelona, Spain, 1763 90
9 Handwritten note in the 1763 edition of the cookbook at the Library of Congress 91

Tables

1 Kitchen positions and their compensation 12
2 Organization of the cookbook 17
3 910 primary food ingredients for recipes in Martínez Montiño's *Arte de cocina* 25
4 4,313 secondary food ingredients for recipes in Martínez Montiño's *Arte de cocina* 26
5 Grains and their by-products (primary) 27
6 Meat, fowl, and fish and shellfish 30
7 Fruit, vegetables, nuts, and seeds 40
8 Sauces 49
9 Editions of *Arte de cocina, pastelería, vizcochería y conservería* 75

Tables in Appendices

Appendix 1. Kitchen Furnishings and Equipment

A.1 A listing of kitchen furnishings in Martínez Montiño's cookbook   621
A.2 A listing of the common cookware in Martínez Montiño's cookbook   621
A.3 A listing of the specialty cookware in Martínez Montiño's cookbook   622
A.4 A listing of the common prepware and serveware in Martínez Montiño's cookbook   622
A.5 A listing of specialty prepware and serveware in Martínez Montiño's cookbook   623
A.6 A listing of utensils in Martínez Montiño's cookbook   625

Figures in Appendices

Appendix 2. On Measurements

A2.1 Detail from a diagram of kitchen equipment and legend in the 1760 edition of *Arte de cocina*. Photo by author, courtesy of Museo Massó, Bueu, Spain, n.p., 2017   631

Appendix 3. Images from Recipes Recreated

A3.1   "Pollos rellenos" [Chicken with stuffing]   635
A3.2   "Un lechón en salchichón" [Suckling pig served sausage style]   636
A3.3.A–B   "Un platillo de pichones" [A squab dish]   637
A3.4   *La flor* [flor]   638
A3.5.A–D   "Artaletes de ave" [Poultry pinwheels] and "Otros artaletes de aves" [Other poultry pinwheels]   639–40
A3.6   "Carnero verde" [Green mutton stew]   641
A3.7.A–B   "Empanadas de liebre" [Hare empanada]   642
A3.8   "Plato de albondiguillas fritas" [Dish of fried meatballs]   643
A3.9   "Torta de orejones" [Dried apricot pie]   643
A3.10.A–G   "Bollo maimón" [Maimon layered pastry]   644–7
A3.11.A–D   "Bollo de rodilla" [Spiral sweet roll]   648–9
A3.12.A–F   "Buñuelos de viento" [Puffs]   650–2
A3.13.A–F   "Quesadillas fritas de cuajada" [Fried cheese curd tarts]   653–5
A3.14   "Quesadillas de horno" [Baked cheese tart]   656
A3.15.A–C   "Platillo de alcachofas" [An artichoke dish]   657–8
A3.16   "Berenjenas rellenas" [Stuffed eggplant]   659
A3.17   "Calabaza rellena en el día de pescado" [Stuffed squash for fish days]   659

A3.18	"Espinacas a la Portuguesa" [Spinach, Portuguese style]	660
A3.19.A–B	"Sardinas rellenas de escabeche" [Pickle stuffed sardines]	660–1
A3.20	"Tortilla blanca" [White omelette]	661
A3.21	"Cómo se puede asar una pella de manteca de vacas en el asador" [How to roast a butterball on a spit]	662
A3.22	"Hinojo conservado" [Preserved fennel]	662

Acknowledgments

For the past ten years, Martínez Montiño's "librito" [little book], as he refers to his masterpiece in the preface, has been the centrepiece of my professional research agenda. And I have enjoyed every minute that I've dedicated to writing this critical edition and translation. Understanding early modern Spain through foodways has been, and continues to be, an exciting journey, and I am fortunate to share the discoveries made along the way with scholars, colleagues, and students both here at Illinois Wesleyan and beyond, with food enthusiasts, and especially with family and friends who have helped along the way. In fact, it is through a long-term collaboration with many of them that this cookbook project has come to be.

First and foremost, I would like to acknowledge the profound impact my partner, Chad Sanders, has had on this critical edition and translation. He has been my first consultant for all my queries regarding these recipes, has recreated, often more than once, dozens of them, read over the manuscript, and provided many valuable insights on contextualizing Martínez Montiño's work within a larger culinary history framework. Your collaboration on this project has been such a source of joy for me. Thank you, friend. Our children, Miranda, Camille, Franklin, and Ethan, have also listened to many discussions both at home and at conferences and weighed in on different tastes and other angles related to these early modern recipes. Miranda also served as the first transcriber of the work in the very early stages and Franklin as the valued indexer in the final stage. I deeply appreciate the enthusiasm and support they have shared with me throughout this entire project. I am also grateful for the love and support of my parents, siblings, and their families as well, in particular my brother, Dan, whose help deciphering a hand-written note in the 1760 edition was key. We have all grown up with an adventurous food curiosity, and although our family gatherings are not as frequent as they once were, food still plays a central role in all our lives, and their genuine interest in my scholarly pursuits has uplifted me on many occasions.

Second, I am honoured to have the support and love of my friend Carmela Ferradáns, who has encouraged me at every step of the process. She has continually lent her optimism and encouragement and, when needed, even brought in

her brother, Rafael, to help better understand certain cooking methods. (¡Gracias, Rafa!) Together with Kathleen Montgomery and Lynda Duke, she formed part of the "Royal Tasters," who tested out many of the dishes from this cookbook. I am so grateful for the many dinners all four of us shared as we were transported back to early modern Spain and discussed the flavours found within Martínez Montiño's pages. Those evenings together reminded me of what matters most as we travel through our professional lives. I would also like to thank my good friends Virginia Bell, Ben Blustein, Carlota Larrea, Cristina Sáenz de Tejada, Joanne Diaz, and Charles Ganelin, who have always taken an interest in my research and provided me with intellectual stimulation. Conversations with each of you have sustained me throughout the years. I would also like to extend my sincerest thanks to our Sunday dinner friends, Laura Edwards, Giovanni Testolin, and Nico Edwards Testolin, and to their family in Italy for taking care of me while I was doing research there. Our Sunday dinners are the source of weekly nourishment and renewal, both mentally and physically, and I am so grateful for this time together. Also, I would like to extend my sincere gratitude to Ana Montoya, Luis Fernández Hebrero, and Concha Valderas, who provided me not only with useful insights into early modern cookware but also with hospitality in Spain and enduring friendship over the years that have filled me with joy.

To understand the impact of Martínez Montiño and the nuances of the many editions of his cookbook, I travelled to libraries, archives, and special collections throughout the United States and Europe. My humble thanks go to the many archivists and librarians at the Archivo General de Palacio in Madrid; the Benson Latin American Collection, at the University of Texas, Austin; the Biblioteca Bertoliana, in Vicenza, Italy; the Biblioteca Nacional de España, in Madrid; the Bibliotequé universitat, in Barcelona; the Biblioteca valenciana Nicolau Primitiu, in Valencia; the British Library, in London; the Library of Congress, in Washington, DC; the Lilly Library, at Indiana University in Bloomington; the Museo Massó, in Bueu, Spain; the New York Academy of Medicine and the New York Public Library in New York City; and the Schlesinger Library, in Cambridge, MA. Even when I wasn't able to travel to places that housed important editions, like the Bibliothèque nationale de France, in Paris, and the Huntington Library in Pasadena, CA, librarians there went out of their way to provide me with editions and help when I had questions about them. In particular, I would like to thank Javier de Diego in the print reserves section of the Biblioteca Nacional de España for pointing out ways to distinguish one edition from the next even when they have the same date and publisher; Covadonga López de Prado Nistal of the Museo Massó, in Bueu, Spain for her generosity and kind assistance when I visited the archives there; Juan José Alonso Martín for his assistance in identifying an additional document in the Royal Palace archives in Madrid that would have gone overlooked without his assistance; and Jessica Pigza in the Brooke Russell Astor Reading Room for Rare Books and Manuscripts at the New York Public Library, who graciously guided me through the necessary steps to access the works

I needed. When undertaking this project, I knew I would visit archives to study the different editions, but having the privilege to work in these spaces, visit these collections, and meet the people dedicated to both preserving history and making it available to researchers today was an added bonus indeed. As an early modern scholar, I deeply value that support.

This labour of love presented many challenges regarding translations of foodstuffs, instruments, and processes so that I could remain faithful to the text and simultaneously find the best way to communicate early modern cooking practices to a twenty-first-century readership. I am deeply indebted to food historian and author Vicky Hayward for her continued support over the years and especially for her valuable assistance in clarifying many of the pressing questions regarding names of different animals and fruit and for her help in deciphering the *flor*. Her insights have been key to resolving many questions I have had throughout this project. Additionally, María del Carmen Simón Palmer graciously offered invaluable assistance with locating Palace archives related to Martínez Montiño. Rachel Laudan kindly provided key sources for tracking down Martínez Montiño's presence in the Americas, and Barbara Ketcham Wheaton generously opened up a world of amazing resources within a wider European context within which I was able to contextualize Martínez Montiño's project during her historic cookbook seminar (2015).

For some of the international references, particularly German ones, I would like to thank Thomas Gloning, who shared my inquiry regarding German fish recipes with the historical cookery and cookbooks listserv, kochbuchforschung. There I met Andreas Klumpp, who went above and beyond to locate many recipes showing how Germans prepared fish in vinegar salt boils, how other preparation styles turned fish blue, and how the napkin was used to serve it. I would also like to thank Richard Fitch, who provided me with useful comparative information on bread baking, court ovens and cob-irons in early modern England. Additionally, I would like to extend my sincere thanks to Carmen Abad Zardoya for providing me with valuable insights into the cookware of the time period, and to Nawal Nasrallah for our exchanges regarding the deep connections between recipes from Martínez Montiño's cookbook and Ibn Razīn al-Tujībī's thirteenth-century Hispano-Muslim cooking manuscript. At the final stages, Ken Albala clarified dozens of details and was helpful in setting the record straight on the use of *pimienta longa*, the presence of *capirotada* in Mexico today, the history of *hochepot*, the use of ambergris and sandalwood in certain recipes, and the popularity of isinglass in the early modern era. He is a generous scholar and I know this critical edition has greatly improved as a result of his feedback. I would also like to express my thanks to the anonymous readers both for their valuable feedback and for reminding me of important bibliographic references regarding Martínez Montiño and professional cooks of the early modern era.

In addition to consulting colleagues, I was also invited to discuss different aspects of Martínez Montiño's work and food in the court of Philip III. In those

gatherings I learned much from the questions and points of discussion that followed. I would like to express my profound gratitude to Montserrat Piera and the Center for Humanities at Temple University; Michelle Hamilton and the Center for Medieval Studies at the University of Minnesota, Twin Cities, and Isidro Rivera and the Spanish Department at the University of Kansas; Lia Markey and the Center for Renaissance Studies at the Newberry Library in Chicago and David Goldstein, Allen Grieco, and Sarah Peters Kernan and the Folger Institute in Washington, DC; Elizabeth Neary and Katie Robiadek and the Graduate Early Modern Student Society of the University of Wisconsin-Madison; Daniela Gutiérrez-Flores and the University of Chicago; Catherine Lambrecht and the Culinary Historians of Chicago; Gina Hunter, Katie Sampeck, and Noha Shawki and the International Seminar series at Illinois State University; Seth Garfield and the Institute for Historical Studies at the University of Texas, Austin; and Jane Hardy at Wabash College.

Researching Martínez Montiño's cookbook also led me to the world of the Society of Creative Anachronism. Donna Green of the West Coast Culinary Symposium not only invited me to one of the SCA events but has also recreated several of Martínez Montiño's recipes. She has worked out the challenges of several dishes, including ones with eggs, roasts, preserves, and even roasted butter on a spit. I am so appreciative of our email exchanges that have been a constant reminder why Martínez Montiño is such an important historic culinary figure. Likewise, Jen Small of the Society of Creative Anachronism in the Midrealm (much of the midwest and parts of Canada) invited me to speak at an event in Chicago where she and others tried recipes from the cookbook. On both occasions it was a pleasure to dress in clothing from the period and exchange ideas with so many who shared a similar passion for early modern cooking and dining habits.

On two different occasions I had the opportunity not only to discuss the food but also to recreate recipes and share them with conference attendees. First, I would like to thank Roy Williams and Daniel Whittington of the Wizard Academy in Austin, who sponsored a Martínez Montiño banquet for the Cervantes Society of America executive board in the fall of 2015. Throughout the years, members of the CSA executive board have supported my culinary pursuits and shared many stories of their own experiences with food as it relates to the early modern kitchen. I would like to especially thank Fred de Armas, Howard Mancing, Adrienne Martin, Steve Hutchinson, Mercedes Álcala-Galán, Cory Reed, David Boruchoff, Bruce Burningham, and Ana Laguna for their friendship and support throughout the project. That evening I was able to receive feedback on the flavours of several of the recipes from many of them as well as from Rosie Hernández, Michael Armstrong-Roche, Sue Byrne, Sherry Velasco, Nacho López, Rachel Schmidt, and Matt Wyszynski. Thank you all for your shared interest in this project. A special thanks go to Luis Laplaza and his wife, Montse, who were visiting from Seville and spent the afternoon preparing the banquet with me.

Second, I would like to express my sincere thanks to the co-host of the International Food Symposium, "Thought for Food in the Luso-Hispanic Translatlantic," Katie Sampeck from Illinois State, and those invited guests who shared their food-related research over the course of two wonderful days in spring 2019. This time with support from Chad Sanders, Tripper Phipps, and his staff in the IWU kitchen, I once again recreated a banquet from Martínez Montiño's cookbook. Engaging with scholars whose collective work spans the globe, I was able to contextualize Martínez Montiño's project within the much larger transatlantic context of the Luso-Hispanic world. Colleagues Rebecca Earle, Ana María Gómez-Bravo, Gregorio Saldarriaga Escobar, Amy Tigner, Rebecca Ingram, Lara Anderson, Rebekah Pite, Lúcio Menezes Ferreira, Ted Fischer, Carla Martin, Emmy Grace (IWU, '11), and William Munro offered enlightening talks on food-related projects spanning from the Middle Ages to modern day and I am so appreciative of their contributions to that stimulating conference.

I am likewise so grateful to many colleagues on the campus of Illinois Wesleyan University. I have worked at this liberal arts institution for almost thirty years and continue to feel support from my colleagues and inspiration from my students. In our close-knit community, my colleagues in Humanities and Social Sciences have shown incredible support, and I would especially like to thank department colleagues Cristina Almeida Vélez, Jessie Dixon-Montgomery, Carmela Ferradáns, Chisato Kojima, Mauricio Parra, Stephanie Porter, Cecilia Sánchez, Suzie Smeeton, and César Valverde for their support throughout the years. I would also like to thank Cristina Isabelli, who generously clarified many of the linguistic terms needed to describe the shifts in language evident in the cookbook. Many other colleagues also shared their enthusiasm for my project. I'd like to express my profound gratitude to Joanne Diaz, whose work ethic and insights have been a huge source of inspiration. I am also grateful to Jim Simeone for keeping the importance of food alive through IWU's Peace Garden. In Ames Library I also want to thank Karen Schmidt for her key role in accessing many of the different editions, archivist Meg Miner, who was always amenable to conversations regarding old documents and ways to respectfully handle and reproduce them, and Tony Heaton, who never failed to locate even the most obscure texts through interlibrary loan.

I look back at my classes over the years and am so appreciative of the wonderful students who have been part of my early modern literature and culture classes. At times we would gather at my house and share early modern dishes that were accompanied by personal stories students would share as if we were all travellers in the novel *Don Quijote*. Most recently, in the fall of 2021, students in the "Reading and Writing Culture" course selected one of the recipes from Martínez Montiño's cookbook, recreated it, and compared it to a recipe from today. In addition to these extraordinary teaching moments, I had the privilege of working with outstanding research assistants. Many thanks go to Melissa Ramirez ('14) and Nathan Douglas ('15), who spent hours converting Martínez Montiño's cookbook into a

working Word document. After my first draft was complete, exchange student Marta Suarez Bravo ('18) read the entire manuscript to make sure the transcriptions were correct and the translations made sense. Her feedback was so valuable at the early stage of the project.

Several institutions also helped support this research project. I am humbly indebted to Illinois Wesleyan for a sabbatical leave, an artistic and scholarly development grant, and a Mellon student research assistant grant; the American Philosophical Society, who awarded me my first grant as I was beginning the project; the Renaissance Society of America for a short-term research grant; and the National Endowment of the Humanities, who awarded me both a fellowship and a summer stipend. While a fellow at the Institute for Research in the Humanities at UW, Madison, I completed the editing process of the manuscript and would like to extend my appreciation for the supportive atmosphere that Steven Nadler, Katie Aspey, Elizabeth Neary, and the amazing group of 2022–23 fellows created. I could not have imagined a better place to finish the project. I'd also like to extend a very heartfelt thank you to Illinois Wesleyan alumnus Byron S. Tucci, who made possible the professorship that has provided me with continual funding to pursue this project. Without his support and the university's, I would not have been able to pursue my research to the extent that I have over this past decade. I would also like to confirm that any views, findings, conclusions, or recommendations expressed in this critical edition do not necessarily reflect those of the National Endowment for the Humanities, Renaissance Society of America, the American Philosophical Society, or Illinois Wesleyan University.

The process of preparing this critical edition also led to the publication of two articles. I sincerely thank Taylor & Francis and the *Bulletin of Spanish Studies* and Vanderbilt University Press for granting me permission to republish parts or all of the information from these articles: "Food Fit for a King: Exploring Royal Recipes in Francisco Martínez Montiño's 1611 Cookbook," *Bulletin of Spanish Studies*: Food Cultural Studies and the Transhispanic World, vol. 97, no. 4, 2020, 615–33, https://doi.org/10.1080/14753820.2020.1699333, and "Furniture and Equipment in the Royal Kitchens of Early Modern Spain," in *Food, Texts and Cultures in Latin America and Spain*, ed. Rafael Climent-Espino and Ana María Gómez Bravo, Vanderbilt University Press, 2020, 115–49.

Finally, I would like to extend my sincere thanks to editorial director Suzanne Rancourt, associate managing editor Barbara Porter, and copy editor Judy Williams for their professionalism and excellent work at every stage of the publishing process. Each one of you makes the final stages of this labour of love that much more enjoyable.

THE ART OF COOKING, PIE MAKING, PASTRY MAKING, AND PRESERVING

Arte de cocina, pastelería, vizcocheria y conserveria

Introduction

I. The Cookbook as Cultural Artefact

On 11 January 1610, Jorge de Tobar, secretary of the Royal Patrimony and member of Council to King Philip III of Spain, signed *per procurationem* the king's privilege and thus set in motion a series of events that would lead to the publication of the most renowned Spanish cookbook from the time printing presses were invented through to the late nineteenth century. This privilege essentially secured a ten-year copyright for Francisco Martínez Montiño, master cook for Philip III, to publish *Arte de cocina, pastelería, vizcochería y conservería* [The art of cooking, pie making, pastry making, and preserving]. Over a year later, the manuscript made its way to the office of the "corrector general," something akin to a combination of copy editor and proof reader today, where a second seal of approval all but guaranteed its pending release. The work was finally passed to Gerónimo Núñez de León, clerk of the king's chamber and resident clerk to his council, who confirmed that the book was guaranteed to be sold at 168 maravedís, and so on the fifteenth of April, 1611, the cookbook was released for publication.

Could Martínez Montiño have known that this collection of over five hundred court recipes would be published throughout Spain ten times in the seventeenth century, fourteen times in the eighteenth century, and five times in the nineteenth century until 1823?[1] What sort of identity did he craft as master cook at court and as author of this key culinary artefact?[2] Today, in what ways can his masterpiece help us discern the construction of culinary culture in Spain?

As we consider these questions, the words of another writer, this time from the twentieth century, provide us with some perspective. In the introduction to her cookbook *La cocina española antigua* [Old Spanish cooking], Emilia Pardo Bazán writes, "la alimentación revela lo que acaso no descubren otras indagaciones de carácter oficialmente científico" [food reveals what, perhaps, no other investigation of scientific inquiry can discover]. She reminds us that "cada época de la Historia modifica el fogón, y cada pueblo come según su alma, antes tal vez que según su

estómago" [each historic moment modifies the hearth, and each nation eats with its heart, perhaps even before eating with its stomach] (III). The Spanish Hapsburg court is no exception, and Francisco Martínez Montiño's cookbook, *Arte de cocina, pastelería, vizcochería y conservería*, gives us direct access to what food and flavours were being prepared in the royal kitchens of the early seventeenth century.

Cooking manuals are key to understanding culinary history because, unlike other discourses such as novels, plays, travel journals, or regulatory decrees that may discuss aspects of food preparation and consumption, cookbooks focus primarily on the preparation and cooking of food. First and foremost, they are cultural artefacts that reveal ingredients and flavours of a certain community and time period. They highlight regional, ethnic, or international cooking practices and tastes. These prescriptive texts allow readers today to visualize kitchen spaces and equipment, often simply evoked by action instead of naming a particular object. They describe in detail forms of presentation, that is, dishware used, colour and shape of arrangements, or detail of garnishes. In other words, cookbooks provide evidence of the values of a specific cultural and historical moment. On another level, cookbooks provide insight into the life of a master cook and others who work in the kitchen and give readers a sense of how cooks think about food. In the case of Martínez Montiño, he fills his recipes with helpful hints, notes of caution, overviews of a product, purposeful visual imagery that help to recreate dishes, and, every once in a while, his own personal sense of humour. His personal comments sprinkled throughout the recipes provide information not only on his skills as master cook but also on the pride he felt for his role in his profession. They provide us a pathway to enter the seventeenth-century kitchen and see, smell, and taste food prepared there.

To understand the culinary literature and history of Spain, one must return to early manuscripts and books, because they provide a foundation for subsequent culinary publications and offer insight into the cultural and social identity of the people of early modern Spain.[3] Martínez Montiño's cookbook is absolutely essential, as it is one of the few printed cookbooks in Spanish of the early modern period and certainly the title with most editions, published at least twenty-nine times. In his study *Printed Cookbooks in Europe 1470–1700*, Henry Notaker explains that "a little more than a hundred different titles and about 650 editions of cookbooks were produced in Europe from the beginning of printing until 1700" (2). He goes on to explain that the number is most likely higher, as several titles and editions may not have been recorded in bibliographies. However, of those hundred titles printed in the first 230 years of cookbooks, at least twenty are compilations or plagiarisms and another twenty to thirty are translations or partial translations of cookbooks in other languages (8). This information is important, as it places Martínez Montiño's cookbook in the category of only fifty to sixty non-plagiarized and non-translated cookbooks published between 1470 and 1700.

Before the release of Martínez Montiño's masterpiece, four cookbooks had been printed in Spanish. The first, *Libro de guisados* (1525), is a translation of

Mestre Robert's (Ruperto de Nola's) 1520 Catalan cookbook, *Llibre del coc*. The second is Miguel de Baeza's *Los quatro libros del arte de la confitería* (1592). This work exclusively treated conserves and confectionery. Next is Diego Granado's *Libro del arte de cozina* (1599). Over 80 per cent of this cookbook is a recompilation of recipes primarily from Bartolomeo Scappi's Italian masterpiece, *Opera dell'arte del cucinare*, and also from Nola. The final Spanish cookbook that appeared before Martínez Montiño's is the university cookbook, also titled *Libro de arte de cocina* (1607). It was penned by Domingo Hernández de Maceras and, like Martínez Montiño's, is neither a translation nor a recompilation of others' works. However, this cookbook saw no additional editions and thus did not impact culinary history in the way that Martínez Montiño's did. After the publication of Martínez Montiño's cookbook, no others were released in Spain in the seventeenth century. It is not until some 130 years later that another is published, when in 1745 Juan de Altamiras writes *Nuevo arte de cocina* [The new art of cooking], a cookbook based on recipes from when he was cook at the convent of San Diego in Zaragoza.[4]

Martínez Montiño's intentions are clear. His goal is to preserve in writing recipes for future cooks so that they do not have to commit them to memory. As Walter Ong noted centuries later, "the text frees the mind of conservative tasks ... and thus enables the mind to turn itself to new speculation" (41). Future cooks would now have this cookbook as a base from which to create dishes. In his prologue Martínez Montiño writes: "El intento que he tenido en escribir este librito ha sido no haber libros por donde se puedan guiar los que sirven el oficio de la cocina, y que todo se encarga a la memoria" [The intention I have had in writing this little book has been that there are no books that can guide those serving in the cooking profession and that everything must be committed to memory] (108; 109). Now, future cooks can both recreate these recipes and adapt them to develop and create new ones.

II. Spain and the Court in the Late Sixteenth and Early Seventeenth Century

Martínez Montiño entered the court in 1586, at the end of the reign of Philip II, a court – now fully established in Madrid – characterized by its maximum global expansion both politically and economically. He stayed on as master cook for Philip III and retired from service at the start of the reign of Philip IV, sometime before 1628. His time in the Hapsburg court is characterized as the peak of the Counter-Reformation, as an era of artistic cultural exploration and innovation, Spain's Golden Age, and yet ever present was the sensation of a pending deterioration of Spain's economic and military power.

Philip II had moved the court to Madrid in 1561, and here poets, playwrights, novelists, painters, and sculptors flourished throughout his reign and those of his descendants Philip III and Philip IV. Martínez Montiño cooked in the age

of Cervantes, Lope, Calderón, and Velázquez. Artists at that time were grappling with dynamism in their works, multiple layers of meaning, characters and settings that mirrored realistic life, and metaphors that inspired imagination and creativity. Although presented in a different medium, Martínez Montiño's *Arte de cocina* shares these same features. It was the Baroque era, and artists often critiqued the tumultuous political and economic landscape of seventeenth-century Spain. Other times they grappled with *desengaño*, disappointment, regarding ideals that had gone unrealized or the bouts of famine and disease that plagued both city and country.[5] Always these artists captured the imagination of the masses and the elite who packed the *corrales* to view theatre, of printers who published hundreds of novels of chivalry, romance, and the picaresque, not to mention the hugely popular first modern novel, *Don Quixote* (1605), and of patrons who constantly commissioned portraits, still lifes, landscapes, and works reflecting both sacred and profane themes. The demand for artistic creativity and renovation was high. In the field of the culinary arts, Martínez Montiño's work is a response to this demand as well. It is his attempt to set the record straight on how to create, inspire, and make an impact on his audience.

Philip II had inherited an expansive empire from his father. Abroad he controlled most of South America, Central America, and what is today the southern United States from California to the Carolinas. Within Europe he was King of Spain and Portugal (and all its territories in the New World, Africa, and Asia), Naples, Sicily, Sardinia, and the Low Countries, and Duke of Milan and Burgundy. In the east the crown also controlled the Philippine Islands. With these expansions came increased trade, particularly with the New World as demand for Spanish products grew in the colonies and silver imports reached their climax. Trade routes, map making, and other technological developments advanced. But, with this expansion also came intense vulnerability, and the crown drained its coffers on warfare abroad. Notable was the victory of the Holy League (of which Spain was a major contributor) against Ottoman forces in the Battle of Lepanto in the Mediterranean (1571) and the loss of the "Invincible" Armada to England in Spain's attempt to stave off the growth of Protestantism, deter England's support of the Netherlands, and reduce disruption that both the English and Dutch were causing in Spain's interests in America (1588).

Within the country, each region had different taxation, privileges, and military quotas. These arrangements strained some regions with heavier taxation and caused resentment among others with less representation and power. The crown also dealt with rebellions, most notably in the Alpujarras, a mountainous region outside Granada where Moriscos suffered daily injustices and were forbidden to use their own language, clothing, or public baths or practise their own ceremonies and celebrations (1568–70). The subsequent expulsion of Moriscos from Granada, and later under Philip III from Spain, also negatively affected Spain's economy. These military campaigns, along with the financial pressures Philip II

had inherited from his father, Carlos I, led to the state's consistent inability to repay loans. Silver coming in from the New World was not enough to maintain solvency, and bankruptcy became a defining feature of the Hapsburg court.

At the end of the sixteenth century, Philip III inherited the crown (1598). Historians have often characterized his reign as a turning point for the Hapsburg dynasty as Spain's economic, political, and military power began to wane. And until recently historians have characterized him as a passive king not interested in politics. However, recent work by Antonio Feros, Patrick Williams, and other historians has methodically examined administrative documents such as registers from council meetings and ambassadors' correspondence; inventories and estate documents; and chronicles, theatrical plays, sermons, and records of artistic sponsorship to argue that the king, with the help of his favourite, the Duke of Lerma, developed strategies to address Spain's problems. Historian Antonio Feros maintains that Philip III's policies of peace with England in 1604 and the Dutch Republic (after four decades of fighting) in 1609 were attempts to avoid costly wars (150–3). Furthermore, he argues that potential criticism of peace with "heretics" in the larger European arena led the king to call for the expulsion of the Moriscos from Spain, which was carried out from 1609 to 1614 (203–4). This edict significantly reduced the pool of skilled workers and merchants. Additionally, those working in the textile industry were forced out of business by steep inflation, which made it impossible to compete with international markets.

Spain in the late sixteenth and early seventeenth centuries was undoubtedly a pastoral-agrarian society. The Mesta, originating in the thirteenth century, was a guild dedicated to the seasonal movement of livestock and maintained a profitable wool industry with Flanders. Even though transhumance numbers had decreased from some three million in the early sixteenth century to two million in the early seventeenth century, the Mesta still held powerful sway at court, since it significantly contributed to the king's coffers (Casey 49). However, the court also earned money from selling arable land, and under Philip II sold between 25 and 30 per cent of the land in Tierra de Campos as arable enclosures (Casey 50). The tensions between herders and farmers, these two major purveyors of foodstuffs for court and country, played out time and again in courts of law as farmers brought suits of property damage and land ownership against herders.

In terms of food, bread was the mainstay of the peasant diet. James Casey in his book *Early Modern Spain: A Social History*, reports:

> The Courts of 1580 noted how reliant the Old Castilians were on gruel or porridge rather than bread – on boiling rather than baking their rye, millet or barley. The same body emphasized that some form of grain or bread was the bulk of the peasant diet: the shepherd would have his "bread crumbs fried in suet or milk, or just bread and water", the villager "bread with some stew of vegetables and a little bacon, or in Lent, chickpeas instead." (35)

Recipes for these village mainstays of porridge, breadcrumbs, and stews appear in Martínez Montiño's cookbook as well, though one can imagine that the quality of ingredients, the seasoning, and the enhanced variety of food choices separated the peasants' meal from the royal household meal. At the turn of the century, meat was consumed in small quantities, "averaging about 50 grams a day per person according to random calculations for Murcia, Valladolid and Valencia" (Casey 36). Given the weight of Counter-Reformation practices throughout the country, rules for abstinence and partial abstinence were enforced a full third of the year. Martínez Montiño's recipes provide a detailed sense of the variety of foodstuffs available at court throughout the year, as the seasoned changed, and as Christian dietary laws allowed.

III. Martínez Montiño's Biography and the Early Modern Spanish Kitchen

As with so many cooks of the early modern period, little is known about Francisco Martínez Montiño's life. He was possibly Galician, though Jorge Guitián has presented several arguments that question the master's Galician roots. Guitián's most compelling argument is that the master cook's last name appears as Martínez Motiño in the earliest editions of the book, 1611, 1617, and the front material of the 1623 edition, without the "n" in Montiño, and that Motiño is not a common name in Galicia but rather in the Basque Country, Madrid, and Extremadura. Regardless of his ancestry, we know from his own testimony in the prologue that Martínez Montiño worked his entire life in kitchens, beginning as a type of humble kitchen hand (*galopín*) and making his way up to head cook for Philip III and Philip IV. In a 1620 petition to the king regarding a personal matter, Martínez Montiño explains that he has been employed in the service of his lordship for thirty-four years, placing his arrival at court in 1586. He also states that prior to his arrival he served the Princess Juana, Philip II's sister, when she resided in Portugal (Archivo de Palacio 634.56). Pérez Samper confirms that Martínez Montiño continued working for Philip IV until his retirement or death in 1629, when records show he was replaced by another cook (*La alimentación* 29–30). It is also notable that in the 1628 edition of his cookbook the licence is no longer granted to Martínez Montiño himself, as it had been in previous editions, but rather to the bookseller/editor, Alonso Pérez.

Nearing the end of his illustrious career and in a petition to secure his retirement and his family's financial stability, Martínez Montiño writes to the king requesting jobs for his two sons and resources for him and his wife. The Duque de Infantado, head chamberlain at court, also writes in support of his request, and, after confirming the nearly four decades of service to the court, the Duque makes Martínez Montiño's case more compelling by referencing the *bizcochos* [sweet biscuits] that Martínez Montiño had made the king for so many years (see Figure 1):

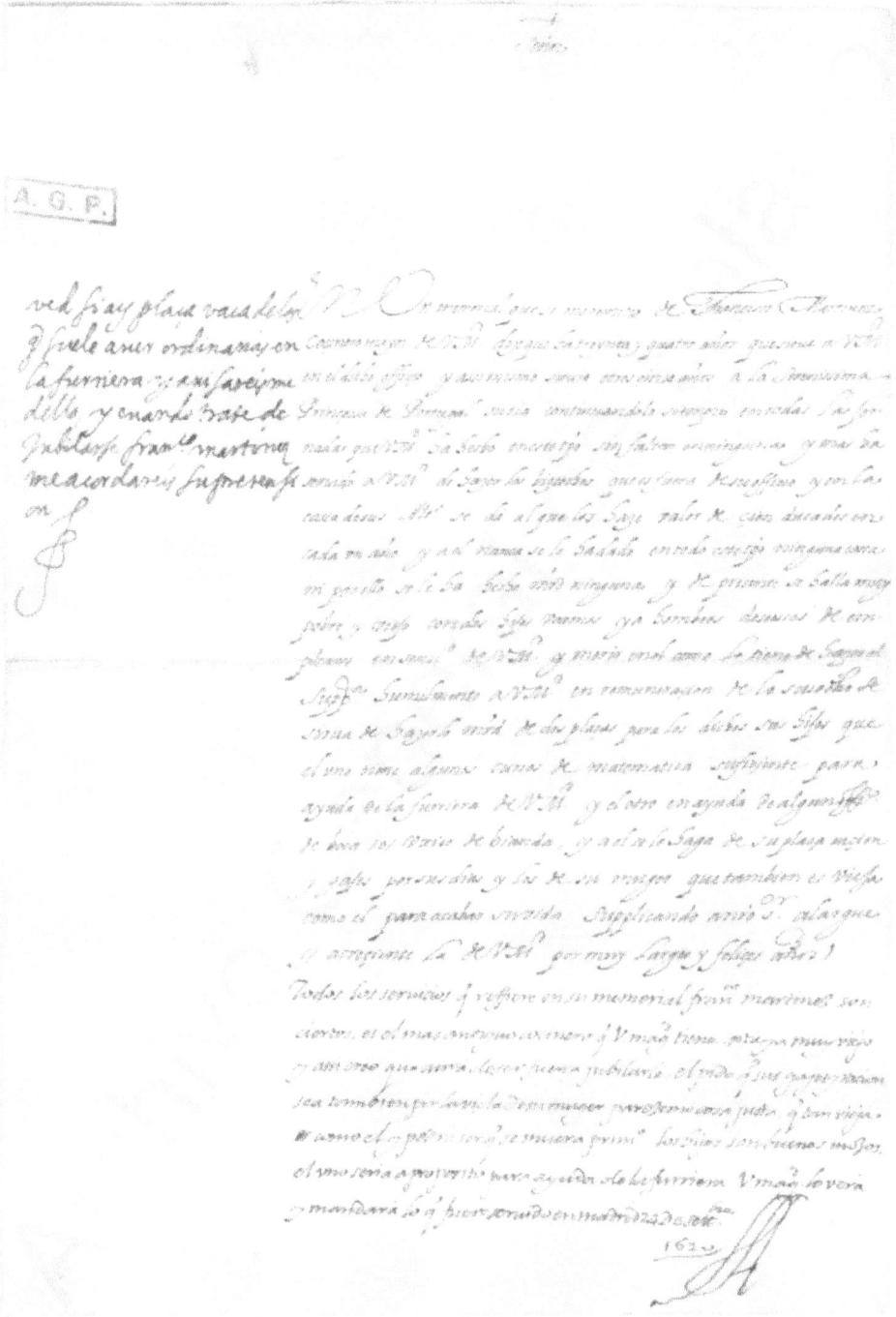

Figure 1. Chamberlain's letter of support for Martínez Montiño's request. Image courtesy of Archivo General de Palacio 634.56, Madrid.

ha treinta y cuatro años que sirve a Vuestra Merced en el dicho oficio y así mismo sirvió otros cinco años a la serenísima Princesa de Portugal su tía continuándolo siempre en todas las jornadas que Vuestra Merced ha hecho en este tiempo sin faltar en ninguna y *más ha servido a Vuestra Merced de hacer los bizcochos que es fuera de su oficio* y en la casa de sus Altísimos se da al que los hace valor de cien ducados en cada un año y a él nunca se le ha dado en todo este tiempo ninguna cosa ni por ello se le ha hecho merced ninguna.... Todos los servicios que refiere en su memorial Francisco Martínez son ciertos, es el más antiguo cocinero que Vuestra Majestad tiene, está ya muy viejo y así creo que habrá de ser fuerza jubilarle, él pide que sus gajes y raciones sea también por la vida de su mujer, paréceme cosa justa. (Archivo de Palacio, my emphasis)

For thirty-four years he had served Your Grace in said office and before that for five years for your aunt, the most serene Princess of Portugal. He worked every day that Your Grace was in attendance throughout this time without ever being absent. *Moreover, he has served Your Grace by making sweet biscuits which is beyond his profession.* In the house of Your Highnesses one hundred ducats a year are given to whoever makes them and in all this time he has never been given anything nor has ever requested anything for them ... All the services to which Francisco Martínez refers in his brief are true. He is the oldest cook that Your Majesty has, he is old and we should insist he retire. He is requesting that his allowance and perquisites also be for his wife. I think it is a fair request.]

As master cook, Martínez Montiño would answer to three officials. The first is the *mayordomo mayor* [head major domo], who is in charge of running the palace. The second is the group of *mayordomos semaneros* [weekly major domos], who are in charge of different parts of the house and, in the case of the kitchen, oversee the menu prepared for the king. Finally, he would answer to the *contralor* [comptroller], who is responsible for the daily expenses at court and, with regard to the kitchen, the rations distributed throughout the kitchen and to other *oficios de boca* [personnel related to food and dining] with whom he intimately worked (Simón Palmer, *La cocina de palacio* 81–2). María del Carmen Simón Palmer provides a list of those palace positions and their responsibilities from 1606:

GUARDAMANGIER: receives and distributes food and beverage provisions
PANETERÍA: supplies and distributes bread, salt, milk, cheese, and table linens
CAVA: supplies and distributes wines and snow, is responsible for the silver, and tastes beverages before they are served to the king
SAUCERÍA: provides vinegar and spices
FRUTERÍA: is responsible for fruit and the corresponding silver dishes
POTAGIER-BUSIER: provides salads, vegetables, and legumes as well as kitchenware like pots, brooms, string, paper, baskets, and coal
FURRIERÍA: is responsible for dining furniture and all wooden things

TAPICERÍA: is responsible for the tapestry decorations

CERERÍA: is responsible for candles and lighting for kitchen, dining room, and hallways. (*La cocina de palacio* 83–91)

Simón Palmer also lists those working directly under the master cook in 1605: four *ayudas de cocina* [cook's assistants], two *portadores* [food runners], four *mozos* [kitchen boys], and one *portero aguador* [water attendant/doorman] (*La cocina de palacio* 99).[6] The *portero* accompanied the master cook to select the provisions for the day from the *guardamangier*. He also made sure that the kitchen was clean and that access was limited to only those allowed.

Simón Palmer also gives us a sense of the earnings of various kitchen positions in her 1982 study *La alimentación y sus circunstancias en el Real Alcázar de Madrid*. In summary, as shown in Table 1, the following positions were compensated monetarily and with food, housing, and access to medical attention (52–3).

In his prologue, Martínez Montiño mentions several kitchen positions. He is specific about who works with him in the king's kitchen and how cooks and other kitchen employees rotate out weekly to work in the state kitchen: "sólo en su cocina de boca no entran más de un oficial, y un portador, y un mozo de cocina y un galopín; y estos están una semana con el cocinero mayor, y el Domingo se mudan a la cocina del Estado, y venían otros tantos por sus semanas" [In the king's kitchen, no more than one cook, one food runner, one kitchen boy, and one *galopín* are allowed to enter. These workers stay with the master cook for a week and on Sunday they switch to the state kitchen, and others are rotated in for their own week] (122; 123). In this way, small groups of apprentices worked closely with the master cook.

Later, for serving food in the dining hall, Martínez Montiño mentions the different roles of *maestresala* [steward], *veedor* [inspector], *pages* [pages], and *mayordomo* [major domo].

son menester seis Mastresalas,[7] y seis personas que sirvan como de Veedores[8] para solo llevar la vianda desde la Cocina a la mesa: (7r)[9] y cada Veedor ha de llevar un servicio, y entregarlo a su Mastresala, porque en tales días no ha de bajar el Mastresala a la cocina, y si bajare la primera vez, no puede bajar las otras; porque se ha de servir la vianda en tres veces. Ha de bajar el mayordomo con sus Veedores. Digo, pues, que el Veedor que tomare el primer servicio, llevará cinco pajes, y estos llevarán diez platos, cada uno dos, y detrás del postrer page irá otro Veedor, con otros cinco pajes, otros diez platos: y desta manera irán los demás, porque cada cinco pajes seguirán a su Veedor, sin que se mezclen unos con otros. (124–6)

[Six stewards are necessary and six people who will serve as inspectors who will solely carry the food from the kitchen to the table. Each inspector should carry with him one place setting and give it to the steward, because on these days, the steward should not go down to the kitchen, and if he does go down the first time, he should not go down any other

Table 1. Kitchen positions and their compensation

Position	Years	Monetary compensation (in maravedís)	Other compensation
Cocinero de la servilleta (exclusively dedicated to meals for the king and/or queen)	1645–70	113.450–107.000	One portion of bread, wine and fish; housing; medicinal needs
Cocinero mayor	1605	60.000–66.000	Two portions of two rolls, pound and a half of mutton; half *azumbre* of wine; and half a cart for clothing and/or linens
Ayudas u oficiales (under supervision of *cocinero de la servilleta*)	1680	30.000–33.000	
Portadores (delivers food to the kitchen from *guardamangier* or other areas)	1605–86	20.000–23.000	
Portero (watches over the security of the kitchen; accompanies *portadores* in their deliveries)		20.000–27.000	
Mozos (responsible for various kitchen jobs)		20.000–29.000	Corresponding rations.
Galopines (cleaning poultry and the kitchens)		none	Annual kitchen clothing

time, because the food will be served three times. The major domo should go down with his inspectors. As I was saying, the inspector who delivers the first course will bring five pages, and they will carry ten dishes, each one two, and after the last page, the next inspector will follow with another five pages and another ten plates. And in this way the rest will follow as each five pages follow their inspector without one group mixing with another.] (125–7)

These tips for future cooks on how food is delivered from the kitchen to the table complement what Miguel Yelgo de Vázquez writes in his 1614 *Estilo de servir a príncipes con ejemplos morales para servir a Dios*. In Chapter 4, he describes in detail the responsibilities of the *maestresala*: "es un oficio muy honrado, de quien cuelgan todas las ceremonias de criança y cortesía de la mesa y de la sala" [it is a very honoured position on which rests all the ceremony of politeness and courtesy of the dining room and hall] (33v) and goes on to explain his significant responsibilities for training the pages, stating that "El maestresala tiene de enseñar al page ... cómo han de servir a la mesa,

en que mano han de llevar la copa, y en que hombro la toalla, con que mano tomará, o pondrá el plato en la mesa, y cómo han de dar agua a manos, y cuándo han de hablar, y cuándo han de callar" [the steward has to instruct the page … how to serve at the table, in which hand he should carry the glassware, on which shoulder the towel, with which hand he should place and remove a plate at the table, how to offer water for handwashing, when to speak and when to remain quiet] (35v–36r).

Yelgo de Vázquez also signals the importance of the *veedores* in the delivery of food from the kitchen to the table. In doing so, he particularly notes that the *veedor* must carefully watch the pages.

> No hay criado que no procure regalar con lo mejor. Quien bien quiere, y tiene obligación: y assí debe abrir los ojos el Veedor, y aún plegue a Dios que baste para que no los hurten, y donde tienen más peligro, es al tiempo de sentarlo en la mesa, que allí se desaparece el page, haziendo espaldas el gentilhombre, y a este tiempo se ha de poner el Veedor detrás de la mesa, apartadico un poco, con la memoria debajo de la capa, y como se fueren sentando, el Veedor echando una raya secretamente, sin que sea echado de ver, porque si no lo haze así, lo mejor se perderá: y si a este tiempo hubiere platos menos, diráselo al mayordomo (138r)

> [There are no servants who wouldn't try to give away the best parts to those to whom they are endeared or have some obligation. So, the steward must keep his eyes open and even say a prayer to God to put a stop to it so they don't steal. The most dangerous moment is when everyone is being seated at the table and the page disappears, when the gentleman's back is turned. It is at this moment that the steward must stand at a slight distance, behind the table, with his notes under his cape, and, while they are being seated, give a sharp glance all around without being noticed, because if he doesn't do this, the best will be lost. And at this point, if there were missing dishes, he should report it to the major domo.]

It is clear, then, that Martínez Montiño worked among a complex network of court staff, reporting to some while in command of others.

Beyond the human resources that fill the early modern kitchen, the physical space of the early modern court kitchen is also very much defined by its equipment and utensils. Martínez Montiño's cookbook offers us a detailed and fascinating look into this world of culinary creativity with its hundreds of different pieces of kitchen equipment, including thirty-five different varieties of pots, pans, and sheets, and 416 references to hand-held tools that can be divided into utensils used to spread and stir, to cut or puncture, to separate, to flatten, and to seal and secure, and other specialty items.[10] In the eighteenth century, editor Juliana Carrasco decided to include a diagram of kitchen equipment found in the early modern court kitchen. This same diagram was later reproduced in the 1800, 1822, and 1823 editions. It can also be found in cookbooks by other authors (see Figure 2), but in 1611 Martínez Montiño

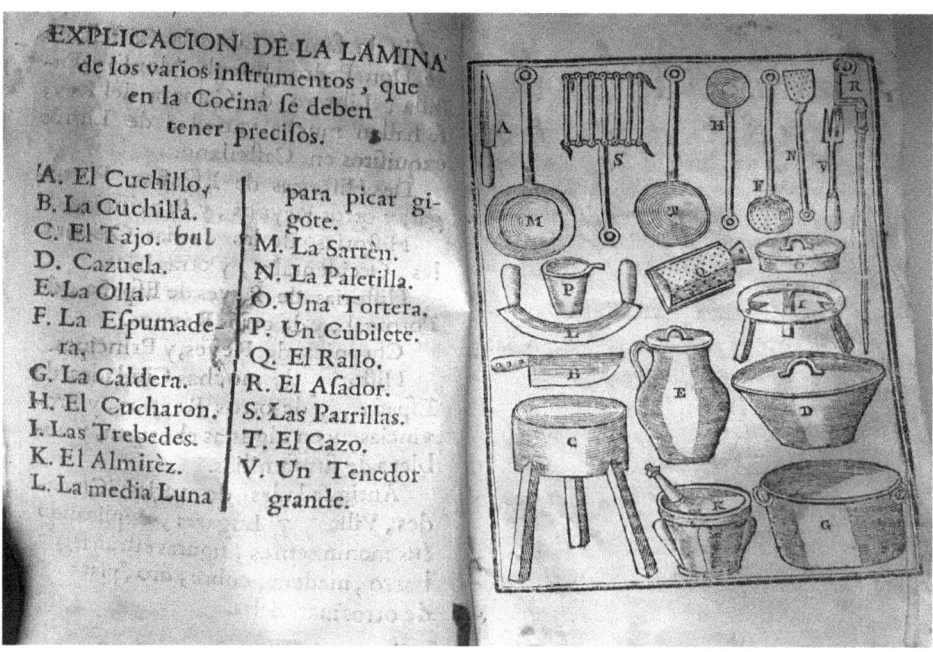

Figure 2. Diagram of kitchen equipment and legend. First reproduced in the edition by Juliana Carrasco, Madrid, 1760. Photo by author, courtesy of Museo Massó, Bueu, Spain, n.p. 2017.

chooses to include just two illustrations of different-sized spoons. As a significant culinary artefact in its own right, this cookbook provides readers today with a deeper appreciation of not only *what* food was prepared but also *how* it was prepared at the early modern Spanish court. For example, we get direct access to heat sources of conduction (grill, fry, sear), convection (boil, bake, braise, deep fry, parbake, parboil, roast, simmer, steam, stew, and warm), and radiation (broil, spit), and the many ways to cook without heat (brine, cure, marinate, pickle, salt, soak).

Second, by studying kitchen appliances and utensils we are able to uncover lost techniques that Martínez Montiño practised and passed on to others. The combination of *vidrio* [glass container] and *puchero* [stew pot] to create a bain-marie for making sustaining broths, the different-sized *ollas* [pots] sealed with dough to build pressure for stewing duck, the series of *plumas* [feathers] for spreading fat to laminate dough and create airy pastries, and the different sizes and types of paper used for cooking *en papillote* (wrapping a foodstuff in greased paper to maintain tenderness) are a few of these examples.

Last, delving into Martínez Montiño's work also brings to light the specialty items required in the preparation of certain dishes. I'll mention the *alcuzcucero*

[couscoussier], *garabato* [spoon hook for puffs], and the *hierro a manera de hongo* [mushroom-shaped iron], as examples of those listed in Tables A.3 and A.5 of Appendix 1, as culinary curiosities that broaden our knowledge of cooking practices. In short, exploring the spaces and instrumentation of the early modern kitchen that Martínez Montiño includes in *Arte de cocina, pastelería, vizcochería y conservería* provides insight into Spain's social history and enables scholars today to delve deeper into understanding the material culture of food preparation at the seventeenth-century court.

IV. Cookbook Organization

The opening words of Chapter 1 bring to the forefront one of the guiding principles of Martínez Montiño's project. He asserts that cleanliness "es la más necesaria, e importante, para que cualquier cocinero dé gusto en su oficio" [is most necessary and important for any cook to please in his profession] (115; 116). To this principle he quickly adds a second priority: order.

The skilled cook should be vigilant and constantly aware of both: "Todas las veces que entrares por la puerta de tu cocina procura tener algo que enmendar; mira si está bien colgada la herramienta, y si está cada cosa en su lugar: y si hay por las paredes o por el techo alguna telaraña, hazlo remediar luego" [Each time you enter through the kitchen door, try to have something to improve on. Check to see if the utensils are hung properly, if everything is where it should be, and if the walls or ceilings have cobwebs; if needed, have it taken care of right away] (120; 121). This cleanliness of course extends to the kitchen staff as well:

> pondrás una costumbre que todos los oficiales y mozos que entraren por la mañana en la cocina, lo primero que han de hacer sea.... lavarse las manos, y limpiarse en una toalla, que estará colgada para esto, y trabajar con mucha limpieza. (122)

> [You should insist as a general habit that the first thing that all cooks and kitchen hands do as they enter the kitchen each morning is ... wash their hands and dry them with a towel, hung for this very purpose, and work with much cleanliness.] (123)

He even reminds his readers that every time a staff member leaves and reenters the kitchen, and after they eat lunch, the same routine should be followed, particularly the hand washing (122–4; 123–5).

While these guiding principles have endured throughout the centuries, early modern cookbooks do not share the same sense of organization as modern cookbooks. More often they are loosely gathered into sections that are, at times, divided by food category and at other times by cooking method, order of service, religious regulations, or even by the consumer's constitution, i.e., a section on food for the

infirm. In the case of Martínez Montiño, we find a deliberate organizational system that is primarily governed by foodstuffs but also includes methods of preparation. The book is organized, much as the title suggests, into various sections on cooking, pies, pastries, and preserves. As outlined below, the cooking section begins with roasts and accompanying sauces, particularly for birds and small game, and continues with one-pot meals, stews, and sops. *Pastelería* [pie making] follows and includes sweet and savoury pies, pastries and puff pastries, empanadas and other wrapped foods, and fried dough. There are also recipes for wild game. Martínez Montiño then includes an abstinence and partial abstinence section for recipes with organ meats, vegetables, fish and shellfish, and nuts. An extensive section, with twenty-seven recipes for eggs, follows. He then returns again to grain-based recipes, including two for couscous (the only ones that appear in a Spanish-language cookbook until Emilia Pardo Bazán rewrites Martínez Montiño's recipes in her 1913 cookbook), game, and other meat and vegetable dishes, before a section on food for the sick and lighter fare. His next section contains a variety of recipe for non-main dishes; for example, sauces, vinegars, and fats. He then includes recipes that fall under the category of *vizcochería* [pastry making], followed by a couple of pickled vegetable recipes. He closes this part of the cookbook with instructions for carving and serving different types of meat. The last section on *conservería* [preserving] includes two memoirs with recipes for jams, jellies, and gelatines. The cookbook closes with a final section of miscellaneous recipes.

Several times throughout his cookbook, Martínez Montiño references different "capítulos" and also includes headers for a few sections. It is not uncommon for him to provide a summary recipe at the beginning or end of a section that provides overviews and tips for preparing certain types of dishes. This is evident, for example, at the start of the fish section with the recipe "Cómo se han de aderezar algunos pescados" [How to prepare some fish] (380; 381), in which he explains the most common ways to prepare fish and other general tips. With the recipe "Otra manera de masa de bollos" [Another way to make pastry dough] (270; 271), which Martínez Montiño includes after his ten different *bollo* [pastry] recipes, he explains how to make an excellent dough for empanadas for the previous recipes and introduces the next section on puff pastry.

For readers today to better understand the sense of order, I have divided the recipes into eighteen sections (see Table 2). My editor's additions are in **bold** and I note with *italics* where Martínez Montiño himself references different chapters. However, readers will note that the rules are soft and that sometimes a section begins with an organization based on foodstuffs but finishes with recipes organized by cooking methods, and that other times the transitions are fluid, leaving the reader to explore several recipes that overlap from one section to another or that are simply grouped into a "miscellaneous" section, perhaps reflecting a handful of recipes that were gathered together after the original grouping had been set.

Table 2. Organization of the cookbook

1. **1–75 Birds and small game [Cocina (cooking)]** *Chapter II. On all types of roasts*
   a. 1–5 **Roasts (and sauces)**
      i. 1 Turkey and capon
      ii. 2 Capon *(reference to chapter on sops)*
      iii. 3 Mutton
      iv. 4 Veal
      v. 5 Wood pigeon
   b. 6–10 **Other birds**
      i. 6 Wood pigeon
      ii. 7 Partridge
      iii. 8 Woodcock
      iv. 9 Crane *(reference to chapter on boar)*
      v. 10 Duck and teal
   c. 11–16 **Game**
      i. 11 Hare
      ii. 12–15 Rabbit
      iii. 16 Beef
   d. 17–24 **Other birds**
      i. 17–18 Chicken
      ii. 19–21 Empanadas filled with partridge, collared doves, wild squab, or farm-raised squab or beef
      iii. 22–3 Partridge
      iv. 24 Duck
   e. 25–33 **Suckling pig and mutton**
      i. 25–7 Suckling pig *(reference to chapter on sops)*
      ii. 28–33 Mutton
   f. 34–51 **Farm-raised birds**: squab, chicken, hen, and capon
      i. 34–8 Squab, chicken, hen
      ii. 39 Capon
      iii. 40–1 Poultry
      iv. 42–4 Hen
      v. 45 Squab
      vi. 46–8 Capon
      vii. 49 Chicken empanadas
      viii. 50 Stuffing
      ix. 51 Poultry pinwheels

   Vegetables (Potagería)
      g. 52–4 Pinwheels with poultry, veal, and kid
      h. 55 Poultry stew
      i. 56 Pinwheel
      j. 57–8 Wild squab *(reference to a previous chapter)*
      k. 59–60 Mutton
      l. 61–2 More chicken

(Continued)

Table 2. *(Continued)*

m.	63–6	Meatballs with poultry, mutton, beef (#66 references discussing meatballs once again later on)
n.	67–70	Hare
o.	71–2	More meatballs
p.	73–4	Marrow
q.	75	Oviduct

2. **76–86 Miscellaneous 1**
   - a. 76–8 — Carrots
   - b. 79 — Fried dough (*reference to chapter on preserves*)
   - c. 80 — Toronja
   - d. 81 — Kid pluck
   - e. 82–4 — Small birds and brenca sauce
   - f. 85 — Mutton essence
   - g. 86 — Veal pinwheels

3. **87–96 Cream-based recipes with a focus on sops and breadcrumbs**
   - a. 87–9 — Sops
   - b. 90–1 — Other cream-based recipes
   - c. 92–4 — Breadcrumb
   - d. 95–6 — Cream pies (overlaps with next section)

4. **97–138 Pies and pastries "*Comienza la masa*" [Pastelería (pie making)]**
   - a. 97–102 — Fruit and nut pies
   - b. 103–4 — Savoury pies: veal or kid, squab
   - c. 105–7 — Fruit pies: apricot, lime, and cherry
   - d. 108–9 — Borage and Swiss chard pie
   - e. 110 — List of quantities for making different pastry dough (*reference to chapter on preserves*)
   - f. 111 — Borage meatballs
   - g. 112–22 — Pastries
   - h. 123–8 — Puff pastry (*reference to chapter on sweet biscuits*)
   - i. 129–32 — Additional sweet rolls, pies, and pastry
   - j. 133–8 — Savoury pies and one recipe for sops

5. **139–170 Meat**
   - a. 139–50 — Boar
   - b. 151–9 — Venison
   - c. 160–5 — Beef and veal
   - d. 166–70 — Empanadas with savoury filling

6. **171–85 Sweet pastries**
   - a. 171–3 — Puffs
   - b. 174–8 — Pastries with curds and fresh cheese
   - c. 179 — Fried dough
   - d. 180–1 — Turnovers
   - e. 182–5 — Fried dough

7. **186–316 Dishes for full and partial abstinence**
   - a. 186–200 — **Offal**
     - i. 186 — Calves' feet
     - ii. 187–92 — Kid head

Cookbook Organization

		iii.	193–5	Beef offal
		iv.	196–9	Sausages
		v.	200	Beef tenderloin
	b.	201–50		**Vegetables**
		i.	201–7	Blancmange
		ii.	208–13	Rice
		iii.	214–16	Artichokes
		iv.	217–19	Fava beans
		v.	220–2	Lettuce
		vi.	223–5	Eggplant
		vii.	226	Green almonds
		viii.	227–8	Garbanzos
		ix.	229–37	Squash
		x.	238–41	Turnips
		xi.	242	Cabbage
		xii.	243	Peas
		xiii.	244–5	Spinach
		xiv.	246	Borage
		xv.	247	Fried dough
		xvi.	248–50	More borage
	c.	251–84		**Fish and shellfish**
		i.	252–60	Sturgeon
		ii.	261	Swordfish
		iii.	262–9	Trout
		iv.	270–6	Tuna
		v.	277–80	Lamprey
		vi.	281	Cuttlefish, squid, and octopus
		vii.	282–4	Snails
	d.	285–93		**More vegetables**
		i.	285–9	Truffles
		ii.	290–2	Cardoons
		iii.	293	Onion
	e.	294–313		**More fish**
		i.	294–8	Carp (one includes tench and barbel)
		ii.	299–301	Eel
		iii.	302–3	Barbel
		iv.	304	Sea bream
		v.	305	Sardines
		vi.	306–7	Lobster
		vii.	308	Crab
		viii.	309–10	Oysters
		ix.	311	Shellfish (crab, barnacles, prawns, and clams)
		x.	312–13	Frog
	f.	314–16		Offal: Pig's feet
8.	**317–43 Eggs**			
	a.	317		Egg and nut pie (*announces section on eggs*)
	b.	318–30		Eggs
	c.	331–6		Omelettes
	d.	337–43		Other egg recipes (ends with sops recipes)

(Continued)

Table 2. *(Continued)*

9. 344–82 **Breads, savoury pies and pastries, grain dishes, some miscellaneous and sweet pastries [Pastelería, continued]**
   - a. 344 — Torrijas
   - b. 345–8 — Sops
   - c. 349–50 — Savoury empanadas
   - d. 351 — Quince pie
   - e. 352 — Veal pastries
   - f. 353 — Ham (a little unrelated)
   - g. 354–5 — Cous cous
   - h. 356–7 — Puff pastry
   - i. 358–70 — **Miscellaneous II**
     - i. 358–61 — Kid
     - ii. 362–4 — Beef sops
     - iii. 365 — Boar udder
     - iv. 366–7 — Rabbit
     - v. 368 — Partridge
     - vi. 369 — Savoury pie (mutton and ham hocks)
     - vii. 370 — Another pinwheel recipe
   - j. 371–82 — **Sweet pastries**
     - i. 371–4 — Sweet pies
     - ii. 375 — Puff pastry pie
     - iii. 376–7 — Rolls and bread
     - iv. 378 — Date Pie
     - v. 379 — Marzipan cheese tart
     - vi. 380–2 — Custard pies

10. 383–405 **For the convalescent and lighter fare**
    - a. 383–5 — Sustaining broths
    - b. 386–8 — Broths
    - c. 389–90 — Almond butter
    - d. 391 — Farro
    - e. 392 — Clear chicken soup
    - f. 393–4 — Panetela (bread soup)
    - g. 395–6 — Ginebradas (clotted milk tarts)
    - h. 397–9 — Poultry (blancmange, capon, hen)
    - i. 400 — Rolls
    - j. 401 — Puff pastries
    - k. 402 — Puffs
    - l. 403 — Wafers
    - m. 404 — Fried dough
    - n. 405 — Mostachon cookie

11. **406–19, 429–30 Sauces, vinegars, fats**
    - a. **Sauces and vinegars**
      - i. 406 — Black mustard
      - ii. 407–10 — Vinegars
      - iii. 411 — Pickles
      - iv. 412–13 — Arugula sauces
      - v. 414 — Liver and sops

    b. **Fats**
        i.   415–16   Butter
        ii. 417   Oil, from hard-boiled yolks
        iii. 418   Almond oil
        iv. 419   Roasted butter

12. 420–8 **Cookies and other baked goods [Vizcochería (pastry making)]**
    a. 420   Ladyfingers
    b. 421   Cinnamon rolls
    c. 422   Cookies
    d. 423–4   Ring-shaped pastries
    e. 425   Meringue frosting for cookies
    f. 426   Wine jelly
    g. 427–8   More cookies

13. 429–30 **Pickles**
    a. 429   Pickled eggplant
    b. 430   Olive marinade

14. 431–45 **More pastries [Vizcochería continued (pastry making)]**
    a. 431–4   Sweet biscuits
    b. 435–7   Marzipan
    c. 438–41   More sweet biscuits
    d. 442   Fried cream
    e. 443   Preserved bread
    f. 444   Twists (*reference to chapter on ring-shaped pastries*)
    g. 445   Sweet cream puff pastry

15. 446–9 **Other savoury recipes**
    a. 446   Partridge
    b. 447   Mutton
    c. 448   Roasted pork fat
    d. 449   Roasted quince

16. **450–3 Carving**
    a. 450–1   Poultry
    b. 452   Suckling pig
    c. 453   Hare

17. **454–82 [Conservería (preserving)]**
    a. *"Memoir of preserves"*
        i.   454   Apricot
        ii.   455–7   Peaches
        iii. 458–9   Pear
        iv. 460   Toronja
        v.   461   Lemon
        vi. 462   Borage root
        vii. 463   Red rose sugar
        viii. 464   Borage blossom
        ix. 465   Rosemary flower syrup
        x.   466   White rose sugar

(Continued)

Table 2. *(Continued)*

xi.	467	Squash
xii.	468	Lettuce
xiii.	469	Squash
xiv.	470	Black salsify
xv.	471	Candied dried pear
xvi.	472	Quince
xvii.	473	Candied citron
b.	474–82	*"Memoir of jellies"*
i.	474	Quince
ii.	475	Pomegranate
iii.	476	Plum
iv.	477	Sour grape
v.	478–9	Quince
vi.	480	Plum
vii.	481	Walnut
viii.	482	Fennel
18.	**483–506 Final recipes Miscellaneous III**	
a.	483	Veal
b.	484	Kid
c.	485	Fish blancmange
d.	486	Sweet cream sauce
e.	487	Green citron pie
f.	488	Poultry for the sick
g.	489	Squab
h.	490	Kid liver and lung
i.	491	Venison or veal liver
j.	492	Kid trotters
k.	493	Porridge
l.	494	Mutton
m.	495	Starch
n.	496	Lettuce
o.	497	Sweet eggs
p.	498	Squab
q.	499	Stockfish
r.	500	Mushrooms
s.	501	Almond pastry
t.	502	Sausage
u.	503	Essence of roast mutton
v.	504	Tenderize poultry
w.	505	Golden thistle
x.	506	Chestnut soup

V. Ingredients

Before delving into what types of foodstuffs and modes of preparation are found in Martínez Montiño's opus, we must note that even the most established court cookbook does not reveal the whole story of cooking and eating in the early modern period.

While essential to understanding food practices and culinary history, these works can potentially be misleading because what happens in the kitchen and the dining room is not exactly the same as what is recorded in cookbooks. Priscilla Parkhurst Ferguson's work on food as material object and food as food discourse proves key to understanding this difference. In her monograph *Accounting for Taste: The Triumph of French Cuisine*, Parkhurst Ferguson explains that while cooking and cuisine are interdependent, the former involves material production in the kitchen and consumption in the dining room, while the latter, and here she defines cuisine as the "reading, talking, and thinking about the intellectualized, aestheticized culinary product," is not limited by space and is only limited by the constraints of writing (21).

Additionally, we must consider that not all food consumed had an accompanying cookbook recipe. We know, for example, that for the feast of Corpus Christi in 1605, the Duke of Lerma hosted a banquet for King James I's ambassador to Spain, Lord Charles Howard, where, as part of the starter course, capers, radishes, and asparagus were served, and later, as part of the dessert course, cheeses (Pinheiro da Veiga 83–4). These foodstuffs would not have made it to the duke's table if they were not signifiers of wealth, abundance, and good taste, but rarely are they found among the pages of *Arte de cocina, pastelería, vizcochería y conservería*. Other staples, bread being the most obvious, were rarely included in cookbooks, since bread bakers and cooks were two different professions.

As a third point, anyone who has cookbooks lining the kitchen shelves knows that not all recipes come off the page in equal proportion. Although in his prologue Martínez Montiño is clear that these recipes are his own invention and that they not only have been tested but also have met with the expressed approval of the king, thus implying that there are no frivolous extras, he does sprinkle throughout the recipes comments on which dishes are the king's favourites. Thus, the recipe for chicken pinwheels, most certainly a favourite of the king, was most likely prepared many more times than the recipe "Cómo se puede llevar la carne de un venado veinte, o treinta leguas, sin que se pierda en las grandes calores" [How to travel twenty or thirty leagues in the heat with venison meat and not spoil it] (304; 305). However, with these caveats in mind, we can delve into Martínez Montiño's work and begin to gather evidence of taste in early modern Spain.

If one were to count individual recipe titles in *Arte de cocina*, 502 would be found. Upon closer examination, there are 4 recipes that fall under one single title. For example, Martínez Montiño's signature recipe for "Carnero verde" [Green mutton stew] falls under the title "Otros palominos ahogados" [Another dish of sautéed wild squab] (197–9; 198–200). At times these recipes embedded into other recipes are referenced as individual recipes in the index found at the back of the cookbook; other times, they appear neither in the table of contents nor with their own title, but it is clear that they act as separate recipes. Thus, I suggest that a total of 506 recipes provides a more accurate account.

Included in these 506 recipes are close to five thousand ingredients, and for each recipe I have provided a food category label that is familiar to today's readers: 1. Grains; 2. Meat and poultry; 3. Fish and shellfish; 4. Fruit, vegetables, nuts, and seeds; 5. Eggs; 6. Dairy products; 7. Sweeteners; 8. Fats; 9. Herbs and spices; 10. Sauces and stocks; and 11. Pickles and preserves. It is important to keep in mind that more often than not a single recipe falls within two different food categories. For example, the recipe "Albondiguillas reales" [Royal meatballs] (208; 209) would fall squarely under the single "meat and poultry" category, while "Una torta de limones verdes" [Green lemon pie] (245; 246) would fall under both "fruit," as green lemons are the main ingredient, and "grain," as it is a pie. Thus, the 506 recipes make up 910 different primary food categories (see Table 3).

These data reveal that, together, grain-based dishes and meat and poultry dishes make up almost half (48 per cent) of the options available in Martínez Montiño's cookbook. We can also note that the religious abstinence practices that use vegetables (which form about 8 per cent of the total), fish (6 per cent), eggs (12 per cent), and butter (<1 per cent) to replace meat and poultry play a significant role in the cookbook as well. A full abstinence day is commonly referred to as "día de pescado" [fish day] or "días de Viernes" [Fridays] and signified abstinence from many different meat products. For example, on fish days, *manteca de vacas* [butter] and *aceite* [oil] replaced *tocino* [fatback]. Other substitutes include vegetables for meat, cheese for bone marrow, and garbanzo broth for meat stock. Unlike in other parts of Europe, eggs could be consumed. In the recipe "Otro plato de cabezuelas, y asaduras de cabrito" [Another kid head and pluck dish], Martínez Montiño writes: "Advierte, que esta sopa es muy buena para días de Viernes con huevos estrellados encima" [Note that these sops are very good for Fridays with fried eggs on top] (334; 335). "Comida de sábado" [Saturday meals] consistently reflected partial abstinence practices in which only limited animal products like offal could be consumed. On Saturdays one could eat *tocino* [fatback], as Martínez Montiño points out in a handful of recipes, like "Torta de ternera, o de cabrito" [Veal or kid pie] (247; 248). On *días de carne* [meat days], no abstinence was practised.[11]

In addition to data on primary food categories, I have also analysed over 4,300 secondary ingredients that make up these 506 recipes and classified them into the same eleven categories. What becomes readily apparent, and what is to be expected, is that the lesser categories of fats, herbs and spices, sauces and stocks, and pickles and preserves, which make up only 6 per cent of the ingredients in the primary categories, take on a more significant role as flavour enhancers to the main ingredients (56 per cent of all ingredients), while fish and shellfish virtually disappear as secondary foodstuffs (see Table 4). This shift provides an additional layer of understanding taste in early modern Spain as these data show

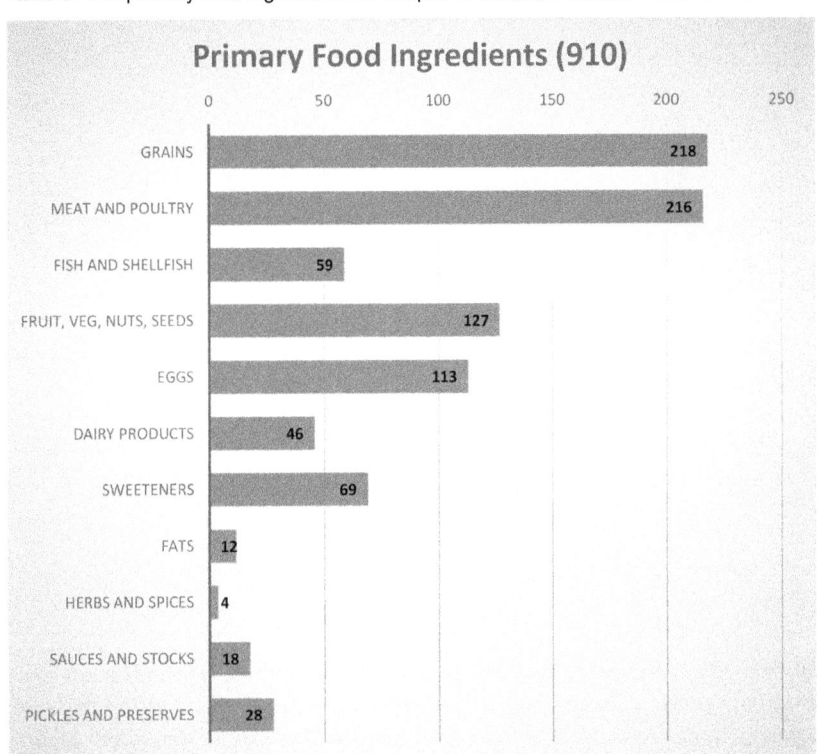

Table 3. 910 primary food ingredients for recipes in Martínez Montiño's *Arte de cocina*

Primary Food Ingredients (910)

GRAINS	218
MEAT AND POULTRY	216
FISH AND SHELLFISH	59
FRUIT, VEG, NUTS, SEEDS	127
EGGS	113
DAIRY PRODUCTS	46
SWEETENERS	69
FATS	12
HERBS AND SPICES	4
SAUCES AND STOCKS	18
PICKLES AND PRESERVES	28

not only what types of dishes were valued and consumed but also how those dishes were flavoured.

Foodstuffs from four hundred years ago and a different continent pose multiple problems. Beginning with vegetables, the many varieties are difficult to identify, and even if we could identify a specific type, how relevant are the flavours of four hundred years ago to today's palette? When Martínez Montiño describes eggplant or carrots, for example, he mentions different varieties by size or colour: "berenjenas, si fueren chicas, que son las mejores" [eggplant, if they are small, which are the best] (358; 359) and "las acenorias para ensalada se han de buscar de las negras" [for carrots for a salad, look for black ones] (220; 221). These clues can point today's reader in the right direction, but selecting the right ingredient is still somewhat of a guessing game. Visual clues from paintings of the same time period can prove useful in targeting a specific variety. The same is true for all animal

Table 4. 4,313 secondary food ingredients for recipes in Martínez Montiño's *Arte de cocina*

GRAINS	444
MEAT AND POULTRY	241
FISH AND SHELLFISH	10
FRUIT, VEG, NUTS, SEEDS	398
EGGS	308
DAIRY PRODUCTS	95
SWEETENERS	358
FATS	447
HERBS AND SPICES	1136
SAUCES AND STOCKS	511
PICKLES AND PRESERVES	365

products. How animals are raised has a tremendous effect on the flavour. One need only consider an egg from a chicken raised on one's own farm to that of a commercial egg to know how different the two are in terms of wateriness, colour, and richness of flavour.

Grains

The following tables provide insight into what foodstuffs were being prepared in the kitchen. In Table 5, we find that Martínez Montiño made his own couscous, prepared different grain-based porridges, and made dough not only from the expected finely sifted, light wheat flour but also from a variety of darker grains. In terms of bakery products, he was particularly proud of the double-baked sweet biscuits that, as I will discuss below, were one of the king's favourites.

Although no recipes for a loaf of bread are found within the pages of this cookbook, bread, breadcrumbs, and sops play a major role in the secondary ingredients. Sops, which appear in over forty different recipes, are described and consumed in a variety of ways.[12] Among those prepared in the royal kitchens, Martínez Montiño discusses white sops, milk sops, golden sops, and cream sops. In the recipe "Capón en Gigote sobre sopa de natas" [Minced capon on cream sops], the sop base

Table 5. Grains and their by-products (primary)

Grains	Bakery product	Bread product
Barley (*cebada*)	Bar (*tabletas*)	Bread (*pan*)
Couscous (*alcuzcuz*)	Biscuit, sweet (*bizcocho*)	Breadcrumbs (*migas*)
Farro (*farro*)	Cake (*torta*)	Empanada (*empanada*)
Rice (*arroz*)	Cookie: mostachon (*mostachones*)	Fried bread (*picatoste*)
Wheat (*trigo*), germ (*salvo*) and semolina (*sémola*)	Fried dough (*frutas de …*)	Rolls (*panecillos*)
	Pastries (*pasteles*)	Sops (*sopa*)
Flour	Pastry, ring-shaped (*bollo roscón*)	Torrijas (*torrijas*)
Flour (*harina*)		Turnover (*empanadilla*)
Rice flour (*harina de arroz*)	Pastry, round (*bollo*)	
Starch (*almidón*)	Puff pastry (*hojaldre*)	
Wheat flour (*harina de trigo*)	Puff pastry pie (*costrada, hojaldrilla, pastel hojaldrado*)	
Dough	Pie (*torta*)	
Dark (*masa negra*)	Puff (*buñuelo de viento*)	
Light (*masa blanca*)	Roll (*bollo*)	
Rye (*centeno*)	Tart, cheese (*quesadilla*)	
Whole wheat or with bran (*cemite*)	Tart, clotted milk (*ginebrada*)	
	Tartlet (*cazolilla*)	
	Twist (*tableta de masa*)	

is made of sweet biscuits instead of slices of bread and soaked in cream, egg yolks, and milk instead of the more common stock or broth (144; 145). And if that weren't rich enough, next the sops are covered in layers of sugar and cream and baked on low. The grilled capon is then served on top. Other recipes call for sweet sops with sugar, cinnamon, and a cottage or ricotta cheese; or drunken sops, soaked in wine, simple syrup, pork fat, and cinnamon. Portuguese-style sops specify hand-torn rolls soaked in beef broth and served with dill, pennyroyal, summer savory, and a lot of cilantro. There are even faux sops that replace the cream with milk and soft cheese, and replace the beef broth with collard greens and their broth. Finally, in "Sopa de calabaza redonda" [Sops of round squash], bread is not used at all; rather, slices of fried squash replace the bread and are again combined with fresh cheese, sugar, and cinnamon (370; 371).

Martínez Montiño includes popular types of breads in different recipes as well. For example, in some recipes for *migas* [breadcrumbs], *torrijas*, and sops, he insists that *mollete* bread be used. *Molletes* are rolls with a soft and often sweet

crumb.[13] And in the recipe "Bollo de mazapán, y manteca fresca" [Marzipan and butter roll], he begins with *mollete* dough (484; 485). The popular candeal bread, known for its characteristic dense, white crumb, light crust, and round shape, is also referenced in his cookbook. For a handful of recipes, he references leaven dough like that for candeal bread. He also cites candeal wheat and candeal rolls in other recipes. Apart from *mollete* rolls and candeal rolls, Martínez Montiño also alludes to Madrid rolls and San Nicolás rolls at different points in his cookbook.

Pastries, the other big contributor to this category, include dough, pie crust, pastry sheets, pastry shells, puff pastry, tarts, and turnovers. In fact, Martínez Montiño is among the first to include instructions for laminating dough, a key step in making puff pastry. Sometimes, as is the case with dough, the ingredient is even used as an instrument in the baking process. In "Ánades estofadas" [Stewed duck], dough is wrapped around the lip of the pot to regulate the amount of steam that is released from the dish: "pondrás un borde de masa a la olla, y asentarás otra ollita llena de agua sobre la olla de los anadones; de manera que ajuste muy bien con la masa" [cover the lip of the pot with an edge made of dough and place on top of this duck pot another pot filled with water so that the dough seals the pot very well] (164; 165). This creative technique of sealing the pot with dough and placing another pot on top is a prototype for the pressure cooker that was designed later in the seventeenth century by French physicist Denis Papin. Martínez Montiño uses this technique in several recipes.[14] We also continue to see a variety of grains and flours, including barley, wheat germ, semolina, and fine wheat bran.

Ten different recipes for sweet biscuits appear in the cookbook, giving them a privileged position within the pastry-making section. The first recipe, "Memoria de los bizcochelos" [Memoir of ladyfingers], contains the basic flour, sugar, and egg combination but is unusual in its flavouring, since most sweet biscuit recipes include anise (526–8; 527–9). Indeed, anise-flavoured *bizcocho* cookies have endured across the centuries and continue to be recognized as a defining part of Spanish cuisine today. Here, however, rose water and musk are added instead. The dough is kneaded a little, rolled out, and cut lengthwise on the diagonal into finger-sized pieces. They are then double baked in the oven. Another version is flourless and does include the standard anise flavouring (537, 538). Another provides the proportion of one ounce of flour for each egg (538–40; 539–41), while another substitutes starch for flour (542; 543), and still others specify without a glaze topping (542–4; 543–5). Other recipes use rice flour or a combination or different flours and different baking techniques (548–50; 549–51). The first recipe for "Bizcochillos secos" [Mini dry sweet biscuits], and there are three of them, is significant because at the end of it Martínez Montiño makes the only note in the entire cookbook that addresses the queen's preferences: "Su Majestad de la Reina nuestra señora suele gustar

destos bizcochillos" [Her Majesty the Queen our lady likes these mini dry sweet biscuits very much] (548; 549).

Meat, Fowl, Fish, and Shellfish

Table 6 gives today's readers a sense of the extensive meat, poultry, and fish options that were prepared in the royal kitchens. To begin, beef and veal appear in dozens of recipes: in twenty-eight, beef or veal is the main ingredient, in twelve, offal is the main ingredient, and an additional thirty-seven recipes include bone marrow. Martínez Montiño includes expected cuts like tenderloin, beef brisket, or veal shank and prepares them in many ways, including roasted, grilled, ground into meatballs or sausage; pounded and rolled up into pinwheels; as main ingredients in empanadas, pies, stews, and salpicon; as stuffing for poultry dishes; and as the main ingredient in one of his couscous dishes or in a handful of recipes for sops. In his recipe "Empanadas de ternera" [Veal empanadas] he provides an overview of the value of veal.

> La carne de la ternera, ya se sabe, que lo mejor es echarla en adobo, y comerla asada con salsa de oruga: de las piernas puedes hacer empanadas frías y calientes, como está dicho atrás en las del jabalí. Los pechos en sal y cocidos son muy buenos, y rellenos, y tostados sobre alguna sopa, o sobre arroz de grasa también son buenos: *la carne de la ternera es la que se acomoda en más cosas de platillos y rellenos, y empanadas Inglesas picadas, y de la carne del pecho entero:* y así no hay para qué comenzar cosa tan larga, sólo pondré aquí un platillo de los huesos. (310, my emphasis)

> [The best way to prepare veal, as is already known, is to marinate it and eat it grilled with an arugula sauce. The meat from the legs can be made into empanadas both cold and hot, as is already explained in the boar (recipes). The breasts, salted and boiled, are very good, or stuffed, or roasted and served on sops or over rice cooked in animal fat are also tasty. *Veal is what most gets used for individual dishes, as stuffing, and in English empanadas, minced or as the whole breast.* So, there's no reason to begin such a long section. I'll just include here an individual bone dish.] (311)

From these instructions, readers today have a sense of how beef and veal were consumed, what cuts were used in what types of recipes, and that in addition to being marinated (in a garlic, oregano, vinegar, and salt mixture), the meat was often accompanied with an arugula sauce.

In addition, Martínez Montiño provides many recipes for offal. Returning again to the religious practices that dictated eating habits, at least once a week, he would prepare brain, head, intestines, kidney, knuckles, udder, liver, tongue,

Table 6. Meat, Fowl, and Fish and Shellfish

Meat	Fowl	Fish/Shellfish
Farm raised	**Farm raised**	**Saltwater**
Beef and veal (*vaca* and *ternera*)	Capon (*capón*)	Conger eel (*congrio*)
	Chicken (*pollo*)	Dogfish (*cazón*)
Goat and kid (*cabra* and *cabrito*)	Hen (*gallina*)	Grouper (*mero*)
	Squab (*pichón*)	Hake, salted (*pescado cecial*)
Mutton (*carnero*)	Turkey (*pavo*)	Sardine (*sardina*)
Pork and suckling pig (*puerco* and *lechón*)		Sea bream (*besugo*)
	Game birds	Shad (*sábalo*)
	Dove/pigeon (*paloma*)	Swordfish (*aguja paladar*)
Big game	Great bustard (*avutarda*)	Tuna (*atún*)
Boar (*jabalí*)	Ground dove (*tortolilla*)	
Venison (*venado*)	Partridge (*perdiz*)	**Fresh water**
	Pheasant (*faisán*)	Barbel (*barbo*)
Small game	Squab (*palomino*)	Carp (*carpa*)
Hare (*liebre*)	Thrush (*zorzal*)	Eel (*enguila*)
Rabbit (*conejo*)	Woodcock (*chorcha*)	Frog (*rana*)
		Lamprey (*lamprea*)
Offal	**Aquatic fowl**	Sturgeon (*sollo*)
	Crane (*grulla*)	Tench (*tenca*)
	Duck (*ánade*)	Trout (*trucha*)
	Geese (*ganso*)	
	Teal (*zarceta*)	**Shellfish**
		Clam (*almeja*)
	Offal	Crab (*cangrejo*)
		Cuttlefish (*jibia*)
		Gooseneck barnacle (*percebe*)
		Lobster (*langosta*)
		Mussel (*mejillón*)
		Octopus (*pulpo*)
		Oyster (*ostión*)
		Prawn (*gámbaro*)
		Snail (*caracol*)
		Squid (*calamar*)

or sweetbreads. Although today's reader might think of offal as a lesser category of food, in *Arte de cocina* there is no indication of any type of inferiority. In fact, Martínez Montiño often offers great detail and expresses genuine excitement in these recipes. For example, he describes *frasia* [frasia], the part of the small intestines attached to the mesentery, as the best veal dish (306; 307). At times, offal is treated as a side dish, for example in serving "Huevos con

comino" [Eggs with cumin] with beef brain (438; 439). Other times, it acts as a substitute ingredient; for example, beef tongue for brisket in an empanada recipe. This type of substitute was common for partial abstinence days, when offal could be prepared and consumed but not animal muscle. Fully one third of the offal references are linked to marrow, the rich, fatty tissue extracted from the interior of bones.

Marrow is a flavour enhancer for poultry and lamb dishes and even beef dishes such as the "Platillo de artaletes de ternera" [A dish of veal pinwheels] (228–30; 229–31) or "Albondiguillas reales" [Royal meatballs] (208; 209). It is used for seasoning between the skin and flesh of capon, squab, and other birds, and very commonly as part of stuffing for poultry dishes. In his recipe "Como se hacen los rellenos" [How to make stuffing], Martínez Montiño explains the essential ingredients: "todos los rellenos que han de ser cocidos, han de ser de carne sazonada en crudo, y procurar que lleven buen tocino, *y algunas cañas de vaca,* y un poquito de riñonada de carnero fresco, y un poco de agrio de limón" [All stuffing that is going to be cooked should have the meat seasoned while it is still raw. Try to include good-quality fatback, *some beef marrow*, a little fresh mutton loin, and a little lemon juice] (190; 191, my emphasis). Martínez Montiño also includes marrow in rice dishes, casseroles, and even vegetable dishes prepared on meat days. It is also added to pie filling, both savoury and sweet. In one sweet recipe on preserved toronja, Martínez Montiño includes marrow along with meat, dried currants, and pine nuts. It appears in other sweet recipes like lime pie, blancmange tartlets, and Lady pie, something akin to the festive Moroccan *b'stilla* [sweet poultry pie]. Finally, beef bone marrow, together with pieces of hard-boiled egg, is often used as garnish for dishes.

Mutton, like veal, appears frequently in the cookbook: in nineteen recipes as the main ingredient, in another three mutton offal recipes, and in seven in which Martínez Montiño suggests either mutton or veal as the meat that can be used. This is particularly true when the cut of meat is the loin and is used as stuffing for another dish. To provide just one example, in "Artaletes asados" [Roasted pinwheels] Martínez Montiño explains that the filling can be made with either one: "pica un poco de riñonada de ternera, o carnero, que esté granujada" [chop up a little veal or mutton loin so that it is very shredded] (370; 371). In fact, the two are so often interchangeable that in a few recipes Martínez Montiño specifically states to *not* use mutton. This is certainly the case in "Pastelillos saboyanos" [Little Savoy pastries], when he finishes the recipe by stating firmly: "no han de ser de carnero, sino de ternera" [These should not be made with mutton, just veal] (462; 463). He includes five different recipes for preparing a leg of mutton; several for stews, including the famous "Carnero verde" [Green mutton stew] seasoned with spearmint, cilantro, and parsley (200; 201); and still others for meatballs, pies, and sops. Leg of mutton is the basis for four different sustaining broth recipes for

feeding the sick. Sheep's head, feet, mesentery, and testicles are other parts of the animal found in various recipes. Fried testicles are used as a garnish in dishes like "Un plato de madrecillas de gallinas rellenas" [A dish of stuffed hen oviduct] (218; 219) or "Otros artaletes de aves" [Other poultry pinwheels] (152–4; 153–5).

Turning to pork and its by-products, it is surprising that pork itself is only included in a handful of recipes – ten, to be exact, for meat and another nine for offal, excluding lard – given its deep ties to old Christian eating habits. Martínez Montiño has two recipes for roasting suckling pig; one for serving suckling pig, sausage style; another for a suckling pig sauce; and another on how to carve it. Pork loin is at the centre of both "Una olla podrida en pastel" [A pie of hodgepodge stew] (284–6; 285–7) and "Sopa de capirotada" [Capirotada sops] (282–4, 283–5). And he writes fairly extensively on how to make pork sausage, including recipes for "Morcillas de puerco dulces" [Sweet pork blood sausage] (338; 339), "Salchichones de carne de puerco" [Pork sausages] (338; 339), "Chorizos de puerco" [Pork chorizo] (340; 342), and "Longanizas" [Longaniza sausages] (340; 342). There are also a handful of recipes for pig's feet, and a couple that specify high-grade pork fat for making pastry. However, by far the overwhelming majority of references to pork by-product are to lard, which appears in hundreds of recipes.

There are really only three recipes that call for goat meat – actually, more specifically, kid – as the main ingredient: "Artaletes de cabrito" [Kid pinwheels] (194–6; 195–7), "Torta de ternera, o de cabrito" [Veal or kid pie] (248; 249), and "Una empanada Inglesa" [An English empanada] (314; 315). Kid is called for when referring to meat options, while goat is only mentioned in reference to goat milk. Four recipes call for kid stuffing in a recipe for another meat: "Pichones ensapados" [Stuffed squab] (184–6; 185–7), "Otros artaletes de aves" [Other poultry pinwheels] (152–4; 153–5), "Otros artaletes de ternera" [Other veal pinwheels] (194; 195), and "Un plato de madrecillas de gallinas rellenas" [A dish of stuffed hen oviduct] (218; 219). Eight recipes are for kid offal and five use goat milk. Then another two include kid meat or offal as an alternative ingredient and four use goat sweetbreads as a garnish. Finally, eight recipes finish with suggested alternative recipes that include kid meat. For example, at the end of "Cazuela de pajarillos" [Small bird stew], Martínez Montiño writes, "Esta cazuela se puede hacer de cabrito, y de pollos, o pichones, y de carnero, y de menudillos de aves, y de mollejas de ternera, y de cabrito, y de muchos pescados, gastando buena manteca en lugar de tocino" [This stew can be made with kid, chicken, squab, mutton, poultry giblets, kid or veal sweetbread, and many fish when good lard would be used instead of fatback] (226; 227). So, while kid is certainly present among the various meat options, it is rarely principal. Readers can once again note Martínez Montiño's enthusiasm for offal in the recipe "Otro platillo de cabezuelas de

cabrito" [Another kid head dish]. He writes, "Este es muy buen platillo, y no ha de llevar agrio ninguno, salvo algún poco de agraz en grano en el tiempo: y si fuere posible, las cabezuelas no han de ser desolladas, sino peladas" [This is an excellent dish and should not have anything sour added except a few sour grapes when they are in season. If possible, these heads should not be skinned but rather scraped] (334; 335). As mentioned above, offal from various quadrupeds, birds, and fish also plays an important role as a secondary ingredient.

In the sections on boar and venison, Martínez Montiño provides instructions on how to dress the animals after harvesting. He includes several recipes for preserving the meat (salting or making jerky) and even transporting it. Attention to game meat is fitting for a court cookbook, as it reflects the courtly status and rights to hunt game. For both venison and boar, Martínez Montiño includes recipes for tenderloin and empanadas, and for boar he adds recipes for pies. In fact, as is seen in recipes for veal, once again he specifies the cut of meat for the type of recipe. For empanadas, the leg is used, and in one recipe for a boar pie, he specifies the loin next to the tail. However, for another type of pie, Martínez Montiño indicates that any part of the animal can be used: "Tomarás pedazos de carne de jabalí con huesos, y cuero, y todo de cualquiera parte, aunque sean de costillas, o de pechos; porque se pueda empanar de todo el jabalí" [Take pieces of boar meat with the bone in and the skin and everything from any part, even the ribs or the upper belly, because you can make an empanada out of any part of the boar] (294; 295). In terms of big game offal, he has recipes for the tips of deer antlers; venison mesentery, liver, and fat; boar head cheese; and boar udder. At times he compares the two meats, stating that venison tenderloin is better than boar but that boar empanadas are tastier than venison empanadas. For both he recommends serving with *salsa negra* [black sauce].

As for the leporids, Martínez Montiño writes six different recipes for rabbit and six for hare, which include recipes for stewed, stuffed, minced, and wrapped small game. He recommends serving rabbit with a caper sauce and hare with a quince sauce. With the exception of rabbit kidney in recipes for stuffed rabbit, offal from these animals is not discussed.

Fowl

Fowl is an especially complex category, as Martínez Montiño includes a wide variety of options. By fowl, I mean any type of bird fit for consumption, but for the purposes of this cookbook, the term is further divided into two categories. Domesticated fowl or poultry includes chicken, hen, capon, turkey, and squab. Wild or game fowl that is hunted includes partridge, dove, pheasant, woodcock, great and little bustards, and small birds such as thrush, and swift. Additionally, water fowl is a subcategory of wild fowl and includes duck, teal, crane, and goose. Some birds

fall into either category. Such is the case with squab, which can be either farm raised (*pichón*) or wild (*palomino*).

Some recipes are generic in nature and simply call for *ave* [bird, fowl, poultry], *volatería* [fowl], or *pajarillos* [small birds]. Others include specific options for poultry but still allow for flexibility. A common example of this is chicken. Although three recipes specifically call for chicken, many more allow for either chicken or squab or, at times, any other farmed bird. For example, in "Platillo con membrillos" [A little dish with quince], Martínez Montiño writes: "tomarás los pollos, o pichones a medio cocer ..." [Take partially cooked chicken or squab ...] (176; 177). In her book on Juan de Altamiras, Vicky Hayward reminds us of how modes of preparation changed with the seasons and the bird's age. Citing Alonso de Herrera's *Obra de agricultura*, she writes, "the first chicks might be killed in July. But the autumn they would have grown into dark-fleshed braising fowl and by mid-winter they would be fat boiling hens" (*New Art of Cookery* 89). Thus, not only the type of bird but also its age would factor into a recipe.

Among the domesticated birds, hen and capon are the ones that most frequently appear. There are a dozen recipes in which hen appears as the main ingredient, another in which it or other birds could be used as the main ingredient, and six different recipes that include hen offal. *Higadillos de gallina* [hen livers] are the most common, but *sesos de la gallina* [hen brain] and *madrecillas de gallinas* [hen oviduct] are other recipe options. Likewise, capon is exclusively featured in eight recipes and is one of a couple of poultry options in others.

One of the few ingredients imported from the New World is turkey. Generally, it is unusual to find references to New World foodstuffs in cooking manuals of the sixteenth and even seventeenth centuries. This is certainly the case in Spain, where the earliest recipes for produce like the tomato and potato do not appear until well into the eighteenth century. But turkey is the exception and appears in the cookbooks of both Diego Granado (1599) and Domingo Hernández de Maceras (1607) as well as in other European works, like the impressive six-book *Opera* by Bartolomeo Scappi (1570).[15] What is worth noting with Martínez Montiño is that he chooses to foreground the turkey in his opening recipe, "De todo género de asado" [On all types of roasts] (142–4; 143–5), thus giving it a privileged position in his cookbook. Here he suggests roasting turkey on a spit, searing it first on the grill then wrapping it with slices of fatback and finally wrapping it in paper – *en papillote* – to maintain its tenderness. For this roast turkey he suggests grinding up the liver and combining it with roasted almonds, thinning it with broth, sweetening it with cinnamon and sugar, and adding a little lemon juice for added flavour. After boiling, the sauce is then strained through a sieve to give it a smooth texture. Later on, he includes a recipe for turkey giblets, "Una empanada de menudos de pavos" [Turkey giblet empanada] (458–60; 459–61), and at the close of the cookbook he has two recipes dedicated to handling turkey:

"Cómo se han de aparar los pavos" [How to present turkey] (558–60; 559–61) and "Cómo se manen las aves en dos horas" [How to tenderize poultry in two hours] (600–2; 601–3). While this latter title addresses all types of birds, Martínez Montiño singles out the turkey in the opening sentence in a similar way to the opening recipe. "Tomarás el capón, o pavo por las dos alas …" [Take a capon or turkey by the wings …] (600; 601).

Squab, which in English refers both to *pichones* [farm-raised squab] and *palominos* [wild squab], is another popular bird, appearing as the main ingredient in eight recipes and as one possible bird in another dozen recipes. In the second edition of the cookbook, Martínez Montiño highlights the options for a specific dish when he changes the title from "Un platillo de pichones" [A squab dish] to "Un platillo de pichones, o pollos o palominos" [A dish of farm-raised squab, chicken, or wild squab] (172–4; 173–5).

Regarding wild fowl, partridge has, by far, the most recipes. In eleven, it is the primary ingredient, and in another four, it appears as a secondary ingredient or a suggested accompaniment. Roasting is the preferred cooking method, as explained in the recipe "Cómo se aderezan las perdices" [How to prepare partridge] (148–50; 149–51), but partridge can also be consumed in empanadas ("Empanadas de perdices" [Partridge empanadas]) (160; 161), with sops ("Sopa de perdices" [Partridge sops]) (162; 163), as a stew ("Una olla podrida en pastel" [A pie of hodgepodge stew]) (284–6; 285–7), and stuffed ("Perdices rellenas" [Stuffed partridges]) (553–5; 554–6). Martínez Montiño also includes a couple of recipes for essence of partridge. One in particular is for the infirm. Pheasant is referenced in the cookbook but does not have a dedicated recipe. Of the small birds, "los pajarillos oncijeros, y vencejos, y zorzales, y tortolillas" [snared birds, swifts, thrushes, and ground doves] are mentioned in the generic recipe "Cómo se han de asar los pajarillos gordos" [How to roast small plump birds] (226; 227).

For water birds, Martínez Montiño includes recipes for duck and teal, and another for crane. All are served roasted. In his recipe for quince sauce, he explains it can be used with a variety of wild fowl. In addition to "ánades y zarcetas" [duck and teal], "sisones, y alcarvanes [sic] y pluvias, y gangas, y otros pájaros salvajes" [little bustards, stone curlews, plovers, pin-tailed sand grouses, and other game birds] (152; 153) are suggested. Likewise, in several individual fowl recipes, quince sauce is suggested. Three recipes include goose, in which interested cooks learn how to carve big-breasted birds like geese, that one can serve goose with turnips, and that, if need be, goose giblets are an effective substitute for turkey giblets. Although goose liver pâté, the famous *pâté de foie gras*, is more than a century away from being revived and served at royal tables, Martínez Montiño does include a variety of options for poultry liver, especially from hen. In a handful of recipes for pies, fried hen liver is an added ingredient; it is also recommended as a garnish. A liver-based filling with egg, breadcrumbs, and seasonings is added to the already mentioned turkey giblet empanada. Likewise, hen liver is the main

ingredient in one of the three "Torta de dama" [Lady pie] recipes. In this recipe, specifically made for Saturdays, hen liver is mashed up with almonds, sugar, and orange blossom water and then added to an egg-cream mixture and flavoured with rosewater (482; 483). Other puff pastry recipes combine hen liver with veal sweetbreads.

Eating fowl was certainly indicative of social capital. In one of his final recipes, "Cómo se manen las aves en dos horas" [How to tenderize poultry in two hours], Martínez Montiño unequivocally places fowl as the most desired food of all things edible. "En los platillos lo más de las veces los pongo de pollos, o pichones, o aves, y es porque son los más regalados; mas con todo eso se pueden hacer de carnero, y de cabrito, y de ternera, guardando la orden de los que están escritos, y de muchos pescados" [For smaller plates, I mostly use young chicken, squab, and adult birds, and it's because they are the most exquisite. But you can also do all this with mutton, kid, and veal, maintaining the instructions that are already written, and with many fish] (600–2; 601–3). Francisco Valles Rojo further prioritizes various fowl served at the dining table. In his research, Valles Rojo has found that among the farm-raised birds the preference from highest to lowest is as follows: "capón cebado, capón, polla cebada, polla, pavo, gallina, gallina cebada, pollo" [fattened capon, capon, fattened (female) chicken, (female) chicken, turkey, hen, fattened hen, (male) chicken] (238), all of which are found among Martínez Montiño's pages. Among game birds, the hierarchy of preferences is "perdices, francolín, perdigón, buchón, ansarón, ánsar, astarna, zorzal" [partridges, francolin, young partridge, pigeon, gosling, goose, grey partridge, thrush] (Valles Rojo 238). Surprisingly, half of these birds never appear in the king's cookbook. Personal preferences of either the cook or the king might be at play here, or perhaps it has to do with hunting practices of those who supplied wild birds to the court.

Fish and Shellfish

Martínez Montiño includes fifty-nine recipes whose primary ingredient falls into the fish and shellfish category. This includes saltwater and freshwater fish as well as snails and frogs. For big fish, like sturgeon or swordfish, or, as he clarifies, those that don't have bones in their flesh and don't have an odour, Martínez Montiño recommends boiling and frying as methods of preparation. He emphasizes that when cooking in water, it is important to use only a little for fear that the fresh fish will fall apart if placed in too much. If we assess taste by the sheer number of recipes that appear in his cookbook, then it is clear that Martínez Montiño's favourite fish, big or small, freshwater or saltwater, is *sollo* [sturgeon], which lives in both fresh and salt water. Martínez Montiño begins the fish section with this fish and includes nine different recipes. He states that it is the fish that most resembles meat, thus implicitly prioritizing the taste of meat above other dishes.

He then repeatedly uses methods of sturgeon preparation as a base for other recipes. For example, the sturgeon marinade, made up of vinegar, water, garlic, oregano, and salt, is the basis for marinating trout, tuna, barbel, and other fish. Furthermore, in sturgeon and other fish recipes and depending on the mode of preparation, he suggests serving them with arugula sauce, green mutton sauce, black sauce, or quince sauce.

Tuna is another popular fish, appearing in seven recipes. In a recipe for grilled tuna belly, Martínez Montiño seasons it with orange, pepper, and the sturgeon marinade. Other tuna flesh can be chopped up, seasoned, and prepared as empanadas. It is also very tasty when prepared as a stew. He says it is versatile and can be prepared in pies, puff pastry pies, or big pies with black sauce. He underscores the importance of the freshness of fish. In a recipe for tuna, for example, he states, "Este pescado, aunque después de salado tiene un rancio, que algunas personas no lo comen de buena gana, cuando está fresco acabado de sacar del agua tiene muy buen gusto, y se pueden hacer muchas cosas dél" [This fish, when salted, can take on a rancid odour and some people don't enjoy eating it. When it is fresh, just caught from the sea, it is very tasty, and you can do many things with it] (394; 395). He notes that its rancidness even when the fish is salted can overwhelm. Another saltwater fish included in the cookbook is swordfish, but Martínez Montiño mentions several times over that it is not as good as sturgeon.

For freshwater fish, Martínez Montiño affirms that trout is the most exquisite and that it is best served boiled, although it is excellent as a fish stew as well. For "Trucha estofada" [Trout stew], he insists on very specific ingredients, including salted butter from Flanders. Once it is cleaned and in the pot, he adds "vino, y vinagre, y pimienta, y jengibre, y nuez, y una cebolla entera, y un manojito de hierbas – mejorana – y hierbabuena, y un pedazo de manteca de vacas fresca por derretir, o manteca salada de Flandes" [wine, vinegar, pepper, ginger, nutmeg, a whole onion, a handful of herbs – marjoram and spearmint – a slab of butter for melting or salted butter from Flanders] (390–2; 391–3). This is one of only two recipes with a specialty item from Flanders. The other is stockfish, not found in Spain but only imported from Flanders. He explains that it requires soaking in a special alkaline water (596–8; 597–9). Returning to trout stew, for Martínez Montiño this recipe serves as a basis for other fish stews. To this and other fish stews, he suggests adding pears, quinces, or dried currants (391; 393).

Lampreys, eel-like vertebrates that, depending on their species, migrate from freshwater larval habitats to the ocean or remain in fresh water, are best served in a stew or as an empanada. Martínez Montiño includes five recipes. For lamprey stew and lamprey empanada, he prefers that no sweetener is added and instead seasons the fish with *todas especias* or all spices (a combination of black pepper, ginger, clove, nutmeg, and saffron), salt, and wine. For roast lamprey, he explains that a sauce is made from the drippings of the skewered fish, salt, pepper, and nutmeg,

to which he adds either lemon or orange juice (400; 401). But, it is in his recipe for "Lamprea en cecina" [Cured lamprey] where he indicates a flavour combination that more closely aligns with the famed *lampreado* style that appears in other recipes. Here he fries onion and seasons the fish with all spices, wine, and vinegar, to which he adds flour and water and continues to braise the fish. In the end he includes the possibility of adding sugar and a little sourer flavour.

> Las lampreas en cecina se han de echar en remojo, y las lavarás muy bien, y hacerlas pedazos, y freír un poco de cebolla con buena manteca de vacas, o buen aceite, y sazonar con todas especias, y una gota de vinagre, y un poco de vino tinto: luego quemarás un poco de harina, y desátala con agua, y échasela de manera que no sea más de cuanto se bañe, y cueza poco a poco cosa de media hora, o más, y SÍRVELA sobre rebanadas de pan tostado. A estas lampreas les podrás echar azúcar (178r) alguna vez; añadiendo algún poco de más agrio para que sea agridulce; porque desta manera suele salir muy buena. (400–2)

> [Set cured lamprey to soak, thoroughly wash it, and chop into pieces. Fry a little onion in good butter, or good oil, and season with all spices, a drop of vinegar, and a little red wine. Then, toast a little flour, thin it with water, and add just enough of this to braise. Let it simmer for about half an hour or a little more. Serve on slices of toasted bread. Sometimes you can add sugar to this lamprey [recipe], adding a little more sourness so that it is sweet and sour. It turns out very tasty this way.] (401–3)

However, the most curious lamprey recipe is "Un capón relleno con ostiones" [A capon stuffed with large oysters]. Here, once the bird is stuffed and placed on a skewer for roasting, it is wrapped with a lamprey: "Luego tomarás una lamprea fresca, y rodearlo has al capón, atándolo muy bien, y ponerlo has a asar" [Next take a fresh lamprey and wrap it around the capon, tying it tight, and put it on to roast] (186; 187). It is an inventive way to combine the land and the sea in a single dish and must have been visually appealing as well.

There are also three recipes, one for turnips, another for tuna, and a third for fried fatback, that are prepared *lamprea* style. Based on Martínez Montiño's recipes, *lampreado* refers to a dish in which the main ingredient is fried or roasted and has added to it a sweet and sour black sauce with all spices and cinnamon. It should be noted, however, that Valles Rojo defines it more generally as a dish in which the main ingredient is fried with fatback and onion and to which a sauce is added. He also explains that it could also refer to a specific style that, in addition to the above, has water or wine added along with sugar or honey and is served with a sour juice on top (420–1). This broader definition of *lampreado* certainly encompasses the way that Martínez Montiño defines this cooking style.

Carp and eel each have a handful of recipes, while barbel, sea bream, and sardines are the main ingredient in one or two recipes. For preparing carp, Martínez Montiño includes a fun fact. After opening them in half and upon placing them

in vinegar, they turn blue: "echa estas carpas en vinagre que se mojen bien, y velas volviendo que se mojen por todos cabos, y se pondrán muy azules" [Place the carp in vinegar and let them soak a while. Turn them often so that all parts of the fish are soaked. They should turn very blue] (412; 413). This cooking process also appears in German cookbooks from the seventeenth century through today.[16]

For shellfish, Martínez Montiño includes recipes for cephalopods (octopus, squid, and cuttlefish), crustaceans (lobsters, crab, prawns, and langoustines), and molluscs (oysters, clams, barnacles, and mussels). For the smaller shellfish, and here he includes crab, barnacles, and prawns, a simple boil in water with salt and pepper is a great way to prepare them. Also, for those whose shells can be removed, like prawns, langoustines, mussels, and more, a quick sauté in butter and onion and seasoning with all spices, green herbs, lemon juice, and salt is perfect when preparing a stew. Furthermore, simply frying and serving them with orange and pepper is also tasty.

In the recipe for cephalopods he does note twice that they have to be treated with care or they will become firm and tough to eat. He also notes the importance of beating octopus as part of the preparation because of its toughness. Three snail recipes, for stew, stuffed snails, and a pie, are included in this section. In all three, the classic all spices combination and green herbs (like those for green mutton stew) are included, but he also suggests adding fennel and thyme to the first, fennel and cumin to the second, and scalded asparagus tips or rampion bellflower shoots to the third. Thus, the snail recipes differ significantly from other savoury dishes in the cookbook, as their flavouring combinations are unique. Lobster is prepared both boiled, where he suggests black pepper and orange as flavourings, and stuffed, where he adds onion, spearmint, and dried currants (if available). He also highlights the enjoyment of cracking the lobster as part of the full dining experience. The pleasure of eating is also noted in the crab recipe, "Cómo se aderezan los cangrejos" [How to prepare crab], in which he explains, "los señores gustan de partirlos con los dientes, y chupar los tuétanos" [Lords like to crack them open with their teeth and suck out the insides] (424; 425). Regarding oysters, Martínez Montiño explains that the best way to eat them is grilled on the half shell with butter, salt, and pepper and finished with a drizzle of orange or lemon juice. He also states that preparing them in a pie is an excellent way to enjoy them and that they are used for stuffing poultry and as filling in English empanadas. Frogs and frog legs are prepared much in the same way as oysters; that is, seasoned with orange and black pepper. In fact, he notes that this is the most common way to prepare frog. Frog can also be used for making meatballs, a pie, or English empanada, and even blancmange.

Fruit, Vegetables, Nuts, and Seeds

In considering what fruits, vegetables, and nuts were eaten at court, readers (and diners) find a rich variety of options within the pages of Martínez Montiño's work (see Table 7). Quince is the fruit most often used throughout the cookbook,

Table 7. Fruit, vegetables, nuts, and seeds

Fruits	Vegetables
Apricot (*albericoque y albérchigo*), dried (*orejón*)	Artichoke (*alcachofa*)
	Arugula (*oruga*)
	Asparagus (*espárragos*)
Cherry/sour cherry (*guinda*)	Borage (*borraja*)
Citron (*citrón*)	Cabbage (*repollo*)
Currants, dried (*pasas de Corinto*)	Capers (*alcaparras*)
	Cardoons (*cardo*)
Date (*datil*)	Carrot (*acenoria*)
Elderberry (*saúco*)	Chicory (*achicoria*)
Gooseberry (*agrazón o grusela o uvas pin*)	Collard greens (*berzas*)
	Cucumber (*pepino*)
Grape (*uvas*)	Eggplant (*berenjena*)
Lemon (*limón*)	Escarole (*escarole*)
Lime (*limoncillo*)	Fennel (*hinojo*)
Orange (*naranja*)	Garlic (*ajo*)
Peach (*Durazno y melocotón*)	Golden thistle (*cardillos*)
Pear (*pera*)	Leafy greens (*hierbas, hojas verdes, verduras*)
Plum (*ciruela*)	Leeks (*puerros*)
Pomegranate (*granada*)	Lettuce (*lechuga*)
Prunes (*ciruelas pasas*)	Mallow blossom (*flor de la malva*)
Quince (*membrillo*)	Mushrooms, wild (*hongos*)
Raisins (*pasas*)	Olive (*aceitunas*)
Toronja (*toronja*)	Onion (*cebolla*)
	Peas (*arveja*)
Nuts and Seeds	Rampion bellflower (*riponces*)
Almond (*almendra*)	Rose (*rosa*)
Chestnut (*castaña*)	Salsify (*escorzonera*)
Green almond (*almendruco*)	Sorrel (*acederas*)
Hazelnut (*avellana*)	Spinach (*espinaca*)
Marzipan (*mazapán*)	Squash (*calabaza*)
Pine nut (*piñón*)	Swiss chard (*acelgas*)
Seeds of squash, melon (*pepitas de calabaza, de melón*)	Truffles (*trufas*)
	Turnips (*nabos*)
Walnut (*nuez*)	Watercress (*berros*)
	Vegetable pickled/preserved (*en escabeche*)
	Legumes
	Fava bean (*haba*)
	Garbanzos (*garbanzos*)
	Lentil (*lenteja*)

appearing as the main ingredient in ten recipes and turning up in several others. He creates quince sauces to accompany duck, chicken, squab, lamb, and even sturgeon and trout. For an abstinence day meal, he includes "Garbanzos dulces con membrillos" [Sweet garbanzos with quince] (362; 363) that is served on a bed of strips of puff pastry. He also makes jam, jelly, and paste with quince, preserves them, and even has a recipe for roast quince with cinnamon, clove, and just the right amount of orange blossom water. Like most of the other fruit, quince also fills pies and puff pastries.

At the time of the publication of Martínez Montiño's cookbook, the fruit *albérchigo*, which today is known as a type of peach, was understood as a type of apricot. Alonso de Herrera, author of *Obra de agricultura* [Treatise on agriculture] (1513) (132), Andrés Laguna, who translated into Spanish and commented on Dioscorides' *De Materia Medica* [On medical substances] (1555) (I.186), and Sebastián de Covarrubias, author of the first vernacular dictionary (1611) (108) all confirm this meaning. Later, in 1726, the *Diccionario de autoridades* explains that the *albérchigo* is a type of peach (Cambra 10–12). In the general instructions for pie making, *albérchigos* are categorized with apricots and peaches. Martínez Montiño explains that for every four pounds of fruit, one of sugar is needed. Peaches, pears, and plums are also candied, preserved, and pureed. He includes two different peaches, *duraznos* and *melocotones*, and three different plums, monk plums, damson plums, and Genoese plums. Prunes are also suggested as alternative ingredients in a number of savoury dishes. Plums and pomegranates have their own recipes for sauces, primarily served with poultry.

Other fruits used in pies include dried apricots, sour cherries, citron, and dates. At times these pies consist of a pie shell and a single layer of filling, similar to pies eaten today, but other times they are layered, alternating fruit with pastry sheets and sometimes sweet scrambled eggs, as is the case with "Torta de dátiles" [Date pie] (484; 485).

Citrus fruit, primarily lemon and orange, but also citron, toronja, and lime, are the most popular secondary fruits. Lemons and oranges are often used interchangeably, especially when they are drizzled over a dish as a finisher. Lemons, which appear 144 times in the cookbook, are prepared as a sauce, in pies, and then as a secondary ingredient either alone, with cinnamon and sugar, combined with egg yolk, or used with wine. Martínez Montiño also mentions specific types of lemon: the Ceutí and the *poncí*. The former refers to a type of small lemon and the latter to a type of lemon with a thick rind. Lemons, oranges, and also citron are often used as garnishes for suckling pig, roast kid, or even stuffed beef tenderloin. They are also added to salads and used in brines and marinades. Citron is dried and stored for later rehydration and is used much like lemon juice. As seen in the section on fish and shellfish, orange (perhaps zest) is often paired with black pepper and served with sturgeon, tuna, trout, or other fish. Although today the *toronja* translates as grapefruit, this translation in inadequate, since the grapefruit is really a cross between two different fruits that grew in the Caribbean in the eighteenth century. Toronja is actually its own type of citrus fruit and appears

here in two recipes for preserved toronja (222–4; 223–5) and another in which the preserved toronja is stuffed with veal or mutton (566; 567).

Sour fruit, like elderberries or *agraz* [sour grapes or, in liquid form, verjuice], are often used as a vinegar. Martínez Montiño includes two recipes for elderberry vinegar and uses *agraz* in a variety of ways in twenty-one recipes in his cookbook. He uses sour grapes for stuffing, either whole or as a mash, as a garnish, and in his delicious sour grape pie. He includes recipes for making verjuice as both a liquid and a solid to reconstitute for future use; for jelly; and for different sauces, one with the grapes intact and one with verjuice. Both whole grapes and verjuice are added to recipes for poultry, mutton, squash, and offal. They can also be found in a recipe for shellfish. Throughout the cookbook, Martínez Montiño brings the growing season for sour grapes more to the readers' attention than he does for other fruits and vegetables. *Pasas de Corinto* [dried currants] appear several times as a secondary ingredient in a tuna and a lobster dish, and as an alternative ingredient in fish, poultry, and goat dishes, but never as a main ingredient.

Reading through his recipes makes it clear that Martínez Montiño is passionate about vegetables, but the one that rises to the top is, without a doubt, *calabaza* [squash or gourd].[17] Not only are there more recipes for squash than for any other vegetable but also, in his introduction to the vegetable section, he writes: "Las calabazas son muy buena potajería, demás de ser muy buena para enfermos, y para platillos de pollos, o pichones, o aves, y para cualquiera desta volatería" [Squash is a very good vegetable, in addition to being very good for the ill, and for young chicken or squab, adult ones, or any fowl dish] (362; 363). He continues with instructions for preparing the poultry and squash and finishes with a note on the excellence of this dish and a promise to include other recipes: "Son los mejores platillos de todo el año. Ahora pondré aquí otros tres, o cuatro platos de la calabaza diferentes" [These are the best dishes of the year. I'll include here another three or four different squash dishes] (364; 365). Although he states he'll include a few more, he goes on to write eleven in total, which include squash in stews, stuffed, fried, and candied. He also addresses their medicinal properties in dishes made specifically for the ill. To get a sense of perspective, each vegetable averages between two and three recipes.

One wonders if the new squash varieties coming in from the Americas may have something to do with Martinez Montiño's enthusiasm. These varieties include squashes from the *curcubita pepo* species such as acorn squash, crookneck, pumpkin, and zucchini, to name the most well known; from the *curcubita moschata*, which includes butternut squash; the *curcubita maxima*, which includes buttercup squash and the *zapallito* summer squash; and the *curcubita ficifolia*, which includes angel hair or spaghetti squash. He does mention different shapes – long and round ones – that seem to indicate varieties that differ from the bottle gourd already in Spain before explorations of the New World began. But, Martínez Montiño never credits the Americas with introducing new culinary wonders to Spain, even as he opens his cookbook with a roast turkey recipe.[18] Other popular vegetables that

are grouped with squash include eggplant and artichoke, which, like many other vegetables, are prepared boiled, roasted, stuffed, baked in a casserole, and pickled. Cardoons, similar to artichokes but used for their stems instead of their flowers, also appear in three recipes as the primary ingredient.

Borage also plays an important role. This versatile vegetable appears as the primary ingredient in ten recipes, and all parts are used, from the root to the blossom, the stem, and the leaves. Data on the secondary ingredients reveal that green-leaf vegetables like arugula, chicory, collard greens, escarole, lettuce, sorrel, spinach, Swiss chard, and watercress also form part of the royal kitchen. Lettuce, for example, appears frequently as wilted leaves used for wrapping a stuffing and served with poultry. It is also eaten raw or the stalks are preserved. After borage, lettuce appears to be the most popular of the leafy greens, which are written as *hierbas* and also *hojas verdes* or *verduras*.

Enthusiastic about squashes as he is, Martínez Montiño is equally unenthusiastic about turnips. In his recipe "Cómo se aderezan los nabos" [How to prepare turnips], he notes, "Los nabos no es muy buena potajería: yo trato dellos de mala gana, porque soy muy enemigo dellos; porque cualquier platillo donde cayere algún caldo de nabos, se hecha a perder" [Turnips are not a very good vegetable. I am grudgingly including them here, because I really don't like them and because any dish that contains any turnip broth will be ruined] (370; 371). He ends by stating that one should only cook with turnips when they are in season and that, at other times of the year, it is preferable to use kale, cabbage, or other leafy vegetables, "porque los más de los señores gustan dél" [because most lords like them] (372; 373).

Onions, like squash in the primary category, are the most frequently cited secondary vegetable. They appear in 108 different recipes. The most common way they are incorporated is fried or sautéed. However, recipes for onions raw, in a boil, and roasted are also included. In terms of their preparation, Martínez Montiño normally minces onions, but at times they are diced, julienned, or simply chopped. In one recipe he specifies *green* onions to be used and, in several others, there is a generic call for onions without specifying any type of onion, cut, or method of cooking. The closest second is garlic, which appears in only 12 recipes. Both often serve as a base, along with fatback, for many of the savoury dishes.

Martínez Montiño incorporates several other vegetables into his cookbook. Leeks, asparagus, and rampion bellflower shoots are used primarily in fish and poultry dishes. Arugula, capers, and garlic are cited for making specific sauces. Carrots appear in different colours. Golden thistle is one of several vegetables noted for its seasonal use; wild mushrooms and truffles, some of the foraged fruits, garlic, olives, and fennel are among several vegetables used in brines and marinades. Finally, several vegetables appear just once in the cookbook. Among those are cabbage, capers, cucumbers, golden thistle, mallow blossom, wild mushrooms, olive, peas, salsify, and Swiss chard.

Regarding legumes, garbanzos are the most cited. The beans appear in two recipes as the primary ingredient and in another five as a secondary ingredient, and garbanzo broth is used in some two dozen recipes, often on fish days as a substitute for meat broth, to lend "exquisite taste" to a recipe, to thin a sauce or liquid, or even as part of the method to thicken liquid. Fava beans appear in three different stew recipes, peas in one, and lentils are referenced but no actual recipe is included.

Eggs

It should be noted that while eggs are but 12 per cent of the primary food categories and 7 per cent of the secondary, they stand alone with no subcategory like the others. Indeed, eggs were readily available, and it cannot be underestimated how essential to the diet they were at all levels of society. Not exclusively relegated to full and partial abstinence days, they were the basis of the popular egg-vinegar sauce used in so many dishes. They were poached in soups, hard-boiled and added to vegetables and empanadas, and scrambled alone or together with virtually any meat or vegetable. It is not uncommon to find a recipe that requires eighteen eggs, or even two dozen; one elaborate recipe, "Bollo maimón" [Maimon layered pastry], uses three dozen eggs in its preparation (258–60; 259–61)! They were used as a batter for meat, fish, and vegetables; bread was dipped in them before being fried; they were, of course, essential to custards, cream-filled pastries, candied yolks, meringues, and cakes; and they were used as a garnish, particularly as "Huevos hilados" [Candied egg yolk threads] (432–4; 433–5). It is fair to say that eggs are one of the most used foodstuffs, if not the most used, in the cookbook.

Dairy Products

Apart from butter, which will be treated in the fat section, the biggest dairy product is milk, which is used extensively in the production of baked goods: pastries, puff pastries, pies, tarts, and turnovers. The well-known blancmange, a poultry dish cooked in milk and thickened with rice flour, has several renditions in the cookbook. Milk is also significant in custards, vegetable casseroles, white blood sausage, and even fish dishes. Another treat, torrijas, which are slices of bread soaked in a sweet egg-milk batter and then fried and sprinkled with cinnamon and sugar, has endured over the years and continues to be a popular treat, especially during Lent and Holy Week. In total, milk appears in some sixty recipes. As an alternative to cow milk, Martínez Montiño uses goat milk in five different recipes. One is for making butter from goat milk. He incorporates both almond milk, in over ten recipes, and pine nut milk, in two. Cream is also popular. Martínez Montiño includes cream-based recipes

for sops, torrijas, breadcrumbs, cream casserole, and three different pies. Cream sops figure into another handful of recipes, and cream is used in several other pastry recipes.

Although butter and milk are frequently used, cheese references are scarce. Throughout the work, when Martínez Montiño uses cheese, it is generally a semi-soft white cheese, *queso fresco* or *requesón*, which today can be translated as cottage cheese (fresh curd cheese), ricotta cheese (whey cheese), or farmer cheese (curd cheese with some or most of the liquid pressed out). *Leche cuajada* [clotted milk] is very similar to *queso fresco*. Both fall under the category of fresh cheeses; the difference lies in the curdling agent and how much the curds are pressed. In his general instructions for making pies, pastries, puff pastry pies, and other baked goods, Martínez Montiño discusses different fresh cheeses such as clotted milk, farmer cheese, and curd cheese, as filling. He also explains how to turn curd cheese into butter by beating it until it begins to coagulate. Although predominately found in sweet pastries, fresh cheese also appears in offal dishes like "Otro plato de cabezuelas, y asaduras de cabrito" [Another kid head and pluck dish] (334–6; 335–7). Overall its presence is not significant.

Sweeteners

Of all the sweeteners, and there are 427 separate references, sugar is by far the most prevalent. Grated, ground, sifted, clarified, in paste form, as simple syrup, and at several different boiling points, sugar is used in virtually all types of recipes, from game meat and fish stews to baked goods and dinner rolls, from food for the sick to the most delicate of pastries, and from meringue to candied egg yolk threads. In "Pastelón de cidra verde" [Big green citron pie], Martínez Montiño ends the recipe describing the various ways in which the two pounds of sugar are used: "Para este pastel son menester dos libras de azúcar, una para conservar la cidra, seis onzas para el vaso, diez onzas para los huevos hilados" [For this pie two pounds of sugar are necessary, one for preserving the citron, six ounces for the crust, and ten ounces for the candied egg yolk threads] (586; 587), thus exemplifying the diversity of this foodstuff.

In one of the final chapters, "Memoria de conservas" [Memoir of preserves], Martínez Montiño employs various techniques to describe different stages of sugar boiling, today known as thread stage (106–112ºC, 230º–235ºF), soft-ball stage (112–116ºC, 235º–240ºF), firm-ball stage (118–121ºC, 245º–250ºF), hard-ball stage (121–130ºC, 250º–265ºF), soft-crack stage (132–143ºC, 270º–290ºF), and hard-crack stage (149–154ºC, 300º–310ºF). The first four stages produce a sticky consistency, while the last two do not. In "Memoria de Jalea de amacenas" [Memoir of damson plum jelly], he vividly describes the texture of the sugar: "ponerlo a cocer, que haga un punto que se pegue a los dos dedos; y entonces está buena, y se puede poner en sus vidrios" [put it on to boil

so that it reaches the stage where it sticks between your fingers] (576; 577).[19] "Flor de borrajas" [Borage blossoms] is another excellent example of the different stages. Here, Martínez Montiño indicates that the sugar should rise from the thread stage to the soft-ball stage. He later continues the cooking process to the hard-ball stage when almost no water remains in the syrup: "has de tomar libra y media de azúcar, y ponerla a cocer, que esté muy subido de punto, y echar dentro una libra de flor de borrajas, y ha de hervir mucho hasta que haga un punto suave en el dedo … y has de poner el azúcar en un punto, que echando una gota en el agua se quiebre" [Take a pound and a half of sugar, put it on to boil to a high thread stage. Add the pound of borage blossoms and let it boil a lot until it's soft to the touch … It should be at the hard-crack stage so that when a drop of it hits water, it breaks] (568; 569). Martínez Montiño's description of the drop breaking is a sign of the highest temperature stage of sugar syrup. Later, in 1747, Juan de la Mata names each of the different sugar stages in Chapter 2 of his book *Arte de repostería* (6–8).[20] Finally, honey, which appears over thirty times, is often suggested as an alternative to sugar, whether it be as part of a sauce, drizzled over puff pastries, or whipped and thinned with water to use as a glaze for tarts and other baked goods.

Fats

In early modern Spain, fat matters. *Tocino* [fatback], which is unrendered fat, *manteca* [lard], which is rendered, uncured fatback and a semi-solid oil, *manteca de vaca* [butter], and olive oil are the most common, but other forms of both vegetable and animal fat are also used. For both fatback, which is in 135 recipes, and lard, in almost 150, Martínez Montiño distinguishes between different subcategories. For example, sometimes he specifies using *tocino gordo* [extra fatty fatback], other times *tocino magro* [meaty fatback], and still other times *tocino de pernil* [ham fat]. *Tocino de redaño* [caul lard], taken from around the digestive organs, is generally used for wrapping meat.

He often gives options of using fatback or other types of fat; for example, fat tissue from capon or from tuna. Fatty tissue from poultry is indeed popular. Martínez Montiño may specify fat from a certain type of bird, like a capon, or even a specific area of the bird's body, as in the recipe "Un pastel de ave para enfermo" [Hen pie for the sick], in which fatty tissue from around the hen's ovaries is minced into the poultry (280–2; 281–3).

Butter is more prevalent than perhaps expected, given that olive oil and lard are more common in Spanish cooking today than butter is. In fact, in her study of the Spanish kitchen of the nineteenth century, María de los Ángeles Pérez Samper explains that butter was no longer a common ingredient (*Mesas y cocinas* 106). But, in Martínez Montiño's cookbook, *manteca de vaca* [butter] – or as he regularly writes, *manteca de vacas fresca* [freshly churned butter], thus reminding other

cooks to use the best quality butter – is still widely accepted.[21] From sauces and sops to vegetable and meat dishes, to pies and pastries, butter appears in some 150 recipes. He specifically mentions that it can replace animal fat on fish days in several recipes. Moreover, the pastry-making section provides some of the most tantalizing and magnificent sweet treats. This rich pastry section benefits from the long-established Muslim pastry traditions passed on over the centuries in Spain. Pastries and puff pastries, spiral sweet rolls and milk bread, strudel, mini rolls filled with preserves, turnovers, tarts, marzipan rolls, ring-shaped pastries (*rosquillas*), sweet biscuits and ladyfingers, dough twists, and more leave cooks in training with many creative options to explore.

Finally, he uses *sebo* [tallow], a product primarily used for making candles and greasing wheels (Gutiérrez Cuadro and Rodríguez 144), only once when he describes how to dress a recently killed deer (see "Como se ha de aderezar un venado" [How to prepare venison (offal)] [298; 299]).

While some critics have signalled the use of butter and puff pastry in Martínez Montiño's cookbook, no one to date has acknowledged the extent of his sections on *pastelería* [pastry making]. Ken Albala, in his book *The Banquet: Dining in the Great Courts of Late Renaissance Europe*, gets it right when he writes, "The court of Spain in the seventeenth century was absolutely insane for little pies, fritters, and similar tidbits. Practically every ingredient he treats gets put into a pastry" (99). Although Albala recognizes the numerous pies and pastries found in Martínez Montiño's masterpiece, historians have yet to fully contextualize Martínez Montiño as one of the first to record how to make puff pastry.

Herbs, Spices, and Flowers

In terms of seasoning, Martínez Montiño's most popular spice mix, which is used in approximately 30 per cent of the recipes, is called *todas especias* [all spices], and, as he states in his cookbook, consists of *pimienta* [black pepper], *jengibre* [ginger], *clavo* [clove], *nuez* [nutmeg], and *azafrán* [saffron] (202; 203). This distinctive combination gives readers today a definite pathway into what flavours were most privileged at the Spanish court. It is noteworthy that Martínez Montiño left cinnamon out of this mixture, since it is commonly used with these other spices in other cookbooks of the day, like Bartolomeo Scappi's 1570 *Opera*. Although Martínez Montiño is clear on which spices make up his most popular spice mix, he never routinizes the quantities.[22] Other spices do indeed include the popular *canela* [cinnamon], which is used in hundreds of sweet and savoury dishes; *comino* [cumin] and *alcarvea* [caraway], which are found in about a dozen recipes each; *cilantro seco* [coriander], which is used in just four recipes; and *galangal* [galangal] and *granos de paraíso* [grains of paradise], each of which is used in just one recipe.

His most popular herb mix, *verduras* or *todas verduras*, is a combination of parsley, spearmint, and cilantro and is used in close to a hundred recipes that also provide us today with sensual (both smell and taste) knowledge of the early modern kitchen. In her 2014 cookbook, *Sunday Suppers*, Karen Mordechai unknowingly recreates Martínez Montiño's famous green sauce and provides a 1:1:2 proportion of mint, cilantro, and parsley (94). In addition to this popular green herb combination, Martínez Montiño uses *mejorana* [marjoram], which is the most popular of the remaining herbs, *salvia* [sage], *hisopillo* [winter savory], and *ajedrea* [summer savory], and less frequently includes *hinojo* [fennel], *laurel* [bay leaf], *orégano* [oregano], and *eneldo* [dill]. When sage and winter savory appear, it is always in conjunction with marjoram. Fennel and oregano sometimes appear as seasoning; however, they are more commonly used as ingredients in marinades or brines. Bay leaf is used in a couple of ham dishes, for wrapping head cheese, as part of the brine for marinating olives, as a garnish, and, curiously, to flavour fried dough. Here, the bay leaf is dipped in batter and deep fried, and when done, the bay leaf is removed and the batter dipped in honey (376; 377). Finally, orange blossom water and rose water are two aromas that enhance a number of pies, puff pastries, and cookies, and even light savoury dishes such as roasted quince or eggs.

Sauces

In this cookbook I have identified twenty-seven different sauces: those made from poultry, pig liver, or boar; fish; herb- or wine- and vinegar-based sauces; fruit-, nut-, or vegetable-based sauces, including a popular quince sauce; lemon, almond, caper, and barberry sauces, as well as the already mentioned egg-based sauces (see Table 8). *Salsa negra* [black sauce] is quite popular, appearing in several different recipes. Generally, fruit sauces tend to accompany poultry and small game.

Pickles and Preserves

The acidic juices play an enormous role in all of Europe's pre-industrial kitchens because they function as a preservative, as seen for example in the pickled vegetables and brined meats, and they are also used as an antiseptic. In "Una liebre enlebrada" [Hare with *lebrada* sauce], Martínez Montiño writes: "si tuviere sangre la liebre, recógesela, enjuagándola por de dentro con un poco de vinagre y échalo donde está la asadura" [If the hare has blood, collect it by rinsing the insides with a little vinegar; also pour some in with the pluck] (210; 211). In terms of flavour enhancers, vinegar is certainly the most common of the acidic juices, but lemon juice is often cited as an alternative, and at times, orange juice or seasonal sour grapes. Added to stocks and sauces, essential to marinades, used in conjunction

Table 8. Sauces

Sauces	Recipes and other recommended uses
Almond sauce (*salsa de almendras*)	De todo género de asado [On all types of roasts]; Palomas torcaces con salsa de Almendras [Wood pigeons with almond sauce]; Also recommended: Pastelones de lenguas de vaca, o pies de puerco, y para ánades, y para otras muchas volaterías salvajes [Beef tongue pie or pig's feet pie or duck and many other game birds]
Arugula sauce (*salsa de oruga*)	La oruga de miel [Arugula and honey sauce]; Oruga de azúcar [Arugula and sugar sauce]; Cómo se hace la ternera [How to prepare fresh veal] Also recommended: Jabalí fresco [Fresh boar]; Empanadas de ternera [Veal empanadas]; Cómo se adereza el sollo [How to prepare sturgeon]; Olla de atún [Tuna stew]
Black pepper sauce (*pebrada*)	Grullas asadas [Roast crane]; Gigote de liebres [Minced hare] Also recommended: Todas las aves salvajes [All game birds]; Gigote de venado [Minced venison]
Black sauce (*salsa negra*)	Empanadas de liebre [Hare empanada]; Pastelones de jabalí picados [Big minced boar pies]; Otros pastelones picados [Other big minced pies]; Pastelón de truchas [Big trout pie]; Pastelón de atún [Big tuna pie]; Atún lampreado [Tuna, lamprea style]; Enguilas de pan [Eel wrapped in bread] Also recommended: Manecillas de cabrito [Goat trotters]
Boar sauces (*salsas de jabalí*)	Empanadas frías de jabalí [Cold boar empanadas]; Empanadas de jabalí calientes [Hot boar empanadas]
Brenca sauce (*salsa brenca*)	Salsa brenca [Brenca sauce] Also recommended: Aves asadas, o pollos, o pichones, ú otra cualquiera volatería [Roasted poultry, chicken, squab, or any other fowl]
Bruguete sauce (*bruguete*)	Sopa de carpas [Carp served on sops]
Caper sauce (*salsa de alcaparras*)	Conejos [Rabbit]
Egg yolk-vinegar sauce for thickening (*salsa a base de yemas de huevo y vinagre para cuajar*)	Capón a la tudesca [Capon, German style]; Una cazuela de ave [Poultry stew]; and many others
Garlic sauce (*ajopollo*)	Cómo se puede freír, y asar, y cocer un pescado todo en un tiempo, sin partirlo [How to fry, roast, and boil a fish at the same time without cutting it up]; Cómo se guisan las enguilas [How to cook eel]
Jadeo sauce (*salsa llamada jadeo*)	Un platillo de jadeo de manos de ternera [A dish of calves' feet with jadeo sauce]

(Continued)

Table 8. *(Continued)*

Sauces	Recipes and other recommended uses
Lamprea sauce (*salsa lampreada*)	Torreznos lampreados [Roasted pork fat, lamprea style] Also recommended: Lenguas de vaca, y ubres de vaca [Beef tongue and beef udder]
Lebrada sauce (*salsa lebrada*)	Una liebre enlebrada [Hare with lebrada sauce]
Lemon sauce (*salsa de limones*)	Cómo se aderezan las Perdices [How to prepare partridge]
Moreta sauce (*salsa moreta*)	Barbos en moreta [Barbel in moreta sauce]
Mustard sauce (*salsa de mostaza*)	Memoria de la mostaza negra [Memoir of black mustard] Also recommended: De cómo se cuece el jabalí fresco [How to boil fresh boar]
Parsley sauce (*salsa de perejil*)	Cómo se puede freír, y asar, y cocer un pescado todo en un tiempo, sin partirlo [How to fry, roast, and boil a fish at the same time without cutting it up]
Partridge sauce (*salsa de perdiz*)	Sopa de perdices [Partridge sops]; Perdices asadas con aceite [Roast partridge with oil]
Plum sauce (*salsa de ciruelas*)	Palomas torcaces con salsa de Almendras [Wood pigeon with almond sauce]
Pomegranate sauce (*salsa de granadas*)	De todo género de asado [On all types of roasts] for capon Also recommended: Cómo se aderezan la ubre de la jabalina [How to prepare boar udder]
Quince sauce (*salsa de membrillos*)	Las ánades, y zarcetas [Duck and teal] Also recommended: con sisones, y alcarvanes [*sic*], y pluvias, y gangas, y otros pájaros salvajes, y con liebres asadas [with little bustards, stone curlews, plovers, pin-tailed sand grouse, and other game birds, and with roasted hare]
Roast chicken sauce (*pollos asados con su salsa*)	Pollos asados con su salsa [Roast chicken with its sauce]
Sauce for suckling pig (*salsa de lechón*)	Salsa de lechón [Sauce for suckling pig]
Sweet and sour sauce (*una salsilla agridulce*)	Cómo se han de asar los pajarillos gordos [How to roast small plump birds] Also recommended: para todo género de asado, y para higadillos de gallina asados, o fritos, y para carbonadillas de ternera, y de aves, y particularmente para enfermos [for all types of roasts, with grilled or fried hen livers, with grilled fillets of veal or poultry, and it is especially good for sick people]
Sweet cream sauce (*papín*)	Otras empanadillas [Other turnovers]
Venison brown sauce (*salsas negras de venazón*)	Grullas asadas [Roast crane] Also recommended: aves salvajes [Game birds]
Zurciga sauce (*zurciga*)	Capirotada de huevos [Eggs, capirotada style]; Otra capirotada de huevos rellenos [Another stuffed egg recipe, capirotada style]

with sugar or honey for the perfect sweet and sour taste, or mixed with wine or oil, vinegar appears in a wide range of meat, poultry, fish, and vegetable dishes. But the combination of four egg yolks and a dash of vinegar that brings a rich texture and a zesty lift to dishes is found in recipes as diverse as "Pollos rellenos cocidos" [Braised stuffed chicken] (174; 175), "Carnero verde" [Green mutton stew] (200; 201), "Sopa de lechugas" [Lettuce sops] (354; 355), and "Platillo de cabezuelas de cabrito, y de las tripillas" [Dish of kid head and intestines] (330; 331). "Pastel de caracoles" [Snail pie] provides standard egg yolk and vinegar instructions: "cuajarás este pastel con yemas de huevos, y un poco de caldo de garbanzos, y su agrio de limón, o un poco de vinagre. Suelen ser muy buenos estos pasteles" [Thicken this pie with egg yolks, a little garbanzo broth, and the right amount of lemon juice or a little vinegar. These pies are typically very tasty] (404; 405). In fact, this popular flavour combination has its own name: *brodete*. For this egg yolk- and vinegar-infused broth, Martínez Montiño explains that the proportions are eight egg yolks to two quarts of broth.

This preliminary information on main ingredients gives us a strong sense of what was being prioritized in Martínez Montiño's kitchen. Additionally, his side comments, sprinkled throughout the cookbook, create a map of selective tastes that guides both future cooks as they stand ready to serve the king and his royal family and contemporary cooks who are working in the service of other nobility or high-ranking families. His comments give shape to a top-down culinary history that, when examined collectively, shows the pre-eminent role of the cookbook in the formation of Spain's culinary identity.

VI. Taste at Court and the Emergence of Spanish Cuisine

In the royal kitchens of early seventeenth-century Spain, we know that Martínez Montiño was certainly aware of the impact of food on the body and how humoral theory explained a person's well-being. Like other cookbook authors, he does include a section of recipes for the infirm. In Martínez Montiño this is a modest section with only a dozen or so recipes. Additionally, in a handful of recipes beyond that section, he provides medical notations of the potential health benefits of a certain dish. For example, in "Migas de la grasa del venado" [Venison fat breadcrumbs], he writes, "Estas tortillas y migas de grasa de venado, dicen que son buenas para los que tienen cámaras' [It is said that these omelettes and breadcrumbs made with venison lard are good for those who have diarrhea] (300; 301). However, he very decidedly leaves these issues to those who are better suited to address them and, in his cookbook, focuses on creating excellent, tasty food for the king. In the prologue he writes, "Mucho más pudiera escribir, mas he ido dejando las cosas que son muy ordinarias. *Tampoco me he querido meter en oficio de nadie*, mas de lo que toca al oficio de la cocina" [I could have written a lot more, but I have left out the most mundane things. *I have also chosen not to get into others' professions*, only that

which is relevant to the cooking profession] (108; 109, my emphasis). Likewise, in the section for the infirm, he reiterates this position as he discusses why mixing two broths together is beneficial for someone who has fallen ill.

> Y esto digo, porque lo he oído decir a muy grandes Médicos, Y así lo que han de llevar dentro las sustancias, lo han de ordenar los Médicos, porque en algunas mandan echar oro, y en otras rajitas de calabazas, y en otras garbanzos negros, y otras cosas convenientes para la enfermedad del enfermo, que no sean de mal gusto: y en algunas mandan echar tortugas y pepitas de calabaza: y en esto no tengo que meterme, más que sacar muy bien la sustancia. (490)

> [I say this because I've heard very great doctors say this. And whatever is added to the sustaining broths is whatever the doctors prescribe, because some prescribe gold to be added, others, squash slices, others, dark garbanzos and other things that do not taste bad and are advisable according to the illness of the patient. Some prescribe turtle and squash seeds, but I won't involve myself in this except to make an excellent sustaining broth.] (491)

In these side comments, it is made clear that Martínez Montiño consciously limits his comments on foods' effects on the body. Instead, he positions himself as an expert cook and signals the importance of that role: he is a cook, not a doctor or health inspector, and takes pride in his contributions as such.

This stated purposefulness leads him time and again to attend to *gusto*, a word that simultaneously signifies taste and pleasure. Similar to Platina, one of the early humanists who asserts that the pleasure of eating in moderation is essential to maintaining good health and happiness, taste and pleasure are central to Martínez Montiño's project. In fact, *Arte de cocina, pastelería, vizcochería y conservería* directly contributes to the humanist debate on the senses and the role of taste in man's intellectual and spiritual pursuits. In addition to his descriptions and side notes, Martínez Montiño weighs in on the role of food and the evolving understanding of *gusto* [taste] as natural and acquired flavour, as aesthetic judgment (likes and dislikes), and in turn, on how those likes and dislikes establish social norms.

Although the eighteenth-century *Diccionario de autoridades* underscores *gusto* as one of the five senses, it is surprisingly never used that way in the cookbook. Rather, Martínez Montiño employs the word in reference to the flavour of a food item, and in this way reflects the *Diccionario*'s second definition: "Se toma tambien por el sabor que tienen en sí las mismas cosas, o natural, o por haberlas sazonado" [It is also understood as the flavour that things themselves have either naturally or by seasoning them] (4.1734).[23] In Martínez Montiño's recipe, *gusto* is employed both to refer to an ingredient's natural flavour and to the flavour achieved through the cooking process. For a recipe for tuna stew, he explains, "Este atún después de

salado, es muy bueno para hacer una olla que tenga el gusto de la olla podrida de carne" [After it's salted, this tuna is very good for making a stew that tastes like the hodgepodge stew made with meat] (398; 399).[24] In describing a type of empanada made on a rotisserie, he notes, "parecerán empanadas Inglesas en el gusto" [they will taste like English empanadas] (162; 163). In another recipe for boar headcheese, Martínez Montiño warns that if bay leaf is used both as wrapping on the sides and on top, the dish may take on "demasiado gusto el laurel" [too much bay leaf flavour] (290; 291). In each of these cases Martínez Montiño highlights the natural flavour of a foodstuff, whether a meat stew, an English pastry, or an aromatic leaf, that enhances the description of a different dish, such as the fish stew, a rotisserie pastry, or a meat jelly.

By far the most common use of the word *gusto* is also related to this second definition but focuses more on *creating* good flavour through cooking choices. Martínez Montiño reiterates phrases such as: "tienen muy buen gusto" [it has very good flavour] (206; 207, 600; 601), "es de muy buen gusto" [it is very tasty] (181; 182), and "da muy buen gusto" [it provides very good flavour] (209; 210, 249; 250, 429; 430, 513; 514). In the early modern period the sweet and sour combination is still highly valued. Several times Martínez Montiño specifies this combination as both particularly tasty and full of flavour: "es muy buen gusto el agrio, y dulce" [the sweet and sour is very tasty] (173; 174). And it is this way of epistemologically thinking about taste – what is considered tasty and how to produce those flavours – that concerns the master cook throughout his cookbook.

In addition to the ideas of taste and flavour, Martínez Montiño also uses *gusto* in the sense of aesthetic judgment, something that produces pleasure for or meets the approval of a person. Much like the third definition of the *Diccionario de autoridades*, "Significa assimismo propria voluntad, determinación, o arbitrio" [It also means one's own will, determination, or judgment] (4.1734), Martínez Montiño uses *gusto* to express the preferences of his diners. Whether it be the king or queen, a lord of a future cook, or the infirm, throughout the manual Martínez Montiño is sensitive to his diners' tastes. For example, in "Como se hacen los rellenos" [How to make stuffing], he insists that the seasoning be adjusted according to the preference of the one eating: "y en lo que se dice de cebollas, hierbas, ajo ú otras cosas, haste de conformar con el gusto de tu señor" [regarding onions, herbs, garlic, and other ingredients, you need to conform to your lord's taste] (190; 191). The seventeenth-century philosopher Baltasar Gracián also takes up this notion of *gusto*. One critic explains, "Gracián's notion of taste marks a formative moment in the history of values and social class – a moment at which the notions of social relations as fixed and the capacity for judgment as inborn were displaced by the notion of aesthetic judgment as socially formed" (Cascardi 262).[25] We can see, with these running comments sprinkled throughout the recipes, that Martínez Montiño is fully aware of taste as aesthetic judgment and advises other cooks to be sensitive to the changing notions of taste.

Among his recipes Martínez Montiño provides his readers with intimate knowledge about the food habits of the king and queen and implicitly encourages others to acknowledge those tastes. As we know from the work of sociologist Pierre Bourdieu, defining taste is a way to distinguish status and class. Individual subjectivities are continually produced in tension with others and practised, mostly unconsciously, in everyday habits like eating. Thus, knowing how to eat like the king becomes a signifier of taste, status, and social class.

As he shares with readers the king's and queen's food preferences, Martínez Montiño provides opportunities to emulate their acquired tastes, thus shaping taste and food choices for the Spanish elite and others on down the hierarchical social ladder. Remember that during Philip III's own lifetime, *Arte de cocina* was published at least three times and then seven more times throughout the seventeenth century. For example, from Martínez Montiño's notes attached to various recipes, readers learn that Philip III regularly ate roast partridge brushed lightly with olive oil instead of lard (476; 477), that he preferred meatballs made from poultry (204–6; 205–7), that he liked his chicken pinwheels – which are normally filled with hard-boiled egg yolk seasoned with mint, pepper, nutmeg, ginger, and a little lemon juice – on the sweeter side (192; 193), and that he liked his cookies with only a light spice flavour (510; 511). Considering all these preferences together, one could surmise that the king had a sensitive or perhaps even bland palate.

The king's taste in food does not go unchallenged. In this pinwheel example, Martínez Montiño suggests that the king's preference may not necessarily agree with his own: "He puesto esta manera de artaletes, no porque son los mejores, sino porque son los que su Majestad come mejor" [I've included this recipe for pinwheels not because they are the best but because they are the ones His Majesty likes to eat] (192; 193). In terms of cookies, which normally were flavoured with anise, Martínez Montiño explains, "A todos los bizcochos se les suele echar anís, aunque yo no lo echo a ningunos, porque su Majestad no gusta dello" [For all these sweet biscuits, anise is generally added, but I never add it, as His Majesty does not like it] (540; 541). Again, he makes the point that the king's taste differs from others. In "Memoria de los mostachones" [Memoir of mostachon cookies], he ends the recipe with the following side note: "Estos son los que más gusto suelen dar a su Majestad, porque están moderados en especia: otros los quieren más picantes de especias" [These are the ones that His Majesty likes most because they are moderately spiced. Others prefer them with a sharper spice flavour] (510; 511).[26]

As mentioned previously, ten different recipes for sweet biscuits appear in the cookbook. The first recipe, "Memoria de los bizcochelos" [Memoir of ladyfingers], is unusual in its flavouring, since most sweet biscuit recipes include anise. Here, however, rose water and musk are added (526–8; 527–9). It is quite possible that Martínez Montiño included this one first in response to the king's

dislike of anise. Likewise, "Bizcochillos secos" [Mini dry sweet biscuits] is significant because at the end of it Martínez Montiño makes the only note in the entire cookbook that addresses the queen's preferences: "Su Majestad de la Reina nuestra señora suele gustar destos bizcochillos" [Her Majesty the Queen our lady likes these mini dry sweet biscuits very much] (548; 549). Undoubtedly, the *bizcochos* that take such a prominent position in the cookbook itself, that define the taste of both king and queen, and that, years later, inform a petition of compensation for Martínez Montiño's life work, play more than just a small role in the shaping of Spanish culinary history. Indeed, anise-flavoured *bizcocho* cookies have endured across the centuries and continue to be recognized as a defining part of Spanish cuisine today.

How should readers today interpret these critiques of taste? Are they simply to call attention to the king's preference so that others know and can react accordingly? Or is Martínez Montiño taking this opportunity to participate in the construction of a national cuisine and exercise his position as author and master cook in that very construction? It certainly would not be the first time that he exercised his authority in his work. Readers know that he is particularly proud of a certain dish when the recipe ends with a superlative. For example, in "Otras empanadillas de criadillas de tierra" [Other truffle turnovers], he concludes: "La masa se decir, que es de las mejores que se hacen" [It is said that this dough is one of the best that is made] (314; 315). Many times, he also underscores what a cook must know with phrases like "es necesario saberlos hacer" [it is imperative to know how to make …] or "el toque de … está en …" [the secret to … is in …]. At times he even states what a stickler he is: "Y no te parezca que soy enfadoso en esto, porque todo el toque de ser oficial uno, está en saber hacer bien los platillos" [Don't think I'm being annoying with this point, because the secret to being number one is in knowing how to make these dishes] (374; 375). This message both shapes the formation of future cooks in Spain and solidifies Martínez Montiño's role in fostering excellence in the Spanish kitchen. He knows that to get to be *oficial uno* one has to be attentive to this level of detail.

Throughout the recipe book Martínez Montiño remains attentive to conforming to the diner's taste. He often provides an either-or variation on a recipe and reminds cooks that their choice of preparation is dependent upon their lord. We see this, for example, in the recipe "Una olla podrida en pastel" [A pie of hodgepodge stew] when he closes with "Se les suelen echar aceitunas fritas, y algunas castañas: mas algunos señores no gustan dello, ni yo soy aficionado a echarlo" [Fried olives and some chestnuts are often included, but some lords don't like them, and I am not a fan of including them] (286; 287). In another example he offers the option of adding dill to a bean stew but cautions once again to heed the taste of the one for whom it is being prepared: "A estas habas se suele echar un poco de eneldo, mas algunos señores no gustan de él" [It is common to add dill to

these beans, but some lords don't like it] (354; 355). Other times, however, he leaves these detail-oriented decisions to the discretion of the head cook. For example, in deciding how to stuff turnovers, how much sugar to add, or whether to include garlic or not, Martínez Montiño insists that it be left up to the discretion of the head cook (312–14; 313–15, 430; 432, 418; 419).

When addressing issues of taste, Martínez Montiño weighs in on issues of class in no uncertain terms. In describing an omelette made with honey and beef fat, he insists that these eggs are better for "frailes, y gente ordinaria, que para señores" [monks and regular people than for lords] (436; 437). Questions of the diner's taste involve decisions not only about ingredients but also how to serve the dishes. In several shellfish recipes, Martínez Montiño includes how to serve them and insists that the shell be left intact. In "Langosta rellena" [Stuffed lobster], the visual image is delightful: "luego harás una sopilla, y pondrás la concha rellena en medio, y pondrás alrededor las piernas con sus conchas, porque gustan los señores de partirlas" [Next, make sops and put the stuffed lobster in the middle and put the legs in their shells around it because lords like to crack them open] (424; 425).

Regional Foodstuffs and Recipes

Let us move beyond the individual preferences of the king and turn to the regional and international dishes Martínez Montiño chooses to include in his cookbook, as they too act as signifiers of taste in addition to being building blocks in creating a consciously Spanish cookbook. Foodstuffs and dishes from a variety of regions promote the idea that Spain's culinary heritage comes from diverse sources and that, as author, Martínez Montiño brings the best of those together. Examples include a scrambled egg dish that, as Martínez Montiño reminds us, is elsewhere called "los huevos de Tolosa" [Tolosa eggs] (442; 443) and "Sopa de Aragón" [Sops, Aragonese style] (520; 521). "Migas de nata" [Breadcrumbs with cream] (238; 239) and "Bollo fitete" [Fitete roll] (268–70; 269–71) both contain *názulas*, which, according to Covarrubias, was a regionalism for *requesón* [curd cheese] used in and around Toledo (690), thus highlighting a product from that area. Although none of these recipes indicate why they are distinctive to their respective region or city, they do serve as markers for Martínez Montiño's comprehensive spirit as he brings to court recipes and ingredients from different areas of the country.

In addition, he notes the quality of specific regional products, like oil from Valencia in "Conejos en mollo" [Rabbit in mollo broth] (154; 155). For this, he first roasts the rabbit, then fries onion seasoned with pepper, nutmeg, and ginger. Next, he combines the rabbit and some stock with the spice mixture. He then adds vinegar and saffron, and as he brings the recipe to a close, he insists, "esto se entiende, que ha de ser con buen aceite de Valencia, o con otro aceite que sea muy bueno" [It is understood that good Valencia oil should be used or another excellent (quality) oil] (154; 155). Likewise, he insists on excellent quality pork fat from the

city of Garrovillas in Extremadura. In his recipe "Pasteles de carnero, y de pernil de tocino" [Mutton and fatty ham pies], he begins, "Tomarás unos torreznos de buen tocino de Garrobillas" [Take some good-quality pork belly from Garrovillas] (478; 479). And in "Sopa borracha" [Drunken sops] he also notes, "asarás torreznos de las Garrobillas o de otra parte que sean buenos, y no tengan sal" [roast pork belly from Garrovillas or from another place with good quality and that is not salted] (454; 455). Like the famous master cook, writers of the day, among them Cervantes, Quevedo, and Tirso de Molina, frequently noted the excellent quality of ham that came from Garrovillas (Nadeau, *Food Matters* 112).

Other times in his cookbook, Martínez Montiño uses lexicon from different regions, again indicating a possible origin for that particular recipe. In providing instructions for "Cazuelas de acenorias, y pescado cecial" [Carrot and salted hake stew], he uses the word *tarazón* to refer to a slice (220; 221). Nuria Polo Cano, in her work on kitchen lexicon from the seventeenth century, points out that *tarazón* is one of the few culinary terms that comes from Leonese and means *a piece of something*, especially of meat or fish (240). Something similar is occurring in the recipe "Empanadas de pollos ensapados" [Stuffed chicken empanadas]. According to Lluis Gimeno Betí, *ensapado*, from the verb *ensapar-se*, means "posar-se fart, replé de menjar, i més de beure aigua" [to become full, from food and more so from drinking] (99). Thus, the adjective is another way of referring to the *stuffed* birds. The Catalan root of the word suggests that the recipe may have its origins in Catalunya.

Muslim/Morisco Heritage

In addition to the regional references scattered throughout, Martínez Montiño also includes a series of dishes that have clear ties to Spain's Muslim heritage and contemporary Morisco communities. Dishes with ties to Islam are nothing new for cooking manuals on the Iberian Peninsula. In fact, essentially all of them, the *Libro de Sent soví* [The book of Sent soví], *Manual de mugeres* [Manual for women], Mestre Robert's *Llibre del coc* [Book on cookery] or its translation (Ruperto de Nola's) *Libro de guisados*, and Hernández de Maceras' *Libro del arte de cocina* [Book on the art of cooking] contain several Muslim or Morisco-inspired recipes.[27] In Martínez Montiño, "Bollo maimón" [Maimon layered pastry] (258–60; 259–61), "Gallina morisca" [Morisco-style hen] (182–4; 183–5), "Gallina a la morisca" [Hen, Morisco style] (504; 505), and "Cazuela mojí de berenjenas" [Moxi eggplant casserole] (358; 359) all contain Muslim or Morisco signifiers in their titles. For example, the word *maimón* comes from the Arabic *maímun* [happy], and *Morisco* of course refers to the Muslim population that was forcibly converted to Christianity. While these two Morisco-style dishes vary little from other poultry dishes in the same section, it is notable that Martínez Montiño includes both wine and lard in the former and lard in the latter, thus emphasizing the Christian elements of the Morisco

dish. More than any single cooking style or ingredient, these recipes acknowledge Muslim influences in Spanish cooking through their very titles.

While meat choices, particularly pork, instantly segregated social groups in the early modern period, an individual's taste for specific vegetables underscored common eating practices across social and ethnic divides. This is certainly the case with eggplant, popular among Muslim, Jewish, and Christian communities. From fictional primary sources of novels and plays in which the lower classes savoured the same vegetable dishes as those recorded in Martínez Montiño's court cookbook, we get a sense of some of the central tastes of Spanish cuisine.

In Francisco Delicado's 1528 picaresque novel, *La lozana andaluza* [Portrait of Lozana], the main character, the Jewish *conversa* Aldonza, reminisces about her grandmother's kitchen. In her culinary catalogue of early modern working-class dishes, she includes "caçuela de berengenas moxíes en perfición; caçuela con su agico y cominico, y saborcico de vinagre, esta hazía yo sin que me la vezasen" [her twice-baked eggplant casserole, to perfection; a casserole with a little garlic, a pinch of cumin and a hint of vinegar, I could make this without anyone having to show me] (Delicado 178).[28] Cervantes would later include this same casserole in his play "Los baños de Argel" [The baths of Algiers], in which a sacristan and a Jew appear on stage, the former holding the dish and both desiring to eat what is truly a taste sensation. In Martínez Montiño's rendition, he also includes cumin but does not suggest either garlic or vinegar, which again indicates the evolution of the dish, or perhaps just personal preference. Martínez Montiño boils slices of small eggplants, drains them, and sets them aside. He then mixes together cheese, breadcrumbs, and eggs, seasoned with cinnamon, caraway, and his favourite spice mix, all spices. To that mixture he adds half of the eggplant in sliced form and half minced. The casserole is then placed in the oven to bake on low, and as a finisher more cheese is added to form a top crust (358; 359).

Recipes that focus on Muslim and now Morisco culinary contributions at a time when the crown is systematically eradicating cultural artefacts such as Arab clothing and language and actively expelling Moriscos from the country brings to the forefront the primacy of food in the formation of Spanish cultural heritage. We can recall that Martínez Montiño's recipes were scrutinized at three different government levels over the course of a year, first by the secretary of the Royal Patrimony, then by the "corrector general," and finally by the clerk of the king's chamber and resident clerk to his council, and at no point were these recipes expunged from the book in ways that would be analogous to the fate of the very people who inspired them. This may, in part, be a result of the fact that, by the dawn of the early modern period, foodstuffs commonly associated with Islam were so deeply entrenched into the food habits of the Iberian Peninsula that recipes containing either these foodstuffs or the very word *Morisco* in their titles would no longer pose a threat to institutional

hegemony, and that food practices more generally were able to rise above the political hostility toward Moriscos.

However, there is one significant feature to Martínez Montiño's cookbook that suggests a greater intentionality to the Morisco recipes he includes. Between the thirteenth century, when two Hispano-Muslim cooking manuscripts, *Fuḍālat-al-Hiwan* by Ibn Razīn al-Tujībī and the anonymous *Kitāb al-tabīj*, were compiled, and the twentieth century, Martínez Montiño is the only author to include couscous recipes in any cookbook authored within the borders of Spain.[29] There is no doubt that couscous was a distinctive marker of Muslim identity. Both Inquisition records and apologists' treatises demonstrate this tacit connection when describing cultural habits of Moriscos.[30] And while these common cultural practices of preparing and consuming couscous were often implicated in demonstrating alleged heretical activity, Martínez Montiño debunks these notions as he celebrates couscous recipes in his cookbook.

The first of two couscous recipes details how to make couscous from scratch, an art form that only survives today in parts of the Maghreb. In his second recipe he describes how to serve meat and vegetables on a bed of couscous. Like his Hispano-Muslim predecessors, Martínez Montiño stresses the importance of preparing couscous by rubbing carefully with one's hands the mixture of *harina floreada* [finely sifted flour] and *cemite* [bran flour]:

> irás trayendo la mano extendida por encima la harina, y siempre a una mano; luego tornarás a echar más agua con el hisopillo, y andar con la mano extendida sobre la harina: y de cuando en cuando meterás la mano y revolverás el harina lo de arriba abajo: y desta manera irás haciendo hasta que el harina ande haciéndose muchos granillos, y que no tenga polvo. (464)

> [Begin pulling your extended hand through the flour, always with one hand. Then sprinkle more water on with the hyssop brush and continue moving your extended hand through the flour. Every once in a while, you must dip your hand into the flour and move it around top to bottom, and in this way, you will continue preparing it until all the flour forms little beads and no flour remains.] (465)

He also notes the specific pot necessary for preparing the dish and, anticipating that his readers may not be familiar with it, he describes it in detail: "luego échalo en su alcuzcucero, que es una pieza de barro, o de cobre con muchos agujerillos en el suelo un poco angosto y romo de abajo, y ancho y abierto de arriba" [then place it in the couscoussier, which is a pot made of clay or copper that has a flat, narrow bottom with many small holes and is wide and open on the top] (464; 465).

Several factors indicate that Martínez Montiño takes great care in preparing this recipe and that he shows no disrespect for its Berber origins. First, these two recipes are among the most extensive and detailed of the entire collection.

He distinguishes the type of grains needed to make couscous, how the water should be sprinkled over the flour, and the care involved in touching the mixture. In addition, his instructions reflect an emotional attachment to the dish not characteristic of his writing. For example, for boiling the liquid, he writes, "pon la olla sobre la lumbre que cueza *amorosamente*" [Put the pot over the flame and let it *(lovingly) gently* boil] (464; 465, my emphasis). This is the only time in his cookbook that Martínez Montiño uses this adverb. Could it be that as master cook he is keenly aware of the important culinary contributions from Spain's Muslim past and is consciously preserving that history within the pages of his Spanish cookbook? Could it be that he is intentionally subverting official ideology because he fundamentally understands that transforming cultural, and specifically culinary, practices into grounds for expulsion threatens the very culinary Spanish identity that he is trying to build? Today, it is impossible to know with any certainty why he included couscous recipes in his work, but their existence is a testament to the culinary diversity and rich cultural heritage that Martínez Montiño outlines in his court cookbook.

International References

The intentionality of both regional and ethnic recipes is also seen at the international level, particularly when Martínez Montiño incorporates Portuguese recipes into his work. The author himself brings to light his connection with Portugal when he reminds the king of his service to Philip II's sister, the Princess Juana of Portugal, whom he served for five years before transferring to the court in Madrid in 1586. In addition, by 1611 Portugal had been part of the Spanish crown for over thirty years. Thus, Portuguese nobles were present at court, particularly serving the king in political and economic affairs that directly affected Portugal. In fact, any decision the king made regarding Portugal was first discussed with his advisors who made up the Council of Portugal.[31] It is within this context that we can understand why Portugal figures so prominently in Martínez Montiño's cookbook.

Recipes *a la Portuguesa* [Portuguese style] include soup (472; 473), fowl (180–2; 182–3), spinach (376; 377), rice (348; 349), and fish (472; 473). Sometimes Portuguese words filter into recipes, as is the case with his use of *pimienta longa*, Portuguese for *pimienta larga* [long pepper], in the recipe "Gilea de vino" [Wine jelly] (532–4; 533–5).[32] What makes them "Portuguese" may be the egg garnishes that finish the dishes – *huevos hilados* [candied egg yolk threads] around the poultry, poached eggs on top of the spinach, and egg yolks scrambled into the rice – or, like many of the regional and ethnic dishes, they may be Portuguese in name alone.

However, in the recipe "Besugos en escabeche al uso de Portugal" [Pickled sea bream, as prepared in Portugal], one can notice the pride Martínez Montiño takes in the Portuguese style as he ends the recipe with the comparison between Portuguese brine and the regular type.

Estos besugos, si los sirves calientes, con un poco del mismo escabeche, son muy buenos: y si los quisieres tener así secos, con sólo aquel poco que estuvieron en el escabeche, les hallarás tanto gusto, como si hubiera un mes que estaban en él, y los puedes llevar muchas leguas en una banasta, o cesta, entre unas pajas de centeno, y está mucho más tierno que el otro escabeche ordinario. (422)

[This sea bream, if served hot with a little of the same brine, is very tasty. If you want to eat it just dry, with only that little amount of time in brine, you'll find it as tasty as if it'd been soaking in it for a month. It can travel in a regular or large basket for many leagues stored with rye straw and is much more tender than (if stored in) other regular brine.] (423)

One of the changes between the 1611 edition and the 1617 edition was the inclusion of an additional recipe, "Sopa de vaca a la portuguesa, contrahecho en día de pescado" [Beef sops, Portuguese style, faux for fish days], which appears in all subsequent editions as well (472; 473). Given Martínez Montiño's connection to Portugal, it seems clear that the author insisted it be included. The dish consists of collard greens seasoned with "cantidad de culantro verde, y unas matas de hierbabuena, y un manojillo de ajedrea, y tres y cuatro cogollos de sándalos" [a large amount of cilantro, some sprigs of spearmint, a handful of summer savory, and three or four shoots of sandalwood] (472; 473).[33] At the close of the recipe he confirms that "Estas sopas a la portuguesa, comen mucho los portugueses" [the Portuguese eat these Portuguese-style sops a lot] (472; 473). And in fact, today, Portugal's national dish, "Caldo verde" [Green soup], also uses kale as its main ingredient.

On two occasions Martínez Montiño references the Portuguese dessert *tijeladas*, an egg custard tart today associated with the region of Abrantes. In "Pasteles de leche" [Custard pies], he explains, "se llaman éstas tigeladas" [these are called *tigeladas*] (488; 489). In another recipe, "De manjar blanco" [Blancmange tartlets], he returns again to this Portuguese custard as he explains how to bake these ultra-rich tartlets: "Hanse de cocer en el horno, y parecerán tijeladas de Portugal, aunque son mejores" [Bake them in the oven. They should turn out like Portuguese custard but better] (346; 347). Another sweet treat are the "Fruta de Fartes" [Fartes fritters], which have a honey and crumbled puff pastry filling (508–10; 509–11). The Real Academia Española (RAE) in its *Diccionario de la lengua española* explains that *fartes* is "frito de masa rellena de una pasta dulce con azúcar, canela y otras especias" [fried dough with a sweet paste filling made from sugar, cinnamon, and other spices]. It was a popular recipe in several European countries, as evidenced by its appearance in an English recipe called "To Make Fartes de Portingale" that appeared in *A Book of Cookrye* originally published in 1584.[34]

The influence of Portugal extends beyond foodstuffs and recipes to include equipment as well. In "Relación de algunas cantidades, para hacer tortas, hojaldres, costradas, y otras cosas" [List of certain quantities for making pies, pastries,

puff pastry pies, and other things], Martínez Montiño describes different cheesecloths and uses the linen ones sold in Portugal as an excellent example.

> Todas las veces que digo que se cuele por estameña, se entiende que la estameña no ha de ser de lana, porque son muy sucias para cosas de grasa. Han de ser las estameñas de unas beatillas de lino gordas y blancas, que las venden los Portugueses para las mozas. Estas son muy limpias, y en manchándose se pueden meter en colada, y se ponen muy blancas. (254)

> [Every time that I discuss straining through a cheesecloth, it should be understood that the cheesecloth isn't wool, because that type is very dirty for things with fat. The cheesecloths should be made from a thick, white fine linen, the kind the Portuguese sell for young women. This type is very clean, and when it gets stained, you can put it in the wash and it will come out clean.] (255)

This is an example of one of the many clarifying points of technique that permeate the text. Martínez Montiño explains that for fatty foods, one should not use a wool strainer and in the process reveals his experience working in Portugal.

We find instances of both foodstuffs and dishes labelled as being from other parts of Europe that in each case remind readers that they are foreign and, by way of juxtaposition, once again build support for his Spanish cookbook. Many times, these products simply support an inclusive approach to taste and an understanding that excellent cuisine is not, nor should be, regulated by limitations imposed by political ideologies. "Ciruelas de Génova" [Genoese plums] (578; 579), "Capón a la Tudesca" [Capon, German style] (180; 181), "Una pierna de carnero a la Francesa" [Leg of young mutton, French style] (170–2; 171–3), "manteca salada de Flandes" [salted butter from Flanders] (392; 393), "Estocafix ... de Flandes" [Stockfish ... from Flanders] (596; 597), and "Empanadas Inglesas" [English empanadas] (314; 315, 386; 387) exemplify this position.

In fact, at times Martínez Montiño adds a side note to correct misunderstandings about certain dishes. For example, in both English empanada recipes, he calls for a sweet dough because, as we learn later, this is the common perception of the type of dough used for an English empanada. However, in "Una empanada de pecho de vaca" [A beef brisket empanada], the dough is made with flour, egg, and a stock seasoned with wine, nutmeg, and ginger, to which is added some of the brisket that has been thoroughly mashed. The dough is then rolled out, and the brisket placed inside, sealed, and baked. Once he finishes with the instructions, Martínez Montiño adds, "Ésta es empanada Inglesa, que las que llamamos Inglesas no lo son, sino empanadas dulces, que éstas no han de llevar dulce" [This is an English empanada. The ones that we call English are not these, rather they are sweet empanadas. These [English ones] shouldn't have anything sweet in them] (306; 307).

Other times, Martínez Montiño juxtaposes other countries' approaches to cooking with Spanish ways. In a recipe for preparing trout, he once again shows his knowledge of another international kitchen when he explains how Germans prepare and serve the dish: "Éstas se suelen servir entre unos dobleces de servilleta a uso de Alemania, mas los señores de España no las quieren sino enteras, un poco más moderado el cocimiento de sal, y vinagre" [These are normally served between folds of a napkin, German style, but lords from Spain only like them whole and with a more moderate salt and vinegar boil] (390; 391). In his discussion of woodcock entrails, he once again distinguishes "the other" from what happens in his kitchen. "Estas chorchas, dicen, que lo que tienen en las tripas no es cosa sucia: y así *los estrangeros* las suelen sacar las tripas con el higadillo, quitando la hiel, y pícanlo asina crudo … Muchos señores gustan dello, mas yo no he usado desta salsa, porque lleva la suciedad de las tripas" [It is said that what these woodcocks have in their intestines is not dirty. Thus, *foreigners* typically take the intestines out with the liver, removing the bile, and chop them all up raw … Many lords like this dish, but I do not make this sauce because it has the filth from the intestines] (150; 151, my emphasis). In rectifying these perceived misconceptions of kitchen protocol, Martínez Montiño also situates Spain in a position superior to that of other nations.

As he brings the cookbook to a close, he once again reiterates his intention of creating a Spanish cookbook that distinguishes itself from other cooking methods: "Con lo cual por ahora doy fin a este Libro, porque en él casi todo lo que hallares es al uso Español" [With this and for now, I'm putting an end to this book. Almost everything that you find in it is the Spanish method] (602–4; 603–5). Martínez Montiño's *Arte de cocina* is a cultural artefact in its own right. His 506 recipes with comments on the king's preferences and regional, ethnic, and international foodstuffs mark the beginnings, if not of a clearly articulated Spanish cuisine, at the very least of a consciousness of its existence. Martínez Montiño frames this project with a clarity of intentionality from the very first words of the prologue – in which he firmly states that no such book exists in Spain that could be advantageous to Spaniards working in the kitchen – to the very last, when he signs off by reminding readers that the recipes and methodology found in his work are purely Spanish. Over four hundred years later, readers can perceive how both its recipes and the author's comments reveal concepts of taste and an emerging culinary identity for Spain.

VII. Curiosities of Martínez Montiño's Cookbook

Recipes and Ingredients

Martínez Montiño's cookbook is filled with exciting recipes that, even for those already familiar with early modern dining, reveal novel cooking techniques, popular flavours, and unique recipes, or suggest an intentionality to highlight his own contributions to excellence in cooking. I have already mentioned his efforts to

preserve recipes from Spain's Muslim past with the inclusion of couscous recipes. In addition to his connection to this culinary heritage, his cookbook also contributes to the evolution of Spanish cooking with original recipes and early references to cooking techniques that today are associated with other cultures or time periods.

First among the defining features of the cookbook are the pastry recipes. Martínez Montiño is often credited with being the first to record puff pastry. For me, it is not so important whether he is first or not, but rather the specificity of his instructions for making what he calls *masa encerada* [elastic dough] and the quantities of pastry-related recipes in his cookbook. His instructions for laminating dough are novel for the time and are part of the recipes "Empanadas de perdices" [Partridge empanadas] (160; 161) and "Bollo fitete" [Fitete pastry] (268–70; 269–71). In both he explains how to roll out the dough, dab it with butter, fold it over on itself, and repeat the process. This application of fat between layers of dough causes the pastry to puff up and has become a standard technique of pastry making.[35]

In several recipes, he also documents cream puff dough or *pâte a choux*, recorded centuries before Antonin Carême popularized it in France. This basic mixture of flour added to boiling water with fat that then has eggs beaten into it is explained in "Buñuelos de viento" [Puffs] (314–16; 315–17), and in two different recipes with the same title, "Otros buñuelos de viento" [Other puffs] (316–18; 317–19). It is today the basis for *buñuelos*, *pepitos*, profiteroles, eclairs, and crullers.

What has also gone relatively unnoticed until now is Martínez Montiño's extensive variety of pastries. Generally, pastries and related recipes make up over a quarter of the entire cookbook and include both sweet and savoury recipes. He includes recipes for round and ring-shaped *bollos* [pastries]; *ginebradas* [clotted milk tarts], *quesadillas* [cheese tarts], and *cazolillas* [tartlets]; *bizcochos* [sweet biscuits], *biscochelos* [ladyfingers], and *mostachones* [mostachon cookies]; *costrada*, *hojaldrilla*, and *pastel hojaldrado* [all names for puff pastry pies], *pasteles* [pastries] and *hojaldre* [puff pastry]; *frutas de* ... [fried dough] and *buñuelos de viento* [puffs]; and *tabletas* [bars] and *tortas* [cakes and pies]. In fact, recreating many of these pastry recipes has been an absolute pleasure.[36]

A second defining feature is the *artalete* [pinwheel], today also known as *roulade*. Pinwheels are usually seasoned with fatback and onion and baked in a *tortera* [covered tart pan]. They are often held together with a brochette or small skewer. Although usually made by rolling up a thin fillet with an egg yolk filling that is then baked, Martínez Montiño also makes them with minced meat, particularly from poultry or veal. Generally, pinwheels accompany a whole bird or fillets of poultry, beef, or other meat. He includes eight different pinwheel recipes in his cookbook.[37]

Among the more than two dozen sauces he includes, two are original to Martínez Montiño. The first is zurciga, which is a type of egg-cheese sauce flavoured with garlic, all spices, and, at times, nuts. It is ladled over egg dishes, as explained in

"Capirotada de huevos" [Eggs, capirotada style] (440; 441) and "Otra capirotada de huevos rellenos" [Another stuffed egg recipe, capirotada style] (440; 441).[38] The second is moreta sauce, which is prepared for serving with the fish *barbo* [barbel] (420; 421). For this sauce, he sautés the fish with onion and lard and then adds a little wine, a little vinegar, all spices, salt, a handful of garden herbs, and enough water to braise. He uses flour as a thickener, boils it and then lets it simmer to reduce the sauce down. As with many recipes, at the end he adds his personal preference for keeping the sauce on the sour side, though he notes that others add cinnamon and sugar to it.

One of the most exciting discoveries while researching the cookbook was the use of the *flor* [flor], a culinary term that refers to the coagulated protein that separates from both the fat and the juices when meat cooks. Martínez Montiño separates out the flor in twelve different recipes and reserves it to then spoon on top of the dish as a finishing touch. After consulting with many experts in the field, several of whom were unfamiliar with the term, in the end I found that the best way to identify the flor was to recreate several dishes.[39]

In addition to these original contributions, Martínez Montiño makes several early references to cooking techniques and food items that are generally associated with later time periods or different countries. For example, although it is very much associated with classic French cuisine from the mid-seventeenth century, Martínez Montiño includes an earlier iteration of the basic thickener, roux. His use of fat and flour as a thickener is explained four decades before its appearance in the cookbook historians often credit for first including it: the 1651 *Le cuisinier François* by La Varenne. This use of heating fat and flour to thicken a dish occurs in several of Martínez Montiño's recipes, including "Otra manera de carnero verde" [Another way of (making) green mutton stew] (200; 201), "Potaje de calabaza" [Squash stew] (364; 365), "Potaje de arvejas" [Pea stew] (374; 375), "Cómo se aderezan los caracoles" [How to prepare snails] (402–4; 403–5), "Platillo de cardo" [A dish of cardoons] (408; 409), and "Gallina a la morisca" [Hen, Morisco style] (504; 505).

This cookbook also provides today's readers with an early example of pre-tomato gazpacho. In the recipe "Sopa de perdices" [Partridge sops], Martínez Montiño categorizes it as a type of gazpacho: "Esta sopa es sopa de gazpacho caliente" [These sops are hot gazpacho sops] (162; 163). Instead of today's *gazpacho andaluz* [Andalusian gazpacho], the refreshing cold soup made with tomatoes, other raw vegetables, and bread, the tradition Martínez Montiño draws from is more closely aligned to the *gazpacho manchego* [Manchegan gazpacho], which is a game-based stew served hot over sops, as he specifies in the recipe.

Another distinctive feature is the appearance of a sandwich recipe. Martínez Montiño calls his creation grilled *empanadillas* [turnovers] because no word yet exists for *sandwiches*, but, in fact, this is exactly what he is creating in this third iteration of the recipe, "Sesos de ternera" [Veal brain]: a grilled sandwich.

Estos sesos podrás picar muy bien después de cocidos, y luego echarles sal, y pimienta, sin otra cosa ninguna, y poner destos sesos sobre una rebanada de pan: y luego poner otra rebanada encima desta, y apretarla un poco, y tener manteca de puerco muy caliente, y freírlos allí de manera, que el pan quede muy tostado: y estas empanadillas de sesos han de ir a la mesa muy calientes. (308)

[This brain also comes out well when finely diced after boiling and then adding salt and pepper without anything else. Spoon it onto a slice of bread and then put another on top and squeeze them together a little. Have some hot lard and fry them so that the bread comes out very toasted. These little brain turnovers should be very hot when they go out to the table.] (309)

This grilled meat sandwich appears an entire century before sandwich recipes appear in English-language cookbooks.[40]

Finally, he has an early recipe for *croquetas de pollo* [chicken croquettes], today standard fare for any tapas bar in Spain. His name for them is "Otros buñuelos de manjar blanco" [Other blancmange puffs] (344; 345). He uses blancmange, which is similar to the béchamel and chicken for croquettes, shapes them bigger than a hazelnut, fries them, and serves them with a little sugar sprinkled on top.

Attentiveness to His Diverse Audiences

One of the features that separates Martínez Montiño from Mestre Robert's 1520 *Llibre del coc*, which was translated five years later into Spanish as *Libro de guisados* by Ruperto de Nola and was the only other early modern cookbook that underwent multiple publications, is that Martínez Montiño regularly includes serving instructions and personal comments on the success of a recipe, while Nola simply provides instructions on how to cook. This attentiveness to the recipients of the final product is one of the defining characteristics of *Arte de cocina, pastelería, vizcochería y conservería*. For example, when considering food presentation for the diner, often Martínez Montiño provides a variety of garnishes and ways to finish off a dish before sending it out to the table. Beyond thinking about those who will eat his food, and we have also seen this when he alludes to the individual taste of lords and the need to adjust flavourings, Martínez Montiño is also very much in tune with those who will be preparing the dishes.

It is not unusual to see this attentiveness to readers in the prologues of early modern prescriptive works, like cookbooks, or even works of fiction, as many authors directly address readers in an effort to frame their writing and ask for their readers' indulgence. This is exactly what Martínez Montiño does in his own prologue as he addresses a variety of different readers.

y si en alguna cosa hubiere falta, suplico al discreto Lector lo supla, que como hombre me habré descuidado, que ya sé que los grandes oficiales no han menester libro: mas con todo eso por ser todos tan amigos míos, tendrán en algo mis cosas, y todavía hallarán alguna cosa nueva: y los aprendices si hicieren lo que yo ordeno, entiendo que no podrán errar. Y así los unos por aprender, y los otros por curiosidad, todos se holgarán de tener mi obrecilla. (108)

[And if there were a mistake somewhere, I beg of my discreet reader to fix it, because as a man I may have been a little neglectful, and I know, of course, that master cooks don't need this book. But, in spite of this and because they are all good friends of mine, I hope they might get something out of my ideas and even find something new. And if apprentices do what I put forth here, I am certain they will not fail. And thus, for those who are learning and for others out of curiosity, all will delight in having my little work.] (109)

From the beginning in his prologue he writes directly to cooks and apprentices. This attentiveness to his readership focuses on those with various levels of culinary knowledge. Other times he specifies different age groups, or gender, economic status, or even specialized areas within kitchen.

In one section he explains, "Quiero poner aquí algunas potajerías de legumbres: y esto hago (como tengo dicho) *para los mancebos, y mujeres, que sirven a algunos señores, y no saben estas cosas*, aunque parecen muy fáciles" [I want to write down here some vegetable stews and I'm going to do this (as I have said) *for apprentices, and women, who serve lords and do not know these things* even though they seem so easy] (342; 343, my emphasis). In another instance he focuses exclusively on women: "Estos Flaones, o pasteles de leche *si hubiere alguna mujer que no los sepa hacer*, podrá echar este batido en una cazuela untada con manteca, y meterla en el horno a fuego manso, y se cuajará como si fuera pastel" [These flaones, or custard pies, *in case some woman does not know how to make them*, she could put this batter into a casserole that has been greased with lard, and put it in the oven on low flame, and it will set as if it were a pie] (486; 487). He approaches the difference in knowledge base directly and unbiased. In "Migas de gato" [Cat breadcrumbs], he acknowledges his diverse readers when he states

no te espantes, porque pongo algunas cosas extraordinarias: esto bien sé que lo saben hacer los oficiales, mas porque sé, que aunque sean muy ordinarias hay mozos y mozas que no lo saben, ni sus amos les han de dar recaudo para los platos regalados, y querría que se aprovechasen todos (240)

[Don't be nervous because I'm including some unusual things here. I know that cooks know how to make this; moreover, I know that even though they might be usual for cooks, there are young men and women who don't know how to prepare them or

their masters don't give them the necessary ingredients to make exquisite dishes, and I want everyone to be able to make the most of their situation]. (241)

Moreover, at times he adds in cost-cutting measures, indicating that he is fully aware he is writing for people with diverse disposable incomes. In one of the recipes, titled "Otro Capón relleno" [Another stuffed capon], he suggests the following: "Por no gastar dos capones podrás sacar la carne de la pechuga deste capón, para hacer los artaletes" [To avoid using two capons, you can take some of the breast meat from the same capon to make the pinwheels] (188; 189). Here, as in other moments throughout the cookbook, he acknowledges the economic realities of acquiring the necessary ingredients to make a dish. In fact, Martínez Montiño often reaches out to cooks working beyond the palace. He often offers great detail, eager for those reading to get it just right. This is certainly the case for the pastry "Rebollo" [Rebollo]. Here he gives descriptive instructions to ensure that the pastry turns out right: "Y advierte, que cuando se pongan los materiales en la hoja, los has de poner a la larga por junto al borde, y has de poner más a la una parte que a la otra, para que cuando esté arrollado parezca lamprea, o enguila, que parezca la una punta cabeza, y la otra cola. Hase de cocer enroscado" [Note that when you are adding the ingredients to the sheet, place them all close to the long edge. Also put more on one end than on the other so that when it's rolled up it looks like lamprey or eel with one end as the head and the other the tail. It should be baked coiled up] (264; 265).

He also writes directly to specific kitchen personnel. In "Como se ha de salar el jabalí" [How to salt boar], he first explains how to debone and cut the meat, then how to salt and dry it, and finally, what to serve it with. As a transition to treating deer meat, he offers the following explanation: "Y esto todo importa mucho saberlo los pasteleros, porque de esto saben mucho menos que los cocineros" [And all of this is very important for the pastry makers to know because they know much less about this than cooks do] (296; 297). This naming of specific types of people is an effective technique to reach his diverse audiences.

Still other times he makes certain assumptions, knowing that his reading audience does have a certain level of culinary knowledge. In the recipe "Otros palominos ahogados" [Another drowned squab dish], he describes how to prepare the herbs and spices by relying on his readers' knowledge of parsley sauce: "picarás un poco de verdura, perejil, hierbabuena, y ciliantro verde, o seco, con un migajoncillo de pan duro, y échale un medio grano de ajo, y unos pocos de cominos, y pimienta, y nuez, y májalo mucho, tanto, como para salsa de perejil" [chop up a few green herbs, parsley, spearmint, and fresh cilantro or dried, with a little piece of stale bread. Add a half clove of garlic, a little cumin, pepper, and nutmeg, and grind it up very fine, as you would for parsley sauce] (198; 199). In this example, Martínez Montiño acknowledges that those reading his recipe will already know how to prepare parsley sauce. In the recipe "Fruta de frisuelos" [Funnel cakes], his attentiveness to his

audience draws upon visual images from beyond the kitchen to facilitate the cook's understanding of how to cook this sweet treat to perfection: "Para estar la fruta como ha de estar … por la parte de abajo ha de parecer un garvín de mujer con muchos granillos redondos, como perdigones de arcabuz, que parecen muy bien" [For this fried dough to turn out as it should … on the bottom it should look like a woman's laced bonnet with many little, round seeds, like buckshot from an harquebus. That would look just right] (378; 379). In this case, Martínez Montiño uses both feminine and masculine images to convey the blistering of the fried dough that indicates it is done. These two very different visual cues allow for increased audience reception to best achieve the outcome of the recipe and demonstrate Martínez Montiño's sensitivity to his readers.

Martínez Montiño's Voice

One final thought on what makes this cookbook so important to Spanish cultural and culinary history. In the early years of cookbook writing, cooks have few models of written instruction on how to create in the kitchen. They do not yet have access to the rich history of recorded recipes, much less entire books dedicated to such instruction. Indeed, conventions are not yet established, and even the language of cooking is still being sorted out. An example of this is Martínez Montiño's recipe for stockfish, which he calls "Estocafix" for lack of any Spanish word for a fish that is shipped from abroad (596). Another is the overlapping of different sections or the grouping of miscellaneous recipes in different parts of the work. Cookbook writers and, I would add, publishers are still grappling with issues of structure, organization, consistency of measurements, cross-referencing of instructions, and attending to accurate descriptions of foodstuffs and kitchen techniques and instrumentation.[41]

Taking a step back, cookbooks are generally thought of as examples of discourse colony, a type of narrative whose individual parts do not depend on one another for their meaning.[42] Although an overall framing context exists, one component may be used without another, and meaning is generally not derived from sequence. This is why today cookbooks are read for specific recipes or clusters of recipes, and generally not from start to finish. But was this the case for contemporary readers of *Arte de cocina, pastelería, vizcochería y conservería*? Might Martínez Montiño have written the cookbook as a manual that others would read start to finish? There are certainly many cross-references that exemplify that he is fully aware of the big project, perceiving his book not just as a collection of recipes but as a whole, unified work. For example, in "Grullas asadas" [Roast crane] he ends by directing his readers to suggested sauces found in another section of the cookbook: "las podrás servir con salsas negras de venazón en potajes, o en pastelones: las cuales salsas hallarás escritas en el capítulo donde se trata del jabalí" [You can also serve them with the venison black sauce either as a stew or a pie; both are written in the chapter that deals with boar] (152; 153). We see this type of

cross-reference throughout the cookbook. In "Otro Capón relleno" [Another stuffed capon] he ends with "Estos bollos adelante diré cómo se hacen" [I will say how to make these pastries later on] (188; 189), which references the recipe "Bollo de rodilla" [Spiral sweet roll] (262; 263). Martínez Montiño expects his readers to be familiar with the entire work. As mentioned above, while he writes for *Spanish* cooks, he is attuned to a diversity of readers with different skill levels and knowledge bases. But, his understanding is that his readership will take in the book from start to finish, not read it in the way that readers today engage with a cookbook.

Throughout the cookbook his tone is disciplined, passionate, and determined as he critiques and corrects previous recipes. In "Pepitoria" [Pepitoria (Stew with poultry offal)], he corrects the use of cinnamon found in a previous cookbook, which he prefers not to name: "Advierte, que todas las veces digo, que sazones con todas las especias, se entiende pimienta, y clavos, y nuez, y jengibre, y azafrán; porque la canela no ha de entrar en cosa que no lleve dulce, y en todos, o en los más dulces ha de entrar canela; porque está puesto al revés en el otro libro" [Note that whenever I say to season with all spices, I mean pepper, clove, nutmeg, ginger, and saffron, because cinnamon should not be added to something that is not sweet. In all sweet dishes, or in the sweetest, cinnamon must be present, unlike the other book that says the opposite] (204; 205).

Other times he expresses genuine excitement about the food he prepares, as is evidenced in concluding remarks about the quality of the final product. For "Un platillo de aves con acederas" [A poultry dish with sorrel], he gives concrete advice on how to best present the dish: "Este platillo no se cuaja con huevos: sírveles sobre rebanadas de pan, y es muy apetitoso" [This dish is not thickened with eggs. Serve it on slices of bread. It is very appetizing] (180; 181).

And still other times, he includes some playfulness in both naming recipes and presenting them. In one of his more decorative salads, Martínez Montiño gives a lot of attention to how the dish should be presented.

> compondrás el plato de tu gigote, y ensalada, haciendo como una rosca en el plato, yendo poniendo montoncillos de carne, y otros de ensalada, y en el medio pondrás un poco de ensalada muy bien puesta, con todas las cosas que se suelen echar sus ruedas de limón, y sazónala de aceite y vinagre; y luego adornarla por la parte de afuera con algunas rajas de diacitrón, y granos de granada, y confites, y todas las cosas que suelen poner a las ensaladas: y en medio pondrás unos cogollos de lechuga enteros en pie, y por encima del gigote, o salpicón, aceitunas quitados los cuescos. Este plato es bueno para meriendas, porque se ha de comer frío. Algunos los llaman conejos en huerta. (156)

> [put together a plate of your minced meat and salad by making a ring on the plate with little piles of meat and others of salad. In the middle arrange some of the salad nicely with all the usual things that are in a salad and lemon wheels. Season with oil and vinegar and then, around the outside, garnish with candied citron, pomegranate

seeds, and other sugar-coated nuts and seeds and everything you usually add to a salad. In the centre place some lettuce hearts standing up and, on top of the minced meat or salpicon, some olives with their pits removed.] (157)

Although the recipe is called "Otro gigote de conejos frío" [Another minced rabbit, (served) cold], at the end of the instructions, he provides readers with the playful alternative name "Conejos en huerta" [Rabbits in the garden], thus highlighting the visual play of rabbit meat and green salad on the plate. By reading his cookbook as a narrative whole, one gets a much more accurate sense of Martínez Montiño's voice, which may get lost in reading just a handful of recipes.

VIII. Martínez Montiño's Legacy

Cookbooks

In the centuries to follow, Martínez Montiño's recipes appeared in several cookbooks, sometimes as exact copies and other times simply as a continuation of a tradition that can trace back to Martínez Montiño. Such is the case with Juan de Altamiras' *Nuevo arte de cocina* (1745), written by a Franciscan monk who wrote for the masses rather than the elite. In his cookbook of 207 recipes, he includes two pepitoria recipes, one of which, entitled "Pepitoria de menudillos de pollos" [Pepitoria with chicken giblets] (78), harks back to Martínez Montiño's "Pepitoria" [Pepitoria (Stew with poultry offal)] (202–4; 203–5). Both recipes are based on the neck, wings, and liver, both include herbs and aromatic spices, and both finish with a note of vinegar or other sour juice. However, where Martínez Montiño expressly excludes cinnamon from this recipe, Altamiras includes it, along with an almond sauce. An example of a more direct copy of Martínez Montiño can be found in Altamiras' "Costrada de asadurillas" [Puff pastry pie filled with pluck] (51). His recipe is almost identical to the 1611 "Costrada de asadurillas de cabrito" [Puff pastry pie filled with kid pluck] (224–6; 225–7), though Altamiras does not specify kid as the animal of choice, nor does he use the multilayers of thin dough on the bottom and top as Martínez Montiño does. Rather, Altamiras lays down only one layer on the top and bottom. However, both add a half pound of sugar and eight eggs, and finish by sprinkling sugar on top, which gives the dish its *costra* (crusty finish). Also, like Martínez Montiño, Altamiras closes the recipe with suggestions of veal, other meat, and fish. Martínez Montiño's recipes for "Una costrada de sollo" [A sturgeon puff pastry pie] (386; 387) and "Costrada de atún" [Tuna puff pastry pie] (396; 397) are also present in Altamiras (92–3). In the latter, Altamiras makes a slight modification when he concedes that, if butter is not available, oil will do, because "los pobres nos componemos con lo más barato" [we poor get by with the cheapest (things)] (93). The only other significant change is the addition of "un baño de huevos deshechos por encima" [an egg wash across the top], again to produce the *costra* in *costrada*.[43]

Later, in 1770, the publisher Josep Bró in Gerona releases an amended version of Altamiras' cookbook, and in that work the editor includes the section "Addición del *Arte de cocina, repostería, bizcochería, confitar frutas, compone aguas y resolis, etc.*," in which he includes the following roasts, stews, empanadas, and other savoury dishes from Martínez Montiño as well as several recipes from other sources.

Perdices asadas con aceite [Roast partridge with oil]
Cómo se han de asar los pajarillos gordos [How to roast small plump birds]
Cazuela de pajarillos [Small bird stew]
Pierna de carnero estofada [Stewed leg of mutton]
Empanadillas de cuajada [Curd turnovers]
Empanadas de perdices [Partridge empanadas]
Pichones ensapados [Stuffed squab]
Empanadas de pollos ensapados [Stuffed chicken empanadas]
Una empanadas de pecho de vaca [A beef brisket empanada]
Empanadillas de masa dulce [Sweet dough for turnovers]
Otras empanadillas de pies de Puerco [Other pig's feet turnovers]
Una empanada de pichones [Squab empanada]
Empanadas de liebre [Hare empanada]
Empanadillas de sardinas [Sardine turnovers]
Un pastel de ave para enfermos [Hen pie for the sick] (see Bró 134–50)

A few pages later, in a section on preserves, the following recipes are likewise selected from Martínez Montiño.

Albérchigos [Apricots]
Duraznos [Clingstone peaches]
Melocotones [Firm peaches]
Bocados de durazno [Morsels of clingstone peach purée]
Peras en almíbar [Pears in simple syrup]
Cajas de perada [Boxes of preserved pear purée]
Toronjas [Toronja]
Limones Ceutíes [Ceuti lemons]
Azúcar rosado blanco [White rose sugar]
Bocados de calabaza [Morsels of squash] (see Bró 168–74)

What is fascinating here is the intentionality of including seventeenth-century court recipes in amending a cookbook whose primary audience has limited resources. This decision brings the flavours and cooking techniques of the highest level of society into kitchens with more modest resources but with the desire to make food enjoyed by royalty.

These recipes for preserving fruit and vegetables also appear in nineteenth-century cookbooks. For example, several of Martínez Montiño's recipes on preserves are in *Libro de confitura para el uso de Elias Gómez Maestro cerero y confitero de la ciudad de Olite* (1818), including "Albérchigos" [Apricots] and "Limones ceutíes" [Ceutí lemons] (see Ciérbide and Corcín 93).

At the close of the nineteenth century, Angel Muro, a food writer who had gained fame for his *Diccionario General de cocina*, went on to publish *El practicón: tratado complete de cocina. Al alcance de todos y aprovechamiento de sobras* (1894). This cookbook was enormously successful, with over thirty editions prior to the outbreak of the Spanish civil war. Among his recipes, he confidently cites Martínez Montiño as the source for the name of a popular oxtail dish, "Rabo de vaca a la Hochepot" [Oxtail, Hochepot style]. He purports, "No hay duda que el nombre *Hochepot* está tomado del *Uspot* de la cocina antigua española, pues el célebre Montiño da la receta que copió a continuación con su misma ortografía" [There is no doubt that the name *Hochepot* is taken from *Uspot* from old Spanish cuisine, because the famous Montiño writes the recipe, copied below, with the same spelling] (167). While Muro correctly singles out Martínez Montino's recipe, the term *hochepot* is first found in an earlier French cooking source, *The manuscript of Sion*, a cooking treatise of 131 recipes dating from around 1300.[44]

It is clear how much Muro admires Martínez Montiño: in the appendixes, Muro includes chapter one of Martínez Montiño from the beginning up to the section on banquets (459–61). In this way, Muro recognizes both Martínez Montiño's authority and the historic traditions from the Spanish Habsburg court that were still popular almost three hundred years later.

Approximately twenty years after Angel Muro's best-selling cookbook comes out, Emilia Pardo Bazán authors two cookbooks dedicated to Spanish cuisine, *La cocina española antigua* (1913) and *La cocina española moderna* (1917). In the former, she establishes the primary role of cookbooks in understanding one's culture. In fact, she argues that through cooking we can understand our history in unique ways: "Hay platos de nuestra cocina nacional que no son menos curiosos ni menos históricos que una medalla, una arma o un sepulcro" [There are dishes from our national cuisine that are no less curious or less historical than a medal, a weapon, or a tomb] (III). In this way she states the importance of collecting recipes from the past to ensure that her contemporaries have a way to remember and continue culinary traditions established centuries ago.[45] Regarding Martínez Montiño, Pardo Bazán cites him in two specific recipes: "Huevos de capirote" [Eggs capirote] (448; 449), which she amends as "Huevos de capirote o tortillejas" [Eggs capirote or little tortillas] (65–6), and his "Salchichas" [Sausages] (600; 601), which she renames "Salchichas antiguas" [Old sausages] (294). In addition, she includes a series of recipes that echo those of Martínez Montiño but for which she has modernized the procedures. In fact, the *costradas* that Altamiras included in his cookbook appear once again in Pardo Bazán's but have evolved to resemble bread sops soaked in a fatty broth to which is added vegetables, meat, or other ingredients differing in each of the seven *costrada* recipes (23–7). Other signature Martínez Montiño's

recipes found here include couscous, which she renames "Alcuzcuz moro" [Moor couscous] (343–4), and "Sopa borracha de torrijas" [Drunken torrija sops] (32), which is similar to Martínez Montiño's "Sopa borracha" [Drunken sops] (454–6; 455–7).

Turning to Martínez Montiño's legacy in the Americas, there is clear evidence that his cookbook also travelled there, as revealed in the inventory of the governor of Santa Fe, Don Diego de Vargas. In her work on the history of the city, Elizabeth West found a copy of Martínez Montiño's cookbook among the belongings recorded in the governor's will (179). Additionally, in the *Manuscrito Ávila Blancas, Gastronomía mexicana del s XVIII*, which Guadalupe Pérez San Vicente has transcribed and edited, over 20 per cent of the entire manuscript of 169 recipes come directly from Martínez Montiño. This manuscript is divided into three parts and contains recipes collected by twenty-three different people that include soups, moles, tamales, salads, pastries, desserts, and beverages (*Gastronomía mexicana* 18–20). A large part of the second section comes from Martínez Montiño. Pérez San Vicente affirms that it was written by one person and also questions if, in fact, the recipes may have been copied from another manuscript, though she does not recognize Martínez Montiño's recipes (*Gastronomía mexicana* 14). In total, forty are included: cream recipes, sweet pie recipes, citrus recipes, one on sugar, others on meat-stuffed lettuce, pig's feet, and an extensive section that includes Martínez Montiño's recipes on boar, venison, beef, and some of the empanadillas (70–120).

The other major Mexican recipe manuscript of the eighteenth century, *Tesoro de la cocina mexicana* by Doña Dominga de Gúzman, also contains one of Martínez Montiño's recipes: "Gallina morisca" [Morisco-style hen] (182–4; 183–5). In fact, here Gúzman includes two "Gallina morisca" recipes. One closely resembles Martínez Montiño's (Pérez San Vicente, *Recetario* 106); the other, less so (Pérez San Vicente, *Recetario* 75). Rachel Laudan has pointed out that in addition to these two recipes the author also includes a third called "Morisco" and that following that one is the recipe "Mestizo"; though similar, it includes tomatoes and chilies, thus showing how Martínez Montiño's recipe transformed across time and space (Pérez San Vicente, *Recetario* 94).

The same recipe, "Gallina morisca," also appears in the anonymous 1817 *Libro de cocina de la gesta de independencia*, showing its popularity across centuries. In fact, in this cookbook it is clear that several recipes – and here I'll only mention a handful, including "Frasía de ternera" [Veal frasia] (41), "Potaje de habas" [Fava bean stew] (50), "Garbanzada de membrillo" [Garbanzos with quince] (50–1), "Nabos lampreados" [Turnips, Lamprea style] (51), and "Nabos cuajados" [Turnips with an egg crust] (51) – all come from Martínez Montiño. There is still much work to be done in understanding how Martínez Montiño's recipes impacted cooking practices for Spaniards who relocated to the Americas in the eighteenth and nineteenth centuries and in turn how what happened in those kitchens both affected and was affected by cooking practices and products in and of the Americas.

IX. Previous Editions

Abbreviations of Archives and Libraries Consulted

BA:	Biblioteca pública del estado en Ávila, Ávila, Spain
BB:	Biblioteca Bertoliana, Vicenza, Italy
BL:	British Library, London, England
BLAC:	Benson Latin American Collection, University of Texas, Austin, USA
BNE:	Biblioteca Nacional de España, Madrid, Spain
BNF:	Bibliothèque nationale de France, Paris, France
BU:	Bibliotequé universitat, Barcelona, Spain
BVNP:	Biblioteca valenciana Nicolau Primitiu
EL:	Eclesiásticas de León, León, Spain
HL:	Huntington Library, Pasadena, CA, USA
HT:	Hathi Trust
LC:	Library of Congress, Washington, DC, USA
LL:	Lilly Library, Indiana University, Bloomington, IN, USA
MM:	Museo Massó, Bueu, Spain
NYAM:	New York Academy of Medicine, New York, NY, USA
NYPL:	New York Public Library, New York, NY, USA
SL:	Schlesinger Library, Cambridge, MA, USA

Table 9. Editions of *Arte de cocina, pastelería, vizcochería y conservería*.

Date	City	Bookseller	Backer	Editions consulted
1611	Madrid	Luis Sánchez	n/a	LL, BNE
1617	Madrid	Juan de la Cuesta	Antonio Rodríguez, mercader de libros	BNE
1620	Madrid	n/a	n/a	no extant
1623	Madrid	La viuda de Alonso Martín	Domingo Gonçalez, mercader de libros	BNF
1628	Madrid	La viuda de Luis Sánchez, impresora del reino	Alonso Pérez	BB
1637	Alcalá	Antonio Vázquez, impresor de la universidad	Manuel López, Puerta de Sol	BNE, BU, BL
1653	Madrid	María de Quiñones	Manuel López, Puerta de Sol	BNE, BU
1662	Madrid	Joseph Fernández de Buendía	Manual López, Mercader de libros	BNE, BL
1674	Madrid	Viuda de Francisco Nieto	Gabriel de León, Mercader de libros	BA

(Continued)

Table 9. *(Continued)*

Date	City	Bookseller	Backer	Editions consulted
1676	Madrid	Julián de Paredes impresor de libros, en la Plazuela del Angel	n/a	BNE, BU, BL
1705	Valencia	Francisco Mestre	Carlos Ducai, mercador de libros	NYPL
1705–23	Valencia	Francisco Mestre	Carlos Ducai, mercader de libro	BVNP, MM
1715	Pamplona	Francisco Picar	n/a	EL
1725	Madrid	Juan de Ariztia	n/a	BLAC
1728	Madrid	Doña Paula Alonso y Padilla y de D. Pedro Joseph Alonso y Padilla.	n/a	BU
1732	Barcelona	Joseph Cormellas	n/a	HL
1754	Barcelona	Carlos Sàera y Jaume Ossèt	Josef Altès y Ignacio Jordi, libreros y compañía	BU
1760	Madrid	Juliana Carrasco	Don Pedro Joseph Alonso y Padilla, librero de Cámara del Rey	SL
1763	Barcelona	María Angela Martí, viuda en la plaza de S Jayme,	n/a	BU
1763	Barcelona	María Angela Martí, viuda en la plaza de S Jayme,	n/a	LL
1763	Barcelona	María Angela Martí, viuda en la plaza de S Jayme,	n/a	NYPL, LC
1778	Madrid	Pantaleón Aznar	Real Compañía de impresores, y Libreros del Reino	BNE, MM LL, HT
1790	Madrid	Joseph Doblado	n/a	BVNP, NYPL, NYAM
1797	Madrid	Joseph Doblado	n/a	BU
1800	Madrid	Barco	n/a	LL
1807	Barcelona	Juan Francisco Piferrer, impresor de S.M.	n/a	BNE, SL
1809	Madrid	Joseph Doblado	n/a	BNE, SL, HT
1822	Madrid	la viuda de Barco Lopez	n/a	BNE, BVNP
1823	Barcelona	Sierra y Martí	n/a	LC, HT

Martínez Montiño's 1611 cookbook follows a small format, the 12mo. This means that each printed sheet has 12 leaves and that the pages are 1/3 the size of the quarto format. The book measures 14.5 x 9 cm. Each page holds up to 24 lines of text. Notaker explains that this size was commonly found throughout Europe, particularly in domestic manuals for women that combined "medicine, confectionery and cookery" (12).[46] Although page sizes vary slightly, this same small format is maintained throughout all subsequent editions. The pages are numbered as folios, recto and verso. By the start of the eighteenth century, page numbers definitively replace folio numbers.

We know from the work of Amalia Sarriá Rueda that the number of books printed with each edition ran between one thousand and three thousand copies (146). Another notable fact is that, once a book left the hands of the author, that person rarely contributed again to the layers of editing and amending that took place. Jaime Moll explains that today we will not know for certain what type of editing happened once the book was submitted to a printer and/or bookseller. Moll continues, "En la mayoría de los casos, lo habitual es que el autor, una vez vendido el privilegio, no se preocupe de la materialidad de la edición, corriendo a cargo del librero editor y del impresor su vigilancia" [In the majority of cases, usually the author, once the privilege has been sold, does not worry about the production of the edition, as this concern is the responsibility of the publisher bookseller and the printer] (51). So, the changes that the book undergoes in its earliest editions may have had input from Martínez Montiño, though it is very likely that Luis Sánchez, bookseller in 1611, Juan de la Cuesta, bookseller in 1617, and the widow of Alonso Martín, bookseller in 1623, may have played a bigger role in changes made.

Notaker also explains that, while decorative elements such as head and tail pieces and ornamental initials, both of which are present in Martínez Montiño's work, are common additions to a cookbook, an illustrated title page is less common. In the 1611 edition, the printer Luis Sánchez chose as an illustration for the title page a well-known emblem, "Vigili labore" [By vigilant labour], from Christóbal Pérez de Herrera's *Proverbios morales, y consejos christianos, muy provechosos* [Very beneficial moral proverbs and Christian advice] (1576).[47] The image consists of a hand with eyes floating above each finger and the phrase "Vigili labore" written above it (see Figure 3). By highlighting the senses of sight and touch, Sánchez weighs in on the humanist debate of the banquet of the senses by privileging touch together with sight as a way to acquire and achieve knowledge. He echoes the thoughts of the humanist Fray Luis de Granada, who wrote, "usando de la industria de las manos en las cosas de naturaleza, habemos venido a fabricar otra nueva naturaleza" [using the industry of the hand in the things of nature, we have come to produce another, new nature] (489). In this way, Luis Sánchez communicates to readers of this court cookbook the task of all who aspire to cook well: through selecting the right ingredients, preparing them under the right conditions, and serving them perfectly, they transform nature into something new and better.

Figure 3. Title page of *Arte de cocina, pastelería, vizcochería y conservería*, 1611. Photo by author, courtesy of the Lilly Library, Indiana University, Bloomington, Indiana.

This same illustration is seen in the next edition as well, but in 1623 the widow of Alonso Martín replaced the emblem with the figure of a hippogriff. In one claw it is holding a ring attached to a block. Later, in 1637, an additional layer of a winged ball chained to the block is added below (see Figure 4). Other seventeenth-century title pages include a cross with vegetation surrounding it in 1628 and 1662, ivy and sickle in 1653, and a small flower pot in 1676. The later editions become less and less concerned with the title page visual.

Additional illustrations are rare in early modern cookbooks and didactic illustrations rarer still (Notaker 13). However, Martínez Montiño's original 1611 edition contains a woodcut of two different-sized spoons in the back of the book, which are discussed both in Chapter 1 and Chapter 2 of his cookbook (for the image see 604). This is the only edition that contains two illustrations of two different-sized spoons. Later, the 1617 edition also contains two spoons, but they are the same size. In the 1623, 1637, 1653, and 1662 editions, one spoon is illustrated in the back. The 1628 and 1676 do not contain any illustrations, nor do other eighteenth- and nineteenth-century editions.

Regarding illustrations, in the mid-eighteenth century, a one-page drawing of kitchen utensils and appliances is included along with a legend that names each of the twenty items (see Figure 2). This added illustration is situated between the end of the prologue and the beginning of Chapter 1, in the editions of 1760, 1800, 1822, and 1823.

It has been a fascinating treasure hunt investigating different editions of the cookbook. From online searches to visits to special collections and rare book rooms across North America and Europe, I have had the pleasure of studying how different printers and booksellers have put their particular mark on Martínez Montiño's cookbook. Changes in title pages, front and back material, order and names of recipes, and evolution of syntax and morphology are abundantly evident as each printer, editor, and publisher partakes in the presentation of Martínez Montiño's masterpiece. I'll point out below a few of the substantial changes in the front material and simply state that comparing these editions lends itself to a fascinating linguistic study of how the language evolved over the centuries as the material essentially remains the same but the nuances of expression evolve over time.

The 1611 edition

The front material includes the following sections:

- *tassa* [certificate of price]
- *fe de erratas* [errata sheet] (unlabelled)
- *El rey (privilegio)* [the king (privilege)]

Figure 4. Detail of title page of *Arte de cocina, pastelería, vizcochería y conservería*, 1637. Photo by author, courtesy of the Bibliotequé universitat, Barcelona, Spain.

- *prólogo al letor* [prologue to the reader]
- *advertencia, acerca de la medida que han de tener los cucharones para hazer bizcochos* [notice, on the size spoons should have for making sweet biscuits], and a
- *tabla de los banquetes que van en este libro* [table on banquets that are in this book]

In the king's section of the front material, the cookbook's title is actually referred to as *De la manera que se habían de aderezar las cosas de comida* [On the way food should be prepared]. This reference raises the possibility that Martínez Montiño (or another figure close to the king) may have discussed the book with Philip III and remembered the work with this title instead of its official one. Whatever the case may be, this reference is later changed in the 1623 edition to *Arte de cocina*.

The index at the back of the book lists recipes in order by page number. In 1617 this will change to an alphabetical index, but at the start of the eighteenth century it switches back to the page number order and remains that way in the following editions.

The 1617 Edition

The front material remains unchanged, and, apart from changes in letter boxes and other small expected changes that occur from one publisher to the next, Juan de la Cuesta makes several notable minor changes to the cookbook, including:

- the order and titles of some of the recipes
- the subtitles "Potajería" [Vegetables] and "Comienza la masa" [The dough section begins] to the corresponding sections of the cookbook
- a new recipe, "Sopa de vaca a la Portuguesa, contrahecha en día de pescado" [Beef sops, Portuguese style, faux for fish days] (472; 473)
- The index is now alphabetized instead of organized by order or appearance.

The 1620 Edition

Although I have not yet found a copy of a 1620 edition, indications from other cookbooks lead me to believe that one was printed at that time. In the 1623 edition, under the "Privilegio del rey" front material, the licenciado writes: "Tiene prorrogación por cuatro años más. Dada en Madrid a 17 de Hebrero de 1620 años, ante Lázaro de Ríos" [It has a four-year extension. Given in Madrid the 17th February, 1620 before Lázaro de Ríos]. This type of paperwork would usually occur when the book is printed, not three years prior to publication. In the 1637 and both 1705 editions the same information is provided.

The 1623 Edition

A significant detail of the 1623 edition is that the author's name on the title page changes from Martínez Motiño to Martínez Montiño. However, in the section on the licensing, dated 20 May 1623, the licenciate Murcia de la Llana still writes the author's name as Francisco Martínez Motiño. This change of name, which begins with this 1623 edition, will be definitive in all other editions, and today he is known as Martínez Montiño. But, in researching who this cook was and where he came from, scholars have begun to debate whether he is from Galicia (based on the accepted "Montiño" spelling of his name) or elsewhere (based on the fact that these early versions, while the author is still alive, have his second last name as Motiño.)

Another interesting fact about this edition is that in the "Tassa" [Certificate of price] section of the front material, the king's clerk, Gerónimo Núñez de León, mentions forty pliegos [sheets] instead of the previous forty-two. This directly affects the pricing of the book, which dropped from the original 168 maravedis to 160.

Finally, in his study *Printed Cookbooks in Europe 1470–1700*, Henry Notaker speculates that there may be two 1623 editions, one from Alonso Martín's widow and another from Pedro Tazo (356). However, in her work on women printers in early modern Spain, Sandra Establés Susán notes that Pedro Tazo married the daughter of Alonso Martín, Beatriz Martín, and began working for his widow in 1623 (362). I've yet to see a copy with the name Pedro Tazo and suspect that it may be the same edition.

The 1628 Edition

This edition is significant because it marks the end of Martínez Montiño's career and possibly indicates the year of his death. Indications of this hypothesis are found in the *Tassa* [Certificate of price] section of the cookbook. The current secretary, Lázaro de Ríos Angulo, references the author only as Francisco Martínez, not Francisco Martínez *Montiño*. Second, Ríos Angulo only addresses him as "cozinero" [cook], not "cocinero mayor del rey nuestro señor" [master cook of the king our lord], as had been the case in earlier editions. Third, the request comes from Alonso Pérez, bookseller, no longer from Martínez Montiño himself. The date of the *tassa* is "a diez días del mes de julio de mil y seiscientos y ventiocho años" [on the tenth of the month of July, in the year sixteen twenty-eight]. This series of substantial changes suggests that perhaps Martínez Montiño has retired, if not passed away, by this time.

This edition brings with it a couple of other points of significance. For example, it is the only edition in which the word *vizchochería* changes to *bizcochería* in the title. The price for the book has been reduced again, as there is one less sheet (thirty-nine in this edition). Moreover, the king's voice is gone and it is clear that the section "Rey (Privilegio)" [The king (privilege)] has been penned by Ríos Angulo. Finally, this edition contains numerous errors in the numbering of folios.

The 1637 Edition

Several data bases and catalogues list this edition as 1634. However, I am confident that it is a recurring typo and that no 1634 edition exists, since each time it would lead to this 1637 edition. Starting with this edition, the *Tassa* indicates that Martínez Montiño is the author but no longer a cook for the king. This is most likely because he died sometime between the last edition and this one. It also includes for the first time an *Erratas* [Errata] header that precedes the "El Rey (privilegio)" [The king (privilege)] section. This section lists a series of page numbers and the typos found within. It is also the last time the "Privilegio" section, which indicates the king's permission to print the book, appears (except in the 1705 editions, which reproduce the front material from the 1623 edition).

The 1653 Edition

The order of the front material is now title page, licence, errata sheet, certificate of price, prologue, notice, and table of banquets. In the title, "cocina" is spelled with a "c" instead of a "z." The price is listed as 124 maravedis. Apart from those minor changes, there is nothing too notable about this edition except for the printer. For the first time, the name is not that of a man or a "widow of" a man but rather a woman: María de Quiñones. She was twice married to printers, first Pedro Madrigal and then Juan de la Cuesta, and a widow twice over. She was active from 1628 until 1666, and from 1633 on, all books she printed carried her name. Included in her publications were pharmaceutical books, guides for nursing, remedies for the sick, and Tirso de Molina's play "El amor medico."[48]

The 1662 Edition

There are no significant changes from the previous edition.

The 1674 Edition

There are no significant changes from the previous edition.

The 1676 Edition

In this edition the price has gone up to 6 maravedis the sheet. It still has thirty-one sheets and thus the cost is 186 maravedies. Another novelty is that at the end of the cookbook, the printer includes an advertisement for other books he is selling. They are primarily religious in content but also include books on science, politics, and the military as well as *comedias* and a book of sayings. It gives readers today an idea of what this printer thought was marketable.

En Madrid Por Julián de Paredes impresor de libros en la Plazuela del Angel, Año de 1676.
En la misma imprenta se venden los libros intitulados:
Obras del P. Estella …
El Abulense ilustrado …
La Corona de Madrid …
Ciclo Espiritual …
Corónica de la vida del santo Pontífice Pío V …
La Vara de Iese, Vida de Jesús y María
Vida del Venerable Siervo de Dios …
Arte de Navegar, Navegación Astronómica …
Política, y Mecánica militar para Sargento mayor de un Tercio.
Additiones, seu observationes …
Parte Quarenta de Comedias de varios autores
Refranes Castellanos antiguos glossados.
[In Madrid by Julián de Paredes book printer in the Plazuela del Angel, Year 1676. The same book printer sells the books entitled:
Works by P. Estella …
The illustrated Abulense …
The Crown of Madrid …
Spiritual Cycle …
Chronicle of the life of the Holy Pontiff Pius V …
The staff of Jesus, Life of Jesus and Mary
Life of the Venerable Servant of God …
Art of Navigating, Astronomical Navigation …
Politics, and Military Goods for a Sergeant Major of a Battalion.
Additions, to be observations …
40th Part of comedies by various authors
Old Castilian Sayings with glosses.

The 1705 (BVNP) Edition (and Museo Massó)[49]

In this edition, the printer recycles the front material from the 1611 edition, but in the *advertencia* [notice] section that appears before the series of seasonal banquet menus, the references to spoon illustrations at the back of the book disappears. For each folio, the verso/recto distinction has disappeared and now each side has its own number. A copy of this same edition is also housed in the Museo Massó in Bueu, Spain but without the cover page.

The 1705 NYPL Edition

Although this edition is from the same year and printer, it is a separate edition. The cover page illustration is the first of many differences as this edition includes a bird and the former, a lion. The two illustrations of the first page of chapter

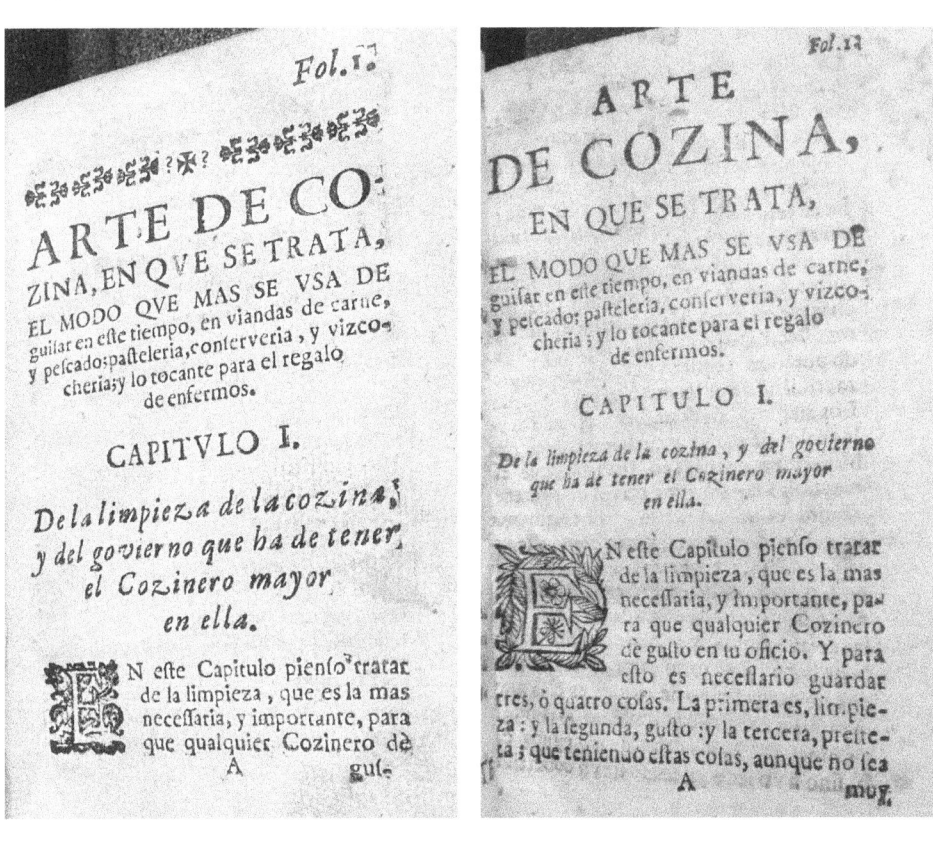

Figure 5. Folio 1 of the distinct 1705 BVNP (left) and NYPL (right) editions. Photos by author, July 2016 and July 2023.

one provide examples of significant difference between the two editions. Note the use/absence of the head piece, the page layout, the distinct inhabited initials, margins, font, and content and placement of signature marks and catchwords.

The 1715 Edition

I have not been able to access this edition, located in Eclesiásticas de León, a library affiliated with the Red de bibliotecas de Castilla y León.

The 1725 Edition

After the title page, what was once some six pages of front material before the prologue is reduced to two pages. There is now a brief "aprobación" [approval] in front of the licence, tassa, and errata sections. This format remains throughout the eighteenth and into the nineteenth century.

The 1728 Edition

One curiosity about this edition is that, right on the title page, it announces that there are thirty-two *pliegos* [sheets of paper]. This is the only time this information is placed on the title page. From here on out, the subtle language changes are numerous. There are many nuances that occur in this edition and those of 1754, 1763, and 1807. Examples include:

Harta sal changes to *mucha sal*
Untada con changes to *untada en*
Echa lumbre changes to *ponle lumbre*
Migajoncillo changes to *pedacito*
Tórnalo changes to *vuélvelo*
Huevos changes to *yemas de huevos*
Trocitos changes to *pedacitos*
Huevos crudos, cosa de cuatro changes to *cuatro huevos duros*
Postrer changes to *último*
Comienza changes to *empieza*

There are also numerous errors in page numbers throughout the cookbook. Moreover, actual chunks of pages were misplaced in the cookbook. For example, pp. 269–70 are erroneously inserted between pp. 260 and 261. This mistake includes part of "Cómo se aderezan las espinacas" [How to prepare spinach], "Espinacas a la Portuguesa" [Spinach, Portuguese style], and "Fruta de borrajas" [Deep-fried borage].

The 1732 Edition

There are no significant changes from the previous edition.

The 1754 Edition

There are no significant changes from the previous edition.

The 1760 Edition

There are a few noteworthy changes to this edition. The first is the inclusion of an ordinal rank of publication, stated on the cover page as the "duodécima impresión" [twelfth printing]. By this time, the 1760 edition is at least the eighteenth, but it does set a standard, and afterward most editions follow its format (all but the 1763 and 1807 editions). Second, this is the first edition to include the illustration of cooking equipment that has been discussed above (see Figure 2). The third difference is the inclusion of other books sold at the

bookshop that has backed the printer to produce the cookbook. The following advertisement is reminiscent of the 1676 edition, although the titles differ substantially.

En la famosa Librería Castellana de don Pedro Joseph Alonso y Padilla, Librero de cámara del Rey, se hallan mucha variedad de Libros exquisitos en Castellano.
De historias de España, Portugal, y otros Reynos, y Provincias.
Historias de las Indias Orientales, Occidentales, y otras Islas.
Historias de Reyes de España, de Portugal, y de otros Reynos.
Chrónicas de Reyes, Príncipes.
Historias de muchas ciudades de España, y de otros Reynos, y Provincias, y en algunas el origen, y nobleza de sus familias.
Antigüedades de varias Ciudades, Villas, y Lugares, explicando sus monumentos, figuras estrañas, de barro, madera, cobre, oro, plata, y de otros materiales.
[In the famous Castilian Bookstore of Don Pedro Joseph Alonso y Padilla, librarian of the king's chamber, you will find a great variety of exquisite books in Spanish.
Of histories of Spain, Portugal, and other kingdoms, and provinces.
Histories of the East and West Indies, and other islands.
Stories of Kings of Spain, Portugal, and other kingdoms.
Chronicles of Kings and Princes
Stories of many cities in Spain, and other kingdoms, and provinces, and in some, the origin and noble lineages of their families.
Antiquities of various cities, villas, and places, explaining their monuments, odd figures made of clay, wood, copper, gold, silver, and other material.

The 1763 Editions

Of all the eighteenth-century editions, this is the most significant, as it was selected for the version to base facsimiles on in the twentieth century. In 1994 and 1997 (Valencia) and in 2006 (Valladolid), book publishers reproduced Martínez Montiño's cookbook using the 1763 edition. Actually, there are at least three different versions of the cookbook printed in 1763. When comparing copies from various institutions, one can see actual changes in words and also in measurements of the text and in how it sits on the page. These are definitive indicators of separate editions of a book.[50] For example, some 1763 copies have a *lema* [lemma or catchword] placed under one part of the last line of the book, while others have it placed under another part, as seen in Figures 5, 6, and 7.

Another exciting discovery related to the 1763 editions was a note found in an edition housed at the Library of Congress. This copy is part of the Elizabeth Pennell collection. While researching the editions, I discovered a handwritten slip of paper inserted into the copy. It read: "A late edition of a book first published in 1617 – Interesting because Martiño was the cook of Philip IV and also because the date shows his popularity as an authority" (see Figure 8).[51]

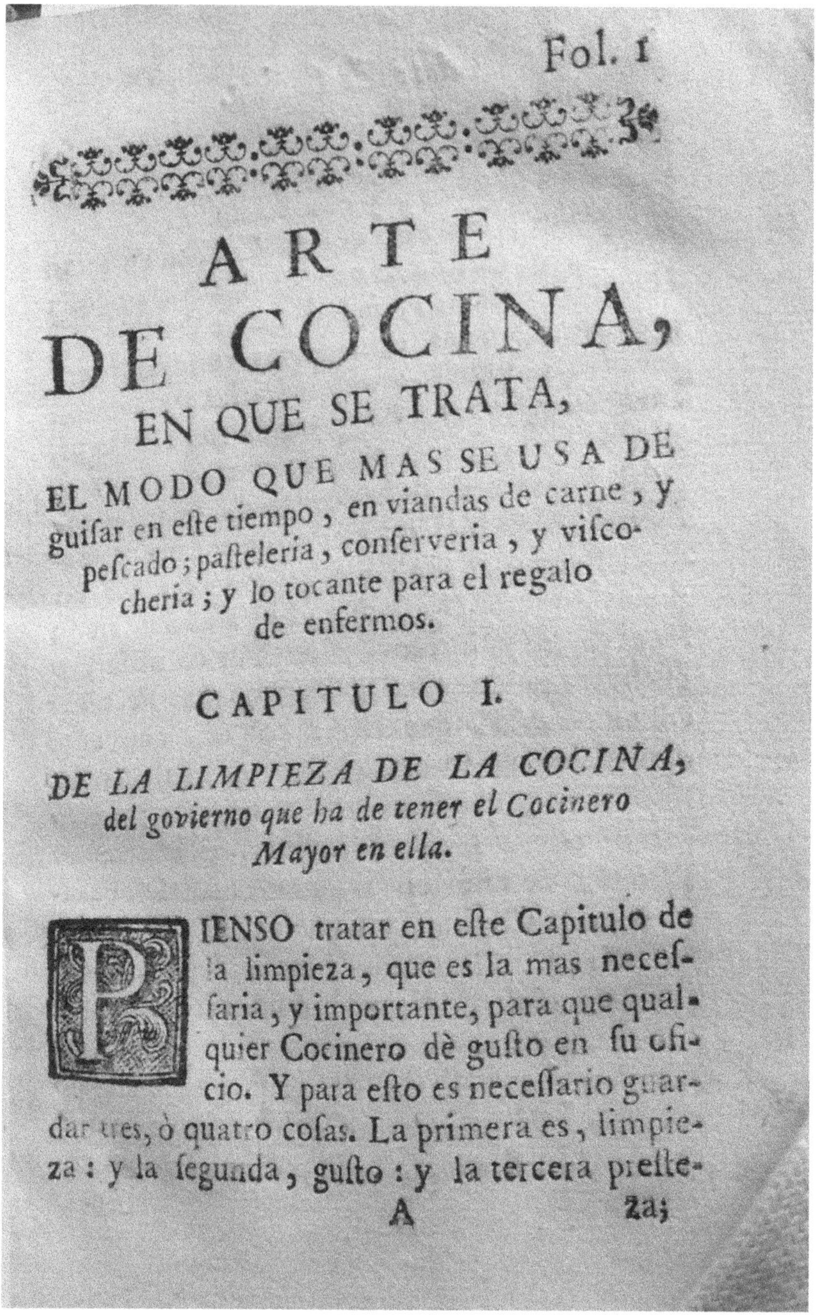

ARTE DE COCINA,

EN QUE SE TRATA,

EL MODO QUE MAS SE USA DE guisar en este tiempo, en viandas de carne, y pescado; pastelería, conservería, y viscochería; y lo tocante para el regalo de enfermos.

CAPITULO I.

DE LA LIMPIEZA DE LA COCINA, del govierno que ha de tener el Cocinero Mayor en ella.

PIENSO tratar en este Capitulo de la limpieza, que es la mas necessaria, y importante, para que qualquier Cocinero dè gusto en su oficio. Y para esto es necessario guardar tres, ò quatro cosas. La primera es, limpieza: y la segunda, gusto: y la tercera presteza;

Figure 6. Folio 1 from the Library of Congress 1763 edition: the "A" sits under the colon. Photo by author, March 2016.

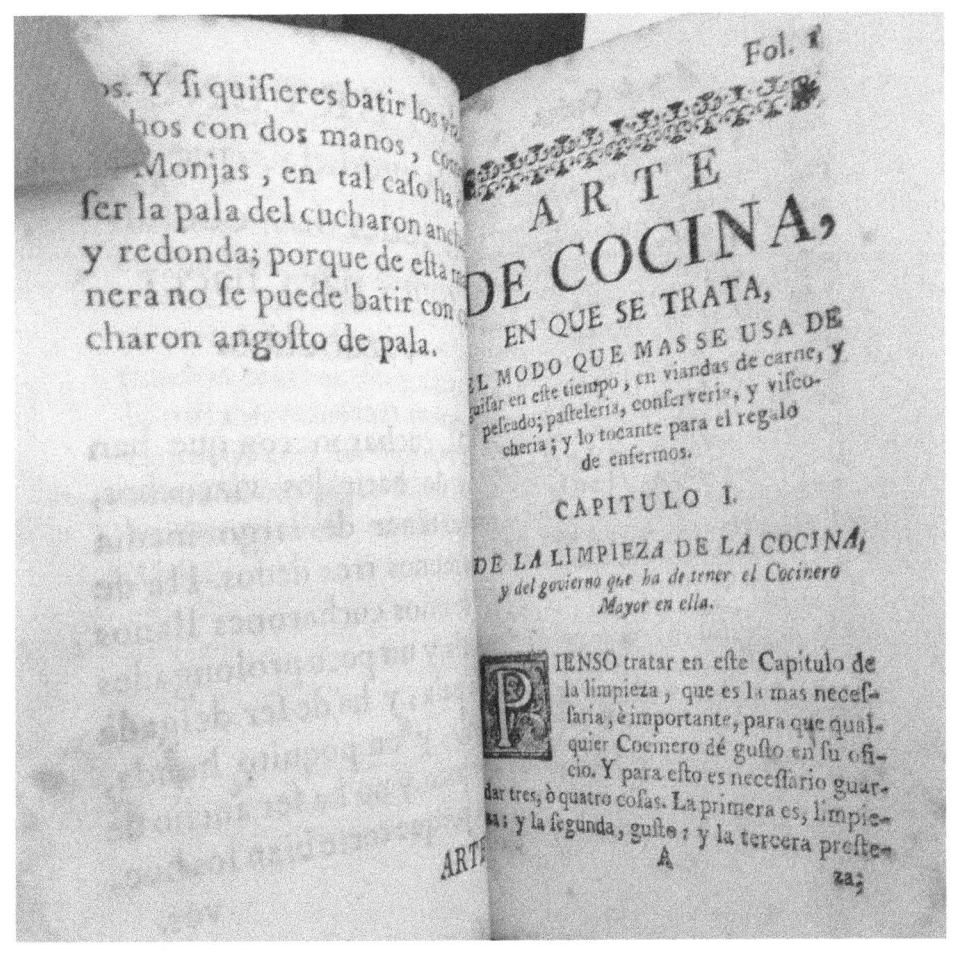

Figure 7. Folio 1 from the Lilly Library, Indiana University 1763 edition: the "A" sits under the "st" of "gusto." Photo by author, July 2016.

Although I have not confirmed the handwriting, it is quite probable that the note was written by author and food writer Elizabeth Pennell (1855–1936), who amassed over four hundred volumes of early modern European cookbooks. In her bibliographic essay *My Cookery Books*, she writes with excitement about Martínez Montiño:

> Few of my treasures do I prize more than the Arte de Cocina, though it is in the fifteenth edition, with the date on the title-page provokingly effaced. The first edition was published in 1617, and its author was Francisco Martínez Montiño, Cocinero Mayor del Rey – this particular Rey being none other than Philip IV. Here, then, you may learn what the Spaniard ate in the days when Velázquez painted. (105)

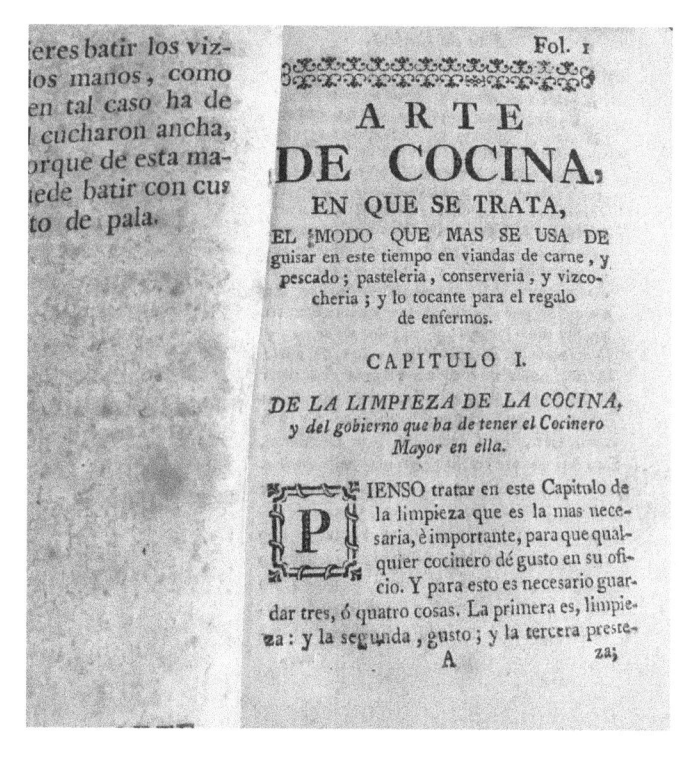

Figure 8. Folio 1 from the Bibliotequé universitat, Barcelona, Spain 1763 edition: the "A" sits under the "u" of "gusto." Also note the difference of the initial P that begins the chapter compared to the other two 1763 versions. Photo by author, July 2016.

Although she misdates the original publication, it is clear that Martínez Montiño's cookbook resonated with foodies well into the twentieth century.

The 1778 Edition

This is the first edition to omit all front material before the prologue. It is also the basis for two twenty-first-century facsimiles, Seville, 2008 and Madrid, 2009.

The 1790 Edition

In this front material for this edition, the king for whom Martínez Montiño cooked is misidentified and his name misspelled: "Don Phelipe II." There are a series of typos and a few significant errors like the recipe title, "Manteca de almendras amarillas" [Yellow almond butter], which is written as "Manteca de vacas amarilla" [Yellow cow butter].

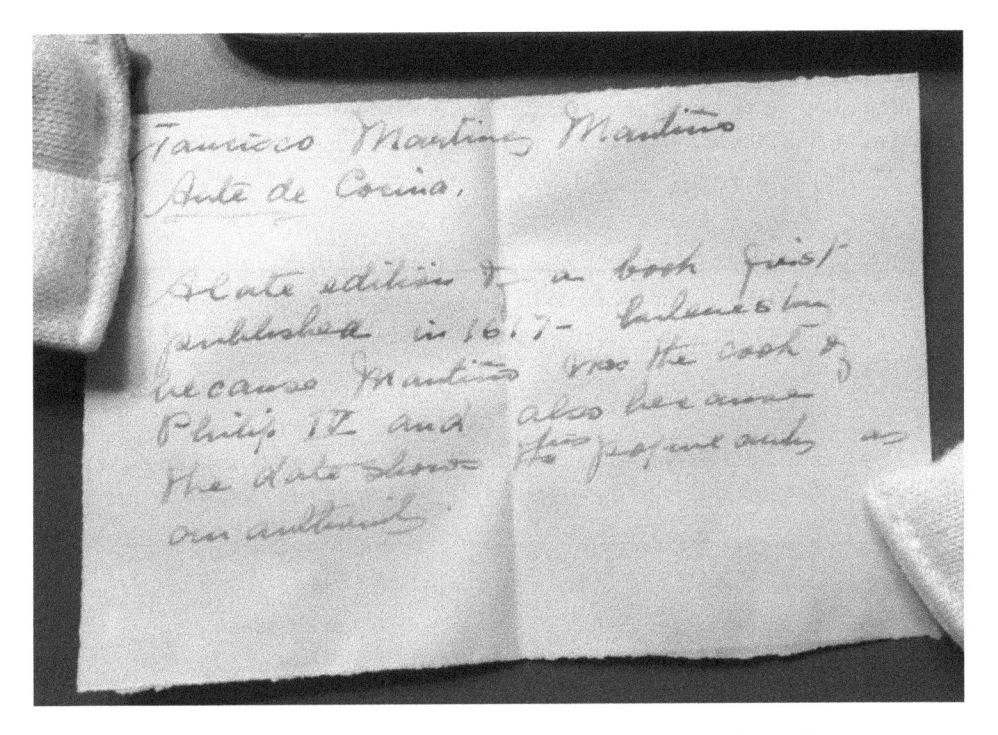

Figure 9. Handwritten note in the 1763 edition of the cookbook at the Library of Congress. Photo by author, March 2016.

The 1797 Edition

One of the significant changes in this late eighteenth-century edition is the exclusion of language that references spoon drawings in the back of the book. In the original version, Martínez Montiño included two spoon illustrations. Even though the spoons disappeared early in the eighteenth century, references to these illustrations did not. In addition to the front material, which includes an entire notice on the size of spoons for making sweet biscuits, the recipe "Bizcochos de harina de trigo" [Sweet biscuits with wheat flour] (also makes a specific reference: "el papelillo, y el batido, y los cucharones, todo irá dibujado al fin de este libro [The little papers, the batter, and the spoons are all drawn at the back of the book] (540; 541). However, in the 1797 edition, this language disappears and is excluded from all of the following editions with the exception of the 1807 one.

The 1800 Edition

By the time the nineteenth century begins, the cookbook has a different, more modern look, but otherwise there are no significant changes from the previous edition.

The 1807 Edition

This is the edition of the 1982 facsimile from Barcelona that Tusquets released as part of "Los 5 sentidos libros perdidos" series. In many ways, this edition follows the patterns of word choice, spelling, and syntax of the eighteenth-century editions.

The 1809 Edition

This edition diverges somewhat from the 1807 edition. Generally, it aligns more with the later two publications, while the 1807 edition aligns more with the eighteenth-century ones.

The 1822 Edition

There are no significant changes from the previous edition.

The 1823 edition

This is last known edition (before the facsimiles of the late twentieth and twenty-first centuries). Generally, it aligns with the previous 1822 edition.

X. This Edition and Commentary

This critical edition is based on the 1611 edition of Martínez Montiño's cookbook from the National Library of Spain in Madrid, which is available online through the National Library. For today's reader, I have made a series of changes to Martínez Montiño's original 1611 publication. First, I have added in brackets a number for each of the 506 recipes. This additional numbering system can be used to locate recipes throughout the work. I have also included the original folios (recto and verso) for those who would like to access the recipes in the original 1611 version. In those cases where two recipes fall under one title, I have supplied a title for the embedded recipe in brackets.

Second, to facilitate access to Martínez Montiño's work, I have added modern-day accent marks, updated punctuation, and made the following orthographic changes:

1. *z* for *ç* (*zumo* instead of *çumo*, *azúcar* instead of *açucar*)
2. *c* for *z* (for example, *veces* instead of *vezes*, *tocino* instead of *tozino*)

3. *c* for *q* (*cuando* instead of *quando*)
4. *u* for *v* (*un* instead of *vn*)
5. *v* for *u* (*aves* instead of *aues*, *huevos* instead of *hueuos*)
6. *v* for *b* (*vuelve* instead of *buelve*)
7. *b* for *v* (*bizcocho* instead of *vizcocho*)
8. *hi* for *y* (*hierbabuena* instead of *yervabuena*)
9. *i* for *y* (*reina* instead of *reyna*)
10. added or removed *h* (*hombre* instead of *ombre*; *ijada* instead of *hijada*)
11. *h* for *g* (*ahora* instead of *agora*)
12. *f* for *h* (*fanega* instead of *hanega*)
13. *j* for *g* (*jengibre* instead of *gengibre*; *majestad* instead of *magestad*)
14. *j* for *x* (*dejar* instead of *dexar*, *mejido* instead of *mexido*, *jengibre* instead of *xengibre*)
15. *x* for *s* (*extranjeros* instead of *estranjeros*)
16. removed double letters (*así* instead of *assi*)
17. *e* for *y* before *i*; *ú* for *o* before a word that begins with *o*
18. joined the clitic to the end of the verb (*meterle* instead of *meter le*)
19. separated *haber* from the end of the verb (*apartarlas has* instead of *apartarlashas*)

However, I have maintained the following orthographic differences:

1. Contractions: for example, *della*, *deste*
2. *por que* (when its meaning is *para que*)
3. The use of capital letters
4. Old verb forms: *vos*: *habiades*, *teniades*; subjunctive: *mandásemos*; *pedistes*, *suplicastes*

And, I have also maintained the following syntactic difference:

1. The pronoun placement after the verb: *iráslos*, *tuvímoslo*

In addition to the orthography, for the translations, I have modernized the punctuation, often replacing the word *y* [and] with a period and the beginning of a new sentence. In the early modern era, lengthy sentences were not uncommon, but to gain clarity for today's readers, I have updated the punctuation to maximize understanding the instructions. This decision also aligns with editors throughout the centuries, since most chose to modernize punctuation (and grammar) to conform to the standards of the day. Finally, with the exception of the first section of Chapter 1, I have remained faithful to the paragraph breaks from the original 1611 version.

The notes in this edition are written with both the specialist and non-specialist in mind. They include explanations for specific lexicon, cooking techniques, cultural

commentary, cross-references, writing style, and other curiosities I thought would be of interest to all readers. In reference to early modern cookbooks, Barbara Ketcham Wheaton explains that "these rich, unreliable, diverting, and moving documents challenge, surprise, and enlighten the careful reader" ("Cookbooks" 295). This is very much the case with Martínez Montiño's masterpiece. Preparing the edition has been a deeply satisfying research project. However, I also recognize my own limitations as I present the multi-faceted ways Martínez Montiño reveals early modern Spanish cuisine to his own readers. My aim is for readers today to get something out of this edition and to learn something new. But, like Martínez Montiño, I too look forward to hearing from you, my discreet reader, on points that still need clarification and details yet to be revealed.

NOTES

1 *Arte de cocina, pastelería, vizcochería y conservería* was published ten times in the seventeenth century (1611, 1617, 1620, 1623, 1628, 1637, 1653, 1662, 1674, 1676), fourteen times in the eighteenth century (1705 [twice] 1715, 1725, 1728, 1732, 1754, 1760, 1763 [three times], 1778, 1790, 1797), and five times in the early part of the nineteenth century (1800, 1807, 1809, 1822, 1823). The cookbook was published again in 1982 when Tusquets printed a facsimile version, and again in Valencia, 1994 and 1997. In the early twenty-first century, three new facsimiles surfaced: Valladolid, 2006; Seville, 2008; and Madrid, 2009. The first is based on the 1807 edition, the following three (1994, 1997, and 2006) on the 1763 edition, and the latter two on the 1778 edition. Later, in 2021, Jesús M. Usunáriz and Magalí Ortiz Martín published their critical edition of the cookbook with the Instituto de Estudios Auriseculares. Other important works before 1700 include Mestre Robert's *Llibre del coc* (1520, published six times in the sixteenth century and also translated into Castilian in 1525 under the name Ruperto de Nola, as *Libro de cozina* or *Libro de guisados* and published seventeen times by 1577 and again some eleven times between 1929 and 2002); Miguel de Baeza's *Los quarto libros del arte de la confitería* (1592; no subsequent edition was released); Diego Granado's *Libro del arte de cozina* (1599; published three times until 1614 and again in 1990 and 1991); and Domingo Hernández de Maceras' *Libro del arte de cozina* (1607; no subsequent edition was released until 1998).
2 I intentionally use the title *master cook* throughout this edition, because I think it retains more of the original feel of *cocinero mayor* than the truncated term *chef*, which was imported into the English language from the French *chef de cuisine* in the late nineteenth century.
3 For a brief history of cooking manuscripts and cookbooks in Spain before 1700, see Nadeau, *Food Matters* 3–44, and for an overview of food's relationship to cultural and social identity in early modern Spain, see Nadeau, *Food Matters*, and Campbell. For a broader view of the role of cookbooks in the formation of Spain's cultural history,

see Moreno, "Beyond the Recipes," Moreno, *De la página al plato*, and Anderson, *Cooking Up the Nation*.

4 For a critical edition of Nola, see Cruz Cruz; for Hernández de Maceras, Pérez Samper, *La alimentación*; and for Altamiras, Hayward, *New Art*.

5 For example, the Castilian plague of 1596–1602 literally decimated the population, claiming some 600,000 lives (Casey 41).

6 José del Corral has a slightly different list but affirms the general sense of who was working with Martínez Montiño in the royal kitchen: "cinco ayudas de cocina, dos portadores, tres mozos de oficio, un potagier, un buxier, un portero de cocina y un pastelero" [five cook's assistants, two food runners, three kitchen boys, a potage maker, a fire attendant, a kitchen porter, and a pastry baker] (50). Also see Martínez Millán and Hortal Muñóz. Scholars are also contextualizing contributions of cooks within a larger socio-historic context. For more information, see Simón Palmer, "El estatuto del cocinero," and for the role of the cook in shaping food discourse in Spain and Latin America, see Gutiérrez Flores.

7 As the name itself indicates, the *mastresala* is the master of the dining room, or *steward*. His chief duty is to attend to the lord at the table by presenting the food, serving it, and ensuring its quality.

8 The *veedor* [inspector] is the person in charge of the pantry and is responsible for purchasing food from different vendors. In addition, and as is noted here in Martínez Montiño's instructions, the *veedor* oversees the delivery of the food from the kitchen to the dining room.

9 Folio numbers include r [recto] and v [verso].

10 See Appendix 1, "Kitchen Furnishings and Equipment," for a complete listing of kitchen furnishings, cookware, prepware, serveware, and utensils. For the most comprehensive work on early modern kitchen spaces and instruments to date, see Brears. For Italian kitchen space, see Krohn's study of Bartolomeo Scappi's *Opera* (1570) in *Food and Knowledge in Renaissance Italy*. For more on the material culture of the early modern court kitchen in Spain, see Nadeau, "Furniture and Equipment."

11 In *Cocina y alimentación en los siglos XVI y XVII*, Julio Valles Rojo explains that privileges and other exceptions to rules of abstinence were often granted. He also notes that, in 1566, Pope Pius V declared null previous bulls that had granted these privileges and established Fridays as an official day of abstinence throughout the year. Meat was forbidden, but animal by-products such as eggs and dairy, as well as fish, were allowed (339). For more on religious regulations concerning food, see Usunáriz and Ortiz Martín 74–91.

12 While we commonly think of *sopa* as *soup*, in this cookbook, and more generally in seventeenth-century Spain and beforehand, *sop* is a piece of bread placed on the bottom of a dish that soaks up the juices of the dish or a piece of bread that has some type of liquid – usually stock, broth, wine, or cream – poured on top of it.

13 For more on the history of *molletes*, see Corbacho, and Yarza 24.

14 For more information, see Carmen Abad Zardoya, "Herramientas curiosas," particularly 89.

15 A few years earlier, in 1607, Domingo Hernández de Maceras includes turkey as one of the ten different animals he highlights in his chapter on butchering animals and parting them out (191–2). He also includes a recipe for roasting turkey that shares some of the features of Martínez Montiño's but also differs in roasting technique and suggested sauce.

16 I am indebted to archaeologist and historian Andreas Klumpp, who has shared with me several recipes that describe this cooking process. For more information, see the recipe "Cómo se aderezan las carpas" [How to prepare carp] (412; 413).

17 I've translated *calabaza* as *squash*, given their popularity across continents, though it is possible that Martínez Montiño also used gourds for any of his recipes. For more information on early years of squash in Europe and Africa, see Gispert Cruells 223–4.

18 For more on squash varieties that arrived in Spain in the early days of the Transatlantic Exchange, see Gispert Cruells, especially 223–4.

19 The *amacena* is another name for *damascena*, or *from Damascus*. Today the fruit is called damson plums. They are dark purple, oval, and have a slightly sour flavour. They are primarily used for jams and jellies.

20 The different sugar stages from lightest to heaviest are *lisa* [smooth] (thread stage), *perla* [pearl] (soft-ball stage), *soplo* [blow] (between soft and firm), *pluma* [feather] (firm ball stage), *caña* [reed] (hard-ball stage), and *caramelo* (caramel stage) (6–8).

21 In early modern Spain and up until the early twentieth century, *manteca de vaca* was the accepted term for *butter*, while the broader *manteca* was used contextually to refer to both butter and lard. *Manteca de vaca* was still the dominant term used at the close of the nineteenth century, as evidenced in Antonio Usero Torrente's 1899 dissertation on the defence of butter. He begins with its definition: "La manteca de vaca es un producto graso extraído de la leche en la que se encuentra en suspensión" [Butter is a fat extracted from milk which is suspended]. It is in the early twentieth century when a certain "manteca dulce de Soria," which was called *mantequilla*, began to replace the term *manteca de vacas* as the common referent for butter (Gutiérrez Cuadro and Rodríguez 159).

22 In recreating recipes from *Arte de cocina*, I have refined the spice blend to the following proportions: four parts black pepper and ginger to two parts nutmeg, to one part clove. For each tablespoon of this mixture, I add several strands of saffron. Of course, both now and then, these proportions could vary slightly from recipe to recipe and according to individual taste.

23 All translations from the *Diccionario de autoridades* are my own.

24 It is curious how even in 1611 some foods were imagined as substitutes for others and evaluated to the degree that the flavour of one dish could imitate that of another.

25 For more on taste as an aesthetic concept and its treatment in Gracián, see Nelson, and Ruan.

26 For more on *mostachón* [mostachon cookie], see the recipe "Memoria de los mostachones" [Memoir of mostachon cookies] (510; 511).

27 I have intentionally excluded Diego Granado's 1599 cookbook, as it is primarily a translation of the Italian Bartolomeo Scappi's opus, *Opera dell'arte del cucinare*.

28 It is not until 1913, with the publication of Emilia Pardo Bazán's *La cocina española Antigua*, in which the author republishes a series of Martínez Montiño's recipes, that couscous appears once again in the recipe books. For a Spanish translation of *Kitāb al-tabīj*, see Huici Miranda.

29 For connections between Aldonza's grandmother's kitchen and the Islamic world, see Corriente Córdoba.

30 For more on the connection between couscous and Muslim/Morisco identity as seen in Inquisitional records, see Cardaillac 27. And, for more on the use of cultural practices ascribed to Moriscos and assimilation of new converts, see Bernabé.

31 Philip III followed in his father's footsteps in terms of maintaining peaceful conditions with the Portuguese. The Council of Portugal existed between 1582 and 1668, several years after Portugal seceded from Spain in 1640. For further information on the relations between Spain and Portugal during the Hapsburg dynasty, see Kamen 243–5.

32 Although a relative of the *piper negrum*, where black pepper comes from, *pimienta larga* has a hotter taste than the round, black pepper. The part used is the dried catkin-shaped stick, which is then ground, not the seeds, which is the case with black pepper. Thanks to Ken Albala for pointing out this distinction.

33 Again, the citation for this recipe is from the 1617 edition.

34 The complete recipe follows: "Take a quart of life Hony, and set it upon the fire and when it seetheth scum it clean, and then put in a certaine of fine Biskets well serced, and some pouder of Cloves, some Ginger, and powder of sinamon, Annis seeds and some Sugar, and let all these be well stirred upon the fire, til it be as thicke as you thinke needfull, and for the paste for them take Flower as finelye dressed as may be, and a good peece of sweet Butter, and woorke all these same well togither, and not knead it."

35 Rosa Tovar reminds us that the process of folding fat into the dough was first recorded in the Hispano-Muslim cookbooks of the thirteenth century.

36 For the recreation of the pastry "Bollo maimón" [Maimon layered pastry], which has clear antecedents in Hispano-Muslim baking, see Appendix 3.10.

37 For more on the fascinating and complex evolution of the *artalete*, see 188n74, and for images on how they are made, see Appendix 3.5.

38 Scholars who study culinary lexicon from this time period have yet to weigh in on this sauce, which is unique to Martínez Montiño. However, for excellent studies on Martínez Montiño's contributions to culinary lexicon, see Torres Martínez, "Léxico culinario autorizado," Soto García, "El arte de cocina" and "Los términos culinarios," and Eberenz.

39 I am grateful to Chad Sanders for recreating dishes from this cookbook that mention flor to discover exactly what Martínez Montiño is referencing. In researching this question, Vicky Hayward also brought to my attention that Corominas' definition of *aflorar* states, "'apurar algo para sacar su flor o parte selecta,' princ. S. XV; 'salir a la superficie, a flor de agua,' 1875" ["to bring something to the surface to highlight

its flower or select part" beg 15th c; "to rise to the surface, at water level," 1875] (Corominas 276). Both are relevant to Martínez Montiño's usage of the word. Hayward notes that *flor* "is still used in food and wine with both meanings, the first to describe the finest olive oil – squeezed out from olives pressed between esparto mats without any grinding between stones or in a mechanical press – and the second to describe the thick layer of yeasts that floats on top of sherry wine while it matures in the cask" (email correspondence, 26 July 2018). This latter meaning visually resembles Martínez Montiño's flor. See Appendix 3.3 for an image of the flor (637), and for a recreation of this dish, with the flor garnish on top of the birds and the egg-enriched sauce, see Appendix 3.4 (638). Finally, I wish to express thanks to both Rafael Ferradáns and Restaurante Arzak for also exploring the possibilities of the significance of flor (email correspondence, 24 July 2018 to 8 September 2018).

40 Prior to the appearance of the sandwich in Europe, recipes existed in medieval Arab cookbooks. For more on the origens of the sandwich, see Nasrallah, "Mediaeval Arabs."
41 In her fascinating work on the development of the early modern cookbook in England, Elizabeth Spiller retraces the intellectual and cultural shifts occurring there that led to the standardization of both the formulaic instructions that make up recipes and the formulaic format of how an entire cookbook should be laid out.
42 For more on discourse colony, see Michael Hoey, especially 77–89.
43 For more information on the evolution of Altamiras' *costradas*, see Hayward's excellent edition and translation of the cookbook (*New Art of Cookery* 18–23).
44 In *Le manuscript de Sion* the recipe is for a poultry stew instead of veal as Martínez Montiño uses. For the complete recipe "Hochepot de poullaile" [Poultry hochepot], see Müllers 20. My thanks to Ken Albala for pointing out this *Sion* reference.
45 For a fuller understanding of Pardo Bazán's contribution to Spanish culinary history, see Ingram 15–43.
46 Notaker's comment on the domestic and largely female audience for smaller books raises the question of whether the bookseller, Luis Sánchez, had in mind a wider audience for selling the cookbook beyond cooks at court. Notations of Martínez Montiño throughout the recipes certainly allude to a wider audience that included women and cooks who served lords and other aristocrats.
47 For more information on the original title page illustration and other illustrations found in subsequent editions, see 100n2.
48 For more information on María de Quiñones and other women printers working in early modern Spain, see "Impresoras en Madrid s. SVII."
49 My thanks to Ángel Soto García for pointing out this BVNP edition and its differences from the other 1705 edition. For more on this and other editions, see Soto García, "*El arte de cozina [...]*."
50 My thanks to Javier de Diego in the print reserves section of the Biblioteca nacional for pointing out ways to distinguish one edition from the next even when they have the same date and publisher.
51 A special thanks to my brother, Dan, for his help in deciphering the handwriting.

ARTE DE COCINA, PASTELERÍA, VIZCOCHERÍA Y CONSERVERÍA

The Art of Cooking, Pie Making, Pastry Making and Preserving

Arte de cocina, pastelería, vizcochería y conservería.
Compuesta por Francisco Martínez Motiño,[1]
cocinero mayor del Rey nuestro señor.

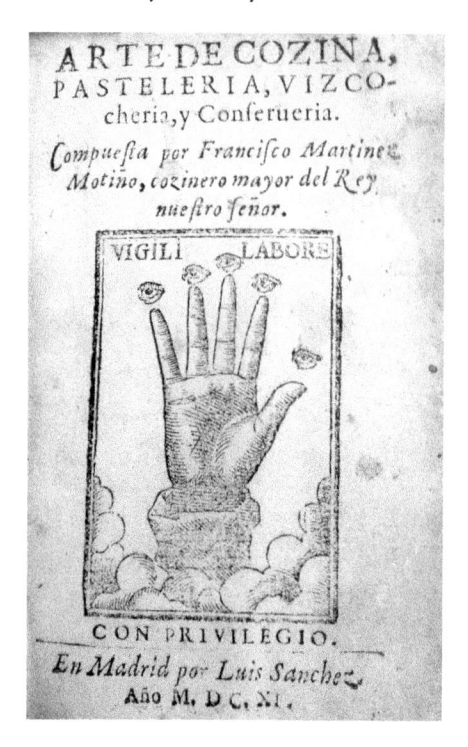

> ARTE DE COZINA,
> PASTELERIA, VIZCO-
> cheria, y Conseruería.
> Compuesta por Francisco Martinez
> Motiño, cozinero mayor del Rey
> nuestro señor.
>
> VIGILI LABORE
>
> CON PRIVILEGIO.
> En Madrid por Luis Sanchez
> Año M. D C. XI.

Con privilegio
En Madrid por Luis Sánchez
Año M. D. C. XI[2]

---

[1] In 1611 and 1617 the author's name appeared as Martínez Motiño, but in the third edition of 1623 it appears as Martínez Montiño, and this has been the accepted spelling of his last name since that date.

[2] This title page illustration was first published as an emblem in Christóbal Pérez de Herrera's *Proverbios morales, y consejos christianos, muy provechosos* [Very beneficial moral proverbs and Christian advice] (1576). By highlighting the senses of sight and touch, Sánchez weighs in on the humanist debate of the banquet of the senses by privileging touch together with sight as a way to acquire and achieve knowledge. He echoes the thoughts of the humanist Fray Luis de Granada, who wrote, "usando de la industria de las manos en las cosas de naturaleza, habemos venido a fabricar otra nueva naturaleza" [using the industry of the hand in the things of nature, we have come to produce another, new nature] (489). This illustration is also found in the 1617 edition. Later in the seventeenth century, the hand is replaced by other objects; for example, a hippogriff in 1623 and 1637, a cross with vegetation surrounding it in 1628 and 1662, ivy and sickle in 1653, and a small flower pot in 1676. The later editions become less and less concerned with the title page visual. However, in both the 1728 and 1760 versions, the cover page has a coat of arms, apparently of the Padilla family. Pedro Joseph Alonso y Padilla was the "Librero de camera del rey" [book collector of the king's chamber] and put up the money for the book's publication.

The Art of Cooking, Pie Making, Pastry Making and Preserving.
Composed by Francisco Martínez Motiño,
Master cook of the King our lord

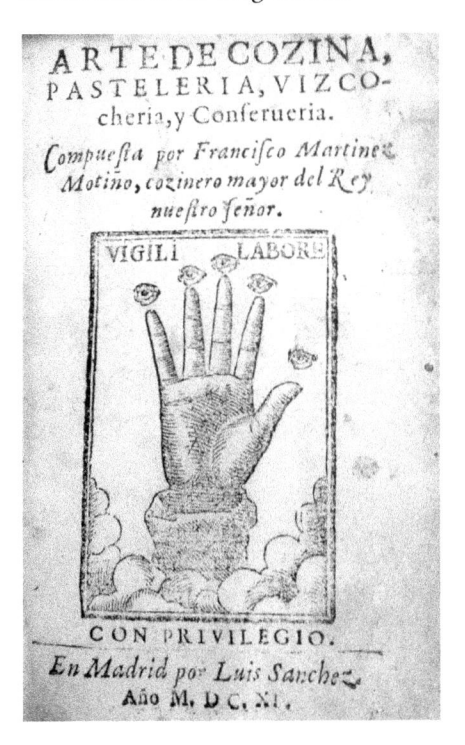

With permission
In Madrid by Luis Sánchez
Year M. D. C. XI

TASA.[3]

Yo Gerónimo Núñez de León, escribano de cámara del Rey nuestro señor, de los que en su consejo residen doy fe, que habiéndose visto por los señores del, un libro intitulado Arte de Cocina: compuesto por Francisco Martínez Motiño [sic], cocinero mayor del Rey nuestro señor, que con licencia de los dichos señores del Consejo fue impreso, tasaron cada pliego de los del dicho libro a cuatro maravedís,[4] y parece tener cuarenta y dos pliegos, que al dicho respeto montan ciento y sesenta y ocho maravedís en papel: y a este precio mandaron se vendiese, y no más: y que esta tasa se ponga al principio de cada libro de los que se imprimieren. Y para que dello conste de mandamiento de los dichos señores del consejo, y de pedimiento del dicho Francisco Martínez Motiño, doy esta fe. En Madrid quince de Abril de mil y seiscientos y once años.

Gerónimo Núñez de León

Tiene este libro cuarenta y dos pliegos, que conforme a su tasa en papel, monta cinco reales menos dos mrs.[5]

He visto este libro de Arte de cocina, compuesto por Francisco Martínez Motiño, cocinero mayor del Rey nuestro señor, y hallo que está conforme a su original por donde se mandó imprimir, y no hay en él errata de consideración que apuntar. Y por ser así verdad lo firmé. En Madrid veinte de Marzo, deste año de mil y seiscientos y once.

El Licenciado Murcia de la Llana.[6]

---

3 During the Hapsburg empire, the court established explicit guidelines for book production. For each publication, it was necessary to include the name of the author, the printer, the city of publication, the certificate of price, the errata sheet, the approval or licence, and royal permission (Escolar Sobrino 20). This section on the *tasa* [certificate of price] appears through the first half of the eighteenth century and then disappears from the cookbook after the 1754 edition. In fact, by 1797 all the front material between the title page and prologue disappears.

4 A *pliego* [sheet] referred to a sheet of paper that was printed on both sides and folded in four, thus forming four separate folios or eight separate pages. In the case of this first edition, there were 336 folios, which included the front material, numbered folios of the different chapters, and the back material.

5 *Mrs.* is one of the common abbreviations for *maravedís*, the recognized monetary unit of the day. Each one of the 42 *pliegos* or sheets was valued at 4 mrs. (which total 168 mrs.). This price is again stated in terms of reals. The *real* was valued at 34 mrs. (5 x 34 = 170). The quoted price of 5 reals less 2 mrs. confirms the price of 168 mrs. With the exception of the 1676 edition, which was priced at 6 mrs. per sheet, every seventeenth-century edition was priced at 4 mrs. per sheet. However, over time the necessary number of sheets diminished, and thus the price of the cookbook actually dropped from 168 mrs. in 1611 and 1617 to 160 mrs. in 1623 and 1637, and to 124 mrs. in 1653 and 1662. Between 1676 and 1760, the book was priced at 6 mrs. per sheet, with the exception of the 1705 editions, which followed the original 1611 pricing. By the mid-eighteenth century, this royal certificate of price disappeared from the front material.

6 Starting in 1628, this last section carries a header: "Fe de erratas" [Erratum]. Subsequent editions vary on whether or not they continue with the 1611 model (no header). In 1653, the header expands to "Fee del Corrector General de Libros por su majestad" [Certificate of the Corrector General of Books on behalf of His Majesty].

CERTIFICATE OF PRICE

I, Gerónimo Núñez de León, clerk of our lord the king's chamber, among those who reside in his council, certify that all Council members, having examined a book entitled *The Art of Cooking*, composed by Francisco Martínez Motiño, master cook of the king our lord, that was printed with the permission of said Council gentlemen, priced each sheet of said book at four maravedis. And it seems to have forty-two sheets, which accordingly adds up to one hundred and sixty-eight maravedis of paper. At this price and no more they have ordered the book to be sold. And this certificate of price should be put at the beginning of each book of however many are published. And so that this is recognized by order of said gentlemen of the Council and as per request of said Francisco Martínez Motiño, I so certify. In Madrid the fifteenth of April of sixteen hundred and eleven.

Gerónimo Núñez de León

This book has forty-two sheets, which, according to the certified paper price, adds up to five reals less two mrs.

I have examined this book, *The Art of Cooking*, composed by Francisco Martínez Motiño, master cook of our lord, the king, and find that it is faithful to the original, which was approved for printing, and there are no noteworthy errors for consideration, and because it is true, I have signed it. In Madrid the twentieth of March of this year, sixteen hundred and eleven.

The Licentiate Murcia de la Llana.

EL REY. (Privilegio)[7]

Por Cuanto por parte de vos Francisco Martínez Motiño [sic],[8] cocinero mayor de nuestra real casa, nos fue fecha relación, que por la larga experiencia que teníades de las cosas tocantes al dicho oficio, habíades compuesto un libro intitulado, *De la manera que se habían de aderezar las cosas de comida*:[9] el cual habíades compuesto con mucho trabajo, y era de mucha importancia para los que usaban el dicho oficio, y nos pedistes y suplicastes os mandásemos dar licencia para le poder imprimir y privilegio por veinte años para le poder vender, o como la nuestra merced fuese. Lo cual visto por los del nuestro consejo, y como por su mandado se hicieron las diligencias que la premática por nos últimamente fecha sobre la impresión de los libros dispone, fue acordado, que debíamos mandar dar esta nuestra cédula para vos en la dicha razón, y nos tuvímoslo por bien. Por la cual por os hacer bien y merced, os damos licencia y facultad para que por tiempo de diez años primeros siguientes, que corren y se cuenten desde el día de la fecha della,[10] vos, o la persona que vuestro poder quiere, y no otro alguno, podáis imprimir y vender el dicho libro que de suso se hace mención por el original que en el nuestro consejo se vio, que va rubricado y firmado al fin del de Christobal Núñez de León nuestro escribano de cámara de los que en el residen, con que antes que se venda lo traigáis ante ellos, juntamente con el dicho original, para que se vea si la dicha impresión está conforme a él, o traigáis fe en pública forma, en como por corretor [sic] por nos nombrado, se vio y corrigió la dicha impresión por su original. Y mandamos al impresor que imprimiere el dicho libro, no imprima el principio y primer pliego, ni entregue más de un solo libro con el original al autor, o persona a cuya costa se imprimiere, y no otro alguno para efeto de la dicha corrección y tasa, hasta que primero el dicho libro esté corregido y tasado por los del nuestro consejo. Y estando así y no de otra manera, pueda imprimir el dicho libro, principio, y primer pliego; en el cual seguidamente se ponga esta nuestra licencia y privilegio, y la aprobación, tasa, y erratas, so pena de caer e incurrir en las penas contenidas en la premática y leyes de nuestros Reinos que sobre ello disponen.

---

7 This "Privilegio" section, which indicates the king's permission to print the book, appears in 1617, 1623, and 1637 and again in the 1705 editions. In the 1628 edition and later in 1653, the "Privilegio" is replaced by a "Licencia" section. By 1778 all the front material that appears between the cover and the prologue disappears from all editions.

8 The controversial name Motiño is used in the 1611, 1617, and 1623 versions, even though the 1623 edition has the name Montiño printed on the cover.

9 After the 1617 edition, this title is never mentioned again, and, as the cover page indicates, it changed when it went to publication.

10 Although Martínez Montiño requests permission to publish and sell his book for twenty years, the court approves that he do so for ten years, which was the court-approved standard amount of time.

The King (Privilege)

On behalf of you, Francisco Martínez Motiño, master cook of our royal household, a petition was made to us that due to your long experience that you have had with matters related to said office, you have composed a book entitled *On the Way Food Should Be Prepared*, which you have worked very hard in composing and which was very important to those who work in said profession, and you asked and requested that we approve for you a licence to print and hold exclusive rights to sell it for twenty years or for however long we deemed. This has been seen by those of our council and, as per your request, the requirements set forth in the decree recently issued by us regarding the printing of books having been met, we should grant you our seal of approval, given the said reasons, and we are in agreement. As such we do you the good favour and grant licence and rights for the immediate next ten years that start and continue from this day forth to you or to whomever in your power you choose and no one else, for printing and selling said book mentioned previously because the original that our council saw and was signed and sealed at the end by Cristóbal Núñez de León, our court clerk, among those who reside in council, with the understanding that before it is sold it be brought before them, together with the original, so that they can see whether said printing complies with it [the original], or that you come with a public figure, an editor named by us, who saw it and proofread said printed copy with its original. And we order that the printer who will print said book not print the beginning and first sheet nor submit more than one single book with its original to the author, or the person at whose expense it will be printed, and not to anyone else, for the purpose of said editing and price setting, until said book is first edited and had its price set by those of our council. And this being the case and no other, the beginning and first sheet of said book can be printed in which will immediately appear our licence and permission, the [censor's] approval, retail price, and testimony, under penalty of fine and subject to liabilities contained in the rules and laws of our kingdoms that are decreed therein.

Y mandamos, que durante el tiempo de los dichos diez años persona alguna sin vuestra licencia no le pueda imprimir, ni vender, so pena que el que lo imprimiere haya perdido y pierda, todos y cualesquier libros, moldes, y aparejos, que del dicho libro tuviere: y más incurra en pena de cincuenta mil maravedís. La cual dicha pena sea la tercia parte para la nuestra cámara: y la otra tercia parte para el juez que lo sentenciare: y la otra tercia parte para la persona que lo denunciare. Y mandamos a los del nuestro consejo, Presidentes y Oidores de las nuestras audiencias, alcaldes, alguaciles de la nuestra casa y Corte, y Chancillerías, y a todos los Corregidores, Asistente, Gobernadores, Alcaldes mayores y Ordinarios y otros jueces y justicias cualesquier de todas las ciudades, villas, y lugares de los nuestros Reinos y señoríos, así a los que ahora son, como a los que serán de aquí adelante, que vos guarden y cumplan esta nuestra cédula: y contra su tenor y forma, y de lo en ella contenido, no vayan ni pasen, ni consientan ir, ni pasar en manera alguna, so pena de la nuestra merced, y de veinte mil maravedís para la nuestra cámara. Fecha en Madrid a once días del mes de Enero de mil y seiscientos y diez años.

YO EL REY
Por mandado del Rey nuestro Señor,
Jorge de Tobar

And we approve that during the span of the said ten years, any person without your licence cannot print or sell it, for whoever prints it will be subject to having lost and losing all and any copies, plates, and equipment that said book had: and will be subject to a fine of fifty thousand maravedis. From said penalty, a third goes to our chamber, another third to the sentencing judge, and another third to the person making the denouncement. And we order those of our council, presidents and judges of our courts, mayors, clerks of the royal house and court and chancery, and all magistrates, assistants, governors, lord mayors, and municipal magistrates, and any and all judges and justices in all the cities, villages, and places of our kingdoms and estates, both those current and those to come forthwith, that you observe and fulfil this our decree, and against its tenor and form and its contents within, do not go or proceed, nor consent to go or proceed in any way, or be subject to our mercy, and [a fine of] twenty thousand maravedis for our chamber. Dated in Madrid on the eleventh day of the month of January of sixteen hundred and ten.

I THE KING
By mandate of the King our lord,
Jorge de Tobar

PROLOGO AL LECTOR

El intento que he tenido en escribir este librito, ha sido no haber libros por donde se puedan guiar los que sirven el oficio de la cocina, y que todo se encarga a la memoria: solo uno he visto, y tan errado, que basta para echar a perder a quien usare de él, y compuesto por un oficial, que casi no es conocido en esta Corte: y así las cosas del libro no están puestas de manera, que ningún aprendiz se pueda aprovechar, a lo menos los Españoles, antes si se siguieren por él, lo errarán y echarán a perder la hacienda, y también por habérmelo pedido algunas personas: y lo que pretendo es, que cualquiera persona que se quiera aprovechar deste, acierte las cosas con muchas facilidad, y todas son cosas mías, y ninguna escrita por relación de nadie, y muchas dellas son de mi inventiva; porque las cosas que son escritas por relación, muy pocas veces salen verdaderas, porque las personas que dan las memorias, nunca las dan cabales: y así no se puede escribir cosa, que no se haya experimentado. Y lo que me ha dado ánimo para escribir es, haber servido tantos años al Rey nuestro Señor, y habérseme encargado las mayores cosas que se han ofrecido en el palacio Real de mi arte, con satisfacción de mis mayores: y por ser yo muy inclinado a enseñar, porque he hecho grandes oficiales de mi mano, y así espero en Dios, que con solo este poco de trabajo, que he tomado en escribir este librito, tengo de hacer oficiales con pocos principios que tengan: y se ha de ahorrar mucha hacienda a los Señores, porque no hay cosas que más hacienda gaste en este ministerio en los banquetes, que trabajar a tiento, porque piensan que por echar mucho recaudo es mejor, y por ahí lo echan a perder más presto, y gastase la hacienda, y no luce: y si en alguna cosa hubiere falta, suplico al discreto Letor lo supla, que como hombre me habré descuidado, que ya sé que los grandes oficiales no han menester libro: mas con todo eso por ser todos tan amigos míos, tendrán en algo mis cosas, y todavía hallarán alguna cosa nueva: y los aprendices si hicieren lo que yo ordeno, entiendo que no podrán errar. Y así los unos por deprender, y los otros por curiosidad, todos se holgarán de tener mi obrecilla. Mucho más pudiera escribir, mas he ido dejando las cosas que son muy ordinarias. Tampoco me he querido meter en oficio de nadie, mas de lo que toca

PROLOGUE FOR THE READER

The intention I have had in writing this little book has been that there are no books that can guide those serving in the cooking profession and that everything must be committed to memory. I have seen only one, and so flawed that whoever uses it will be ruined. It is written by a cook who is not even really known at this court. And thus, the matters of that book are not organized in a way that any apprentice could use to his advantage, at least not Spaniards, who, if faced with using it, will err, and their fortune will be ruined. I have also written it because several have asked that I do so, and my intention is that any person who wants to benefit from it can easily get things right. And all these recipes are my own, not written or belonging to anyone else; I have invented many of them, since the ones written down from another's account very often don't turn out as they should, since people, when recalling them by memory, never get it completely right. And likewise, nothing should be written down that hasn't first been tested. And what has encouraged me to write is, having served the king our lord for so many years and having been entrusted with the utmost responsibilities within my art that the Royal Palace has offered me and to the satisfaction of my superiors, and because I am inclined to teach, as I have successfully trained so many skilled cooks, thus I put my faith in God that with just the little work I have done in writing this little book, I can train even those with as little initial experience as they may have to become cooks. And, a lot of the lords' finances will be saved, because nowhere is more money spent in this profession of banquets than in working slowly because they [cooks] think that it is better to be extra careful, but that is where things are easily spoiled and money is wasted and it doesn't turn out impressive. And if there were a mistake somewhere, I beg of my discreet reader to fix it, because as a man I may have been a little neglectful, and I know, of course, that master cooks don't need this book. But, in spite of this and because they are all are good friends of mine, I hope they might get something out of my ideas and even find something new. And if apprentices do what I put forth here, I am certain they will not fail. And thus, for those who are learning and for others out of curiosity, all will delight in having my little work. I could have written a lot more, but I've left out the most mundane things. I have also chosen not to get into others' professions, only that which is relevant

al oficio de la cocina, por no enfrascar mucho al Lector, antes advierta, que en el capitulo de las tortas, que está escrito en el otro libro, hay muchas suertes de tortas, que no solo no son buenas, ni se deben hacer, mas antes es impertinencia escribirlas, como son las de castañas, y otras de higos, y de turmas de tierra, y de nabos, y de zanahorias, y de patatas,[11] *ni de cerezas, ni se ha de echar agrio en cosas que lleve leche, ni queso, porque son materiales muy contrarios, y hacen mucho daño a las personas que lo comen. Y esto advierto, porque en el otro libro se manda echar en muchas cosas queso y agraz, hasta la torta de manzanas dulces, ni de camuesas, no son buenas, sino les echan al conservar zumo de membrillos, que con esto serán buenas.*

---

11 The mention of *patata* here is one of the few times Martínez Montiño references New World products in his cookbook. Most critics assume that Martínez Montiño is critiquing Diego Granado's cookbook in his prologue, and while he could be, it is worth noting that Granado's cookbook has no recipes for potato pies.

to the cooking profession so the reader won't get bogged down. But I must warn that in the chapter on pies that is written in the other book, there are many kinds of pies that are not only no good but also should not be made. Moreover, it was impertinent to write them at all, like those with chestnuts, others with figs, truffles, turnips, carrots, potatoes, or cherries, nor should one add anything sour to recipes with milk or cheese, as they are contrary ingredients and would be very upsetting to whoever ate them. I am warning this because the other book often adds cheese and sour grapes to many things, even to sweet apple or to sour apple pies; this is no good, unless you first preserve them in quince juice because with this they will turn out good.

Advertencia, acerca de la medida que han de tener los cucharones para hacer bizcochos, que están figurados al fin de la obra.[12]

El cucharón con que han de batir los bizcochos, ha de tener de largo media vara menos tres dedos.[13] Ha de ser de unos cucharones llanos de pala, y un poco prolongados de la pala, y ha de ser delgada la pala, y un poquito honda, muy poco, y no ha de ser ancho de pala, porque corte bien los huevos. Y si quisieres batir los bizcochos con dos manos, como las monjas: en tal caso ha de ser la pala del cucharón ancha y redonda; porque desta manera no se puede batir con cucharón angosto de pala.[14] El cucharoncillo pequeño que va aquí dibujado al fin del libro, es, para poner el batido en los papelillos, que no ha de servir de otra cosa.[15]

---

12 Editors treated this notice differently. For example, in the 1725 edition, the subtitle disappears for the first time. It simply reads "Advertencia," as is the case in subsequent editions, with the exception of four editions: 1754, 1763, 1807, and 1822. These continue to use the complete subtitle.

13 A *vara*, or a *yard*, was a standard unit of measurement used in early modern Spain, though, according to the Real Academia Española, the length varied between 768 and 912 millimetres or between 2.5 and 3 feet. A half *vara* would measure anywhere from 38 to 46 cm or 15 to 18 inches, and Martínez Montiño's spoon approximately 33 to 40 cm or 13 to 16 inches.

14 This reference to nuns stirring batter with two hands refers specifically to holding the spoon between the palms of two hands and quickly rubbing them together to create an airy batter. I am indebted to Vicky Hayward, who shared with me the image of Marcela Osoro de Mendaro and Mari José "batiendo huevos, por el antiguo sistema llamado 'a dos manos de las monjas'" [Beating eggs the old-fashioned way called "with two hands, nun style"] from José María Gorrotxategi Pikasarri (271). In the *Diccionario general de bibliografía española*, the author also notes the peculiar comment on nuns using two hands to beat the batter. "De lo antedicho pueden los gastrónomos deducir una importantísma consecuencia, y es, que la hondad del bizcocho de monja debe consistir en hallarse batido a dos manos" [From the above, gastronomes can deduce a very important consequence, and that is that the thickness of the nun's sponge cake is the result of having been beaten with two hands] (Hidalgo 144).

15 This last sentence, which references a drawing in the back of the book, is only in the seventeenth-century editions. It disappears from the 1705 edition and all subsequent editions. However, between the end of the prologue and the beginning of Chapter 1, in the editions of 1760, 1800, 1822, 1823 a one-page drawing of kitchen utensils and appliances is included, along with a legend that names each of the twenty items. Although they were not part of Martínez Montiño's original work, I have included a copy of them in Appendix 1, since the visual image helps in understanding what each kitchen utensil looked like.

Notice on the size that spoons for making sweet biscuits should be, which are illustrated at the end of the book

The big spoon with which you mix the sweet biscuits should be a half-yard less three fingers long. It should be one of the flat wooden types with an extra-long paddle, and the paddle should be thin and fairly shallow and it should not be a wide paddle so that it will beat the eggs well. And if you want to beat the sweet biscuits with two hands, as nuns do, then the spoon should have a wide, round paddle, because you cannot beat this way with a spoon with a narrow paddle. The small spoon that is drawn at the back of the book is for spooning the batter onto the little papers and should not be used for anything else.

TABLA DE LOS Banquetes que van en este libro.[16]

Capitulo Primero De la limpieza de la cocina, y del gobierno que ha de tener el cocinero mayor en ella. I.

>   Tratado, como se ha de servir en los banquetes. 6.
>   Como se ha de servir la vianda en la cocina. 8.
>   Banquetes por Navidad. 9.
>   Segunda vianda. 9.
>   Tercera vianda. 10.
>   Las frutas que se han de servir en esta vianda. 10
>   Una comida por el mes de Mayo. 10.
>   Segunda vianda. 11.
>   Tercera vianda. 11.
>   Las frutas que se han de servir en esta vianda. 11.
>   Una comida por Setiembre. 12.
>   Segunda vianda. 12.
>   Tercera vianda. 12.
>   Una merienda.[17] 13.
>   La demás Tabla va al fin.

---

16 This table of contents for seasonal banquets found at the beginning of Chapter 1 is moved to the end of the book in the 1754, 1763, and 1807 editions, together with the table for Chapter 2 and the two memoirs on preserves and jellies.

17 "Una merienda" [supper] refers to a late afternoon or early evening meal, something akin to a high tea in England.

Table on the banquets that are in this book

Chapter One. On cleanliness in the kitchen and the governance that the master cook should have therein

   Treatise, how to serve during banquets. 6.
   How to serve food in the kitchen. 8.
   Christmas banquets. 9.
   Second course. 9.
   Third course. 10.
   Fruit that should be served with this food. 10.
   A meal for the month of May. 10.
   Second course. 11.
   Third course. 11.
   Fruit that should be served with this food. 11.
   A meal for September. 12.
   Second course. 12.
   Third course. 12.
   A supper. 13.
   The remaining table is in the back.

(1r) ARTE DE COCINA; En que se trata el modo que más se usa de guisar en este tiempo, en viandas de carne y pescado, pastelería, conservería, y bizcochería; y lo tocante para el regalo de enfermos.

Capitulo primero. De la limpieza de la cocina, y del gobierno que ha de tener el Cocinero mayor en ella.[18]

EN ESTE CAPITULO pienso tratar de la limpieza, que es la más necesaria, e importante, para que cualquier cocinero dé gusto en su oficio. Y para esto es necesario guardar tres, o cuatro cosas. La primera (1v) es, limpieza: y la segunda, gusto: y la tercera, presteza; que teniendo estas cosas, aunque no sea muy grande oficial, gobernándose bien, dará gusto a su señor, y estará acreditado.

Ha de procurar que la cocina esté tan limpia y curiosa, que cualquiera persona que entrare dentro, se huelgue de verla: y ha de tener buenas herramientas curiosas, para cosas particulares y trasordinarias, como son cazolillas, y barquillas, y gubiletes, torteras, piezas llanas, y moldes, y otras muchas piezas para hacer diferencias de platos.[19] Puesto todo muy bien, lucio y colgado por buena orden, que no anden las piezas rodando por las mesas, ni por el albañar:[20] los asadores en su lancera muy lucios, y los palos de masa, y cucharones de manjar blanco. Has de tener en una tabla, que estará colgada con unos clavos de palo torneados, como los tienen los Boticarios, que sean mucho mayores, y otro como éste, para cedacillos y estameñas. Esto ha de estar (2r) en la parte más desembarazada de la cocina: y si puedes allí acomodar la mesa para las cosas de masa, y ponerle encima un cielo de lienzo, o un zaquizamí de tablas, porque no caiga polvo de arriba: es cosa muy necesaria.[21] Si fuese posible no había de estar ninguna cocina

---

18 The term *cocinero mayor* [master cook] was widely used throughout Europe prior to the use of the word *chef* in the nineteenth century. This entire first section, until "Tratado, de cómo se ha de servir en los banquetes," is reproduced in Angel Muro's monumental book *El practicón* (1894), showing both the relevance and enormous influence of Martínez Montiño at the start of the twentieth century (459–61). Finally, although the seventeenth-century editions do not include paragraph breaks in this first section of Chapter 1, I have decided to use the paragraph breaks that first appear in the 1705 editions for increased clarity for today's reader.
19 *Barquilla* is a boat-shaped petit-four mould used for making pastries. *Gubileta*, or *cubilete*, is another pastry mould that is wider at the top than at the bottom; it could be round or boat-shaped.
20 While today *albañal* refers to a sewer or storm drain, for Martínez Montiño it refers to a large earthenware vat or basin for washing pots and pans and other kitchen utensils.
21 *Zaquizamí* usually refers to an attic, but here it refers to a wooden overhead covering.

[ART OF COOKING, in which is treated the ways most commonly used to cook at this time, meals of meat and fish, pie making, preserving, and pastry making and that which involves caring for the sick.

Chapter one. On the cleanliness of the kitchen and the governance that the master cook should have in it.

In this chapter I plan to discuss cleanliness, as it is most necessary and important for any cook to please in his profession. And to do this, it is necessary to observe three or four things. The first is cleanliness; the second, taste; and the third, celerity. By observing these three things, even if you are not a high-ranking official, and by running it [the kitchen] well, you will please your lord and gain a favourable reputation.

One should try to have such a clean and tidy kitchen that when anyone enters, they will delight in seeing it. One should try to have good, well-organized tools, both for regular use and for special occasions, such as little saucepans, boat-shaped petit four moulds, wide-mouthed pastry moulds, covered tart pans, flat dishes, moulds, and many other pieces for making different dishes. Everything should be shining and hanging it its proper place; pieces should not be left around on the tables or the wash area: the spits on their rack, shining brightly, and the rolling pins and big spoons for blancmange. You should have [them] on a board hanging from wooden pegs, like the ones found in pharmacies, but much bigger, and another one like this for sieves and cheesecloths. This should be in the most open part of the kitchen, and if you could have the pastry table there with a canvas covering or a panelled hood overhead, so that no dust falls from above, this is a necessary thing. If it were possible, no kitchen should be

debajo de ninguna casa, sino a un lado debajo de un cobertizo, de madera, que no hubiese encima vivienda de gente, salvo si es de bóveda, que con eso, y buena luz estará bien.[22]

Has de procurar que la blanqueen,[23] y no las de consentir a los mozos, ni oficiales, que la manchen pegando velas, aunque sean de cera. Hánse de poner unos saetines, hincados en las paredes, para poner las velas, y que no peguen enjundias de gallina en las paredes, porque una enjundía que no sea mayor que un real de a cuatro, hace una mancha en la pared blanca tan grande como un plato, y parece mal.[24]

El agua tendrás en tinajas, o en tinacos, con sus cobertores: y tendrás cuatro o seis cántaros (2v) en una cantarera de palo,[25] que no lleguen con los suelos al de la cocina. Estos sean vedriados con sus tapadores: del agua destos cántaros echarás a cocer todo lo que se hubiere de guisar: y la otra será para lavar y fregar las herramientas. No consientas que se corte ninguna cosa sobre las mesas, sino sobre un tajo que tendrás hincado en el suelo a una punta de la mesa donde embarace menos: allí cortarán toda la carne, y quebrarán los huesos: y las mesas las harás de pino blanco, y que las frieguen cada día con agua hirviendo, y ceniza, y estarán muy blancas, y como no estén acuchilladas parecerán mejor que de nogal. La carne picarás en tajos de trozos del álamo negro, que aunque parece que tendrá la madera negra, no la tiene sino blanca. Han de ser aserrados desde el tronco en unos trozos de ocho dedos de cantero, que parezcan ruedas de limón; porque adonde picares la carne esté la hebra derecha arriba, que desta manera (3r) no sueltan género de madera: y si la picas en tableros, aunque sean blancos de fresno, que son los mejores, si no picas con mucho tiento, sacarás madera.

---

22 For more on the layout of court kitchens in the early modern era, see León Tello and Sanz Sanz. In their book, *Estética y teoría de la arquitectura en los tratados españoles del siglo XVIII*, they include M. Losada's royal palace proposal that he designed after the Alcázar burned down in 1734. Although this design was conceived over one hundred years after Martínez Montiño's tenure at the palace, it provides a sense of what the layout of the palace kitchen space may have been (994–5).

23 The object pronoun, *la*, could be referring to the pastry table or to the kitchen itself.

24 The *enjundía* normally refers to the fatty tissue that surrounds the ovaries of fowl or, more generally, fatty tissue from fowl. Martínez Montiño uses this type of *enjundia* in three recipes: "Albondiguillas de ave" [Poultry meatballs] (204; 205), "Un pastel de ave para enfermo" [Hen pie for the sick] (280–2; 281–3), and "Una cazolilla de ave para enfermo" [Poultry in a saucepan for the sick] (586–8; 587–9). But it can also refer to pig fat tissue, and Martínez Montiño uses it this way in two recipes. See "Hojaldre con enjundia de puerco" [Puff pastry with pork fat] (274; 275) and "Lo que se ha de hacer del redaño del venado" [What to do with venison caul fat] (300; 301). For more, see Gutiérrez Cuadro and Rodríguez.

25 A *canterera* is a table with holes in it for placing the *cántaros* [jugs]. As suggested here, the tables are often made of wood.

below house level, but rather off to the side, under a wooden shelter, with no living quarters above it, unless it is vaulted and has good light, and if so, it would be good.

You should insist on bleaching it, and don't allow kitchen boys or cooks to dirty it with candles, even ones made from wax. They should nail some headless nails into the walls and hang the candles there and they shouldn't stick fatty tissue from poultry on the walls, because that fatty tissue in an amount no bigger than a four-real piece makes a stain on the wall bigger than the size of a plate and it looks bad.

Keep water in large earthenware vessels or in covered water tanks. You should have four to six jugs in a wooden pitcher stand so that the bottoms do not touch the kitchen floor. These should be glazed and have lids. The water from these jugs is used for all cooking, and the other water, for cleaning and scrubbing kitchen tools. Do not allow anyone to cut anything on the tables, but rather on a chopping block that should be attached to the floor at the end of the table where it least gets in the way. This is where all meat should be cut and bones split. The tables should be made of white pine and should be scrubbed daily with boiling water and ashes and this way they will stay white, and since they won't have knife marks in them, they will look better than walnut ones. You should chop meat on chopping blocks made from black poplar. Although it seems as if the wood should be black, it is actually white. They should be sawed from the trunk in pieces eight fingers thick and should look like lemon wheels so that, however you cut the meat, the grain will be standing up, and this way no wood will come out. If you chop on cutting boards, even if they are from white ash, which is the best, if you don't chop very carefully, you will get wood [in your food].

Los tableros de mesa[26] es forzoso que sean de nogal, y sean de poco más de una pulgada de cantero, y échales unas cantoneras de hierro por los bordes; de manera que vengan a cercar casi todo el tablero: y en la una punta una sortija de hierro en la bisagra con un botoncillo embebido en la madera, que se anda al derredor para colgar el tablero. Estos tableros se han de colgar a la parte a donde está la mesa de la masa. Algunos son amigos de tener algún aposentillo, o recocina dentro de la cocina; mas yo no soy deste parecer, sino que no haya ningún rincón en la cocina, que no se vea en entrando por la puerta, salvo el albañar.

A una parte de la cocina en lo más desembarazado, se pondrá un palo muy bien acepillado para poner las capas, y unos clavos para las espadas de los oficiales:[27] (3v) y con eso véase toda la cocina, que cuando estuvieres al tablero, o en otra mesa haciendo algo puedas gobernar y mandar, y ver todo lo que pasa. No consientas que haya cenicero en la cocina, sino que lleve la ceniza la lavandera cada día, o se eche a mal, porque se pueda barrer el fogón, y la basura: tener un esportón,[28] y cada vez que se barriere la cocina, que echen la basura fuera, porque no huela mal, o lleguen moscas. Todas las veces que entrares por la puerta de tu cocina, procura tener algo que enmendar: mira si está bien colgada la herramienta, y si está cada cosa en su lugar: y si hay por las paredes o por el techo alguna telaraña, hazlo remediar luego sin dejarlo para después, porque se olvidará el mozo de cocina, o portador, y tendrás que tornar a mandar, y con esto tendrán cuidado, y te temerán.[29] Y si el mozo no fuere muy aficionado a tener la cocina limpia, no lo tengas en ella, sino despídelo luego, porque no andes cada día riñendo (4r) con él: y más, si no se precia de hacer bien su oficio de mozo de cocina, nunca será oficial. Si fuere posible no tengas pícaros sin partido:[30] y si los tuvieres, procura con el señor que les dé algo, o con el limosnero, porque puedan tener camisas limpias que se mudar; porque no hay cosas más asquerosas que pícaros rotos y sucios. Más que es una simiente que el Rey don Felipe II, que Dios tiene, con todo su poder no pudo echar esta gente de sus cocinas: aunque mandó añadir mozos de cocina, y otra suerte de mozos de cocina, que se llaman galopines;[31] todo porque no hubiese

---

26 In the original 1611 edition, "tableros de masa" [dough boards] is written instead of "tableros de mesa" [table-top cutting boards], which is the phrase used in all other editions.
27 *Oficial* is a position for someone who has completed an apprenticeship but not attained the position of master in a given profession. In the kitchen, that person today is called *cook*.
28 *Esportón* is a large basket made of esparto grass. This grass is native to Iberia and is used for making baskets, cords, and espadrille shoes.
29 Note the attitude of governing the kitchen through fear.
30 *Sin partido* refers to boys without a master or someone else looking after them.
31 This is the first time the term *galopín* appears in Spanish. As Martínez Montiño describes, it refers to a position comparable to a kitchen boy. Elena Varela Merino provides additional

It is mandatory that tabletop cutting boards be made of walnut and be at least an inch thick. They should be reinforced with metal edging on the corners so that the metal encloses almost the entire cutting board edge, and, [have] on one end, an iron ring on a hinge with an embedded button in the wood that can move around to hang the board. These boards should be hung in the part [of the kitchen] near the pastry table. Some like to have a small room or scullery in the kitchen but I am not one of them. Rather, there should be no corner of the kitchen that can't be seen upon entering, except the wash area.

In some uncluttered part of the kitchen, there should be a finely polished pole for capes and some hooks for swords for cooks. And thus, you can see the entire kitchen, so that when you are at a cutting board or at another table doing something else, you can run the kitchen, give orders, and see everything that is going on. Don't allow any ashcans in the kitchen; the laundress must remove them daily or it will be a disaster. In order for the fireplace to be swept, and the garbage, have a large basket available, and every time the kitchen is swept, the trash must also be taken out, so that it won't smell bad or attract flies. Each time you enter through the kitchen door, try to have something to improve on. Check to see if the utensils are hung properly, if everything is where it should be, and if the walls or ceilings have cobwebs; if needed, have it taken care of right away and don't leave it for later because the kitchen boy or the food runner might forget and you will have to tell them again. In this way, they will be careful and fear you. And if the kitchen boy was not big on keeping the kitchen clean, don't keep him; rather, fire him immediately so that you won't have to run around yelling at him every day. Moreover, if he does not appreciate doing the job of a kitchen hand well, he will never become a cook. If possible, don't hire a scullion without patronage, but if you do, make sure that the lord, or whoever is in charge of distributing charity, gives him something so that he has clean shirts to change into. Because there is really nothing more disgusting than dirty, ragged scullions. But, it's really just the beginning. King Philip II, God rest his soul, with all his power, could not get rid of these rascals from his kitchens. Even though he ordered more kitchen boys and a different type of kitchen boy called a *galopín* to

pícaros, y nunca se pudo remediar: sólo en su cocina de boca no entran más de un oficial, y un portador, y un mozo de cocina, y un galopín; y estos están una semana con el cocinero mayor, y el Domingo se mudan a la cocina del Estado, y venían otros tantos por sus semanas. Con todo me crié yo en una cocina que no tuvo pícaros, como tenía testigos vivos (4v) que la conocieron, como es el cocinero mayor de su Majestad de la Reyna Juan de Mesones, y Amador de la Aya, su ayuda, que la conocieron muy bien. Sólo esta cocina entiendo que se ha librado desta gente, que fue la cocina de la serenísima Princesa de Portugal doña Juana. Si ellos dan en ser virtuosos, y se aficionan a deprender, en muy poco tiempo toman principio, y estos se hacen oficiales; mas lo que son pícaros bellacos nunca son cocineros, antes dan en otras cosas muy malas. Esto se entiende en las cocinas de los grandes señores, que en las cocinas chicas más fáciles son de gobernar y tener limpias.

Otra cosa tengo experimentada, que hombre que sea torpe, o patituerto, nunca salen oficiales, ni son bien limpios. Procúrese que sean de buena disposición, liberales, de buen rostro, y que presuman de galanes, que con eso andarán limpios, y lo serán en su oficio, que los otros por ser pesados tienen pereza, y nunca hacen (5r) cosa buena: que el oficio de la cocina, aunque parece que es cosa fácil, no es sino muy dificultoso; porque hay tantas cosas que hacer, y cada cosa tiene su punto, y todo se ha de encargar a la memoria: que los Boticarios, y los Médicos, y Letrados, cuando se les ofrece alguna duda, con estudiarla en sus libros, salen della con facilidad. Y por eso digo, que la gente de la cocina ha de ser de buen talle y disposición y entendimiento. Has de procurar, que en la cocina haya cada día ropa blanca para cubrir la mesa y los asadores con la vianda, y para que se limpien las manos; y pondrás una costumbre que todos los oficiales y mozos que entraren por la mañana en la cocina, lo primero que han de hacer sea quitarse sus capas y espadas, y colgarlas en el palo, y los clavos que están puestos para ello, y quitarse los puños,[32] y lavarse las manos, y limpiarse en una toalla, que estará colgada para esto, y trabajar con mucha limpieza. Si alguno tomare su (5v) capa, y saliere fuera, cuando tornare a entrar, se torne a quitar los puños, y lavarse las manos, y limpiarse en la toalla.

---

instances of the word in other seventeenth-century texts and explains that the word derives from the French *galopin*, a name given to those who had to run errands. She notes that in French from the fourteenth century, it was used to describe boys working in the kitchen (2.1311–12).

32 The *puño* [cuff] refers not only to the end of the sleeve, as it does today, but also to a decorative addition to the cuff generally made of linen or embroidered cloth. It can be one piece with the sleeve or, as Martínez Montiño explains here, removed from the sleeve. For a complete definition, see *Diccionario de autoridades* (5.1737), http://web.frl.es/DA.html.

be hired, he did all of this just so that there wouldn't be any scullions, but it was an impossible situation. In the king's kitchen, no more than one cook, one food runner, one kitchen boy, and one *galopín* are allowed to enter. These workers stay with the master cook for a week and on Sunday they switch to the state kitchen, and others are rotated in for their own week. However, I was raised in a kitchen that didn't have scullions, as many witnesses still alive today can attest, such as the master cook to her Majesty the Queen, Juan de Mesones, and his assistant, Amador de la Aya, who knew this kitchen well. This is the only kitchen I know, free from that type of help, and that was the kitchen of the most serene princess of Portugal, Dona Juana. If they have the calling to be virtuous and are truly interested in learning, then in very little time they will become apprentices and in turn cooks. But, those who are unscrupulous scullions will never become cooks but will end up doing very bad things. This is to be understood for large kitchens of grandees, but in smaller kitchens, it is easier to run them and keep them clean.

Another thing I know to be true, if a man is clumsy, bow-legged, or unkempt, he will never become a cook. Make sure they have a good disposition, are kind-hearted, clean cut, and are proud of their good looks, because with these [qualities] they will stay clean and will act so in their profession. The others, because they are heavy, are also lazy, and will never do anything right. The kitchen profession, although it may seem easy, is actually very difficult, because there are so many things to do, each one different for reaching perfection, and everything has to be done by memory. When pharmacists, doctors, and lawyers are confronted with doubt and consult their books, they easily figure it out. For this reason, I state that kitchen staff must have a good body, disposition, and sense of understanding. You must ensure that every day in the kitchen there are clean linens for covering tables and spits with food and for cleaning hands. You should insist as a general habit that the first thing that all cooks and kitchen hands do as they enter the kitchen each morning is remove their capes and swords and hang them on the pole and hooks intended for this very purpose, remove their cuffs and wash their hands and dry them with a towel, hung for this very purpose, and work with much cleanliness. If one were to put his cape back on and go out, then upon returning, he should remove his cuffs once again, and wash his hands and dry them on a towel.

A una parte de la mesa grande, harás poner unos manteles limpios, y pondrás sobre ellos la plata. Y cuando fuere hora de hacer los gigotes,[33] háganse sobre los manteles, porque los platos estén limpios por los suelos: y no consientas hacer gigote ninguno a ningún mozo, ni oficial, sin su toalla al hombro, y su tenedor: y tomará la pieza, o pierna, o ave con tenedor muy bien, y picará en el aire con mucha gracia. Y advierta el que picare que entretanto que picare no ha de toser, ni hablar, ni ha de hacer otra cosa ninguna, sino estar con mucha compostura; porque es mucho descomedimiento picar y hablar. No consientas que en la cocina entretanto que se trabaje haya conversaciones, ni almuerzos. La gente de la cocina antes que se ponga a trabajar, en acabando de tomar recaudo, luego ha de hacer un almuerzo, y almuercen (6r) todos, y ninguno ande comiendo por la cocina, que parece mal: y en acabando de almorzar lávense las manos, y cada uno acuda a lo que tiene a cargo.

Tendrás un cofre en la cocina para guardar algunas cosas que sobran, y tener las especias, y un cajoncillo para tus toallas, y algunos regalillos del señor. La llave del cofre darás al oficial, o ayudante más antiguo. Las especias anden en sus bolsas o cajas, cada cosa aparte, y una cucharita en ellas para sazonar con ella. Hínchanse de una vez de especias molidas y cernidas; porque aprovechará más una libra desta manera, que libra y media si se moliese a remiendos. Las cuchillas se amuelen los Viernes, o Sábados, que hay menos que cortar con ellas.[34]

(6v) *Tratado, de cómo se ha de servir en los banquetes.*

AQUI Pondré tres, o cuatro comidas, y una merienda, y no pondré ningún plato fantástico, sino todo cosas que se hayan de comer: y daré a entender cómo se han de servir; porque en los banquetes todo el toque está en saberlos servir; porque aunque se gaste mucho dinero en un banquete, si no se sirve bien, no luce, y se afrenta el señor mucho habiendo desórdenes en él: y algunas veces las está mirando el señor desde su asiento en la mesa.

Hagamos cuenta que estas comidas son de seis platos de cada cosa: hánse de poner seis bufetes, y si ponen los bufetes ancho por largo, serán menester siete bufetes para seis servicios: son menester seis Mastresalas,[35] y seis personas que

---

33 Normally *hacer gigotes* refers to cutting meat into very small pieces, i.e., chopping, pulling, or even mincing, but, in this context, it appears that Martínez Montiño uses the word to refer to *carving* meat, and he does this in the air. This technique is described in more detail in the recipe "Cómo se han de aparar las aves en la cocina" [How to present poultry in the kitchen] (556–8; 557–9).

34 Martínez Montiño does not elaborate on other essential pieces of kitchen furniture, like grain bins and other storage units for dried goods and kitchen equipment. For a complete list of kitchen furnishings and equipment, see Appendix I and for more information, see Nadeau, "Furniture and Equipment," and Abad Zardoya, "Herramientas" 98–9.

35 As the name itself indicates, the *mastresala* or today *maestresala* is the master of the dining room, or *steward*. His chief duty is to attend to the lord at the table by presenting the food, serving it, and ensuring its quality.

At one end of the big table, lay out clean tablecloths and put the silverware on them. And when it is time to chop up the meat, do so over the tablecloth so that the plates stay clean on the bottom. And do not allow any kitchen hand or cook to chop up any meat without a towel over his shoulder and without his fork. He should take hold of the cut or leg or whole bird with his fork and cut it in the air gracefully. Note that whoever is chopping, while doing it, he should not cough, speak, or do anything else but rather be very composed, because it is very rude to chop and talk. Do not ever allow people in the kitchen to chat or eat a meal while they are working. The kitchen staff, before beginning work and after taking precautions, have a meal all together and no one will be eating while in the kitchen because it is bad practice. After finishing the meal, everyone will wash their hands and then attend to whatever they are in charge of.

In the kitchen, there should be a chest for storing leftover material and for the spices, and there should be a small crate for towels and for some of the master's treats. Give the key to the chest to the oldest cook or cook's assistant. Spices should be in their bags or boxes, each one separate, and a teaspoon in each for seasoning with them. Immediately fill them all up with spices that have been ground and sifted because you will get more from a pound this way than if you grind a pound and a half as needed. Knives are sharpened on Fridays or Saturdays because there is less to cut those days.

Treatise on how to serve at banquets

Here I will include three or four main meals, and a supper, and I won't include any fantastic dishes, but rather everything that can be eaten. I will also explain how they should be served, because at banquets it's all about knowing how they are served. Even if a lot of money is spent on a banquet, if it is not well served, it won't be impressive, and the lord feels very ashamed when there is disarray at the banquet. Sometimes the lord is watching it from his seat at the table.

Let's do the numbers for meals that have six of each dish. Six sideboards should be set, and if they are placed widthwise then it will be necessary to have seven sideboards for six services. Six stewards are necessary and six people who

sirvan como de Veedores[36] para solo llevar la vianda desde la Cocina a la mesa: (7r) y cada Veedor ha de llevar un servicio, y entregarlo a su Mastresala, porque en tales días no ha de bajar el Mastresala a la cocina, y si bajare la primera vez, no puede bajar las otras; porque se ha de servir la vianda en tres veces. Ha de bajar el mayordomo con sus Veedores. Digo, pues, que el Veedor que tomare el primer servicio, llevará cinco pajes, y éstos llevarán diez platos, cada uno dos, y detrás del postrer page irá otro Veedor con otros cinco pajes, y otros diez platos: y desta manera irán los demás, porque cada cinco pajes seguirán a su Veedor, sin que se mezclen unos con otros: y en llegando a la mesa el primer Veedor con sus diez platos, se arrimará al Mastresalas de la cabecera de la mesa, y los demás vayan cada uno a su Mastresala, y hagan alto sin asentar plato ninguno en la mesa, hasta que llegue el Veedor postrero: y en viendo que están todos los Veedores con toda la vianda junta a la mesa, (7v) arrimados a sus Mastresalas, alcen todos los principios,[37] salvo algunos perniles, o cabezas de jabalí, que como son platos que van enramados parecen bien en la mesa;[38] además, que entre la comida gustan algunas personas de comer un poco pernil para beber. Desta manera estará la mesa muy llena, y no se perderá plato ninguno.[39] En asentando la vianda en la mesa, volverán los Veedores por la segunda; y harán lo mismo que hicieron en la primera, y levantarán la vianda del primer servicio, salvo algunos platos regalados que no hayan llegado a ellos, y los perniles, y asentarán la segunda vianda. Y desta manera harán la tercera. Y cuando alzaren la tercera, levantarán toda la vianda, sin dejar cosa ninguna, y asentarán los postres: y desta manera no puede faltar plato ninguno, que más presto se echa de ver la falta de un plato, que de un servicio todo.

---

36 The *veedor* or *inspector* [*supervisor*] is the person in charge of the pantry, and here, in Martínez Montiño's instructions, oversees the delivery of the food from the kitchen to the dining room.
37 For two useful graphics that capture Martínez Montiño's explanation on how to serve dishes at the table, see Usunáriz and Ortiz Martín 100–1.

   Typical foodstuffs that were served as "principios" [starters] included "vino bastardo con bizcochos, perniles de tocino de Garrovillas, o Aracena, o Rute, que son las mejores cecinas, guindas garrafales, limas dulces, melones, uvas, brevas, ensaladas labradas, manteca de vacas labrada, salchichón de Flandes, naranjas dulces, frescas [*sic*], mora, amacenas, y ciruelas, y las demás frutas" [sweet wine (from raisins) with sweet biscuits, fatty ham from Garrovillas, or Aracena, or Rute, which are the best cured meats, sweet sour cherries, sweet limes, melons, grapes, figs, arranged salads, sculpted butter, sausages from Flanders, sweet oranges, strawberries, blackberries, damson plums, and plums, and other fruits] (Yelgo de Vázquez 138r–139v).
38 *Enramado* refers to a decorative technique that involved intertwining branches, for example laurel branches, as a garnish for the meat. In Chapter 2, Martínez Montiño uses this word only twice, in "Como se ha de beneficiar un jabalí" [How to dress boar] (286–8; 287–9) and "Queso de cabeza de jabalí" [Boar head cheese] (288–90; 289–91). In both cases they refer to serving boar.
39 In Chapter 17, "Del modo de servir del veedor, y sus obligaciones," of *Estilo de servir a príncipes*, Yelgo de Vázquez cautions how food can "go missing" between the kitchen and the table (137v–138r). Martínez Montiño reiterates this cautionary note a second time later in this section on serving banquets.

will serve as inspectors, who will solely carry the food from the kitchen to the table. Each inspector should carry with him one place setting and give it to the steward, because on these days, the steward should not go down to the kitchen, and if he does go down the first time, he should not go down any other time, because the food will be served three times. The major domo should go down with his inspectors. As I was saying, the inspector who delivers the first course will bring five pages, and they will carry ten dishes, each one two, and after the last page, the next inspector will follow with another five pages and another ten plates. And in this way the rest will follow as each five pages follow their inspector without one group mixing with another. When the first inspector arrives with his ten dishes, he will stand next to the steward at the head of the table and each of the others should direct themselves to their steward and wait without placing any plate on the table until the last inspector arrives. Upon seeing that all the inspectors are there next to their stewards with all the food next to the table, all the starters are removed, except some boar legs or boar head, since they are dishes that are decorated with branches and look good on the table. Moreover, between courses, some people like to nibble on ham while they drink.

This way, the table will be very full and no dish will go missing. After placing the food on the table, the inspectors will return for the second course and do the same as they did with the first, and they will remove the food from the first course, except some of the exquisite dishes that have not yet been touched and the hams, and they will place down the second course. And in this same way, the third. And when they remove the third (course), they will also remove all the food, without leaving anything, and then they will serve dessert. This way, no dish will go missing, as it is easier to notice that a single dish is missing than a whole course.

(8r) *Como se ha de servir la vianda en la cocina*

Ya tengo dicho como se ha de llevar la vianda desde la cocina a la mesa, y como se como ha de servir; ahora me falta decir, como se ha de servir en la cocina. Para un servicio de a seis se ha de hacer una mesa tan ancha, que quepan seis platos a lo ancho: y porque en las cocinas nunca hay mesas tan anchas, ni son menester, para este día podrás hacer esta mesa de prestado en medio de la cocina, si es ancha, o a la puerta debajo de algún cobertizo: y si no hubiere comodidad para esto en una cocina muy pequeña, lo podrás hacer teniendo una mesa en que quepan tres platos por ancho en hilera, y diez por largo: y para los otros tres platos pondrás unas tablas en la pared, como las tienen los confiteros, y boticarios, y suplirán por mesa, y pondrás seis platos por lo ancho en hilera. (8v) Ahora pondrás seis pavos en la cabecera de la mesa, los tres en la mesa, y los otros tres en las tablas que están en la pared. Luego pondrás seis platos de ollas, y luego irás poniendo todos tus diez, o doce servicios de a seis. Ahora, para servir esta vianda, que son sesenta platos, hallarás seis hileras de a diez platos por lo largo, y cada hilera es un trozo. La primera hilera darás al primer Veedor, y esta vaya al primer Mastresala: y luego otra hilera al segundo: y desta manera vayan unos tras otros, sin que se mezclen unos con otros: y cada uno llevará un trozo, que es de cada cosa un plato. Y después que esté asentada la vianda en la mesa, tendrá cada caballero delante de sí de todo cuanto hubiere en la mesa, y que lo pueda alcanzar todo desde su asiento; que eso han de tener los banquetes, que cada caballero que estuviere en la mesa, tenga en su bufete de todo cuanto hubiere en la mesa, que aunque la mesa sea muy larga, y la mirare (9r) toda, no vea cosa que no tenga delante de sí, que si el caballero viese alguna cosa en la mesa que no la tuviese delante de sí, no estaría bien servido el banquete; porque la mayor falta que puede haber en los banquetes es servirse mal, o faltar algún plato; que claro está, que si habían de ser seis pavos, y hurtasen uno desde la cocina a la mesa, y no pareciesen allá más de cinco, que quedaría un bufete sin pavo, y se echaría luego de ver: y si faltase todo un servicio, que son seis platos , no se echaría de ver en la mesa; si no fuese quien supiese de toda la vianda: y por eso se ha de tener muy grande cuenta, y hacer mucha diligencia para que entren los servicios enteros en la mesa, pues es todo el toque de que parezca muy buen el banquete, o se haga una falta muy grande. Y con esto me parece que está dado a entender como se han de servir los banquetes.

Chapter one

How to serve food in the kitchen

I have already explained how to carry the food from the kitchen to the table and how it should be served. Now I need to explain how to serve in the kitchen. For service for six, one needs a table wide enough for six dishes to fit widthwise. Since there is never a table this wide in the kitchen nor a need for one, on this day you can place a borrowed table in the middle of the kitchen, if it is wide, or right next to the door under a cover. If there is not enough space in a small kitchen, you can make do with a table wide enough for three dishes in a row and ten dishes long, and for the other three plates, you can put up some boards next to the wall, as candy makers or pharmacists do, and they can be in place of the table; that way you can have six dishes laid out in a row widthwise. Then place six turkeys at the head of the table, three on the table and three on the boards next to the wall. Then place six stew dishes and then begin laying out service for ten or twelve in six rows. Now, to serve the food, which consists of sixty dishes, you will have six rows ten dishes in length, each row making up a section. Give the first row to the first inspector that goes to the first steward, then the next row to the second, and so on one after another without mixing up one set of dishes with another. Each inspector will be in charge of one section, which contains one of each dish. After the food in placed on the table, each gentleman will have in front of him everything that is on the table, and can reach everything from his seat. This is what banquets should be, that each gentleman who is at the table has within his own buffet section everything that is on the table. Even if the table is very long and he can see the whole thing, he won't see anything that he doesn't have right in front of him. If a gentleman does see something that is not within his reach, it would not be a successful banquet, because the worst error in a banquet is poor service or a missing dish. It is entirely clear that if there should be six turkeys and one disappears between the kitchen and the table and only five appear, then one buffet section is without any turkey and it would be very noticeable. But if one entire service were missing, that is six dishes, it would not be as noticeable at the table, unless someone was aware of all the dishes being served. And, for this reason, one has to keep all this in mind and be very careful so that the entire six services arrive at the table. Because this is the special touch that either makes a banquet look so good or turns it into a big mistake. And with this I think it is well understood how to serve banquets.

(9v) **BANQUETES por Navidad.**

PERNILES, con los principios.
Ollas podridas.
Pavos asados con su salsa.
Pastelillos Saboyanos de ternera hojaldrados.
Pichones, y torreznos asados.
Platillo de artaletes de aves sobre sopas de natas.
Bollos de vacía.
Perdices asadas con salsa de limones.
Capirotada con solomo, y salchiches [sic],[40] y perdices.[41]
Lechones asados con sopas de queso, y azúcar, y canela.
Hojaldres de masa de levadura, con enjundia de puerco.
Pollas asadas.

SEGUNDO

CAPONES asados.
Ánades asadas con salsa de membrillos.
(10r) Platillo de pollos con escarolas rellenas.
Empanadas Inglesas.
Ternera asada con salsa de oruga.
Costrada de mollejas de ternera, y higadillos.
Zorzales asados sobre sopas doradas.
Pastelones de membrillos, y cañas, y huevos mejidos.
Empanadas de liebres.
Platillo de aves a la Tudesca.
Truchas fritas con tocino magro.
Ginebradas.

TERCERO.

POLLOS rellenos con picatostes de ubres de ternera asados.
Gigotes de aves.
Platillo de pichones ahogados.

---

40 This typographical error, which is most likely a printer's error, is corrected in the following edition in 1617.
41 This menu suggestion corresponds to the recipe "Sopa de capirotada" [Capirotada sops] (282–4; 283–5).

Christmas banquet

FRESH hams with starters
Hodgepodge stews
Roast turkey with sauce
Little Savoy veal pastries wrapped in puff pastry dough
Roast squab and roasted pork belly
Dish of poultry pinwheels over cream sops
Airy pastry
Roast partridge with lemon sauce
Capirotada with tenderloin, sausages, and partridge
Roast suckling pig on cheese sops with cinnamon and sugar
Leaven dough puff pastries with pork fat tissue
Roast young hen

Second course

ROAST capons
Roast duck with quince sauce
Chicken with stuffed escarole
English empanadas
Roast veal with arugula sauce
Puff pastry pie with sweetbreads and hen liver
Roast thrush over golden sops
Quince pie with marrow and sweet scrambled egg yolks
Hare empanadas
Poultry dish, German style
Fried trout with meaty fatback
Ginebradas [clotted milk tarts]

Third course

STUFFED chicken served with cow udder over slices of fried bread
Minced poultry
A squab dish sautéed with onion and fatback

Cabrito asado y mechado.
Tortas de cidras verdes.
Empanadas de pavos en masa blanca.
Besugos frescos cocidos.
Conejos con alcaparras.
Empanadillas de pies de puerco.
Palomas torcaces con salsa negra.
(10v) Manjar blanco.
Buñuelos de viento.

Las frutas que se deben servir en esta vianda son,
UVAS, melones, limas dulces, o naranjas, pasas, y almendras, orejones, manteca fresca, peras, y camuesas, aceitunas, y queso, conservas y suplicaciones.

Una comida por el mes de Mayo.

PERNILES con los principios.
Capones de leche asados.
Olla de carnero, y aves, y jamones de tocino.
Pasteles hojaldrados.
Platillo de pollos con habas.
Truchas cocidas.
Gigotes de piernas de carnero.
Torreznos asados, y criadillas de carnero.
Cazuelas de natas.
(11r) Platillos de artaletes de ternera, y lechugas.
Empanadillas de torreznos con masa dulce.
Aves en alfitete frío con huevos mejidos.
Platos de alcachofas con jarretes de tocino.

SEGUNDA.

GAZAPOS asados.
Morcillas blancas de cámara, sobre sopas de bizcochos, y natas.
Pastelones de ternera, y cañas, y pichones, y criadillas de tierra.
Ternera asada y picada.
Empanadas de palominos.
Platillo de pichones con criadillas de carnero y cañas.
Empanadas Inglesas de pechos de ternera, y lenguas de vaca.
Hojaldres rellenas de masa de levadura.
Fruta de cañas.
Pollos rellenos, sobre sopas doradas.

Roast kid, larded
Green citron pie
White dough turkey empanadas
Fresh sea bream, boiled
Rabbit with capers
Pig's feet turnovers
Wood pigeon with black sauce
Blancmange
Puffs

Fruit that should be served with this meal are
GRAPES, melons, sweet limes or oranges, raisins, almonds, dried apricots, fresh butter, pears, Camuesa apples, olives, cheese, conserves, and wafers.

A meal for the month of May

FRESH hams with starters
Roasted milk-fed capons
Lamb-poultry stew with fatty ham
Puff pastry pies
Chicken dish with fava beans
Boiled trout
Minced leg of young mutton
Roast pork belly and sheep testicles
Cream casserole
Dish of beef pinwheels with lettuce
Fried pork fat turnovers with sweet dough
Stuffed hen with sweet scrambled egg yolks on puff pastry, cold
Artichoke dish with fatty ham shanks

Second course

ROASTED young rabbit
White blood sausage with large intestine casing over cream and sponge cake sops
Big pies of veal, marrow, squab, and truffle
Roast veal, minced
Wild squab empanadas
A squab dish with sheep testicles and marrow
English empanadas of breast of veal and beef tongue
Puff pastry, stuffed, made with leaven dough
Fried dough with marrow filling
Chicken with stuffing over golden sops

Empanadas de venado.
Pastelillos de conservas y huevos mejidos.

11v Tercera vianda

SALMÓN fresco.
Pollas asadas sobre arroz de grasa.
Pichones ensapados sobre hojuelas.
Pastelones de salsa negra.
Cabrito asado, y mechado.
Tortas de dama.
Lechones en salchichones.
Empanadas frías.
Barbos fritos con tocino, y picatostes de pan.
Manjar blanco.
Fruta de piñas.
Bollos maimones.

Las frutas que se han de servir en esta vianda, son,
Albaricoques, fresas, cerezas, y podría ser que hubiese guindas si fuese el banquete al cabo del mes de Mayo, natas, y limas, pasas, y almendras, aceitunas, queso, conservas, y confites, suplicaciones. (12r) En esto no hay que decir, porque se ha de servir de toda la fruta que hubiere, y requesones.

Una comida por Setiembre.

PERNILES con los principios.
Pavillos nuevos asados con su salsa.
Ollas podridas en pastelones de masa negra.
Pasteles hojaldrados gubiletes.
Platillo de palominos con calabaza rellena.
Perdigones asados.
Bollos sombreros.
Ternera asada y picada.
Empanadas de pichones en masa dulce con torreznos.
Tortas de ternera, y cañas, y almendras.
Pajarillos gordos con pan rallado, sobre sopas doradas.
Truchas frescas cocidas.
Conejos gordos asados.

Venison empanadas
Little pastries filled with preserves and sweet scrambled egg yolks

Third course

FRESH salmon
Roast chicken over rice cooked in fat
Stuffed squab on puff pastry
Big pies with black sauce
Roast kid, larded
Lady pies
Suckling pig served sausage style
Empanadas, cold
Fried barbel with fatback and slices of fried bread
Blancmange
Pine nut fried dough
Maimon layered pastry.

Fruit that should be served with this meal are
   Apricots, strawberries, cherries, and there might be sour cherries if the banquet took place at the end of May, cream, limes, raisins, and almonds, olives, cheese, preserves, sugar-coated nuts and seeds, and wafers.
   Regarding this, nothing more be said because all available fruit and curd cheese should be served.

A meal for September.

FRESH hams with the starters
Roast new turkey poults with their gravy
Hodgepodge stew in a dark-crust pie
Puff pastry pies [baked in] moulds
Dish of wild squab with stuffed squash
Roast partridge chicks
Hat pastries
Roast veal, minced
Squab empanadas with pork belly in a sweet crust.
Beef pie with marrow and almonds
Small plump birds with breadcrumbs over golden sops
Fresh boiled trout
Roasted rabbit, with its fat

(12v) Segunda vianda

CAPONES asados.
Platillo de ternera, con albondiguillas de ternera, mollejas, y higadillos.
Tórtolas asadas.
Platos de membrillos, y pollos rellenos rebozados.
Cazuelas mojís de berenjenas.
Platos de salchichones, y cenizas.
Platos de capones rellenos, cocidos con artaletes sobre sopas blancas.
Pasteles de tetilla.
Quesadillas de marzapán.
Empanadas de liebres en figura de leones.
Bollos de rodilla.
Pichones asados con costillas de carnero, y pan rallado.

Tercera vianda

POLLAS asadas.
Platillos de cañas con huevos encañutados.
Pollos asados con salsa de agraz.
Tortas de albérchigos en conserva.
(13r) Empanadas frías.
Cabrito asado y mechado.
Platillos de palominos con lechugas.
Manjar blanco.
Piernas de carnero en gigote.
Cazolillas de natas y cañas, y manjar blanco.
Salchichones de lechones cortados en ruedas, mezclados con otros salchichones, y lenguas.
Fruta de piñas.

Las frutas desta vianda, han de ser, uvas, melones, higos, ciruelas, natas, pasas, y almendras; melocotones, confites, y conservas, aceitunas, y queso, y suplicaciones.

Una merienda.

PERNILES cocidos.
Capones, o pavos asados calientes.
Pastelones de ternera, y pollos, y cañas calientes.
Empanadas Inglesas.
Pichones y torreznos asados.
(13v) Perdices asadas.

Second course

ROAST capon
Beef dish, with beef, sweetbreads, and hen liver meatballs
Roast collared doves
Dish of stuffed chicken coated in quince sauce
Moxi eggplant casserole
Dish of black pepper sausages with ash
Dish of stuffed capons, cooked with pinwheels served over white sops
Teat pies
Marzipan cheese tarts
Hare empanadas in the shape of a lion
Spiral sweet rolls
Roast squab with lamb ribs and breadcrumbs

Third course

ROAST chicken
Beef marrow dish with sweet egg canutos
Roast chicken with sour grape sauce
Apricot preserve pie
Cold empanadas
Roast kid, larded
Dish of wild squab with lettuce
Blancmange
Leg of young mutton, minced
Tartlets of cream, marrow, and blancmange
Suckling pig sausages, sliced and served with other black pepper sausages and tongue
Pine nut fried dough

Fruit served with this food should be grapes, melons, figs, plums, creams, raisins, almonds, peaches, sugar-coated nuts and seeds, preserves, olives, cheese, and wafers.

Late afternoon supper

BOILED ham
Roast capon or turkey [served] warm
Big pies of veal, chicken, and marrow [served] warm
English empanadas
Roast squab and roasted pork belly
Roast partridge

Bollos maimones, o de vacía.
Empanadas de gazapos en masa dulce.
Lenguas, y salchichones, y cecinas.
Gigotes de capones sobre sopas de natas.
Tortas de manjar blanco, y natas, y mazapán [sic].
Hojaldres rellenas.
Salchichones de lechones enteros.
Capones rellenos fríos, sobre alfitete frío.
Empanadas de pavos.
Tortillas de huevos, y torreznos, y picatostes calientes.
Empanadas de venazón.
Cazuelas de pies de puerco con piñones.
Salpicones de vaca, y tocino magro.
Empanadas de truchas.
Costradas de limoncillos, y huevos mejidos.
Conejos de huerta.[42]
Empanadas de liebres.
Fruta de prestiños.
(14r) Truchas cocidas.
Ñoclos de masa dulce.
Panecillos rellenos de masa de levadura
Platos de frutas verdes.[43]
Gileas blancas, y tintas.
Fruta rellena.
Empanadas de perdices en masa de bollos.
Buñuelos de manjar blanco, y frutillas de lo mismo.
Empanadillas de cuajada, o ginebradas.
Truchas en escabeche.
Plato de papín[44] tostado con cañas.
Solomos de vaca rellenos.
Cuajada en platos.
Almojábanas.

---

42 In Chapter 2, this recipe is called "Otro gigote de conejos frío" [Another minced rabbit, (served) cold] (156; 157). Its playful name here, "Conejos de huerta" [Rabbits in the garden], refers to rings of minced rabbit meat and heavily garnished salad.

43 Martínez Montiño explains that *fruta verde* refers to firm fruit, like quince, pears, and sour apples (252; 253).

44 *Papín* is a sweet cream sauce, similar to today's *crème anglaise*. Recipes for making it are found in "Un plato de papín tostado, con cañas, huevos mejidos, y hojuelas" [Toasted sweet cream with marrow, sweet scrambled egg yolks, and puff pastry] (552; 553) and "Papín de harina de trigo" [Sweet cream sauce made with wheat flour] (584–6; 585–7).

Maimon-layered pastries or airy pastries
Young rabbit empanadas in a sweet crust
Tongue, black pepper sausage, and dried beef
Minced capon over cream sops
Blancmange, cream, and marzipan pies
Puff pastries, stuffed
Whole suckling pig sausages
Stuffed capon, served cold over puff pastry
Turkey empanadas
Warm egg and fried pork fat omelettes and slices of fried bread
Venison empanada
Pig's feet casserole with pine nuts
Beef and meaty fatback salpicon
Trout empanadas
Lime puff pastry pie with sweet scrambled egg yolks
Rabbit in the garden
Hare empanadas
Prestiño fried dough
Boiled trout
Bite-sized wafers made with sweet dough
Little rolls, stuffed, made with leaven dough
Dish of firm fruit
White and red [wine] jelly
Sweet puffs, stuffed
Partridge empanadas made with pastry dough
Blancmange puffs and fried dough, also from blancmange
Clotted milk turnovers or *ginebradas*
Pickled trout
Toasted sweet cream with marrow
Stuffed beef tenderloin
Dishes of clotted milk
Fried cheese pastries

Si la merienda fuere un poco tarde, con servir pastelones de ollas podridas, pasará por cena. Ensaladas, fruta, y conservas, no hay para que ponerlas aquí, pues se sabe que se ha de servir de todo lo que se hallare, conforme al tiempo en que se hiciere la merienda. Y adviértase, (14v) que todos los platos que van escritos en estas viandas, los hallarán escritos en el libro: y la orden de cómo se han de hacer, y los recaudos que son menester para ellos.

Las volaterías, ninguna se ha de pelar en agua, y si se pelare sean pichones, porque esta volatería no tiene casi hebra, y así no pierde mucho pelándose en agua. Y si se hubieran de rellenar pollos, o pichones, es forzoso pelarse en agua, porque no se pueden rellenar en otra manera. Las palomas torcaces, y chorches [sic], y sisones, y otras aves salvajes, si estuvieren bien limpias, y bien tratadas, bien se pueden asar sin lavarse, aunque yo no uso dello por asegurar la limpieza. Cuanto a lo de pelar en agua, defiendo de manera, que no se pela cosa en agua en las cocinas de su Majestad, sino es para rellenos, como tengo dicho.[45]

---

45 In the cookbook, only three times does Martínez Montiño suggest wet plucking fowl: for squab in "Pichones ensapados" [Stuffed squab] (184–6; 185–7), as referenced here, for wings and necks in "Pepitoria" [Pepitoria (Stew with poultry offal)] (202–4; 203–5), and for turkey wings in "Una empanada de menudos de pavos" [Turkey giblet empanada] (458–60; 459–61). Other times he includes wet plucking for boar, deer antlers, and goat heads. For more information on wet plucking and dry plucking birds, see Shaw.

If supper were a little later, by serving hodgepodge stew pies, it could also be dinner. It is not necessary to include salads, fruit, and preserves here because everyone knows that any and all of that should be served according to the season whenever you have the supper. Also note that every dish written for these food items is found written in this book, instructions on how to make them, and the required sauces for them.

Regarding fowl, none should be wet plucked, but if you must, let it be squab, because this type of fowl has almost no muscle fibre and so you won't lose much when you wet pluck. And if you were to stuff chicken or squab, it is absolutely necessary to wet pluck because they cannot be stuffed in any other way. Wood pigeons, woodcocks, little bustards, and other wild birds, if they are well cleaned and taken good care of, then you can roast them without washing them, although I don't do that, so as to ensure cleanliness. Regarding wet plucking birds, I stand by not wet plucking any fowl in His Majesty's kitchens except when it's for stuffed birds, as I've already said.

[1]¹ (15r) *Capítulo II. De todo género de asado.*

Un pavo² se ha de perdigar sobre las parrillas, después de bien limpio, y se ha de embroquetar con dos broquetas de caña, o de otra madera que no amargue: luego espetarlo en su asador, y empapelarlo,³ poniéndole debajo del papel unas lonjas de tocino delgadas, y echarle has sal, y se podrán hincar algunos clavos en las pechugas, aunque algunos no lo usan. Para la salsa deste pavo, tomarás dos onzas de almendras mondadas, y tostadas en la sartén, y majarlas has, y asarás dos higadillos de gallina, o el del pavo, que estén bien secos, y majarse ha todo junto, y echarle has dos onzas de azúcar, y de que esté todo bien molido, desatarlo has con caldo,⁴ que no tenga grasa, y echarlo has en un cacillo, y ponlo a cocer de manera, que dé dos, o tres hervores, meneándolo siempre con un cucharón, y luego colarlo por (15v) un cedacillo, o estameña, y echarle una poca de canela molida, y un poco de zumo de limón. Hase de servir fría esta salsa.

Un capón se asa de la misma manera, salvo que no se ha de perdigar, ni empapelar, ni meter clavos. La salsa más ordinaria que se sirve para capones, es de granadas. Esta se hace desta manera, tomarás dos granadas acedas para cada capón, y desgranarlas has: y poner los granos en una estameña, o cedacillo, y estrujarlos con un cucharón hasta que suelten toda la tinta, y agrio que tienen; luego echarle dos onzas de azúcar, y un poco de vino tinto, y unas ragitas de canela, y tres clavos enteros, y cueza hasta que esté en punto, y sírvela en su platillo, o escudilla, fría.

---

1 The numbers in brackets are not part of Martínez Montiño's cookbook. I have inserted them here for easier reference for today's readers.

2 While there is no indication whether *pavo* refers to a New World turkey or a medieval peacock, Barbara Ketcham Wheaton gave her expert opinion that turkey replaced peacock almost instantly, was in fashion, and most certainly would be the bird referenced for this recipe ("Reading Historic Cookbooks"). Apart from the social, fashionable reasons for the switch, Ketcham Wheaton also hypothesized that flavour was another reason. Peacocks are not as flavourful and were most certainly served for their magnificent plumage. Nuria Polo Cano also documents that the word *pavo* from the sixteenth century on refers to the Mexican *guajalote* (240). Finally, L. Jacinto Garcia also affirms that the first appearances of the American turkey are in Martínez Montiño's and Hernández de Maceras' cookbooks (48). In the original edition, the publisher chose to capitalize the first word or two of each recipe, until 57v, when just the first two or three letters are capitalized. In the 1617 edition, the publisher, Juan de la Cuesta, takes great care to capitalize the first word of each recipe. In later editions, through the seventeenth and eighteenth centuries, just the first two letters of the first word are capitalized, and with that usually the first letter is as big as two lines and the second letter is as big as one line. By 1807, the words are written as they are today with the first letter capitalized and all others small.

3 This process of wrapping the turkey in paper to maintain tenderness is called *en papillote*. It figured prominently in the days of haute cuisine's ceremonious service in the late twentieth century. This roasting technique also appears in other early modern cookbooks such as in the recipe "Cook capon in a sheet," in the 1590 Hungarian cookbook, *The Science of Cooking* (*The Prince* 48) or in "Cómo se ha de aderezar un pavo" [How to prepare a turkey] found in Domingo Hernández de Maceras' 1607 cookbook, *Libro del arte de cocina* (209).

4 *Caldo* translates both as *broth* and as *stock*. The difference is that the former is made from meat or vegetables while the latter is made with bones. Martínez Montiño notes that using bones will produce a richer result in his recipe "Platillo de artaletes de ternera" [A dish of veal pinwheels] (228–30; 229–31). Throughout the cookbook I try to maintain this distinction. However, when it is not clear whether he is using one or the other, I translate the word as whatever fits best according to the context.

Chapter two. On all types of roasts

Sear a turkey on a grill after cleaning it very well and skewer it with two reed skewers or another type of wood that doesn't give off a bitter flavour. Then, place it on its spit and wrap it in paper, placing thin strips of fatback under the paper. Salt it and you can stick some cloves into the breast, although some prefer not to. For sauce for this turkey, take two ounces of shelled almonds that have been toasted in a pan; grind them. Roast two hen livers or the turkey liver that have been thoroughly cooked and grind everything together. Add two ounces of sugar, and when everything is ground together, thin with broth that has no fat and pour it all into a saucepan and bring to a boil two or three times, always stirring with a big spoon. Then strain it through a sieve or a cheesecloth. Add a little ground cinnamon and a little lemon juice. This sauce should be served cold.

A capon is roasted the same way, except that it is not seared, wrapped in paper, or seasoned with cloves. The most common sauce that is served with capon is pomegranate sauce. It is made in this way. Take two sour pomegranates for each capon and deseed them. Place the seeds in a cheesecloth or sieve and squeeze them with a big spoon until all the colour and acidic juice are released. Then add two ounces of sugar, a little red wine, some slivers of cinnamon stick, and three whole cloves and boil until the flavour is perfect. Serve cold on a small plate or

Con esta salsa se puede servir un capón asado, y hecho carbonadas tostadas en las parrillas, y asentadas sobre unas rebanadas de pan tostado.[5] Luego hacer la salsa de granadas (como está dicho) añadiendo más granadas, (16r) y más azúcar, y echárselo por encima, y sírvase caliente.

[2] *Capón en Gigote sobre sopa de natas.*[6]

Este capón después de asado podrás picar las pechugas, y hacer carbonadas de las piernas y las caderas, luego hacer una sopa de natas con bizcochos. Está adelante en el capítulo de las sopas la hallarás escrita como se ha de hacer.[7] Después de hecha la sopa, y cocida, asentarás las carbonadas del capón sobre ella, y lo picado de la pechuga en medio, sazonado de sal, y un poquito de agrio, de manera que el agrio no llegue a la sopa, y sírvase caliente.

[3] *Gigote de una pierna de carnero.*[8]

Una pierna de carnero en gigote se ha de asar, y picarse muy menuda: (16v) luego tener el zumo de otra pierna, que sea recién muerta. Ésta se ha de asar, que no sea muy seca, y luego punzarla muchas veces, y apretarla con el tenedor, y la misma canilla de la pierna, o con una prensa, y sacará medio cuartillo de zumo, o sustancia.[9] Ésta se

---

5 Placing prepared meat or poultry on a bed of toasted bread is one of the most common ways to serve roasts. It comes from the medieval use of trenchers, which were originally bread plates and later evolved into dishes made of wood or metal.

6 While we commonly think of *sopa* as *soup*, in this cookbook and, more generally, in seventeenth-century Spain and beforehand, it is understood as *sop*, a piece of bread placed on the bottom of a dish that soaks up the juices of the dish or a piece of bread that has some type of liquid – usually, stock, broth, wine, or cream – soaked into it.

7 While recipes are grouped by food item or method of preparation, Martínez Montiño excludes actual chapter titles, with a handful of exceptions. However, in different recipes throughout the cookbook, he references chapters, as he does here regarding a chapter on sops. Other mentions include a chapter on boar, on sponge cakes, and on ring-shaped pastries.

8 The translation of the word *carnero* is complicated. First, Martínez Montiño never uses the word *cordero* in the recipe book, in contrast to other meats for which he clearly distinguishes the young from the adult: *ternera/vaca*; *cabrito/cabra*; even *lechón/cerdo*. Thus, the question of whether he used the term *carnero* for both *mutton* and *lamb* comes into play. Additionally, in early modern Spain *carnero* often refers to *mutton* that is about a year old, while for today's standard, *carnero* is the term for meat from a sheep at least eighteen months of age. For meat from a one-year-old sheep, the term *cordero pascual* [hogget] is used today. Thus, for the early modern period, *carnero* can come from an animal that is only a year old. However, food critic Vicky Hayward has noted that the age of the animal is difficult to determine and the meat could have been from "two-year-old wethers or ewes up to six or eight years old" (email correspondence, 26 July 2018). For the purposes of this cookbook, I will use the term *mutton*, but the reader should be made aware of the difference of terminology across both space and time. It is also worth noting that Martínez Montiño does not include *oveja* [ewe] or any of its related words.

9 Measurements are tricky to translate, as the sizes that correspond to words used today do not always correspond to that same measurement. Also, in early modern Spain, measurements varied from region to region. A *cuartillo* is approximately the equivalent of a half litre or one pint (two cups),

in a bowl. This sauce can be served with a roasted capon, which can be cut up and grilled on the grill and set on top of slices of toasted bread. Then make the pomegranate sauce (as stated), adding more pomegranates and sugar. Ladle on top and serve hot.

Minced capon on cream sops

After roasting this capon you can chop up the breast meat, and finish the legs and thighs by grilling them. Next, prepare cream sops with sweet biscuits. You will find [this recipe] later on in the chapter on sops where it is written how to make it. After the sops are made and cooked, set the grilled capon on them with the chopped breast in the middle. Season with salt and a little sour juice, but the sour juice shouldn't reach the sops. Serve hot.

Minced leg of mutton

A minced leg of mutton should be roasted and chopped very fine. Have juice from another leg of a recently slaughtered sheep. This should be roasted, but not too well done, and then pricked all over. Hold the shinbone itself with a fork or a press, and squeeze out a half pint of juice or essence. Ladle this over the minced meat of

ha de echar sobre el gigote de la pierna manida,[10] que está picada, sazonándolo de sal. Hase de servir caliente, sin echarle otra cosa ninguna. Y si no hubiere otra pierna de qué sacar la sustancia cuando se hace la pierna del gigote, póngase debajo della una graserilla, o un plato con un poco de agua, y un poco de sal: y váyase recogiendo la sustancia que cayere de la pierna: y con esto se cebará el gigote, y servirá de sustancia. Y si acaso se asaren más piernas con la del gigote, con hacer lo que está dicho, y sacarlas todas juntas sobre la sustancia de la graserilla, y dejarlas estar un poco destilarán lo que bastara para hacer el gigote del señor, pues que las otras serán para el tinelo,[11] o para (17r) el estado. Este gigote con sustancia es bueno para servir con perdigones, asando los perdigones, y asentándolos sobre unas rebanadillas de pan tostado: luego echar el gigote con mucha sustancia por encima, sazonándolo de un poquito de especia, y un poco de zumo de limón, y una gota de vino. Adviértase, que en ningún gigote ha de caer gota de caldo, porque se echa a perder.

[4] *Cómo se hace la Ternera.*

La ternera lo más ordinario es echarla en adobo de ajo y orégano, y vinagre, y sal, y asarla para ella, que esté en adobo, o no, la salsa ha de ser de oruga: ésta se hace tostando un poco de pan, de manera que esté negro, y echarlo en remojo en vinagre; luego moler un poquito de la oruga, y echar cuatro o cinco partes de pan remojado sobre ella, y molerlo junto con un cuarterón de azúcar, de manera que no esté muy fuerte la oruga, y desatarlo con un poco de (17v) vinagre, y pasarla por un cedacillo, o estameña, y echarle un poquito de canela. Esta salsa se sirve fría. Otra oruga se hace de miel, y se puede guardar muchos días. Adelante diré cómo se hacen entrambas, y pondré las cantidades, y la miel, y cómo se ha de beneficiar.

[5] [*Palomas torcaces asadas.*][12]

Las palomas torcuaces [sic] se asan de manera, que no estén muy asadas, y se sacan y señalan por sus juntas,[13] y se les echa mucho zumo de naranjas, y un poquito de pimienta y sal, y se vuelven las pechugas abajo, y se ponen un poquito sobre las brasas, de manera que no cuezan. Sírvanse calientes.

---

so here *medio cuartillo* can be translated as a *half pint* or *one cup*. For more on measurements, see Appendix 2, "On Measurements," Castaño Álvarez, and "Antiguas pesas y medidas."

10 *Una pierna manida* [a dry aged leg] refers to a process of tenderizing meat in which the meat is left to hang, thereby allowing enzymes to break down tissues, making the meat more tender, allowing water to evaporate, and concentrating the flavour.

11 *Tinelo* is the dining room for servants in the house of a grandee (RAE). *Estado* refers to the state room where government officials would dine. The food for the state room was prepared in a separate space from the food for the king. In Chapter 1, Martínez Montiño discusses rotating the kitchen staff for both these kitchens so that everyone can experience the different levels of preparation and responsibility.

12 Although there is no title to introduce what follows, it is clearly a separate recipe. Additionally, Martínez Montiño does include this title in the index at the end of the cookbook.

13 The joint is crucial for indicating how far along the poultry has cooked.

the dry-aged leg of mutton, seasoning it with salt. Serve hot without adding anything else. If you don't have another leg from which to get the essence, then when preparing the minced mutton, have a drip pan underneath or a plate with a little water and salt in it, and catch the essence that drips from the leg. This will enrich the minced mutton and will act as [a substitute for] the essence. If you roast other legs with the minced leg, and do what has been stated and place all of them together over the drip pan to catch the essence and leave them there, they will drip enough [juices] for the minced meat for your lord; then the rest will be for those who eat in the kitchen or for the state room. This minced meat with its essence is good to serve with partridge chicks. Roast the chicks and then place them on top of slices of toasted bread. Next, ladle over the top the minced meat with a lot of essence. Season it with a little bit of spice and a little lemon juice and a drop of wine. Note that in no minced meat dish should there be a drop of broth because it will ruin it.

How to prepare veal[1]

Veal: the most common way is to marinate it in garlic, oregano, vinegar, and salt and grill it. Whether marinated or not, for veal the sauce must be arugula. This is made by toasting a little bread until it is black and soaking it in vinegar. Then, grind a little arugula and add four to five times the amount of soaked bread, and grind it all together with a quarter pound of sugar so that the arugula flavour is not too strong. Thin it with a little vinegar and strain it through a sieve or cheesecloth. Add a little cinnamon. This sauce should be served cold. You can also make arugula sauce with honey and it will last many days. Later on, I will say how to make both and will list the amounts and the honey and how to prepare them.

[*Grilled wood pigeon*]

Wood pigeons should be partially roasted; take them off and check their joints. Ladle a lot of orange juice on them and sprinkle with a little salt and pepper. Turn the bird breasts down and return to finish them over red-hot embers but do not let them overcook. Serve hot.

---

1 Although today *ternera* is often translated as *beef*, Martínez Montiño clearly distinguishes between the two. For most recipes he uses *ternera* [veal], but for some he specifically uses *vaca* [beef]. Today, *veal* refers to the meat from a calf less than a year old, although the exact age and weight vary from one country to another. For the European Union, veal has sub-designations depending on the age of the animal: Class V for calves younger than eight months and Class Z for calves between eight and twelve months. Any meat from animals older than twelve months is classified as beef. For more information, see European Commission. Although the title refers to veal, the actual instructions focus more on making arugula sauce.

También se sirven asándolas mechadas, y poner debajo dellas un poco de caldo, y recoger el zumo dellas, y de otras asadas: luego tostar unas rebanadas de pan, y asentarlas en el plato, y señalar las palomas, y asentarlas sobre el pan, y sazonar el caldo, y el zumo de los asados, echándoles sus especias, pimienta, nueces y jengibre, y zumo de limón y (18r) echarlo has por encima de las palomas: y pondrás el plato sobre un poco de lumbre antes que se sirva, y vaya caliente a la mesa.

[6] *Palomas torcaces con salsa de Almendras.*

Asarás cuatro palomas, y apartarlas has, y ahógalas con un poco de tocino gordo, y un poco de cebolla cortada muy menuda: y luego échales caldo cuanto se bañen, y vayan cociendo poco a poco, y sazona con todas especias,[14] y tomarás un cuarterón de almendras, y tostarlas las con su cáscara, y májalas has muy bien en el almirez: luego las desatarás con un poco de caldo, y pasarlas has por un cedacillo, o estameña. Echarás estas almendras dentro la vasija donde están las palomas, y echarle has seis onzas de azúcar, y un poco de agrio; y vaya cociendo poco a poco: y has de sazonar con todas especias, (18v) y canela: sírvelas sobre rebanadas de pan tostado. Estas palomas estofadas son buenas con salsa de ciruelas. Esta salsa de ciruelas se hace desta manera. Cocer las ciruelas, y pasarlas por un cedacillo, de manera que no quede por pasar más de los cuescos,[15] y con la misma agua donde se cocieren las ciruelas, se puede hacer la salsa, y sazonarla con todas especias, y canela, y echarle azúcar de manera, que esté bien dulce, y agria, y que esté un poco encorporada, como salsa negra de harina:[16] ha de llevar su vino,[17] ni más ni menos que la de harina quemada, y es muy buena para pastelones de lenguas de vaca, o pies de puerco, y para ánades, y para otras muchas volaterías salvajes.

[7] *Cómo se aderezan las Perdices.*

En las perdices no hay que decir para ellas, porque lo más ordinario se comen asadas. La salsa de éstas se suele (19r) hacer, señalándolas por las junturas, echando un poco de limón, y un poco de vino, y pimienta, y nuez de especie, y estofarlas un poquito, de manera que no cuezan, y si le [sic] quisieres echar un poco de manteca, de vaca fresca, será buena.[18] Otra salsa de limones se suele servir con las perdices,

---

14 In the recipe "Pepitoria" [Stew with poultry offal], Martínez Montiño explains that *todas especias* means black peppers, clove, nutmeg, ginger, and saffron (204; 205). For more on *todas especias*, see the Introduction (47).
15 By 1617 *cuesco* is replaced with *hueso*.
16 Instructions on how to make *salsa negra* are found in "Empanadas frías de jabalí" [Cold boar empanadas] and "Empanadas de jabalí calientes" [Hot boar empanadas] (290–2; 291–3).
17 The use of the possessive pronoun before a food ingredient – here, literally, *its wine* – indicates the amount that is right for that dish. I have translated it here and often elsewhere as *the right amount of*; at other times, for example with *su sal*, as *to taste*.
18 *Manteca de vaca fresca* is a common term for *freshly churned butter*. Martínez Montiño uses it in many recipes, and by using the adjective *fresca* he is reminding other cooks to use the best-quality butter. However, by the eighteenth century, butter is no longer a common ingredient in Spanish kitchens (Pérez Samper, *Mesas y cocinas* 106).

They can also be prepared by larding and roasting them. Place a little broth under them and collect the juice from the birds and other roasted birds. Then toast slices of bread, set them on a plate, and check the pigeons and set them on the bread. Season the broth and juice from the roasted birds by adding in spices – black pepper, nutmeg, and ginger – and lemon juice. Ladle this over the wood pigeons. Put the plate over low heat before serving it so that it arrives at the table hot.

Wood pigeon with almond sauce

Roast four wood pigeons, part them, and sauté them with a little fatback and a little minced onion. Then pour enough broth over them to braise them and continue cooking them slowly. Season with all spices. Take a quarter pound of almonds, toast them in their shells, and thoroughly grind them in a mortar. Then thin them with some broth and strain through a sieve or cheesecloth. Add the almond sauce to the pot where the wood pigeons are and add six ounces of sugar and a little acidic fruit juice and continue to cook slowly. Season with all spices and cinnamon and serve them on slices of toasted bread. These stewed wood pigeons are good with plum sauce. Plum sauce is made this way. Cook plums and strain them in a sieve so that nothing but the pit remains, and, in the same water in which the plums were cooked, make the sauce. Season it with all spices and cinnamon. Add sugar so that it is very sweet, and some acidic fruit juice; it should be slightly thick like black sauce [made] from flour. It should have the right amount of wine, no more or less than the toasted flour sauce. It goes very well with beef tongue pie or pig's feet pie or duck and many other game birds.

How to prepare partridge

Regarding partridges, there is not much to say about them because the most common way to eat them is roasted. The sauce for them is usually prepared by checking the joints and adding a little lemon, wine, pepper, and nutmeg, and stewing them a little but not so much that it comes to a boil. If you want to add a little fresh butter, it would be good. Other lemon sauces are also served with partridge.

tomando limones, y mondarlos, y cortarlos menudos,[19] y echar un poquito de vinagre, y pimienta y sal, y una gota de vino blanco, y echarlo por encima de las perdices, así como salen del asador: y no se ha de calentar más, porque amargaría: y si le quisieres echar alguna vez azúcar, de manera que vaya agridulce no será malo.

[8] *Cómo se aderezan las Chorchas.*

Las chorchas se sirven de la manera que tengo dicho en las palomas, y los sisones, y otras aves salvages, añadiéndoles un poco de vino, y hierbas,[20] como es mejorana, y salvia, e hisopillo. (19v) Estas chorchas, dicen, que lo que tienen en las tripas no es cosa sucia: y así los estrangeros[21] las suelen sacar las tripas con el higadillo, quitando la hiel, y pícanlo asina[22] crudo, y échanlo en una cazuela, sazonándolas de especia y sal, y un poco de vino, y un poquito de vinagre, y un poquito de caldo, y pónenlo debajo las chorchas, cuando se están asando, y con la sustancia que cae dellas, y de otros asados hacen una salsa, y sirven las chorchas sobre unas rebanadas de pan tostado muy bien aparadas, y échanle salsa por encima, añadiéndolas un poco de zumo de limón. Muchos señores gustan dello, mas yo no he usado desta salsa, porque lleva la suciedad de las tripas.

[9] *Grullas asadas.*

Las grullas asadas se suelen servir haciendo gigote de la mitad de la grulla, y la otra media mechada y asada: asentarás la media grulla entera en (20r) el plato sobre rebanadas de pan tostado; y pondrás el picado al lado: luego harás pebrada, echando en una sartén un cuarterón de azúcar molido, medio cuartillo de vino tinto, la mitad de medio cuartillo de vinagre, un poco de caldo;[23] sazonarás con

---

19 The use of lemon rind in preparing sauces echoes Hispano-Muslim practices. Even so, Martínez Montiño's use is original, because in the Hispano-Muslim cookbooks lemon rind is either dried or brined, but here he minces rind and adds it to the sauce (Eléxpuru 132).
20 For Martínez Montiño, *hierbas* [herbs] mostly mean *mejorana* [marjoram], *salvia* [sage], *hisopillo* [winter savory], and *ajedrea* [summer savory], but sometimes also include *hinojo* [fennel] and *oregáno* [oregano]. Marjoram is the most popular. When present, sage and winter savory always appear in conjunction with it. While fennel and oregano sometimes appear with these herbs as seasoning, they are more commonly used as an ingredient in marinades or brines. *Hierbas* are different from *verduras*, which are generally a combination of parsley, spearmint, and cilantro.
21 Martínez Montiño comments on foreigners' "misconception" of cleanliness and proper food preparation. It is one of several moments when he distinguishes between what happens in a Spanish kitchen and what happens in other kitchens.
22 *Asina* is an old form for *así* [thus]. By 1617 it is replaced with *assí*.
23 *Pebrada* [pepper sauce] first appeared in Mestre Robert's 1520 *Llibre del coc*, later translated into Castilian, *Libro de guisados*, under the name, Ruperto de Nola. In the Spanish translation of his recipe, Nola specifies "esta salsa quiere ser fortezuela de pimienta, y asimismo el color, y no se pone otra cosa; porque poniéndole otra cosa no se llamaría pebrada" [this sauce should have a strong pepper flavour and have the same colour. Nothing more is added, because if you add something else it won't be called pepper sauce] (336). Of course, here, Martínez Montiño adds other spices. In a later recipe he clarifies that the spices used are ginger, cinnamon, and clove. See "Gigote de Liebres" [Minced hare] (154; 155).

They are made by taking lemons, peeling and mincing them. Add a little vinegar, salt and pepper, and a drop of white wine. Ladle this over the partridges as soon as they come off the spit. Do not heat it up because it will turn bitter, and if you sometimes want to add sugar to it so that it is sweet and sour, it won't taste bad.

How to prepare woodcock

Woodcocks are served in the same fashion as I have stated for wood pigeons, little bustards, and other game birds by adding a little wine and herbs like marjoram, sage, and winter savory. It is said that what these woodcocks have in their intestines is not dirty. Thus, foreigners typically take the intestines out with the liver, removing the bile, and chop them all up raw. They place them in a casserole, seasoning them with spices, salt, and a little wine, vinegar, and broth and put it [the sauce] under the woodcocks when they are roasting, and with the essence that drips down from them and other roasts, they make a sauce. Woodcocks are served opened up, on slices of toasted bread. Ladle the sauce on top, finishing it with a little lemon juice. Many lords like this dish, but I do not make this sauce because it has the filth from the intestines.

Roast crane

Roast crane is usually served by making minced meat of one half of it and the other half larded and roasted. Set the entire half crane on a plate over slices of toasted bread and place the minced part on the side. Then make a black pepper sauce by putting in a frying pan a quarter pound of ground sugar, a half pint of red wine, half of a half pint of vinegar, and a little broth. Season with all spices

todas las especias y canela, y cueza hasta que empiece a tomar punto,[24] y echarla has por encima de la media grulla picada, y ponla a estofar un poco.

Si quieres servir esta grulla picada con un poco de adobo de ternera, y un poco de pimienta, y un poco de zumo de limón sin dulce, ni otra cosa ninguna; es muy buena. Las mollejas de las grullas son muy grandes y muy tiernas. Éstas limpiándolas, y echándolas en adobo, luego abrir las tripas, y lavarlas, y echarlas también en adobo. Luego espetar las mollejas en un asadorcillo, y las tripas revueltas: luego asarlas y servirlas con un poco del mismo adobo, y un poco de zumo de limón, o naranja: es cosa muy regalada.

(20v) También son buenas estas grullas partidas por medio, y perdigadas en las parrillas, y mechadas, y echarlas en adobo, luego empanarlas en masa negra, que sea gruesa: y cuando estén acabadas de cocer, hacerle un agujero, y echarle un poco de adobo dentro, y dejarlas cocer otra media hora, suelen salir muy buenas.[25] Desta manera se sirven las avutardas,[26] las tripas se han de revolver a la molleja. Todas las aves salvajes podrás servir con estas salsas picantes, añadiéndoles algunas hierbas del jardín, como es salvia y mejorana, y las podrás servir con salsas negras de venazón en potajes, o en pastelones: las cuales salsas hallarás escritas en el capítulo donde se trata del jabalí.[27]

[10] *Las Ánades, y zarcetas.*[28]

Las ánades y zarcetas, servirás asadas con salsa de membrillos. Tomarás los membrillos, y mondarlos has, y (21r) pártelos por medio, y córtalos en rebanadillas delgadas, y tomarás tocino en dados, y freírlo has hasta que esté blanco: y luego echarás dentro un poco de cebolla picada, y los membrillos, y los ahogarás hasta que estén blandos. Luego sazonarás con especia negra y canela, y echarás un poco de vino y vinagre y azúcar, y un poco de caldo: y tendrás las ánades asadas y mechadas, y aparadas, y asentarlas has sobre unas rebanadas de pan tostado: luego echarás la salsa por encima. Esta salsa puede servir con sisones, y alcarvanes [*sic*], y pluvias, y gangas, y otros pájaros salvajes, y con liebres asadas, si son tiernas: y si no son tiernas picarlas has descarnándolas, y juntando la carne de la liebre con otra poca de ternera, o carnero: y sazonarás con todas especias, y su tocino picado, y huevos, y tornarás a armar la liebre en una cazuela grande, y pondrásla al fuego con lumbre abajo, y arriba: y de que esté cocida asentarla has sobre rebanadas de pan tostadas, (21v) y echarás por encima, y por los lados la salsa de membrillos. Y advierte, que si no hubiere membrillos, podrás hacer esta salsa con peros agrios.

---

24 Today cooks talk about coating the back of the spoon to check for the desired consistency.
25 In Martínez Montiño's cookbook, cooking times are given in fractions of the hour, never in minutes. For more on cooking times, see Appendix 2, "On Measurements."
26 *Las avutardas* [great bustards] are related to cranes. Both are from the gruiformes order of birds, have long legs, and are approximately the size of the turkey.
27 These cross-references exemplify that Martínez Montiño is fully aware of the big project, perceiving his book not just as a collection of recipes but as a whole, unified work.
28 *Zarceta* or today *cerceta* [Eurasian teal or common teal] is a member of the duck family.

and cinnamon, boil until it begins to thicken, ladle over the minced meat, and let it stew for a while.

If you would like to serve this minced crane meat with a little of the veal marinade and a little pepper, a little lemon juice, with no additional sweetener or anything else, it is very tasty. Crane gizzards are very big and tender. Clean them and marinate them, then open and clean the intestines and also add to the marinade. Next, skewer the gizzards with the intestines wrapped around them on a small spit. Next, roast them and serve them with a little of the same marinade, and a little lemon or orange juice. It is exquisite.[2]

These cranes are also very good split in half, seared on the grill, larded, and marinated. Then wrap them in a dark, thick dough and when they are done baking, make a little hole and spoon in some marinade and let them bake another half an hour. They are usually very tasty. This is the way to serve great bustards. The intestines should be wrapped around the gizzards. All game birds can be served with these pungent sauces, adding some garden herbs like sage and marjoram. You can also serve them with the venison black sauce either as a stew or a pie; both are written in the chapter that deals with boar.

Duck and teal

Duck and teal are served roasted with quince sauce. Take quince, peel them, cut them in half, and cut them into thin slices. Cube some fatback and fry it until it turns white. Then add in some diced onion and the quince, sauté them until they are soft. Then season with black pepper and cinnamon and add a little wine, some vinegar and sugar, and a little broth. Have the ducks larded, roasted, and opened up and set them on slices of toasted bread. Then, ladle the sauce on top. This sauce can also be served with little bustards, stone curlews, plovers, pin-tailed sand grouses, and other game birds, and with roasted hare, if they are tender. But if they are not tender, mince them up by pulling the meat off, and mix the hare meat with some veal or mutton and season it with all spices, the right amount of minced fatback, and eggs, and then assemble the hare in a large casserole and place it on the fire with heat above and below it. Once it's cooked, set it on slices of toasted bread and ladle over the top and on the sides the quince sauce. And, note, if there aren't any quinces, you can also make this sauce with sour apples.

---

[2] I have translated the word *regalado* as *exquisite* but want to mention Covarrubias' definition to fully capture its meaning: "el que se trata con curiosidad y con gusto, especialmente en su comida" [that which deals with curiosity and pleasure, especially regarding food] (900).

[11] *Gigote de Liebres.*

Las liebres también son buenas asadas y picadas en gigote, con aceite y vinagre, y pimienta: a estas liebres si quisieres, echarles has una pebrada en lugar del aceite y vinagre, echando en la sartén un poco de vino tinto, y un poco de vinagre, y azúcar un cuarterón para cada plato, y poco de caldo, y sazonarás con pimienta y jengibre y canela, y algunos clavos enteros, y cueza hasta que el azúcar vaya tomando punto.[29] Luego échela por encima del gigote de la liebre, y ponla a estofar un poco. Esta pebrada puede servir también para echar por encima de las liebres armadas: y para encima de gigote de palomas, o sisones, o ánades, y para encima de gigote de venado.

[12] (22r) *Conejos.*

Los conejos, lo más ordinario es servirlos con aceite y vinagre. Si los quisieres servir con salsa de alcaparras, tomarás un poco de buen aceite, y freirás cebolla picada muy menuda, y tendrás las alcaparras bien desaladas, y cocidas, y échalas en una sartén con la cebolla y el aceite, y echa pimienta, y un poco de vinagre, y denle un hervor, y señalarás los conejos, y asentarlos has en el plato, y echarás la salsa de las alcaparras por encima, y si le quisieres echar dulce alguna vez, bien podrás.

[13] *Conejos en mollo.*[30]

Los conejos en mollo asarlos has, y cortarlos has en pedazos, y freirás cebolla cortada larga con aceite, y echarás los conejos dentro, y dejarlos has ahogar bien. Luego sazonarás con pimienta, nuez, y jengibre, y echarás caldo de la olla, cuanto se cubran los conejos, (22v) y cuezan muy poco a poco hasta que estén bien cocidos, y échale un poco de vinagre y azafrán, y servirlos has sobre rebanadas de pan blanco. Esto se entiende, que ha de ser con buen aceite de Valencia, o con otro aceite que sea muy bueno.[31]

---

29 In the section "Memoria de conservas" [Memoir on preserves], Martínez Montiño describes various stages of sugar boiling. For more information, see 561–75. This black pepper sauce is also explained in the recipe "Grullas asadas" [Roast crane] (150–2; 151–3).

30 *Mollo* is related to the Portuguese *molho* [sauce]. Given Martínez Montiño's deep connections to Portugal, this could be another recipe with Portuguese origins.

31 This is the only time in the cookbook that Martínez Montiño specifies using oil from Valencia. Today Spain is the world's largest producer and exporter of olive oil and one of the twenty-eight "Designations of Origin" comes from Valencia: DO Aceite de la Comunitat Valenciana. For more information, see "Información sectorial" and "Denominaciones de origen." This recipe is also reproduced by Doña Dominga de Guzmán in her mid-eighteenth century Mexican cookbook (Pérez San Vicente, *Recetario* 108).

Minced hare

Hare is also good roasted and chopped into minced meat with oil, vinegar, and pepper. If you like you can replace the oil and vinegar with a pepper sauce by putting in a frying pan a little red wine, a little vinegar, and a quarter pound of sugar, for each plate. Add a little broth and season with black pepper, ginger, and cinnamon, and some whole cloves. Boil until the sugar begins to thicken. Then pour over the minced hare and allow it to stew a while. This pepper sauce is also good for reassembled hare and on top of minced wood pigeon, little bustard, or duck and on top of minced venison.

Rabbit

Rabbits: the most common way to serve them is with oil and vinegar. If you want to serve them with a caper sauce, take some good oil and fry up minced onion and take some capers that have been thoroughly desalted and boiled and add them to the pan with the onion and oil. Add black pepper and a little vinegar and bring to a boil. Check the rabbits and set them on the plate and ladle caper sauce on top. If sometime you want to sprinkle some sweetener on it, it would be good.

Rabbit in mollo broth

For rabbit in mollo broth, roast them and cut them up into pieces. Fry onion that has been cut lengthwise in oil, add the rabbit pieces to it, and sauté them well. Then season with black pepper, nutmeg, and ginger and add stock to the pot, enough to cover the rabbit, and slowly simmer until it is well cooked. Add a little vinegar and saffron and serve over slices of white bread. It is understood that good Valencia oil should be used or another excellent [quality] oil.

[14] *Gigote de Conejos.*

Asarás dos conejos, y después de asados picarás las piernas, y los lomos, y asentarás este picado sobre unas rebanadillas de pan blanco, y pondrás las espaldillas, y las cabezas de los conejos al derredor y luego mezclarás un poco de caldo con un poco de aceite, vinagre, pimienta, y sal, y echarlo has por encima del gigote, y ponle a estofar un poco, y sírvelo caliente: y si quieres guardar el lomo de un conejo, y hacerlo rebanadillas, y asentarlo por encima del gigote parece muy bien.

[15] (23r) *Otro Gigote de conejos frío.*[32]

Asarás los conejos, y picarás toda la carne de los lomos y piernas, sin dejar más de las cabezas, y sazonarás de sal, y pimienta: y luego harás una ensalada de todas hierbas, y compondrás el plato de tu gigote, y ensalada, haciendo como una rosca en el plato, yendo poniendo montoncillos de carne, y otros de ensalada, y en el medio pondrás un poco de ensalada muy bien puesta, con todas las cosas que se suelen echar sus ruedas de limón, y sazónala de aceite y vinagre; y luego adornarla por la parte de afuera con algunas rajas de diacitrón, y granos de granada, y confites, y todas las cosas que suelen poner a las ensaladas: y en medio pondrás unos cogollos de lechuga enteros en pie, y por encima del gigote, o salpicón, aceitunas quitados los cuescos. Este plato es bueno para meriendas, porque se ha de comer frío. Algunos los llaman conejos en huerta.

[16] (23v) *Salpicón de Vaca.*

Pues que tratamos de salpicón, quiero avisar, que cuando te pidieren salpicón de vaca, que procures tener un poco de buen tocino de pernil cocido,[33] y pícalo, y mézclalo con la vaca, y luego su pimienta, sal, y vinagre, y su cebolla picada, mezclada con la carne, y unas ruedas de cebolla para adornar el plato es muy bueno, y tiene buen gusto.

---

32 This is a highly decorative salad. Martínez Montiño gives a lot of attention to how the dish should be presented. At the end of the recipe he also provides readers with the playful alternative name: "conejos en huerta" [rabbits in the garden].

33 *Tocino* [fatback] actually includes several different types, depending on what part of the pig it is cut from. When Martínez Montiño specifies *tocino de pernil* he is referring to *ham fat*, which is acquired from the leg of the animal. Based on his recipes, it seems to have more meat attached to it than the generic *tocino* [fatback], which is primarily taken off the back under the skin. A third type, *tocino de redaño* [caul lard], is the mesentery found around the digestive organs and is generally used for wrapping meat.

Minced rabbit

Roast two rabbits and after roasting, mince the legs and lower back and set the minced meat on slices of white bread. Place the head and shoulders of the rabbit around [the meat] and then mix a little broth with a little oil, vinegar, salt, and pepper, and pour over the minced meat and let stew for a while. Serve hot. If you want to reserve the rabbit loin and slice it and set it on top of the minced meat, it will look really good.

Another minced rabbit, [served] cold

Roast [some] rabbits and mince all the meat from the back and legs, leaving nothing but the head. Season with salt and pepper. Then, make a salad with all types of leafy greens and put together a plate of your minced meat and salad by making a ring on the plate with little piles of meat and others of salad. In the middle arrange some of the salad nicely with all the usual things that are in a salad and lemon wheels. Season with oil and vinegar and then, around the outside, garnish with candied citron, pomegranate seeds, and other sugar-coated nuts and seeds and everything you usually add to a salad. In the centre place some lettuce hearts standing up and, on top of the minced meat or salpicon, some olives with their pits removed. This dish is good for late afternoon suppers because it is eaten cold. Some call it "rabbits in the garden."

Beef salpicon

Now that we are discussing salpicon, I must advise that when asked to prepare beef salpicon, have a small amount of good fat from boiled ham, dice it, and mix it in with the beef. Then add salt and pepper to taste, vinegar, and the right amount of diced onion mixed with the meat and some onion rings to garnish. The dish is very good and it is very tasty.

[17] *Pollos asados con su salsa.*

Los pollos asados pocas veces se sirven con salsa, salvo si hay agraz.[34] Para esta salsa tomarás los granos de agraz, y tendrás en una sartén tocino frito en dados, que estén bien fritos, y sacarlos has fuera de la sartén, echarás los granos del agraz a freír, y darles has dos, o tres vueltas sobre el fuego, y no más, porque no se cuezan demasiado, y echarás azúcar y canela, y pimienta, y un poco de vinagre, y asentarás los pollos sobre (24r) rebanadas de pan tostado, y echarás la salsa de agraz por encima.

[18] *Pollos rellenos.*[35]

Si quisieres rellenar pollos tomarás un poco de tocino en rebanadillas, y freírlo has, y cuando esté medio frito echarás un poco de cebolla cortada a lo largo, y freírla has a medio freír; luego echarás un poco de carne cruda picada, y freírlo has todo, revolviéndolo con una paleta, hasta que esté la carne perdigada, y echarás allí hierbabuena, y cilantro verde, y un poco de mejorana. Luego batirás media docena de huevos para cuatro pollos, y echarlos has en la sartén, y revolverlo has con la paleta hasta que esté bien seco, y sacarlo has al tablero, y picarlo has muy bien, y meterle has cuatro huevos crudos, y sazonarás con especia negra, y azafrán, y agrio de limón, o naranja y sal. Este relleno es lo más ordinario. Si no tuvieres carne para este relleno con higadillos de gallinas, (24v) y los demás materiales, lo podrás hacer. Si quisieres rebozar estos pollos rellenos, podrás echar en el relleno agrio, y dulce: y cuando tengas los pollos rellenos, y espetados en el asador, tomarás los pies de los pollos cortados por la junta, y aguzarás el hueso del pie, y meterlo has por la cabeza del pollo: en cada cabeza de pollo pondrás los pies de manera, que parezcan cuernos de venado, y asarlos has: y cuando estén asados rebózalos con yemas de huevos, de manera que estén bien cubiertos yéndolos asando, y dando con unas plumas, y las yemas rebozando también los pies, que están puestos en las cabezas de los pollos. Cuando estén bien cubiertos tomarás un poco de manteca caliente, y echársela has por encima, y esponjará el rebozado, y echarás un poco de azúcar por encima, sacarlos has y servirlos has con unas hojuelas, porque no se sirven sobre sopa, porque abultan mucho, que con cuatro pollos henchirás un plato. (25r) Las cabezas destos pollos han de estar puestas por la rabadilla, que vengan a quedar los cuernos sobre las espaldas.

---

34 Martínez Montiño uses *agraz* [sour grapes, verjuice] in a variety of ways in twenty-one recipes in his cookbook. For more information on *agraz*, see 42.
35 This recipe was recreated and a photo of the finished product, chicken with "antlers," can be found in Appendix 3.1.

Roast chicken with its sauce

Roast chicken is rarely served with sauce unless there are sour grapes. For this sauce, take sour grapes and have cubed, fried fatback that has been well fried in a frying pan. Remove it from the pan and fry the sour grapes and flip them two or three times over the fire and no more so they won't get overcooked. Add cinnamon and sugar, pepper, and a little vinegar. Set the chicken on slices of toasted bread and ladle the sour grape sauce on top.

Chicken with stuffing

If you want to make chicken with stuffing, take a few slices of fatback and fry them and when they are partially fried, add some onion chopped lengthwise and continue to fry. When the onion is partially cooked, add in some raw minced meat and fry it, stirring it all with a spatula until the meat is browned. Add in spearmint, cilantro, and a little marjoram. Then, for four chickens, beat half a dozen eggs and add them to the frying pan and stir with the spatula until the eggs are thoroughly cooked. Turn it out onto a cutting board and chop it finely. Add four raw eggs and season with black pepper, saffron, lemon or orange juice, and salt. This is the most common stuffing. If you don't have meat for the stuffing, you can also use hen livers with the other ingredients. If you want to coat the stuffed chickens, you can add sweet and sour flavours to the stuffing. When the chickens are stuffed and skewered on the spit, take the chicken legs, cut at the joints, and sharpen the leg bone, and stick it on the chicken's head. You will do this for each chicken so that they look like deer antlers and roast them that way. While they are roasting, coat them with egg yolks so that they are totally coated as you continue to roast and brush on the egg yolk. You should also coat with egg yolk the legs that are on the chickens' heads. When everything is thoroughly coated, take a little hot lard and ladle it on top; it will aerate the coating. Sprinkle a little sugar on top, take them off [the spits] and serve them on pastry sheets. They should not be served on sops because they take up a lot of space; four chickens will fill up the whole plate. They should be arranged head to back so the antlers will be over the backs.

[19] *Empanadas de Perdices.*

Empanadas de perdices con masa de bollos, tomarás las perdices después de peladas y limpias, y perdigarlas has en las parrillas, y darles has un golpe en las pechugas, de manera que estén medio asadas, y ponlas en una pieza con un poquito de vino, y de todas especias, y su sal, y tendrás unas lonjas de tocino gordo muy delgadas y otras chiquitas de tocino magro muy remojadas, y déjalo estar desta manera por media hora, y toma harina, y haz una masa encerada con huevos y agua y sal,[36] y un poquito de manteca, y tiende una hoja un poco larga y gorda, y tendrás manteca fresca de vaca lavada, y sobada,[37] pondrás muchos pedacitos de manteca por la hoja de masa que tome la mitad della, y (25v) rociarla has con un poco de harina, y doblarla has que caiga encima de la manteca del otro pedazo que no la tiene, y tornarla has a tender larga, y tornarás a poner otros bocaditos de manteca por toda ella, y echarás otro poco de harina, y arrollarla has como hojaldrado. Luego cortarás cerca de un palmo de este rollo de masa, y recogerás las puntas, y harás una torta redonda. Luego tomarás unas lonjas de tocino gordo, y pondráslo sobre la masa: luego pondrás sobre ellas otras chiquitas de tocino magro. Luego pondrás una perdiz, la pechuga para abajo, y luego le pondrás en las espaldas otra lonja de tocino gordo: é irás recogiendo la masa de manera, que todas las orillas vengan a juntarse en las espaldas de la perdiz, mojándolas con un poco de agua, porque quede cerrado, como cerradero de bolsa.[38] Luego volverás la perdiz la pechuga hacia arriba, y amoldarla has de manera, que no se vea por donde se cerró, y tomarás dos pies (26r) de la perdiz, e hincarlos has en la empanada, las uñas afuera, y dorarla has con yemas de huevo, y ponlo sobre un papel, y métela en el horno. Son muy buenas empanadas, y llámanse Empanadas sin repulgo.

[20] *Empanadas en asador.*

Ya que habemos comenzado a decir destas empanadas trasordinarias, pondré aquí otras dos maneras de empanar en asador. Tomarás tórtolas, o perdices, o palominos, o pichones, y córtales has los alones muy a raíz, y las piernas recogérselas has de manera, que queden muy redondas, y espetarlas has, y asarlos has: y cuando

---

36 *Masa encerada* is a phrase Martínez Montiño uses to describe a soft, elastic dough. The following instructions explain how to laminate dough and are key to making puff pastry and other flaky pastry doughs.

37 In this phrase, Martínez Montiño includes a couple of the stages for processing butter. When converting milk to butter, rinsing it helps remove the remaining buttermilk from the butter solids. Likewise, kneading it also releases liquid.

38 *Cerradero de bolsa* [purse strings] is a wonderful visual image of how to seal the edges of the empanada and a good example of how Martínez Montiño reaches out to his readership so that they will understand how to finish the empanada.

Partridge empanadas

Partridge empanadas in pastry dough: after plucking and cleaning the partridges, sear them on the grill and pound the breasts once so that they are partially grilled. Put them in a bowl with a little wine, all spices, and salt to taste. Have some thin slices of extra fatty fatback and other small slices of meaty fatback that have been well soaked. Let everything soak for a half hour. Then take flour and make an elastic dough with eggs, water, salt, and a little butter. Roll the dough out into a long, thick piece. Take fresh butter that has been rinsed and kneaded and dot half of the dough with the butter and then sprinkle on a little flour. Fold the dough over so that the unbuttered side is on top of the buttered side and roll it out into a long piece again. Once again dot the entire dough with butter and sprinkle on a little flour and roll it up like puff pastry dough. Then cut about a palm's length from this rolled-up dough, pinch the ends, and make a round pie. Then take the slices of extra fatty fatback and lay them on the dough. On top of them lay the smaller pieces of meaty fatback. Then put in the partridge, the breast facing down, and then on the back place another slice of the extra fatty fatback. Then pick up the dough so that all the edges meet on the partridge back. Wet [the edges] with water so that it [the dough] stays closed, as if it were closed purse strings. Then turn the partridge over, the breast right side up, and shape it so that you can't see where it was closed. Take two partridge feet and stick them in the empanada, with the claws out. Coat it with egg yolk, place on a piece of paper, and finish in the oven. These empanadas are very good and they are called "seamless empanadas."

Empanadas on a spit

Now that we've started to talk about these unique empanadas, I will include here two ways to make empanadas on a spit. Take collared doves, partridges, wild squab, or farm-raised squab, cut their wings off right at their bodies, and fold up their legs so the birds take a round shape. Skewer them and roast them. As they

estén asados tendrás hecho un batido con harina de arroz y azúcar, y yemas de huevos, y una gota de vino: luego echarás a lo que se asa un poco de sal y especias: luego irás dorando con el batido lo que se está asando: y cuando este baño estuviere bien seco, echarle has un poco de manteca, y (26v) dejarlo has secar más, y luego dale otro baño con unas plumas: y desta manera irás haciendo hasta que no se vea nada de la volatería. Luego lo tornarás a rociar con manteca, y échales azúcar molido por encima, y quedarán redondas como empanadas, y parecerán empanadas Inglesas en el gusto.[39]

[21] *Otras empanadas en asador.*

Tomarás carbonadillas de pierna de ternera muy delgadas,[40] y batirlas has con la vuelta del cuchillo, y mecharlas has, y échalas en adobo de la misma ternera, añadiéndole especias, y luego espetarlas has en un asador delgado, y que vayan muy juntas y apretadas, y en un asador puedes hacer tres empanadas, apartando unas de otras dos dedos: y cuando estén asadas harás una masa fina, sin azúcar, y sobarla has mucho, que haga correa, y tenderla has delgada, y harás levantar el asador a la mesa, (27r) y tomarás aquella hoja de masa, y untarla has con manteca, y revuélvela, sobre él un tercio de las chulletas [*sic*], que dé tres, o cuatro vueltas. Luego le pondrás un papel por encima, untado con manteca, y átalo por las puntas, y por el medio: luego haz otro tanto a las otras dos empanadillas. Y después que esté todo hecho, ponlas a asar hasta que esté la masa bien cocida, y que tenga color. Luego quítales el papel, y rocíalas con manteca, y échales azúcar raspado por encima.

[22] *Sopa de Perdices.*

Asarás las Perdices, y luego las cortarás, apartando toda la carne de los huesos, y hacerla has tajadillas pequeñas: luego harás una sopa de pan blanco cortado con la mano a bocadillos, de manera que esté la sopa bien alta. Luego pondrás por encima la carne de las perdices. Luego tomarás caldo de (27v) la olla, y échale un poco de buen aceite y vinagre, que esté bien agrio, y pimienta, y un poco de sal, y échalo por encima de la sopa, y de la carne, y ponla a calentar, y sírvela caliente. Esta sopa es sopa de gazpacho caliente.[41] Esta misma sopa podrás hacer de conejos, beneficiándola como la de las perdices.[42]

---

39 The recipe for English empanadas is written below on 314; 315.
40 The *Diccionario de autoridades* cites this recipe to define *carbonadilla*.
41 Instead of today's *gazpacho andaluz* [Andalusian gazpacho], the refreshing cold soup made with tomatoes, other raw vegetables, and bread, the tradition that Martínez Montiño's recipe draws from is more closely aligned to the *gazpacho manchego* [Manchegan gazpacho], which is a game-based stew served hot over sops, as he specifies in the recipe.
42 The verb *beneficiar* is no longer used in Spain to mean *to slaughter and dress* an animal, although this usage is still common in various Latin American countries.

are roasting, you'll have a batter made of rice flour, sugar, egg yolks, and a drop of wine. Then sprinkle salt and spices on what is roasting. Next you will slowly coat what is roasting with the batter until it's golden. And when this coat is crispy, brush on a little lard and let it crisp a little longer and then brush on another coat with a feather brush. Continue doing this until you can no longer see the fowl. Finish with a lard glaze and sprinkle ground sugar on top. These empanadas will turn out round and will taste like English empanadas.

Other empanadas on a spit

Take thin cuts of veal shank ready for grilling and pound them with the back of the knife. Lard them and let sit in a marinade made from the same veal to which spices have been added. Then skewer them on a thin spit so that they are tightly packed together. On one skewer you can make three empanadas that are each two fingers apart. Once [they are] roasted, make a delicate dough, without sugar. Knead it a lot so it becomes elastic and roll it out thin. Bring the spit to the table. Smear lard on the sheet of dough and wrap it around a third of the cuts three or four times. Then put paper, which has been greased with lard, over the top of it. Tie it up on the ends and in the middle. Then repeat with the other two turnovers. After all are done, put them on to roast until the dough is cooked through and browned. Remove the paper, dot with lard, and grate sugar over the top.

Partridge sops

Roast partridges, then cut them up, pulling all the meat off the bones and slicing into thin strips. Then, make sops by ripping up bite-sized pieces of white bread and stacking them up tall. Place the partridge meat on top. Then take stock from the pot, add to it a little good [quality] oil and vinegar, that is very pungent, pepper, and a little salt. Pour this over the sops and meat. Heat it up and serve hot. These sops are hot gazpacho sops. You can also make these sops with rabbits, dressing them the same way as with the partridges.

[23] *Perdices asadas con aceite.*

Pondrás a asar las perdices, luego tomarás un poco de buen aceite, echarle has dos partes de agua, y échale sal de manera, que esté salada, y bátelo mucho hasta que se ponga blanca: y con esta salsa irás untando las perdices cuando se van asando; luego hará otra salsa como ésta, y sírvela con las perdices así fría en su trinchero. Esta salsa ha de llevar harta sal.

[24] *Ánades estofadas.*

Perdigarás las ánades en las parrillas, de manera que estén medio (28r) asadas; luego dales a cada una un golpe en la pechuga, luego freirás tocino en dados con un poco de cebolla, y asentarás las ánades en una olla, y echa el tocino, y la cebolla por encima, y ahóguense un poco; luego échale un poco de vino blanco, y un poco de vinagre, y échale agua caliente, cuando se cubran las ánades; luego sazona con todas especias, y sal, y échale dentro dos, o tres membrillos en cuartos: luego pondrás un borde de masa a la olla, y asentarás otra ollita llena de agua sobre la olla de los anadones; de manera que ajuste muy bien con la masa,[43] y ponla sobre un poco de rescoldo, de manera que cueza poco a poco: y cuando estén cocidos, sírvelos sobre unas rebanadas de pan tostado con su salsa por encima, y no eches los membrillos, que como no llevan dulce, no saben bien. Si quieres echar dulce en estos anadones bien podrás, y podrás servir los membrillos con ellos: y si no hubiere membrillos, podrás echar ciruelas pasas, (28v) cociéndolas, y pasándolas por un cedacillo, y desatarlas con el mismo caldo de los anadones, y échaselo dentro, y un poco de azúcar, o buena miel, y canela molida, y dejarás algunas ciruelas enteras, quitados los cuescos para que vayan por encima de las ánades: y sírvanse como está dicho.

[25] *Lechones asados.*

Los lechones lo más ordinario es asarse, y servirse con sopa de queso: de sopas; no digo por ahora nada, porque adelante haré un capítulo que trate della.

---

43 This technique of sealing the pot with dough and placing another pot on top helps to prevent steam from escaping and keeps the moisture, and the flavour, from escaping. It is a technique found in other European cookbooks and is associated with the *dum pukht* cooking technique of the early modern Moghul Empire of South Asia. Scholars have noted that it anticipates the modern pressure cooker that was designed later in the seventeenth century by French physicist Denis Papin. Martínez Montiño uses this technique in several recipes. For more information, see Abad Zardoya ("Herramientas" 89).

Roast partridge with oil

Put partridges on to roast. Then take a little good oil, add two parts of water and enough salt so that it's salty, and mix it very well until it turns white. Baste the partridges with this sauce while they are roasting. Then make another sauce like the first one and serve it cold with the partridge, right on the carving platter. This sauce should be very salty.

Stewed duck

Sear ducks on the grill so that they are partially grilled. Then pound each of the breasts once. Next, fry some cubed pieces of fatback with a little onion. Set the ducks in the pot and put the fatback and onion on top and lightly sauté. Then add in a little white wine and vinegar, and enough hot water to cover the ducks. Next, season with all spices, salt, and add two or three quinces that have been quartered. Cover the lip of the pot with an edge made of dough and place on top of this duck pot another pot filled with water so that the dough seals the pot very well. Set over grey embers so that it slowly simmers and when it is cooked, serve on slices of toasted bread with the right amount of sauce on top. Do not include the quince because they have not been sweetened and will not taste good. If you want to add sweetener to the ducks, you can, and then serve the quince with them. If you don't have quince available, you can use prunes. Boil them, strain them in a sieve, and thin them with broth from the duck. Add to this a little sugar or good honey, and ground cinnamon. Also leave some of the prunes whole, without the pit, so that they can go on top of the duck and serve as was already explained.

Roast suckling pig

Suckling pig: the most common [way to prepare it] is to roast it and serve it on cheese sops. Regarding sops I won't say anything right now as I have a chapter on it later on.

[26] *Salsa de Lechón*.

Tomarás el hígado del lechón asado, y majarlo has con unas almendras tostadas con cáscara, y una rebanada de pan tostado y remojado con caldo, y majarse ha todo muy bien, pasarlo has por un cedacillo, o estameña: y sazonarás de todas especias y canela, y cueza un hervor, echándole cuatro onzas (29r) de azúcar, y un poco de zumo de limón. Y si quisieres hacer esta salsa sin dulce, echarle has un grano de ajo asado, un poquito de queso, y sus especias, y no has de echar género de agrio adonde entrare queso.

[27] *Un Lechón en Salchichón*.

Tomarás un lechón que sea grande, mayor de los que se suelen asar, y después que esté muy bien pelado cortarle has los pies, y abrirlo has por la barriga: y después de destripado iráslo descarnando de manera, que toda la carne vaya pegada en el pellejo, arrimando el cuchillo a los huesos. Hase de desollar cabeza y todo, que no quede en los huesos ninguna carne, y echarás el pellejo con su carne en agua que se desangre, y luego escurrirlo has, y pondráslo sobre el tablero, la carnaza cara arriba. Tomarás sal molida en cantidad, y sembrárselo has por encima de manera, (29v) que esté bien salado; luego tendrás pimienta, y clavo, y nuez, y jengibre todo mezclado, y echarlo has por encima de manera, que quede todo negreando, y arrollarlo has, comenzando por la cabeza; y después que esté arrollado, atarle has las puntas muy recio, porque no se salga la sazón; luego lo irás liando con hilo de bala muy apretado, y dejarlo has un poco enarqueado, como verga de ballesta, y pondráslo a cocer con tocino, y vino, y vinagre, y salvia, y mejorana, y otras hierbas, y un poco de agua, cuanto se cubra, sazonándolo de sal y especias, que esté un poco subido, y servirlo has frío con algunas flores, o ruedas de limón, quitándole primero todos los hilos con que estuvo atada. Y si quisieres servirlo en ruedas de limones, parece muy bien, y es muy buen plato. Cortando este lechón en ruedas parece hojaldrado, y sírvelas sobre algunas hojas verdes, y adórnalas con ruedas de limones.

[28] (30r) *Una pierna de Carnero estufada.*[44]

Tomarás una pierna de carnero, que sea recién muerto, y golpearla has con la mano del almirez, de manera que estén quebrantados los huesos, y mecharla has con mechas gordas de tocino, que la atraviesen todo por de dentro, derecho por la hebra, y ponle unos clavos de especia hincados, y algunos ajos, luego métela en

---

44 *Estufada* is a printer's error that does not appear in any other edition or at any other time in this edition.

Sauce for suckling pig.

Take the liver from the suckling pig and mash it with almonds toasted in their shell and a slice of toasted bread soaked in stock. Thoroughly grind everything together and strain through a strainer or a cheesecloth. Season with all spices and cinnamon, and bring to a boil. Add four ounces of sugar and a little lemon juice. If you'd like to make this sauce with no sweetener, add a clove of roasted garlic, a little cheese, and the appropriate spices, but no type of sour flavour should ever be added when cheese is included.

Suckling pig served sausage style

Take a suckling pig, it should be big, bigger than what is normally roasted. After all the hairs have been removed, cut off its feet and open up its belly. After the guts have been removed, begin deboning it so that the meat remains attached to the skin. Keep the knife very close to the bone. Skin the head and everything so that no meat remains on any bones. Then soak the skin with its flesh in water to remove the blood. Then rinse it and place it on the table top fleshy side up.[3] Take a lot of ground salt and sprinkle it over the top so that it is completely salted. Then mix together pepper, clove, nutmeg, and ginger and spread it all over so that the whole surface is almost black. Roll it up starting with the head. Once the animal is rolled up, tightly tie the ends together so that none of the seasoning is lost. Then begin tying it tightly together with twine and make it somewhat arched, like a crossbow. Bake it with fatback, wine, vinegar, sage, marjoram and other herbs, and enough water to cover it. Season it with salt and all spices. It should be a little lifted up. Serve cold with some flowers or lemon wheels, but first remove all the string that was tying it together. If you want to serve it with lemon wheels, it will look good and it's a very tasty dish. When you cut the suckling pig in rolled slices, it will look like puff pastry dough. Serve over some leafy greens and garnish with lemon wheels.

Stewed leg of mutton

Take a leg of mutton, recently slaughtered, and pound it with the pestle so that you break the bones. Lard it with thick pieces of fatback that are threaded throughout, straight through the grain. Stick in some whole cloves and some garlic. Then place it in a pot and add as much vinegar as fits in the rind of a half

---

3 Martínez Montiño uses the term *tablero* primarily to indicate *cutting board* but also for *table top*. When the item referred to is large or if the context dictates, I translate *tablero* as *table top* instead of *cutting board*. For a modern-day version of how to roll and tie up the suckling pig, see Appendix 3.2.

una olla, y échale tanto vinagre como quepa en una cáscara de media naranja,[45] y otra tanta agua, y un poco de pimienta, y nuez de especia, no ha de llevar otra especia: échale un poquito de sal, y tomarás un poco de masa, y harás un rollito, y pondrásle por el borde de la olla: luego pondrás encima otra ollita que ajuste en la boca de la olla grande, de manera que con la masa no pueda respirar: y desta manera la pondrás al fuego que sea un poco de rescoldo, y la ollita que está sobre la (30v) olla grande, ha de estar llena de agua; porque de otra manera se secaría la olla de la pierna. Cuando haya estado al fuego hora y media, sacarla has del fuego, y quita la ollita, y vuelve la pierna, y torna a poner la ollita sobre la olla, y vacía el agua caliente de la ollita, y tórnala a henchir de agua fría, y déjala acabar de cocer, y hallarla has muy tierna, y con dos escudillas de sustancia, sírvela sobre unas rebanadillas de pan tostadas, y echa la sustancia por encima. Si la quisieres servir picado como gigote, también es buena. Y advierte, que si no quisieren ajos en ella, que importa poco que no los lleve, que sin ajos se puede hacer.

[29] *Otra pierna estofada de otra manera.*

Golpearás la pierna muy bien, y perdigarla has sobre las parrillas, y de que esté bien perdigada métele unos clavos, y unos ajos, y métela (31r) en una olla, échale un poco de vino tinto, y un poco de vinagre, y sazona con especia negra, y échale tocino en dados frito con un poco de cebolla picada, y su sal y agua, o caldo, hasta que se cubra la pierna, y tápala con una cobertera, podrás echar dentro, si quisieres, algunos membrillos, o peros agrios, o almendras tostadas: y si alguna vez la quisieres hacer dulce podrás, añadiéndole más agrio y canela: y si la salsa estuviere muy rala, espesarla has con un poquito de harina quemada, desatándolo con el mismo caldo de la pierna.

[30] *Otra pierna estofada, de otra manera.*

Echarás a cocer una pierna de carnero, y cuando esté medio cocida sacarla has, y déjala enfriar, y picarla has como para gigote: y pondrás allí también los huesos, y échale un poco de caldo, y un poquito de vino blanco, y una gota de (31v) vinagre y pimienta, y nuez, y jengibre, y un poco de manteca de vacas fresca,[46] y media cebolla cruda entera, y un poco de orégano molido, y ponla sobre una poca de lumbre en un plato, o cazuela de barro, y tápala, y déjala estofar media hora a poca

---

45 Measurements are most times given in traditional units but sometimes, as is the case here, specified in terms of other, often edible, common objects. For more on measurements, see Appendix 2, "On Measurements."

46 In early modern Spain and up until the early twentieth century, *manteca de vacas fresca* was the accepted term for *butter* and the broader *manteca* was used contextually to refer to both butter and lard. For more on the use of butter and other fats, see 46–7.

orange and the same amount of water, a little pepper, and nutmeg. It shouldn't have any other spices. Add in some salt. Take a little bit of dough, roll it out, and stick it around the edge of the pot. Then place another, smaller pot on top that fits tightly on the top of the big pot so that, with the help of the dough, no air escapes. Place it this way on the fire that should be from grey embers. The smaller, top pot should be full of water; if not, the bottom pot with the leg in it will dry out. Let this cook for an hour and a half, remove it from the fire, and take the small pot off. Turn the leg and put the top pot back on the bottom pot again. Empty out the hot water and refill it with cold water. Let it finish cooking and it will come out very tender. You should have about two bowlfuls of essence. Serve it on toasted slices of bread and ladle the essence over the top. If you want to serve it chopped up, like minced dishes, it is also delicious. Note that if you don't want to include garlic, it will not matter too much; it can also be made without garlic.

Another stewed leg, made another way

Pound the leg a lot and sear it on the grill. Once seared, stick in some cloves and garlic and put it in a pot. Add a little red wine and a little vinegar and season with black pepper. Add in some fried, diced fatback with a little chopped onion, salt to taste, and enough water or stock to cover the leg. Cover the pot with a lid. If you like, you can also add some quince, or sour apples, or toasted almonds. And, if you ever want to make it sweet, you can, adding more sour juice and cinnamon. If the sauce is too thin, you can thicken it with a little toasted flour that has been thinned with the same meat stock.

Another stewed leg, made another way

Begin cooking a leg of mutton and when it is partially cooked, take it off, let it cool, and chop it into minced meat. Add the bones as well and a little stock, a splash of white wine, a drop of vinegar, pepper, nutmeg, ginger, a little butter, half a raw onion, and a little ground oregano. Place on a plate or in a terracotta casserole on low flame, cover, and let stew for half an hour on low flame. Cut very

lumbre, y corta unas rebanadillas de pan muy delgadas, y asiéntalas en un plato, y compón los huesos de la pierna encima, y luego echarás el picado con su salsa, y la media cebolla echarás a mal, y échale un poco de zumo de limón, o de naranja encima, y sírvela caliente. Desta manera puedes estofar carbonadas de cabrito con sus huesos y carbonadas de pierna de ternera, añadiéndoles más caldo después que estén estofadas, para que se puedan cocer bien.

[31] *Una pierna de Carnero rellena.*

Tomarás una pierna de carnero, que no sea manida,[47] y desuéllala, abriéndola (32r) por la parte de adentro, de manera que no se rompa: luego descárnala, y pica la carne, y de la mitad harás un relleno, perdigando la carne con su cebolla y tocino, como está dicho, para los pollos rellenos,[48] echando allí unas hojas de hierbabuena, y mejorana, y cuatro huevos, y desque esté bien seca, júntala con la otra carne que está cruda, y pícala junta, y sazona con todas especias, y un par de huevos y sal, y el zumo de un limón, y un poco de mejorana picada: luego tendrás el pellejo de la pierna sobre el tablero asido al jarrete, y ponle un poco de redaño por la parte de adentro,[49] y tórnala a coser con una mechadera, y un poco de hilo de bala, y espétala en un asador, atándola muy bien, porque no se ande, y ponla a asar, y pondrás debajo una pieza con un poco de caldo, adonde caiga la sustancia de la pierna, y tostarás unas rebanadillas de pan, y ponerlas en un plato, y saca la pierna, y asiéntala sobre ellas, y toma la sustancia, échale (32v) zumo de limón, y un poquito de especia, y dale unos cortes a la pierna por encima, y échale la sustancia.

[32] *Una pierna de Carnero a la Francesa.*[50]

Has de desollar la pierna, y descarnarla, y picar la carne, echando con ella tocino y cebolla cruda, y un poco de mejorana, y ajedrea, hisopillo, y cuatro huevos crudos y especias, y un poquito de vinagre, y sal, y ponle un redaño sobre el pellejo

---

47 For more information on what *manida* means, see 146n10.
48 Here is another example of Martínez Montiño's cross-referencing and awareness of the project as a whole.
49 *Redaño* [mesentery] is a membranous tissue that holds the stomach and small intestines within the abdominal cavity; it has a white, lacy look. In the culinary world the common term is *caul fat*. Martínez Montiño uses it in some dozen recipes. Depending on the context, I've translated the term as both *mesentery* and *caul fat*.
50 In his monograph *The Banquet*, Ken Albala cites similar preparation styles, as found in the recipe "To boyle a legge of Mutton after the French fashion" in Théodore Turquet de Mayerne's 1658 cookbook, *Archimagirus anglo-gallicus: or, Excellent & approved receipts and experiments in cookery* (131). However, it is clear that tastes change from one country to the next, because the actual stuffing in the later version is quite different and includes bread, cream, marrow, currants, raisins, and dates.

thin slices of bread, put them on a plate, and arrange the leg bones on top and then ladle the minced meat with the right amount of sauce, discard the half onion, and drizzle a little lemon or orange juice on top. Serve hot. In this same way you can braise grilled leg of kid with its bones and grilled leg of veal, adding more stock after braising so they can cook more fully.

Stuffed leg of mutton

Take a leg of mutton that has not been dry aged. Skin it, opening up the insides so that nothing tears. Then remove the meat from the bone and chop it up. With half of it you will make a stuffing, first browning the meat with the right amount of onion and fatback as was stated above for "Chicken with stuffing." Add spearmint leaves and marjoram, four eggs, and once the egg is cooked through, mix it with the other, raw meat and chop it all together. Season with all spices, a couple of eggs, salt, juice from one lemon, and a little minced marjoram. Then, place the skin of the leg that is attached to the shank on top of the table, lay caul fat on the inside of the skin. Close it up again with a larding needle and a little twine and skewer it on a spit, securely tying it up so that it doesn't move around. Begin roasting and put a pan with a little stock in it underneath to catch the leg's juices. Toast some slices of bread and put them on a plate. Remove the leg and set it on the bread. Take the essence and add lemon juice and a little bit of spice to it. Make some cuts across the top of the leg and ladle the essence on top.

Leg of mutton, French style

Skin the leg, remove the meat, and chop it up, adding in fatback, raw onion, a little marjoram, summer savory, winter savory, four raw eggs, spices, a little vinegar, and

por la parte de adentro, y luego echarás la carne sazonada, y coserla has con una mechedera, una hebra de hilo de bala: y después atarás la pierna con unas vueltas de hilo, y ponla en un perol, o en una olla, y échale allí caldo cuanto se cubra, y échale tocino frito en dados, y un poco de cebolla cruda, cortada a lo largo, y un poco de manteca de vacas fresca, y vino, y vinagre, y salvia, y mejorana, e hisopillo, (33r) y cuézase con todo esto hasta que esté cocida: y luego échale un poco de harina quemada, que no esté muy negra, desatada con el mismo caldo, de manera que no esté muy espesa, ni muy negra, sino un poco parda, y asentarla has sobre rebanadas de pan tostadas, y darle has unos cortes: echa la salsa por encima.

[33] *Otra pierna de otra manera.*

Otra pierna se hace armada, descarnando toda la pierna, y picar la carne con su tocino, sazonarla con sus especias, y cuatro, o seis huevos, y sal, y un poquito de agrio, y armarla en una cazuela grande, de manera que parezca la misma pierna, y ponerla por encima algunos trozos de cañas de vaca, y algunos piñones hincados, algunas yemas de huevos duros, y cuézase con lumbre abajo y arriba, y sírvela sobre una sopa. Desta manera se arman gallinas, y pichones, y cabrito, salvo que los (33v) corpanchones de las gallinas se han de cocer primero, y después armar sobre ellos, y se ha de perdigar la mitad de la carne, y hacer un relleno, y mezclarlo con la otra mitad de carne cruda, porque esté más tierno.

[34] *Un platillo de Pichones.*[51]

Un platillo de pichones, o pollos, o palominos, tomarás media docena de pollos pelados, y limpios, cocerlos has a medio cocer, y luego asiéntalos en un cacillo, o cazuela de barro, y tomarás unas lechugas perdigadas, y asentarlas has sobre los pollos, y luego pica un poco de verdura, hierbabuena, y perejil, y cilantro verde: y luego toma tocino en dados muy menudos, y freírlo has hasta que esté bien frito, y luego echa la cebolla cortada muy menuda, y fríela con el tocino, y échala sobre los pollos: luego sazona con pimienta, nuez, y jengibre, y échale caldo hasta que

---

51 This recipe is not just for farm-raised squab but also for chicken and wild squab. In fact, beginning in 1617, the title expands to the first phrase of the recipe: "Un platillo de pichones, o pollos o palominos" [A dish of farm-raised squab, chicken, or wild squab]. The recipe then begins with "Tomarás media docena de …" [Take a half dozen …]. See Appendix 3.3 for images of preparing this dish. Also note that throughout the cookbook the term *platillo* appears 123 times, of which over 80 per cent refer figuratively to the small portion size, i.e., *a single serving* or *a little dish*, as it does here. Other times it refers simply to the literal size of the plate; that is, one that is smaller than the *plato*. Likewise, the term *plato* appears over 300 times and is used to designate a physical plate, obviously bigger than the *platillo*, that would be used to serve items that are shared at the table. This physical reference for *plato* occurs over 80 per cent of the time.

salt. Lay caul fat on the inside of the skin and then the seasoned meat. Sew it up with a larding needle and a strand of twine. Afterward wrap the twine around the leg several times and place it in a big, round-bottom cooking pot or stew pot and pour in enough stock to cover it. Add in cubes of fried fatback, a little raw onion, sliced lengthwise, a little fresh butter, wine, vinegar, sage, marjoram, and winter savory. Cook with everything until it's done and add in some toasted flour that is not too black and that's been thinned with some of the same stock so that it doesn't end up too thick or too black but rather a light brown. Set it on toasted slices of bread and make some cuts and ladle the essence on top.

Another leg, made another way

Another leg is assembled by removing all the meat. Mince the meat with the right amount of fatback, and season it with its spices, four to six eggs, salt, and a little sour juice. Assemble it in a large casserole so that it looks like the same leg. Sprinkle little bits of marrow on top, stick in some pine nuts, and add in some hard-boiled egg yolks. Simmer on low with the heat below and above. Serve over sops. You can also assemble hens, squab, and kid this way, but with large hens you must first cook them and then put the finishing touches on top of them. First brown half the meat, make the filling, and mix it together with the other half of raw meat so that it will come out more tender.

A squab dish

A dish of farm-raised squab, chicken, or wild squab: take a half dozen plucked, cleaned chickens and partially cook them. Then set them in a saucepan or a terracotta casserole. Take some wilted lettuce leaves and set them on the chicken. Next, chop up some green herbs – spearmint, parsley, and cilantro. Then take finely minced cubes of fatback, fry them until they are well done, add in some minced onion, and fry it with the fatback. Pour this over the chicken and season with pepper, nutmeg, and ginger. Pour in enough broth to braise the chickens or

se bañen los pollos, o palominos, y ponlos (34r) a cocer, y hazlos apurar hasta que queden con poco caldo, y luego batirás cuatro yemas de huevos, y una gota de vinagre,[52] y sacarás primero de la flor del platillo en un plato:[53] luego cuajarás el platillo, llégalo al fuego, y no cueza, porque no se corte, y pondrás unas rebanadillas de pan en el plato: luego echa el platillo sobre las rebanaditas con el mismo cacito, y echa la flor por encima, y un poco de zumo de limón, o naranjas. Advierte, que todas las veces que puedas hacer cada platillo de por si, que es mejor que no hacer muchos juntos, y van con mejor gracia: y luego buscarás algunas cosillas con que adornar los platillos, como son mollejuelas de cabrito, o de ternera: y con sólo agraz y verdura son buenos sin lechugas y sin huevos.

[35] *Pollos rellenos cocidos.*

Los pollos rellenos cocidos con lechugas rellenas con carne sazonada, (34v) como para albondiguillas, que no tengan más de carne, tocino, y huevos, y de todas especias sin perdigar, y rellena los pollos entre cuero y carne, y asiéntalos en un cazo, o cazuela: y luego perdiga las lechugas, y quítalas el cogollo de medio, y en su lugar se henchirá de la carne del mismo relleno de los pollos, y átalas por las puntas, y asiéntalos con los pollos rellenos, y échales cebolla frita con tocino, y todas especias, y échale un poco de verdura picada, y caldo, hasta que se cubran las lechugas, y cuezan hasta que se apure el caldo, cuanto se bañen los pollos. Luego cuajarás este platillo con cuatro yemas de huevos batidas con un poco de vinagre, sacando primero la flor,[54] y podrás sacar los pollos y partirlos por medio, e ir armando el plato, poniendo entre pollo y pollo lechuga rellena. Y después que esté el plato compuesto echarás la flor por encima, porque le da mucha gracia.

En este relleno de pollos y lechugas (35r) podrás echar yemas de huevos duras, y cañas de vaca al tiempo que se rellenan. También podrás echar algunas veces a estos platillos de azúcar y canela por encima, añadiéndole más agrio de limones, o naranjas.

Advierte, que el dulce no se ha de echar cuando cueza, sino cuando está ya puesto en el plato, y es muy buen gusto el agrio y dulce. Cuando tuvieres muchos platos de cada cosa; harás estos platillos desta manera. Las lechugas rellenas harás aparte en una pieza grande, y los pollos rellenos en otra, y cuajarás el platillo de los pollos, o el de las lechugas: y cuando vayas sirviendo mojarás las sopas, o rebanadas con el caldo que está cuajado, e irás componiendo tus platos de pollos rellenos y lechugas, echando de la flor por encima.

---

52 This egg yolk and vinegar mixture added to broth and thickened is a common sauce that Martínez Montiño uses in many poultry dishes as well as other savoury recipes.

53 *Flor* is a culinary term unique to this cookbook that refers to the coagulated protein that separates from both the fat and the juices when meat cooks. For more information on *flor*, see 65 and for an image of it, see Appendix 3.4.

54 For more information on the flor, see 65.

squab and bring to a boil. Let them finish cooking until only a little broth remains. Then, beat four egg yolks and a drop of vinegar. But, first take out the flor for this dish and set it a on a plate. Let the dish set, bringing it close to the fire without bringing it to a boil so that it won't break. Put some slices of bread on a plate, set this little dish from the saucepan over the bread, and sprinkle the flor on top with a little lemon or orange juice. Note that whenever you can, make each individual plate separately; it's better than making them all together and they will look better. Then look around for things to garnish the individual plates, like kid or veal sweetbreads or it's good with just sour grapes and herbs without lettuce or eggs.

Braised stuffed chicken

Braised stuffed chicken with stuffed lettuce [filled] with meat seasoned like meatballs, without anything more than meat, fatback, eggs, and all spices and without searing: Stuff the chickens between the skin and the flesh and set them in a large saucepan or casserole. Then wilt the lettuce and remove the hearts from the middle and replace with the same meat stuffing used for the chickens. Tie off the ends, set them in with the stuffed chicken. Add in fried onion and fatback, all spices, and a little bit of chopped green herbs. Add broth, enough to cover the lettuce, and boil until the broth reduces to a level for braising chicken. Then set the dish with four egg yolks beaten together with a little vinegar, but first remove the flor. When you take the chicken out, split them in halves and begin assembling the plate by putting the stuffed lettuce between each chicken. Once the plate is arranged, sprinkle the flor on top, because it will give it a nice touch.

In the stuffing for the chicken and lettuce, you can add hard-boiled egg yolks and beef marrow when you are stuffing them. You could also add to these dishes sugar and cinnamon on top and if so, also add lemon or orange juice.

Note that the sweetener should not be added while it is cooking, rather once it's placed on the plate. The sweet and sour is very tasty. When you have a lot of plates of each, make these dishes this way. You'll make the stuffed lettuce separately in a big bowl and the stuffed chicken in another. Thicken the chicken dish and the lettuce dish. When serving, soak the sops or slices of bread in the broth that has been thickened and then put the plates together with stuffed chicken and lettuce, sprinkling the flor on top.

Esto basta para entender que lo mismo es hacerse de pollos, como pichones, o gallinas; porque aunque tengo dicho, que partan los pollos por medio, parecen bien enteros: las lechugas entremetidas (35v) entre pollo y pollo: y luego echarás azúcar y canela por encima, y la flor del platillo: y añadirás más agrio de limón, o naranja: y si acaso no tuvieres pollos, ni pichones recién muertos, y no los pudieres rellenar, rellénalos por de dentro: y si acaso no hubiere lechugas, puedes rellenar escarolas.

[36] *Platillo con Membrillos.*

Estos platillos podrás hacer sin rellenos; tomarás los pollos, o pichones a medio cocer, y partirlos has en medios, o en cuartos, y asentarlos has en un cacillo, o cazuela, y freirás tocino en dados, que sea muy menuda, y esté bien frito. Luego echa cebolla picada muy menuda, y fríela, y echarás membrillos cortados delgados, como quien corta cebolla larga,[55] y echarlos has en la sartén con cebolla, y el tocino, y fríelo hasta que los membrillos estén blandos, y échalo todo en el cacillo, de manera que queden cubiertos los pollos, (36r) o pichones: luego sazonarás con pimienta, y nuez, y jengibre, y canela, y echarás un poco de vino, y un poquito de vinagre, y cosa de seis onzas de azúcar, y echarle has caldo hasta que se bañen por encima, y cueza hasta que se apure, que quede como conservado. Sírvelo sobre rebanadas de pan tostado, y componlo con algunas torrijas, o algunas ubres de ternera tostadas. No los saques con cuchara, sino con el mismo cacito lo puedes echar en el plato, porque quede de la misma manera que está en el cacito. Estos platillos no es bueno hacerse muchos juntos, porque no se anden cuchareando, sino cada plato de por sí, en cazuelas o en cacillos. En lugar de los pollos, échense lenguas de vaca cocidas.

[37] *Otro platillo con hierbas.*[56]

Para hacer platillo de pollos, pichones, o gallinas, ú otra cualquiera cosa, tomarás los pollos, o pichones, (36v) y cocerlos has a medio cocer, y asentarlos has en un cazo, o cazuela, y tomarás las hierbas perdigadas, como son lechugas, o escarolas, o riponces, o chicorias dulces, o amargas, que todas son buenas, e irás mudando cada día su manera de hierbas y volatería: y asentarás las hierbas sobre los pollos, o pichones, y freirás cebolla con tocino, y echársela has por encima, y echarás

---

55 Martínez Montiño is referencing the julienne knife cut that cuts into the onion parallel to the stem and the root (as opposed to crosswise). Although the technique is used here, the term *julienne* does not appear until the eighteenth century.

56 Although *hierbas* often translates as *herbs*, here it means *leafy green vegetables*. Riponces or *rapónchigo* [Rampion bellflower] is a common plant throughout Europe. Its leaves were used like spinach, its root like radish or parsnip, and its shoots like asparagus. Medicinally it was used as an astringent. Curiously, Rapunzel is named after this plant.

This is enough to understand that the same thing is done for chicken as for squab or hen. Even though I've said to split the chickens in half, they also look good whole. The lettuce should be placed between each chicken. Then sprinkle on top sugar, cinnamon, and the flor from the dish. Add either lemon or orange juice. If you don't have recently slaughtered chicken or squab and you couldn't stuff them [between the skin and flesh], stuff them inside [the cavity]. And if you don't have lettuce, you can stuff escarole.

A little dish with quince

These little dishes you can make without stuffing. Take partially cooked chicken or squab and split them in half or in quarters and set them in a saucepan or casserole. Fry cubed fatback that has been minced. Make sure it's well done. Then add in some minced onion, continue frying. Add quince cut thin, as one would cut onion lengthwise, add them to the frying pan with the onion and fatback, and fry until the quince is soft. Add it all to the saucepan so that the chickens or squab are covered. Next, season with pepper, nutmeg, ginger, and cinnamon, and add a little wine, a little vinegar, and about six ounces of sugar. Add on top enough stock to braise and boil until it has thickened up to the consistency of preserves. Serve over slices of toasted bread and assemble it with some torrijas or some roasted cow udder.[4] Don't take it out with a spoon, just slide it out directly from the saucepan so that it comes out as it is in the saucepan. It's not good to make a lot of these little dishes together so that you don't have to ladle them out. Each serving should have its own casserole or saucepan. As a substitute for chicken, you can use boiled beef tongue.

Another dish with leafy greens

To make a dish of chicken, squab, or hen or any other bird, take the chickens or squab and partially cook them. Set them in a saucepan or casserole. Take some wilted leafy greens, like lettuce, escarole, rampion bellflower, sweet or bitter chicory, all of them are good. You should vary the leafy greens and the fowl daily. Place the greens on the chickens or squab. Fry onion with fatback and pour over

---

[4] *Torrijas* are slices of bread soaked in a sweet egg-milk batter or some other liquid that are then fried and sprinkled with cinnamon and sugar. The recipe for them is found on 454; 455. In the English translation, I maintain the name *torrija* as it is a famous Spanish dish, much like *paella* or *gazpacho*.

caldo hasta que se bañen; y picarás un poco de verdura, perejil, y hierbabuena, y échaselo por encima, y sazona con todas especias: y de que esté el platillo cocido, cuajarlo has con yemas de huevos batidas, y un poco de vinagre, apartando primero la flor:[57] y no cueza más de medio hervor, porque no se corte. Sacarlo has en el plato sobre rebanadillas de pan, y echarle has la flor por encima, pongo aquí esta manera de cuajar los platillos, porque es lo mejor. También se pueden hacer de otra manera, que es hacer un brodete:[58] y (37r) después de hechos sus platos, echarle del brodete por encima, y luego echarle un poco de la flor del platillo: y es muy acomodado cuando hay muchos platos que servir; mas con todo eso aconsejo que se cuaje cada una de por sí. Ya tengo dicho que a estos platillos se les puede echar dulce cuando quisiere, mas no han de cocer con él, sino echárselo cuando lo sirvieren en el plato, y ha de ser azúcar, y canela, añadiendo más agrio de limón, o naranja. Este brodete para servir los platillos se hace, batiendo yemas de huevos, y un poco de vinagre, y echar caldo conforme la cantidad que fuere menester, y ponerlos sobre el fuego, trayéndolo a una mano,[59] de manera que no se corte, y dejarlo un poco ralo. Suélenle echar un poquito de azafrán. Serán menester ocho yemas de huevos para una azumbre de caldo: y este servirá para cuatro, o cinco platos.

[38] (37v) *Platillos sin verduras.*

Si no hallares verduras, toma carnero, o ternera, y pícala, y sazónalo, como para albondiguillas con sus huevos, y especias, y tocino: y luego échalo en un cacito, y échale caldo, y desátalo, y ponlo sobre el fuego, y velo meneando, y harás un pastel en bote,[60] y mete allí los pollos, o pichones: y sazónalo todo, y podrás poner en ello algunas cañas de vaca. La volatería que entrare en estos platillos, ha de estar cocida del todo, y sacarlo has en los platos, y pondrás yemas de huevos duros por encima, y

---

57 For more information on the flor, see 65.
58 *Brodete* is an egg yolk and vinegar infused broth. Martínez Montiño explains that the proportions are eight egg yolks to two quarts of broth. *Brodete* comes from *brodio* or today *bodrio*, which, although it has negative connotations today, was originally a stock with scraps still in it, typically prepared for the poor. In *La cocina española antigua*, Pardo Bazán includes a recipe for "Burete" or "Bodrio" in which she explains that the Spartans feed bodrio to children to teach them the importance of austerity (22). However, her bodrio has nothing to do with Martínez Montiño's. Another source (Telingen) mentions *brodete* and *brodo* as sixteenth-century Italianisms (cited in Ayala Simón 42n6).
59 I have translated "trayéndolo a una mano" with the phrase "stirring it with one hand," though I sense there might be a more accurate way to translate this phrase. It is used about a dozen times in the cookbook. In his definition of the term, Soto García explains in more detail "remover con un cucharón de manera constante para homogeneizarla o para que no se corte, agarre o queme" [stir constantly with a spoon to thoroughly blend or so that it doesn't separate, stick or burn] ("Los términos culinarios, 75).
60 *Un pastel en bote* or *embote* refers to minced meat or fish served over slices of bread in the shape of a pie. Ruperto de Nola in his 1520 recipe collection also includes "pastel en bote" made with minced mutton and extra fatty fatback, but instead of egg yolks and lemon juice, he uses bread and grated cheese to make it take shape (329).

the top. Add in enough broth to braise. Chop some green herbs – parsley and spearmint – and add on top. Season with all spices. Once the dish is cooked, set it with whipped egg yolk and a little vinegar but first take out the flor. Only bring to a half boil so that it doesn't break. Place over slices of bread on a plate and ladle the flor on top. I've written here how to set the little dish this way because it's the best. You can also make this another way, which is to make a *brodete*. Once the dishes are done, ladle the *brodete* over the top, then finish by ladling over it some of the flor from the dish. This is very easy to do when there are a lot of plates to serve, but I still advise to thicken each one individually. I've already stated that you can add sweetener to these dishes anytime you want, but do not add it while cooking, rather to the plate when serving. It should be cinnamon and sugar with some lemon or orange juice. To make *brodete* for serving these dishes, beat egg yolks with a little orange or lemon juice and the appropriate amount of broth. Put on the fire, stirring it with one hand so that it doesn't break, and it should be somewhat thin. A little saffron is normally added. Eight egg yolks are necessary for two quarts of broth and this is enough for four or five plates.

Dishes without green-leaf vegetables

If you have no green-leaf vegetables, take mutton or veal, chop it up, and season it as you would for meatballs with eggs, spices, and fatback. Then put it all into a saucepan and add broth to thin it out. Put it over the fire and stir continually. It will be like crustless pie and in it add the chicken or squab. Season the whole thing and you can also add some beef marrow to it. Fowl for these little dishes should be thoroughly cooked and put on plates with hard-boiled eggs on

adornarás el plato con algunas torrijas cortadas angostas. Estos pollos con ternera, o cabrito, podrás hacer con albondiguillas, asentando los pollos en un cacillo, y sazonar con todas especias, y un poco de verdura picada, y freirás un poco de cebolla con tocino, y échaselo dentro, y echarle has caldo, hasta que se cubran bien: y luego harás albondiguillas (38r) sobre los pollos, y cuezan dos hervores, y cuájalos con yemas de huevos batidos con un poco de vinagre, y sírvelos sobre rebanadas de pan, y zumo de limón, o naranjas por encima. Advierte, que antes que venga el agraz un mes vienen los agrazones, que se llaman por otro nombre grusela, y por otro se llama uvas pin. Estos nacen en una manera de espinos, que sirven de agraz para los platillos. Para cada platillo son menester cuatro pollos, y seis huevos, sin los demás adherentes que se suelen echar por encima, como son mollejas, higadillos, y carbonadillas mechadas.

[39] *Capón a la Tudesca.*

Tomarás un capón que esté cocido, y pondráslo en un cazo con caldo, y tendrás cosa de libra y media de ternera de pierna medio cocida, y picarla has sobre el tablero, y echarla has en una pieza, y échale doce yemas de huevos crudas, y un poco de vinagre, y sazonarás (38v) con todas sus especias, y échale donde estuviere el capón; de manera que el capón esté bien cubierto: y advierte, que el caldo estuviere el capón, ha de tener buena grasa. Demás deso le echarás dos, o tres cañas de vaca, hechas trozos, y ha de cocer el capón con la ternera poco a poco, cosa de una hora. Luego sacarás el capón sobre rebanadas de pan, componiéndole aquella ternera al derredor, y por encima: y pondrásle yemas de huevos duras por encima para adornar el plato con las cañas.

[40] *Un platillo de Aves con Acederas.*

Tomarás las aves, o pollos, o lo que quisieres, y cocerlo has, y asentarlos has en un cacito, o cazuela, y echarle has encima muchas acederas crudas, y tomarás tocino en dados muy chicos, y fríelos mucho hasta que estén blancos, y échales cebolla cortada muy (39r) menuda, y fríela, y échalo todo encima de las acederas, y sazonarás con todas especias, y échale caldo cuanto se bañe, y ponlo a cocer: y en dando un par de hervores sacarlo has del fuego. Este platillo no se cuaja con huevos: sírveles sobre rebanadas de pan, y es muy apetitoso.

[41] *Un ave a la Portuguesa.*

Tomarás una ave cocida y rellena salpimentada, y asentarla has sobre hojuelas, y cercarla has con huevos hilados[61] y conservas, como son cermeñas,[62] y diacitrón cortado, y otras conservas y hojuelas. Este plato se sirve frío.

---

61 To make *huevos hilados* [candied egg yolk threads] see the recipe on 432–4; 433–5; to make *hojuelas* [pastry sheets], see the next recipe, "Una gallina rellena en Alfitete" [Stuffed hen served on fried pastry sheets] (182; 183).

62 *Cermeñas* [Cermeña pears] are small and harvested earlier than most pears.

top. Garnish the plate with thickly sliced torrijas. This chicken with veal or kid can be made into little meatballs. Set the chicken in a saucepan. Season with all spices and a little chopped green herb. Fry a little onion in fatback and add it. Add enough broth to fully cover it. Then make little meatballs around the chicken. Bring it to a boil two times and thicken with beaten egg yolk and a little vinegar. Serve on slices of bread with lemon or orange juice sprinkled on top. Note that a month before sour grapes arrive, gooseberries come in; some call them white currants, others, pin grapes. These are grown like hawthorn and work like sour grapes on the dishes. For each dish four chickens and six eggs are needed, without the additional items that are usually placed on top, like gizzards, poultry livers, and larded grilled meat.

Capon, German style

Take a cooked capon and put it in a pan with broth. You should have about a pound and a half of partially cooked veal shank. Chop it up on the cutting board and place it in a bowl. Add twelve raw egg yolks and a little vinegar. Season with all spices and pour it all in with the capon so that it entirely covers the capon. Note that the capon broth should have a high fat content. In addition, add two or three pieces of beef bone marrow, broken up. The capon and veal should cook slowly, taking about an hour. Then put the capon over slices of bread, arranging the veal around and on top of it. Then place hard-boiled egg yolks and the pieces of marrow on top to garnish the plate.

A dish of poultry with sorrel

Take poultry or chicken, or whatever you might like, and cook it. Set it in a small pan or casserole and add on top a lot of uncooked sorrel. Take minced fatback, fry it until it turns white, add in some minced onion, and continue frying. Add all this on top of the sorrel. Season with all spices and add broth for braising and set to simmer. Once it has boiled a couple of times, remove it from the fire. This dish is not thickened with eggs. Serve it on slices of bread. It is very appetizing.

Poultry, Portuguese style

Take a cooked, stuffed bird that has been salted and peppered and set it on some pastry sheets. Place all around it candied egg yolk threads and preserves like Cermeña pears, candied citron, and other preserves and pastry sheets. This dish is served cold.

[42] *Una Gallina rellena en Alfitete.*[63]

Harás una masa con sólo huevos y sal, y un poco de manteca, de manera que no ha de llevar agua, ni vino, mas de solos los huevos, y harás hojuelas un poco gordas, y freírlas has con manteca de puerco, y tendrás una ave rellena y (39v) cocida, y asentarla has sobre las hojuelas, y tendrás hecho un brodete con buen caldo y grasa,[64] y echarás alrededor del ave un poco dello, de manera que no se mojen todas las hojuelas, y echarás azúcar y canela por encima de todas las hojuelas: y sírvase caliente.

[43] *Otra Ave en Alfitete frío.*

Tomarás las hojuelas de la misma manera que está dicho atrás, y cortarlas has redondas, unas mayores que otras antes de freírse, y tendrás huevos mejidos, é irás echando en el plato una hoja de la masa frita, y luego huevos mejidos encima,[65] y luego otra hoja encima de los huevos mejidos, é irás echando hojas y huevos mejidos, hasta que esté bien alto el plato, poniendo los mayores debajo, y luego tendrás unas almendras rajadas muy menudas, y tomarás un poco de almíbar que esté muy subido de punto, echarlo has por encima (40r) de todas las hojuelas: luego echarás las almendras cortadas por encima del plato, y pegarse han al almíbar: luego tendrás una gallina cocida, rellena, y salpimentada, y pondrásla en medio del plato. Este plato se sirve frío.

[44] *Gallina Morisca.*[66]

Asarás un par de gallinas, y luego haráslas cuartos, y cortarás un poco de tocino en dados muy menudos, y freírlos has muy bien hasta que estén blancos, y échale

---

63 *Alfitete* [fried pastry sheet]. As Martínez Montiño explains in the recipe, *alfitetes* are made with just flour, egg, salt, and lard and are deep fried. In the anonymous *Treatise of Portuguese Cuisine from the 15th Century*, a similar recipe appears that explains both how to make the pastry sheet and how to serve poultry on top ("Alfitete").

64 For more on *brodete*, see 178n58.

65 The recipe for *huevos mejidos* [sweet scrambled egg yolks] is found later in the cookbook, "Plato de huevos mejidos" [Dish of sweet scrambled egg yolks] (436; 437). Today *huevos mejidos* are usually scrambled eggs sweetened with sugar instead of cooked in simple syrup.

66 This Morisco-style dish varies little from the other poultry dishes in this section. It is notable, however, that Martínez Montiño includes both wine and lard in the recipe, whose very title suggests its Muslim origins. Later in eighteenth-century Mexico, this recipe appears in Doña Dominga de Gúzman's recipe collection. For more information, see Pérez San Vicente (*Gastronomía mexicana* 106). There is also another recipe in the same collection with the same title and prepared in a similar way (75). In addition, "Gallina morisca" also appears in the anonymous 1817 *Libro de cocina de la gesta de independencia*. My thanks to Rachel Laudan for pointing out these connections.

Stuffed hen served on fried pastry sheets

Make a dough with just eggs and salt and a little lard but no water or wine, just eggs. The pastry sheets should be relatively thick. Fry in lard. With an already cooked stuffed bird, set it on the pastry sheets. Have prepared some *brodete* from good broth and fat and ladle some around the bird so that only some of the pastry sheets get wet. Sprinkle cinnamon and sugar on top of all the pastry sheets and serve hot.

Another stuffed hen on fried pastry sheets, cold

Take pastry sheets as stated above and cut them into different sized round shapes before frying. Have ready some sweet scrambled egg yolks. On a plate, place a fried pastry sheet and then some sweet scrambled egg yolks and another sheet on top of the sweet scrambled egg yolks and repeat pastry sheet and sweet scrambled egg yolks until you have built up several layers. The larger round shapes should be on the bottom. Then have some finely shaved almonds and some simple syrup at the late thread stage. Sprinkle the syrup over all the pastry sheets. Next sprinkle the chopped almonds on top of the plate so that they stick to the syrup. Then place the hen that has been salted and peppered, stuffed, and cooked in the middle of the plate. This dish is served cold.

Morisco-style hen

Roast a couple of hens and quarter them. Mince some fatback into small cubes and fry them until they turn white. Throw in some minced onion and

un poco de cebolla picada muy menuda, y ahogarás las gallinas con este tocino, y cebolla; échale caldo cuanto se cubran, y échale un poquito de vino, un poco de vinagre: y si hubiere un poco de manteca fresca se le puede echar. Sazona con todas especias. En este platillo no se echan huevos. Ha de salir un poco agrio. Si le quisieres echar un poco de verdura picada podrás.

[45] (40v) *Pichones ensapados.*

Tomarás cuatro pichones recién muertos, y pélalos en agua caliente,[67] y ábrelos por las espaldas, desde la cabeza hasta la cola, sólo el pellejo: luego los irás desollando: de manera que no se rompa el pellejo, y cortarás las piernas, de manera que queden los muslillos en el pellejo, y los alones, cortándolos por las juntas. Luego pondrás el pellejo sobre el tablero, y rellenarlo has con relleno de la misma carne de los pichones, y ternera, o cabrito, y picarás la carne, y freirás tocino en rebanadillas delgadas: y en estando medio fritas, echa un poco de cebolla cortada a lo largo, y freírlo has con el tocino. Luego echarás un poco de hierbabuena, y cilantro verde, y mejorana, si la hubiere; perejil muy poco, porque si es mucho da mal gusto en los rellenos: y si no hubiere hierbabuena, y cilantro verde, échaselo seco, y molido. Echarás en la sartén la carne (41r) picada, y freírlo has: luego echa ocho huevos crudos, y revuélvelo todo con la paleta, hasta que esté bien seco el relleno. Luego tórnalo al tablero, y pícalo muy bien, y métele otros cuatro, o seis huevos crudos, y sazona con todas especias y agrio de limón, y pondrás yemas de huevos duras en el pellejo, y cañas de vaca en trozos: luego echarás el relleno encima, y coserás el pellejo del pichón con una aguja, y una hebra de hilo larga, de manera que en la costura no haya más de una hebra,[68] y pondrás los pichones en una cazuela con lonjas de tocino debajo y encima, y pondrásla al fuego, y tápala con una cobertera, y échale lumbre debajo y encima:[69] y después de asados tirarás por la punta del hilo, y saldrá todo, y sírvelo sobre unas hojuelas muy delgadas, y échales un poco de almíbar por encima, sin tocar a los pichones. Luego corta una docena de almendras en ragitas muy menudas, y échales por encima las hojuelas. Si quisieres (41v) hacer este relleno dulce, échalo azúcar y canela, añadiéndole más agrio. También podrás mezclar a este relleno, si fuere amigo de dulce tu señor, un poco de pasta de mazapán, mezclado con yemas de huevos duros, y mezclado con el relleno de la carne. Si no quisieres servir estos pichones sobre hojuelas, sírvelos sobre una sopa de natas, o sobre

---

67 This is one of only three poultry recipes in which Martínez Montiño suggests wet plucking. He generally advocates for dry plucking. Today, when one wet plucks, water temperatures between 60º and 65ºC or 140ºF and 150ºF are recommended. For more on plucking fowl, see 140n45.

68 Martínez Montiño's comment on a single thread brings to mind thread production in pre-industrial Spain and the aesthetic importance here of not using multiple threads to sew up the bird.

69 The *cobertera* [lid] was designed for coals to be placed on top and thus create heat from both above and below. For more information, see Abad Zardoya, "Herramientas" 89.

sauté the hens with the fatback and onion. Pour in enough broth to cover them. Add in a little wine, a little vinegar, and if you have a little fresh butter, you could add that. Season with all spices. No eggs are added to this dish. It should come out a little sour. If you want to add some chopped green herbs, you can.

Stuffed squab

Take four recently slaughtered squab and pluck them in hot water. On the back side, split open just their skin from the head to the tail and skin them, but don't let the skin break. Cut the legs so that the thighs stay attached to the skin. Also cut off the wings at the joint. Place the carcass on a cutting board and stuff it with meat from the bird itself, and veal or kid. Mince the meat. Fry thin slices of fatback and, once they are partially cooked, add some onion, cut lengthwise, and continue frying. Then add some spearmint, cilantro, and marjoram and if you have some, also add in just a little parsley; too much does not taste good in stuffing. If you don't have spearmint or cilantro, use dried, ground versions. Add the minced meat into the frying pan and continue frying. Then add eight raw eggs, stirring it all with a spatula until the filling is cooked through. Turn out onto the cutting board, chop it all up, and add in another four to six raw eggs. Season with all spices and lemon juice. Place boiled egg yolks and bits of bone marrow on the skin and then put the stuffing on top and sew up the squab with a needle and a long strand of thread so that the seam is only from a single thread. Place the squab in a casserole with slices of fatback above and below them. Put it [the casserole] on the fire, cover it with its lid, and add heat below and above. After it's roasted, pull the thread from one end and it will all come out. Serve on thin sheets of pastry and sprinkle on some simple syrup, but without getting any on the squab. Then shave a dozen almonds in thin slices and sprinkle on the pastry sheets. If you want to have a sweet filling, add in cinnamon and sugar but also more sour juice. If your lord has a sweet tooth, you can also mix into this stuffing a little bit of marzipan paste mixed with hard-boiled egg yolks and then mixed into the meat stuffing. If you don't want to serve the squab over pastry sheets, serve them over some cream-soaked sops or over golden

una sopa dorada. No se dice como se han de hacer las sopas, porque adelante las hallarán escritas. Esta suerte de pichones pongo aquí, porque es el ave que mejor se acomoda desta manera; porque también se pueden hacer de pollos, o de gallinas.[70]

[46] *Un capón relleno con Ostiones.*

Porque voy tratando de rellenos, quiero poner aquí un plato de carne y pescado: y si te hallares adonde lo hubiere fresco, aparejarás un capón para relleno, y tomarás ostias frescas, y harás un relleno con un poquito de ternera, (42r) y ostias, y friéndolo todo en la sartén con tocino, echarle has un poquito de verdura, y cuatro huevos crudos, revolverlo has sobre la lumbre con la paleta, hasta que esté bien seco, y sazona con pimienta y jengibre, y nuez, y pícalo sobre el tablero, y échale otro par de huevos crudos, y tendrás otros pocos de ostiones ahogados, y mézclalos con el relleno, así enteros como están, y échale un poco de agrio de limón, y rellena el capón con este relleno, y embroquétalo, y perdíguese un poco, y espétalo en el asador.[71] Luego tomarás una lamprea fresca, y rodearlo has al capón, atándolo muy bien, y ponerlo has a asar, y pondrás debajo un plato que recoja el zumo del capón, y lamprea: echarás allí un poquito de caldo, y un poco de pimienta, y nuez, y una migaja de clavo, y tostarás rebanadas de pan, y ponlas en el plato, y el capón encima con su lamprea, y échale la salsa por encima, y un poco de agrio de limón, o naranja: y si no (42v) hubiere lamprea, harás el capón con ostias, y sírvelo sobre una sopa dorada, o de natas: y sírvelo caliente.

[47] *Otro Capón relleno.*

Tomarás un capón, y rellenarlo has entre cuero y carne con ternera, y algunas cañas de vaca de la manera que está dicho en los pollos rellenos, y dejarle has el pescuezo con su pico, y cortarás el medio pico de la parte de arriba: y después de relleno pondrásle de manera, que entre la rabadilla por el pico, y el pescuezo venga por el lomo, y embroquetarlo has, y ponle una lonja de tocino en la pechuga, y ásalo, y después de asado toma una docena de yemas de huevos, y rebozarlo has con ellas, de manera que esté bien cubierto: luego echa un poco de manteca caliente,

---

70 The word *receta* was historically used for medical prescriptions, while cooking manuals used *suerte* [type], as is the case here, or *orden* [instruction]. *Procedimiento* [procedure] is found in other cookbooks but is not a term Martínez Montiño uses. The first appearance of *receta* in a cookbook with instructions only for food that doesn't include medical recipes is later in the eighteenth century.

71 *Embroquetar* and *espetar* are two verbs generally used to mean to skewer an animal or animal product on a brochette or spit respectively. The verb *embroquetar* is used in just three recipes; all have to do with securing a bird and searing it before putting it on the spit to roast.

sops. I won't explain how to make sops because they are written down later on. I've written here this kind of squab [recipe] because it is the best poultry to make this way, but you can also make it with chicken or hen.

A capon stuffed with large oysters

Because I am dealing with stuffings, I want to include here a meat and fish dish. If you were in a place where there was fresh fish, then prepare a capon for stuffing, take fresh oysters, and make a stuffing with a little veal and oysters. Fry everything together in a frying pan with fatback, add a little herbs, and four raw eggs. Stir with a spatula over the flame until the egg is completely cooked. Season with pepper, ginger, and nutmeg. Chop it up on a cutting board and add another couple of raw eggs. You should have a few other sautéed oysters. Mix them into the stuffing, whole just as they are, and add in a little lemon juice. Stuff the capon with this stuffing, skewer them on a brochette, sear them a little, and place them on the spit. Next take a fresh lamprey and wrap it around the capon, tying it tight, and put it on to roast. Place underneath a pan to catch the capon and lamprey juices. Ladle over it a little broth, sprinkle a little pepper and nutmeg, and a pinch of clove. Toast some slices of bread and put them on a plate with the capon and its lamprey on top. Ladle on the broth and a little lemon or orange juice. If there weren't any lamprey, you could make the capon with oysters and serve over golden sops or cream sops. Serve hot.

Another stuffed capon

Take a capon and between its skin and flesh, stuff it with veal and some beef marrow the way that is explained in the stuffed chicken (recipe). Leave the neck and the beak and cut off the upper part of the beak. After it's stuffed, arrange it so that the tail is inserted into the beak and the neck is alongside the loin. Put it on a brochette and put a slice of fatback over the breast and roast it. Once it's done, take a dozen egg yolks and coat the bird with them so that it is totally covered. Then brush hot lard on to make the coating more airy. Take some spiral

y esponjará el rebozado, y tomarás unos bollos de rodilla, y armarás el plato con ellos, y con el capón. Estos bollos adelante diré cómo se hacen.[72]

[48] (43r) *Otro Capón relleno.*[73]

Aparejarás un capón para relleno, y cortarle has el pescuezo, y los pies: este relleno ha de ser de ternera, o de cabrito, y no ha de ser perdigado en la sartén, sino carne picada cruda con su tocino, y huevos, y especias, como para albondiguillas, echándole algunos trozos de cañas de vaca, y yemas de huevos cocidas: y si quisieres echar piñones, bien puedes: rellenarás el capón entre cuero y carne, y por lo hueco; y echarlo has a cocer: y luego harás artaletes de otro capón del relleno que sobrare, añadiendo yemas de huevos cocidas y picadas, y cocerás los artaletes en una tortera,[74] cuando esté el capón cocido, y los artaletes, harás una sopa de pan de leche, o de lo más blanco que hubiere, y mojarlo has con sólo caldo: y después que esté bien esponjada; asentarás el capón en ella, de manera que se entierre casi la mitad: luego darás unos (43v) cortes por la pechuga, e irás metiendo los artaletes por aquellas cuchilladas, y los demás pondrás alrededor del capón, y echarle has un poco de zumo de limón, o de naranja por encima, y unos higadillos de aves fritos, o mollejas de cabrito, o de ternera. Si quisieres echar algunas ruedas de limón, puedes, quitándole la cáscara, porque no amargue. Por no gastar dos capones podrás sacar la carne de la pechuga deste capón para hacer los artaletes.

---

72 The recipe for "Bollo de rodilla" [Spiral sweet roll] is found on 262; 263.
73 Of all of the stuffed poultry recipes, this one is the most extravagant and visually complex.
74 Martínez Montiño introduces here the *artalete* [pinwheel], today similar to the *arrollado* or *flamenquín* [roulade or roll up]. I've chosen the word *pinwheel* to highlight the uniqueness of the word *artalete* while maintaining the imagery of the rolled-up meat. In these first recipes, there is an assumption that the reader is familiar with them, as he does not specify what they are until "Artaletes de ave" [Poultry pinwheels] a few recipes later. Although they are usually made by rolling up a thin fillet with an egg yolk filling that is then baked, he also allows that they can be made with minced meat, particularly from poultry or veal. Pinwheels are usually seasoned with fatback and onion and baked in a *tortera* [covered tart pan]. They are often held together with a brochette or small skewer. Generally, pinwheels accompany a whole bird or fillets of poultry, beef, or other meat. For more on the fascinating and complex evolution of its meaning, see Varela Merino, who documents that the first use of *artalete* is in Martínez Montiño (1.516–20) and Torres Martínez, "Léxico culinario en el libro," pp. 127–9. This is also the first time in the cookbook that Martínez Montiño makes use of a *tortera*, a covered tart pan, deeper than today's tart pans, with a lipped lid designed for holding coals or other forms of heat on top. It is the fourth most common piece of cookware in Martínez Montiño's kitchen after the *sartén* [frying pan], *cazuela* [casserole], and *olla* [pot].

sweet rolls and arrange them on the plate with the capon. I will say how to make these pastries later on.

Another stuffed capon

Prepare a capon for stuffing, chop off the neck and feet. The stuffing should be made out of veal or kid and don't sear it in a frying pan. Instead, mince the raw meat with the right amount of fatback, eggs, and spices as you would for meatballs. Add in bits of beef marrow and hard-boiled egg yolk. And, if you'd like to add pine nuts, that would also be good. Put the stuffing between the skin and flesh and in the cavity. Put it on to cook. Then make some pinwheels with leftover stuffing from another capon. Add chopped egg yolk and cook the pinwheels in a covered tart pan. When the capon and the pinwheels are done, make sops from milk bread or from the whitest bread you have and soak it just with broth. When it has become very spongy, set the capon on it so that the bird is half way buried in it. Then make some slits in the breast and place the pinwheels in those slits and the remaining ones around the capon. Sprinkle on top some lemon or orange juice and add some fried poultry liver or some veal or kid sweetbreads. If you want to garnish with lemon wheels you can, but first remove the peel so it won't be too bitter. To avoid using two capons, you can take some of the breast meat from the same capon to make the pinwheels.

[49] *Empanadas de Pollos ensapados.*⁷⁵

Aparejarás los pollos, abriéndolos por las espaldas, y rellenarlos has (como tengo dicho atrás en los pichones) y coserlos has con la hebra de hilo larga, y tomarás hojaldrado, y harás una hoja grande y gorda, y pondrásla sobre el tablero, y sobre ella un pollo, la pechuga para arriba, y ponle otra hoja de hojaldrado por encima, y repúlgala, y harás (44r) de manera, que quede la punta de la hebra de hilo con que está cosido fuera; porque después que esté cocida la empanada, puedas tirar por ella, y saldrá toda, y cuécela en el horno, y ráspale un poco de azúcar por encima. Y advierte, que esta empanada ha de llevar una lonja de tocino delgada en las espaldas del pollo. También se pueden empanar estos pollos y pichones ensapados en masa dulce, mas hanse de comer calientes. A todos estos rellenos se les podrá echar agraz cuando está pequeño, y se pueden echar pasas de Corinto: y el agrio que les echarás dentro no sea de vinagre, si es posible, sino de limón, o de agraz. Esta empanada de hojaldrado se hace muy buena de un capón relleno, porque con sola una se hinche un plato, y podrásle poner el pescuezo de fuera, que vuelva hacia la pechuga con una cubierta de hojaldrado, que quede la cabeza fuera.

[50] (44v) *Cómo se hacen los Rellenos.*⁷⁶

Porque voy tratando de rellenos, digo, que todos los que han de ser asados, han de ser friendo tocino, y cebolla, y luego echarle la carne picada, y echarle huevos crudos, y freírlo hasta que esté seco, como huevos revueltos: y luego echarlo en el tablero, y picarlo, metiendo más huevos crudos, y sazonar, y rellenar: y en lo que se dice de cebollas, o hierbas, o ajo, ú otra cosa, haste de conformar con el gusto de tu señor; porque aunque quites algún material de lo que va escrito, no por eso dejará de estar bueno: y todos los rellenos que han de ser cocidos, han de ser de carne sazonada en crudo, y procurar que lleven buen tocino, y algunas cañas de vaca, y un poquito de riñonada de carnero fresco, y un poco de agrio de limón.

---

75 According to Lluis Gimeno Betí, *ensapado*, from the verb *ensapar-se*, means "posar-se fart, replé de menjar, i més de beure aigua" [to become full, from food and more so from drinking] (99). Thus, the adjective is another way of referring to the *stuffed* birds. The Catalan roots of the word suggests that the recipe may have its origins in Cataluña.

76 This recipe is categorized as a master recipe, as it is the basis for stuffing found in most of the recipes of this section. Finishing a section with a recipe that includes generalities about the previous recipes is common in Martínez Montiño's cookbook. For today's reader, it would be more logical to place this type of recipe at the beginning of the section.

Stuffed chicken empanadas

Prepare chickens by cutting them open down the back, stuffing them (as I previously explained for squab), and stitching them up with a long strand of thread. Take puff pastry dough and shape into a big, thick sheet. Place it on the table top and put the chicken on it with the breast up. Place another sheet of puff pastry dough on top. Crimp it so that the end of the strand of thread used to sew the bird up is on the outside and thus can be entirely pulled out once the empanada is cooked. Bake in the oven and grate a little sugar on top. Note that this empanada should have a thin slice of fatback on the backside of the chicken. You can also wrap these stuffed chickens or squab in a sweet dough, but they must be eaten hot. To all of these stuffings you can add sour grapes, when they are small. You can also add dried currants.[5] If you add sour juice, it should not be vinegar if at all possible, rather from lemon or verjuice. These puff pastry empanadas are great with a stuffed capon because with just one you will fill the whole plate. You can leave the neck out, turned toward the breast, covered with puff pastry dough so that [just] the head sticks out.

How to make stuffing

As I am discussing stuffing, I will note that all that are roasted should be made by first frying the fatback and onion and then adding the minced meat and raw eggs and frying all of it until dry, as you would for scrambled eggs. Then turn it out on a cutting board, mince it, and add more raw eggs. Season and stuff. Regarding onions, herbs, garlic, and other ingredients, you need to conform to your lord's taste. Even if you leave out some of the ingredients written here, there's no reason it still can't turn out tasty. All stuffing that is going to be cooked should have the meat seasoned while it is still raw. Try to include good-quality fatback, some beef marrow, a little fresh mutton loin, and a little lemon juice.

---

5 Today's reader needs to distinguish between currants grown on a bush, like the common red and black currants, and *pasas de Corinto* [Corinthian raisins], which are also known as currants. I have used the translation *dried currants* to signal that Martínez Montiño was using currants, but they are more like small raisins.

[51] (45 r) *Artaletes de Ave.*

Tomarás para un plato dos pechugas de aves, y harás las chulletas [sic] muy delgadas; de manera, que de cada pechuga hagas ocho, o diez chulletas, y golpearlas has con la vuelta del cuchillo: y tendrás dos docenas de huevos cocidos duros, y sacarles has las yemas, y pícalas sobre el tablero, y picarás un poco de hierbabuena, y echársela has; y sazonarás con pimienta, y nuez, y jengibre, y cuatro yemas de huevos crudos, y un poco de zumo de limón, y un poco de sal. Luego pondrás las chulletas tendidas sobre el tablero, y picarás un poco de tocino gordo muy picado, y pondrás un poquito sobre cada una dellas, y tenderlo has por toda la chulleta; luego echarás del batido de las yemas de huevos, y arrollarlas has cada una de por sí: y así harás todos los artaletes. Luego tomarás unas broquetillas de caña muy delgadas, e íraslos (45v) metiendo de cuatro en cuatro, y ponlos en una tortera untada con manteca, y cúbrela con su cobertera: y echa lumbre abajo y arriba, y cuézanse. A este relleno podrás echar azúcar, y canela, si quisieres, y un poco de pasta de mazapán, mezclados con los huevos, y sírvelos sobre una sopilla dorada: y si no fueren dulces basta mojar la sopilla con un poco de caldo, y un poco de agrio, sin huevos, ni otra cosa. He puesto esta manera de artaletes, no porque son los mejores, sino porque son los que su Majestad come mejor.[77]

POTAJERÍA[78]

[52] *Otros Artaletes de Aves.*[79]

Aparejarás las chulletas de las aves, y tomarás carne de pierna de cabrito, y picarla has, y freirás un poco de tocino gordo en rebanadillas, y un poquito de cebolla, y picarás la carne, y echarla has en la sartén con el tocino, y fríase bien, y échala un poquillo de (46r) hierbabuena, y seis huevos crudos, y freírlo has todo, revolviendo con la paleta; de que esté bien seco, sacarlo has al tablero, y pícalo muy bien,

---

77 This type of closing note reminds his readers for whom he is cooking and that he knows the king's taste better than anyone.
78 This subtitle and others throughout the cookbook appear for the first time in 1617 (45v). Although not included in the 1611 edition, I have added it here to give additional structure to the work and because it is part of all subsequent editions. It is also important to note that in Martínez Monitño's day, *potage* referred both to the final product of a vegetable stew and to the vegetables themselves and *legumbre*, as a term that encompassed a wide variety of vegetables. The *Diccionario de autoridades* defines *potage* as follows: "Por antonomásia se llaman las legumbres guisadas para el mantenimiento de los días de abstinéncia [Typically, the stewed vegetables eaten on abstinence days]. *Legumbre* has an expansive definition beyond dried beans: "Algunos le extienden a significar algunas hortalizas" [Some extend its meaning to some leafy green vegetables].
79 See Appendix 3.5 for images of preparing this dish.

Poultry pinwheels

For one plate, take two poultry breasts and slice them into very thin fillets. From each one you should get eight to ten fillets. Pound them out with the back of your knife. Take two dozen hard-boiled eggs, remove the yolks, and chop them on a cutting board. Mince a little spearmint and add it in. Season with pepper, nutmeg, and ginger. Add four raw egg yolks, a little lemon juice, and a little salt. Then, spread the fillets out on a table top, mince a little extra fatty fatback, put some on each one, and spread it over the entire fillet; then, the egg yolk batter. Roll up each one and this is how you make all the pinwheels. Then take very thin reed skewers and put four on each one. Place them in a covered tart pan greased with lard and cover it with its lid. Add heat above and below and let cook. You can add cinnamon and sugar to the filling, and if you like, a little marzipan paste mixed into the hard-boiled egg yolks. Serve over golden sops. If they aren't sweet, just soak the sops in a little stock with a little sour juice but no eggs or anything else. I've included this recipe for pinwheels not because they are the best but because they are the ones His Majesty likes to eat.

Vegetables

Other poultry pinwheels

Prepare fillets of poultry. Take some leg of kid and mince it. Fry some slices of extra fatty fatback and a little onion. Mince the meat and add it to the frying pan with the fatback and continue frying. Add in a little spearmint and six raw eggs. Continue frying and stirring it well with a spatula. Once everything is cooked, place on a cutting board and chop it all up. Add in another two or three raw eggs and season with all spices. Then take four hard-boiled egg yolks chopped up with

y métele otros dos, o tres huevos crudos, y sazonarás con todas especias. Luego tendrás otras cuatro yemas de huevos duras, picadas con un poquito de verdura.[80] Luego arrollarás los artaletes, como está dicho en los de atrás, y meterlos has en sus broquetillas. Luego asentarlo has con las puntas sobre las yemas duras picadas: y luego asentarlos en su tortera untada con manteca, y cúbrelo con su cobertera, y ponlos a cocer con lumbre abajo y arriba, y sírvelos sobre alguna sopa. Este plato no dejes de adornarle con algo, como son mollejas de cabrito, o algunas turmas de carnero fritas: y si no tuvieres nada desto, deja un poco del relleno de los artaletes, y échale más huevos crudos, y un poco de leche, y échalo a cuajar en una tortera: y de que esté cocido córtalo en rebanadillas, y (46v) irás metiéndolas entre los artaletes, y parecerán muy bien; porque si es posible nunca se ha de servir ningún plato de platillería sin que se le pongan algunos adherentes para adornarle.

[53] *Otros Artaletes de Ternera.*

Picarás carne de ternera con tocino gordo, y sazonarás con huevos, y todas las especias, como para albondiguillas, y tomarás un tablero mojado con vinagre y agua, y tomarás la carne picada, y asentarla has por el tablero, del anchor de seis dedos, y de largo lo que alcanzare. Luego ternás una docena de yemas de huevos duras, y picadas con verdura, perejil, y hierbabuena, y echarlo has por encima de la carne, que está también por el tablero, de manera que se cubra toda con las yemas y verdura, y échale algunas cañas de vaca picadas, y un poco de especia. Luego cortarás esta carne al través del (47r) ancho de tres dedos. Luego arrollarlo has, e irás haciendo artaletes, asentándolos en una tortera: para esto no son menester broquetas, porque no se abre. Adviértase, que de la ternera se pueden hacer artaletes, haciendo carbonadillas muy delgadas de la misma ternera, y hacer el relleno, como está dicho en los artaletes de ave y cabrito, y adornarlos con unas carbonadillas, mechadas de la misma ternera: han de ser muy delgadas, y golpeadas con el cuchillo, y mechadas y asadas en las parrillas: luego echarles sal y pimienta, y zumo de naranjas: y con esto se han de adornar los artaletes de ternera.

[54] *Artaletes de Cabrito.*

Echarás a cocer las piernas de cabrito, y cuando esté más de medio cocido, sácalo al tablero, y pícalo muy bien, y mézclale tocino gordo picado, y algunas cañas de vaca en pedacillos. (47v) Luego échale media docena de yemas de huevos, y un poco de verdura, hierbabuena, y mejorana, y sazona de todas especias y sal, y cuatro yemas de huevos duras, y picadas, y échale un poco de zumo de limón, o naranja, y toma

---

[80] With the mention of *verdura*, Martínez Montiño is referring to green herbs, not vegetables. Here, he suggests spearmint and marjoram and leaves it up to whoever is preparing the *artaletes* to decide how much of these fresh herbs to use.

some herbs. Next, roll up the pinwheels, as is stated in those previous [recipes], and place them on small skewers. Then dip the ends in the chopped-up yolks and set them in a covered tart pan greased with lard. Cover them with a lid and bake with the heat above and below. Serve them over sops. Do not forget to garnish this plate with something like kid sweetbreads or fried sheep testicles. If neither of these are available, then set aside some of the filling from the pinwheels, add to it more raw egg and a little milk, and let it set in a covered tart pan. Once cooked, cut it into slices and place them between the pinwheels. They will look good. If possible, never serve any dish on dishware without putting on some extras to garnish it.

Other veal pinwheels

Mince veal with extra fatty fatback and season with eggs and all spices as you would for small meatballs. Moisten a cutting board with water and vinegar and take the minced meat, set it on the board, [making it] at least six fingers wide and as long as it can be. Then take a dozen hard-boiled egg yolks chopped up with herbs – parsley and spearmint – and add it to the meat that is also on the board so that the eggs and herbs cover all the meat. Add in some minced beef marrow and a little spice. Then cut the meat widthwise into strips three fingers wide. Then roll them up and make the pinwheels, setting them in a covered tart pan. For this (recipe) you don't need skewers because they won't open up. Note that with veal you can also make pinwheels by grilling very thin strips of the same veal and then make the stuffing as stated for the poultry and kid pinwheels. Garnish them with grilled pieces of the same veal that have been larded. They should be very thin and pounded with a knife and larded and grilled on the grill. Then add salt, pepper, and orange juice and with this the veal pinwheels can be garnished.

Kid pinwheels

Begin cooking a leg of kid and when it is a little more than halfway cooked, put it on the cutting board and mince it up. Mix in some minced extra fatty fatback and bits of beef marrow. Then add in a half dozen egg yolks and a little bit of green herbs – spearmint and marjoram – and season with all spices and salt and four hard-boiled, chopped egg yolks. Add in some lemon or orange juice. Take a

un redaño de carnero delgado, y ve haciendo con él los artaletes, y asiéntalos en una tortera untada con manteca, y cuézanse con lumbre abajo y arriba, y sírvelos sobre una sopa: y advierte, que del cabrito se pueden hacer los artaletes, haciendo de las piernas las chulletas muy delgadas, y descarnando lo demás podrás sacar carne, y picarla: y luego freír tocino y cebolla, y la misma carne picada, y échale sus verduras de hierbabuena, y mejorana, y un poco de perejil,[81] y echarle media docena de huevos crudos batidos, freírlo hasta que esté muy seco. Luego sácale al tablero y picarlo muy bien, y meterle otros tres o cuatro huevos crudos. Sazona de todas especias, y un poco de agrio de limón, (48r) y poner las chulletas de cabrito sobre el tablero, y ponerle el relleno, y arrollarlas como está dicho en los de atrás. Y a todos estos artaletes de carne, que sean dulces, o no lo sean, se les pueden echar a todos pasas de Corinto, y a todos los rellenos de aves. Los artaletes con redaño se pueden hacer de la carne de las albondiguillas y cañas de vaca.

[55] *Una cazuela de Ave.*

Tomarás una ave, y cocerla has, y después de cocida, cortarla has en pedacitos: luego freirás un poco de tocino en dados muy menudo, y echarle has un poco de cebolla picada muy menuda. Luego asentarás el ave en una cazuela, y echa sobre ella el tocino, y la cebolla frita. Y advierte, que es esta cazuela de ave, le puedes echar criadillas de tierra cocidas y ahogadas con el tocino, y la cebolla, o algunos cogollos de lechuga cocidos: y si no hubiere nada (48v) desto, échale puntas de espárragos perdigados, o riponces: cualquiera destas verduras han de ser primero cocidas. Luego sazonarás con todas especias, y échale caldo de la olla cuanto se bañe, y cueza dos, o tres hervores no más. Luego sacarás un poco de la flor,[82] cuajarás la cazuela con cuatro yemas de huevos batidos con un poquito de vinagre, y póngase al fuego, y no cueza más de medio hervor, porque no se corte, o se cuaje demasiado. Luego ponle unas rebanadillas de pan angostillas, hincadas al derredor de los bordes de la cazuela, y échale la flor por encima: y si la quisieres hacer agridulce, échale un poco de azúcar y canela, un poco antes que la cuajes: y añadirás un poco de más agrio.

[56] *Un platillo de Artaletes.*

Después de hechos los artaletes, y cocidos en las torteras, o cazuelas, sacarlos has, y asentarlos has en un (49r) cacillo, y mezclarás con ellos algunos pichones, o pollos, o aves en cuartos, y algunas criadillas de carnero, o de tierra, y su verdura picada, y freirás tocino gordo, cortado muy menudo: y cuando esté bien frito

---

81 Here is a clear example of the use of *verduras* to mean *herbs*.
82 For more information on the flor, see 65.

thin piece of sheep caul fat and begin making the pinwheels with it. Place them in a covered tart pan greased with lard and cook with the heat above and below. Serve them over sops. Note that with kid you can also make pinwheels by slicing very thin fillets from the leg and removing the rest of the meat and mincing it. Then fry some fatback, onion, and the minced meat. Add in some herbs of spearmint, marjoram, and a little parsley. Add in half a dozen beaten eggs and fry until they are thoroughly cooked. Then turn it out onto the cutting board and mince it. Add another three or four raw eggs. Season with all spices and a little lemon juice. Put the kid fillets on the table and spread the filling on them and roll up as stated in the previous (recipes). For all these meat pinwheels, whether they are sweet or not, you can add dried currants to all of them as well as to the poultry ones. The pinwheels with caul fat can be made with meat from the meatball (recipe) and beef marrow.

Poultry stew

Take a bird, cook it, and, once cooked, chop it into little pieces. Then fry up a little diced fatback and add to it a little minced onion. Then set the bird in a casserole and put on top the fatback and onion. Note that in this poultry stew you can add some truffles that have been sautéed and smothered with fatback and onion or some cooked lettuce hearts. But if there weren't any of these, add in some parboiled asparagus tips or rampion bellflower shoots. Any of these green vegetables should be boiled first. Then season with all spices. Add enough stock from the pot to braise and bring it to a boil two or three times and no more. Then take out a little of the flor. Thicken the stew with four beaten egg yolks and a little vinegar. Put it on the fire and only bring it to simmer so that it doesn't break or thicken too much. Then put some thin slices of bread around and up the sides of the casserole, and sprinkle the flor on top. If you want it to be sweet and sour, add a little cinnamon and sugar right before you thicken it and add a little more sour juice.

A dish of pinwheels

After the pinwheels are made and baked in covered tart pans or casseroles, take them out and set them in a saucepan. Add in some quartered squab, young chicken, or adult ones, sheep testicles or truffles, and the right amount of chopped herbs. Fry some minced extra fatty fatback and when it's well done, add in some minced

échale cebolla picada muy menuda, y fríelo muy bien: y échalo sobre los artaletes, y sazona con todas especias, y échale caldo hasta que se bañe, y cueza dos, o tres hervores. Luego batirás cuatro yemas de huevos con un poco de agrio, y cuajarás este platillo, apartando primero la flor dél:[83] y sírvelo en un plato sobre rebanadillas de pan blanco, y échale un poco de zumo de limón por encima, o naranja, y la flor: y sírvase caliente.

[57] *Palominos ahogados.*

Tomarás seis palominos después de limpios, y hazlos cuartos, o medios: luego freirás un poco de tocino en dados muy menudos, y écharle un poco (49v) de cebolla picada muy menuda, y echa allí los palominos, y ahóguese un poco. Luego échalos en una cazuela de barro, y échale caldo cuanto se cubran. Toma seis yemas de huevos duros, y majarás las en el almirez con un poco de verdura picada, y con un poquito de pimienta, y nuez, y jengibre, y unos poquitos de cominos, y tanto pan como media castaña. Todo esto se ha de majar muy bien en el almirez, y desatarlo con un poco de caldo de los palominos, y una gota de vinagre, y échese en la cazuela, y cuezan dos, o tres hervores, habiéndola sazonado de sal, y sírvelo sobre rebanadillas de pan, o en la misma cazuela.

[58] *Otros Palominos ahogados.*

Aparejarás los palominos de la manera que está dicho en el capítulo atrás,[84] y picarás un poco de verdura, perejil, hierbabuena, y ciliantro verde, o seco, con un migajoncillo de pan duro, (50r) y échale un medio grano de ajo, y unos pocos de cominos, y pimienta, y nuez, y májalo mucho, tanto, como para salsa de perejil,[85] y desátalo con un poco de caldo, y un poquito de vinagre, y échalo en la cazuela con los palominos, y cueza dos, o tres hervores, y sírvelos sobre rebanadillas, o en la misma cazuela. Este platillo ha de salir muy verde, y el otro de las yemas cocidas, ha de ser entre verde y amarillo.

---

83 For more information on the flor, see 65.

84 Here, Martínez Montiño uses the word *capítulo* [chapter] to refer to a specific recipe. This use of the term is not unusual and is also seen, for example, in Hernández de Maceras' 1607 cookbook, *Libro del arte de Cocina* [Book on the art of cooking]. In other parts of the cookbook, however, *capítulo* does refer to a specific section of recipes.

85 Although a specific recipe for parsley sauce is not part of this cookbook, the ingredients of spearmint, pepper, and a little oil are referenced in the recipe "Cómo se puede freír, y asar, y cocer un pescado todo en un tiempo, sin partirlo" [How to fry, roast, and boil a fish at the same time without cutting it up] (414–16; 415–17).

onion and fry it well. Add this to the pinwheels, season with all spices, and add enough stock to braise and bring to a boil two or three times. Then beat four egg yolks with a little sour juice and thicken this dish, but first remove the flor. Serve on a plate over slices of white bread, sprinkle the flor over it, and drizzle a little lemon or orange juice. Serve hot.

Sautéed wild squab

Take six wild squab and after cleaning them, quarter or halve them. Fry some minced fatback and add a little minced onion. Then add the squab and sauté it a little. Next, put everything in a terracotta casserole and add enough broth to cover it. Take six hard-boiled egg yolks; mash them in the mortar with a little bit of minced green herbs, a little pepper, nutmeg, ginger, and a dash of cumin, and about a half-chestnut amount of bread. All this should be ground together in the mortar and thinned with some of the squab broth and a drop of vinegar. Add it to the casserole and bring to a boil two or three times, having seasoned it with salt. Serve over slices of bread or in the same casserole.

Another dish of sautéed wild squab

Prepare squab the way it was stated in the previous chapter. Chop up a few green herbs, parsley, spearmint, fresh cilantro or dried, with a little piece of stale bread. Add a half clove of garlic, a little cumin, pepper, and nutmeg, and grind it up very fine, as you would for parsley sauce. Thin it with a little broth and a little vinegar and add it to the casserole with the squab. Bring it to a boil two or three times and serve it over slices (of bread) or in the casserole itself. This dish should be very green, and the other one with the hard-boiled yolks should have a yellow-green colour.

[59] [*Carnero verde.*]⁸⁶

Desta manera harás el carnero verde, cociendo primero el carnero, hecho pedacitos como nueces: y después que tengas la salsa molida en el almirez, desátala con el caldo que se coció el carnero, y echarás el carnero en una olla, o cazuela, y échale la salsa encima: luego freirás un poco de tocino gordo muy menudo, y un poco de cebolla, y échasela dentro, y dé dos, o tres hervores, y sírvelos sobre rebanadillas de pan, y cuatro yemas de huevos duras encima. Has de advertir una cosa, que todas las (50v) veces que frieres tocino y cebolla para platillos, que ha de ser en dados muy menudos, y el tocino muy frito, antes que eches la cebolla en la sartén, porque en entrando la cebolla en la sartén, o cazuela, no se fríe más el tocino, sino así se queda: y como son platillos que no han de cocer más de dos o tres hervores, quédase el tocino crudo, y siéntase cuando se come en el platillo.⁸⁷ Desta manera son buenos los conejos, y el cabrito asándolo primero y haciéndolo pedazos, y ahogándolo como los palominos. Con esta salsa se aderezan las ranas, y otros pescados.

[60] *Otra manera de Carnero verde.*

Pondrás a cocer el carnero, como está dicho, cortando el carnero a pedacitos, tamaños como nueces, y échalo a cocer con agua y sal, y un pedazo de tocino gordo; y una cebolla entera: y cuando el tocino, y la cebolla esté (51r) cocido, sácalo al tablero, y échale cantidad de verdura, perejil, hierbabuena, y cilantro verde, y pícalo todo junto así caliente como está: y después que esté bien picado, y el carnero bien cocido, echa la verdura, y el tocino picado dentro de la olla: y si vieres que tiene mucho caldo, sácale dello, antes de echar la verdura, y sazona con todas especias, y échale un poco de agraz, si fuere tiempo, y cueza dos, o tres hervores: luego batirás tres, o cuatro yemas de huevos desatadas con un poco de vinagre, y sacarás toda la flor del platillo con la verdura,⁸⁸ y cuajarlo has con las yemas de huevos, y sírvelo sobre rebanadillas de pan. Luego échale aquella flor toda por encima: y si hubieres de hacer muchos platos juntos, no los cuajes con huevos,

---

86 This explanation for green mutton stew is part of the squab recipe in every edition. However, in the index, Martínez Montiño does include a title for it. I have added it here in brackets to signal to the reader today that this second part is a whole new recipe, not simply a variation of a recipe like those Martínez Montiño includes in many others. Additionally, he titles the next recipe "Otra manera de …" [Another way …], thus implying that the first recipe was included above. And later, in "Cazuela de pajarillos" [Small bird stew] (226; 227), he references both of these recipes as if they were two separate recipes. For a picture of this stew, see Appendix 3.6.
87 This detailed explanation on the correct way to fry fatback and onion is significant because this combination is used for so many dishes. Martínez Montiño is also expressing concern not only for time and order in the cooking process but also for the texture of the final product.
88 For information on the flor, see 65.

[*Green mutton stew*]

In this same way you can prepare green mutton stew by first boiling the mutton that has been cut up into walnut-sized pieces. Then once you have the sauce ground up in the mortar, thin it with the broth in which you cooked the mutton. Place the mutton in a pot or casserole and pour the sauce on top. Then fry a little extra fatty fatback that has been diced and a little onion and add it. Bring to a boil two or three times. Serve over slices of bread with four hard-boiled egg yolks on top. You should note one thing. Each time you fry fatback and onions for dishes, the fatback should be diced very small and fried until well done before adding the onion in the frying pan, because once the onion is in the pan or a casserole, the fatback stops frying and stays as it is. And since these are dishes that shoudn't come to a boil more than two or three times, the fatback will be undercooked and it will feel like that when the dish is eaten. This is a good way to prepare rabbit or kid that has first been roasted and chopped into pieces and sautéed like squab. You can also use this sauce for frog and other fish.

Another way of (making) green mutton stew

You can start boiling the mutton as is stated, by cutting the mutton into walnut-sized pieces. Bring it to a boil in salted water, [with] a piece of fatback, and a whole onion. When the onion and fatback are done, take them out and put them on a cutting board and add a good amount of herbs, parsley, mint, and cilantro, and chop it all up while still hot. After it is well chopped, and the mutton well cooked, add the herbs and the minced fatback to the pot. If you see that there is a lot of broth, take some out before adding the herbs. Season with all spices, and add a little verjuice if it's in season. Bring to a boil two or three times. Then beat three or four egg yolks thinned with a little vinegar. Remove all flor and the herbs from the dish and thicken the dish with the egg yolks. Serve it over sliced bread. Then pour all the flor on top. And if you were plating up a lot at once, do not thicken them

sino toma una poca de buena manteca de puerco, y caliéntala bien, y echa dentro un poquito de harina, y fríela un poco, de manera que no se ponga negra, no más de cuanto haga unas ampollitas blancas, (51v) y échala en el potaje,[89] y échale un poquito de azafrán, y un poco de agrio, y viene a quedar muy bueno: y cuando lo sirvieres échale de la flor por encima.

[61] *Plato de Pollo rellenos con Membrillos.*

Rellenarás cuatro pollos, como está dicho atrás, y asarlos has y rebozarlos has con yemas de huevos: luego tendrás seis membrillos enteros, conservados y rellenos de huevos mejidos, y armarás los pollos sobre hojuelas, y pondrás los membrillos entre pollo y pollo un membrillo, compuestos con hojuelas entre los pollos y los membrillos, y pedacitos de jilea [*sic*] de los membrillos por encima de las hojuelas. Éste es plato de merienda.

[62] *Pepitoria.*[90]

Pelarás las aves, y cortarles has los alones, y los pescuezos: estos alones (52r) y pescuezos, pélalos en agua, porque salgan blancos, y cortarás las puntas a los alones, y a los pescuezos les quitarás los picos, y los gaznates, y les darás dos golpecitos, sin acabarlos de cortar: el uno en medio del pescuezo, y el otro en la cabeza; porque cuando se coman puedan comer los sesos de la gallina: y los pies se pelen también en la misma agua caliente. Todo esto se echará a cocer con agua, y sal, y un pedazo de tocino gordo, y unas cebollas enteras: y en estando cocido el tocino y cebollas, sácalo al tablero, y pícalo con mucha verdura, así caliente: y después que esté muy bien picado tórnalo a echar en la olla, y sazona con pimienta, jengibre, y nuez, y cueza. Luego toma un poco de buena manteca de puerco en una sartén, o cacito, y ponla a calentar: y cuando esté bien caliente échale un poco de harina floreada, y sea tan poca la harina que no se haga masa en la sartén, sino que haga unas ampollitas blancas, y que se (52v) quede muy blanca, y échala así con la sartén dentro en la olla de la pepitoria, y échale un poco de vinagre, y un poco de azafrán. A estas

---

89 Martínez Montiño's use of lard and flour as a thickener is an early explanation of roux. For more on roux, see the Introduction (65).

90 Today *pepitoria* refers to a poultry dish made with egg, added in either raw or already cooked. In this recipe, possibly the first recorded version, you can see the origins of the dish which is made from offal, the head, neck, wings, and feet of the bird. It also includes a roux-based sauce finished with saffron and then garnished with liver, stuffed oviduct, and hard-boiled egg yolks. In Altamiras' 1745 cookbook, he continues in the tradition of Martínez Montiño in his recipe "Pepitoria de menudillos de pollos" [Pepitoria with chicken giblets], in which he also includes neck, wings, and liver (78). A popular saying is "Con gallina en pepitoria bien se puede ganar la gloria" [By preparing hen pepitoria style, you can get into heaven].

with eggs. Instead, take a little good-quality lard, heat it up well, and mix in a little flour. Fry it but don't burn it, only until it forms little white bubbles. Pour it into the stew and add a little saffron and a little sour juice. It is going to be delicious. And when you serve it, pour the flor on top.

A dish of chicken stuffed with quince

Stuff four chickens, as stated previously, roast them, and coat them in egg yolk. Then take six whole quince that have been preserved and filled with sweet scrambled egg yolks. Arrange the chicken on pastry sheets and put a quince between each chicken and pastry sheets between each chicken and quince. Then place little slices of quince jelly on top of the pastry sheets. This is a dish for a late afternoon supper.

Pepitoria [Stew with poultry offal]

Pluck the birds and cut off the wings and necks. Pluck the wings and necks in water so that they come out white. Cut off the tips of the wings and from the neck remove the beak and the gullet. Give the neck two blows without cutting it open, one to the middle of the neck and the other to the head, so that when you eat them, you can eat the hen brains. Pluck the feet in the same hot water. Then put everything on to boil in salted water, with a piece of extra fatty fatback and some whole onions. When the fatback and onion are cooked, put them on a cutting board and chop while still hot with a lot of herbs. After it is minced up, return it to the pot and season with pepper, ginger, and nutmeg and let simmer. Next, put some good lard in a frying pan or saucepan and heat it up. When it's very hot, add in some finely sifted flour, but just a little so that it won't form into dough in the frying pan. Rather, you want it to form little white bubbles and turn very white. Add what's in the frying pan to the pot with the *pepitoria*. Add in a little vinegar

pepitorias no se han de echar huevos batidos, sino cocerlos, y asentar las yemas duras encima del plato. Y advierte, que los higadillos no se han de cocer, sino asarlos, o freírlos, y asentarlos por encima de los platos, y las madrecillas de las gallinas las podrás rellenar, y adornar los platos con ellas, y con los higadillos. Este plato ha de estar un poco subido de sal y especias, y vinagre, porque de otra manera está la carne dulce. Advierte, que todas las veces digo, que sazones con todas las especias, se entiende pimienta, y clavos, y nuez, y jengibre, y azafrán;[91] porque la canela no ha de entrar en cosa que no lleve dulce, y en todos, o en los más dulces ha de entrar canela; porque está puesto al revés en el otro libro.[92]

[63] (53r) *Albondiguillas de Ave.*

Has de picar la pechuga que sea muy buena, y tendrás un migajoncillo de pan blanco, tanto como una castaña remojado en agua fría. Luego picarás otro tanto tocino gordo como el pan: y si fuere para enfermo, en lugar del tocino echará una enjundia[93] del capón que sea fresca, y picarse ha con el pan: y luego mezclarás el pan y tocino, o enjundia, y echarle has dos yemas de huevos, y mézclalo con la carne, y échale otras dos yemas de huevos, y píquese todo junto muy bien: sazona con pimienta, y nuez, y jengibre, y cilantro seco, y tendrás caldo de gallina colado, que no tenga ningún género de verdura en una ollita,

---

91 This side note is significant because Martínez Montiño specifies exactly what he means by *todas especias* [all spices]. In Bartolomeo Scappi's 1570 Italian cookbook, *Opera dell'arte del cucinare*, the author also specifies a premixed spice mixture which includes 2 oz. clove, 1 oz. nutmeg, 1 oz. ginger, and ½ oz. saffron, but substitutes ½ oz. of grains of paradise for black pepper. Scappi's mixture diverges drastically from Martínez Montiño's spice mix, because his main ingredient is, in fact, 4½ oz. cinnamon, and he also includes 1 oz. sugar (114). In recreating several of Martínez Montiño's recipes, I have found that the following proportions are suitable to today's palate: ¼ tsp clove, ¼ tsp nutmeg, ½ tsp ginger, ½ tsp black pepper, and 4 strands saffron.

92 Cinnamon appears in over 130 recipes, and all but a handful do contain sugar or some other sweetener. The exceptions are recipes for pork or marinade: "Como se ha de beneficiar un jabalí" [How to dress boar] (286–8; 287–9). "Empanada de pernil de tocino" [Fatty ham empanada], "Un pernil cocido sin remojar" [Leg boiled without soaking], "Memoria de la mostaza negra" [Memoir of black mustard], and "Memoria del adobo de aceitunas" [Memoir of olive marinade]. *El otro libro* [the other book] is another disparaging comment Martínez Montiño makes regarding the book he referenced in his prologue. Here, he corrects what the author indicated regarding sweet dishes and cinnamon. It is true that in Diego Granado's *Libro del arte de cozina* (and by extension, Scappi's cookbook), cinnamon appears in many of the savoury dishes without the support of sugar. A few examples from Granado include "Platos de trigo o cebada sin corteza" [Wheat or barley dishes, without the hull] (cinnamon and saffron) (99–100), "Para freír los fríjoles (guisantes) frescos con la vaina o camisa y sin ella" [To fry fresh beans (peas) with or without the pod or covering] (pepper, cinnamon, and saffron) (101), or "Para hacer platos de repollo" [To make cabbage dishes] (grated cheese, pepper, and cinnamon) (104).

93 *Enjundia* is the fat or fatty tissue that surrounds the bird's ovaries, but it can also mean more generally the fatty tissue of the bird, which is the case here. For more, see 118n24.

and a little saffron. Don't add whipped eggs to these *pepitorias*, instead boil them and set the egg yolks on the plate. Note that the liver shouldn't be boiled but rather roasted or fried and set on top of the plate. You can stuff the hen's oviduct and use as a garnish with the livers. This dish should have a good amount of salt, spices, and vinegar; otherwise the meat will be sweet. Also note that whenever I say to season with all spices, I mean pepper, clove, nutmeg, ginger, and saffron, because cinnamon should not be added to something that is not sweet. In all sweet dishes, or in the sweetest, cinnamon must be present, unlike the other book that says the opposite.

Poultry meatballs

Chop up a poultry breast of good quality and have the inside of white bread, about the size of a chestnut, soaked in cold water. Then chop up the same amount of extra fatty fatback. If this is for a sick person, instead of fatback, use fresh fat tissue from the capon, chop it up with the bread, and add salt. Then mix the bread and fatback or fat tissue, add in two egg yolks, and mix it all together with the meat. Add another two egg yolks and mince it up all together. Season with pepper, nutmeg, ginger, and coriander. Put some strained hen stock, without any herbs at all, in a little pot or casserole. Make meatballs the size of small Cermeña pears.

o cazuela, y harás las albondiguillas de tamaño de cermeñas: y no han de cocer más de dos hervores, ni han de estar hechas, sino tener aparejado el recado: y cuando tu señor pidiere la comida, (53v) entonces se han de hacer; porque si se hacen antes se ponen morenas un poco, y si se sirven en acabándose de hacer, van muy blancas. Estas albondiguillas no han de llevar ningún género de verdura, ni azafrán; porque lo que se pretende es, que salgan muy blancas: has de tener una buñolera con que las hacer,[94] como quien hace buñuelos, que de la misma manera se pueden hacer. Hase de cuajar con dos yemas de huevos, y un poco de zumo de limón. Estas son las que se sirven más ordinariamente al Rey nuestro señor.[95]

[64] *Otras Albondiguillas.*

Si quisieres hacer otras albondiguillas de ternera, que parezcan de ave, pica la ternera: luego echa un poquito de pan blanco en remojo en leche: luego pica un poco de tocino gordo, y un poquito de riñonada de carnero que sea fresca del día: luego echa el pan con ello, y pícalo todo junto: y luego echarás un par (54r) de huevos, y píquese muy bien, y mézclese con la carne, y píquese mucho, y échale otro par de huevos, o los que fueren menester, y sazona con pimienta, y nuez, y jengibre, y echa unas gotas de leche en la carne, y echarás caldo colado en una olla, o cazuela, y harás albondiguillas, mojando la buñolera en leche, mezclado con un poco de caldo, y echarás unas gotas de leche dentro de las albondiguillas: con sólo esto saldrán tan blancas como las de las pechugas de aves. A estas no se ha de echar ningún género de agrio, ni se han de cuajar con huevos, porque sin ello tienen muy buen gusto. Desta carne puedes hacer relleno con redaño[96] de carnero, y asarlos en tortera.

---

94 Here, Martínez Montiño points out that the same instrument used for making *buñuelos* [puffs] should be used for forming the meatballs.
95 Note how Martínez Montiño once again specifies the king's taste.
96 For more information on *redaño* [mesentery/caul fat], see 170n49.

They shouldn't be brought to a boil more than twice. Actually, they shouldn't even be made, rather have the mixture ready to go, and when your lord is ready to eat, then make them. If you make them beforehand, they will turn a little brown, but if you serve them right after you make them, they are still white. These meatballs (with poultry) should not have any type of herb or saffron, because the idea is for them to turn out as white as possible. You should have a puff scoop to make them, the one used for making puffs, because these can be made the same way. Thicken it with two egg yolks and a little lemon juice. These are what are most commonly served to our lord the king.

Other meatballs

If you want to make meatballs from veal so that they look like meatballs (made) from poultry, chop up the veal. Then soak a little bit of bread in milk. Then chop up the extra fatty fatback and a little mutton loin that is fresh that day, add the bread to it and chop it all up together. Then add a couple of eggs, dice it all up, and add it all to the meat and mince it all. Add in a couple more eggs, or however many necessary, and season with pepper, nutmeg, and ginger. Add a few drops of milk to the meat and some strained stock from a pot or a casserole. Make meatballs and dip the puff scoop in milk mixed with a little stock. Add a few drops of milk to the meatballs and with just these (steps) they will turn out as white as meatballs made with poultry breast. Do not add any sour juice nor thicken with eggs because without either they taste great. With this meat you can also make stuffing with mutton caul fat and roast in a covered tart pan.

[65] *Albondiguillas Castellanas.*

Toma una pierna de carnero, y pica la carne con tocino, y verdura, y cebolla cruda, y échale cuatro huevos con claras, y sazona con todas especias, (54v) y sal, y haz las albondiguillas, y pica verdura, y échasela dentro, y cueza cosa de hora y media, porque se cueza la verdura y cebolla que tiene: y cuando las quisieres servir, cuájalas con huevos y acedo, apartando primero la flor:[97] y después que estén en el plato, echa la flor por encima.

[66] *Albondiguillas Reales.*

Picarás carne de ternera con un pedazo de tocino gordo, y sazónalo con todas especias, y cuatro huevos crudos. Luego tendrás yemas de huevos cocidas duras, hechas cuarterones y cañas de vaca en trozos, y hazlas albondiguillas tan grandes, como membrillos grandes, poniendo dentro de cada una unas pocas de cañas, y yemas de huevos, y ponlas a cocer en mucho caldo: y cuando las quisieres servir, sácalas en el plato, y ábrelas por medio, porque se parezcan las cañas y yemas. Éstas se han de cuajar con yemas de huevos y acedo:[98] (55r) y si rellenases un par de pollos desta misma carne, y los cocieses, y después los asentases en el plato, partidos también por medio, componiendo el plato con albóndigas, y los pollos, no sería menester otros adherentes. Y con esto no es menester tratar más desta materia; porque de cualquiera carne las podrás hacer: a su tiempo, tornaremos a tratar otro poco de otras albondiguillas.[99]

---

97 Although Covarrubias has translated *acedo* in more general terms as "lo áspero, desabrido que tiene punta, como el vinagre" [harsh, unpleasant with a sharp finish, like vinegar] (173), I have specifically translated it as *sorrel juice*, given the linguistic connection between *acedo* and *acedera*. I wish to thank Vicky Hayward for first making this connection. Also, in the recipe "Un platillo de cabrito" [A kid dish], Martínez Montiño qualifies the type of *acedo* with the adjective *agrio*, again leading me to belief that *acedo* is a specific juice and not another generic term for *sour juice*: "échale acedo que esté un poquito agrio" [add sorrel juice that is a little sour] (582; 583). Martínez Montiño uses this term in fourteen recipes, unlike the more general *agrio* [sour, sour juice] that appears one hundred times. For more information on the flor, see 65.

98 These instructions for thickening with egg yolk and sorrel juice refer to adding them to the leftover juices and broth to create a sauce for the meatballs.

99 At the close of this recipe, Martínez Montiño references other parts of the cookbook. He also seems to close this section out, designating it as the end of a chapter.

Castilian meatballs

Take a leg of mutton and mince the meat with fatback, herbs, and raw onion. Add in four whole eggs and season with all spices and salt. Make the meatballs, mince more herbs, and put a little in the centre. Cook for about an hour and a half so that the herbs and onion inside get cooked. When you want to serve them, thicken with eggs and sorrel juice; first remove the flor. After they are on the platter, sprinkle the flor on top.

Royal meatballs

Mince leg of veal with a piece of extra fatty fatback and season with all spices. Add four raw eggs. Then take four hard-boiled eggs that have been quartered and bits of beef marrow and make meatballs as big as large quince. Put in each centre some beef marrow and hard-boiled egg yolk. Put them on to boil in a lot of broth. When you are ready to serve them, put them on the plate and cut them in half so that you can see the marrow and yolk. These should be thickened with egg yolk and sorrel juice. If you stuff a couple of chickens with this same meat, cook them, set them on the plate, also split in half, and put the plate together with meatballs and chicken, you won't need to add anything else. With this I have nothing further to add on this subject because you can do this with any meat. A little later on we will return with a few other types of meatballs.

[67] *Una Liebre enlebrada.*[100]

Tomarás una liebre que sea recién muerta, y desollarla has muy limpiamente: y luego le sacarás la asadura,[101] y la echarás en un poco de agua: y si tuviere sangre la liebre, recógesela, enjuagándola por de dentro con un poco de vinagre, y échalo donde está la asadura. Luego harás la liebre pedazos, y échalos también con el [*sic*] asadura, porque se desangre. Luego sácalos de allí, y échalos en agua clara, adonde se lave muy bien. Luego tomarás un poco de tocino cortado (55v) en dados, y fríelo en la sartén con un poco de cebolla. Luego echa allí los pedazos de la liebre, y ahóguense un poco. Luego échalos en una olla. Luego colarás el agua y vinagre adonde estuvieron los pedazos de la liebre, y asadura, por un cedacillo, o estameña, y échalo en la olla, y échale un poco de vino, y sazona con todas especias, y canela, y sal, y échale más agua si fuere menester, cuanto se cubra la liebre, y échale un cuarterón de azúcar, o un poco de miel que esté bien dulce, y cueza hasta que esté bien cocida: y con sólo esto estará la salsa bien negra y espesa, sin echarle otra cosa ninguna: y si la liebre no tuviere sangre, quemarás un poco de harina, y desatarla has con caldo. A esta lebrada le podrás echar un poco de ajo, unos pocos de cominos si quisieres: y si quieres hacer esta lebrada agria, has de aparejar la liebre, como está dicho, y sazonar con todas especias, salvo canela, y echarle has un poco de (56r) ajo, y cominos. Hanse de servir estas lebradas sobre rebanadas de pan tostados y si quisieres tostar unas pocas de almendras con cáscara, y majarlas, y desatarlas con el caldo de la lebrada dulce, será bueno, porque le da muy buen gusto.

[68] *Olla de Liebre.*[102]

Cortarás la liebre en pedazos, y lavarse has muy bien, y freirás tocino en dados, y luego echarás los pedazos de la liebre en la sartén, y darle has dos vueltas sobre la lumbre, y échala en una olla, y échale agua que se cubra, y sazona de sal, y échale unos garbanzos: y cuando esté la liebre a medio cocer, échale de todas verduras,[103] y dos cebollas enteras, y una cabeza de ajos, y unos pocos de cominos, y de todas

---

100 *Lebrada* is a sauce or condiment for hare. Before Martínez Montiño, it also appeared in Nola, but the ingredients differ substantially.
101 *Asadura* or *asadurilla* [pluck] refers to the internal upper organs of an animal, specifically to the heart, liver, and lungs. Today this term is sometimes mistakenly used to mean all organ meats and sometimes all variety meats. Later, in the recipe "Otro platillo de cabezuelas de cabrito" [Another goat head dish], *asadurilla* refers only to the lungs and liver (332; 333).
102 In his work on the Navarrese cook Antonio Salsete, Fernando Serrano Larráyoz points out the similarities between this recipe and the one that opens Salsete's cookbook, *El cocinero religioso instruido en aprestar las comidas de carne, pescado, yerbas y potajes a su comunidad* (162).
103 *Todas verduras* refers to a mixture of spearmint, cilantro, and parsley as indicated in his recipe "Cazuela de truchas" [Trout stew] (392; 393).

Hare with lebrada *sauce*

Take a hare that has recently been slaughtered, cleanly skin it and then remove the pluck. Place it in water. If the hare has blood, collect it by rinsing the insides with a little vinegar; also pour some in with the pluck. Next, chop the hare into pieces and toss them in with the pluck so the blood can drain. Take them out and place them in clean water and wash everything well. Next, take some cubed fatback and fry it in a frying pan with a little onion. Then add all the pieces of hare and lightly sauté them. Then put everything in a pot. Next, drain the water and vinegar where you had the hare and pluck through a sieve or cheesecloth and add it to the pot with a little wine. Season with all spices, cinnamon, and salt and add more water if necessary so that the hare is covered. Add in a quarter pound of sugar and some honey so that it is very sweet. Boil until it's well done. With just this you will have a thick, dark sauce; there's no need to add anything else. If the hare has no blood, then burn a little flour and thin it with stock. You can add garlic and a little cumin to this *lebrada* sauce if you like. If you want to give the *lebrada* sauce a sour touch, prepare the hare as stated above and season with all spices, but not with cinnamon, and add in a little garlic and cumin. You should serve this hare with *lebrada* sauce on toasted slices of bread, and if you want to toast some almonds in their shells, grind them, and then thin with some stock from the unseasoned hare, it will turn out well because it will make it taste really good.

Hare stew

Chop the hare into pieces and thoroughly wash it. Fry cubed pieces of fatback and then add the hare to the frying pan and turn it over a couple of times over the flame. Then transfer to a pot and cover with water. Season with salt, add in some garbanzos, and when the hare is half cooked, add in all types of green-leaf vegetables, two whole onions, a head of garlic, a little cumin, and all spices. When it

especias, y de que esté cocida, sácala sobre una sopa blanca.[104] Esta liebre podrás cocer con nabos, y sazonarás con todas especias, y alcaravea y verdura con tocino: y si fuere en tiempo que no hubiere nabos, échale (56v) de todas verduras enteras con sus cebollas, y ajos, hierbabuena, y perejil, y sazona con todas especias.

[69] *Gigote de Liebre.*[105]

Asarás la liebre, y después de asada descarnarla has toda la carne, y picarla has sobre el tablero, y asentarás la cabeza de la liebre con los cuatro delanteros en el plato sobre unas rebanadas de pan tostadas. Luego pondrás lo picado a un lado, de manera que esté acomodado con la otra media liebre: luego harás una pebrada en una sartén, echando medio cuartillo de vino tinto, un poco de vinagre, un poco de caldo, y cuatro onzas de azúcar, y sazonarás con pimienta, y un poquito de clavo y jengibre, y canela, y cueza un poco hasta que el azúcar comience a tomar punto, y échala por encima de la liebre picada, y échale un poquito de sal, y pon el plato sobre una poca de lumbre, y sírvelo caliente. Este gigote es muy bueno (57r) con aceite y vinagre, y pimienta, y un poco de caldo en lugar de la pebrada.

[70] *Empanadas de Liebre.*[106]

Ya se sabe que las liebres son buenas empanadas muy bien mechadas, y empanadas de masa negra. Si quieres empanar esta liebre picada, descarnarla has toda la carne, y picarla has con tocino gordo, y sazonarás con todas especias, y un poquito de vinagre, y un poco de mejorana, é hisopillo, picado todo. Luego tiende una hoja de masa negra, y asentarás la liebre descarnada, y encima della acomodarás la carne picada sobre los huesos de la liebre, de manera que torne a estar en su misma forma, como si estuviera entera. Luego tender otra hoja, y echársela encima de la liebre, y cerrarla con su repulgo, y cocella en el horno. Ésta se come fría, y si quisieres echarle unos pocos de cominos, no estaría mala.

---

104 There is no recipe for "Sopa blanca" [White sops] in the cookbook, most likely because it was such a basic sauce for sops. In the recipe "Perdices asadas con aceite" [Roast partridge with oil], Martínez Montiño describes a white sauce that is most likely the same one used for "sopa blanca": "luego tomarás un poco de buen aceite, echarle has dos partes de agua, y échale sal de manera, que esté salada" [then take a little good oil, add two parts of water and enough salt so that it's salty, and mix it very well until it turns white] (164; 165).

105 This recipe is very similar to the earlier "Gigote de Liebres" [Minced hare] (154; 155). Both include instructions for pepper sauce. Here, Martínez Montiño gives additional instructions on presentation of the dish.

106 For images of this recipe, see Appendix 3.7.

is done, ladle over white sops. This hare can be cooked with turnips and seasoned with all spices, caraway, and some green-leaf vegetables with fatback. If turnips are not in season, add in whole green-leaf vegetables with onion, garlic, spearmint, and parsley, and season with all spices.

Minced hare meat

Roast a hare and once roasted, pull off all the meat and chop it up on the cutting board. Set the hare head with its four feet on a plate over toasted slices of bread. Then put the minced part on one side so that it goes well with the other half of the hare. Next, make a pepper sauce in the frying pan by adding a half pint of red wine, a little vinegar, a little broth, and four ounces of sugar. Season with pepper, a little clove and ginger, and cinnamon. Boil a little, until the sugar begins to thicken. Ladle on top of the minced hare and sprinkle a little salt. Put the plate over a low flame and serve hot. This minced meat is really good with oil and vinegar, pepper, and a little broth instead of the pepper sauce.

Hare empanada

It is well known that well-larded hares make good empanadas, the dark dough empanadas. If you want to make minced hare meat into an empanada, pull off all the meat and mix in extra fatty fatback. Season it with all spices, a little vinegar, a little marjoram, and winter savory all minced together. Then roll out a layer of dark dough and set the hare with the meat removed on it and on top place the minced meat over the hare bones so that it returns to its same shape, as if it were whole. Then roll out another layer and place it on top of the hare. Crimp the seams and bake it in the oven. This is eaten cold and if you want to add in some cumin, it wouldn't taste bad at all.

Esta liebre podrás empanar picada y (57v) sazonada (como está dicho) y meterla en un vaso de masa negra, o blanca, como quisieres.[107] Esto no ha de llevar hueso ninguno, antes ha de llevar en medio de la carne unas mechas de tocino algo gordas a lo largo: y si la quisieres servir caliente échale salsa negra, como si fuera pastelón de venado.[108]

[71] *Plato de Albondiguillas fritas.*[109]

Tomarás cuatro libras de ternera de pierna, las dos harás carbonadillas muy delgadas, y golpeadas con la vuelta del cuchillo, y mecharlas muy bien, y échalas en adobo. Luego picarás las otras dos libras, y sazonarás como para albondiguillas con sus especias y huevos, y tocino. Luego harás albondiguillas enharinadas con harina, y iraslas poniendo sobre un tablero. Luego pondrás a asar las carbonadillas sobre las parrillas: y entretanto que se asa freirás las albondiguillas, así enharinadas como están en buena manteca de puerco: y (58r) luego freirás picatostes, de pan blanco angostos, y de todo esto irás armando el plato con picatostes, y albondiguillas, y carbonadillas, entremetiendo uno con otro: y luego echarle por encima zumo de limón, o naranja: y adornar el plato con algunos higadillos fritos. Desta misma carne, sazonada para albondiguillas podrás freír rebozándola con huevos, y con unas torrijas: y desta carne frita harás de presto un plato, y echarle has agrio de limón por encima: y si quisieres echarle azúcar y canela, podrás, añadiendo más agrio de limón, o naranja, y tendrá muy buen gusto. No han de ser albondiguillas, sino unos bocados un poco largos.

[72] *Albondiguillas de pan rallado y grasa.*

Echarás a cocer un riñón de ternera, y cuando esté medio cocido, sácalo, y pica la grasa,[110] y un poco de tocino gordo muy picado: y luego le echarás (58v) tres partes de pan rallado, y sazonarás con todas especias y sal, y echarle has cantidad de yemas de huevos: y desto harás unas albondiguillas un poco grandes, cuájalas con yemas de huevo, y un poco de acedo, y sírvelas sobre rebanadillas de pan blanco.

---

107 *Un vaso de masa* refers to a crust or a piece of dough shaped in the form of a pie. The size may vary.
108 Martínez Montiño includes a recipe for venison empanadas but not specifically a venison pie (300; 301). However, he does state that the boar recipes, which include a pie, can be used for venison as well and also explains how to make *salsa negra* (292; 293). Likewise, in "Grullas asadas" [Roast crane], he discusses sauces and modes of preparation similar to those for venison pie as well (150–2; 151–3).
109 For an image of this recipe, see Appendix 3.8.
110 Although he says "pica la grasa" [mince the fat], I believe he meant to say "pica el riñón" [mince the kidney], to which he then adds minced fatback.

You can also make minced and seasoned hare empanada (as stated above) and stuff it in a crust of dark or light dough, whichever you prefer. This shouldn't have any bones in it; rather, in the middle of the meat, lay some fatty strips of fatback across it. If you want to serve it hot, add in black sauce, as if it were venison pie.

Dish of fried meatballs

Take four pounds of leg of veal, two for grilling very thin slices, which are pounded out with the back of the knife, well larded, and marinated. Then mince the other two pounds and season them like meatballs with their spices, eggs, and fatback. Shape into little meatballs dredged in flour and place them one by one on the cutting board. Next, start grilling the meat on the grill and while that is cooking, fry the meatballs as they are with the flour in a good-quality lard. Then fry slices of white bread, cut thinly. Arrange all of these on a plate, interspersing slices of fried bread, meatballs, and slices of grilled meat, one after another. Sprinkle with lemon or orange juice and garnish the plate with fried poultry livers. With this same meat with meatball seasoning, you can fry them by first dredging them in egg and (serving) with torrijas. Immediately arrange this fried meat on a plate and sprinkle with lemon on top, and if you want to sprinkle with cinnamon and sugar, you can, but also add a little more lemon or orange juice and it will turn out very tasty. These should not be tiny meatballs but rather a little larger than bite-sized.

Meatballs with breadcrumbs and fat

Put on to boil a veal kidney and when it is parboiled, remove it, mince the kidney and a little bit of minced extra fatty fatback. Then add in three parts of breadcrumbs and season with all spices and salt. Add in several egg yolks and from this you will make bigger-sized meatballs. Thicken with egg yolks and a little sorrel juice. Serve over slices of white bread.

[73] *Platillo de cañas de Vaca.*

Tomarás los tuétanos de tres, o cuatro cañas de vaca, y harás los trocitos de una pulgada de largo, y pondráslos en un cacillo, y echarle has media libra de azúcar, y un poquito de verdura picada, y un poquito de vino blanco, y el zumo de medio limón, y sazonarás con todas especias y canela, y echarle has dos cucharadas de caldo, y un poco de azafrán, y una migaja de sal, y cueza dos o tres hervores. Luego tendrás un poco de pan rallado, y batirás dos docenas de huevos con claras, y echarlos has sobre las cañas, y echa un poco de pan rallado (59r) y azúcar y canela, todo revuelto por encima de los huevos, y ponlo al fuego sobre un poco de brasa, y cúbrelo con una cobertera, y échale lumbre abajo y arriba, y cueza poco a poco hasta que esté cuajado con buena color encima. Luego tomarás una paleta, y desapegarlo [*sic*] has del cazo, y tendrás en el plato un poco de hojaldrado frito, o hojuelas, y echarás el platillo sobre ello; de manera que quede la flor hacia arriba:[111] y tendrás tres o cuatro cañutos de huevos encañutados,[112] y meterlos has por el bollo de las cañas para adornarle: y si no tuviere cañutos, ni hojaldrado, con unas torrijas lo podrás adornar. Cómese caliente, porque frío no vale nada.

[74] *Fruta de Cañas.*

Tomarás dos cañas de vaca, que sean buenas, y saca los tuétanos dellas, y pártelas en trocitos, y dales un hervor: y luego sácalos, y toma una docena de yemas de huevos duros, échalas con (59v) las cañas, y échale un cuarterón de azúcar molido, y canela, y mézclalo todo muy bien. Luego harás una masilla fina sin dulce, y tenderla has sobre el tablero, y harás empanadillas chiquitas deste batido de cañas sin repulgo, sino cortarás con la cortadera al derredor de la empanadilla, mojándola primero con las plumas, y un poco de agua, y golpearle has los bordes con el sello de la cortadura,[113] y picarle has con un alfiler por encima: y luego fríelas con mucho cuidado que no se rompa ninguna en la sartén, porque echará a perder la manteca, y ponlas en el plato, y échales por encima un poco de almíbar, o una poca de buena miel, y su azúcar raspado. Este plato se sirve caliente.

---

111 For more information on the flor, see 65.
112 Martínez Montiño includes the recipe for "Huevos encañutados" [Sweet egg canutos] later in the cookbook (596; 597). They are deep-fried pastry tubes, similar to cannoli, but with a candied egg yolk thread filling instead of a cream-based one.
113 *El sello de la cortadura* [the seal of the trimmer]. Think of a pie server with a decorative hole in it. That seal would then be pushed into the edge of the dough to make a decorative pattern and seal the empanada at the same time. For a visual, see "Los cuchillos en la historia de Albacete."

A dish of beef marrow

Remove the marrow from three or four beef marrow bones and chop into one-inch-long pieces. Place them in a saucepan and add half a pound of sugar, a little minced green herbs, a little white wine, and juice from half a lemon. Season with all spices and cinnamon, add two tablespoons of stock, a little saffron, a pinch of salt and bring to a boil two or three times. Next, have some breadcrumbs, beat two dozen whole eggs and pour over the marrow. Sprinkle on top of the eggs the breadcrumbs mixed with some cinnamon and sugar. Put it on the fire over a little bit of red-hot embers, cover it with a lid, and add heat above and below. Slowly cook until the eggs are set and it has good colouring on top. Then take a spatula and unstick it from the pan. Have a plate with some fried puff pastry dough or pastry sheets and place the little dish on it so that the flor is face up. Have three or four canutos of sweetened eggs and stick them in the holes of the bone marrow as a garnish. If you don't have canutos or puff pastry, you can garnish them with torrijas. Eat them hot because they don't taste good at all when they are cold.

Fried dough with marrow filling

Take two beef marrow bones of good quality, remove the marrow, chop it into pieces, and boil them. Then remove them. Take a dozen hard-boiled eggs and add them to the marrow. Add in a quarter pound of ground sugar and cinnamon and mix it all very well. Then make a fine, unsweetened dough and roll it out on the table top. Make mini turnovers with the marrow filling, but don't crimp it; rather, cut around the turnover with a trimmer, but first, using feathers, wet the edges with a little water. Press the seal of the trimmer into the edges and with a pin stick some holes on top. Then fry them very carefully so that nothing falls apart in the frying pan, because the lard will spoil. Put them on a plate and drizzle some simple syrup or a little bit of good honey on top and the right amount of grated sugar. This dish should be served hot.

[75] *Un plato de madrecillas de Gallinas rellenas.*

Tomarás las madrecillas, y cortarle has un poquito por la parte de adonde (60r) son más anchas, que es la overa, y meterás por allí el dedo con mucho tiento, y irás arrollando la madrecilla en el dedo, rompiéndole unas telillas que tiene, y tornarás a lavar: y luego irás metiendo el relleno por lo más ancho con mucho tiento, porque son muy fáciles de romper, y luego con las puntas que sobrare darás un ñudo, y quedará redondo como rosquilla, y echarlas has a cocer por espacio de una hora. Luego tostarlas has sobre las parrillas, y asentarlas has sobre una sopa dorada, y adornarás el plato con algunas mollejas de cabrito, o higadillos, o turmas de carnero fritas. Este plato es bueno para el día de Sábado,[114] haciendo el relleno con higadillos de gallina, o asadurillas de cabrito. Ha de ser este relleno hecho de la manera que se hace para pollos asados, y por tenerlo dicho, no digo aquí de la manera que se ha de hacer.[115]

[76] *Potaje de Acenorias.* (60v)

Las acenorias es una potajería, que para solas no son muy buenas: en día de pescado[116] las podrás cocer con agua y sal; y luego hacerlas rajitas, y ahogarlas con manteca de vacas, o buen aceite con su cebolla, y echarlas en una olla o cazuela, y sazonarlas con todas especias, y sal, y echarle agua caliente cuanto se cubran, y echarle dulce de miel, o azúcar, y vinagre, que estén bien dulces y agrías. Luego freirás un poco de harina, de manera que esté bien quemada, y desátala con el mismo caldo de las acenorias, y trábalas con ella: y si quisieres haz unos huevos estrellados duros, de uno en uno y échaselos dentro, y cuezan un poco. Luego sirve acenorias y huevos todo revuelto.

---

114 Saturday meals consistently reflected *partial* abstinence practices in which limited animal products like offal could be consumed. This practice contrasted to those in place for "fish days," when full abstinence was practised, and "meat days," when no abstinence was practised. For more information, see the Introduction (16).

115 Martínez Montiño is referring to the recipe "Pollos rellenos" [Chicken with stuffing] that explains how to make standard stuffing and provides a few variations as well (158; 159).

116 *Día de pescado* refers to those days in which meat and many meat products are not consumed. As one can see in the recipe, *manteca de vacas* [butter] and *aceite* [oil] are substitutes for *tocino* [fatback]. Other substitutes include vegetables or some by-products for meat, cheese for bone marrow, and garbanzo broth for meat stock. In fact, garbanzo broth is mentioned in almost two dozen different recipes, leading one to believe that garbanzos were most likely part of a regular diet, possibly more for the staff than for royalty.

A dish of stuffed hen oviduct

Take the oviduct and make a slit in the widest part, which is the uterus. Carefully insert your finger and begin rolling your finger on the inside of the oviduct, detaching the little membranes that are there. Clean it out once again. Then begin inserting the stuffing at the widest opening, being very careful as it is very easy to rip. Then, with the ends left over, make a knot and it will look round like a ring-shaped pastry. Let it boil for about an hour. Then finish on the grill and set them on golden sops. Garnish the plate with some kid sweetbreads, poultry liver, or fried sheep testicles. This is a good dish for a Saturday because the stuffing is made out of hen liver or kid pluck. This stuffing should be made the same way as it is for roast chicken, and since I've already written it down, I won't explain here how to make it.

Carrot stew

Carrots are a vegetable that by themselves are not very tasty. On a fish day, you can cook them in salted water. Then cut into thin slices and sauté them in butter or good oil and the right amount of onion. Then put them in a pot or a casserole and season them with all spices, salt, and add in enough hot water to cover them. Add in sweetener, either honey or sugar, and vinegar so that it is really sweet and sour. Next, fry a little flour so that it burns and thin it with some of the carrot broth. Then thicken the carrots with it. If you want, make some hard, fried eggs, one by one you can add them and let everything cook. Next, serve the carrots and eggs all mixed together.

[77] *Cazuelas de Acenorias, y pescado Cecial.*

Cocerás las acenorias con agua y sal; luego las harás rajitas, dejando (61r) el corazón: luego cocerás pescado cecial en tarazones,[117] y enharinarlo has, y fríelo, y luego enharina las acenorias, y fríelas también: luego asienta el pescado y acenorias en una cazuela, y pica un poco de verdura, perejil, hierbabuena, y cilantro verde,[118] y májalo en el almirez con un migajón de pan tostado, y remojado en vinagre, y echa allí de todas especias, y canela, y desata esta salsa con agua caliente, y échale miel, o azúcar y vinagre, que esté bien dulce y agria. Luego echa esta salsa en un cazo, y dale un hervor, y échala en la cazuela del pescado, y cueza un poco, y pruébala de sal, y sírvela en la misma cazuela: y si quisieres echar huevos estrellados duros en esta cazuela con el pescado y las acenorias, no será malo. Esta suerte de acenorias, y pescado, se llama sobrehúsa:[119] y si hubiere muchos platos que hacer, se puede hacer en una pieza grande, y de allí ir haciendo los platos. Y advierte, que cuando tuvieres las acenorias, y el pescado (61v) frito que has de freír un poco de cebolla muy menuda en el mismo aceite, y echarla en la salsa de la cazuela.

[78] *Ensalada de Acenorias.*

Las acenorias para ensalada se han de buscar de las negras,[120] y lavarlas, y mondarlas de las barbillas, y cortarles el pezón, y la colilla, y meterlas en una olla las colas para bajo, y que estén muy apretadas, y poner la olla en el rescoldo, y echarle lumbre al derredor, y por encima, y se asarán muy bien. Luego sácalas y móndales unas cascaritas que tienen muy delgadas, y sazónalas de sal, y sírvelas con aceite y vinagre, y sírvelas calientes: y si las quisieres echar azúcar del azucarero podrás.[121] La olla ha de estar boca abajo.

Hanse de poner estas acenorias adonde están las borrajas; y hanse de hacer rajitas.

---

117 For more on the origins of *tarazón*, see the entry in the Glossary.
118 In recipes that include both herbs and spices, Martínez Montiño almost always adds herbs first, then spices, and then salt, as is the case here. Herbs and spices are never mixed together before being added to a dish. Today, spices are normally added first, since they need time to develop, and herbs later, since they lose their flavour the longer they are cooked.
119 For Covarrubias, whose work was first published the same year as this cookbook, *sobrehúsa* is described as a sauce that is ladled on top of a dish, very different from what Martínez Montiño is describing here (Covarrubias 942). Today *sobrehúsa* is typically known as an Andalusian fish stew with onions, garlic, paprika, and other spices. However, there are other versions today with beans, sausage, and eggs, and no fish. For more on the history of this dish, see Arteaga.
120 The mention of black carrots raises the question of different varieties. Andrés Laguna, in his 1555 commentary on Discórides' entry for carrots, mentions the rich variety of carrot colours: "Hallanse entre la hortense quatro especies, o diferencias: porque una produce la raíz blanca pro todas partes, otra roja, otra de color naranjado; y finalmente otra por defuera negra, y por dedentro sanguinea" [Among this garden vegetable there are four species, or differences: because one produces an entirely white root, another red, another orange; and finally another one that is black on the outside, and blood red on the inside] ("De la pastinaca" III.LV). For a fascinating study on carrot varietals that continued to be readily available in early twentieth-century Spain, see Guillot Ortiz.
121 The *azucarero* was a container designed for storing sugar. It had holes on the top so that sugar could be sprinkled onto a dish, much like a salt shaker today.

Carrot and salted hake stew

Boil the carrots in salted water. Then cut into thin slices, leaving the core. Then boil salted hake in pieces, dredge in flour, and fry it. Then dredge the carrots in flour and fry them too. Next set the fish and carrots in a casserole and chop up a few green herbs – parsley, spearmint, and cilantro – and grind them together in a mortar with the toasted insides of bread that has soaked in vinegar. Add to the mortar all spices and cinnamon. Thin this sauce with hot water, add honey or sugar and vinegar so that it is very sweet and sour. Next, put this sauce in a pan, bring it to a boil, and then add it to the casserole with the fish and let it simmer. Adjust the salt and serve in the same casserole. If you want to add some hard, fried eggs to the casserole with the fish and carrots, it wouldn't taste bad. This kind of carrot and fish [recipe] is called *sobrehúsa*. If you had to make many plates, you can make it all as one big dish and from there serve it onto plates. Also note that after you have fried the carrots and fish, you should sauté up a little minced onion in the same oil and add it to the sauce in the casserole.

Carrot salad

For carrots for a salad, look for black ones, wash them, scrub off the fine root threads, cut off the tops and bottoms, and place in a pot bottom-side down and all packed together. Place the pot in grey embers, spread the heat around and on top, and they will roast up well. Then remove them, peel off the fine outer layer, and season with salt. Serve hot with oil and vinegar. If you like, you can sprinkle them with sugar from the sugar shaker. The pot should be face down.

Carrots should be plated with borage and cut into little strips.

[79] *Fruta rellena.*[122]

(62 r) Harás un batido de huevos, y harina, y leche, como está dicho en la fruta de hierros:[123] y tendrás un hierro a manera de hongo, y harás muchas frutas con él, calentándolo en la manteca, o aceite donde se ha de freír la fruta. Luego tener un paño de lienzo doblado dos o tres veces, y enjugar el hierro en él. Luego mojarlo en el batido, y meterlo en la sartén, y desapegarse ha del hierro, y fríase: estas frutas de hongos rellénalas de todas conservas y huevos hilados, y luego les pondrás otros hongos encima, como coberteras: y destos hongos rellenos armarás el plato con hojuelas y huevos hilados. Luego harás una espuma de claras de huevos, y leche, y azúcar, y cubrirás con ella unas ramitas de romero, y hincarlas has en un poco de masa: ponlas a enjugar en el horno: hincarlas has por entre las frutas rellenas, y ráspale un poco de azúcar por encima, o échale un poco de maná en lugar de azúcar, y parecerá muy (62v) bien.[124] Advierte, que en lugar de la fruta podrás rellenar toronjas conservadas. Éstas en el capítulo de las conservas las hallarás escritas, como se han de conservar.[125]

[80] [*Toronja rellena.*][126]

Estas toronjas rellenas podrás hacer de carne, endulzándolas, como para conservar. Luego hacer un relleno de carne de ternera, o carnero, picando la carne muy bien con tocino: y luego perdigarla en un cacillo con una gota de caldo, y sacarla,

---

122 As has been noted in a couple of other instances, this recipe is really two recipes under one title. The first part, as the title suggests, deals with stuffed sweet fritters, but the majority of the recipe explains how to make candied toronja and what to fill them with.
123 Although no recipe has the title "Fruta de hierro" [Fried dough with an iron rosette], in "Fruta de borrajas" [Deep-fried borage], Martínez Montiño explains that the same batter is used for both (376; 377).
124 *Maná* [manna] is the food God provided the Israelites in the desert for forty days and nights (Ex. 16:11–36), but in the seventeenth century it was "una especialidad de confiteros, más pequeña que la gragea" [a speciality of candy makers, smaller than sprinkles] (Valles Rojo 423).
125 The recipe referred to is called "Toronjas" [Toronjas] (222–4; 223–5), but he also explains how to prepare them in the last paragraph of this very recipe.
126 Although today *toronja* translates as *grapefruit*, this translation is inadequate, because the grapefruit is really a cross between two different fruits that occurred in the Caribbean in the eighteenth century. Covarrubias explains that the toronja is a type of citron (969), though perhaps, more accurately, it is simply its own type of citrus fruit. Thus, I have decided to leave the word in its original to note that it is not grapefruit as we think of it today. In addition, this recipe for "Toronja rellena" [Stuffed toronja] is part of the "Fruta rellena" [Stuffed fried dough] recipe in every edition. I have added a title in brackets to signal to the reader today that this second part is a whole new recipe, not simply a variation of a recipe like those Martínez Montiño includes in many others.

Stuffed fried dough

Mix up a batter of eggs, flour, and milk as explained in the (section on) fried dough made with an iron rosette. Take a mushroom-shaped iron and make a lot of fried dough. First heat up the lard or oil in which you will fry the fried dough. Then fold up a cloth two or three times and wipe the iron dry with it. Then dip it in the batter, drop it into the frying pan, and the batter should come off the iron and fry. This mushroom-shaped fried dough can then be filled with all types of preserves and candied egg yolk threads, and then place other mushrooms on top of them as lids. These stuffed mushrooms are arranged on a plate with sheets of pastry and candied egg yolk threads. Next make a froth of egg whites, milk, and sugar and use it to coat some sprigs of rosemary. Stick them in some dough and place in the oven to dry. Stick them between each of the stuffed fried dough [pieces] and grate a little sugar on top or use a little manna instead of sugar and it will look really good. Note that instead of fried dough you can fill preserved toronja. In the chapter on preserves, you will find this [recipe] and how to preserve them.

[*Stuffed toronja*]

These stuffed toronjas can be made with meat, sweetening them as if preserving them. Then make the filling with veal or mutton, mincing it with fatback. Brown it in a saucepan with a drop of broth, remove it, mince again, and season with

y tornarla a picar, y sazonarla de especias, y sal, y meterle unos trocitos de cañas mezclados con la carne, y métele huevos los que pareciere ser necesario, y que esté la carne como para pasteles de tetilla, o pasteles de escudilla,[127] y échale dulce de azúcar y agrio de limón, y rellena toronjas, y ráspales azúcar por encima, y mételas en el horno sobre unas rebanadas de pan, y dale lumbre abajo y arriba, y déjalas cuajar muy bien, y ráspales azúcar por encima. (63r)

Advierte, que este relleno de las toronjas podrás hacer, como se hace para rellenar pollos, haciéndolo agridulce, y le podrás meter pasas de Corinto, y piñones, y cañas de vaca.

También lo podrás hacer con yemas de huevos duras, mezclados con otros tanto de pasta de mazapán, y cañas de vaca, todo majado junto: luego meterle unas yemas de huevos crudas, y sazonarlo de especias, y canela, y zumo de limón, y las toronjas han de ser conservadas. Estas se podrán endulzar y conservar, y rellenar todo en medio día, aunque sean acabadas de cortar del árbol. Hase de hacer una lejía, y aclararla, y darles un cocimiento en ella: luego darles tres, o cuatro cocimientos en agua dulce: y con esto se pondrán tiernas y dulces. Luego tener almíbar, y cocerlas en él, y luego rellenarlas de lo que quisieres.

[81] (63v) *Costrada de asadurillas de Cabrito.*[128]

Tomarás tres asadurillas de cabrito, y envolverlas has en los redaños, y ásalas: luego pícalas muy bien, y sazona con todas especias, y zumo de limón, y seis onzas de azúcar, y métele huevos crudos, cosa de cuatro, o los que fueren menester, y una caña de vaca picada: y si la quisieres echar dos, o tres onzas de almendras tostadas con cáscara y muy bien majadas, le dará muy buen gusto. Luego harás tu costrada, haciendo un poco de masa fina con yemas de huevos, y manteca, y un poco de

---

127 The recipe for "Pasteles de tetilla" [Teat pies] can be found on 278; 279. While there is no recipe for "Pasteles de escudilla" [Bowl-shaped pies], Martínez Montiño does explain how to make them in "Platillo de asadurillas de cabrito" [A dish of kid liver and lung]: "Estos se hacen cortando unos trocitos de un rollo de hojaldrado, y hacer unas como cubiertas de pastelillos, y ponerlos dentro en las escudillas, e irlos subiendo con el dedo pulgar, e igualarlos con los bordes de las escudillitas: luego henchirlos …" [These are made by cutting a sheet of pastry dough into small sections and making some as tops for little pies. Put them into bowls and, with your thumb, begin raising the edges and evening them out on the tops of the bowls. Then fill them …] (590; 591).

128 This recipe and all of Martínez Montiño's *costrada* recipes appear in Juan de Altamiras' 1745 cookbook, *Nuevo arte de cocina* (69). While Altamiras does include the instructions for making the *costrada* crust with grated sugar on top, he uses only one layer on the top and bottom and not the many layers of thin, flaky crust that Martínez Montiño uses. In only one other *costrada* recipe does Altamiras discuss the crust. For his other recipes, the *costrada* seems to refer to a whipped egg topping that is baked and thus forms the crust. For more information on Altamiras' *costradas*, see Hayward (*New Art of Cookery* 18–19).

spices and salt. Mix into the meat small bits of marrow and as many eggs as you think necessary. The meat should be like the meat for teat pies or bowl-shaped pies. Add in sugar as sweetener and lemon juice and stuff the toronjas. Grate sugar on top and place them in the oven over some slices of bread with the flame above and below and let them set nicely. Grate sugar on top.

Note that this toronja filling can be made like the stuffing for chickens, making it sweet and sour, and you can also add dried currants, pine nuts, and beef marrow.

You can also make it with hard-boiled egg yolks mixed with the same amount of marzipan paste and beef marrow all mashed together. Then add in some raw egg yolk, season with spices, cinnamon, and lemon juice. The toronja must be preserved. You can sweeten, preserve, and fill them all in a half day even if they were just picked from the tree. You should make a lye solution, dilute it, and boil them in it. Then boil them in fresh water three or four times. This is how they will turn out tender and sweet. Have some simple syrup and cook them in it. Then you are ready to fill them with whatever you like.

Puff pastry pie filled with kid pluck

Take three pieces of kid pluck, wrap them in caul fat, and roast them. Then chop them up very well and season with all spices, lemon juice, and six ounces of sugar. Add in raw eggs, about four or as many as needed, and minced marrow from one beef bone. If you want to add two to three ounces of almonds roasted in their shell and ground up, it will give it a very nice flavour. Next, make your puff pastry crust by mixing a delicate dough with egg yolk, lard, a little sugar, and a little

azúcar, y un poco de vino: y sóbala muy bien, hasta que haga correa. Luego unta una tortera, y ponle tres, o cuatro hojas abajo, y dos o tres arriba, y úntala con manteca, y ráspale azúcar por encima: de manera que la costrada ha de venir a llevar media libra de azúcar, y ocho huevos. (64r) Esta costrada podrás hacer de las asadurillas cocidas y picadas con tocino, y ahogadas, y sazónalas como está dicho en las otras.

Estas costradas se pueden hacer de ternera, y de cabrito, y de carnero, y de muchos pescados, poniendo buena manteca en lugar del tocino, y de las cañas de vaca.

[82] *Cómo se han de asar los Pajarillos gordos.*

Los pajarillos oncijeros[129] y vencejos, y zorzales, y tortolillas, y otros pajarillos tiernos se han de asar en asador delgado atravesados, o ponerlos en unas broquetas de hierro, o de caña, que quepan seis en cada una. Luego atarlas en el asador y han de llevar entre pájaro y pájaro una rebanadilla de tocino gordo, y pónganse a asar: y cuando estén asados, échales pan rallado, y sal por encima, de manera que queden bien cubiertos, y sírvelos con sus ruedas (64v) de limón: y podrás hacer una salsilla agridulce con un poco de azúcar y zumo de limón, y un poco de canela, y un poquito de pimienta y sal, y un poco de caldo. Esta salsilla es muy buena para todo género de asado, y para higadillos de gallina asados, o fritos, y para carbonadillas de ternera, y de aves, y particularmente para enfermos; porque los más dellos gustan desta salsilla; porque todo lo que es agridulce, es muy buen gusto.

[83] *Cazuela de Pajarillos.*

Freirás un poco de tocino en dados muy menudo: luego echa los pajarillos limpios y partidos por medio, o enteros, como quisieres, y échale un poco de cebolla picada muy menuda, y ahóguese todo junto, de manera que no se queme la cebolla. Luego échale caldo cuanto se cubran, o agua caliente: luego sazona con todas especias, y sal, y échales un poco de verdura picada, perejil, (65r) hierbabuena, y cilantro verde, o seco: y de que estén los pájaros cocidos, bate cuatro yemas de huevo, y un poco de vinagre, y cuaja la cazuela: y si no quisieres echar huevos, maja un poco de verdura con un migajoncillo de pan, como está dicho en los palominos ahogados, y en el carnero verde.

Esta cazuela se puede hacer de cabrito, y de pollos, o pichones, y de carnero, y de menudillos de aves, y de mollejas de ternera, y de cabrito, y de muchos pescados, gastando buena manteca en lugar de tocino, y se le puede echar algunas veces dulce, añadiendo más agrio.

---

129 The *Diccionario de autoridades* explains that the *oncejera* is a "cierto lazo que usan los cazadores, que llaman chucheros, para prender los páxaros pequeños, y cogerlos" [certain type of snare that hunters use, which they call *chucheros*, to snare the small birds, and catch them].

wine. Knead it a lot until it's elastic. Next, grease a covered tart pan, place three or four sheets on the bottom and two or three on top. Cover with lard and grate sugar on top. When done the puff pastry should have about half a pound of sugar and eight eggs. You can also make this puff pastry pie with boiled pluck that has been chopped up with fatback, sautéed, and seasoned as is explained in the other (recipes).

These puff pastry pies can be made of veal, kid, mutton, and many types of fish, using good lard instead of fatback and beef marrow.

How to roast small plump birds

Snared birds, swifts, thrushes, ground doves, and other tender small birds should be pierced with a thin spit and roasted or placed on iron or wooden skewers, which should fit six on each. Tie them to the spit and place a chunk of fatback between birds; then begin roasting. When they are done, sprinkle breadcrumbs and salt on top so that they're completely covered and serve with lemon wheels. You can make a sweet and sour sauce with a little sugar and lemon juice, a little cinnamon and broth, and very little salt and pepper. This sauce goes very well with all types of roasts, with grilled or fried hen livers, with grilled fillets of veal or poultry, and it is especially good for sick people. Most of them really like this sauce because everything sweet and sour is very tasty.

Small bird stew

Fry minced pieces of cubed fatback, then add in little birds that have been cleaned and are either halved or whole, however you prefer. Add in some minced onion and sauté everything together but don't let the onions burn. Then add in enough broth or hot water to cover it, season with all spices and salt, and add in some chopped green herbs – parsley, spearmint, and fresh cilantro or dried. Once the birds are cooked, whip four egg yolks with a little vinegar and thicken the stew. If you don't want to put in eggs, grind together some of the green herbs with the inside of bread as instructed in "Sautéed wild squab" and in "Green mutton stew."

This stew can be made with kid, chicken, squab, mutton, poultry giblets, kid or veal sweetbread, and many fish when good lard would be used instead of fatback. If at times you want to add sweetness, (also) add more sour.

[84] *Salsa Brenca.*[130]

Tomarás aves asadas, o pollos, o pichones, ú otra cualquiera volatería, y partirla has en cuartos: luego cortarás cebolla a lo largo, y fríela con manteca de vacas: luego echa dentro la volatería, y ahóguese todo muy bien: luego (65v) échale un poco de vino blanco y especias, y un poco de sal, y zumo de limón, y sírvela sobre rebanadillas de pan.

[85] *Sustancia asada.*

Esta sustancia después de sacada se le ha de quitar toda la grasa.

Asarás una pierna de carnero que sea recién muerto: y cuando esté asada, y no esté seca, sácala, y púnzala por muchas partes, de manera que pase el cuchillo de una parte a otra. Luego métela en una prensilla de nogal, y apriétala de manera que se quebranten los huesos, y sacarás más de medio cuartillo: y desta manera se hace de capones, y de aves.

[86] *Platillo de artaletes de Ternera.*

Tomarás tres libras de ternera de la pierna, y cortarás ocho, o diez chulletas della muy delgadas de dos dedos de ancho, y una ochava de largo,[131] y batirlas has con la vuelta del cuchillo, de manera (66r) que queden muy delgadas. Hanse de cortar al través de la hebra. En esto se gastará una libra de la ternera; ahora toma las otras dos libras, y pícalas muy bien en el tablero, como para pasteles,[132] y pica media libra de tocino con la carne de las dos libras de ternera, y métele tres huevos con claras, y sazona con todas especias, y sal: y de las dos partes desta carne sazonada, harás un albondigón grande, metiendo en medio dél cuatro yemas de huevos duras, hechas cuartos, y una caña de vaca hecha trocitos, y esto ha de quedar en medio del albondigón, y échalo a cocer en caldo, de manera que se cubra ahora de la una parte de la carne picada y sazonada que quedó, harás el relleno de los artaletes, tomando cuatro onzas de tocino gordo en rebanadillas, y échalo en la sartén, y fríase, y a medio freír échale media cebollita cortada a lo largo, y fríase un poco. Luego echa la carne picada en la sartén, y revuélvela con la paleta sobre (66v) la lumbre, hasta que esté bien perdigada. Luego échale tres huevos con claras, y

---

130 Today *brenca* refers to the stamens of saffron and formerly referred to *culantro*, a herb similar to cilantro, but neither of these ingredients is part of this poultry dish with lemon-wine sauce.

131 In early modern Spain an *ochava* referred to an eighth of a *vara*, which measured somewhere between three and three quarters and four and a half inches. For more on measurements, see Appendix 2, "On Measurements," Castaño Álvarez, and "Antiguas pesas y medidas."

132 By explaining that the meat should be minced in the same way it is for pie, Martínez Montiño attempts to clarify how the meat is prepared. This explanation also exemplifies the common knowledge his readers would have shared.

Brenca sauce

Take roasted poultry, chicken, squab, or any other fowl and quarter it. Slice an onion lengthwise and fry it in butter. Then add the fowl and thoroughly sauté everything. Add in some white wine and spices, a little salt, and lemon juice. Serve over slices of bread.

Essence from a roast

After this essence is strained off, all the fat should be removed.

Roast a leg of recently slaughtered mutton. When it's done but not dry, take it out, prick it all over so the knife goes straight through from one side to the other. Then put it in a walnut press and press it enough to break the bones. You should extract more than a half pint. You can do the same thing with capons and [other] poultry.

A dish of veal pinwheels

Take three pounds of veal shank and cut eight to ten thin fillets about two fingers wide and an *ochava* long. Pound them with the back of the knife so that they end up very thin. Cut across the grain. This will use up one pound of veal. Now take the remaining two pounds, mince them on the cutting board, as you would for pies, and add in half a pound of minced fatback. Add three whole eggs and season with all spices and salt. With two-thirds of this prepared meat, make one large meatball, adding into the middle of it four hard-boiled, quartered egg yolks and minced marrow from one beef bone. This should stay in the middle of the meatball. Then cook it in broth so that it's covered. Now, with the remaining part of minced and seasoned meat, you can make the filling for the pinwheels by taking four ounces of sliced fatback and putting it in the frying pan. Let it fry and when it's half-way cooked, add in half an onion, sliced lengthwise, and continue frying. Then add the minced meat to the pan, stirring it over the flame with a spatula until the meat is browned. Then add in three whole eggs, a little minced herbs,

un poquito de verdura picada, y revuélvelo todo sobre la lumbre hasta que esté bien seco. Luego sácalo al tablero, y pícalo muy bien, y métele dos huevos crudos, y mézclese bien, y échale un poco de zumo de limón, y pruébalo de sal y especias: y si le faltare algo échaselo, y echa sobre cada chulleta de la ternera un poco deste relleno, y arrollarla, y harás un artalete: y cada tres artaletes pondrás en una broquetilla de caña: y en teniendo hecho los artaletes ponlos en una cazuela untada con manteca, y ponla sobre brasas: y cuando los artaletes estuvieren tostados por de abajo, vuélvelos, porque se tuesten de la otra parte: luego sácalos de allí, y échalos en la vasija donde está cociendo el albondigón, y cuézase todo junto, sazonando el caldo de especias, y un poquito de verdura picada. Todo esto ha de cocer una hora. Luego cuájalo con dos (67r) huevos batidos con un poco de acedo. Luego saca el albondigón en el plato sobre unas rebanadillas de pan, y dale dos cortes, o tres, y abrirse ha como granada. Luego saca los artaletes de las broquetillas, y velos asentando por entre los cortes, y por en medio. Sírvelo caliente. Es buen plato y muy abultado, que si fuese el plato no muy grande con dos libras de ternera se podría hacer. Este platillo se podrá hacer de otra manera: harás el albondigón, como está dicho. Luego tomarás una gallina cocida, o unos pollos, o pichones, y hazla pedacitos, y ahóguese en una sartén con un poco de tocino picado, menudo, y un poquito de cebolla muy picada: y de que esté bien ahogado todo, échalo en la vasija donde está cociendo el albondigón, y sazónalo de especias y verdura, como está dicho: y cuando esté cocido, cuájalo con dos huevos con claras, o cuatro yemas, y un poco de acedo. Luego saca el albondigón, y dale los dos, o (67v) tres cortes, y abrirse ha, y echa el platillo de la gallina, o pichones en medio, y parecerá muy bien.

Y adviértase, que de la manera que está dicho que se ha de sazonar la carne para los albondigones, se ha de hacer para las albondiguillas chicas de ternera, o de carnero, y de gallina: y también cuando la carne estuvo sazonada para albondiguillas, podrás desatarla con un poco de caldo, de manera que esté ralo, y ponerlo sobre la lumbre, y andarlo a una mano con un cucharón, y harás de presto un pastel embote, o una cazuelilla, cuajándola con dos huevos, y un poco de acedo. Y adviértase, que aunque se dice, que se eche caldo en los platillos, no ha de haber caldo todas las veces, mas con echar a cocer los huesos de la carne que picaste con agua y sal, y cueza una hora, y es mejor caldo para platillos que el de la olla.[133]

Y adviértase también, que no digo en ninguna parte que hagan los platillos ahogando la carne, o pollos, o pichones, (68r) o cabrito, o conejos, es, porque salen los platillos morenos, y cociéndose un poco, y espumándolos: y luego sacarlos y ahogarlos con su tocino y cebolla, y especias, y luego echarle del mismo caldo en que se coció; salen de buen color: y si no los quisieres cocer, ásense: y cuando estén medio asados se podrán cortar y ahogar.

---

133 *Caldo* translates into English as both *broth* and *stock*. However, here, Martínez Montiño is signalling the difference between the two. Stock is made from boiling bones and produces a richer base with which to flavour dishes than the more common broth from the pot.

and stir it over the flame until the eggs are cooked through. Then turn it out onto the cutting board and chop it all up well. Add in two raw eggs, mix it in, and add in a little lemon juice. Test for salt and spices. If anything is missing, add it in. Put a little of this filling on each veal fillet, roll it up, and you'll have the pinwheel. Put three pinwheels on a small, wooden skewer. Once all are done, put them in a casserole greased with lard and place over red-hot embers. When they are browned on the bottom, flip them over so that the other side will brown. Then remove them and add them to the pot where the big meatball is cooking and cook it all together, adding spices to the broth and a little bit of chopped herbs. This should cook for about an hour. Then thicken it with two beaten eggs and a little sorrel juice. Place the big meatball on a platter with slices of bread and slice it two or three times, and open it like a pomegranate. Then take the skewers of pinwheels and arrange them around the meatball slices and in the middle. Serve hot. This is a tasty dish that fills the plate. If the plate isn't very big, then you can also make it with just two pounds of veal. This little dish can also be made another way. Prepare the big meatball as explained. Then take a cooked hen, or chicken, or squab, and chop it into pieces. Sauté it in the frying pan with a little minced fatback and onion. Once everything is thoroughly sautéed, add it to the pot where the meatball is cooking and season with spices and herbs as explained. When done cooking, thicken it with two whole eggs or four yolks and a little sorrel juice. Then take the meatball out, slice it two or three times, open it up and put the little dish of hen or squab right in the middle and it will look very good.

Note that this same way of seasoning meat for big meatballs can also be used for small meatballs made out of veal, mutton, or hen. Also, when the meat for the little meatballs has its seasoning, it can also be thinned with a little broth so that it's loose. Place over the flame and stir continually with a big spoon. It will turn into a moulded pie or (the shape of) a little casserole, setting it with two eggs and a little sorrel juice. Note that although it may say to ladle broth into the dishes, there won't always be broth. Moreover, if you cooked the meat bones that you sprinkled with salted water, and boiled that for an hour, you will have a richer stock for the dishes than what you'll get out of the pot.

Also note that nowhere do I say to make these dishes by sauteéing meat, chicken, squab, kid, or rabbit. This is because the dishes will turn out brown. Rather, if you first let the dish simmer and skim it and then take (the meat) out and sauté it with the right amount of fatback and onion and spices and then add to it the stock in which it cooked, it will have a better colour. If you prefer not to boil them, you can also roast them and when they are half roasted you can then cut them up and sauté them.

[87] *Sopa Dorada.*

Tomarás rebanadas de pan tostadas, y armarás la sopa, y pon el plato sobre un poco de lumbre así en seco, y échale un poco de azúcar molido por encima. Y cuando el plato esté bien caliente, échale caldo cuanto se bañe la sopa, y échale más azúcar por encima, y atápalo con otro plato, y déjalos estofar muy bien: y cuando el caldo esté bien embebido en el pan, batirás ocho yemas de huevos, y echarle has un poquito de caldo, el zumo de un medio limón, o una gota de vinagre, y échalo por encima (68v) de toda la sopa, y échale más azúcar por encima, y ponla una cobertera, que esté un poco levantada de la sopa, y échale un poquito de lumbre arriba, y déjala que se cuaje: y si quisieres echarle un poquito de manteca muy caliente por encima, para que se cuaje más presto, bien podrás, mas yo no lo uso, porque soy enemigo de manteca, si no es muy demasiado de buena. Esta sopa se puede hacer de otra manera. Batirás las ocho yemas de huevos, y echarás caldo sobre ellas, lo que fuere menester para mojar la sopa, y armarás el plato con las rebanadas tostadas, y echarás su azúcar por encima: luego echarás el caldo con las yemas, y su acedo de manera, cuanto se bañe bien la sopa, y échales azúcar molido por encima, y un poco de canela: y luego échale un poco de manteca muy caliente, y ponle al fuego con lumbre abajo y arriba. Desta misma manera podrás hacer otra sopa dorada sin agrio, sino con huevos, y azúcar, y canela, (69r) todo mezclado: y cuando fueres asentando el pan en el plato, has de ir echando del azúcar, y canela, y queso entre las rebanadas, y después por encima, y echar su caldo con las yemas de huevos, y echar más azúcar: luego ponla al fuego a cuajar: y cuando esté medio cuajada, échale un poco de manteca muy caliente por encima.

[88] *Sopa de Natas.*

Batirás una libra de natas con ocho yemas de huevos, y un poquito de leche, y tendrás armado el plato con las rebanadas de pan tostado, y untado el plato con un poco de manteca fresca, y echarás azúcar molido encima de las rebanadas: luego echarás las natas con las yemas de huevos, y pondrás más azúcar por encima, y pondrásla al fuego dentro de un horno con fuego manso: y si las natas se metieren todas entre el pan, echarás más natas, y echarás encima de todo unas pocas de natas sin huevos, y su azúcar: y con esto la (69v) puedes cuajar en el horno. Esta misma sopa de natas se hace muy buena, echando bizcochos en lugar de pan.

[89] *Otra sopa de Natas.*

Batirás cuatro huevos con claras, y medio cuartillo de leche, y tomarás una libra de natas, y echarás la mitad con los huevos y la leche, y tomarás una libra de queso fresco, y haráslo rebanadillas muy delgadas. Luego harás otras tantas rebanadillas de pan blanco sin tostar, y tendrás media libra de azúcar molido y untarás un plato

Golden sops

Take slices of toasted bread and assemble the sops. Put the plate over a low flame, dry, and sprinkle a little ground sugar on top. When the plate is very hot, add in enough broth to cover it half way and sprinkle more sugar on top. Cover it with another plate and let the bread stew. When the bread has soaked up all the broth, beat eight egg yolks, add in a little broth, juice from half a lemon, or a dash of vinegar and pour over the sops. Sprinkle more sugar on top and cover with a lid. The sops will puff up. Add a little heat on top and let the sops set. If you want to add a little very hot lard over the top so that it sets quicker, you can, but I don't, because I don't like lard if it's not excellent quality. These sops can be made another way. Beat eight egg yolks and ladle broth over them, enough to soak the sops. Arrange the plate with toasted slices and sprinkle the right amount of sugar on top. Then, ladle enough broth with egg yolk and the right amount of sorrel juice so it half covers the sops. Sprinkle sugar on top and a little cinnamon and then spoon on a little very hot lard and put it on the fire with heat above and below. In this same way you can make golden sops without the sour flavour, just eggs, cinnamon, and sugar all mixed together. When placing the bread on the plate, sprinkle on the cinnamon and sugar and some cheese between the slices and then on top. Then ladle on the right amount of broth with egg yolks and sprinkle more sugar. Put it on the fire to set and when it's half set, ladle a little hot lard on top.

Cream sops

Beat a pound of cream with eight egg yolks and a little milk. You'll have slices of toasted bread arranged on a plate that has been greased with butter. Sprinkle ground sugar over the bread. Next, pour on top the cream and egg yolks and sprinkle more sugar on top. Place it in an oven on the fire with low flame. If the cream falls between the slices of bread, add more cream. Then add, on top of everything, cream without any egg but with the right amount of sugar. In this way, it will set in the oven. This cream sops dish turns out really good using sweet biscuits instead of bread.

Other cream sops

Beat four eggs and a half pint of milk. Take a pound of cream and add half of it to the eggs and milk. Take a pound of farmer cheese and cut it into very thin slices. Next cut the same number of slices of untoasted, white bread. Have half

con un poco de manteca fresca: y pondrásle un lecho de rebanadas de pan en el plato, y echarle has un poco de los huevos, y las natas y azúcar. Luego echarás otro lecho de rebanadas de queso: y hecha, tornarás a echar de los huevos, y las natas por encima y azúcar molido, y unos bocadillos de manteca fresca: y desta manera irás haciendo hasta acabar los materiales. El (70r) postrer lecho ha de ser de rebanadas de queso; ha de quedar la sopa muy bien empapada: y luego ponla a cocer en un horno: y cuando esté medio cocida, échale la otra mitad de las natas por encima sin huevos, y ponla azúcar, y acabala de cocer.

Advierte, que si no tuvieres natas,[134] y tuvieres buena manteca fresca, bate los huevos con leche sola, y harás torrijas de pan, y untarás el plato con manteca de vacas. Luego irás mojando las torrijas en los huevos, y leche, asentándolas en el plato por la misma orden con las rebanadas de queso, y entre lecho y lecho echarás su azúcar molido, y unos bocadillos de manteca fresca: y desta manera vendrá a salir, que parezca que es de natas. A esta sopa podrás echar canela con el azúcar.[135] En las sopas de natas hase de echar poca vianda encima; porque sola la sopa hace plato. Has de poner alguna ave de leche,[136] o algunos pollos rellenos, o algunas morcillas blancas, (70v) que adelante diré cómo se han de hacer: y si fuere día de pescado algunos artaletes de algún pescado, o huevos estrellados, o tortillas de agua, cosa que no manche la sopa.

[90] *Una cazuela de Natas.*[137]

Tomarás libra y media de natas, y batirlas has con seis huevos con claras, y un cuartillo de leche. Tendrás doce onzas de azúcar molido, libra y media de queso fresco en rebanadas, y harás otras tantas rebanadas de pan blanco sin tostar: untarás una cazuela con manteca de vacas, e irás haciendo, con la misma orden que está dicho en la sopa de natas y queso fresco: irás echando lechos de pan mojado en las natas, y huevos, y leche, echando su azúcar entre lecho y lecho, y sus rebanadas de queso, y unos bocadillos de manteca de vacas fresca: y si no lo hubiere bueno, no eches ninguna, que las natas lo suplirán: el postrer lecho de arriba ha de ser de rebanadas

---

134 This attention to lack of *nata* [cream] may reflect the sumptuary laws put into place in late sixteenth-century Spain. Alvar-Ezquerra points out that in 1592 *nata* became another prohibited item (317).
135 Today's readers will most certainly recognize this recipe as a version of what we call *French toast*. Variations of bread soaked in egg and milk and then fried appear in the first century in Apicius' *De re coquinaria* as well as in several medieval recipe collections across Europe.
136 *Ave de leche* refers to a young pigeon or dove that is fed crop milk, a secretion from the crop of parent birds that is regurgitated to young birds. For more, see Mayntz.
137 This recipe [90] and the following on cream, breadcrumbs, and a series of pies, through recipe [99], appear in the eighteenth-century recipe collection, *Manuscrito Ávila Blancas* (Pérez San Vicente, *Gastronomía mexicana* 78–92).

a pound of ground sugar. Grease a plate with a little butter. Put a bed of sliced bread on the plate, pour over the top a little of the egg mix, cream, and sugar. Next, place on top a layer of sliced cheese. Once again pour over the top some egg mix, the cream, ground sugar, and some dabs of butter. Continue doing this until all the ingredients have been used. The last layer should be sliced cheese. The sops should be well soaked. Then, bake in the oven and when it is half done, spread the other half of the cream on top, without any eggs. Sprinkle some sugar and finish baking.

Note that if you don't have any cream but have good, fresh butter, you can beat together just the eggs and milk and make some torrijas. Grease the plate with butter. Dip the torrijas in the eggs and milk and arrange them on the plate in the same order with the slices of cheese. And between each layer, sprinkle the right amount of ground sugar and dabs of butter. This is how they will turn out as if they had cream. You can also add cinnamon with the sugar to these sops. For these cream sops, you should serve little food on top of them because the sops are really a dish in themselves. You can serve with some baby birds, stuffed chicken, or white blood sausage. I will explain how to make them later on. If it is a fish day, some fish pinwheels or fried eggs or plain omelette, things that won't colour the sops.

Cream casserole

Take a pound and a half of cream and beat it with six whole eggs and a pint of milk. Have ready twelve ounces of ground sugar, a pound and a half of sliced farmer cheese, and make just as many slices of untoasted, white bread. Grease a casserole with butter and begin layering with the same instructions as explained with cream sops and farmer cheese. Put together layers of bread soaked in the cream, eggs, and milk and slices of farmer cheese. Sprinkle the right amount of sugar between each layer and dab with butter. If you don't have good butter, don't use any. The cream

(71r) de queso. Cuécela en un horno a poca lumbre, porque no se queme, que tarda mucho en cuajarse: y si no hallares queso fresco, tomarás de lo más frescal que hallares, que no sea de cuajo, sino de hierba,[138] y rallarlo has, y echarlo has en lugar de las rebanadas del queso fresco, y echarás menos cantidad, y más de azúcar.

[91] *Torrijas de Natas sin pan.*

Tomarás unas pocas de natas, que no lleven leche ninguna, y echarlas has un poco de azúcar, y yemas de huevos crudos en cantidad, y batirlo has todo junto: han de ser tanta las yemas que venga a estar el batido un poco ralo, y echarlo has en unas torteras que no tenga el batido de alto más del grueso de un dedo chiquito de la mano. Untarás un poco la tortera, porque no se pegue, y ponle al fuego con poca lumbre abajo y arriba, y cuajaráse: sácala del fuego, y déjala enfriar: y cuando esté fría, dale tres cortes en la tortera: (71v) luego otros tres atravesados, de manera que queden torrijas cuadradas. Luego sácalas con la paleta muy sutilmente, y pondráslas sobre el tablero: luego bate huevos con claras, y rebózalas como torrijas de pan, y fríelas en buena manteca, y pásalas por un poco de almíbar, y sírvelas calientes, echándolas un poquito de canela por encima: y podrá ser que no las hayas visto desta manera a otro oficial.[139] Estas torrijas de natas, si les quisieres echar un poquito de pan rallado, o un poquito de harina, no por eso dejarán de salir buenas: y si no hallares natas, tomarás cosa de cuatro onzas de harina de trigo, o arroz, y un cuarterón de azúcar molido, y mezclado todo junto, ponlo en un cacillo: luego echa un poquito de leche, de manera que se haga un batidillo espeso: échale después huevos hasta una docena, la mitad con claras, y echa las yemas primero, y bate muy bien el batido con el cucharón: y de que esté bien batido, que no tenga (72r) ningún burujo, ve echando los demás huevos, y bátelo mucho: y luego ve echando leche cosa de media azumbre antes más que menos, y échales sazón de sal, y unta una tortera, o dos con manteca, y echarás el batido que quede del grueso de un dedo, y ponlo al fuego con lumbre abajo y arriba, y cuájese, y sácalo al tablero, y déjalo enfriar, y cortarás las torrijas de la manera que está dicho en las de natas, y rebózalas con huevos, y fríelas, y si no tuvieres almíbar, sírvelas con buena miel, y azúcar, y canela por encima.

---

138 *Hierba* is short for *hierba de cuajar* or *herbal rennet*, such as cardoons, whose dried flowers have enzymes that are often used to *curdle* milk. Martínez Montiño insists on this type of cheese in a handful of other recipes: "Cazuela mojí de berenjenas" [Moxi eggplant casserole] (358; 359), "Cebollas rellenas" [Stuffed onions] (410–11; 412–13), and "Otra sopa de vaca" [Another beef sops (dish)] (474; 475). He also explains how to make it in "Relación de algunas cantidades, para hacer tortas, hojaldres, costradas, y otras cosas" [List of certain quantities for making pies, pastries, puff pastry pies, and other things] (252–4; 253–5).

139 Here is a great example of Martínez Montiño asserting his originality and authority.

will make up for it. The top layer should be slices of cheese. Bake in the oven on low so that it doesn't burn, as it takes long to set. If you can't find any farmer cheese, use the most lightly preserved [cheese] that you have. It shouldn't be made from animal rennet, rather from herbal rennet. Grate it and sprinkle it on instead of slices of farmer cheese. You'll need less of it but more sugar.

Torrijas made with cream but without bread

Take a little heavy cream, just the fat-rich part of the milk, and add in a little sugar and a lot of egg yolks and beat everything together. You should add enough eggs so that the batter is fairly thin. Pour it into covered tart pans so that the batter is about the thickness of a little finger. Grease the covered tart pan a little so that it doesn't stick and put it on the fire with low heat above and below. When it's done, remove it from the fire and let it cool. When it has cooled, slice it three ways in the covered tart pan and then slice it crossways three more times so that the pieces of torrijas come out square. Then carefully take them out with a spatula and place them on the cutting board. Next, beat whole eggs, coat (the squares) in them like bread torrijas, fry them in good lard, dip them in a little simple syrup, and serve hot. Sprinkle a little cinnamon on top. It's possible that you have never seen (torrijas made) this way by any other cook. If you want to add some breadcrumbs or a little flour to these torrijas made with cream, they would still turn out really good. If you don't have any cream, take about four ounces of wheat or rice flour and a quarter pound of sugar, mix it all together, and put it in a saucepan. Then add a little milk so that the batter is still thick. Next, add up to a dozen eggs, first the yolks and just half with whites. Mix well with a big spoon. Once it is well mixed and has no lumps, add in the rest of the eggs and beat well. Then slowly add about one quart of milk, better more than less and add salt. Grease one or two baking pans with lard. Add one finger-width of batter and put it on the fire with heat above and below. When it's done, put it on the cutting board and let it cool. Cut the torrijas the same way as explained for the ones made with cream. Coat with egg batter and fry. If you don't have simple syrup, you can serve it with good honey and cinnamon and sugar on top.

[92] *Migas de Natas.*

Tomarás seis escudillas de natas,[140] y desharás tres panecillos de leche, que sean molletes,[141] y harás los bocadillos del tamaño de media nuez, cortadas con la mano; porque para ningún género de migas, no se ha de cortar el pan con cuchillo, salvo las migas de gato, que han (72v) de ser de las cortezas del pan. Y teniendo estos panecillos cortados, como digo, échales las natas, y seis onzas de azúcar molido, y revuélvelo todo así en frío, porque se mezclen las natas, y el azúcar con el pan: luego pon el cacillo sobre brasas, y velas revolviendo con un cucharón, porque no se peguen, y ha de ser sin aporrear mucho el pan, porque se haría una pasta. Y cuando las natas fueren derritiéndose, harás un bollito, acomodándolo con el cucharón, de manera que no se pegue, ni se aplaste el pan: y cuando estuvieren tostadas por abajo, vuélvelas de la otra parte; de manera que de ambas queden tostadas: luego sírvelas calientes. Estas migas las quieren algunos señores que estén tostadas por la parte de afuera: y que por de dentro no estén derretidas las natas, sino que estén blanqueando: y para que salgan desta manera, mezclarás en frío muy bien el pan, y el azúcar, y las natas: y en poniendo el cacillo al fuego no le revuelvas, (73r) sino comienza luego a acomodar el bollito: y desta manera lo sacarás tostado por de fuera, y por de dentro blanco. Estas migas se llaman por otro nombre heces.

Desta propia manera podrás hacer heces de requesones, salvo que les has de echar un poco de manteca fresca por derretir, porque las názulas son muy secas; aunque adelante enseñaré cómo has de sacar manteca de názulas.[142]

[93] *Migas de Leche.*

Desharás tres panecillos molletes de leche, como tengo dicho con la mano, y los bocadillos sean mayores, con todas sus cortezas, y ponlo en un plato, y échale cerca de medio panecillo de sal,[143] y luego echa la leche hasta que se bañe, y ponlo

---

140 The quantity for measuring cream presents certain difficulties. Although José Castaño Álvarez in his book *El libro de los pesos y medidas* mentions the *escudilla* as a container and a unit of measure for dry goods and liquids, he does not say what quantity is contained within (177). Later, Martínez Montiño explains that six portions equal one plate (248; 249) and in another recipe states that if four *escudillas* of cream is not available, you can substitute a half pound of marzipan paste (346; 347). For measurement of *nata*, see 242n149 and Appendix 2, "On Measurements."

141 *Molletes* are a soft, sweet roll. For more on their history, see Corbacho, and Yarza 24.

142 *Názula* is another word for *requesón* (curd cheese, like ricotta or cottage cheese). For more information, see 690.

143 A *panecillo de sal* [bread roll amount of salt] gets its name from how the salt was stored. Though the exact quantity of salt is unknown, based on other recipes where he uses this measurement, it may be that one *panecillo* is equivalent to one ounce. For more information, see the entry in the Glossary.

Breadcrumbs with cream

Set aside six bowls of cream. Tear up three soft rolls; they should be *molletes*. Break them into pieces about half the size of a walnut. This should be done by hand, because no type of breadcrumb recipe should use a knife for cutting the bread, with the exception of the cat breadcrumbs, which are made with the crust of the bread. Once the rolls are torn up as I've explained, mix them with the cream and six ounces of ground sugar and stir it all together cold so that the cream and sugar blend with the bread. Then place the saucepan over red-hot embers and stir with a big spoon so that nothing sticks. But try not to beat the bread too much so that it doesn't turn into a paste. When the cream has been absorbed, make a little ball, adjusting it with the big spoon so that it doesn't stick and the bread doesn't get squashed. When the underside is browned, flip it over so that both sides are browned. Then, serve hot. Some lords prefer this breadcrumb recipe to have the outside browned but the cream not fully absorbed and white on the inside. For this to turn out, you need to mix together very well the bread, sugar, and cream while cold. Once the saucepan is on the fire, don't stir it anymore, just get ready to shape the ball. In this way, it will come out toasted on the outside and white on the inside. These breadcrumbs are also known by another name: *turds*.

In this same way you could make curd cheese *turds* except that you must have a little fresh butter for melting because curd cheese is very dry. Further along I will teach how to express the fat out of curd cheese.

Breadcrumbs with milk

Tear up three soft *mollete* rolls, as I have said, by hand, but in bigger pieces and with the crust intact. Put them on a plate and sprinkle on about half a bread roll worth of salt. Then pour enough milk on them to half cover them. Place it over

sobre un poquito de fuego, y tápalo con otro plato: y en calentándose por la parte de abajo, vuelve los platos el de arriba para bajo, y tórnense a calentar por la otra parte: luego pon la sartén al fuego con un poco de (73v) manteca de vacas: y cuando esté caliente fríe en ella un par de granos de ajos: y luego sácalos, y echa las migas, y dales dos, o tres vueltas con la misma sartén, o con un cucharón; luego velas acomodando, y haciendo un bollo redondo, como una tortilla, y grueso cerca de dos dedos, y menearlas has con la sartén, porque no se peguen hasta que estén tostadas por una parte, y luego vuélvelas por la otra, y tuéstense también: y sírvelas calientes sin dulce: y si las quisieres echar dulce, échaselo después de tostadas, y no importará que no lleven ajos. Advierte, que estas migas no se han de andar mucho meneando con el cucharón, porque se hacen mazacote como migas de pastores,[144] sino que quede la torta de las migas muy bien tostadas, y muy juntas, y más que queden los bocados de pan enteros.

[94] (74r) *Migas de Gato.*[145]

Las migas de gato se hacen de cortezas de pan cortadas con cuchillo muy delgadas: henchirás el plato deste pan, y tendrás un poco de agua cociendo, sazonada de sal y pimienta, y un poquito de ajo, y azafrán, y remojarás las migas con ello: y cuando estén bien estofadas calentarás un poco de aceite bien caliente, un poco de manteca de vacas, y echárselo has por encima. Sobre estas migas, se suelen poner huevos frescos escalfados, o estrellados blandos, y se les suele echar unas veces una poca de alcaravea: y no te espantes porque pongo algunas cosas extraordinarias: esto bien sé que lo saben hacer los oficiales, mas porque sé, que aunque sean muy ordinarias hay mozos y mozas que no lo saben, ni sus amos les han de dar recaudo para los platos regalados, y querría que se aprovechasen todos.[146] Con esto dejo las migas, aunque faltan otras para su tiempo, (74v) y trataré de algunas cosas de masa, y comenzaré por las tortas y bollos, y luego por los pasteles y frutas, y otras cosas trasordinarias.

---

144 There is no recipe for "migas de pastor" in Martínez Montiño's cookbook, but this reference implies that everyone was familiar with their consistency.
145 There is no explanation for the title of this recipe. However, it differs from other *miga* recipes for two reasons. First, it uses only the crust of the bread, and second, the breadcrumbs don't go into the frying pan, rather hot fat is poured over them.
146 This is one of several occasions throughout the cookbook that Martínez Montiño references women as part of the kitchen staff, and it serves as a reminder of their important role in the workforce. For further information, see Bravo Lozano.

a low flame and cover it with another plate. When the bottom part is warm, flip the plates over so the top is on the bottom and warm that side. Then put a frying pan on the fire with a little butter. When it is hot, fry a few cloves of garlic, remove them and add the breadcrumbs. Flip them over two or three times either with the pan itself or with a big spoon. Then begin arranging them in the shape of a round pastry, like an omelette, and about two fingers thick. Shake them in the frying pan so that they don't stick but do brown on one side, and then flip them and brown on the other. Serve hot without any sweetener. If you want to add sweetener, do so after they are browned and it won't matter if there isn't any garlic. Note that you shouldn't stir these breadcrumbs too much with a big spoon or they will get too sticky, like shepherd's breadcrumbs. Here the breadcrumb pie should be nicely toasted and all together so that all the bite-sized pieces of bread are as one.

Cat breadcrumbs

Cat breadcrumbs are made by cutting very thin slices of crust with a knife. Fill a plate with this bread. Have some water boiling with salt, pepper, a little garlic, and saffron and soak the breadcrumbs in this. When the bread is well soaked, heat up some oil with a little butter and pour it over the top. These breadcrumbs are usually served under either poached eggs or soft, fried eggs on top and sometimes sprinkled with a little caraway. Don't be nervous because I'm including some unusual things here. I know that cooks know how to make this; moreover, I know that even though they might be usual for cooks, there are young men and women who don't know how to prepare them or their masters don't give them the necessary ingredients to make exquisite dishes, and I want everyone to be able to make the most of their situation. I'll end the section on breadcrumbs here, although there are others that will come up in due time. Now I'll explain some things about dough and will start with pies and round pastries and then other pastries and fried dough and other special things.

COMIENZA LA MASA[147]

[95] *Tortas de Natas.*[148]

Tomarás ocho natas, o un plato dellas, que será lo mismo,[149] y échalas en un cacillo, y echarles has una docena de yemas de huevos, y cerca de media libra de azúcar molido, y cosa de dos onzas de harina de trigo, o un poco de pan rallado, y un poquito de clavo molido, y una gota de agua rosada, y ponlo al fuego, y ándalo a una mano, hasta que venga a hacerse una crema un poco espesa: luego sácalo, y déjalo enfriar, y métele otras seis yemas de huevos crudos, y harás tu torta de no más de dos hojas, aunque no haya inconveniente.[150] Si quisieres echar más por la parte de abajo, y por la parte de arriba con unas tiras harás unas celogías, cortándolas (75r) con la cortadera: y con este propio batido podrás hacer pastelillos muy chiquitos, y sírvelos entre hojuelas muy menudas, o tallarines un poco grandecillos, echando primero almíbar a las hojuelas: y luego asentar los pastelillos entre ellas.

Y si quisieres hacer estos pastelillos un poco mayores, les podrás echar unos pocos de huevos mejidos, y algunas conservas cortadas, todo revuelto con el batido. También podrás hacer frutillas chicas rellenas, como las de las cañas de vaca.[151] También podrás hacer empanadillas chiquitas cocidas en el horno, y la masa destas empanadillas hallarás escritas las cantidades de harina, y azúcar, y huevos, y de manteca, adonde están escritas las empanadillas de torreznos,[152] porque pienso escribir muchas suertes de vianda, que se empanan en esta masa; porque cada una se sazona de diferente manera, y la masa es toda una, y de las mejores que se hace.

---

147 This subtitle is not in the original 1611 edition but it is added in 1617 and then remains in all following editions. I added it here to give additional clarity to the different sections.
148 This recipe is similar to an old-fashioned sugar cream pie but with rosewater and clove added as flavouring. For a modern version, see Spraker.
149 The question of how much is a portion or a plate of *nata* is a challenging one. But, by comparing proportional references to quantities of *nata* to quantities of egg yolks used in the various cream pie recipes, one may surmise that one plate of *nata* is equivalent to eight portions of *nata* (stated here), which in turn is equivalent to six *escudillas* of *nata* (stated in the recipe "Torta de pichones y nata" [Squab pie with cream] (248; 249) and to three cups of *nata* (inferred in "Torta de dama" [Lady pie] and the two "Otra torta de dama" [Another lady pie] recipes based on the similar portions of *nata* to egg yolks (478–82; 479–83). However, this hypothesis has yet to be tested in the kitchen.
150 Here and in other pie recipes Martínez Montiño often describes multiple layers, usually two but other times three or even four, for forming the bottom of a pie crust. This technique differs greatly from the *masa quebrada* [short crust] technique used today for pies that requires just one single layer.
151 This recipe, "Fruta de cañas" [Fried dough with marrow filling], is located above on 216; 217.
152 Martínez Montiño is referring to the recipe "Empanadilla de masa dulce" [Sweet dough for turnovers] (310–12; 311–13).

[The dough section begins]

Cream pies

Take eight (portions of) cream or a plate of it, which is the same, and place it in a saucepan. Add a dozen egg yolks, about half a pound of ground sugar, around two ounces of wheat flour or a little bit of grated breadcrumbs, a little ground clove, and a drop of rose water and put it over the fire. Stir continually until it becomes creamy and begins to thicken. Then remove it and let it cool. Add six raw egg yolks. Make your crust with no more than two sheets, even though you may have more. If you want you can add more underneath, and on top make latticework out of strips, trimming them with the trimmer. With this same batter you can make bite-sized pastries and serve them between very small pieces of puff pastry or strips that are a little bigger, but first ladle some simple syrup on the puff pastry and then set the little pastries between them.

If you want to make the little pastries a little bigger, you can fill them with some sweet scrambled egg yolks and some chopped preserves all mixed into the batter. You can also make little filled puffs, like the ones with beef marrow. You can also make mini turnovers baked in the oven. You'll find the quantities for flour, sugar, eggs, and lard written down for the dough for these turnovers where the turnovers with roasted pork belly are. I plan to include a lot of kinds of food that are wrapped with this dough, because each one is seasoned differently and the dough is the same for each and is one of the best there is.

[96] (75v) *Otra torta de Natas.*

Tomarás un plato de natas,[153] y echarle has una docena de yemas de huevos crudos, y media libra de azúcar molido, y un poco de pan rallado: luego harás la torta deste batido, así frío, echándole dos, o tres hojas de masa debajo, y otras dos, o tres encima. Con estas natas, y un poco de manjar blanco, se hacen muy buenas tortas.

[97] *Torta de Agraz.*

Desgranarás cosa de seis libras de agraz, y tendrás un cazo con agua cociendo, echa el agraz dentro, y déjalo cocer dos, o tres hervores; luego vacíalo en un colador, y déjalo escurrir un poco; luego pasa este agraz por un cedacillo, de manera que no quede arriba mas de los granos; y tendrás una libra de azúcar en punto subido,[154] y echa aquel agraz pasado dentro, y cueza hasta que apure bien: y si estuviere algún (76r) poquito ralo, échale un poquito de pan rallado, y sácalo del fuego, y échale cantidad de canela molida, y un poco de olor, y haz tu torta, echando dos o tres hojas debajo. Y advierte, que el agraz es unas veces más agrio que otras: y cuando estuviere más agrio, ha de llevar más azúcar, y que esté bien subido de punto. Esta torta no ha de llevar huevos, sino es en la masa, y tiene muy buen gusto de agridulce.

[98] *Una torta de Cidra verde.*

Tomarás una cidra, o dos, que pesen cuatro libras, y rallarla has toda la carne con la cáscara que no quede por rallar más de lo agrio:[155] y esta cidra la echarás en un cazo que esté lleno de agua, y cueza tres, o cuatro hervores: luego sácalo del fuego, y echa el agua, y la cidra en una servilleta, y colará toda el agua, y quedará toda la cidra en la servilleta. Torna a poner el cazo lleno de (76v) agua en el fuego, y torna a echar la cidra, y cueza otros dos, o tres hervores. Tórnala a colar por la servilleta: y desta manera la darás tres, o cuatro caldas: y probarás las cidras: y luego verás si está dulce, si lo está tendrás una libra de azúcar en punto bien subida, y echa dentro

---

153 For measurement of *nata*, see 242n149 and Appendix 2, "On Measurements."
154 When discussing simple syrup and uses of sugar in his cooking, Martínez Montiño most commonly uses the following phrases: *azúcar en punto, almíbar en punto, azúcar clarificado en punto, azúcar en buen punto*. All of these refer to early thread stage when the temperature is only slightly above boiling point (100ºC, 212ºF). Here, the phrase *en punto subido* also refers to the thread stage but at a higher temperature, although it would not exceed 112ºC, 234ºF, which would put the sugar stage into another category. For more information on sugar temperatures, see the Introduction (45–6).
155 Martínez Montiño is referring to the white part of the fruit, which is the most bitter. The filling for this pie is made much the way marmalade is.

Another cream pie

Have a plate of cream and add a dozen raw egg yolks, half a pound of ground sugar, and some breadcrumbs. Next, make the crust for this batter, as is, cold, with two or three sheets of dough below and another two or three on top. With this cream and a little bit of blancmange, you will make excellent pies.

Sour grape pie

Separate some six pounds of sour grapes from the stalk, have a pot of boiling water and place them in it. Bring it to boil two or three times. Then, pour into a colander and let it strain a little. Next place the sour grapes into a sieve and let nothing but the seeds remain. Have a pound of sugar at the late thread stage, add the strained sour grapes, and let cook until it is well done. If it turns out a little thin, add a little bit of breadcrumbs. Remove from the fire and add a good amount of ground cinnamon and some rose water. Make the crust by placing two or three sheets below. Note that sour grapes vary in sourness. When they are really sour, add more sugar and make sure it's at the late thread stage. This pie shouldn't have any eggs, unless they're in the crust. It has an excellent sweet and sour flavour.

Green citron pie

Take one or two citrons that weigh about four pounds and grate all the fruit with its rind so that none but the most sour part is left. Put this citron in a pan that is full of water and bring to a boil three or four times. Remove from the fire and pour the water and fruit onto a napkin to strain out all the water so that only the citron remains on the napkin. Put a full pan of water back on the fire and again put the citron in it and bring it to a boil two or three more times. Strain it through the napkin once again and repeat this cooking process three or four times. Try the citron to see if it's sweet. If it is, use a pound of sugar that has been brought to a rolling

la cidra rallada, bien exprimida del agua, y consérvala muy bien: y luego sácala del fuego, y échale tanta canela que quede bien parda; y échale un poco de olor, y haz tu torta con dos hojas debajo, y encima un rejadillo a modo de celogía.

[99] *Una torta de Limones verdes.*

Buscarás limones poncís,[156] que tengan la cáscara gorda, y partirlos has, y sacarles has toda la cáscara, y cortarla has delgada, como quien corta cebolla a lo largo, y échalas en agua fría de un día para otro. Luego darles has tres, o cuatro caldas, con otras tantas aguas de la manera que se caldeó la cidra rallada, (77r) y probarás los limones si están dulces: y si lo estuvieren, exprímelas muy bien el agua, y échalos en el azúcar. Y advierte, que para esto ha de estar el azúcar más delgado de punto, para que se vayan conservando los limones: y cuando estén bien conservados, sácalos fuera, y échales su canela, y un poco de olor, y haz tu torta.

[100] [*Una torta de cidra.*]

De cidra se hace esta torta, beneficiándola de la misma manera que los limones, cortada muy delgada, y dándoles sus caldas como a los limones, y la cidra ha de ser agria, si es posible; porque las cidras agrias tienen la carne mejor y más tierna: ha de estar en remojo veinticuatro horas si hubiere lugar: y si no, caldeándola muchas veces, la harás endulzar. Destas cidras o limones, podrás hacer pastelillos, añadiéndoles huevos mejidos, y cañas de vaca, si fuere día de carne; y si no con sola la cidra y huevos mejidos se puede hacer.

[101] (77v) *Torta de Orejones.*[157]

Tomarás una libra de orejones, y pondráslos en remojo, de la noche a la mañana: luego dales un hervor, y tendrás una libra de azúcar clarificado, y echa los orejones dentro, y váyanse conservando poco a poco: luego sácalos, y déjalos enfriar: luego haz tu torta echándole un poco de olor, un poco de agua de azahar, y un poquillo de canela: y después de cocida la torta procura de tener un poco de almíbar que le echar por encima. La masa para esta torta la podrás hacer fina con un poquito de azúcar, y echarás dos o tres hojas abajo, y un par dellas arriba, que parezca a modo de costrada. Advierte, que si los orejones están bien remojados, no es menester cocerlos, y hanse de remojar en vino aguado.

---

156 *El limón poncí* refers to a type of lemon with a thick rind.
157 For an image of this pie, see Appendix 3.9.

boil and add the grated citron to it, making sure all the water has been expressed, and preserve it very well. Remove it from the fire and add in enough cinnamon so it has a nice light brown colouring. Add in a little rose water and make your pie with two sheets on the bottom and latticework on top.

Green lemon pie

Look for *ponci* lemons that have a thick rind. Cut them open, remove the entire rind, and slice them thin, the same way you would for an onion cut lengthwise. Soak them in water overnight. Next heat them in water three or four times, changing the water each time, the same way that the grated citron was heated. Taste the lemons for sweetness. If they are sweet, then express all the water and put them in the sugar. Note that for this recipe the sugar is a little lower than boiling point so that the lemons are preserved. When they are well preserved, remove them and sprinkle on them the right amount of cinnamon and rosewater and make the crust.

[A citron pie]

You can make this same pie in the same way with citrons, slicing them thin and heating them up like the lemons. If possible, the citron should be sour because the sour ones have the best and most tender flesh. If there is time, they should soak for twenty-four hours, and if not, you can sweeten them by heating them up many times. With these citrons or lemons, you can make little pastries by adding sweet scrambled egg yolks and beef marrow if it's a meat day and, if not, then you can make them with just the citron and sweet scrambled egg yolks.

Dried apricot pie

Take a pound of dried apricots and soak them overnight. Then bring them to a boil and have reserved a pound of clarified sugar and put the dried apricots in it so that they are slowly preserved. Then, remove them and let them cool. Next, make your crust, adding in a little rosewater, a little orange blossom water, and a tiny bit of cinnamon. Once the crust is cooked, try to reserve a little simple syrup to brush on top. The dough for this pie should be made very thin with a little sugar. Place two or three layers on the bottom and a couple on top, so that it looks like a puff pastry pie. Note that if the dried apricots are well soaked, it is not necessary to [first] boil them. They should soak in watered-down wine.

[102] *Torta de Almendras.*

Majarás tres cuarterones de almendras (78r) muy bien, y echarle has media libra de azúcar, y májese todo muy bien: luego échale seis huevos con claras, y mézclase bien, y harás tu torta de dos hojas, una abajo, y otra arriba, y úntala con manteca de vacas por encima, y ráspale un poco de azúcar. Y advierte, que las tortas de almendras siempre han de llevar los huevos con claras, y que esté el batido muy blando; porque desta manera salen buenas, y de otra manera salen muy apelmazadas.

[103] *Torta de Ternera, o de Cabrito.*

Tomarás cosa de media libra de ternera de pierna, y ponla a cocer: y cuando estuviere medio cocida sácala al tablero, y pícala muy menuda. Luego tomarás media libra de almendras mondadas, y majarlas has mucho con otra media libra de azúcar. Luego echarás la ternera picada dentro en el almirez con las almendras, y el azúcar, y májalo (78v) todo junto muy bien: luego échale huevos con claras, hasta que esté ralo: luego tiende dos hojas de masa, y ponlas en la tortera debajo, y echa el batido en ella: luego tendrás dos cañas de vaca, y velas poniendo en la torta; de manera que quede bien empedrada con ellas: y echarle has un poco de canela, y una migaja de clavo, y cierra tu torta, y cuécela a fuego manso. Si quisieres picar las cañas de vaca menudas, y mezclarlas con el batido bien puedes. Esta torta se sirve caliente, y se puede hacer de livianos en Sábado con tocino.

[104] *Torta de Pichones, y Natas.*

Asarás cuatro pichones, y descarnarlos has todos, y picarás la carne: luego tomarás seis natas,[158] y batirlas has con doce yemas de huevos, y mezclarlo has todo junto, y echarle has media libra de azúcar, un poquito de clavo (79r) con un poco de canela, y haz tu torta, y sírvela caliente.

[105] *Torta de Albérchigos.*[159]

Tomarás albérchigos conservados, y tiende una hoja de masa muy delgada, y ponla en la tortera, ha de ser tan delgada, que se traspariente por ella la tortera, y úntala con manteca, y échale otras dos encima, untándolas entre hoja y hoja: luego pon los albérchigos de manera, que sean muy pocos, no más de cuanto cubran el suelo de la tortera: luego échale otra hoja muy delgada encima, y cierra la torta, haciéndole

---

158 For measurement of *nata*, see 242n149 and Appendix 2, "On Measurements."
159 At the time of the publication of Martínez Montiño's cookbook, *albérchigo* is understood as a type of apricot. For more on the evolution from apricot to peach, see the Introduction (41).

Almond pie

Grind very well three quarters of a pound of almonds. Add half a pound of sugar and continue grinding it very well. Next, add six whole eggs and mix well. Then make your pie with two sheets, one on the bottom and the other on the top. Grease with butter on top and then sprinkle some sugar on. Note that almond pies should always contain eggs with their whites and that the batter should be very light because this way it will turn out great and any other way they will turn out very dense.

Veal or kid pie

Have about half a pound of veal shank and put it on to boil. When it is parboiled, place it on the cutting board and mince the meat. Then take half a pound of shelled almonds and grind them well together with half a pound of sugar. Then add the minced veal to the mortar with the almonds and sugar and grind it all well together. Add in eggs with the whites until it has thinned. Roll out two sheets of dough and place them in the bottom of a covered tart pan and pour in the batter. Then take two beef marrow bones and dot them over the pie so that it is well-speckled with them. Sprinkle a little cinnamon, a pinch of clove, and close up the pie. Bake with a low flame. If you want to mince the beef marrow and add it to the batter, that would work well. This pie is served hot and can also be made with lung and fatback on Saturdays.

Squab pie with cream

Roast four squab, remove all the meat, and dice it up. Then take six [portions of] cream, beat them with twelve egg yolks, and mix it all together. Add in half a pound of sugar, a little clove and cinnamon, and make your pie. Serve hot.

Apricot pie

Take some preserved apricot and roll out a very fine layer of dough and put it in a covered tart pan. The dough should be so thin that you can see the covered tart pan through it. Grease with lard and put two more layers on, greasing with lard between each one. Then spread the apricots out so that there is a fine layer, no more than one layer on the bottom of the covered tart pan. Then put another thin layer of

unas ondecillas por el borde, y úntala con un poquitico de manteca: y cuando esté cocida toma un poco de agua rosada, y rociarás la torta, y échale azúcar raspado por encima, y tórnala a echar lumbre para que tome color y costra muy buena.

[106] (79v) *Una costrada de Limoncillos, y Mazapán.*[160]

Tomarás media libra de almendras, y media de azúcar, y harás mazapán: luego sacarás el mazapán del almirez, y echarás media docena de limoncillos en almíbar de los secos en el almirez,[161] y májalos: y si quisieres echar algún poco de diacitrón, también da muy buen gusto. Luego torna a echar el mazapán en el almirez, y májalo todo, y échale seis ú ocho huevos con claras, y mézclalo todo. Luego harás docena y media de huevos mejidos, y haráslos pedacitos, y echarlos has en el batido de la torta, de manera que se queden así sin deshacerse más. Luego harás la masa fina, y harás tu costrada, echando tres o cuatro hojas debajo, y encima unas tiras cortadas con la cortadera. Advierte, que los huevos mejidos siempre han de ser pasados por la espumadera, estando el (80r) azúcar en buen punto, y cociendo muy aprisa, porque no salgan apelmazados.[162]

[107] *Una torta de Guindas.*

Tomarás cuatro libras de guindas, y sacarlas has los cuescos, y ponlas en un cacillo, y échale una libra de azúcar, y una gota de vino, y ponlas a la lumbre, y cuécela hasta que echen de sí harto zumo, y hase de cocer poco a poco hasta que estén bien conservadas. Luego harás tu torta con tres, o cuatro hojas debajo, y una encima: y si sobrare algún almíbar, después que esté la torta cocida, se lo pondrás echar por encima, si no es que ella tenga todo lo que ha de menester.

[108] *Torta de Borrajas.*

Cocerás las borrajas que te pareciere, y luego échalas en un colador, y exprímelas muy bien del agua: luego pícalas, y ahógalas con un poco de manteca (80v) fresca, y sácalas a enfriar, y métele huevos hasta que esté blando este batido: sazona con pimienta y jengibre, y nuez, y canela, y échale media libra de azúcar molido, y harás tu torta desta manera. Podrás hacer torta de espinacas, y de otra cualesquiera hierbas: si quisieres añadir a estas tortas un poco de queso bueno, podrás.

---

160 *Limoncillo* is also one of the more than dozen names for the *Melicoccus bijugatus* tropical fruit from the New World. It looks like a lime but has a creamy pulp inside, a relatively large pit, and is not a citrus fruit. Because Martínez Montiño treats the limoncillo as a citrus fruit, I am inclined to believe this is an Old World foodstuff.
161 *Seco* [dry] refers to the amount of juice in a piece of fruit but can also refer to the size (due to dehydration).
162 Note that pushing the egg yolks through a skimmer is the technique also used for "Huevos hilados" [Candied egg yolk threads] (432–4; 433–5).

dough on top and seal the pie with a wavy border. Dab a little lard on it. When it is cooked, take some rose water and sprinkle it on the pie. Grate some sugar on top and return it to the heat so that it browns and creates an excellent crust.

Lime and marzipan puff pastry pie

Combine half a pound of almonds and another of sugar to make marzipan. Remove it from the mortar. Put a half dozen candied limes, the dried ones, into the mortar and grind them up. If you want to add a little candied citron it will taste really good too. Put the marzipan back into the mortar and grind everything. Add six to eight whole eggs and mix everything together. Then make a dozen and a half of sweet scrambled egg yolks, chop them up, and add them to the pie batter so that the chopped-up pieces don't fall apart. Then make a fine dough and make the puff pastry pie by putting three or four sheets on the bottom and some strips cut with the trimmer on top. Note that the sweet scrambled egg yolks should always be made by pouring them through a skimmer and having the simple syrup at boiling point so that they cook very fast and don't get too mushy.

Sour cherry pie

Take four pounds of sour cherries and remove the pits. Put them in a saucepan, add a pound of sugar and a drop of wine. Put them on the flame and cook until a lot of juice is released. Cook slowly until they turn to preserves. Then make a pie with three or four (pastry) sheets on the bottom and one on top. If you have some cherry syrup left over, after the pie is cooked brush it on top if it doesn't already have everything it needs.

Borage pie

Boil as much borage as desired and then place in a strainer and thoroughly express the excess water. Then chop it and sauté with a bit of fresh butter and set aside to cool. Add eggs until it makes a thin batter. Season with pepper, ginger, nutmeg, and cinnamon and add in half a pound of ground sugar and you will make your pie this way. You can also make spinach pie or pie from any other leafy greens this way. If you would like to add some good cheese to these pies, you can.

[109] *Torta de Acelgas.*

Cortarás las acelgas muy menudas, y tomarás pan rallado, y queso, por iguales partes, y échale huevos hasta que esté blando: luego échale media libra de azúcar molido, y sazona con todas especias, y canela: luego échale las acelgas cortadas muy menudas como están, y échale un poco de manteca de vacas, y un poquito de sal, y tendrá el gusto de cazuela mojí. Destas mismas acelgas cortadas muy menudas, harás una torta, que llaman gatafura:[163] tomarás una libra de cuajada muy exprimida, y que esté (81r) muy agria, hecha del día antes y deshacerla has muy menuda, como para ginebradas, y mezclarla has con las acelgas, y echarla has pimienta, y un poco de aceite que sea muy bueno: y haz tu torta con una hoja muy delgada abajo, y otra arriba. Esta torta no ha de llevar azúcar, ni huevos, sino solo las acelgas crudas, y la cuajada, y pimienta, y aceite, y un poco de sal.

[110] (314r) *Relación de algunas cantidades para hacer tortas, hojaldres, costradas, y otras cosas.*[164]

No he puesto las cantidades de harina que han de llevar los hojaldres, porque unas veces son grandes, y otras pequeñas.
    Para cada hojaldre que sea buena, llevará libra y media de harina.
    Cada torta media libra de harina.
    (314v) Cada costra una libra de harina.
    Las tortas de fruta verde, como son membrillos, peras, o peros; tres libras de fruta, y tres cuarterones de azúcar: hanse de mondar, y hacer rebanadillas, y echar azúcar y fruta, y cuartillo y medio de agua, y ponerse a cocer, y espumarse, y consérvese poco a poco.
    Las tortas de albericoques y melocotones, y albérchigos y duraznos, para cada libra de azúcar cuatro de fruta, porque se va la mitad en cuescos y mondaduras. Para esta fruta se ha de poner el azúcar en un punto como para huevos mejidos. Este punto se da desta manera: Echar una libra de azúcar, [en este azúcar se ha de echar cuartillo y medio de agua] en un cacillo en pedacillos: luego echarle una clara de huevo batida dentro, y ponerlo a cocer, y no se espume hasta que quiera

---

163 Exactly as Martínez Montiño describes, the *Diccionario de autoridades* defines *gatafura* as "Torta, hecha de hierbas y leche cuajada aceda" [pie made with leafy greens and milk curds made with sour juice].

164 In the original edition, this section is found at the very end of the text (314r–316r). In all subsequent editions, it appears here at the end of the *tortas* section. I have moved it here because I believe this was Martínez Montiño's decision in 1617. Note also that general instructions for pie crusts come at the end of the pie section, not at the beginning as they would in cookbooks today.

Swiss chard pie

Finely chop chard. Take equal parts of breadcrumbs and cheese and add eggs to thin it out. Then add half a pound of ground sugar and season with all spices and cinnamon. Then add the finely chopped chard just as it is, a little butter, and a little salt. It will taste like a moji-style casserole. With this same finely chopped chard you can make a pie that is called *gatafura*. Take a pound of well-pressed, very sour clotted milk that was made the day before and crumble it up, as if you were making *ginebradas*. Mix it with the chard, add pepper and a little oil of excellent quality. Make your pie with a thin pastry sheet on the bottom and another one on top. This pie shouldn't have any sugar or eggs, just the raw chard, the pressed clotted milk, pepper, oil, and a little salt.

List of certain quantities for making pies, pastries, puff pastry pies, and other things

I have not written down quantities of flour for pastries because some are big and others small.

For each pastry to turn out good, it should have a pound and a half of flour.
Each pie, half a pound of flour.
Each puff pastry pie, a pound of flour.
Pies made with green fruit like quince, pears, and sour apples: three pounds of fruit and three quarters of a pound of sugar. You should peel, slice, and add the fruit and sugar to a pint and a half of water. Bring to a boil, skim off the foam, and simmer until thick.
Pies made with apricots, firm peaches, *albérchigos*, and clingstone peaches: for each pound of sugar, four of fruit because half of it will be pits and peels. For this type of fruit bring the sugar to the same boiling point you would for sweet scrambled egg yolks. You reach this stage in the following way. Break up a pound of sugar into small pieces and place them in a saucepan with a pint and a half of water. Add a beaten egg white and bring to a boil. Do not skim until it reaches

tomar punto,[165] porque recoja toda la espuma del azúcar: luego espúmalo con la espumadera, y si no quedare bien claro, cuélalo por la estameña, y tórnalo al fuego, y moja la punta del cuchillo en el (315r) azúcar, y deja caer una gota en la cabeza de un dedo, y aprieta con el otro dedo, y si hiciere un hilito, es el punto de los huevos mejidos: y estando desta manera está bueno para echar la fruta de cuesco, porque se conserva muy presto.[166] Esto se entiende para tortas, que para guardar, en el capítulo de las conservas está escrita la orden que se ha de tener. Y advierte, que todas las veces que digo, que se haga almíbar para algún plato, o para pasar alguna fruta, se entiende, que es el punto de huevos mejidos, porque es el punto más blando que se da al azúcar.

Las tortas de cuajada, o queso fresco, o requesones, lo más ordinario es, llevar dos libras de cuajada, o requesones, y ocho huevos, los seis mezclados con la cuajada, y los dos para hacer la masa: para esta cantidad será menester media libra de azúcar y un cuarterón de manteca, el azúcar ha de ir molido, y mezclado con la cuajada y los seis huevos. Estas tortas se pueden hacer con una (315v) libra de miel en lugar de azúcar.

Para una torta de leche son menester tres cuartillos de leche, y ocho huevos, los dos para hacer la masa, y con los cuatro harás una crema como para pasteles de leche, y con su media libra de azúcar, y un poco de manteca de vacas, y cocerla en un cacillo hasta que espese: luego meter los otros dos huevos crudos, y hacer tu torta.

Si no tuvieres cuajada, y quisieres cuajar leche, ponla a entibiar: luego toma un poco de hierba de cuajar, que es la flor de cardo, de los que parecen alcachofas, y lávala en agua tibia muy bien, y pásala en otro poquito de agua tibia: y luego toma un guijarrillo blanco y áspero, y estrega en él la hierba hasta que se ponga el agua morena: luego cuélala por una punta de estameña, o servilleta, y menea la leche: luego echa aquella agua dentro, y ponla al ardor de la lumbre, y cuajarse ha: y si no tuvieres hierba, con desatar un poquito de cuajo con (316r) un poco de agua tibia, y echarla en la leche, se cuajará.

Todas las veces que digo que se cuele por estameña, se entiende que la estameña no ha de ser de lana, porque son muy sucias para cosas de grasa. Han de ser las estameñas de unas beatillas de lino gordas y blancas, que las venden los Portugueses para las mozas.[167] Estas son muy limpias, y en manchándose se pueden meter en colada, y se ponen muy blancas.

---

165 In 1617, an additional phrase was added and is shown here in brackets. It appears in most other editions as well.

166 Martínez Montiño is describing the thread stage of boiling sugar. For more on the different sugar stages, see the section "Sweeteners" in the Introduction (45–6).

167 This is an example of one of the many clarifying points of technique. Martínez Montiño explains that for fatty foods, one should not use a wool strainer. Here he also reveals his experience working in Portugal when he reminds his readers of the type of linen to use. Carmen Bernis explains that in women's clothing, *beatilla* was a more expensive linen and was used for veils, *gorgueras*, and shirt sleeves (281).

the thread stage so that all the sugar foam can be skimmed at once. Skim with a skimmer and if it isn't clean, strain it through a cheesecloth and put it back over the fire. Dip the tip of a knife in the sugar and let a drop fall onto the tip of your finger. Squeeze it with another finger and if it makes a thread, it has reached the stage for making sweet scrambled egg yolks. This stage is good for stone fruit because it preserves it quickly. This is meant for pies. To preserve fruit long term, the instruction for how to do so is written in the chapter on preserves. Also note that every time I say to make simple syrup for a dish or for dipping fruit, it should be at the stage for making sweet scrambled egg yolks, because this is the softest sugar stage.

Pies made from clotted milk, farmer cheese, or curd cheese: the most common [preparation] is to use two pounds of clotted milk or curd cheese and eight eggs. Six eggs are mixed with the clotted milk and two [are] for the dough. For this quantity, half a pound of sugar and a quarter pound of lard are necessary. The sugar should be ground and added to the clotted milk and six eggs. These pies can be made with a pound of honey instead of sugar.

For a milk pie, you will need three pints of milk and eight eggs, two of them for making the dough. And with four eggs, make a cream as you would for making milk pastries with half a pound of sugar and a little butter. Cook it in a saucepan until thick, then add the remaining two eggs and make your pie.

If you don't have any clotted milk and you want to make some, warm up some milk. Take a little bit of herbs for curdling, which is the cardoon flower, the ones that look like artichokes, and wash it well in warm water and then rinse in other warm water. Next take a rough, white stone and scrub the cardoon in the warm water until the water turns brown. Then strain it with the tip of a cheesecloth or napkin. Agitate the milk. Then add that water and heat it over the flame and it will curdle. If you don't have any of this herb, then put a little rennet in a little warm water and add it to the milk and it will curdle.

Every time that I discuss straining through a cheesecloth, it should be understood that the cheesecloth isn't wool, because that type is very dirty for things with fat. The cheesecloths should be made from a thick, white fine linen, the kind the Portuguese sell for young women. This type is very clean, and when it gets stained, you can put it in the wash and it will come out clean.

[111] *Albondiguillas de Borrajas.*

Cocerás las borrajas, y luego las exprimirás muy bien del agua, y pícalas en el tablero, y échales un poco de pan rallado, y un poco de hierbabuena picada, y yemas de huevos, hasta que esté el batido un poco blando, y sazona con todas especias: y tendrás en un cacillo, o cazuela, caldo de garbanzos, sazonado con buena manteca de vacas, y cebolla frita, y harás las albondiguillas, como si fuesen de carne, y cuezan dos (81v) hervores, y cuájales con yemas de huevos, y agrio, y sírveles sobre rebanadillas de pan.

[112] *Un plato de todas frutas.*

Tomarás cosa de media libra de guindas en conserva, y algunas perillas, o albérchigos, y albercoques, y algunas ciruelas de monje.[168] Todo esto has de conservar por tu mano, porque todos los materiales con que has de trabajar, es necesario saberlos hacer. Y en cuanto toca a las conservas, adelante diré suertes dellas, cómo se han de hacer. Harás docena y media de huevos mejidos, y con estas conservas y huevos mejidos, y unas hojuelas muy delgadas, armarás un plato, componiéndole muy bien, entremetiendo las conservas con las hojuelas; de manera que se vea todo. Este plato se hace de muchas maneras, mudando las conservas, como son cermeñas, y limoncillos, y membrillos en su tiempo; mas en todo tiempo han (82r) de entrar los huevos mejidos, o encañutados, porque es lo que más adorna este plato.

[113] *Bollo de vacía*

Has de tomar dos libras de azúcar y clarificarlo; luego hacer en él veinte huevos hilados, y cuatro yemas doradas que sean duras, y ponerlo todo en una pieza. Luego tomarás dos libras de almendras mondadas, y majarás la una libra y un cuarterón, y los tres cuarterones harás unas rajitas muy menudas, de manera que salgan de cada almendra más de veinte rajillas. Luego apartarás la mitad del almíbar, y echarás las almendras majadas en la otra mitad, y cuécelo sobre el fuego meneándolo con un cucharón hasta que se haga un mazapán muy seco, que se desborone todo como pan rallado, y échale allí un poco de canela molida, y un poco de jengibre: y puesto todo desta manera toma dos libras de manteca fresca de vacas, y (82v) cuécela, y espúmala: y con esto tienes aparejado todos los materiales: ahora harás un poco de masa con agua, y sal, y dos huevos con claras, y sobarla has mucho, hasta que haga empollas,[169] y quede un poco blanda, como para hojaldrado: y harás el bollo desta manera: Tomarás una tortera, que sea un poco honda, y tiende una hoja de la masa muy delgada que se

---

168 According to Andrés Laguna, the *ciruelas de monje* [monk plum] was the best of the many plum varieties: "Entre las Ciruelas de España tienen el principado las que se dicen de Monge" [Among plums in Spain, the best are those called monk plums] (1.194).
169 *Empolla*, today *ampolla* [blister], refers to the bubbling of the dough.

Borage meatballs

Cook borage and squeeze out all the water. Chop it on a cutting board and add in some breadcrumbs, minced spearmint, and egg yolks until the batter is fairly smooth. Season with all spices. Have some garbanzo broth seasoned with good butter and fried onion in a saucepan or casserole. Make the balls, as if they were made from meat, and bring them to a boil twice. Thicken (some of the broth) with egg yolk and sour juice and serve it on slices of bread.

A dish of all kinds of fruit

Take about half a pound of preserved sour cherries, some small pears or *albérchigos*, apricots, and monk plums. This should all be preserved by hand because it is imperative to know how to make all the ingredients you work with. With respect to preserving, further on I will talk about many kinds of them [fruit] and how to preserve them. Make a dozen and a half of sweet scrambled egg yolks and with these preserves, sweet scrambled egg yolks, and some very thin pastry sheets. Arrange the dish very thoughtfully by interspersing preserves and pastry sheets so that you can see everything. This dish can be made several ways, changing up the preserved fruit seasonally for small pears, sweet limes, or quince. But in any season you should have sweetened egg yolks either scrambled or in canutos because they are the best garnish for this dish.

Airy pastry

Take two pounds of sugar and clarify it. Then make twenty eggs of candied egg yolk threads in it and four hard-boiled golden egg yolks and set it all aside in a dish. Next, take two pounds of shelled almonds. Grind up one and a quarter pounds and with the remaining three quarters, slice so thin that you get over twenty slivers from each almond. Then set aside half the simple syrup and add to the other half the ground almonds. Cook them over the fire, stirring them constantly with a big spoon until you have a very dry marzipan that crumbles as if it were breadcrumbs. Add a little ground cinnamon and a little ginger. Now that everything is set, take two pounds of fresh butter, boil it, and skim it. Now you have all your ingredients ready. Next make a little dough with water, salt, two eggs and knead it a lot until it makes little blisters and is soft like puff pastry dough. Make the pastry this way: Take a covered tart pan that is fairly shallow. Roll out a very thin sheet of dough

extienda con las manos, como hojaldrado, y ponla en la tortera, untándola primero con manteca, y ha de ser la hoja tan delgada, que se trasluzga la tortera por la masa;[170] luego úntala con manteca, y ponle otra y otra, hasta tres: luego echarás un lecho de mazapán desmoronado, que parezca pan rallado; luego toma un manojo de plumas, y rocía este lecho con manteca, y tiende otra hoja delgada, y échasela encima, y échale un lecho de huevos hilados, y torna a rociarlo con manteca. Luego echarás otro lecho de rajitas de almendras y rocíalo con manteca: y desta manera (83r) irás haciendo lechos, y metiendo hojas de masa muy delgadas entre lecho y lecho, hasta que se acaben los materiales, y cerrarás tu bollo con otra hoja de masa muy delgada, y cortarle has los bordes a la redonda, y hazle el borde ondeado, y rocíalo con manteca, y ponlo a cocer dentro de un horno: y cuando te pareciere que esté bien cocido, échale por encima del bollo la otra mitad del almíbar que tienes guardado, y échaselo caliente, y como se mezcle con la manteca que tiene el bollo cocerá muy recio a borbollones: y no tornes a cubrir el horno sino déjalo cosa de dos credos,[171] y sácalo de presto con un paño, y échalo en un plato, porque si te descuidares, y se aferrase el almíbar, no lo sacarías, sino haciéndolo pedazos. Y después que lo tengas en el plato, ponle encima las cuatro o cinco yemas doradas, y en cada yema tres, o cuatro rajitas de las almendras. Estas yemas han de quedar medio enterradas en el bollo, y échale por encima (83v) unos polvos de canela. Este plato puede durar un mes si fuere menester, unos le comen caliente, y otros, frío. A mi parecer es mejor caliente por amor de la manteca.[172]

[114] *Bollo Maimón.*[173]

Has de cocer treinta y seis huevos duros, y sácales las yemas, y deshazlas con un cucharón muy bien, de manera que parezcan hormigos,[174] y tendrás libra y media de almendras muy bien majadas, de manera que no se enaceite; y mézclalas con las

---

170 Although Martínez Montiño is using *hojaldrado* (puff pastry dough), his method of stretching the dough out by hand and his description of a layer so thin you can see through it are more closely aligned with phyllo dough. Another note of interest, this layering of thin dough, fat, and crumbled nuts and sugar, finished with simple syrup poured on top, is reminiscent of baklava. Here, however, it is also layered with candied egg yolk threads and topped with candied egg yolks.
171 The creed, by anyone who knows it, takes less than thirty seconds to recite. Martínez Montiño then is suggesting that the finishing touch on the pastry should take less than a minute to brown in the oven.
172 Martínez Montiño finishes the recipe with his personal preference, though he concedes that the dish can be served either warm or cold. His comment on its lasting a month reminds readers of the long-term preservation characteristics of sugar.
173 The word *maimón* comes from the Arabic, *maímun* [happy]. The spelling in Spanish varies from *maimón* to *maymón*, depending on the edition. This recipe was recreated using hard red spring wheat from Janie's Mill (Ashkum, IL). It is stone milled and sifted, a milling technique that would better approximate the production process of early modern Spain than that of commodity wheat, which is roller milled with the bran and germ removed. For images of recreating this recipe, see Appendix 3.10.
174 *Hormigos* is a sweet dish made with breadcrumbs, almonds, and honey. In Delicado's novel *La lozana andaluza*, the character Aldonza includes *hormigos* in the catalogue of great foods that came from her grandmother's kitchen (177–9).

that is stretched by hand, like puff pastry dough, and place it in the covered tart pan, greasing it first with butter. The sheet should be so thin that you can see the covered tart pan through the dough. Then grease with butter and put on another and another, up to three. Sprinkle on a layer of crumbly marzipan so that it looks like breadcrumbs. Next take a handful of feathers and sprinkle the layer with butter and roll out another thin sheet and lay it on top. Add a layer of candied egg yolk threads and sprinkle some butter on again. Then add another layer of grated almonds and sprinkle them with butter. In this way, continue making these layers, adding very thin pastry sheets between each layer until you've used up all the ingredients. Close up the pastry with another thin pastry sheet. Trim it, rounding out the edges and making a wavy edge. Sprinkle with butter and bake it in an oven. When it seems done, baste the pastry with the reserved simple syrup; make sure it's hot. When it mixes with the butter on the pastry it will cook rapidly and form bubbles. Leave the lid off the oven and leave it there for about the length of two creeds. Remove it immediately with a kitchen cloth and put it on a plate. If you get distracted and the sugar hardens, you will only be able to get it out in pieces. Once it's on the plate, place on top the four or five golden yolks and on each yolk, three or four almond slivers. These yolks should be nestled in the pastry. Sprinkle cinnamon powder on top. This dish can last up to a month if needed. Some eat it hot, others cold. My opinion is that it's better hot because the butter is better that way.

Maimon layered pastry

Hard boil thirty-six eggs and take out the yolks and crumble them with a big spoon so they look like *hormigos*. Then take a pound and a half of well-crushed almonds that are not too oily, and mix them with the egg yolks. Add enough

yemas de huevos, y echarle has canela molida hasta que vengan a quedar pardos. Luego tendrás dos libras de azúcar en punto, y harás masa como para bollo de vacía; y echarás tres hojas debajo como al otro, y tendrás dos libras de manteca de vacas fresca, cocida y espumada. Luego harás un lecho de aquellas yemas, y rociarla has con un poco de manteca, y otro poco de almíbar, de manera que lleve más azúcar (84r) que manteca. Luego echarás otra hoja de masa encima muy delgada, y otro lecho de yemas de huevos y almendras, y rocíala con manteca y azúcar: y desta manera irás haciendo lechos, hasta que se acaben los huevos y almendras, y cierra tu bollo con otra hoja muy delgada, y corta los bordes, y hazlos ondeados, y rocíalo con manteca, y cuécelo en un horno: y cuando te pareciere que está bien cocido: si tuvieres almíbar de sobra échaselo por encima de todos los bordes y si no tuvieres no le hará falta, porque lo tendrá dentro.

[115] *Otro Bollo Sombrero.*

Tomarás media libra de limoncillos en conserva, y media libra de diacitrón y majarlo has todo junto muy bien; luego echarás en el almirez cuatro pellas de manjar blanco, y majarlo has todo junto, y echarle has huevos hasta que esté blando, y sácalo en una pieza, y harás (84v) una docena y media de huevos hilados, y mézclalos con el batido de los limoncillos, y manjar blanco hecho pedacitos: y con este batido harás el bollo desta manera: Harás una masa fina sin azúcar, y tiende una hoja un poco gorda en que se ha de armar el bollo: luego harás unas hojuelas redondas, del ancho de la copa de un sombrero, unas mayores que otras, y fríelas en manteca de vacas, y ve armando el bollo sobre la hoja de masa gorda: y pondrás sobre ella una hojuela de las más anchas: y luego echarás del batido del manjar blanco, y limoncillos, y rocíala con manteca de vacas si fuere buena, y si no en su lugar unas pocas de natas; porque si la manteca no es buena, todo lo echa a perder: y desta manera irás poniendo hojas de masa frita, y encima della del batido hasta que se acabe, poniendo las hojuelas más pequeñas en lo más alto. Luego tiende otra hoja de masa un poco gorda, y cubrirás el bollo con ella, y juntarla has (85r) con la hoja de abajo muy bien, y cortarla has con la cortadera; de manera que queden dos dedos de falda, que parezca sombrero. Luego cortarás de la misma masa una pluma que sea ancha de abajo y puntiaguda de arriba, dándole unos cortecitos con la cortadera: y asiéntala en el bollo como pluma: luego harás de la misma masa su toquilla a modo de cordón, y ponle una roseta de la misma masa, y dorarla has con una yemas de huevos desatadas con un poquito de agua, y ponlo sobre unas obleas, y sobre un pliego de papel[175] untado con manteca, y ponlo a cocer en un horno

---

175 According to various *pliegos* at the Royal Palace, a *pliego de papel* [sheet of paper] at the seventeenth-century court measured approximately 17 x 8.25 in. Later in the cookbook, Martínez Montiño explains how to cut a single sheet to make up sixteen individual sheets for baking. Common sizes he uses are both the *medio pliego* [half sheet] and the *cuartilla* [quarter sheet]. For his instructions on folding and making different sizes, see the recipe "Bizcochos de harina de trigo" [Sweet biscuits with wheat flour] (539–41; 540–2).

ground cinnamon so that they turn brown. Then have ready two pounds of sugar at the early thread stage and make dough as you would for "Airy pastry." Place three sheets on the bottom, same as for the other [recipe], and have two pounds of fresh butter that has been cooked and skimmed. Next, make a layer from those yolks, sprinkle a little butter on them and some of the simple syrup so that there is more sugar [syrup] than butter. Then place another very thin sheet of dough on top, another layer of the egg yolks and almonds, and brush with butter and sugar. Continue layering in this way until there aren't any more eggs and almonds. Cover your pastry with another thin dough layer, trim the edges, and make them wavy. Brush with butter and bake in the oven. When it seems done, if you have extra simple syrup, put it around all the edges, but if you don't have extra, it won't need any because it will be inside.

Another hat pastry

Take half a pound of preserved limes and half a pound of candied citron and thoroughly grind them both together. Then, add to the mortar four scoops of blancmange and continue to mash everything together. Add eggs until it becomes smooth and put it in a bowl. Make a dozen and a half of candied egg yolk threads and mix them into the lime batter with blancmange as little pieces. With this batter you can make the pastry in the following way: Make a fine dough with no sugar and roll out a fairly thick sheet on which the pastry will be assembled. Then, make a few round pastry sheets, the width of a hat brim, some bigger than others, and fry them in butter. Begin assembling the pastry on the sheet of thick dough by placing on top one of the widest pastry sheets. Next spoon on some of the blancmange-lime batter and, if it's good, dot with some butter, and if it's not, then in its place some cream, because if the butter isn't good, the whole thing will be spoiled. Continue this way, placing fried pastry sheets and, on top of them, the batter until it is all used up, making sure the smallest [sheets] are on top. Then roll out another slightly thick sheet of dough and cover the pastry with it, joining the top and bottom tightly together, and trim the edges with a trimmer so that you are left with a border about two fingers wide and it looks like a hat. Then cut out of the same dough a feather that is wider below and pointy on the top and make little slits with the trimmer and place it on the pastry like a feather. Next from the same dough make a hat band in the form of a cord and add to it a rosette also made from the same dough. Brush on it a little egg yolk diluted with water and place it on some wafers which are on a piece of paper greased with butter. Place it

sobre una hoja de cobre: y cuando estuviere cerca de cocido, úntalo con manteca, y échale un poco de azúcar raspado por encima, porque haga costra. Este bollo las más veces se sirve frío.

Este bollo sombrero lo podrás hacer con los mismos materiales de otra manera: tendrás cosa de dos libras de conservas en almíbar, y cuatro pellas de manjar blanco, y docena y media de huevos hilados, (85v) y armarás el bollo de la misma manera que el de atrás salvo que todos los materiales han de ir distintos; pondrás una hoja de masa cruda, y luego una hoja de masa frita, y pondrás sobre ella de todas conservas, y bocaditos de manjar blanco, y huevos hilados, y rociarla has con un poco de manteca de vacas, que sea buena: si no la hubiere buena, no eches ninguna. Desta manera irás echando lechos hasta que se acaben los materiales, y cerrarás tu bollo, de la manera que dije en el otro.

También podrás hacer este bollo sin las hojas fritas con las conservas, y manjar blanco, y huevos hilados: y en lugar de las hojas echarás lechos de tallarines fritos muy delgados, y echarle has azúcar y canela, y rociarlos has con manteca de vacas: y desta manera harás el bollo.

[116] *Bollo de Rodilla.*[176]

Tomarás masa de levadura de los panecillos candeales, que esté un poco (86r) dura, y sobarla has mucho, hasta que esté más blanda, y haga empollas.[177] Luego tendrás una hoja como hojaldrado de masa delgada, y rociarla has con manteca de vacas, y arróllala en un trozo de caña: luego corta la masa, y saca ese hojaldrado de la caña; de manera que cuando salga de la caña, se pueda hacer como cubierta de pastel hojaldrado, salvo que ha de estar más gordo, y ha de tener un agujero en medio: echarlo has a freír en manteca de vacas: y cuando esté frito tendrás yemas de huevos batidas, y échalas por encima del bollo con una cuchara muy poco a poco por todo el bollo, y ellas, se irán metiendo por todas las hojas, y esto ha de ser en la misma sartén: luego vuélvelo, y fríelo un poco, y torna a echar de las yemas de huevos por la otra parte, y acábalo de freír: tendrás almíbar en punto, y pásalos por ella: de cuatro bollos harás un plato. Advierte, que en esta masa podrás echar yemas de huevos, aunque se haya de hojaldrar: (86v) la manteca ha de ser vacas, porque se pueda comer en día de pescado. Estos bollos se podrán hacer sin echar yemas de huevos al freír, que sin eso serán muy buenos.

---

176 *Rodilla* comes from the late Latín *rotella* (*ruedecita*), the diminuitive form of *rota*, which means *rueda* [circle]. Therefore, I've translated the title as sweet *spiral* roll, to capture the circular meaning of the origin of the word. For images of this recipe, see Appendix 3.11.
177 Candeal bread is a popular Spanish bread made from candeal wheat. It is known for its characteristic dense, white crumb, light crust, and round shape.

in the oven on a copper sheet. When it is almost done, grease the top with butter and sprinkle a little grated sugar so that it makes a sugar-coated crust. This pastry is most often served cold.

This hat pastry can also be made a different way with the same ingredients. Have about two pounds of preserves in simple syrup, four scoops of blancmange, and a dozen and a half of candied egg yolk threads. Assemble the pastry in the same way as the previous one, except that all the ingredients will go on separately. Place a sheet of uncooked pastry dough and then a sheet of fried dough and place on top all the preserves, little mounds of blancmange, and the candied egg yolk threads. Dot a little butter on top; make sure it's good quality. If it isn't, don't use any at all. Continue layering this way until all the ingredients are used up, and seal the pastry the same way I explained in the previous one.

You can also make this pastry with no fried pastry sheets and with [just] preserves, blancmange, and candied egg yolk threads. Instead of the sheets, build layers with very thin fried strips and sprinkle cinnamon and sugar and dot with butter. This is the way you can make the pastry.

Spiral sweet roll

Get leaven dough that is used for candeal rolls and is a little stiff. Knead it a lot until it is softer and blisters. Then roll out a sheet as you would for a thin puff pastry dough and dot it with butter. Roll it up on a piece of reed. Then, cut the dough and remove the puff pastry dough from the reed so that when it comes off the reed, you can make a puff pastry top, except it should be thicker and with a hole in the middle. Fry it in butter and when it's ready, have some beaten egg yolk ready and spoon it on top of the entire pastry little by little. The yolk should run between all the layers and this should happen in the same frying pan. Then flip it over and spoon the egg yolk over the other side and finish frying it. Have on hand some gently boiling simple syrup and dip the pastry in it. Four pastries make up one plate. Note that you can use egg yolk in the dough even if you treat it as puff pastry dough. The animal fat should be butter so that you can eat it on a fish day. It is possible to make these pastries without spooning on any egg yolk when frying and they will still turn out good.

[117] *Un Rebollo.*[178]

Otro bollo se hace, que se llama rebollo, es como el bollo sombrero, salvo que se diferencia en la hechura: Harás una masa fina, y tiende una hoja un poco larga, y de tres cuartas de ancho,[179] y pon por un borde todas las cosas que se echan en el bollo sombrero; y luego rociarás esta hoja de masa con manteca de vacas, y arrollarlo has como rollo de hojaldrado, y asentarlo has en un plato untado con manteca, y cuécelo en el horno: y cuando estuviere cocido dale una costra de azúcar por encima. Y advierte, que cuando se pongan los materiales en la hoja, los has de poner a la larga por junto al borde, y has de poner más a la una parte que a la otra, para que cuando esté (87r) arrollado parezca lamprea,[180] o enguila,[181] que parezca la una punta cabeza, y la otra cola. Hase de cocer enroscado.

[118] *Bollo Roscón.*

Harás una masa fina sin azúcar, y tiende tres hojas redondas del tamaño de la falda de un sombrero grande muy delgadas, y úntalas con manteca, y pon una sobre otra, y tiéndelas un poco más con el palo de la masa, de manera que todas tres parezcan una. Esta hoja ha de ser redonda, y compondrás de todas conservas, y huevos mejidos, y unos pocos de tallarines fritos, y un poco de manjar blanco alrededor: esto ha de ser en ruedo, que parezca una corona, y le pondrás pedacitos de mazapán cocido en el cazo, como está dicho atrás, y rocíalo con un poco de manteca: y luego harás otra hoja de tres hojas, como la de abajo, y pónsele encima, mojando primero con agua los bordes, y el hueco de la corona, y (87v) asentarla has un poco floja, de manera que se pueda juntar por enmedio la una hoja con la otra, y apretarlas muy bien con los dedos, de manera que se pegue bien: luego cortarás aquella masa de en medio en dos cruces, una por otra,[182] que venga a hacer ocho puntos, e irás levantando una a una, y pegándolas al bollo, y harán una corona redonda, redondearlo has por la parte de afuera, que no quede más borde de cuanto se pueda hacer un repulgo, untarlo has con manteca, y ráspale un poco de azúcar por encima: y si lo quisieres dorar, y después echar su costra de azúcar,

---

178 I've decided to leave the original title but want to add that the *re-* prefix signifies an intensification of the thing or action. In this way, we could think of this recipe as "an intense sweet roll." From the instructions, Martínez Montiño's recipe should look like coiled puff pastry with filling that consistently decreases from one end to the other.
179 For more on measurements in seventeenth-century Spain, see Appendix 2, "On Measurements."
180 *Lamprea* [lamprey] is an eel-like vertebrate with a round sucking mouth that feeds on the blood of others. As is apparent in the cookbook, it makes a valued fish dish. Today different municipalities in Galicia celebrate lamprey with a "Festa da Lamprea" [Lamprey festival].
181 In the original 1611 edition, *anguila* is written as *enguila*. All subsequent editions use *anguila*.
182 These two cross marks will end up looking like an asterisk.

Rebollo

You can make another pastry called *rebollo*. It's like hat pastry except that its shape is different. Make a fine dough and roll out an extra long sheet, three quarters [of a yard] wide. Spread on one edge everything that goes into the hat pastry and then dot the sheet with butter. Roll it up as you would a roll of puff pastry dough and set it on a plate greased with butter. Place it in the oven. When it is done, make a sugar coating on the crust. Note that when you are adding the ingredients to the sheet, place them all close to the long edge. Also put more on one end than on the other so that when it's rolled up it looks like lamprey or eel with one end as the head and the other the tail. It should be baked coiled up.

Ring-shaped pastry

Make a fine dough with no sugar and roll out three very thin, round sheets the size of the brim of a big hat. Grease with lard and place one on top of the other. Roll them out a little more with a rolling pin so that all three are now one. This sheet should still be round. Arrange all types of preserves, sweet scrambled egg yolks, a few strips of fried pastry dough, and a little blancmange all around. It should all be placed around the edge and look like a crown. Sprinkle little pieces of marzipan that has been cooked in a saucepan as previously explained and dot with a little lard. Next make another sheet with three sheets like the bottom one and place it on top, wetting first the edges with water and the inside of the crown. Loosely lay it on top so that you can join the two sheets in the centre, squeezing them with your fingers so they stick well together. Next, cut the dough in the centre in the form of two crosses, one on top of the other so that there are eight points, and pull each one up one by one and stick them on the pastry and they will form a round crown. Round out the outside so that no edge is left except what's left for crimping the edge. Grease with lard and grate some sugar over the top. If you want to first make it golden and then sugar coat it, that will turn out really well.

parecerá muy bien. Con estos mismos materiales podrás hacer otro bollo redondo, que parezca empanada de enguila, y echándole sus dos, o tres hojas fritas que sean grandes y redondas, echando los materiales sobre ellas. A todos estos bollos podrás echar natas, mezcladas con yemas de huevos, que sirven al bollo de manteca, y es uno de los mejores materiales que lleva.

[119] (88r) *Un pastelón de Mazapán.*

Has de hacer una hoja de masa fina, que sea un poco gorda, y has de tener aparejados los materiales, que serán manjar blanco, mermelada, mazapán cocido en el cazo, que esté bien seco, albérchigos en conserva, cascos de membrillos, que sean todas conservas blandas en almíbar. Luego tendrás dos libras de pasta de mazapán hecha en el almirez, y harás un rollito largo y redondo: y con esto formarás un pastelón sobre la hoja de la masa fina, untándolo por debajo con una gota de agua, y levantarle has con los dedos cosa de una pulgada, a modo de borde de pastel: y pondrás dentro una hostia blanca, cortada de las esquinas: y sobre esta hostia pondrás de todos los materiales que están dichos, de manera que cargue todo sobre la hostia: luego harás otro rollito de pasta de mazapán, e irásle poniendo sobre el otro borde, mojándolo primero (88v) con una gota de agua: y subirás el borde con los dedos otro tanto como el otro, o más: y tornarás a meter dentro otra hostia, y tornarla has a cargar con los mismos materiales: y desta manera irás haciendo hasta que tengas un pastelón muy abultado. Luego harás unos rollitos de la misma pasta muy delgados: y harás sobre el pastelón un enrejadillo, y repulgarlo has: con esto queda cerrado. A este pastelón no se le ha de echar ningún género de manteca. Y advierte, que cuando comenzares a hacer este pastelón, has de cortar un suelo de la masa, no mas de lo que fuere menester para armar el pastelón, y haslo de poner luego sobre dos, o tres obleas; porque después de hecho lo puedas pasar desde el tablero a la hoja del horno: y si lo quisieres armar luego sobre la hoja, ahorrarás trabajo. Y advierte, que esto de hacer el pastelón de tantas piezas, es más seguro, que levantarlo de una; porque desta manera el peso no hace (89r) fuerza en las paredes, y siempre sale muy derecho, y de la otra manera nunca deja de salir tuerto: y ya algunas veces se cae, porque yo lo tengo experimentado. Cuando este pastelón estuviere cocido, tomarás un poco de azúcar molido y cernido, y desatarlo has con una gota de agua; de manera que quede espeso, y vedriarlo has así caliente como está con unas plumas, y quedará con muy buen lustre.

With these same ingredients you can make another ring pastry that will look like an eel empanada. Put together two or three fried sheets that are round and fairly big and put the ingredients on them. To all of these pastries you can add cream mixed with egg yolk that will act as the lard for the pastry. It [the cream] is one of the best ingredients it can have.

A big marzipan pie

Roll out a sheet of fine dough that is a little thick and have ready all your ingredients, which are blancmange, jam, very dry marzipan cooked in a pan, preserved *albérchigos*, and quince rind. All the preserves should be soft, soaked in simple syrup. Next, have two pounds of marzipan that was made in the mortar and roll it out into a long, round piece. This will be the base of the pie that sits on the sheet of fine dough, dabbing it with a drop of water. Lift the edges up with your fingers to form an inch-deep pie border. Place inside a white wafer that has been trimmed in the corners. On top of this wafer, place all of the ingredients already mentioned so that they all stay on top of the wafer. Then roll out another piece of marzipan and place that on top of the edge, first wetting it with a little water. Once again make an edge with your fingers as deep as the one before or deeper and set another wafer inside and load it up with the same ingredients. Do this until it is overflowing. Next make some skinny rolls with the same marzipan and place them on top of the pie in the form of lattice work, crimp it, and with this, the pie will be sealed. No animal fat should be added to this pie. Note that when you begin making the crust, you should cut out the bottom only to the size necessary for assembling it. Then you should put it on top of two or three wafers so that you can easily transport it from the cutting board to the baking sheet. If you want to assemble it right on the baking sheet, you will save yourself some work. Also note that making this big pie in multiple pieces is safer than making it all as one. This way the weight won't push against the walls and it will always come out right, while the other way it always comes out uneven and sometimes even collapses. I've experienced this. Once the pie is cooked, take a little sifted ground sugar and add a few drops of water to it so that it is thick. Glaze it while still hot with a feather brush and it will give it a nice lustre.

[120] *Bollos Pardos.*

Tomarás media libra de almendras dulces mondadas, y majarlas has en el almirez, y después de majadas échalas media libra de azúcar, y harás pasta de mazapán. Luego pondrás en el tablero media libra de harina de trigo floreada,[183] y sobre ella media libra de manteca de vacas fresca, y media docena de yemas de huevos, y la pasta de mazapán, y un poquito de sal: y con esto harás una masita encerada, sin echar agua, ni vino, (89v) ni otra cosa; y echarle has canela molida, y cernida, hasta que esté la masa muy parda; luego harás unos bollitos a modo de mostachones,[184] haciéndoles unas raitas con la vuelta del cuchillo. Cuézanse sobre obleas a fuego manso: y con estas cantidades podrás hacer un plato destos bollos.

[121] *Bollo Fitete.*

Harás una masa de agua, y sal, y huevos encerada, y sobarla has un poco, y tenderla has que quede un poco gorda:[185] y tendrás manteca de vacas fresca, y que esté muy bien lavada y sobada, y pondrás en la mitad de la hoja de la masa muchos bocadillos de manteca, y polvorearla has con un poco de harina, y echarás la media hoja que no tiene manteca sobre la que lo tiene, y tornarás a tender la hoja que quede un poco gorda: y pondrás bocadillos de manteca en la mitad, y tornarás a doblarla como la primera vez, y tornarás a tender (90r) la hoja, y echarás manteca por toda ella, y arrollarla has apretándola muy bien. Luego cortarás este rollo de masa en trozos, y a cada trozo recogerás las puntas, y harás una tortita redonda de cada una, tendido con las manos, de manera que de seis destos bollitos se haga un buen plato: y si quisieres hacer de cada bollo un plato, harás un rollo gordo, y cortarás los trozos un poco grandes, y harás las tortas gordas y anchas, del gordor de un dedo. Hará cada bollo un plato, y dorarlos has con unas yemas de huevos, desatadas con una gota de agua, y pondráslos sobre papeles untados con manteca. Cuécelos en el horno, y sírvelos con buena miel por encima, y azúcar raspado. Desta masa de bollos podrás hacer muchas suertes de frutas: y ya está dicho que puedes hacer de cada bollo un plato, y de seis bollitos un plato:[186] y podrás hacer destos bollitos chicos más delgados, rellenos de názulas[187] con sus yemas de huevos y azúcar, o (90v) de peros conservados,

---

183 *Trigo floreado* refers to a high-quality, finely sifted flour. There would be very little bran left in the flour.

184 For more on *mostachón* [mostachon cookie], see the recipe "Memoria de los mostachones" [Memoir of mostachon cookies] (510; 511).

185 Although Martínez Montiño does not specify flour for this dough, it is understood that it is part of the recipe.

186 Martínez Montiño regularly suggests that the same recipe can be used for making six small baked goods that fit onto a plate or one big one.

187 *Názula* is another word for *requesón* [curd cheese, like ricotta or cottage cheese]. For more information, see 690.

Brown pastries

Have half a pound of shelled, sweet almonds and grind them in the mortar. After they are ground, add half a pound of sugar and make marzipan paste. Next, put on the pastry board half a pound of finely sifted wheat flour and on top of that half a pound of fresh butter, a half dozen egg yolks, the marzipan, and a little salt. Make an elastic dough without adding any water, wine, or anything else. Add some ground cinnamon so that the dough is brown. Then make little pastries like mostachon cookies, scoring them with the back of the knife. Bake them on wafers on low flame. With these quantities you can make a whole plate of these pastries.

Fitete pastry

Make an elastic dough with water, salt, and eggs and knead it a little. Roll it out so that it is slightly thick. Have fresh butter that is well washed and kneaded and put several dabs of it on half of the dough. Sprinkle with a little flour and fold the unbuttered half over on top of the buttered half. Roll it out again so that it is still a little thick, dab butter on half of it and fold it over again like the first time. Roll it out again and add butter over all of it. Roll it all up, squeezing it tightly. Then, cut this roll of dough into pieces, and tuck in the tips of each piece and with your hands stretch them into little round pies so that six of them fill up a plate. If you prefer to make one big, plate-sized pastry, then make a thicker roll and cut each piece bigger. Make the pies thicker and wider, about the thickness of a finger. Each pastry will fit on a plate. Add a golden glaze with a wash of yolk egg and a drop of water and place them on paper greased with butter. Bake them in the oven and serve with good honey and grated sugar on top. With this pastry dough you can make many kinds of fried dough. Making big plate-sized pastry and six little ones has already been explained. You can make very thin mini pastries, filled with curd cheese, and the right amount of egg yolks and sugar, or with sour apple preserves,

o del relleno de fruta de cañas, o de otra cualquiera cosa, has de hacer dos bollitos, y poner el relleno sobre el humo: y luego poner el otro encima: luego cerrarlo como pastel de dos hojas sin repulgo. Otras veces les podrás dar unos cortes por encima, que lleguen hasta el medio, y abrirán muchas hojas, aunque no levantarán tanto.[188] Y también podrás hacer fruta de masa haciendo bollos un poco más delgados: y luego cortarlos de la manera que te pareciere unas eses como rosquillas, otras cortadas al sesgo: y estas frutillas pondrás sobre medios pliegos de papel, y cuéceles en el horno, y dorándolas primero, sírvelas por fruta de postre con su miel, y azúcar raspado por encima. Es muy buena fruta. Esta masa es muy buena para hacer todo género de tortas, porque deshoja muy bien, y es masa muy suave: y si quisieres hacer algunas empanadillas de pescado, o de otras cosas tiernas, son muy buenas.

[122] (91r) *Otra manera de masa de Bollos.*

Para hacer las empanadas que están atrás escritas, harás la masa desta manera, echarás harina de trigo floreada sobre el tablero, y harás una presa redonda, y dentro della echarás yemas de huevos, y sal, y un poco de vino: y tomarás la manteca fresca bien lavada, y sobada, y harás muchos bocadillos, y pondráslos alrededor de la presa en la propia harina: y luego amasarla has sin sobarla no más de cuanto se mezcle la harina con los materiales. Luego harás tus empanadillas, y deshojarán casi tanto como la masa de los bollos, ha de ir un poco más salada que la otra; porque no ha de llevar dulce ninguno. Quiero dejar ahora los bollos, porque se pueden hacer de tantas maneras, que sería cosa muy larga: y sabiendo hacer los que tengo dicho, siempre el oficial hace algo más de lo que le enseñan. Ahora pondré (91v) aquí media docena de hojaldres de los mejores que se hacen.

[123] *Hojaldre de Torreznos.*[189]

Hará una masa con buena harina floreada, y agua, y sal, y huevos con claras un poco dura, y sobarla has mucho: luego irás metiendo manteca de puerco fría, hasta que la masa haga mucha correa: luego irás metiendo azúcar molido y cernido,

---

188 Martínez Montiño is signalling that the top cuts should be deeper than a simple scoring and should go all the way through the crust.
189 Generally, *torreznos* are roasted pork *belly*, but as seen here and in one other recipe, "Torreznos lampreados" [Roasted pork fat, lamprea style] (554; 555), Martínez Montiño also uses the term for fat from other parts of the pig. For this reason, here, I have translated *torreznos* as *roasted pork fat*.

or with filling from "Fried dough with marrow filling," or really with anything. You will make two pastry crusts. Smoke the (one with the) filling and then put the second pastry crust on top. It should be sealed like a double-crusted pie without crimping. You can also cut slits on top that cut to the centre and a lot of layers will open, although they'll rise just a little. You can also make a fried pastry dough [by] making even thinner pastries and then cutting them into the shapes you wish, like S-shaped pastries, [or] others cut diagonally. Place these little pastries on half sheets of paper and bake them in the oven, first brushing them with egg wash. Serve them as a fried pastry dessert with the right amount of honey and grated sugar on top. It makes a very good fried dough. This dough is very good for making all sorts of pies because the layers separate well and the dough is smooth. If you want to make turnovers with fish or with other delicate fillings, they will also turn out very good.

Another way to make pastry dough

To make the empanadas that are written in earlier pages, make the dough this way. Spread finely sifted wheat flour on the pastry board and make a round well. Pour inside it egg yolks, salt, and a little wine. Take some fresh butter that has been well rinsed and kneaded and separated into many small pieces and cut them into the dough. Bring it together with only as much kneading as is necessary to mix all the ingredients together. Then make the turnovers. They should flake out almost as much as the dough for pastries does and it [this dough] should be a little more savoury than the other because it has nothing sweet in it. I am going to end the pastry section now because there are so many ways to make them that it would end up being too long. And, knowing how to make the ones I have explained, the cook always makes something beyond what he is taught. Now I'll record here a half dozen puff pastry (recipes) from among the best that are made.

Puff pastry with roasted pork fat

Make a slightly thick dough with good, finely sifted flour, water, salt, and eggs and knead it a lot. Add in cold lard until the dough is very elastic. Next mix in sifted ground sugar until the dough becomes very sweet. It will lose its elasticity

hasta que la masa esté bien dulce: ella perderá la correa con el azúcar, mas sobándola mucho tornarála a cobrar. Tendrás tocino de pernil, que sea bueno cortado al través de la hebra, y muy delgadas las rebanadillas, y tendráslas en agua tibia dos, o tres horas, y no sea más de tibia, porque se echarán a perder. Luego las escurrirás desta agua, y lavarlas has en dos o tres aguas frías, y a la postre las lavarás en un poco de vino, y apretarlas has muy bien, que no les quede ninguna agua, ni vino. Tomarás un poco de la masa, y harás un rollito, y (92r) darás con él en el tablero, y la harás tender mucho. Luego lo cogerás por medio, y harás della un cordón, torciendo las dos puntas, y tendrás papeles untados con manteca: y deste cordón harás una rosquilla, de manera que lo torcido se vea por las orillas. Luego toma de las rebanadillas del tocino, y asentarle has cinco o seis en medio de la hojaldrilla, de manera que haga el hoyo en medio redondo, y queden los bordes libres, y más altos que el tocino, y cuécelas en el horno, y no les eches otra cosa ninguna: de cuatro, o cinco destas se hace un plato: y si quisieres hacer una hojaldre grande que haga plato, de la misma manera lo podrás hacer. Con la propia masa de las hojaldrillas puedes hacer unos hojaldres grandes, cortando un poco más gordo el tocino, y cociéndolo con agua y vino, y mejorana, e hisopillo. Cuando el tocino esté blando saca las hierbas, y el cocimiento, dejando un poco: luego échale un poco de azúcar: y esto cueza (92v) un poco, y déjalo enfriar, y échalo en la hojaldre por toda ella, y échale un poco de canela, y échale un enrejadillo de la misma masa. Éstas se hacen bien en torteras. Las hierbas no importará mucho que las lleven.

[124] *Hojaldre relleno.*

Tomarás masa de levadura, como para pan candeal, y sobarlo has, y harás dellas hojaldrado con manteca de puerco, que sea un poco gordo: luego tomarás media libra de almendras, y harás pasta de mazapán con otra media libra de azúcar, y echarle has un poquito de agua de aza[h]ar, y un poco de canela molida, y un poquito de clavo, y una migaja de nuez de especias, y darle has una vuelta sobre el fuego en un cacillo; y luego harás una hoja de hojaldrado muy ancha y gorda, tendiéndola sobre el tablero con los dedos, dejándole buenos bordes, y asentarla has sobre un pliego de papel, y harás una torta de mazapán, (93r) casi tan ancha como la hojaldre, y asentarla has sobre ella. Luego harás otra hoja del hojaldrado, y echársela has encima, mojando los bordes con agua, y cerrarás tu hojaldre de manera, que queden los bordes muy iguales y gordos, rocíala con manteca, y ponla a cocer en el horno: y cuando la hojaldre estuviere cocida del todo, toma un poco de miel que sea muy buena, y échasela por encima de toda la hojaldre; luego échale mucho azúcar, y canela, y tórnala al horno hasta que se embeba toda la miel, y se enjugue el azúcar: luego sácala, y sírvela caliente.

with the sugar, but if you knead it a lot, it will return. Have some ham fat of good quality and cut against the grain in very thin slices. Soak them in warm water for two or three hours. The water should just be warm or it will ruin the fat. Remove from water, strain them, and rinse two or three times in cold water. The last time they should be rinsed in a little wine. Squeeze them out a lot so that no wine or water is left. Take a little of the dough and roll it into a small ball. Place it on the pastry board and roll it out a lot. Next, pick it up in the middle and make a rope, twisting the two ends. Have papers greased with lard and with the rope make a ring so that the twisted part is on the outside edge. Next, take the slices of fat and place five or six of them in the centre of the pastry ring so that the centre has a round hole, the edges have nothing touching them, and they are taller than the fat. Bake in the oven and don't add anything else. Four or five of these fit on a plate. If you want to make one big puff pastry that fits on a plate, you can make it in the same way. With the same dough for the little puff pastries, you can make big ones by cutting the fat a little thicker and boiling it in water, wine, marjoram, and winter savory. When the fat is soft, remove the herbs and [most of] the liquid, leaving just a little. Then add a little sugar, let it boil a little, cool, and place it over the whole puff pastry. Sprinkle on some cinnamon and make lattice from the same dough. These cook well in covered tart pans. It is not essential to include the herbs.

Stuffed puff pastry

Take leaven dough, like for candeal bread, knead it, and make puff pastry dough with lard; it should be a little thick. Next, take half a pound of almonds and make marzipan paste with another half pound of sugar. Add in a little orange blossom water, a little ground cinnamon, a little clove, and a pinch of nutmeg and stir it all around in a saucepan over a flame. Then roll out a very wide and thick sheet of puff pastry dough, spreading it out on the pastry board with your fingers. Make nice edges and place it on a sheet of paper. Make your marzipan pie almost as wide as the puff pastry and place it on the dough. Next, make another sheet from the puff pastry dough and place it on top, wetting the edges with water. Seal up the puff pastry so that the edges end up thick and even. Dot with lard and set it in the oven to bake. When the puff pastry is all the way cooked, take a little honey of excellent quality and drizzle it over the entire puff pastry. Then sprinkle a lot of cinnamon and sugar and put it back in the oven until it soaks up all the honey and the sugar has crystallized. Remove it and serve hot.

[125] *Hojaldre con enjundia de Puercos.*

Tomarás dos libras de masa de pan con levadura: y si fuere posible ha de ser pan de leche, y de pan candeal, y meterla has cuatro, o seis huevos, y tomarás enjundia de puerco fresca, y desvenarla has, y majarla has muy bien en el almirez, e irásle quitando las venillas que salieren,[190] (93v) irás mezclando con la masa, sobarla has mucho hasta que haga mucha correa: y cuando vieres que tiene harta manteca, irásle metiendo azúcar molido, y cernido. Esto ha de ser poco, porque ha de llevar después almíbar por encima. Esta masa ha de quedar bien blanda. Luego untarás una tortera con enjundia, y pondrásle unas obleas debajo, y por los bordes, y echarás la masa dentro, y ponla al fuego en un horno: y cuando la hojaldre estuviere cuajada, tomarás un poco de agua fría, y mojarás los dedos, y harás unos picos por toda la hojaldre, los más altos que pudieres: y si te quemares ve metiendo la mano en el agua: y luego torna la tortera al horno, y acaba de cocer la hojaldre. Luego tendrás media libra de azúcar en almíbar, y échasela por encima de toda la hojaldre, y cueza un poco, y sácala, y haz unas rosquillas de melindres, y pondrás en cada pico de la hojaldre una rosquilla. Estos melindres hallarás escritos, como (94r) se han de hacer, en el capítulo de los bizcochos. Esta hojaldre se sirve caliente.

Otra hojaldre se hace de la misma manera en día de pescado, sólo en lugar de la enjundia se ha de echar manteca de vacas fresca que sea muy buena, lavándola primero, y sobándola muy bien. Esta hojaldre ha de llevar tres cuarterones de azúcar: y si fuere muy grande llevará más. Es muy buena suerte de hojaldres. Advierte, que la masa con levadura, si no hicieses luego las hojaldres acedarse ha la masa, y estarían agrias las hojaldres, échales sus melindres, y sírvelas calientes.

[126] *Hojaldre de Mazapán.*

Harás una masa con agua y sal, y cuatro huevos con claras, de manera que quede un poco dura, y vela sobando con manteca hasta que esté la masa blanda, y tenga mucha correa. Luego tomarás pasta de mazapán, hecha de media libra de almendras, y media de azúcar, (94v) de manera que venga a ser tanta cantidad de pasta como de masa, y mézclalo todo, y sóbalo todo muy bien, porque se mezcle el mazapán con la masa; luego tendrás cuartillas de papel,[191] untadas con manteca, y harás una hojaldrillas llanas y redondas, y cuécelas en el horno: y tendrás un poco de buena miel caliente, y pásalas por ello, y ponlas en su plato, y enjugarse han muy presto, y échales un poco de azúcar, y canela por encima. Estas son muy buenas para día de Sábado con manteca de puerco: y en día de pescado con manteca de vacas.

---

190 The deveining of an animal is a Jewish practice, but here performed on pork.
191 For more on the size of paper sheets used for baking, see 260n175.

Puff pastry with pork fat

Take two pounds of leaven bread dough, and, if possible, it should be from milk bread and from candeal bread. Add to it four to six eggs. Take fresh pig fat tissue, devein it, and mash it up in a mortar, removing the little veins as they surface. Mix this with the dough, knead it a lot until it is very elastic. When you see it has enough lard, begin adding sifted ground sugar. This should just be a little, because simple syrup goes on top later. This dough should be very soft. Then grease the covered tart pan with the pig fat tissue and lay some wafers on the bottom and around the sides. Put the dough in and place it on the fire in the oven. When the pastry sets, take a little cold water, wet your fingertips, and raise peaks all over the top of the pastry. Make them as tall as possible. If you burn yourself, dunk your hand in water. Return the covered tart pan to the oven and let the pastry finish baking. Next, take half a pound of simple syrup and pour it on top of the entire pastry, let it cook a little, and remove it. Make some frosted ring-shaped pastries and place a ring-shaped pastry on top of each of the peaks. [The recipe] for making these frosted treats is written in the chapter on sweet biscuits.[6] This pastry is served hot.

Another pastry can be made the same way on a fish day if, instead of pork fat, you use good-quality fresh butter that has first been rinsed and then kneaded very well. This pastry should have three quarters of a pound of sugar and more if it's very big. It's an excellent kind of pastry. Note that with leaven dough, if you don't make the pastry right away and the dough turns sour, the pastries will turn out sour. Add frosting on the top and serve them hot.

Marzipan puff pastry

Make a dough with water, salt, and four eggs so that it is fairly firm. Knead lard into it until it becomes soft and fairly elastic. Then take some marzipan paste made with half a pound of almonds and a half [pound] of sugar so that you have as much marzipan as dough. Mix it all together and knead it well so that the marzipan is incorporated into the dough. Then have quarter sheets of paper greased with lard. Make some flat, round little puff pastries and bake them in the oven. Have a little good-quality hot honey and dip them in it. Put them on a plate; they will rapidly soak up (the honey). Sprinkle a little cinnamon and sugar on top. For Saturdays, these are very good with lard, and on fish days, with butter.

---

6 Martínez Montiño has two *rosquilla* recipes: "Memoria de las rosquillas" [Memoir of ring-shaped pastries] (530; 531) and "Otra suerte de rosquillas" [Another kind of ring-shaped pastries] (530; 531).

[127] *Hojaldre con leche.*

Tomarás media azumbre de leche, y ponlo al fuego en un cazo, y échale un poco de manteca fresca de vacas, y un poco de sal: y cuando comience a cocer, échale harina de trigo floreada, y menéalo con un cucharón, y ha de quedar una masa un poco dura, y cuécela muy bien sobre la lumbre, y sácala luego (95r) al tablero, y métele media docena de huevos. Luego irás sobándola, y metiéndole manteca hasta que esté blanda. Luego métele media libra de azúcar molido y cernido. Luego pondrás unas obleas en una tortera, y echa la masa dentro, y pon tu hojaldre a cocer en un horno: y cuando esté quejada harás los picos, como está dicho en los de atrás, y acábala de cocer, y échale un poco de almíbar por encima, y tórnala otro poquito al horno para que se acabe de enjugar. Son de muy buen gusto estos hojaldres. Y advierte, que en cualquiera hojaldre podrás meter, si quisieres, en lugar de torreznos algunas cosas de conservas, como son cascos de membrillos, o cermeñas, o albérchigos, o albericoques.

[128] *Una Hojaldre tropezada.*[192]

Echarás en el tablero harina de trigo floreada, la que te pareciere que será menester para una hojaldre, cosa de libra y media, y harás una presa redonda, y (95v) echa dentro della cinco, o seis huevos, y la manteca que pareciere será menester: luego echarás otra tanta cantidad de pasta de mazapán, como hay de harina, y un poquito de vino, y un grano de sal, y amásala, sin que la sobes mucho, no más de cuanto se embeba la harina con los materiales, y harás tu hojaldre grande, que haga un plato, o seis chicas. Estos no se han de pasar por miel, ni se les ha de echar otra cosa más de un poco de azúcar raspado por encima. Salen enjutas[193] y desboronan[194] mejor que las otras. Desta misma masa se pueden hacer unas rosquillas chiquitas, y unos panecillos redondos muy chiquillos, suelen salir muy buenos.

---

192 The idea of *tropezada* refers to how the ingredients are loosely blended together, almost as if, as the adjective suggests, they just bump into one another. In his instructions, Martínez Montiño specifies this delicate kneading process and insists that the result is a flakier product.

193 Although *enjuto* [dry] is often associated with scrawniness, Martínez Montiño generally uses the term in a neutral or positive way. See, for example, "Como se aderezan las espinacas" [How to prepare spinach] (376; 377), "Huevos con cominos" [Eggs with cumin] (438; 439), and "Mazapanes secos" [Dry marzipan] (546; 547).

194 *Desboronar* or today *desmoronar* means *to collapse* or *to crumble*. Given the context of puff pastry, I have translated it here as *flaky*.

Milk puff pastry

Take one quart of milk and place it in a pan over the fire. Add a little fresh butter and a little salt. When it begins to boil, add finely sifted wheat flour and stir it with a spoon. The dough should end up a little firm. Cook it thoroughly over the flame and then turn it out onto the pastry board and add a half dozen eggs. Next, continue kneading it and adding butter until it is soft. Add half a pound of sifted, ground sugar. Place some wafers in a covered tart pan and put the dough in. Place your puff pastry in the oven to cook and when it sets, make some peaks as previously explained and finish baking. Add some simple syrup on top and briefly return it to the oven so that it finishes drying. These puff pastries are very tasty. Note that for any puff pastry, if you want, instead of adding roasted pork belly you can add preserves, such as quince rind, Cermeño pears, *albérchigos*, or apricots.

A puff pastry, loosely pulled together

Put finely sifted wheat flour on the pastry board, enough for making your puff pastry, about a pound and a half, and make a round well. Pour in five or six eggs and the amount of lard you think necessary. Then add in the same amount of marzipan paste as flour, a little wine, and a pinch of salt. Knead it, but not too much, only enough to pull together the flour with the other ingredients. Either make your puff pastry big, the size of a plate, or [make] six small ones. Do not dip these in honey or add anything to them except a little grated sugar on top. They will turn out a little dry and flakier than the others. With this same dough you can make mini doughnuts and mini round rolls. They usually turn out very good.

[129] *Panecillos rellenos de conservas.*

Tomarás masa de levadura de panecillos candeales, cosa de dos libras, y meterle has cinco, o seis huevos: luego vele metiendo manteca de vacas, hasta (96r) que haga mucho correa: luego meterás media libra de azúcar molido y cernido: y desque la masa estuviere bien hecha, tomarás escudillas untadas con manteca, y pondrás dentro dellas unos pedacitos de obleas: luego hinche las escudillas de masa, y métalas a cocer en un horno, y hacerse han unos panecillos redondos, y déjalos cocer muy bien. Luego sácalos, y hazles a cada uno un agujero en el suelo, y sácale por allí todo el migajón, y tendrás un poquito de almíbar, y echarás dentro la mitad del migajón, guardando las coronitas para tornar a tapar los agujeros después que se rellenan: luego harás una pasta del migajón, y el almíbar, y un poco de canela molida, cociéndolo sobre el fuego: y luego lo sacarás, y mezclarás con huevos mejidos, y conservas cortadas muy menudas, que tornarás a rellenar los panecillos, y tapa los agujeros con las coronillas, y tórnalos al horno, y déjalos calentar bien, y dales un vidriado con un poco (96v) de baño blanco. Este baño adelante dirá como se ha de hacer. Estos mismos panecillos podrás rellenar con carne perdigada y sazonada, echando a la carne unas yemas de huevos, y un poquito de agrio: y harás los agujeros en lo alto de los panecillos, y no han de ser vedriados, y la masa se ha de hacer con manteca de puerco.

[130] *Pasteles de Tetilla.*

Los pasteles de tetilla se hacen con la misma masa de los hojaldres de torreznos, salvo que ha de quedar un poco más dura: y hase de sazonar la carne perdigada, carnero, y ternera, todo mezclado: y ha de llevar sus yemas de huevos batidas, y sus yemas cocidas, y sus cañas de vaca: y si quisieres hacer la carne agridulce podrás, has de poner un poco de masa sobre un papel untado con manteca caliente, y luego poner un poco de carne sobre aquella masa; luego irás recogiendo todos los bordes de la (97r) masa, y vendrás a juntarlos sobre la carne, y arróllala allí muy bien de manera, que haga una punta hacia arriba, y métalos en el horno con buena lumbre, y vendrán a quedar de la hechura de un pecho de mujer, que por esto se llaman pasteles de tetilla.

[131] *Otros panecillos rellenos.*

Agujarás los panecillos molletes por el suelo,[195] y sácales todo el migajón, y échalo en un cazo, y échale allí buena miel, y un poco de aceite que sea bueno, y harás una pasta sobre la lumbre, y échale un poco de canela, y tórnalos a rellenar, y tapa los

---

195 *Molletes* are soft, sweet rolls. For more on their history, see Corbacho, and Yarza 24.

Little rolls filled with preserves

Take about two pounds of leaven dough for candeal rolls and add five or six eggs. Then, begin adding butter until it is very elastic. Next, add a pound and a half of sifted, ground sugar. When the dough is well mixed, take some bowls greased with lard and place inside them some wafer pieces. Then fill the bowls with dough and put them in the oven to bake. This will make little round rolls. Let them bake until done. Then take them out and in each one, make a hole in the bottom and scoop out all the crumb. Have some simple syrup and place about half the crumb in the syrup but leave the top crown out so that you can later cover the hole with it after you've added your filling. Next, make a paste of the crumb and simple syrup and a little ground cinnamon, cooking it over the flame. Remove it and add in sweet scrambled egg yolks and diced preserves. Fill the rolls again and cover the hole with the top crown and bake in the oven once again so they warm through. Ice them with a little meringue. The (recipe) for meringue is given later on. These same rolls can be filled with meat that has been seared and seasoned. Add egg yolks and a little sour juice. Make the hole in the tall part of the rolls. They should not be iced and you should use lard in the dough.

Teat pies

Teat pies are made with the same dough as the one for "Puff pastry with roasted pork fat," except that it should be a little firmer. Season seared meat, mutton and veal all mixed together. It should include scrambled egg yolks, and boiled egg yolks, and bone marrow. If you want the meat to be sweet and sour, that's fine. Place a little of the dough on paper greased with hot lard. Put a little meat on the dough. Next, pick up the dough edges and close them up over the meat. Twist them together so that they end up with a point on top. Place them in the oven on high and they should come out in the shape of a woman's breast. That is why they are called teat pies.

Other stuffed rolls

Make a hole in the bottom of *mollete* rolls and remove all the crumb. Place them in a pan and add good-quality honey and a little good-quality oil. Make a paste over the flame and add in a little cinnamon. Fill the *mollete* rolls, cover the hole

agujerillos con las coronillas que quitaste, y ponlos en el cazo, y échales por encima miel y aceite, y tenlos al fuego que estén bien calientes, y cuando los sirvieres ráspales un poco de azúcar por encima.

[132] *Hojaldres bizcochados.*[196]

Batirás ocho huevos frescos, y échales (97v) tres cuarterones de azúcar molido y cernido, bátelo mucho, como para bizcochos: y cuando estuviere bien blanco, y espeso, échale cosa de media libra de manteca de vacas, que sea muy buena, derretida y espumada; luego échale harina de trigo floreada, de manera que quede el batido un poco blando, como para bizcochos, y echárselo has poco a poco, cerniéndolo con un cedacillo, porque no haga borujones, y échale un poco de anís, y unta una tortera, y ponle unas obleas en el suelo, y en los bordes, y echa el batido encima, y mete la tortera en un horno a fuego manso: y cuando esté bien cocido sácala de la tortera, y ponla a bizcochar un poquito, y sírvela así entera.

[133] *Pasteles hojaldrados.*

De cosa de pasteles no pienso decir sino muy poco, porque cuando un hombre viene a saber hacer un pastel, ya sabe lo que se ha de echar dentro. (98r) Ya se sabe, que los pasteles hojaldrados son mejores no cebarlos con cosa ninguna, sino que vayan a la mesa con sólo el caldo que sale dellos. Y para esto es necesario que la carne entre muy jugosa, que cuando se sazona le echen un poco de más agua: y digo agua, porque lo tengo por mejor que echarle caldo, pues se puede sazonar con buen tocino, y con cañas de vaca, y buenas especias. Has de perdigar la mitad de la carne, y tomarla a picar muy menuda, y mezclarla con la cruda, y sazona, y cierra tus pasteles. Y también tengo por mejor que no lleven hojaldrado más que en las cubiertas, porque se embebe mucho el caldo y la grasa en los pasteles que son todos hojaldrados: y si se hubiere de cebar, y cuajar, es necesario perdigar toda la carne: y en tal caso se pueden cebar con caldo, y yemas de huevos, y un poquito de agrio.

[134] (98v) *Un pastel de Ave para enfermo.*

Echarás a cocer una pechuga de ave, y cuando estuviere casi cocida, sácala, y pica toda la carne muy menuda sobre un tablero blanco, porque salga muy blanca, y picarás un poco de enjundia fresca de la misma gallina, y mézclala con la carne, y sazónala de sal, y muy poca especia, unas gotas de caldo, y harás tu pastelillo, y cuécelo, y cebarlo has con dos yemas de huevos, y un poco de caldo, y agrio

---

196 Even though *hojaldre* is usually translated as *pastry* or *puff pastry*, I've translated it here as *cake*, as this is what the recipe most resembles.

with the top crown you removed, and put them in the pan. Drizzle over the top honey and oil and warm them up over the fire. When you are ready to serve, grate a little sugar over the top.

Sponge cakes

Beat eight fresh eggs and add to them three quarters of a pound of sifted, ground sugar. Beat a lot, as you would for sweet biscuits. When it is very white and thick, add about half a pound of excellent-quality butter that has been melted and skimmed. Then add finely sifted wheat flour so that the batter is somewhat soft, as it is for sweet biscuits. This flour should be added very slowly and should be well sifted in a sifter so that there are no lumps. Add a little anise, grease the covered tart pan, and put wafers on the bottom and around the sides. Pour the batter on top. Place the covered tart pan in the oven on low heat. When it's done, take it out of the covered tart pan and return it to the oven to double bake a bit longer. Serve it whole as is.

Puff pastry pies

I am not going to say much about pies, because when a man comes to know how to make a pie, he knows what he wants to put inside. It is already known that puff pastry pies are better without adding anything else to enrich them. They should be served at the table just with the juices that are baked in them. And for this, it is necessary for the meat to be juicy, so when it is seasoned, add a little more water. I say water here because for me it is better than any broth you could add, since it can be seasoned with good fatback, bone marrow, and good spices. You should sear half the meat, shred it, mix it in with the raw meat, season it, and seal up your pies. Also, I think it's best to not use puff pastry dough except for the top because the ones that are made entirely of puff pastry dough soak up too much juice and fat. If you were to enrich and thicken it, it is necessary to sear all the meat first. In this case you can enrich it with broth, egg yolk, and a little sour juice.

Hen pie for the sick

Put poultry breast on to boil and when it's almost done, remove it, and dice up all the meat on a white cutting board so that it comes out white. Mince a little of the fresh fatty tissue from around the same hen's ovaries and add it to the meat. Season with salt, very little spices, and a few drops of broth. Make your little pie, cook it, and enrich it with two egg yolks, a little broth, and lemon juice. Sometimes

de limón. Algunas veces le podrás dar agrio y dulce, y podrás otras veces echarle crestas y turmas de pollos todo cocido, y otras veces mollejas de cabritos fritas.

[135] *Pastel de Pollos, o Pichones.*

Cocerás primero los pollos, o pichones, o aves,[197] que estén medio cocidas, y cortarlas has en cuartos, o en medias, (99r) y picarás tocino, y verdura, perejil, cilantro, y hierbabuena, y tomarás este tocino, y los pollos o pichones, y ponlo todo en una pieza, y allí lo sazona todo: y luego harás el vaso que sea un poco grande, y pondrás la mitad del tocino por todo el suelo del pastel: y luego pon los pollos: y luego por encima de todo la otra parte del tocino: y cuando estuviere el pastel cocido, cébalo con caldo, y yemas de huevos, y zumo de limón, y déjalo cuajar un poco. En estos pasteles podrás echar cañas de vaca, y algunas criadillas de tierra, o de carnero, y les podrás echar tantas cosas, que los podrás llamar pasteles podridos; porque a vuelta de[198] los pollos, o pichones, o aves, podrás hacer artaletes de ternera, o de aves, y cocerlos, y ponerlos en el pastel. Algunas veces se ponen albondiguillas, alcachofas, riponces, e higadillos fritos. Y si estos pasteles hubieren de llevar carne picada de ternera, o carnero, con las aves, o sin ellas, el tocino ha de (99v) ir en la carne picada, y ha de ser perdigada, y no ha de llevar género de verdura, sino sazonar con todas especias, y cañas de vaca, y ponerle yemas de huevos duras: y cuando estuvieren cocidos cuajarlos con su caldo, y sus yemas de huevos crudos batidos con agrio de limón. Para ningún género de pasteles no es bueno poner zurciga cocida, sino batir las yemas de huevos, y agrio, y cebar los pasteles antes que salgan del horno.[199]

[136] *Sopa de Capirotada.*

Tomarás lomo de puerco, y salchichas, y perdices todo asado, y harás torrijas de pan, e irás armando tu sopa con torrijas y solomo, y salchichas y perdices: han de ser hechas cuartos las perdices, y el solomo hecho pedazos: é irás poniendo todo este recaudo en lechos: y como fueres echando las torrijas, y la carne, irás echando queso rallado, y en el queso echarás pimienta, y nuez, y jengibre, (100r) é irás poniendo lechos hasta que la sopa esté bien alta. Luego estrellarás unos huevos que

---

197 Sometimes *aves* [poultry] refers to poultry, but other times Martínez Montiño uses the term to refer to the adult age of the bird, as is the case here, where it's contrasted with the young birds.
198 The RAE explains that the phrase *a vueltas de* means "juntamente, a la vez, además" but is no longer used today. I have translated it here as *besides*.
199 Zurciga is a type of egg-cheese sauce flavoured with garlic, all spices, and, at times, nuts that is unique to Martínez Montiño. In the recipes "Capirotada de huevos" [Eggs, capirotada style] (440; 441) and "Otra capirotada de huevos rellenos" [Another stuffed egg recipe, capirotada style] (440; 441), he explains how to make it.

you can add sweet and sour. Other times you can add boiled chicken crests and testicles, and other times, fried kid sweetbread.

Chicken or squab pie

First, parboil young chicken, squab, or adult ones and cut them in quarters or halves. Mince together fatback and herbs – parsley, cilantro, and spearmint – and take this fatback with the chicken or squab, put everything in a bowl, and season it. Next, make a fairly big crust. Spread half the fatback on the entire bottom of the pie. Then add the chicken and on top of that the other half of the lard. When the pie is cooked, enrich it with broth, egg yolks, and lemon juice and let it thicken a little. In these pies, you can add bone marrow, some truffles, or sheep testicles. Really you can add so many things that you could call these hodgepodge pies, because besides young chickens, squab, or adult ones, you could make veal or poultry pinwheels, bake them, and add them to the pie. Sometimes mini meatballs, artichokes, rampion bellfower, or fried hen liver. If these pies had minced veal or mutton with the poultry or even without it, the fatback should go in the minced meat and it should be seared. There shouldn't be any herbs added but rather [the pie should be] seasoned with all spices and bone marrow. Add in hard-boiled egg yolks. When everything is cooked, thicken it with the right amount of broth and raw egg yolk beaten with lemon juice. For all type of pies, it is no good to add cooked zurciga sauce; rather beat the egg yolk and sour juice and enrich the pies before they come out of the oven.

Capirotada sops

Take pork loin, sausages, and partridge, all roasted. Make torrijas from bread and assemble sops with the torrijas, tenderloin, sausages, and partridge. The partridge should be quartered and the tenderloin sliced. Layer all of these ingredients. When you're adding the torrijas and the meat, also add grated cheese. In the cheese, add pepper, nutmeg, and ginger. Continue layering until the sops are very high.

no sean muy duros, y asentarlos has por encima la sopa: luego majarás un poco de queso con un grano de ajo, y desátalo con caldo: luego batirás en un cacillo ocho huevos, cuatro con claras, y los otros cuatro sin ellas, y batirlos has mucho, y desatarlos con caldo; luego echarás el caldo, y el queso majado, que está en el almirez con los huevos, y echarás el caldo que te pareciere que será menester para mojar la sopa, y ponla sobre la lumbre, y tráela a una mano porque no se corte: y cuando esté espeso, sácalo del fuego, y velo echando por encima de la sopa poco a poco, de manera que se embeba muy bien, y échale queso por encima. Ha de venir a quedar la carne, y lo demás cubierto con la salsa, ha de llevar azafrán, que quede un poco amarillo: y cuando la sopa estuviere medio cocida, échale manteca de puerco por encima bien caliente, (100v) y queso rallado, y luego acábalo de cocer en un horno. En estas capirotadas se meten también aves, y ánades, como sean tiernas, porque es como olla podrida que han de hallar muchas cosas en ellas, y han de ser todas asadas primero.

[137] *Una olla podrida en Pastel.*[200]

Has de cocer la vianda de la olla podrida, cociendo la gallina, vaca, y carnero, y un pedazo de tocino magro, y toda la demás volatería, como son palomas, perdices, zorzales, y solomo de puerco, longanizas, salchichas, liebre, morcillas:[201] esto todo ha de ser asado primero que se echen a cocer. En otra vasija has de cocer cecina,

---

200 The *olla podrida* is one of the best-known recipes of the day and one that has endured to the present in the form of *cocido*. Although its beginning as a simpler stew with humbler ingredients is generally agreed upon, no one really knows its point of origin. Some postulate that it is originally Gallic or perhaps Visigoth; others theorize that the *olla podrida* comes from the Jewish *adafina*, a stew prepared on Fridays to avoid cooking on the Sabbath. See, for example, Gómez Laguna (13) and Rodríguez Marín (424–9). However, the Spanish recipe also bears a striking resemblance to the recipe "On Cooking a Dish Called Ṣinhājī" found in Ibn Razīn al-Tujībī's *Fiḍālat al-Khiwān fī Ṭayyibāt al-Ṭaʿām wa-l-Alwān* (*Best of Delectable Foods and Dishes*) (around the second half of the thirteenth century). My thanks to Nawal Nasrallah for pointing out this connection. For more information, see Nasrallah, *Best of Delectable Foods* (353–4.) Here, Martínez Motiño creates his unique interpretation by turning it into a pie.

201 Stuffed meats are often made of pork, but other meats are also possible. They can be either dry cured or cooked and are eaten both as is or cooked. *Chorizo* (ground pork prepared with paprika, garlic, and oregano), *salchichón* (ground pork prepared with black pepper and sometimes nutmeg together with garlic and oregano), and *sobrasada* (minced meat prepared with both paprika and black pepper) are the three most popular cured sausages. Today, *longaniza* is very similar to *chorizo*. It differs primarily in its packaging, since *longaniza* is usually one long, thinner piece while *chorizo* is partitioned in smaller portions. Later in the cookbook, Martínez Montiño has recipes for stuffing *chorizo*, *longaniza*, *salchica*, and *salchichón*. For him, *chorizo* is made with lean pork and *longaniza* with pork tenderloin. *Chorizo* is marinated in wine, vinegar, and salt, while *longaniza* contains all of that and is seasoned with pepper, clove, ginger, and cumin. He does not reference paprika in his cookbook. See 338–41; 600–1 for the recipes.

Next fry some eggs with the yolk broken and not too well done. Place them on top of the sops. Next, mash together a little cheese and a clove of garlic and thin it with some broth. Next, beat eight eggs in a saucepan, four with the whites and four without. After they are well beaten, thin them with broth. Next, add the broth, the ground cheese that is in the mortar with the eggs, and enough additional broth to moisten the sops. Cook it over a flame and stir with one hand so it won't curdle. When it is thick, remove it from the flame and little by little ladle it over the sops so that they soak up a lot of liquid. Sprinkle cheese on top. The meat and everything else should be covered with sauce. It should have saffron in it so that it's a yellow colour. When the sops are halfway cooked, ladle some very hot lard on top and grated cheese and finish cooking it in the oven. In these *capirotadas* you can use poultry and duck, if they are tender, because this dish is like a hodgepodge stew in which you find a lot of things, all of which should first be roasted.

A pie of hodgepodge stew

Cook the ingredients for a hodgepodge stew including hen, beef, mutton, a piece of meaty lard, all other fowl like pigeons, partridges, and thrushes, pork loin, *longaniza* sausage, *salchicha* sausage, hare, blood sausage. All of this should first be roasted then put on to boil. In another pot, cook cured beef, beef and pork

lenguas de vaca, y de puerco, pies de puerco, orejas, y salchichones, y del caldo de entrambas ollas echarás en una vasija, y cocerás allí las verduras, berzas, y nabos, perejil, y hierbabuena, y los ajos, y las cebollas han de ser asados primero. Sacarás toda esta vianda en piezas, que esté (101r) dividida una de otra, y las verduras en otra pieza, de manera que no esté nada deshecho, y déjalo enfriar, y harás un vaso muy grande, y muy gordo de masa negra de harina de centeno, o de cemite,[202] y asentarlo has sobre una hoja de horno, e irás asentando de toda la vianda que tienes cocida dentro en el pastel e irás sazonando con todas especias y alcaravea, y echarás de las verduras, ni más ni menos. Y cuando estuviere lleno el pastelón, ciérralo, y métalo en el horno de pan, porque no habrá horno de cobre tan grande que se pueda cocer dentro, y pondráslo sobre una hoja de horno de cobre, y no lo quites de la hoja donde está, hasta que se cueza: y cuando la masa del pastel estuviere más de medio cocida, agujerá [sic] el capirote de la cubierta, e hínchelo de caldo, y cueza en el horno por espacio de una hora.

Respecto desto, no ha de ir la vianda del pastel muy deshecha cuando entrare en él, porque ha de estar en el horno, por lo menos (101v) hora y media; y desta manera ha de ir a la mesa con todo su caldo y vianda, y allá lo sacarán con cuchara de plata. También se les suelen echar aceitunas fritas, y algunas castañas: mas algunos señores no gustan dello, ni yo soy aficionado a echarlo.

[138] *Pasteles de cabezas de Carnero.*

Cocerás las cabezas poco más de medio cocidas: luego las descarnarás, y picarás la carne, y las lenguas, y picarás tocino, y mezclarlo has con la carne, y sazona con todas especias: luego harás una masa fina dulce, casi tan dulce como la de las empanadas Inglesas, salvo que no ha de llevar tanta manteca, y harás unos pastelillos de medio talle, e hínchelos de la carne, y ciérralos, y cuézanse, y cébalos con el caldo de las cabezas y yemas de huevos, y agrio y dulce: y cuando estén a medio cocer úntalos con un poco de manteca, y ráspales (102r) azúcar por encima, y suelen salir muy buenos: y aunque llevan la masa dulce, y parece que se han de caer, no salen sino muy derechos.

[139] *Cómo se ha de beneficiar un jabalí.*

Quiero poner aquí como has de beneficiar un jabalí, y un venado, y lo que se puede hacer de todos estos despojos destas reses. El jabalí, si no está abierto chamuscarse ha, o pelarse con agua caliente: y si estuviere abierto sácale una correa por la una

---

202 *Cemite* or *acemite* refers to bran and *harina de cemite* refers to *flour with bran*, or, as I have translated it here, *whole-grain wheat flour*. Martínez Montiño uses this heavier flour when making crusts for heavy meat dishes such as boar empanadas and hotchpodge stew pie.

tongue, pig's feet, ears, and *salchichon* sausage. Fill another pot with stock from the first two and in that cook greens like collard and turnip greens, parsley and spearment and garlic and onions, which should first be roasted. Put all the ingredients in bowls, each one separate from the other, and the greens in another bowl, and don't let anything fall apart. Let them cool. Make a big, thick crust from a dark dough of rye or whole-grain wheat flour. Place it on a baking sheet and fill the pie with all the cooked ingredients. Season with all spices and caraway. Add in all the greens, no more, no less. When the pie is full, seal it and place it in the bread oven, because no copper oven would be able to hold it. Place it on a copper baking sheet and don't remove it from the sheet until it's done baking. When the crust is more than half baked, poke a hole in the top layers and fill it with stock and let it continue baking in the oven for an hour.

Regarding this, the ingredients that fill the pie should not be falling apart when it goes into the oven, because it should cook at least an hour and a half. It should be brought to the table with all its ingredients and juices and should be served with a silver serving spoon. Fried olives and some chestnuts are often included, but some lords don't like them, and I am not a fan of including them.

Sheep's head pie

Boil the sheep heads a little beyond half-boiled. Then, pull the meat off the head, chop the meat up with the tongues, chop up some lard, and mix it with the meat. Season with all spices. Next, make a fine, sweet dough, almost as sweet as the dough for English empanadas, except that it shouldn't have as much lard. Make pastry shells, about half sized, and fill them with meat. Seal them and bake them. Enrich them with stock from the sheep head, egg yolks, and sweet and sour. When they are half baked, grease the top with lard and grate sugar on top. They usually come out very good. And although they're made with sweet dough and look as if it they might collapse, they will still turn out with a nice crust.

How to dress boar

I want to record here how to dress boar and venison, and what to do with the extremities from these carcasses. Boar: if not yet cut open, singe it or remove the hair with scalding water. If it is open, cut out a strip from the opening,

parte de la abertura, desde la cola hasta la degolladura, y cóselo con ella, que parezca que no está abierta; porque de otra manera se ahumaría, y chamúscalo: y después que esté chamuscado córtale toda aquella correa, y déjale enfriar: luego córtale la cabeza con todo el pescuezo, de manera que llegue a la punta de las espaldas; luego sácale la lengua, y lávala, muy (102v) bien, y envuelve la cabeza en un angeo, y la lengua vaya dentro, y échala a cocer en un caldero que se pueda cubrir: y échale tres cuartillos de sal, antes más que menos; porque cuando salga del cocimiento ha de amargar de salada, y échale salvia, y mejorana, e hisopillo, y una azumbre de vino, y media de vinagre, y cueza hasta que esté bien cocida: y sácala, y desenvuélvela: y tendrás dos onzas de canela molida, y mezclada con un poco de pimienta, y nuez, y échaselo por encima que esté como salpimentada, y tápala con un paño por media hora. Sírvela entera muy enramada. Si quisieren carbonadas del pescuezo, corta unas rebanadas, y tuéstalas en las parrillas, y sírvelas con un poco de vino tinto, y zumo de limón, y un poco de canela y nuez de especia. Sírvelas calientes. De lo que quedare podrás hacer un queso.

[140] (103r) *Queso de cabeza de jabalí.*

Este queso harás desta manera, sacarás toda la carne que pudieres de la cabeza, y el pescuezo, después de cocida, de manera que no lleve ningún pellejo, y harás unas rebanadillas delgadas, y cortarás también la lengua: y si quisieres echar un par de lenguas más, bien puedes, y echarás esto en un cazo, y échale caldo hasta que se bañe, y échale un cuartillo de vino blanco antes más que menos, y medio cuartillo de vinagre, antes menos que más, y un manojo de hierbas, que tenga salvia y mejorana, e hisopillo, y cueza hasta que mengue la cantidad del vino, y vinagre, y un poco más: y luego harás un aro de una pleita de esparto: y pondrás una estameña, o lienzo sobre un tablero de nogal, y sobre esta estameña pondrás el aro, y harás una especia que tenga pimienta, y un poco de clavo, y jengibre, y nuez, y un (103v) poco de sal. Echarás un poco desta especia dentro en el aro sobre la estameña. Luego echarás una cucharada de carne con una espumadera, y tornarás a echar por encima de la especia, y apretarla has con una paletilla, o cucharón; luego echa otra cucharada de la carne, y echa otro poco de especia por encima, y tórnala a apretar con la paleta, o cucharón: y desta manera irás haciendo hasta henchir el aro de la pleita; luego echarás la otra punta de la estameña por encima, y ponla una cobertera, ú otra cosa llana, y cárgala encima con cosa que pese dos arrobas,[203] y déjale estar así hasta que se enfríe: luego saca el queso, y sírvelo frío: y si quisieres servir algunas rebanadas deste queso calientes, derrite tocino gordo, y echa en una

---

203 *Arroba* is a unit of weight (it could also measure mass or volume) that, in Spain, was equivalent to twenty-five pounds. So, here, Martínez Montiño weighs down the head cheese with a fifty-pound weight.

from the tail to the slit throat, and sew it up with it so that it doesn't seem cut open. If you don't do this, it will begin to smoke when you singe it. Once it's singed, cut out that whole strip and let it cool. Next, remove the head and neck right to the top of the back. Remove the tongue and wash it well. Wrap the head in coarse linen and keep the tongue in it. Put the head on to boil in a cauldron with a lid. Add in twelve cups of salt, better more than less, so that when it comes out, it is extremely salty. Add sage, marjoram, winter savory, two quarts of wine, and one of vinegar. Boil it all until it is well cooked. Remove and unwrap it. Have two ounces of ground cinnamon, mix with a little pepper and nutmeg, and sprinkle it over the head as if it were salt and pepper. Cover with a kitchen cloth for half an hour. Serve it whole decorated with a lot of branches around it. If you want the neck grilled, cut some slices, toast them on the grill, and serve them with a little red wine, lemon juice, and a little cinnamon and nutmeg. Serve hot. With the leftovers, you can make head cheese.

Boar head cheese

Make this head cheese this way. Remove all the meat that you can from the head and neck after it has boiled and has no hair left on it. Cut into thin slices and also slice the tongue. If you want to add a couple of other tongues, that would be good. Place this in a pan with stock, enough to braise them. Add in a pint of white wine, better more than less, a half pint of vinegar, better less than more, and a handful of herbs that includes sage, marjoram, and winter savory. Boil until the wine and vinegar is reduced, and then (reduce) a little more. Next, make a ring from braided esparto. Place cheesecloth or linen on a walnut cutting board and put the ring on this. Make a spice mix with pepper, a little clove, ginger, nutmeg, and a little salt. Sprinkle a little of this over the cheesecloth inside the ring. Next, using a skimmer, place a spoonful of meat and again sprinkle spices on top. Press it down with a spatula or big spoon. Then place another spoonful of meat and sprinkle spices on top and press it down with the spatula or big spoon again. Continue this way until the plait ring is full. Cover it with the other end of the cheesecloth and place a lid on it or any flat object. Place on top something that weighs two *arrobas*. Let it stand until cool. Then remove the cheese and serve it cold. If you want to serve some slices of this headcheese hot, melt some extra fatty fatback and add the slices into

sartén desta grasa, como para una tortilla, y allí podrás tostar las rebanadas del queso. Las hierbas que se echaron al cocimiento del queso, han de estar atadas, y se han de echar a mal. Si cuando hiciste el queso (104r) pusieras dentro en el aro unas hojas de laurel: y cuando la acabaste pusieras otras encima, parecería muy bien; mas toma algunas veces demasiado gusto el laurel como está caliente: y por eso uso pocas veces dél, y de romero ninguno, sino es para enramar, porque son cosas muy fuertes, y suelen echar a perder la vianda.

[141] *Adobos de Solomillos.*

Estos solomillos se han de echar en agua que se desangren muy bien: luego harás un adobo con agua, y sal, y vinagre, é hisopillo picado muy menudo, y mejorana también picada menuda, y un poco de vino blanco: y si quisieres echar un poco de ajo, bien podrás: sazonarlo has con todas especias. Estos solomillos se han de servir asados: y si quisieres echarlos en adobo ordinario de ajos y orégano, y agua y sal, haslos de perdigar primero en las parrillas. Sírvense (104v) asados los unos, y los otros; y algunas veces en empanadas de masa blanca. Advierte, que los lomos del jabalí, si el es nuevo, son muy buenos asados.

[142] *Empanadas frías de jabalí.*

Partirás el jabalí por medio, y de las piernas harás cuatro empanadas, dos para frías, y dos para calientes: las frías perdigarás en las parrillas: luego las mecharás con tocino gordo, con una mechadera grande, que las mechas sean tan gordas, como el dedo pequeño de la mano: y estas mechas han de ir derechas con la hebra de la carne, y se han de salpimentar con especias, y sal: y luego mechar, y las mechas han de atravesar toda la pieza de parte a parte por en medio, y muy espesas: y luego las echarás en vinagre, que se cubran, y estarán en él seis horas: luego las empanarás en masa negra de cemite, o de harina de trigo por cerner, como viene del molino.[204] Ha (105r) de ser de dos hojas cada empanada, y muy gordas: sazonarás con toda especia, y has de procurar que el repulgo sea muy fuerte: y cuando estén cocidas échales la salsa para frías. Esta salsa se hace desta manera: Tomarás rebanadas de pan, y ponlas en las parrillas sobre la lumbre, adonde hubiere mucho llama, y quémese de manera, que quede muy negro: y luego pásalo por un poco de agua fría, porque luego desechará el humo que tomó de la llama, y échale caldo cuanto se bañe, y échale vino y vinagre, y un manojo de las hierbas del jardín, salvia,

---

204 Different levels of sifting led to different flour qualities. The first sift would remove the larger bits of bran and germ and leave a lighter, tan flour. Subsequent siftings would remove more and more of the bran and germ, and the flour would become increasingly whiter and finer. Here, Martínez Montiño insists on using flour that still includes bran.

the frying pan, that is greased as you would for an omelette, and brown the headcheese slices. The herbs added to the headcheese boil should be tied together and discarded. When you made the headcheese, if you used bay leaves in the ring and finished it with others on top, it would look good. But, sometimes it takes on too much bay leaf flavour because it's warm. For this reason, use it sparingly and don't use any rosemary, unless it is for decorating with its sprigs, because both have such a strong flavour and can ruin the food.

Marinade for boar tenderloin

These tenderloins should soak in water to remove a lot of the excess blood. Then make a marinade with water, salt, vinegar, minced winter savory, minced marjoram, and a little white wine. If you want to add a little garlic, you can. Season with all spices. These tenderloins should be served grilled. If you want to marinate them in the most common marinade of garlic, oregano, water, and salt, you should first sear them on the grill. Both ways you should serve [them] grilled, or sometimes you can bake them wrapped in a white dough. Note that boar tenderloins, if they are fresh, are very tasty grilled.

Cold boar empanadas

Saw the boar in half. With the legs you can make four empanadas, two cold and two hot. For the cold ones, sear them [the legs] on the grill. Then, with a big larding needle, lard them with extra fatty fatback. The strips of lard should be as thick as a pinky finger. They should be placed with the grain of the meat. First sprinkle with spices and salt, then lard. The lard should go through the entire piece of meat, from one end to the other, right through the middle, and they [the strips of lard] should be very thick. Submerge them [the larded meat] in vinegar for six hours. Wrap them with a dark dough of whole-grain wheat flour or unsifted wheat flour right from the mill. Each empanada should have two thick layers. Season with all spices and try to make a strong, crimped edge. When they are cooked, add some sauce for the cold ones. The sauce is made this way. Take slices of bread and place them on the grill over a high flame so that they burn and are black. Then dip them in a little cold water to get rid of the smoke they picked up from the flames. Put them in some stock, enough to half cover them, and add wine, vinegar, a handful of garden herbs – sage, marjoram, winter savory,

mejorana, hisopillo, y ajadrea, y cebollas, y hierbabuena, y cueza poco a poco, hasta que el pan se ablande bien: luego todo esto se ha de pasar por un cedacillo, o estameña: y cuando las empanadas estuvieren bien cocidas, échales la salsa, y cuezan con ella una hora: luego sácalas, y atapa los agujeros, por donde entró la salsa, y menéalas muy bien, porque se mezcle la salsa con la (105v) especia, y la carne. Estas se sirven frías. La salsa no ha de llevar especias, porque en las empanadas se ha de echar un poco de más especias, y ellas se mezclarán dentro con la salsa. Desta manera se hacen también estas empanadas de piernas de carnero.

[143] *Empanadas de jabalí calientes.*

Estas empanadas se han de empanar en pastelones, y hanse de mechar, y sazonar ni más ni menos que las frías, salvo que la salsa ha de llevar dulce, y se han de servir calientes: para esta salsa de pastelones calientes, ha de ser la salsa muy negra: y podrás quemar harina, y desatarla con un poco de vinagre: luego echarle caldo, y vino, y un manojo de hierbas del jardín, y un poco de cebolla frita con tocino muy menudo, y echarle canela, porque las otras especias ya las tiene la empanada. Y esta salsa ha de ser, como digo, bien negra, y bien agria (106r) y dulce. Ha menester cada pastelón media libra de azúcar. Han de ser picantes, y sírvense calientes.

[144] *Pastelones de jabalí picados*

De las espaldas del puerco harás pastelones picados, picando la carne muy bien, y metiéndole sus especias, y sal, y harás tus pastelones a modo de barcos, y échales una cama de carne: luego les echarás cuatro o cinco mechas de tocino gordo, como las de las empanadas: luego pondrás otra cama de carne, y otras tantas mechas, y acomodarás la carne en el pastelón de masa negra: y cuando lo quisieses servir, hínchelo de la salsa negra, ni más ni menos que a la de los pastelones calientes de la pierna.[205]

[145] *Otros Pastelones picados.*

También podrás hacer estos pastelones de otra manera, picando carne, (106v) como tengo dicho, salvo que el tocino que había de ir en las mechas, ha de ir picado, mezclado con la carne. Luego tendrás salsa negra sazonada, y en el mismo tablero sazonarás la carne, é irásle metiendo de aquella salsa hasta que la carne esté blanda. Luego ponla en el vaso, y cuézase: y cuando lo quisieres servir, no tienes que hacer más salsa que ella echará de si.

---

205 Instructions on how to make *salsa negra* [black sauce], the sauce used here and in the next two recipes, are found in "Empanadas frías de jabalí" [Cold boar empanadas] and "Empanadas de jabalí calientes" [Hot boar empanadas] (290–2; 291–3).

and summer savory – onions, and spearmint and slowly simmer until the bread is fairly soft. Place all this in a sieve or cheesecloth. When the empanadas have been cooking for a while, add the sauce to them and cook for another hour. Remove them and cover up the holes where you added the sauce. Shake it [the empanada] well so that the sauce mixes with the spices and the meat. These should be served cold. The sauce shouldn't have any spices because the empanadas should already have more than enough and they will mix in with the sauce. In this same way you can make mutton empanadas.

Hot boar empanadas

These empanadas should be made into large pies and larded and seasoned no more or less than the cold ones, except that the sauce should be sweet and they are served hot. This sauce for hot pies should be a very black sauce. Burn the flour and thin it with a little vinegar. Then add stock and wine and a handful of garden herbs and a little fried onion with minced fatback. Add cinnamon, because the other spices are already in the empanada. And this sauce, as I have said, should be very black and very sour and sweet. For each pie, a half a pound of sugar is needed. They should be pungent and served hot.

Big minced boar pies

From the back of the boar, you can make minced pies, mincing the meat and adding spices and salt. Make the pies boat-shaped and have the meat on the bottom. Then lay on top four or five strips of extra fatty fatback, like the ones for the empanadas. Add another layer of meat, another of the strips, and arrange it all in a dark dough pie. When you are ready to serve it, fill it with black sauce, no more or less than for the hot empanadas made with meat from the leg.

Other big minced pies

You can make these pies another way using minced meat, as I have explained above, except that the fatback that was in strips can be minced and mixed in with the meat. Then you will have seasoned black sauce, and on the same cutting board you will season the meat and continue adding in enough black sauce until the meat is soft. Put it in a crust and bake it. When you're ready to serve, there's no need to make any more sauce; there'll be enough in the pie itself.

[146] *Otra suerte de Pastelones de jabalí.*

Tomarás los dos pedazos de jabalí, los primeros de los lomos junto a la cola, y échalos a cocer con agua y sal, y vino y vinagre, y salvia, y mejorana, y de las otras hierbas: y cuando estén casi cocidos, sácalos, y enfriénse. Luego métalos en pastelones de masa negra, sazonados con todas especias, y tocino picado por encima, y por debajo, y cierra tus pastelones, y cuézanse: y luego quemarás (107r) pan, como para las empanadas frías, y pásalo por un poco de agua fría, porque se le quite el humo, que esto tiene el pan que al punto se le quita, y cocerás este pan con caldo del cocimiento de las piezas del jabalí, y pásalo por un cedacillo, o estameña, y saldrá una salsa un poco parda, y ha de ser agridulce. Y advierte, que en todas estas salsas negras, no digo que sazones con especias, porque las empanadas que han de llevar salsa, han de llevar siempre un poco de más especias; porque la salsa no lo ha de llevar, que allá dentro se mezcla ella con las especias de la empanada, salvo que a la dulce se le ha de echar canela: y digo, que cuando estuvieren cocidos estos pastelones se les ha de echar desta salsa, y se han de servir calientes.

[147] *Otros pastelones de jabalí.*[206]

Tomarás pedazos de carne de jabalí con huesos, y cuero, y todo de cualquiera parte, aunque sean de costillas, (107v) o de pechos; porque se pueda empanar de todo el jabalí, aunque lleve cada pastelón dos, o tres pedazos, que para estas empanadas no importa nada echar la carne en pedazos. Echa esta carne en adobo de orégano y sal, agua, y ajos, y vinagre sin otra cosa. Hase de echar en adobo crudo, y sin perdigar: han de estar veinte y cuatro horas en él: luego perdigarlas en las parrillas, o en un asador, como si se asase: y cuando estén bien perdigadas, si el jabalí fuere flaco, métales unas mechas de tocino, así sin orden; porque como tienen todos sus huesos, no podrás mechar con orden: y si el jabalí fuere gordo no lo ha menester, empánanse en pastelones redondos, echando dos pedazos, o más en cada uno, y sazona con todas especias, y sal: y en la cubierta del pastelón, harás luego un agujero que quepa un dedo, porque no levante cuanto se cueza, porque es necesario que quede la cubierta del pastelón asentada sobre la carne en este modo (108r) de empanar: échalos a cocer en horno de pan: y cuando estén cocidos tomarás del adobo en que han estado, y échales a cada uno un par de cucharadas del mismo adobo, y cuezan con él una hora. Este adobo no se ha de colar, sino así como está con su orégano, y ajos: y cuando echares el orégano al adobo, májalo con la sal, y los ajos, porque no se vean las hojas en las empanadas: son muy buenas, y cómense

---

206 This recipe [147] and the following on boar, venison, beef, and a series of empanadas through to recipe [169] appear in the eighteenth-century recipe collection *Manuscrito Ávila Blancas* (Pérez San Vicente, *Gastronomía mexicana* 96–120).

Another kind of boar pies

Take the two pieces of boar meat, the first cuts from the loins next to the tail, and put them on to boil with water, salt, wine, vinegar, sage, marjoram, and some other herbs. When they are nearly done, remove them and let cool. Then place them into big pies of dark dough seasoned with all spices and with minced fatback both on the bottom and on the top. Seal the pies and bake them. Next, burn some bread as you would for the cold empanadas. Then dip them [the pieces of bread] in a little cold water to get rid of the smoke; whatever is coming off the bread will instantly stop. Boil this bread in some broth from the boil that the pieces of boar meat were cooked in, and strain through a sieve or cheesecloth. A sauce will come through that is light brown and sweet and sour. Note that with all these black sauces, I say not to season with spices because the empanadas with sauce inside always have more than enough spices in them. The sauce should not have spices because it will mix with the spices inside the empanada, with the exception of the sweet one, which should have cinnamon added to it. And I'll say that when these pies are baked, they should have sauce added to them and they should be served hot.

Other big boar pies

Take pieces of boar meat with the bone in and the skin and everything from any part, even the ribs or the upper belly, because you can make an empanada out of any part of the boar. Even if each pie has two or three pieces, for these empanadas it is fine to have (the meat) in pieces. Marinate this meat in a marinade of oregano, salt, water, garlic, and vinegar and nothing else. Place the meat in raw, without searing it, and let it marinate for twenty-four hours. Then sear them [the pieces of meat] on the grill or on a spit as if you were roasting them. When they are well singed, if the boar meat is lean, lard it with some strips of fatback without any particular order. With the bones in, you can't lard systematically. If the boar meat is fatty, there is no need (to lard it). Shape them into round pies, adding two pieces or more to each one, and season with all spices and salt. On the top of the pie, make a hole big enough for a finger to fit in so that the crust doesn't rise. For this type of crust, it is important for the pie crust to stay next to the meat. Place in the oven to bake, and when the crust has formed, take the marinade they [the pieces of meat] have been in and ladle on each [pie] a couple of spoonfuls of that same marinade and let bake for an hour. This marinade should not be strained, rather used just as it is with its oregano and garlic. When you add the oregano to the marinade, grind it with salt and the garlic so that you can't see the leaves in the empanadas. These

calientes: y también se pueden comer frías; porque aunque se les echa el adobo, no se vea la salsa en ellas, sino muy poco. Advierte, que estos pastelones han de tener la masa muy gorda; porque de otra manera romperse hian [*sic*], por cuanto llevan el adobo al cocer.

[148] *Otras empanadas de jabalí.*

Estas empanadas puedes hacer sin ningún género de salsa, y serán muy buenas, tomando carne de la pierna del (108v) jabalí, y perdígalas en las parrillas, y méchalas con muchas mechas de tocino, salpimentadas como está dicho, derechas con la hebra, y por medio de la empanada: y luego échalas en vinagre, y sal, y ajos, y orégano, y un poco de vino blanco sin agua ninguna, y estén en el adobo ocho, o diez horas, y empánalas en masa negra, y las empanadas sean de dos hojas, y sazona con todas especias y sal, y cuézanse muy bien; porque todo el toque de las empanadas para que salgan buenas, está en saberlas mechar bien, y que estén bien cocidas, que sin estas dos cosas ninguna valdrá nada.

[149] *De cómo se cuece el jabalí fresco.*

Tomarás un pedazo de jabalí del lomo, o del pecho fresco, sin sal, y échalo a cocer con agua, y sal, y vino, y vinagre, y de todas hierbas del jardín: y cuando la pieza estuviere casi cocida, (109r) échale unos clavos enteros, y un poco de pimienta, y acábese de cocer, y sírvelo sobre una sopa blanca, y quitarle has a la mitad de la pieza el cuero, y la otra mitad vaya con él: y en la parte que quitaste el pellejo, darás dos, o tres cortes al través de la hebra, y meterle has entre los cortes unas rebanadas de pan: y en lo demás echarás perejil en rama. Sírvelo con mostaza, ú oruga.[207]

[150] *Cómo se ha de salar el jabalí.*

Si quisieres salar este jabalí, sálalo luego antes que esté manido: descárgalo bien de los huesos gordos, como son el espinazo, y las espaldas, y las cañas, y hazlo piezas pequeña. Si estuviere muerto de algún día, irás mojando estas piezas en vinagre, y salándolas: y esténse con la sal dos días, y cuélgalas adonde las dé el aire. Es muy bueno después de seco para servir con nabos, y con otras verduras. Y con esto dejaré de tratar (109v) del jabalí, y diré algo del venado. Y esto todo importa mucho saberlo los pasteleros, porque desto saben mucho menos que los cocineros.[208]

---

[207] Early modern mustard differs significantly from today's. Martínez Montiño includes a recipe on how to make it later in the cookbook, "Memoria de la mostaza negra" [Memoir of black mustard] (512–14; 513–15). For more on this condiment, see its entry in the Glossary.

[208] Here is a strong example of how Martínez Montiño is conscious of his readership. He highlights the section for pastry makers, who know less about game than cooks.

are very tasty and are eaten hot. You can also eat them cold, because even though they have the marinade in them, you don't really see it at all or very little. Note that these pies should have a very thick crust, because otherwise with the marinade they will fall apart when they are baking.

Other boar empanadas

These empanadas are made without any type of sauce and they are very good. Take the meat from the boar's leg, sear it on the grill, and lard it with a lot of strips of fatback. Season it as explained above, with the grain, and right through the middle of the empanada. Then place them in vinegar, salt, garlic, oregano, and a little white wine without any water and let them marinate eight to ten hours. Wrap in dark dough. The empanadas should have two sheets (of dough) and be seasoned with all spices and salt. Bake thoroughly. The secret to having the empanadas turn out well is in knowing how to lard them and baking them well. Without these two basics, they will never turn out well.

How to boil fresh boar

Take a piece of fresh boar loin or from the upper belly, unsalted, and put on to boil in water, salt, wine, vinegar, and all herbs from the garden. When the piece is almost boiled, add in some whole cloves and a little pepper and finish cooking. Serve over white sops. Half of it should be served with the skin and the other half without it. In the piece with no skin, make two or three slits against the grain and fill them in with slices of bread. Also add springs of parsley. Serve with mustard or arugula [sauce].

How to salt boar

If you want to salt boar, salt it right away before it is dry aged. Remove all the big bones like the spine, shoulder and pelvis, and leg bones and cut it into small pieces. If the boar was killed more than a day ago, soak the pieces in vinegar and salt them. Leave them salted for two days, hanging where there is a lot of air. Once it's dry, it's good to serve with turnips and other green-leaf vegetables. With this I am finishing [the section] on boar and will now discuss venison. All of this is very important for pastry makers, because they know a lot less about this than cooks.

[151] *Cómo se ha de aderezar un venado.*

En matando el venado se ha de abrir y guardar el redaño, y la tripa grande, que se dice del cagalar.[209] La tripa la lavarás en muchas aguas, de manera que el sebo quede muy blanco. Luego échale un poco de agua tibia, y ablandará, y la podrás volver, atarle has las puntas muy bien, y luego lávala con sal, y luego en muchas aguas, y échala a cocer con agua y sal, y un poco de tocino hasta que esté bien cocida: luego sácala, y córtala en pedacillos, y métela en una cazolilla, y échale allí un poco de caldo, y una gota de vino, y un poco de manteca fresca de vacas, y sazona con pimienta, nuez, y jengibre, sin otra especia ninguna: y (110r) con esto cueza un poco. Luego tuesta rebanadillas de pan, y sírvelas sobre ellas: y si le quisieres echar un poquito de verdura picada, bien podrás: y también la podrás cuajar con unas yemas de huevos, y acedo, aunque no es mucho menester. Advierte, que en la cazolilla donde se sazonó la tripa, se ha de echar también un manojito de hierbas, mejorana y ajedrea, e hisopillo;[210] si no hubiere manteca de vacas, sea tocino derretido: y si no quisieres servir la tripa en platillo,[211] echarás las hierbas, y vino, y vinagre en el primer cocimiento: y cuando estuviere bien cocida, sácala y envuélvela en un poco de pan rallado, así caliente como está: y luego tuéstala en las parrillas, y sírvela sobre una sopilla dorada.

[152] *Platillo de las puntas de cuernos de venado.*

Los cuernos de venado, o gamo, cuando están cubiertos de pelo, tienen (110v) las puntas muy tiernas.[212] Estas se han de cortar de manera, que quede hacia la punta todo lo tierno, y pelarlos en agua caliente, y quedarán muy blancos, y hanse de

---

209 *Cagalar* [caecum or blind gut] is a part of the large intestine that is attached to the appendix and is located where the small intestine meets the large. In English it is also known as the bung and is used as casing for sausages and such. I've translated *redaño* here as *mesentery* because this recipe deals more with the butchering of the animal parts.
210 These two ingredients, the herb *jedrea* or today *ajedrea* [*Satureja hortensis*, summer savory] and the evergreen *hisopillo* [Satureja Montana, winter savory] are often used together.
211 Depending on the context, *platillo* can refer to *serving a dish on a small plate* or *a side dish* or *a small late-night dinner-size portion*. Additionally, in his *Diccionario general de cocina*, Ángel Muro writes that it also refers to a specific type of preparation: "a cierto guisado, compuesto de carnes, verduras y otras cosas también se le llama *platillo,* como se verá en las siguientes formulas de la cocina antigua" [certain stews, made up of meat, vegetables, and other things, are also called *platillo*, as you will see in the following old cuisine recipes] and provides about a dozen examples from Martínez Montiño (2.731–5). It is most often used in reference to vegetable dishes, and sometimes, as is the case with this recipe, Martínez Montiño offers an alternative of serving the dish as a main course; for example, over sops, as indicated here.
212 *Venado* is both a generic term for *deer* and *venison meat* and, as is the case here, a specific name for the species *cervus elaphus* of the genus *cervus*. Apart from *venado*, another name for the species is *ciervo común* or *ciervo rojo*, or *red deer* in English. The *venado* differs from the *gamo* in several ways, including its bigger size and uniform reddish colour.

How to prepare venison [offal]

When you kill a deer, it should be opened and the mesentery and large intestines – that's the name for the caecum – should be set aside. Wash the intestines with water many times so that the fat turns white. Next flush with some warm water and it will soften and you can turn it inside out. Tie up the ends very well and wash with salt and then with a lot of water. Put it on to boil with water, salt, and a little fatback until it is well cooked. Remove it and chop it into little pieces. Place it in a saucepan and add a little broth, a drop of wine, and a little butter. Season with pepper, nutmeg, and ginger without any other spices and let simmer. Next, toast slices of bread and serve (the offal) on them. If you want to add in some minced herbs, you can. Also, you can have it set with some egg yolks and sorrel juice, although it's really not necessary. Note that in the saucepan in which you seasoned the intestines, you should also add a handful of herbs – marjoram, summer savory, and winter savory. If you don't have any butter, you can use melted fatback. And if you don't want to serve it as an individual dish, add the herbs, wine, and vinegar to the first boil and when it's done, roll it in some breadcrumbs, while it's still hot, then toast it on the grill and serve on top of golden sops.

Dish of the tips of deer antlers

Antlers from red deer or from fallow deer, when they are velvety, have very delicate tips. These should be cut so that all the tender part remains in the tip. Peel them in hot water and they will turn white. Prepare them the same way as the

aderezar como la tripa del venado, salvo que no se han de tostar, sino cocerlos con un poco de caldo, y sazonar con pimienta, nuez, y jengibre, y échale un poquito de vino, y vinagre, y un poco de manteca de vacas fresca: y con esto cuezan cosa de una hora: y no se ha de cuajar con huevos, ni se le ha de echar género de verdura. Es muy buen platillo, sólo el nombre tiene malo.

[153] *Lo que se ha de hacer del Redaño del venado.*

Echarás en agua el redaño para que se desangre bien; luego lo exprimirás del agua, y córtalo a pedazos, y ponlo en un cazo a derretir, como se derrite la enjundia de puerco: y cuando anden casi fritos los chicharrones, tendrás camuesas en cuarterones, y echarselas dentro, y (111r) fríanse allí: y cuando estuvieren fritas, sácalas, y echa en el almirez cosa de medio cuartillo de agua, y echa allí la grasa del redaño sobre la agua, y déjalo un poco enfriar, y harás una torta muy blanca, y guárdala.[213] Luego trataré lo que se ha de hacer della. Con la grasa que quedare en los chicharrones, has de hacer una tortilla de huevos muy gorda, y muy esponjada, y los chicharrones, se han de secar mucho, y echarles sal que estén bien salados, y se han de echar encima de la tortilla con las camuesas, todo hecho un montoncillo, y unos picatostes de pan blanco a la redonda: has de enviar la tortilla a la mesa muy caliente, y bien apuntada de sal. También se suelen hacer torrijas desta grasa de venado sin dulce, sino bien apuntadas de sal.

[154] *Migas de la grasa del venado.*

Desta grasa del redaño del venado podrás hacer migas: remoja el pan con (111v) agua y sal, que esté cociendo: luego pon en la sartén una poca de grasa del redaño, y freirás en ella un par de granos de ajo: luego saca los ajos, y echa las migas, y fríelas de manera que estén bien tostadas por entrambas partes. Estas tortillas y migas de grasa de venado, dicen que son buenas para los que tienen cámaras.

[155] *Empanadas de venado.*

Las empanadas deste venado, o gamo, se han de beneficiar de la manera que he dicho del jabalí, salvo la manera que dije que se cociese el jabalí, porque las del venado no salen tan bien cocidas como las del jabalí: y si el jabalí no es bueno, o gordo, tampoco salen bien cocidas.

---

213 As the caul fat heats up, part will melt and another part will remain solid. Here Martínez Montiño removes the melted part and pours it over cold water to solidify and save for later. The solid parts are chopped up and will be placed on top of the egg omelette, while the grease remaining in the pan will be used to cook the omelette. For more on caul fat/mesentery, see 170n49.

venison intestines, except that instead of toasting them, boil them in a little broth. Season with pepper, nutmeg, and ginger, and add in a little wine and vinegar and a little fresh butter. Boil everything for about an hour. Do not thicken with eggs or add any type of green herb. This is a very good dish; the only thing bad about it is its name.

What to do with venison caul fat

Place the caul fat in water so that all the blood is drained. Then squeeze out the water and chop it into pieces. Place in a pan to melt as pork fat tissue melts. When the fatty pieces are almost fried, have some sour apples quartered and add them in to fry. When they are fried, take them out. Put in a mortar about a half pint of water and place the [melted] fat from the caul fat on top of the water and let it cool. Shape into a white cake and reserve it. I'll explain what to do with that later. With the leftover caul fat from the fried fatty pieces, make a thick and very fluffy egg omelette. The fried fatty pieces should be dried off and salted so that it is very salty. Layer it on top of the omelette with the apples, all stacked up. Add some slices of fried white bread around it. The omelette should be sent out to the table very hot and very salty. It is also common to make torrijas with this venison caul fat, but without anything sweet and plenty of salt.

Venison fat breadcrumbs

With the venison caul fat, you can make breadcrumbs. Soak the bread in salted water that is boiling. Then put in the frying pan a little of the caul fat and fry a couple of cloves of garlic. Remove the garlic and add in the breadcrumbs and fry them so that they are well toasted on both sides. It is said that these omelettes and breadcrumbs made with venison lard are good for those who are have diarrhea.

Venison empanadas

Empanadas made with meat from red deer or fallow deer should be prepared in the same way as I explained for the boar, except for the way I explained to bake the boar because venison (empanadas) don't bake as well as the boar ones do. And if the boar meat is not that good or that fatty, they won't bake up well either.

[156] *Solomillos de venado.*

Los solomillos de venado son mejores y mayores que los de jabalí: (112r) y así aderezados con los adobos que tengo dicho en el jabalí, y mechados y asados, y la lengua cocida, luego echada en adobo, y después frita con tocino derretido, hendida por medio es muy buena.

[157] *Cómo se ha de salar el venado, y se pueda comer fresco.*

Si quisieres salvar el venado gordo, o vaca gorda, muerta por el mes de Otubre, y que se pueda comer fresca todo el Invierno, como si no se hubiera salado, y la grasa que esté fresca como si se acabara de matar. Harás desta manera: Tomarás piezas grandes de a cuatro, o seis libras cada una, y quítales los huesos grandes, como es el espinazo, y las espaldas, y las cañas de las piernas, y salarlas has, estregándolas mucho con la sal, é irás asentando en un dornajo[214] de barro muy bien salados, y déjales estar allí cinco, o seis días, hasta que se vayan (112v) purgando, y haciendo salmuera: luego sácales de allí, sacudiendo muy bien la sal: y luego toma toda aquella salmuera, y más sal, y ponla en un barquillo,[215] o caldera, y échale agua tanta cantidad que se puedan cubrir las piezas del venado, y échale más sal, y menéala con un cucharon de manjar blanco hasta que esté bien deshecha la sal. Luego toma un huevo fresco, y échalo en la salmuera: y si se hundiere échale más sal, meneando con el cucharón hasta que esté deshecha, y torna a poner un huevo fresco en la salmuera: y si se tuviere encima, que no se hunda, y se descubra la mitad del huevo, está buena la salmuera; porque el huevo fresco en agua dulce se va al suelo como una piedra. Esta salmuera has de cocer y espumar muy bien: luego apártala, y déjala enfriar, y quedará tan clara como agua de la fuente: luego asienta las piezas del venado en el dornajo, y échale la salmuera por encima: y entiéndase que ha de estar bien fría, y (113r) ha de cubrir las piezas muy bien, que tenga un palmo de salmuera por encima, y déjale estar así otros ocho días:[216] luego mirarla has, y si estuviere algo revuelta, torna a sacar las piezas, andando lo menos que pudieres en ellas con las manos, y torna a hacer la prueba del huevo fresco, y torna a cocer la salmuera,

---

214 The RAE explains that *dornajo* [terracotta trough] is a "especie de artesa, pequeña y redonda, que sirve para dar de comer a los cerdos, para fregar o para otros usos" [type of small, round trough used to feed pigs, wash dishes or other uses]. In Cuenca it is called *tornajo*. Thanks to Ana Montoya for pointing this regionalism out.
215 The *Gran encyclopedia de Navarra* [Great encyclopedia of Navarra] defines *barquillo* [boat-shaped vessel] as a silver container generally used either for serving wine during festivals or for storing salt for baptisms ("Barquillo").
216 Although *ocho días* [eight days] is a common euphemism for a week, like from Sunday to Sunday with both days included, Martínez Montiño intends the cooking process to take place over eight days.

Venison tenderloin

Venison tenderloin is bigger and better than boar tenderloin. Thus, prepared with the marinade I explained for boar, larded, grilled, and the tongue boiled, then marinated and fried with melted fatback and slit open in the middle, it is very tasty.

How to salt venison and eat it fresh

If you want to save the high-fat meat from venison or from beef that is slaughtered in October and eat it fresh all winter long, as if it hasn't been salted, and the fat, as if it had just been slaughtered, do the following: Take big pieces, four to six pounds each, and remove the big bones – the spine, the shoulder and pelvis – and the leg bones. Salt them, rubbing on a lot of salt, place them, very salted, in a round terracotta trough, and leave them five or six days as they release moisture and create brine. Remove them, shaking off all the salt. Then take all of the brine and more salt, and put it in a boat-shaped vessel or cauldron and add in enough water to cover the pieces of venison. Add more salt and stir it with the blancmange spoon until all the salt has dissolved. Then take a fresh egg and add it to the brine. If it sinks, add more salt, stirring it with the spoon until it dissolves, and put a fresh egg in the brine once again. If it stays on top and doesn't sink and half the egg is exposed, the brine is good, since a fresh egg in fresh water drops to the bottom like a rock. This brine should be brought to a boil and skimmed a lot. Then, take it off the flame, let it cool, and it should be as transparent as water from a fountain. Next, place the pieces of venison in the trough and pour the brine on top. Understand that it must be cold and must completely cover the pieces with at least a hand span of brine on top. Let it sit for another eight days. Check it, and if it is cloudy, take the pieces out again, touching them as little as possible with your hands. Do the egg test again, boil the brine again, let cool, and put the pieces back in.

y tórnase a enfriar, y torna a meter las piezas dentro, y puédeslas dejar por todo el Invierno, que la salmuera estará siempre muy clara, y la carne muy fresca. Cuando se hubiere de cocer, échala en agua dulce de la noche a la mañana, mudándole el agua un par de veces, y estará como si acabara de venir de la carnicería, y cuécela, y sírvela sobre una sopa blanca con perejil en rama por encima.

[158] *Cómo se hacen los tasajos de venado.*

Para salar un venado en tasajos, en matando la res hasla de desollar luego, (113v) y hazla piezas pequeñas y largas, que tengan poco hueso, o ninguno, y estrégalas con la sal medio quebrantada, y cuélgalas adonde les dé el aire, y no es menester más. Si quisieres hacer las piezas de a cuatro libras ponlas en sal tres o cuatro días, habiéndoles quitado los huesos grandes.

[159] *Cómo se puede llevar la carne de un venado veinte, o treinta leguas, sin que se pierda en las grandes calores.*

Harás las piezas del tamaño que quisieres, y harás un cocimiento de agua y sal, y vino, y vinagre, y hierbas del jardín, salvia, y mejorana, e hisopillo, y cuece las piezas del venado en este cocimiento, hasta que tengan muerta la sangre, y luego sácalas, y déjalas enfriar: y luego embanástalas en una banasta, poniendo un lecho de pajas de centeno, (114r) luego otro lecho de las piezas del venado, o gamo: y desta manera irás poniendo lechos hasta que se hincha la banasta, de manera que la carne no llegue una a otra, sino que cargue todo sobre las pajas de centeno: y desta manera puede ir, aunque sea camino de treinta leguas con buena diligencia. Luego se puede ir cociendo, como si se acabara de matar: la carne de las empanadas perdígalas en las parrillas, y méchalas muy bien con las mechas salpimentadas, y échales en vinagre por espacio de cuatro, o seis horas: y luego sácalas, y déjalas escurrir del vinagre, y embanástalas, poniendo un lecho de pajas de centeno, y luego otro de empanadas, y luego otro de pajas de centeno: y desta manera se pueden llevar: y en llegando adonde se han de comer, se podrán empanar, y durarán después tanto como si se acabara de matar.

[160] (114v) *Una empanada de pecho de vaca.*

Tomarás un pecho de vaca, que sea muy gordo, y dejarlo has manir, y luego cuécelo con buen rato de sal, y cuando estuviere cocido sácalo en una pieza así caliente como está, y échale y un poquito de vino por encima, y un poquito de vinagre, y de todas especias: y si te pareciere que no tendrá harta sal, échale un poco, y dale unas cuchilladas para que tome mejor la sazón, y déjalo estar allí hasta que se enfríe: y luego harás la masa desta manera: Echa en un cacillo un poco de caldo, y un poco de vino, y un poco de nuez y jengibre: luego toma riñonada de ternera, y si no la

You can leave them there the entire winter. The brine should always be clear and the meat will stay fresh. When it is time to cook them, place them in fresh water overnight, changing the water a couple of times. It will taste as if it just came from the butcher's. Cook it and serve with white sops and a sprig of parsley on top.

How to make venison jerky

To make venison jerky, after killing the beast, skin it right away. Make large and small pieces that have little or no bone. Rub them with large chunks of salt and hang them in the air to dry. There's no need for anything else. If you'd like to make four-pound pieces, have them hang with salt three or four days, having first removed the big bones.

How to travel twenty or thirty leagues in the heat with venison meat and not spoil it

Cut pieces of whatever size you want and prepare a boil of water, salt, wine, vinegar, and garden herbs: sage, marjoram, and winter savory. Boil the venison pieces in this boil until all the blood is cooked through. Next, remove the pieces and let them cool. Then package them in a woven basket by placing a layer of rye straw, then another layer of pieces of red deer or fallow deer meat. Continue layering in this way until the basket is full. Make sure the pieces of meat don't touch one another, rather that they only touch the straw. (Packed) this way, they can travel well even if the route is thirty leagues long at a fast pace. Then, you can cook it as if (the deer) had just been killed. For empanada meat, sear it on the grill, lard it well with strips [of fatback] that have been salted and peppered, and soak them in vinegar for four to six hours. Remove them and let the vinegar drain off. Then pack them in the basket by first laying down a bed of rye straw, then another of empanada meat, then another of rye straw. They can be transported this way. When you arrive to where you will eat them, wrap them in dough, and they will last as long as if the deer had just been killed.

A beef brisket empanada

Take fatty beef brisket and hang it to age. Then boil it in heavily salted water and when it has boiled put it in a bowl while still hot, sprinkle a little wine on top with a little vinegar and all spices. If you think it doesn't have enough salt, add in a little and make several slits on top so that the seasoning works in better. Leave until it cools. Next, make the dough in the following way: Put in a pan a little broth and wine with a little nutmeg and ginger. Then take some veal loin and, if you don't have any, beef loin, and finely shred it. Mash

tuvieres sea de vaca, y desuéllala muy bien, y májala en el almirez, hasta que esté como manteca, y échale dentro del cacillo donde tienes caldo sazonado, y ponlo a cocer: y entre tanto que cuece (115r) pon harina floreada sobre el tablero, y harás una presa redonda, échale ocho yemas de huevos, y un poquito de sal: luego harás la masa con el caldo que tienes en el cacillo sazonada, y hasla de masar y tender muy aprisa, y poner el pecho, y cerrar la empanada antes que se enfrié, porque si se enfriase no la podrías juntar: ponla sobre un papel untado con manteca, y ponla a cocer en el horno: y cuando vaya tomando color ponle un redaño de carnero encima, y acábalo de cocer: luego ábrela por lo alto, y cébala con el adobillo que quedó adonde estuvo el pecho, y cueza con él un poco, y sírvela caliente. Ésta es empanada Inglesa, que las que llamamos Inglesas no lo son, sino empanadas dulces, que éstas no han de llevar dulce. Esta suerte de empanar se puede hacer de lenguas de puerco, o ternera, añadiéndoles un poco de tocino picado, porque el pecho no lo ha de menester. También lo podrás hacer por medios pavos cocidos.

[161] (115v) *Cómo se adereza una frasia de Ternera.*[217]

El mejor plato de la ternera es la frasia. Esta se hace desta manera: Harás apartar las tripas gordas a una parte, y luego las pequeñas, así como están pegadas al entresijo, ponlas en una bacía grande llena de agua, o en un arroyo, y tomarás un palillo como un huso, que esté un poquito romo de la punta, y meterlo has por una punta de la tripa, e irásla llamando con el cuchillo, y como se vaya hinchendo [*sic*] el palillo,[218] iráslo cortando a lo largo hasta que halles el otro cabo de la tripa; de manera que han de quedar todas las tripas abiertas, y pegadas en su lugar en el entresijo: luego las lavarás mucho en agua, luego en sal, y quedarán muy blancas: estas has de echar a cocer con un poco de agua y sal: y cuando estén perdigadas sácalas, y córtalas a pedazos, y ponlas a cocer (116r) con un poco de tocino gordo, y una cebolla, con su sazón de sal: y cuando estén cocidas saca el tocino, y la cebolla, y pícalo sobre el tablero, y tórnalo a echar en la olla, y sazónalo con pimienta y nuez y jengibre, y cueza otro poco, y cuájalo con yemas de huevos y vinagre, saldrá un platillo muy blanco y muy gustoso: y si a esta frasia quisieres echar un poco de perejil picado por encima, después de servido en el plato, bien podrás, porque parece muy bien: y también podrás picar verdura con el tocino cocido, y la cebolla cocida, y echárselo dentro: y cuando lo cuajares aparta un poco de la flor:[219] y

---

217 In his book *Cocina y alimentación en los siglos XVI y XVII*, Francisco Valles Rojo defines *frasia* as "la parte de tripas de vaca y ternera pequeñas pegadas al entresijo" [the part of beef or veal small intestines attached to the mesentery] (414).
218 The original version uses *el palillo*, but in later editions it changes to *platillo* or, in one edition, *platito* (1763).
219 For more information on flor, see 65.

it in a mortar until it looks like lard. Add it to the pan with the seasoned broth and bring it to a boil. While it is simmering, put finely sifted flour on a pastry board, make a well, and add in eight egg yolks with a little salt. Make a seasoned dough with the broth from the pan, quickly knead it, and roll it out. Put the brisket in and seal it before it cools, because if it cools first, you won't be able to seal it. Place on a paper greased with lard and put it in the oven to bake. When it begins to brown, put a piece of mutton caul fat on top and finish baking. Then open the top and enrich it with the marinade remaining from the brisket. Bake it a little more and serve hot. This is an English empanada. The ones that we call English are not these, rather they are sweet empanadas. These [English ones] shouldn't have anything sweet in them. This way of making empanadas can be used with pork or beef tongue, adding a little bit of minced fatback. The brisket doesn't need any. You can also make it with parboiled turkey.

How to prepare veal frasia

The best veal dish is *frasia*. It is made this way: Separate and put aside the large intestines. Then place the small intestines that are attached to the mesentery in a big basin full of water, or in a stream, and take a stick, like a spindle, that has a rounded tip, and stick it into one end of the intestines and follow it with a knife, and as the stick fills in the intestines, cut them lengthwise until you reach the other end of the intestines. This way the whole intestine is opened up but still attached to the mesentery. Next, wash them [the intestines] with a lot of water and then with salt so that they come out very white. Put them in salt water to boil and when they are parboiled, take them out and cut them into pieces. Put them on to boil with a little extra fatty fatback, onion, and the right amount of salt for seasoning. When they are done, remove the fatback and onion and dice it up on a cutting board and then return them to the pot. Season with pepper, nutmeg, and ginger and let simmer. Thicken with egg yolk and vinegar and you will have a very white, very tasty dish. If you want to add some minced parsley on top of this *frasia* once it is served on the plate, you can, because it will look very good. You could also add some minced green herbs to the boiled fatback and onion and mix it up. When you go to thicken it, first set aside the flor. When plated, then sprinkle it

cuando esté en el plato échaselo por encima. De las tripas gordas harás morcillas de cámara: las cuales dejo para adelante, porque pienso escribir otras dos o tres suertes de morcillas de puerco.

[162] *Cómo se adereza una cabeza de Ternera.*

(116v) La cabeza de ternera cocerás con agua, y sal, y sacarla has en el plato, y quitarle has las quijadas, y abrirla has por encima de los sesos, y quitarle has aquellos huesos, y tendrás hecha una pebrada desta manera: Freirás tocino de la papada en dados, y un poco de cebolla muy menuda: luego echa allí vino y vinagre, y un poco de azúcar, y de todas especias, y canela, y cueza un poco, y échala por encima de la cabeza. Otras se sirven hendida la cabeza en dos medias, y cocida, y enharinada, y frita, y con la pebrada encima. Otras se sirven en medias, y tostadas con pan rallado sobre alguna sopa: y también la podrás servir, no más de cocida blanca, con pimienta, y un poco de vinagre, y perejil en rama.

[163] *Sesos de Ternera.*

De los sesos podrás hacer picatostes, cociéndolos primero, y luego picarlos, y echarles pan rallado, y azúcar, (117r) y canela, y de todas especias, y echale algunas yemas de huevo, de manera que esté un poco blando, y pondrás deste relleno sobre rebanadas de pan, y ponlas en una tortera, untada con manteca, y cuézanse con poca lumbre abajo y mucha arriba. Estos picatostes puedes hacer picantes sin dulce, y algunas veces les podrás echar queso y dulce. Destos sesos se pueden hacer buñuelos, picándolos como está dicho, y mezclándole pan rallado, y sus huevos, y unas pocas de especias, y freírlos. Estos sesos podrás picar muy bien después de cocidos, y luego echarles sal, y pimienta, sin otra cosa ninguna, y poner destos sesos sobre una rebanada de pan: y luego poner otra rebanada encima desta, y apretarla un poco, y tener manteca de puerco muy caliente, y freírlos allí de manera, que el pan quede muy tostado: y estas empanadillas de sesos[220] han de ir a la mesa muy calientes. Son muy buenas para quien come poco dulce.

---

220 Martínez Montiño calls these creations grilled *empanadillas* [turnovers] because no word yet exists for *sandwiches*, but, in fact, this is exactly what he is creating in this third iteration of the recipe: a grilled sandwich. This recipe is one of the first appearances of a sandwich in a European cookbook, an entire century before sandwich recipes appear in English cookbooks. Prior to the appearance of the sandwich in Europe, recipes existed in medieval Arab cookbooks. For more on the origins of the sandwich, see Nasrallah, "Mediaeval Arabs."

over the top. With large intestines, you can make tubes of blood sausage, which I am leaving for later because I plan on writing two or three other kinds of pork blood sausage [recipes].

How to prepare veal head

Boil veal head in salted water. Put it on a plate and remove the jawbone. Split open the top above the brains and remove all those bones. Have ready a pepper sauce made this way: Fry cubes of fatback from the jowls and some minced onion. Then add some wine, vinegar, a little sugar, all spices, and cinnamon and bring to a boil. Pour this on top of the head. Others are served with the head split in half, boiled, dredged in flour, and fried with the pepper sauce on top. Others are served halved, toasted with breadcrumbs over sops. And it can also be served just boiled white with pepper, a little vinegar, and a sprig of parsley.

Veal brain

You can make slices of fried bread with brain by first boiling it and then dicing it up. Add breadcrumbs, sugar, cinnamon, all spices, and some egg yolk so that it is soft. Put this filling on slices of bread and put them in a covered tart pan greased with lard. Let it bake with a low flame below and high flame above. These slices of fried bread can be made just with spices and no sweetener, and other times you can add cheese and sweetness. You can also make puffs with this brain, dicing it as explained; mixing it with breadcrumbs, the right amount of eggs, and a little bit of spices; and frying them. You can mince this brain after boiling and then add salt and pepper without anything else. Spoon it onto a slice of bread and then put another on top and squeeze them together a little. Have some hot lard and fry them so that the bread comes out very toasted. These little brain turnovers should be very hot when they go out to the table. They are very good for whoever doesn't eat a lot of sweet food.

[164] (117v) *Empanadas de Ternera.*

La carne de la ternera, ya se sabe, que lo mejor es echarla en adobo, y comerla asada con salsa de oruga: de las piernas puedes hacer empanadas frías y calientes, como está dicho atrás en las del jabalí. Los pechos en sal y cocidos son muy buenos, y rellenos, y tostados sobre alguna sopa, o sobre arroz de grasa también son buenos: la carne de la ternera es la que se acomoda en más cosas de platillos y rellenos, y empanadas Inglesas picadas, y de la carne del pecho entero: y así no hay para qué comenzar cosa tan larga, sólo pondré aquí un platillo de los huesos.

[165] *Uspot.*[221]

Tomarás los jarretes de la ternera hechos pedazos, y échalos a cocer con agua y sal, y cuando estén medio cocidos sácalos, y ponlos en un cazo, y toma tocino en dados, y fríelo, y tendrás cantidad (118r) de cebolla picada a lo largo, y fríela en el tocino, y échala en un cazo sobre la carne, y sazona con pimienta, nuez y jengibre: luego échale caldo hasta que se bañe, y cueza poco a poco: y luego tendrás para cada plato destos huesos, seis yemas de huevos cocidos duros, y un migajón de pan blanco, remojado todo en vinagre, y pasarlo has todo por un cedacillo, o estameña, y con esto cuajarás el platillo: y cuando lo sirvieres tendrás un poquito de verdura picada, y échasela por encima. Es muy buen platillo. Y si fuere tiempo de zanahorias, cuécelas primero, y luego hazlas rajitas, y fríelas con el tocino y cebolla, y échalas en el platillo. Ha de salir un poco agrio. Volvamos ahora a tratar otro poco de cosas de masa.

[166] *Empanadilla de masa dulce.*[222]

Pondré aquí cuatro, o cinco suertes de empanadillas de masa dulce, que (118v) aunque las viandas sean diferentes, la masa siempre ha de ser de una manera: Tomarás una libra de harina de trigo floreada, y ponla sobre el tablero, y harás una presa redonda, y échale dentro media libra de azúcar molido y cernido, y un cuarterón de manteca de puerco, y echarás ocho huevos, los dos con claras, y los seis sin ellas, y un poquito de vino, y un poquito de sal, y amasa tu masa, y vendrá a quedar encerada: y desta masa has de hacer cuatro empanadillas, que no ha de haber más ni menos: y por esta cuenta podrás hacer masa para muchas. Lo que has de echar dentro, ha de estar cocido, o asado o frito. Harás unas de torreznos que sea tocino bueno y tierno, y harás unos torreznos pequeños un poco delgados, y ásalos en las parrillas, de manera que no se sequen: luego échalos así calientes en un poco

---

221 For more on the origins and legacy of this recipe, see the Introduction (73) and the Glossary.
222 The first part is the basic recipe for making sweet dough for turnovers. It continues with a recipe for roasted pork belly turnovers.

Veal empanadas

The best way to prepare veal, as is already known, is to marinate it and eat it grilled with arugula sauce. The meat from the legs can be made into empanadas both cold and hot, as is already explained in the boar (recipes). The breasts, salted and boiled, are very good, or stuffed, or roasted and served on sops or over rice cooked in animal fat are also tasty. Veal is what most gets used for individual dishes, as stuffing, and in English empanadas minced or as the whole breast. So, there's no reason to begin such a long section. I'll just include here a bone dish.

Uspot

Take chopped-up pieces of veal shanks and put them on to boil in water with salt. When they are parboiled, take them out and put them in a pot. Take cubes of fatback and fry them. Have a lot of onion cut lengthwise and fry it in the fatback. Add it to the meat in the pot and season with pepper, nutmeg, and ginger. Next, add in enough stock to braise and let it simmer. Then for each plate of these bones (with meat), take six hard-boiled egg yolks and the crumb of white bread soaked in vinegar and strain it all through a sieve or cheesecloth. You will thicken the dish with this. When you serve it, have a little minced green herb to sprinkle on top. It is a very tasty dish. If carrots are in season, boil them first then slice them into thin pieces and fry them with the fatback and onion and serve them on the plate. It should come out a little sour. Let's turn again to a couple of things on dough.

Sweet dough for turnovers

I will include here four or five kinds of sweet dough for turnovers. Even though the fillings differ, the dough should always be made this way: Take a pound of finely sifted wheat flour and put it on the pastry board. Make a round well and put in it half a pound of sifted, ground sugar, a quarter pound of lard, eight eggs – two with the whites and six without – a little wine, and a little salt. Knead it until it is smooth. With this dough you can make four turnovers. There shouldn't be any more or less. With these calculations you can make dough for many more. What you put inside should be boiled, grilled, or fried. Make some with roasted pork belly; the fat should be good and tender. Make the small [pieces of] roasted pork belly somewhat thin and grill them on the grill such that they don't dry out.

de vino blanco, y déjalos estar media hora. Luego harás de la masa ocho torticas redondas, y destas harás cuatro empanadillas de (119r) a dos hojas, y en cada una un torrezno partido por medio: han de ser tan iguales estas tortitas de la masa, que no las has de cercenar, ni las has de mojar con ninguna cosa para repulgarlas ni has de echar especia ninguna. El tocino esté bien desalado. No se han de dorar, ni echar azúcar por encima.

[167] *Otras empanadillas de pies de Puerco.*

Cocerás los pies de puerco, y de que estén bien cocidos, quítales los huesos mayores, y sazónalos con un poco de especia, y haz tus empanadillas, echando en cada una dos medios pies, y sean redondas como las del tocino. Estos pies de puerco, si los quisieres sazonar dulces, tendrás un poquito de almíbar, y pásalos por él. Luego échales un poco de especias, y déjalos enfriar, y haz tus empanadillas: si las quieres hacer, de buen solomo de puerco podrás, beneficiándolo, como las de los torreznos.

[168] (119v) *Empanadillas de Sardinas.*

Tomarás sardinas frescas, escámalas y fríelas, de manera que no se sequen mucho, y luego fríe un poco de cebolla con un poco de buen aceite, y échalo sobre las sardinas, y sazónalo con un poquito de pimenta y sal si no la tuvieren las sardinas, y echa tres sardinas, y un poquito de la cebolla frita encima, escurrida del aceite en cada empanadilla, y cierra tus empanadillas de la manera que está dicho en las otras, y en la masa no has de echar aceite sino manteca de vacas fresca, porque con aceite no saldrán bien.

[169] *Otras empanadillas de criadillas de tierra.*

Cocerás las criadillas con agua y sal: luego ahógalas con un poco de buen aceite, y sazónalas con un poco de pimienta y nuez, y jengibre, y una migaja (120r) de azafrán, y sal: luego ve haciendo tus empanadillas: Y advierte, que estas empanadillas se han de servir calientes. Estas empanadillas es mejor tenerlas hechas dos o tres días antes que se hayan de servir, porque estará muy revenida, y calentándose estará muy tierna, y con diferente gusto,[223] y las puedes hacer de otras muchas cosas, como son pajarillos gordos, y gazapillos, todo esto queda al albedrío del

---

223 Preparing the turnovers in advance should cause the dough to form a dry skin on the outside and begin to slightly ferment. When cooked, the dryness disappears and the flavour will change.

Then, drop them hot into a little white wine and let them soak for a half hour. With the dough make eight little round pies, and from those, four turnovers of two sheets each. In each one, a slice of roasted pork belly cut in half. Each of these little dough pies should be exactly the same size, so it isn't necessary to trim them. You don't need to wet them with anything for crimping. Don't add any spices either. The fat should be well desalted. These should not be browned or have sugar sprinkled on top.

Other pig's feet turnovers

Boil pig's feet and once thoroughly cooked, remove the big bones and season with a little spice. Make the turnovers and put, in each one, two half feet. They should be round like the fatback ones. If you want to make these pig's feet sweet, have some simple syrup and dip them in it. Then, sprinkle on a little bit of spices, let them cool, and make the turnovers. If you want to make them with some good pork tenderloin, you can, preparing it like the ones with roasted pork belly.

Sardine turnovers

Take fresh sardines, scale and fry them such that they do not dry out a lot. Then, fry a little onion in some good-quality oil and pour it over the sardines. Season with a little salt and pepper if the sardines don't already have it. Place three sardines and a little of the fried onion without much of the oil in each of the turnovers and seal the turnovers as previously explained. The dough should not have oil, rather butter, because it won't turn out well with oil.

Other truffle turnovers

Boil the truffles in salted water. Then sauté them with a little good oil and season with a little pepper, nutmeg, ginger, a pinch of saffron, and salt. Next, begin making the turnovers. Note that these turnovers are served hot. It is better to have these turnovers made two or three days in advance, because they will dry out and heating them will soften them up and give them a different taste. You can make them out of many things like small, plump birds and young rabbits. All of this is

oficial. La masa se decir, que es de las mejores que se hacen. Advierte, que estas empanadillas no han de llevar dentro ningún género de caldo, que no es masa que lo puede sufrir.

[170] *Una empanada Inglesa.*

Si quieres hacer una empanada Inglesa con esta masa de las empanadillas podrás, añadiendo la tercera parte de más harina y huevos, porque no esté tan fina, sino que tenga un poco de más fuerza: echarle has cuatro huevos con claras, (120v) y cuatro sin ellas; y con esto podrás hacer de la masa que habías de hacer ocho empanadillas, hacer una empanada Inglesa: y con esto podrás hacer empanada de un pecho de ternera cocido hecho pedazos, o entero, como quisieres: picarás un poco de tocino con un poco de verdura, y después que tengas tendida una hoja desta masa dulce, que esté un poquito gorda, ponle un poquito de tocino picado en el suelo hacia la una parte; luego tendrás el pecho sazonado de todas especias y sal, y asienta la carne sobre el tocino, y ponle por encima otro poco de tocino picado, y cierra tu empanada en media luna, y úntala por encima con un poco de manteca por derretir, y ráspale un poco de azúcar por encima, y si no quisieres echarle tanta manteca, bien le podrás echar un poco de agua con un hisopillo, y ráspale el azúcar encima, y será lo mismo que con la manteca. Algunos les dan después de cocidas una costra con espuma de claras (121r) de huevos, y azúcar: y porque no es bueno, no lo pongo aquí: en estando cocida cuájala con cuatro yemas de huevos y caldo, batidas con un poco de agrio de limón: y si quisieres hacer esta empanada Inglesa de carne picada, picarás dos libras y media, o tres de carne de ternera, o cabrito, muy bien con su tocino gordo, y un poquito de verdura: y cuando esté bien picada métele huevos crudos, cosa de cuatro, y sazona con todas especias, y sal, y una gota de vinagre, o zumo de limón, porque enternece la carne. Y si le quisieres echar un poquito de pan rallado mezclado con la carne, no es malo como sea poco: luego tiende la hoja para la empanada, y asienta esta carne picada sobre ella, de manera que sea la empanada un poco ancha; ciérrala en media luna con su repulgo, y ponle su manteca, y su azúcar por encima. Y advierte, que todo el azúcar que se hubiere de echar en las empanadas Inglesas, y en las empanadillas, y en los hojaldres (121v) ha de ser cernido por cedazo de cerdas, porque todos los granillos que queden enteros no se derritan en la masa: y así no se mezclen bien el azúcar con el [sic] harina.

[171] *Buñuelos de viento.*[224]

Tomarás un poco de harina floreada cosa de media libra, y desátala con agua fría, y un poquito de sal, y hará un batido como para hacer hostias: luego calentarás un poquito

---

[224] This recipe is an early documentation of cream puff dough, also known as *pâte a choux*, centuries before Antonin Carême popularized it in France. Here, instead of heating the liquid and fat first and then adding the flour, he mixes together the flour and liquid before adding it to the hot fat. This and the following two recipes were made in the test kitchen. For images of the process, see Appendix 3.12.

up to the discretion of the cook. It is said that this dough is one of the best that is made. Note that these turnovers should never have any broth as part of the filling, since the dough would not hold up.

An English empanada

If you want to make an English empanada using this dough for turnovers, you can by adding a third more of flour and eggs so the dough isn't as fine but rather somewhat strong. Add four eggs with the whites and four without. With this dough, which is meant for making eight turnovers, you can make one English empanada. And with this dough you can make an empanada with boiled breast of veal, chopped or whole, whichever you prefer. Dice up some fatback with a little bit of green herbs, and once you have rolled out a thicker sheet of this sweet dough, put a little of the fatback on one side of the bottom. Then have your breast, seasoned with all spices and salt, and place the meat on the fatback and spread on top a little more of the diced fatback. Seal the empanada in (the shape of) a half moon. Grease the top with a little unmelted lard and grate a little sugar on top. If you prefer not to use so much lard, you can sprinkle a little water on with a hyssop brush, grate the sugar on top, and it will be the same as the lard. Once it's baked some (cooks) brush the crust with egg whites and sugar, but because it isn't any good, I'm not including it here. Once baked, thicken it with four egg yolks and broth beaten with a little lemon juice. If you want to make this English empanada with minced meat, mince two and a half or three pounds of veal or kid with the right amount of extra fatty fatback and a little bit of green herb. When it's all minced, add raw eggs, about four, and season with all spices, salt, and a drop of vinegar or lemon juice to tenderize the meat. If you want to mix in a little bit of breadcrumbs with the meat, it is okay as long as it is just a little. Then roll out the dough for the empanada and place the minced meat on top so that the empanada is a little wide. Seal it in (the shape of) a half moon, crimp the edges, then spread the right amount of lard on top and sprinkle with sugar. Note that all sugar used in English empanadas, turnovers, and in puff pastry should be sifted in a sieve made with horsehair so that all the little sugar granules that remain whole don't melt in the dough and thus the sugar doesn't mix in with the flour.[7]

Puffs

Take about half a pound of finely sifted flour and thin it with cold water and a little salt. Make a batter for making wafers. Then heat a little lard in a frying pan

---

[7] To clarify these instructions, Martínez Montiño is sifting sugar through a fine sieve and using the chunks that remain to sprinkle on top of the empanada.

de manteca en una sartén como para hacer una tortilla de huevos: y cuando esté caliente echa el batido dentro en la sartén, y menéalo con un cucharón sobre unas brasas, y vendráse a hacer una masita encerada, y cuécela muy bien, meneándola siempre, porque no se pegue a la sartén, ni haga cortezas, porque todo el toque desta masa está en que salga muy bien cocida de la sartén, porque si sale bien cocida, en ninguna manera pueden salir malos los buñuelos. En estando cocida la masa, échala (122r) en el almirez, y májala muy bien, y vele metiendo huevos poco a poco y majándola mucho hasta que esté blanda, y los huevos no han de ser todos con claras sino la mitad, porque no esponjen demasiado, y se hagan resquebrajados. Estos buñuelos si los pasares por almíbar, y les echares un poco de canela molida por encima, haciendo los buñuelos un poco grandes, entiendo que es la mejor suerte de buñuelos que se hacen.

[172] *Otros Buñuelos de viento.*

Si quieres hacer los buñuelos de viento de tortillas, harás el batido como está dicho en los de atrás: Tomarás una sartén, y calienta un poquito de manteca, y cuando esté caliente vacíala, que no quede más de untada la sartén, y echa un poquito del batido dentro, y hazlo correr por toda la sartén, de manera que se haga una tortilla muy delgada: y en estando cuajada, vuélvela de la otra (122v) parte para que se cuaje, y luego échala en el almirez, y así irás haciendo todo el batido en tortillas: luego májalas muy bien en el almirez, y vele metiendo huevos como está dicho en los de atrás, y viene a ser una misma cosa. Esta suerte de buñuelos, y estoros de atrás, fríelos y pásalos por almíbar si lo tuvieres, y si no échales miel por encima y azúcar raspado.

[173] *Otros Buñuelos de viento.*[225]

Si hubieres de hacer muchos platos de buñuelos de viento, y te pareciere que son muy embarazosos los que quedan referidos atrás, pon un cazo al fuego con agua, y sal, y un poco de manteca, y cuando esté cociendo échale harina dentro sin quitar el cazo del fuego, y menéala con un cucharón de manjar blanco, y harás embeber toda la harina que pudieres, de manera que quede la masa encerada, y cuécela mucho sobre (123r) el fuego; porque todo el toque desta masa está en escaldarse bien la harina, y cocerse bien en el cazo sobre la lumbre, meneándola mucho, porque no se pegue al cazo; y aunque se pegue algo, lo pegado se quedará en el suelo del cazo: luego echarás esta masa en un librillo,[226] o en el tablero, y sobarla

---

225 This version of the dough recipe most matches the basic cream puff dough also known as *pâte à choux*.
226 *Librillo* or today *lebrillo* is a bowl whose top is wider than its bottom that was used for kitchen chores like kneading dough, cleaning insides of pig, or washing dishes. In the early eighteenth century, editors changed the term to *barreño*.

as if to make an egg omelette. When it is hot, pour the batter into the frying pan and stir it with a spoon over red-hot embers. It will turn into a smooth dough. Continue to cook, constantly stirring so that it doesn't stick to the pan or form a crust. The secret to this dough is that it is thoroughly cooked in the frying pan, because if it is thoroughly cooked, there's no way the puffs are going to turn out bad. Once the dough is cooked, put it in a mortar and mash it up. Slowly add eggs and continue mashing until it is very soft. The eggs shouldn't all have their whites, just half of them so it doesn't get too spongy or crack too much. I am told that these puffs, if you dip them in simple syrup and sprinkle them on top with a little ground cinnamon, making them a little bigger, are the best kind of puffs that are made.

Other puffs

If you want to make tortilla puffs, make the batter as explained above. Take the frying pan and heat it up with a little lard. When it's hot, empty the pan so that it's just greased. Then pour in a little batter and spread it over the whole pan so that it makes a single, thin tortilla. When it's setting, flip it over so the other side sets. Put it in the mortar and continue making tortillas with the batter. Then mash them well in the mortar, adding eggs as explained above, and it will come out the same. [For] this type of puff, and those above, fry them, dip them in simple syrup if available, and if not, sprinkle honey and grated sugar on top.

Other puffs

If you have to make a lot of plates with puffs and what was previously written seems too cumbersome, put a pot on the fire with water, salt, and a little lard. When it's boiling, add flour without removing the pot from the flame and stir it with the blancmange spoon. Allow the flour to absorb all the liquid so that it forms an elastic dough. Continue cooking on the fire. The secret to this dough is to add the flour to water at a rolling boil. Cook it over the flame, stirring it constantly so that it doesn't stick to the pot, and even if it sticks a little, the stuck part should stay in the bottom of the pot. Then, put the dough in a terracotta bowl or on a pastry board and knead it very well with your hands. Add

has muy bien con las manos, e irás metiendo huevos, y sobando, y harásle embeber huevos hasta que esté blanda, y échala sobre una tablilla, o sobre una cobertera: y de allí irás haciendo buñuelos con la buñolera, o con un garabato de cuchara.[227] Esta masa sirve para almojábanas, y para fruta de jeringa.[228]

[174] *Almojábanas de Cuajada.*

Cuajarás una azumbre de leche con hierba de cuajar,[229] y ponla a calentar un poco: luego irásla juntando, que se venga a hacer una pella, y si no se quisiere juntar bien, caliéntala un poco más, (123v) y juntarse ha: exprímela muy bien, y ponla sobre el tablero, y sóbala con un poco de harina, de manera que no le quede burujón ninguno: luego métele yemas de huevos hasta que esté blanda, que se puedan hacer las almojábanas sobre el tablero con harina, y fríelas poco a poco, y cuando lo saques de la sartén, tendrás aparejado un poco de almíbar hecho, y cociendo, y tendrás un poco de suero en otra vasija, e irás pasando las almojábanas por el suero, y luego por el almíbar, y veles echando su canela molida: y suelen salir muy buenas. De queso fresco también podrás hacer almojábanas,[230] sobando el queso con un poco de harina: luego métele huevos como está dicho: a éstas echarás un poco de hierbabuena picada, o seca molida, y beneficiarlas has como está dicho el las de atrás.

[175] *Otras almojábanas de cuajada diferentes.*

(124r) Cuajarás la leche, y luego echa la cuajada en una servilleta, y exprímele un poco, de manera que quede blanda: luego échala en un cacillo, o cazuela, y échale dos, o tres yemas de huevos y un poquito de harina, y menéala con un cucharón, de manera que quede blanda, y bien rala, y pon la sartén al fuego con manteca, o buen aceite, y ve haciendo las almojábanas desta manera: Mojarás la palma de la mano con agua, y harás allí la almojábana con un agujero en medio, y velas

---

227 *Buñolera* is a kitchen instrument designed for making *buñuelos*. The batter is placed in the scoop and dropped into the heated oil to form uniform puff balls. *Garabato de cuchara* is a semicircular hook, usually made of iron, that is hung on the wall and typically used to hang kitchen equipment; in this case, a spoon hook. While the *buñolera* makes round puffs, the *garabato de cuchara* would make looped ones.
228 *Fruta de jeringa* refers to fried dough much like what you would find at a summer fair or like today's churros. It is named *de jeringa* because the batter is placed into a large syringe or some type of pastry bag and piped into the hot oil to fry.
229 *Hierba de cuajar* refers to *cardoons*, whose dried flowers have enzymes that are often used to *curdle* milk.
230 *Queso fresco* [farmer cheese] and *leche cuajada* [clotted milk] are very similar. Both fall under the category of fresh cheeses, as do *queso de Burgos* [Burgos cheese], mozzarella, feta, and ricotta. The difference lies in the curdling agent and how much the curds are pressed.

eggs as you knead and incorporate them until it is soft. Move it to a smaller board or a lid and from there begin making the puffs with a puff scoop or a spoon hook. This dough can also be used for fried cheese pastries or for fried dough made with a puff syringe.

Fried cheese pastries made with curds

Curdle two quarts of milk with curdling herbs and warm it up. It will slowly come together in the shape of a ball, and if it doesn't want to come together, turn up the heat and it will. Express it, turn it out onto a pastry board, and knead it with some flour until there are no lumps left. Then, add egg yolks until it is soft. You can make the fried cheese pastries on the pastry board with flour, frying them a few at a time. When you take them out of the frying pan, have prepared some simple syrup that is boiling. Have some whey in another pot. Dip the fried cheese pastries in the whey and then in the simple syrup and then sprinkle the right amount of ground cinnamon on top. They will turn out very tasty. You can also make fried cheese pastries with farmer cheese, kneading the cheese with some flour, then add eggs as described above. Also add to these a little [fresh], minced spearmint, or dried and ground, and prepare them as explained above.

Other different fried cheese pastries made with curds

Curdle the milk and then put the curds in a napkin and squeeze them a little so that they are soft. Put them in a saucepan or casserole and add two or three egg yolks and a little flour. Stir with a spoon so that it is soft and thin. Put a frying pan on the fire with lard or good oil and continue making the fried cheese pastries in this way: Wet the palm of your hand with water and make the fried cheese pastries there with a hole in the middle and let them drop into the frying pan. If they break

dejando caer en la sartén: y si se desparramare en la sartén, échales un poquito de más harina, y salgan redondas muy delgadas. Este batido ha de estar tan ralo, que apenas se puedan hacer las almojábanas, y han de salir coscuradas, como buñuelos picados:[231] hanse de pasar por almíbar, y no se han de pasar por el suero, porque lo que pretendo en las otras en pasarlas por el suero, es, que salgan muy tiernas, y en éstas pretendo que salgan muy tiesas, (124v) porque algunos señores gustan de las unas, y otros de las otras.

[176] *Buñuelos de Queso fresco.*

Tomarás el queso hecho del propio día, o un día antes, y quítale las cortezas, y sóbalo en el tablero, de manera que no le quede burujón ninguno: luego échale un poquito de harina, y métele yemas de huevos hasta que esté un poco blando: luego pondrás una sartén al fuego con mucha manteca, de manera que no se caliente mucho. Luego harás unos buñuelos grandes y redondos, y deja estar la sartén con poca lumbre, que ellos se irán volviendo sin que lleguen a ellos. Cuando estén fritos pásalos por un poco de almíbar, o miel, y échale su canela molida por encima: y deste mismo queso, o cuajada bien (204) exprimida, podrás hacer buñuelos majándola en el almirez, o echándola (125r) allí un poco de harina, y sus huevos, de manera que venga a estar bien blanda, y has tus buñuelos con una cuchara.[232]

[177] *Quesadillas fritas de Cuajada.*[233]

Cuajarás la leche, y cuando esté cuajada, ponle sobre la lumbre, de manera que se caliente, y luego vela juntando con las manos poco a poco, y la vendrás a juntar toda: y luego sácala fuera del suero, y exprímela muy bien, y échala en el almirez, y májala bien, y échale un poco de harina, y vele echando huevos hasta que esté blanda, y échala un poco de hierbabuena picada, o seca molida, y sazona de sal, y luego amasa una masita fina sin azúcar, y tiende una hoja grande y delgada, y extiendela sobre el tablero, y con una cucharita irás echando cucharadillas sobre la hoja de la masa deste (125v) batido apartadas las unas de las otras, y mojarás los dedos de las manos en agua; e irásalas aplanando todas que vengan a estar anchuelas: luego toma la cortadera, y velas cortando alrededor, que no se arrime mucho la cortadera al batido: luego saca las cercenaduras, y ve haciendo sus quesadillas como candilejas, que tenga cada una cinco o seis piquitos: y para hacer estos no las has

---

231 *Buñuelos picados* refers to puffs made with some type of chopped meat or poultry in them. Readers today can infer that these puffs also came out bumpy.
232 Martínez Montiño is contrasting these *buñuelos* [puffs] made with a spoon with the previous recipe for *almojábanas* [fried cheese pastries], which are made with one's hands.
233 See Appendix 3.13 for images of making this recipe.

up in the pan, add in more flour so that they come out round and very thin. This batter should be so thin that it is almost too thin to make fried cheese pastries, and they should come out bumpy like puffs with minced meat. Dip them in simple syrup but not in whey. What I am trying to do in the others by dipping them in whey is to have them come out tender, and with these, I want them to come out firm because some lords like them one way and others, the other way.

Farmer cheese puffs

Take cheese made the same day, or the day before, and remove the rind. Knead it on a pastry board so that no bumps are left. Then, add in a little flour and enough egg yolks to make it soft. Then, put a frying pan on the flame with a lot of lard but don't heat it too much. Then make some big, round puffs and leave them in the frying pan on low flame. They will turn over without you having to touch them. When they are fried, dip them in simple syrup or honey and sprinkle the right amount of ground cinnamon on top. With this same cheese or curds that have been well expressed, you can make puffs by mashing them in the mortar or adding a little flour and the right amount of eggs to make it very soft. Make these puffs with a spoon.

Fried cheese curd tarts

Curdle some milk and when it's done, put it on the fire so that it heats up. With your hands slowly bring it all together. Remove it from the whey and thoroughly squeeze it. Put it in a mortar and mash it up. Add in some flour and then eggs until it turns soft. Add in some [fresh] minced spearmint, or dried and ground, and season with salt. Then knead a fine dough with no sugar and roll out a big, thin sheet across the pastry table. With a teaspoon, place spoonfuls of the filling onto the sheet of dough, separated one from the other. Wet your fingers with water and flatten them so they become wide. Then take the pastry cutter and cut around them, but don't let the pastry cutter get too close to the filling. Take the trimmed edges and begin making cheese tarts in the shape of oil lamps with five or six little points. To make these it is not necessary to wet them; rather, when

de mojar, porque es mejor cuando hacen esos picos, que los juntes con el mesmo batido, y con esto pegan muy bien: y después que tengas hechas una sartenada, pon la sartén al fuego, de manera que la manteca no se caliente mucho, y velas echando dentro boca abajo, y fríanse poco a poco, y velas volviendo de manera, que no se tuesten mucho: y en sacándolas tendrás un poco de miel espumada, y pásalas por ella, y velas asentando en el plato, y con cada lecho irás echando azúcar y canela. Es fruta que se puede guardar muchos días, y la miel ha de tener un poquito (126r) de agua al espumarse, y las quesadillas no han de ser mayores que un real de a ocho.[234] Y advierte, que cuando acabares de hacer el batido, has de hacer una quesadilla, y probarla en la manteca: y si el batido se esparramare por la sartén, échale un poquito de más harina.

[178] *Quesadillas de horno.*[235]

Has de majar el queso fresco, y meterle huevos hasta que esté blando, y échale un poco de hierbabuena molida, y echa a cada libra de queso un cuarterón de azúcar, y un poco de manteca de vacas, y harás unos vasitos anchuelos y bajos, e hínchelos deste batido: y después de cocidos échalos un poco de buena miel por encima.

[179] *Fruta de Cañas.*[236]

Tomarás dos o tres cañas de vaca, y hazlas trozos, y perdígalas en agua (126v) y sal, que den dos hervores; luego sácalas, y tendrás doce yemas de huevos cocidos, y pondrás las cañas y las yemas de los huevos, y un cuarterón de azúcar molido, y un poco de canela molida: y juntos todos estos materiales, deshazlo todo con un cucharón, de manera que se haga una pasta, y amasarás un poco de masa fina frita sin azúcar, y tiende una hoja delgada de la masa: y pondrás tres, o cuatro cucharadillas de la pasta de las cañas, y mojarás la hoja con un poquito de agua por la una parte con unas plumas, y también entre la pasta porque pegue bien la masa: luego volverás una punta de la hoja por encima de todos aquellos montoncitos de pasta, y asentarla has muy bien con la mano por el borde, y por entremedias dellas: y luego con el sello de la cortadera irás dando alrededor, y vendrán a quedar hechas empanadillas: luego tomarás la cortadera, y córtalas, y pícalas con un alfiler: en cada una darás (127r) cinco, o seis picadas, y pondrás la manteca al fuego, y fríanse con mucha cuenta, porque no se rompe ninguna, que si se rompiese una, echaría a

---

[234] This coin, *real de a ocho* [eight-real], was a silver coin first minted in the late sixteenth century, approximately 38 mm (or an inch and a half) in diameter. It is slightly larger than an American fifty-cent piece.
[235] See Appendix 3.14 for an image of this recipe.
[236] Although this recipe is written differently from the earlier "Frutas de caña" [Fried dough with marrow filling] (216; 217), the two are essentially the same.

making these points, stick them together with the filling itself, because they will stick well together with it. Once you have enough made to fill a frying pan, put the pan on the flame so that the lard doesn't heat up too much. Lower them in face down, fry them a little, and turn them over so that they don't get too brown. When you take them out, have some whipped honey ready and dip them in it and put them on the plate. With each layer you should sprinkle cinnamon and sugar. This fried dough can be kept for several days. The honey should have a little water added to it for whipping and the cheese tarts should not be bigger that an eight-real coin. Note that when you're done making the filling, you should make one cheese tart to test the lard. If the filling breaks apart in the frying pan, add a little more flour.

Baked cheese tarts

Mash some farmer cheese and add eggs until it's soft. Add in some ground spearmint and, for every pound of cheese, a quarter pound of sugar and a little butter. Make some wide, shallow crusts and fill them with this filling. After they're baked, drizzle some good honey on top.

Fried dough with marrow filling

Take two or three pieces of bone marrow and break them into pieces and prepare in salted water by bringing them to a boil two times. Remove them and have twelve hard-boiled egg yolks. Add together the bone marrow, egg yolks, a quarter pound of sugar, and a little ground cinnamon. Combine all this together, mixing with a big spoon so that a paste is formed. Knead a fine fried dough with no sugar and roll out a thin sheet of dough. Place three or four spoonfuls of the marrow paste and, with a feather brush, wet one side of the sheet with a little water. Also brush between the pieces of paste so that they will stick to the dough. Next, turn over one end of the sheet onto the top of all the little piles of filling and with your hand adjust it on the edge and between the piles. Then, with the seal of the pastry cutter go around all of them and they will turn out like turnovers. Then take the pastry cutter and trim them. With a pin, prick five or six holes in each one. Heat up some lard on the fire and carefully fry them so that none of them fall apart. If one were to fall apart, the lard would be spoiled.

perder la manteca: y desta manera podrás freír las demás. A estas empanadillas les podrás echar un poco de almíbar en lugar de miel.

[180] *Empanadillas de Quajada.*

Unas empanadillas podrás hacer de cuajada, exprimiéndola bien, y sobándola bien: luego meterás dos huevos, y otras dos yemas a la cuajada que saliere de una azumbre de leche, y échale un cuarterón de azúcar, y un poco de manteca de vacas: y si estuviere muy rala, échale un poquito de harina; harás un poco de masa fina, que tenga un poco de azúcar, luego tiende una hoja larga y delgada; luego pondrás un montoncillo del batido en la una punta de la masa, que sea un poquito largo, (127v) y ha de estar un poco desviado del borde de la hoja: luego le darás tres cortecitos con la cortadera que sean cortos, y mojarás la masa con unas plumas, y dóblala por encima del batido, de manera que parezca empanadilla, y los cortecillos vengan a caer en medio del batido, de manera que se vea el batido por en medio dellos: luego redondéala con la cortadera dos dedos desviado del batido: y asiéntala con el sello, y levanta aquel borde, y harás un doblez en la una punta, y otros en medio, y otro en la otra punta, y entre doblez y doblez que junte la masa a la empanadilla, como cuando haces empanada Inglesa con picos. Éstas son buenas para meriendas, aunque se sirvan frías, porque han de llevar poca manteca, y poco azúcar, al cocerlas has de untar con un poco de manteca derretida, y no les has de echar azúcar por encima, ni las has de dorar, sino así blancas: el batido subirá y abrirá: los golpes que tiene encima parecen muy (128r) bien. Si no tuvieres leche para hacer estas empanadillas, podrás hacer un poco de almidón con leche de almendras bien incorporado. Luego le podrás echar los huevos, y un poco de manteca, (209) porque el azúcar ha de ir desecho en el almidón cuando se cociere: y con este batido podrás hacer empanadillas, como las de la cuajada.

[181] *Otras empanadillas.*

Si quisieres hacer unas empanadillas muy chiquitas, harás un poco de papín[237] con harto azúcar y yemas de huevos, y un poco de manteca de vacas fresca, y su sazón de sal, y leche de cabras,[238] y déjalo enfriar, y harás un poco de masa dulce, por cuenta de las empanadillas de torreznos, y pies de puerco, que está escrita atrás, y

---

237 *Papín* is a sweet cream sauce very similar to today's *crème anglaise*.
238 Juan Huarte de San Juan, author of *Examen de ingenious para las ciencias* [The examination of men's wits], considers *leche de cabra* [goat milk] to be one of the most exquisite food products that exist: "en opinion de todos los médicos, es el mejor y más delicado de cuantos usan los hombres" [in the opinion of all doctors it is the best and most delicious of all things that men consume] (160).

Continue frying the rest this way. You can drizzle simple syrup over these turnovers instead of honey.

Curd turnovers

You can make turnovers from curd, thoroughly squeezing it and kneading it well. Then add two eggs and another two egg yolks to the curds that came out of two quarts of milk. Add in a quarter pound of sugar and a little butter. If it's very thin, add in a little flour. Make a little fine dough that has a little sugar and roll it out into a long, thin sheet. Then put a little scoop of filling on one end of the dough; it should be a little long and it should be a little away from the edge. Then make three short slits with the pastry cutter. Wet the dough with a feather brush and fold it over the filling so that it looks like a turnover. The little slits should be in the middle so that you can see the filling through the slits. Round it [the turnover] out with the pastry cutter two-fingers length away from the filling and mark it with the seal. Lift that edge and make a fold, one on the edge, others in the middle, and another on the other edge. Between each fold the turnover filling should come together just as when you make an English empanada with points. These are good for late afternoon supper even if they are served cold. Because they have little butter and sugar, when they are baking you should spread some melted butter on top. Don't add any sugar or make the crusts golden. Just leave them white. The filling will rise and come out. The marks on top will look good. If you don't have milk to make these turnovers, you can make them with a little starch and almond milk mixed well together. Then you can add eggs and a little lard. The sugar will disintegrate into the starch when it's baking. With this filling you can make turnovers like the ones for curds.

Other turnovers

If you want to make mini turnovers, make a sweet cream sauce with a lot of sugar and egg yolks, a little fresh butter, and the right amount of salt, and goat milk. Let cool. Make a sweet dough, with the calculations for turnovers for roasted pork belly or for pig's feet that are written earlier. They should not be bigger than an

no sean mayores que un real de a ocho. Para hacer este batido echarás seis onzas de azúcar, y media azumbre de leche, y seis huevos, y tres onzas de harina.

[182] (128v) *Fruta de Fillos.*

Batirás doce yemas de huevos: luego echa allí un poco de harina cuanto quede un poco encorporada, y bátelo muy bien, que se mezcle bien la harina con las yemas de huevos: luego échale un poquito de leche, y sazona de sal, y pon la sartén al fuego con mucha manteca: y cuando esté bien caliente echarás un poquito del batido para probar: si el batido se cuajare como buñuelo, echarás algunas yemas más, y un poquito de leche: y cuando ello se hiciere como una esponjita, que esté un poquito cuajado en medio, y a la redonda esté como una esponja, entonces está bueno: y harás destas frutillas dos o tres en cada sartenada, y han de salir morenas, y hanse de pasar por almíbar, y echarles su canela por encima; y aunque no es muy galana, es de muy buen gusto. Lo que tiene es, que gasta mucha manteca. Y si cuando probares el batido en (129r) la sartén se desparramare todo por la manteca, con echar un poquito de más harina despolvoreada, y batirlo muy bien se emendará, y hará la esponjita que tengo dicho.

[183] *Fruta de Chicharrones.*

Para hacer una fruta que se llama chicharrones, has de batir diez huevos con claras, y todos muy bien batidos: luego tomarás un poco de harina, véselo despolvoreando por encima de los huevos, y bátelos mucho, hasta que se deshagan todos los burujoncillos, y ha de quedar un batido un poco más incorporado que el batido de la fruta de borrajas: y luego echarle medio panecillo de sal,[239] porque esta fruta ha de salir un poco salada, porque no ha de llevar dulce. Luego pondrás la sartén al fuego con un poquito de manteca fresca, y cuando esté caliente echarás la mitad del batido dentro, trayéndolo por toda la sartén, de manera que se haga como una tortilla, y no (129v) la dejes tostar, sino en estando cuajada por la una parte, volverle por la otra, y cuájese, y luego échale sobre un tablero, y harás la otra del batido que queda, y luego cortarás estas tortillas en pedacitos, unos cuadradillos, otros más larguitos, otros como eses, otros de las hechuras que te pareciere: luego tomarás la manteca de vacas la más fresca que tuvieres, y cocerla has, y freirás estos chicharrones, que así se llaman, poco a poco, dándoles vuelta con la misma sartén, de manera que cuando tomaren color, estén bien calados, y parezcan bizcochados. Estos se sirven sin dulce, porque tienen el gusto de chicharrones de puerco, y no son buenos, sino con manteca de vacas fresca.

---

239 A *panecillo de sal* [bread roll worth of salt]. Though the exact quantity of salt is unknown, based on other recipes where he uses this measurement, it may be that one *panecillo* is equivalent to one ounce. For more information, see the entry in the Glossary.

eight-real coin. To make this filling, use six ounces of sugar, a quart of milk, six eggs, and three ounces of flour.

Fried dough with spongy edges

Beat twelve egg yolks. Then add in a little flour, enough so that it turns out slightly thick. Beat a lot so that the eggs and flour are mixed well together. Then add a little milk and season with salt. Put a frying pan on the fire with a lot of lard. When it's heated, drop a little batter in to test. If the batter sets like a puff, add in more egg yolks and a little milk. When the batter looks like a little sponge, set in the middle but spongy on the edges, then it's the right consistency. With this batter, make two or three fried doughs at a time. They should come out brown. Dip them in simple syrup and sprinkle the right amount of cinnamon on top. Even if it's not (visually) stunning, it is very tasty. One thing about it is that it uses up a lot of lard. When you test the batter in the pan, if it breaks apart in the lard, add a sprinkling of a little more flour and beat it in well. It should rectify the problem and come out spongy as explained.

Crackling fried dough

To make a fritter called *crackling* you need to beat ten eggs with their whites very well. Then take some flour and sift it on top of the egg batter, mixing a lot until all the lumps disappear. The batter should be a little thicker than the batter for making deep-fried borage. Then add in half [the amount] of a bread roll worth of salt, because this fritter should be a little salty and it shouldn't have any sweetener in it. Then put in the frying pan a little fresh lard and when it is hot, add in half the batter, spreading it out across the whole pan so that it's like a tortilla. Don't let it brown; rather, once it has set, flip it over, let it set on that side, and turn it out onto a pastry board. Repeat with the remaining batter. Then cut these tortillas into small pieces, some into little squares, others rectangles, others like an S, others in whatever shapes you'd like. Then take the freshest butter possible, melt it, and fry these *cracklings*, that is what they're called, slowly, turning them over in the same pan so that when they begin to brown, they have soaked up a lot of butter and look crusty. These are served without any sweetener because they should have the flavour of pork rinds. They only turn out good when made with fresh butter.

[184] *Fruta de Prestiños*.

Batirás doce huevos en un cazo con claras, y échale canela molida, hasta que estén los huevos pardos, y échale un poco de sal; luego ve echando harina, (130r) e iráslo revolviendo con un cucharón de manjar blanco, y hazle embeber toda la harina que pudieres, de manera que quede una masa encerada, y sácala al tablero, y sóbala un poco; luego ve haciendo rollitos delgados, como cera hilada;[240] luego tomarás uno de estos rollitos, y ve torciendo con los dedos, cogiendo la puntilla, y torciendo saldrá un prestiño de la hechura de un piñón, de manera que no venga a tener más bulto que un piñón con cáscara: y si te pareciere que es cosa muy prolija, ve cortando el rollito de la mesa con un cuchillo al sesgo, unos bocaditos del tamaño del piñón, y despacharás más presto, mas no saldrán tan bien hechos, y veles echando harina, porque no se peguen unos con otros: y cuando tuvieres muchos hechos pon la sartén al fuego con mucha manteca, o buen aceite, y velos friendo con mucha cuenta; porque se cansa la manteca muy presto: y dé que estén bien fritos tendrás miel espumada y muy subida (130v) de punto: y para ver si está la miel en punto, echa unas gotas en un poco de agua, y si hicieren correa, no está harto: y si en sacándolas del agua se quebraren como vidrio, está buena la miel, echa los prestiños dentro en ella, y dales una vuelta, y tendrás un tablero de masa mojado con agua fría, y trastornarás los prestiños encima con su miel: y tendrás un poco de agua en que mojar las manos, e irás apartando montoncillos, y acomodándolos a modo de piñas, o de la manera que te pareciere: y entretanto que no se enfriaren, ellos se irán desmoronando: mas yéndose enfriando los harás quedar como quisieres, mojando siempre las manos en el agua: luego armarás tu plato destas piñas. Si los quisieren enviar fuera los podrás echar en unas ollas que estén mojadas con agua, así como salen los prestiños del cazo, y pegarse han unos con otros, y no en la olla.

[185] *Fruta de Piñas.*[241]

(131r) Tomarás cosa de media libra de harina, antes menos que más, y desatarla has con un poco de vino blanco y agua, y échale ocho huevos, y ha de quedar el batido bien batido, y un poco grueso, como el de los chicharrones, y échale un poco de sal, y untarás una tortera, y echa el batido dentro, y cúbrelo con su cobertera: y ponla con lumbre abajo y arriba: y en estando cuajada saca la torta sobre

---

240 *Cera hilada* [strings of wax], wrapped around a wooden paddle, were commonly used to provide light for the deceased during the month of November. For more information, see "Tablillas de difunto."

241 In this recipe, and the one above, Martínez Montiño recreates the look of a pine cone. Here he does so by frying pieces of a cake that has been cut on the side.

Prestiño fried dough

Beat twelve eggs with their whites in a pan, add in enough ground cinnamon to turn the eggs brown. Add a little salt. Then slowly add flour, stirring continually with a blancmange spoon. Make sure as much flour as needed is absorbed, and it forms an elastic dough. Turn it out onto a pastry board and knead it a little. Then make little, thin rolls, like string wax. Take one of these rolls and begin bending it with your fingers by taking one end. As you bend it, a *prestiño* will come out in the shape of a pine nut and in a way that doesn't have any more volume that a pine nut with its shell. If you find this takes too long, then cut the roll diagonally on the table with a knife into bite-sized pieces about the size of a pine nut. You will make them quickly but they won't turn out as well. Sprinkle some flour so they won't stick to one another. When you have a lot made, put the frying pan on the fire with a lot of lard or good oil and begin frying a lot at once, because the oil quickly turns old. Once they are fried, have some whipped honey at the high boiling point. To see if it's at this point, dribble a few drops of it in water. If it runs, it is not ready. If you take them [the drops] out of the water and they break like glass, the honey is ready. Dip the *prestiños* in it and turn them over. Have a pastry board wet with cold water. Then place the *prestiños* with their right amount of honey on it and have a little water to wet your hands. Begin separating them into little piles and arrange them to look like a pine cone or whichever way you prefer. If they aren't cold enough, they will start to collapse. But, as they cool down, they will take whatever shape you want. Always keep your hands wet with water. Then arrange the plate with these pine cones. If you want to send them elsewhere, you can put them in a pot that is damp with water just as you take them out of the pan and they will stick to one another and not to the pot.

Pine cone fried dough

Take about half a pound of flour, better less than more, and thin it with a little white wine and water. Add eight eggs. The batter should be well beaten and a little thick, like the crackling batter. Add in a little salt, grease a covered tart pan, pour the batter in, and cover it with a lid. Bake with heat above and below. Once it's set, place the cake on a pastry board and cut it into square pieces like torrijas

un tablero, y córtala en pedazos cuadrados como torrijas, y dale unos cortecitos cruzados unos por otros, y quedarán unos cuadradillos como garbanzos, y fríelos echando los cortes para bajo en la manteca, y fríanse poco a poco, y esponjarán, y parecerán a modo de piñas. Sírvelos con miel y azúcar raspado por encima. Si quisieres servir la torta entera dale los cortecitos, y fríela en un cazo con mucha manteca, los cortes hacia abajo, y cárgala en medio con una cuchara para que se amolde con el cazo, y de una sola podrás hacer (131v) un plato, y parecerá un morrión, échale miel, y algún poco de gragea por encima.

[186] *Un platillo de jadeo de manos de Ternera.*

Tomarás las manos de ternera cocidas, y las rebozarás con huevos, y freírlas has: luego tendrás hecha una salsa, que se llama jadeo. Para un plato desta salsa tomarás seis yemas de huevos crudos, y batirlos has en un cacillo, y echarle has medio cuartillo de vino blanco, y un poco de vinagre, y echarás pimienta, y nuez, y jengibre, y canela, y un cuarterón de azúcar, y media libra de manteca fresca de vacas, y un par de cucharadas de caldo, y sazonarlo has de sal, y ponlo al fuego, y tráelo a una mano como almendrada:[242] y cuando esta salsa comenzare a cocer, estará como ha de estar: luego meterás dentro las manos de ternera, o cabezuelas de cabrito rebozadas, (132r) y ponlo con un poquito de rescoldo cuanto no de un hervor recio, porque no se corte. Sírvelo con rebanadillas debajo, o con torrijas. Este plato se puede hacer de pollos, pichones, o aves, y no han de ser rebozadas, sino cocido blanco, y se puede hacer de manecillas de cabrito, o de carnero rebozadas. Este caldo de jadeo es bueno para tomar a las mañanas sin carne cuando hace frío.

[187] *Platillo de cabezuelas de Cabrito, y de las Tripillas.*

Para este platillo has de pelar las cabezuelas en agua caliente, y las manecillas, y de las tripillas harás una frasia,[243] como está dicho en la de la ternera, que aunque ésta es chiquita es una misma cosa: luego cocerás todo esto en una olla con un poco de tocino, y una cebolla: y cuando esté cocido picarás el tocino, y la cebolla, con un poco de verdura, (132v) y sazonarás con todas especias: y después cuajarlo has con tres, o cuatro yemas de huevos, y un poco de vinagre: y apartarás primero un poco de la flor:[244] y sírvelo sobre rebanadillas de pan, y échale la flor por encima, y un poco de zumo de limón. En este platillo no has de echar las asadurillas de cabrito.

---

242 For further information on *almendrada*, see the recipe "Una escudilla de almendrada" [A bowl of almond broth], in which Martínez Montiño explains how to make it (492–4; 493–5).
243 For an explanation of *frasia*, see 306n217.
244 For more information on the flor, see 65.

and make a series of cross slits. They will look like little scored garbanzos. Fry them, slits down, in lard. They should fry slowly and get spongy and come out looking like pine cones. Serve with honey and grated sugar on top. If you want to serve the cake whole, make the slits and fry it in a pan with a lot of lard, the slits face down, and hold it down in the middle so it moulds to the pan. A single one fits onto a plate. It will look like a helmet. Drizzle honey and add some sprinkles on top.

A dish of calves' feet with jadeo *sauce*

Take boiled calves' feet, coat with egg, and fry them. Then have made a sauce called *jadeo*. For dishes with this sauce, take six raw egg yolks and whip them in a saucepan. Add in a half pint of white wine, a little vinegar, pepper, nutmeg, ginger, cinnamon, a quarter pound of sugar, half a pound of butter, a couple of ladlefuls of stock, and season it with salt. Put it on the fire and continue stirring with one hand as you would for almond sauce. When this sauce comes to a boil, it is done. Then add in the calves' feet or kid head that has been coated in egg and fried. Reduce heat to grey embers, so that it isn't a rolling boil and doesn't break the sauce. Serve over slices of bread or torrijas. This dish can be made with young chicken, squab, or adult ones, but they should not be coated in egg and fried; instead they should just be boiled. You can also make this dish with kid or sheep feet coated in egg and fried. This *jadeo* sauce is good without meat in the mornings when it's cold.

A dish of kid head and intestines

For this dish, peel the heads and trotters in hot water and make a *frasia* with the small intestines as explained in the veal *frasia* recipe. Even though these intestines are small, it will come out the same. Then boil all of this in a pot with fatback and onion. When it's done, dice up the fatback and onion with a little bit of green herbs and season with all spices. Then let it thicken with three or four egg yolks and a little vinegar, but first, remove a little of the flor. Serve this on slices of bread, sprinkle the flor on top, and drizzle a little lemon juice. This dish should not have any kid pluck.

[188] *Otro platillo de cabezuelas de Cabrito.*

Con las cabezuelas y asadurillas de cabrito podrás hacer un platillo, cociéndolo todo salvo el hígado: y después de cocidas las cabezuelas, asentarlas has en un cacillo en medias, y cortarás los livianos, y el hígado en rebanadillas delgadas,[245] y freirás tocino en dados: y luego echarle has cebolla cortada muy menuda, y fríelo un poco, y luego echa allí las asadurillas, y ahóguense, y échalo todo sobre las cabezuelas, y sazona con todas (133r) especias, y échale caldo hasta que se bañen, y cuezan, y échales un poco de verdura picada, y un poco de agraz en grano, si fuere tiempo, y si no un poco de vinagre: y si lo quisieres cuajar, bien podrás, mas no es mucho menester; antes si le quisieres echar un poquito de mostaza,[246] cuando se quiera servir, podrás; porque es como fricasea, y en ellas dice bien la mostaza. Desta manera puedes hacer la fricasea de las cabezuelas, quitándoles los huesos, y mezclando la carne con las asadurillas, y sazonándola en la sartén.

[189] *Fricasea de cosas fiambres.*

Las fricaseas se hacen de muchas cosas, de algunas aves fiambres, o pollos, o pichones que estén cocidos, o asados, y esto ha de ser en sartén cuando lo quisieres servir, porque no es bueno estar hecho antes: freirás tocino en dados que esté bien frito, luego échale cebolla picada, (133v) y los pollos, o pichones, o aves cortadas en pedacitos, y fríelo todo junto en la sartén, y luego échale vinagre aguado con caldo, y un poco de verdura picada. Sazona con todas especias, y sal, y déjalo cocer dos hervores, y échalo en el plato sobre rebanadillas de pan: y si quisieres echar un poco de mostaza podrás, porque dice muy bien; particularmente si la fricasea es de cabezuelas de cabrito, o de callos de vaca, o de panzas de carnero. Estas fricaseas son muy buenas cuando se camina con algún señor, que hay poco espacio para aderezar de comer, que con llevar algunas aves fiambres: entre tanto que se le asa otra cosa, se hace la fricasea, pues que en un mesón no ha de faltar una sartén.

[190] *Cabezuelas de Cabrito rellenas.*

Echarás a cocer las cabezuelas partidas por medio: luego freirás un poco de tocino en rebanadillas, y echarás allí los sesos, y un poco de carne picada, (134r) o los livianos del cabrito picados después de cocidos: luego echarle has media docena de

---

245 Normally the *asadura* includes the heart, but in this recipe Martínez Montiño is using just the liver and lungs.
246 Early modern mustard differs significantly from today's. Martínez Montiño includes a recipe on how to make it later in the cookbook, "Memoria de la mostaza negra" [Memoir of black mustard] (512–14; 513–15). For more on this condiment, see its entry in the Glossary.

Another kid head dish

With kid head and pluck you can make a dish, boiling everything except the liver. After the heads are boiled, place them halved in a saucepan. Cut the lungs and liver in thin slices. Fry cubes of fatback. Add minced onion and fry. Next, add in the pluck and sauté it. Ladle it over the heads and season with all spices. Add in enough stock to braise and bring to a boil. Add a little minced green herb, and a few sour grapes if they are in season. If not, use a little vinegar. If you want to thicken it, you can, but it is not really necessary. Or if you would like to add a little mustard when you serve it, you can, because it's like a fricassee and it is said that mustard goes well with them. You can also make the kid head fricassee this way by removing all the bones and mixing meat with the pluck and seasoning it in the frying pan.

Cold meat fricassees

Fricassees can be made from a lot of things, poultry meat served cold, or from chicken or squab that have been boiled or roasted. When you are ready to serve, it should be right from the frying pan, as they should not be made in advance. Fry cubes of fatback until well done and add in diced onion, the pieces of young chicken, squab, or adult ones that have been cut up and fry everything together in the pan. Then, add vinegar diluted with broth and a little minced green herb. Season with all spices and salt and bring it to a boil two times. Put in on a plate on slices of bread. If you want to add some mustard, you can, because it is said it goes very well, especially if the fricassee is kid head, beef tripe, or mutton stomach. These fricassees are very good when travelling with a lord because there is not a lot of time to prepare a meal, but by including some already cooked poultry, while roasting something else, you can make the fricassee, because at any roadside inn there will always be a frying pan.

Stuffed kid head

Put on to boil kid heads chopped in half. Then fry some slices of fatback and add the brains, a little minced meat, or kid lung minced after it has been boiled. Then add half a dozen raw eggs and stir them in the frying pan until thoroughly

huevos crudos, y revolverlo has todo en la sartén, hasta que esté bien seco: luego sazona de todas especias, y échale otros dos, o tres huevos crudos, y un poco de agrio, y un poco de sal, y rellena las medias cabezuelas, y asiéntalas en una tortera untada con manteca, y ponla al fuego con lumbre abajo y arriba. También se ha de echar en el relleno un poquito de verdura picada. Y si alguna vez las quisieres hacer agridulces, podrás: y si llevaren dulce, sírvelas sobre una sopa dulce; y si no sobre una sopa de queso.

[191] *Otro platillo de cabezuelas de Cabrito.*

Henderás las cabezuelas por medio y lávense muy bien: luego tendrás un poco de perejil, y hierbabuena, unas hojas de mejorana: luego pondrás (134v) desta verdura encima de media cabezuela, mezcladas con unas rebanadillas de tocino muy delgadas, y un poco de toda especia: luego ponle otra cabezuela encima, y átala muy bien con un hilo: y desta manera puedes hacer las demás, y échales a cocer con agua, y sal, y un poco de tocino, y unos garbanzos, y los livianos de las asadurillas enteros, y sazona con un poco de especias: y de que estén cocidas sácalas, y desátalas los hilos, y sírvelos sobre una sopa blanca, abiertas las cabezuelas, y la verdura hacia arriba, y echa allí los livianos enteros, y unos pocos de garbanzos a modo de olla. Este es muy buen platillo, y no ha de llevar agrio ninguno, salvo algún poco de agraz en grano en el tiempo: y si fuere posible, las cabezuelas no han de ser desolladas, sino peladas.[247]

[192] *Otro plato de cabezuelas, y asaduras de Cabrito.*

(135r) Cocerás las cabezuelas de cabrito partidas por medio, y después de cocidas pásalas por un poco de manteca, y luego échales mucho pan rallado, y azúcar, y canela todo revuelto, y asiéntalas en una tortera untada con manteca, y ponlas al fuego con lumbre abajo y arriba: y cuando estén medio tostadas tendrás unas yemas de huevos batidas, y echarás con un manojo de plumas destas yemas por encima las cabezuelas, y luego échale más pan rallado, y azúcar y canela, y unas gotas de manteca caliente, y déjalas acabar de tostar: y luego sírvelas sobre una sopa de leche. Ésta harás desta manera: Harás unas torrijas de pan blanco, luego batirás cuatro huevos con un cuartillo de leche, y untarás un plato con manteca de vacas, e irás mojando las torrijas en la leche, y los huevos, y asentándolas en el plato, y tendrás seis onzas de azúcar molido, e irásselo echando por encima, y unos bocadillos de manteca fresca: y así acabarás de hacer la sopa, (135v) y echarle has toda la leche, y los huevos y manteca fresca por encima, y ponla a cocer en

---

[247] This suggested method of preparation helps to retain the skin on the head when the hairs are being removed.

cooked. Season with all spices and add in another two or three raw eggs, a little sour juice, and a little salt. Fill the half heads and place them in a covered tart pan greased with lard. Heat with the flame above and below. You should also add some minced green herb to the filling. If you ever want to make them sweet and sour, you can. If sweetener is added, then serve them on sweet sops, and if not, on cheese sops.

Another kid head dish

Split the heads in half and wash them well. Have a little parsley and spearmint and some marjoram leaves. Then sprinkle this green herb mix on top of a half head mixed in with some very thin slices of fatback and a little bit of all spices. Then put the other half on top and tie them together with a string. You can make the others this way. Put them on to boil in salted water with a little fatback, some garbanzos, the whole lungs from the pluck, and season with a little bit of spices. Once boiled, remove them, untie the string, and serve over white sops with the heads open and the green herbs facing up. Place the whole lung and some garbanzos as they were in the pot. This is an excellent dish and should not have anything sour added except a few sour grapes when they are in season. If possible, these heads should not be skinned but rather scraped.

Another kid head and pluck dish

Boil the kid heads split in half and when they are done, dip them in a little lard. Add a lot of breadcrumbs, sugar, and cinnamon, all mixed together, and place them in a covered tart pan greased with lard. Put them in to bake with the flame above and below. When they are partially browned, have some whipped egg yolks and, with a bunch of feathers, brush the yolk on the heads. Then sprinkle on more breadcrumbs, sugar, and cinnamon and some drops of hot lard. Finish browning and then serve them on milk sops. Make these this way: Make torrijas from white bread. Beat four eggs with a pint of milk. Grease a plate with butter and soak the torrijas in the eggs and milk. Arrange them on the plate and take six ounces of ground sugar and sprinkle on top with some dabs of fresh butter. You'll finish making the sops this way. Pour on top the remaining milk and eggs and (dab on the remaining) fresh butter.

un horno a fuego manso, y luego sirve las cabezuelas encima. Es buen plato para Sábado.[248] Advierte, que esta sopa es muy buena para días de Viernes con huevos estrellados encima, y con el recado desta sopa, y unas rebanadas de queso fresco, o unos requesones, se puede hacer una cazuela, y poner en el postrer lecho unos huevos estrellados, parécese mucho a la cazuela de natas. Y si quisieres servir las cabezuelas de cabrito asadas sobre la sopa, partirás las cabezuelas por medio, y después de lavadas les echarás un poco de sal en los sesos, y un poco de pimienta: luego le pondrás una lonjilla de tocino delgada encima, y átalas muy bien con un hilo y espétalas en el asador, y envuelve la asadurilla del cabrito con un poco de redaño, y su sal, y ponlas a asar, y sírvela sobre la sopa de leche.

[193] (136r) *Unos picatostes de ubre de Ternera.*

Cocerás la ubre con agua y sal, y desvenarla has muy bien, y májala en el almirez, y échale allí dos tantos de pan rallado como es la ubre, y échale cosa de cuatro, o seis onzas de azúcar, y yemas de huevos, hasta que esté un poco blando: y si lo estuviere mucho échale más pan rallado: y asiente este batido sobre unas rebanadas de pan blanco, y ponlas en una tortera, untada con manteca, apartadas unas de otras, y échale un poco de azúcar por encima, y ponlas al fuego a poca lumbre abajo, y mucha encima. En estos picatostes dice muy bien un poco de manjar blanco, mezclado con la ubre. Y advierte, que deste batido se puede hacer una muy buena torta, echándole más huevos, y más azúcar.

[194] (136v) *Otros Picatostes de Riñones de Ternera.*

Asarás los riñones de ternera, y pícalos así calientes, y sazona con especias, y échales un poco de azúcar, y pan rallado, y huevos: y si les quisieres echar un poco de verdura picada podrás, y asiéntalos sobre sus rebanadas de pan, y cuézanse como los de atrás en su tortera. Éstos son mejores para adornar platos, que para servir solos.

[195] *Morcillas blancas de cámara.*[249]

Tomarás riñonada de ternera, y si no la hubiere sea de vaca, y desvénala de las venas y pellejitos que tiene, y pícala con cuchillo chico muy menuda; y échala otra tanta

---

248 Unlike in many parts of the Christian world, where eggs were not consumed on abstinence and partial abstinence days, this is clearly not the case in Martínez Montiño's day in Spain. For more on Saturday meals and rules for partial abstinence, see introduction (24).

249 *Morcillas* by definition include blood as the main ingredient, usually from a cow, but it could also come from other animals. However, *morcillas blancas* implies that no blood is used in the preparation, hence the different colour. That is the case here. In *Manual de mugeres* (1475–1525), a similar recipe appears, "Reçueta para hazer morçillas finas" [Recipe for making fine blood sausages]. There, similar ingredients are used, but instead of any meat or coagulated blood, almonds and pine nuts are used (77–8).

Place in the oven to bake on low and serve the kid head on top. This is a good dish for Saturdays. Note that these sops are very good for Fridays with fried eggs on top. With the ingredients for these sops and some slices of farmer cheese or curd cheese you can make a casserole. Put some fried eggs on the last layer. It will look a lot like a cream casserole. If you want to serve these kid heads roasted on sops, split the heads in the middle and, after washing them, sprinkle some salt and a little pepper on the brains. Then lay a slice of thin fatback on top, tie them tightly together with string, and skewer them on the spit. Wrap the pluck using a little caul fat, salt to taste, and roast them. Serve them on milk sops.

Cow udder over slices of fried bread

Boil the udder in salted water, devein it well, mash it in the mortar, and add two parts of breadcrumbs to one part udder. Add four to six ounces of sugar and enough egg yolks to get somewhat soft. If it's too soft, add more breadcrumbs. Place this batter over slices of white bread and place them in a covered tart pan greased with lard, one separated from the other. Sprinkle a little sugar on top and broil them with a little flame below and a lot on top. A little bit of blancmange mixed with the udder goes really well with these slices of fried bread. Note that this batter makes a great pie, adding more eggs and sugar.

Another [recipe] for veal kidney over slices of fried bread

Grill veal kidney and chop it up while hot. Season with spices and add in a little sugar, breadcrumbs, and eggs. If you want to add a little minced green herb, you can. Arrange on slices of bread and cook like the ones above in a covered tart pan. This is better for garnishing plates than as a dish to serve by itself.

White blood sausage with large intestine casing

Take veal loin, and if you don't have any, beef loin. Remove any bits of skin and veins it may have. With a small knife, mince the meat. Add in as many

cantidad de pan rallado, como hay de grasa, y pica un poco de tocino gordo muy menudo, y freirás allí un poco de cebolla picada muy menuda, y échala con la grasa, y échale azúcar molido, de manera que esté bien dulce, (137r) y sazona con todas especias, y canela, y échale huevos hasta que esté como batido de buñuelos de pan rallado:[250] luego echarás un poco de leche hasta que esté bien blando, y sazona de sal, y luego hinche las tripas grandes de la ternera, y pon un cazo al fuego con agua, y sal: y de que esté cociendo echa dentro las morcillas, e irásslas picando con un alfiler, o aguja muchas veces, porque no se revienten: y cuando estén cocidas sácalas, y tuéstelas en las parrillas, y sírvelas sobre sopas de natas, o sopa contrahecha con leche, y queso fresco. Estas morcillas harás también con los livianos de la ternera cocidos, y muy picados, y mezclarlos has con la grasa, y el pan rallado, aunque el pan no ha de ser tanto para estas morcillas, como para las blancas, y sazonarse han como las otras, y saldrán entre blancas y pardas, y son muy buenas.

[196] *Morcillas de Puerco dulces.*

(137v) Tomarás la sangre del puerco colada, y no se menee cuando se cogiere, porque se cuaje luego: déjala cuajar bien, y tendrás un cazo de agua cociendo, y echarás allí la sangre, y déjala cocer hasta que esté dura: luego sácala, y ponla en un paño, o estameña, y ponla sobre un tablero, y cárgala como queso, y déjala estar así hasta que se enfríe, y se escurra del agua: luego rállala, y échale un poco de pan rallado, y azúcar, que esté bien dulce. Luego tomarás enjundia de puerco,[251] y desvenarla has muy bien, y májala en el almirez, y mezclarás la que te pareciere con la sangre, y deshazlo todo muy bien, hasta que esté bien mezclada la grasa con la sangre, y sazona con todas especias y canela, y un poquito de anís, y harás tus morcillitas muy chiquitas, y perdígalas. Estas no son para guardar mucho.

[197] *Salchichones de carne de Puerco.*[252]

Tomarás carne de pernil de puerco (138r) fresco, y picarla has con otra tanta carne gorda del mismo puerco: y luego le echarás la tercia parte del pernil añejo, bien picada, y mézclalo todo muy bien, y sazona con todas especias, y sal, y échale zumo de limón, y un poquito de vino, y henchirás las tripas que sean un poco gordas, y harás tus salchichones pequeños, y haslos de perdigar en agua y sal: y luego los freirás, o asarás en las parrillas. No son para guardar mucho, mas son buenos para frescos.

---

250 *Buñuelos* [puffs] are most commonly made with flour, but occasionally Martínez Montiño substitutes breadcrumbs for the flour. This substitution produces a heavier result. See, for example, "Otra manera de borrajas" [Another way (of making) borage] (380; 381) or "Sesos de ternera" [Veal brain] (308; 309).
251 For more information on *enjundia*, see 118n24.
252 For more information on *salchichón* and *chorizo*, see 284n201.

breadcrumbs as fat. Mince a little extra fatty fatback, fry a little minced onion, and add it to the fat. Add ground sugar so that it is very sweet. Season with all spices and cinnamon. Add eggs until you have the consistency of batter for puffs made with breadcrumb. Then add in a little milk until it's soft. Season with salt. Then, fill large intestines with the veal. Put a pot with salted water on the fire. Once it's boiling, put the blood sausages in. Prick them with a pin or needle several times so that they don't explode. When they're done boiling, remove them and roast them on the grill. Serve over cream sops or faux cream sops made with milk and farmer cheese. You can also make this blood sausage with minced, boiled veal lung. Mix it with fat and breadcrumbs, though you don't need as many breadcrumbs as you do for the white sausage. Season like the other one and they will come out between white and brown and are very tasty.

Sweet pork blood sausage

Take strained pig blood but don't shake it too much when collecting it so that it will then coagulate. Let it thoroughly coagulate. Have a pot of boiling water and put the blood in it. Let it boil until it's hard. Remove it and put it in a cloth or cheesecloth on a cutting board and weigh it down as you would for cheese. Leave it like this to cool and for the water to drain. Next, grate it and add in breadcrumbs and sugar until it is sufficiently sweet. Then, take some pork fat, devein it well, and mash it up in the mortar. Mix however much you want with the blood, mix it all together until the fat and blood are well blended together. Season with all spices, cinnamon, and a little anise. Make mini blood sausages and parboil them. These are not meant to keep very long.

Pork sausages

Take fresh ham meat and mince it with an equal amount of a fatty piece of meat from the same pig. Then, add a third of that amount of well-minced, aged ham and mix everything together very well. Season with all spices and salt. Add lemon juice and a little wine. Fill the intestines, which should be a little thick, and make small sausages. You need to parboil them in salted water. Then fry them or grill them on the grill. These are not meant to keep very long but are tasty when fresh.

[198] *Chorizos de Puerco.*

Tomarás carne de puerco que sea más magra que gorda, y echarla has en adobo de sólo vino, y un poco de vinagre, y la carne ha de ser cortada en rebanadas: el adobo ha de ser corto, no más de cuanto se cubra: sazónalo de especias, y sal, y estése en ello venticuatro horas: y luego hinche los chorizos, las tripas que sean un poco gordas, y pásalos por agua cociendo. Estos se guardan (138v) todo el año, y se comen cocidos, y la vinagre ha de ser tan poca, que no se sienta después al comer.

[199] *Longanizas.*

Unas longanizas pondré aquí, porque las suele comer bien Su Majestad: Tomarás carne de los solomos de puerco, que no tenga mucho gordo, y cortarla has en rebanadillas menudas, y echarla has en adobo, en agua, y sal, y un poco de vinagre; y sazonarás con todas especias, salvo nuez, que no ha de llevar sino pimienta, clavo, y jengibre, y echarle has unos pocos de cominos, de manera que sepan bien a ellos, y esté en adobo venticuatro horas: luego henchirás las longanizas, y ponlas a enjugar. Éstas no llevan ajos, ni orégano: y si le quisieres echar algún poco de ajo, han de ser asados y pocos.

[200] *Un Solomo de vaca relleno.*[253]

Para un plato es menester dos solomos. (139r) Abrirás estos solomos por medio a lo largo, de manera que no llegue la abertura a la otra parte: luego le darás otras dos cuchilladas a lo largo, una en cada parte, de manera que venga a estar el solomo casi tan ancho como largo: luego pondrás las dos puntas de los lomos una sobre otra, y harás de los lomos uno largo: luego picarás carne, y tocino, y sazonarlo has, como para salchichas, echándole de todas especias, y anís: y sazonada esta carne de especias, y sal, y un poquito de vinagre: meterle has unos huevos, y rellenarás los solomos, y coserlos has con un hilo y una aguja, o mechadera, y harás dellos una rosca, y ponla en una tortera grande a cocer con lonjas de tocino debajo, y otras encima, y mete la tortera en un horno con lumbre abajo y arriba, y de la carne sazonada que te sobrare del relleno, harás unas torrijuelas rebozándolas con huevos, y fríelas en manteca de puerco: y con estas torrijas, y el caldo (139v) que saliere del roscón, harás la sopa, y asentarás el roscón sobre ella, y echarle has zumo de limón por encima: y después que hayas quitado todos los hilos, pondrás ruedas de limón por encima.

---

253 The *solomo* is the cut of meat between the ribs and the loin of the animal. Today we say *solomillo* [tenderloin].

Pork chorizo

Take pork meat that is on the lean side and marinate it with just wine and a little vinegar. The meat should be cut in slices and the marinade should only just cover the meat. Season it with spices and salt and let it rest twenty-four hours. Then fill the sausages. The intestine should be a little thick. Rinse them in boiling water. These will last all year and are eaten cooked. There should only be a little vinegar, so little that you don't notice it afterward while eating.

Longaniza sausages

I'm including longaniza sausages here because His Majesty often eats them. Take pork loin that is not too fatty and slice it very thin. Marinate in salted water and a little vinegar. Season with all spices, except nutmeg. Use only pepper, clove, and ginger. Also add in a little cumin so that they take on that flavour. Let it rest twenty-four hours. Then fill the sausages and set them to dry. These sausages do not have garlic or oregano. If you do want to add a little garlic, it should first be roasted and it should only be a little.

Stuffed beef tenderloin

For one plate, two tenderloins are necessary. Slice open lengthwise but without slicing through to the other side. Then make two slits lengthwise, one on each part, so that the tenderloins are almost as wide as they are long. Then place the two ends of the tenderloin one on top of the other to make one long tenderloin. Next, mince meat and fatback and season it as you do for sausages, adding all spices and anise. Once seasoned with spices, salt, and a little vinegar, add some eggs and stuff the tenderloin. Sew it with thread and needle or a larding needle and make a big roll with them. Put it in a big covered tart pan to cook with strips of fatback both under and on top. Place the covered tart pan in the oven with the heat above and below. With the seasoned meat left over from the filling, make little mini torrijas and coat with egg. Fry them in lard and, with these torrijas and the drippings that came off the roll, make sops and set the roll on them. Drizzle some lemon juice on top. After you've removed all the threads, place lemon wheels on top.

[201] *Manjar Blanco.*

Quiero poner aquí algunas potajerías de legumbres:[254] y esto hago (como tengo dicho) para los mancebos y mujeres, que sirven a algunos señores, y no saben estas cosas, aunque parecen muy fáciles. El manjar blanco para una pechuga, sacarla has de una gallina acabada de matar, y tendrás la olla cociendo, y échala dentro, y cueza hasta que esté casi acabada de cocer: luego deshílala muy menuda, y échala en un cazo, y échale medio cuartillo de leche, y bátela con el cucharón, de manera que no se corte: luego échale una libra de harina de arroz, y échale otro poquito de leche, y bátelo muy bien: luego vele echando (140r) leche, y trayéndolo a una mano hasta que tenga cinco cuartillos, y echa una libra de azúcar, y si le echares cinco cuarterones será mejor: échale un poco de sal blanca, cantidad de un panecillo de los de Madrid, y pon el cazo sobre unas trébedes con buena lumbre de tizón de carbón,[255] y tráelo a una mano con mucho cuidado, porque no se queme, ni se ahúme: y cuando comenzare a cuajar bátelo muy bien: tardará en cocerse tres cuartos de hora, poco más, o menos. Para ver si está cocido, toma un poco en la punta de un cuchillo, y déjalo enfriar un poco, y llégalo a la mano, si no se pegare estará cocido. Advierte, que si haces muchas pechugas juntas, como si fuesen seis, no pueden llevar tanta leche, que a seis pechugas bastarían siete azumbres de leche,[256] si no fuesen muy buenas las pechugas, aún sería mucha leche, porque trabajan más las pechugas, y se deshacen más, y no pueden llevar tanta leche, porque saldría el manjar (140v) blanco blando. Otro manjar blanco se hace con más leche, y más azúcar, mas yo me atengo a éste.

[202] *Buñuelos de Manjar blanco.*

De este manjar blanco aprovecharás lo que sobrare para regalar a tu señor: Harás unos buñuelos, echando un poco de manjar blanco en almirez, y majarlo has muy bien: y luego le echarás un poquito de harina, y yemas de huevos, hasta que esté blando: luego pondrás una sartén al fuego con un poco de manteca: y cuando esté caliente, ve echando buñuelos con una cucharita, y velos friendo: y cuando estén

---

254 Although Martínez Montiño writes "potajerías de legumbres," based on the recipes that follow, which include rice, artichoke, lettuce, eggplant, squash, turnips, spinach, and borage in addition to legumes, it seems that he is using the word *legumbre* to mean *vegetables* more generally and does not limit it to the pod-based legumes.

255 *Carbón* [charcoal] is made from hardwood that is carbonized with minimal exposure to air. It gives off a lot of heat, produces less ash than regular wood, and has little or no smoke. Of course, it does release carbon monoxide and thus could not be used in an unventilated space. For more on the production of charcoal, see Wright (esp. 28–31).

256 An *azumbre* is approximately equivalent to 2.05 litres or a little more than two quarts, or four pints.

Blancmange

I want to write down here some vegetable stews and I'm going to do this (as I have said) for apprentices, and women, who serve lords and do not know these things even though they seem so easy. Blancmange: for one breast of a hen, get it from a recently slaughtered hen. Have a pot with boiling water and place it in it. Cook it until it is almost completely cooked through. Then, finely shred it and place it in a pan. Add a half pint of milk and beat with a big spoon so that the milk doesn't curdle. Then add a pound of rice flour and a little more milk and beat well. Then, continue adding milk, stirring with one hand, until there are five pints. Add one pound of sugar, and if you add a pound and a quarter, even better. Add a little white salt, the amount of a bread roll from Madrid, and place the pan on a trivet with a good flame of charcoal coals. Stir constantly with one hand so that it doesn't burn or get smoky. When it begins to thicken, beat it very quickly. It will take approximately three quarters of an hour. To see if it is done, put a little on the tip of a knife, let it cool a little, and when you touch it, if it doesn't stick, it is done. Note that if you cook a lot of breasts at once, for example, six, you cannot add as much [corresponding] milk. For six breasts, seven *azumbres* of milk is enough. But if the breasts are not that good, even that would be a lot of milk. Because the breasts need to cook longer, they fall apart more, and cannot use as much milk because the blancmange would end up weak. Another blancmange uses more milk and more sugar but I stand by this one.

Blancmange puffs

With this blancmange you can use what's left over to give your lord a treat. Make some puffs by putting some blancmange in a mortar and mashing it up well. Add a little flour and egg yolks until it becomes soft. Then put a frying pan with a little lard on the flame. When it is hot, drop the puffs in with a small spoon and begin

casi fritos, velos apretando con la paleta de manera, que queden todos despachurrados: luego sácalos, y pásalos por un poco de almíbar, y échales por encima un poco de canela. Estos se llaman buñuelos despachurrados. Y advierte, que se han de freír con muy poca manteca.

[203] (141r) *Otros Buñuelos de Manjar blanco.*[257]

Tomarás tres, o cuatro pellas de manjar blanco, y harás unos rollitos del tamaño, o gordor del dedo chico en la mano, e iráslos cortando en trocitos, un poco mayores que avellanas, y échales harina por encima, y ve haciendo dellos unos bodoquillos,[258] y échalos harina por que no se peguen, y pon a calentar la manteca que esté bien caliente en la sartén, y échalos dentro, y ponlos al fuego a buena lumbre, y meneando siempre la sartén a una mano: y en tomando color sácalos luego con la espumadera, y no te descuides, porque se quemarán, o se despachurrarán. Escúrrelos bien de la manteca, y sírvelos sobre unas hojuelas, y ráspales un poco de azúcar por encima. Deste manjar blanco podrás hacer unas pellas tostadas, poniendo cada pella sobre una rebanada de pan: y luego asentarlas has en una tortera untada (141v) con manteca, y échale por encima un poco de azúcar raspado sin otra cosa ninguna: y ponlas con un poco de lumbre abajo y arriba: y en estando doradas sácalas, y sírvelas que son mucho mejores que tostadas en sartén, ni en parrillas.

[204] *Picatostes de manjar blanco.*

Echarás las pellas de manjar blanco en el almirez, y échales yemas de huevos, majándolas hasta que esté un poco blando: luego ve poniendo sobre unas rebanadas de pan deste manjar blanco, que tengan más manjar blanco que pan, ponlas en una tortera untada con manteca, y ráspale un poco de azúcar por encima, y ponle lumbre moderada abajo y arriba: y de que estén dorados sácalos: Estos son buenos para componer platos de pollos rellenos, o pichones: y también se suelen servir solos.

[205] *Frutillas de manjar blanco.*

(142r) Deste manjar blanco puedes hacer frutillas, haciendo una masa fina sin azúcar: y luego hacer unos rollitos de manjar blanco del gordor del dedo chico,

---

257 This recipe, "Otros buñuelos de manjar blanco" [Other blancmange puffs], is a seventeenth-century version of *croquetas de pollo* [chicken croquettes]. They are served on puff pastry with sugar sprinkled on top.
258 Bodoquillo is the diminutive of *bodoque*, which means *small ball or pellet*.

frying. When they are almost done, begin pressing them with a spatula so that they become flattened. Take them out and dip them in a little simple syrup. Sprinkle some cinnamon on top. These are called flattened puffs. Note that you should use very little lard when frying.

Other blancmange puffs

Take three or four balls of blancmange and roll them out to the size or thickness of a pinky finger. Cut them into little bits a little bigger than the size of hazelnuts and dust them on top with flour. Make little pellets and sprinkle with flour so they don't stick together. Heat up some lard and, when it's hot in the frying pan, drop them in and make sure the flame is high. Constantly shake the frying pan with one hand, and when they begin to turn brown, remove them with a skimmer. Don't neglect them, because they will burn or deflate. Thoroughly drain off the lard and serve them on puff pastry and grate a little sugar on top. With this blancmange you can also make toasted balls by placing each ball on a slice of bread. Then, put it in a covered tart pan greased with lard and sprinkle on top a little grated sugar without anything else. Put a little heat above and below them and once golden, remove them. Serve them. They are much better than if they were toasted in a frying pan or on the grill.

Blancmange over slices of fried bread

Put the blancmange balls in the mortar and add egg yolks, mashing them until it's somewhat soft. Then spoon blancmange onto slices of bread so that there's more blancmange than bread. Place them in a covered tart pan greased with lard and grate a little sugar on top. Use moderate heat above and below. Remove them once they're golden. These are good when making plates of stuffed chicken or squab and they are also often served by themselves.

Blancmange fried dough

With this blancmange you can also make fried dough. Make a fine dough with no sugar. Then make little blancmange rolls the width of a pinky finger. Roll out

y tender la masa muy delgada, y hacer unas frutillas como medias herraduras, y unas empanadillas muy chiquitas, y otras como candilejas: y puedes hacer unos pastelillos de hojaldrados de dos hojas, y fritos, y pasados por almíbar. El manjar blanco destos pasteles no ha de llevar huevos.

[206] *Cazolillas de manjar blanco.*

Del manjar blanco podrás hacer unas cazolillas, echándole yemas de huevos, y natas, y cañas, y las cazolillas han de ser muy pequeñas. Hanse de cocer en el horno, y parecerán tijeladas de Portugal,[259] aunque son mejores. Deste manjar blanco podrás hacer unos pastelillos de masa llana, metiéndoles dentro manjar blanco, y huevos mejidos, y (142v) algunas cañas de vaca, y conservas, y si no fuere día de carne, se harán sin las cañas: para estos podrás hacer los vasos de pasta de mazapán, perdigándolos primero, porque no se caigan cuécelos en el horno, y sírvelos con unos tallarines fritos a la redonda.

[207] *Torta de Manjar blanco.*

Tomarás cinco, o seis pellas de manjar blanco, y echarle has yemas de huevos hasta que esté un poco blando: luego harás tu torta con dos hojas, una abajo, y otra arriba, y rocíala con manteca, y raspa el azúcar por encima. Advierte, que esta torta para ser muy buena ha de llevar cuatro escudillas de natas mezcladas con manjar blanco, y si no las tuvieres toma media libra de pasta de mazapán, y una caña de vaca en trozos todo mezclado con manjar blanco, y mézclalo todo muy bien, y será muy buena torta.

[208] (143r) *Cómo se va de hacer el Arroz.*

Tomarás el arroz, y aventarlo has de las pajas, y las hojitas: luego lávalo con agua tibia, hasta que salga el agua clara: luego arrópalo en un colador cerca de la lumbre, y enjugarse ha presto, y esponjará algo: luego ponlo en el tablero, y móndalo, y tendrás tantas azumbres de agua caliente, como son libras de arroz, y échalo dentro en el cazo, y cueza dos hervores, y apártalo, y tápalo cerca de la lumbre, y ello irá esponjando, y embeberá toda el agua: luego échale otras tantas azumbres de leche, como hay libras de arroz, y échale el azúcar, a media libra de azúcar para cada libra de arroz, y sazónalo de sal, y ponlo al fuego de brasa, y cueza poco a poco, y menéalo muy pocas veces porque no se deshaga el grano: y con esto saldrá

---

259 *Tijeladas* are a regional dessert from Abrantes that are essentially egg custard tarts.

the dough very thin and shape the little fried dough into half horseshoes, mini turnovers, and others like oil lamps. You can make these pastries from two sheets of puff pastry dough, fried and then dipped in simple syrup. The blancmange for these pastries should not have any eggs.

Blancmange tartlets

With blancmange you can make tartlets by adding egg yolks, cream, and marrow. These tarts should be very small. Bake them in the oven. They should turn out like Portuguese custard but they are better. With this blancmange you can make little pastries with a smooth dough, filling them with blancmange, sweet scrambled egg yolks, bone marrow, and preserves. If it isn't a meat day, you can make them without the marrow. For these you can make the crust with marzipan paste, parbaking them first so that they won't fall. Bake them in the oven and serve with strips of fried pastry dough around them.

Blancmange pie

Take five or six blancmange balls and add egg yolks until it is somewhat soft. Then make a pie with two pastry sheets, one below and one above. Dot with lard and grate sugar on top. Note that for this pie to be great, it should have four bowls of cream mixed with the blancmange. If you don't have that, take half a pound of marzipan paste, one bone marrow in pieces, and mix it all together with the blancmange. Thoroughly mix it and it will be a very tasty pie.

How to make rice

Take rice and winnow it to remove the stalk and little leaves. Then rinse in warm water until the water comes out clear. Cover it in a strainer near the heat and it will dry quickly and get a little fluffy. Next, place it on a cutting board and continue cleaning it. For every pound of rice, have two quarts of hot water and place [the rice and water] in a large saucepan. Bring it to a boil twice, take it off the heat, cover it, and leave near the heat. It will continue to fluff up and absorb all the water. Then for each pound of rice, add in two quarts of milk. Also add sugar: for every pound of rice, half a pound of sugar. Season with salt and put it on red-hot coals and slowly bring to a boil, but do not stir it much, so that the grain doesn't fall apart. This is how the grains will stay intact and firm. And if the rice is for an

granado y duro:[260] y si el arroz fuere para mesa muy regalada, podrás echar (143v) tres cuarterones de azúcar a cada libra de arroz: y entiéndese, que el arroz ha de ser bien granado, porque de otra manera nunca sale bueno.

[209] *Buñuelos de Arroz.*

De este arroz podrás hacer buñuelos, apartando un plato dello, y déjalo enfriar: luego échale un puñado de harina, y dos huevos con claras, y revuélvelo con un cucharón, no más de cuanto se embeba la harina, y los huevos, porque si los revuelves mucho, se echará a perder. Luego pondrás la manteca al fuego, y echarás buñuelos con un cucharón, que sean un poco grandes, y fríelos bien, que salgan morenos, y sírvelos con miel, y azúcar, y canela por encima. Son mejores de lo que parecen. La harina échasela de una vez, y antes pequen de mucha harina que de poca.

[210] *Cazuela de Arroz.*

Deste arroz podrás apartar un plato, (144r) y echarle media docena de yemas de huevos, y dos con claras, y un poco de pan rallado, y un poco de canela molida, y revuélvelo todo, y echa un poco de manteca de vacas en una cazuela, y echa el arroz dentro, y ráspale un poco de azúcar por encima, y cuécelo en un horno, y de que esté bien cocida, sírvelo en la misma cazuela. En lugar del pan rallado podrás poner requesones si quisieres. Deste mismo arroz de la cazuela podrás hacer una torta, y podrás hacer también unos picatostes sobre rebanadas de pan, y ráspales azúcar por encima, y cuécelos en una tortera con lumbre abajo y arriba.

[211] *Arroz a la Portuguesa.*

Harás una libra de arroz con leche de la manera que está dicho arriba: y cuando lo quisieres servir, batirás una docena de yemas de huevos muy batidos, y pondrás el arroz sobre la lumbre, e irás echando estas yemas de huevos, y (144v) revolviéndolo muy aprisa: y en dando un hervor, sácalo, y échalo en los platos, y echa el azúcar y canela por encima, y sírvelo caliente.

[212] *Arroz de grasa.*

El arroz de grasa se ha de limpiar como está dicho en el de leche: échale a cada libra azumbre y medio de caldo, o algo menos, y sus caña de vacas, y tres cuarterones

---

260 Martínez Montiño uses the adjective *granado* in just two recipes; both describe the finished quality of rice.

exquisite table, you can add three quarters of a pound of sugar for each pound of rice. Understand that the rice has to come out with the grain intact, because any other way never turns out well.

Rice puffs

With this rice you can make rice puffs, separating out a plate of rice and letting it cool. Then add in a handful of flour and two eggs with their whites. Stir it with a spoon just long enough for the flour and eggs to be incorporated, because if you stir it a lot, it will be ruined. Heat up the lard and drop the puffs in with a spoon. They should be on the big side, and fry them well so they turn out brown. Serve with honey, sugar, and cinnamon on top. They are better than they look. Add in all the flour at once and better to err by adding a little more than a little less.

Rice casserole

You can separate a plateful of this rice and add to it a half dozen egg yolks, two eggs with their whites, a little bit of breadcrumbs, and a little ground cinnamon. Stir it all together. In a casserole, add a little butter and then add the rice. Grate a little sugar on top. Bake in the oven. Once it is done, you can serve it in the same casserole. Instead of breadcrumbs, you can add curd cheese if you prefer. With this same rice from the casserole, you can make a pie or you can shape it into pieces of fried bread served over slices of bread. Grate sugar on top and bake in a covered tart pan with heat above and below.

Rice, Portuguese style

Make a pound of rice with milk as explained above. When it's ready to be served, beat very well a dozen egg yolks. Put the rice on to cook and slowly add the egg yolks, stirring very quickly. When it comes to a boil, remove it and serve on plates. Sprinkle cinnamon and sugar on top. It should be served hot.

Rice [cooked] in fat

Rice [cooked] in fat should be cleaned as explained for rice [cooked] in milk. For each pound, add three quarts of broth, or a little less, bone marrow, and three

de azúcar, porque el de la leche ha menester algo menos de azúcar, por cuanto la leche es más dulce que el agua, y el de la leche de almendras ha de llevar también más azúcar: y si mezclas leche de almendras con la leche de cabras, y le echas una libra de azúcar a una libra de arroz, es el mejor arroz de todos y más gustoso. Deste arroz de grasa podrás hacer todas las cosas que tengo dicho del arroz de leche, y te saldrán mejores. El arroz de aceite, y de manteca de vacas, se ha de hacer por el orden que está dicho en (145r) el de grasa: y por eso no hay que tratar dello.

[213] *Cazuela de arroz sin dulce.*

Mondarás el arroz de parte de noche, y lávalo mucho en agua caliente, y en la postrer agua déjalo estar un poco: y luego así caliente escurrido del agua, échalo en unos manteles que estén doblados dos, o tres veces y arrópanlo muy bien, y déjalo allí hasta la mañana, o desde la mañana hasta las once del día,[261] y hallarlo has esponjado y tierno: luego échalo en unas cazolillas con un poco de agua caliente, cuanto se bañe, sazonado de sal y pimienta, y un poco de aceite que sea bueno, y métele en un horno con poca lumbre, y embeberse ha el agua, y quedará el arroz muy granado, que no se pegue un grano con otro, y muy tierno, y de buen gusto.

[214] *Platillo de Alcachofas.*

Las alcachofas se aderezan desta manera: (145v) Limpiarlas de las hojas más viejas y de la cáscara del pezón, y córtales las puntas hasta cerca del medio: luego perdígalas en agua, que se les quite el amargor: luego sácalas y exprímelas, y métalas en una olla, o asiéntalas en un perol o cazuela con los pezones hacia bajo: y si tuvieres manteca fresca échasela así cruda, y sazónalas con pimienta, y nuez, y jengibre, y unos clavos enteros, y échales un poco de vino blanco, y un poco de vinagre y agua caliente, o caldo, hasta que se bañen, y ponle dentro un manojo de perejil, y hierbabuena, y cilantro verde, y unas cebollas enteras, y sazona de sal, y un poco de azafrán, y con esto se pueden cocer: y tuesta unas rebanadas de pan, y sírvelas sobre ellas, pon los pezones hacia arriba, y echarás a mal las hierbas todas, y las cebollas, que con la manteca se hará un caldo espeso que parezca cuajado: si no tuvieres manteca fresca, y fuere día de carne, freirás cebolla con tocino, y échaselo, y verdura (146r) picada, y la demás sazón que se echa a las de la manteca, y cuajarlas has con unas yemas de huevos, y un poco de agrio.

---

261 This is an unusual reference to a specific hour of the day, which is seldom seen in recipe manuals. For more on the concept of time in Martínez Montiño's kitchen, see Appendix 2 (632–3).

quarters of a pound of sugar. The milk recipe requires less sugar because milk is sweeter than water. Rice with almond milk should also have more sugar. If you mix almond milk with goat milk, add a pound of sugar for each pound of rice. This is the best rice and the tastiest. With this rice [cooked] in fat you can make every dish that I've explained for rice [cooked] in milk and they will come out better. Rice [cooked] in oil and in butter should be prepared with the instructions explained for rice [cooked] in fat, so it's not necessary to deal with that here.

Unsweetened rice casserole

Clean the rice at night. Rinse it in warm water, and on the last rinsing, let it sit a while. Then, while still warm and the water is drained off, put it on a cloth doubled over two or three times, cover it well, and let sit until morning, or from early morning until eleven a.m. It will be soft and fluffy. Next, place it in some tartlet pans with a little warm water, enough to braise. Season with salt and pepper and some good-quality oil. Place in the oven on low and it will absorb all the water. The grains will be intact, won't stick to one another, and it will be tender and very tasty.

An artichoke dish

Artichokes are prepared this way: Clean off the oldest leaves and the peel on the stem. Cut off the tips to almost halfway down and parboil in water to remove any bitterness. Then remove and drain them. Put them in a deep pot or arrange them in a round-bottom pot or a casserole with the stems down. If you have butter, put some in as is and season with pepper, nutmeg, ginger, and some whole cloves. Add in a little white wine, a little vinegar, and some hot water or broth, enough to braise. Add a bunch of parsley, spearmint, and cilantro and some whole onions. Season with salt and a little saffron and put on to boil. Toast some slices of bread and serve them on them. Place them stems up, discard all the herbs and onions, and with the butter make a thick sauce that looks as if it has set. If you don't have butter or if it's a meat day, fry onion with fatback and add it with minced green herbs and all the other seasonings that were in the butter sauce and thicken with egg yolks and a little sour juice.

[215] *Alcachofas asadas.*

Perdigarás las alcachofas con agua y sal, cortándolas primero cerca la mitad hacia las puntas, y exprímelas del agua, y échalas a cocer en caldo que tenga buena grasa, o en agua, y sal, y harta manteca de vacas, y ponlas en un hornillo, los pezones hacia abajo sobre unos pedacillos de masa, y échales dentro por las puntas un poco de sal, pimienta, y aceite que sea bueno, y dales lumbre que sea moderada abajo y arriba, e iránse calando: y cuando estén asadas, sácalas, y asiéntalas en el plato, y échales zumo de naranja por encima, aunque parezcan que están secas, por de dentro estarán muy tiernas y muy gustosas.

[216] *Platillo de Alcachofas.*

(146v) Las alcachofas cuando están tiernas, todo lo tierno dellas es muy bueno para aderezar en platillos. Perdigarás las alcachofas con agua, y sal, de manera que estén casi cocidas: luego le quitarás todo el tierno, y lo ahogarás con un poco de manteca de vacas fresca, hechas pedacitos: luego le echarás un poquito de vino blanco, y el zumo de un limón, y sazonarás con todas especias, y un poquito de verdura picada, y un poco de azafrán, y echarle has un par de cucharadas de agua, y un poco de sal: luego batirás deziocho, o veinte huevos, y echarlos has dentro en el cacillo sobre las alcachofas, y échale un poco de pan rallado por encima. Este platillo ha de llevar media libra de azúcar juntamente con las alcachofas: luego pondrás el cacillo al fuego, con un poco de lumbre abajo, y otra poca encima de una cobertera, y cueza poco a poco, hasta que esté bien cuajada, y dorado por la parte de arriba, y sírvelos sobre rebanadillas (147r) de pan tostado, y azúcar, y canela por encima. Estas alcachofas son buenas para platillos de pichones, o de pollos, y para pasteles de criadillas de tierra, y pollos, y para otros muchos platillos.[262]

[217] *Potaje de Habas.*

Las habas en día de pescado buscarlas has que sean muy tiernas, y mondarlas has y echarás aceite que sea bueno en una cazuela de barro, o en una olla, y ponla sobre brasas: y cuando esté caliente echa las habas dentro, y así crudas como están, y tendrás lechugas lavadas, y deshojadas y torcerlas has en las manos, y haráslas lo más menudo que pudieres sin llegar cuchillo a ellas, y exprímelas del agua, y velas echando con las habas, y váyanse ahogando habas y lechugas: ellas irán echando de sí agua, que casi bastará para servir de caldo: échale de todas especias y verdura, cilantro verde más que de las otras, y sazona de sal, y échales un poquito de agua

---

262 At the end of this recipe we have an example of the master cook's suggestions for food pairings. For images of recreating this dish, see Appendix 3.15.

Roasted artichokes

Parboil the artichokes in salted water, first cutting off about half of the tips and squeezing out the water. Put on to boil [again] in a fatty broth or in salted water with a lot of butter. Put them in a small oven, stems down, on little pieces of dough. Sprinkle on the tips some salt, pepper, and good-quality oil. Heat them with moderate heat above and below. They will soak it all up. When they are roasted, remove them and arrange them on a plate. Sprinkle orange juice on top. Even if they look dry, inside they will be tender and very delicious.

An artichoke dish

When artichokes are tender, all the tender part is really good to prepare as individual dishes. Parboil the artichokes in salted water so that they are almost cooked. Then remove all the tender part, chop into little pieces, and sauté them with a little butter. Then add a little white wine and the juice of one lemon. Season with all spices, a little minced green herbs, and a little saffron. Add in a couple of tablespoons of water and a little salt. Then whip eighteen or twenty eggs and pour them into the saucepan over the artichokes. Sprinkle some breadcrumbs on top. This dish should have half a pound of sugar together with the artichokes. Then put the saucepan on the flame on low and also have low heat on the lid on top and cook slowly until it has set and the top is golden. Serve over slices of toasted bread with cinnamon and sugar on top. These artichokes are good for squab or chicken dishes, for truffle or chicken pies, and for many other dishes.

Fava bean stew

On a fish day, look for fava beans that are very tender and shuck them. Put some good-quality oil in a terracotta casserole or in a pot and place it over red-hot embers. When it is heated, put in the beans, raw just as they are. Have some lettuce washed, with the leaves separated. Tear them with your hands and make them as small as you can without using a knife. Squeeze out the water, add to the beans, and sauté the beans and lettuce in oil. They will exude their own water, perhaps enough for the broth. Add all spices and green herbs, more cilantro than

caliente, y (147v) un poco de vinagre, y cuezan hasta que estén blandas: échale unos huevos crudos para que salgan escalfados en las mismas habas: y sirve las habas y los huevos todo junto en la misma cazuela. A estas habas se les suele echar un poco de eneldo, mas algunos señores no gustan dél.

[218] *Otras Habas.*

Mondarás las habas, y perdígalas en agua, y ahógalas en aceite con manteca fresca, y su cebolla: y después de bien ahogadas échales caldo de garbanzos, o agua caliente cuanto se cubran, y sazona de sal, y de todas especias, y verdura picada, y mucho cilantro verde, y si quisieres echar lechugas perdigadas primero, y medio picadas, échaselas dentro, y cuájalas con huevos y acedo: y si las quisieres hacer sin lechugas con sola la verdura son buenas. Estas habas son buenas con sábalo en cazuela.

[219] *Habas en día de carne.*

(148r) Las habas en día de carne se han de guisar con tocino frito en dados, y en lo demás guardar la orden que está dicho en las de pescado, las unas ahogadas sin perdigar, y lechugas también crudas desmenuzadas con las manos, y han de llevar de todas verduras,[263] y las otras se han de perdigar y cuajar con huevos y agrio. Estas habas cuando están tiernas son muy buenas para echar en los platillos de carne, y en pasteles de pollos, o pichones.

[220] *Sopa de Lechugas.*

Perdigarás las lechugas, y luego asentarás los cogollos en el cacillo, todas las puntas cara dentro, y picarás las demás medio picadas, y échalas dentro en el cacillo: luego freirás un poco de cebolla muy menuda con manteca de vacas, y échasela dentro en el cacillo: sazona con todas especias, y canela, y échale un cuarterón de azúcar dentro, y agua caliente cuanto se bañen las lechugas, (148v) y sazona de sal, y cuezan, y den dos, o tres hervores: luego cuájalas con cuatro yemas de huevos, y un poco de vinagre, y tendrás rebanadas de pan tostado asentadas en un plato, y echarás las lechugas con el mismo cacito, de manera que caigan en el plato todas sin descomponerse: échale azúcar y canela por encima y zumo de limón, o naranja: luego harás seis, u ocho huevos, escalfados, o estrellados blandos, y ponlos encima de la sopa de lechugas: y si no hubiere lechugas, se puede hacer de borrajas, de berros, o escarolas, y de otras muchas verduras.

---

263 For an explanation of *todas verduras*, see *hierbas* (682–3).

others, and season with salt. Add a little hot water and a little vinegar and cook until everything is soft. Add in raw eggs that will poach with the beans themselves. Serve the beans and the eggs together in the same casserole. It is common to add dill to these beans but some lords do not like it.

Other fava beans

Shuck the beans, parboil them in water, and sauté in oil and butter with the right amount of onion. After they are thoroughly sautéed, add garbanzo broth or hot water to cover, season with salt and all spices, add minced green herbs with a lot of cilantro. If you want to add in lettuce that has first been wilted and chopped up, do so. Thicken with eggs and sorrel juice. If you want to make them without lettuce, they are very good with just the green herbs. These fava beans are good with stewed shad.

Fava beans on a meat day

Fava beans on a meat day should be cooked with fried cubes of fatback. For everything else, follow the instructions for those for fish days. Some should be sautéed without parboiling. The lettuce should also be raw and shredded by hand and they should have all green herbs. The others should be parboiled and thickened with eggs and sour juice. When these fava beans are tender, they go great with individual meat dishes, and with chicken and squab pies.

Lettuce sops

Wilt the lettuce and then place the hearts in a saucepan with the tops face down. Dice up the rest and place them in the pan. Then, fry a little minced onion in butter and add it to the saucepan. Season with all spices and cinnamon, and add in a quarter pound of sugar and enough hot water to braise the lettuce. Season with salt and bring to a boil two or three times. Then thicken it with four egg yolks and a little vinegar. Have slices of toasted bread on a plate and place the lettuce hearts from the saucepan itself in such a way that they go onto the plate without falling apart. Sprinkle sugar and cinnamon on top, and lemon or orange juice. Then take six or eight poached eggs, or soft fried eggs, and place them on top of the lettuce sops. If you don't have lettuce, you can make this dish with borage, watercress, or escarole and many other green-leaf vegetables.

[221] *Lechugas rellenas.*

Perdigarás las lechugas, que estén medio cocidas, enteras, o en medias, porque poniendo debajo media lechuga, y luego el relleno, y otra media encima, viene a juntar el pezón, que parece una lechuga entera. Digo pues, que picarás unas pocas destas lechugas cocidas a medio picar, (149r) y exprímelas muy bien: luego pondrás un poco de manteca fresca a calentar en una sartén, y freirás allí un poco de cebolla cortada larga, y echa allí las lechugas picadas, y den una, o dos vueltas en la sartén: luego échale huevos en cantidad en la misma sartén, y ponla sobre el fuego, y ve revolviendo como huevos revueltos hasta que esté bien seco: luego échalo sobre el tablero, y pícalo todo junto muy bien, y échale huevos crudos, y un poco de pan rallado, y queso rallado, y azúcar, que esté bien dulce, sazona con todas especias y canela: el relleno no ha de quedar muy blando, ni ha de llevar género de agrio: rellena tus lechugas asentando primero las medias lechugas en una tortera untada con manteca, y acomodándolas que no lleguen unas a otras: luego asienta encima el relleno muy bien puesto, y luego pon las otras medias encima sobre el relleno, de manera que quede todo cubierto, y úntalas con manteca, y pon la tortera al fuego con poca (149v) lumbre, para que se cuaje el relleno, y no se quemen las lechugas. Éstas servirás sobre una sopilla dulce, o con torrijas, y su azúcar y canela por encima, y un poquito de queso rallado. Las lechugas son muy dejativas[264] para hacer platillos en día de pescado, mas para en día de carne son muy buenas.

[222] *Lechugas rellenas en días de carne.*[265]

Aparejarás las lechugas como está dicho en las de atrás: luego picarás carne de ternera, o carnero con su tocino, y sazonarla has de sal, y de todas especias, y meterla has huevos, de manera que esté un poco blanda, como para albondiguillas, y meterle has algunas pocas de cañas de vacas, y un poco de zumo de limón, y rellenarás las lechugas en la tortera, poniendo la media lechuga debajo, y asentarás la carne encima; y pondrás la otra media lechuga encima, (150r) y úntala con manteca, y cuézase en la tortera a fuego manso, porque no se tuesten las lechugas, y sírvelas sobre una sopa con unos pedazos de pechos de ternera, cocidos y tostados en las parrillas con pan rallado entre lechuga y lechuga un pedazo del pecho, o con palominos cocidos.

---

264 *Dejativo* means *lazy* or *weak*. In a food context I've translated it as *delicate*, but it could also mean *easily digested*. In *Lozana andaluza*, the protagonist also uses the adjective to insult a character, Lombarda, and makes a pun with her name and red cabbage: "vuestra Lombarda, qu'es más dejativa que menestra de calabaza" [Your Lombardy, she's weaker than squash stew] (Delicado 305).

265 This recipe appears in the eighteenth-century recipe collection *Manuscrito Ávila Blancas* (Pérez San Vicente, *Gastronomía mexicana* 93).

Stuffed lettuce

Wilt lettuce heads until they are half-cooked, whole or halved, because if you put one half down, fill it, and the other half on top, the stems will connect and it will seem like a whole lettuce head. As I was saying, dice some of the cooked lettuce and squeeze it out well. Then heat up some butter in a frying pan and fry some onion chopped lengthwise, and add in the diced lettuce. Stir it around once or twice in the frying pan. Then, add a lot of eggs to the same frying pan, return it to the fire, and stir as for scrambled eggs until they are thoroughly cooked. Then turn it out onto the cutting board, mince it all up, and add raw eggs, a little bit of breadcrumbs, grated cheese, and sugar so that it is very sweet. Season with all spices and cinnamon. The stuffing should not be too soft, nor should it have any type of sour flavour added. Stuff the lettuce by first setting one half in a covered tart pan greased with lard and adjusting them so that one is not touching the other. Then, set the stuffing on top so that it is just right and then put the other half on top of the stuffing so that everything is covered. Dab with lard and put the covered tart pan on low heat so that the filling sets but the lettuce doesn't burn. These can be served over sweet sops or with torrijas with the right amount of sugar and cinnamon sprinkled on top and a little grated cheese. Lettuce is very delicate for making dishes on a fish day, moreover, for meat days it is [also] very good.

Stuffed lettuce on meat days

Prepare the lettuce as explained in the previous recipes. Then chop up some veal or mutton with the right amount of fat and season with salt and all spices. Add eggs so that it is soft, as for meatballs. Add some bone marrow and a little lemon juice. Stuff the lettuce in the covered tart pan by putting one half down. Set the meat on top, place the other lettuce half on top, and grease with lard. Bake in the covered tart pan on low flame so that the lettuce doesn't turn brown. Serve them on sops with a few pieces of breast of veal boiled and seared on a grill, with breadcrumbs. Each piece of breast, or [you could also use] boiled squab, should be placed between lettuce heads.

[223] *Cazuela mojí de Berenjenas.*

Las berenjenas se aderezan en platillos, y se sirven con queso rallado por encima, y de otras muchas maneras, mas yo no quiero poner aquí más de dos, o tres maneras.[266] Para una cazuela mojí son menester dos, o tres docenas de berenjenas si fueren chicas, que son las mejores. Tomarás tres docenas, y quítales los platillos de los pezones,[267] e hiéndelas por medio, y ponlas a cocer en una olla con agua y sal, y ponles en la boca de la olla unas hojas de parra, o lechugas, porque no estén descubiertas. (150v) Después que estén cocidas, sácalas en un colador, y escúrrelas del agua una a una, y aparta la mitad dellas para picar: luego tomarás una libra de queso de hierba,[268] que sea bueno, y rállalo, y mézclalo con otro tanto, o poco menos de pan rallado, y échalo todo en una pieza, y sazónalo con todas especias, y canela, y alcaravea, y échale media libra de azúcar, y un poco de miel, porque el dulce desta cazuela no es bueno, todo azúcar, ni todo miel, sino con miel y azúcar: luego échale dos docenas de huevos batidos, y bátelo todo muy bien con un cucharón; y luego echarás dentro las berenjenas picadas, y las que están en medias, y revuélvelo muy bien: sazona de sal, y un poco de azafrán: y con esto harás dos cazolitas medianas, o una buena: echa un poco de aceite, no más de cuanto se unte la cazuela, porque éstas no han de llevar más aceite de lo que fuere menester para untarlas, que será menos de dos onzas, que echándole más recaudo,[269] las echarás a (151r) perder: luego echa el batido en las cazuelas que estén bien llenas, y ponle encima una yema de huevo cruda, o las que quisieres, y mételas en un horno, y cuézase a fuego manso: y cuando estén medio cocidas úntalas con un poco de aceite, y échales un poco de queso rallado por encima, y harán una costra. Estas cazuelas se hacen sin género de dulce, y en lo demás han de llevar todo lo que llevan éstas, y mas han de llevar unos pocos de cominos.[270] Cuando tuvieres muchos platos que hacer, y no tuvieres cazuelas, echa el batido destas cazuelas dulces en unas torteras grandes, y sírvelas en rebanadas con su azúcar y canela por encima: y para diferenciar platos harás las rebanadas, y rebozarlas has con huevos, y fríelas, y sírvelas con torrijas de pan mezcladas con las rebanadas, y tendrás azúcar y canela, y un poquito de queso rallado, echárselo por encima. Estas cazuelas se hacen también de carne, con cañas de vaca, y berenjenas, o alcachofas.

---

266 This first sentence serves as a general introduction to Martínez Montiño's eggplant section, which, as indicated, includes three recipes. Later, in the pickled vegetable section, he has a fourth eggplant recipe.
267 In this context, the *platillos* are the sepals that protect the fruit while blossoming. In the case of eggplant, this green leafy part remains as the fruit matures.
268 For more on *queso de hierba* made from herbal rennet, see 236n138.
269 *Recaudo* in a culinary context refers to *seasoning* or, here, to the fat used for greasing the pan.
270 This section begins an alternative version to the recipe that does not include sweetener but does add cumin to the seasoning.

Moxi eggplant casserole

Eggplants are prepared as individual dishes and served with grated cheese on top and in many other ways, but I won't include more than two or three ways here. To make a moxi casserole, two or three dozen eggplants are required if they are small, which are the best. Take three dozen and remove the sepals from the stems, slice them down the middle, and put them on to boil in a pot of salted water and place grape leaves or lettuce on top of the pot so that the eggplant is covered. After they are cooked, put them in a strainer and drain the water off one by one and set half aside for chopping. Then take a pound of cheese made from herbal rennet, make sure it's good, and grate it and mix it with the same amount, or a little less, of breadcrumbs, and put it all together in a bowl and season with all spices, cinnamon, and caraway. Add in half a pound of sugar and a little bit of honey, because the sweetener for this casserole shouldn't be all sugar or all honey, rather both honey and sugar. Then add two dozen whipped eggs and beat it all together with a big spoon. Then add in the chopped eggplant and those that are halved, and stir it well. Season with salt and a little saffron. With this you will make two medium casseroles or one large one. Add in a little oil, not more than to grease the casserole, because these shouldn't have any more oil than what is needed for greasing the casserole. It should be less than two ounces; if you add any more fat it will spoil the dish. Then add the mixture to the casseroles so that they are fairly full, and place on top one raw egg yolk, or as many as you like. Place them in the oven and bake with a low flame. When they are half-baked, drizzle with a little oil on top and then add grated cheese to form a crust. These casseroles can be made without any type of sweetener and in all other respects have everything else the same, but also have a little cumin. When you have to make a lot of dishes and don't have casseroles, spread the mixture of the sweet casseroles into large covered tart pans. Serve sliced with the right amount of sugar and cinnamon on top. To distinguish one dish from the other, you can take the slices, coat them with egg, fry them, and serve them with torrijas mixed with the [eggplant] slices, which will have cinnamon and sugar and a little grated cheese sprinkled on top. These casseroles can also be made with meat and bone marrow and eggplant or with artichokes.

[224] (151v) *Berenjenas rellenas*.[271]

Cocerlas has partidas por medio: luego exprímelas, y luego sácalas lo que tienen dentro, de manera que quede cada una hueca como media nuez, y picarás unas pocas de berenjenas cocidas, y freirás un poco de cebolla con un poco de manteca de vacas, o con buen aceite, y luego echa allí las berenjenas, y un poco de hierbabuena y cilantro verde, y huevos crudos, y ponlos sobre el fuego, y revuélvelos hasta que esté bien seco: luego sácalo al tablero, y pícalo todo muy bien, y métele huevos crudos, y un poco de pan rallado, y un poco de queso, y sazona con todas especias y canela, y un poquito de alcaravea, y un poco de azúcar: luego hinche las medias berenjenas, y rebózalas con huevos, y fríelas, y sírvelas con azúcar y canela por encima. A estas berenjenas les puedes hacer el relleno en día de carne con carne, y de las mismas berenjenas, y en (152r) día de Sábado con livianos de carnero, y de ternera, muy bien picados, y con berenjenas: y en lo demás guardarás la orden que está dicho en las de pescado.[272]

[225] *Plato de Berenjenas en día de carne.*

Cocerás las berenjenas en medias, luego sácalas y exprímelas del agua y ahógalas con un poco de tocino y cebolla, y sazona con todas especias, y un poco de alcaravea, y échales caldo hasta que se bañen, y tendrás un poco de tocino cocido, y pícalo con un poco de todas verduras,[273] y échaselo dentro, y cuezan un poco, y sírvelas sin cuajar, y échales por encima un poco de queso mezclado con un poco de alcaravea.

[226] *Platillo de Almendrucos.*[274]

Tomarás los almendrucos antes que se cuajen los cuescos, y estregarlos has con un paño para que se les quite el (152v) vello, y luego ponlos a cocer con agua, sin otra cosa: luego échalos en el colador, y fríe cebolla picada con tocino, o con buena manteca de vacas, y ahogarás los almendrucos con ella, y échales caldo cuanto se bañen, y sazona con todas especias y canela, y un poco de dulce de azúcar, y cuezan dos, o tres hervores, y échales un poquito de verdura picada, y no los cuajes con huevos, sino así como fricasea. Sírvelos sobre unas rebanadillas de pan blanco. Este platillo es muy bueno.

---

271 For an image of this recipe, see Appendix 3.16.
272 This last phrase exemplifies well the importance of abstinence and partial abstinence days for Martínez Montiño. Here he includes three different recipes to accommodate the Christian diet.
273 For an explanation of *todas verduras*, see *hierbas* (682–3).
274 *Almendruco* is a green almond. The outside shell is still green, and the seed has a soft fuzz surrounding it and is still tender.

Stuffed eggplant

Cook them sliced in half. Then squeeze the liquid out and remove the insides so that they are hollowed out, like a half walnut. Chop some of the cooked eggplant and fry a little onion in a little butter or in good oil. Then, add the eggplant, a little spearmint and cilantro, and raw eggs and cook over the flame, stirring until all is thoroughly cooked. Then turn it onto a cutting board, mince it up, and add raw eggs, a little bit of breadcrumbs, and a little cheese. Season with all spices and cinnamon, a little caraway, and a little sugar. Then fill the half eggplants, coat them in egg, fry them, and serve them with cinnamon and sugar on top. The filling for these eggplants can also be made with meat and the same eggplant on a meat day. On a Saturday, with minced mutton and calf lung and eggplant. With respect to the rest, follow the same instruction that is explained for eggplant for fish days.

Eggplant dish for a meat day

Boil eggplant halves, take them out, and drain off the water. Then, sauté with a little fatback and onion and season with all spices, and a little caraway. Add enough broth to braise them. Have a little cooked fatback and chop it with green herbs. Add it [to the pan] and let it boil a little. Serve without thickening and sprinkle on top a little cheese mixed with a little caraway.

A green almond dish

Take green almonds, before the nut is fully formed, rub them with a cloth to remove the fuzz. Then, bring to a boil in water without anything else. Then strain them in a colander. Fry diced onion with fatback, or with good butter, and sauté the green almonds with them. Add enough broth to braise them, and season with all spices, cinnamon, and a little sugar sweetener. Bring to a boil two or three times. Add in a little chopped green herbs and don't thicken with eggs; rather, as is, like a fricassee. Serve on slices of white bread. This dish is very tasty.

[227] *Garbanzos dulces con Membrillos.*

Echarás los garbanzos a cocer, y cuando estén cocidos tomarás membrillos tanta cantidad como los garbanzos, y móndalos, y quítales las pepitas, y córtalos por medio: luego del medio cortarás rebanadillas delgadas a lo largo, y a lo ancho del membrillo: luego tomarás (153r) manteca de vacas fresca, y freirás cebolla, y los membrillos, hasta que estén bien blandos: luego échalos con los garbanzos, y sazona con todas especias y canela, y un poco de vinagre, y échales dulce de azúcar que estén bien dulces, y tengan poco caldo: luego harás unos tallarines muy delgados, y fríelos, y echarás en un plato un lecho de tallarines (aunque se puede servir sin ellos) y otro de garbanzos, y azúcar, y canela: y desta manera hinchirás el plato.[275] Y advierte, que este plato ha de ser bien dulce, y bien agrio: y si no hubiere buena manteca, hágase con buen aceite: si no hubiere membrillos, hágase con peros agrios.

[228] *Otros Garbanzos dulces.*

Cocerás los garbanzos con agua y sal, y aceite bueno, y unas cebollas enteras, y pícalas mucho, y ahógalas con aceite, o manteca fresca, y échalas en la olla de los garbanzos, y tendrás pan tostado, (153v) remojado en vinagre, y sacarás algunos garbanzos al almirez, y májalos con un poco de verdura picada, y toma el pan remojado, y exprímelo de la vinagre y échalo en el almirez, y májalo todo muy bien, y desátalo con un poco de vinagre donde se remojó el pan, y con caldo de los garbanzos, y échalo en la olla, y sazona con todas especias, y canela, y azafrán, y dulce de azúcar, o miel, que estén bien agridulces, y sírvelos sobre una sopa de canteros de pan.

[229] *Cómo se adereza la Calabaza.*[276]

Las calabazas son muy buena potajería, demás de ser muy buena para enfermos, y para platillos de pollos, o pichones, o aves, y para cualquiera desta volatería: Perdigarla has que esté medio cocida, y la calabaza también ha de estar perdigada,

---

275 Martínez Montiño frequently uses this technique of layering ingredients.
276 *Calabaza* [*squash* and *gourd*] are members of the *Cucurbitaceae* family of plants. They are fruit-bearing, flowering vines that grow close to the ground. Gourds were cultivated in Africa, Asia, Europe, and the Americas for thousands of years before Columbus' arrival in the Americas. Squashes originated in the Americas and by the mid-sixteenth century were cultivated throughout Europe and Africa. I've translated *calabaza* as *squash*, given their popularity across continents, though it is possible that Martínez Montiño also used gourds for this and any of the following recipes. For more information on early years of squash in Europe and Africa, see Gispert Cruells 223–4.

Sweet garbanzos with quince

Put the garbanzos on to boil, and when they are done, get some quince, the same amount as the garbanzos, peel them, remove the seeds, and cut them in half. Then cut thin lengthwise and widthwise slices from the quince halves. Next, take fresh butter and fry onion and the quince until they are soft. Then add this to the garbanzos and season with all spices and cinnamon and a little vinegar and add simple syrup so that they are very sweet and have little broth. Then make some very thin strips of pastry dough, fry them, and put a layer of strips on a plate (although this can be served without them) and another of garbanzos with cinnamon and sugar. In this way you will fill the plate. And note that this dish should be sufficiently sweet and sufficiently sour. If you do not have good butter, make it with good oil; if you do not have quince, make it with sour apples.

Other sweet garbanzos

Cook garbanzos in salted water and good oil and with whole onions. Mince [the onions] and sauté them with oil or fresh lard and return them to the garbanzo pot. Have some toasted bread, soaked in vinegar. Put a few garbanzos into the mortar, mash them with minced green herbs. Take the soaked bread, and squeeze out the excess vinegar. Add to the mortar and mash everything all together well. Thin it with a little vinegar in which you soaked the bread and with garbanzo broth. Add it to the pot and season with all spices, cinnamon, saffron, and sweetener of sugar or honey, so that it has a good sweet and sour flavour. Serve over sops [made from] the crusty ends of bread.

How to prepare squash

Squash is a very good vegetable, in addition to being very good for the ill, and for dishes of young chicken or squab, adult ones, or any fowl. Sear [the bird] until half cooked. The squash should also be seared and cut into small pieces. Arrange this

y cortada, y menuda: armarás el platillo en un cacito, o cazuela, poniendo la volatería debajo: luego freirás un poco de cebolla con tocino, (154r) y echa allí la calabaza, y ahóguese un poco, y échalo todo en un cacillo sobre los pollos, o pichones, y échale un poco de caldo cuanto se bañe, y sazona con todas especias, y un poco de verdura picada: y si tuvieres alguna caña de vaca, échasela dentro en trozos, y échale un poco de agraz en grano; porque las calabazas y el agraz todo viene en un tiempo, y déjalo apurar: y luego cuájalo con yemas de huevos, y un poco de agrio. Son los mejores platillos de todo el año. Ahora pondré aquí otros tres, o cuatro platos de la calabaza diferentes.

[230] (252) *Potaje de Calabaza.*

Tomarás las calabazas largas, que sean tiernas, y ráspalas de toda la cáscara, y córtala un poco menuda, y ponla a perdigar en agua, y sal, y luego échala en el colador a que se escurra, y pon en un cazo, o cazuela, un poco de manteca de vacas, o buen aceite, y freirás un poco de cebolla, y echa allí la calabaza, y (154v) ahógala un poco: luego échale caldo de garbanzos, o agua caliente, cuanto se bañe, y échale verdura picada, y sazona con todas especias, y échale un poco de leche dentro, y toma un poco de manteca, y ponla a calentar en una sartén: y cuando esté caliente échale un poquito de harina, y fríela de manera que no se ponga negra, ni espesa en la sartén, sino que haga unas empollitas blancas,[277] y échala sobre el platillo de la calabaza, y échale un poquito de azafrán, y un poco de agrio, y con esto no es menester cuajarse con huevos. Si le quisieres echar dulce, bien podrás, y azúcar y canela por encima. Sírvela sobre rebanadillas de pan, y adórnala con algunas torrijas.

[231] *Calabaza rellena en el día de Pescado.*[278]

Cortarás la calabaza en trozos, del tamaño de pastelillos de medio talle, (155r) y quítale todo lo de adentro, no acabándolos de agujerear por la una parte, y perdígalos en agua, y sal, y echarás allí un poco de la cabeza en pedacitos para el relleno, y de que esté perdigado sácalo en el colador, y fríe un poco de cebolla cortada larga con un poco de manteca de vacas: luego echa allí la calabaza que está en pedacitos, y ahóguese todo en la sartén, y echa un poco de verdura entera. Y de que esto esté bien ahogado échale huevos crudos en cantidad, y revuélvelo con la paleta sobre el fuego hasta que esté bien seco: luego sácalo en el tablero, y pícalo

---

[277] For more information on this early instruction for roux, see the Introduction (65).
[278] Society for Creative Anachronism member Jen Small recreated this dish for the "Culinary Tour through the History of Spain" banquet at the "Twelfth Night" event in Schaumberg, IL, January 2020. An image can be found in Appendix 3.17.

little dish in a saucepan or casserole, placing the fowl on the bottom. Then fry a little onion with fatback, add the squash, and lightly sauté it. Add it all to the casserole on top of the chicken or squab and add enough broth to braise it. Season with all spices and some chopped green herbs. If you have some bone marrow, add it in pieces and add a few sour grapes, because squash and sour grapes grow in the same season. Let it finish and then thicken with egg yolks and a little sour juice. These are the best dishes of the year. I'll include here another three or four different squash dishes.

Squash stew

Take long squashes that are tender, peel the skin, and cut them into fairly small pieces. Parboil them in salted water and then place them in a strainer to drain. Put a little butter or good oil in a saucepan or casserole and fry a little onion. Add the squash and lightly sauté it. Then add enough garbanzo broth or hot water to braise the squash. Add chopped green herbs, season with all spices, and add a little milk. Take a little lard and heat it up in a frying pan. When it's hot, add in some flour and fry it up so it doesn't burn or get too thick in the pan but rather forms little white blisters. Pour it over the individual squash dish. Add a little saffron and a little sour juice. With this, it is not necessary to thicken with eggs. If you want to add sweetness, you certainly can, as well as sugar and cinnamon on top. Serve over slices of bread and garnish with some torrijas.

Stuffed squash for fish days

Slice the squash into pieces, the size of medium-sized tartlets, and remove the insides without perforating the sides. Parboil them in salted water and add in some of the chopped squash from the head for the filling. Once parboiled, put it in a strainer. Fry onions sliced lengthwise in a little butter. Add the squash that was cut into small pieces and sauté it all in the frying pan and add a little bit of whole green herbs. Once everything is thoroughly sautéed, add in a lot of raw eggs and stir with a spatula over the flame until the eggs are well cooked. Turn it out onto the cutting board and mince it all. Add a little bit of breadcrumbs and cheese,

muy bien, y échale un poco de pan rallado, y queso que sea bueno, y sazónalo con todas especias, y un poco de azúcar y canela, y métele huevos crudos, de manera que no esté muy ralo, y rellena tus pastelillos, y échales un poco de queso rallado por encima, y asiéntalos en una tortera untada con manteca, y échales un poquito de manteca por encima, y pon la tortera (155v) al fuego con lumbre abajo y arriba, y cuézanse así en seco,[279] y sírvelos sobre una sopa dulce que lleve queso. Si la quisieres servir en platillo, cuando estuviere acabada de cocer, echa en la misma tortera caldo de garbanzos que llegue a igualar con los pastelillos, y sazona este caldo con verduras y especias: y si le quisieres poner agraz, con no echar queso al relleno, será muy bueno, y parecerá relleno de pollos, y el agraz no lo has de echar hasta que tengas hecho el relleno del todo; porque los granos quedan enteros: y si tu señor no fuere amigo de agraz en grano, échale al relleno agraz sacado, y será una misma cuenta. Y también podrás al rellenar estas calabazas cortar algunas largas hendidas por medio, que queden a manera de tejas, y asentarlas has en la tortera, y rellenarlas, y ponerlas unas yemas de huevos duras encima, y servir de las redondas, y de las largas todo junto con algunas torrijas entre medias, parece bien.

[232] (156r) *Calabaza en día de carne.*

La calabaza en platillo ha de ser como la del día de pescado, salvo que en lugar de manteca de vacas, o aceite, ha de ser tocino frito en dados, y en lo demás todo ha de llevar una cuenta. La calabaza rellena en el día de carne, como está dicho, no ha menester llevar calabaza dentro, ni queso, ni dulce, sino carne, y haz tu relleno como para rellenar pollos friendo unas lonjitas de tocino, y un poco de cebolla cortada a lo largo, y un poco de verdura, y échale carne picada, y fríelo un poco, y échale huevos crudos, y revuélvelos sobre la lumbre hasta que esté bien seco: luego sácalo al tablero, y pícalo muy bien, y métele huevos crudos, y sazona con todas especias, y rellena tus pastelillos, y ponle una yema de huevo encima de cada uno con algunas cañas de vaca, y pica un poco de tocino gordo, y unta la tortera, y asiéntalos dentro, y cuezan (156v) así en seco. Y advierte, que estos pastelitos de calabaza, que se cuecen en seco, es mejor que sean bajitos; lo que había de ir en una, vaya en dos: y no importa mucho aunque estén agujereados: por entrambas partes, que como el relleno es seco se cuajan luego los suelos, y se quedan con su sazón. Sírvelos sobre alguna sopa, y adórnalos con algunas torrijas.

---

279 *Cocer en seco* refers to cooking without any liquid in the cooking vessel. It is sometimes translated as *bake*.

make sure it's good. Season with all spices and a little sugar and cinnamon. Add raw eggs, but don't make it too thin. Fill the squash tartlets and top with a little grated cheese. Place them in a covered tart pan greased with butter, dab the tops with a little butter, and place the covered tart pan on the fire with heat above and below it; let it bake like this and serve on sweet cheese sops. If you want to serve it on an individual plate when it's done cooking, add to the covered tart pan itself garbanzo broth, enough to reach the tops of the squash tartlets. Season the broth with green herbs and spices. And if you want to include sour grapes, and not add cheese to the filling, it will be very tasty and look like stuffing for chicken. The sour grapes should not be added until the stuffing is completely finished so that the grapes remain intact. And if your lord does not like whole sour grapes, then add sour grape mash to the stuffing. It will turn out the same. When filling the squash, you can also make deep slits in the middle so that they look like tiles. Set them in the covered tart pan, fill them, and add hard-boiled egg yolks on top. Serve the round ones and the long ones all together with some torrijas in between them. It will look good.

Squash for meat days

Squash as an individual dish should be like squash for fish days, except, instead of butter or oil, it should have fried, cubed fatback. The rest should be the same calculations. Stuffed squash for meat days, as explained, does not need to be filled with squash, cheese, or sweetener but rather, meat. Make the stuffing like stuffing for chicken by frying slices of fatback, some onion cut lengthwise, a little bit of green herbs, and ground meat. Fry it a little. Add raw eggs and stir over the fire until they are well done. Then turn it out onto a cutting board and mince it. Add raw eggs, season with all spices, and fill your squash tartlets. Put an egg yolk and some bone marrow, from a cow, on top of each one. Mince a little fatback and grease the covered tart pan and place them in it and bake this way. Note that for these baked squash tartlets it is better to have them shallow; what would normally go in one should go in two, and it will be okay even if both have holes, because, since the stuffing is cooked through, the bottoms will congeal and the flavour will remain intact. Serve over sops and garnish with some torrijas.

[233] *Calabaza rellena en platillo.*

Hanse de rellenar los gubiletes[280] de la calabaza con carne cruda: picada con su tocino gordo, y sazonada con todas especias y huevos, como si fuera para hacer albondiguilla y mezclado dentro de la carne algunas cañas de vaca, y algún agraz en grano, o un poco de agraz sacado, e hinche tus pastelillos, y asiéntalos en un cazo, que estén muy juntos unos con otros: luego échales caldo hasta que se (157r) cubran, y echa allí verdura picada: y si no tuvieres harta grasa, freirás un poco de tocino en dados muy menudos, y échale un poco de cebolla cortada muy menuda, y échalo sobre el platillo de los gubiletes de la calabaza, y échale un poco de verdura picada, y sazónalo de especias. Y cuando quisieres servir el plato, cuájalo con unas yemas de huevos, y un poco de acedo: y si le quisieres echar un poco de azúcar y canela por encima, podrás; y aparta primero la flor, y después échasela por encima.[281]

[234] *Plato cuajado de Calabazas.*

De la calabaza larga, o redonda, podrás hacer platos, cociendo la calabaza con agua, y sal; luego sácala en el colador, y escúrrase, y échala sobre el tablero, y pícala muy bien, y mézclale pan rallado, y queso, y azúcar, y sazona con todas especias y canela, y métele huevos (157v) crudos, hasta que esté bien blanda: unta un plato, o una tortera con manteca, e hínchelo de aquel batido, y ponles por encima unas rebanadillas de queso, y si fueren en día de carne, en lugar de queso sean cañas de vaca: y también podrás echarle un suelo de hojaldrado, y hacerle buenos bordes, y cuézanse en el horno, y parecerá costrada: y si no le quisieres echar queso, lo podrás hacer agridulce, y tendrá muy buen gusto.

[235] *Calabaza frita.*

De la calabaza redonda podrás hacer platos, quitándole la cáscara, que es muy recia, y de lo blando de dentro harás rebanadillas muy delgadas, y enharínense, y fríanse muy bien, y parecerán hojarascas; y se han de servir con azúcar y canela, y zumo de limón, o naranja: y si son para freír mucho mejores que las largas, y para otra cosa ninguna no son tan buenas: y si fuere día de carne freirás estas calabazas redondas con manteca (158r) de puerco, y échales azúcar, y canela, y agraz, y no se frían hasta que se quieran servir; de manera que vayan calientes a la mesa. Son de mucho gusto. Y advierte, que estas calabazas antes que se frían, se han de sazonar de sal.

---

280 *Cubilete*, formerly *gubilete*, is a copper or tin, round or curved (abarquillado) receptacle with a top wider than the bottom used in the kitchen as a mould. Here it refers to the shell of a pumpkin or squash.
281 For more information on the flor, see 65.

A stuffed squash dish

Fill the squash shells with raw, ground meat minced with the right amount of fat and seasoned with all spices and eggs as if it were for making meatballs. Mix in some beef bone marrow and some whole sour grapes or a little sour grape mash and fill the shells and place them in a pot so that one is right next to the other. Add in enough broth to cover them and add in some chopped green herbs. If you don't have enough fat, fry some minced cubes of fatback and some minced onion and sprinkle it on top of the squash shells dish. Add a little chopped green herbs and season with spices. When you want to serve the dish, thicken it with egg yolks and a dash of sorrel juice. And if you want to sprinkle some sugar and cinnamon on top, you can. First, take out the flor and later sprinkle it on top.

Squash with egg crust

With long or round squash you can create a dish by boiling the squash in salted water. Next, place it in a strainer and drain it. Turn it out onto a cutting board and mince it. Add in breadcrumbs, cheese, and sugar. Season with all spices and cinnamon and add raw eggs until it is soft. Grease a dish or a covered tart pan with lard and fill it with that mixture. Put slices of cheese on top. If it were a meat day, instead of cheese, it should be beef bone marrow. Also, you can have a bottom of puff pastry dough and make nice edges. Bake in the oven and it will look like a puff pastry pie. If you don't want to add cheese, you can make it sweet and sour and it will be very tasty.

Fried squash

With round squash you can make dishes by removing the skin, which is very tough, and from the soft inside cut very thin slices, flour them, and fry them well. They will look like fallen leaves. They should be served with cinnamon and sugar and lemon or orange juice. If they are for frying, [these] are much better than the long ones. And for anything else they are not as good. And if it were a meat day, fry the round squash in pork lard and add sugar, cinnamon, and verjuice. Don't fry them until you are ready to serve them. In this way, they will arrive hot to the table. They are very tasty. And note that these squashes should be seasoned with salt before they are fried.

[236] *Potaje de Calabaza redonda.*

Perdigarás la calabaza en agua y sal; y luego sácala al colador a que se escurra, y ahogarla has en su cazuela, u olla, con su cebolla picada con manteca de vacas, o buen aceite, y sazona con todas especias, y canela, y dulce de azúcar, o miel: échale un poco de agua caliente cuanto se bañe: y cuando esté bien cocida revuélvela con el cucharón hasta que se deshaga bien, que parezcan puches, y puédesle echar un poco de pan rallado, y luego cuajarlo con unos huevos y agrio, de manera que sean agridulces, y sírvela en escudillas, y su azúcar y canela por encima. Este platillo no es (158v) muy bueno para mesas regaladas, mas es bueno para conventos, y personas particulares en sus casas:[282] y si los sirvieres en plato no se deshagan mucho.

[237] *Sopa de Calabaza redonda.*[283]

Freirás la calabaza redonda en rebanadillas, como está dicho, y armarás una sopa de calabaza frita, y rebanadas de queso fresco, y azúcar, y canela: y entremedias pondrás unos huevos rellenos, y unos bocadillos de manteca fresca: luego batirás cuatro huevos con claras, y echarle un cuartillo de leche, y mojarás la sopa con esta leche, de manera que quede bien empapada, y ponla a cocer en un horno. Suele salir muy buen plato.

[238] *Cómo se aderezan los Nabos.*

Los nabos no es muy buena potajería: yo trato dellos de mala gana, (159r) porque soy muy enemigo dellos; porque cualquier platillo donde cayere algún caldo de nabos, se hecha a perder; con todo esto diré tres, o cuatro maneras de nabos. Hanse de escoger que sean delgados y lisos, y de tierra fría:[284] ráspalos, y perdígalos un poco, sácalos en el colador, y luego fríe tocino en dados, y cebolla menuda, y echa allí los nabos, y ahóguense un poco: luego échales caldo de la olla hasta que se cubran, y échale allí un poco de tocino gordo: y cuando los nabos estén cocidos, saca el tocino en el tablero, y pícalo con verduras, y tórnalo a echar dentro en los nabos, y sazona con todas especias, y un poco de alcaravea, y déjalos apurar que no quede más caldo de lo que ha de llevar en el plato, y echa un poco de zumo de naranjas por encima. Sobre estos nabos has de poner siempre alguna cosa salada, como es cecina de vaca, o gansos, lenguas, o salchichones: y si no tuvieres nada

---

282 This side commentary shows that Martínez Montiño was writing for a wider audience than only the cooks in the king's kitchen.
283 *Calabaza redonda* could refer to pumpkin, acorn squash, patty pan squash, or any of the round varieties.
284 In his chapter on turnips, Alonso de Herrera also notes the importance of cold earth for growing turnips. Like Martínez Montiño, he discusses two types of turnips: thin and round (244).

Round squash stew

Parboil the squash in salted water and then place it in a strainer to drain. In a casserole or pot, sauté with the right amount of diced onion in butter or good oil. Season with all spices, cinnamon, and a sweetener of sugar or honey. Add enough hot water to braise, and when it is cooked, stir it with a big spoon until it begins to fall apart and looks like porridge. You can add in a little bit of breadcrumbs and thicken with some eggs and sour flavouring so that it will be sweet and sour. Serve in bowls with the right amount of sugar and cinnamon on top. This dish is not very good for exquisite tables, but it is good for convents and individual people in their homes. And if you serve it on a plate, don't let it separate too much.

Sops of round squash

Fry the round squash in slices, as is explained [above], and you will put together a sop of fried squash, slices of fresh cheese, sugar, and cinnamon. Place stuffed eggs and dollops of butter throughout. Then whip four eggs with the whites, add a pint of milk, and soak the sops with this milk so that it is all absorbed. Place it in the oven to bake. This dish usually comes out very good.

How to prepare turnips

Turnips are not a very good vegetable. I am grudgingly including them here, because I really don't like them because any dish that contains any turnip broth will be ruined. In spite of this I'll explain three or four ways for [making] turnips. Choose the ones that are thin and smooth, from cold ground. Peel them, parboil them, and place them in a strainer. Next, fry cubes of fatback and minced onion. Add the turnips and lightly sauté them. Then add enough broth from the pot to braise them. Add in a little extra fatty fatback. When the turnips are cooked, remove the fatback to the cutting board and chop it up with green herbs, then return it to the turnips. Season with all spices, a little caraway, and let them finish until no more broth remains except what you need for the dish. Drizzle a little orange juice on top. You should always put something salty on top of these turnips, like cured beef, goose, tongue, or black-pepper sausage. If you don't have

desto, ponle un jarrete de pernil (159v) que sea bueno el tocino. Y advierte, que este plato de nabos con cecinas, ha de ser ordinario en la temporada de los nabos: y después en su lugar berzas, o repollos, u otras verduras, porque los más de los señores gustan dél.

[239] *Nabos cuajados.*

Cocerás los nabos en buen caldo hasta que estén bien cocidos; luego sácalos, y pícalos muy bien en el tablero con un poco de tocino gordo cocido, y sazona de todas especias: y si le quisieres echar un poco de dulce podrás, y échale media docena de yemas de huevos; y unta un plato con un poco de tocino gordo picado, y echa allí los nabos, y ponle cañas de vaca por encima, y ponlo a cuajar en el horno, y sírvelo en el mismo plato caliente.

[240] *Nabos lampreados.*[285]

Cocerás los nabos, y luego ahógalos con manteca de vacas y cebolla: (160r) y después que estén medio fritos échales agua caliente cuanto se bañen, y sazona con todas especias y canela: luego quema un poco de harina en seco, y desátala con el mismo caldo, y harás una salsa un poquito espesa y negra, y échales azúcar, o miel, que estén bien dulces: y cuando los quisieres servir, entonces les has de echar el agrio, porque los nabos no requieren mucho agrio. Cocidos estos nabos con toda su sazón sin dulce, y luego fritos con tocino, hasta que estén dorados, y luego echarles pimienta y naranja son muy buenos, mas para mí ningunos son tan buenos como los que son echados en la olla de carne sin perdigar, ni especia, ni agrio, sino buena vaca gorda, y carnero, y tocino.

[241] *Sopa de Nabos.*

Cocerás los nabos en la olla con buena grasa, y luego sácalos y pícalos bien menudos, y harás una sopa del mismo caldo, y ve echando los (160v) nabos picados sobre la sopa, y entre lecho y lecho irás echando azúcar, y canela, y zumo de naranja, o limón, y un poco de pimienta. Y desta manera henchirás el plato de los nabos, y encima de todo echarás su azúcar, y canela, pimienta, y agrio, como está dicho, y échale de la grasa de la olla, y sírvelo caliente.

---

285 Based on Martínez Montiño's recipes, *lampreado* refers to a dish in which the main ingredient is fried or roasted and has added to it a sweet and sour black sauce seasoned with all spices and cinnamon. Valles Rojo defines it more generally as a dish in which the main ingredient is fried with fatback and onion and to which a sauce is added. He also explains that it could also refer to a specific style that, in addition to the above, has water or wine added along with sugar or honey and that it is served with a sour juice on top (420–1).

any of these, use ham shank with good fat on it. Note that this dish of turnips with cured beef is the most common in turnip season. Afterwards, you can replace them with collard greens, cabbage, or other green-leaf vegetables because most lords like them.

Turnips with an egg crust

Boil turnips in good broth until they are well cooked. Remove them and chop them up on a cutting board with a little extra fatty fatback that has already been cooked. Season with all spices. If you want to add sweetener, you can. Add in a half dozen egg yolks. Grease a plate with some of the minced fatback, place the turnips there, and add bone marrow on top. Bake them in the oven until the egg sets. Serve them on the same hot plate.

Turnips, Lamprea style

Boil turnips and sauté them with butter and onion. Once they are partially fried, add enough hot water to braise and season with all spices and cinnamon. Then burn a little flour, dry. Thin it with some of the same broth and make a thick, black sauce. Add sugar or honey so that it is very sweet. When you are ready to serve, add in the sour flavour, because turnips don't require a lot of sour flavour. These boiled turnips with their seasoning and no sugar that are then fried in fatback until golden brown and seasoned with pepper and orange juice are very good. But, for me, none are as good as the ones that are added to a meat stew without parboiling, without any spices or sour flavouring, just good, marbled beef, mutton, and fatback.

Turnip sops

Boil turnips in a pot with good fat. Then turn them out and mince them up. Make sops with the same broth and place the minced turnips on the sops. Between each layer be sure to sprinkle sugar, cinnamon, lemon or orange juice, and a little [black] pepper. In this way you will fill the plate with turnips. On the top layer sprinkle the right amount of sugar, cinnamon, pepper, sour juice, as is already explained, and some of the fat from the pot. Serve hot.

[242] *Cómo se adereza el Repollo.*

El repollo lo más ordinario es guisado con buena grasa, y con un poco de queso, y alcaravea por encima. Para rellenar este repollo, buscarás los repollos que sean pequeños, y muy apretados, y agujerarlos has por el pezón, y quitarles has todo lo que tienen dentro, que quedan huecos como calabaza: luego picarás un poco de carne con tocino, y meterle has huevos, y sazonarás de especias, y sal, y un poquito de alcaravea: y meterás en esta carne unos trozos de cañas de vaca, y unas yemas de huevos (161r) duros en cuarterones, y rellenarás los repollos con esta carne, y tórnales a tapar los pezones, y échalos a cocer en buen caldo con buena grasa, y sazona con un poco de alcaravea, sin otra cosa ninguna: y cuando los quisieres servir sácalos, y harás de cada repollo cuatro cuartos, y asentarlos has en el plato, la carne hacia arriba: y pondrás encima deste repollo algún tocino magro cocido, o algunos salchichones, u otras cecinas, y en día de pescado el relleno de las lechugas.

[243] *Potaje de arvejas.*

Las arvejas, es muy buena potajería cuando son tiernas. Éstas mondarás, y ahogarlas has con manteca de vacas, o tocino, si fuere día, y pondrás a cocer las cáscaras: y cuando estén cocidas que será muy presto, velas echando en una estameña, y velas estregando allí, y echando del agua donde se cocieron, y (161v) pasará mucha verdina dellas: y cuando las arvejas estén bien ahogadas, échales desta agua, y sazónalas con todas especias, y un poco de verdura picada: y cuando estén bien cocidas, freirás un poco de harina en manteca, de manera que se fría, y quede muy blanca y rala, y échala sobre las arvejas, de manera que queden un poco trabadas con poco caldo y su agrio. Advierte, que a todos los platillos sueltos de calabazas, berenjenas, o alcachofas, y habas, que de mi parecer nunca se han de cuajar con huevos, ni las pepitorias,[286] sino freír un poco de harina con manteca que esté caliente, y no de manera que queme la harina, ni has de echar mucha harina que se haga engrudo en la sartén, sino que quede bien rala, y blanca: y cuando ella hiciere unas empollitas meneándolo un poco, y échala con la sartén en la potajería.[287] Y no te parezca que soy enfadoso en esto, porque todo el toque de ser oficial uno, está en saber hacer bien los platillos.[288] Estas arvejas has de servir (162r) sobre rebanadillas de pan, y adornar el plato con algunas torrijas cortadas: y si las arvejas estuvieren enjutas, pon encima del plato una tortilla de agua. Estas arvejas son muy buenas con platillos de carne, como son pollos, o pichones, o aves.

---

286 For more on *pepitoria*, see 202n90.
287 For more information on this early instruction for roux, see the Introduction (65).
288 Here is a moment of self-realization for Martínez Montiño. He is very aware that he is being a stickler on this point, but he knows that to get to be *oficial uno* [number one in the kitchen] one has to be attentive to this level of detail.

How to prepare cabbage

Cabbage: the most common is cooked with good fat, a little cheese, and caraway on top. To stuff this cabbage, look for small, tight cabbages. Make a hole in the base of the stem and remove all the insides so that it's hollow like a squash. Then mince a little meat with fatback, add eggs, and season with spices, salt, and a little caraway. Add bits of bone marrow to this meat and some quartered, hard-boiled egg yolks. Stuff the cabbage with this meat, and cover the hole with the base of the stem. Set it to boil in a good broth with good fat. Season with a little caraway and nothing else. When you are ready to serve them, remove them and quarter each cabbage. Set them on a plate with the meat side up. Place some boiled meaty fatback, black-pepper sausage, or other cured meat on top of the cabbages. On fish days, use the filling for [stuffed] lettuce.

Pea stew

Peas are a very good vegetable when they are tender. Shuck them, sauté them with butter or fatback, depending on the day, and put the pods on to boil. When they're done, and this will happen quickly, put them in a cheesecloth, rub them in it, and pour in the water they were cooked in. A lot of green will come off. When the peas are sautéed, add in some of this water and season with all spices and a little bit of minced green herbs. When they're done, fry some flour in lard so that when it's frying it turns out white and thin. Pour this over the peas so that they thicken with just a little broth and the right amount of sourness. Note that for all these squash, eggplant, artichoke, or fava beans dishes, it is my view that they should never be thickened with egg or [prepared] like *pepitoria* stews. Rather, one should fry just a little flour in hot lard. Not so much as to burn the flour or so much that it becomes pasty in the frying pan; it should be very thin and white. When it begins to form little bubbles while [you are] shaking it a little, add it to the frying pan with the vegetables. Don't think I'm being annoying with this point, because the secret to being number one is in knowing how to make these dishes. These peas should be served over slices of bread and garnished with some slices of torrijas. If the peas were dry, put a plain omelette on top. These peas go very well with individual meat dishes like young chicken, squab, or adult birds.

[244] *Cómo se aderezan las Espinacas.*

Las espinacas, lo más ordinario es guisarlas dulces, enjutas con pasas y piñones, cociéndolas primero, y picarlas, y exprimirlas del agua, y ahogarlas con un poco de buen aceite, y cebolla, y sazonar con todas especias, y sal, y un poco de agrio, y luego echarles su dulce de miel, o azúcar, y sus pasas, o piñones, y algunas veces garbanzos, y éstas no han de llevar casi caldo, porque han de ir muy enjutas.

[245] *Espinacas a la Portuguesa.*[289]

Echarás el aceite en una cazuela: y cuando esté caliente tendrás las espinacas (162v) mojadas y lavadas, y quitadas todos los pezones, y muy exprimidas del agua, e iráslas echando en el aceite, meneándolas con un cucharón, y ellas se irán allí ahogando de manera, que vendrán a caber muchas en la cazuela, y ellas mismas harán un caldillo, y echarás allí mucho cilantro verde: y después que estén bien ahogadas, sazónalas de especias y sal, y échales un poco de más agua caliente que se bañen bien, y échales vinagre que estén bien agrias: luego échales allí cuatro, o seis huevos crudos que se escalfen en las mismas espinacas, y cubre la cazuela para que los huevos se pongan duros, y sírvelos en la misma cazuela.

[246] *Fruta de Borrajas.*

Harás un batido de leche, y harina, y huevos, y sal, de manera que quede un poco ralo: y si no hubiere leche bien se puede hacer con agua, y tomarás la hoja de la borraja lavada y escurrida, y (163r) mójala en el batido, y échala en la sartén: y si el batido se desparramase por la sartén, tiene poca harina: y si saliere muy grueso, es señal que tiene demasiada: y emendarla has con echar más huevos, y una gota de leche: y la que estuviere rala, se enmendará con echar un poco de harina: freirás luego las borrajas, mojando en el batido cada hoja de por sí, e irlas echando en la sartén: y de que estén bien fritas sírvelas con miel y azúcar raspado por encima. Deste mismo batido podrás hacer fruta de laurel, encorporándolo un poco más, y mojando las hojas del laurel, de manera que queden los pezones de las hojas enjutos: y cuando estén fritas, tomarlas has en la mano izquierda, y tira con la otra por el pezón, y saldrá la hoja y quedará la fruta hueca, y sírvela con miel y azúcar raspado por encima.[290] Deste mismo batido podrás hacer fruta de hierros.

289　This recipe was recreated and a photo of the finished product can be found in Appendix 3.18.

290　This technique of frying a bay leaf that has been dipped in batter and then removing the leaf so that just the aroma remains is unique to Martínez Montiño. However, in Libro de Arte Culinaria (~1450–60), Martino da Como also includes a recipe, "Buñuelos con ramas de laurel" [Bay leaf puffs], in which he first fries the bay leaf, then dips it in batter and fries it again (Cruz Cruz 190). This version does not include quickly removing the bay leaf before consuming the fried dough.

How to prepare spinach

Spinach: the most common is to cook it as a sweet, dry dish with raisins and pine nuts. First, boil the spinach, chop it up, and squeeze out the extra water. Sauté it with a little good olive oil and onion. Season with all spices, salt, and a little sour juice. Then add the right amount of sweetener, honey or sugar, and the right amount of raisins and pine nuts, and sometimes garbanzos. This spinach dish needs no more than a bit of broth, because the spinach should be very dry.

Spinach, Portuguese style

Heat some oil in a casserole, and when it's hot, have some wet spinach that has been washed, with stems removed, and most of the water squeezed out. Begin adding the spinach in the oil, stirring it with a spoon. The spinach will be sautéed in a way that a lot will fit in the casserole and it will create its own liquid. Add a lot of cilantro, and once everything is well sautéed, season with spices and salt and add in a little more hot water, enough to braise. Add vinegar so that the spinach is sufficiently sour. Next, add four to six eggs that will poach right in with the spinach. Cover the casserole so that the eggs get done. Serve them in the casserole itself.

Deep-fried borage

Make a batter of milk, flour, eggs, and salt so that it turns out fairly thin. If there is no milk, you can make it with water. Take borage leaves that have been washed and drained, dip them in the batter, and put them in the frying pan. If the batter breaks apart in the pan, it has too little flour, and if it turns out too thick, then it's a sign there's too much. Fix it by adding more eggs and a drop of milk. If it's too thin, fix it by adding a little more flour. Then fry the borage, dipping each individual leaf in the batter and dropping in the pan. Once they're fried, serve them with honey and grated sugar on top. With this same batter you can make bay leaf fried dough, thickening it a little more and dipping the bay leaves in so that the stems remain dry. When they are fried, grab them with the left hand, and with the other, pull the stem, and the leaf will come off and the hollow fried dough will remain. Serve with honey and grated sugar on top. With this same batter you can make fried dough with an iron rosette.

[247] *Fruta de Frisuelos.*[291]

(163v) Harás un batido como el de la fruta de las borrajas atrás escrito, con leche, o un poco de vino blanco: el batido ha de estar un poco más incorporado: tomarás una sartén con harta manteca, ponla al fuego, y caliéntese bien: y tomarás una cuchara cerrada, e hínchela deste batido, velo echando en la sartén, colando por otra cuchara espumadera que tenga los agujeros un poco grandes, y esto ha de ser andando por toda la sartén hasta que parezca que está la sartén llena, porque ha de hacer unas espumas: y cuando te pareciere que esté frita por un cabo, toma una paleta, y mira si la puedes volver entera, y si no pudieres, volverla has en pedazos: y para estar la fruta como ha de estar, ha de estar lisa por la una parte, que es la parte de arriba, y por la parte de abajo ha de parecer un garvín de mujer con muchos granillos redondos, como perdigones de arcabuz, que parecen muy bien:[292] y si los granillos estuvieron muy menudos, (164r) y se desparramasen algunos por lo sartén, tiene poca harina, y se puede remediar como está dicho en la fruta de borrajas. Ésta es muy buena fruta, sírvela con miel y azúcar raspado por encima.

[248] *Borrajas con caldo de Carne.*

Las borrajas es una hierba, que dicen que es muy sana: y así acostumbran algunos señores comerlas: y lo más ordinario es cocer las borrajas, y picarlas sobre el tablero, de manera que no estén muy picadas, y ponerlas en una ollita, o cazuela, y echar allí caldo de la olla del señor,[293] que no tenga berzas, ni nabos, y que no lleven demasiada grasa, sin especias, ni otra cosa ninguna, y cuézanse allí con aquel caldo, y sírvela al principio que se han de comer antes que la fruta verde.[294]

---

291 The word *frisuelo* comes from the Latin *foliolum*, diminutive of *folium*, meaning *hoja* [leaf or sheet]. This type of "large-leaf" fried dough is still commonly made in Asturias. In some regions it still looks like a funnel cake and in other regions is similar to a crepe. Given Martínez Montiño's description, *funnel cake* is the better translation.

292 A *garvín* is a *laced cap* or *bonnet* that women wore on their heads. Martínez Montiño's attentiveness to his audience draws upon visual images from beyond the kitchen to facilitate the cook's understanding of how to cook this sweet treat to perfection. Here, he compares his fried dough to the feminized object of a cap with little round seeds (bumps) but then immediately adds the comparison of the masculine image of pellet shot to convey the blistering of the fried dough that indicates it is done. These two very different visual cues allow the audience to understand the recipe and achieve the best outcome.

293 Although Martínez Montiño describes the stock used to boil the borage by what it doesn't have, based on the title of the recipe and the fact that the stock comes from *the lord's* pot, one can assume that it is made with high-quality products. This recipe is also unique in that it signals the health properties advantageous to the consumer.

294 Martínez Montiño rarely includes instructions on the order for consuming specific dishes, but here he notes that this borage dish should be eaten before any of the firm fruits are served.

Funnel cakes

Make a batter, like the one for deep-fried borage written above, with milk or with a little white wine. The batter should be a little thicker. Take a frying pan with a lot of lard, put it on the flame, and heat it well. Take a rounded spoon, fill it with batter, and begin ladling it into the frying pan via a skimmer with large holes. Do this over the whole pan until the pan looks full. It should bubble up. When it seems fried on one side, use a spatula and see if you can flip the whole thing over. If you can't, turn it over in pieces. For this fried dough to turn out as it should, it should be smooth on one side, which is the top, and on the bottom it should look like a woman's laced bonnet with many little, round seeds, like buckshot from an harquebus. That would look just right. If the little bubbles are really small and begin breaking off in the pan, then it has too little flour. This can be remedied as explained in [the recipe for] deep-fried borage. This is very good fried dough. Serve with honey and grated sugar on top.

Borage with meat stock

Borage is a leafy green vegetable that is said to be very healthy. So, some lords get in the habit of eating it. The most common [method of preparation] is to boil borage and chop it up on a cutting board, but not too much. Place in a small pot or a casserole and add stock from the lord's pot that doesn't have any collard greens or turnips and that doesn't have too much fat. Don't add any spices or anything else. Let boil in that stock and serve as a starter, as it should be eaten before any of the firm fruits.

[249] *Sopa de Borrajas.*

Cocerás las borrajas, y picarlas has (164v) muy menudas, y exprimirlas has que no tengan ningún género de agua, y tendrás leche de almendras, sazonada con su azúcar, ni más ni menos que para almendrada,[295] y ponla al fuego, y cuécela andando a una mano con un cucharón: y cuando la almendrada esté cocida, échale dentro las borrajas picadas, y den dos hervores: luego tendrás una sopilla hecha de pan tostado, y encima della unos huevos frescos escalfados: luego echa las borrajas por encima con su leche de almendras, y tomarás un poco de manteca fresca de vacas, y échasela por encima. Es muy buena sopa, y se puede dar a enfermos.

[250] *Otra manera de Borrajas.*

Cocerás las borrajas, y pícalas muy bien, y exprímelas mucho, y échalas en el almirez, y májalas un poco con un poco de pan rallado, y un poco de azúcar molido, y unas poquitas de especias, pimienta, y canela, y unas yemas de (165r) huevos crudos. De todo esto harás unas tortillas cada una del tamaño de un as de oros,[296] sobre el tablero, que sean un poco delgadas: luego tendrás la sartén con muy poca manteca de vacas, y rebozarás estas tortillas de borrajas con yemas de huevos, y fríelas que estén bien tostadillas: y sírvelas sobre unas torrijuelas de pan, y su azúcar, canela, y zumo de limón. Destas borrajas cocidas, y picadas, puedes hacer buñuelos echándoles un poco de pan rallado, y sus huevos: son muy buenos y baratos.[297] También puedes picar las borrajas cocidas, y mezclarlas con huevos y pan rallado, y sazonar de sal, y unas poquitas de especias, y hacer una tortilla: y si le quisieres echar dulce podrás.

[251] *Cómo se han de aderezar algunos Pescados.*

Trataré un poco de pescados, aunque no me pienso detener mucho en (165v) ello, porque los pescados cuanto toca a cocimientos y frituras, que son las dos maneras más ordinarias, casi todos van por un camino: una cosa tienen los pescados frescos que no quieren ser cocidos en mucha cantidad de agua sino muy poca, que sean como estofados, porque en mucho agua se ponen desabridos.

---

295 For *almendrada* instructions, see the recipe "Una escudilla de almendrada" (492–4; 493–5).
296 This card reference to explain the size of the tortilla exemplifies Martínez Montiño's vibrant descriptions as he finds different ways to connect with his audiences. A Spanish deck of cards is made up of four suits, *bastos* [clubs], *oros* [gold coins], *copas* [cups], and *espadas* [swords]. These tortillas, then, would be small in contrast to the full-size tortilla he describes at the end of the recipe.
297 This rare comment about the cost of a dish reinforces the idea that Martínez Montino's project went beyond court to other cooks, in particular those who had to watch their budgets more carefully.

Borage sops

Boil borage, mince it, and squeeze it so no drop of water remains. Have some almond milk, flavoured with the right amount of sugar, no more or less than what is used for almond broth. Put it on the flame and bring to a boil while constantly stirring with one hand with a big spoon. When the almond broth has boiled, add the minced borage and let it come to a boil twice. Then, have a small amount of sops made with toasted bread and on top of them some fresh eggs, poached. Then ladle the borage in its almond milk on top. Take a little bit of butter and place on top. These are very good sops and can be given to those who are ill.

Another way [of making] borage

Boil borage, mince it, and thoroughly squeeze it out. Put it in the mortar and mash it a little with a little bit of breadcrumbs, a little ground sugar, a bit of spices, pepper, cinnamon, and some raw egg yolks. With all this on the cutting board, make tortillas, each one the size of the ace of gold coins and fairly thin. Then have a frying pan with just a little butter, coat the borage tortillas in egg yolk, and fry them until they are browned. Serve them on little pieces of torrijas, with the right amount of cinnamon and sugar and lemon juice. With this boiled and minced borage, you can also make puffs by adding a little bit of breadcrumbs and the right amount of eggs. They are tasty and cheap. You can also mince the boiled borage, mix it with eggs and breadcrumbs, season with salt [and] a little bit of spices, and make a tortilla. If you want to add sweetener, you can.

How to prepare some fish

I'm going to address fish, although I don't plan on detaining myself for too long on this, because fish, when it comes to boils or fries, which are the two most common modes [of preparation], are almost all prepared the same way. One thing about fresh fish, they shouldn't be boiled in a lot of water, rather just a little, as for stews, because in a lot of water they lose their flavour.

[252] *Cómo se adereza el Sollo.*

Quiero empezar por un sollo, que es el pescado que tiene mucha apariencia con la carne, más que otro ninguno. A este sollo cortarás la cabeza, y sazonarás un cocimiento de agua y sal, y vino, y vinagre, y échale buena manteca de vacas fresca, y échale de todas especias y cantidad de jengibre, y de las hierbas del jardín, mejorana, e hisopillo, y un poco de hinojo, y un poco de orégano: y con todo esto la cocerás y mojarás una sopa con el mismo caldo, y sírvela sobre ella, como cabeza de ternera, (166r) y servirás oruga con ella, porque es su salsa.[298] Adelante diré cómo se ha de hacer la oruga: y si hubieres de cocer algún pedazo del sollo, ha de ser el cocimiento como el de la cabeza. Este sollo tiene cinco hileras de conchas.[299] Antes que se parta es necesario quitar todas estas conchas. Puédeslas cocer en un cocimiento como el de la cabeza: y también las puedes hacer un platillo, friendo cebolla con buena manteca de vacas, y ahogar allí las conchas, y luego echarle un poco de vino, y un poquito de vinagre, y sazonar con todas especias, y majar un poco de verdura, y hacerle una salsa como carnero verde. Son muy buenos platillos. Las huevas del sollo se han de perdigar un poco, y luego echarlas en adobo de ajos, y orégano, y vinagre, y agua, y sal: luego sacarlos del adobo y enharinarlas, y freírlas, y sírvelas con unos picatostes, y pimienta, y naranja: y si hallares criadillas de tierra fríelas también, y sírvelas revueltas con las huevas, (166v) y sus picatostes, y naranja, y pimienta, que es muy buen plato. Ahora podrás hacer del sollo de la manera que si fuera carne de pierna de ternera: y en esto no había para qué detenerme, pues está dicho en la carne; con todo eso diré dos o tres platos: Cortarás el sollo en ruedas, y de ahí se irá haciendo la diferencia de los platos.

[253] *Sollo asado.*

El sollo de ninguna manera es tan bueno como asado, y echarás las ruedas del sollo en adobo, y harás este adobo desta manera: Tomarás orégano, y sal, y ajos, y majarlo has todo junto: luego desatarlo has con vinagre, y échalo en una olla de barro, de manera que esté bien cubierto, y échale vino blanco que sepa bien a ello, y unos clavos enteros, y no eches otra especia ninguna, y pruébalo de sal, y que esté un poco agrio, y mete el sollo en ruedas en el adobo, y échale un poco de aceite encima (167r) que sea buena. Este sollo se ha de asar en las parrillas, untándolo con aceite y adobo, o con manteca fresca y si quisieres hacer gigote dél, podrás hacer un

---

298 Martínez Montiño provides two recipes for *oruga* [arugula sauce], one made with honey and another with sugar. He also clearly states that the sauce made with sugar is more elite than the one made with honey (518; 519).
299 Sturgeon are covered with dermal denticles instead of scales. The bodies are sectioned into five bony plates. When Martínez Montiño describes *cinco hileras de conchas*, he is referring to these plates.

How to prepare sturgeon

I want to begin with sturgeon because it's the fish, more than any other, that most resembles meat. With sturgeon, cut off the head. Prepare a boil of salted water, wine, and vinegar and add in some good butter, all spices, a lot of ginger, and garden herbs: marjoram, winter savory, a little fennel, and a little oregano. Boil the head in this; soak the sops with this same stock, and serve it on them, like veal head. Serve arugula sauce with it, as it is its sauce. Later on, I will explain how to make arugula sauce. If you were to boil a piece of sturgeon, it should be the same boil [recipe] as for the head. Sturgeon has five rows of bony plates. Before parting, it is necessary to remove these plates. You can boil them in the boil like the one for the head. You can also make a dish by frying some onion in good butter and sautéing the plates. Then add a little wine and vinegar, season with all spices, mash some green herbs, and make a sauce like the [one for] green mutton stew. They are very tasty dishes. Sturgeon roe should be quickly parboiled and then marinated in garlic, oregano, vinegar, and salted water. Next, remove it from the marinade, dredge it in flour, and fry it. Serve it with slices of fried bread, pepper, and orange. If you can find truffles, fry them too and serve them tossed together with the roe and its slices of fried bread, pepper, and orange. It makes a very tasty dish. Now you can prepare the sturgeon as if it were meat from a veal shank. There's no reason to detain myself with this, as it is explained in the meat [section], but with all that I will explain two or three dishes. Cut the sturgeon in steaks and from there you can make the different dishes.

Grilled sturgeon

There is no better way to prepare sturgeon than grilled. Put the sturgeon steaks in marinade. Make the marinade this way: Take oregano, salt, and garlic, and grind it all together. Then thin it with vinegar and put it in a terracotta pot so that it is totally covered. Add some white wine so that it takes on its flavour, some whole cloves, and no other spices at all. Taste for salt and make sure it's a little sour. Add the sturgeon steaks to the marinade and pour some good oil on top. This sturgeon should be grilled on the grill, greasing it with oil and marinade or with butter. If you want to make minced sturgeon, you can make it as white as minced squab. Put

gigote tan blanco como de capón, y pondrás en el plato unas rebanadillas de pan muy delgadas, y asentarás allí una rueda del sollo, y al lado le echarás otra pieza picada en gigote que no sea muy menudo, y échale por encima un poco del adobo, y un poco de zumo de limón. Si no lo hubieres de servir en gigote tomarás unos panecillos hendidos por medio, y fríelos en manteca, y sirve el sollo entre ellos como torreznos con sus limones al lado, y pimienta y sal por los bordes del plato.

[254] *Albondiguillas del Sollo.*

Picarás la carne del sollo muy bien, así cruda como está; luego le meterás huevos, y un poquito de pan rallado: sazonarás con pimienta y jengibre, y nuez: y tendrás caldo de garbanzos, sazonado con buena manteca de vacas, (167v) y harás tus albondiguillas, y échale un poquito de verdura picada: luego cuajarás con cuatro yemas de huevos, batidas con un poco de vinagre. Sírvelas sobre rebanadillas de pan.

[255] *Pastel de Sollo.*

Picarás la carne del sollo cruda: luego tendrás un poco de manteca de vacas en una cazuela al fuego, y echarás dentro la carne picada, y revolverla has con un cucharón hasta que se perdigue, y quede muy granujada: luego sácala del fuego, y sazona con todas especias y sal, y déjalo enfriar: luego harás tu pastel, y cerrarlo has ni más ni menos que de carne: y cuando esté cocido cebarlo has con caldo de garbanzos, y yemas de huevos batidos, y zumo de limón, y vendrá a salir un pastel que parecerá de pechuga de capón. Y advierte, que en estos pasteles de pescados dicen bien pasas de Corintio, y algunas veces piñones.

[256] (168r) *Un pastel embote de Sollo.*[300]

Picarás el sollo, y perdigarlo has en la cazuela, como está dicho para el pastel, salvo que has de freír primero un poco de cebolla muy menuda en la manteca: y luego perdigar la carne que quede muy granujada: sazona de todas especias y sal, y échale un poquito de verdura picada, y un poco de agua caliente cuanto se bañe, y cueza un poco, y cuájalo con unas yemas de huevos batidas con un poco de zumo de limón, y sírvelo sobre rebanadillas de pan, y asarás un poco del sollo, y haráslo rebanadas, y adornarás el pastel embote con él, y otras veces con torrijas, y yemas de huevos duras.

---

300 For more information on *un pastel embote* [a crustless pie], see 178n60.

on the plate some very thin slices of bread and set the sturgeon steak there. Next to it put another piece minced, but not too finely, and ladle on top a little of the marinade and a little lemon juice. If you don't serve any minced, take some rolls slit in half, fry them in lard, and serve the sturgeon between them, as you would with roasted pork belly, with lemons next to it. Sprinkle salt and pepper around the edge of the dish.

Sturgeon balls

Finely mince some raw sturgeon, just as it is. Then add some eggs and a little bit of breadcrumbs. Season with pepper, ginger, and nutmeg. Have some garbanzo broth seasoned with good butter and make little balls. Add in some minced green herbs and thicken them with four egg yolks beaten with a little vinegar. Serve them on slices of bread.

Sturgeon pie

Mince some raw sturgeon. Then have a little butter in a casserole on the flame and add the minced meat. Stir with a big spoon until it is seared and is very shredded. Then remove it from the flame, season with all spices and salt, and let cool. Then make your pie and close it up with the meat, nothing more or less. When it's baked, enrich it with garbanzo broth, whipped egg yolk, and lemon juice. The pie will turn out looking like a breast of squab [pie]. Note that in these fish pies dried currants and sometimes pine nuts go well.

Crustless sturgeon pie

Mince the sturgeon and sear it in a casserole as explained for the pie, except that you should first fry a little minced onion in lard. Then sear the meat until it's shredded, season with all spices and salt, and add in a little chopped green herbs and enough hot water to braise. Let boil a little and let it set with whipped egg yolks and a little lemon juice. Serve over slices of bread. Grill a little of the sturgeon and cut it into slices. Adorn the crustless pie with it and other times with torrijas and hard-boiled egg yolks.

[257] *Una costrada de Sollo.*[301]

Picarás la carne, y perdigarla has con buena manteca, como está dicho en los pasteles, y sacarla has en una pieza que se enfríe, y sazonarás con todas especias, (168v) y canela, y un poco de zumo de limón, y un cuarterón de azúcar molido, y échale cuatro huevos crudos muy bien batidos, y harás una masa fina, que tenga un poco de azúcar, y harás tu costrada, echando tres, o cuatro hojas debajo muy delgadas, untando primero la tortera: luego echarás el batido del pescado, y cerrarás la costrada con otras dos hojas, y úntalo con manteca, y cuécelo a fuego manso. Suele ser tan buena como la carne.

[258] *Una empanada Inglesa de Sollo.*

Picarás el pescado así crudo, y después de muy bien picado meterle has huevos crudos hasta cuatro, y sazonarás con todas especias, y un poco de agrio, y sal, y echarle has un poco de manteca de vacas: y después de mezclado todo esto, harás una masa con dos libras de harina, y tres cuarterones de azúcar molido, y cernido, y un cuarterón de manteca (169v) de vacas antes más que menos, y ocho yemas de huevos, y un poco de sal, y amásala con un poco de vino: y con esta masa harás tu empanada Inglesa, y untarla has con manteca, y échale un poco de azúcar por encima: y después de cocida abrirla has por lo alto, y cebarla has con un poco de caldo de garbanzos, y cuatro yemas de huevos batidos, y agrio de limón.

[259] *Empanada de Sollo.*

Tomarás un pedazo de sollo, y perdigarlo has un poquito en las parrillas, y échalo en adobo de vino y vinagre, y sal, y un poquito de hinojo, y estése en él dos horas: luego empánalo en masa blanca, sazonando de pimienta y sal, y un poco de manteca de vacas. Estas empanadas suelen salir un poco secas, porque el pescado no tiene mucha grasa, que por mejores tengo las empanadas de atún fresco, que éstas si ellas se hubiesen de comer en día de carne, (169v) mechándolas con tocino son muy buenas: y si se matara el atún en el tiempo que muere el sollo, mechándolas con el gordo del atún, también son muy buenas.

---

301 Juan de Altamiras also includes this recipe in his cookbook, *Nuevo arte de cocina*. While the ingredients are the same, Altamiras' recipe is a crustless dish (92). In another, "Costrada de carne, y huevos" [Meat and egg *costrada*], Altamiras specifies that the "costra" or crusty finish comes from the eggs whipped with cinnamon and sugar that are poured over the dish before baking (53). In her edition of Altamiras' cookbook, Vicky Hayward discussed the evolution of the costrada (*New Art of Cookery* 18–19). For more information, see 224n128.

A sturgeon puff pastry pie

Mince the meat and sear it with good lard as explained for the pies. Put it all in a bowl and let it cool. Season with all spices, cinnamon, a little lemon juice, and a quarter pound of ground sugar. Add in four raw eggs that are thoroughly whipped. Make a fine dough with just a little sugar. Make the crust by placing three or four very thin [pastry] sheets on the bottom. First grease the covered tart pan. Then add the fish mixture and close up the puff pastry pie with two more sheets. Grease with lard and bake it on a low flame. It normally turns out as good as the meat one.

English empanada with sturgeon

Mince raw sturgeon, and once it's finely minced, add up to four raw eggs and season with all spices, a little sour juice, and salt. Add in a little butter. After it's all mixed, make a dough with two pounds of flour, three quarters of a pound of sifted ground sugar, a quarter pound of butter, better more than less, eight egg yolks, and a little salt. Knead it with a little wine. With this dough make the English empanada, grease with lard, and add a little sugar on top. After it has baked, open the top up and enrich it with a little garbanzo broth, four whipped egg yolks, and some lemon juice.

Sturgeon empanada

Take a piece of sturgeon, quickly sear it on the grill, and place it in a marinade of wine, vinegar, salt, and a little fennel. Let it rest two hours. Then wrap it in white dough, seasoning it with salt, pepper, and a little butter. These empanadas usually turn out a little dry because the fish doesn't have much fat. Better are the empanadas made with fresh tuna. These, if they are eaten on a meat day and you can lard them with fatback, are very tasty. If tuna is caught when you've caught sturgeon and you lard it [sturgeon] with tuna fat, it is also very tasty.

[260] *Artaletes del Sollo.*

Picarás un pedazo de carne de sollo, luego freirás un poco de cebolla en manteca, cortada a lo largo, y échale el pescado picado encima, y perdígalo en la sartén, y échale un poco de hierbabuena: luego batirás media docena de huevos, y échaselos dentro, y revuélvelos sobre la lumbre con la paleta hasta que esté bien seco, y sácalo al tablero, y pícalo muy bien, y échale otros tres, o cuatro huevos crudos, y sazona con todas especias y zumo de limón: luego tomarás otro pedazo de sollo, y harás rebanadillas delgadas, y batirlos has con la vuelta del cuchillo, como chulletas de pechos de gallinas, y rellenarlas has con el relleno que está hecho, y meterlas has (170r) en sus broquetas de cuatro en cuatro, y asiéntalos en una tortera, untándola primero con manteca de vacas: y después de cocidos, sírvelos sobre una sopa dulce. En este plato no ha de entrar aceite, todo ha de ser con buena manteca. Y advierte, que no se dice más deste pescado por excusar prolijidad, porque se puede hacer dél todas las cosas que se pueden hacer de carne, como son pasteles calientes de salsa negra, y empanadillas dulces, y otros rellenos en las torteras, también con salsas negras, y con salsas de membrillos: y esto se entiende con la aguja paladar, y otros pescados grandes que no tienen espinas en la carne, y no tienen humo, que los que tienen humo como es el congrio, y la merluza, y el cazón.[302] De todos estos no se pueden hacer estos platos que están dichos del sollo, sino asados y fritos, y estofados, y empanados: estos son sus aderezos, y en cazuela son muy buenos: y por esto no pienso decir mucho de los pescados. El (170v) sollo hecho pedazos, y en pastel con buena manteca es bueno.

[261] *Aguja Paladar.*[303]

Este pescado se parece algo al sollo, mas no es tan bueno, que es más blando, podrás hacer dél lo mismo que está dicho del sollo; aunque como digo es pescado blando, y también salen las empanadas un poco secas; de ninguna manera es tan buena como asada, y también es buena en cazuela: y no se puede tener en adobo tanto como el sollo.

[262] *Cómo se aderezan las Truchas.*

Las truchas es el pescado del río más regalado, y lo más ordinario es comerlas cocidas: y si ellas estuviesen acabadas de matar, no es menester para cocerse más

---

[302] Martínez Montiño's description of fish with or without odour refers to the smell of the fish, which is related to levels of uric acid in the fish. He uses this same description for dill in the recipe "Sopas a la Portuguesa" [Sops, Portuguese style] (472; 473).

[303] *Aguja paladar* is another name for *swordfish*, though it is not used today. In Spanish, swordfish is also called *pez espada* or *emperador*.

Sturgeon pinwheels

Chop up a piece of sturgeon. Fry it with a little onion, cut lengthwise, in lard. Place the chopped-up fish on top and sear it in the frying pan. Add in a little spearmint. Next, beat half a dozen eggs and add them. Stir over the flame with a spatula until [the eggs] are well cooked. Turn it onto the cutting board, mince it, and add three or four raw eggs. Season with all spices and lemon juice. Then, take another piece of sturgeon and slice it very thin. Pound them [the slices] with the back of the knife, as for hen breast cutlets, and fill them with the filling that is made. Put them on a skewer four at a time and set them in the covered tart pan, first greasing it with butter. After they've cooked, serve them on sweet sops. This dish shouldn't have any oil; it should all be made with good butter. Note that nothing more is explained about this fish to avoid lengthiness, because, with sturgeon, you can do anything that you can do with meat, such as hot pies with black sauce, sweet turnovers or other fillings in covered tart pans also with black sauces or quince sauces. This is also understood for swordfish and other big fish that don't have bones in their flesh and don't have an odour, rather than fish that have odour, like conger eel, hake, or dogfish. With all these fish you can't make the dishes explained for sturgeon, only those grilled or fried, stewed or wrapped. That is the way you can prepare them. In casseroles they are also very tasty. For this reason, I don't plan on saying much about fish. Sturgeon, cut into pieces and made into a pie with good butter, is tasty.

Swordfish

This fish is similar to sturgeon, but it's not as good and it's softer. You can prepare it the same way as is explained for sturgeon, even though, as I've said, it's a soft fish. Also, the empanadas turn out a little dry. In no other way is it as good as grilled and it is also good stewed. It should not marinate as long as sturgeon.

How to prepare trout

Trout is the most exquisite river fish, and the most common way to eat it is boiled. If they are recently caught, it is not necessary to boil them in anything but salted

de agua y sal, y unas ramas de perejil, y no más agua de cuanto se cubran: y si después de cocidas las quisieres echar algún acedo por encima podrás, (171r) y del caldo de las trucas se pueden hacer sopas. Y si las cocieres en caldo de carne, serán mejores.

[263] *Otro cocimiento de Truchas.*

Tomarás agua y sal, y vinagre, y ramas de perejil, y cuando cociere echa las truchas dentro, y al servir, échales más vinagre por encima y pimienta, y ramas de perejil.

[264] *Otro.*

Escamarás las truchas, y partirlas has por medio, hendidas de arriba abajo, que se hienda también la cabeza, y harásla pedazos, y ponla en una pieza, y échale allí vinagre que se cubra, y échale vino: luego pondrás agua al fuego con mucha sal, y un poco de cebolla; y cuando esté cociendo echa las truchas dentro con el vinagre, y el vino, y ponle una cobertera encima del cazo. Éstas se suelen servir entre unos dobleces de servilleta a uso de Alemania,[304] mas los señores de (171v) España no las quieren sino enteras, un poco más moderado el cocimiento de sal, y vinagre. Para este plato han de ser las truchas grandes.

[265] *Truchas estofadas.*

Tomarás las truchas lavadas y escamadas, y partirlas has como está dicho, y asiéntalas en una cazuela, o cazo, y échale allí vino, y vinagre, y pimienta, y jengibre, y nuez, y una cebolla entera, y un manojito de hierbas, mejorana, y hierbabuena, y

---

304 In this recipe Martínez Montiño shows his knowledge of another international kitchen when he explains how Germans prepare and serve the dish. Archaeologist and historian Andreas Klumpp has kindly shared with me several early modern German recipes that include similar cooking and serving procedures. In "Saelbling haiß abzusieden" [To hotly seeth charr], the fish is cooked in salted water, quenched in a wine vinegar broth, and placed on a table napkin before serving (*Ein Koch- und Artzney-Buch* [Graz, 1686], 110). In "Die Ferchen schoen blau abzusieden in dir Sultzen" [To poach trout finely blue in aspic], the trout is prepared in a similar manner but once cooked is covered with a thick cloth so that the steam is not released (*Ein Koch- und Artzney-Buch* 110–11). Klumpp also stated that many similar recipes are found in German culinary history, from medieval manuscripts through to the twentieth century. Regarding Martínez Montiño's access to knowledge of German cooking techniques, Thomas Gloning theorizes that it may very well have come from personal exchanges with other cooks. As there were also several courtiers of Germanic descent at the Spanish court, they could have provided background knowledge of German fish preparation. Martínez Montiño may have exchanged ideas with other cooks and colleagues who ate in the kitchens and thus learned about different preparation and presentation styles from different sources.

water with a few sprigs of parsley and only enough water to cover them. If after they are cooked you want to drizzle some sorrel juice on top, you can. With the trout stock you can make sops. If you want to boil them in meat stock, they will be even better.

Another trout boil

Take salted water with vinegar and sprigs of parsley and when it is boiling, put the trout in. When serving, drizzle more vinegar on top with pepper and parsley sprigs.

Another

Scale the trout and split it in half, slit from end to end, splitting the head too. Cut into pieces and place it in a bowl. Pour in vinegar, enough to cover, and add wine. Then, put on the fire some water with a lot of salt and a little bit of onion. When it's boiling, add the trout with the vinegar and wine and put a lid on the pan. These are normally served between folds of a napkin, German style, but lords from Spain only like them whole and with a more moderate salt and vinegar boil. For this dish it should be big trout.

Trout stew

Take washed and scaled trout and split them as already explained. Set them in a casserole or pan and add wine, vinegar, pepper, ginger, nutmeg, a whole onion, a handful of herbs – marjoram and spearmint – a slab of butter for melting or salted

un pedazo de manteca de vacas fresca por derretir, o manteca salada de Flandes,[305] y sazona de sal, y echa agua cuanto se bañen no más, y ponlo al fuego con su cobertera, y estófese allí, y tostarás rebanadas de pan, y sírvelas sobre ellas, que vaya bien bañado de caldo. Y advierte, que los más de los pescados, o todos son buenos desta manera: y así si dijere de algún pescado estofado, se entiende, que ha de ser desta (172r) manera. A estos pescados estofados se les suelen echar algunas veces peras, o membrillos, y algunas pasas de Corinto.

[266] *Sopa de Truchas.*

Tomarás una trucha que sea grande, y harásla pedazos hendida por medio, y freírla has con tocino, si fuere día de carne, y si no con manteca de vacas: luego tomarás vino tinto en una sartén, y un poco de agua, y un poco de vinagre, y échale azúcar que esté bien dulce, y sazona con todas especias y canela, y un poco de sal: y pondrás a cocer esta pebrada hasta que comience a tomar punto con el azúcar, y echa las truchas dentro: luego harás una sopa con pan tostado, y asienta las truchas encima, y échales la salsa que se moje bien la sopa, y échale un poco de manteca fresca por encima, o un poco de grasa de tocino, y déjalas estofar un poco, y sírvelas calientes.

[267] (172v) *Cazuela de Truchas.*

Freirás las truchas en buen aceite: luego picarás de todas verduras, perejil, y hierbabuena, y cilantro verde: y majarás esta verdura en el almirez tan molida, como para hacer salsa de perejil:[306] luego echarle has un poco de pan remojado en agua fría, y májalo todo, y sazona con todas especias y canela: luego desátalo con un poco de vinagre y agua, y échale dulce de buena miel, o azúcar, de manera que esté agridulce, y ponlo al fuego, y trayéndolo a una mano, hasta que cueza, y échale un poco de cebolla frita muy menuda en buen aceite: luego asienta las truchas en una cazuela, y échales la salsa por encima, y cuezan un poco con la salsa, y sírvela caliente.

[268] *Platillo de Truchas, y Berzas.*

Tomarás una trucha que sea grande, y escamarla has, y henderla has por (173r) medio de cabo a cabo, y harás pedazos della, y freírlos has con tocino magro y

---

305 This specialty item, salted butter from Flanders, is noted in several early modern plays and, even as late as 1840, is cited as a superior product. For more, see Boy 22.

306 The ingredients for this parsley sauce – spearmint, pepper, and a little oil – are included in the recipe "Cómo se puede freír, y asar, y cocer un pescado todo en un tiempo, sin partirlo" [How to fry, roast, and boil a fish at the same time without cutting it up] (414–16; 415–17).

butter from Flanders. Season with salt and add in enough water to braise, no more. Put it on the flame with its cover on and let stew. Toast slices of bread and serve them on them, they'll be good soaked in broth. Note that all other fish are good to prepare this way, so if some fish stew were mentioned, it is understood that it be made this way. Sometimes it is normal to add pears, quince, or dried currants to these fish stews.

Trout sops

Take a trout, it should be big, cut it into pieces split down the middle, and fry it in fatback on a meat day or, if not, in butter. Then put red wine in a frying pan, with a little water and a little vinegar. Add sugar so that it gets very sweet and season with all spices, cinnamon, and a little salt. Put this pepper sauce on to boil until the sugar begins to thicken and add the trout to it. Then make sops with toasted bread and place the trout on top. Pour the sauce on so that the sops are well soaked. Add a little butter on top or a little fat from fatback and let stew a little. Serve them hot.

Trout casserole

Fry trout in good oil. Then, chop all green herbs: parsley, spearmint, and cilantro. Finely grind the green herbs together in a mortar, as if you were making parsley sauce. Next, add a little bread soaked in cold water and grind everything up. Season with all spices and cinnamon. Then thin it with a little vinegar and water. Add sweetener, either good honey or sugar, so that it's sweet and sour. Put it on the fire and stir with one hand until it comes to a boil. Add in a little minced onion, fried in good oil. Then, set the trout in a casserole and pour the sauce on top. Let it simmer a while with the sauce and serve hot.

A dish of trout and collard greens

Take trout, make sure it's big, scale it, slit it down the middle from end to end, and cut it into pieces. Fry them in meaty and fatty fatback. Next, take the hearts

gordo: y luego tendrás cogollos de berzas que estén blancos, y han de ser cocidos con su sazón: y en acabando de freír la trucha, freirás picatostes de pan blanco: luego echarás los cogollos de berzas en la sartén, y freírlos de manera que no se sequen, y sácalos: luego irás armando tu plato: pondrás un lecho de picatostes, luego otro de cogollos de berzas, y pedazos de truchas, e irás echando pimienta y naranja, y entremetiendo picatostes y tocino magro entre medias de las berzas, y truchas. Sirve este plato caliente. Es plato de mucho gusto. Si quisieres hacer este plato en día de pescado, lo que se había de hacer con tocino, harás con buena manteca fresca.

[269] *Pastelón de Truchas.*

Estas truchas grandes son buenas hechas pedazos, empanadas con rebanadillas (173v) de tocino magro en un pastelón: y después que esté cocido hacer una salsa negra, y echársela dentro: y si no quisieres hacer la salsa negra, harás una pebrada, y será lo mismo:[307] y si fuere en día de pescado, en lugar del tocino sea un poco de buena manteca fresca de vacas, y cueza con la salsa un poquito, y sírvela caliente. Estas truchas grandes, también son buenas hechas pedazos, y echados en adobo de sollo, y asadas en las parrillas, y servirlas con pimienta y naranja, y un poquito de adobo.

[270] *Cómo se adereza el Atún.*

El atún fresco es muy buen pescado, y lo mejor es tomar las ijadas y echarlas en adobo de sollo, y asarlas en las parrillas. Es un pescado muy regalado, sirviéndolo con su naranja y pimienta, y un poco de adobo: y tomando de la otra parte magra del atún en pedazos mezclados con pedazos de la ijada, y (174r) empanarles con salpimienta son muy buenas empanadas. Este pescado fresco es muy bueno en cazuela, haciendo pedazos dél, y ahogar un poco de cebolla con buen aceite, y echar allí del atún los pedazos que te pareciere que son menester, y ahógalos muy bien, y sazona con todas especias y sal, y échales un poco de agua caliente cuanto se bañen, y échale un poco de verdura picada, y su agrio, y déjalo cocer un poco tapada la cazuela, que sea medio estofado. Este pescado, aunque después de salado tiene un rancio, que algunas personas no lo comen de buena gana, cuando está fresco acabado de sacar del agua tiene muy buen gusto, y se pueden hacer muchas cosas dél, como son pasteles y costradas, pastelones de salsa negra: y esto se ha de mezclar atún de la ijada con lo demás, porque fuera de las ijadas no tiene género de gordura.

---

307 Instructions on how to make *salsa negra* are found in "Empanadas frías de jabalí' [Cold boar empanadas] and "Empanadas de jabalí calientes" [Warm boar empanadas] (290–2; 291–3); for *pebrada* sauce, see "Gigote de Liebres" [Minced hare] (154; 155, 212; 213).

of collard greens, they should be white, and boil them with their seasoning. Once the trout is fried, fry some pieces of white bread. Then add the collard green hearts to the frying pan and fry them, but don't let them get dry. Remove them. Begin arranging your plate. Make a layer of slices of fried bread, then another of collard green hearts and pieces of trout. Continue by sprinkling pepper and orange and placing slices of fried bread and meaty fatback between the collard greens and trout. Serve this dish hot. This is a very tasty dish. If you are going to make this dish on a fish day, when you were going to use fatback, use good, fresh butter.

Big trout pie

These big trout are good cut into pieces and wrapped with slices of meaty fatback in a big pie shell. After it's baked, make a black sauce and add it inside. If you don't want to make black sauce, make a pepper sauce and it will work. If it is a fish day, instead of fatback, use some good, fresh butter, cook the sauce a little, and serve hot. These big trout are also good cut into pieces, marinated in the sturgeon marinade, and grilled on the grill. Serve them with pepper and orange and a little of the marinade.

How to prepare tuna

Fresh tuna is very good fish. The best is to take tuna belly, marinate it in the sturgeon marinade, and grill it on the grill. It is an exquisite fish; serve it with the right amount of orange and pepper and a little marinade. From the lean part of the tuna, cut pieces and mix them with pieces from the belly. Wrap them in dough with salt and pepper and they are very good empanadas. This fresh fish is very tasty as a stew. Cut it into pieces, sauté a little onion in good oil, add in as many tuna pieces as you think necessary, thoroughly sauté them, and season with all spices and salt. Add a little hot water, enough to braise, and a little chopped green herb and the right amount of sour juice. Let simmer, partially covered, until it is braised. This fish, when salted, can take on a rancid odour and some people don't enjoy eating it. When it is fresh, just caught from the sea, it is very tasty, and you can do many things with it such as pies, puff pastry pies, or big pies with black sauce. For these you have to mix fish belly with other parts, because apart from the belly, there is no fat at all.

[271] *Costrada de Atún.*[308]

(174v) Para hacer una costrada picarás de la carne magra del atún, y echarle has un poco de la hijada en lugar de tocino, en la cantidad que te pareciere, y picándolo todo junto muy bien: tomarás un poquito de manteca de vacas en un cacito, o en una cazuela, y cuando esté caliente echarás allí el pescado picado, y perdigarse ha de manera que quede muy granujado, como si fuera carne, y sazona con todas especias y canela, y zumo de limón, y échale unas pasas de Corintio, y échale cuatro o seis onzas de azúcar, y métele unos huevos crudos, cosa de cuatro, y harás tu costrada con tres, o cuatro hojas debajo, y dos encima, y úntalo con manteca, y azúcar raspado por encima, y cuécela, y sírvela caliente. Y entiéndese, que ha de ir sazonada de sal.

[272] *Pastelón de Atún.*

Para hacer un pastelón de atún con salsa negra,[309] has de perdigar el atún (175r) en las parrillas, o freírlo un poco con buena manteca de vacas, porque salga el atún un poco moreno, y hacer tu pastelón de masa blanca: y en estando cocida la masa harás la salsa negra como está dicho en los pastelones del jabalí. Y advierte, que si la quisieres hacer de ciruelas, es muy buena. Para pescados has de tomar ciruelas pasas, y cocerlas muy bien, y luego pasarlas por una estameña, y servirán de harina quemada, y darán muy buen gusto de agrio: luego sazonarás (como está dicho) de todas especias y azúcar, y ha de venir a quedar la salsa bien agridulce. Si quisieres hacer plato con esta salsa de ciruelas, picarás el pescado crudo con sus verduras, y sazonarás con todas especias, y meterle has huevos, y armarás unos albondigones grandes y largos, o unos roscones, o como te pareciere, en unas torteras untadas con manteca de vacas, y pondráslas a cocer con lumbre abajo y arriba: y cuando estén cocidas échales la salsa de (175v) las ciruelas, y sírvelas sobre rebanadas de pan tostado, y échales la salsa por encima: y esta salsa ha de llevar un poco de vino.

---

308 Juan de Altamiras includes his version of this recipe in his cookbook with a couple of slight modifications. Altamiras concedes that if butter is not available, oil will do, because "los pobres nos componemos con lo más barato" [we poor get by with the cheapest (things)] (93). The only other significant change is the addition of "un baño de huevos deshechos por encima" [an egg bath across the top], which would have the effect of a baked egg crust on top. Once again, although *costrada* is mentioned in Altamiras, there is no reference to any crust made from dough.

309 Instructions on how to make *salsa negra* are found in "Empanadas frías de jabalí" [Cold boar empanadas] and "Empanadas de jabalí calientes" [Warm boar empanadas] (290–2; 291–3).

Tuna puff pastry pie

To make the puff pastry pie, chop up lean tuna meat, add in some of the belly instead of fatback, however much you think necessary, and mince it all together. Take a little butter in a small saucepan or a casserole and when it's hot, add the minced fish, sear it so that it stays shredded, just like meat, and season with all spices, cinnamon, and lemon juice. Add dried currants, four to six ounces of sugar, and some raw eggs, about four. Make the puff pastry crust with three or four sheets on the bottom and two on top. Grease with lard and sprinkle grated sugar on top, bake it, and serve hot. It's understood that it should be seasoned with salt.

Big tuna pie

To make a big tuna pie with black sauce, sear the tuna on the grill or fry it in a little butter so that the tuna is a little browned. Make your crust with white dough. Once it's baked, make the black sauce as explained in the boar pie [recipe]. Note that if you want to make it with prunes, it is very tasty. For fish, take prunes, boil them well, and then run them through a cheesecloth. They will serve as [a substitute for] toasted flour and will give a good sweet and sour flavour. Then season (as explained above) with all spices and sugar. The sauce will turn out with a strong sweet and sour flavour. If you want to make a dish with this prune sauce, chop up the raw tuna with its green herbs, season with all spices, and add eggs. Assemble big, long balls or rings, or whatever you like, in a covered tart pan greased with butter. Bake it with heat above and below and when it's baked, ladle on the prune sauce. Serve over slices of toasted bread and ladle sauce on top. This sauce should have a little wine in it.

[273] *Salpicón de Atún.*

Este atún después de salado es muy bueno si es de ijada y gordo, cocido, y hacer unas rebanadas de lo más gordo, y de lo más magro hacer un salpicón con su cebolla, y pondrás las rebanadas gordas por las orillas del plato, y el salpicón en medio: luego otras rebanadas por encima, y ruedas de cebolla, y luego echarles aceite y vinagre por encima de todo.

[274] *Atún lampreado.*[310]

Este atún es bueno lampreado: cocerás el atún, y luego lo freirás un poco con manteca de vacas, y tomará un colorcito negro, y tendrás hecha la salsa negra con harina quemada, como se hace para los pastelones de carne,[311] y sazonarás (176r) con vino y vinagre, y con dulce, y de todas especias y canela: luego echarle has el atún dentro, y un manojito de salvia y mejorana, y mondarás unas almendras, y tostarlas has, y echárselas has dentro.

[275] *Olla de Atún.*

Este atún después de salado es muy bueno para hacer una olla que tenga el gusto de la olla podrida de carne. Cocerás el atún, y luego freírlo has un poco a pedazos grandes, y tendrás caldo de garbanzos, y echarle has cogollos de berzas que estén bien perdigadas, y de todas las verduras, y sazonarás con todas especias y alcaravea, y freirás un poquito de harina que quede muy blanca, y échasela dentro, y sírvelo sobre una sopa blanca, y servirás salsa de oruga con ella.

[276] *Escabeche de Atún.*

Este atún fresco en escabeche lo podrás hacer lonjas de dos libras, y sazonar (176v) de sal, y asarlo has, y déjalo enfriar: y puedes hacer escabeche con su vino, y vinagre, y especias, y un poco de hinojo, y asienta el atún en el barril, y cébalo con escabeche, y tápalo: y desta manera podrás hacer el sollo.

---

310 For more on the meaning of *lampreado*, see the note in the recipe "Nabos lampreados" [Turnips, Lamprea style] (372n285).

311 Instructions on how to make *salsa negra* are found in "Empanadas frías de jabalí" [Cold boar empanadas] and "Empanadas de jabalí calientes" [Warm boar empanadas] (290–2; 291–3).

Tuna salpicon

Tuna belly fat, after it's salted, is very tasty boiled. Slice the fattiest part and with the meatiest part make the salpicon with the right amount of onion. Place the thick slices on the edges of the plate and the salpicon in the middle. Then more slices on top and onion rings. Then drizzle oil and vinegar on top of everything.

Tuna, lamprea style

Tuna made *lamprea* style is tasty. Boil the tuna, then fry it in a little butter and it will turn a dark colour. Have some black sauce made with toasted flour, as it is made for big meat pies. Season with wine and vinegar, sweetener, all spices, and cinnamon. Then add the tuna to this with a handful of sage and marjoram. Shell almonds, toast them, and add them too.

Tuna stew

After it's salted, this tuna is very good for making a stew that tastes like the hodge-podge stew made with meat. Boil the tuna, then quickly fry big pieces of it. Have some garbanzo broth and add to it hearts of collard greens that have been par-boiled and all green herbs. Season with all spices and caraway. Fry a little flour, but keep it white, and add it to the stew. Serve on white sops, and serve it with an arugula sauce.

Pickled tuna

You can pickle fresh tuna in two-pound slices. Season with salt, grill it, and let it cool. Make the pickling brine with the right amount of wine, vinegar, spices, and a little fennel. Set the tuna in a barrel, enrich it with the pickling brine, and cover it. You can do the same with sturgeon.

[277] *Cazuela de Lamprea.*

Ya se sabe que la lamprea en cazuela, o empanada, es lo mejor, y así tomarás la lamprea después de bien lavada, y quitada de la hiel,[312] que la tiene en la boca, y cortarla has en tarazones, y asiéntala en una cazuela, echando allí un poco de cebolla frita con buena manteca fresca, o un poco de buen aceite, y un poco de vino, y un poquito de vinagre, y sazona con todas especias y sal, y échale un poco de agua caliente cuanto se bañe, y cueza más de media hora: y no será menester otra cosa, que ella echará de sí una salsilla un poco espesa, porque la lamprea no ha menester más salsa, (177r) que la que echare de sí: el vino ha de ser tinto, si fuere posible. Si quisieres hacer esta cazuela dulce bien podrás, mas yo tengo por mejor que no lo lleve.

[278] *Empanada de Lamprea.*

Para empanar esta lamprea hasla de lavar muy bien, y ráspale los dientes, y abrirla, y quitarla todo lo que tiene dentro, y quitarle la hiel que está en la boca, y un nervio que tiene arrimado al lomo por la parte de dentro, y darla dos o tres cuchilladitas por el lomo, y arrollarla, y meterla en un vaso de masa negra, y echarla allí de todas especias, y su sazón de sal, y una gota de vino, y cerrar tu pastel, y ella misma hará su salsa. Esta lamprea se come fría, y se empana en masa negra, porque dure más días, porque si es para comer luego, bien se puede empanar en masa blanca.

[279] *Lamprea asada.*

(177v) La lamprea si es acabada de sacar del agua la puedes limpiar, y espetarla en un asador enroscada, y ponla a asar, y ponla debajo una pieza con un poco de agua y sal, y pimienta y nuez, y con lo que destilare de la lamprea, se hará una salsilla: y cuando la lamprea esté asada, sácala en el plato, y echa la salsa por encima, y agrio de limón, o naranja.

[280] *Lamprea en cecina.*

Las lampreas en cecina se han de echar en remojo, y las lavarás muy bien, y hacerlas pedazos, y freír un poco de cebolla con buena manteca de vacas, o buen aceite, y sazonar con todas especias, y una gota de vinagre, y un poco de vino tinto: luego quemarás un poco de harina, y desátala con agua, y échasela de manera que no sea más de cuanto se bañe, y cueza poco a poco cosa de media hora, o más, y sírvela

---

312 Martínez Montiño is referring to sulphated bile salts, which are produced and released by sexually mature males to attract ovulating females (Morii 83).

Lamprey stew

It is well known that lamprey as a stew or empanada is the best. As such, take lamprey after it's been washed very well and the bile removed, which is located in its mouth. Cut it into steaks and place them in a casserole, adding a little onion fried in good, fresh butter or some good oil, with a little wine and a little vinegar. Season with all spices and salt. Add in enough hot water to braise and cook for more than a half hour. Nothing else is necessary. It will produce its own sauce, somewhat thick, so lamprey doesn't need any other sauce except the one it makes itself. The wine should be red if possible. If you want to make this a sweet stew, you can easily do it, but I prefer it without sweetener.

Lamprey empanada

To wrap lamprey in dough, you must thoroughly wash it, scrape the teeth, open it, remove the insides, remove the bile salts that are in the mouth and the nerve that runs down the inside of the loin. Make two or three slices in the loin, roll it out, and put it in a dark dough crust. Add all spices, season with the right amount of salt and a drop of wine, and close up the pie. It will produce its own sauce. This lamprey is eaten cold and breaded with dark dough so that it lasts longer. If it's for eating right away, you can wrap it in white dough.

Roast lamprey

If it has just come from the water, you can clean lamprey and skewer it by wrapping it around the spit. Put it on to roast and place underneath it a bowl with salted water, pepper, and nutmeg. With this and whatever drippings there may be from the lamprey, make a sauce. When the lamprey is roasted, put it on a plate and ladle the sauce on top with some lemon or orange juice.

Cured lamprey

Set cured lamprey to soak, thoroughly wash it, and chop into pieces. Fry a little onion in good butter, or good oil, and season with all spices, a drop of vinegar, and a little red wine. Then, toast a little flour, thin it with water, and add just enough of this to braise. Let it simmer for about half an hour or a little more.

sobre rebanadas de pan tostadas. A estas lampreas les podrás echar azúcar (178r) alguna vez, añadiendo algún poco de más agrio para que sea agridulce; porque desta manera suele salir muy buena.

[281] *Jibia,*[313] *y Calamares, y Pulpo.*

Estos tres pescados hay, que casi tienen un natural, porque la jibia, y el calamar tienen una bolsa de una tinta muy negra: ésta es menester quitarla con mucho cuenta, porque no se rompa; porque aunque la laven en muchas aguas, nunca se le acabaría de quitar la tinta: y estos tres pescados después que se hayan limpiado muy bien en entrando en el agua a cocer, nunca más han de salir del agua caliente, porque se pondrían muy duros, y muy crudíos. Si quisiere hacer una cazuela, que es el mejor aderezo que tienen, en la misma agua caliente los has de limpiar, porque son muy blancos. Después de limpios para hacerlos en cazuela, freirás la cebolla en la misma cazuela, y sacarás el pescado del agua caliente, (178v) y echarlo has dentro en la cazuela, y ahógalo allí, y sazónalo con sus especias, y su verdura, y échale su agua caliente cuanto se bañe, y no le eches agrio hasta que lo quieras servir, porque son pescados que se encrudecen con mucha facilidad: y si los aderezan con cuidado son muy tiernos y muy blancos. El pulpo es un poco más duro: éste se suele azotar dando con él en una piedra, o golpeándolo con un palo: las cazuelas destos pescados son buenas agridulces.

[282] *Cómo se aderezan los Caracoles.*

Los caracoles lo más ordinario es aderezarlos en potaje: Tomarás los caracoles, y lavarlos has en muchas aguas: luego los pondrás en una vasija que sea ancha, y tenga agua cuanto se bañen bien: y esta pieza la pondrás sobre lumbre, de manera que se vaya calentando poco a poco, y ellos se irán saliendo de las conchas, y se irán muriendo con todo (179r) el cuerpo fuera dellas: y en estando muertos sacarlos has, y lávalos muy bien con sal, y con más aguas: luego échalos a cocer con agua y sal, otros dos, o tres hervores; porque se les acabe de quitar la verdina[314] que tienen, y tórnalos a sacar, y échalos en el colador que se escurran: luego freirás cebolla con buen aceite, y echarás allí los caracoles, y ahogarlos has muy bien, y échalos en su olla, y échales agua caliente y sal, y cuezan tres, o cuatro horas: luego picarás verduras y majarlas has con un poco de pan, como quien hacer carnero verde, sazona con

---

313 *Jibia* is also known as *sepia* in Spanish.
314 The *verdina* refers to the green film that can build up on objects in the water, like film in a fish tank. However, it is probable that Martínez Montiño is referring to both this and the snail slime. Javier Bartolomé, head chef at El Brezo, discusses removing both *verdín* [green film] and *baba* [slime] when preparing snails for the Romería de San Marcos in Palencia (see Herrero).

Serve on slices of toasted bread. Sometimes you can add sugar to this lamprey [recipe], adding a little more sourness so that it is sweet and sour. It turns out very tasty this way.

Cuttlefish, squid, and octopus

There are these three fish that are almost identical, because the cuttlefish and squid have a sac of ink that is very black. It is necessary to remove it very carefully so that it doesn't break, because even if you wash it in several rounds of water, you'll never be able to remove the ink. And these three fish, after they've been thoroughly washed, once they've been put into water to boil, can never come out of the hot water because they'll turn firm and tough. If you want to make a stew, which is the best way to prepare them, you should wash them in the same hot water because they are very white. After cleaning them for stew, fry some onion in the same casserole, take the fish out of the hot water, put it in the casserole, and sauté it. Season it with the right amount of spices and herbs and add just enough hot water for braising. Don't add any sour flavour until you're ready to serve, because these are fish that get tough very quickly. If you prepare them carefully they are very tender and white. Octopus is a little firmer. Normally you pound it against a rock or beat it with a rolling pin. Stews made with these fish are very tasty sweet and sour.

How to prepare snails

Snails are normally prepared as a stew. Take snails and wash them in several rounds of water. Then place them in a water bath in a wide pot. Place this pot over the flame so that it slowly heats up. The snails will come out of their shells and will be completely out when they die. Then you can remove them, rub them thoroughly with salt, and rinse them in several rounds of water. Then bring them to a boil in salted water two or three times so that they will lose all the green film they have. Remove them again and drain them in a strainer. Next, fry onion in good oil and add the snails. Sauté them well. Put them in a pot, add hot salted water, and let them simmer three or four hours. Then chop up green herbs, mash them with a

todas especias, y con hinojo, y con un poco de tomillo salsero,[315] y desatarlo has con el caldo de los caracoles: y si estuviere algo ralo freirás un poquito de harina, y échaselo dentro: y si quisieres echar algún poco de ajo bien podrás, y al tiempo del servir les podrás echar un poco de agrio.

[283] *Caracoles rellenos.*

(179v) Saltearás los caracoles, como está dicho, en agua caliente, y luego los lavarás con sal, y después con muchas aguas: y luego échalos a cocer con agua y sal, hasta que estén bien cocidos: luego sácalos de las cáscaras, y quítales todo lo blando que son las tripas, y ve guardando las conchas mejores y más blancas: después que estén todos sacados freirás un poco de cebolla muy menuda con buena manteca de vacas: luego echa allí los caracoles, y ahóguense bien: luego maja unas verduras con un poco de pan bien majadas, y sazona con todas especias, y un poco de hinojo, y esta salsa echarás sobre los caracoles que se están ahogando con la cebolla, de manera que sea la salsa corta, y cueza con los caracoles un poco: sazona de sal y zumo de limón: luego irás tomando las conchas, y metiendo dos, o tres caracoles en cada una, e irlos has componiendo en la tortera por su orden, arrimados unos a otros, y que queden llenos (180r) de la salsa, y ponles lumbre abajo y arriba, y tuéstense un poco: luego sácalos, y asiéntalos en el plato, arrimando unos a otros sin rebanada ninguna, y échales de la salsa por encima. Y advierte, que a esta salsa se le puede echar ajo, y comino, si gustaren dél.

[284] *Pastel de Caracoles.*

Estos caracoles podrás cocer como está dicho: luego sacarlos de las conchas, y quitarles lo blando, que son las tripas, y ahogarlos con un poco de manteca, y sazónalos con todas especias, y un poquito de verdura picada, y un poco de sal, y puedes hacer dellos un pastel: y podrás echar en este pastel algunas puntas de espárragos perdigadas, o algunos riponces[316] cocidos primero con agua y sal, y cuajarás este pastel con yemas de huevos, y un poco de caldo de garbanzos, y su agrio de limón, o un poco de vinagre. Suelen ser muy buenos estos pasteles.

[285] (180v) *Cómo se guisan las Criadillas de Tierra.*

Las criadillas de tierra se guisan de muchas maneras en platillo: Cocerás las criadillas con agua y sal muy bien mondadas de las cáscaras: y luego las ahogarás con

---

315 *Tomillo salsero* (*Thymus zygis*) [Spanish thyme] is very similar to *tomillo* (*Thymus vulgaris*). Today, it is commonly used for brining olives and for seasoning roasts.
316 For more information on *riponces*, see 176n56.

little bread, as if you were making green mutton stew, season with all spices, fennel, and a little brining thyme. Thin it with broth from the snails. If it's too thin, fry a little flour and add it. If you want to, you could add a little garlic. When it's time to serve, you can add a little sour flavour.

Stuffed snails

Pan fry the snails as explained with hot water. Then rub with salt and rinse in several rounds of water. Then put them on to boil in salted water until they are well cooked. Take them out of their shells, remove all the soft part, which is their intestines, and set to one side the best and whitest shells. Once all are removed, fry diced onion in good butter. Then, add the snails and sauté them well. Next, mash well some green herbs with a little bread. Season with all spices and a little fennel. Pour this sauce over the snails sautéed with onion so that there is just a little sauce and let it simmer. Season with salt and lemon juice. Then take the shells and fill each with two or three snails and begin placing them in a covered tart pan in an organized way, one right next to another, and all filled with sauce. Bake them with heat above and below and brown them a little. Then, remove them, set them on a plate, one right next to the other, without any slices [of bread], and ladle sauce on top. Note that you can add garlic and cumin to this sauce if [some lords] like them.

Snail pie

These snails can be boiled as already explained. Then, take them out of their shells, remove all the soft part, which is their intestines, sauté them with a little lard, and season with all spices, a little chopped green herb, and a little salt. You can make a pie with them. You can also add to the pie some parboiled asparagus tips or rampion bellflower shoots that have been boiled in salted water. Thicken this pie with egg yolks, a little garbanzo broth, and the right amount of lemon juice or a little vinegar. These pies are typically very tasty.

How to cook truffles

Truffles are cooked in many ways as a dish. Boil truffles that have been carefully peeled in salted water. Then sauté them in good oil and a little minced

buen aceite, y un poco de cebolla menuda: luego les echarás caldo de garbanzos, y sazona con todas especias, y un poquito de azafrán, y un poquito de verdura muy picada, y échasela dentro, y cueza un poco; sazonarlas de sal, y luego cuájalas con unas yemas de huevos, y zumo de limón, o vinagre: y sírvelas sobre rebanadillas, o en una cazolilla.

[286] *Otro platillo de Criadillas de Tierra.*

Cocerás las criadillas con agua y sal; luego ahógalas con buen aceite y cebolla, como está dicho en las de atrás, y harás una salsa majando de todas (181r) verduras, y un migajón de pan, que salga la salsa muy verde, como carnero verde, y sazona con todas especias, y un poquito de cominos, y un granillo de ajo, y desátala con caldo de garbanzos, o agua caliente, y un poquito de agrio de vinagre, y sazona de sal; luego échala sobre las criadillas, y ponlas al fuego, échales dentro tres, o cuatro huevos crudos que se escalfen allí hasta que estén duros, y sírvelas sobre rebanadillas las criadillas, y los huevos todo junto, y échales por encima un poco de agrio de limón, o naranja.

[287] *Cazuela de Criadillas de Tierra.*

Estas criadillas puedes aderezar de cualquier destas maneras que están dichas, y tengan poco caldo, y échalas en una cazuela, y cuájalas con huevos con claras, y que sean en cantidad, y échales un poco de pan rallado, y métclas en un (181v) horno que se cuajen, y cuájense. Estas criadillas son buenas fritas en naranja y pimienta: y si hubiere algunas huevas de algún pescado, fríanse también; y sírvelas con las criadillas con pimienta y naranja.

[288] *Criadillas de Tierra con huevos revueltos.*

Las criadillas de tierra podrás freír, y luego batir una docena de huevos, y echarles unos pocos de cominos y sal, y echar estos huevos sobre las criadillas, y hacer huevos revueltos: y si le quisieres echar un poco de ajo podrás friendo primero los ajos en la manteca, o aceite de las criadillas, para que quede allí un poco de gusto. Y advierte, que esto de ajo se ha de echar con mucha moderación: y lo mejor es asar primero, o freír los ajos: y luego freír las criadillas, y echar los ajos a mal. Otras muchas maneras pudiera poner aquí, como son tortas y costradas con su dulce; mas (182r) fuera de las suertes que van aquí escritas, no me contenta ninguna.

[289] *Pastel de Criadillas de Tierra.*

Estas criadillas ahogadas, como está dicho atrás, y sazonadas con todas especias, y sal, y un poquito de verdura y metidas en un pastel: y en estando la masa cocida

onion. Next add garbanzo broth. Season with all spices, a little saffron, and a little minced green herb. Add all that in and let simmer. Season with salt and thicken with egg yolks and lemon juice or vinegar. Serve over slices [of bread] or in a tartlet pan.

Another truffle dish

Boil truffles in salted water, then sauté them with good oil and onion as explained for truffles in the previous [recipe]. Make a sauce by mashing together green herbs and the centre of a [loaf] of bread. The sauce should be very green, like [the sauce for] green mutton stew. Season with all spices, a little cumin, and a clove of garlic. Thin with garbanzo broth or hot water and a little vinegar and season with salt. Then, pour this over the truffles, put on the fire, and add three or four raw eggs to poach until they are hard. Serve the truffles and the eggs together over slices [of bread] and drizzle on top a little lemon or orange juice.

Truffle stew

These truffles can be prepared in any of the ways already explained that have a little broth. Put in a casserole, thicken with eggs including their whites, you will need a lot, and add in a little bit of breadcrumbs. Place them in an oven to set and let them set. Truffles are also good fried in orange and pepper. If you had any fish roe, fry that too and serve it with the truffles with pepper and orange.

Truffles with scrambled eggs

You can fry truffles, then beat a dozen eggs and add in a little cumin and salt. Pour the eggs over the truffles and scramble them. If you want to add a little garlic, you can by first frying the garlic in lard or truffle oil, so that its flavour stays there. Note that garlic should be used sparingly. It's best to first roast or fry the garlic, then fry the truffles, and discard the garlic. I could include many other ways [to prepare truffles], such as pies and sweet, puff pastry pies, but apart from the kinds that are written down here, I'm not happy with any other.

Truffle pie

These sautéed truffles, as previously stated, [are] seasoned with all spices, salt, and a little green herb, and placed in a pie. Once the crust has baked, beat egg yolks

podrás batir unas yemas de huevos, y un poco de caldo de garbanzos, y su agrio, y cebado el pastel suele salir muy bueno: y si echares la mitad de criadillas, y la mitad de ostias frescas sería muy buen pastel. Empanadas son también buenas: y ya ay [sic] dicho atrás como se han de hacer en empanadillas, o empanada Inglesa. Estas criadillas en platillo de muchos riponces, y cuajadas con sus yemas de huevos, y zumo de limón, es muy buen platillo. Y advierte que si echares riponces con las criadillas y las ostias frescas que dicen muy bien, y es un pastel muy regalado.

[290] (182v) *Platillo de Cardo*.

Mondarás el cardo, y desvenarlo has lo más que pudieres, y cuécelo con agua y sal, y luego ahógalo con buena manteca de vacas, y su cebolla menuda, que esté bien ahogado, sazónalo de pimienta, y nuez, y jengibre, y échale un poco de verdura picada, y agua caliente cuanto se bañe, y cueza en cosa de barro, y si fuere cobre, sea bien estañado: y de que esté el cardo bien cocido échale un poco de leche, y cueza un poco, y cuájalo con huevos: y si no quisieres gastar huevos, calienta un poco de manteca, y fríe en ella un poco de harina, de manera que no se queme, sino que salga rala y blanca: y cuando ella hiciere unas ampollitas, trastórnala con la sartén dentro del platillo: y yo tengo por mejor estos platillos cuajados con la harina, que con los huevos: y cuando sirvas el cardo, le podrás echar azúcar y canela por encima. Y si quisieres hacer (183r) este platillo sin leche, sazónalo como está dicho en lo demás, y échale un poco de azafrán, y échale su dulce, y zumo de limón para que salga agridulce: el agrio sea poco.

[291] *Otro platillo de Cardo*.

Mondarás el cardo de manera que quede lo más tierno, aunque gastes más cardos, y desvenarlo has mucho, y cuécelo con agua y sal, hasta que esté bien cocido: luego ahógalo con manteca de vacas sin ninguna cebolla, y échale un poquito de agua, y un poquito de vino, y el zumo de medio limón, y media libra de azúcar, y sazona con pimienta, y nuez, y canela, y un poquito de verdura picada, y una migaja de sal, y otra de azafrán, y cueza un poco: luego batirás veinte huevos con claras,[317] y échales dentro en el cacillo donde está el cardo, y échale por encima un poco de pan rallado, y pon el cacito al fuego con un poco de lumbre abajo, y tápalo con (183v) su cobertera, y échale lumbre encima, y cuájese de manera, que no se queme, y por la parte de arriba esté dorado: luego sácalo sobre unas torrijas delgadas, y haz de manera que salga este platillo entero, como está en el cacillo, la flor hacia arriba, y échale por encima un poco de azúcar y canela. Y advierte, que todos

---

317 In the 1617 edition, Martínez Montiño changes "veinte huevos" [twenty eggs] to "diez y seis huevos" [sixteen eggs]. This substantive change remains throughout all the other editions.

and a little garbanzo broth with the right amount of sour juice, and this enriched pie is typically very tasty. If you make it half with truffles and half with fresh oysters, it would make a very tasty pie. Empanadas are also tasty, and it was already explained how to make turnovers or English empanadas. A dish of truffles with a lot of rampion bellflower shoots that is thickened with egg yolk and lemon juice is a very tasty dish. Note that if you add rampion bellflower shoots to the truffle and fresh oyster [pie] they go very well, and it is an exquisite pie.

A dish of cardoons

Peel the cardoons and devein them as much as you can. Boil in salted water and then sauté with good butter and the right amount of minced onion. Once it's sautéed, season with pepper, nutmeg, and ginger. Add in some diced green herb and enough hot water to braise. Cook in a terracotta dish, but if it's copper, it must be well tinned.[8] Once the cardoons are done, add a little milk, simmer, and thicken with egg. If you don't want to use eggs, heat up some butter and fry a little flour in it, but don't let it burn. It should be thin and white, and when it begins to bubble, flip it from the frying pan onto the individual plate. I think these dishes thickened with flour are better than those thickened with eggs. When you serve the cardoons, you can sprinkle sugar and cinnamon on top. If you want to make this dish without milk, season as explained in the other [recipes] and add a little saffron, the right amount of sweetener, and lemon juice so that it turns out sweet and sour. The sour flavour should be light.

Another individual cardoon dish

Peel the cardoons so that only the tender part is left, even if you use up most of it. Thoroughly devein them and boil in salted water until they're done. Then sauté them in butter without any onion. Add a little water, a little wine, juice from half a lemon, and half a pound of sugar. Season with pepper, nutmeg, cinnamon, a little chopped green herbs, a pinch of salt, and another of saffron, and let it all simmer. Then whip twenty eggs with their whites, add them to the saucepan with the cardoons, and add on top a little bit of breadcrumbs. Put the saucepan on the fire on low. Cover it with its cover and add heat on top. Let it set but don't let it burn. The top should be golden brown. Next, place it on thinly sliced torrijas in such a way that this whole dish comes out of the pan as is and with the essence on top. Sprinkle a little sugar and cinnamon on top. Note that it is understood

---

8 Tinning copper is necessary to avoid a reaction between the food and the copper.

los platillos que tengo dicho que se han de hacer con manteca de vacas, o buen aceite, se entiende que en día de carne ha de ser tocino en lugar de la manteca, y caldo de carne en lugar de caldo de garbanzos.

[292] *Pastel de Cardos.*

Cocerás el cardo como está dicho, y luego ahógalo con manteca de vacas, y sazónalo con sus especias: luego échale un poco de leche, y una poquita de verdura, y un poquito de sal, y ahóguese muy bien, y échale más leche cuanto fuere menester para el pastel, o (184r) pasteles, y para cada uno seis onzas de azúcar: y cuando está el cardo cocido sácalo con una espumadera, y déjalo enfriar, y échalo en los pasteles con su manteca: y cuando esté la masa cocida, batirás huevos con claras, para cada pastel cuatro, y dejarlo has con la leche en que se sazona el caldo, y henchirás los pasteles desta leche, y cuájense los pasteles descubiertos: y cuando estén cuajados les podrás poner las coberteras encima: y si los quisieres servir abiertos, podrás perdigar primero los vasos de los pasteles: y podrás echar leche, y el cardo con los huevos. Y advierte, que cuando ahogares el cardo, ha de tener manteca en cantidad: y si quisieres hacer este pastel sin leche, podrás henchir el pastel de solo cardo, y sazonado con especias, y su verdura, y su azúcar molido: y después cebarle con caldo de garbanzos y yemas de huevos batidas: y en los pasteles que llevan leche, puedes ahogar el cardo, y echar la leche al cuajar.

[293] (184v) *Cebollas rellenas.*

Las cebollas cocidas y ahogadas con manteca de vacas, y sazonadas de sal, y todas especias, y servidas con queso rallado por encima son buenas. Las cebollas rellenas, tomarás dos, o tres cebollas grandes para un plato, y cortarles has el pezón, y las raíces, y échalas a cocer: y cuando estén medio cocidas sácalas, y mete el dedo por en medio, y sacarás el tallo de en medio [de] la cebolla: y luego sacarás otra un poquito mayor: luego irás sacando todas las telas enteras de manera, que cada una parezca una cebolla entera: luego pícalas chicas, y fríelas con manteca, y un poco de verdura: luego echarás allí en la sartén seis, u ocho huevos batidos, y revolverlo has sobre la lumbre, hasta que esté bien seco: luego sácalo al tablero, y pícalo muy bien, y échale queso rallado que sea bueno de hierba,[318] que el de cuajo no se ha de echar en cosa ninguna que (185r) se haya de guisar, si fuere posible, y echarás otro tanto pan rallado, como queso, y échale huevos crudos hasta que el relleno esté un poco blando, y échale un poco de azúcar, y sazona con todas especias y canela, y rellena los cascos de las cebollas, y asiéntalas en una tortera untada con manteca, tápala con su cobertera, y ponla al fuego con lumbre abajo y arriba, tostarse han un

---

318 For more on *queso de hierba* made from herbal rennet, see 236n138.

that, for all these dishes which I've explained are made with butter or good oil, fatback should be used on meat days instead of butter and meat stock instead of garbanzo broth.

Cardoon pie

Boil the cardoons as explained and then sauté them in butter and season with their spices. Then add a little milk, a little bit of green herbs, and a little salt and sauté it very well. Add more milk, the amount needed for a pie or pies. For each one, six ounces of sugar. When the cardoons are done, remove them with a skimmer and let cool. Add them to the pies with the right amount of butter. When the crust is baked, beat eggs with their whites, four for each pie, and add them to the milk with the seasoned broth. Fill the pies with this milk and let them set uncovered. When they're set, you can put on a top crust. If you want to serve them open, first parbake the pie crust and then add milk, and cardoons and eggs. Note that when you sauté the cardoons, you must use a lot of butter. If you want to make this pie without milk, you can fill it with just cardoons, seasoned with the right amount of spices, herbs, and ground sugar. After, enrich it with garbanzo broth and whipped egg yolks. In the pies that do have milk, sauté the cardoons and add the milk when it's setting.

Stuffed onions

Boiled onions sautéed in butter, seasoned with salt and all spices, and served with grated cheese on top are tasty. Stuffed onions: take two or three big onions per plate, cut off the tops and bottoms, and put on to boil. When they are par-boiled, take them out, put your finger in the middle, and take out the stem in the middle of the onion. Then take out another section that's a little bigger, then take out a little bit more. Then, take off all the membrane layers; each should look like its own onion. Next, mince and fry it in lard with a little bit of green herbs. Then add to the frying pan six or eight beaten eggs, stir over the flame until all the egg is cooked. Turn it out onto a cutting board and mince it all. Add grated cheese that is from good cheese made with herbal rennet because cheese from animal rennet shouldn't be added to anything being cooked, whenever possible. Add the same amount of breadcrumbs as cheese, and enough raw eggs to make the filling a little soft. Add a little sugar, season with all spices and cinnamon, and fill the onion shells. Set them in a covered tart pan greased with lard, cover it with a lid, and put it on the fire with heat above and below. Toast it a

poco, y cuajarse ha el relleno, y harás una sopa dulce con azúcar y canela, y queso, todo revuelto, y mojarse ha con caldo de garbanzos, y media docena de yemas de huevos, y asienta las cebollas encima de la sopa: luego échale un poco de manteca de vacas bien caliente por encima, y queso rallado: y pon esta sopa dentro en un horno para que se cuaje, y tome color el queso rallado que va por encima.

[294] *Cómo se aderezan las Carpas.*

Las carpas para ser buenas han de (185v) venir vivas a la cocina. Éstas no se han de escamar, sino abrirlas por un lado, como lechón, y sacarle las tripas, y la hiel: y si tuviere muchas huevas, sácalas, y echa estas carpas en vinagre que se mojen bien, y velas volviendo que se mojen por todos cabos, y se pondrán muy azules,[319] y pon el cazo al fuego con agua y sal, y alguna cebolla y perejil en rama: y cuando esté cociendo echas las carpas y la [sic] vinagre todo junto en el cazo en que estaba, y atapa el cazo, y cuando estén cocidas sírvelas con vinagre y ramas de perejil y pimienta. Estas carpas han de salir muy azules, porque parecen así muy bien.

[295] *Sopa de Carpas.*

Escamarás las carpas, y lávalas muy bien, ábrelas por la barriga, y sacarás las tripas, y la hiel, y guarda las huevas, y el hígado, y la sangre que tuvieren dentro: luego partirás estas carpas por medio desde la cola a la cabeza, y haráslas (186r) pedazos, que estarán corriendo sangre, y asiéntalas en un cacillo así sin lavar, porque se aproveche la sangre: luego corta cantidad de cebolla larga, y échala por encima de los pedazos de carpa, así cruda sin freír, y sazona de sal y especias, y échale un poco de vino tinto y vinagre, que estén un poco agrias, y un poco de agua cuanto se bañen, y echa allí las huevas, y el hígado: luego pon al fuego una sartén con manteca de vacas, y déjala calentar tanto hasta que se queme, y se ponga bien negra: y así caliente como está, la echarás por encima de las carpas, y ponlas a cocer a mucha furia hasta que se apure: y con sólo esto se hará una salsilla negra, y trabada, que

---

319 I am indebted to archaeologist and historian Andreas Klumpp, who has shared with me several recipes from the seventeenth century through to today that mention the blue that results from adding vinegar to the cooking process. He confirms that blued fish has remained a classic staple of German cuisine throughout the centuries and that there are still many regional and national varieties. Examples include "Die Ferchen schoen blau abzusieden in dir Sultzen" [To poach trout finely blue in aspic] (*Ein Koch- und Artzney-Buch* [Graz, 1686], 110–11), "Forellen blau zu sieden" [To seethe trout blue] and "Hecht blau zu sieden" [To seethe pike blue] (Johann Albrecht Grunauer, *Das vollständige und vermehrte, auf die neueste Art eingerichtete Kochbuch* [Nürnberg, 1733], ed. Wolfgang Protzner [Würzburg, 2008], 239 and 244), and "Blaue gesottene Forelle. Truite au bleu" [Trout seethed blue] (Johann Rottenhöfer, *Anweisungen in der feineren Kochkunst* [Munich, 1866], 521). When I tried this recipe with local carp, the fish did turn a hazy blue.

little, and let the filling set. Make sweet sops with sugar, cinnamon, and cheese, all mixed together. Moisten with garbanzo broth and a half dozen egg yolks. Set the onions on top of the sops. Then add a little hot butter and grated cheese on top. Put the sops in the oven to set and to brown a little. Grate cheese on top.

How to prepare carp

For carp to be tasty, they must arrive live to the kitchen. You don't scale this fish, just open them on their side like suckling pig. Remove their guts and bile and if there are a lot of eggs, remove them too. Place the carp in vinegar and let them soak a while. Turn them often so that all parts of the fish are soaked. They should turn very blue. Put the pot on the fire with salted water, some onion, and sprigs of parsley. When it's boiling, add the carp and vinegar all together to the pot it was all in, cover it, and when it's done, serve them with vinegar, parsley sprigs, and pepper. These carp should turn out very blue, because they look really good that way.

Carp served on sops

Scale the carp and wash them well. Open the belly, remove their guts and bile, and reserve the roe, liver, and whatever blood is inside. Then split the carp down the middle from head to tail and cut into pieces. There will be blood running, so place the carp in a saucepan as is, without rinsing, so as to use the blood. Then cut a lot of onions lengthwise and place them raw on top of the carp without frying. Season with salt and spices, add a little red wine and vinegar so they're somewhat sour, and enough water to braise. Add in the roe and liver. Then put some butter in a frying pan and place it on the flame. Let it heat until it begins to burn and turn black. With it this hot, pour it over the carp and cook them vigorously until it's done. With just this you'll make a black sauce, and it will be thick as if you had

parecerá que se le echó pan tostado, o harina quemada. Sírvela sobre rebanadas de pan tostado, y échala con el mismo cacito en el plato, porque no se han de revolver: y si tuvieres más de un plato procura que cada plato se haga de por sí, si fuere posible. Estas carpas hechas (186v) pedazos, y fritas, y asentadas sobre una sopilla de pan tostado: y luego tomar en un plato un poco de manteca fresca en pella, un poco de vinagre bien aguado, y pimienta, y jengibre, y nuez, y póngase a calentar sobre brasas: y cuando la manteca esté derretida, y la salsa está blanca, échala por encima de las carpas, de manera que ande bien bañada la sopa. Ésta se llama salsa de brugete: y si cocieses unos espárragos, y luego freírlos, y asentarlos entre las carpas, y la sopa, suele salir muy buen plato. Si echases dulce a la sopa de las carpas, estarán buenas.

[296] *Pastel enbote de Carpas.*

Tomarás dos carpas grandes, porque de chicas no se puede hacer este plato, y desollarlas has, y descarnarás toda la carne que pudieres, dejando quedar el espinazo, y las costillas, y todas las espinas grandes, y picarás esta carne muy picada: luego ahogarás un poco de cebolla (187r) muy menuda con manteca de vacas, y echarás allí la carne de las carpas, y perdigarla has revolviendo con un cucharón, y vendrá a quedar granujada que parecerá carne de pechuga de ave, y sazona de todas especias, y un poquito de verdura picada y sal, y échale un poco de agua caliente cuanto se bañe, y cueza un poco: y luego cuájalo con yemas de huevos batidas, y zumo de limón, y tendrás las cabezas de las carpas cocidas en un cocimiento de agua y sal, y cebolla y vinagre: y pondrás estas cabezas en el plato sobre rebanadillas de pan, y echarás el pastel en bote al derredor, porque se eche de ver que es de carpas, que en el gusto parecerá de carne, si la manteca es buena.

[297] *Unas Albondiguillas de Carpas.*

Descarnarás las carpas, como está dicho, y picarás la carne cruda, y meterle has media docena de yemas de (187v) huevos, y un poquito de pan rallado, y sazona con pimienta y nuez, y jengibre, y sal, y tendrás caldo sazonado con buena manteca de vacas, y harás tus albondiguillas cuando las quisieres servir: y tendrás las cabezas de las carpas cocidas, y asiéntalas en el plato, y echa las albondiguillas al derredor: y entiendo que son mejores que de ningún pescado: porque este pescado no tiene ningún género de humo.

[298] *Cómo se puede freír, y asar, y cocer un pescado todo en un tiempo, sin partirlo.*

No soy amigo de escribir platos fantásticos, mas con todo eso quiero poner aquí cómo se puede freír, cocer y asar un pescado entero todo en un tiempo. Tomarás la carpa, o tenca, o barbo, u otro cualquiera pescado que sea un poco largo, y espetarlo

added toasted bread or burnt flour. Serve it over slices of toasted bread, adding the whole pan at once to the plate so it doesn't get all stirred up. If you had more than one plate, try to make each one separately if possible. Cut these carp into pieces, fry them, and set them over sops of toasted bread. Next, put on a plate a little bit of butter in a ball, a little well watered down vinegar, pepper, ginger, and nutmeg, and heat it up over red-hot embers. When the butter has melted and the sauce is white, pour it over the carp so that the sops are very soaked. This sauce is called *bruguete*. If you boil asparagus, fry it, and set it between the carp and the sops; it is normally a very tasty dish. If you want to add sweetener to the carp sops, they will be tasty.

Crustless carp pie

Take two big carp, because you can't make this dish with small ones. Skin them, and remove as much meat as you can, leaving behind the spine, ribs, and all the small bones. Mince the meat, thoroughly sauté minced onion in butter, and add in the carp meat. Sear it by stirring it around with a big spoon. It should turn out shredded like meat from poultry breast. Season with all spices, a little bit of minced green herbs and salt, and add in a little hot water to braise. Let it simmer a little. Then thicken with whipped egg yolks and lemon juice. Have the carp heads boiling in a boil of salted water, onion, and vinegar. Place the heads on a plate over slices of bread. Place the crustless pie around so that you can see it's carp, because it will taste like meat if the butter is good.

Carp balls

Remove the meat from the carp as explained, mince the raw meat, add a half dozen egg yolks, a little bit of breadcrumbs, and season with pepper, nutmeg, ginger, and salt. Have some broth flavoured with butter, and make balls when you are ready to serve them. Have the carp heads cooked, place them on the plate, and place the carp balls around. I am told that they are better than any others made with fish because this fish has no odour whatsoever.

How to fry, roast, and boil a fish at the same time without cutting it up

I am no fan of writing fantastical dishes, but with that said, I'd like to record here how to fry, boil, and roast a whole fish at the same time. Take carp, tench, barbel, or any other fairly long fish and skewer it on a spit after it has been well cleaned

has en un asador, después de bien limpio y escamado, (188r) y harás el abertura muy pequeña: el asador ha de entrar por la cola, y ha de salir por la cabeza: luego tomarás unas sedeñas, o lino rastrallado,[320] y echarás sal en un pedazo de la cola: luego envuelve aquel pedazo con las sedeñas, y mójalas por encima con aceite que quedan bien empapadas: luego tomarás otras sedeñas, y pondráslas anchas, y pon allí perejil en rama, y cebolla cortada, y sal, y envuelve la cabeza hasta las alas con aquellas sedeñas, de manera que las cebollas y el perejil queden arrimadas a la cabeza, y moja estas sedeñas con agua, y harás un cocimiento de agua, y sal, y vinagre, y moja las sedeñas muy bien, y acomódala, porque no es menester atarlas con ningún hilo, que ellas se pegan muy bien: luego has de poner este cocimiento sobre un poco de lumbre, de manera que esté cociendo, y en otra cazuela un poco de aceite, que esté también muy caliente al lado del asador: has de poner a asar el pescado, y has de (188v) ir echando de aquel cocimiento por encima de las sedeñas, que están en la cabeza, de manera que nunca se venga a secar, y el pedazo de en medio ha de estar descubierto, y has de tener un poco de aceite en otra vasija con un poco de sal, y un poquito de ajo, y una gota de agua, y un poco de orégano molido, y una gota de vinagre, y hazlo de ir untando con unas plumas, y el tarazón[321] de en medio viene a ser asado: la otra vasija de la cola has de tener solo con aceite bien caliente: y de cuando en cuando le has de ir echando deste aceite caliente por encima de las sedeñas de la cola; porque desta manera se freirá, como si se friera en la sartén, y la parte de la cabeza se cocerá, como si se cociera en un cazo, y vendrá a estar frito, cocido, y asado todo en un tiempo. Ahora sacarás el pez del asador en una pieza llana, o en un plato grande, y cortarás las sedeñas con las tijeras muy sutilmente, porque no se deshaga la cabeza, que lo otro bien tieso estará: y (189r) después de quitadas todas las sedeñas, asiéntalo en un plato grande, y quedará la cabeza tan naturalmente cocida, y azul, como si se cociera en su cocimiento, y lo demás quedará asado y frito. Ahora pondrás tres salserillas en el plato con tres salsas; a la parte de la cabeza pondrás perejil que tenga hierbabuena, y pimienta, y un poco de aceite; y en la de en medio pondrás una salserilla con una salsa, al modo de ajopollo,[322] mezclado con un poquito de adobo con que se asó el pescado: y en la de la cola pondrás un poco de escabeche muy bien hecho: y con esto será el pescado frito, cocido, y asado con sus salsas.

---

320 Making linen from flax is a complicated process of retting (soaking), drying, breaking, scutching (pounding/scraping), and heckling (combing) before spinning into thread. Heckling occurs in stages with different-sized combs, and in each, *estopa* [tow], the short fibres that are combed out of the longer flax fibres, is produced. As Martínez Montiño mentions, *sedeña* [fine tow] comes from fibres that remain from the second combing and is less coarse than the fibres from the first combing.

321 For more on the orígens of *tarazón*, see the Glossary entry.

322 *Ajopollo* sauce is made with oil, garlic, fried bread soaked in vinegar, and toasted almonds; notably, there is no chicken in the sauce. Because Martínez Montiño has no need to explain how to make it, readers today can infer that it was a well-known sauce in the early modern era. Today it is associated with the regions of Almería and Granada.

and scaled. Make just a small opening. The spit should enter through the tail and come out at the head. Then, take some fine tow or combed linen and put salt on the tail. Wrap that piece in the fine tow and wet it with oil on top so that it is soaked through. Then take other pieces of fine tow, turn them wide, and put sprigs of parsley, chopped onion, and salt in them. Wrap the fish from the head to the fins with these pieces of fine tow so that the onions and parsley lie next to the head. Thoroughly soak the fine tow with water. Make a boil of salted water and vinegar and get the fine tow really wet and adjust it. Wet the fine tow really well because it isn't necessary to tie it with string; it sticks on well. Then, put the boil over a low flame enough so it's boiling and, in another casserole, a little oil that is also hot next to the spit. Put the fish on to roast and ladle [liquid] from the boil on top of the fine tow that is on the head so that it never dries out. The piece in the middle should be unwrapped, and, in another pot, you should have some oil with a little salt, a little garlic, a little ground oregano, and a drop of water and another of vinegar. Use feathers to smear it on. The piece in the middle should be roasted. The other pot for the tail should only have hot oil in it. From time to time ladle this hot oil over the fine tow on the tail. This way it will be fried, just as if it were in a frying pan. The head will be boiled, as if it were boiling in a pot. It will end up being fried, boiled, and roasted all at once. Next, remove the fish from the spit and onto a flat dish, or a big plate. Carefully cut the fine tow with scissors so that the head doesn't fall apart underneath. The other parts should be firm. Then, after removing the fine tow, set [the fish] on a big plate, and the head should turn out perfectly boiled and blue, as if had just been boiling in its boil. The rest will be roasted and fried. Now place three small sauce dishes on the plate with three sauces. For the head, have parsley [sauce] with spearmint, pepper, and a little oil. For the middle, place a sauce dish with a sauce like garlic sauce but mixed with a little marinade with which the fish was roasted. And, for the tail, put some excellent brine. This is the way to fry, boil, and roast fish with its sauces.

[299] *Cómo se guisan las Enguilas.*

Las enguilas es un pescado que se tiene alguna sospecha de que no es muy sano, y así siempre se acostumbra echarle un poco de ajo, eso queda al albedrío del oficial, o al gusto del señor: lo más ordinario es comerlas asadas: y para esto es necesario hacerlas trozos (189v) después de desolladas y abiertas, y echarlas en adobo de agua, y sal, y orégano molido, y un poco de vinagre: y digo el orégano molido, porque a los adobos siempre se ha de moler el orégano con la sal gorda, que de otra manera no tomarán bien el gusto. Estarán estas enguilas en adobo un par de horas: luego las asarás en las parrillas, y sírvelas con un poco de adobo, y zumo de limón, y un poco de pimienta. También las podrás servir con un poco de ajo pollo.[323] Y si has hubieres de freír, las has de echar también en adobo, como está dicho: y ha de ser el adobo un poco más fuerte, porque después no ha de llevar más de un poco de zumo de naranja por encima, y un poco de pimienta.

[300] *Cazuela de Enguilas.*

Las enguilas también son buenas en cazuela, haciéndoles trozos, y ahogándolas con buen aceite, y cebolla menuda, (190r) y luego echarle agua caliente cuanto se bañen, y luego majar un poco de verdura con un migajoncillo de pan, y echarlo en la cazuela, y sazona con todas especias, y su agrio. Estas cazuelas comen algunos agridulces, y son muy buenas así.

[301] *Enguila en pan.*

Estas enguilas son muy buenas empanadas enroscadas como lampreas, y dadas unos cortes por los lomos, porque suelen romper la masa del pastel. A estas no es menester echar más de sal, y pimienta, y unas rajitas de un grano de ajo. Y advierte, que para empanar pescados no es menester otra especia que pimienta y sal, sino es para las lampreas: o si quisieres empanar algún pescado que no tenga espinas, y le quisieras echar salsa negra,[324] u otra salsa de otra manera; en tal caso podrás sazonar con todas especias, mas para empanadas secas no es menester más de sal y pimienta.

[302] (190v) *Un Barbo estofado.*

El barbo si es fresco, lo mejor es comerlo cocido; mas para diferenciar se hace de otras maneras: Escamarás el barbo, y ábrelo, y echa a mal las tripas, y la hiel, y

---

323 Ingredients for this sauce are explained in the note above.
324 Instructions on how to make *salsa negra* are found in "Empanadas frías de jabalí" [Cold boar empanadas] and "Empanadas de jabalí calientes" [Warm boar empanadas] (290–2; 291–3).

How to cook eel

Eel is a fish that is suspected of being unhealthy and thus people are always in the habit of adding a little garlic. This is up to either the discretion of the cook or the likings of the lord. Normally they are eaten grilled, and for this it is necessary to chop them into pieces after skinning them, opening them, and marinating them in salted water, ground oregano, and a little vinegar. I mention ground oregano because for marinades oregano should always be ground with coarse salt; otherwise the flavour won't be picked up. These eels should marinate for a couple of hours. Then grill them on the grill and serve them with a little marinade, lemon juice, and a little pepper. You can also serve them with a little *ajopollo* sauce. If you want to fry them, you should also soak them in marinade as explained. The marinade should be a little stronger because afterward it shouldn't have anything but a little orange juice on top and a little pepper.

Eel stew

Eel is also tasty stewed, cutting it into pieces and sautéing it with good oil and diced onion. Then, add enough hot water to braise, mash a little bit of green herbs with the inside of bread, and add it to the casserole. Season with all spices and the right amount of sour juice. This stew is sometimes eaten sweet and sour and is very tasty that way.

Eel wrapped in bread

This eel is very tasty as an empanada, coiled around like lamprey and with slits in the loins because they often break through the dough. For this [dish] nothing more is necessary than salt, pepper, and a few slivers of a clove of garlic. Note that, to wrap fish in dough, no other spices other than salt and pepper are needed, unless it's for lamprey. Or, if you want to wrap a fish with no bones in dough and add black sauce or another similar sauce, then you could season with all spices, but for empanadas with no sauce, nothing more than salt and pepper.

Stewed barbel

If barbel is fresh, it's best to eat it boiled. But, to vary it, you can make it other ways. Scale the barbel, open it, discard the guts and bile, and reserve the liver and roe.

guarda el hígado, y las huevas, y harás el pez pedazos, y échalo en una olla, y échale un poco de vino tinto, un poco de vinagre, y pimienta, y nuez, y sal, y un poquito de agua, que apenas se bañe el pescado, y echa las huevas dentro,[325] y un poco de cebolla entera, y un poco de manteca de vacas fresca: luego pondrás un borde de masa en la olla, y ponle encima una escudilla llena de agua que se ajuste con la masa, y pon la olla sobre el rescoldo, y cueza allí media hora, o más, y hallarás el pescado estofado con una salsilla muy buena, y echa la cebolla fuera, y sírvelo sobre rebanadas tostadas.

[303] (191r) *Barbos en moreta.*[326]

Escamarás los barbos, o carpas, u otro cualquier pescado que sea grande, porque de ninguno que sea chico no se hace bien: harás los barbos pedazos, y ahogarás cebolla en un cazo, y echa allí los pedazos de los barbos, y darles has una vuelta con la cebolla, y la manteca, y luego echarles has un poco de vino, y un poco de vinagre, y de todas especias, y sal, y un manojo de hierbas del jardín, y agua cuanto se bañen, y desatarás un poco de harina quemada desatada: y con todo este recaudo lo pondrás a cocer a mucha furia, y no cueza más de media hora, antes menos que más. Esta moreta se suele hacer, como está dicho, y se le añade azúcar y canela en la misma salsa, mas yo me atengo a la agria. Estos barbos grandes son buenos cortados en ruedas, y echados en adobo de sollo, y asados en las parrillas, y sírvelos con un poquito del adobo, o zumo de limón, o naranja.

[304] (191v) *Besugos en escabeche al uso de Portugal.*[327]

Los besugos de ninguna manera son tan buenos como cocidos con pimienta y naranja; con todo se comen asados, en cazuela, y empanados. Una manera de escabechar besugos pondré aquí, que quizá no la habrás visto: Has de escamar los besugos, y hacerlos trozos, si no los quieres freír enteros tomarás el zumo de una docena de naranjas agrias que sean buenas, y echarle has encima media azumbre de vinagre, y un cuartillo de agua, y un poco de sal y pimienta, y clavo, y jengibre, y un poco de azafrán: pon este escabeche en una cazuela de barro, o una pieza de plata adonde esté caliente, y no cueza, y ponte a freír los besugos: y en estando fritos velos sacando del aceite: y así como salen de la sartén caigan en el escabeche que se cubran todos,

---

325 If you recreate this dish, please note that barbel roe is poisonous and should not be consumed.
326 Martínez Montiño is cited in Esteban Terreros y Pando, *Diccionario castellano con las voces de ciencias y artes y sus correspondientes de las tres lenguas francesa, latina e italiana*, as the source for moreta sauce (619).
327 In this recipe one can notice the pride Martínez Montiño communicates for the Portuguese style as he ends the recipe with the comparison between the Portuguese marinade and the regular type.

Chop the fish up into pieces, put them in a pot, and add a little red wine, a little vinegar, pepper, nutmeg, salt, and a little water, just enough for the fish to braise. Add in the roe, a small, whole onion, and a little fresh butter. Then put dough around the edge of the pot and place a bowl full of water on top so it fits nicely with the dough. Put the pot on the grey embers and simmer for a half hour or more. The stewed fish will have a very tasty little sauce. Discard the onion and serve over slices of toast.

Barbel in moreta sauce

Scale the barbels or carp or any other big fish; no small one will be any good. Cut the barbel into pieces, sauté onion in a pan, and add the pieces of barbel. Stir together with the onion and lard and then add a little wine, a little vinegar, all spices, salt, a handful of garden herbs, and enough water to braise. Add a little toasted flour that's been thinned. With all these ingredients, put it on to boil vigorously and don't let it simmer more than half an hour, maybe less and [certainly] no more. This moreta sauce is normally made as explained, and sugar and cinnamon are added to the sauce itself, but I stand by the more sour [version]. These big barbels are good cut as steaks, marinated in the sturgeon marinade, and grilled on the grill. Serve with a little marinade or lemon or orange juice.

Pickled sea bream, as prepared in Portugal

There is no better sea bream that when it's boiled with pepper and orange; even so, it can be eaten grilled, stewed, or wrapped in dough. I'll include here one way to brine sea bream that perhaps you haven't yet seen. Scale the sea bream and chop it into pieces. If you don't want to fry them whole, take the juice of a dozen good-quality sour oranges and add one quart of vinegar, one pint of water, a little salt and pepper, clove, ginger, and a little saffron. Put this brine in a terracotta casserole or a silver bowl and heat it up, but don't bring it to a boil. Put the sea bream on to fry. When done, begin taking them out of the oil and as soon as they are out, dunk them in the brine to cover all of them. Then quickly take them

y luego sácalos (192r) presto en un plato, y tápalos con otro, de manera que estén bien ajustados, y déjalo estar así hasta que tengas otra sartenada frita, y entonces desembaraza los platos para echar los otros, y harás otro tanto con ellos, como con los primeros. Estos besugos, si los sirves calientes, con un poco del mismo escabeche, son muy buenos: y si los quisieres tener así secos, con sólo aquel poco que estuvieron en el escabeche, les hallarás tanto gusto como si hubiera un mes que estaban en él, y los puedes llevar muchas leguas en una banasta, o cesta, entre unas pajas de centeno, y está mucho más tierno que el otro escabeche ordinario.

[305] *Sardinas rellenas de escabeche.*[328]

Tomarás sardinas frescas, o a lo menos que sean frescales, escámalas, y quítales las agallas, que no les quede más del testuz: luego ábrelas por medio hasta la cola, arrimando el cuchillo a la (192v) espina del lomo: luego saca la espina del lomo toda, dejando el testuz de la cabeza, y velas quitando unas raspillas que tienen en las ijadas, y si no son frescas del todo, échalas abiertas así en remojo lo que te pareciere. Y advierte, que no han de estar abiertas por el lomo, sino por la barriga: luego echarás a cocer para doce sardinas, seis, o siete huevos duros, y mondarlos has, y echarlos has en el almirez con clara y todo, y májalos mucho que estén como esponja, que no se conozca la yema de la clara: luego sazónalo con todas especias, y un poco de cilantro seco: y si quisieres echar un poquito de comino, podrás, como quien sazona una morcilla: échale un poco de sal, y échale huevos crudos, cosa de dos, o tres; de manera que no esté muy blando el relleno, e irás rellenando las sardinas, poniendo un poco de relleno en la sardina a la larga: luego cerrarla que torne a estar en la misma forma de sardina: y aunque no llegue a juntar (193r) la sardina bien por la barriga por amor del relleno no importa, porque no se abrirá: luego batirás otros tres, o cuatro huevos, y rebozarás estas sardinas, y fríelas en buen aceite, y desde que tengas fritas las sardinas, harás un escabeche con vinagre, agua, y especias, y azafrán, y dulce de miel, o azúcar, y cocerlo has, y espúmalo, y déjalo enfriar: y pon las sardinas en una olla con algunas ruedas de limón, y echa el escabeche encima, y puédeslas guardar un mes, o cerca dél: y si las quisieres enviar fuera podrás hacer el escabeche de los besugos a la Portuguesa, con mucho zumo de naranjas: y cuando se acabaren de freír pásalas por el escabeche, y estófalas entre los platos como los besugos, y así se podrán enviar fuera en seco en alguna olla, o cesta.

[306] *Cómo se guisan las Langostas.*

Las langostas se comen cocidas en un cocimiento de agua, y sal, pimienta: (193v) lo que está dentro en la concha mayor, dicen, que son los sesos.[329] Esta concha

---

328 For images of this recipe, see Appendix 3.19.A–B.
329 With the phrase "dicen," Martínez Montiño recognizes that the inner nervous system probably is not a brain, but he calls it this to simplify the situation.

out, [put them] on a plate, cover them with another in a way that they fit tight, and let them be until you have another frying pan full of fried fish. Then clear off the plate to put the others on and do the same thing with them as for the first round. These sea bream, if served hot with a little of the same brine, are very tasty. If you want to eat them just dry, with only that little amount of time in brine, you'll find it as tasty as if it'd been soaking in it for a month. It can travel in a regular or large basket for many leagues stored with rye straw and is much more tender than other regular brine.

Pickled stuffed sardines

Take fresh sardines or at least lightly salted ones. Scale them and remove the gills so nothing else is left on the back of the head. Then open down the middle all the way to the tail, placing the knife right next to the spine. Next, remove the whole spine, leaving the head and neck. Remove the little bones that are on the sides and if they aren't completely fresh, let them soak for as long as you think necessary. Note that you shouldn't open them through the back, rather through the belly. For twelve sardines, cook six or seven hard-boiled eggs, peel them, place them, whites and all, in a mortar, and mash them until they become fluffy and you can't tell the white from the yolk. Season with all spices and a little coriander and if you want to add a little cumin, you can, like for seasoning blood sausage. Add a little salt and raw eggs, about two or three. The filling shouldn't be too soft. Begin stuffing the sardines by putting a little filling in the sardine lengthwise. Then close it up so that it looks like a sardine. Even if it doesn't fully close around the belly because there's too much stuffing, it's okay because it won't open up. Whip three or four eggs, dip the sardines in them, and fry them in good oil. Once fried, make brine with vinegar, water, spices, saffron, and sweetener, either honey or sugar. Boil it, whip it, and let it cool. Put the sardines in a pot with some lemon wheels and pour the brine over them. You can store them for a month or close to a month, and if you want to deliver them elsewhere, you can make the brine for sea bream Portuguese style, with a lot of orange juice. Right when they're finished frying, dunk them in the brine, and pack them tight between plates, like the sea bream, and this way they can travel dry in a pot or basket.

How to cook lobster

Lobster is eaten boiled in a boil of water, salt, and pepper. It is said that what is inside the big part of the shell are the brains. After it's been boiled, open

después que haya cocido abrirla has, y con una cucharita desharás un poco de aquellos sesos, y echarle has un poco de vino dentro, y un poco de pimienta y nuez, y un poquito de manteca fresca, y zumo de limón, y una migaja de sal, y ponlo sobre las parrillas, y dé un hervor.[330] Desta manera son de buen gusto, y los demás tuétanos se comen así, descascarándolos con pimienta, y naranja.

[307] *Langosta rellena.*

Si quisieres rellenar la concha de la langosta harás un relleno con los mismos sesos, y un poco de la cola picada, que es carne muy blanca: Freirás un poco de cebolla con un poco de manteca de vacas, y echarás allí la carne picada de la cola, y los sesos, y darle has una vuelta en la sartén: luego échale huevos crudos, y fríelas que estén secos, (194r) y échale un poquito de hierbabuena, y sácalo al tablero, y pícalo todo, y échale un poquito de pan rallado, y huevos crudos hasta que esté un poco blando, y sazona con todas especias, y échale pasas de Corintio, si las hubiere, y un poco de zumo de limón, e hinche la concha deste relleno, y ponla dentro de un hornillo sobre un poquito de masa, porque no se trastorne, y ponle lumbre abajo y arriba, y cuajarse ha: luego harás una sopilla, y pondrás la concha rellena en medio, y pondrás alrededor las piernas con sus conchas, porque gustan los señores de partirlas, y éstas tendrás en su cocimiento calientes, hasta que se hayan de poner en el plato: y también podrás poner un poco de la carne de la cola alrededor de la concha, porque es carne muy blanca, aunque es muy poco dura: de la carne de la cola podrás hacer pasteles, y pastel en botes, y otros cualesquier platillos, como tengo dicho en el sollo, y en las carpas, y los tuétanos de las (194v) piernas pondrás como cañas de vaca. Desta carne de la cola de las langostas se puede hacer manjar blanco, porque tiene hebra, por la cuenta del de carne.[331]

[308] *Cómo se aderezan los Cangrejos.*

Los cangrejos grandes, que algunas veces son mayores que langosta, también se aderezan echándoles dentro un poco de vino, y pimienta, y nuez, y un poco de manteca fresca, y zumo de limón, y se pone sobre las parrillas a estofar: y entiéndese que ha de estar cocido primero: este cangrejo se puede rellenar como langosta, y poner las piernas alrededor: los cangrejos chiquillos se han de estofar vivos con agua y sal, y vino, y un poquito de vinagre y pimienta, y los señores gustan de partirlos con los dientes, y chupar los tuétanos.

---

330 Both here and with crab, Martínez Montiño gives specific instructions to boil the shellfish on the grill.
331 The term *cuenta* [account] is another example of the ways Martínez Martiño references a recipe.

this part of the shell and, with a small spoon, loosen up the brains a little and add a little wine, a little pepper and nutmeg, a little butter, lemon juice, and a pinch of salt. Put on the grill and let it boil. They are delicious this way. The rest of the meat is eaten this way: with pepper and orange and removing it from the shell.

Stuffed lobster

If you want to fill the lobster shell, make a filling with the brains themselves and a little minced tail meat, which is very white. Fry a little onion in a little butter, add to it the minced meat and brains, and stir it in the frying pan. Add some raw eggs and fry them until done. Add some spearmint, turn it onto the cutting board, and chop it all up. Add a little bit of breadcrumbs and raw eggs, until it's somewhat soft. Season with all spices and add in dried currants, if available, and a little lemon juice. Fill the shell with this filling and place it in a small oven with a little dough so it doesn't move. Put the heat above and below and let it set. Next, make sops and put the stuffed lobster in the middle and put the legs in their shells around it because lords like to crack them open. These should stay hot in the boil until you are ready to serve them on the plate. You can also put a little tail meat around the shell because it's very white meat even though it's a little tough. With tail meat you can also make pies, crustless pies, and any other dishes, as I have explained for sturgeon and carp. You can put on the leg meat as you would beef marrow. With lobster tail meat you can make blancmange, with the same calculations as for the meat [blancmange recipe], because it is fibrous.

How to prepare crab

Big crabs, which at times are bigger than lobsters, are also prepared by adding inside them a little wine, pepper, nutmeg, a little butter, and lemon juice. Put it on the grill to simmer [in its shell] slowly. It is understood that it should be boiled first. The crab can be stuffed like lobster with the legs placed around it. Smaller crabs should be simmered live in salted water, wine, and a little vinegar and pepper. Lords like to crack them open with their teeth and suck out the insides.

[309] *Cómo se aderezan los Ostiones.*

Tomarás los ostiones mayores, y (195r) lava las conchas muy bien, y ábrelas con la punta de un cuchillo, porque son muy fuertes de abrir; mas si metes la puntilla del cuchillito, y llegares a herir en el ostión, luego se abrirá la concha con mucha facilidad: luego descarnarlos has, y pondrás en las conchas más hondas dos o tres ostiones en cada una, y ponlos sobre las parrillas, y echarás en cada uno un poquito de manteca de vacas fresca en pella, y un poquito de salpimienta, y ellas se ahogarán allí, y volverlas has para que se ahoguen de la otra parte, y echarle has encima un poco de zumo de naranja, o limón, y han de ir calientes a la mesa en las mismas conchas. Desta manera son mejores que de otra ninguna.

[310] *Pastel de Ostiones.*

De estos ostiones frescos podrás hacer buenos pasteles, ahogándolos con buena manteca de vacas, y sazonándolos con todas especias, y un poquito (195v) de verdura y sal, y de que estén cocidos los pasteles cebarlos con huevos y agrio. También son muy buenos para rellenar pollos, o capones, ahogándolos, y sazonándolos con todas especias, y rellenar los pollos sin otra cosa ninguna: y si quisieres hacer un relleno de pollos, o capones de carne: después de hecho, echarás en él ostiones enteros, porque éstos de cualquiera manera que vayan han de ir enteros: en empanadas Inglesas son muy buenos, ahogándolos, y sazonando con todas especias, y un poco de verdura: y si hubiere criadillas de tierra que mezclar con ellos son muy buenos. Estos ostiones fritos con naranja y pimienta, también son buenos.

[311] *Cómo se aderezan los mariscos.*

Estos pescadillos de conchas, que se llaman mariscos, como son los cangrejos, y pesebres,[332] y gámbaros, y a[l]mejas,[333] y otros muchos, todos son buenos (196r) cocidos con agua, y sal, y pimienta, porque es mucho gusto descascarlos, y comer los tuétanos: y descascando los gambaros, y langostines, y los mejillones, y otros muchos que hay son buenos ahogados con su manteca, y cebolla, y sazonando con todas especias, y aderezándolos en su cazuela, echarás su verdura picada, y su agrio de limón, y agraz, sazonándolo de sal, son muy buenas cazuelas, y fritos con naranja y pimienta son buenos.

---

332 *Pesebre* or today *percebe* [gooseneck barnacle] is a shellfish that traditionally attaches to coastal rocks. It is primarily associated with Galician gastronomy.

333 In the 1611 version, "almejas" [clams] is written without the *l*: "amejas." I have included it here because all other versions do include it.

How to prepare oysters

Take big oysters and wash the shells well. Open them with the tip of a knife because they are hard to open, but if you slip the tip of the knife in and injure the oyster, the shell will easily open. Remove the oysters and in the deepest shells, put two or three oysters in each. Put them on the grill and, in each one, add a little ball of butter, a little salt and pepper, and they will be sautéed in it. Turn them over to sauté the other side and drizzle some orange or lemon juice on top. They should go to the table hot in the shell itself. This way is the best way of all to serve them.

Oyster pie

With these fresh oysters you can make tasty pies by sautéing them in good butter, seasoning them with all spices and a little bit of herbs and salt, and once the pie is baked, enrich it with eggs and sour juice. These are also very good for stuffing chickens or capons, sautéing them, and seasoning with all spices. Stuff the chickens without anything else and if you want to make a stuffing with chicken or capon meat, once it's done, add whole oysters, because any way you prepare them they should be whole. In English empanadas they are very tasty, sautéing them and seasoning them with all spices and a little bit of green herbs. If truffles are available to mix in with them, they are very tasty. These oysters fried with orange and pepper are also tasty.

How to prepare shellfish

These small fish with shells that are called shellfish, like crab, barnacles, prawns, and clams, and many others, are all good boiled in water with salt and pepper, because it is a lot of fun to shell them and eat the meat inside. When shelling prawns, langoustines, mussels, and many others that exist, they are good sautéed in the right amount of butter and onion, seasoning them with all spices. When preparing them in their shell, add the right amount of chopped green herbs, lemon juice, and verjuice and season with salt. They are very tasty stewed and fried with orange and pepper.

[312] *Ranas.*

Estas ranas ya se sabe que su comer más ordinario es fritas con naranja y pimienta: y también se hacen buenas albondiguillas dellas, quitando los huesos, y picando la carne de las piernas, porque no tienen otra, y sazonando con todas especias, y echarle un poquito de pan rallado, y echarle has yemas de huevos crudos, y sazona de sal, y tendrás aparejado caldo de garbanzos con buena manteca, (196v) y harás tres albondiguillas un cuarto de hora antes que las hayas de servir, y cuájalas con sus yemas de huevos, y agrio de limón. También son buenas estas ranas ahogadas con buena manteca, y cebolla menuda, y luego hacer una salsa como para carnero verde.

[313] *Pastel de Ranas.*

De estas ranas podrás hacer un pastel, ahogarlas has con un poco de manteca fresca, y echarles has encima un poco de agua caliente, y un poquito de verdura, y sal, y den un hervor: luego sácalas con la espumadera, y sazónalas con todas especias, y sal, y métalas en el vaso con un poco de manteca de vacas: y cuando esté cocido batirás unas yemas de huevos con zumo de limón, y echa del caldo adonde se han perdigado las ranas, y ceba tu pastel, y cuájese: y desta misma manera se han de sazonar para empanadas Inglesas de ranas, ahogando (197r) estas ranas con su manteca, y cebolla, se les puedes echar de todas especias, y un poquito de vino, y un poco de agrio, y estofarlas.

Destas ranas se hace muy buen manjar blanco, perdigando las ranas en agua, que den un par de hervores, y quitarles unas venillas negras que tienen: y luego tomar cantidad destas ranas, como de pechuga, y media de gallina, y deshacerlas con los dedos muy blandamente, porque son muy tiernas: y luego batirlas con un poquito de leche con el cucharón de manjar blanco: y luego echar la harina del arroz por la cuenta del manjar blanco de carne.

[314] *Pasteles de pies de Puerco.*[334]

Cocerás los pies de puerco, y luego les quitarás los huesos grandes, y rebozarlos has con huevos, y fríanse: y luego picarás un poco de tocino gordo, (197v) y sazonarás los pies con todas especias, y pondrás un poco del tocino picado, y asentarás los pies en el pastel, y echarás otro poco de tocino por encima, y cierra tu pastel: y cuando esté cocido batirás cuatro huevos con claras, y echarle has leche lo que fuere menester para henchir el pastel, y echarle has un cuarterón de azúcar molido, y mezclarlo has todo, y cebarás el pastel, déjalo cuajar, y sírvelo así caliente: y si tuvieres muy buena manteca fresca, bien la podrás poner en lugar del tocino picado.

---

334 This recipe and the next appear in the eighteenth-century recipe collection *Manuscrito Ávila Blancas* in reverse order (Pérez San Vicente, *Gastronomía mexicana* 94–5).

Frog

It is already known that the most common way to prepare frog is fried with orange and pepper. Good meatballs are also made with them, removing bones, chopping up the meat from the legs, because there isn't any other meat, and seasoning with all spices. Add a little bit of breadcrumbs, raw egg yolk, and season with salt. Have garbanzo broth with good lard prepared and make three big balls a quarter of an hour before serving them. Thicken with egg yolk and lemon juice. They are also good sautéed in good lard with diced onion and then make a sauce like the one for green mutton stew.

Frog pie

With these frogs you can make a pie. Sauté them with a little fresh lard and pour on top a little hot water, a little bit of green herbs and salt, and bring to a boil. Then remove them with a skimmer, season with all spices and salt, and put them in a crust with a little butter. When it's baked, whip egg yolks with lemon juice and add some broth in which you parboiled the frogs, enrich the pie, and let it set. You can season an English empanada made with frog this same way, sautéing the frog with the right amount of lard and onion, adding all spices, a little wine, and a little sour juice, and let them stew.

These frogs make a very good blancmange if you parboil them in water that is boiled twice. Remove the little dark veins they have. Next, take frog, the same amount as a breast and a half of hen, and gently pull the meat with your fingers, because the meat is tender. Next, beat in a little milk with a blancmange spoon. Then add in rice flour as calculated in the meat blancmange [recipe].

Pig's feet pie

Boil pig's feet, remove the big bones, coat them in egg, and fry them. Then mince a little extra fatty fatback, season the pig's feet with all spices, add a little of the minced fatback, and place the feet in a pie crust. Add a little more fatback on top and seal the pie. When it's baked, beat four eggs with their whites, add enough milk to fill the pie, add a quarter pound of sugar, and mix it all together. Enrich the pie, let it set, and serve it hot. If you have good, fresh butter, you could easily use it in place of the minced fatback.

[315] *Cazuela de pies de Puerco.*

Estos pies de puerco los podrás hacer en cazuela untándola con manteca de vacas, o tocino picado, y sazona los pies con todas especias: luego tomarás cuatro, o seis huevos, y bátelos muy bien, y échales leche lo que fuere menester para henchir la cazuela, y échale cuatro o seis onzas de azúcar, y un poco (198r) de canela, y asienta los pies rebozados en la cazuela, y échale los huevos y la leche sobre los pies de puerco, de manera que esté bien mezclado, y échales su manteca fresca por encima, y métela en el horno a cuajar. Y advierte, que en esta cazuela de pies de puerco, y en el pastel atrás escrito podrás echar unos pocos de piñones majados y revueltos con la leche, y los huevos, le dan muy buen gusto: y esto que digo de echarle cuatro, o seis onzas de azúcar, se entiende para un pastel mediano, que si fuese para un pastelón grande, sería menester media libra. Esto se queda al albedrío del oficial.

[316] *Cazuela verde de pies de Puerco.*

Cocerás, y rebozarás los pies de puerco, como está dicho en los dos servicios de atrás,[335] y asentarlos has en la cazuela: luego picarás verdura, y majarla (198v) has en el almirez con un migajón de pan muy majado, como para salsa de perejil, y desatarlo has con un poco de vinagre y agua caliente: luego freirás un poco de tocino en dados muy menudo, y un poco de cebolla, y sazona con todas especias, y canela, y échale cuatro, o seis onzas de azúcar de manera que esté bien agridulce: luego ponlo a cocer trayéndolo a una mano con el cucharón, y dando dos hervores échalo en la cazuela, y cueza otro poco, y sírvela caliente. Las cazuelas de pies de puerco, y pasteles de leche, que llevan leche de cabras, los podrás hacer con leche de piñones: y cuando sacares la leche de los piñones (si fuere posible) sácala con otra leche de cabras, y si no sea con agua: y en sacando la leche, aquel orujo que queda de los piñones, la mitad dello tornarás a echar con la leche, y los huevos para cuajar el pastel, o cazuela; porque el orujo de los piñones no es sequerón como el de las almendras, antes es muy blando, (199r) y da muy buen gusto: y con esto quedará el pastel muy bien cuajado, y sabrá a los piñones.

[317] *Pasteles de Piñones, y Huevos mejidos.*

Majarás una libra de piñones remojados, e irás echando unas gotas de leche de cabras en el almirez, y cuando estuvieren bien majados las piñones desatarlo has con

---

335 Although in Chapter 1 *servicio* translates as *service* to explain how to serve different dishes, in Chapter 2 it is better translated as *recipe*, as seen both here and later in "Cómo se manen las aves en dos horas" [How to tenderize poultry in two hours] (600–2; 601–3). Throughout the cookbook Martínez Montiño uses various words to stand in for *recipe*: *suerte* [kind], *cuenta* [account], *memoria* [memoir], and *orden* [instruction] are other examples.

Pig's feet casserole

You can make these pig's feet in a casserole, greasing it with butter or minced fatback. Season the feet with all spices. Then, take four to six eggs and beat them very well. Add enough milk to fill the casserole and add four to six ounces of sugar and a little cinnamon. Place the coated pig's feet in the casserole. Pour the milk and eggs over the pig's feet so that it's all well mixed together. Add the right amount of fresh lard on top and put it in the oven to set. Note that to this pig's feet casserole and to the pie previously written down you can add a few ground pine nuts to the milk and eggs and it will give it a very nice flavour. And when I say to add four to six ounces of sugar, I mean for a medium-sized pie. If it's a big pie, half a pound is necessary. This is up to the discretion of the cook.

Green pig's feet stew

Boil and coat pig's feet as explained in the two previous recipes and place them in a casserole. Then chop herbs and thoroughly grind them in a mortar with the crumb of a loaf of bread, as you would for parsley sauce, and thin it with a little vinegar and hot water. Then fry a few minced cubes of fatback and a little onion, and season with all spices and cinnamon. Add in four to six ounces of sugar so that it is very sweet and sour. Next, put on to boil and, using a big spoon, stir it with one hand. Once it has come to a boil twice, add it to the casserole and cook it a little longer. Serve hot. The pig's feet casserole and milk pies made with goat milk can also be made with pine nut milk. When you make pine nut milk (if it's possible), make it with goat milk and if not, water. When making the milk, half the pulp that comes from the pine nuts should be added back into the milk and eggs to set the pie or casserole. Because the pine nut pulp isn't dry, as almond pulp is, but actually very soft, it provides a very tasty flavour. This is how the pie will set well and taste like pine nuts.

Pine nut pie with sweet scrambled egg yolks

Grind a pound of soaked pine nuts and slowly add goat milk to the mortar. When the pine nuts are well ground, thin them with more goat milk, about one quart.

más leche de cabras, cosa de media azumbre; luego batirás media docena de huevos, y mezclarlo has todo, luego le echarás cosa de seis onzas de azúcar, y una migaja de sal: luego harás gubiletes de masa llana un poco anchuelos, y no muy altos, y perdígalos en el horno, echándolos una migaja de manteca a cada uno, y pícalos con la punta del cuchillo en el suelo, porque no hagan empollas: y en estando tiesos échales del batido, de manera que les falte una pulgada para henchirse: luego tendrás docena y media de huevos hilados (199v) y alguna caña de vaca en trozos: y con esto acabarás de henchir los gubiletes, que luego subirá batido, y se mezclará con los huevos y las cañas, y ponlos a cocer, y ellos subirán una pulgada cada uno por encima del borde, y no tornarán a bajar. Es un plato que parece muy bien: y si quisieres exprimir la leche de los piñones, y quitarle la mitad del orujo de los piñones, bien podrás, que con el demás recaudo cuajarán muy bien: y con este recaudo harás ocho, o diez pasteles de los que tengo dicho: parecen muy bien en las meriendas. Ahora quiero tratar un poco de algunas maneras de huevos.[336]

[318] *Huevos hilados.*[337]

Harás almíbar de una libra de azúcar, y tomarás dos docenas de yemas de huevos, y batirlos has muy bien, y luego los echarás en una punta de estameña, o servilleta, y apretarlos has, y colarán todos, y quedarán en la servilleta (200r) las telillas de las yemas de los huevos, y las galladuras, y luego tomarás una cucharita que no tenga más de un agujero, y pondrás el azúcar sobre buena lumbre que alce el hervor, y echarás de las yemas batidas en la cucharita, e irás echando sobre el azúcar, andando alrededor siempre por encima del hervor del azúcar, y aprisa porque no se pegue la una hebra con la otra, y que salga muy delgado, y harás una hilla que parezca de seda, y harás tres o cuatro dellas: y luego tomarás unas rebanadillas de pan, y armarás un plato, y si sobrare algún almíbar echarlo has por encima, porque se mojen las rebanadas: y si no tuvieres cucharita de un agujero, con un cascarón de huevo, lo podrás hacer, y si no con un pucherito chiquillo, agujerado por el suelo se hace muy bien. Y si alguno dijere, que sin tantas diligencias los podrás hacer, bien lo creo; mas como los que yo hago no los hará, si no lo hace desta manera. Si tuvieres (200v) muchos platos de huevos hilados que hacer, claro está que no los estarías haciendo con un cascarón de huevo, sino que tomarás una cuchara espumadera, y otra cerrada, y seis, u ocho libras de azúcar en almíbar: y así cuando

---

336 This closing sentence that introduces eggs exemplifies the intentionality of Martínez Montiño's design of specific sections within Chapter 2.
337 In the early nineteenth century, "Huevos hilados" [Candied egg yolk threads] were still found in recipe books like *Libro de confitura para el uso de Elias Gómez maestro cicero y confiero de la ciudad de Olite*. While the cooking process is still very similar, when the sweet threads are removed from the boiling sugar, they are placed in a big tub of water and then drained (Ciérbide and Corcín 87).

Then beat a half dozen eggs and mix everything well together. Then add about six ounces of sugar and a pinch of salt. Then make flat, somewhat wide, shells of dough, not very tall, and parbake them in the oven. Add a dab of lard to each one. With the tip of the knife poke the bottom so that it doesn't bubble up. When firm, add the batter, leaving an inch open on the top. Next, have a dozen and a half of candied egg yolk threads and some pieces of beef bone marrow. Finish filling the shells with this and the batter will rise and mix with the eggs and marrow. Put them in to bake and they will rise an inch over the edge and won't fall again. This dish is very attractive. If you want to express milk from the pine nuts and remove half the pine nut pulp, you can, because with the rest they will set very well. And with the rest you can make eight to ten pies of those I've explained. They are attractive at late afternoon suppers. Next, I'd like to take up a few ways of preparing eggs.

Candied egg yolk threads

Make a simple syrup with a pound of sugar. Take two dozen egg yolks and whip them. Then pour them into the tip of a cheesecloth or napkin, squeeze, and strain it all. The yolk membrane and red dots will remain behind in the napkin. Then, take a small spoon with only one hole, put the sugar over a high flame so that it comes to a boil, place the whipped egg yolks in the spoon, and begin dropping them over the sugar, always moving around on top of the boiling sugar. Move quickly so that the threads don't stick to one another and come out very thin. Make a little skein that looks like silk; make three or four of them. Then, take slices of bread and assemble a plate. If some simple syrup is left over, drizzle it over the top so that the slices soak it up. If you don't have a spoon with a hole, you can make these with an eggshell, and if not, a small cooking pot with a hole in the bottom works very well. If someone were to say that you could make this without so much care, I think you could. But the way I make them that person couldn't, unless he does it this way. If you had a lot of candied egg yolk threads to make, of course you wouldn't use an eggshell; rather take a skimmer and a regular spoon and six to eight pounds of simple syrup. When it is at the early thread

estuviere en punto, lo pondrás sobre unas trébedes que tengan buena lumbre, e irás echando con la cuchara cerrada sobre la espumadera, y trayéndolo por el hervor del azúcar alrededor aprisa, se harán muy buenos huevos hilados; mas con todo eso serán como hilo, o seda. Para armar estos platos de huevos hilados, para que levanten, y se puedan deshilar harás unas hojuelas muy delgadas, y armarás el plato sobre ellas, o harás una madeja muy grande que vayan en ella todos los huevos que tocan a un plato, y asiéntalos sobre las hojuelas, y en medio pondrás algunas guindas conservadas, y algunas cermeñas, u otras conservillas menudas.

[319] (201r) *Otro plato de Huevos hilados*.[338]

Harás huevos hilados de la manera que está dicho atrás, y harás unas parrillas de pasta de mazapán, y cocerlas has sobre un pliego de papel, polvoreado de harina: hanse de cocer estas parrillas en el horno, y los pies hacia arriba, y asiéntalas sobre los huevos hilados, y sacarás de las hebras de los huevos por entre las varillas de las parrillas, parecerán llamas de fuego, y del mazapán que te sobró, a la mitad dél le echarás unos polvos de sándalo, que es un palo de la India escofinado, que se halla en las boticas, y pondráse colorado. Luego harás dos rollitos de mazapán blancos, y otros dos de colorado, y pon uno blanco debajo, y otro colorado encima, luego otro blanco, luego otro colorado: luego los apretarás un poco que se peguen unos con otros, y queden de ancho de dedo y medio, y cortarás destos (201v) rollitos al través, y saldrán unos torreznillos, o cosa que lo parezca, y estos cocerás como cociste las parrillas: luego asiéntalos sobre las mismas parrillas, y parecerá tocino que se está asando: luego toma unas rebanadas de pan tostadas, y remojadas en vino, y conservadas en azúcar de las que están escritas atrás,[339] y compondrás el plato a la redonda, y parecerán rebanadillas de diacitrón. Este plato parece muy bien, porque todo lo que lleva es otra cosa de lo que significa. Y si otro día quisieres adornar algún plato con unos huevos cocidos duros, que no sean huevos, sacarás leche de almendras, y échale su azúcar y cuécela, como almendrada, y toma un poco de colapege derretida,[340] y échala dentro en la almendrada: luego tomarás

---

338 This recipe is for food art that was familiar to other cooks throughout Europe. At the close of his cookbook, Martínez Montiño promises another one that focuses on this type of fantastic food. In addition, using certain ingredients to pose as foods other than what they were was a technique used during Lent. For example, in *Ordinance of Pottage*, a fifteenth-century codex, a similar recipe can be found for making hard-boiled eggs out of almonds, sugar, and a fish-based gelatin, "Brawn ryall in lentyn" (Hieatt 177–8). Readers might notice the commonality with creative techniques of today's chefs.
339 Martínez Montiño is referring to the recipe "Unas rebanadas de pan conservadas" [Preserved bread slices] (550–2; 551–3).
340 *Colapege* or today *cola de pescado* is *isinglass*, a gelatin-like substance that comes from sturgeon bladder. For more on the history of gelatin, see Albala, *The Great Gelatin Revival*.

stage, put it on a trivet with a strong flame and, with the spoon, begin pouring [the yolks] on the skimmer and quickly passing it through the boiling sugar. The candied egg yolk threads will come out very good. Moreover, made like this they will turn out like threads or like silk. To assemble these plates of candied egg yolk threads so that they stand up and can be untangled, make some very thin pastry sheets and assemble the threads on top of them. Or, you can make one very big skein of all the eggs that can fit onto one plate and set them on the pastry sheets. Place in the middle some preserved sour cherries, some Cermeña pears, or other small preserved fruit.

Another dish of candied egg yolk threads

Make candied egg yolk threads as explained earlier and make grills out of marzipan paste. Bake them on a sheet of paper that is dusted with flour. These grills should be baked in the oven, with the legs up. Set them on the candied threads of egg yolk and pull the threads of the eggs through the bars of the grills. They will look like flames. With the leftover marzipan, use half of it and mix in sandalwood powder, which is a filed stick from India that you can find in pharmacies and that will colour the marzipan. Next, make two small rolls of white marzipan, and two more of the coloured marzipan, and put one white one below, then a coloured one on top, then another white and another coloured. Squeeze them a little so they stick together and are about a finger and a half wide. Cut them across and you'll have little pieces of fried pork fat, or something that looks like it. Bake it the way you baked the grills. Then set them on the grills themselves and it will look like fatback being grilled. Then, take some toasted slices of bread, soaked in wine, and preserved with sugar as is previously explained. Put together a plate in the round and it will look like slices of candied citron. This plate looks really good because everything on it is something other than what it signifies. On another day, if you want to decorate a plate with some hard-boiled eggs, that aren't eggs, get some almond milk and add the right amount of sugar to it and boil it like for almond broth. Take a little melted isinglass and add it

unos cascarones de huevos muy limpios, y asiéntalos sobre un poco de sal, y les tendrás hecho un agujero que sea pequeño, por donde habrás sacado lo que tiene el huevo dentro, tan ancho como una (202r) avellana mondada, e hínchelo desta almendrada, y déjalo cuajar: luego tomarás pelotillas de mazapán, que tengan un poco de azafrán, y una yema de huevo, y hase de cocer en un cacillo: y luego hacer las pelotillas, y meterlas en los cascarones, que vengan a quedar en medio del huevo: luego derrite la almendrada, de manera que no esté caliente, ni tibia, no más de cuanto no esté cuajada, y luego acaba de henchir los cascarones, y déjalos helar, y después de helados les podrás quitar las cáscaras: y aunque los tenga una persona en la mano, si no los prueba es imposible conocer que no son huevos, y si los prueba es una almendrada muy buena. Esos son para adornar algunos platos, y para hacer burla. Advierte, que cuando echares la yema del huevo al mazapán, que se le ha de dar una vueltecilla para que se cueza la yema: y luego sacarlo así caliente, y hacer las pelotillas: el punto del almíbar, ha de ser mojando el dedo, y que haga un hilo.

[320] (202v) *Plato de Huevos mejidos.*

Para hacer un plato de huevos mejidos, harás almíbar de una libra de azúcar, y batirás venticuatro yemas de huevos, y pondrás el azúcar donde cueza muy aprisa: luego echarás todos los huevos juntos sobre el almíbar; de manera que suba el almíbar por encima de todos los huevos, y así irás haciendo el bollito de los huevos mejidos: y si los quisieres servir juntos con el mismo cacito, lo podrás echar sobre el plato, poniendo debajo unas hojuelas, o unas rebanadillas de pan, y sino sírvelo en pellitas, adornando el plato con algunas conservas.

[321] *Huevos esponjados.*

Tomarás media libra de miel, y otra media de manteca de vacas, y ponlo todo en un cacito al fuego: entre tanto batirás docena y media de huevos con claras: y cuando esté cociendo la miel, (203r) y manteca, echa los huevos dentro, y ponles una cobertera encima con un poco de lumbre, y cuajarse ha que parezcan huevos mejidos, y sírvelos sobre rebanadillas de pan. Estos huevos más son para frailes, y gente ordinaria, que para señores, que con ocho maravedís de miel y un poquito de manteca, podrá hacer una moza seis, u ocho huevos: y con esto contentará a su amo. A estos huevos se les suele echar un poquito de azúcar y canela por encima. Estos mismos huevos podrás hacer revueltos, echando la miel y la manteca en un cazo, o en una cazuela, y batir los huevos, mezclados con un poco de pan rallado, y échalos sobre la miel, y la manteca, y revuélvelos con un cucharón, y se vendrán a hacer unos huevos revueltos muy buenos, y sírvelos sobre rebanadillas de pan, y azúcar, y canela por encima.

to the almond broth. Then take some very clean eggshells and set them on some salt. You should have a small hole in the shell from which you drained everything inside, the size of a shelled hazelnut. Fill it with the almond sauce and let set. Then take some little marzipan balls that have a little saffron and an egg yolk and boil them in a saucepan. Make little balls and place them in the shells so that they're in the middle of the egg. Melt the almond broth so that it's not hot or warm, no more than what is was before it set. Then, finish filling the shells and let them chill. After they've chilled you can take them out of their shells. Even if a person were holding them in their own hands, if they didn't try them, it would be impossible to know they weren't really eggs. If the person tastes them, it tastes like a very tasty almond broth. These are for garnishing dishes and for playing a joke. Note that when you add the egg yolk with the marzipan, you should turn it over so that the yolk cooks. Then remove it hot as is and make the little balls. The early thread stage is when you wet your finger [with the simple syrup] and it makes a thread.

Dish of sweet scrambled egg yolks

To make a dish of sweet scrambled egg yolks, make the simple syrup with a pound of sugar and whip twenty-four egg yolks. Bring the sugar to a rolling boil. Then drop the egg batter all at once into the simple syrup so that the syrup goes over the top of all the egg yolks. This is the way you'll make the little ball of sweet scrambled egg yolks. If you want to serve them together, with the same pan you can turn them onto the plate, putting under them some pastry sheets or bread slices. Or you could also just serve them as balls, garnishing the plate with some preserves.

Fluffy eggs

Take half a pound of honey and another half of butter and put them in a saucepan on a flame. Meanwhile, beat a dozen and a half eggs with their whites, and when the honey and butter are boiling, add in the eggs, put a lid on it, and cook on low. It should set so it looks like sweet scrambled egg yolks and [should be] serve[d] on slices of bread. These eggs are really more for monks and regular people than for lords. With eight maravedis worth of honey and a little butter, a girl can make six or eight eggs, and with this her master will be happy. Normally a little sugar and cinnamon is sprinkled on top. You can make scrambled eggs with these same eggs by putting the honey and butter in a pan or a casserole. Beat the eggs mixed with a little bit of breadcrumbs and pour this over the honey and butter and stir with a spoon. This will make some very tasty scrambled eggs. Serve over slices of bread with cinnamon and sugar on top.

[322] *Huevos de Alforja.*

Harás dos docenas de huevos hilados (203v) como está dicho en los de atrás, y ha de estar el azúcar bien subido de punto, que haga hilo: y después que estos huevos estén hechos, harás cinco o seis partes dellos, y harás de cada parte un bollito un poco larguillo a manera de mostachón, y apretarlos has muy bien, y desta manera harás los demás, y pondráslos sobre el tablero a que se enjuguen: luego los pondrás sobre la hoja del horno sobre un papel polvoreado de harina, y métetelos en el horno a fuego manso, y déjalos tomar una colorcilla dorada, que parezcan panecillos bizcochados: y desta manera pueden ir en cajas adonde quisieren. A estos huevos se les suele echar en el almíbar agua de azar [sic], o algún otro olor. Otros se hacen batiendo las yemas de huevos, y echando un poco de almíbar en una tortera ancha: luego echar las yemas de huevos de manera, que se extiendan por toda la tortera, y que tengan de grueso medio dedo, cubre la tortera, y échale lumbre (204r) abajo y arriba, y cuajarse ha, y luego sacarla has; y harás unas tiras del ancho de dos dedos, y cortarlas has que queden como tabletas, y déjalas enjugar, y ponlas sobre la hoja del horno sobre unas cañitas, y darle has un poco de fuego que se sequen bien: luego las vidriarás con un poco de azúcar, o les darás un baño blanco. Este baño y vidriado hallarás escrito donde se trata de bizcochos.[341]

[323] *Huevos con Cominos.*

Pondrás una olla con un poco de agua, sal, y un poco de verdura picada, perejil, y hierbabuena, y échale un poco de buena manteca de vacas fresca, o buen aceite, y sazonarás con todas especias, y unos pocos de cominos, y un grano de ajo, y batirás otra tanta cantidad de huevos como hay de agua, y bátelos bien, y échalos dentro en la olla, o en una cazuela de barro, que esté el agua cociendo, y velo revolviendo con un (204v) cucharón hasta que estén los huevos cuajados, que parezcan huevos revueltos, y pondrás en el plato rebanadillas de pan, y sírvelos encima. Estos huevos de cominos los podrás hacer, batiendo los huevos con unos pocos de cominos, y sal, y pondrás la sartén al fuego con un poco de buena manteca, o aceite: y cuando esté bien caliente freirás en ella dos, o tres granos de ajo, y saca los ajos, y echa los huevos, y revuélvelos con un cucharón hasta que estén enjutos, y sírvelos sobre unos picatostes. Estos huevos con cominos son buenos con sesos de ternera, o de carnero, cociendo primero los sesos: y luego freírlos, y tener los huevos batidos con sal, y cominos, y echar los sesos dentro: y luego tomar un poco de manteca limpia, y calentarla, y freír los ajos en ella: y luego echar los ajos a mal, y echar los huevos en la sartén, y revolverlos con un cucharón hasta que estén secos todos estos huevos con cominos. Si tu señor (205r) no fuere amigo de ajos, no será mucha falta no llevarlos.

---

341 Martínez Montiño is referencing "Memoria de los bizcochos de almidón" [Memoir of sweet biscuits with starch] (542; 543).

Saddlebag eggs

Make two dozen candied egg yolk threads as explained in the previous [recipes]. The sugar needs to be at a high boiling point, so that it makes threads. After the eggs are done, divide into five or six parts and, with each one, make little extended balls, as for mostachon cookies, and squeeze them tightly. Make the others this way and put them on a cutting board so that they dry out. Next, put them on a baking sheet on paper dusted with flour and put them in the oven to bake on low flame. Let them turn a golden brown; they should look like little sponge cake rolls. They can go into boxes this way and be sent wherever. For these eggs, the simple syrup normally has some orange blossom water added to it or some other fragrance. Others are made by whipping the egg yolks and putting a little simple syrup in a wide covered tart pan. Then add the egg yolks so that they cover the entire covered tart pan and are about a half finger thick. Cover the covered tart pan, add heat above and below, let it set, and then remove it. Make some strips, about two fingers wide, cut them so that they look like tablets, and let them dry. Place them on a baking sheet on some little reeds and put some heat on them to really dry out. Then glaze them with a little sugar or dip them in meringue. This meringue and glaze are found where sponge cakes are treated.

Eggs with cumin

Put a pot on with a little water, salt, chopped green herbs – parsley and spearmint – and add a little good butter or oil. Season with all spices, a little cumin, and a clove of garlic. Beat as many eggs as there is water, and beat them well. Add them to the pot or the terracotta casserole. Have the water boiling and constantly stir with a spoon until the eggs are set and look like scrambled eggs. Put some slices of bread on a plate and serve them on top. You can also make these eggs with cumin by beating the eggs with cumin and salt. Put the frying pan on the flame with some good butter or oil and, when it's hot, fry two or three cloves of garlic and then remove them. Add in the eggs, stirring them with a spoon until they're dry. Serve them on slices of fried bread. These eggs with cumin are good with veal or mutton brains, first boiling the brains. Then fry them and have the beaten eggs with cumin and salt and add the brains. Then take some clean lard, heat it up, and fry garlic in it. Then discard the garlic, add the eggs to the frying pan, and stir with a spoon until all the eggs with cumin are done. If your lord isn't a friend of garlic, it wouldn't matter too much if there weren't any.

[324] *Capirotada de Huevos.*

Harás torrijas con manteca de vacas, y huevos estrellados duros, y tendrás queso rallado cosa de una libra; luego harás una zurciga majando un poco de queso y un grano de ajo, y echarás allí media docena de huevos crudos, y desatarlo has con caldo de garbanzos, o agua tibia, y sazonarás con pimienta, jengibre, y nuez, y azafrán, y echarle has un poco de manteca de vacas, y ponlo a cocer, trayéndolo a una mano por que no se corte, y armarás tu sopa con las torrijas, y los huevos estrellados, e irás echando queso rallado entre lecho y lecho, y las torrijas han de ir de esquina, y luego le echarás la zurciga por encima, y dos pares de huevos estrellados blandos, y su queso rallado por encima, y un poco de manteca muy caliente, y ponlo a cuajar en un horno.

[325] (205v) *Otra capirotada de Huevos rellenos.*

Cocerás una docena de huevos duros, y luego partirlos has por medio, y sacarás las yemas, y destas yemas y un poco de queso rallado, y un poco de pan rallado, picado todo: luego le echarás yemas de huevos crudas hasta que esté blando el relleno, y sazona con todas especias, y sal, y torna a henchir los huecos donde salieron las yemas, y todo lo que pudiere caber en el medio huevo: luego batirás cuatro huevos, y rebózalos, y fríelos, y luego majar piñones, y queso, y un grano de ajo, y seis yemas de huevos, y desátalo con caldo de garbanzos, y sazona con todas especias, y cuece la zurciga: luego tendrás torrijas hechas, y armarás la sopa con ellas, y los huevos rellenos, y queso rallado: luego echar la zurciga por encima, y su queso, y manteca bien caliente: luego métela en el horno a cuajar. Esta (206r) sopa de huevos rellenos podrás hacer echando en el relleno unos pocos de piñones majados, y un poco de azúcar, y todo el demás recado, salvo ajos que no han de entrar aquí: y para hacer la zurciga majarás piñones, y sacarás leche dellos con un poco de agua tibia: luego echarás media docena de huevos, los tres con claras, y harás tu zurciga con dulce de azúcar, y armarás la sopa con torrijas y huevos rellenos, y en lugar de queso, azúcar, y canela revuelto con un poquito de queso rallado que sea muy bueno: y luego que tengas la zurciga cocida échasela a la sopa, como está dicho en las atrás, y échale su manteca muy caliente por encima, y ponla a cuajar en el horno. Y advierte, que los piñones majados han de ir envueltos con la leche, y saldrá espesa, que es lo que se pretende.

[326] *Otros Huevos rellenos.*

Estos huevos rellenos podrás hacer (206v) sacando las yemas, partiéndolos por medio, y picarlas con un poco de verdura, y un poco de pan rallado, y sazonar con todas especias y canela, y un poco de azúcar, y échale huevos crudos cuanto esté un poco blando el relleno: luego rellena los huevos, y rebózalos, y fríelos, y luego sírvelos sobre torrijas con azúcar y canela, y zumo de limón. Estos no han de llevar queso, leche, ni piñones.

Eggs, capirotada style

Make torrijas with butter and hard, fried eggs. Have about a pound of grated cheese. Then make a zurciga sauce by mashing a little cheese and a clove of garlic together. Add in a half dozen raw eggs and thin it with garbanzo broth or warm water. Season with pepper, ginger, nutmeg, and saffron. Add a little butter and put it on to boil, stirring it with one hand so that it doesn't break. Assemble your sops with the torrijas and fried eggs. Sprinkle grated cheese between each layer. The torrijas should be squared, then ladle the zurciga sauce on top, place two pairs of soft, fried eggs and sprinkle the right amount of grated cheese on top, and drizzle on a little hot butter. Put it in the oven to set.

Another stuffed egg recipe, capirotada style

Hard boil a dozen eggs, split them down the middle, and remove the yolks. Mince together these yolks with a little bit of grated cheese and a little bit of breadcrumbs. Then add raw egg yolks until the stuffing becomes soft. Season with all spices and salt. Fill the hole in the eggs where the yolk was with as much as can fit in the half egg. Next, beat four eggs, dip them in the egg batter, and fry them. Then grind together pine nuts, cheese, a clove of garlic, and [mix in] six egg yolks. Thin it with garbanzo broth, season with all spices, and let this zurciga sauce simmer. Have some torrijas made and assemble sops with them, the stuffed eggs, and grated cheese. Then ladle the zurciga sauce on top with the right amount of cheese and hot butter. Place in the oven to bake. These stuffed eggs on sops can also be made by adding to the filling some ground pine nuts, a little sugar, and the rest of the mixture except garlic, which shouldn't be included. To make the zurciga sauce, mash pine nuts and use some warm water to release some milk from them. Then add a half dozen eggs, three with the whites, and make your zurciga sauce with sugar as a sweetener. Assemble the sops with torrijas, stuffed eggs, and instead of cheese, mix in sugar and cinnamon to the grated cheese, which should be good quality. Once the sauce is done, ladle it on the sops as explained above, add the right amount of hot butter on top, and put it in the oven to bake. Note that the ground pine nuts should be mixed in with the milk and it should turn out dense. That's what you're aiming for.

Other stuffed eggs

These stuffed eggs can be made by removing the yolks, slicing them down the middle, and mincing a little bit of green herbs and a little bit of breadcrumbs. Season with all spices, cinnamon, and a little sugar, and add in raw egg yolks to soften the filling. Then fill the eggs, dip them in batter, and fry them. Serve over torrijas with cinnamon and sugar and lemon juice. These shouldn't have any cheese, milk, or pine nuts.

[327] *Huevos crecidos.*

Tomarás doce huevos, e irás quitándoles las claras, dejando las yemas en los medios cascarones: estas claras batirás con otros cuatro huevos, y un poco de verdura picada y especias y sal, y un poco de pan rallado, y pondrás una sartén al fuego con manteca: y cuando esté caliente echa las yemas dentro así enteras, y fríanse: luego sácalas y rebózalas con las claras, y tórnalas a echar en la sartén, y fríelas: luego sácalas, y tórnalas (207r) a rebozar con más claras: y desta manera irás haciendo hasta que se acaben las claras, y vendrán a quedar los huevos muy grandes: luego harás unas torrijas, y una sopa con ellas, y los huevos, entremetiendo uno con otro, y tomarás caldo de garbanzos, sazonando con especias, y un poco de agrio y su manteca de vacas, y media docena de yemas de huevos, y desátalos con el caldo, o brodete.[342] Y advierte, que esta sopa ha de llevar azúcar y canela entre los huevos y torrijas.

[328] *Huevos en escudilla.*

Tomarás medio cuartillo de agua clara, ponla a cocer con sólo sal, que esté un poco más salada del ordinario, y batirás seis, u ocho huevos, echarlos has en la cazuela donde está el agua cociendo, y revuélvelos con un cucharón muy bien hasta que se vayan cuajando, y harás huevos revueltos, de manera que no estén muy cuajados, y sírvelos así en su cazuela, si es nueva, sino (207v) en un platillo sobre unas rebanadillas. Y si no quisieres hacer más de cuatro, se podrán hacer en una escudilla de plata.

[329] *Huevos revueltos con vino.*[343]

Tomarás seis onzas de azúcar, y echarlo has en medio cuartillo de agua en un cacito, y echarle has la cuarta parte de vino, y ponlo al fuego: y cuando cociere échale doce huevos batidos y revuélvelos con un cucharón hasta que se cuajen, y vengan como huevos revueltos, de manera que no estén muy cuajados, y sírvelos sobre unas rebanadillas de pan, y échales un poco de azúcar y canela por encima. Estos huevos son buenos, porque no llevan manteca ni aceite, y se pueden hacer en una escudilla de plata cuatro huevos con dos onzas de azúcar, y una gota de vino. Estos huevos se llaman por otra parte, los huevos de Tolosa.[344]

---

342 For more on *brodete*, see 178n58.
343 After the 1617 edition, the title of this recipe was edited to simply "Huevos revueltos."
344 With this closing comment, Martínez Montiño recognizes the importance of regional dishes. Tolosa is a city in Guipúzcoa (Basque Country).

Expanded eggs

Take twelve eggs and begin separating the whites and leaving the yolks in their half shell. Beat the whites with four other eggs, a little chopped green herbs, spices, salt, and a little bit of breadcrumbs. Put a frying pan on the fire with some lard. When it's hot, put the yolks in whole, fry them, take them out and dip them in the egg white batter. Then return them to the frying pan and fry them. Remove them and dip them in the egg white batter again. Continue this way until all the batter is gone. The eggs will turn out huge. Then make some torrijas. Make sops with them and the eggs, layering one and then the other. Take some garbanzo broth, seasoning it with spices, a little sour juice, and the right amount of butter. Take a half dozen egg yolks and thin them with the broth or *brodete*. Note that these sops should be sprinkled with sugar and cinnamon between the eggs and the torrijas.

Eggs in a bowl

Take a half pint of clear water, put it on to boil with just salt so that it's a little saltier than normal. Beat six to eight eggs, add them to the casserole where the water is boiling, and stir them well with a spoon until they begin to set. You'll make scrambled eggs that are not too dry. Serve them in the casserole, if it's new, and if not, on an individual plate over slices [of bread]. If you don't want to make more than four, you can do it in a silver bowl.

Scrambled eggs with wine

Put six ounces of sugar in a saucepan, add in a half pint of water and a quarter cup of wine, and put it on the fire. When it's boiling, add in twelve beaten eggs and stir them with a spoon until they set and look like scrambled eggs that are not too dry. Serve them on some slices of bread and sprinkle a little sugar and cinnamon on top. These eggs are tasty because they don't have lard or oil. You can make them in a silver bowl with four eggs, two ounces of sugar, and a drop of wine. Elsewhere, these eggs are called *Tolosa eggs*.

[330] (208r) *Huevos arrollados.*

Tomarás un cuarterón de almendras y otro de azúcar, y harás pasta de mazapán, y desta pasta harás unos rollitos delgados, y de una ochava de largo:[345] luego harás seis huevos, u ocho en tortillas muy delgadas, que no lleve cada tortilla más de un huevo, y que tome toda la sartén; y envolverás un rollito de la pasta en cada tortilla, y harás della una rosquilla, y trabarla has con un palillo de orégano: luego batirás media docena de huevos, y rebozarás estas rosquillas, y fríelas en manteca de vacas, y quítales los palillos, y sírvelas con miel, azúcar, y canela por encima. Estos huevos arrollados se pueden hacer sin pasta de mazapán, echando sobre las tortillas azúcar, y canela, arrollarlas, y rebozarlas, y freírlas, y sírvelas con su miel, y azúcar, y canela por encima.

[331] *Tortillas de Agua.*

(208v) Batirás cuatro huevos muy bien batidos con su sal: luego pon la sartén al fuego con aceite, o manteca, que para éstas no importa que sea bueno, o malo el aceite, porque no ha de llevar ninguno: en estando caliente el aceite en la sartén, vacíalo, y echa de presto unas gotas de agua en la sartén, y tórnalo a volver cara abajo que se caiga también el agua: luego echa los huevos de presto, y revuélvelos con un cucharón, como quien hace huevos revueltos: y cuando se vayan cuajando arróllalos al medio de la sartén, recogiéndolos que venga a quedar redonda la tortilla, y gorda, a modo de un panecillo, y luego vuélvela con la punta del cucharón: y desta manera harás cuantas quisieres. Y advierte, que estas tortillas han de llevar un poco de más sal que las otras, y han de quedar tiernas por de dentro: y cuando se hacen, ha de andar la sartén bien caliente: y cuando se echare el agua no han de ser más de unas gotas: y hase de vaciar (209r) esta agua, y echar los huevos con tanta presteza que no se enfríe la sartén, porque se pegaría la tortilla si se enfriase.

[332] *Tortillas Cartujas.*[346]

Las tortillas cartujas has de hacer ni más ni menos que las de agua, salvo que no han de llevar agua, sino calentar la manteca, o aceite: y cuando esté caliente vaciarlo todo, y echar los cuatro huevos bien batidos, y revolverlos con un cucharón, como la tortilla de agua: y cuando se vayan cuajando irlos recogiendo al medio de la

---

345 For *ochava* (approximately 10 cm or 4 in) and other measurements, see Appendix 2, "On Measurements," Castaño Álvarez, and "Antiguas pesas y medidas."

346 Today known as the *tortilla francesa* [French omelette], a name acquired after the War of Independence of 1808, this omelette is made with the simplest of ingredients: eggs and fat. Its name reflects the austere lifestyle and meatless diet of the Carthusian monks.

Eggs in a ring

Take a quarter pound of almonds and another of sugar and make marzipan paste. Roll this dough out into thin rolls, an ochava long. Then, from six or eight eggs, make thin omelettes; each one should only have one egg and take up the whole frying pan. Roll up a marzipan roll in each omelette and then make it ring-shaped. Fasten it with a sprig of oregano. Beat half a dozen eggs, dip the ring shapes in them, and fry them in butter. Remove the sprig and serve with honey, sugar, and cinnamon on top. These eggs in a ring can be made without marzipan paste and by adding cinnamon and sugar to the omelette. Roll them, dip them, fry them, and serve with the right amount of honey, sugar, and cinnamon on top.

Water omelette

Whip four eggs together with the right amount of salt. Then put the frying pan on the fire with oil or lard. For this [recipe] it doesn't matter if the oil is good or bad because it won't have any. Once the oil in the pan is hot, empty it out and quickly add some drops of water to the frying pan. Turn the pan upside down so the water comes out. Then quickly cook the eggs, stir them with a spoon as if you're making scrambled eggs, and when they begin to set, gather them into the centre of the pan, gathering them up into a round, fluffy omelette so that it looks like a roll. Then flip it with the end of the spoon. Make as many as you want this way. Note that these omelettes should have a little more salt than the others and should be soft inside. When you make them, the pan should be really hot. Also, when you put the water in, use only a few drops. You must get rid of this water and put the eggs in quickly so the pan doesn't cool down because the omelette will stick if it gets cool.

Carthusian omelette

A Carthusian omelette should be made exactly the same way as the water omelette, except it shouldn't have any water; rather, heat up some lard or oil and when it's hot, empty it all out. Add the four well-beaten eggs and stir them with a spoon [as you would] for the egg omelette [made] with water. When they begin to set, begin

sartén: y luego volverla con la punta del cucharón, y ha de quedar tierna por de dentro, y gordita. Para éstas es menester que sea el aceite, o manteca buena, y no eches más de cuatro huevos en cada una, que no saldrán buenas si echas más.

[333] *Tortillas dobladas.*

Batirás doce huevos con su sal, y pondrás (209v) la sartén al fuego con buena manteca, y has de echar un poco de más manteca que la que se suele echar para las tortillas ordinarias, y echarás la tercia parte de los huevos en la sartén, y harás una tortilla redonda pequeña: luego vuélvela con la paleta, y echa encima la otra tercia parte de los huevos, y acomódalos a la otra tortilla, de manera que se venga a cubrir la tortilla, tórnala a volver, y echa la otra tercia parte de los huevos, y torna a hacer otro tanto: tórnala a volver, y tostar por entrambas partes. Esta tortilla ha de salir sabrosa de sal.

[334] *Tortilla blanca.*[347]

Tomarás ocho, o diez huevos frescos conforme fuere la sartén, y aparta las claras todas, y deja las yemas en los medios cascarones, y bate estas claras mucho, hasta que haga una espuma muy blanca, y toda sea espuma, entonces pondrás la sartén al fuego, con cosa de media (210r) libra de manteca de vacas, que esté bien caliente: luego echa las claras dentro, y hacerse ha como una esponja: luego ve echando las yemas sobre las claras, que quede la tortilla empedrada, y podrás echar algunas yemas más de otros huevos, aunque no sean frescos: y con la manteca que anduviere por los bordes de la sartén irás echando con la paleta por encima de la tortilla hasta que se cuajen las claras, y las yemas: sírvelas sobre unas rebanadillas de pan. Ha de ir muy caliente a la mesa, y con harta sal.

[335] *Una tortilla con agua y sal.*[348]

Echarás un poco de agua en la sartén, y un poco de zumo de limón: luego echarás media docena de huevos batidos, y velos recogiendo poco a poco, y se vendrá a hacer un bollito como tortilla de agua, y se habrá embebido el agua y el limón en los huevos: luego vuélvela con la paleta, y sírvela caliente. (210v) Hase de calentar primero la sartén con aceite.

---

347 For an image of this dish, see Appendix 3.20.
348 Although Martínez Montiño does not specify adding salt to the eggs, given the title, it can be assumed that one adds salt to either the eggs or the water before cooking.

gathering them together in the centre of the pan. Then, fold it with the end of the spoon. It should be soft inside and fluffy. For this you need good oil or lard, and don't use more than four eggs in each one, because it won't turn out good if you use more.

Folded omelette

Beat twelve eggs with the right amount of salt. Put some good lard in a frying pan on the fire. Use a little more lard than what is normally used for regular omelettes. Add a third of the eggs to the frying pan and make a small, round omelette. Flip it with a spatula and add on top another third of the eggs, adjusting them to the omelette so that they cover it. Flip it again. Add the other third and adjust it and flip it again so that both sides are toasted. This omelette should turn out perfectly salty.

White omelette

Take eight to ten fresh eggs, as many as you need for the size of your frying pan. Separate all the whites and leave the yolks in their half shell. Whip the whites into a white foam; all of it should be foamy. Then, put the frying pan on the fire with about half a pound of butter. It should be really hot. Next, add the whites, and they should come out foamy. Then begin adding the yolks on top of the whites. The omelette should look like cobblestone. You can add more yolks from other eggs even if they're not freshly opened. With the butter on the edge of the pan, use the spatula to begin ladling it over the omelette until the whites and the yolks set. Serve on slices of bread. It should be served hot at the table and with a good amount of salt.

Omelette [made] with water and salt

Put a little water in a frying pan with a little lemon juice. Then add in a half dozen beaten eggs and begin gathering them slowly. They will come together in a small ball like a water omelette and the eggs will have absorbed the water and lemon. Then flip it with a spatula and serve it hot. You should first heat up the frying pan with oil.

[336] *Tortilla con Queso fresco.*

Tomarás una docena de huevos, o docena y media: Tendrás una libra de queso fresco hecho rebanadas: luego picarás un poco de hierbabuena, y mejorana, y un poco de jadrea, picarlo has todo muy bien, y échalo en los huevos, y échale un poco de sal y especias: luego pon la sartén al fuego con un poco de buena manteca de vacas, y echa los huevos dentro con las rebanadas de queso, y velas recogiendo lo más presto que pudieres, porque no se derrita mucho el queso: luego vuélvela de la otra parte, y sírvela caliente con unos picatostes encima.

[337] *Huevos de Capirote.*[349]

Tomarás docena y media de huevos, y partirás los cascarones por (211r) junto a las coronillas cerca de en medio, y quitarles has toda la clara, y quédense las yemas en los cascarones, y echarás un poco de sal, y anís en cada uno: luego pondrás la sartén al fuego con media libra de manteca de vacas, y menearás las yemas con un palillo, e irás echando en la sartén estos cascarones boca abajo: y luego veles echando de la manteca caliente por encima con la paleta, y vendrán a hacer una tortilleja en la boca de cada cascarón: sácalos de la sartén que se escurran, y harás unos picatostes angostos, y sírvelos entre los huevos. Son huevos secos, y de buen gusto.

[338] *Platillo de Huevos dulces.*

Harás unas torrijas de pan blanco, remojadas en leche, y fríelas en manteca de vacas: luego córtalos en dados, y toma media libra de azúcar, y ponlo en un cacillo, y échale medio cuartillo de agua sobre el azúcar, y picarás un poquito (211v) de verdura, y échalo dentro, y un poquito de vino, y zumo de medio limón; sazona con todas especias, y canela, y azafrán, y un poquito de sal, y echa los dados de las torrijas dentro y media libra de manteca fresca, y cueza un cuarto de hora, o menos: luego batirás deziocho huevos con claras, y échalos dentro el cacillo, y menéalo que se mezclen los huevos con los demás materiales, y no lo toques más, sino échale un poco de pan rallado por encima, y ponlo con un poco de lumbre abajo y arriba sobre una cobertera, y váyase cuajando poco a poco, hasta que esté bien cuajado, y esté dorado por arriba y por abajo: luego pondrás unas rebanadillas de pan en un plato: luego deja caer el bollo desde el cacito al plato, sin que se vuelva, sino que caiga como está en el cacillo, y échale zumo de medio limón por encima, y un poco de azúcar y canela. Este plato adornarás con cuatro o cinco cañutos de huevos encañutados (212r) cortados en trocitos, y clavados en el bollo: y si no los tuvieres con unas rebanadillas de las torrijas metidas por el borde del

---

349 Emilia Pardo Bazán includes this recipe in her book *La cocina española antigua* (65–6).

Omelette with farmer cheese

Take a dozen eggs or a dozen and a half. Have a pound of sliced farmer cheese. Chop up a little spearmint, marjoram, and a little summer savory. Mince it all up and add it to the eggs. Add a little salt and spices. Then put the frying pan on the fire with some good butter. Add the eggs with the slices of cheese and begin gathering them as fast as possible so that the cheese doesn't melt too much. Then, flip it over. Serve hot with some pieces of fried bread on top.

Eggs capirote

Take a dozen and a half eggs, and spilt the shells between the middle and the top. Remove the whites and leave the yolks in their shells. Add a little salt and anise to each one. Then put the frying pan on the fire with half a pound of butter. Stir the egg yolks with a small stick and begin adding them to the frying pan with the shells face down. Then with a spatula begin ladling the hot butter on top. A mini omelette will appear at the opening of each shell. Take it out of the pan and let it drain. Make some thin slices of fried bread and serve them between the eggs. The eggs are dry and very tasty.

A dish of sweet eggs

Make some torrijas with white bread soaked in milk. Fry in butter and cube. Take half a pound of sugar, put it in a saucepan, and add a half pint of water to the sugar. Chop up a little bit of green herbs and add it in with a little wine and the juice of half a lemon. Season with all spices, cinnamon, saffron, and a little salt. Add in the cubes of torrijas and half a pound of butter and cook for a quarter of an hour or less. Then beat eighteen eggs with their whites and add them to the pan. Stir so that the eggs mix with all the other ingredients and then don't touch it again. Sprinkle breadcrumbs on top. Put low heat below and above on the lid and let it slowly set until it's done and golden on top and below. Place some slices of bread on a plate. Then place the sweet bun right from the saucepan onto the plate without flipping it and without it falling, just as it is in the pan. Sprinkle some lemon juice on top and a little cinnamon and sugar. You can garnish this dish with four or five canutos of sweetened eggs cut into pieces and stuck on top of the sweet bun. If you don't have any, [garnish] with little slices of torrijas placed around the

bollo, y unas ruedas de limón a la redonda. Este plato es para día de pescado, porque derechamente es platillo de cañas contrahecho: y si hay buena manteca fresca, es tan bueno como el de las cañas.[350] Advierte, que este plato se puede hacer con cimas de cardo, que sean tiernas con alcachofas, quitadas las hojas, y se puede hacer con mollejas de cabrito, beneficiándole como está dicho.

[339] *Huevos dorados.*[351]

Para este plato es necesario que sean los huevos frescos, porque si no lo son no salen bien: Tomarás una libra de azúcar, y harás almíbar que no esté demasiado grueso, y apartarlo has, que esté bien frío, o frío del todo: luego echarás en él venticuatro yemas de huevos crudos y enteras,[352] y cuando lo quisieres (212v) servir, pon el cazo sobre buena lumbre: y cuando el azúcar subiere que cubra los huevos, déjale dar un medio hervor, y entonces estarán buenos, porque están cuajados, y están tiernos: y si las yemas de los huevos dorados salen duros no son buenos.[353] Éstos servirás sobre unas rebanadillas de pan muy delgadas, y vayan calientes a la mesa, y el azúcar que sobrare échaselo por encima; las rebanadillas que vayan bañadas en el almíbar. Si no quisieres hacer los venticuatro huevos juntos, podrás hacerlos en dos veces, aunque bien se pueden hacer de una vez: y si fuere para algún enfermo que ha menester pocos, con tres, o cuatro onzas de azúcar, podrás hacer seis huevos: y porque trato de que las yemas doradas vayan enceradas, te quiero dar un aviso para hacer los huevos en cáscara, que salgan encerados, que nunca salgan más duros, ni más blandos: echa los huevos frescos en un cacito con agua fría, y ponlos sobre buena lumbre, (213r) entonces ten cuenta cuando alzare hervor, que entonces están encerados, ni más, ni menos: y si los quisieres más que encerados, con dejarlos estar un poquito más sobre la lumbre, estarán buenos: y aunque tengas el cacito junto al fuego con los huevos, y el agua se entibiare no importa, que cuando te pidieren la vianda, pondrás el cacito al fuego, y cocerá más presto, y será la misma cosa.

[340] *Fricasea de Huevos.*

Tomarás dos docenas de huevos, y cocerlos has duros: luego móndalos de las cáscaras, y cortarlos has por el medio a lo largo: luego los cortarás en rebanadillas delgadas,

---

350 Martínez Montiño is referencing the recipe "Platillo de cañas de vaca" [A dish of beef marrow] (216; 217).
351 In *Libro de confitura para el uso de Elias Gómez maestro cicero y confiero de la ciudad de Olite*, the recipe for "huevos dorados" is very similar (Ciérbide 87).
352 An interesting combination of feminine and masculine adjectives to describe the egg yolks: "yemas de huevos crudos y enteras" [whole yolks from raw eggs].
353 *Duros* is amended to *duras* in 1617 and all other editions.

edge of the sweet bun and some round lemon wheels. This dish is [made] for a fish day because it is truly a faux marrow dish. If you use good, fresh butter, it is as tasty as the marrow dish. Note that this dish can be made with cardoon tops that are very tender, with artichokes with the leaves removed, and also with kid sweetbreads prepared as already explained.

Golden eggs

For this dish it's necessary to have fresh eggs; if not, it won't turn out well. Take a pound of sugar and make simple syrup that is not too thick. Remove it and have it cool somewhat or cool completely. Then add to it twenty-four raw, whole egg yolks, and when you are ready to serve, put the pan over a strong flame. When the sugar rises and covers the eggs, let it boil a little and the eggs will be done because they'll be set and tender. If the golden egg yolks are hard, they're no good. Serve these over very thin slices of bread. They should be hot when they go to the table. With the leftover sugar, ladle some on top. The slices should be soaked in simple syrup. If you don't want to make twenty-four eggs together, you can make two batches, even though you can easily make them all at once. If they're for someone ill who needs only a few, with three or four ounces of sugar, you can make six eggs. Since I am discussing golden eggs, which are soft boiled, I want to offer you advice on making eggs in their shells that come out soft boiled and that are never too hard or too soft. Place the fresh eggs in a saucepan with cold water and place them over strong flames. Then, pay attention to when it comes to a boil, which is when they will be soft boiled, no more and no less. If you want them a little more than soft boiled, then leave them a little longer over the heat, and they will turn out good. Even if you keep the saucepan with the eggs next to the fire and the water warms, it doesn't matter. When they ask for the food [to be served], put the saucepan on the fire and it will quickly come to a boil and turn out the same.

Egg fricassee

Take two dozen eggs and hard boil them. Then peel the shells and cut them lengthwise down the middle. Then cut them into thin slices, just as you would cut

como quien corta cebolla menuda a lo largo: y de que tengas deshechos todos los huevos, freirás un poco de cebolla menuda con buena manteca de vacas, y de que esté frita echa dentro los huevos, y un poquito de verdura picada, y sazona con todas especias, y ahogarás estos huevos con la manteca, (213v) y la cebolla: y cuando quisieres servir, échale un poquito de caldo de garbanzos, y vinagre, que estén un poco agrios, y échales un poco de mostaza:[354] sírvelos sobre unas rebanadillas de pan.

[341] *Huevos en puchero.*[355]

Batirás una docena de huevos con un poco de sal: y luego pondrás media docena de gubiletes de cobre al fuego con un poco de manteca en cada uno, y déjalos calentar muy bien: luego echa en cada uno cosa de un huevo de aquellos batidos, y hacerse han como esponjas: y cuando te pareciere que se podrán volver, que será muy presto vuélvelos con la punta del cuchillo, y fríanse por el otro lado, y saldrán unos huevos redondos, y parecerán esponjas: sácalos a que se escurran de la manteca, y sírvelos con miel y azúcar y canela por encima.

[342] (214r) *Sopa de Huevos escalfados con leche.*

Para esta sopa es necesario que los huevos sean frescos, porque si no lo son, no salen bien, porque se desparraman las claras, y quedan las yemas descubiertas: y así pondrás agua a calentar en una sartén grande, o en otra pieza de cobre ancha, y quebrarás doce huevos frescos en un plato, con cuidado que no se quiebre alguna yema, y cuando la pieza del agua esté cociendo, tomarás una cuchara limpia, y métela en el agua, y traerla has alrededor aprisa, para que mueva el agua:[356] luego saca la cuchara, y echa los huevos dentro, y no tornes a meter la cuchara, sino da unas puñaditas con la mano en el astil de la pieza, y deja cuajar los huevos, de manera que las claras estén cuajadas, y las yemas blandas; luego sacarás la pieza del fuego, y ve echando agua fría por un ladito de (214v) la pieza, e irá saliendo la caliente por encima del borde, y echarás agua fría, hasta que esté tibia la en que

---

354 Early modern mustard differs significantly from today's. Martínez Montiño includes a recipe on how to make it later in the cookbook, "Memoria de la mostaza negra" [Memoir of black mustard] (512–14; 513–15). For more on this condiment, see its entry in the Glossary.

355 In the seventeenth century, the *puchero* [tall stew pot] usually had one handle and was made from terracotta, either glazed or not. And, like the *cazuela*, it was available in a variety of sizes. For today's audience, a *puchero* looks more like an oversized pitcher than a pot. For an image, see Nadeau, "Furniture and Equipment" (131). It's unclear why the title references the *puchero* when the eggs are cooked in *gubiletes* [moulds].

356 This technique of agitating the water prevents the eggs from dropping straight to the bottom. It also helps maintain the heat, so there are no cold spots in the water.

thin lengthwise slices of onion. Once all the eggs are peeled, fry a little diced onion with good butter. Once it's fried, add the eggs with a little chopped green herb. Season with all spices and sauté the eggs in the butter and onion. When you're ready to serve, add a little garbanzo broth and vinegar so that they're a little sour, and add a little mustard. Serve over slices of bread.

Eggs in a stew pot

Beat a dozen eggs with a little salt. Then put half a dozen copper moulds on the fire with a little lard in each one and let them get hot. Then, add in each one about one egg from the beaten eggs. They should become fluffy. When they look as if you can flip them, which will happen quickly, then flip them with the tip of the knife and fry them on the other side. They will end up as little round eggs and look like a sponge. Remove them and let the lard drain off. Serve them with honey, sugar, and cinnamon on top.

Milk sops with poached eggs

For these sops it is necessary to have fresh eggs, because if they're not it won't turn out well, as the whites will spread out and the yolk will be exposed. Put water on to heat up in a big frying pan or in another pot that's wide and copper. Carefully crack the twelve fresh eggs on a plate so that the yolks don't break. When the water in the pot is boiling, take a clean spoon, place it in the water, and quickly stir it up so the water is moving. Then, take the spoon out and add the eggs. Don't put the spoon back in, but, using your hand, shake the pot handle. Let the eggs set so that the white is set and the yolk soft. Then take the pot off the heat and begin adding cold water to one side of the pot as the hot water pours over the edge. Continue adding cold water until the water in which the eggs are poached is lukewarm. Then toast slices of bread and assemble the

están los huevos escalfados: luego tostarás rebanadas de pan, y armarás una sopa, y echarás en un cacito un poquito de harina floreada, y un cuarterón de azúcar, y desatarlo has con cerca de media azumbre de leche, y un granillo de sal, y échale un poquito de buena manteca fresca, y ponlo sobre un poco de lumbre, y velo trayendo a una mano hasta que dé un hervor: luego sácalo, y moja la sopa que esté bien empapada, e irás sacando de los huevos escalfados con la espumadera, o paleta, e iráslos asentando sobre la sopa, y tornarás a echar más leche de la del cacillo sobre la sopa, y los huevos, y cúbrelo con otro plato, y estófese un poquito.

[343] *Sopa de Huevos estrellados con leche.*

(215r) Harás unas poquitas de torrijas, y luego córtalas que sean un poco largas y angostas, y estrellarás una docena de huevos un poco duros: luego batirás cerca de media azumbre de leche con cuatro huevos con claras: luego armarás una sopa de los huevos estrellados y torrijas, de manera que vayan mezclados los huevos con las torrijas, y entre lecho y lecho un poco de azúcar y canela, y un poco de manteca de vacas, y échale de la leche con los huevos, de manera que se empape bien la sopa, y luego échale su azúcar y canela, y ponlo a cuajar en el horno.

[344] *Torrijas de Pan.*

Tomarás pan blanco mollete,[357] y que sean los panecillos tiernos y redondos, cortarás una docena de torrijas redondas, que sean un poquito gordas, y pásalas por un poquito de leche, y luego ráspales un poco de sal por encima: luego pondrás la sartén al fuego con (215v) harta manteca, y harás cada torrija de por sí, y batirás docena y media de huevos, y mojarás una torrija en ellos, y tomarla has con una cuchara cerrada, de manera que vaya la cuchara llena de huevos, y echa la torrija, y los huevos todo junto en la sartén, y hacerse ha como una esponja: luego carga la torrija con la cuchara cerrada, y con la paleta ve recogiendo los huevos encima la torrija, y luego vuélvela con la paleta, y fríase bien hasta que esté un poco morena: y destara [*sic*] manera podrás hacer las doce torrijas con los deziocho huevos, y luego pásalos por almíbar: y si no lo tuvieres, sírvelas con miel y azúcar raspado por encima.

[345] *Sopa Borracha.*

Asarás torreznos de las Garrovillas[358] o de otra parte que sean buenos, y no tengan sal: luego harás torrijas de pan blanco, y sean un poco grandes, y tendrás hecho

---

357 *Molletes* are soft, sweet rolls. For more on their history, see Corbacho, and Yarza 24.
358 *Torreznos* [roasted pork belly] and other pork products from Garrovillas were well known for their excellent quality.

sops. In a saucepan put in a little finely sifted flour and a quarter pound of sugar. Thin it with almost one quart of milk, a pinch of salt, and a little good, fresh butter. Put it over the flames on low and begin stirring until it comes to a boil. Next, remove it, thoroughly soak the sops, and then take the poached eggs out with a skimmer or spatula and begin setting them on the sops. Ladle more milk from the saucepan over the sops and eggs. Cover them with another plate and let them stand for a little while.

Milk sops with fried eggs

Make a few pieces of torrijas and cut them into long, narrow slices. Fry a dozen eggs, medium well. Then beat about one quart of milk with four eggs with their whites. Assemble sops with the fried eggs and torrijas so that the eggs and torrijas are layered. Between layers, sprinkle cinnamon and sugar and dab a little butter. Ladle the egg-milk mixture so that the sops are soaked. Sprinkle the right amount of cinnamon and sugar and put it in the oven to set.

Torrijas

Take white mollete bread. They should be soft, round rolls. Cut up a dozen round torrijas. They should be fairly thick. Dip them in a little milk and grate a little salt on top. Then put the frying pan on the fire with a lot of lard and make each torrija individually. Beat a dozen and a half eggs and soak the pieces of torrijas in them. Pick up one piece with a spoon so that the spoon is full of egg batter. Place the torrija together with the egg batter in the frying pan. It should come out like a sponge. Then hold the torrija with the spoon and with a spatula gather up the eggs on top of the torrija and flip it with the spatula. Fry until it is a little browned. This is how to make twelve torrijas with eighteen eggs. Dip them in simple syrup. If you don't have any, serve them with honey and grated sugar on top.

Drunken sops

Roast pork belly from Garrovillas or from another place with good quality and that is not salted. Then, make torrijas from thick slices of white bread. Have ready half a pound of sugar turned into simple syrup. Soak the torrijas in red

media libra de azúcar en almíbar, (216r) y mojarás las torrijas en vino tinto: luego las pasarás por el almíbar que den un hervor en él: luego harás otro tanto al tocino: luego untarás un plato con manteca fresca de vacas, y harás un lecho de torrijas, y échale canela por encima, y asentarás los torreznos, y echarle has canela, y echarás torrijas encima, de manera que se vean las puntas de los torreznos, y mezclarás un poco de vino con el almíbar, lo que vieres que podrá embeber la sopa; mójala con este vino, y almíbar, déjala estofar: es menester para cada sopa borracha media libra de azúcar: y si el plato fuere un poco grande, serán menester tres cuarterones.

[346] *Otra Sopa Borracha.*

Asarás los torreznos, y un lomo de carnero que sea muy tierno, y harás unos pocos de torrijos [*sic*]: luego harás los torreznos en rebanadas pequeñas y larguillas, y cortarás el carnero cada (216v) costilla de por sí: luego untarás el plato con manteca fresca de vacas, y harás un lecho de torrijas, y echarás azúcar y canela por encima: luego irás armando sobre este lecho la sopa, poniendo una rebanada de tocino de cantera: y luego una torrija también de cantera: luego una costilla de carnero, todo esto muy junto uno con otro, y algunas rebanadas de tocino en el medio, y unas yemas de huevos duras: luego echar azúcar y canela por encima, y moja la sopa con vino blanco, y échale su azúcar y canela, y déjala estofar.

[347] *Otra Sopa borracha.*

Asarás cabrito, pollos, o aves, o perdices, o pichones, y haráslo pedazos, y si son aves en cuartos, y rebózalos con huevos, y fríelos: luego harás torrijas, y mójalas en un poco de vino, que tenga un poco de azúcar: luego tomarás el rebozado, y échale un poco de pimienta, (217r) y zumo de limón, y dale una vuelta que tome el gusto del limón, y de la pimienta: luego arma la sopa de torrijas y cabrito, o aves rebozadas mezclado uno con otro, y vayan algunas torrijas de cantero, y entre torrija y torrija un pedazo de cabrito, o cuarto de ave, y su azúcar y canela, y luego échale lo que sobró de mojar las torrijas: y si no hubiere harto échale más vino tinto, o blanco, como quisieres, y echa el azúcar y canela por encima, y déjala estofar. Esta sopa ha de llevar media libra de azúcar, y estos materiales que se van señalando, se van poniendo respeto de un plato mediano: y si fuese un plato grande, claro está que no se podría hacer sin añadir más recaudo. Y si lo quisieren hacer en una flamenquilla, no sería menester tanto.[359]

---

359 The RAE defines the *flamenquilla* in the following way: "Plato mediano, de forma redonda u oblonga, mayor que el trinchero y menor que la fuente" [a medium-sized dish, either round or oblong, bigger than a trencher but smaller than a platter].

wine. Then, dip them in the simple syrup while it's boiling. Next make the same amount with the fat. Then grease a plate with butter and make a bed of torrijas. Sprinkle cinnamon on top, set the pork belly [on top], sprinkle on more cinnamon, put more pieces of torrijas on top so that you can see the tips of the pork belly. Mix a little wine into the simple syrup, enough so that the sops can soak up all the wine and simple syrup, and let it simmer. Half a pound of sugar is necessary for each [plate of] drunken sops. If it's a big plate, then three quarters of a pound.

Other drunken sops

Roast pork belly and a loin of mutton that is very tender and make a few slices of torrijas. Then cut the pork belly into small, long slices and cut the mutton ribs into single chops. Then grease a plate with fresh butter, make a bed of torrijas, and sprinkle cinnamon and sugar on top. Then continue assembling the sops on this bed by putting an end slice of fatback, then a heel slice of torrija, and then a mutton chop. All of this should be close together, one next to the other, with some fatback slices in the middle and some hard-boiled egg yolks. Then, sprinkle sugar and cinnamon on top. Soak the sops in white wine, sprinkle on the right amount of sugar and cinnamon, and let it simmer.

Other drunken sops

Roast kid, young chicken or adult ones, or partridges, or squab, and chop them up. If the poultry is quartered, dip them in eggs and fry them. Then make torrijas and dip them in a little wine with a little sugar. Next, take the poultry that was coated and fried and sprinkle it with a little pepper and lemon juice. Turn it over so it picks up the lemon and pepper flavour. Next, assemble the sops of torrijas, kid or fried poultry, layering them one by one. Add in some heels of torrijas and between each one a piece of kid or a quarter of poultry with the right amount of sugar and cinnamon. Then ladle on the leftover liquid from soaking the torrijas. If there isn't enough, add more red wine, or white, whichever you prefer, and sprinkle sugar and cinnamon on top and let it simmer. These sops should use half a pound of sugar, and the other ingredients mentioned here are for a medium-sized plate. If it were for a big plate, then of course you couldn't make it without adding more of the ingredients. If you want to make it for a *flamenquilla*, then you wouldn't need as much.

[348] *Otra Sopa Borracha, fría.*

Ésta me parece que es la fina sopa borracha, pues no lleva más de pan, y (217v) vino, y azúcar, tostarás unas rebanadas de pan mollete,[360] que sean un poco gordas, y redondas: luego tendrás media libra de azúcar molido, y mezclado con canela, y tomarás media azumbre de vino que sea bueno, y suave, y ha de ser blanco, e irás remojando estas rebanadas de pan, y asentándolas en el plato, y echarás azúcar y canela por encima, y sea harto: y desta manera irás haciendo tu sopa, y echando el azúcar y canela hasta que se acabe el pan, y esté lleno el plato, y échale mucho azúcar y canela por encima. Ésta toda ha de ser fría, y se puede comer en las colaciones.[361]

[349] *Empanada de Pernil de Tocino.*

Echarás el pernil en remojo que esté bien remojado, y cuécelo, y echa en el cocimiento una azumbre de vinagre: y cuando vieres que el tocino está más de medio cocido: sácalo, y asiéntalo (218r) en un cazo, y échale del cocimiento en que se coció cuanto se bañe, y échale media azumbre de vino blanco, y salvia, y mejorana, e hisopillo, y ponlo sobre lumbre que cueza, y un poco antes que lo quieras sacar, échale unas hojas de laurel, y no cueza más de un hervor con ellas, y sácalo, y enfríese, y sazona con todas especias y canela, empánalo en masa negra, y la empanada sea de dos hojas, y harásle su facción en el jarrete que se eche de ver que es pernil: cuando salga del cocimiento, ha de salir entero un poco teniente. Y advierte, que el azumbre de vinagre que se le echó, es, porque la vinagre encrudece la carne, y no le deja hacer hebras, que si fuera para servir así fiambre, no le habías de echar vinagre ninguno hasta que lo estofaras, mas el vino si le echares una azumbre, o dos al cocer le hiciera mucho provecho, mas la vinagre no se le ha de echar hasta el estofado, y ha de ser poca, no siendo para empanar.

[350] (218v) *Una empanada de menudos de Pavos.*

Tomarás un menudo de pavo, que son los alones, el pescuezo, y los pies, y la molleja: luego desollarás los pescuezos, y harás un relleno con higadillos de los mismos pavos, o de aves, friendo un poco de tocino, y cebolla, y los higadillos y échales un poco de hierbabuena, y luego echa cuatro huevos crudos, y revuélvelo sobre la lumbre, hasta que esté bien seco: luego sácalo al tablero, y pícalo muy

---

360 *Molletes* are soft, sweet rolls. For more on their history, see Corbacho, and Yarza 24.
361 *Colación* [collation] is a light meal allowed on days of fasting. It is usually eaten once a day and in the evening. In the early seventeenth century, it was also a term used for a light afternoon or early evening meal.

Other drunken sops served cold

For me this one is the fine drunken sops [recipe], since it isn't anything more than bread, wine, and sugar. Toast slices of mollete rolls that are fairly thick and round. Then take half a pound of ground sugar and mix it with cinnamon. Take one quart of good, smooth wine – it should be white – and begin soaking the slices of bread. Set them on the plate and sprinkle sugar and cinnamon on top, a lot of it. And in this way make your sops, sprinkling sugar and cinnamon on top until all the bread is gone and the plate is full. Sprinkling a lot of sugar and cinnamon on top. This [dish] should be served cold and can be eaten during collation.

Fatty ham empanada

Soak the leg and when it's thoroughly soaked, boil it. Add to the boil two quarts of vinegar. When the fat is more than half cooked, remove it and set it in a large pan. Add enough of the liquid from its boil to braise. Add one quart of white wine, sage, marjoram, and winter savory and bring it to a boil. Just before you're ready to take it out, add bay leaves and don't let it boil more than once with them. Remove it and let it cool. Season with all spices and cinnamon. Wrap it in a dark dough; the crust should have two layers. Expose the features of the shank so that one can see it's a ham. When you take it out of the boil, it should come out whole, a little underdone. Note that the two quarts of added vinegar are to tenderize the meat and not allow it to become sinewy. If it were for eating as cold meat, you wouldn't need to add any vinegar until you were ready to stew it. Moreover, if you added two to four quarts of wine when it was boiling, it would be very advantageous. Also, don't add the vinegar until it's time to stew. It should be very little if you're not wrapping it in crust.

Turkey giblet empanada

Take the giblets of a turkey, which are the wings, neck, feet, and gizzard. Skin the necks and make a filling from the liver of the same turkeys or other poultry by frying a little fatback, onion, and livers. Add in a little spearmint, then four raw eggs, and stir it over the fire until the eggs are well cooked. Then turn it out

bien, y échale un poquito de pan rallado, y échale dos huevos crudos, y sazona con todas especias y agrio de limón, y sal: y con este relleno henchirás la morcilla del pescuezo: luego tomarás los alones, y pelarlos has en agua, y cortarles has las puntas, y cuézanse así enteros, y cortarás el pescuezo por medio, y cuézase todo junto con la molleja, y los pies, y la morcilla con (219r) un poco de agua y sal, y tocino: y después de cocido sacarlo has que se enfríe, y harás una masa dulce como de empanada Inglesa, y empánalo con ella, y echando unas lonjas de tocino debajo, y sazonarlo de sal, y especias, y echa otras lonjas de tocino encima, y cierra tu empanada, y cuézase: y advierte, que para cada empanada son menester dos menudos con sus dos morcillas de los pescuezos: y si no hubiere pavos, se puede hacer de gansos, aunque no son tan buenas, y si fuere en día de carne podrás hacer el relleno con carne en lugar de los higadillos.

[351] *Un pastel de Membrillos.*

Tomarás dos libras de azúcar, y harás almíbar dello: luego harás docena y media de huevos hilados en este almíbar: luego echarás ocho, o diez membrillos sobre el almíbar, y echarle has agua de manera que se cubra, y echarle has unas rajas de canela dentro, y (219v) dos pares de clavos enteros, y un poco de vino: luego ponlo a cocer todo poco a poco, que se vayan conservando los membrillos, y tápalos con una cobertera, y de cuando en cuando dales una vuelta con el cazo: y cuando estén bien conservados, y con buena color, sacarlos has del almíbar que se enfríen: luego harás un pastelón de masa blanca, y meterás membrillos dentro: luego meterás los huevos mejidos entre membrillos y membrillos, y dentro dellos porque se han de conservar enteros: y luego cierra tu pastel: y en estando cocida la masa abre el pastel, e hínchelo de almíbar, y mételo en el horno así destapado para que los huevos se tuesten un poco y tomen una colorcilla dorada. Y advierte, que si fuere día de carne le podrás echar una caña de vaca hecha trozos: y si no le quieres echar huevos mejidos con sola la caña de vaca que le eches, y unas yemas de huevos duras parecerá bien: a estos pasteles que no (220r) llevan huevos mejidos, has de echar unas rebanadas de pan blanco tostadas entre membrillo y membrillo: y después de lleno el pastel con el almíbar parecen muy bien.

[352] *Pastelillos Saboyanos.*

Tomarás carne de ternera, y picarla has muy bien con su tocino, y luego la perdigarás, y sazónala con pimienta, nuez, y jengibre, y un poquito de azafrán, y sazona de sal: luego harás unos gubiletillos muy pequeños, e hínchelos desta carne, mezclando alguna caña picada con ella: luego cúbrelos con hojaldrado, y cuézanse: batirás unas yemas de huevos con un poco de zumo de limón, y un poco de caldo, y cebarás los pastelillos muy sutilmente, de manera que no se eche de ver que se han abierto. Y si alguna vez quisieres hacer éstos agridulces podrás, y raspa un poco

on a chopping board, mince it all, add a little bit of breadcrumbs, two raw eggs, and season with all spices, lemon juice, and salt. With this filling fill the neck skin sausage. Then, take the wings, pluck them in water, cut off the tips, and boil them whole. Cut the neck in half and boil it along with the gizzard, feet, and neck sausage in a little salted water and fatback. Once they're boiled, take them out to cool. Make sweet dough, as for English empanada, and wrap [the filling] in it, placing strips of fatback underneath. Season with salt and all spices. Add more strips of fatback on top, seal the empanada, and bake. Note that for each empanada it is necessary to have two [sets of] giblets with two neck sausages. If there are no turkeys, you can make it with goose, although it won't turn out as good, and if it's a meat day, you can make the filling with meat instead of poultry liver.

Quince pie

Take two pounds of sugar and make simple syrup with it. Then make a dozen and a half of candied egg yolk threads in this syrup. Next, put eight or ten quinces in the simple syrup and add enough water to cover them. Add pieces of cinnamon stick, two pairs of whole cloves, and a little wine. Then put it all on to boil slowly, so the quince becomes preserved, cover it with a lid, and every once in a while, stir it with the ladle. When the quinces are well preserved and have a good colour, take them out of the simple syrup and let them cool. Then make a big pie crust with white dough, fill with quince, then fill with sweet scrambled egg yolks between the quinces and inside them, because the preserved quinces are whole. Next, seal the pie. Once the crust is baked, open the pie up and fill it with simple syrup. Put it back in the oven uncovered so that the eggs brown a little and take on a golden colour. Note that if it's a meat day, you can add pieces of beef bone marrow. If you don't want to add sweet scrambled egg yolks, then with just the added beef bone marrow and some hard-boiled yolks it will turn out well. For these pies that don't have sweet scrambled egg yolks, add toasted slices of white bread between the quinces. Once the pie is filled with the simple syrup they will look very good.

Little Savoy pastries

Take some veal and mince it with the right amount of fatback, then sear it and season with pepper, nutmeg, ginger, and a little saffron, and season with salt. Then make some very small shells and fill them with the meat and some minced marrow. Cover this with puff pastry dough and bake. Beat some egg yolks with a little lemon juice and a little broth and delicately enrich the little pastries so that you can't tell they've been opened. If you want to make these pastries sweet and sour,

de azúcar por encima del hojaldrado. Éstos han (220v) de ser muy chiquitos, y no han de ser de carnero, sino de ternera.

[353] *Un pernil cocido sin remojar.*

Cocerás este pernil en agua sola, y que sea la pieza donde se cuece bien grande, que ande nadando en el agua: y cuando vieres que está medio cocido, hinche una bacía de agua fría, y ponla junto al caldero donde se está cociendo el pernil, y sácalo del caldero, y échalo en el agua fría así cociendo como está, y déjale estar medio cuarto de hora, y tórnalo al caldero, y cueza; y de ahí a otra media hora tórnale a hacer otro tanto, y se enternece, y se corta la hebra, y después lo podrás acabar de cocer, y estofarlo has con harto vino, y un cuartillo de vinagre, y las hierbas del jardín, salvia, y mejorana, e hisopillo en un cazo, y echarle del cocimiento en que se coció hasta que se bañe, y taparlo has con una cobertera, y cueza media (221r) hora: y cuando lo quisieres sacar échale unas hojas de laurel, y no cueza con ellas más de un hervor, y sácalo, y levántale el pellejo, y arróllaselo al jarrete muy bien, y métele unos clavos enteros por el pernil, y échale harta canela por encima, y un poco de pimienta. La carne destos perniles después de remojados los torreznos es bueno echarlos en leche, o en vino, media hora antes que se hayan de asar.

[354] *Cómo se hace el Alcuzcuz.*[362]

Tomarás medio celemín de harina floreada, y echarle has medio cuartillo de cemite cernido que sea de tahona,[363] si fuere posible, y mezclarlo has todo junto; y esta harina la has de echar en una pieza de cobre ancha y llana, o en una artesilla de

---

362 This recipe for couscous is unique to cookbooks in Spain. In fact, after the publication of two Hispano-Muslim cookbooks in the thirteenth century, no other cookbook includes any references to this dish with clear ties to the Muslim and Morisco communities of Spain. When Martínez Montiño published this work, consuming couscous had long been a recognized sign of Islamismo and a practice that ecclesiastical authorities sought to eliminate. For more, see Gallego Burín and Gámir Sandoval (73). Similar recipes do not appear again until 1817 with the publication of the anonymous New World cookbook, *Libro de cocina de la gesta de independencia*. The first two recipes, "Alcuscuz de trigo" [Wheat couscous] and "Modo de guisarlo" [The way to cook it], have clear ties with Martínez Montiño's cookbook, while the third, "Alcuscuz de maíz" [Corn couscous], brings together New World and Old World food sensitivities (90–1). My thanks to Rachel Lauden for making this connection. As a side note, what is written as *corn couscous* is in actuality a recipe for preparing hominy grits.

363 Flour milled by the *tahona* process, that is, powered by a draft animal, is clearly the most valued, as it is finer. Martínez Montiño references it in six different recipes, and in the recipe "Panecillos de colaciones" [Collation rolls] directly compares "de tahona" [animal-powered mill] to "de molino" [grinder] (504–6; 505–7). For more on *tahonas*, see Arjona. And for more on dry measures, see Appendix 2, "On Measurements," Castaño Álvarez, and "Antiguas pesas y medidas."

you can. Grate a little sugar on top of the puff pastry dough. These should be really small and should not be made with mutton, just veal.

Leg boiled without soaking

Boil this leg in just water. The pot in which it boils should be very big so that the leg is swimming in the water. When you see that it is half cooked, fill a basin with cold water, put it next to the pot in which the leg is cooking, and take the leg out of the pot and put it right from boiling into the cold water. Let it sit half of a quarter of an hour, return it to the pot, let it boil, [and] before another half hour do it once again. This will make it tender and break up the sinew. Then you can finish cooking. Stew it in a pan with a lot of wine, a pint of vinegar, and garden herbs: sage, marjoram, and winter savory. Add in enough of the boil in which it was boiling to braise. Cover with a lid and cook for half an hour. When you're ready to remove it, add some bay leaves and don't let it boil more than once with them. Remove it, lift the skin, and roll it tightly around the shank. Stick some whole cloves in the leg and sprinkle a lot of cinnamon and a little pepper on top. After the fat has soaked, it is good to put the meat from these legs in milk or wine a half hour before roasting.

How to make couscous

Take half a celemin of finely sifted flour and add two cups of sifted bran; if possible, it should be milled. Mix it all together. This flour should be in a wide, flat copper bowl or in a wooden trough, or in a round, woven basket, the Valencian

palo, o en una serilla redonda de las de Valencia,[364] que tan bien se puede hacer allí como en el cobre, y aun mejor: luego tendrás en una (221v) pieza agua tibia, y tendrás un hisopillo, y esta agua ha de estar salada, como para hojaldrar, y ve echando con el hisopillo de aquel agua sobre la harina, de manera que las gotas del agua cayan [sic] muy menudas sobre el harina, que en esto está el toque de torcer bien el alcuzcuz,[365] e irás trayendo la mano extendida por encima la harina, y siempre a una mano; luego tornarás a echar más agua con el hisopillo, y andar con la mano extendida sobre la harina: y de cuando en cuando meterás la mano y revolverás el harina lo de arriba abajo: y desta manera irás haciendo hasta que el harina ande haciéndose muchos granillos, y que no tenga polvo: luego tendrás dos harnerillos, el uno ha de tener los agujeros que no pase por ellos mayor grano que de mijo, y el otro ha de ser que pase por él del tamaño de un grano de rábano, o un poquito mayor: luego cernerás este alcuzcuz con el harnerillo chico sobre una pieza, y todo lo que quedare (222r) arriba échalo sobre el harnerillo grande, y ciérnelo sobre unos manteles limpios, de manera que no haga montón: y desta manera irás cerniendo todo el alcuzcuz, y todo lo menudo que hubiere pasado por el harnecillo chico: y lo que no hubiere pasado por el harnero grande, lo junta otra vez todo junto en la pieza donde se tuerce el alcuzcuz, y estregarlo has entre las manos, y tornarás a torcer, trayendo la mano extendida por encima: y si vieres que tiene polvo, échale unas gotas de agua con el hisopillo, y tuerce con fuerza: y cuando el alcuzcuz se comienza a torcer ha de andar la mano muy liviana: y cuando no tiene ya polvo ha de andar con mucha fuerza: y desta manera lo irás torciendo y cerniendo sobre los manteles, y déjalo secar: luego échalo en su alcuzcucero, que es una pieza de barro, o de cobre con muchos agujerillos en el suelo un poco angosto y romo de abajo, y ancho y abierto de arriba: y luego (222v) tomarás una olla un poco grande, media de agua, y ponle un borde de masa, mezclada con unas estopas, y mójalo con un poquito de agua, y asentarás el alcuzcurero sobre esta olla con su alcuzcuz: luego echarle masa a la redonda, y más estopas;[366] porque en ninguna manera ha de resollar la olla, sino es por dentro del alcuzcucero, y pon

---

364 *Una serilla de Valencia* is a small *sera* [straw basket with no handles]. In *Vida del escudero Marcos de Obregón* [The life of the squire Marcos de Obregón] (1618) by Vicente Espinel, the protagonist cleverly discovers the identity of a thief who stole "una serilla de higos" [a basket of figs], reflecting its common use for storing fruit and dried goods (252–4). My thanks to Carmen Abad-Zardoya for clarification on its usage.

365 The choice of the verb *torcer* [twist] signals the unique process of treating the flour. I believe the process involves a hand motion of mixing or twisting the flour front to back and, as Martínez Montiño later indicates, then rubbing the flour. The intensity with which this process is done, gently at first and then more firmly, varies according to how the flour is responding.

366 *Estopa* [tow] are the short fibres combed out when processing flax into linen. They produce a *coarse linen* but when wet are expanded and become almost impermeable. This explains why Martínez Montiño uses it when he needs no steam to escape out the sides. For more on *estopa*, see 416n320.

type, where it can be made just as well as in the copper bowl or even better. Then have warm water in a bowl with a hyssop brush. This water should be salty, as for puff pastry, and begin sprinkling the water on the flour with the hyssop brush so that very tiny drops fall onto the flour, because this is the secret to twisting the couscous. Begin pulling your extended hand through the flour, always with one hand. Then sprinkle more water on with the hyssop brush and continue moving your extended hand through the flour. Every once in a while, you must dip your hand into the flour and move it around top to bottom, and in this way, you will continue preparing it until all the flour forms little beads and no flour remains. Then take two small sieves. One should have holes no bigger than a grain of millet, the other should have [holes] the size of a radish seed or a little bigger. Then sift the couscous over a bowl through the small sieve. Whatever is left above, pour it into the big sieve and sift it over a clean tablecloth so that it doesn't pile up. Continue sifting all the couscous in this way and all the small pieces should pass through the small sieve. And whatever doesn't pass through the big sieve, gather it all together again in the bowl in which you twisted the couscous and rub it between your hands, twist it again, by extending your hand over the top. If you notice that there's flour, sprinkle some drops of water with the hyssop brush and twist forcefully. When the couscous begins to twist together, you should lighten your touch, and when the flour disappears, be more forceful. This is the way you should twist and sift over the tablecloth. Let it dry. Then place it in the couscoussier, which is a pot made of clay or copper that has a flat, narrow bottom with many small holes and is wide and open on the top. Then take a big pot half full of water and make an edge with dough mixed with coarse linen. Wet it with a little water and set the couscoussier with couscous on top of the pot. Next add more dough around it and more coarse linen, because no steam at all should be released from the pot except through the couscoussier. Put the

la olla sobre lumbre que cueza amorosamente: y luego comenzará a salir el vaho de la olla por el alcuzcuz: y si sintieres que no sale bien, mete un cuchillo por el alcuzcuz abajo hasta llegar al suelo, y menea la punta del cuchillo en el suelo del alcucero [sic], y luego saldrá bien, y cueza por espacio de más de una hora: luego sácalo y échalo sobre un tablero, y toma un poco de manteca, o aceite, y moja las manos, y estrega el alcuzcuz, porque desta manera se desgranará muy bien: y si acaso tuviere algunos burrujoncillos será menester cernerlo por otro harnerillo un poco más ancho (223r) que ninguno de los dos con que se cernió. Ahora resta decir como se ha de guisar este alcuzcuz.

[355] *Cómo se guisa el Alcuzcuz.*

Para guisar este alcuzcuz has de moler azúcar, y poner un poco de canela, y tomarás el alcuzcuz, e irlo has echando en una almofía,[367] o cazuela de barro, o en alguna pieza de plata, e irásle echando azúcar y canela entre lecho y lecho, y no has de henchir la pieza, porque crecerá la tercia parte: y cuando lo tengas en este punto, tendrás una olla de caldo, adonde se haya cocido un pedazo de vaca, y una gallina, y un poco de carnero y tocino de pernil, porque lo gordo no vale nada para esto, y ha de tener esta olla sus verduras ordinarias, perejil, y cilantro, y hierbabuena: y con la grasa deste caldo mojarás el alcuzcuz, y él empapará luego el caldo, y tornarlo has a mojar, y también se tornará a empapar: y esta almofía, o porcelana, ha de estar (223v) sobre una olla que esté cociendo poco a poco, y taparás el alcuzcuz con un plato: y cuando el alcuzcuz esté remojado y granujado le podrás poner alguna cosa encima, como es una cola de carnero cocida y tostada, o un ave enterrada en el alcuzcuz, y sus yemas de huevos duras por encima, o unos cogotes de carnero, cocidos y tostados: la gallina si la hubieres de servir con el alcuzcuz, es necesario que esté cocida cuando asentares el alcuzcuz, y ponerla en el almofía, e ir echando el alcuzcuz por encima hasta que se cubra, y luego remojarlo con caldo, y adornarlo con las yemas de huevos. Este alcuzcuz se puede hacer sin dulce, no más de remojado con su caldo: y si no fuere día de carne, remojarlo has con caldo de garbanzos, sazonado con buena manteca de vacas fresca.

[356] *Hojaldrillas de manteca de vacas.*

Harás un rollo de hojaldrado con manteca (224r) fresca de vacas: luego harás unas cubiertas, como para tapar pasteles, un poco más gorditas de los bordes: luego tendrás hecha una pasta de yemas de huevos duras, y azúcar molido y canela, de manera que esté bien dulce, y echarás un poco desta pasta encima de una de aquellas hojas de hojaldrado, y cubrirla has con otra: y harás un pastelillo de dos hojas,

---

367 *Almofía*, another word for *jofaina*, is a basin or a type of wide, shallow receptacle.

pot over the flame and let it gently boil. Next, the steam from the pot will begin to go through the couscous. If you feel it's not going through, insert a knife through the couscous until you reach the bottom and jiggle the knife on the bottom of the couscoussier and it will turn out well. Steam for a little over an hour, then remove it, and turn it out onto a cutting board. Take a little lard or oil, wet your hands, and rub the couscous, because this way the grains will separate nicely. If you find any lumps, it will be necessary to sift it through another sieve that is wider than the first two already used for sifting. Now saying how to cook this couscous is the only thing left.

How to cook couscous

To cook this couscous, grind sugar and add a little cinnamon. Take the couscous and put it in a basin or terracotta casserole or a silver bowl. Begin sprinkling sugar and cinnamon between each layer. Don't fill the bowl, because it will expand by a third. When this is done, have a pot of stock in which was cooked a piece of beef, a hen, a little mutton, and ham fat, because the fatty fatback is not right for this. Basic herbs, parsley, cilantro, and spearmint, should also be in the pot. Moisten the couscous with the fat from this stock, and it will soak up the stock; moisten [with fat] again, and it will soak up the stock again. This basin or porcelain should be on top of a pot that is simmering. Cover the couscous with a plate, and when the couscous is soaked and granular, you can add something else on top like a boiled and toasted tail of mutton or a bird buried in the couscous with some hard-boiled egg yolks on top or some boiled and toasted neck of mutton. If you're going to serve hen with the couscous, it is necessary that it's already cooked when placing on the couscous. Put it in the basin and begin spooning the couscous on top until it covers it. Then soak it with stock and garnish with the egg yolks. This couscous can be made without sweetener, just using stock. If it's not a meat day, soak up with garbanzo broth and season with good butter.

Puff pastry with butter

Roll out puff pastry dough with butter. Then make tops, the kind you use for covering pies, a little thicker around the edges. Then have a paste made of hard-boiled egg yolks, ground sugar, and cinnamon so that it's very sweet. Dab some of this paste on top of one of the puff pastry sheets and cover it with another. Make

de manera que queden los bordes muy redondos, iguales, y gorditos, y cuécelas en el horno sobre papeles, y después de cocidas pásalas por buena miel, o por almíbar. Estas mismas hojaldrillas podrás hacer en día de carne con manteca de puerco el hojaldrado: y añadirás a la pasta cañas de vaca cocidas y cortadas muy menudas, y mezcladas con las yemas de huevos duras, y azúcar y canela, que viene a ser derechamente como la fruta de cañas. Pásalos por el almíbar, y sírvelas con un poco de azúcar y canela por encima.

[357] (224v) *Otras Hojaldrillas chicas.*

Estas hojaldrillas podrás hacer de dos hojas de hojaldrado de manteca de puerco: el relleno ha de ser de pasta de mazapán, como tengo dicho en las hojaldres rellenas: de masa de levaduras harás pasta, o mazapán con media libra de almendras; y media de azúcar, y échale una poco de agua de azahar, y un poco de clavo molido, y un poco de canela, y una migaja de nuez: y a esta pasta le darás un hervor sobre la lumbre en un cacillo, revolviendo con un cucharón: luego sácalo, y harás unas tortitas redondas y delgadas desta pasta, luego otras del hojaldrado que sean más anchas: y pondrás entre dos hojas de hojaldrado, una de la pasta, y cerrarla has que queden los bordecillos gordos: y desta manera harás las demás, y úntalas con manteca, y cuécelas sobre cuartillas de papel: y cuando estuvieren cocidas échales (225r) un poco de buena miel por encima de toda la hojaldrilla, y échale azúcar y canela por encima la miel, y tórnalas al horno un poco cuando se embeba la miel y se tueste un poco el azúcar y canela, y sírvelas calientes.

[358] *Cabrito relleno asado.*

Freirás una rebanadillas de tocino gordo, y echarle has un poco de cebolla cortada a la larga y delgada, y freírla has con el tocino, cuando esté el tocino, y la cebolla medio frito: luego tendrás el hígado del cabrito perdigado en agua, y los livianos cocidos, y cortarlos has en rebanadillas muy delgadas, y ahogarlo has con la cebolla y el tocino de la sartén, y echarle has un poco de verdura entera, y ahóguese todo, y batirás seis huevos con claras, y échalos dentro en la sartén, y ponla sobre la lumbre hasta que esté bien seco: luego sácalo al tablero, y pícalo muy bien, y sazona (225v) con todas especias y sal, y zumo de limón, y métele otros dos o tres huevos crudos, y una migaja de azafrán: luego rellena el cabrito, tomando medio cabrito, y cortándole el pescuezo a cercén: y por entre las espaldillas, y el pescuezo, has de hacer un agujero entre la tez del cabrito, y las costillas, de manera que venga a quedar todo hueco hasta la pierna: y luego ve metiendo el relleno que se hincha todo aquel hueco hasta la pierna: y luego coserás la boca del agujero, y perdígalo en agua, y méchale la pierna, y la espalda muy bien frisada, y lo de en medio rebózalo con un pliego de papel untado con manteca, y ásalo, y sírvelo con sus rebanadillas de pan blanco, y unas ruedas de limón.

a pastry with two sheets so that the edges are round, even, and thick. Bake in the oven on paper, and once they're cooked, dip them in good honey or simple syrup. On a meat day you can make these same little pastries with lard [in] the puff pastry dough. Add beef bone marrow that's been boiled and diced to the paste, mixed in with the hard-boiled eggs, sugar, and cinnamon. It will turn out just like the "Fried dough with marrow filling." Dip in simple syrup and serve with a little sugar and cinnamon on top.

Other little pastries

You can make these little pastries with two sheets of puff pastry dough made with lard. The filling should be a marzipan paste, as explained in "Stuffed puff pastry" with leaven dough. Make the paste, or marzipan, with half a pound of almonds and a half of sugar. Add a little orange blossom water, a little ground clove, a little cinnamon, and a pinch of nutmeg. Bring this paste to a boil in a saucepan over the fire, constantly stirring with a spoon. Then, remove it, and make little round thin tartlets from this paste, then others from the puff pastry dough. They should be a little wider. Between two sheets of puff pastry dough, place one of paste, and seal it so the edges are thick. Make the rest this way. Grease them with lard, bake them on quarter sheets of paper, and when they're done, drizzle a little good honey on top of the whole puff pastry. Sprinkle sugar and cinnamon over the honey, put back in the oven for a little so that the honey gets absorbed and the sugar and cinnamon get toasted. Serve hot.

Stuffed kid, roasted

Fry slices of extra fatty fatback. Add long, thin slices of onion and fry it with the fatback. When the fatback and onion are partially fried, then have parboiled kid liver and boiled lung and cut them into thin slices. Sauté them with the onion and fatback in the frying pan. Add a little bit of green herbs, whole, and sauté everything. Beat six eggs with their whites and add them to the frying pan. Put it on the flame until the eggs are well done. Then, turn it out onto a cutting board, mince it, and season with all spices, salt, and lemon juice. Add in another two or three raw eggs and a pinch of saffron. Then stuff the kid by taking half a kid at a time, severing the neck, and between the shoulders and the neck, make a hole between the skin of the kid and the ribs so that there's a hole all the way to the leg. Then begin placing the stuffing to fill the hole down to the leg. Next, sew the opening of the hole, parboil in water, lard the leg, and the back should be well rubbed. Coat the middle part with a sheet of paper greased with lard, roast it, and serve with slices of white bread and some lemon wheels.

[359] *Cabrito relleno cocido.*

Si quisieres hacer este cabrito relleno en platillo, picarás carne de ternera, o de cabrito con tocino, y un poco (226r) de riñonada de carnero, o de ternera, y meterle has huevos hasta que esté blando, y sazonarás con todas especias y agrio de limón y sal, cortarás una caña de vaca en trozos, y mezclarlo has todo, y dos o tres yemas de huevos duras partidas en cuartos, y tomarás medio cabrito, cortarásle la pierna, y harás un agujero por la punta de la cintilla, y meterás el cuchillo entre las costillas, y la tez del cabrito, y harás de manera que quede todo hueco hasta debajo la espaldilla, y rellénala, y cierra el agujero, y pondrás a cocer esta cintilla de cabrito en buen caldo con especias, y un poco de verdura picada, y la piernecilla la tendrás picada juntamente con el relleno, y de lo sobrare harás un albondigón muy grande, que lleve en medio yemas de huevos en cuartos, y trozos de cañas de vaca, que sean un poco largos, y cueza con caldo: y cuando esté cocido cuajarás el caldo donde se coció el albondigón con dos o tres yemas de (226v) huevos, y su agrio, y sacarás el albondigón, y haráslo cuatro cuartos, y asentarlo has sobre unas rebanaditas de pan en el plato, a modo de cruz, que salgan las puntas hasta el borde del plato, como rebanadas de melón, y asentarás la cintilla rellena encima, y echarles has del caldo que tienen huevos por encima, y unas ruedas de limón alrededor suele parecer muy bien, y se le pueden echar algunas veces cogollos de lechugas.

[360] *Platillo de Cabrito.*

Este plato de cabrito relleno en platillo que está escrito atrás, podrás hacer de la carne que te sobró del relleno algunas veces un poco de pastel en bote, y servirlo has sobre rebanadas de pan: y luego asentarás la cintilla sobre el pastel en bote, y otras veces podrás hacer albondiguillas, y asentarás la cintilla rellena en plato, y las albondiguillas alrededor, y otras veces podrás armar la (227r) piernecilla del cabrito, y adornarla con piñones y yemas de huevos, y algunas pasas de Corintio: y luego tostarás la cintilla rellena sobre las parrillas con un poco de pan rallado, y harás una sopilla dulce, y asentarás la cintilla, y la piernecilla sobre ella, y adornarás el plato con algunas ruedas de limón.

[361] *Otro plato de medio Cabrito.*

Cortarás la pierna del cabrito, y picarla has, y sazonarla has como está dicho en el cabrito relleno en platillo,[368] y lo demás del medio cabrito asarlo has, y cortarlo

---

368 Although there is no recipe called "Cabrito relleno en platillo" [Stuffed kid on an individual plate], in the recipe "Cabrito relleno cocido" [Stuffed kid, boiled] Martínez Montiño opens with the phrase "Si quisieres hacer este cabrito relleno en platillo" [If you want to make this stuffed kid an individual plate] (470; 471). For this reason, I believe he is referring to this recipe.

Stuffed kid, boiled

If you want to make this stuffed kid an individual dish, chop veal or kid with fatback, a little mutton or veal loin, and add enough eggs until it is soft. Season with all spices, lemon juice, and salt. Cut beef bone [marrow] into pieces and mix it all together with two or three hard-boiled egg yolks sliced in quarters. Take half a kid, cut off the leg, and make a hole at the tip of the loin. Put the knife between the ribs and the skin, and open to make a hole to the shoulder blade. Fill it and close it up. Put this loin on to boil in good broth with spices and a little bit of chopped green herbs. The leg should also be minced together with the stuffing. And with what is left over, make a big meatball with quartered egg yolks and fairly long pieces of beef bone marrow inside. Boil in the broth. When it's done, thicken the broth in which you made the big meatball with two or three egg yolks, and the right amount of sour juice. Remove the meatball and cut into quarters. Set it crosswise over slices of bread on a plate so that the tips point toward the edge of the plate like slices of melon. Set the stuffed loin on top and ladle some of the broth with egg yolk on top. Lemon wheels around usually look really good. You can also add lettuce hearts.

An individual kid dish

This dish of an individual plate of the stuffed kid that is written above can sometimes be made, with the leftover meat from the stuffing, into a little crustless pie, and served over slices of bread. Then set the loin over the crustless pie, and other times you can make little meatballs and set the stuffed loin on the plate and the meatballs around it. Other times you can assemble the kid leg and garnish it with pine nuts, egg yolks, and dried currants. Then toast the stuffed loin on the grill with a little bit of breadcrumbs. Make sweet sops and set the loin on them and the leg on it and garnish the plate with lemon wheels.

Another dish of half a kid

Cut off the leg of the kid, mince it, and season as explained in "Stuffed kid on an individual plate." Roast the rest of the kid, chop into pieces, and season

has en pedazos, y salpimentarlo has con sal y especias: luego rebózalo con huevos, y fríele con manteca de puerco, y la carne que tienes picada de la pierna, vela tomando a pedazos un poco largos, y rebózala con huevos, y fríela, y sírvelo con azúcar y canela, y zumo de naranja todo junto con unas torrijas.

[362] (227v) *Sopas a la Portuguesa.*

Echarás a cocer vaca, que sea manida y gorda, y echarle has un ave, y un pedazo de tocino de pernil con sus garbanzos, y algún brazuelo de carnero: y cuando esté cocida la vaca échale de todas verduras,[369] y una rama de eneldo, y un cogollo de poleo, y un poco de jadrea, y mucha cantidad de ciliantro [sic] verde. No ha de llevar ninguna especia. Has le de echar tanto vinagre como quepa en una cáscara de avellana, y pruébala de sal. Luego harás las sopas en una porcelana grande, o almofía. El pan ha de ser mollete, y no se ha de cortar con cuchillo, sino con la mano, unos pedacitos grandes como nueces y mayores, y mojarla has con el caldo de la vaca, de manera que no estén muy empapadas las sopas, y servirás encima unas rebanadas de vaca gorda. Algunos señores no quieren eneldo, porque tiene (228r) mucho humo: y en su lugar podrás echar unos cogollitos de berzas.

[363] *Sopa de vaca a la Portuguesa, contrahecho en día de pescado.*[370]

La sopa de vaca se contrahace en día de pescado desta manera. Tomarás berzas crudas, que sean repolludas, e hinche una olla dellas, y échale dentro cantidad de culantro verde,[371] y unas matas de hierbabuena, y un manojillo de ajedrea, y tres, y cuatro cogollos de sándalos,[372] y échale un poco de buena manteca de vacas: luego échale el agua, que pudiere entrar, hasta que se hincha: sazónala de sal, y ponla a cocer, hasta que estén las berzas cocidas, y tendrán las sopas el gusto, como las de vaca. Estas sopas a la Portuguesa, comen mucho los Portugueses.

---

369 For an explanation of *todas verduras*, see *hierbas* (682–3).
370 This recipe does not appear until the 1617 edition (229v–230r). Given Martínez Montiño's connection to Portugal, it seems clear that the author insisted it be included. Because it appears in all subsequent editions as well, I have included it here.
371 While *culantro* [*Eryngium foetidum*] is an entirely different plant from *cilantro* [*Coriander sativum*], in early modern cookbooks the words are often used interchangeably. Different editions of Martínez Montiño's cookbook show a preference for one over the other. For example, *culantro* appears here and in seven other editions in the seventeenth and eighteenth centuries, while *cilantro* appears in ten editions in the seventeenth and eighteenth centuries and all the nineteenth-century editions.
372 Sandalwood appears only twice in the cookbook. Here, its woody fragrance and reddish-brown colour help to provide these faux beef sops with a "meaty" flavour and look.

with salt and other spices. Then, coat it with eggs and fry with lard. Begin taking the minced meat from the leg in long chunks and coat with egg. Fry it and serve with sugar and cinnamon and orange juice all together with some torrijas.

Sops, Portuguese style

Put on to boil beef that is dry aged and marbled. Add a bird, a piece of ham fat with the right amount of garbanzos, and a mutton shank. When the beef has boiled, add in all green herbs, a sprig of dill, a shoot of pennyroyal, a little summer savory, and a lot of cilantro. It shouldn't have any spices. Pour in as much vinegar as fits in the shell of a hazelnut and salt to taste. Then, make the sops in a big porcelain bowl or a basin. The bread should be mollete rolls and should not be cut with a knife but rather torn by hand into pieces as big as walnuts or bigger. Soak them in the beef broth so that the sops aren't too soaked and serve slices of marbled beef on top. Some lords don't like dill because it has a strong odour. Instead you can add collard green shoots.

Beef sops, Portuguese style, faux for fish days

Faux beef sops are made for fish days in this way. Take raw collard greens, ones that are thick, and fill a pot with them and add in a large amount of cilantro, some sprigs of spearmint, a handful of summer savory, and three or four shoots of sandalwood. Add in a little good butter. Then add in as much water as possible, until it is full, season with salt, and put it on to boil until the greens are cooked. The sops will taste like other beef sops. The Portuguese eat these Portuguese-style sops a lot.

[364] *Otra Sopa de vaca.*

Cocerás vaca de pierna, y de la cadera que sea gorda, y harás rebanadas della: luego tostarás una rebanadas de pan, y untarás un plato con la grasa de la misma olla, y tendrás queso rallado que sea muy bueno, y échale de la grasa de la olla, y mézclalo todo que esté como papín un poco ralo, y ve mojando las rebanadas del pan en el queso, y la grasa, y velo asentando en el plato: luego harás otro tanto a las rebanadas de la vaca, y asentarlas has sobre las del pan, y échale más queso por encima, y de la grasa de la olla. En este queso se ha de echar un poco de pimienta, y un poco de nuez, y ponlo dentro en el horno: déjalo cuajar un poquito, y sírvela caliente. Esta sopa de vaca harás de otra manera, picando la vaca después de cocida (228v) con cuchillo chico, como quien hace gigote, y tomarás queso rallado, y grasa de la olla, que tenga pimienta, y nuez, como está dicho, y mojarás las rebanadas en el queso, y la grasa de la olla, y asentarlas has en el plato: luego tomarás rebanadas de vaca, y harás otro tanto, poniéndolas junto al borde del plato: luego echa queso rallado en la vaca picada con su pimienta, y nuez, y caldo con muchas grasa, y una migaja de azafrán, y échale dos yemas de huevos no más: todo esto junto échalo en el plato, y ponle por encima unas rebanadillas de queso y una caña de vaca, también hecha rebanadillas, y mete el plato en un horno, y tuéstese allí un poco: y entiéndese que el queso ha de ser muy bueno de hierba.[373]

[365] *Cómo se aderezan la ubre de la jabalina.*

La ubre de la jabalina, cuando está criando, o está preñada, cocerás esta (229r) ubre, y de que esté cocida échala en adobo de sal, y orégano, y un poco de vino, y de todas especias, y un poco de hisopillo y mejorana: hase de echar la ubre en el adobo, en sacándola de la olla así caliente, porque lo tomará en dos, o tres horas: y luego mecharla has, y asarla has en el asador, y si no abrirla has por medio, y tuéstala en las parrillas, y servirla has con un poquito del adobo, y un poco de agrio de limón. También podrás servir esta ubre tostada y asentada sobre unas rebanadas de pan tostadas: y luego harás una pebrada con vino tinto, y un poco de vinagre y azúcar, y pimenta, canela, jengibre, y unos clavos enteros, y un poquito de caldo, y cueza hasta que comience a tomar punto el azúcar, y échalo por encima la ubre, y las rebanadas de pan, de manera que se bañen bien, y ponlo a estofar un poquito, y sírvela caliente. También podrás servir esta ubre con salsa de guindas, tomando dos libras de guindas, quitados (229v) los cuescos, y los pezones, y echarle media libra de azúcar, y un poco de vino tinto, y dos pares de clavos enteros, y unas rajitas de canela, y déjalas cocer hasta que estén conservadas, y podrás echar las guindas sobre

---

[373] With the phrase "de hierba," Martínez Montiño is referencing a fresh cheese made with cardoons instead of rennet. For more on *queso de hierba* made from herbal rennet, see 236n138.

Another beef sops [dish]

Boil a beef shank and a fatty piece of the round and slice them. Then toast slices of bread and grease a plate with the fat from the same pot. Have some good grated cheese and add some fat from the pot and mix it all together until it is like a thin, sweet cream sauce. Begin soaking the slices of bread in the cheese and fat and setting them on the plate. Then make as many with the slices of beef and set them over the bread slices. Ladle more cheese and fat from the pot on top. This cheese sauce should have a little pepper and nutmeg. Put it in the oven to set for a while and serve hot. You can make this dish of beef sops another way by chopping the beef after it has boiled with a small knife, the way one makes minced meat. Take grated cheese and fat from the pot that has pepper and nutmeg, as has been explained, and soak the slices in the cheese and fat from the pot and set them on the plate. Then take slices of beef, as many as before, placing them around the edge of the plate. Then add grated cheese to the minced beef with the right amount of pepper, nutmeg, and fatty broth and a pinch of saffron. Add two egg yolks, no more. Ladle this entire mix on the plate and put some slices of cheese on top and beef bone marrow, also sliced, and put the plate in the oven. It should toast there a little while. Understand that the cheese must be very good cheese made with herbal rennet.

How to prepare boar udder

The udder of a boar when it's breastfeeding or pregnant: boil this udder and once it's done, put it in a marinade of salt, oregano, a little wine, all spices, and a little winter savory and marjoram. The udder should go into the marinade directly from the pot still hot, because it will take two to three hours. Then lard it and roast it on a spit. If not, split it open down the middle and toast it on the grill. Serve it with a little marinade and a little lemon juice. You can also serve this grilled udder placed on some toasted slices of bread. Next, make a pepper sauce with red wine, a little vinegar, sugar, pepper, cinnamon, ginger, some whole cloves, and a little broth. Boil until the sugar begins to enter the thread stage. Ladle it on top of the udder and the slices of bread so they braise and put it on to stew a little. Serve hot. You can also serve this udder with a sour cherry sauce by taking two pounds of sour cherries without pits or stems. Add half a pound of sugar, a little red wine, two pairs of whole cloves, and some slivers of cinnamon. Let boil until they are preserved. Spoon the cherries over the slices and set the udder on top of it all. You

las rebanadas, y asentar la ubre encima de todo. Esta ubre podrás servir, como está dicho, sobre rebanadas de pan tostadas, y salsa de agraz por encima, y otras veces con salsa de granadas. Estas salsas de agraz, y de granadas hallarás escritas, adonde se trata de capones, y pollos asados: y en lugar de ubre de jabalina, podrás hacer todas las cosas que están dichas con ubre de vaca, y de lechonas mansas.

[366] *Conejos rellenos.*

Los conejos rellenos se han de pelar como lechones en agua caliente: y luego hacer su relleno de la manera que está escrito atrás para cabrito relleno asado, y se ha de rellenar por dentro del hueco, y coserlo, y ponerle una (230r) broquetilla en las piernas, y meter el asador por debajo desta broqueta, y vaya por de fuera de la barriga hasta los pechos, y torne a entrar por los pechos, y salga por la cabeza, a ásese yéndolo lardando a la redonda con manteca que haga sus cueros como lechón: y si el conejo fuere muy gordo, y tuviere grasa en los riñones, en lugar del relleno le pondrás unos granos de agraz con un poco de sal y pimienta: y luego cose tu conejo, y ponle su broqueta, y ponle una longita de tocino ancha y muy delgada encima del lomo, y ásese; sácalo y descóselo, cortándole todas las hijadas, y sírvelo barriga arriba, descubierta la grasa del conejo, y los agraces: y si quisieres servir el conejo gordo, y que no se derrita la grasa de los riñones, sino que salga entera y blanca, como cuando está cruda: desuéllalo, y lávalo de manera, que no se desperdicie la grasa, y ponlo barriga arriba, y échale un poco de sal, y una longita de tocino gordo, que (230v) cubra los riñones, y espétalo, y cóselo de manera que el asador no entre por el hueco de la barriga, y ponle otra longa de tocino en el lomo, o la mecha, y ásese, y descóselo cortando la cosedura, y parte de las hijadas, y quita la lonja de tocino, y hallarás el conejo con sus riñones cubiertos de grasa, como cuando estaba crudo.

[367] *Conejos en empanada.*

Estos conejos gordos son muy buenos empanados, y masa dulce, y puestos boca arriba con una lonja de tocino gordo sobre los riñones, y sírvelo caliente, y quítale la lonja del tocino, y hallarás el conejo con toda su gordura. Estos conejos asados no tienen otra salsa mejor que aceite y vinagre.

[368] *Perdices asadas con Aceite.*

Pondrás a asar la perdiz que sea tierna, y tomarás un poco de aceite con (231r) dos tanto de agua, y un poco de sal, y bátelo como huevos hasta que esté un poco blanco, y luego ponlo junto al fuego, e irás lardando la perdiz con las plumas en lugar de manteca: y cuando esté asada, hasla de servir con esta misma salsa, que esté un poco salada. Tiene muy buen gusto, y su Majestad las come desta manera muy ordinariamente.

can serve this udder, as already explained, over toasted slices of bread with a sour grape sauce on top or other times with a pomegranate sauce. You can find these sour grape and pomegranate sauces written down where capons and roasted chickens are discussed. Instead of boar udder, you can do all these already explained with cow udder or one from a domesticated sow.

Stuffed rabbit

Stuffed rabbits should be scraped like suckling pigs in hot water. Then make the stuffing the way it's previously written for roasted stuffed kid. The stuffing should go inside the cavity and be sewn up. Stick a small skewer through the legs and place the roasting spit under this skewer so that it goes on the outside from the belly to the chest, goes in again at the chest, and exits through the head. Roast, turning it while basting it with lard. Its skin should turn out like suckling pig. If the rabbit were fat and had fatty kidneys, instead of stuffing, add some sour grapes with a little salt and pepper. Then sew up the rabbit, skewer it, and put a wide, thin strip of fatback on top of the loin and roast. Unstitch it by cutting along the sides and serve it belly up with the rabbit fat and sour grapes exposed. If you want to serve the rabbit with its fat, without the kidney fat melting, and served whole and white as when it's raw, then skin it, and when you're washing it, don't let the fat go to waste. Put it belly up and sprinkle on some salt, add a slice of extra fatty fatback so that it covers the kidneys. Skewer it and sew it up so that the skewer doesn't go into the cavity of the belly. Add another slice of fatback to the loin or lard it and roast. Open it up by cutting the stitching and part of the sides. Remove the slice of fatback and you will have a rabbit with its kidneys covered in fat just as if it were raw.

Rabbit in an empanada

These rabbits with fat are very good as empanadas, with a sweet dough and placed face up with a strip of fatback around the kidneys. Serve hot. Remove the slice of fatback and you will have a rabbit with all its fat. These roasted rabbits have no better sauce than oil and vinegar.

Roast partridge with oil

Put the partridge on to roast. Make sure it's tender. Take a little oil, and about twice as much water, and a little salt. Beat it like eggs until it turns a little white. Then put it next to the fire and with feathers begin larding the partridge [with it] instead of with lard.[9] When it's roasted, serve it with this same sauce that should be a little salty. It is very tasty and His Majesty eats it this way very often.

---

9 With this instruction, Martínez Montiño means to soak feathers in the emulsion and then pull the feathers through the bird, as if they were a larding needle. This will have the effect of drawing the salty oil emulsion through the bird.

[369] *Pasteles de Carnero, y de pernil de Tocino.*

Tomarás unos torreznos de buen tocino de Garrovillas, o de otra parte que sean buenos, que tenga quitado el cuero, de manera que quede lo gordo del torrezno con lo magro, y remójese muy bien: y cuando esté bien desalado y escurrido del agua: pícalo muy bien: y luego pica dos tanta carne de pierna de carnero, y mézclalo todo, y ponlo en un cacito, y échale un poquito de caldo, (231v) y perdígalo muy bien que esté bien granujado: luego tendrás un poco de azúcar en almíbar, y echa esta carne dentro, y dale allí unas vueltas sobre el fuego, y sazona con muy poca especia y sal, y échale un poco de canela molida: luego déjalo enfriar, y haz tus pastelillos anchuelos y bajos de borde de masa dulce, e hínchelos y cuécelos: y cuando los quisieres servir échales un poco de caldo de la olla sin otra cosa ninguna. Estos se pueden guardar ocho, o diez días: y cuando los quisieres servir caliéntalos, y échales un poco de caldo, por que no estén muy enjutos. Advierte, que si son para guardar, que no se les ha de echar caldo cuando se cuezan, sino cuando se hubieren de servir, porque ellos están como conservados. Habrá menester un plato destos dos libras de carnero, y una de tocino magro, y media libra de azúcar.

[370] *Artaletes asados.*

(232r) Adonde traté de los artaletes no pase de los que se pueden asar en el asador: Para estos harás unas chulletas de ternera muy delgadas, y un poco más largas que las de los otros, y bátelas con la vuelta del cuchillo, y échales un poco de sal, y pica un poco de tocino gordo muy picado, y pon en cada una un poquito, cuando se unte toda la chulleta, y pica un poco de riñonada de ternera, o carnero, que esté granujada, y pica un poco de verdura, y mézclalo todo con docena y media de yemas de huevos duros: y de que esté todo mezclado, sazona con todas especias y sal, y zumo de naranja, y ve echando por encima de las chulletas que no sea mucha cantidad: luego velas arrollando como hojaldrado, y tendrá un poco del relleno a una parte: y en acabando de arrollar el artalete, ponlos cabos en el relleno, y aprieta un poco, y pegarse ha dello, y velos espetando en un filete, que es un asadorcillo delgado, y si no en una (232v) broqueta de hierro, o de caña: y pondrás los artaletes en dos destas, y atarlas has a un asador gordo, una de una parte, y otra de otra, y asarlos has, y harás una sopa la que te pareciere, y asiéntalos encima, y adórnalos con algunas ruedas de limón mondado, porque la cáscara en calentándose amarga.

[371] *Torta de Dama.*

Tomarás una libra de almendras con su cáscara, y tostarlas has, y majarlas con una libra de azúcar muy majadas: y luego tendrás la carne de cuatro pichones asados y descarnados, y quitados los pellejos, y se picará muy bien, y se majará con las almendras, y se ha de pasar por la estameña, echándole en el almirez onza y media de agua

Mutton and fatty ham pies

Take some good-quality pork belly from Garrovillas or from elsewhere as long as it's good quality. Remove the skin so that just the fat of the pork belly and the meat is intact. Soak it well. When it is desalted and drained, mince it up. Then chop up twice as much meat from a leg of mutton and mix it all together. Put it in a saucepan, add a little stock, and sear it until the meat is shredded. Then take a little bit of simple syrup and add the meat to it. Stir it over the fire and season it with just a little bit of all spices and salt. Add a little ground cinnamon. Next, let it cool and make little, wide and shallow pastry shells with sweet dough. Fill them and bake them. When you are ready to serve, add a little stock from the pot without anything else. You can keep these for eight to ten days. When you want to serve them, heat them up and add a little stock so that they are not too dry. Note that if you plan to keep them, don't add stock when you cook them; rather, wait until you serve them, because they will be preserved. For this dish, you will need two pounds of mutton, one of meaty fatback, and a half a pound of sugar.

Roasted pinwheels

When I discussed pinwheels, I did not include those you can roast on a spit. For these, make very thin veal chops, a little longer than the other ones, and pound them out with the backside of the knife. Sprinkle a little salt. Mince a little extra fatty fatback and put a little bit on each one. When each one is dabbed, chop up a little veal or mutton loin so that it is very shredded, chop up some green herbs, and mix it all together with a dozen and a half hard-boiled egg yolks. Once it's all mixed together, season with all spices, salt, and orange juice. Spoon it onto the chops, but not too much. Then begin rolling them up like puff pastry dough. Have a little filling set aside. When finished rolling the pinwheel, put them bottom side down in the filling and squeeze them a little. They should stick to it. Then skewer them on a *filete*, which is a small thin skewer, and if not, then on an iron or a reed skewer. Put the pinwheels on two of these and tie them to a thick spit, one on one side and the other on the other, and roast them. Make sops, any kind you like, and set them on top. Garnish with some lemon wheels, peeled, because the rind becomes bitter when heated.

Lady pie

Take a pound of almonds in their shells, toast them, and grind them with a pound of sugar until well ground. Then have the meat of four deboned and skinned roasted squab and mince it. Grind up with the almonds and strain in cheesecloth. In the mortar add an ounce and a half of orange blossom water,

de azahar, y cuatro yemas de huevos, y medio cuartillo de natas, y un poco de olor, y con esto lo acabarás de majar, y pásalo por la estameña, o cedacillo de cerdas (233r) de manera que pase toda, salvo algunos granillos de las almendras que quedarán en el cedacillo: y luego harás una masilla muy fina, y tendrás una hoja de masa muy delgada, y la asentarás un una tortera, y echarás en la pasta un poco de canela, y una migaja de clavo, y echarás esta pasta dentro, que será negra, y córtala a la redonda por un poco más arriba de la pasta, porque no ha de llevar cubierta, y tendrás un poquito de manteca de vacas fresca, o un poco de agua de azahar, y untarla has por encima con un hisopillo de plumas sin llegar a la pasta, y rasparle has un poco de azúcar por encima, y cuézase a fuego muy manso, y saldrá morena, más de muy buen gusto. Y advierte, que si no tuvieres natas, podrás majar con las almendras un par de cañas de vaca, y echar en el batido más agua de azahar, y unas gotas de leche. Esto es para desleír el batido: y para que pase por la estameña. Esta torta se ha de servir caliente, y la (233v) canela ha de ser media onza, y el clavo muy poquito.

[372] *Otra Torta de Dama.*

Tomarás una libra de almendras mondada, y májalas en el almirez, y picarás la pechuga de un capón asado, y majarla has en el almirez, y una libra de azúcar: y de que esté bien majado todo échale medio cuartillo de natas, y las cuatro yemas de huevos crudas, y la onza y media de agua de azahar, y pásalo por la estameña, o cedacillo, echándole la media onza de canela, y un poquito de clavo: y después que esté pasado todo tiende una hoja de masa muy delgada, y la asentarás en la tortera, y echarás el batido que será blanco un poco mosqueteado[374] por la canela y clavo, y rociarla has con un poco de agua de azahar, y echa el azúcar raspado por encima, y cercena la masa por un poco más arriba del batido, y cuécela a fuego manso. Y advierte, que han de (234r) llevar estar tortas de dama olor de almizcle, o ámbar:[375]

---

374 This adjective probably comes from *mosquete* [musket] to describe an effect similar to the spray of pellets that dotted the surface of the target.

375 Musk is seldom used today in Spanish cooking, but it was an ingredient found in Hispano-Muslim cookbooks in both sweet and savoury recipes. According to the recipe "Ŷuwāriš de almizcle" [Electuary of musk] in *Kitāb al-tabīj fī l-Magrib wa-l-Andalus fī 'asr al-muwahhudin li-mu'allif mayhul (Tratado sobre cocina en el Magrib y al-Andalus en época almohade, de autor desconocido)* [The book of cooking in Maghreb and Andalus in the era of Almohads, by an unknown author], it was known to delight one's soul and improve the smell of the breath. It also stimulates appetite and digestion, helps to expel gas and dissolve phlegm, aids in dropsy, and induces urine and menstruation (cited in Huici Miranda 306). Martínez Montiño uses it here, in a cookie recipe, "Memoria de los bizcochelos" [Memoir of ladyfingers] (526–8; 527–9), and in his preserved fennel recipe (581–3; 582–4). Ambergris, also found in just these same two recipes, is a substance from the intestines of the sperm whale. In her translation of Ibn-Razín's thirteenth-century Hispano-Muslim cookbook, *Best of Delectable Foods and Dishes from al-Andalus and al-Maghrib: A Cookbook by Thirteenth-Century Andalusi Scholar Ibn Razín al-Tujībī (1227–1293)*, Nawal Nasrallah explains: "Based on al-Himyarī, *al-Rawḍ al mi'ṭār* 339, the best of ambergris from the western zone … came from the coasts of Shadhūna (Medina-Sidonia) in southern Spain … It was generally believed to benefit the entire nervous system" (653).

four egg yolks, a half pint of cream, and a little rosewater. Finish grinding with all of this and strain in the cheesecloth or horsehair sieve so that all goes through except little bits of almond that will remain in the sieve. Then make a fine dough. Have a sheet of thin dough and set it in a covered tart pan. Put in the [almond] paste, a little cinnamon, and a pinch of clove. Put this paste inside, it should be black, and cut it into a circle a little higher than the [pastry] dough, because it will not be covered. Have a little fresh butter or a little orange blossom water and sprinkle on top with a hyssop brush without [the brush] touching the paste. Grate a little sugar on top and bake on low. It should come out brown and be very tasty. Note that if you don't have cream, you can mash the almonds with a couple of pieces of beef bone marrow and add more orange blossom water to the batter and a few drops of milk. This is for thinning the batter and so it goes through the cheesecloth. This pie is served hot. You should use a half ounce of cinnamon and just a little clove.

Another lady pie

Take a pound of shelled almonds and grind them in a mortar. Mince the breast of a roasted capon and grind it in the mortar with a pound of sugar. Once it's all ground together, add a half pint of cream, four raw egg yolks, and one and a half ounces of orange blossom water. Pass it all through cheesecloth or a sieve, and also add a half an ounce of cinnamon and a pinch of clove. Once it is all strained, roll out a very thin sheet of dough and place it in a covered tart pan. Pour in the batter, which should be white and speckled with cinnamon and clove. Sprinkle a little orange blossom water and grated sugar on top and trim the dough a little higher than the batter. Bake on low flame. Note that these lady pies should have added a musk or

y si no hallares natas se le podrá echar una poca de manteca de vacas buena en su lugar: y cuando esté el batido en la tortera, ráspale su azúcar por encima: y para que esté el batido un poco líquido, y se pueda pasar por la estameña se le ha de echar un poco de más agua de azahar, y unas gotas de leche en lugar de las natas.

[373] *Otra Torta de Dama.*

Esta torta se puede hacer en día de Sábado con una libra de almendras tostadas con su cáscara, y una libra de azúcar: y majado todo esto échale una docena de higadillos de gallina cocidos, y májalos mucho con almendras y el azúcar, y la onza y media de agua de azahar, y las cuatro yemas de huevos crudas, y el medio cuartillo de natas, y un poco de canela molida, y una migaja de clavos, y su olor, y pásalo (234v) por la estameña, o cedacillo, y harás tu torta descubierta, como está dicho; porque todas estas tortas de dama han de ir descubiertas, y rocíala con su agua de azahar, o manteca de vacas, y raspa el azúcar por encima. Y advierte, que si lleva natas, no ha menester manteca de vacas.

[374] *Torta Blanca.*

Harás mazapán de media libra de almendras, y media de azúcar, y echarle has tres pellas de manjar blanco, y májalo todo muy bien, y échale dos, o tres natas,[376] y un poco de olor, o un poco de agua de azahar, y échale seis yemas de huevos crudas, y harás tu torta con cuatro, o cinco hojas muy delgadas debajo, y otras dos, o tres encima: y si le quisieres echar dentro un par de cañas de vaca, podrás; y si no fuere día de carne, con sólo almendras, y natas, se podrá hacer.

[375] (235r) *Costrada de mollejas de Ternera, y Menudillos.*

Tomarás dos, o tres mollejas de ternera, y ocho, o diez higadillos de gallinas, y cuécelo todo, y sácalo que se enfríe, y pícalo muy menudo: y luego freías un poco de tocino en dados muy menudo, y un poco de cebolla muy menuda, y échalo sobre los menudillos, y tórnalo a picar más, y sazónalo con pimienta y clavo y jengibre, y sazona de sal, y échale un cuarterón de azúcar molido, y un poco de agrio de agraz, o de limón, y seis yemas de huevos: luego harás tu masa fina, y echarás en la tortera media docena de hojas muy delgadas y encima otras tres, o cuatro, y cierra tu costrada, y úntala con manteca, y ráspale un poco de azúcar por encima, y cuézase: y después de cocida, si la quisieres cubrir con huevos hilados, y un poco de almíbar bien subido, de manera que haga (235v) hilas, podrás: y suele ser muy buen plato.

---

376 For measurement of *nata*, see 242n149 and Appendix 2, "On Measurements."

ambergris aroma, and if you don't have any cream, you can use some good butter instead. When the batter is in the covered tart pan, grate the right amount of sugar on top. For this batter to be thin enough and pass through cheesecloth, you should add a little more orange blossom water and some drops of milk in place of cream.

Another lady pie

This pie can be made on Saturdays with a pound of almonds toasted in their shells and a pound of sugar. Mash everything together and add a dozen boiled hen livers and thoroughly mash them together with the almonds and sugar, an ounce and a half of orange blossom water, four raw egg yolks, a half pint of cream, a little ground cinnamon, a pinch of clove, and the right amount of rosewater. Strain it all through cheesecloth or a sieve. Make an open-faced pie as explained above, as all of these lady pies are open faced. Sprinkle with the right amount of orange blossom water or dot with butter, and grate sugar on top. Note that if you use cream, you don't need butter.

White pie

Make marzipan with half a pound of almonds, a half of sugar, and add three balls of blancmange. Mash it all together and add two or three [portions of] cream, a little rosewater, a little orange blossom water, and six raw egg yolks. Make this pie with four or five very thin pastry sheets on the bottom and two or three on top. If you want to add in a couple of pieces of beef bone marrow, you can. And if it's not a meat day, you can make it with just almonds and cream.

Puff pastry pie with sweetbreads and giblets

Take two or three veal sweetbreads and eight to ten hen livers and boil them all. Remove them, let them cool, and mince them up. Then fry some fatback minced into small cubes and a little minced onion and add it to the giblets. Mince it even more and season with pepper, clove, and ginger. Season with salt, and add a quarter pound of ground sugar, a little bit of sour juice, either from sour grapes or from lemon, and six egg yolks. Then, make a fine dough and put in a covered tart pan a half dozen very thin pastry sheets, and, on top [of the sweetbread mixture], another three or four, and close up your puff pastry pie. Grease with lard and grate a little sugar on top and let bake. After it's cooked, if you want to cover it with candied egg yolk threads and sugar at a thread stage so high it makes spun sugar, you can. It usually turns out very tasty.

[376] *Bollo de Mazapán, y Manteca fresca.*

Hase de tomar libra y media de masa de molletes de leche que esté leuda, y luego majar una libra de almendras con otra de azúcar, y hacer pasta de mazapán, y mezclarlo todo, y echarle media libra de manteca de vacas fresca, y sobar la masa mucho, y echar allí ocho huevos, y sobarla hasta que haga correa: y luego untar una tortera con manteca fresca, y échale obleas por el suelo, y por los bordes, y ponla a cocer en un horno, y échale su costra de azúcar por encima.

[377] *Pan de Leche.*

Tomarás una azumbre de leche, y échale media libra de azúcar molido, y un poco de olor, y ponla a calentar, (236r) que esté un poco más de tibia: luego harás una presa de harina floreada de tahona, y echarle has un poco de levadura, y desatarla has con un poco de leche: luego echarás toda la leche, y amasarás la masa muy sutilmente, y harás los panecillos, y cuézanse en el horno de pan, que esté muy templado. A esta masa se le ha de echar media libra de manteca de vacas: y si le quisieres echar un poco de olor, podrás. Y advierte, que la levadura ha de ser de heces de cerveza, si es posible, y ha de llevar esta masa ocho huevos.

[378] *Torta de Dátiles.*

Tomarás dos libras de dátiles, y picarlos has quitándoles los cuescos, y consérvalos, y luego harás docena y media de huevos mejidos, y harás tu torta echándole un poco de agua de olor, y un poca de manteca fresca, y harás unas hojas muy delgadas de la manera que se hace para el bollo de vacía: y echarás (236v) un par de hojas debajo, y luego un lecho de dátiles, y huevos mejidos, y rociarla con manteca, y echar otra hoja, y hacer lo mismo: y desta manera irás haciendo hasta que se acaben los materiales, y cierra tu torta con otra hoja delgada, y cuécele en un horno: y después de cocida échale un poco de almíbar por los bordes, y sírvela caliente. Advierte, que estos dátiles los podrás conservar enteros, quitados los cuescos, y rellenarlos con los huevos mejidos, y armar un plato sobre unas hojuelas, y adornarlo con rebanadas de diacitrón, o calabazate.

[379] *Quesadillas de Mazapán.*

Tomarás una libra de almendras, y májalas con otra libra de azúcar, y harás pasta de mazapán, y tomarás media libra de queso asadero,[377] o de queso frescal, que sea mantecoso, y májalo muy bien, y revuélvelo con el mazapán, y échale cuatro

---

377 *Queso asadero* [asadero cheese] is a mild, chewy cheese that is both creamy and sliceable.

Marzipan and butter roll

Take a pound and a half of mollete dough that is yeast-raised and has milk. Then grind a pound of almonds with another of sugar and make marzipan paste. Mix it all together and add a half a pound of butter, knead the dough a lot, and add eight eggs. Knead until it is smooth. Then grease a covered tart pan with butter and put wafers on the bottom and around the edges. Place in the oven to bake and sprinkle a sugar crust on top.

Milk bread

Take two quarts of milk, add a half a pound of ground sugar and a little rosewater, and heat it up until it's a little warmer than lukewarm. Then, make a well of finely sifted mill flour, add a little leavening agent, and thin it with a little milk. Then, add all the milk and gently knead the dough. Make the rolls and bake them in a bread oven that is a moderate temperature. You should add half a pound of butter to the dough, and if you want to add a little more rosewater, you can. Note that the leavening agent should be from beer dregs if possible and the dough should also have eight eggs.

Date pie

Take two pounds of dates, pit them, mince them, and preserve them. Next, make a dozen and a half of sweet scrambled eggs. Make your crust and add to it a little rosewater and a little butter. Make long, thin sheets in the way they are made for "Airy pastry." Lay a couple of sheets on the bottom, then a layer of dates and sweet scrambled eggs, and dot with lard. Place another sheet on top and repeat. Continue this way until you've used up all the ingredients and seal the pie with another thin sheet. Bake in the oven. Once it's baked, brush a little simple syrup around the edge and serve hot. Note that these dates can be preserved whole once the pit is removed and stuffed with sweet scrambled egg yolks. Assemble a dish on top of pastry sheets and garnish with slices of candied citron or squash.

Marzipan cheese tarts

Take a pound of almonds and grind them up with another of sugar and make a marzipan paste. Take half a pound of asadero cheese, or farmer cheese, that is creamy, mash it up, and mix it in with the marzipan. Add four eggs with their whites. Then

huevos con claras: y luego (237r) echa yemas hasta que esté un poco blando: luego harás las quesadillas, y perdigarlas has en el horno, y echarle has media libra de manteca fresca de vacas al batido, y hinche las quesadillas, y no vayan muy llenas: y cuando estén a medio cocer rocíalas con un poco de manteca de vacas, y échale su costra de azúcar.

[380] *Pasteles Flaones.*

Para hacer un pastel de estos que haga plato, has de echar doce yemas de huevos en una pieza, y echarle allí media libra de azúcar molido, y cosa de dos, o tres onzas de harina, y unas gotas de leche: y bate esto mucho que se deshaga bien la harina: luego irás echando leche poco a poco hasta cerca de tres cuartillos, y echarle has un poquito de sal: y luego harás un vaso de masa, en que quepa toda esta cantidad. Ha de ser este pastel ancho, que no sea muy alto, pero muy delgado, y con su repulguillo por (237v) los bordes, y ponlo a perdigar en el horno, y échale dentro un poco de manteca de vacas fresca, tanto como una nuez, y dale unas punzadillas en el suelo con la punta del cuchillo, porque no empolle: y cuando esté bien perdigado, y que esté la masa tiesa, échale el batido dentro, y lo podrás henchir bien, porque no ha de crecer ninguna cosa, y ha de quedar así raso, y cuézase, y sírvelo caliente: y algunas veces se suelen servir fríos.

[381] *Otros Flaones.*

Harás el batido, como está dicho en el de atrás, y en lugar del pastel untarás un plato con manteca de vacas, y echarásle este batido dentro, y ponlo sobre unas brasas, y calienta una cobertera de cobre que esté bien caliente, y tómala con un garabato, y ponla sobre el plato así en el aire, y tomará color por encima, y se cuajará con mucha facilidad, y se puede servir así, raspándole un poco de azúcar por encima.

[382] (238r) *Pasteles de Leche.*

Estos pasteles podrás hacer como los flaones, salvo que en lugar de las doce yemas de huevos, puedes echar seis huevos con claras: y será lo mismo añadiendo un poquito de más harina, porque tenga fuerza, porque han de subir mucho, y porque no tornen a bajar mucho, que parecen mal. Estos flaones o pasteles de leche, si hubiere alguna mujer que no los sepa hacer, podrá echar este batido en una cazuela untada con manteca, y meterla en el horno a fuego manso, y se cuajará como si fuera pastel: y si quisieres echar este batido en un cacito con un poco de manteca de vacas, ponlo sobre brasas, y tráelo a una mano con un cucharón, y vendrá a hacerse una crema: luego tórnale a meter dos o tres huevos crudos, o cuatro yemas, y unta la cazuela, y échalo dentro, y métela en el horno, y te saldrá muy buena y muy

add yolks until it is fairly soft. Then make the tart shells and parbake them in the oven. Add half a pound of butter to the batter, fill the cheese tarts but not too full, and when they are half baked, dot with a little butter and make a sugar crust.

Custard pie

To make a pie of this type that fills a whole plate, put twelve egg yolks in a bowl and add half a pound of ground sugar and about two or three ounces of flour and a few drops of milk. Mix all of this well so that the flour dissolves. Then slowly add up to three pints of milk and a little salt. Then make a pie shell so that all the batter fits. It should be a wide crust and not too tall, but very thin and with a small crimped edge. Put it in the oven to parbake and put in a little fresh butter, about as much as a walnut, and prick the bottom with the tip of a knife so it does not bubble up. When it is parbaked and the crust is crisp, add in the batter filled to the top because it won't expand at all. It should be level. Bake and serve hot. Sometimes it is served cold.

Other custard

Make this batter as explained in the previous one [recipe], and instead of a pie, grease a plate with butter, add the batter to it, and put it over red-hot embers. Warm a copper lid so that it gets very hot, grab it with a hook, and hang it over the plate in the air. It will begin to brown and quickly set. It can be served as is, grating a little sugar on top.

Custard pies

These pastries can be made like custard pies, except, instead of twelve egg yolks, you can add six eggs with the whites. It will be the same by adding a little more flour so that it's stronger, because it has to rise a lot, and so that it won't later fall, because that looks bad. These flaones, or custard pies, in case some woman does not know how to make them, she could put this batter into a casserole that has been greased with lard and put it in the oven on low flame, and it will set as if it were a pie. If you want to put this batter in a saucepan with a little butter, put it over red-hot embers and stir it with one hand with a spoon. It will turn into a cream. Then add again two or three raw eggs or four egg yolks. Grease the casserole and add it in. Place it in the oven and it will come out easily and look good. Instead

fácil, y en lugar de la (238v) cazuela podrás echar esta crema en unas escudilletas muy chicas, o cazuelitas de barro, o de plata, y meterlas has en un horno, y harás que se tuesten un poco por encima: y antes que entren en el horno ponles unas rajitas de almendras blancas, que parecen muy bien y se llaman éstas tigeladas.[378]

[383] *Sustancias para enfermos.*[379]

Para sacar una sustancia en vidrio, has de tomar una gallina vieja y gorda, acabada de matar, y pélala, y sácale el menudillo, y golpéala muy bien con la vuelta del cuchillo, de manera que se quiebren los huesos: luego hazla pedacitos, de manera que quepan por la boca de una redomilla, y échalos en agua por espacio de medio cuarto de hora para que se desangre:[380] luego lávalos y exprímelos del agua, de manera que queden un poco húmedos, y mételes uno a uno en la redoma, y tápala con un (239r) corcho, y ponle un poco de masa por encima, y asiéntala sobre un ladrillo con un poco de masa por debajo: y pondrás este ladrillo en el suelo con su redoma encima, y échale un cerco de brasas alrededor, que por ninguna parte llegue al ladrillo con un pie, y déjala estar un poco, e irasle acercando un poco más la lumbre, y verás que se va calentando el vidrio, y vele llegando un poco más la lumbre que esté igual por todas partes: y desta manera irás llegando la lumbre a la redoma hasta que comience a cocer: y si vieres que cuece con mucha furia, vele apartando la lumbre de manera, que no deje de cocer, y que cueza igualmente por todas partes: y ha de estar cociendo cosa de dos horas y media; y con esto estará cocida la sustancia: luego calentarás un paño, y arroparás con él la redoma, y levantarla has sobre la mesa con su ladrillo, y destaparla has, y echarás la sustancia en una ollita de plata, colándola (239v) por una estameña, y echarle has un granito de sal, y ponla a calentar: y desta manera la darás al enfermo. Esta sustancia como se saca en el vidrio, al fuego, se puede sacar en agua, metiéndola en la redoma, como está dicho, y henchirás un barquino, o caldero de agua con un poco de bálago, o heno dentro: luego atarás la redoma con un cordel, y atravesarás un palo en la boca de un caldero, y colgarás de allí la redoma que esté metida en el agua hasta el collete, y que esté entre el bálago, o heno, porque no tope en el caldero: y desta manera estará cociendo tres horas, antes más, que menos: y la sustancia estará hecha: y pondrás la estameña sobre una ollita, y echarás en ella la sustancia sin

---

378 *Tigelada* is a Portuguese custard similar to flan. Two recipes for *tigeladas* appear in the fifteenth-century Portuguese cookbook *Um tratado da cozinha portuguesa do século XV* [A treatise on Portuguese cooking from the fifteenth century]. One is ascribed to Isabel de Vilhena. In this recipe Martínez Montiño finishes the pies with almond slivers.
379 While Martínez Montiño has made references to certain recipes being good for the ill, in this section a handful of recipes are written specifically to nurture the sick.
380 "Por espacio de medio cuarto de hora" [the period of half of a quarter of an hour] is an excellent example of how the language of minutes is not yet current.

of the casserole, you can put this cream into very small bowls or little casseroles made of clay or silver, and place them in the oven. They will turn brown on top. Before you put them in the oven, shave some white almond slices on top. They will look very nice. These are called *tigeladas*.

Sustaining broth for the ill

To make a sustaining broth in a glass container, take an old, fat hen, recently slaughtered, pluck it, and remove its giblets. Hit it well with the back side of the knife so that the bones break. Then cut it into pieces so that they can fit through the mouth of a carafe. Put them in water for the period of half of a quarter of an hour to bleed them. Next, wash them, squeeze out the excess water so that they are just a little damp, put them one by one into the carafe, and close it up with a cork. Put a little dough on top and set it on a brick with a little dough underneath. Put this brick on the floor with the carafe attached and place a circle of red-hot embers around it that is no closer than a foot distance all around. Leave it like this for a while and slowly move the heat closer and you'll see how the glass heats up. Get the heat closer evenly all around. Continue this way with the heat getting closer and closer until it begins to boil. If you notice that it's boiling too rapidly, move the heat back, but don't let it stop boiling and let it cook evenly all around. It should cook for about two and a half hours. After this the sustaining broth will be done. Then, heat up a dish cloth and wrap it around the carafe. Pick it up with the brick, place it on a table, uncork it, and pour the sustaining broth into a silver pot, straining it through cheesecloth. Add a pinch of salt and heat it up. Give it to the sick person in this form. This sustaining broth that is made in glass over fire can also be made in water by placing it in the carafe as already explained. Fill a leather skin or a big cooking pot with water and a little straw or hay. Tie the carafe with a cord and place a stick through the top of the pot and hang the carafe from it so that it is in the water up to its neck and in the straw or hay so that it doesn't bump against the pot. Let it cook this way for three hours or more, but no less, and the sustaining broth will be done. Put the cheesecloth over a small pot and pour it through without squeezing it, because

exprimirla; porque cuanto menos grasa tuviere será mejor para el enfermo: luego la podrás sazonar de sal, y calentarla: desta manera se podrá dar al enfermo. Advierte, que si no tuvieres redomilla para sacar la sustancia, podrás sacarla en un (240r) orinal nuevo, o en una ventosa grande, o en otro vidrio cualquiera, que tenga la boca angosta. La sustancia que está dicho del vidrio en seco, y de la del vidrio en agua, la podrás sacar en un puchero en agua vidriado un poco altillo: pondrás tu gallina como está dicho, y taparás el puchero con un corcho, y con un poco de masa, y ponlo en un perol, o caldero, con unas piedras a la redonda, porque no se trastorne: y luego hínchelo de agua hasta el cuello del puchero: luego dale lumbre, y cueza tres horas, y hallarás la sustancia hecha. Estas tres suertes de sustancias toda es una misma cosa, no se diferencian sino es en las vasijas. Una sustancia cocida se hace quebrantando la gallina como para sustancia, y metiéndola en una olla que lleve una azumbre de agua, y echándole allí media docena de garbanzos y unas ramas de perejil, y haciéndola cocer hasta que esté muy cocida, y el caldo muy apurado que no venga a quedar de una (240v) gallina más de escudilla y media de caldo. Colando esta sustancia cocida, y la otra de vidrio, y mezclando las entrambas, es la mejor sustancia que se puede hacer, porque la de vidrio, aunque parece clara como agua, es más fuerte y más recia para desistir que la cocida. Y esto digo, porque lo he oído decir a muy grandes Médicos, Y así lo que han de llevar dentro las sustancias, lo han de ordenar los Médicos, porque en algunas mandan echar oro, y en otras rajitas de calabaza, y en otras garbanzos negros, y otras cosas convenientes para la enfermedad del enfermo, que no sean de mal gusto: y en algunas mandan echar tortugas y pepitas de calabaza: y en esto no tengo que meterme, más que sacar muy bien la sustancia.

[384] *Sustancia de Pobres.*

Para hacer esta sustancia si no hubiese más de un cuarto de ave, y hubiere (241r) poca lumbre, Tomarás este cuarto de ave quebrantado, y hecho pedacitos, y una libra de carnero de pierna, que sea recién muerto, y golpearlo has mucho, y haráslo rebanaditas, y ponlo con el cuarto de ave en agua por medio cuarto de hora, y meterlo has en una ollita de barro vidriada, exprimiéndolo primero del agua; y pondrásla sobre rescoldo, y pondrás un borde de masa en la ollita en la boca, y luego le pondrás una escudilla llena de agua encima, de manera que asiente bien en la masa: y cuando vieres que el agua de la escudilla se calienta derrámala, y tórnala a henchir, y en estando caliente otra vez torna a hacer otro tanto. Esta sustancia ha de estar a la lumbre hora y media, y hallarás una escudilla de sustancia: y cuando la saques la sazonarás de sal, y ha de ser muy poca la sal, porque no hay más mala cosa para enfermos que hallar sal en las viandas.

the less fat in it, the better for the sick person. Then, season with salt and heat it up, and this is how you give it to the sick person. Note that if you don't have a carafe to make the sustaining broth, you can make it in an unused chamber pot, a big cupping glass, or any type of glass container with a narrow opening. The sustaining broth explained with or without water can also be made in a tall glazed stew pot in water. Put the hen in as explained, cork the pot with a cork and a little dough, put it in a round-bottom pot or cauldron. Place some stones around it so it doesn't move and fill it with water up to the neck of the stew pot. Put it on to cook and let it cook for three hours and the sustaining broth will be done. These three kinds of sustaining broth are really all the same; their only difference is the cookware. A "boiled sustaining broth" is made by breaking the bones of the hen as for sustaining broth, putting it in a pot with two quarts of water, adding in a half dozen garbanzos, springs of parsley, and letting it boil until it is thoroughly cooked and little stock remains. From a whole hen, you should only be left with a bowl and a half of stock. By straining this "boiled sustaining broth" and the other "glass sustaining broth," and mixing the two, you will get the best sustaining broth, because the glass sustaining broth, even though it looks as clear as water, is stronger and more intense for stopping [an illness] than the boiled one. I say this because I've heard very great doctors say this. And whatever is added to the sustaining broths is whatever the doctors prescribe, because some prescribe gold to be added, others, squash slices, others, dark garbanzos and other things that do not taste bad and are advisable according to the illness of the patient. Some prescribe turtle and squash seeds, but I won't involve myself in this except to make an excellent sustaining broth.

Sustaining broth for the poor

To make this sustaining broth when you have only a quarter of a bird and a little fire, take a quarter of a bird with the bones smashed and cut into pieces, and a pound of leg of mutton that has recently been slaughtered, pounded and sliced. Put it with the poultry in water for half of a quarter of an hour. Place it in a glazed terracotta pot, but first squeeze off all the water. Place it over grey embers and place dough around the rim of the pot and then place a bowl full of water on top so that it sits over the dough perfectly. When you notice that the water in the bowl is hot, remove it and fill it up again. When it warms up again, do the same thing. This sustaining broth should be cooking for an hour and a half and it will make a bowl of sustaining broth. When you take it out, season with salt, but it should be very little, because there is nothing worse for sick people than to have salt in their food.

[385] *Sustancia asada.*

(241v) Asarás una pierna de carnero, y cuando esté casi asada, sacarla has en un plato, y picarla has con el cuchillo, de manera que la pase de parte a parte muchas veces: luego le doblarás el jarrete, apretándola con el tenedor, y sacarás medio cuartillo de sustancia. La pierna ha de ser de carnero muerto de aquel día. Esta sustancia se saca de aves, y de perdices: éstas es necesario haber prensa para ellas, y si no la hubiere, en acabándola de sacar del asador, se apretarán entre dos platos muy apretados, punzándolas también con el cuchillo. Estas sustancias se han de poner en un plato sobre un poco de nieve,[381] y helarse ha toda la grasa que tuviere; luego la apartarás con unas plumas grandes de gallina al borde del plato, y echarás la sustancia en otro vaso, y sazonarla has de sal, y calentarla has, de manera que no cueza: y así se ha de dar al enfermo.

[386] (242r) *Una escudilla de Caldo.*

Para hacer una escudilla de caldo para una persona enferma, o regalada. Tomarás media gallina vieja y gorda, acabada de matar, y golpearla has mucho con la vuelta del cuchillo, y échala en un poco de agua por un cuarto de hora, para que se desangre: y luego échala a cocer en una ollita nueva con cuatro garbanzos, y un granillo de sal, y cueza poco a poco hasta que esté la gallina bien cocida, y el caldo apurado: y cuando el señor se hubiere sentado a la mesa, batirás una yema de huevo fresco en la escudilla, y esté el caldo cociendo, y ve echando caldo, y meneándolo con una cucharita, trayéndolo a una mano hasta que se hinche la escudilla, y este caldo ha de salir de una colorcilla blanca, al modo de almendrada, y no ha de cocer más; porque si el caldo está cociendo cuando se eche en la escudilla, basta, y no ha de llevar otra cosa más de lo dicho, (242v) ni tocino, ni verdura, ni carnero, no más de sólo la gallina: es de las mejores suertes de caldo que se hacen.

[387] *Una escudilla de Almendrada.*

Para hacer una escudilla de almendrada son menester cuatro onzas de almendras, y mondarlas has en agua caliente, y echarlas has en agua fría, por espacio de media hora: y luego majarlas has en el almirez, mojando a menudo la mano del almirez es

---

381 This is the first time Martínez Montiño specifically references *nieve* [snow] for chilling a dish. The only other time it appears in the cookbook, it is for this same recipe, repeated later in the book (600; 601). Snow would be from the mountains, packed in straw and placed in cold storage. There also existed several treatises dedicated to snow and ice and their medicinal property; for example, Nicolás Monardes' *Libro que trata de la nieve y de sus propiedades, y del modo que se ha de tener en bever enfriado con ella y de los otros modos que ay de enfriar* (1571). For more on the use of snow in early modern Spain, see Herrero-García 147–76.

Essence from a roast

Roast a leg of mutton and when it's almost done, remove it onto a plate and pierce it with a knife from one side to the other several times. Then, fold the shank over, squeeze it with a fork, and extract a half pint of essence. The leg must be from ram slaughtered that day. This essence can also be made from poultry or partridges. For the latter, it is necessary to have a press, but if you don't have one, right after you have taken them off the spit, squeeze them very tightly between two plates, also stabbing them with a knife. The essence should go on a plate that is on snow and all the fat should congeal. Then with some big hen feathers, separate it to the side of the plate and pour the essence into another container, season with salt, warm it up, but do not bring it to a boil. Serve it to the sick person this way.

A bowl of [hen] broth

To make a bowl of broth for a sick or delicate person: Take half of an old, fat hen, recently slaughtered, and hit it several times with the back of a knife. Put it in some water for a quarter of an hour to bleed it. Then put it in a different small pot with four garbanzos, and a pinch of salt, and let it slowly simmer until the hen is done and the broth reduced. When the lord is sitting at the table, beat a fresh egg yolk in a bowl. As the broth is simmering, begin adding the broth, stirring with a small spoon, with one hand until the bowl is full. The broth should take on a whitish colour, like an almond sauce, and don't cook it any more, because if the broth is boiling when it goes into the bowl, that's enough. It doesn't need anything more than what is already explained, no fatback, no herbs, no mutton, nothing but hen. It is one of the best kinds of broth that is made.

A bowl of almond broth

To make a bowl of almond broth, four ounces of almonds are needed. Peel them in warm water and place them in cold water for about half an hour. Then, grind them in a mortar, wetting the pestle often with warm water. Once they are

agua tibia: y después de bien majadas irlas echando agua tibia, cantidad de medio cuartillo, antes más que menos: y luego se ha de colar por una estameña, o servilleta, y exprimirlo muy bien, y tornar a echar las granzas en el almirez, y majarlas muy bien, y tornar a echar la leche dentro poco a poco,[382] y tornarla a pasar por la estameña, y exprimirla muy bien, y echarle tres onzas de azúcar, y un granillo de sal, y ponla a cocer en un cacito (243r) chico, trayéndolo a una mano, y con dos o tres hervores que dé, estará hecho, y no se le ha de echar almidón, ni otra cosa que la pueda espesar, antes se echen más almendras, y sacar la leche más gruesa, que ayudarla con otra cosa ninguna. Y esto digo, porque sé que en algunas partes echan almidón a la almendrada, y algunos un migajoncillo de pan blanco remojado en la misma leche de almendras, o de cabras. Esto hacen para encorporar la almendrada, mas no sólo no es menester, sino que se puede hacer la leche tan gruesa, que con el recaudo que tengo dicho, añadiendo otras tres onzas de más almendras, y otras dos onzas de azúcar, aunque se añada un poquito de más agua la podrás hacer, que en dando dos o tres hervores recios, estará tan gruesa, que en enfriándose la puedan apellar como manjar blanco: y esta se llama manteca de almendras: a las cuales se suelen echar muchas cosas por orden de los Médicos, como (243v) son pepitas de calabaza, y de melón, o avellanas: todas éstas se han de mondar las cáscaras, y ponerlas en remojo dos horas, y juntarlas luego con las almendras, y sacar de todo esto junto a la leche, y hacer la almendrada que no esté muy trabada, ni muy rala.

[388] *Una escudilla de Borrajas.*

Para hacer una escudilla destas borrajas con leche de almendras, sacarás la leche que no sea muy gruesa, sino como para almendrada, y un poquito más suelta, y harás almendrada: y en dando dos hervores tendrán las borrajas cocidas, y picadas, y exprímelas del agua, y échalas dentro en el almendrada, y cuezan otros dos hervores: y luego las podrás servir en la escudilla. Han de llevar el mismo azúcar, que suele llevar el almendrada.

[389] *Manteca de Almendras amarilla.*

(244r) Tomarás cuatro onzas de almendras y échalas en un poco de agua que esté cociendo, y en soltando ellas el pellejo las sacarás sin echarlas en agua fría y mondarlas has, y ponlas en una pieza limpia sin agua; y luego tomarás un cedacillo de cerdas, y ponlo sobre un plato: e irás tomando las almendras una a una, y estregándolas sobre las cerdas del cedacillo un poco recio, e iránse deshaciendo las almendras, y cayendo en el plato, y en deshaciendo aquella toda, tomarás otra: y desta

---

382 The water first used in the recipe is now referred to as *leche* [milk] because it has passed once through the almonds, but it is the same liquid.

well ground, begin adding warm water, about a half pint, better more than less. Then, strain it through cheesecloth or a napkin, thoroughly squeezing it. Return the solids to the mortar and grind them again, slowly add milk again, strain it through the cheesecloth again, and thoroughly squeeze it. Add three ounces of sugar and a pinch of salt, and put it in a small saucepan to boil, stirring with one hand. When it comes to a boil two or three times, it is done. You don't need to add starch or anything else to thicken it; rather, for a thicker milk, adding more almonds is better than anything else. I am saying this because in some places starch is added to almond broth, or [in] some, the crumb of white bread soaked in almond milk or goat milk. This is done to thicken the almond broth. But it is not only not necessary, it can also make the milk too thick. With the ingredients I have explained, adding another three ounces of almonds and another two ounces of sugar, even if you add a little more water, you can make it. When it comes to a rolling boil two or three times it will be so thick that when it cools you can shape it into balls like blancmange. This is called almond butter, and doctors often prescribe many things to be added to it like squash or melon seeds, or hazelnuts, all of which should have their skins removed and be soaked for two hours and then added to the almonds. The milk should come from all of them together. Make the almond broth so that it's not too thick or too thin.

A bowl of borage soup

To make a bowl of borage soup with almond milk, make milk that is not too thick, like for almond broth or even a little thinner. Make the almond broth; when it comes to two boils, have the borage boiled and chopped and the water squeezed out. Add it to the almond broth and boil it twice. Then you can serve it in a bowl. It should have the same [amount of] sugar as the almond broth.

Yellow almond butter

Take four ounces of almonds and put them in a little boiling water. Once the skin falls off, remove them without putting them in cold water and peel them. Put them in a clean bowl without water. Then, take a horsehair sieve and place it over a plate. Begin taking the almonds one by one and firmly rubbing them over the sieve. The almonds will be falling apart and onto the plate. Once one almond is completely crumbled, pick up another and continue this way until,

manera las irás gastando todas, una a una, y hacerse ha un montoncillo en el plato de una manteca amarilla, y no se ha de llegar a ello con cuchillo, ni con cuchara, ni con otra cosa, porque se apelmazaría de manera, que no se pudiese hacer como se pretende, sino tomar otra tanta cantidad de azúcar molida, y cernida, e irásla echando sobre la manteca, revolviéndolo muy sutilmente y cuando estuviere bien mezclado, estará todo amarillo y granujado. (244v) Esta manteca es buena para algunas personas que tienen malo el pecho: y hase de tomar fría a cucharadillas. Y advierte, que el azúcar ha de ser otra tanta cantidad como las almendras: y así se ha de tener respeto a lo que se desperdicia de las almendras para quitarle del azúcar otro tanto.

[390] *Otra Manteca de Almendras blanca.*

Tomarás media libra almendras, y mondarlas has en agua caliente, y como fueres mondándolas las irás echando en agua fría, y déjalas estar allí media hora: luego irás majándolas en el almirez poco a poco, y mojando la mano del mortero en agua tibia, y májalas mucho, e irás echando gotas de agua hasta cerca de un cuartillo: luego la colarás por la estameña, o servilleta, y apretarla has muy bien: y luego torna a echar las almendras en el (245r) almirez, y májalas mucho tornando a echar la misma leche poco a poco en las almendras,[383] y majarlo hasta echarla toda: y luego tórnala a pasar por la estameña, apretándola mucho: y a esta leche echarás seis onzas de azúcar, y ponla a cocer, y cueza cuatro, o cinco hervores, y se vendrá a espesar que se eche de ver que está muy gorda: luego sácala, y échala en alguna vasija de vidrio, o de plata, y déjala enfriar, y cuajarse ha que parezca cuajada. Esta manteca blanca es buena para una persona que tiene malo el pecho, o la garganta, como está dicho atrás, porque es muy blanda y muy suave.

[391] *FARRO.*[384]

Este farro es de cebada, y es muy fresco, y así lo ordenan para muchos enfermos: Sacudirás el farro de las pajas, y lavarlo has en muchas aguas tibias, y luego lo echarás a cocer en un puchero (245v) con caldo de ave, y cueza poco a poco hasta que parezca que está cocido, y el farro esté un poco espeso: luego tomarás cuatro o cinco almendras mondadas, y echarlas has en el almirez, y májalas con una gota de agua: y luego echarás el farro dentro, y darle has unos golpes, y echa

---

383 As seen in the earlier recipe "Una escudilla de almendrada" [A bowl of almond broth] (492–4; 493–5), the water first used in the recipe is now referred to as *leche* [milk] because it has passed once through the almonds, but it is the same liquid.

384 For Martínez Montiño, farro is a generic dish, something akin to porridge and made with barley. Today it refers to three ancient wheat species: einkorn, emmer, and spelt. For more information, see the entry in the Glossary.

one by one, they are done and formed into a little pile of yellow butter on the plate. Don't put a knife or even a spoon to it or anything else, because it would solidify that way. It can't be made how one would expect; rather, take the same amount of ground sugar that has been sifted and begin pouring it over the butter, gently stirring it. When it is all mixed together it should be yellow and granular. This butter is good for people who have chest pains. It should be taken cold by the teaspoon. Note that the sugar should be the same quantity as the almonds, always being careful about how much almond is lost so as to remove that same amount of sugar.

Another white almond butter

Take half a pound of almonds and peel them in hot water. As soon as they are peeled, put them in cold water and let them stand a half hour. Then slowly grind them in the mortar, wetting the pestle with warm water. Thoroughly grind them and slowly add drops of water, almost a pint. Then strain it through cheesecloth or a napkin and squeeze it tightly. Return the almonds to the mortar and thoroughly grind them, slowly adding again the same [amount of] milk to the almonds. Grind until all has been added. Strain it through the cheesecloth again and tightly squeeze it. Add six ounces of sugar to this milk and put it on to boil. Bring it to a boil four or five times and it will begin to thicken and you will notice that it is thick. Then, remove it and put it in a container made of glass or silver and let it cool. It should set so it looks like pressed clotted milk. This white [almond] butter is good for a person who has chest pains or a sore throat as explained above, because it is soft and very gentle.

Farro

This farro is made from barley and is fresh and thus it is prescribed for many people who are sick. Shake the chaff off the farro and rinse it many times in warm water. Then put it in a tall stew pot to boil with poultry stock and let simmer until it appears to be done and the farro somewhat thick. Then take four or five shelled almonds and put them in the mortar. Grind them up with a drop of water and add them to the farro. Pound it a little and add a little stock. Then strain it

un poco del caldo: y luego pásalo por la estameña, que no quede en ella sino algunos granillos, y tórnalo a echar en su ollita, y échale azúcar que esté bien dulce, y no cueza más de un par de hervores, porque se hará un poco moreno, que por eso se echan las cuatro o cinco almendras, para que con aquella leche se blanquee. Este farro suelen mandar hacer con leche de almendras, y sale mejor, porque con caldo siempre sale un poco moreno, si no se tiene mucha cuenta con él, y con leche de almendras sale blanco, aunque no tan sustancial: y para hacerse con la leche de almendras se ha de cocer primero con agua, o con caldo: y para un (246r) cuarterón de farro será menester un cuarterón de azúcar, y otro de almendras. Este farro suelen comer algunos sin pasarlo por la estameña, sino cocido con caldo, o con leche, las almendras; mas a mí paréceme que lo que se pasa por la estameña es lo mejor, porque va más líquido y no se sienten los granillos al comer.

[392] *Pistos para enfermos.*[385]

De estos pistos no había para tratar, porque es cosa que se usa mucho, y me parece que lo saben todos. Para una escudilla de pisto, cocerás media gallina que sea buena en una ollita nueva: y cuando esté bien cocida, tomarás la media pechuga, y pícala un poquito, y échala en el mortero, y májala mucho, y tendrás un migajoncillo de pan remojado en el mismo caldo, y májalo mucho con la carne: y luego desátalo con el caldo de la gallina, de manera que (246v) venga a hacerse una escudilla del pisto: y luego cuélalo, y échalo en una ollita, y ponlo al fuego cuanto se caliente: luego pruébalo de sal, y se puede dar al enfermo, revolviéndolo con una cucharita, porque se suele asentar la mitad, o parte de la carne en el suelo de la olla, aunque sea cosa pasada por la estameña: y por esto, y porque los caldos y sustancias han de ser muy frescas, principalmente en Verano que se corrompen muy presto, lo que se había de echar a cocer de una vez se ha de echar en dos: y cuando el enfermo está muy desganado, que no come cosa mascada, sino cosas liquidas con cuchara, es bueno picar alguna pechuga de perdigón muy menuda, y mezclarla con el pisto, y dársela a cucharaditas: y desta manera les harán comer lo que no comieran si lo sintiesen. Otras veces se saca una sustancia en el vidrio, y luego se hace el pisto con ella; porque aunque el enfermo tome poco, sea bien sustancial.

---

[385] Although Martínez Montiño explains that *pistos* are incredibly common, they have nothing to do with the now famous *pisto manchego*. As you can deduce from this recipe, seventeenth-century pisto was a strained soup that included ground poultry as the main ingredient.

through cheesecloth so that nothing remains except a few small grains. Return it to the small pot and add sugar so that it's very sweet. Don't let it come to a boil more than a couple of times because it will turn a little brown. That's why you add the four or five almonds so that its milk whitens it a little. It is normally suggested to make this farro with almond milk, and it does come out better, because with stock it always turns out a little brown if you're not paying attention to it. With almond milk it comes out white, even though it's not as nourishing. To make it with almond milk, cook it first with water or with stock. For each quarter pound of farro, a quarter pound of sugar and another of almonds are necessary. Some eat this farro without being strained through cheesecloth but rather boiled in stock or almond milk. However, it seems to me that what is strained through the cheesecloth is the best, because it is thinner and you don't feel the little grains when eating.

Pisto soup for the ill

I don't need to touch on these pisto soups because they are so common and I believe everyone knows them. For a bowl of pisto soup, boil half a good-quality hen in a small, new pot. When it's done, take half the breast and chop it up a little. Place it in the mortar and thoroughly grind it. Have the crumb of some bread soaked in the same stock and grind it up together with the meat. Then thin it with hen stock so that it makes enough for a pisto bowl. Strain it, pour it into the pot, and put it on the fire to heat it up. Taste for salt. It can be given to the sick but must be stirred with a spoon, since half, or at least some, of the meat usually sets on the bottom of the bowl even if it has been strained through cheesecloth. For this reason and because stocks and sustaining broths have to be very fresh, especially in summertime because they'll go bad so quickly, what is normally put in together all at once is put in two times. When the sick person has no appetite and does not eat food [that has to be] chewed, but only liquids with a spoon, it is good to mince up some breast from a partridge chick and mix it in with the pisto soup and give it [to the person] in little spoonfuls. This way they will be made to eat what they wouldn't eat if they were able to feel it. Other times a sustaining broth can be made in glass [cookware] and the pisto soup can be made with it. This way, even though the sick person eats just a little, it will be very nourishing.

[393] (247r) *Una Panetela.*[386]

Para una escudilla de panetela, cocerás media gallina con un poco de carnero, y picarás la carne de la pechuga en parte que salga muy blanca, y tendrás pan rallado que esté de un día para otro, y echarás dos partes de pan rallado, y una de gallina de pechuga, y sacarás caldo de gallina, y échalo en una ollita, y luego pon el pan rallado, y la pechuga, revolviéndolo con un cucharón, de manera que quede rala, y dale dos hervores, y sírvela así caliente, digo así blanca sin dulce, ni otra cosa más de que el caldo ha de estar muy sazonado. A esta panetela se lo suele echar algunas veces dulce: lo cual ha de ser a gusto del enfermo. Advierte, que esta panetela no se ha de hacer hasta que se quiera servir, porque vaya granujada, que por eso se dice, que el pan esté bien seco, o se tueste en el horno, con que no se ponga moreno; porque (247v) todo el toque desta panetela está en que ha de salir muy blanca. Algunas veces se les suelen echar dos yemas de huevos frescos; mas yo me atengo a la blanca. Otras veces se hacen estas panetelas dejando cocer mucho el pan, y el azúcar con el caldo: y luego se cuajan con unas yemas de huevos, y un poco de zumo de limón, que vengan a salir agridulces.

[394] *Otra Panetela.*

Otra se hace en día de pescado para personas sanas: para ésta no es menester otra cosa más de rallar el pan, como está dicho, y poner un poco de agua, y sal, y azúcar al fuego, y echarle un poco de manteca fresca de vacas, y su pan rallado, de manera que quede rala, y cueza dos hervores: luego bate dos o tres yemas de huevos, y desátalos con la misma panetela, y échaselas dentro, y dé un hervor. Y advierte, que las cosas que hicieras para enfermos, te han de (248r) moderar en la sal; porque siempre se quejan que está salada la vianda, porque la calentura les hace tener mucha sed, y con eso sienten mucho la sal.

[395] *Ginebradas.*

Cuajarás dos azumbres de leche, y pondráslas a escurrir, habiéndola recogido en el suelo caliente, y déjala escurrir bien: luego échala sobre el tablero, y deshacerla has con las manos, de manera que no le quede ningún burujón: luego métele una libra poco menos de harina de trigo muy blanca floreada, y tendrás dos libras de manteca fresca derretida y espumada, y bien clara, y echarle la mitad, antes más que menos, y libra y media de azúcar molido y cernido, y un poquito de sal, y harás

---

386 Once again, Martínez Montiño's recipe for panetela has nothing to do with modern-day versions of panetela found in Cuba or Puerto Rico. This recipe recreates another soup dish for the infirm.

Panetela (Hen and mutton bread soup)

For a bowl of panetela, boil half a hen with a little mutton and chop up the meat from the breast so that it's very white. Have some breadcrumbs left over from the day before and add two parts of breadcrumbs and one part of hen breast. Take some of the hen stock and put it in a small pot, then add the breadcrumbs and breast and stir it with a spoon so that it becomes thin. Bring it to a boil twice and serve it hot as is, that is, white without any sweetener or anything other than the seasoning for the stock. Sometimes sweetener is added to this panatela. It should depend on the taste of the sick person. Note that this panetela should not be made until it's ready to serve so that it comes out granular. This is why it is explained that the bread should be very dried, or toasted in the oven as long as it doesn't turn brown, because the secret to this panatela is that it is very white. Sometimes fresh egg yolks are added, but I stick to keeping it white. Other times these panatelas are made by boiling the bread, sugar, and stock a lot, then thickening it with egg yolks and a little lemon juice. This way it turns out sweet and sour.

Another panatela

Another one can be made for fish days for healthy people. For this one, nothing else is necessary but to grate the bread, as already explained, and put a little water, salt, and sugar on to boil. Add a little fresh butter and the right amount of breadcrumbs so that it's thin. Bring it to a boil twice. Then beat two or three egg yolks and thin them with the panatela itself. Add it and bring it to a boil. Note that things made for sick people should have a moderate amount of salt because they also complain that their food is too salty and because fever makes a person very thirsty. That is why they are sensitive to salt.

Ginebradas (Clotted milk tarts)

Curdle four quarts of milk and set it up to drain after having gathered it up while hot on the bottom [of the pan]. Let it thoroughly drain. Then turn it out onto a cutting board and crumble it by hand so that no lumps remain. Then add a little less than a pound of white, finely sifted flour. Have two pounds of melted, skimmed, very clear, fresh butter. Add half of it, better more than less, a pound and a half of sifted, ground sugar, and a little salt. Make two medium-sized crusts

tus vasitos de medio talle, de una masa fina con la misma manteca sin azúcar, y métoslos en el horno, e hínchelos deste batido, habiéndolos primero perdigado: y cuando estén cocidos úntalos con un (248v) poco de manteca. Advierte, que en estas ginebradas se han de echar ocho huevos, cuatro con claras, y cuatro sin ellas: y si las quisieres hacer en masa dulce, harás una masa dulce con la misma manteca, y con azúcar molido, y cernido: y en lugar de agua echarás suero de lo de la cuajada, y harás una masa encerada, y sobarla has muy bien que esté muy suave, y tendrás una hoja del grueso de un real de a dos, y cortarás una tortitas redondas, y mojarlas has las orillas con un poco de suero con unas plumas, y harásles unos picos, como a las quesadillas de los pasteleros, pero han de ser más altas de borde: luego harás unos rollitos de masa de cemite, y harinarlos has, y ponlos al rededor de la ginebrada por la parte de adentro, arrimándolos a los bordes porque no se caigan, y ponlos a perdigar en el horno:[387] y en estando perdigados sácales los rollitos de la masa, e hínchelos del batido, y cuézanse: y cuando estén casi cocidos, rocíalos con (249r) manteca, y échales azúcar por encima, y acábense de cocer.

[396] *Otras Ginebradas.*

Cuajarse ha la leche, y apretarse ha mucho, de manera, que no tenga suero ninguno: luego la echarás sobre un tablero, sobarla has mucho, de manera que estará bien desgranujada: y luego tomarás azúcar molido y cernido, y tendrás harina de tahona muy floreada, y tendrás manteca fresca que sea muy buena exprimida: luego tomarás una cucharita de hierro, y medirás la cuajada con ella, y verás cuántas cucharadas has echado, y échala en un cazo, y echarás otras tantas de harina, y otras tantas de azúcar, y otras tantas de manteca, y pondrás el cazo sobre las brasas, y velo mezclando todo, de manera que no cueza: y cuando esté bien mezclado apártalo del fuego, y sazónalo de sal, y amasa una masa con suero de lo de la cuajada, y huevos, y manteca, y harás unos vasillos a (249v) modo de quesadillas con sus picos, y déjalas secar: luego perdígalas en el horno: y cuando estén tiesos hínchelos del batido, y ponlos a cocer: y cuando se vayan acabando de cuajar, échales buen rato de azúcar por encima, y acábalos de cocer. Estas ginebradas no llevan huevos en el batido: suelen salir muy buenas.

[397] *Conserva de manjar Blanco.*

Tomarás una libra de almendras, y échalas en agua cociendo: luego pélalas, y májalas, mojando la mano del mortero, porque no se enaceiten: y cuando estén bien majadas, tendrás una pechuga de gallina cocida, y deshilada como para manjar blanco, y echarla has dentro del mortero con las almendras, y májalo todo junto

---

387 These *rollitos* [little rolls] act as weights to keep the dough from puffing up too much.

with a fine dough and the same butter and no sugar. Place them in the oven and fill them with the batter, having first parbaked them. When they are baked, brush with a little butter. Note that eight eggs, four with the whites and four without them, should be added to these *ginebradas*. If you want to make them with sweet dough, make a sweet dough with the same butter and sifted, ground sugar, but instead of water, add the whey from the clotted milk and make an elastic dough. Thoroughly knead it so that it's smooth. You'll have a [pastry] sheet the thickness of a two-real coin, and cut out some round tarts. With some feathers, wet them on the edges with a little whey and make some points, like bakers' cheese tarts, but they should be taller around the edge. Then make some little rolls from dough made with whole-grain wheat flour, dust with flour, and place them around the *ginebrada* on the inside, lean them next to the edges so that they don't fall. Place them in the oven to parbake. When they are parbaked, remove the little rolls, fill them [the shells] with the batter, and bake. When they are almost done, dot with butter and sprinkle sugar on top and finish baking.

Other ginebradas (Other clotted milk tarts)

Curdle milk and squeeze it a lot so no whey remains. Then turn it out onto a cutting board and knead it a lot so that it becomes smooth. Then take sifted, ground sugar and have finely sifted mill flour, and fresh butter that has been well pressed. Then take an iron teaspoon and measure the clotted milk with it so you'll see how many spoonfuls you've put in. Put them in a large saucepan and add the same amount of flour, sugar, and butter. Put the saucepan over red-hot embers and begin mixing it all together, but don't let it boil. When it's all mixed together, take it off the heat and season with salt. Make a dough with the whey from the clotted milk, eggs, and butter. Make some little crusts with points, like the ones for cheese tarts with their points. Let them dry and then parbake them in the oven. When they are firm, fill them with batter and bake them. When they have finished setting, sprinkle a good amount of sugar on top and finish baking. These *ginebradas* don't have any eggs in the batter. They are usually very tasty.

Blancmange preserves

Take a pound of almonds and put them in boiling water. Then peel them and grind them, wetting the pestle so that they don't get too oily. When they are well ground, have a boiled breast of hen and shred it as you would for blancmange. Add it to the mortar with the almond and grind it all together. Have a pound and a half

un poco: y tendrás libra y media de azúcar en almíbar un poco delgada, y echa dentro las almendras, y la pechuga, y cuezan unos tres, o cuatro hervores: y si se espesare mucho, (250r) échale otro cuarterón de azúcar en almíbar. Esta conserva ha de salir un poco blanda, y échala en sus vidrios: y si le quisieres echar unas gotas de agua de azahar, bien podrás: y si se le echare un par de limones en conserva majados, es bueno.

[398] *Un Capón que sea medio cocido, y medio asado.*

Pondrás a cocer un capón en una olla, y cuando estuviere un poco más de medio cocido, sácalo, y déjalo enfriar, y méchalo por un lado con mechas muy menudas, que vaya muy frisado: luego harás una sopa de las natas, o de leche, contrahecha a la de las natas, o una sopa dorada: y así cruda como está pon encima el capón, del lado que no está mechado hacia abajo, y apriétalo, que se entierre la mitad en la sopa: y luego ráspale un poco de sal encima de lo mechado, y métela en un horno con (250v) lumbre abajo y arriba, y váyase tostando poco a poco, y se irá cuajando la sopa, y tostando el capón, y se acabará de cocer la parte de abajo, y se tostará el tocino, y la parte de arriba: y así parecerá el uno asado, y el otro cocido.

[399] *Gallina a la Morisca.*[388]

Tomarás un par de pollas, o cuatro pollos, y ásalos, y luego cortarlos en cuartos, y freirás un poco de cebolla con un poco de tocino en dados, y ahóguese muy bien: y luego échale caldo de la olla, y sazona con todas especias, salvo clavos, y cueza poco a poco: échales un poco de vinagre que estén bien agrias, y si tuvieres un poco de manteca de vacas fresca, échasela dentro, y podrás freír un poquito de harina en esta manteca de la suerte que está dicho atrás, porque este platillo no ha de llevar huevos: y si le quisieres echar un poquito de verdura picada podrás. Este platillo ha de salir un poquito amarillo.

[400] (251r) *Panecillos de colaciones.*[389]

Tomarás tres libras y media de harina de tahona, muy floreada, y si no la hubiere de tahona, sea de molino de trigo candeal, y ponla sobre el tablero, y harás una presa redonda, y echarás allí un poco de levadura, y deshazla con una gota de vino

---

[388] The title calls for *gallinas* [hens], but the recipe states *pollas* or *pollos* [young hens or male chickens]. Martínez Montiño also includes a roux thickener in this recipe.

[389] The *panecillo* [small loaf of bread or roll] weighed 0.227 kilograms or half a pound and was baked by *panaderos de corte* [court bakers], in contrast to *pan* [standard loaf bread], which weighed 0.9 kilograms or 2 pounds and was baked by *panaderos de villa* [village bakers] (Andrés Ucendo and Lanza García 69). For more on collation, see 458n361.

of fairly thin simple syrup and add it to the almonds and breast, and boil three or four times. If it gets too thick, add another half cup of simple syrup. This preserve should come out a little soft. Pour it into glass [containers]. If you want to add a few drops of orange blossom water, you certainly can. If a couple of preserved mashed lemons are added, it will taste good.

Capon, half boiled, half roasted

Put a capon on to boil in a pot and when it's a little more than half cooked, remove it, let it cool, and lard it on one side with very fine slices [of fatback], very tight together. Next, make cream sops or faux cream sops made from milk, or golden sops. And place the capon on top, raw, just like it is, with the unlarded side face down. Press it down so that half is buried in the sops. Then, grate a little salt over the larded part and place it in the oven with the heat above and below so that it slowly browns, the sops set, and the capon is browned. The bottom part will finish cooking and the fatback will brown as well as the top part. In this way it will seem like part is roasted and the other part boiled.

Hen, Morisco style

Take a couple of young hens or four young chickens, roast them, and cut them into quarters. Fry a little onion with cubes of fatback and thoroughly sauté it. Then add some stock from the pot, season with all spices, except clove, and gently boil. Add a little vinegar so that they are sour and if you have a little bit of fresh butter, add that in. You can fry a little flour in this butter the way that was previously explained, because this dish shouldn't have any eggs. If you want to add some chopped green herbs, you can. This dish should come out a little yellow.

Collation rolls

Take three and a half pounds of finely sifted mill flour; if there isn't any from an animal-powered mill, it should be candeal bread flour from a grinder. Put it on the cutting board and make a round well. Add in a little yeast and have it dissolve

tibio, y echa encima una libra de azúcar molido y cernido: y luego échale media escudilla de aceite que sea buena, tibia, y un poco de anís, y un poco de sal: luego tendrás cosa de un cuartillo de vino tibio, y echa un poco en la presa de la harina, y ve amasando tu masa con el vino, de manera que quede encerada: y luego así caliente la envolverás en unos manteles calientes, y la pondrás en una cestilla, o en otra cosa al amor de la lumbre para que se leude: y cuando esté leuda vela sacando al tablero poco a poco para hacer los panecillos, y lo demás quedará arropado: y como vayas hiñendo la masa, y haciendo (251v) los panecillos, tendrás una cama hecha adonde los poner entre los dobleces de unos manteles limpios, y en medio de otra ropa donde estén bien abrigados: y desta manera los irás haciendo de a cuatro onzas cada uno: y entre tanto que se acaban de leudar se caliente el horno de pan, de manera que esté muy bien templado, y cocerlos has sobre papeles polvoreados de harina: y si no tuvieres horno de pan, bien se podrán cocer en un horno de cobre, teniendo cuenta cuando entraren los panecillos en el horno no esté frío, ni muy caliente por abajo; porque si se resfrían, no crecen; y si tiene mucha lumbre el horno se quema por el suelo con mucha facilidad. Estos se pueden comer en las colaciones. Y advierte, que cuando hicieres los panecillos, has de heñir muy bien la masa, porque importa mucho.

[401] *Hojaldrillas fritas.*

Tomarás un par de panecillos de candeal (252r) crudos, y pondráslos sobre el tablero, y sobarlos has con un poquito de harina para que se incorporen un poco más: y luego meterles has cuatro yemas de huevos, y un poco de manteca de puerco, o de vacas, y sobarla has hasta que haga correa: luego echarás un poco de azúcar molido y cernido, y sobarla has hasta que tome correa, e irás haciendo unas hojaldrillas delgadas del tamaño de un real de a ocho, y tendrás la manteca caliente, y como las vayas haciendo, velos echando en la sartén: y en friéndolas pásalas por almíbar, y échales un poco de canela por encima: y no te espantes porque digo que eches azúcar en la masa que se ha de freír, porque antes es muy bueno. De la masa de las empanadas Inglesas podrás hacer unos tallarines, o unos cuadrillos, y fríelos. Son muy buenos para componer platos, como son platos de pastelillos de conservas. Y advierte, que si la masa estuviere un poco dura, que de (252v) los cuatro huevos que está dicho, podrás echar los dos con claras.

[402] *Buñuelos de Queso asadero.*

Tomarás una libra de queso asadero, que sea bueno, y mondarlo has de la corteza, y majarlo has en el almirez con un cuarterón de azúcar, y ponle cuatro huevos batidos, y cosa de tres onzas de harina, y májalos mucho: y luego harás tus buñuelos, y sírvelos con miel, y azúcar, y canela por encima.

in a drop of warm wine. Add a pound of sifted, ground sugar on top. Then add a half bowl of good-quality warm oil and a little anise and a little salt. Next, have about a pint of warm wine and add a little to the flour well. Begin kneading your dough with the wine so that it becomes smooth. Then, while warm, wrap it in a warm tablecloth and put it in a small basket or something else near the heat so that it rises. When it has risen, begin putting it little by little on the cutting board to make rolls. The rest should remain covered. As you are kneading the dough and making the rolls, have a couche made where you can put them between the folds of clean tablecloths and between another cloth so they are well covered. Continue making them this way, each one four ounces. While they are rising, heat the bread oven so that it is thoroughly warmed and bake them on paper dusted with flour. If you don't have a bread oven, you can easily make them in a copper oven, remembering that when you put the rolls in, the oven cannot be either cold or too hot below, because, if they are cold, they will not rise, and if it's too hot, the bottoms will quickly burn. You can eat these as [part of] collation. Note that when you make these rolls, the dough should rise a lot, because it is very important.

Little fried puff pastries

Take a couple of uncooked candeal rolls and put them on the cutting board. Knead them with some flour so that they become a little thicker. Then, add four egg yolks, a little lard or butter, and knead it until it becomes elastic. Then, add a little sifted, ground sugar and knead it until it becomes elastic. Begin making thin puff pastries the size of an eight-real coin. Have some hot lard and, as you make them, drop them into the frying pan. Once fried, dip them in simple syrup and sprinkle a little cinnamon on top. Don't be frightened when I say to add sugar into the dough before frying because it is really very good. With English empanada dough you can make strips or little squares and fry them. They are great for arranging plates, like a plate of little pastries with preserves. Note that if the dough is a little stiff, you can add two egg whites from the four egg yolks mentioned.

Puffs of asadero cheese

Take a pound of asadero cheese, it should be good, and peel off the rind. Grind it up in a mortar with a quarter pound of sugar. Add four whipped eggs and about three ounces of flour. Thoroughly grind them all up. Then make your puffs and serve them with honey, sugar, and cinnamon on top.

[403] *Ñoclos de masa.*

Tomarás una libra de harina muy floreada, y échale media libra de azúcar molido y cernido, y tres onzas de manteca fresca de vacas, y un poquito de vino blanco, y una migaja de sal, y seis huevos sin claras, y dos con claras, y un poquito de anís: y de todo esto harás una masa encerada; y luego tiende una (253r) hoja gorda como un dedo: luego tomarás un dedal, e irás cortando con él, y saldrán los panecillos redondos, poco mayores que avellanas, y cuécelos en un horno sobre papeles polvoreados de harina. También se pueden hacer con la mano redondillos como cermeñas.

[404] *Fruta de Fartes.*[390]

Harás hojuelas delgadas, y fríelas en buen aceite, que estén bien fritas, y sácalas en un colador que se escurran del aceite: y luego las echarás en el almirez, y muélanse muy bien: luego tendrás miel que sea muy buena, espumada, conforme a la cantidad de las hojuelas que tuvieres, harás el almíbar de miel, que esté subido de punto, y echa dentro las hojuelas muy molidas, y échale un poco de clavo molido, y canela, y un poco de pimienta, y un poquito de nuez: y si quisieres echarle un poco de pan rallado tostado primero, bien podrás, mézclalo con las hojuelas: y de todo esto (253v) harás una pasta en el cacito de miel: y luego harás una masita con yemas de huevos, y vino, y una gota de manteca fresca, o buen aceite, y una migaja de sal: y esta masa se ha de sobar mucho, y tender muy delgada: y luego harás los fartes de la hechura que quisieres redondos con unos piquitos, e irás envolviéndolos en una masita muy delicadamente, y mojarás el bordecillo con una pluma, y asentarás el otro borde encima, de manera que después de cocido el farte, no se ha de ver por donde se pegó la masa: luego pondrás unos papeles en la hoja del horno, y los irás poniendo dejando los piquitos para arriba, e henchirás la hoja del horno dellos, y cuécelos: y si quisieres hacerlos aprisa tiende una hoja de masa: y luego harás un rollito largo de la pasta, que tome toda la hoja: luego pon aquel rollito sobre el borde de la masa, y arróllalo con la masa, una vuelta no más: corta la masa, y cierra el borde mojándolo con una pluma, (254r) y asiéntalo sobre el otro borde, y apriétalo un poco: luego ve cortando al sesgo con el cuchillo unos trocitos, un poco más largos de una pulgada: y desta manera los podrás hacer. No parece tan

---

390 The RAE explains that *fartes* is "frito de masa rellena de una pasta dulce con azúcar, canela y otras especias" [fried dough with a sweet paste filling made from sugar, cinnamon and other spices]. Here, Martínez Montiño combines honey and crumbled puff pastry filling to make the filling. For more information, see "International References" in the Introduction (61).

Bite-sized wafers made with dough

Take a pound of very finely sifted flour and add half a pound of sifted, ground sugar, three ounces of butter, a little white wine, a pinch of salt, six eggs without their whites and two with their whites, and a little anise. From all of this, make an elastic dough. Next, roll out a sheet a finger-width thick. Then take a thimble and begin cutting out with it. Little round rolls should come out, a little bigger than hazelnuts. Bake them in an oven on paper dusted with flour. You can also make little round ones, like Cermeño pears, by hand.

Fartes fried dough

Make thin pastry sheets and fry them in good oil. Once they're done, remove them to a colander so the oil drains off. Then put them into a mortar and thoroughly grind them up. Then take honey, it should be excellent, whipped, and the right amount for the pastry sheets you have. Make a simple syrup from honey cooked beyond the boiling point and add the ground-up pastry sheets to it. Add a little ground clove, cinnamon, a little pepper, a little nutmeg, and, if you want to add breadcrumbs that were first toasted, you can. Mix it all with the pastry sheets. With all this make a filling in the honey pan. Then make a dough with egg yolks, wine, a touch of fresh lard or good oil, and a pinch of salt. Knead this dough a lot and roll it out thin. Next make the fartes in whatever round shape you want with little points. Begin carefully wrapping them in dough. Wet the edges with a feather and place the other edge on top so that once the farte is baked you won't see where you sealed the dough. Then put some paper on the baking sheet and begin placing them on it with the little points facing upward. Fill the baking sheet with them and bake them. If you want to make them quickly, roll out a sheet of dough. Then, make a long roll of the filling, the length of the sheet. Then place the roll over the edge of the dough and roll it up with the dough, just once. Cut the dough and seal the edge by wetting it with a feather and placing it over the other edge, and gently squeeze it. Then with a knife cut pieces on the diagonal, a little longer than an inch, and this is how you make them. They don't turn out looking as nice but it's the same thing. If you knead the dough with

bién,[391] mas es la misma cosa. Si sobares esta masa con aceite muy bien, y le echases un poquito de azúcar molido y cernido, y no les echases huevos, se podrían comer en las colaciones: y si fuere Verano por amor de la calor, podrás hacer la pasta con azúcar, y un poquito de miel, y moderarte en las especias. Y si no quisieres freír las hojuelas, cuécelas en el horno, y muélelas, y será los mismo.

[405] *Memoria de los Mostachones.*[392]

Tomarás cosa de medio celemín de harina floreada,[393] y harás una presa sobre el tablero un poco larga, y echarle has dentro una libra, y un cuarterón de azúcar molido, y cernido, y dos onzas (254v) de canela molida y cernida, y siete onzas de agua clara, y una de agua rosada: y con esto batirás el azúcar dentro en la presa hasta que haga ampollitas: luego irás metiendo harina hasta que la masa esté encerada: luego quitarás el harina que sobrare a una parte del tablero, y sobarás un poco la masa, y harás tus mostachones de cosa de dos onzas cada uno, un poquito largos, y cuécelos sobre papeles bien polvoreados de moyuelo,[394] que es un cemite muy menudo, y muy áspero: y tendrás caliente el horno, como para pan, y que esté reposado, y no los dejes cocer demasiado, porque se pondrás muy duros: y también si los sacas antes que se embeba la humedad, quedarse han muy blandos, que en el cocer está el toque de que salgan buenos. Y advierte, que si les metieses más harina de lo necesario, saldrían muy secos y ásperos: y si los dejases muy blandos se te despachurrarían, y se irían (255r) por el horno, y no serían de provecho: la masa ha de quedar encerada, y con esto saldrán bien.

Advierte más, que si no hallares moyuelo, los podrás poner sobre obleas, y saldrán muy bien, y después de cocidos les podrás raspar los suelos. Estos son los que más gusto suelen dar a su Majestad, porque están moderados en especia: otros los quieren más picantes de especias.

---

391 In 1611, the phrase *tan bien* is written as *también* but in 1617, it changes to *tan bien* and stays that way in all subsequent editions. I've made the change here, since the context reveals that the use of *también* is most likely a typo.

392 I have used the word *memoir* to translate *memoria* in order to remain faithful to its definition in the *OED*: "A note, a memorandum; a record; a brief testimonial or warrant; (in pl.) records, documents" ("Memoir"). Today *mostachón* is a spongy finger cake, something similar to a madeleine. Martínez Montiño's recipe is for a long cookie flavoured with cinnamon and rosewater but with no butter or eggs. The *mostachones de Utrera* from a town near Seville are well known throughout Spain today. Also, *mostachón* is what is used today to make strawberry shortcake.

393 Used for dry ingredients, a *celemín* is one twelfth of a *fanega* and measures 4.625 litres, approximately a gallon. Thus, *medio celemín* would measure two quarts or eight cups. However, based on basic dough recipes today, I believe this recipe is calling for four cups of flour (to one cup of liquid).

394 *Moyuelo* as described by the RAE: "Salvado muy fino, el último que se separa al apurar la harina" [very fine bran, the last part that is separated when sifting flour].

excellent oil and add a little sifted ground sugar and don't use eggs, you can eat them (as part of) collation. And if it's summer, because of the heat, you can make the paste with sugar, a little honey, and moderate spices. If you don't want to fry the pastry sheets, you can bake them in the oven and grind them and it will turn out the same.

Memoir of mostachon cookies

Take about a half of a celemin of finely sifted flour and make a well on a long cutting board. Add a pound and a quarter of sifted, ground sugar, two ounces of sifted, ground cinnamon, seven ounces of fresh water, and one of rosewater. Beat the sugar in the well until little beads form. Then begin mixing in the flour until the dough is smooth. Then put to the side of the board any extra flour and knead the dough a little. Make the mostachons a little long with about two ounces for each one. Bake them on paper well dusted with *moyuelo*, which is a very small and rough bran. Have the oven heated as if to [bake] bread, let them rest, and don't bake them too long, because they will get very hard. If you take them out before all the moisture is absorbed, they will turn out very soft, because the secret to turning out well is in the baking. Note that if you put in more flour than required, they'll turn out dry and rough. And if they are very soft, they will flatten and when in the oven won't turn out. The dough should be smooth and this is what they need to turn out fine.

Also note that if you can't find any *moyuelo*, you can bake them on wafers and they will turn out good. After they're done, you can scrape off the bottom. These are the ones that His Majesty likes most because they are moderately spiced. Others prefer them with a sharper spice flavour.

[406] *Memoria de la Mostaza negra.*[395]

Tomarás cuatro arrobas de uvas negras,[396] y desgranarlas has, y echarás los granos en un caldero, o perol de cobre, y ponlos sobre las trébedes con lumbre, y cueza una hora: luego apártalo del fuego, y déjalo enfriar, y escurre todo el mosto que saliere: y luego estruja las uvas todo lo que pudieres en una estameña de lino; y después de sacado el mosto, ponlo a cocer, y cueza (255v) hasta que mengue la mitad, y un poco más: y luego déjalo enfriar, y tomar una libra de polvo de mostaza muy fina, y desátala con vinagre muy fuerte, de manera que se haga una masilla, y déjala estar así cosa de seis horas, y luego ponla en un barreñón, o perol, y ve echando mosto poco a poco, y desatando la mostaza hasta que esté bien deshecha, y echarás mosto hasta que esté bien rala: luego échala en una olla vidriada, y déjala estar un día destapada: luego tápala con un corcho, y ponle por encima un pergamino, y el mosto que te sobrare guárdalo en una olla vidriada, muy bien tapada: y cuando la mostaza se endureciere y perdiere la fortaleza, con el arrope que te sobró podrás desatar un poco de polvo de mostaza, habiendo hecho la masilla con la vinagre, como está dicho, y aderezarás la mostaza, de manera que no esté dura, y esté picante: y si esta mostaza se te espesare mucho entre año, y no tuvieres arrope, desatarás (256r) un poco de polvo de mostaza con un poco de vinagre, y un poco de agua, y dejarlo has estar dos, o tres horas para que pierda la verdina: aderezarás una ollita de mostaza, cosa que pueda durar diez, o doce días: y en acabándose ésta aderezar otra para otros tantos días: y esto se puede hacer porque el arrope con que se hizo la mostaza estaba tan negro y tan subido de punto que se vendrá a endulzar a los cuatro o cinco meses, mas tiene buen remedio en lo que tengo dicho, que si esta mostaza se hiciera con mosto de uvas tintas sacado en lagar, sale la mostaza morada: y si la aderezases con mostaza y vinagre, quedaría parda: y si no apurases tanto el arrope, también se corrompería a cosa de tres, o cuatro meses después de hecha: y así más vale aderezarla entre año, que no que se eche a perder, de manera que no se pueda remediar. En el arrope con que se hace la mostaza podrás poner membrillos cuando se cuece, para que tome (256v) aquel gusto: y también se suele echar clavo y canela, mas yo lo he experimentado: y es mejor hacer el arrope, como está dicho, sin echar ninguna cosa más del polvo de la mostaza: y si quisieses hacer esta mostaza sin hacer la masita del polvo de la mostaza con vinagre, sino echar el polvo en una pieza, y desatarlo con el mismo arrope, sin echar gota de

---

395 In the seventeenth century, *mostaza* had a black or brown colour, nothing like the popular yellow mustard or even Dijon mustard of today. The name *mostaza* comes from grape must (*mosto*), to which seeds from any of the mustard plants in the family *Brassicaceae* are added. This recipe takes weeks to make, and Martínez Montiño explains how to prevent it from going bad or even turning sweet. He uses it in dishes with strong flavours such as boar or kid head.

396 *Arroba* is a unit of weight (it could also measure mass or volume) that, in Castile, was equivalent to 25 pounds. Here, he calls for 100 pounds of grapes.

Memoir of black mustard

Take four *arrobas* of black grapes and deseed them. Put the grapes in a cauldron or a round-bottom copper pot and place it on a trivet to boil. Let it boil for an hour. Then take it off the fire and let it cool. Drain off all the must that comes out. Then, squeeze the grapes as much as you can in a linen cheesecloth. Once the must is collected, put it on to cook and let cook until half remains and a little more. Then let it cool. Take a pound of very fine mustard powder and thin it with strong vinegar so that it makes a paste. Let this rest for about six hours then place it in a large tub or round-bottom pot and begin adding the must, thinning the mustard until it's all dissolved. Add the must until [the mixture] is thin. Then pour it into a glazed pot and let it rest uncovered for a day. Then cork it and place a piece of parchment on top. Reserve the leftover must in a glazed pot that is well sealed. When the mustard hardens and loses its strength, with the leftover grape syrup you can thin some mustard powder, having made a paste with vinegar as explained above. Prepare the mustard so that it isn't hard and it is pungent. If the mustard thickens throughout the year and you don't have any grape syrup left, you can thin some mustard powder with a little vinegar and water and let it sit two or three hours so that it loses its green film. Prepare a small pot of mustard, something that can last ten or twelve days. Once it's done, prepare another for the same amount of days. This should be done when the grape syrup, with which you made the mustard, is so dark and its flavour so intense that it turns sweet over four or five months. Moreover, there's a good solution for what I have explained. If the mustard is made with must from red grapes fresh from the press, the mustard turns out purple. If you adjust it with mustard and vinegar, it will turn brown. And if you don't squeeze the grape syrup tightly enough, it will also go bad in three or four months after it's made. So, it's really worth it to adjust it throughout year so it doesn't go bad and you'll have no way of fixing it. You can add quince to the syrup you use for the mustard when it's boiling so that it takes on that flavour. Clove and cinnamon are also often added, but I've tried this and the syrup turns out better as explained above without adding anything except the mustard powder. If you want to make this mustard without the mustard powder and vinegar paste but by putting the powder into a bowl and thinning it with the

vinagre, estará más segura de que no se pierda entre año: haciéndola desta manera echarla has en una olla vidriada, y dejarla has destapada veinte y cuatro horas para que eche la verdina fuera: hará una espuma, y quitársela has con un cucharón, y taparás la olla con un corcho que esté muy justo, y luego un pergamino encima, porque no pierda la fuerza: y si entre año se endulzare se tornará a aderezar como está dicho atrás.

[407] *Vinagre de Saúco.*

Cogerás la flor del saúco y echarla (257r) has en una cesta, y déjala estar en ella veinte y cuatro horas, que esté bien apretada: luego pondrás un paño, o manteles, e irás sacudiendo aquella flor encima, y caerá la florecilla sobre los manteles, y quedarán los palillos mondados sin ninguna flor: luego pondrás la flor adonde se seque sin que le de el sol, porque le quitaría el gusto: y cuando la flor esté bien seca, tomarás las redomas de vidrio de a tres azumbres, y echarle has dentro la flor que pudieres tomar con las dos manos, e hínchelas de vinagre blanco que sea bueno, y tápalas con sus corchos y con sus pergaminos, y ponles adonde les dé el sol, y el sereno, y esténse allí hasta que la flor toda se abaje toda al suelo de la redoma: luego trasiega la vinagre en otras redomas, y tápalas con unos corchos que vengan muy justos, y ponle unos pergaminos encima mojados, y átalos muy bien porque no se salga la fortaleza de la vinagre: luego podrás tornar a henchir las redomas adonde (257v) está la flor del saúco, y taparlas has con sus corchos y pergaminos, y de ahí a dos meses tendrán otro tanto vinagre de saúco, casi tan bueno como el primero: puédese guardar todo el año: si le quisieres echar a cada redoma tres, o cuatro claveles, estén bien secos. Sabrá un poco a clavos:[397] y si le quisieres echar tres o cuatro botoncillos de rosa seca, también se los puedes echar que da muy buen gusto.

[408] *Otro vinagre de Saúco.*

Si hubieres de andar caminos, y no pudieres llevar el vinagre de saúco: lleva un poco de flor seca en una taleguilla, y adonde quisieres hacer vinagre de saúco, pon a calentar el vinagre en una cazuela de barro, o en alguna pieza de plata: y cuando la vinagre comenzare a alzar hervor, échale dentro un poco de la flor de saúco, y apártala, y tápala poniendo encima una servilleta, y luego un plato, y déjala estar

---

397 Although it may seem strange, carnations were known to emit a clove aroma. Andrés Laguna explains, "se dice clavel en España por ser olorosa su flor, como los clavos de especias" [it is called *clavel* in Spain because the flower has the fragrance of the spice, clove] (4.4). The relationship between the two (*clavel/clavo*) is also found in German (*Nelke/Gewurznelke*), Arabic (*krenfel* for both), and Greek (Γαρύφαλλο for both).

syrup itself and not adding a drop of vinegar, it is more likely not to go bad within the year. If you make it this way, pour it into a glazed pot and leave it uncovered for twenty-four hours so that it loses its green film. It will foam and you should skim this off with a spoon. Then cork the pot tightly and place parchment on top so that it doesn't lose its strength. If it turns sweet during the year, adjust it again as explained above.

Elderberry vinegar

Gather elderberry flowers and put them in a basket. They should be packed together, and let them rest twenty-four hours. Then over a cloth or tablecloth, begin shaking the flowers over it and the little flowers should fall off and the bare stems with no flower should remain. Then, set the flowers aside to dry, but without direct sunlight, because that takes away its flavour. When the flowers are thoroughly dry, take six-quart glass carafes and put as many flowers inside as you can hold in two hands. Fill with good white vinegar and seal it with the appropriate cork and parchment paper. Then set it where it will be exposed to sun and evening dew and leave it until all the flowers are on the bottom of the carafe. Next, decant the vinegar into other carafes, tightly cork them, put damp parchment paper on top, and tightly tie them up so none of the vinegar's sharpness escapes. Then, you can refill the carafes where the elderberry flowers are, seal them with cork and parchment, and two months later, you'll have another batch of elderberry vinegar that is almost as good as the first. This will last all year. If you want to add to each carafe three or four carnations, they should be thoroughly dry. This will give it a clove flavour. If you want to add three or four little dried rose buds, you can also add them, and it will give it a very good flavour.

Another elderberry vinegar

If you were travelling and couldn't bring elderberry vinegar with you, pack a little bit of dried flowers in a small sack. Whenever you want to make elderberry vinegar, heat up some vinegar in a terracotta casserole or in a silver bowl and, when the vinegar begins to boil, add a little bit of the elderberry flower. Take it off the heat and cover it with a napkin and then a plate. Let it rest for a quarter of an hour.

un cuarto (258r) de hora: luego destápala, y ponla a enfriar, y hallarás vinagre de saúco, con tan buen gusto como la que se curó al sol. Y advierte, que el mandar que se eche esta flor del saúco en una cesta aprestada, y en parte fresca, es, porque se escalde un poco, y suelte bien las florecillas; porque si se secase suelta con los palillos, son tan tiernos como las flores, y se quiebran y se mezclan con la flor, que no hay quien los pueda apartar: y después sabe el vinagre a ellos, no tiene buen gusto.

[409] *Agraz para todo el Año.*[398]

Tomarás el agraz cuando esté bien crecido, y bien verde, y májalo, y saca todo el agraz que pudieres, y cuélalo por un cedacillo, y ponlo en una pieza, y déjalo asentar, y quedará muy claro como agua, trasiégalo en unas redomas, que tengan unas canillas junto al suelo, y no ha de llevar ningún poso, (258v) sino muy claro, y no se hinchan las redomas mucho, porque se ha de echar en cada redoma un poco de aceite, cosa de medio cuartillo, y se ha de ir sacando el agraz por la canilla, el aceite estará siempre encima, y no le dejará criar nada, porque de otra manera la criará, y se echará a perder el agraz: y si quisieres sacar mucho agraz, podráslo poner en una tinaja que tenga su canilla, y echarás cantidad de aceite, de manera que tenga siempre el grueso de un dedo de aceite encima, e iráse sacando el agraz por abajo, como está dicho.

[410] *Otra manera de Agraz.*

Sacarás el agraz, como está dicho, y colarlo has por cedacillo, y echarás este agraz en unos vidrios anchos y bajos de borde así, sin dejarlo asentar, y pondrás estos vidrios en parte adonde les dé el sol todo el día: y con esto se vendrán a cuajar y a secar de manera que se pueda moler, y tendrás este agraz guardado (259r) en una caja: y cuando quisieres usar dél, desatarlo has con un poco de agua, o caldo de la olla, y tendrá el propio gusto del agraz, y lo podrás tener todo el año. El zumo de las cidras agrias se puede guardar para todo el año, secándolo en los vidrios como el agraz cuando se cogen las cidras para hacer diacitrón por el mes de Abril, que hace ya buen sol: y este agrio que queda de las cidras lo puedes exprimir, y echarlo en los vidrios, y ponerlo a secar, y se cuajará como el agraz, y después de seco lo podrás tener guardado: y cuando quisieres usar dél, desátalo con un poco de caldo del hervor de la olla, y sabrá a zumo de limón.

---

398 For more on *agraz* [sour grape], see the Introduction (42). Food historian and journalist Vicky Hayward has recreated this and the following recipe for a sun-dried verjuice paste. For a detailed explanation of the process, see her article "Spanish Dried Agraz."

Then, uncover it, let it cool, and you'll have elderberry vinegar with a flavour as good as if it had been cured in the sun. Note that the step for pressing the elderberry flowers together in a basket when they are fresh is so that they will become a little chafed and easily release their flowers, because if you dry them separately while still connected to the stems, which are as tender as the flowers, they will break off and mix in with the flowers and they will be impossible to separate. Then the vinegar will taste like the stems and the flavour won't be as rich.

Verjuice for the whole year

Take some sour grapes when they're full sized but still very green. Grind them up and remove as much juice as you can. Strain through a sieve, put in a bowl, and let rest. It should be as clear as water. Decant it into some carafes with little spouts on the bottom. It shouldn't have any dregs; rather it should be very clear. Don't over-fill the carafe because you should add a little oil, like about a half pint, to each one. When you pour the verjuice out through the spout, the oil will always stay on top. It should prevent it from turning, because otherwise it will turn and the verjuice will be ruined. If you want to make a lot of verjuice, you can put it in a large terracotta jar with a spout. Add a lot of oil so that there is always a finger-thick layer of oil on top. Take the verjuice out from below as explained.

Another way of [making] verjuice

Make verjuice as explained and strain it through a sieve. Put the verjuice in wide, shallow glass containers without letting it rest. Place these glass containers where they will be exposed to the sun the whole day. This way, it will set and dry out enough to be ground; store this verjuice in a box. When you want to use it, thin it with a little water or stock from a pot, and it will have the flavour of verjuice. It will keep for a whole year. Sour citron juice can keep for the whole year by drying it in glass like verjuice. You pick citron to make candied citron in the month of April when it's becoming sunny. The sour juice that remains in the citron can be squeezed and poured into the glass containers and put out to dry. It will set like verjuice and once dried out you can keep it. When you want to use it, thin it with a little stock from a boiling pot and it will taste like lemon juice.

[411] *Pepinos en vinagre para todo el Año.*

Tomarás los pepinos que sean muy chicos, de manera que no tengan dentro hueco ninguno, y henchirás una olla vidriada dellos: luego henchirás esta olla (259v) de vinagre, y echarle has un poco de sal y un poco de hinojo en rama, y tápala con un corcho que venga muy justo, y ponla en parte fresca donde le dé el aire, y estarse han todo el año verdes, como si estuvieran en las matas.

[412] *La Oruga de Miel.*

Tomarás una parte de oruga para ocho partes de miel que sea buena, y la oruga la molerás y cernerás por cedazo, y harás una masita de la oruga con vinagre tinto: ha de estar la masilla bien blanda: déjala estar así veinte y cuatro horas, porque deseche la verdina de la oruga: luego tomarás las ocho partes de la miel, y échale un poco de agua y cueza hasta que esté bien espumado: luego ve desatando la oruga con esta miel, y vendrá a estar bien rala, y tórnala a echar en el cazo, y tórnala al fuego, y cueza dos, o tres hervores, para que se acabe de consumir el agua de la miel: y luego (260r) sácala, y échale un poco de canela molida, y déjala enfriar en su vasija: y de que esté fría tápala con corcho y su pergamino, y durará muchos días. Esta oruga es buena para donde hay mucha gente, como son conventos, o algún banquete que ha de durar muchos días, porque esta oruga no es la mejor que se hace, porque la buena se ha de hacer con azúcar y con pan tostado, mas no se guarda de ocho días arriba.[399]

[413] *Oruga de Azúcar.*

Tomarás un panecillo de oruga,[400] y molerlo has muy bien: luego tendrás seis onzas de pan tostado, remojado en vinagre blanco, y exprímelo de la vinagre, y échalo en el almirez, y májalo todo junto con seis onzas de azúcar, antes más que menos, y desátalo con la vinagre en que estuvo el pan en remojo, hasta que esté ralita como mostaza, y échale un poco de canela molida: y luego (260v) pásala por un cedacillo. Esta oruga se puede guardar ocho o diez días a lo más largo, y no ha de llegar al fuego, y es la mejor de todas, y la que se sirve más ordinariamente a los grandes señores: y si la hallares muy fuerte, que podría ser que lo estuviese, podrás añadir más azúcar molido, y con eso se remediará.

---

399 *Ocho días* [eight days] is a common euphemism for a week.
400 "Un panecillo de oruga" [bread roll worth of arugula] Though the exact quantity is unknown, based on this and the previous recipe, it may be that one *panecillo* is equivalent to one ounce. For more information, see the entry in the Glossary (691).

Pickles for the whole year

Take very small cucumbers that have no hole in the middle. Fill a glazed pot with them and then fill the pot with vinegar. Add a little salt and some sprigs of fennel. Seal it tightly with a cork. Place it in a fresh spot when air flows and they will stay green all year as if they just came off the plant.

Arugula and honey sauce

Take one part arugula to eight parts of excellent honey. Grind up the arugula and strain it through a sieve. Make a paste of arugula and red wine vinegar. It should be very soft. Let it set twenty-four hours so that it loses its green film from the arugula. Then take the eight parts of honey and add a little water and boil until it is very foamy. Then begin thinning the arugula paste with this honey. It should be very thin. Return it to the pot on the fire and bring it to a boil two or three times so that all the water from the honey is gone. Then, remove it, add a little ground cinnamon, and let it cool in the container. Once it's cool, seal it with a cork and parchment and it will last many days. This arugula sauce is good in places with a lot of people, like convents or a banquet over several days, because it is not the best that is made. The good one is made with sugar and toasted bread, but it won't last more than a week.

Arugula and sugar sauce

Take a bread roll worth of arugula and thoroughly grind it up. Then take six ounces of toasted bread soaked in white vinegar and squeeze off the vinegar. Add it to the mortar and grind it together with six ounces of sugar, better more than less. Thin it with the vinegar the bread soaked in until it is as thin as mustard. Add a little ground cinnamon and then strain it through a sieve. This arugula sauce will last eight to ten days at the most. It should not be heated and it is the best of all of them and the one more commonly served among grandees. If it is too strong, which is a possibility, you can add more ground sugar and that will fix it.

[414] *Sopa de Aragón.*

Tomarás un hígado de ternera, y cocerlo has, y luego rállalo con el rallo, que salga bien menudo: luego échale otro tanto queso rallado, y un poco de pimienta, y mézclalo todo: luego tomarás buen caldo de la olla, y echaráslo sobre el hígado, y el queso, de manera que esté un poco ralo: luego harás una sopa de rebanadas de pan tostado, y pondrás a cocer la salsa del hígado, y en cociendo échala por encima la sopa, de manera que quede bien cubierta, y bien empapada: luego échale buena grasa de la (261r) olla por encima, y échale un poco de queso: luego métela en un horno a tostar. Esta sopa viene a ser poco más o menos morteruelo:[401] puédese ayudar con pan tostado remojado en caldo, y majado.

[415] *Manteca de Názulas.*

Tomarás las názulas,[402] o requesones, que todo es uno, y pruébalos que no estén ahumados, y déjalo estar dos días, o a lo menos uno, porque acabados de hacer no sale bien la manteca, y echa estos requesones en una vasija redonda, que esté bien limpia, y deshazlo con un cucharón, y tendrás agua caliente, e irás echando unas gotas de agua caliente sobre los requesones, y velos batiendo muy recio con el cucharón, e irás echando más gotas de agua caliente, e irás batiendo apriesa a una mano: y esta agua se ha de ir echando muy poco a poco, porque haya lugar de batir los requesones, y no has de echar más agua caliente, de cuanto los requesones estén como (261v) puches; y has de estar batiendo cosa de media hora, o más, como fuere la cantidad de los requesones: y cuando vieres que los requesones hacen muchos granillos muy blancos, entonces está sacada la manteca: tendrás agua muy fría, e irás echando della poco a poco sobre los requesones, y trayéndolos a una mano con un cucharón, y cuando ellos vengan a estar muy ralos podrás echar cantidad de agua fría, y la manteca se subirá toda arriba, y se arrima al cucharón: luego arrímala a un borde de la pieza, y vacía toda aquella agua, y echa otra agua clara fría sobre la manteca, y deshazla con un cucharón, arrimándola a un borde de la pieza, y lávala muy bien, deshaciéndola muchas veces: y cuando esta agua esté enlechada, tórnala a vaciar: y esto harás hasta que la manteca no eche de sí ninguna cosa de leche, que aunque la laven quede el agua muy clara, y entonces está buena la manteca, y puedes hacer tus mantequillas, o rosquillas, (262r) de la manera que

---

401 This is an early reference to what is still today a dish that resembles a pâté-like spread. In Mestre Robert's 1520 *Llibre del coc*, he also includes a *morteruelo* recipe, but his is prepared with leg of lamb instead of veal liver. Today, the dish is most associated with the regions of Cuenca and Albacete and is made with pig liver and sometimes poultry or small game meat. The name is derived from the *mortero* [mortar] in which all the ingredients are mashed together.

402 *Názula* is another word for *requesón* [curd cheese, like ricotta or cottage cheese]. For more information, see 690.

Sops, Aragonese style

Take veal liver and boil it. Then grate it with a grater so that it is shredded. Then add the same amount of grated cheese and a little pepper and mix it all together. Then take good stock from the pot and add it to the liver and cheese so that it becomes fairly thin. Next, make sops with slices of toasted bread and put the liver sauce on to boil. Once it has boiled, pour it over the sops so that they are completely covered and soaked. Drizzle some good fat from the pot on top and sprinkle on a little cheese. Put it in the oven to brown. These sops are a little like morteruelo. They can be improved with toasted bread soaked in broth and mashed.

Nazulas butter

Take some nazulas curd cheese, or regular curd cheese, they're really the same thing, and check to make sure it doesn't smell bad. Let sit for two days, or at least one, because if it's freshly made, the butter doesn't turn out well. Place this curd cheese in a round container that is very clean and crumble it up with a spoon. Have hot water and sprinkle some drops of hot water on the curd cheese. Begin beating it vigorously with a spoon and sprinkling more drops of hot water and continue beating it quickly with one hand. The water should go on very slowly so that there's room to beat the curd cheese. Don't add any more hot water after the curd cheese is like porridge. It should take about a half an hour or more depending on the amount of curd cheese. When you see that the curd cheese has a lot of little granules that are very white, then you've made the butter. Have some very cold water and sprinkle it little by little on the curd cheese, stirring with a spoon with one hand. When it is very thin, pour on a lot of cold water and the butter will rise to the top and stick to the spoon. Then scrape it on the edge of the bowl, empty out all the water, and pour more fresh cold water on the butter. Dissolve it with the spoon, scrape it on the side of the bowl, thoroughly wash it, and dissolve it again many times over. When the water turns milky, empty it again, and do this until the butter doesn't release any more milk. Even when you wash it, the water will come out clear. Now the butter is good and you can make little butter patties

te pareciere, que aunque parece que en los requesones no habrá manteca, por ser hechos del suero de la leche, con todo eso ha de salir tanta cantidad de manteca, como la mitad de los requesones: y esto se entiende en el bulto, que en el peso saldrá la tercia parte. Es muy buena manteca para comer así fría.

[416] *Cómo se hacen las Mantequillas de Leche de Cabras.*

Tomarás la leche que sea acabada de ordenar, y así caliente como está la echarás en un barquino de cuero, de manera que esté la mitad del vacío: y luego hínchele de aire, que esté casi lleno, y átalo muy bien, y luego tómalo por los dos cabos, y bátelo mucho que ande la leche de una parte a otra, y se vendrá a hacer una pella de manteca: y luego vacía la leche, y echa esta manteca en agua fría, y lávala: y luego harás (262v) las mantequillas, unas rosquillas, o de la manera que te pareciere.

[417] *Aceite de Huevos.*

Tomarás una docena de huevos frescos, y ponlos a asar que estén bien duros, y luego móndalos, y sácales las yemas, y échales en una sartenilla muy limpia, y ponla sobre unas pocas de brasas, y ve deshaciendo allí las yemas con una cucharilla, o paleta, y velas tostando, y meneando hasta que veas que van mostrando señal de aceite: luego tendrás un pañito nuevo y delgado de una cuarta de largo, y una sesma de ancho con dos palillos cocidos en las puntas,[403] y echarás estas yemas de huevos dentro en este pañito: y luego torcerás con los palillos, y darle has garrote,[404] y saldrá aceite: luego tornarás a calentar las yemas en la sartén, y a tostarlas más, meneándolas con la paleta, y tornarlas has a echar en el lienzo, y a darles garrote con los palillos, y sacarás un aceite muy (263r) claro: los huevos han de ser frescos en todo caso. Este aceite es bueno para los empeines,[405] y las mujeres lo estiman en mucho, aunque yo no sé en qué lo gastan.

---

403 A *sesma* is equivalent to one sixth of a *vara castellana*, and measures between five and six inches. A *cuarta* is equivalent to one quarter of a *vara castellana* or between seven and a half and nine inches. For more on measurements, see Appendix 2, "On Measurements," Castaño Álvarez, and "Antiguas pesas y medidas."

404 *Dar garrote* is best known in the context of execution, in which a collar was placed around the condemned person's neck and tightened until the person was strangled to death or his/her neck was broken. Here it refers to tightening the rods as much as possible to release the oil from the yolks.

405 In the 1611 edition, the word is *buena*. However, this is corrected in the 1617 edition and all subsequent editions. I have made the change here as well.

or little butter rings or whatever form you like because even though it seems there's no butter in curd cheese, because they're made with whey from milk, a certain amount of butter does come out, about half of the curd cheese. This is by bulk; by weight it's a third. This butter is very good to eat cold.

How to make butter from goat milk

Take milk that has just come from the goat, and while still warm, pour it into a leather skin so that it is half full. Then fill it with air so that it's almost full and tie it up tightly. Then take the two ends and shake it up a lot so the milk goes from one side to the other. Soon it will form into a butter ball. Then empty out the milk, put this butter in cold water and wash it. Then make little butter patties, little butter rings, or whatever form you like.

Egg oil

Take a dozen fresh eggs and put them on to roast until they're hard. Then peel them, remove the yolks, and put them in a small, very clean frying pan. Place it over a few hot coals and begin crumbling the yolks with a small spoon or spatula and brown them by stirring them until you can see some oil being released. Then, have a fresh, thin dishcloth that is 8¼ in long and 5½ in wide with two rods sewn into the ends. Put the eggs into this cloth and twist the rods as much as possible and twist it tight so that oil is released. Then heat the yolks once again in the frying pan and brown them more, stirring with a spatula. Return them to the linen and twist them tight with the rods and a very clear oil will come out. The eggs must always be fresh. This oil is good for eczema, and women think very highly of it, although I'm not sure what they use it for.

[418] *Aceite de Almendras sin fuego.*

Pondrás las almendras en un poco de agua fría al fuego, y en calentándose, de manera que suelten las almendras el pellejo, sácalas, y móndalas, y échalas en el almirez, y májalas mucho, y ellas se irán enaceitando: y cuando vieres que salpica mucho el aceite, saca las almendras poco a poco, y échalas en el pañito (como está dicho en el aceite de huevos) y dales garrote con los palillos, y sacarás muy bien aceite, y torna a majar las almendras, y tornarás a darle garrote, y sácalas más aceite. Advierte, que las almendras si las echases en agua cociendo para pelarlas, se escaldarían, y no podrías sacar aceite dellas: y así, para hacer los mazapanes, es bueno echar las (263v) almendras en agua cociendo, porque se escalden, y se puedan majar sin aceitarse, aunque los boticarios no se guardan deso; porque aunque escalden las almendras sacan mucho aceite porque lo sacan con fuego y más violentamente: y así este aceite sin fuego es más saludable para los niños cuando son chiquitos, es bueno moler azúcar piedra blanco: y con este aceite hacer unas como papillas, y darles unas cucharaditas, y es bueno para las flemas. Tiene una cosa que se enrancia muy presto, y así es menester sacar poquito, y sacar cada día lo que fuere menester.

[419] *Cómo se puede asar una pella de Manteca de vacas en el asador.*[406]

Tomarás una pella de manteca fresca, y espetarla has de punta a punta en un asador de palo que sea muy derecho y cuadrado, y en la punta redondo. Este asador atarás en la punta del asador (264r) de tornillo muy bien, porque no se puede asar en asador de hierro, porque se calentaría y derretiría la manteca por de dentro: y tampoco se puede asar en asador que no tenga tornillo, porque no andaría redondo, y haría derretir la manteca, y como la tengas espetada como está dicho: pon los caballos,[407] y haz una lumbrecilla de carbón, que no sea más ancha que la manteca, poniendo unos ladrillos a los lados, de manera que quede un claro que no sea más ancho que la manteca: luego tendrás cantidad de pan rallado mezclado

---

406 Similar recipes appear in Gervase Markham's *The English Housewife* (1615) and later cookbooks. Society for Creative Anachronism member Donna Green successfully recreated this recipe and noted that people loved it. "Butter, sugar and breadcrumbs … how can that not be tasty? … The center was harder than the exterior that was closer to the fire, but it was soft enough all the way through to eat. Turning wasn't hard. I kept it moving fairly often so it didn't fall apart from the heat." For an image of Green's recreation of this recipe, see Appendix 3.21.

407 *Los caballos*, also know as *caballitos* or *caballitos de hierro* [cob irons], are a vertical structure whose primary purpose is to support a crossbar or spit. They usually have a variety of hooks that provide flexibility for how far the skewer is placed from the heat source. *Caballos* were still commonly used in rural Spain up to the twentieth century. My thanks to both Richard Fitch and Carmen Abad Zardoya for clarifying its usage. For further information, see Abad Zardoya, "Herramientas" (86n5).

Almond oil, without cooking

Put the almonds in a little cold water on the fire and heat so that the skin falls off. Remove them, peel them, put them in the mortar, and finely grind them. They will become very oily. When you see that there's a lot of oil, slowly remove the almonds and place them in a little cloth (as explained for the egg oil) and twist with the rods. Excellent oil will come out. Grind the almonds again, twist them with the rods again, and get more oil. Note that if you were to put almonds in boiling water to peel them, they would be scalded and you wouldn't be able to get any oil from them. So, for making marzipan, it's good to put the almonds in boiling water so they are scalded. You can grind them without releasing any oil even though pharmacists don't keep this type in stock, because even if the almonds are scalded they produce a lot of oil as it is released faster with fire. So, this fireless oil is healthier. For children when they are young, it's good to grind white rock sugar, and with this oil you can make a type of porridge and feed it to them in small spoonfuls. It's good for [treating] phlegm. It has something that quickly goes rancid so it is necessary to make a small amount and every day make just what you need.

How to roast a butterball on a spit

Take a fresh butterball and skewer it from one end to the other with a wooden skewer that is straight and square and has a round tip. Tie this skewer tightly to the end of the rotating spit, because you can't roast it with an iron skewer, because it will heat up and melt the butter from the inside. You also can't use a spit without a screw, because it would not turn around and it would melt the butter. When you have it skewered as explained, set up the cobb irons and make a small coal fire that is no wider than the butter by placing bricks on both sides so that a space remains that is no wider than the butter. Then have a lot of breadcrumbs

con azúcar, y pon a asar la manteca, y ha de andar el asador muy redondo, y ha de estar echando uno siempre pan rallado, y azúcar por encima, teniendo una pieza debajo para recoger el pan rallado que se cayere, porque la lumbre que ha de asar la manteca no ha de estar debajo, sino adelante, y ha de haber buena lumbre clara de tizos de carbón: y desta manera irás asando la manteca: y si te das buena maña (264v) a echar el pan, la asarás sin que se derrita gota de manteca, más de la que se empapare en el pan: y cuando vieres que se va abriendo haciendo unas aberturas o grietas, la darás buena lumbre para que tome color el pan, y la podrás sacar. Siempre quedará en medio un poquito de manteca sin derretir; porque como el asador es de palo, nunca se habrá calentado en medio de la manteca lo que no se pudiera hacer con el asador de hierro. Y advierte, que cuando la manteca vaya más de medio asada, si abriese mucho, sería necesario sacarla, y ponerla en una barquilla, o en un plato hondo con mucho pan rallado, y azúcar debajo, y encima: y luego calentar un horno de cobre con mucha lumbre: y cuando esté muy caliente mete la manteca dentro de su plato, y luego tomará color; y si se desbaratare algo, toma una paleta, y acomódala que esté de la hechura de pella de manteca fresca, y échale más pan rallado: y desta manera quedará buena. Esta manteca (265r) asada no es más de para averiguar si se puede asar en asador, o no: y es verdad que se puede asar de la manera que tengo dicho, porque yo lo he hecho algunas veces; mas si quisieres hacer esta manteca que venga a estar de la misma manera, como si se asase en asador. Tomarás la manteca así cruda, y mezclarla has con mucho pan rallado y azúcar, de manera que venga a estar como una masa dura, que parezca que es todo pan: luego échala en una barquilla, y ponla sobre unas brasas, y vela acomodando con la paleta, que quede la hechura de una pella de manteca: y si vieres que se rezuma, échale más pan rallado, y cuando esté tostado por un cabo, vuélvela con la paleta, y tuéstala por el otro, y la sacarás que parezca a la otra que se asó en el asador.

[420] *Memoria de los bizcochelos.*[408]

A tres libras de azúcar molido y cernido, tomarás docena y media (265v) de huevos, quitando la mitad de las claras, dos onzas de agua rosada, y un poco de almizcle, harás una presa de harina redonda, que tenga más harina de lo que será menester: echarás dentro las tres libras de azúcar molido y cernido, y la docena y media de huevos, quitando la mitad de las claras, como está dicho, batirás este azúcar, y estos huevos muy bien con las dos onzas de agua rosada dentro de la presa: luego irás juntando la harina que pudiere entrar por la parte de adentro de la presa, de manera que quede la masa encerada, y la demás harina la podrás guardar. Esta

---

[408] I have translated these smaller-sized sweet biscuits as *ladyfingers* because Martínez Montiño describes how to shape them based on the length of a finger.

mixed with sugar and put the butter on to roast. The spit should be constantly rotating and you should be continually adding breadcrumbs and sugar on top. Place a bowl below to catch the breadcrumbs that fall, as the heat for roasting should not be directly below but rather in front of it. It should be a good, clean flame of charcoal coals. This is the way to roast butter. If you're good at putting the breadcrumbs on, you will roast it without a drop of butter melting except for what melts into the bread. When you see any holes or cracks opening up, heat it up enough for the breadcrumbs to brown, and you can take it off. There will always be a little left in the middle that doesn't melt because the skewer is wooden and it will never heat up as an iron skewer would. Note that when the butter is half roasted, if it opened up a lot, you'll have to take it off the heat and put it into a barquette mould or in a bowl with a lot of breadcrumbs and sugar underneath and on top. Then heat a copper oven with a lot of heat and when it is very hot, put in the butter in its bowl and let it brown. If it starts to fall apart, use a spatula to keep it in place. It should maintain the shape of a butterball. Add more breadcrumbs and it will turn out fine this way. There's nothing more to this roasted butter than finding out if it's possible to roast on a spit or not. The truth is that it is possible to roast the way I've explained, because I have done it several times. But, if you want to make this butter so that it comes out the same as if it were roasted on a spit, take raw butter as it is, mix it with a lot of breadcrumbs and sugar so that it turns into a hard dough and looks like the whole thing is bread. Then place it in a barquette mould and place it over red-hot coals and begin shaping it with a spatula so that it is the shape of a butterball. If you see that it begins to ooze out, add more breadcrumbs, and when it's toasted on one side, turn it with the spatula and toast the other. When you take it off, it will look just like the other that you roasted on a spit.

Memoir of ladyfingers

For three pounds of sifted, ground sugar, take a dozen and a half eggs, removing half of the whites, two ounces of rose water, and a little musk. Make a round well of flour. It should have more flour than necessary. Add the three pounds of sifted, ground sugar, a dozen and a half eggs, removing half of the whites as explained. Thoroughly beat the eggs and the sugar together with the two ounces of rose water inside the well. Then begin adding flour into the middle of the well so that the dough becomes elastic. Reserve the rest of the flour. This dough should

masa se ha de sobar un poco, luego labrarla como para rosquillas muy delgadas, del gordor de un dedo de la mano: luego lo partirás al sesgo del largor de un dedo, y se han de juntar unos con otros, como sarticas de peces,[409] y se han de poner en unas torteras, polvoreadas con mucha harina, y cocerse en un horno: y cuando estén a medio cocer partirlos (266r) con un hilo gordo uno a uno, y luego tórnalos a acabar de cocer. También les has de echar un poco de anís molido, cernido, y una migaja de sal: y porque no los andes partiendo con hilo, los podrás poner un poco apartados unos de otros, y desta manera se acabarán de cocer de una vez.

[421] *Bollitos Pardos.*

Toma una libra de azúcar molido y cernido, y otra de harina, y otra de manteca fresca de vacas, y una docena de yemas de huevos, y una libra de almendras: hase de hacer del azúcar y de las almendras mazapán, y luego echar lo demás todo junto sobre el tablero, y de todo esto se ha de hacer una masa; hace de echar canela molida, hasta que esté la masa muy parda, y échale un poco de olor. Hanse de hacer unos bollitos chiquitos, a modo de mostachones. Hánsele de hacer unas raitas con la vuelta del cuchillo, y ponerlos sobre unas obleas, (266v) y cocerlos en horno de cobre a fuego manso.

[422] *Tortillas delgadas de Aceite.*[410]

Batirás seis huevos frescos con media libra de azúcar molido y cernido, hasta que esté muy blanco y espeso como para bizcochos: y luego tendrás onza y media de vino blanco, y un poco de aceite que sea bueno, y échalo en la pieza donde están los huevos batidos con el azúcar, y echa harina hasta que se haga una masa encerada, y échale un poco de anís molido, y un poco de sal, y sácalo sobre el tablero, y sóbalo muy bien, y tomarás el palo de la masa, y harás hojas delgadas del grueso de un real de a dos: luego cortarlas has con la cortadera, del tamaño que quisieres, y cocerlas has en un horno sobre papeles polvoreados de harina a fuego manso, y de que estén cocidos hanse de limpiar muy bien, y vidriar con azúcar, o bañarse con baño blanco de azúcar, y claras (267r) de huevos, como las rosquillas. También son buenas así, sin vedriar, ni bañar.

---

409 Martínez Montiño most likely includes this suggestion to maximize how many fit on the baking pan at once. It is also most likely that, when it's time to separate them with the string, he would be able to do all of them in a single column at once.

410 *Tortilla* is usually translated as *omelette*, but this recipe, like the others before and after, is for baked goods. The shape and size are emphasized in its name. It also differs by including white wine and oil. Several of the others have no fat but are also variations of egg, sugar, and flour.

be kneaded a little. Then work it as you would for little, very thin ring-shaped pastries, the thickness of a finger. Then cut on the diagonal, lengthwise, into finger-sized pieces. Join together some pieces with others as if they were little strings of fish. Put them in covered tart pans that are dusted with a lot of flour, then bake them in the oven. When they are half baked, separate them one by one with a thick string and return them to finish baking. You should also add some sifted, ground anise and a pinch of salt. If you don't want to separate them with a string, you can place them a little separate from one another and they will bake all at once this way.

Cinnamon rolls with marzipan

Take a pound of sifted, ground sugar, another of flour, and another of fresh butter, a dozen egg yolks, and a pound of almonds. Make marzipan out of the almonds and sugar and then put the rest together on a cutting board and mix them into a dough. Add some ground cinnamon so that the dough turns very brown and add a little orange blossom water. Make little balls, as for mostachon cookies. With the back of the knife, make some small lines and place them on top of wafers. Bake in a copper oven on low heat.

Thin, frosted cookies

Beat six fresh eggs with a half a pound of sifted, ground sugar until it turns very white and thick, as for sweet biscuits. Then, have an ounce and a half of white wine and a little oil that is good quality and put them in the bowl with the whipped eggs and sugar. Add flour until it makes an elastic dough. Add a little anise, a little salt, and turn it out onto a cutting board. Knead it a lot. Take the rolling pin and make thin sheets about the thickness of a two-real coin. Then cut them with a trimmer to whatever size you'd like and bake them in an oven on top of papers dusted with flour on low heat. Once they've baked, you should clean them, ice with sugar, or dip them in a meringue of white sugar and egg whites, as you would for ring-shaped pastries. They are also tasty without icing or adding meringue.

[423] *Memoria de las Rosquillas.*[411]

A una libra de azúcar se han de echar veinte y cuatro huevos, quitando cinco claras: hanse de batir los huevos con este azúcar, como para bizcochos, hasta que esté blanco: hásele de echar un poco de anís quebrantado: luego le echarás cosa de media libra de manteca de vacas fresca, y cosa de dos maravedís de vino blanco de lo caro: y luego bátelo un poco más con mucha fuerza, y luego échale harina floreada lo que el batido pudiere embeber, de manera que quede una masita un poco dura: luego sobarla has mucho hasta que haga empollas, y que quede la masa encerada: luego haz tus rosquillas, y pon un cazo con agua al fuego: y cuando esté cociendo echa las rosquillas dentro, y cuezan hasta que ellas mismas suban arriba encima (267v) del agua, y como vayan subiendo las irás sacando en una cesta, dentro unas toallas, porque no se peguen unas con otras; hanse de sudar allí como ocho horas, y luego llevarlas al horno de pan, y cuando las traigan las has de dar lustre, si no las quisieres dar baño: y si las quisieres blanquear con vidriado será mejor.

[424] *Otra suerte de Rosquillas.*

Para seis docenas de rosquillas tomarás una libra de azúcar molido y cernido, y seis docenas de huevos, los seis con claras, y los demás no más de las yemas, y échale dos maravedís de anís, y un cuarterón de manteca de vacas, y tanto vino blanco como quepa en un cascarón de huevo: ha de ser bueno. Todo esto se ha de batir junto, y luego ir metiendo harina floreada, hasta que se haga una masa encerada, trayéndolo siempre a una mano con el cucharón, y no se ha de sobar mucho: (268r) luego guardar la orden que está escrita en las de atrás. Y adviértese, que en las unas y en las otras, se ha de echar la manteca tibia.

[425] *Baño blanco para Rosquillas, y otras cosas.*

El blanqueado se hace desta manera: Tomarás una libra de azúcar blanco molido y cernido, y echarle has las cinco claras de huevos que quitase de las rosquillas, y échale un poco de agua, y revuélvelo con un cucharón, de manera que esté espeso como mostaza, y ponlo al fuego, y tráelo muy apriesa, hasta que todo el azúcar quede deshecho: luego échalo en una albornía,[412] y bátelo mucho hasta que esté espeso, y échale un poco de zumo de limón, y tórnalo a batir mucho, y se pondrá muy blanco: luego toma un hisopillo de plumas, o de cerdas, y ve bañando las rosquillas, y hanse de secar al sol, y si no (268v) hubiere buen sol, al amor de la lumbre sobre un tablero. Con este baño podrás bañar tabletas, y bizcochos, y otras muchas cosas.

---

411 *Rosquillas* are one of the long-standing traditional sweet pastries in Spain. For more information, see the entry in the Glossary.
412 *Albornía* is a "vasija grande de barro vidriado de forma de taza" [big, glazed terracotta pot in the shape of a cup] (RAE).

Memoir of ring-shaped pastries

Add twenty-four eggs, separating out five whites, to a pound of sugar. Beat together the eggs and sugar, as if [you were making] sweet biscuits, until it turns white. Add a little cracked anise. Then add about half a pound of fresh butter and about two maravedis' worth of expensive white wine. Quickly whip it all together and then add as much finely sifted flour as needed so that a rather firm dough comes together. Knead it a lot until it blisters and the dough becomes elastic. Then make your ring-shaped pastries. Put a pot with water on the fire. When it's boiling, add the ring-shaped pastries and let them cook until they float to the top of the water. As they come to the top, begin removing them to a basket lined with towels so that they don't stick together. They should sweat there for about eight hours. Then put them in the bread oven and when you take them out, drizzle with a sugar glaze if you don't want to dip them in whole. And if you want to completely glaze them with white glaze, even better.

Another kind of ring-shaped pastries

For six dozen ring-shaped pastries, take a pound of sifted, ground sugar and six dozen eggs, six with the whites and the rest with only the yolks. Add two maravedis of anise, a quarter pound of butter, and as much white wine as fits into an eggshell. It has to be good quality. Beat all of this together and then begin adding finely sifted flour until the dough becomes elastic, constantly stirring it with a spoon with one hand. It should not be kneaded very much. Then follow the instructions written in the previous ones. Note that in both these and the others the butter is added warm.

Meringue for ring-shaped pastries and other things

Meringue is made in the following way: take a pound of sifted, ground white sugar and add the five egg whites that you reserved from the ring-shaped pastries. Add a little water and stir it all together with a spoon so that it is as thick as mustard. Put it on the flame and beat it quickly until all the sugar has melted. Then transfer it to a glazed terracotta pitcher and beat it until it thickens. Add a little lemon juice and continue beating. It will turn very white. Then take a little hyssop brush made of feathers or horsehair and begin brushing the ring-shaped pastries. They should dry in the sun, but if there isn't any, on a pastry board, close to the flame. With this meringue you can frost bars, sweet biscuits, and much more.

[426] *Gilea de vino.*

Tomarás una azumbre de vino blanco, que sea muy claro y muy bueno, y échale libra y media de azúcar, y dos onzas de canela que sea muy buena, medio molida, y un grano de jengibre, y cuatro maravedís de pimienta todo quebrantado, y más de medio cuartillo de leche: todo esto junto ha de estar en infusión en una olla nueva, por espacio de ocho o diez horas, y menearlo has después de las ocho horas, y échalo a colar en la manga: y cuando esté la mitad pasado, tórnalo a echar en la manga: y esto harás hasta que salga claro, y luego déjalo ir pasando poco a poco, y de que esté todo pasado, póngase junto al fuego cuanto se entibie, y esté la olla tapada con un papel: luego tomarás dos onzas (269r) de colapege,[413] y deshágase muy menudo, y lávalo en muchas aguas, y ponlo al fuego en una cazolilla nueva con medio cuartillo de vino blanco, y cueza muy poco a poco, hasta que la colapege esté toda deshecha, y luego cuélala por una punta de servilleta muy limpia dentro en la olla del vino,[414] y échale zumo de medio limón y ponlo a enfriar, y podráslo sacar en pellas con una cuchara de plata. Y si quisieres hacer esta gilea colorada, toma un par de zanahorias negras, y ráspalas, y luego quítales una rajitas de lo negro, y échalas en una cazolilla nueva de barro, y derrite la gilea, y echa un poco sobre las zanahorias, y pon la cazuela sobre unas brasas cuanto venga a alzar hervor, y saldrá la tinta, y tórnalo a echar en la olla colado por estameña, o por una punta de servilleta, y saldrá la gilea de color de granada. Advierte, que esta gilea nunca se ha de cocer, ni se ha de calentar, sino tibia. Si la quisieres hacer colorada sin zanahorias, con poner vino tinto bueno, en lugar del (269v) blanco, la manga le quitará la mitad del color, y quedará de la misma color de granadas. Si quisieres servir esta gilea blanca sobre cosa de carne, pelarás un lechón, y haráslo cuartos, y échalo en agua que se desangre muy bien: luego échalo a cocer en una olla nueva con un poco de agua, y un poquito de sal, y un grano de jengibre que sea muy blanco, mondada la cáscara, y échale un poco de pimienta longa entera,[415] y un

---

413 For information on *colapege* [isinglass], see 434n340.
414 When referring to the *punta* [tip] of the napkin, I believe Martínez Montiño is describing a napkin folded into a conical shape. This part is most likely understood by his reader, so, for him, there is no need to explain how to shape it.
415 *Pimienta longa*, Portuguese for *pimienta larga* [long pepper] (*Piper longum*), is native to Java. Although a relative of the *Piper negrum*, where black pepper comes from, it has a hotter taste than the round black pepper. The part used is the dried catkin-shaped stick, which is then ground, not the seeds, which is the case with black pepper. However, Nicolás Monardes writes a chapter about the characteristics of *pimienta luenga*, a plant from the coasts of Tierra Firme, in his *Historia medicinal* (see *Segunda parte del libro* 106r–110r). Monardes notes that "Vn cauallero me dio vn plato della porque trae muncha cantidad para el seruicio de su Cozina, porque vsan della en lugar de Pimienta negra: y la tienen por de mejor gusto, y por mas sana" [a gentleman gave me a plate of it because he was bringing so much for use in his kitchen. Instead of black pepper, they use it. And, they also understand that it has a richer flavour and it's healthier] (106v). It is uncertain which one Martínez Montiño may be referring to.

Chapter 2

Wine jelly

Take two quarts of very good and clear white wine. Add a pound and a half of sugar, two ounces of good, partially ground cinnamon, a piece of ginger, four maravedis of completely crushed pepper, and more than a half pint of milk. All of this should steep together in a new pot for about eight to ten hours. Stir it after eight hours and put it in a jelly bag to strain. When half has passed through, put it back in the jelly bag again and this should make it come out clear. Then let it slowly strain and when all has been strained put it near the fire to keep warm. Cover the pot with paper. Then take two ounces of isinglass and shred it up fine. Wash it in a lot of water and put it in a new small pan with a half pint of white wine. Slowly boil until the isinglass is completely dissolved. Then strain it through a tip of a very clean napkin in the pot of wine. Add juice from half a lemon and let it cool. You'll be able to take it out in balls with a silver spoon. If you want to make this jelly a dark colour, take a couple of black carrots, grate them, and then remove some of the grated strips of black and put them in a new small terracotta casserole, melt the jelly, and add a little to the carrots. Put the casserole on the red-hot coals and bring to a boil. The colour will come out. Return it to the pot that was strained with a cheesecloth or the tip of a napkin. The jelly will come out the colour of a pomegranate. Note that this jelly should never come to a boil, or even get hot. It should just get warm. If you want to add colour without carrots, you can use good red wine instead of white. The jelly bag will remove half of its colour and it will end up the same pomegranate colour. If you want to serve this white jelly over some meat, skin a suckling pig, quarter it, and put it in water to thoroughly bleed it. Then put it in a new pot to cook with a little water, a little salt, a piece of very white ginger with its skin peeled, and add a little bit of whole long pepper, a little galangal, and a little

poco de galanga,[416] y un poco de grano de paraíso,[417] y cuézase el lechón con todo esto: y si no hallares estas especias trasordinarias, cuécelo con sólo el jengibre, y pimienta redonda entera: y cuando esté cocido el lechón, saldrá muy blanco: asiéntalo en un plato, la cabeza en medio, y los cuartos a la redonda: y luego hinche el plato de la gilea de vino que se cubra todo el lechón, y ponle unas rajitas de almendras a la redonda: y si quisieres servir esta gilea de vino sin carne, sírvelas en pellas, la mitad de las pellas (270r) blancas, y la mitad coloradas. Se han de adornar las pellas con hojas de laurel doradas, y con unas florecillas que están dentro en los piñones remojados: no se trata de otras colores ni moldes, porque no son buenas. Y si quisieres servir esta gilea en que se coció el lechón, con dejar enfriar el caldo, y echarle el azúcar y la canela que está dicho en la del vino, y dejarla estar en infusión cinco o seis horas al amor de la lumbre, de manera que no se caliente, ni esté frío, y hasle de echar un poquito de vino, y la leche que está dicho atrás, y échala a colar en la manga junto al fuego, y después de colada, échale la mitad de la colapege, que se echó a la otra, y su zumo de limón, y saldrá muy buena. Ésta se puede hacer de gallinas, o capones, echando muchos alones dentro al cocer, y puédese dar a enfermos: también se puede hacer de manos de cabrito, y de ternera. Y advierte, que esta gilea de carne ha de salir muy clara sin ningún género de grasa: (270v) y cuando se colare por la manga, ha de ser cerca del fuego: y si le sintieres algún poco de grasa, con echar unos cascarones de huevos muy limpios dentro en la manga se apegará toda la grasa, y quedará la gilea muy clara. La manga para colar esta gilea ha de ser de media grana blanca, o de muy buen cordellate blanco,[418] y ha de ser ancha de boca y muy aguzada de abajo, y la costura ha de ser a dos costuras muy fuertemente. Cuando la gilea de vino se acaba de colar, es hipocrás, quitándole la tercia parte de azúcar, y añadir especias.[419]

[427] *Melindres de Azúcar.*

Tomarás media libra de azúcar molido y cernido, y luego batirás clara y media de huevo, y echarlo has sobre este azúcar, e irás haciendo una masilla como masa

---

416 *Galanga* or *galangal* is similar to ginger and today is used in many different Asian cuisines.
417 *Aframomum melegueta* [*Grano de paraíso*, grains of paradise], also from the ginger family, is native to West Africa. The seeds resemble black pepper and have a nutty flavour more closely related to cardamom. For more on this intriguing spice, see Nabhan 126–7.
418 According to the *gremio de pañeros* [clothier's guild], *media grana* refers to a medium wool weave; in other words, neither too coarse nor too fine, and very practical. *Cordellate* [grosgrain] is a firm, close-woven fabric. The wool for grosgrain was generally of a lesser grade. My thanks to Carmen Abad Zardoya for clarifying these differences. For more on different types of weaves, see Abad Zardoya, "Ratas, cenizas y perlas."
419 *Hipocrás* [hippocras] is a beverage consisting of three parts excellent wine to one part sweetener, either honey or simple syrup, and mixed with spices. The spices varied but often included cinnamon, clove, and ginger.

grain of paradise. Cook the suckling pig in all this. If you can't find these unusual spices, cook it with just ginger and whole peppercorns. When the suckling pig is done, it will be very white. Set in on a platter with the head in the middle and the quartered pieces all around. Then fill the platter with the wine jelly so that it covers the entire pig. Put some sliced almonds all around. If you want to serve this wine jelly without meat, serve it in balls, half of them white, the other half with colour. The ball should be garnished with toasted bay leaves and with the little flowers inside pine nuts that have been soaking. Don't try to use other colours or moulds because they aren't any good. If you want to serve this jelly with what the suckling pig was cooked in, then let the broth cool, add sugar and cinnamon as explained in the wine jelly, and let it steep five or six hours near the heat so that it doesn't get too hot or too cold. Add a little wine and milk as previously explained and strain it through a jelly bag next to the fire. After it's strained, add half of the isinglass that was added to the other one with the right amount of lemon juice and it will come out well. You can do this with hens or capons by putting on to boil a lot of wings. You can give this to the ill. You can also make it with kid or calf feet. Note that this meat jelly should come out very clear without any type of fat and when it is strained through the jelly bag, it should be close to the fire. If you feel any fat, you can add very clean eggshells to the jelly bag and they will draw out all the fat and the jelly will be clear. The jelly bag for straining this jelly should be made of a white medium weave [cloth] or from very fine white grosgrain. It should be wide at the mouth and very narrow below. The seam should be a strong, double seam. When the wine jelly is just finished straining, it is hippocras if a third of the sugar is removed and spices are added.

Sugar cookies

Take half a pound of sifted, ground sugar and then beat one and a half egg whites and add it to the sugar. Begin making a little dough like elastic dough. Next, make

encerada: luego harás unos rollitos a modo de rosquillas delgadas, y pondráslas sobre unas obleas, y métalas en el horno a fuego manso, y crecerán mucho. Advierte, que estos melindres han de llevar un poco de anís molido: y si los quisieres rellenar, harás el rollito un poco ancho: y luego harás otro rollito de mazapán muy delgado, y ponlo encima del melindre, y arróllalo como quien hace fruta de manjar blanco, y harás tus rosquillas, y cuézanse sobre obleas. Éstos suelen salir muy buenos.

[428] *Bizcochos sin Harina.*

Tomarás ocho onzas de azúcar molido y cernido: luego echarle has ocho yemas de huevos crudas, y un poquito de anís molido, y batirlo has muy bien con un cucharón hasta que esté muy blanco y muy espeso; luego harás una masita muy fina con manteca de vacas y yemas de huevos, y tendrás una hoja muy delgada: luego cortarás unas tortitas redondas con la cortadera del tamaño de un as de oros:[420] luego harásle unos piquitos muy menudos a modo de quesadillas, (271v) y henchirlas has deste batido, y cuézanse en el horno a fuego manso. Y advierte, que el batido se ha de echar en la tortita redonda, antes que se hagan los picos, porque con el mismo batido se pegan muy bien. Estos bizcochos sin harina podrás hacer sobre obleas, echando en cada una cuatro o cinco montoncillos del tamaño de una castaña, y métela en el horno a fuego manso: y si ellos se arrugaren, bátanlos más hasta que salgan lisos, como panecillos de San Agustín.[421] Puédeseles echar un poco de olor.

[429] *Memoria de las Berenjenas en escabeche.*

Tomarás doscientos berenjenas que sean pequeñas, y que estén encapulladas, y córtales un poquito de pezón, y hazles una cruz por en medio, y échalas a cocer, y de que estén bien cocidas sácalas y ponlas a escurrir en el colador: (272r) luego toma dos azumbres de miel, y una de agua, y esta miel y agua ha de cocer toda junta, y de que esté bien espumada, échale las berenjenas, y cuezan dos, o tres hervores, y luego sácalas a que se escurran, y echa en la miel tres cuartillos de vinagre después que las berenjenas estén fuera, y has de tomar una onza de canela, y otra de clavos, y ocho maravedís de pimienta, y un cuarto de alcaravea: todo esto se ha de moler y mezclar junto, y echar en cada berenjena un poquito en la cruz, y asentarlas en

---

420 For more on this reference to the gold coin suit in a deck of cards, see 380n296.
421 In the 1617 version, "panecillos de San Agustín" changes to "panecillos de San Nicolás de Tolentino" and remains that way in all subsequent editions. The confusion may have been due to the fact that San Nicolás was of the Augustinian order. For more on "panecillos de San Nicolás de Tolentino" and their continued popularity in the Philippines, see Nochesada.

little rings the way you would for the thin, ring-shaped pastries. Place them on some wafers and bake them in the oven on low heat. They will rise a lot. Note that these cookies only have a little ground anise. If you want to fill them, make a roll, somewhat wide, and then make a very thin roll of marzipan and place it on top of the cookie. Roll it up as one does when making blancmange fried dough. Then make your ring-shaped pastries and bake them on wafers. These are usually very tasty.

Flourless sweet biscuits

Take eight ounces of sifted, ground sugar. Then, add to it eight raw egg yolks and a little ground anise and thoroughly beat it with a spoon until it's very thick and very white. Then make a fine dough with butter and egg yolks and roll it out into a thin sheet. Next, cut some mini round pies with a trimmer about the size of the ace of the gold coin suit. Then make very small points the way [you did for] curd cheese tarts and fill them with this filling and bake in the oven on low heat. Note that this filling should go into the round pie before the points are made, because they will stick together very well with this filling. These flourless sweet biscuits can be made on wafers by adding to each one four or five little mounds the size of a chestnut. Put it in the oven on low heat. If they wrinkle, beat them more until [the batter] is very smooth, like little St. Augustine rolls. You can add a little orange blossom water.

Memoir of pickled eggplant

Take two hundred small eggplants with the base of the flower still enclosing them. Cut a little off the top and make a cross right in the middle. Put them on to boil. Once they're done, remove them and rinse them in a strainer. Then take four quarts of honey and one of sugar and cook the honey and sugar down together. Once it is very foamy, add the eggplant and bring it to a boil two or three times and then remove them and drain them. Add three pints of vinegar to the honey after the eggplant has been removed. Take an ounce of cinnamon, another of cloves, eight maravedis of pepper, and a quarter of caraway. All this should be ground and mixed together. Put a little on the cross of each eggplant and place them in

una olla vidriada, y luego echarles allí el escabeche así caliente como está, y no las cubras hasta que estén bien frías: luego tápalas con su corcho, y durarán todo el año.

[430] *Memoria del adobo de Aceitunas.*

Hanse de coger las aceitunas del árbol, cuando veas alguna morada, (272v) que es indicio que tienen el grueso que han de tener, darles has cuatro o cinco cuchilladas a cada una, y échalas en agua dulce mudándosela cada dos días, hasta que todas las aceitunas se hundan en el agua: luego échalas en adobo en agua y sal, echando a una fanega un celemín de sal:[422] y cuando tengan tomado el adobo de agua y sal, toma una vasija de dos azumbres, e hínchela de aceitunas, echando las ruedas de limón, y hojas de laurel, y de oliva, e hinojo, y luego hínchela del mismo adobo de agua y sal, y échale media cuarta de canela y medio de clavos, y la mitad de pimienta, y un poquito de azafrán, todo desleído con el mismo adobo: y por esta cuenta podrás hacer las demás. Este adobo de las especias no dura mucho tiempo, porque se pone agrio con los limones, que por eso se dice que se haga una olla de dos azumbres, y porque en acabándose aquella se pueda hacer otra: y si quisieres tener las aceitunas enteras en el adobo (273r) de agua y sal: y cuando quisieres hacer las del adobo de las especias, acuchillarás no más de las que fueren menester para henchir la olla de dos azumbres, y estarán más seguras las enteras. Y advierte, que las aceitunas desde el día que entran en el agua dulce, nunca más han de estar descubiertas, porque se echan a perder: y si las quisieres machacar con una piedra, será lo mismo.

[431] *Bizcochos de harina de Trigo.*[423]

Batirás doce huevos frescos, quitándoles tres claras, y en batiéndolos un poco échales una libra de azúcar molido y cernido, y bátelo hasta que esté espeso, y blanco como miel blanqueada: luego tendrás tres cuarterones de harina, respeto

---

422 The *fanega* is a Spanish bushel or today the equivalent is a little bigger: 1.5 bushels or 55.5 litres or 14.6 gallons. A *celemín*, one twelfth of a *fanega*, is equivalent to 4.625 litres or a little more than one gallon. For more on measurements, see Appendix 2, "On Measurements," Castaño Álvarez, especially 329, and "Antiguas pesas y medidas."

423 This is a signature recipe for Martínez Montiño. First, it is historically important, because it is an early recording of what will later be known as Genoise sponge cake. He is careful to explain in detail the quantities, consistencies, and techniques used at every stage of the process, and it is the basis for other *bizcocho* recipes. Second, to complement the extensive details on beating the eggs and baking the batter, he includes the only references to illustrations at the back of the cookbook. Third, he notes the king's preference for flavour added, and at the end of his (Martínez Montiño's) life, the head chamberlain presents to the king a letter of support on his behalf which mentions his signature sweet biscuits. For more information, see "Martínez Montiño's Biography," 8–13.

a glazed pot and add the already hot pickling broth. Don't cover them until they have thoroughly cooled. Then cork them and they will last all year.

Memoir of olive marinade

Pick the olives from the trees when you notice them turning purple, which is an indicator that they are the thickness they should be. Hit each one four or five times with a knife and put them in fresh water, changing it every other day until all the olives sink in the water. Next, put them in a saltwater marinade. For every bushel, one gallon of salt. When they have soaked up the saltwater marinade, take a four-quart pot and fill it with olives. Add lemon wheels, bay leaf, olive leaf, and fennel. Then fill it with the same saltwater marinade. Add an eighth of a cup of cinnamon, an eighth of clove, half that of pepper, and a little saffron. It should all dissolve in the marinade itself. You can use these calculations for the rest. This spice marinade won't last long, as the lemons will make it bitter. This is the reason for a four-quart pot and why, when one is done, you can make another. If you want to have the olives whole in the saltwater marinade and when you want to marinate them with spices, hit with a knife only the ones you're going to put in the four-quart pot. The whole ones will last longer this way. Note that olives, from the moment they go into fresh water, should not be exposed again, because they will spoil. If you want to crush them with a rock, it will produce the same effect.

Sweet biscuits with wheat flour

Beat twelve fresh eggs, removing three egg whites. While beating, add in a pound of sifted, ground sugar and continue beating until thick and white like whipped honey. Then take three quarters of a pound of flour, for each egg

de cada huevo una onza de harina, y ésta ha de ser de tahona si fuere posible muy floreada, y échasela dentro acabada de cerner, o ciérnela sobre el batido con un cedacillo de cerdas, (273v) porque no haga burujones, y échale un poco de anís, y no se ha de batir con la harina, mas de cuanto se mezcle el harina con el batido: y esto de la harina podría ser que no fuese menester tanta algunas veces por ser los huevos muy pequeños, y otras veces podría ser que fuese menester algo más, por ser los huevos mayores: y así has de tener cuenta cuando se echare el batido en los papelillos, que se quede como un verduguito correoso,[424] y que no se extienda por el papel, y así verás si tienen más necesidad de echarle más harina. A todos los bizcochos se les suele echar anís, aunque yo no lo echo a ningunos; porque su Majestad no gusta dello. Estos bizcochos se cuecen en horno de pan con pala de hierro delgada a horno manso con lumbrera, echando sobre unos papelillos con un cucharoncito chiquito, que irá dibujado la medida al fin deste libro:[425] y tiende un poco del batido a lo largo del papelillo, del grueso de un dedo de (274r) la mano, y échale un poco de azúcar molido por encima, y luego toma el papelillo por una punta para que se caiga el azúcar, salvo lo que quedare pegado al batido, que será muy poco, y mételo en el horno, y así irás metiendo unos, y sacando otros, como se vayan cociendo,[426] y después les quitarás los papelillos, que se quitan con mucha facilidad, y tórnalos a bizcochar en el horno. Estos bizcochos se baten con un cucharón, que sea un poco angosto de pala, y bátense, como quien bate tortilla de huevos, y hase de batir con mucha fuerza. Los papelillos han de ser todos de un igual: han de salir de un pliego diez y seis,[427] doblando el papel cuatro veces, y cada vez ir cortando el doblez: y la tercera vez se ha de doblar ancho por largo: y desta manera vendrán a salir los deziseis [sic] papelillos, y no han de llevar doblez ninguno sino lisos, y el batido ha de caer en el medio a lo largo, que como se echan con presteza en el horno, luego se queda el (274v) batido, y va esponjando, y así no son menester bordes: el papelillo, y el batido, y los cucharones, todo irá dibujado al fin deste libro.[428] Advierte, que ningunos bizcochos has de batir con dos manos,

---

424 *Verduguito correoso* [leather whipping paddle]: Martínez Montiño uses the imagery of the leather paddle with which the executioner whipped the accused in miniature. For a visual representation of it, see "Azotes."

425 With the phrase "que irá dibujado la medida al fin deste libro," Martínez Montiño includes a reference to one of the two spoon images that are found in the back of the 1611 edition. The inclusion of these images and their reference in this recipe are defining factors for future editions. For more information, see the Introduction, "Previous Editions" (74–92).

426 This part of the instructions provides a cycle for the timing of baking the sweet biscuits. Without a mechanical timer, Martínez Montiño explains how to put the sweet biscuits in the oven, rotate them around, and remove them for proper baking time.

427 For more information on the *pliego*, see 260n175.

428 Here is a second reference to illustrations at the back of the book: "el papelillo, y el batido, y los cucharones, todo irá dibujado al fin deste libro" [The little papers, the batter, and the spoons are all drawn at the back of the book]. This reference is included in all seventeenth- and eighteenth-century editions except for 1797. It appears in none of the nineteenth-century editions. For more information on the visuals in the back of the book, see the Introduction, "Previous Editions" (74–92).

an ounce of flour, and it should be milled and if possible very finely sifted flour. Add it right after sifting or sift it over the batter with a horsehair sieve so that there are no lumps. Add a little anise, but don't add it to the flour but rather, as soon as it's folded, into the batter. Sometimes it is possible that you won't need as much flour if the eggs are smaller and other times you might need a little more if the eggs are bigger. When you pour batter onto the paper, take note that it looks like a leather whipping paddle and does not run over the paper, and this way you'll see if you need more flour. For all these sweet biscuits, anise is generally added, but I never add it, as His Majesty does not like it. These sweet biscuits are baked in a bread oven on a thin iron peel with low temperature and an exhaust port. Put [the batter] on the papers with a small spoon that is drawn at the back of this book and roll a little of the batter across the paper the thickness of a finger. Sprinkle a little ground sugar on top, then pick up the paper by a corner so that all the sugar falls off except what sticks to the batter, which will be just a little. Put it in the oven and continue putting ones in while taking others out as they are baking. Afterwards, remove the paper, which will come off easily, and put the sweet biscuits back in the oven to double bake. These sweet biscuits are beaten with a big spoon that has a narrow handle. Beat them as you would beat eggs for an omelette. They should be vigorously beaten. The papers should all be one size. Sixteen should come from one sheet by folding the paper four times and cutting on the folds each time. The third time, fold it widthwise and lengthwise, and this way you'll have sixteen little papers and none will have any folds; they will all be smooth. Drop the batter in the middle lengthwise. As you immediately put them in the oven, the batter will stay in place and get spongy so you don't need edges. The little papers, the batter, and the spoons are all drawn at the back of the book. Note that no sponge cake is beaten with two hands, as the nuns do,

como las monjas, sino con una mano, como quien bate tortilla de huevos:[429] y si quisieres hacer estos bizcochos redondos, toma medias cuartillas de papel, y echa deste batido en cada uno el grueso de un huevo, que quede redondo, y échale su azúcar por encima, como a los demás, y métetelos en el horno, y saldrán unos bizcochos redondos muy buenos.

[432] *Memoria de los bizcochos de Almidón.*

Batirás once huevos, y luego les echarás una libra de azúcar molido y cernido, y batirlo has hasta que esté blanco y espeso: luego le echarás diez onzas de almidón, y un poco de anís, y (275r) no lo batas mas de cuanto se mezcle el almidón con los huevos y azúcar: luego harás una cajitas de medios pliegos de papel, y echarás dentro deste batido el grueso de un dedo, y cuécelos a horno manso de cobre, porque no se pongan colorados, ni empollados, sino lisos y blancos: y en estando cocidos, abrirás los papeles, y cortarás los bizcochos, de manera que de cada caja salgan cosa de diez bizcochos, y tórnalos a bizcochar, y ráspales los suelos si estuvieren quemados: y luego tendrás azúcar clarificado, en punto que no sea muy grueso, y échale un poco de agua de azahar, y torna a cocer hasta que torne a su punto: luego tendrás unos pocos de bizcochos en el horno calientes, y tendrás el azúcar sobre un poquito de rescoldo, e irás tomando los bizcochos con un tenedorcillo, y con un manojito de plumas los irás vidriando con el azúcar, y poniéndolos en un tablero que tengan la una punta sobre unas cañitas, e íraslos (275v) remeciendo, porque no se peguen. Y advierte, que el vidriado ha de ser muy delgado, que sea trasparente, y se vea la color del bizcocho, que si tiene mucho azúcar no vale nada: y si los quisieres bañar con el baño de rosquillas podrás. Y advierte, que cuando vidriares los bizcochos, si el azúcar estuviere muy blando, se mojará el bizcocho: y así lo podrás subir un poco más: y en todo caso ha de estar el bizcocho caliente para que tome bien el vidriado, y el tablero donde se van poniendo ha de estar al amor de la lumbre para que se enjugue el vidriado.

[433] *Batido de los bizcochos de Almidón sin vidriado.*

Si Quisieres hacer los bizcochos de almidón sin vidriarlos son muy buenos: Harás el batido que está dicho con las cantidades que se dice atrás, y pondrás el horno de cobre al fuego con (276r) lumbre mansa, e henchirás la hoja de obleas, muy bien compuesta: luego echarás del batido en cuatro, o cinco partes, ciérralo, y déjalo estar un poco, y el batido se habrá extendido por todo el horno; y de que estén bien cuajados, saca la hoja fuera, y corta los bizcochos en pedazos cuadrados, o como salieren, y tórnalos a poner en el horno a bizcochar, y échales un poco de azúcar

---

429 For more on beating the batter with two hands, see 112n14.

but with one hand, as one does for beating an omelette. If you want to make these sweet biscuits round, take half of a quarter sheet of paper and put an egg-sized amount of batter on it and keep it round. Add the right amount of sugar on top, as for the others, and place them in the oven. Very tasty, round sweet biscuits will turn out.

Memoir of sweet biscuits with starch

Beat eleven eggs, then add one pound of sifted, ground sugar and beat it until it's thick and white. Then, add ten ounces of starch, a little anise, and don't beat it any more than folding the starch into the eggs and sugar. Then with half sheets, make liners and fill with batter about the thickness of a finger. Bake in a copper oven on low so that they don't turn brown or blister, just white and even. Once baked, open up the paper liner and cut the sweet biscuits so that you get about ten sweet biscuits from each liner. Put them back to double bake and scrape off the bottom if they're a little burnt. Then have enough clarified sugar, at thread stage but not too thick. Add some orange blossom water and boil until it reaches thread stage again. Then, have some hot sweet biscuits in the oven and have sugar over the embers. Begin picking up the sweet biscuits with a small fork, icing them with sugar using a feather brush, and putting them on a pastry board that has some reeds underneath one side, and rock them so they don't stick. Note that the glaze should be very thin. It should be transparent so you still see the colour of the sweet biscuit. It's no good if it has too much sugar. Or, if you want, you can dip them in [the] meringue for ring-shaped pastries. Note that when you glaze the sweet biscuits, if the sugar is too soft, the sweet biscuit will become soggy, so you can raise [the heat of the sugar] a little bit. Whatever you do, the sweet biscuit should be warm so that the glaze adheres well. The pastry board where you're placing them should be in a warm spot near the heat so that the glaze dries.

Batter for sweet biscuits with starch and no glaze

If you want to make sweet biscuits with starch and no glaze, they are tasty. Make the batter as explained with the quantities as explained above and place the copper oven on the flame with low heat. Completely cover the sheet with wafers. Spoon the batter into four or five parts [on the wafers], close [the oven], let it cook, and the batter should have thoroughly spread out in the oven. Once it's set, remove the sheet, and cut it up into squares or leave as is. Return them to the oven to double bake. Sprinkle a little grated sugar on top and once they're

raspado por encima, y de que estén bien bizcochados sácalos. Son muy buenos bizcochos. También los bizcochos de almidón vidriados, cuando los echaste a cocer en las cajitas de papel, si los echaras un poquito de azúcar molido por encima, y después que estaban cocidos los cortaras y bizcocharas, sin hacerles otra cosa ninguna, son muy buenos bizcochos. Advierte, que si les echares azúcar por encima, ha de ser no más de un polvito, porque si echas mucho los echarás a perder, que harán una costra, y no los dejará cocer.

[434] (276v) *Otra suerte de bizcochos secos.*

Batirás doce huevos con una libra de azúcar, y cuando esté el batido blanco y espeso, échale harina que esté bien incorporado, y pondrás unas obleas en los suelas de las torteras, y sin otra cosa ninguna echarás allí del batido del grueso de una pulgada, y luego cubrirás las torteras, y dales lumbre abajo y arriba, que sea fuego manso, y de que esté bien cuajado sácalo, y sacarás de cada tortera una torta,[430] y harás dellas unas rebanadillas muy delgadas, y pondráslas a bizcochar en el horno sobre unos papeles hasta que se pongan un poco tostados. Son unos bizcochillos secos y muy buenos.

[435] *Mazapanes de dos pastas.*[431]

Majarás media libra de almendras dulces, como se suelen majar para los otros mazapanes, mojando la mano (277r) en agua de azahar, y échale media libra de azúcar, y májalo muy bien, y ha de quedar la pasta dura, y desta pasta harás unos mazapanes del tamaño que quisieres, redondos, altillos, de los bordes muy delgados en los suelas, que parezcan a modo de pastellillos, y luego harás otra pasta con otra media libra de almendras, y tres cuarterones de azúcar, y majarla has con onza y media de agua de azahar: y esta pasta ha de salir muy blanda, y ha de ser mucho más majada que la otra, y échala en un cacito, y dale una vuelta sobre la lumbre, de manera que dé un hervor, meneándola con un cucharón: y con esta pasta henchirás los vasitos de la otra, y asiéntalos sobre obleas, y cuécelos a fuego manso. Son muy buenos mazapanes. Algunas veces a la pasta postrera, se le suele echar el azúcar doblado, a media libra de almendras una libra de

---

430 Those familiar with Genoise cake, or, as it is sometimes called in Italy, *pan di Spagna* [sponge cake], will recognize the similarities between it and the beginning of this recipe. Although Genoise is associated with both French and Italian cooking, it is clear from this and the other *bizcocho* recipes included here that it was also popular in early seventeenth-century Spain. Krystina Castella notes that the technique of vigorously beating eggs, which produces air bubbles, and their raising the cake into a light and airy sponge cake most likely originated in Spain (6–7).
431 These marzipan pastries are still made today in Middle Eastern bakeries.

double baked, take them out. These are very tasty sweet biscuits. Also, for sweet biscuits with starch and glaze, when you cook them in the paper liners, if you sprinkle a little ground sugar on top and, after they've baked, cut them up and double bake them without doing anything else, they are very tasty sweet biscuits. Note that if you sprinkle sugar on top, it should just be a little dusting, because if you put too much on, you will ruin them. They will become crusted over and won't bake right.

Another kind of dry sweet biscuits

Beat twelve eggs with one pound of sugar. When it is thick and white, fold in flour so that it's well incorporated. Put wafers on the bottom of covered tart pans and without anything else pour out the batter an inch thick and cover the covered tart pans. Add heat above and below; make sure it's a gentle fire. Once it is set, remove it, and from each covered tart pan you'll have one cake from which you'll cut very thin slices. Return them to the oven to double bake on paper until they have browned a little. These are dry sweet biscuits and are very tasty.

Two-dough marzipan

Grind a half a pound of sweet almonds, just as you would for other marzipan, wetting the pestle with orange blossom water. Add a half a pound of sugar and thoroughly grind it up into a hard dough. With this dough make marzipans whatever size you wish, round, tall, with thin edges around the bottom so they look like little pastries. Then make another dough with another half pound of almonds and three quarters of a pound of sugar. Grind it with an ounce and a half of orange blossom water. This dough should be very soft and a lot finer than the other. Put it into a small saucepan and stir it over the flame until it comes to a boil. Stir it with a spoon. With this dough fill the pastry cups [made] from the other marzipan. Place them on wafers and bake them on low heat. They are very tasty marzipans. Sometimes for the second dough, double the amount of sugar is added: for half a pound of almonds, a pound of sugar. But,

azúcar; mas yo hallo que saben poco a las almendras, y quítoles un cuarterón de azúcar, echando a media libra (277v) de almendras tres cuarterones de azúcar, y me salen mejores. Probarás de entrambas maneras, y los que supieren mejor a tu señor, desos harás.

[436] *Mazapanes secos.*

Majarás una libra de almendras, mojando la mano en un poco de agua, y echarle has otra libra de azúcar, y májala muy bien, de manera que no se enaceite, y ha de quedar la pasta un poco dura, y luego echarla has en un cacito, y dales dos, o tres hervores, meneándolo con un cucharón hasta que esté la pasta blanquecina, y bien enjuta: luego sácala al tablero, y sóbala un poco, y tiende una hoja delgada de la gordor de un real de a cuatro, y harás tus mazapanes de cuatro picos, y prolongados, y hazle sus bordecitos repulgados: luego toma un poco de azúcar molido y cernido, y échale un poco de agua de azahar, de manera que estén como puches, cuanto se puedan untar los mazapanes, y vidríalos (278r) con un manojito de plumas, y cuécelos sobre hostias blancas en horno de cobre: y si estos mazapanes fueren para persona que no los quisiere tan duros, échale a esta pasta dos yemas de huevos cuando la sacares del fuego, y haz tus mazapanes y saldrán tiernos, mas yo a los duros me atengo: y si fueren para enfermo que no pueda comer, cocerás una pechuga de ave, y pícala muy bien, y luego májala en el almirez muy majada, mézclala con las almendras y el azúcar, y harás tus mazapanes como está dicho, y serán más sustanciales.

[437] *Mazapanes en Almíbar.*

Majarás una libra de almendras, mojando la mano en un poco de agua, luego tendrás tres cuarterones de azúcar en almíbar, y ponlo en un cacillo al fuego, y echa las almendras dentro, y cuezan dos, o tres hervores, hasta que esté un poco espeso: luego sácalo (278v) del fuego, y déjalo enfriar un poco: luego ve sacando cucharadas dél, y echándolas sobre obleas unos montoncillos redondos, y cuécelos en el horno, de manera que se tuesten un poco. A estos se les suelen echar un poco de olor, o un poco de agua de azahar en almíbar, y azúcar molido por encima.

[438] *Bizcochillos secos.*

Todas las suertes de bizcochos que he dicho, como son los de almidón, y los de harina de trigo, si quisieres incorporarlos un poquito más de harina, y luego echar unas cucharadillas en unos papelillos, o echar seis en un medio pliego de papel, que no tenga cada uno más bulto que una nuez grande, y no le eches azúcar por encima, sino es muy poquito, que no tenga que sacudir, y cuécelos en horno de

I have found that the almond flavour is lost and so I have removed a quarter pound of sugar and left a half a pound of almonds to three quarters of sugar. For me, they come out better this way. Try both ways and, whichever your lord prefers, make them that way.

Dry marzipan

Grind a pound of almonds, wetting the pestle with a little water, and add a pound of sugar. Thoroughly grind it together so that it's not oily. The dough should be a little hard. Then place it in a saucepan and bring it to a boil two or three times, stirring it with a spoon until the dough is milky in colour and very dry. Turn it out onto a pastry board, knead it a little, and roll out a thin sheet as thick as a four-real coin. Make your marzipan with four long points and with crimped edges. Then take a little sifted, ground sugar and add a little orange blossom water so that it's like porridge, enough to spread over the marzipans, and glaze them with a feather brush. Bake them on white wafers in a copper oven. If these marzipans were for someone who doesn't like them so hard, add two egg yolks to this dough as you take it off the heat and then make your marzipan and it will come out softer. But, I stand by the hard ones. If they are for a sick person who can't eat, boil a breast of poultry and shred it. Then thoroughly mash it in the mortar, mix in the almonds and sugar, and make your marzipans as explained, and they will be more nutritious.

Marzipan in simple syrup

Grind a pound of almonds, wetting the pestle with a little water. Then have three quarters of a pound of simple syrup and put it in a saucepan on the fire. Add the almonds in and bring to a boil two or three times until it's rather thick. Then remove it from the flame and let cool a while. Then begin taking out spoonfuls and dropping little round piles on wafers. Bake them in the oven so that they are a little toasted. Rose water or orange blossom water is often added to the simple syrup, and ground sugar is sprinkled on top.

Mini dry sweet biscuits

For all kinds of sweet biscuits that I've included, like those made with starch and wheat flour, if you want, you can incorporate a little more flour and then put small spoonfuls on the pieces of paper or put six on a half sheet of paper. None should be bigger than a big walnut. Don't sprinkle any sugar on top, unless it's very little, so you don't have to shake it off. Bake them in a

barro,[432] y saldrán tiesecillos, que parezcan tabletas, y saldrán llanos, y redondos como tortillas, y no esponjarán; y serán como digo a modo (279r) de tabletas. Su Majestad de la Reina nuestra señora, suele gustar destos bizcochillos.

[439] *Otros bizcochos.*

Estos mismos bizcochos de harina de trigo se batirán con las cantidades de los bizcochillos larguillos, [433] y en lugar de los papelillos echarás el batido en unas cajitas de medios pliegos de papel, que tenga el batido de grueso una pulgada, y cuécelos a horno manso, y luego sácalos de las cajitas, y córtalos, que salgan de cada pan diez, o doce bizcochos, y tórnalos a bizcochar, y son muy buenos: y a todos estos bizcochos se les suele echar un poco de anís.

[440] *Otros bizcochos.*

De harina de arroz puedes hacer bizcochos, guardando la orden de las cantidades de los bizcochos de almidón: la harina ha de ser fresca, sacada del día, y se ha de enjugar primero, porque (279v) es muy húmeda cuando se acaba de sacar, y después de enjuta es muy seca. Estas cajas de medios pliegos de papel salen bien; más como el arroz es pesado, no es muy a propósito para enfermos, y más que si el arroz tuviese algún sabor de húmedo se sentiría en los bizcochos.

[441] *Bizcochos de harina de Trigo, y Arroz todo revuelto.*

Tomarás un cuarterón de harina de arroz, y otro de harina de trigo, y revuélvelo todo con media libra de azúcar molido y cernido, y échale yemas de huevos hasta que esté un poco blando, y batirlo has mucho hasta que esté espeso, y haga muchas empollitas, y échale un poco de anís quebrantado, y haslos de batir con un cucharón que sea gordito, hecho a modo de remo, y has de batir con la punta del cucharón, como quien da puñadas: y cuando tenga muchas ampollitas esta batido, haslos (280r) de cocer sobre papelillos larguillos, como está dicho en los de harina de trigo, que son los que su Majestad suele comer más de ordinario; más estos no han de esponjar tanto, antes has de echar en los papelillos muy poco batido, y un poquito extendido, porque salgan delgadillos y anchuelos, y háseles de echar azúcar por encima al enhornar, y tomar el papelillo por la punta para que se caiga el azúcar, como está dicho en los de harina de trigo, se ha de cocer en horno de barro.

---

432 Martínez Montiño notes the importance of a terracotta oven, as the copper oven would hold the moisture in more.

433 Martínez Montiño is referring to the recipe "Memoria de los bizcochelos" [Memoir of ladyfingers] (526–8; 527–9). Given the instructions and references to the previous recipe, these should also come out looking like ladyfingers.

clay oven and they'll come out a little firm and look like tablets. They will be flat and round like tortillas and not spongy. As I've said, they will look like tablets. Her Majesty the Queen our lady likes these mini dry sweet biscuits very much.

Other sweet biscuits

These same wheat flour sweet biscuits are beaten with the [same] quantities as the mini long sweet biscuits, and instead of [flat] paper, put the batter in liners made from half sheets of paper. The batter should be about one inch high. Bake on low in the oven. Take them out of the liners and cut them so that from each loaf you have ten or twelve sweet biscuits. Return them to double bake. They are very tasty. A little anise is normally added to all these sweet biscuits.

Other sweet biscuits

You can also make sweet biscuits with rice flour, maintaining the instructions for quantities in the sweet biscuits with starch. The flour should be fresh, milled the same day. It should first be dried, as it's very moist when it's recently milled. Once it's dried, it will be very dry. The liners made with a half sheet of paper work well. Furthermore, as the rice is dense, it is not appropriate for sick people. Also, if the rice felt a little moist, you would note it in the sweet biscuits.

Combined wheat and rice flour sweet biscuits

Take a quarter pound of rice flour and another of wheat flour and stir it all together with half a pound of sifted, ground sugar. Add egg yolks until it's fairly smooth and whip it until it's thick and has little bubbles. Add a little crushed anise. Fold it in with a wide spoon that's made like a paddle. Fold it with the tip of the spoon like someone pounding. When the batter has a lot of bubbles, bake them on long pieces of paper as explained in [the recipe] for ones with wheat flour, which are the ones His Majesty eats most often. But these should not puff up as much; rather, put just a little batter on each paper and drag it a little so that they turn out thin and wide. When you bake them, sprinkle sugar on top and pick up the corner of the paper so the sugar falls off as explained in the ones with wheat flour. They should bake in a clay oven.

[442] *Una fruta de Natas.*

Tomarás un plato de natas, o seis escudillas, que todo será uno,[434] y echarle has doce yemas de huevos, y media libra de azúcar molido y cernido: y luego echarle has pan rallado hasta que esté trabado como batido de bizcochos y un poquito más, y harás unas cajitas de medios pliegos de papel, y úntalas por de dentro con un poco de manteca (280v) de vacas, y echa el batido en las cajas de papel, del grueso de pulgada y media, y métalas en el horno, y cocerse han como bizcochos, y después que estén cocidas, sácalas, y haz rebanadas, y rebózalas con huevos, y fríelas, y pásalas por otra media libra de azúcar en almíbar, y harás un plato de unas torrijas muy regaladas, y échale un poco de canela molida por encima, y azúcar raspado.

[443] *Unas rebanadas de pan conservadas.*

Tomarás una libra de azúcar, y harás almíbar que esté un poco grueso, y harás unas rebanadas de pan de leche mollete cuadradas, que sean un poco gordas, y tuéstalas en las parrillas, de manera que queden doradas, y mójalas en vino blanco aguado, de manera que se remojen de parte a parte, y no se empapen demasiado: y como el azúcar esté cociendo, echa dentro dos o tres, o las (281r) que cupieren sin que estén una sobre otra, y cuezan dos, o tres hervores: luego vuélvelas con la paleta, y tornen a cocer otro poco, y esto ha de ser metiendo el cacito en el fuego, y apartándole muchas veces, porque el azúcar no se empanice, y luego velas sacando en el tablero, y mete otras en el azúcar, y harás otro tanto, y sácalas en el tablero, y torna a cocer las primeras: y con esto se acabarán de calar, y tórnalas a sacar al tablero, y échales canela molida y cernida por encima, de manera, que estén cubiertas, y déjalas enfriar un poco: luego vuélvelas con la paleta, y échales otra tanta canela por el otro lado, y harás otro tanto a las otras, y has de hacer de manera, que las rebanadas cuando se remojen no quede nada por remojar, y que estén tiernas y muy bien conservadas, y que no esté el azúcar empanizado por encima dellas, sino que parezca diacitrón; porque si no se calase la rebanada con el vino, no se caláría tampoco (281v) con el azúcar: y si se empapase demasiado con el vino, haríase pedazos en el azúcar; y si quisieses subir mucho el azúcar para trabarla se empanizaría, y no tienen buen comer: han de quedar enteras y tiernas y secas, que todo se puede hacer, que aunque son un poco dificultosas, después que hayas hecho la experiencia, las harás con mucha facilidad: y cuando las hicieres no te duela el azúcar, que lo que te quedare en el cazo se puede aprovechar para otra cosa. También te pudiera aconsejar, que las hicieras en una tortera ancha, porque se hicieran mejor, y con menos azúcar; mas como la tortera no se puede poner y

---

434 For measurement of *nata*, see 242n149 and Appendix 2, "On Measurements."

Fried cream

Take a plate of cream or six bowlfuls; they are the same. Add twelve egg yolks and half a pound of sifted, ground sugar. Then add breadcrumbs until it's thick, like batter for sweet biscuits or a little more. Make liners with half sheets of paper and grease the inside with butter. Add the batter to the liners an inch and a half high. Put them in the oven and bake as for sweet biscuits. Once they're done, remove them, slice them, coat them with eggs, and fry them. Dip them in half a pound of simple syrup and make a plate of exquisite torrijas. Sprinkle a little ground cinnamon on top and grated sugar.

Preserved bread slices

Take a pound of sugar and make syrup that is fairly thick. Cut slices of mollete bread made with milk into squares; they should be fairly thick. Toast them on the grill so that they turn golden brown. Dip each side in watered-down white wine and don't let them soak too long. When the sugar is boiling, put two or three in at a time, or however many will fit without being on top of one another, and bring to a boil two or three times. Then turn them over with a spatula and let them cook a while longer. You need to repeatedly move the saucepan in and out of the flame so the sugar doesn't crystalize. Then remove them onto a pastry board, put other ones in the syrup, and make another batch. Remove them to the pastry board and put the first batch back to cook. This way they will finish soaking up the syrup. Return them to the pastry board, sprinkle sifted, ground cinnamon so that they're covered, and let them cool a little. Then flip them with a spatula and sprinkle the same amount of cinnamon on the other side. Do the same thing for the second batch. Do this so that the slices, after the second time, have nothing left to soak up. They should be tender and well preserved. The sugar should not crystalize on top of them; rather it should be like candied citron. If it [the bread] didn't soak up enough wine, it won't soak up enough sugar either, and if it soaked up too much wine, the sugar will ball up. And, if you cook the sugar too long to thicken it, it will crystalize and they won't be good to eat. [The slices] should be whole, soft, and dry. It can be done, and although they are a little tricky, once you have experienced it, you'll make them much more easily. And when you do it, don't worry about the sugar, because whatever is left over in the pan can be used for something else. I could also advise you to make these in a wide, covered tart pan so they come out better and use less sugar. However, since you can't take the covered tart pan on and off the flame as

quitar tantas veces en el fuego, como el cazo que tiene astil con mucha facilidad se te empanizará el azúcar, y se te echarán a perder las rebanadas, harás un cacito que sea un poco ancho de suelo, y con él las harás con mucha facilidad.

[444] *Tabletas de Masa.*

(282r) Batirás seis huevos frescos, quitándole una clara, y echarle has media libra de azúcar molido y cernido, y batirlo has, como quien bate bizcochos, hasta que esté muy blanco y muy espeso: luego échale un poco de manteca de vacas cosa de un cuarterón, y una gota de vino, y un poco de olor, y un poco de anís quebrantado: luego echa harina de trigo floreada, toda la que pudiere embeber el batido, de manera que quede una masa encerada, y sobada muy bien: luego harás una hoja desta masa, teniéndola con el palo de masa, y quede del gordor de un real de a dos, y corta con la cortadera tiras tan anchas como cuatro dedos, y tórnalas a cruzar de manera que queden quebradas, y cuécelas sobre papeles polvoreados de harina en horno de cobre a fuego manso: y si quisieres bañar algunas, la memoria del baño hallarás escrita en el capítulo de las rosquillas. Hanse de secar al sol. Desta misma masa podrás hacer tabletas con canela, (282v) echándoles canela molida en cantidad, hasta que se pongan bien morenas, y échales algún poco de olor. También puedes hacer unos panecillos redonditos, del tamaño de una cermeña: no se han de bañar. También podrás tender esta masa muy delgada, como hojuelas muy delgadas, y éstas no se han de bañar, y son muy buenas.

[445] *Un plato de Papín tostado, con cañas, huevos mejidos, y hojuelas.*

Freirás una hoja de masa delgada redonda, y luego asiéntala en un plato untado con manteca de vacas: y luego harás un papín con una azumbre de leche, y media libra de harina de arroz, o de trigo, y un par de cañas de vaca en trozos, y ocho yemas de huevos, y un poquito de sal, y media libra de azúcar: luego cuajarás este papín, y echarlo has en un plato sobre la hoja de masa frita, y harás docena y media de (283r) yemas de huevos mejidos, y echarlos has por encima del papín, y otras pocas de cañas de vaca desmenuzadas, y echarle has azúcar molido por encima, de manera que haga costra, y ponlo en un horno a que se tueste un poco, y sírvelo caliente: antes de echar los huevos mejidos se han de hinchar muchas hojuelas por el papín. Sobre este plato se podrá poner un gigote de capón, si quisieres.

[446] *Perdices rellenas.*

Tomarás las perdices, y descarnarlas has las pechugas, y picarás la carne con buen tocino, y luego tomarás la tercia parte desta carne, y freírla has con un poquito de tocino, de la manera que se hace para los pollos rellenos, y echarle has huevos crudos, y revuélvelos sobre la lumbre hasta que esté bien seco: luego sácalo al tablero, y

much as the saucepan that has a handle, the sugar will crystallize much quicker and the slices will be ruined. Use a saucepan that is wide-bottomed and with this you will easily make them.

Dough twists

Beat six fresh eggs, removing one of the whites and adding half a pound of sifted, ground sugar. Whip it as one does for sweet biscuits until it is very white and thick. Then add a little butter, about a quarter pound, a drop of wine, a little rose water, and a little cracked anise. Then add finely sifted wheat flour as much as needed to absorb the batter so that you get an elastic, well-kneaded dough. Next, make a sheet with this dough, rolling it out with a rolling pin so that it's as thick as a two-real coin. With the trimmer cut it into strips four fingers wide and cross them over so that they're twisted. Bake them on paper dusted with flour in a copper oven on low heat. If you want to frost some, the memoir for the meringue can be found in the chapter on ring-shaped pastries. They should dry in the sun. With this same dough you can make cinnamon tablets. Add a lot of ground cinnamon until they turn brown. Add a little rose water. You can also make little round buns the size of a cermeña pear. These shouldn't be frosted. You can also roll this dough out very thin, like thin sheets of pastry. These shouldn't be frosted and they are very tasty.

Toasted sweet cream with marrow, sweet scrambled egg yolks, and puff pastry

Fry a thin, round sheet of dough and then set it on a plate greased with butter. Then make a sweet cream sauce with two quarts of milk, half a pound of rice flour or wheat flour, a couple of pieces of beef bone marrow cut into pieces, eight egg yolks, a pinch of salt, and half a pound of sugar. Let this sweet cream thicken and put it on the plate on the sheet of fried dough. Make a dozen and a half of sweet scrambled egg yolks and put them on top of the sweet cream with some flakes of beef bone marrow. Sprinkle on top some ground sugar, enough to make a crust, and put it in the oven to brown a little. Serve hot. Before adding the sweet scrambled egg yolks, cover many sheets with sweet cream. If you want, you can also serve this with minced capon on top.

Stuffed partridges

Take partridges, remove the meat from the breasts, and chop it up with good fatback. Then take a third of the meat and fry it with a little fatback the way it is prepared for "Chicken with stuffing." Add in some raw eggs and stir it over the flame until the eggs are done. Then turn it out onto a cutting board and mince

pícalo muy bien, luego mézclalo con la otra carne, y mézclese todo, y échale yemas de (283v) huevos hasta que esté un poco blando, y sazona con todas especias, y sal, y zumo de limón, y torna a poner esta carne con las pechugas de las perdices: luego métele unas broquetas para que se tengan en el asador, y empapélalas con medios pliegos de papel untados con manteca, y átalas con hilo bien atadas, y luego espételas en el asador, y ponlas a asar; y cuando estén asadas, córtales todos los hilos, y quítales el papel, y tendrás aparejados yemas de huevos batidas, y rebozarlas has con un manojo de plumas, de manera que estén bien cubiertas: y luego échales un poco de manteca caliente por encima, y sírvelas con ruedas de limón.

[447] *Un plato de Carnero adobado.*

Tomarás carnero que sea de pecho, y haráslo pedazos, y luego échalo a cocer con agua y sal, y un poco de tocino; y cuando esté cocido sácalo en el (284r) colador que se escurra, y pon un poco de miel al fuego en una sartén y cuando esté caliente echa el carnero dentro, y fríase en la miel hasta que esté un poco colorado: luego échale un poquito de vino, y un poco de caldo, y unas almendras mondadas y tostadas: luego sazónalo de todas especias y canela, y un poquito de azafrán, y échale un poco de zumo de limón, o de naranja, y sírvelo sobres unas rebanadas de pan tostado.

[448] *Torreznos lampreados.*[435]

Tomarás tocino de pernil que sea bueno, que esté bien remojado, que no tenga sal, y cortarás unos torreznos un poco grandes, y ponlos a asar en las parrillas que estén medio asados: luego córtalos en rebanadas delgadas, atravesada la hebra, y ponlos en una olla, o en una cazuela, y échales un poco de vino tinto, y caldo, o agua hasta que se bañen, y sazónalos de especia y canela, y cuezan (284v) hasta que estén tiernos, y échale un manojo de hierbas, mejorana, e hisopillo, y jadrea – y échale dulce de miel, o azúcar, que estén bien dulces: y si estuviere la salsa rala, podrásla espesar un poco con un poco de harina quemada, o un poco de pan tostado, y remojado en vinagre, y majado en el almirez, y pasado por un cedacillo: y si le quisieres echar unas hojas de laurel, podrás, mas no ha de dar más de un hervor: y esto es cuando quieran servir los torreznos: y a este tiempo se les ha echar un poquito de agrio, que sea muy poco. También les podrán echar a estos torreznos almendras mondadas y tostadas, o ciruelas pasas, quitados los cuescos, y partidas por medio. Con estas salsas lampreadas[436] podrás servir lenguas de vaca, y ubres de vaca, cociéndolas primero, y luego tostarlas, y luego lamprearlas, y se les puede echar membrillos, y peros agrios, y todo lo demás que está dicho.

---

435 Generally, *torreznos* are roasted pork *belly*, but as seen here and in one other recipe, "Hojaldre de torreznos" [Puff pastry with roasted pork fat] (270–2; 271–3), Martínez Montiño uses the term for fat from other parts of the pig as well. For this reason, here, I have translated *torreznos* as *roasted pork fat*.
436 For more on lamprea sauce, see 372n285.

it. Mix it with the other meat and thoroughly mix it. Add egg yolks until it's soft, season with all spices, salt, and lemon juice, and then put this meat back into the partridge breasts. Push some skewers through so they can go on the spit and wrap them with half sheets of paper greased with lard. Tie them tightly with string and then skewer them on the spit and roast them. When they are roasted, cut the strings, remove the paper, and have prepared whipped egg yolks. Coat them with a feather brush so they're well covered. Then put a little hot lard on top and serve them with lemon wheels.

A dish of marinated mutton

Take some mutton, it should be the brisket, and chop it up. Then put it on to boil in salted water with a little fatback. When it's cooked, put it in a strainer to drain. Put a little honey in a frying pan and when it's hot, add the mutton. Fry it in the honey until it turns a little brown. Then add a little wine, a little broth, and some toasted, shelled almonds. Season with all spices and cinnamon and a pinch of saffron. Add a little lemon or orange juice and serve it over slices of toasted bread.

Roasted pork fat, lamprea style

Take some good ham fat that has been soaking and has no salt. Cut it up into good sized pieces of roasted pork fat and put them on the grill. When they are partially roasted, cut them against the grain into thin slices. Put them in a pot or a casserole, add a little red wine and broth or water, enough to braise, and season with all spices and cinnamon. Boil until tender. Add in a handful of herbs – marjoram, winter savory, and summer savory – and add some sweetener, either honey or sugar, so that it's very sweet. If the sauce is thin, thicken it a little with toasted flour or a little toasted bread soaked in vinegar, mashed in the mortar, and strained through a sieve. If you want to add bay leaf, you can, but don't boil it more than once. This is when you want to serve the roasted pork fat. Now, add a little sour juice, but just a little. You can also add some toasted, shelled almonds to the roasted pork fat, or prunes, with the pits removed and sliced in half. With these lamprea sauces you can serve beef tongue and beef udder. First boil them, then toast them, then prepare them lamprea style. You can also add quince or sour apples and everything else explained above.

[449] (285r) *Membrillos asados.*

Escogerás los membrillos que sean grandes y sanos, y cortarles has un poquito del pezón para que haga asiento, que se pueda tener derecho en el horno: luego por la parte de arriba, le quitarás una coronilla muy pequeña, y por allí le harás un agujero por donde le quitarás todas las pepitas, y que quede el membrillo por de dentro muy limpio: luego la lavarás con un poco de vino, y échale unas gotas de agua de azahar, y hínchelo de azúcar molido: luego tórnale a asentar la coronilla que quitaste encima, y envuélvelo en medio pliego de papel, de manera que quede la coronilla descubierta, y ponlos a asar en el horno: y cuando estén asados los hallarás llenos de almíbar: vacíalo todo en un plato, y échale más azúcar molido, y un poco de agua, y pon el plato sobre las brasa, de manera que dé dos, o tres hervores: y luego después de mondados los (285v) membrillos, asiéntalos en un plato, y tórnalos a henchir deste almíbar, de manera que vayan llenos, y más sobre para que vaya en el plato. Estos membrillos podrás asar de otra manera, mondándolos como está dicho, y echarles sus gotas de agua de azahar, y luego henchirlos de azúcar y canela molido, y tórnales a poner sus coronitas, y clavarlas a cada una con tres clavos de especias: luego hacer un poco de masa de cémite, y tender una hoja un poco gorda y redonda, y asentar el membrillo en medio en pie, y luego recoger la masa que se venga a juntar sobre la coronilla del membrillo, y pegarla muy bien, mojándola con un poco de agua, de manera que no se abra: luego pon a cocer estos membrillos empanados en el horno, y cuando esté bien cocida la masa como empanada, sácalos muy derechos, y parte la masa de manera que no se rompa el membrillo, hallarlos has bien asados, y llenos de almíbar. Estos se suelen servir enteros (286r) sin mondar, para que en la mesa los monde el maestresala.[437] Es muy buena suerte de asar membrillos.

[450] *Cómo se han de aparar las aves en la cocina.*[438]

Tomarás un capón acabándolo de sacar del asador, y vuélvelo la pechuga abajo, y meterle has el tenedor por medio del lomo, de manera que lleguen las puntas del

---

437 For the general responsibilities of the *maestresala* [steward], see Chapter 4 of Miguel Yelgo de Vázquez's *Estilo de servir a príncipes con ejemplos morales para servir a Dios* (1614), especially 35r–44r. Chapter 5 deals with carving poultry and meat but does not include information on peeling fruit at the table (44r–47v). For more on the role of the *maestresala*, see the Introduction (11–13).

438 This recipe and the ones that follow focus on slicing meat after it has been cooked. For poultry, Martínez Montiño describes in detail how to slice birds in the air. Detailed instructions are also found in Yelgo de Vázquez's *Estilo de servir a príncipes con ejemplos morales para servir a Dios* (1614), Chapter 5 (44r–47v). This practice is still found in Angel Muro's 1894 publication, *El practicón*, although he speaks disparagingly of it: "es un jugueteo muy propio de gentes de educación incompleta. Y sin embargo, es muy frecuente este procedimiento, que todo buen gastrónomo cuidará de evitar" [It's a silly trick typical of people with poor education. And yet this procedure is very common, one that any good gastronome should be careful to avoid] (509).

Roasted quince

Choose quince that are big and in good shape. Cut a little off the bottom so that they stand on their own and can be upright in the oven. Then right on top remove the little stem end and make a small hole from which you can remove all the seeds. The inside of the quince should be very clean. Rinse it with a little wine and add a few drops of orange blossom water. Fill with ground sugar. Then set them down again with the stem side up and wrap them in a half sheet of paper so that the stem opening is exposed. Put them in the oven to roast. When they are done, they will be filled with syrup. Empty it onto a plate and add more ground sugar and a little water and put the plate on red-hot coals so that it comes to a boil two or three times. Then, after the quinces are peeled, set them on a plate and fill them again with the syrup so that they're full, even overflowing so that there's some on the plate. These quinces can be roasted another way, peeled as explained above and sprinkled with a few drops of orange blossom water. Then, fill them with sugar and ground cinnamon, put the stems back on, and insert three cloves into each one. Then, make a dough from whole-grain wheat flour, and roll out a round, thick sheet. Place the quince standing up in the middle and then gather the dough so that it comes together at the stem of the quince and stick it firmly, wetting it with a little water so that it doesn't open up. Then put these wrapped quinces in the oven to roast, and when the dough is cooked like an empanada, take it out immediately. Remove the dough without cutting into the quince. They should be nicely roasted and full of syrup. These are usually served whole without peeling so that the steward can peel them at the table. This is a very good way to roast quince.

How to present poultry in the kitchen

Take a capon that has just come off the spit, turn it breast down, and insert a fork into the loin so that the fork tines are touching the breastbone. Then

tenedor a tocar en el hueso de la pechuga: luego vuelve el tenedor hacia arriba, y dale un corte en la pierna derecha por la parte de adentro: luego dale otro por la parte de afuera, de manera que venga a juntar el uno con el otro, de manera que no quede la pierna asida más de en la junta del hueso de la cadera: luego le da otro cortecillo, apartando la carne del muslo también hasta la junta de la cadera: luego le da otro en el artejo de la pierna: luego le da otro corte por la junta del alón, (286v) que vaya por la pechuga abajo, de manera que la junta quede bien desasida: luego volverás la mano con el tenedor, y harás otro tanto del otro lado: luego le darás otro corte en la cabeza de la pechuga, de manera que no atraviese ninguno de los otros cortes, y apartarás un huesezuelo que tiene allí: luego le darás otro corte, apartando la punta de la pechuga de las caderas: luego le darás otros dos cortes por los lados de la rabadilla que lleguen hasta las caderas: estos cortes todos se han de dar en el aire, sin que el capón llegue al plato, y ha de haber en el plato unas rebanadillas de pan en que caiga la sustancia del capón: luego volverás el tenedor las puntas hacia abajo, y darle has una cuchillada en medio de los lomos: y con esta cuchillada cortarás el lomo al capón, y lo harás soltar del tenedor, y luego vuélvelo la pechuga arriba, y échale sal por los cortes, y de aquellas rebanadillas de pan también metidas por entre (287r) los cortes: tápalo con otro plato, y ponlo sobre un poco de lumbre un poquito, y sírvelo así caliente.

Las perdices se han de aparar de la misma manera que los capones.

Las palomas, y las gangas, y pluvias, y otros pájaros pequeños se han de aparar desta manera, tomándolo con el tenedor por el lomo, y darle dos cortecillos en las piernas hasta la cadera, y luego un corte por el encuentro del alón derecho, que baje por toda la pechuga abajo: y luego otro por la otra parte de la misma manera, y luego otro corte que cruce estos dos: luego volver el tenedor las puntas abajo, y darle una cuchilladilla en el lomo, y con eso se soltará el tenedor: luego volver las pechugas arriba, y echarles sal, o la salsa que le tocare.

[451] *Cómo se han de aparar los Pavos.*

Tomarás el pavo con el tenedor, y le darás un corte en la pierna derecha por la parte de adentro, y otra por (287v) la parte de afuera, que vengan a juntar entrambos en la junta del hueso de la cadera, y otro corte por la pulpa de la pierna, que vaya arrimado por el hueso abajo, y otro por la parte de afuera por el artejo: luego otro corte por el encuentro del alón derecho, que baje por toda la pechuga abajo, y otro junto a éste también por la pechuga abajo: luego le harás otro tanto del otro lado; porque estas aves grandes han de llevar cuatro cortes en la pechuga, porque son grandes las pechugas, y con dos sería poco: luego le darás otros dos cortes por los dos lados de la rabadilla, que lleguen hasta el medio del espinazo, y otros dos a los dos lados del pescuezo, que vengan a juntar casi con estotros, y luego una cuchillada en medio del lomo, y con ésta soltará el tenedor: luego vuelve el pavo la pechuga arriba, y échale sal por los cortes, y unas rebanadillas de pan metidas entre ellos.

turn the fork facing upward and slice the right leg on the inside. Then slice it again on the outside so that one [cut] connects to the other and the attached leg is only attached at the joint of the hipbone. Then, make another small cut to separate the thigh at the hip joint. Then make another at the knuckle of the leg. Then, make another cut at the joint of the wing that goes from the breast downward so that the joint is well separated. Then, turn the fork in your hand and do the same on the other side. Next, make another cut at the top of the breast, but don't cross any of the other cuts. Separate the little bone that is there. Then, cut it again and separate the end of the breast from the hips. Make two more cuts on the sides of the rump up to the hips. All of these slices should be done in the air without the capon touching the plate. There should be little slices of bread on the plate onto which the capon essence will drip. Then turn the tines of the fork facing downward and slice down the middle of the loins. With this slice you will cut the loins of the capon and it will come off the fork. Next, turn the breast upwards and sprinkle salt on the slits. Also insert the slices of bread in between the slits as well. Cover it with another plate and place it over a little flame. Serve it hot.

Partridges can be presented the same ways as capons.

Doves, pin-tailed sand grouses, plovers, and other small birds should be presented this way. Put the fork in the loin and make two slices in the legs up to the hip. Then make a slit at the right wing all the way under the breast. Make another the same way on the other side and another that crosses the two. Then turn the fork tines down and slice the loin. This will release the fork. Next, turn the breasts upward, sprinkle with salt, or drizzle over [them] any accompanying sauce.

How to present turkey

Pick up the turkey with a fork. Make a cut in the right leg on the inside and another on the outside so that both meet at the joint of the hipbone. Make another cut through the flesh, underneath, close to the bone, and another on the outside near the knuckle. Then another cut at the right wing from the breast down, and other right next to this one, also from the breast down. Next, do the same on the other side. Because these birds are big, they require four slits in the breasts, as the breasts are big and two would be too few. Then make another two slits on both sides of the rump that go up to the middle of the backbone and another two on both sides of the neck that almost come together with the other ones. Then make a cut in the middle of the loin and with this it will release from the fork. Next, turn the turkey breast side up, sprinkle salt in the slits, and stuff bread slices between them.

Desta misma manera se cortan los (288r) gansos, y las avutardas, y los faisanes, y todas las aves que tienen grandes pechugas.

[452] *Corte de Lechón.*

Pondrás el lechón en el plato boca abajo: luego le darás un corte, hincando el cuchillo bajo de una oreja: y luego ir cortando hasta la cola por un lado del espinazo, y otro desde junto al degolladero, que vaya alrededor de la espaldilla, y venga a parar en bajo del codillo, de manera que quede la espaldilla medio desasida: luego le darás otro desde la cola, que venga dando vuelta alrededor del muslo, que venga a acabar entre las piernas, de manera que quede la pierna casi toda cortada, y luego dale otros tantos cortes del otro cabo, luego híncale la punta del cuchillo en medio de la cabeza, y abrirás los cascos a una parte y a otra, de manera que queden los sesos bien descubiertos, y échales un poco de sal y pimienta, y toma el (288v) lechón con el tenedor, y el cuchillo, y asiéntalo sobre su sopa.

[453] *Cómo se aparan las Liebres.*

Pondrás la liebre en un plato boca abajo, y métele el tenedor por medio los lomos, y dale un corte desde la cola hasta la espaldilla, de manera que se rompa bien el hueso, y vuelve la pierna de la liebre que venga a tocar en la espaldilla, porque ha de venir a parecer flor de lis: luego dales dos cortes en la carne de la pierna a raíz del hueso, uno por de dentro, y otro por de fuera: luego dale otro corte por encima la espaldilla: de manera que quede casi toda desasida: luego le harás otro tanto por el otro lado: luego le da una cuchillada en el pescuezo, de manera que pueda volver la cabeza a asentarse sobre las espaldillas: luego alza el tenedor las puntas abajo, y dale una cuchillada en medio del lomo, de manera que corte todo el espinazo, y con eso caerá la liebre en el plato, (289r) y parecerá una flor de lis, como tengo dicho. Los conejos se han de cortar desta misma manera.

You carve geese, great bustards, pheasants, and all big-breasted birds this same way.

Carving suckling pig

Put the suckling pig face down on the plate. Then make a cut, driving the knife under the ear. Then begin cutting down to the tail on one side of the backbone and another from next to where you slit the throat, around the shoulder, and end up under the elbow so that the shoulder is half separated. Then make another from the tail coming around the thigh and ending up between the legs so that the leg is almost entirely cut off. Next, make as many cuts on the other side. Then drive the tip of the knife into the middle of the head, opening up the skull from front to back so that the brains are well exposed. Sprinkle a little salt and pepper and pick up the suckling pig with fork and knife and set it over sops.

How to present hare

Place the hare face down on a plate and stick the fork between the loins. Make a cut from the tail to the shoulder so that the bone completely breaks. Turn the leg of the hare so that it touches the shoulder, because it should end up looking like a fleur de lis. Then make two cuts in the meat of the leg at the base of the bone, one on the inside and one on the outside. Then make another cut on top of the shoulder so that it is almost entirely separated. Then do the same on the other side. Next, make a cut on the neck so that the head can turn and rest on the shoulders. Then turn the fork tines down and make a cut in the middle of the loin so that it cuts the entire backbone. With this the hare will fall to the plate and will look like a fleur de lis as I have explained. Rabbits are carved the same way.

Memoria de conservas.[439]

[454] *Albérchigos.*[440]

Tomarás los albérchigos, y mondarlos has, y sácales los cuescos, y luego pásalos por un poco de agua caliente hasta que estén tiernos: y luego sácalos, y ponlos en un barreñón, u olla, y tendrás el azúcar clarificado,[441] y echárselo hasta que se cubran, y al otro día sacar el azúcar, y ponerlo a hervir hasta que haya cocido un par de hervores, y luego tórnaselo a echar, y esto ha de ser ocho días hasta que esté el azúcar en punto, y hase de ir añadiendo el azúcar, porque se ha de ir menguando, de manera que estén siempre cubiertos los albérchigos: y si hicieren alguna espuma en este tiempo pondráslos a la lumbre a que den un hervor. Y advierte, que estos albérchigos (289v) nunca han de cocer con el azúcar, ni han de llegar a la lumbre, sino es que a caso hicieren la espuma que tengo dicho, que con solos los cocimientos del azúcar se conservarán muy bien.[442] El azúcar siempre ha de echarse frío.

[455] *Duraznos.*

Tomarás los duraznos, y mondarlos has, y cocerlos has en agua hasta que estén tiernos, y luego has de hacer con ellos lo propio que a los albérchigos, salvo que le has de cocer el azúcar más subido de punto, y pasarlos por él que den un hervor, y echarlos en su barreñón, y darle los primeros días los hervores muy suaves, porque no se arruguen, y en allegando a los cuatro cocimientos irlos subiendo de punto hasta ocho cocimientos en todo: y esto se entiende, que los cocimientos han de ser en el azúcar, que los duraznos no han de volver al fuego más de aquella primera vez que hirvieron en el azúcar.

---

439 In this section Martínez Montiño describes various stages of boiling sugar. We find specific names for these stages in Juan de la Mata's *Arte de repostería* (1747). For more on the different stages of caramelizing sugar, see the section on "Sweeteners," in the Introduction, 45–6.

440 This exact recipe and all others through "Limones ceutíes" [Ceuti lemons] also appear in the amended version of Altamiras' *Nuevo arte de cocina* (1770). In addition, "Azúcar rosado blanco" [White rose sugar] and "Bocados de calabaza" [Morsels of squash] appear (168–74). Several of Martínez Montiño's recipes on preserves also appear in the *Libro de confitura para el uso de Elias Gómez Maestro cerero y confitero de la ciudad de Olite* (1818), including this one and "Limones ceutíes" (see Ciérbide and Corcín 93).

441 Clarifying sugar is a process of transforming raw sugar into loaf sugar that involves beating egg white in water, adding it to the sugar, boiling it, and then skimming off the impurities. What is left is simple syrup that crystallizes once again. Martínez Montiño explains this process in his recipe "Azúcar rosado blanco" [White rose sugar] (568–70; 569–71) and uses it in many of his preserved fruit recipes (from here to "Hinojo conservado" [Preserved fennel] [581–3; 582–4]).

442 This note of caution focuses on keeping the fruit intact, hence only heating up the syrup so that the fruit doesn't fall apart or dissolve, and also eliminating the foam, that is, killing any bacteria that might spoil the fruit.

Memoir of preserves

Apricots

Take apricots, peel them, remove the pits, and soak them in a little hot water until they become tender. Then, remove them and put them in a tub or a pot. Have clarified sugar and pour in enough to cover. The next day, remove the syrup and put it on to boil until it comes to a boil a couple of times. Then, put it back in [with the apricots], and it should be eight days before the sugar is at the early thread stage. You should continue adding sugar as it [the syrup] reduces so that the apricots are always covered. If at any time it [the apricots in syrup] begins to foam, put it [the syrup] on the fire and bring it to a boil. Note that these apricots should never be cooked in the sugar or even get close to the flame, but in case they begin to foam up as I've indicated, then only by boiling [the syrup] will they be preserved. The sugar should always be cold when added.

Clingstone peaches

Take clingstone peaches, peel them, and boil them in water until they are tender. Then do the same thing as for the apricots, except that the sugar should be at a later thread stage. Put them in the water while boiling and move them to a tub. The first few days it should be a gentle boil so they don't wrinkle, but on the fourth boil and through the final eighth, the sugar should be at an increasingly higher thread stage. It is understood that only the sugar boils and that the peaches do not return to the flame after that first time they were boiled in sugar.

[456] (290r) *Melocotones.*

Los Melocotones has de hacer ellos lo propio que con los duraznos.

[457] *Bocados de Durazno.*

Has de tomar los duraznos, y ponerlos a cocer en agua con su cáscara y todo, hasta que estén blandos, y después mondarlos y machacarlos, y pasarlos por un harnero después de machacados, y tomar para cada libra de durazno una libra y dos onzas de azúcar, y clarificarlo y ponerlo en punto, hasta que haga unas vejigas, y en viendo que está bien cocido el azúcar echarle dentro la pasta del durazno, y cueza hasta que tome un punto que no se escurra a una parte, ni a otra, ni se pegue al dedo después de frío, y echarlo después en sus vidrios, o en sus tablas, a donde hubiere de estar: y si fuere para cajas hase de tomar dos onzas más de azúcar en cada (290v) libra, que vendrá a ser una libra y un cuarterón a cada libra de duraznos.

[458] *Peras en Almíbar.*

Hanse de tomar las peras, y echarlas en agua fría, y ponellas al fuego, y dalles un hervor,[443] y luego echarlas en agua fría, porque no se manchen, y después mondallas, y punzarlas por dos partes, y tomar azúcar clarificado frío, y echar las peras en un barreñón, y echar el azúcar encima, y darle ocho días hervor al azúcar,[444] hasta que esté espeso, y siempre se le ha de echar frío.

[459] *Cajas de Perada.*

Hanse de tomar las peras y cocerse echándolas en agua fría, y después de cocidas mondallas, y machacarlas, o rallarlas, y tomar para cada libra de pera una libra de azúcar molido, y revolverlo con la pasta, y ponerlo a la lumbre que cueza hasta que espese, y se (291r) eche un poco en un plato, o en una tabla que se enfríe, y en no pegándose a la tabla, ni al dedo, echarlo fuera de la lumbre: y si no lo quisieren hacer desta manera,

---

443 Although these grammar forms have not appeared in previous sections of the cookbook, in this "Memoria de conservas" [Memoir of preserves] section, Martínez Montiño provides several examples of the assimilation of the enclitic pronoun, which commonly occurred with the final 'r' of an infinitive before an attached pronoun that started with 'l'. In this recipe, "*ponellas* al fuego, y *dalles* un hervor" and "*mondallas*" examplify this usage. In the recipe "Raiz de borraja" [Borage root], he uses both forms: *echalla* and *arropalla* but *tomarla, ponerla, sacarla, echarla,* and *darle* (566; 567). This formation does not appear in any of the other editions.

444 Although *ocho días* [eight days] is a common euphemism for a week, like from Sunday to Sunday with both days included, Martínez Montiño really intends the cooking process to take place over eight days. In other recipes Martínez Montiño explains that fruit is boiled and then rests and is boiled each day for eight days. In this recipe he skips that explanation, knowing that other cooks will understand the meaning.

Firm peaches

Firm peaches are prepared the same way as the clingstone peaches.

Morsels of clingstone peach purée

Take clingstone peaches and put them on to boil with skin and all until they're soft. Afterwards, peel them, mash them, and strain them in a sieve. Once mashed, for every pound of peaches, take a pound and two ounces of sugar, clarify it, and turn it into syrup at the soft-ball stage until it begins to blister. When you see that the sugar is ready, add the peach mash and cook until it doesn't move one way or the other and doesn't stick to your finger once it's cold. Afterwards, put it into glass jars or onto boards or wherever it's going. If it's for boxes, add two more ounces of sugar for each pound so that it will be a pound and a quarter for each pound of peaches.

Pears in simple syrup

Take pears and place them in cold water, put them on the fire, and bring them to a boil. Then place them in cold water so they won't discolour. Afterwards, peel them and prick a hole in them in two spots. Take cold clarified sugar and put the pears in a tub and put the sugar on top. Boil the sugar [once a day] for eight days until it's thick, and always pour it on cold.

Boxes of preserved pear purée

Take pears, boil them, and put them in cold water. After they're boiled, peel them and mash them or grate them. For each pound of pear, take a pound of ground sugar and stir it into the mash. Put it on the flame and cook until thick and when you put a little on a plate or board to cool it doesn't stick to either the board or your finger. Then, take it off the flame. If you don't want to make it this way, clarify the sugar and cook it until the stage that makes a little ball in your finger, then add it to the mash. If it were for single servings, use three quarters of a pound of sugar and put it on to clarify or grind it up, and bring it to the same stage as the [one for] mashed pears.

clarificar el azúcar, y ponerle en un punto que haga una bolita en el dedo,[445] y entonces se podrá echar la pasta. Y si fuere para bocados, hase de tomar a tres cuarterones de azúcar, y ponerlos a clarificar, o molido, y ponerlo en el mismo punto que la perada.

[460] *Toronjas.*[446]

Hanse de tomar, y ponerlas a la lumbre, sacados los agrios en una lejía muy fuerte, hasta que estén muy cocidas, y luego sacarlas y echarlas en agua, y tenerlas allí ocho, o nueve días, mudando cada día el agua: y en estando bien dulces ponellas a escurrir del agua, y luego meterlas en conserva como a los limones, y darle los mismos cocimientos, y estos adelante los hallarás escritos.

[461] (291v) *Limones ceutíes.*

Hanse de tomar los limones de los chicos, y hacer una lejía muy fuerte, y ponerlos a cocer en ella hasta que estén muy tiernos, y sacarlos fuera de la lumbre, y echarlos en agua clara por espacio de nueve días, y mudándosela cada día, una, o dos veces, y luego echarlos en sus ollas, y darles nueve cocimientos; los cuatro que no haga más de hervir el azúcar, y ha de ser a segundo día; porque si se diera cada día, se arrugarían los limones, y en pasando de los cuatro cocimientos se cocerá más el azúcar hasta que esté en su punto.

[462] *Raíz de Borraja.*

Has de tomar las raíces de borrajas, y hase de raer: y así como se va rayendo, se ha de ir echando en agua fría, y luego echalla a cocer en agua que esté cociendo: y cuando esté tierna irla (292r) sacando, y arropalla en unos manteles, o paño de lienzo, y luego tomarla, y ponerla a dar un hervor en el azúcar clarificado, y sacarla del perol, y echarla en un barreño, o en una olla: y luego darle dos, o tres cocimientos, y con eso estará acabado de conservar.

[463] *Azúcar Rosado colorado.*[447]

Has de tomar una libra de rosa, después de haberle cortado el pie de abajo, y machacarla en el mortero: y así como la vayas machacando, le has de ir echando su azúcar molido, hasta que esté muy bien machacado, y ha de ser la cantidad del azúcar dos libras para una de rosa, y ponerlo a la lumbre hasta que cueza un poco. Si es para bocados ponerlo al sol, y si es para vidrio, u ollitas cocello un ratito más.

---

445 Martínez Montiño is referring to the firm-ball sugar stage.
446 For more information on the toronja, see 222n126. This recipe and the next appear in the eighteenth-century recipe collection *Manuscrito Ávila Blancas* in reverse order (Pérez San Vicente, *Gastronomía mexicana* 89–90).
447 This recipe appears in the eighteenth-century recipe collection *Manuscrito Ávila Blancas* (Pérez San Vicente, *Gastronomía mexicana* 92).

Toronja

Take them and put them on the flame. Remove the sourness with very strong alkaline water until they are done. Then, remove them and set them in water for eight or nine days, changing the water every day. Once they are very sweet, drain them of the water and then put them in a preserve like the one for lemons and boil the same way. You can find these [recipes] written down below.

Ceuti Lemons

Take lemons, the small ones, and make very strong alkaline water and put them in to boil until they are very tender. Remove them from the heat and put them in clear water for a period of nine days, changing the water once or twice a day. Then put them in their pots and boil them nine times. Four are just to bring the sugar to a boil, and it should be every other day, because if you add [boiling sugar] every day, the lemons will wrinkle. After the fourth boil, the sugar should continue cooking until it comes to the thread stage.

Borage root

Take borage roots and scrape them. As you scrape it [the root], put it in cold water and then put it on to boil in already boiling water. When it is tender, take it out and wrap it in a tablecloth or linen towel. Then take it and put it on to boil in clarified sugar. Remove it from the round-bottom pot, put it in a tub or a pot. Then, boil it two or three times, and with this you will finish preserving it.

Rose coloured sugar

Take a pound of roses and, after cutting off the base, mash them in the mortar. As you are mashing it, add in the right amount of ground sugar until it's well mashed. The amount should be two pounds of sugar for every pound of roses. Put it on the flame and let it boil a little. If it's for bite-sized pieces, let it dry in the sun, and if it's for storing in glass or little pots, let it boil a while longer.

[464] *Flor de Borrajas.*

Tomarás una libra de flor de borrajas, (292v) y pasarla por un poco de agua tibia, y luego sacarla, y has de tomar libra y media de azúcar, y ponerla a cocer, que esté muy subido de punto, y echar dentro una libra de flor de borrajas, y ha de hervir mucho hasta que haga un punto suave en el dedo,[448] y luego echarla fuera: y si es para en hoja, para una libra de flor has de echar media libra de azúcar, y has de poner el azúcar en un punto, que echando una gota en el agua se quiebre,[449] y ésta se entiende que no se ha de machacar, sino échalla así entera. La flor en hoja quedará como vidriada.

La flor de la malva se puede conservar de la misma manera que la flor de borraja.

[465] *Flor de Romero.*

Has de tomar una libra de flor, y libra y media de azúcar, y poner el azúcar en punto subido, y echar dentro la flor de romero, y no ha de dar más de dos, o tres hervores, y echarlo fuera, y ponerlo en su vidrio, u olla vidriada.

[466] (293r) *Azúcar Rosado blanco.*

Hanse de tomar cuatro libras de azúcar, y media azumbre de agua con cuatro claras de huevos, y batirlas con aquel agua: conforme el azúcar que echaren, se ha de echar a cada libra una clara de huevo, y medio cuartillo de agua, y cueza luego con esta agua, y estas claras de huevo sobre la lumbre para que se clarifique, y no se saque espuma ninguna: y hase de tomar y colar el azúcar por un paño, y poner en un cacito hasta cantidad de media libra de azúcar, y hase de cocer, e ir meneando aquel azúcar con un cucharón hasta que haga unos ojos,[450] y luego echarle un poquito de zumo de limón, y menearlo, y echar un poco de rosa dentro, y echarlo sobre unos papeles blancos en dos tortas. Y advierte, que el azúcar

---

448 Martínez Montiño is indicating that the sugar should rise from the thread stage to the soft-ball stage. He later continues the cooking process to the hard-ball stage when almost no water remains in the syrup.

449 Martínez Montiño's description of the drop breaking is a sign of the highest temperature stage of sugar syrup. Normally the sugar reaches 300°–310° F and almost no water remains in the syrup.

450 Martínez Montiño's description of cooking the sugar "hasta que haga unos ojos" [until eyes form] refers to the density of the sugar. There will appear bubbles that surface to the top.

Borage blossoms

Take a pound of borage blossoms, quickly dip it in a little warm water, and then remove it. Take a pound and a half of sugar, put it on to boil to a high thread stage. Add the pound of borage blossoms and let it boil a lot until it's soft to the touch. Then take it out. If it includes leaves, for a pound of blossoms, add a half a pound of sugar. It should be at the hard-crack stage so that when a drop of it hits water, it breaks. It is understood that you don't mash this, just add them [the blossoms] whole. The blossom and leaf will come out like glass.

Mallow blossom is preserved in the same way as the borage blossom.

Rosemary flower syrup

Take a pound of blossoms and a pound and a half of sugar. Bring the sugar to an advanced thread stage. Add in the rosemary blossom and don't boil it more than two or three times. Remove it and put it in its glass container or glazed pot.

White rose sugar

Take four pounds of sugar and one quart of water with four egg whites. Beat them together with the water. According to the amount of sugar used, for every pound, add one egg white and a half pint of water. Then boil it with this water and egg whites over the heat so that it will clarify it and no foam is released. Take the sugar and strain it through a cloth. Put up to half a pound of sugar in a saucepan. Boil it and begin stirring that sugar with a spoon until eyes form. Then add a little lemon juice and stir it. Add a little bit of rose. Pour it onto white papers in two pies. Note that for white rose sugar, retamen sugar is very

de retamen es muy blando,[451] para el azúcar rosado blanco, y el azúcar de pan es muy seco, (293v) y se resquebrajan mucho las tortas del azúcar rosado: y así es necesario echar la mitad del uno, y la mitad del otro: y con esto saldrán las tortas esponjadas y lisas.

[467] *Calabazate.*

Hase de tomar la calabaza, y quitarle la corteza, y lo que tiene dentro, y echarlo en sal, y de que esté salado sacarlo de la sal, y echalla en agua clara hasta que esté desalado, y ponerlo a cocer hasta que esté bien cocido, y tomar un alfiler, e hincarlo en la calabaza: y si se cayere del alfiler echarlo fuera de la lumbre y ponerla a escurrir, y luego ponello en su vasija, y tomar azúcar clarificado, y echárselo hirviendo como sale de la lumbre, y luego darle nueve cocimientos hasta que haga el azúcar un punto, que haga hilos entre los dedos. Cúbrase como el diacitrón.

[468] *Tallos de Lechugas.*

(294r) Hanse de tomar y mondarlos, y después de mondados echarlos en sal, y conservarlos de la misma manera que la calabaza.

---

451 To understand what *azúcar de retamen* [retamen sugar] is, Miguel de Baeza's explanation of sugar processing found in *Los quatro libros del arte de confitería* [Four books on the art of confection] (1592) proves useful: "aunque es verdad quel azúcar sale todo de una caña y es todo uno tiene diferentes nombres, que es azúcar de pilón blanco de la primera cocha, y lo segundo pilón de guitas, y lo tercero es retame, y esto es azúcar blanco menudo, y es algunos pilones que se deshacen de lo entero, lo cuarto se llama quebrado, y esto es lo que sale de pilón de guitas, y otro más cabado, que se hace de todas las mieles, que salen del azúcar, y esto se llama quebrado, lo postrero llaman espumas, y destas espumas queda una miel, que llaman miel de cañas, que esto ya no se puede cuajar, y en estos azúcares puede haber en cada suerte uno, que sea mejor que otro por razón de una de dos cosas, o por la naturaleza de las cañas o por falta de los maestros, que lo hacen" [even though it's true that all sugar comes from one cane and it's all the same, it does have different names. White sugar loaf is from the first reserve. The second is *guitas* loaf, the third is *retame* and this is small [pieces] of white sugar. It is [from] some loaves that come off the whole. The fourth is called *broken* and this is what comes off the *guitas* loaf. Another, more refined, is made from all the syrup that comes off the sugar and this is [also] called *broken*. The last is the foam and from this foam is a syrup called molasses. This cannot crystallize. In all these sugars there can be in each type one that is better than another for one of two reasons: Either due to the nature of the cane or due to an error by the masters who process it] (cited in Martínez Llopís 45).

soft and loaf sugar is very dry and the rose sugar pies will crack a lot. Thus, it is necessary to add half of one and half of the other, and this way the pies with come out spongy and smooth.

Sweetened dried squash

Take squash and remove the rind. Put the insides in salt and once it's well salted, remove it and put it in clear water. Once it's desalted, put it on to boil until it's well boiled. Take a pin and stick it into the squash. If it falls off the pin, remove it from the heat and drain it. Then put it in its container and take clarified sugar that has been boiling and pour it over it right off the heat. Boil it nine times until it reaches the thread stage, when it makes threads between your fingers. Cover it as for candied citron.

Lettuce stalks

Take them and peel off the outer layer. After peeling them, put them in salt and preserve them the same way as for squash.

[469] *Bocados de Calabaza.*

Si quisieres hacer bocados de calabaza, hase de tomar y cocer la calabaza, y rallarla, o machacarla, y pasarla por una criba,[452] y a cada libra de calabaza, después de escurrida, has de tomar una libra y un cuarterón de azúcar, y ponerlo a clarificar sobre la lumbre, y en estando espeso echar la pasta de la calabaza dentro, y menearla con un cucharón, y cueza unos hervores, y en estando bien espeso, echarlo fuera, y hacer los bocados con un cucharón, y ponerlos en una tabla, y ponerlos a secar al sol hasta que estén secos, y luego volverlos con un cuchillo, y ponerlos que se sequen por otra parte.

[470] *Raíces de Escorzonera.*[453]

(294v) Hase de lavar, y ponerla a cocer en agua fría, y en haciendo una espumita echarla a fuera del agua, y echarla en otra agua fría, e irla rayendo muy sutilmente, y echarla en otra agua limpia, y luego echalla en otra agua clara a cocer, y cueza hasta que esté tierna, y luego echarla en un barreñón, o en una olla. Tomar azúcar clarificado, y echarlo sobre la escorzonera, y darle sus cocimientos ocho días hasta que esté espeso el azúcar, y en su punto.

[471] *Peras secas cubiertas.*

Hanse de tomar, y sacarse del almíbar, y ponellas a escurrir, y tomar el azúcar, y clarificarlo, y ponello en punto como para huevos mejidos, y echar las peras dentro, y poner el azúcar a hervir con las peras, e irlas quitando la espuma que hicieren, e irlas meneando con la espumadera, y cuezan, y váyales tomando el punto hasta que (295r) hagan unas verrugas por la espumadera, y luego quitarlas de la lumbre, y tomar una berguera,[454] y sacar lo que quisiere poner: y en estando un poquito fuera de la lumbre, tomar y batir un poco el azúcar hasta que esté como blanco del color de las propias peras: y luego revolverlo, e irlas echando fuera del perol: hasta que se enfríe no se han de quitar de la berguera.

---

452 Similar to the *cedazo*, the *criba* is used for sifting. For more information, see the entry in the Glossary. However, its holes are generally bigger, and in the seventeenth century, it was used for cleaning grains and legumes, while the *cedazo* was finer and used for removing impurities from flour (Morala Rodríguez 312).

453 *Escorzonera* [black salsify or Spanish salsify] is a root vegetable native to southern Europe. As its English name suggests, it is generally thought to have spread through Europe from Spain.

454 A *berguera* [fruit sieve] was a specialty piece of equipment designed specifically for candied fruit. According to Carmen Abad Zardoya, it consisted of a rectangular frame with esparto fabric or wire screen in the middle and a metal plate on the bottom ("Herramientas" 112n107).

Morsels of squash

If you want to make morsels of squash, take and boil the squash, grate it or mash it, and strain it through a wide-hole sieve. For each pound of squash, after it's strained, have a pound and a quarter of sugar. Put it on the flame to clarify, and when it's thick, add the squash mash to it, stir it with a spoon, bring it to a boil a few times, and once it's very thick, take it out, make bite-sized pieces (morsels) with a spoon, put them on a board, and put them in the sun to dry until they are dry. Then, turn them over with a knife and dry the other side.

Black salsify root

Wash and put it on to boil in cold water. Once it begins to foam, take it out of the water and put it in cold water and begin carefully scraping it. Put it in another [pot of] clean water and then put it on to boil in other clear water. Boil until tender and then put it in a tub or a pot. Take clarified sugar, pour it over the salsify, and boil it [each day] for eight days until the sugar is thick and at thread stage.

Candied dried pear

Take [pears], remove from simple syrup, and drain them. Take sugar, clarify it, and bring it to the stage for sweet scrambled egg yolks. Place the pears in it and bring the sugar to a boil with the pears. Begin removing the foam that rises. Stir with a skimmer, continue cooking, and let them come to the stage where they begin to wrinkle through the skimmer. Then remove them from the heat. Take a *berguera* sieve, and take out however much you want to put in. Once they're removed from the heat, take and whip a little sugar until it's white like the colour of the pears themselves. Then stir it back in and begin removing them from the round-bottom pot. Until they cool, they should not be removed from the sieve.

[472] *Membrillos para la Mermelada.*

Hase de tomar el membrillo, y ponerse a cocer en agua fría hasta que esté muy blando, y luego sacarlo del agua, y mondarlo, y cortarlo hasta el corazón, y machacarlo, o rallarlo, y para cada libra de membrillo se ha de echar libra y cuarterón de azúcar, si es para cajas, y si es para bocados libra por libra, y se ha de tomar el azúcar, y clarificarlo, y ponerlo en un punto que metiendo el dedo dentro, mojado primero en (295v) agua, y luego tornarlo a meter en agua: si se hiciere una pelotilla el azúcar,[455] echar luego la pasta del membrillo, y darle una vuelta, y deshacerlo mucho con el cucharón, y tórnallo a la lumbre, hasta que hierva, y luego echarlo fuera.

[473] *Diacitrón.*

Hase de tomar la cidra, y mondarla de la cáscara, y de los agrios, y luego salarlo, y de que haya tomado la sal echarlo en agua clara, que esté fría, hasta que cueza, y esté muy tierno, y sacarlo, y echarlo en agua clara, y tenerlo dos días, mudándole las aguas: luego echarlo en conserva en el azúcar, clarificado con sus huevos, y echarlo en las ollas, o barreñones donde hubiere de estar el diacitrón, y esté frío el azúcar, e irle sacando cada día el azúcar, e írselo cociendo: y si faltare azúcar irle añadiendo hasta que esté el azúcar espeso que se pegue en los dedos, e irle cociendo, y dejarlo en su almíbar, y para cubierto (296r) sacallo del almíbar, y ponello a escurrir en un harnero, y lavarlo con un poco de agua tibia, y tomar el propio azúcar clarificado, y ponerlo un poco más cocido que para huevos mejidos, y echarlo dentro del azúcar, que lo cubra el azúcar por encima, y cueza con el azúcar hasta que por una espumadera soplando salgan unas vejigas, y ponerlo a enfriar un poco, y luego darle un poco de lumbre, y echarlo fuera sobre unos espartos, o sobre una berguera. El almíbar siempre se ha de echar frío.

Memoria de Jaleas

[474] *Jalea de Membrillo.*

Hase de tomar el membrillo, y mondarlo, y sacarle el corazón, y hacerle pedazos, y ponerlo a cocer, y conforme el membrillo le echarás el agua que se cubra, y dé que esté bien cocido, quítalo de la lumbre, y toma (296v) un paño grueso, y cuela

---

455 Martínez Montiño is describing what happens at the soft-ball stage.

Quince for jam

Take quince, put it on to cook in cold water until it's very soft. Then remove it from the water, peel it, cut to its core, and mash it or grate it. For each pound of quince add a pound and a quarter of sugar if it's to store in boxes; if it's for bite-sized pieces, a pound for each pound. Take the sugar, clarify it, and bring it to the stage that, when inserting your finger after first dipping it in water and then putting it back in water, the sugar forms a little ball. Then add the quince paste, stir it, and mix it well with the spoon. Put it back on the heat until it boils and then take it off.

Candied citron

Take citron and peel the rind off and any bitter parts, then salt it, and, once salted, put it in clear, cold water until it boils and is very soft. Remove it, put it in clear water, and keep it there two days, changing the water. Then preserve it with sugar, clarified with the right amount of eggs, and put it into pots or tubs where the candied citron should be. The sugar [syrup] should be cold. Every day remove the sugar [syrup] and boil it. If you need sugar, add it until the sugar [syrup] is thick enough to stick between your fingers, continue boiling. Return to the simple syrup and leave it covered. Take it out of the simple syrup and let it drain in a sieve. Rinse it in a little warm water. Take the clarified sugar itself and boil it more, as if for sweet scrambled egg yolks. Add it in with the sugar [syrup]. It should cover the sugar [syrup] on top and boil with the sugar [syrup] until when you blow [it] through a skimmer you'll get little blisters. Let it cool a little and then put it back on the heat. Take it off and put it on esparto fabric or in a *berguera* fruit sieve. The simple syrup should always be added cold.

Memoir of jellies

Quince jelly

Take quince, peel it, remove the core, and chop it into pieces. Put it on to boil with the water needed to cover it. Once it's thoroughly cooked, take it off the flame, take a thick cloth, and strain the water and quince, squeezing it tightly. For each

aquella agua y membrillo, exprimiéndolo muy bien, y a cada cazo de zumo que saliere dello echar dos cazos de azúcar en un punto que haga un hilo en el dedo, y ponerlo a cocer todo junto hasta que haga otro punto, que haga otro hilo como el de arriba; luego échalo en sus vidrios.

[475] *Memoria de Jalea de Granadas.*

Has de tomar la granada, y sacar el grano, y ponerlo con muy poca cantidad de agua a cocer, no más de cuanto se cubra, y de que esté bien cocida sacar aquel zumo y agua, y exprimirlo por un cedazo de cerdas, y a dos cazos de aquel zumo, has de echar uno de azúcar clarificado, que tenga el punto como para huevos mejidos, y juntarlo, y ponerlo a cocer hasta que suba un punto que haga unas gotas, que echándolas en una (297r) tablilla, no corran a una parte, ni a otra: y estas gotas se han de echar con una espumadera, que sean las gotas como lentejas: y entonces está buena la jalea, y se puede echar en sus vidrios.

[476] *Memoria de Jalea de Amacenas.*[456]

Hase de tomar media arroba de amacenas,[457] y ocho libras de azúcar clarificado, y ponerlo a cocer con las amacenas, y echarle poco más de azumbre y media de agua, y ponerlo a hervir todo junto, y cuezan hasta que estén deshechas, y echarlas a escurrir en un paño, o un cedazo, y sacar aquel almíbar, y ponerlo a cocer que haga un punto que se pegue a los dos dedos; y entonces está buena, y se puede poner en sus vidrios.

[477] *Memoria de la Jalea de Agraz.*

(297v) Hase de tomar el agraz, y desgranarlo media arroba, o seis libras, lo que quisieres,[458] y ponerlo a cocer con la cantidad de agua que se cubra, y luego colarlo por el paño, o el cedazo, y tener azúcar clarificado, y a tres partes del zumo de agraz echar dos de azúcar clarificado, que tenga muy poco punto cuando se eche en el zumo, y ponlo a hervir hasta que haga un punto como las amacenas.

---

456 The *amacena* is another name for *damascena*, or *from Damascus*. Today the fruit is called *damson plums*. They are dark purple, oval, and have a slightly sour flavour. They are primarily used for jams and jellies.

457 *Arroba* is a unit of weight (it could also measure mass or volume) that, in Spain, was equivalent to 25 pounds. In this recipe, Martínez Montiño requires 12.5 pounds of plums.

458 See previous note. Here, Martínez Montiño suggests using 12.5 pounds of sour grapes or halving the recipes and using only six pounds. But, he is careful to give the amount of sugar proportionally to adapt to the amount of sour grapes used.

saucepan of juice that comes out, add two saucepans of sugar at the stage that makes threads between your fingers. Put it all on to boil together to the same stage, another thread stage as explained above. Then put it into its glass jars.

Memoir of pomegranate jelly

Take pomegranate, remove the seeds, and put just a little water on to boil, only enough to cover, and once it has boiled, remove the juice and water and squeeze it through a horsehair sieve. For every two saucepans of that juice, add one of clarified sugar that is at the stage for sweet scrambled egg yolks. Add the two together and put it on to boil until it reaches the stage where drops form and, when dropped on a board, they won't run off one way or the other. Drop these drops through a skimmer so that they are lentil size. At this point, the jelly is done and can be put into glass jars.

Memoir of damson plum jelly

Take about half an *arroba* of damson plums and eight pounds of clarified sugar and put it on to boil with the plums. Add a little more than three quarts of water, and put all on to boil. Boil until they're falling apart and strain them through a cloth or a sieve. Remove the simple syrup, put it on to boil so that it reaches the stage where it sticks between your fingers. Then it's done and you can put it into glass jars.

Memoir of sour grape jelly

Take sour grapes, deseed about half an *arroba*, or six pounds, whatever you like. Put them on to boil with enough water to cover them. Then strain them through a cloth or sieve. Have clarified sugar, and for three parts of verjuice, add two of clarified sugar with a minimum thread stage when it's added to the juice. Put it on to boil until it reaches that same stage as the damson plums.

[478] *Cuartos de Membrillos.*

Hanse de tomar membrillos crudos y cortarse por medio, y sacar el corazón antes que se monde, y después de mondados ponerlos a cocer poquito cuanto se caliente bien el agua, y sacarlos del agua, y ponerlos a enfriar en un perol, y tomar para cada libra de aquel membrillo otra de azúcar clarificado, y tomar aquella agua donde se cocieron, y echar tanta agua como azúcar, (298r) y antes más que menos, y ponerlo a cocer en una lumbre muy suave, que vaya rociando, y taparlos cuando van a medio cocer con una tabla, y cocerlos hasta que haga un punto espeso, y luego quitarlos de la lumbre.

[479] *Carne de Membrillos delicada.*

Hase de tomar el membrillo el mejor que hubiere, y ponerlo a cocer en agua fría, y cocerlo muy bien, hasta que esté muy blando: y después de cocido tomar y mondarlo, y cortarlo de manera que no se llegue al corazón, y machacarlo, y pasarlo por un cedazo muy espeso de cerdas: y a cada libra de membrillo que se pasare una libra y un cuarterón de azúcar clarificado con huevos, y colado por un paño, y luego ponerlo a cocer hasta que haga unos ojos grandes el azúcar: y de que haya hecho estos ojos, sacarlo de la lumbre, y menearlo con un remo de manjar blanco, o con (298v) un cucharón de palo, y de que esté un poco meneado echar el azúcar fuera de la lumbre, y echarle el membrillo, y ponerlo a cocer todo junto en la lumbre, hasta que cueza, y esté un poquito espeso: y estando espeso sacarle fuera del perol: y con eso esté acabado de hacer.

[480] *Ciruelas de Génova.*

Tomarás las ciruelas, y pasarlas has por agua caliente, y sacarlas has luego al punto, y ponellas a escurrir, y de que estén escurridas, ponellas en unos barreñoncillos pequeños vidriados, y moler azúcar, e ir polvoreando cada lecho de ciruelas que fueren echando, y echarán deste azúcar, y dejarle estar hasta otro día que se escurra aquella aguaza: y luego tomar azúcar clarificado, y cocerlo que tenga gran punto.[459]

---

459 Although not written in this recipe, based on how he perserves fruit in earlier recipes, like "Albérchigos" [Apricots] and "Duraznos" [Clingstone peaches] (562; 563), the probable finish to the recipe is to take the sugary juice and bring it to a boil, cool it, and return it to the plums. Then, make this additional simple syrup, and once cooled, add as much is necessary to the plums, each day over the course of a week.

Quartered quince

Take raw quince and cut them in half. Remove the core before peeling them. Once peeled, put them on to cook briefly, as long as it takes to heat the water. Remove them from the water and put them in a round-bottom pot to cool. For each pound of that quince, take another of clarified sugar, and from the water in which it was cooked, take as much water as sugar, maybe a little more than less. Put it on low heat to simmer, and when they are half cooked, cover them with a board. Boil until they thicken and then take them off the heat.

Delicate quince paste

Take the best quince possible and put it on to boil in cold water. Boil it a lot until it's very soft. After it's boiled, take it, peel it, cut it up, all but the core, and mash it. Strain it through a very fine horsehair sieve. For each pound of quince that is strained, [add] a pound and a quarter of sugar clarified with eggs and strained through a cloth. Then, put it on to boil until the sugar forms big eyes. Once it forms eyes, remove it from the heat, stir it with a blancmange paddle or with a wooden spoon. Once it's stirred a bit, take the sugar off the heat, add in the quince, and put it on to cook near the heat until it boils and is a little thick. Once it thickens, take it out of the round-bottom pot and it is finished being made.

Genoese plums

Take plums and dunk them in hot water. Remove when tender and drain them. Once they're drained, put them in small glazed tubs. Grind sugar and begin sprinkling each layer of plums as you layer them. They will exude juice. Let it rest another day while the juices drain. Then, take clarified sugar and boil it until it reaches a high thread stage.

[481] *Nueces en conserva.*

Tomarás las nueces, cuando están tiernas, (299r) que no estén cuajadas, que será quince días antes de San Juan,[460] poco más, o menos, conforme la tierra donde están los nogales, y punzarlas has con un punzón dos, o tres veces: luego échalas en agua por nueve días, mudándoles el agua cada día: luego harás una lexía fuerte con ceniza, y déjala asentar, y cuélala por un cedazo, y echa las nueces dentro, y dales dos hervores, y luego sácalas en un poco de agua tibia, y déjala estar allí un poco, y échalas en agua fría: luego sácalas, y ponlas en unas alorzas,[461] o barreños, y harás el azúcar que te pareciere en almíbar, de manera que las cubra, y échaselo tibio: luego déjalas hasta otro día, y tórnalo a cocer, y tórnaselo a echar tibio, y déjalo estar hasta otro día: luego echa las nueces y almíbar todo junto en el cazo, o perol, y ponlas a cocer, acábalas de conservar: luego déjalas enfriar un poco, y sácalas en sus ollas, y sazona de especias, clavo, y canela, a cada cien nueces una onza (299v) de cada cosa.

Y si las quisieres hacer con miel a cada cien nueces se ha de echar una azumbre de miel, y otra de agua: hase de cocer y espumar: y de que las nueces estén cocidas y tiernas, échese en la miel, y consérvense, y a cada azumbre de miel se le ha de echar una onza de canela y otra de clavo, y cuando se quisieren sacar de la lumbre se les ha de echar un poco desta especia, que den un par de hervores son ella: y después de quitadas de la lumbre se les ha de echar la demás especia, dejando un poco para ir echando en lechos cuando se van echando en la olla: y esta sazón se entiende también con las de azúcar. Y adviértese, que si las nueces fuesen muy chicas, que se podrían echar ciento y cincuenta nueces a cada azumbre de miel.

[482] *Hinojo conservado.*[462]

Se han de tomar las cogollas del hinojo dulce, que estén bien granadas, (300r) y verdes, y cogerlas con su pezón, algo largas: y luego atarlas, que estén muy recogidas, porque no hagan mucho bulto, y tomarás azúcar clarificado en almíbar muy subido de punto, y pon las dichas cogollas de hinojo dentro, y allí se estén todo el tiempo que quisieres, porque se irá esponjando, y cociendo en el propio almíbar: y cuando lo quisieres servir a la mesa saca una, o dos cogollas, o lo que quisieres, y tendrás azúcar molido y cernido, con ámbar, o almizcle, y échaselo por encima a

---

460 St John's Day is 24 June and celebrates the birthday of John the Baptist.
461 Today *alorza* or *alhorza* refers to a pleat in a cloth, but an *orza* is a *glazed terracotta jar with no handles*. It was typically used to store preserved foodstuffs.
462 Society for Creative Anachronism member Jen Small recreated this sweet dish for the Society for Creative Anachronism banquet "A Culinary Tour through the History of Spain" at the "Twelfth Night" event in Schaumberg, IL, January 2020. An image can be found in Appendix 3.22.

Preserved walnuts

Take walnuts that are tender and not fully ripe; it should be about two weeks before Saint John's day, more or less, depending on the region where the walnut trees are. Puncture them two or three times with an awl. Then soak them in water for nine days, changing the water every day. Then make strong alkaline water with ashes, let it rest, and strain it through a sieve. Add the walnuts to it and bring it to a boil twice. Then remove them to warm water, let them rest a while, and then put them in cold water. Next, remove them, put them in some glazed terracotta jars or tubs. Make syrup with the amount of sugar you need to cover them, and pour it on warm. Let them rest another day, boil them again, put them in warm water again, and let them rest another day. Then put the walnuts and simple syrup together in a pot or a round-bottom pot and put them on to boil. This will finish preserving them. Let them cool a little, remove them to their pots, and season with spices, clove and cinnamon; for each one hundred walnuts, an ounce of each.

If you want to use honey, for every one hundred walnuts add two quarts of honey and one of water. Boil and skim. Once the walnuts are boiled and tender, add the honey and preserve them. For every two quarts of honey, add an ounce of cinnamon and another of clove. When you want to take them off the heat, add a little of these spices and bring it to a boil a couple of times. Once removed from the heat, add the rest of the spices, leaving a little to sprinkle between layers when you put them in the pot. This seasoning should also be used for the ones made with sugar. Note that if the walnuts are very small, use one hundred and fifty walnuts for every two quarts of honey.

Preserved fennel

Take the hearts of sweet fennel that are green and ripe. Keep the longish stem on. Next, tie them up and make sure they are bunched tight so that they are not bulky. Take clarified sugar made into simple syrup at a high stage. Put said fennel hearts in and leave them as long as you like, because they will begin absorbing and cooking in the simple syrup itself. When you are ready to serve at the table, remove one or two hearts, or as many as you like. Have some sifted, ground sugar with ambergris or musk, and sprinkle it on top of the hearts that you're going to

las cogollas que hubieres de servir, y con la humedad que tienen tomarán el azúcar, y quedarán blancas, y sírvelas por plato de postre, y comerán el hinojo, y servirán los palillos para mondar los dientes.[463]

[483] *Carbonadillas de Ternera estofadas.*

Tomarás tres libras de ternera de pierna, y cortarla has en carbonadillas (300v) muy delgadas, al través de la hebra, y batirlas has con la vuelta del cuchillo: luego picarás media libra de tocino gordo con un poco de verdura muy picada, y untarás el plato con él, o una cazuela de barro, y asentarás un lecho de las carbonadillas, y échale un poco de especia, y un poco de tocino por encima de todas ellas, y un poco de sal: luego echa otro lecho de carbonadillas, y un poco del tocino picado con la verdura, y tornar a sazonar con especias y sal, y desta manera gastarás todas las carbonadillas, y tocino: luego pon el plato, o cazuela, sobre una palada de lumbre, y tápalo con otro plato, y déjalo estofar por cosa de media hora: luego destapa el plato, y hallarás las carbonadillas todas pegadas unas a otras; vuélvelas así juntas como están, y torna a tapar el plato, y tórnalo a poner sobre lumbre por otra media hora, y tórnalo a sacar de la lumbre, y despégalas unas de otras todas, y échales un poco de caldo (301r) de la olla cuanto se bañen, y déjalas cocer poco a poco por espacio de otra media hora, y hallarlas has cocidas, y échales un poco de azafrán y zumo de limón: y si fuere tiempo de agraz podrás echarle algunos granos de agraz un cuarto de hora antes que se saquen, y sírvelas sobre rebanadillas de pan. Este platillo no ha de llevar huevo ninguno, ni verdura, más de lo que se picó con el tocino, que será perejil, y cilantro, y hierbabuena: y si no hubiere plato se podrán estofar en una cazuela, y taparlo con un plato de barro al estofar.

[484] *Un platillo de Cabrito.*

Cortarás el cabrito en pedacitos, y ahogarlo has con tocino y cebolla, y échalo en una olla, y échale caldo, o agua caliente cuanto se cubra: luego sazona de especias, pimienta, y nuez, y un poco de jengibre, y sal, y un poco de verdura picada, y tendrás seis yemas de huevos (301v) cocidos duras, y un migajoncillo de pan todo remojado en caldo: luego májalo, y desátalo con el caldo del platillo, y pásalo por un cedacillo, y cuajarás el platillo con esta salsa, y échale acedo que esté un poquito agrio. El cabrito han de ser dos cuartos delanteros para un plato: sírvelos sobre rebanadillas de pan. Este platillo se hace de carnero, y de pajarillos, y de pecho de ternera, y de muchas cosas.

---

463 Given the fibrous nature of fennel, Martínez Montiño acknowledges its use as a toothpick after eating this dish. In the anonymous picaresque novel *Lazarillo de Tormes*, the character of the hidalgo uses a toothpick to feign his long-lost prestigious social position. For more on the history of the toothpick, see Petroski.

serve. With their moistness, they will absorb the sugar and will be white. Serve as a dessert dish. They will eat the fennel and the thin stalks can serve to clean their teeth.

Thinly sliced veal, stewed

Take three pounds of leg of veal and cut it against the grain into thin slices as if for grilling. Pound it with the back of the knife. Next mince half a pound of extra fatty fatback with a little bit of green herbs. Spread this on the plate or in a terracotta casserole and set a layer of the thinly sliced meat. Sprinkle with spices, dab a little fatback on top of all of them, and sprinkle with salt. Then add on another layer of thinly sliced meat, a little minced fatback with herbs, and season again with spices and salt. Continue this way until all the meat and fatback are used. Next put the platter or a casserole on a shovelful of heat [hot coals] and cover it with another plate. Let it cook for about half an hour, then uncover it and you'll see that all the slices of thinly sliced meat have stuck to one another. Flip them over all as one and cover with the plate again. Return to the heat for another half hour and take it off the heat again. Separate each piece from the other, add enough stock from the pot to braise, and let it simmer for a period of another half hour. They will be done. Sprinkle a little saffron and lemon juice. If sour grapes are in season, add some sour grapes about a quarter of an hour before it's done. Serve over slices of bread. This dish has no eggs or green herbs, just what was added to the fatback, which was parsley, cilantro, and spearmint. If no plate is available, you can stew these in a casserole and cover it with a terracotta plate when stewing.

A kid dish

Chop the kid into pieces and sauté it with fatback and onion. Put it in a pot and add enough broth or hot water to braise. Then season with spices – pepper, nutmeg, and a little ginger – and salt, and a little bit of chopped green herbs. Have six hard-boiled egg yolks and the inside of bread soaked in broth. Mash it, thin it with the broth from the dish, and strain it through a strainer. Thicken the dish with this sauce and add sorrel juice that is a little sour. The kid should consist of two front legs quartered for each plate. Serve over slices of bread. This dish can be made with mutton, small birds, breast of veal, and many other things.

[485] *Manjar blanco de Pescado.*

Tomarás una pescada cecial remojada,[464] y cortarle has los lomos, y échalos a cocer en harta agua: y cuando esté cocido sácalo, y límpialo de las escamas y el pellejo, y de todo lo que tuviere que no sea blanco, y de las espinas, y luego deshazlo muy bien con los dedos, y echa este pescado en una servilleta, y vele echando agua fría, y estregándolo con una mano dentro la servilleta, y (302r) deshaciendo todo el pescado, de manera que no quede nada entero, sino como una felpa: luego tomarás tanta cantidad deste pescado, como si fuera una buena pechuga de gallina deshilada, y un poco más, y échalo en un cazo, y échale un poquito de leche, y bátelo con el cucharón de manjar blanco, de manera que no quede ningún burujón: luego échale una libra de harina de arroz, y vele echando leche poco a poco, y revolviéndolo con el cucharón hasta cantidad de un azumbre y cuartillo, y échale una libra de azúcar, y ponlo a cocer sobre las trébedes, y velo revolviendo a una mano con el cucharón de manjar blanco. Tardará en cocerse tres cuartos de hora. Deste manjar blanco podrás hacer todas las cosas que estén escritas en el manjar blanco de carne: y con las mismas cantidades podrás hacer papín de arroz, y apellarlo en pellas como el manjar blanco: y si lo quisieres servir blando, con echarle un cuartillo más de leche, (302v) y cuatro huevos, y sazonarlo de sal, saldrá muy bueno. Y advierte, que este manjar blanco de pescado lo podrás hacer de las colas de las langostas, y de ranas: y también se puede hacer de puerros blancos, aunque no es tan bueno. Puédese hacer con leche de almendras, sacando tres cuartillos de leche de cada libra de almendras.

[486] *Papín de harina de Trigo.*[465]

Tomarás tres cuarterones de harina floreada de trigo, y una libra de azúcar molido todo junto en un cazo: luego échale medio cuartillo la leche, y desata la harina, y el azúcar, de manera que no tenga burujón ninguno, y esté el batido como puches: luego batirás seis huevos con claras, o doce yemas muy bien batidas, y échalas con la harina, y bátelo muy bien: luego ve echando leche hasta una azumbre y un cuartillo antes más que menos, que sea cerca de azumbre y media, y sazónalo de

---

464 Today, *pescada* (*Merluccius gayi* or *Merluccius merluccius*) [hake] are two members of the hake family (*Merlucciidae*). The former is fished off the coast of Chile while the latter is fished off the coasts of Europe and North Africa. Taking into account these differences, I assume that Martínez Montiño is referring to the latter.

465 This recipe is a pastry cream, like today's *crème anglaise*, that is still used to fill *buñuelos* and all sorts of pastries. Today corn starch often replaces flour and gives the cream a glossier look. Historians often credit François Massialot's "Crême pâtissiere" from his 1691 cookbook *Le cuisinier roïal et bourgeois* [The royal and bourgeois cook] as being the first recipe, but Martínez Montiño's predates that recipe by eighty years.

Fish blancmange

Take salted hake that's been soaking, cut the loins, put them on to boil in a lot of water. When it's done, remove it, scale and skin the fish and take off everything that isn't white and remove the bones. Then shred it with your fingers and put this fish into a napkin and begin adding cold water. Rub it with one hand inside the napkin. The whole fish should be broken up so that no whole pieces are left and it looks like plushy fabric. Then take some of this fish, like the amount of a shredded hen breast and a little more, and put it into a pan. Add a little milk and mix it with a blancmange spoon so that no bubbles remain. Then add a pound of rice flour and continue adding milk little by little. Stir with a spoon until you have two quarts and one pint. Add a pound of sugar and put it on a trivet to cook, constantly stirring with the blancmange spoon using one hand. It should take about three quarters of an hour to cook. With this blancmange, you can do all the things mentioned in the meat blancmange [recipe]. With these same amounts you can make a sweet cream from rice and shape it into balls as with blancmange. If you want to serve it soft, add one more pint of milk, four eggs, and season with salt. It will turn out very tasty. Note that this fish blancmange can also be made with lobster tails or from frogs. You can also make it with white leeks, but it would not be as tasty. You can use almond milk, getting three pints from each pound of almonds.

Sweet cream sauce made with wheat flour

Put three quarters of a pound of finely sifted wheat flour and a pound of ground sugar all together in a pan. Then, add a half pint of milk and thin the flour and sugar so that there aren't any lumps and the batter is like porridge. Then whip six eggs with their whites or twelve egg yolks and add them to the flour and thoroughly beat together. Then begin adding milk, up to two quarts and one pint, better more than less; it can be up to three quarts. Season with salt. If you have

sal: y (303r) si tuvieres una poca de buena manteca fresca de vacas échasela dentro, y si la manteca no fuere muy buena, no eches ninguna, y ponlo a cocer sobre las trébedes, y velo andando a una mano con un cucharón de manjar blanco, porque no se pegue, ni se ahúme: y en dando dos o tres hervores sácalo, e hinche los platos, y sírvelo caliente con unas hojuelas muy pequeñitas hinchadas en el papín, o unas rebanadas de pan blanco, cortadas en dados menudos, y fritos en manteca de vacas, y échalos por encima del papín.

[487] *Pastelón de Cidra verde.*

Majarás media libra de almendras dulces muy bien majadas, y échale seis onzas de azúcar, y harás pasta de mazapán, que esté muy bien majada, y ponla sobre el tablero, y mézclale un poco de harina, y desta pasta levantarás un vaso de un pastelón, y déjalo hecho desde la noche para la mañana: luego (303v) tendrás cidra rallada, y conservada como está dicho en la torta de cidra rallada,[466] y la misma cantidad de la torta antes más que menos, y tendrás diez y ocho huevos hilados, y revolverás los huevos, y la cidra, y trozos de cañas de vaca todo revuelto, y de todo esto henchirás el pastelón, y ha de estar todo frío: luego tendrás el horno bien caliente, y asienta el pastelón sobre la hoja del horno sobre dos, o tres obleas, y échale un poco de alcorza molido por encima,[467] y métele en el horno, y déjalo estar por un cuarto de hora sin descubrir el horno, y hallarás el vaso muy tieso, y cocerá lo que está dentro con la grasa de las cañas. Para este pastel son menester dos libras de azúcar, una para conservar la cidra, seis onzas para el vaso, diez onzas para los huevos hilados, y diez y ocho huevos.

[488] *Una cazolilla de ave para enfermo.*

(304r) Descarnarás la carne de una buena pechuga de ave, o de capón, y picarla has sobre un tablero blanco, de manera que salga muy blanca la carne, y picarás con ella una enjundia del ave recién muerta, o un poquito de tocino: y en estando picada echarle has cuatro yemas de huevos, o dos con claras, y sazona con un poquito de pimienta y una migaja de nuez, y un poco de cilantro seco molido: luego desata esta carne en una cazolilla de barro, o plata, con buen caldo de la olla muy bien desatada, de manera que esté bien rala, y pon la cazolilla sobre unas brasas, y vela revolviendo con una cuchara hasta que cueza, y no le dejes hacer burujón ninguno, y se vendrá a hacer un pastel embote muy blanco, y tendrás

---

466 Martínez Montiño is referring to la receta "Una torta de cidra verde" [A green citron pie] on 244–6; 245–7.

467 *Alcorza* is a sugar-starch mixture used as a hard sugar coating; for example, the outside of a Jordan almond, or a hard-coated sweet in its own right. Quevedo references the latter in his novel *El buscón* in the scene at the inn on the way to Alcalá when local pranksters replace a traveller's *alcorzas* with pebbles (138).

some good, fresh butter, add it, but if the butter isn't that good, don't add any. Put it on a trivet to cook and begin stirring it with one hand with a blancmange spoon so that it doesn't stick or get scorched. Once it's boiled two or three times, remove it and fill the plates. Serve hot with little pastry sheets sticking in the sweet cream sauce or slices of white bread chopped into small cubes and fried in butter. Sprinkle them on top of the sweet cream.

Big green citron pie

Thoroughly grind up half a pound of sweet almonds and add six ounces of sugar. Make a marzipan paste that is well mashed. Put it on a pastry board and mix in a little flour and with this paste build up a big pie crust. Let it sit overnight. Then, have some preserved grated citron, which is explained in the grated citron pie [recipe], the same amount as that pie, or even a little more. Have eighteen [eggs' worth of] candied egg yolk threads and stir them into the citron with pieces of beef bone marrow all mixed in. Fill the pie with all this. It should all be cold. Then have the oven well heated and set the pie on a baking sheet on two or three wafers. Sprinkle a little ground-up candy coating and place it in the oven. Let it rest a quarter of an hour before putting it in the oven. The crust should be firm. The filling will bake with the fat from the marrow. For this pie two pounds of sugar are necessary, one for preserving the citron, six ounces for the crust, and ten ounces for the candied egg yolk threads from eighteen eggs.

Poultry in a saucepan for the sick

Separate the meat from a breast of poultry or capon and chop it over a white cutting board so that the meat stays white. Mince a little of the fatty tissue from around the recently slaughtered bird's ovaries or a little fatback. Once it's minced, add four egg yolks or two with the whites and season with a little pepper, a pinch of nutmeg, and a little ground coriander. Then, in either a small terracotta casserole or silver saucepan, thin this meat with a lot of good stock from the pot so that it is very liquidy. Put the saucepan over red-hot coals and begin stirring with a spoon until it comes to a boil. Don't let it have any lumps and a very white, crustless pie will turn out. Have boiled chicken crests and

crestas de pollos cocidas, y las turmillas de los pollos, y echarlo has en la cazolilla, y cuezan dos hervores, y cuájalo con dos yemas de huevos, y zumo de limón, y ponle unas rebanadillas de pan muy chiquitas, como (304v) una uña de un dedo, todo alrededor de la cazolilla, y sírvela en la misma cazuela: y si la quisieres echar un par de alones de pollos bien cocidos blancos, en lugar de las crestillas, podrás: y si la quisieres alguna vez hacer agridulce, con echarle un poquito de azúcar molido al cuajar, y añadir un poco de más agrio tiene muy buen gusto: y si lleva dulce, le has de echar un poquito de canela: y si quisieres servir este pastel embote en un platillo, podrás, con sus rebanadillas de pan, y algunas mollejitas de cabrito asadas encima: y si fuere para sanos, con añadirle un poco de más especias, y echar otra pechuga de ave, es muy buen platillo en cazuela, o en plato.

Y advierte, que lo que tengo dicho que se puede hacer de ave, se puede hacer también de ternera, con ponerlo con carbonadillas de ternera, asadas, y mechadas: y si fuere para sanos echarle sus cañas de vaca, y sus yemas de huevos duras.

Mas advierte, que cuando tengas (305r) la carne picada cruda, y sazonada de especias, sal, y huevos, que podrás untar una tortera, o cazuela, con un poquito de manteca, y hacer en ella unas rosquillas de aquella carne con sus trocitos de cañas por encima, o una rosca grande, y poner la tortera sobre un poco de lumbre, y cubrirla con una cobertera, y ponerle otro poco de lumbre encima, y se cocerán en un cuarto de hora, y sírvela sobre una sopilla dorada, o sobre una sopilla de lechugas. Y si quisieres mezclar un poco de pasta de mazapán con esta carne de las rosquillas, podrás; mas hasle de echar media docena de yemas de huevos duras majadas: y de todo esto hacer las rosquillas, o rosca grande. Todo esto se puede hacer de carnero de pierna.

[489] *Palominos armados.*

Picarás carne de dos libras de ternera, o de cabrito, con media libra de tocino gordo, y de que esté bien picada, (305v) métele cuatro huevos, y sazona con todas especias, y sal, y un poco de zumo de limón, o una gota de vinagre. Tomarás los pescuezos de cuatro palominos con sus picos, y harás de la carne picada cuatro palominos contrahechos, poniendo los pies y pescuezos, y unas yemas de huevos duros en cuartos por encima, y algunos trocitos de cañas: luego de la carne que te sobrare rellenarás cuatro lechugas, o escarolas, y pondráslo luego todo en una tortera untada con manteca, y ponlo con fuego abajo y arriba, y tendrás los palominos cocidos y salpimentados con pimienta, y sal, y pan rallado, y ponlos en otra tortera con lumbre abajo y arriba, y tostarse ha el pan: luego pondrás unas rebanadas de pan en un plato, y con palominos armados, y palominos salpimentados y lechugas, o escarolas rellenas armarás tu plato: y otras veces sin palominos, sino con la ternera, y lechugas rellenas, y una buena cola de carnero tostada con pan (306r) rallado, y algunas carbonadillas podrás armar el plato, y echarle zumo de limón, o de naranjas por encima. Con la carne de las lechugas podrás hacer rellenos con redaño de carnero.

testicles and add them to the saucepan. Bring to a boil twice and thicken with two egg yolks and lemon juice. Sprinkle little pieces of bread about the size of a fingernail around the saucepan. Serve in this same casserole. If you want to add a couple of white, boiled chicken wings instead of the crests, you can. And if sometime you want to make it sweet and sour, add a little ground sugar when thickening and add a little more sour juice. It will turn out very tasty. If it does have sweetener, add a little cinnamon. If you want to serve this crustless pie as an individual dish, you can, garnished with slices of bread and some roasted kid sweetbreads on top. If it's for the healthy, you can add a little more spice and another breast of poultry, and it will be a very tasty dish served either in the casserole or on a plate.

Note that what I have explained for poultry can also be made with veal using slices of veal that have been larded and grilled. If it's for the healthy, add beef bone marrow and hard-boiled egg yolks.

Also note that when you have the raw meat minced and seasoned with spices, salt, and eggs, grease a covered tart pan or a casserole with a little lard and make small rings with that meat with pieces of bone marrow dabbed on top or one large ring. Put the covered tart pan on low flame, cover it with a lid, and put some heat on top. Let it cook for a quarter of an hour and serve over golden sops or lettuce sops. If you want to mix a little marzipan paste into the meat for the ring, you can. But also add a half dozen mashed hard-boiled egg yolks and with this make the little rings or the big one. You can also make this with leg of mutton.

Dressed squab

Mince two pounds of veal or kid with half a pound of extra fatty fatback. Once it is well minced, add four eggs, season with all spices, salt, a little lemon juice, and a drop of vinegar. Take the necks of four squab with their beaks and with the minced meat make four faux squab by putting on the head and feet and some hard-boiled egg yolks quartered on top and some bits of bone marrow. With the leftover meat stuff four [pieces of] lettuce or escarole and put everything in a covered tart pan greased with lard. Put fire above and below. Sprinkle the boiled squab with salt and pepper and breadcrumbs. Put them in another covered tart pan with heat above and below and toast the bread. Then put slices of bread on a plate and with the dressed squab, the salt and peppered squab, and the stuffed lettuce or escarole, arrange the platter. Other times you can assemble the plate without squab and just have veal, stuffed lettuce, a good mutton tail toasted with breadcrumbs, and some sliced, grilled meat. Sprinkle lemon or orange juice on top. You can wrap the meat filling for the lettuce with mutton caul fat.

[490] *Platillo de asadurillas de Cabrito.*[468]

Tomarás cuatro asadurillas de cabrito, y perdigarlas has en agua cociendo: luego mecharás los hígados muy menudos, o los rebozarás con un redaño, y los espetarás en un asador, y echar a cocer los livianos con agua, y sal: y después de cocidos pícalos sobre el tablero muy bien con buen tocino gordo, y un poco de redaño, y sazonarás de sal y especias, y echarle has cuatro huevos crudos, y un poquito de agrio: y tomarás un redaño, e irás haciendo unos rellenos, envolviendo un poco de relleno en un poco de redaño, y asentándolos en una tortera, y pon lumbre abajo y arriba, y cuézanse hasta que estén dorados, (306v) y sírvelos sobre una sopa con los hígados asados entre ellos. Advierte, que cuando tuviste estos livianos sazonados de especias, sal, y huevos, y acedo, podrías hacer dellos unos pastelillos de escudilla, añadiéndole un par de huevos más, y un poco de azúcar y canela. Estos se hacen cortando unos trocitos de un rollo de hojaldrado, y hacer unas como cubiertas de pastelillos, y ponerlos dentro en las escudillas, e irlos subiendo con el dedo pulgar, e igualarlos con los bordes de las escudillitas: luego henchirlos de los livianos, y ponerle media yema de huevo encima de cada uno, y cuézanse así descubiertos: y si los quisieres cubrir con una cubierta de hojaldrado, podrás: y al servir ráspales por encima azúcar, y un poco de canela: y si los quisieres hacer en pastelillos de masa dulce, como los de las cabezas de carnero, podrás, y son muy buenos: y si quisieres hacer destos livianos pastel embote, cuando los acabas de picar, (307r) freirás un poco de cebolla muy menuda con manteca de puerco, y echarás allí los livianos, y ahogarlos has, y échalo todo en una cazuela, y échales agua caliente cuanto se bañen, y sazona de todas especias, y sal, y cueza un poco: luego cuájala con cuatro huevos, y un poco de agrio. Y advierte, que cuando tuviste los livianos aderezados para pastel embote, pudiéraslos echar en una cazuela ancha de suelo, y echarle su cebolla frita, y un poco de dulce de azúcar, o miel, y sazonarás de todas especias, y canela: y luego batir seis huevos con claras, y echarlos dentro, y darles una vuelta que se mezclen, y poner la tortera al fuego, con lumbre abajo y arriba, y cuajarse ha. Luego cortarla has como torrijas, y sírvelas con azúcar y canela, y zumo de naranja. Y advierte, que todo lo que se ha dicho de los livianos de cabrito, mucho mejor se puede hacer con livianos de ternera, o carnero, con sus hígados asados y mechados.

[491] *Cómo se aderezan los hígados de Venado, y de Ternera.*

Los Hígados de venado, y de ternera, son muy buenos, perdigados en agua cociendo, no más de cuanto pasen por ella: luego cortarlos en unas rebanadillas grandes,

---

468 Although *asadurillas* commonly refers to the pluck, the upper organs of the heart, lungs, and liver, in this recipe Martínez Montiño only uses the lungs and liver.

A dish of kid liver and lung

Take four sets of kid liver and lung and parboil them in boiling water. Then, lard the livers a lot or coat them with the caul fat and skewer them on a spit. Put the lungs on to boil in salted water, and after they're done, mince them on a cutting board with good extra fatty fatback, and a little caul fat. Season with salt and spices, and add four raw eggs and a little sour juice. Take one whole piece of caul fat and begin making stuffed caul fat by wrapping a little of the filling in a little caul fat. Place them in a covered tart pan and heat them above and below. Cook until golden and serve over sops with the grilled liver between them. Note that when the lung is seasoned with spices, salt, eggs, and sorrel juice, you can make little pies in a bowl by adding a couple more eggs and some sugar and cinnamon. These are made by cutting a sheet of puff pastry dough into small sections and making some as tops for little pies. Put them into bowls and, with your thumb, begin raising the edges and evening them out on the tops of the bowls. Then fill them with the lung mixture and put half an egg yolk on top of each one. Bake as is, uncovered. If you want to cover them with puff pastry dough, you can. When serving, grate some sugar and a little cinnamon on top. If you want to make the pies with sweet dough, like the ones for mutton head, you can. They are very tasty. And if you want to make crustless pies from this lung mixture, when you've finished mincing, fry a little minced onion with lard. Add the lung mixture to it and sauté it. Put it all into a casserole, add enough hot water to braise, season with all spices and salt, and let simmer. Then thicken it with four eggs and a little sour juice. Note that when the lung is prepared for crustless pie, you can put it in a wide-bottomed casserole and add the right amount of fried onion with a little sweetener of sugar or honey and season with all spices and cinnamon. Then, beat six eggs with their whites and add them. Stir it around to mix and put the covered tart pan on the fire with heat above and below. Let it set. Then, cut it like *torrijas* and serve with cinnamon and sugar and some orange juice. Note that all that I've explained for kid liver and lung can be done even better with liver and lung from veal or mutton, with the liver larded and grilled.

How to prepare venison or veal liver

Venison or veal livers are very tasty quickly parboiled in boiling water, just dipped in the water. Then cut big, very thin slices. Put some lard in a frying pan and get

y muy delgadas, y tomar un poco de manteca en una sartén, y calentarla mucho, y echar allí las rebanadas del hígado, que no se fría más de cuanto esté la sangre muerta, y sácala, y échale sal y pimienta, y zumo de naranja. Desta manera están tiernos y sabrosos, porque si el hígado se fríe mucho, o se cuece, se pone duro.

[492] *Manecillas de Cabrito.*

Las manecillas de cabrito, has de limpiar muy bien, y echarlas a cocer con una cebolla entera, y un poco de tocino: y cuando estén cocidas pica el tocino y cebolla con verdura, perejil, y (308r) hierbabuena, y cilantro verde, y quita del caldo de las manecillas, que no quede más de cuanto se cubran: luego echa el tocino y verdura, y sazona de todas especias y sal, y cuajarlas has con yemas de huevos, y acedo, apartando primero de la flor,[469] y échasela por encima después de servidas en el plato. Estas manecillas podrás hacer en pastel, cociéndolas; y luego sacarle los huesos de las canillas, y picar un poco de tocino con verdura, y sazonar las manecillas de especias y sal, y luego poner un poco de tocino, y verdura en el suelo del pastel, y poner las manecillas, y poner encima de todo otro poco de tocino y verdura, y cierra tu pastel: y de que esté cocido bate cuatro yemas de huevos con un poco de vinagre, y caldo de las mismas manecillas, y cébalo. Y si quisieres hacer este pastel con salsa negra, has de cocer las manecillas, y rebozarlas, y hacer tu pastel, y el tocino no ha de llevar verdura: y cuando esté cocido tendrás (308v) hecha una salsa negra como la de los pastelones de jabalí, e hinche el pastel desta salsa, y si no hínchelo de una pebrada, que por estar atrás dicho como se ha de hacer, no lo digo aquí.[470] Adonde se trata de los gigotes de grullas lo hallarás, y en otras partes. Estas manecillas se pueden cocer, y luego salpimentarlas con pimienta y pan rallado, y azúcar, y canela, y tostadas en una tortera, y servidas sobre una sopa dulce, adornadas con algunos higadillos de gallina son muy buenas. Puédense hacer estos pasteles de pies de puerco, y de ternera, rebozadas y fritas, y hacer los pasteles.

[493] *Potaje de Trigo.*

Tomarás un cuartillo de trigo limpio, que no tenga otras semillas, y rociarlo has con agua muy bien rociado, de manera que se humedezca bien la cáscara: luego échalo en el almirez y velo majando poco a poco, y se irá descascando (309r) hasta que tenga quitada toda la casca: luego sácalo y aviéntalo de las cascas, y quedará todo el trigo sin casca y entero: luego échalo a cocer con agua y sal, y buena manteca de

---

469 For more on the flor, see 65.
470 Instructions for making *salsa negra* [black sauce] are found in "Empanadas frías de jabalí" [Cold boar empanadas] and "Empanadas de jabalí calientes" [Warm boar empanadas] (290–2; 291–3), and for making *pebrada* sauce in "Gigote de Liebres" [Minced hare] (154; 155, 212; 213).

it very hot. Put the slices of liver in and fry only enough for the blood to congeal. Remove it and sprinkle with salt and pepper and drizzle some orange juice. This way they turn out tender and flavourful, because if liver is fried or boiled too long, it gets tough.

Kid trotters

You need to wash kid trotters very well and put them on to boil with a whole onion and a little fatback. When they have boiled, mince the fatback and onion with herbs – parsley, spearmint, and cilantro – [and] remove stock from the trotters so that there remains only enough to cover them. Then add the fatback and herbs, season with all spices and salt, and thicken with egg yolks and sorrel juice. First, remove the flor to put on top after it's served up on the plate. These trotters can be made into a pie by boiling them and then removing the shinbone. Mince a little fatback and herbs and season the trotters with spices and salt. Then put a little fatback and herbs on the bottom of the pie, put the trotters in, and put on top of everything a little more fatback and herbs. Close up the pie. Once it's baked, beat four egg yolks with a little vinegar and stock from the same trotters, and enrich it. If you want to make this pie with black sauce, boil the trotters, coat them, and make your pie. The fatback should not have any herbs. When it's baked, you'll have black sauce like the one for boar pies, and [you can] fill the pie with this sauce or, if not, fill it with a pepper sauce. Since it's previously explained, I won't explain it here. You'll find it where minced crane meat is explained and elsewhere. These trotters can be boiled and then seasoned with pepper and breadcrumbs, sugar, and cinnamon, and toasted in a covered tart pan. They are very tasty served over sweet sops and garnished with some hen livers. You can also make these pies with pigs' feet or calves' feet, coated and fried, and made into a pie.

Wheat porridge

Take four cups of clean wheat without any other seeds and sprinkle it well with water so that the hull is moist. Then put it in the mortar and slowly begin grinding it so the hull begins to fall off, until all of it has been removed. Then take it out and winnow it so that the whole wheat is left without the hull. Next, put it on to boil in salted water with good, fresh butter and spices. [Use] a lot

vacas fresca y sus especias: la manteca ha de ser buena y mucha para que se empape bien el trigo. Si le quisieres echar dulce de azúcar bien podrás, añadiéndole canela: y si lo quisieres echar leche como al arroz podrás; mas la manteca siempre la ha de llevar. Desta manera se adereza el farro gordo, y la sémola, salvo, que no se ha de descascarar, porque ello está ya aderezado.

[494] *Colas de Carnero con agraz.*

Tomarás un par de colas de carnero, y perdigarlas has en las parrillas, de manera que estén medio asadas: luego échalas a cocer con agua y sal, y tocino gordo, y cuando estén cocidas tomarás dos libras de agraz, y desgránalo, y échalo a cocer con agua, y cuando (309v) estén cocidos échalos en el colador, y déjalos escurrir: luego pásalos por un cedacillo, de manera que no quede por pasar más de los granos, yéndole echando del caldo de las colas, y sacarás las colas de la olla, y ponlas en una cazuela, y échale el agraz pasado, y sazona con todas especias, y un poquito de azafrán, y cuezan un poco con la salsa, y sírvelo sobre rebanadas tostadas.

[495] *Una escudilla de Almidón.*

Tomarás cuatro onzas de almendras y pélalas en agua caliente, y échalas en agua fría por espacio de media hora: y luego májalas en el almirez, mojando la mano a menudo en agua caliente: y cuando estén bien majadas, ve echando agua tibia cantidad de un cuartillo, algo menos: y luego pásala por una estameña, o servilleta, y torna a majar las granzas, y torna a echar la leche en el almirez, y tórnala a colar, y échale tres (310r) o cuatro onzas de azúcar: y digo tres, o cuatro, porque son menester cuatro; mas los pobres no echan todo lo necesario, y con tres bastará, y tendrás echado en remojo una onza, o menos de almidón en un poco de agua fría: luego derramarás el agua muy quedito, y quedará el almidón en el suelo de la escudilla, y deshazlo muy bien con una cucharita, y échalo en el cacillo con la leche, y un granillo de sal, y ponlo a cocer, y cueza dos, o tres hervores, y sírvelo acabado de cocer, porque no se cuaje mucho: y por esta orden podrás hacer las que quisieres.

[496] *Platillo de Lechugas, y otras hierbas.*

Perdigarás las lechugas en agua cociendo, porque echándose estando el agua cociendo, quedan las verduras siempre verdes, y después de perdigadas las lechugas sacarlas has en el colador, (310v) y exprimirlas has: luego tendrás tocino frito en dados, o buena manteca de vacas, y freirás en ella cebolla picada menuda, y ahogarás las hierbas muy bien: luego le echarás agua caliente, o caldo, cuanto se bañen, y sazónalas de especias, y sal: y si las quisieres cuajar con huevos, y su acedo, podrás; mas yo no las querría cuajadas, sino así: y si las quisieres picar, medio picadas son muy buenas. Y advierte, que no se trata de otras verduras por

of good-quality butter so that the wheat soaks it up. If you want to add sugar as a sweetener, you can, also adding cinnamon. And if you want to add milk as with rice, you can, but it should always have butter. You can prepare farro with fat, semolina, and wheat germ this way, except that you don't shell it because it's already prepared.

Mutton tail with verjuice sauce

Take a couple of mutton tails and sear them on the grill so that they are half grilled. Then put them on to boil in salted water with extra fatty fatback. When they have boiled, take two pounds of sour grapes and separate them from the stalk. Put them on to boil in water and when they are done, put them in a strainer and let them drain. Then, strain them in a sieve so that nothing remains but the seeds. Begin adding some of the stock from the tails. Remove the tails, put them in a casserole, add the strained verjuice, season with all spices and a little saffron, and let it simmer a while with this sauce. Serve over slices of toast.

A bowl of starch

Take four ounces of almonds, peel them in hot water, and then soak in cold water for a period of half an hour. Then, grind them in the mortar, wetting your pestle often in warm water. When they're well ground, begin adding warm water, about a pint or less. Then strain through a sieve or a napkin and mash the meal again, pour the milk back into the mortar, strain again, and add three or four ounces of sugar. I say three or four because four are necessary, but the poor don't add all that's necessary and three will be enough. Have an ounce of starch, or less, soaking in a little cold water. Then slowly pour out the water and the starch will remain at the bottom of the bowl. Mix it all up with a little spoon and add it to the saucepan with the milk, and a pinch of salt. Put it on to boil two or three times. Serve it immediately so that it doesn't thicken too much. With this instruction, you can make as many [bowls] as you want.

A dish of lettuce and other leafy greens

Wilt lettuce in boiling water because when you add them to boiling water, the green-leaf vegetables maintain their greenness. After the lettuce leaves are wilted, remove them to a colander and squeeze [the water out of] them. Then take fried, cubed fatback or good butter and fry diced onion in it. Sauté the leafy greens very well. Then add hot water or broth, enough to braise, and season with spices and salt. If you want to thicken it with eggs and the right amount of sorrel juice, you can. However, I don't like them thickened, rather just as is. And, if you want to chop them up, they are very tasty partially chopped. Note that I am not dealing

evitar prolijidad, porque todas se aderezan casi de una manera, como son lechugas, y escarolas, borrajas, achicorias, riponces, y otras muchas hierbas: y si fuere día de carne con perdigarlas, y picarlas medio picadas, y ahogarlas, y echarles su caldo, y sazonarlas de especias, estarán buenas echándoles su agrio. Cuando las quisieres servir, si las quisieres cuajar, es bueno echarles dulce de azúcar y canela, y zumo de naranja.

[497] (311r) *Huevos encañutados.*

Tomarás una libra de azúcar en almíbar, que esté un poco subido de punto: luego batirás dos docenas de yemas de huevos, y echarlos has en el almíbar poco a poco, pasándolos por una espumadera cociendo el azúcar a mucha furia: y después de hechos los huevos hilados, harás una masa fina sin azúcar: y luego tendrás unos cañutos de cañas aparejados, untados con manteca o aceite: luego tiende una hoja de la masa larga y delgada de una ochava de ancho,[471] y córtale los bordes con la cortadera: luego pon un cañuto en la punta de la masa, y arróllalo hasta que se cubra toda la caña, y córtalo con la cortadera, y ajusta los bordes del cañuto, y luego échalo a freír con manteca, o aceite: y en estando frita la masa, sácala fuera, y tira por la caña, y quedará hecho el cañito de masa: y desta manera podrás hacer los demás. Luego hínchelos (311v) de los huevos hilados, y asiéntalos sobre unas hojuelas, y echa un poco de almíbar encima de todo, y pondrás unos pocos de huevos mejidos encima de los cañutos. Este plato se sirve frío.

[498] *Una empanada de Pichones.*

Tomarás cuatro pichones del nido, que sean tiernos, y después de pelados y limpios, tomarás tocino de pernil, cortado en rebanadillas muy delgadas, y remójalas que no tengan sal: y luego exprímelos del agua, y sazona los pichones con especias y sal, y tiende una hoja de masa dulce de empanadas Inglesas, y asienta los pichones sobre ella, y echa las rebanadillas de tocino debajo y encima, y cierra la empanada, y sírvela caliente.[472]

[499] *Estocafíx.*

Este estocafíx es un pescado trasordinario, que no lo hay en España, sino se trae de Flandes; no se puede remojar (312r) en agua clara, aunque esté muchos días en

---

471 For more on the *ochava* (approximately 10 cm or 4 in), see 228n131, and for more on measurements, see Appendix 2, "On Measurements," Castaño Álvarez, and "Antiguas pesas y medidas."

472 Although he does not explicitly write the instructions for baking the empanada, Martínez Montiño knows that cooks will understand this final step.

with other green-leaf vegetables to avoid being long-winded, because all of them are prepared in practically the same way as lettuce: escarole, borage, chicory, rampion bellflower leaves, and many other leafy greens. If it were a meat day, when you wilt them, chop them into big pieces, sauté them, add the right amount of broth, and season with spices; they will turn out tasty with the right amount of sour juice added. When you're ready to serve it and you want it thickened, it's good to add a sweetener of sugar and cinnamon and orange juice.

Sweet egg canutos[10]

Take a pound of simple syrup that is at a high thread stage. Then beat two dozen egg yolks and, using a skimmer, slowly put them in the simple syrup. The syrup should be rapidly boiling. After the candied egg yolk threads are done, make a fine dough with no sugar and have ready some reed tubes greased with lard or oil. Then roll out a long, thin sheet of pastry dough an *ochava* wide. Cut the edges off with a trimmer. Then put a tube on the edge of the dough and roll it up until the tube is covered. Cut it with a trimmer and adjust the edges of the tube. Then fry it in lard or oil. Once the dough is fried, remove it, pull it off the tube, and you'll have your pastry tube. Make the rest this way. Then fill them with candied egg yolk threads, place them over pastry sheets, and drizzle a little simple syrup over all of them. Garnish with a little candied egg yolk thread on top of the tubes. This dish is served cold.

Squab empanada

Take four squabs from the nest; they should be tender. Once plucked and cleaned, take ham fat cut into very thin slices and soaked to remove the salt. Then squeeze out the water, season the squab with spices and salt, and roll out a sheet of sweet pastry dough used for an English empanada. Set the squab on it and place the slice of leaf lard above and below. Seal the empanada and serve hot.

Stockfish

This stockfish is a special fish that isn't found in Spain but brought in from Flanders. It cannot be soaked in clear water even if it sits over many days. An

---

10 North Americans might be more familiar with the Italian word for this tubed pastry shell: cannoli shell.

ella: hase de hacer una lejía que no sea muy fuerte, y dejarla enfriar, y luego colarla que quede clara, y echar el pescado en ella, que esté tibia, y luego dejarlo estar de la noche a la mañana, y estará remojado y muy blando. Advierte, que este pescado antes que se eche en mojo [*sic*] se ha de aporrear con un mazo, o con un palo, y después de remojado se ha de echar a cocer: luego deshacerlo, que tiene unas lonjas como abadejo, y freír un poco de cebolla con un poco de manteca, y echar allí el pescado, y ahogarlo muy bien, y echarle un poco de pimienta, y nuez, y jengibre; y luego echarle leche cuanto se bañe, y dale unos hervores, y sírvelo caliente. Advierte, que este pescado podrás servir con solo manteca y mostaza y sus especias, y con esto tiene buen gusto.

[500] *Hongos.*

Los hongos son muy buenos cociéndolos (312v) primero con agua y sal, y luego ahogarlos con buen aceite y cebolla, y echallos en una cazuela de barro: luego picar un poco de verdura, y majarla en el almirez con un migajón de pan, de manera que esté muy majado como salsa de perejil: luego sazona con todas especias, y un poco de cominos y un grano de ajo, y desata esta salsa con un poco de caldo de garbanzos, y cueza con ella: y cuando los sirvieres echa un poco de zumo de limón por encima. Estos hongos se pueden ahogar con manteca de vacas, y luego echarles un poco de vino, y una gota de vinagre, y sazónalo con todas especias, y un poquito de azafrán, y con sólo eso sin verduras estará bien. También podrás estregar un grano de ajo dentro de un plato, y luego echarle un poco de aceite: y cuando esté bien caliente echar allí los hongos crudos, y tapar con otro plato, y dejarlos allí ahogar muy bien: y de cuando en cuando revolverlos, y sazonallos (313r) de sal, y cuando estén bien ahogados sacarlos, y servirlos con naranja y pimienta. Éstos perdigados y escurridos puestos en un barril con sal e hinojo son buenos, y duran mucho.

[501] *Fruta de Almendras.*

Majarás media libra de almendras muy majadas, de manera que no se enaceiten: luego les echarás dentro cuatro yemas de huevos, y un polvito de harina: luego echa más yemas, y velo meneando hasta que esté bien blando: luego tomarás una sartén con manteca de vacas que sea poca, y ponla a calentar: luego echa de aquel batido dentro con una cucharita, y harás unas torrijitas muy delgadas, que parezca calabaza frita: y luego pásalas por almíbar, y sírvelas con azúcar raspado por encima.

alkaline water that isn't too strong must be prepared and cooled. Then strain it so that it's clear and put the fish in it. It should be warm. Then, let it sit overnight and it will be soaked and very soft. Note that before soaking this fish you must pound it with a mallet or a rolling pin. After it has soaked, put it on to boil. Then flake it apart into slices as for codfish. Fry a little onion in some lard and add the fish, sauté it well, add a little pepper, nutmeg, and ginger. Then, add enough milk to braise, bring it to a boil a few times, and serve it hot. Note that this fish can be served with just lard, mustard, and its spices. This way it will be very tasty.

Wild mushrooms

Wild mushrooms are very tasty, boiling them first in salted water and then sautéing them with good oil and onion. Put them in a terracotta casserole. Then, chop up some green herbs and mash them in the mortar with the crumb of a loaf of bread so that it turns out as mashed as parsley sauce. Then season with all spices, a little cumin, and a clove of garlic. Thin this sauce with a little garbanzo broth and boil it. When you serve them, drizzle a little lemon juice on top. These mushrooms can be sautéed with butter and then add a little wine and a drop of vinegar. Season with all spices and a little saffron. With just this and no green herbs it will turn out well. You can also rub a clove of garlic on a plate and then add a little oil. When it's heated, add the raw wild mushrooms and cover with another plate. Let them sauté there and, from time to time, stir them. Season with salt and when they're well sautéed, remove them, and serve with orange and pepper. [When] these are parboiled, drained, and put into a barrel with salt and fennel, they are good and last a long time.

Fried almond pastry

Thoroughly mash half a pound of almonds so that they don't get oily. Then add four egg yolks and a dusting of flour. Next, add more yolks and begin stirring until it's soft. Then take a frying pan with just a little butter and heat it up. Next, with a spoon, put the batter in and fry some very thin pieces that will look like fried squash. Dip them in simple syrup and serve with grated sugar on top.

[502] *Salchichas.*[473]

Tomarás carne de puerco tanta cantidad de magro, como de gordo, y (313v) pícala muy picada, y sazona con pimienta, y jengibre, e hinojo, y sal, y échale un poco de vinagre bien aguado, para que entre más cantidad, y se humedezca la carne, y tomarás tripas de puerco de las angostas, y hínchelas, y pásalas por agua cociendo, y ponlas a enjugar. Hanse de servir asadas, y no se pueden detener muchos días. Advierte, que si en lugar del hinojo les echases anís, tienen muy buen gusto.

[503] *Sustancia asada.*[474]

Asarás una pierna de carnero, y cuando esté casi asada, sacarla has en un plato, y picarla has con el cuchillo, de manera que la pase de parte a parte muchas veces; luego doblarás el jarrete, y apriétala con el tenedor, y sacarás medio cuartillo de sustancia. La pierna ha de ser de carnero muerto de aquel día. Esta sustancia se saca de aves, y de perdices: éstas es necesario haber prensa (314r) para ellas, y si no la hubiere, en acabándolo de sacar del asador, se apretarán entre dos platos, muy apretadas, punzándolas también con el cuchillo. Estas sustancias se han de poner en un plato sobre un poco de nieve, y helarse ha toda la grasa que tuviere; luego la apartarás con unas plumas grandes de gallina al borde del plato, y echarás la sustancia en otro vaso, y sazonarla has de sal, y calentarla has de manera que no cueza, y así se ha de dar al enfermo.

[504] *Cómo se manen las aves en dos horas.* (316r)[475]

Tomarás el capón, o pavo por las dos alas, y con la otra mano le tomarás los dos pies, y se los meterás en el fuego, y tenlo hasta que se quemen bien: luego le henchirás la boca de sal, de manera que parezca que se ahoga, y entonces lo degollarás, y lo atarás por los pies, y lo meterás en un pozo, de manera que llegue la cabeza al agua, y déjalo estar allí dos horas, y lo hallarás manido y tierno.

(316v) En los platillos lo más de las veces los pongo de pollos, o pichones, o aves, y es porque son los más regalados; mas con todo eso se pueden hacer de carnero,

---

473 Under the name "Salchicas antiguas," Emilia Pardo Bazán includes this recipe in her book *La cocina española antigua* (294–5).

474 This recipe is the same as the one that first appears on 228; 229 and later on 492; 493. It is unusual that, in subsequent editions, this recipe was not removed, since it duplicates the second version.

475 While the first part of the recipe aligns with its title, the second part includes more general comments about adjusting recipes and assumed quantities. Also, in the 1611 edition, this is where Martínez Montiño inserted *Relación de algunas cantidades para hacer tortas, hojaldres, costradas, y otras cosas* [List of certain quantities for making pies, pastries, puff pastry pies, and other things] (314r–316r) However, in all other editions it was moved above. See 252–4; 253–5.

Sausages

Take pork, as much meat as fat, and mince it. Season with pepper, ginger, fennel, and salt. Add in a little vinegar that's been watered down so more goes into it and moistens the meat. Take pork intestines from the wide section and fill them. Dip them in boiling water and let them dry. For serving, they should be grilled, and they won't keep many days. Note that instead of fennel, you can add anise and they will be very tasty.

Essence from a roast

Roast a leg of mutton and when it's almost done, remove it onto a plate and pierce it with a knife from one side to the other several times. Then, fold the shank over, squeeze it with a fork, and extract a half pint of essence. The leg must be from ram slaughtered that day. This essence can also be made from poultry or partridges. For the latter, it is necessary to have a press, but if you don't have one, right after you have taken them off the spit, squeeze them very tightly between two plates, also stabbing them with a knife. The essence should go on a plate that is on snow and all the fat should congeal. Then with some big hen feathers, separate it to the side of the plate and pour the essence into another container, season with salt, warm it up, but do not bring it to a boil. Serve it to the sick person this way.

How to tenderize poultry in two hours

Take a capon or turkey by the wings and with the other hand by the feet and put it in the fire until it's scorched. Then fill its mouth with salt so that it looks like it's choking and then slit its throat, tie its feet, and put it into a well so that it's up to its head in water. Let it sit there for two hours and it will come out wrinkled and tender.

For smaller plates, I mostly use young chicken, squab, and adult birds, and it's because they are the most exquisite. But you can also do all this with

y de cabrito, y de ternera, guardando la orden de los que están escritos, y de muchos pescados, como es con la salsa de carnero verde se pueden aderezar ranas, y mero, y congrio, y cazón, y pulpo, y otros muchos pescados, ahogándolos primero con buen aceite, o buena manteca con su cebolla, luego echarle la salsa del carnero verde.

Todas las veces que en algún servicio se dicen cantidades de materiales, como son huevos, o azúcar, ú otros cualesquier materiales, y no se dice para cuántos platos, se entiende que es para un plato, porque lo más ordinario es hacer el servicio sencillo de un plato de cada cosa.

[505] *Platillo de Cardillos*.[476]

Los cardillos siempre vienen por Cuaresma, (317r) y entre Pascua y Pascua:[477] éstos se aderezan desta manera: Mondar los cardillos, y cortarles las puntas, y henderlos por el pezón: luego freír un poco de cebolla cortada menuda con manteca de vacas, o buen aceite, y perdigar los cardillos con agua y sal, y sacarlos en un colador a que se escurran: luego echarlos con la cebolla frita, y ahóguense un poco: luego échales agua caliente cuanto se bañen, y sazona con todas especias y sal, y échales un poco de verdura picada, y un poco de leche: y si no hubiere leche cuájalos con unos huevos y acedo: y si fuere día de carne, en lugar de manteca de vacas sea tocino y grasa de la olla, y las cebolla sean de las nuevas, y mezcla con ellas ajetes, porque les dan muy buen gusto. Sobre estos cardillos se suelen servir cecinas, y salchichones, o cosas saladas. Desta manera se aderezan las ortigas, y las romazas, y otras hierbas.

[506] (317v) *Potaje de Castañas*.

Las castañas apiladas suélense gastar por Cuaresma. Echarás a cocer las castañas con agua y sal, y cuando estén bien cocidas tendrás un poco de pan tostado y remojado en vinagre: luego picarás un poco de verdura, perejil, hierbabuena, y cilantro verde, y échala en el almirez, y májala muy bien: luego echa el pan remojado, y unas pocas de castañas, y májese todo, y sazona con todas especias y canela, y desátalo con un poco de vinagre, y caldo de las castañas, y échales dulce de miel, que estén bien dulces, y un poco espesas y morenas. Con lo cual por

---

476 *Cardillos* (*Scolymus hispanicus*) [golden thistle or Spanish oyster thistle] continues to be eaten throughout Spain in spring when it's harvested. In Castilla it is eaten both as part of a salad and incorporated into *cocido*.

477 *Pascua* references not only Easter but also three other important Christian holidays, Christmas, the Epiphany, and the Pentecost, in addition to the Jewish Passover. Given both the harvest season for thistles and the dominance of Christianity in Spain, here Martínez Montiño is referencing Easter and the Pentecost.

mutton, kid, and veal, maintaining the instructions that are already written, and with many fish. Just like the green mutton sauce that can accompany frog, grouper, conger eel, dogfish, octopus, and many other fish, first sauté them in good oil or lard with the right amount of onion, and then ladle on green mutton sauce.

Every time in any recipe that mentions quantities of ingredients, like eggs or sugar or any other ingredient, and it doesn't specify how many plates, it should be understood that it is for one plate, because the most common thing is to make a single serving for one plate of each thing.

A dish of golden thistle

Golden thistle always comes around Lent, and between Easter and Pentecost. It is prepared in the following way. Peel the thistle, cut off the tops, and split open the bottoms. Then fry a little diced onion in butter or good oil and parboil the thistle in salted water. Remove them to a colander to drain. Then, add them to the fried onion and lightly sauté them. Then add enough hot water to braise, season with all spices and salt, and add in a little minced green herb and a little milk. If you don't have any milk, thicken them with eggs and sorrel juice. If it's a meat day, instead of butter, use fatback and fat from the pot. The onions should be green onions and mixed with green garlic, because they provide very good flavour. Cured beef, black-pepper sausage, and other savoury items are often served over golden thistle. You can prepare nettles, sorrel, and other early spring greens this way.

Chestnut soup

Stored chestnuts are usually used by Lent. Put the chestnuts on to boil in salted water and when they're boiled, have a little bread toasted and soaked in vinegar. Then mince a little bit of green herbs – parsley, spearmint, and cilantro – put it in a mortar and thoroughly grind it up. Then add the soaked bread and some of the chestnuts and grind it all up. Season with all spices and cinnamon and thin it with a little vinegar and chestnut broth. Add in honey as sweetener; it should be very sweet and a little thick and brown. With this and for now, I'm

604   Capítulo II

ahora doy fin a este libro, porque en él casi todo lo que hallares es al uso Español; pero siendo Dios servido, y teniendo salud, entiendo sacar a luz y ampliar este libro con algunas cosas extranjeras: y también pondré algunas cosas fantásticas que sirven para banquetes: las cuales son más de curiosidad y ostentación, que de necesidad.[478,479]

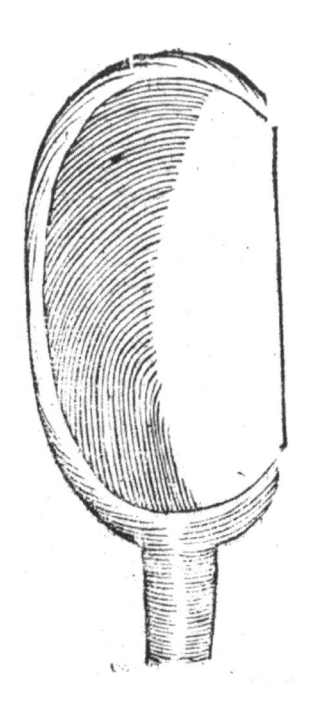

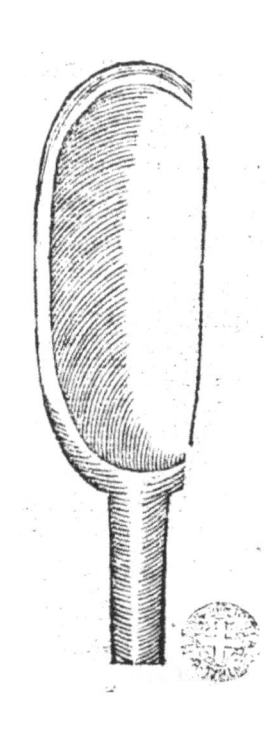

---

478 The recipes end here. In all other editions the word FIN [end] finishes the recipe section before the "tabla" [table] section begins.
479 References to these drawings occur three times in the cookbook, but only in the 1611 version do we have examples of both spoon sizes. While cookbooks often included decorative elements, woodcut illustrations were rare in printed books and rarer still in cookbooks (Notaker 13). In later seventeenth-century editions, only the big spoon is reproduced (in spite of the fact that it is the smaller of the two that Martínez Montiño signals twice in his work). In the editions from 1676 to 1778, the references are intact, but there are no visuals in the back of the book. Finally, from 1790 to 1823, both the references and the visuals have disappeared.

putting an end to this book. Almost everything that you find in it is the Spanish method. However, if God is willing and having good health, I plan to publish and expand this book with some foreign recipes and I will also include some fantastic recipes to use in banquets. Such things are more points of curiosity and show than necessity.

Capitulo II

TABLA, O INDICE de los guisados y cosas de cozina, y conservas que en este libro se contienen.[480] [Table or index of the food, kitchen tips and preserves that this book contains.]

[1] ^[481] De Todo género de asado de un pavo, y de un capón. [On all types of roasts, on turkey and on capon] folio 15 [142–4; 143–5]
[2]^ Gigote de un capón sobre sopa de natas. [Minced capon on cream sops] 16 [144; 145]
[3] Gigote de una pierna de carnero. [Minced leg of mutton] 16 [144–6; 145–7]
[4]^ Cómo se asa la ternera. [How to roast veal] 17 [146; 147]
[5]# Palomas torcaces asadas. [Grilled wood pigeon] 17 [146–8; 147–9]
[6] Palomas torcaces con salsa de almendras. [Wood pigeon with almond sauce] 18 [148; 149]
[7] Cómo se aderezan las perdices. [How to prepare partridge] 18 [148–50; 149–51]
[8] Cómo se aderezan las chorchas. [How to prepare woodcock] 19 [150; 151]
[9] Grullas asadas. [Roast crane] 19 [150–2; 151–3]
[10] Ánades y zarcetas. [Duck and teal] 20 [152; 153]
[11] Gigote de liebres. [Minced hare] 21 [154; 155]
[12] Conejos. [Rabbit] 22 [154; 155]
[13] Conejos en mollo. [Rabbit in broth] 22 [154; 155]

---

480 Differences between editions with respect to the back material include the title itself, the order of presentation of recipes, the inclusion of all chapters or only Chapter 2, and the occasional appearance of the publisher's name (this occurs only in 1617 and 1760) or publisher's advertisements for other titles (this occurs only in 1676). Regarding the title, in 1617 it changes to "Tabla de lo que se contiene en este libro" [Table of what is contained in this book] and stays that way until the nineteenth century, when several editions prefer the work *índice* [index] over *tabla* [table]. In terms of the order of presentation and beginning in 1617, the back matter is arranged alphabetically, like an index, instead of chronologically, by page number, like a traditional table of contents. This trend continues until about the mid-eighteenth century, when it returns to the 1611 "table of contents" format. Notaker explains that throughout Europe the alphabetized and page number systems of tables of contents were both commonly used and that the latter was cheaper for the printer, since there was less work involved (11). Curiously, in the case of the editions for Martínez Montiño's cookbook, the alphabetized versions were more common in the seventeenth century and the cheaper, page-number versions in the eighteenth and nineteenth centuries. Another structural change is that beginning in 1728, most, if not all, editions place the index for both Chapters 1 and 2 at the back of the book; previously the indexes were found at the end of each chapter.
481 To clarify differences between this index, or table of contents, and recipes in the cookbook, I have added symbols for the index in the following way.
   ^ The title in the index differs slightly from the title in the main text.
   # The title exists here but doesn't have a title in the main text. It falls under another recipe.
   * The title does not exist in the index or in the main text but it is clearly a separate recipe.
   • Not listed in the index but yes, in the main text.
   ° Listed in the index but does not have a corresponding recipe in the main text.
   § Does not appear in the cookbook until the 1617 edition.

Chapter 2

[14] Gigote de conejos. [Minced rabbit] 22 [156; 157]
[15]^ Otro gigote. [Another minced (dish)] 23 [156; 157]
[16] Salpicón de vaca. [Beef salpicon] 23 [156; 157]
[17] Pollos asados con salsa. [Roast chicken with its sauce] 23 [158; 159]
[18] Pollos rellenos. [Chicken with stuffing] 24 [158; 159]
[19] Empanadas de perdices. [Partridge empanadas] 25 [160; 161]
[20] Empanadas en asador. [Empanadas on a spit] 26 [160–2; 161–3]
[21]^ Otras en asador. [Other on a spit] 26 [162; 163]
[22]• Sopa de perdices. [Partridge sops] 26 [162; 163]
[23] Perdices asadas con aceite. [Roast partridge with oil] 27 [164; 165]
[24] Ánades estofadas. [Stewed duck] 27 [164; 165]
[25] Lechones asados. [Roast suckling pig] 28 [164; 165]
[26] Salsa de lechón. [Sauce for suckling pig] 28 [166; 167]
[27] Un lechón en salchichón. [Suckling pig served sausage style] 29 [166; 167]
[28] Una pierna de carnero estofada. [Stewed leg of mutton] 30 [166–8; 167–9]
[29]^ Otra pierna estofada. [Another stewed leg] 30 [168; 169]
[30]^ Otra. [Another] 31 [168–70; 169–71]
[31] Pierna de carnero rellena. [Stuffed leg of mutton] 31 [170; 171]
[32] Pierna de carnero a la Francesa. [Leg of mutton, French style] 32 [170–2; 171–3]
[33] Otra pierna de otra manera. [Another leg, made another way] 33 [172; 173]
[34] Un platillo de pichones. [A squab dish] 33 [172–4; 173–5]
[35] Pollos rellenos cocidos. [Braised stuffed chicken] 34 [174–6; 175–7]
[36] Platillo con membrillos. [A little dish with quince] 35 [176; 177]
[37] Otro platillo con hierbas. [Another dish with leafy greens] 36 [176–8; 177–9]
[38] Platillos sin verduras. [Dishes without green-leaf vegetables] 37 [178–80; 179–81]
[39] Capón a la tudesca. [Capon, German style] 38 [180; 181]
[40] Un platillo de aves con acederas. [A dish of poultry with sorrel] 38 [180; 181]
[41] Una ave a la Portuguesa. [Poultry, Portuguese style] 39 [180; 181]
[42] Gallina rellena en alfitete. [Stuffed hen served on fried pastry sheets] 39 [182; 183]
[43]^ Otra ave en alfitete. [Another stuffed hen on fried pastry sheets] 39 [182; 183]
[44] Gallina Morisca. [Morisco-style hen] 40 [182–4; 183–5]
[45] Pichones ensapados. [Stuffed squab] 40 [184–6; 185–7]
[46] Un capón relleno con ostiones. [A capon stuffed with large oysters] 41 [186; 187]
[47] Otro capón relleno. [Another stuffed capon] 42 [186–8; 187–9]
[48]^ Otro. [Another] 43 [188; 189]
[49] Empanadas de pollos ensapados. [Stuffed chicken empanadas] 43 [190; 191]
[50] Cómo se hacen los rellenos. [How to make stuffing] 44 [190; 191]
[51] Artaletes de Ave. [Poultry pinwheels] 45 [192; 193]
   • Potajería [Vegetables]

[52] Otros artaletes de aves. [Other poultry pinwheels] 45 [192–4; 193–5]
[53] Otros artaletes de ternera. [Other veal pinwheels] 46 [194; 195]
[54] Artaletes de cabrito. [Kid pinwheels] 47 [194–6; 195–7]
[55] Cazuela de ave. [Poultry stew] 48 [196; 197]
[56] Un platillo de artaletes. [A dish of pinwheels] 48 [196–8; 197–9]
[57] Palominos ahogados. [Sautéed wild squab] 49 [198; 199]
[58] Otros palominos ahogados. [Another dish of sautéed wild squab] 49 [198; 199]
[59]# [Carnero verde.] [(Green mutton stew)] 50 [200; 201]
[60] Otra manera de carnero verde. [Another way of (making) green mutton stew] 50 [200–2; 201–3]
[61] Plato de pollo rellenos con membrillos. [A dish of chicken stuffed with quince] 51 [202; 203]
[62] Pepitoria. [Pepitoria (Stew with poultry offal)] 51 [202–4; 203–5]
[63] Albondiguillas de ave. [Poultry meatballs] 53 [204–6; 205–7]
[64] Otras albondiguillas. [Other meatballs] 53 [206; 207]
[65] Albondiguillas Castellanas. [Castilian meatballs] 54 [208; 209]
[66] Albondiguillas Reales. [Royal meatballs] 54 [208; 209]
[67] Liebre enlebrada. [Hare with lebrada sauce] 55 [210; 211]
[68] Olla de liebre. [Hare stew] 56 [210–12; 211–13]
[69] Gigote de liebre. [Minced hare meat] 56 [212; 213]
[70] Empanadas de liebre. [Hare empanada] 57 [212–14; 213–15]
[71] Plato de albondiguillas fritas. [Dish of fried meatballs] 57 [214; 215]
[72] Albondiguillas de pan rallado y grasa. [Meatballs with breadcrumbs and fat] 58 [214; 215]
[73]^ Platillo de cañas de vaca. [A dish of beef marrow] 58 [216; 217]
[74] Fruta de cañas. [Fried dough with marrow filling] 59 [216; 217]
[75] Platillo de madrecillas de gallinas rellenas. [A dish of stuffed hen oviduct] 59 [218; 219]
[76] Potaje de acenorias. [Carrot stew] 60 [218; 219]
[77]^ Cazuelas de acenorias. [Carrot stew] 60 [220; 221]
[78] Ensalada de acenorias. [Carrot salad] 61 [220; 221]
[79] Fruta rellena. [Stuffed fried dough] 62 [222; 223]
[80]* [Toronja rellena.] [Stuffed toronja] [222–4; 223–5]
[81] Costrada de asadurillas de cabrito. [Puff pastry pie filled with kid pluck] 63 [224–6; 225–7]
[82] Cómo se han de asar los pajarillos gordos. [How to roast small plump birds] 64 [226; 227]
[83] Cazuela de pajarillos. [Small bird stew] 64 [226; 227]
[84] Salsa brenca. [Brenca sauce] 65 [228; 229]
[85] Sustancia asada. [Essence from a roast] 65 [228; 229]
[86] Platillo de artaletes de ternera. [A dish of veal pinwheels] 65 [228–30; 229–31]
[87] Sopa dorada. [Golden sops] 68 [232; 233]

Chapter 2

[88] Sopa de natas. [Cream sops] 69 [232; 233]
[89] Otra sopa de natas. [Other cream sops] 69 [232–4; 233–5]
[90] Una cazuela de natas. [Cream casserole] 70 [234–6; 235–7]
[91] Torrijas de natas sin pan. [Torrijas made with cream but without bread] 71 [236; 237]
  ° Migas de pan [Breadcrumbs] 72
[92] Migas de natas. [Breadcrumbs with cream] 72 [238; 239]
[93] Migas de leche. [Breadcrumbs with milk] 73 [238–40; 239–41]
[94] Migas de gato. [Cat breadcrumbs] 74 [240; 241]
  • COMIENZA LA MASA [The dough section begins]
[95] Tortas de natas. [Cream pie] 75 [242; 243]
[96] Otra torta de natas. [Another cream pie] 75 [244; 245]
[97] Torta de agraz. [Sour grape pie] 75 [244; 245]
[98] Torta de cidra verde. [Green citron pie] 76 [244–6; 245–7]
[99] Torta de limones verdes. [Green lemon pie] 76 [246; 247]
[100]* [Una torta de cidra.] [A citron pie] 77 [246; 247]
[101] Torta de orejones. [Dried apricot pie] 77 [246; 247]
[102] Torta de almendras. [Almond pie] 77 [248; 249]
[103]^ Torta de ternera. [Veal pie] 78 [248; 249]
[104]^ Torta de pichones. [Squab pie with cream] 78 [248; 249]
[105] Torta de albérchigos. [Apricot pie] 79 [248–50; 249–51]
[106] Costrada de limoncillos y mazapán. [Lime and marzipan puff pastry pie] 79 [250; 251]
[107] Torta de guindas. [Sour cherry pie] 80 [250; 251]
[108] Torta de borrajas. [Borage pie] 80 [250; 251]
[109] Torta de acelgas. [Swiss chard pie] 80 [252; 253]
[110] Relación de algunas cantidades, para hacer tortas, hojaldres, costradas, y otras cosas. [List of certain quantities for making pies, pastries, puff pastry pies, and other things] [252–4; 253–5]
[111] Albondiguillas de borrajas. [Borage meatballs] 81 [256; 257]
[112] Plato de todas frutas. [A dish of all kinds of fruit] 81 [256; 257]
[113] Bollo de vacía. [Airy pastry] 82 [256–8; 257–9]
[114] Bollo maimón. [Maimon layered pastry] 83 [258–60; 259–61]
[115] Otro bollo sombrero. [Another hat pastry] 84 [260–2; 261–3]
[116] Bollo de rodilla. [Spiral sweet roll] 85 [262; 263]
[117] Un rebollo. [Rebollo] 86 [264; 265]
[118] Bollo roscón. [Ring-shaped pastry] 87 [264–6; 265–7]
[119] Un pastelón de mazapán. [A big marzipan pie] 88 [266; 267]
[120] Bollos pardos. [Brown pastries] 89 [268; 269]
[121] Bollo fitete. [Fitete pastry] 89 [268–70; 269–71]
[122] Otra manera de masa de bollos. [Another way to make pastry dough] 91 [270; 271]

[123] Hojaldre de torreznos. [Puff pastry with roasted pork fat] 91 [270–2; 271–3]
[124] Hojaldre relleno. [Stuffed puff pastry] 92 [272; 273]
[125] Hojaldre con enjundia de puerco. [Puff pastry with pork fat] 93 [274; 275]
[126] Hojaldre de mazapán. [Marzipan puff pastry] 94 [274; 275]
[127] Hojaldre con leche. [Milk puff pastry] 94 [276; 277]
[128] Hojaldre tropezada. [A puff pastry, loosely pulled together] 95 [276; 277]
[129]^ Panecillos rellenos. [Little rolls] 95 [278; 279]
[130] Pasteles de tetilla. [Teat pies] 96 [278; 279]
[131] Otros panecillos rellenos. [Other stuffed rolls] 97 [278–80; 279–81]
[132] Hojaldres bizcochados. [Sponge cake] 97 [280; 281]
[133] Pasteles hojaldrados. [Puff pastry pies] 97 [280; 281]
[134] Un pastel de ave para enfermo. [Hen pie for the sick] 98 [280–2; 281–3]
[135] Pastel de pollos, o pichones. [Chicken or squab pie] 98 [282; 283]
[136] Sopa de capirotada. [Capirotada sops] 99 [282–4; 283–5]
[137] Olla podrida en pastel. [A pie of hodgepodge stew] 100 [284–6; 285–7]
[138] Pasteles de cabezas de carnero. [Sheep's head pie] 101 [286; 287]
[139] Cómo se ha de beneficiar un jabalí. [How to dress boar] 102 [286–8; 287–9]
[140] Queso de cabeza de jabalí. [Boar head cheese] 103 [288–90; 289–91]
[141] Adobos de solomillos. [Marinade for boar tenderloin] 104 [290; 291]
[142] Empanadas frías de jabalí. [Cold boar empanadas] 104 [290–2; 291–3]
[143] Empanadas de jabalí calientes. [Hot boar empanadas] 105 [292; 293]
[144] Pastelones de jabalí picados. [Minced boar pies] 106 [292; 293]
[145] Otros pastelones picados. [Other minced pies] 106 [292; 293]
[146] Otra suerte de pastelones de jabalí. [Another kind of boar pies] 106 [294; 295]
[147] Otros pastelones de jabalí. [Other boar pies] 107 [294–6; 295–7]
[148] Otras empanadas de jabalí. [Other boar empanadas] 108 [296; 297]
[149] Cómo se cuece el jabalí fresco. [How to boil fresh boar] 108 [296; 297]
[150] Cómo se ha de salar el jabalí. [How to salt boar] 109 [296; 297]
[151] Cómo se ha de aderezar un venado. [How to prepare venison (offal)] 109 [298; 299]
[152] Platillo de las puntas de cuernos de venado. [Dish of the tips of deer antlers] 110 [298–300; 299–301]
[153] Lo que se ha de hacer del redaño del venado. [What to do with venison caul fat] 110 [300; 301]
[154] Migas de la grasa del venado. [Venison fat breadcrumbs] 111 [300; 301]
[155] Empanadas de venado. [Venison empanadas] 111 [300; 301]
[156] Solomillos de venado. [Venison tenderloin] 111 [302; 303]
[157]^ Cómo se ha de salar el venado, y se puede comer fresco por muchos días. [How to salt venison and eat it fresh for many days] 112 [302–4; 303–5]
[158] Cómo se hacen los tasajos de venado. [How to make venison jerky] 113 [304; 305]

Chapter 2

[159] Cómo se puede llevar la carne de un venado veinte, o treinta leguas, sin que se pierda en las grandes calores. [How to travel twenty or thirty leagues in the heat with venison meat and not spoil it] 113 [304; 305]

[160] Una empanada de pecho de vaca. [A beef brisket empanada] 114 [304–6; 305–7]

[161] Cómo se adereza una frasia de ternera. [How to prepare veal *frasia*] 115 [306–8; 307–9]

[162] Cómo se adereza una cabeza de ternera. [How to prepare veal head] 116 [308; 309]

[163]• Sesos de ternera. [Veal brain] 116 [308; 309]

[164] Empanadas de ternera. [Veal empanadas] 117 [310; 311]

[165]^ Uspote de ternera. [Veal uspot] 117 [310; 311]

[166] Empanadilla de masa dulce. [Sweet dough for turnovers] 118 [310–12; 311–13]

[167]^ Empanadillas de pies de puerco. [Pig's feet turnovers] 119 [312; 313]

[168] Empanadillas de sardinas. [Sardine turnovers] 119 [312; 313]

[169] Otras empanadillas de criadillas de tierra. [Other truffle turnovers] 119 [312–14; 313–15]

[170] Empanada Inglesa. [English empanada] 120 [314; 315]

[171] Buñuelos de viento. [Puffs] 121 [314–16; 315–17]

[172] Otros buñuelos de viento. [Other puffs] 122 [316; 317]

[173] Otros buñuelos de viento. [Other puffs] 122 [316–18; 317–19]

[174] Almojábanas de cuajada. [Fried cheese pastries made with curds] 123 [318; 319]

[175] Otras almojábanas de cuajada diferentes. [Other different fried cheese pastries made with curds] 123 [318–20; 319–21]

[176] Buñuelos de queso fresco. [Farmer cheese puffs] 124 [320; 321]

[177]^ Quesadillas de cuajada fritas. [Fried cheese curd tarts] 125 [320–2; 321–3]

[178] Quesadillas de horno. [Baked cheese tarts] 126 [322; 323]

[179] Fruta de cañas. [Fried dough with marrow filling] 126 [322–4; 323–5]

[180] Empanadillas de cuajada. [Curd turnovers] 127 [324; 325]

[181] Otras empanadillas. [Other turnovers] 128 [324–6; 325–7]

[182] Fruta de fillos. [Fried dough with spongy edges] 128 [326; 327]

[183] Fruta de chicharrones. [Crackling fried dough] 129 [326; 327]

[184] Fruta de prestiños. [*Prestiño* fried dough] 129 [328; 329]

[185] Fruta de piñas. [Pine nut fried dough] 131 [328–30; 329–31]

[186] Un platillo de jadeo de manos de ternera. [A dish of calves' feet with *jadeo* sauce] 131 [330; 331]

[187] Platillo de cabezuelas de cabrito, y las tripillas. [Dish of kid head and intestines] 132 [330; 331]

[188] Otro platillo de cabezuelas de cabrito. [Another kid head dish] 132 [332; 333]

[189] Fricasea de cosas fiambres. [Cold meat fricassees] 133 [332; 333]

[190] Cabezuelas de cabrito rellenas. [Stuffed kid head] 133 [332–4; 333–5]

[191] Otro platillo de cabezuelas de cabrito. [Another kid head dish] 134 [334; 335]
[192]^ Otro plato de cabezuelas. [Another kid head dish] 134 [334–6; 335–7]
[193] Unos picatostes de ubre de ternera. [Cow udder over slices of fried bread] 136 [336; 337]
[194] Otros picatostes de riñones de ternera. [Another (recipe) for veal kidney over slices of fried bread] 136 [336; 337]
[195] Morcillas blancas de cámara. [White blood sausage with large intestine casing] 136 [336–8; 337–9]
[196] Morcillas de puerco dulces. [Sweet pork blood sausage] 137 [338; 339]
[197] Salchichones de carne de puerco. [Pork sausages] 137 [338; 339]
[198]^ Chorizos de carne de puerco. [Pork chorizo] 138 [340; 341]
[199] Longanizas. [Longaniza sausages] 138 [340; 341]
[200] Solomo de vaca relleno. [Stuffed beef tenderloin] 138 [340; 341]
[201] Manjar blanco. [Blancmange] 139 [342; 343]
[202] Buñuelos de manjar blanco. [Blancmange puffs] 140 [342–4; 343–5]
[203] Otros buñuelos de manjar blanco. [Other blancmange puffs] 141 [344; 345]
[204] Picatostes de manjar blanco. [Blancmange over slices of fried bread] 141 [344; 345]
[205] Frutillas de manjar blanco. [Blancmange fried dough] 142 [344–6; 345–7]
[206] Cazolillas de manjar blanco. [Blancmange tartlets] 142 [346; 347]
[207]^ Tortada de manjar blanco. [Big blancmange pie] 142 [346; 347]
[208] Cómo se va de hacer el arroz. [How to make rice] 143 [346–8; 347–9]
[209] Buñuelos de arroz. [Rice puffs] 143 [348; 349]
[210] Cazuela de arroz. [Rice casserole] 143 [348; 349]
[211] Arroz a la Portuguesa. [Rice, Portuguese style] 144 [348; 349]
[212] Arroz de grasa. [Rice (cooked) in fat] 144 [348–50; 349–51]
[213]^ Cazuela de arroz. [Rice casserole] 145 [350; 351]
[214] Platillo de alcachofas. [Artichoke dish] 145 [350; 351]
[215] Alcachofas asadas. [Roasted artichokes] 146 [352; 353]
[216]^ Otro de alcachofas. [Another artichoke dish] 146 [352; 353]
[217] Potaje de habas. [Fava bean stew] 147 [352–4; 353–5]
[218] Otras habas. [Other fava beans] 147 [354; 355]
[219] Habas en día de carne. [Fava beans on a meat day] 148 [354; 355]
[220] Sopa de lechugas. [Lettuce sops] 148 [354; 355]
[221] Lechugas rellenas. [Stuffed lettuce] 148 [356; 357]
[222] Lechugas rellenas en días de carne. [Stuffed lettuce on meat days] 149 [356; 357]
[223] Cazuela mojí de berenjenas. [Moxi eggplant casserole] 150 [358; 359]
[224] Berenjenas rellenas. [Stuffed eggplant] 151 [360; 361]
[225]^ Plato de berenjenas. [Eggplant dish] 152 [360; 361]
[226] Platillo de almendrucos. [Green almond dish] 152 [360; 361]

Chapter 2

[227]^ Garbanzos con membrillos. [Garbanzos with quince] 152 [362; 363]
[228]^ Otros garbanzos. [Other garbanzos] 153 [362; 363]
[229] Cómo se adereza la calabaza. [How to prepare squash] 153 [362–4; 363–5]
[230] Potaje de calabaza. [Squash stew] 154 [364; 365]
[231] Calabaza rellena en día de pescado. [Stuffed squash for fish days] 154 [364–6; 365–7]
[232] Calabaza en día de carne. [Squash for meat days] 156 [366; 367]
[233] Calabaza rellena en platillo. [A stuffed squash dish] 156 [368; 369]
[234] Plato cuajado de calabazas. [Squash with egg crust] 157 [368; 369]
[235] Calabaza frita. [Fried squash] 157 [368; 369]
[236] Potaje de calabaza redonda. [Round squash stew] 158 [370; 371]
[237] Sopa de calabaza redonda. [Sops of round squash] 158 [370; 371]
[238] Cómo se aderezan los nabos. [How to prepare turnips] 158 [370–2; 371–3]
[239] Nabos cuajados. [Turnips with an egg crust] 159 [372; 373]
[240] Nabos lampreados. [Turnips, Lamprea style] 159 [372; 373]
[241] Sopa de nabos. [Turnip sops] 160 [372; 373]
[242] Cómo se adereza el repollo. [How to prepare cabbage] 160 [374; 375]
[243] Potaje de arvejas. [Pea stew] 161 [374; 375]
[244] Cómo se aderezan las espinacas. [How to prepare spinach] 162 [376; 377]
[245] Espinacas a la Portuguesa. [Spinach, Portuguese style] 162 [376; 377]
[246] Fruta de borrajas. [Deep-fried borage] 162 [376; 377]
[247] Fruta de frisuelos. [Funnel cakes] 163 [378; 379]
[248] Borrajas con caldo de carne. [Borage with meat stock] 164 [378; 379]
[249] Sopa de borrajas. [Borage sops] 164 [380; 381]
[250] Otra manera de borrajas. [Another way (of making) borage] 164 [380; 381]
[251] Cómo se han de aderezar algunos pescados. [How to prepare some fish] 165 [380; 381]
[252] Cómo se adereza el sollo. [How to prepare sturgeon] 165 [382; 383]
[253] Sollo asado. [Grilled sturgeon] 166 [382–4; 383–5]
[254] Albondiguillas de sollo. [Sturgeon balls] 167 [384; 385]
[255] Pastel de sollo. [Sturgeon pie] 167 [384; 385]
[256] Un pastel embote de sollo. [Crustless sturgeon pie] 168 [384; 385]
[257] Costrada de sollo. [Sturgeon puff pastry pie] 168 [386; 387]
[258] Empanada Inglesa de sollo. [English empanada with sturgeon] 168 [386; 387]
[259] Empanada de sollo. [Sturgeon empanada] 169 [386; 387]
[260] Artaletes del sollo. [Sturgeon pinwheels] 169 [388; 389]
[261] Aguja paladar. [Swordfish] 170 [388; 389]
[262] Cómo se aderezan las truchas. [How to prepare trout] 170 [388–90; 389–91]
[263] Otro cocimiento de truchas. [Another trout boil] 171 [390; 391]
[264]• Otro. [Another] 171 [390; 391]
[265] Truchas estofadas. [Trout stew] 171 [390–2; 391–3]

[266] Sopa de truchas. [Trout sops] 172 [392; 393]
[267] Cazuela de truchas. [Trout casserole] 172 [392; 393]
[268] Plato de truchas y berzas. [Dish of trout and collard greens] 172 [392–4; 393–5]
[269] Pastelón de truchas. [Big trout pie] 173 [394; 395]
[270] Cómo se adereza el atún. [How to prepare tuna] 173 [394; 395]
[271] Costrada de atún. [Tuna puff pastry pie] 174 [396; 397]
[272] Pastelón de atún. [Big tuna pie] 174 [396; 397]
[273] Salpicón de atún. [Tuna salpicon] 175 [398; 399]
[274] Atún lampreado. [Tuna, lamprea style] 175 [398; 399]
[275] Olla de atún. [Tuna stew] 176 [398; 399]
[276] Escabeche de atún. [Pickled tuna] 176 [398; 399]
[277] Cazuela de lamprea. [Lamprey stew] 176 [400; 401]
[278] Empanada de lamprea. [Lamprey empanada] 177 [400; 401]
[279] Lamprea asada. [Roast lamprey] 177 [400; 401]
[280] Lamprea en cecina. [Cured lamprey] 177 [400–2; 401–3]
[281] Jibia, y calamares, y pulpo. [Cuttlefish, squid, and octopus] 178 [402; 403]
[282] Cómo se aderezan los caracoles. [How to prepare snails] 178 [402–4; 403–5]
[283] Caracoles rellenos. [Stuffed snails] 179 [404; 405]
[284] Pasteles de caracoles. [Snail pies] 180 [404; 405]
[285] Cómo se guisan las criadillas de tierra. [How to cook truffles] 180 [404–6; 405–7]
[286]^ Otro platillo de criadillas. [Another truffle dish] 180 [406; 407]
[287]^ Cazuela de criadillas. [Truffle stew] 181 [406; 407]
[288] Criadillas de tierra con huevos revueltos. [Truffles with scrambled eggs] 181 [406; 407]
[289]^ Pastel de criadillas. [Truffle pie] 182 [406–8; 407–9]
[290] Platillo de cardo. [A dish of cardoons] 182 [408; 409]
[291]^ Otro diferente. [Another, different one] 183 [408–10; 409–11]
[292] Pastel de cardos. [Cardoon pie] 183 [410; 411]
[293] Cebollas rellenas. [Stuffed onions] 184 [410–12; 411–13]
[294] Cómo se aderezan las carpas. [How to prepare carp] 185 [412; 413]
[295] Sopa de carpas. [Carp served on sops] 185 [412–14; 413–15]
[296] Pastel enbote de carpas. [Crustless carp pie] 186 [414; 415]
[297] Albondiguillas de carpas. [Carp balls] 187 [414; 415]
[298]^ Cómo se puede freír, asar, y cocer un pescado todo en un tiempo. [How to fry, roast, and boil a fish at the same time] 187 [414–16; 415–17]
[299] Cómo se guisan las enguilas. [How to cook eel] 189 [418; 419]
[300] Cazuela de enguilas. [Eel stew] 189 [418; 419]
[301]^ Enguilas en pan. [Eel wrapped in bread] 190 [418; 419]
[302] Un barbo estofado. [Stewed barbel] 190 [418–20; 419–21]
[303] Barbos en moreta. [Barbel in moreta sauce] 191 [420; 421]
[304] Besugos en escabeche a uso de Portugal. [Pickled sea bream, as prepared in Portugal] 191 [420–2; 421–3]

[305] Sardinas rellenas de escabeche. [Pickled stuffed sardines] 192 [422; 423]
[306] Cómo se guisan las langostas. [How to cook lobster] 193 [422–4; 423–5]
[307] Langosta rellena. [Stuffed lobster] 193 [424; 425]
[308] Cómo se aderezan los cangrejos. [How to prepare crab] 194 [424; 425]
[309] Cómo se aderezan los ostiones. [How to prepare oysters] 194 [426; 427]
[310]^ Pasteles de ostiones. [Oyster pies] 195 [426; 427]
[311] Cómo se aderezan los mariscos. [How to prepare shellfish] 195 [426; 427]
[312] Ranas. [Frog] 196 [428; 429]
[313] Pastel de ranas. [Frog pie] 196 [428; 429]
[314] Pasteles de pies de puerco. [Pig's feet pie] 197 [428; 429]
[315] Cazuela de pies de puerco. [Pig's feet casserole] 197 [430; 431]
[316] Cazuela verde de pies de puerco. [Green pig's feet stew] 198 [430; 431]
[317] Pasteles de piñones y huevos mejidos. [Pine nut pie with sweet scrambled egg yolks] 199 [430–2; 431–3]
[318] Huevos hilados. [Candied egg yolk threads] 199 [432–4; 433–5]
[319] Otro plato de huevos hilados. [Another dish of candied egg yolk threads] 201 [434–6; 435–7]
[320] Plato de huevos mejidos. [Dish of sweet scrambled egg yolks] 202 [436; 437]
[321] Huevos esponjados. [Fluffy eggs] 202 [436; 437]
[322] Huevos de alforja. [Saddlebag eggs] 203 [438; 439]
[323] Huevos con cominos. [Eggs with cumin] 204 [438; 439]
[324] Capirotada de huevos. [Eggs, capirotada style] 205 [440; 441]
[325] Otra capirotada de huevos rellenos. [Another stuffed egg recipe, capirotada style] 205 [440; 441]
[326]^ Otros. [Other (eggs)] 206 [440; 441]
[327] Huevos crecidos. [Expanded eggs] 206 [442; 443]
[328] Huevos en escudilla. [Eggs in a bowl] 207 [442; 443]
[329] Huevos revueltos con vino. [Scrambled eggs with wine] 207 [442; 443]
[330] Huevos arrollados. [Eggs in a ring] 208 [444; 445]
[331] Tortillas de agua. [Water omelette] 208 [444; 445]
[332] Tortillas cartujas. [Carthusian omelette] 209 [444–6; 445–7]
[333] Tortillas dobladas. [Folded omelette] 209 [446; 447]
[334] Tortilla blanca. [White omelette] 209 [446; 447]
[335]^ Una tortilla con agua, y sal, y zumo de limón. [Omelette (made) with water, salt, and lemon juice] 210 [446; 447]
[336] Tortilla con queso fresco. [Omelette with farmer cheese] 210 [448; 449]
[337] Huevos de capirote. [Eggs capirote] 210 [448; 449]
[338] Platillo de huevos dulces. [Dish of sweet eggs] 211 [448–50; 449–51]
[339] Huevos dorados. [Golden eggs] 212 [450; 451]
[340] Fricasea de huevos. [Egg fricassee] 213 [450–2; 451–3]
[341] Huevos en puchero. [Eggs in a stew pot] 213 [452; 453]

[342] Sopa de huevos escalfados con leche. [Milk sops with poached eggs] 214 [452–4; 453–5]
[343] Sopa de huevos estrellados con leche. [Milk sops with fried eggs] 214 [454; 455]
[344] Torrijas de pan. [Torrijas] 215 [454; 455]
[345] Sopa borracha. [Drunken sops] 215 [454–6; 455–7]
[346] Otra sopa borracha. [Other drunken sops] 216 [456; 457]
[347] Otra sopa borracha. [Other drunken sops] 216 [456; 457]
[348]^ Otra. [Another] 217 [458; 459]
[349] Empanada de pernil de tocino. [Fatty ham empanada] 217 [458; 459]
[350] Empanada de menudos de pavos. [Turkey giblet empanada] 218 [458–60; 459–61]
[351] Un pastel de membrillos. [Quince pie] 219 [460; 461]
[352] Pastelillos Saboyanos. [Little Savoy pastries] 220 [460–2; 461–3]
[353] Un pernil cocido sin remojar. [Leg boiled without soaking] 220 [462; 463]
[354] Cómo se hace el alcuzcuz. [How to make couscous] 221 [462–6; 463–7]
[355] Cómo se guisa el alcuzcuz. [How to cook couscous] 223 [466; 467]
[356] Hojaldrillas de manteca de vacas. [Puff pastry with butter] 223 [466–8; 467–9]
[357]^ Otras hojaldrillas. [Other little pastries] 224 [468; 469]
[358] Cabrito relleno asado. [Stuffed kid, roasted] 225 [468; 469]
[359] Cabrito relleno cocido. [Stuffed kid, boiled] 225 [470; 471]
[360] Platillo de cabrito. [An individual kid dish] 226 [470; 471]
[361] Otro plato de medio cabrito. [Another dish of half a kid] 227 [470–2; 471–3]
[362] Sopas a la Portuguesa. [Sops, Portuguese style] 227 [472; 473]
[363]§ Sopa de vaca a la portuguesa, contrahecho en día de pescado. [Beef sops, Portuguese style, faux for fish days] [472; 473]
[364] Otra Sopa de vaca. [Another beef sops (dish)] 228 [474; 475]
[365] Cómo se adereza la ubre de la jabalina. [How to prepare boar udder] 228 [474–6; 475–7]
[366] Conejos rellenos. [Stuffed rabbit] 229 [476; 477]
[367] Conejos en empanada. [Rabbit in an empanada] 230 [476; 477]
[368] Perdices asadas con aceite. [Roast partridge with oil] 230 [476; 477]
[369] Pasteles de carnero y de pernil de tocino. [Mutton and fatty ham pies] 231 [478; 479]
[370] Artaletes asados. [Roasted pinwheels] 232 [478; 479]
[371] Torta de dama. [Lady pie] 232 [478–80; 479–81]
[372]^ Otra torta. [Another pie] 233 [480–2; 481–3]
[373]^ Otra de dama. [Another lady (pie)] 234 [482; 483]
[374] Torta blanca. [White pie] 234 [482; 483]
[375]^ Costrada de mollejas de ternera. [Puff pastry pie with sweetbreads] 235 [482; 483]
[376] Bollo de mazapán y manteca fresca. [Marzipan and butter roll] 235 [484; 485]

[377] Pan de leche. [Milk bread] 235 [484; 485]
[378] Torta de dátiles. [Date pie] 236 [484; 485]
[379] Quesadillas de mazapán. [Marzipan cheese tarts] 236 [484–6; 485–7]
[380] Pasteles Flaones. [Custard pie] 237 [486; 487]
[381] Otros Flaones. [Other custard] 237 [486; 487]
[382] Pasteles de leche. [Custard pies] 238 [486–8; 487–9]
[383]^ Sustancias. [Sustaining broths] 238 [488–90; 489–91]
[384] Sustancia de pobres. [Sustaining broth for the poor] 240 [490; 491]
[385] Sustancia asada. [Essence from a roast] 241 [492; 493]
[386] Una escudilla de caldo. [A bowl of (hen) broth] 242 [492; 493]
[387] Una escudilla de almendrada. [A bowl of almond broth] 242 [492–4; 493–5]
[388] Una escudilla de borrajas. [A bowl of borage soup] 243 [494; 495]
[389] Manteca de almendras amarilla. [Yellow almond butter] 244 [494–6; 495–7]
[390] Otra manteca de almendras blanca. [Another white almond butter] 244 [496; 497]
[391] Farro. [Farro] 245 [496–8; 497–9]
[392] Pistos para enfermos. [Pisto soup for the ill] 246 [498; 499]
[393] Una panetela. [Panatela (Hen and mutton bread soup)] 247 [500; 501]
[394] Otra panetela. [Another panatela (Another bread soup for fish days)] 247 [500; 501]
[395] Ginebradas. [Ginebradas (Clotted milk tarts)] 248 [500–2; 501–3]
[396] Otras ginebradas. [Other ginebradas (Other clotted milk tarts)] 249 [502; 503]
[397] Conserva de manjar blanco. [Blancmange preserves] 249 [502–4; 503–5]
[398] Un capón que sea medio cocido y medio asado. [Capon, half boiled, half roasted] 250 [504; 505]
[399] Gallina a la morisca. [Hen, Morisco style] 250 [504; 505]
[400] Panecillos de colaciones. [Collation rolls] 251 [504–6; 505–7]
[401] Hojaldrillas fritas. [Little fried puff pastries] 251 [506; 507]
[402] Buñuelos de queso asadero. [Puffs of asadero cheese] 252 [506; 507]
[403] Ñoclos de masa. [Bite-sized wafers made with dough] 252 [508; 509]
[404] Fruta de Fartes. [Fartes fried dough] 253 [508–10; 509–11]
[405] Memoria de los mostachones. [Memoir of mostachon cookies] 254 [510; 511]
[406] Memoria de la mostaza negra. [Memoir of black mustard] 255 [512–14; 513–15]
[407] Vinagre de saúco. [Elderberry vinegar] 256 [514; 515]
[408]^ Otro. [Another] 257 [514–16; 515–17]
[409] Agraz para todo el año. [Verjuice for the whole year] 258 [516; 517]
[410]^ Otro. [Another] 258 [516; 517]
[411]^ Pepinos en vinagre. [Pickles] 259 [518; 519]
[412] La oruga de miel. [Arugula and honey sauce] 259 [518; 519]
[413] Oruga de azúcar. [Arugula and sugar sauce] 260 [518; 519]

Capítulo II

[414] Sopa de Aragón. [Sops, Aragonese style] 260 [520; 521]
[415] Manteca de názulas. [Nazulas butter] 261 [520–2; 521–3]
[416] Cómo se hacen las mantequillas de leche de cabras. [How to make butter from goat milk] 262 [522; 523]
[417] Aceite de huevos. [Egg oil] 262 [522; 523]
[418] Aceite de almendras sin fuego. [Almond oil, without cooking] 263 [524; 525]
[419] Cómo se puede asar una pella de manteca de vacas en asador. [How to roast a butterball on a spit] 263 [524–6; 525–7]
[420] Memoria de los bizcochelos. [Memoir of ladyfingers] 265 [526–8; 527–9]
[421] Bollitos pardos. [Cinnamon rolls with marzipan] 266 [528; 529]
[422] Tortillas delgadas de aceite. [Thin, frosted cookies] 266 [528; 529]
[423] Memoria de las rosquillas. [Memoir of ring-shaped pastries] 267 [530; 531]
[424] Otra suerte de rosquillas. [Another kind of ring-shaped pastries] 267 [530; 531]
[425] Baño blanco para rosquillas, y otras cosas. [Meringue for ring-shaped pastries and other things] 268 [530; 531]
[426] Gilea de vino. [Wine jelly] 268 [532–4; 533–5]
[427] Melindres de azúcar. [Sugar cookies] 270 [534–6; 535–7]
[428] Bizcochos sin harina. [Flourless sweet biscuits] 271 [536; 537]
[429] Memoria de berenjenas en escabeche. [Memoir of pickled eggplant] 271 [536–8; 537–9]
[430] Memoria del adobo de aceitunas. [Memoir of olive marinade] 272 [538; 539]
[431] Bizcochos de harina de trigo. [Sweet biscuits with wheat flour] 273 [538–42; 539–43]
[432] Memoria de los bizcochos de almidón. [Memoir of sweet biscuits with starch] 274 [542; 543]
[433] Batido de los bizcochos de almidón sin vidriado. [Batter for sweet biscuits with starch and no glaze] 275 [542–4; 543–5]
[434] Otra suerte de bizcochos secos. [Another kind of dry sweet biscuits] 276 [544; 545]
[435] Mazapanes de dos pastas. [Two-dough marzipan] 276 [544–6; 545–7]
[436] Mazapanes secos. [Dry marzipan] 277 [546; 547]
[437] Mazapanes en almíbar. [Marzipan in simple syrup] 278 [546; 547]
[438] Bizcochillos secos. [Mini dry sweet biscuits] 278 [546–8; 547–9]
[439] Otros bizcochos. [Other sweet biscuits] 279 [548; 549]
[440]• Otros bizcochos. [Other sweet biscuits] [548; 549]
[441]^ Bizcochos de harina de arroz, y de trigo. [Combined wheat and rice flour sweet biscuits] 279 [548; 549]
[442] Una fruta de natas. [Fried cream] 280 [550; 551]
[443] Unas rebanadas de pan conservadas. [Preserved bread slices] 280 [550–2; 551–3]
[444] Tabletas de masa. [Dough twists] 281 [552; 553]

[445] ^Plato de papín tostado. [Dish of toasted sweet cream] 282 [552; 553]
[446] Perdices rellenas. [Stuffed partridges] 283 [552–4; 553–5]
[447]^ Carnero adobado. [Marinated mutton] 283 [554; 555]
[448] Torreznos lampreados. [Roasted pork fat, lamprea style] 284 [554; 555]
[449] Membrillos asados. [Roasted quince] 285 [556; 557]
[450]^ Cómo se han de aparar las aves. [How to present poultry] 286 [556–8; 557–9]
[451] Cómo se han de aparar los pavos. [How to present turkey] 287 [558–60; 559–61]
[452] Corte de lechón. [Carving suckling pig] 288 [560; 561]
[453]^ Cómo se ha de aparar la liebre. [How to present hare] 288 [560; 561]

Memoria de conservas 289 [560; 561]

[454]• Albérchigos [Apricots] 289 [562; 563]
[455]^ Duraznos en conserva. [Clingstone peaches] 289 [562; 563]
[456]^ Melocotones en conserva. [Firm peaches] 290 [562; 563]
[457] Bocados de duraznos. [Morsels of clingstone peach purée] 290 [564; 565]
[458] Peras en almíbar. [Pears in simple syrup] 290 [564; 565]
[459] Cajas de perada. [Boxes of preserved pear purée] 290 [564; 565]
[460] Toronjas. [Toronja] 291 [566; 567]
[461] Limones Ceutíes. [Ceuti lemons] 291 [566; 567]
[462] Raíz de borraja. [Borage root] 291 [566; 567]
[463] Azúcar rosado colorado. [Rose coloured sugar] 293 [566; 567]
[464] Flor de borrajas. [Borage blossoms] 292 [568; 569]
[465]^ De romero. [Rosemary (flower syrup)] 292 [568; 569]
[466] Azúcar rosado blanco. [White rose sugar] 293 [568–70; 569–71]
[467] Calabazate. [Sweetened dried squash] 293 [570; 571]
[468] Tallos de lechugas. [Lettuce stalks] 293 [570; 571]
[469] Bocados de calabaza. [Morsels of squash] 294 [572; 573]
[470] Raíces de escorzonera. [Black salsify root] 294 [572; 573]
[471] Peras secas cubiertas. [Candied dried pear] 294 [572; 573]
[472] Membrillos para la mermelada. [Quince for jam] 295 [574; 575]
[473] Diacitrón. [Candied citron] 295 [574; 575]

Memoria de jaleas

[474]^ Memoria de jalea. [Memoir of jelly] 296 [574–6; 575–7]
[475]^ Jalea de granadas. [Pomegranate jelly] 296 [576; 577]
[476]^ Jalea de amacenas. [Damson plum jelly] 297 [576; 577]
[477]^ Jalea de agraz. [Sour grape jelly] 297 [576; 577]
[478] Cuartos de membrillos. [Quartered quince] 297 [578; 579]
[479]^ Carne de membrillos. [Quince paste] 297 [578; 579]
[480] Ciruelas de Génova. [Genoese plums] 298 [578; 579]
[481] Nueces en conserva. [Preserved walnuts] 298 [580; 581]

620 Capitulo II

[482] Hinojo conservado. [Preserved fennel] 299 [580–2; 581–3]
[483] Carbonadillas de ternera estofadas. [Thinly sliced veal, stewed] 300 [582; 583]
[484] Un platillo de cabrito. [A kid dish] 301 [582; 583]
[485] Manjar blanco de pescado. [Fish blancmange] 301 [584; 585]
[486] Papín de harina de trigo. [Sweet cream sauce made with wheat flour] 302 [584–6; 585–7]
[487] Pastelón de cidra verde. [Big green citron pie] 303 [586; 587]
[488] Una cazolilla de ave para enfermos. [Poultry in a saucepan for the sick] 303 [586–8; 587–9]
[489] Palominos armados. [Dressed squab] 305 [588; 589]
[490] Platillo de asadurillas de cabrito. [A dish of kid liver and lung] 306 [590; 591]
[491] Cómo se aderezan los hígados de venado y de ternera. [How to prepare venison or veal liver] 307 [590–2; 591–3]
[492] Manecillas de cabrito. [Kid trotters] 307 [592; 593]
[493] Potaje de trigo. [Wheat porridge] 308 [592–4; 593–5]
[494] Colas de carnero en agraz. [Mutton tail in verjuice sauce] 209 [*sic*] [594; 595]
[495] Una escudilla de almidón. [A bowl of starch] 309 [594; 595]
[496]^ Platillo de lechugas, y otras muchas hierbas. [A dish of lettuce and many other leafy greens] 310 [594–6; 595–7]
[497] Huevos encañutados. [Sweet egg canutos] 311 [596; 597]
[498] Una empanada de pichones. [Squab empanada] 311 [596; 597]
[499] Estocafíx. [Stockfish] 311 [596–8; 597–9]
[500] Hongos. [Wild mushrooms] 312 [598; 599]
[501] Fruta de almendras. [Fried almond pastry] 313 [598; 599]
[502] Salchichas. [Sausages] 313 [600; 601]
[503] Sustancia asada. [Essence from a roast] 313 [600; 601]
[504]§ Cómo se manen las aves en dos horas. [How to tenderize poultry in two hours] [600–2; 601–3]
[505] Platillo de cardillos. [A dish of golden thistle] 316 [602; 603]
[506] Potaje de castañas. [Chestnut soup] 317 [602–4; 603–5]

Fin de la Tabla. [End of the table.]

Appendix 1
Kitchen Furnishings and Equipment[1]

Table A.1. A listing of kitchen furnishings in Martínez Montiño's cookbook

Kitchen furnishings	Translation	Count
caballos	cobb irons	1
hornillo	small oven	2
horno	oven	61
horno de barro	terracotta oven	2
horno de cobre	copper oven	6
horno de pan	bread oven	4
horno de pan o de cobre	bread or copper oven	1
ladrillo	brick	2
mesa	table	1
parrilla o asador	grill	1
parrillas	grill	33
pozo	well	1
tabla	board	2
trébedes	trivets	5
Grand total		**117**

Table A.2. A listing of the common cookware in Martínez Montiño's cookbook

Common cookware	Translation	Count
sartén	frying pan	67
cazuela	casserole	55
olla	pot	49
tortera	covered tart pan	46
cazo	large saucepan	41
cacillo	saucepan	24
cacito	saucepan	16

(Continued)

---

1 For more information on kitchen furnishings and equipment, see Nadeau, "Furniture and Equipment."

Table A.2. *(Continued)*

Common cookware	Translation	Count
cobertera	lid	14
ollita	small pot	10
perol	big, round-bottom cooking pot	9
cazolilla	small saucepan or tartlet pan	6
hoja del horno	baking sheet	6
pieza de plata	silver piece	6
vidrio	glass	5
cajitas de papel	paper boxes	4
caldero	cauldron	4
Grand total		**362**

Table A.3. A listing of the specialty cookware in Martínez Montiño's cookbook

Specialty cookware	Translation	Count
alcuzcucero	couscousier	1
almofia	basin	1
barquilla	barquette mould	1
barquillo	funnel-shaped vessel	1
barquino	leather flask	1
barreñón	tub	1
caldera	cauldron	1
cazolita	little saucepan	1
cazuelilla	little pot	1
cazuelita	little pot	1
escudilleta	small bowl	1
graserilla	drip pan	1
gubiletes de cobre	copper moulds	1
redoma	flask	1
redomilla	small flask	1
sartenilla	small frying pan	1
Grand total		**16**

Table A.4. A listing of the common prepware and serveware in Martínez Montiño's cookbook

Common prepware	Translation	Count
tablero	cutting board	75
almirez	metallic mortar	43
pieza	piece	20
escudilla	bowl	12
vidrio	glass	8

(Continued)

Table A.4. *(Continued)*

Common prepware	Translation	Count
vasija	vessel	8
perol	round-bottom bowl	7
barreñón	tub	5
caja	box	5
olla	pot	5
mortero	mortar	3
tabla	board	3
Common serveware		
plato	plate/platter	86
platillo	small plate/platter	11
cesta	basket	4
Grand total		**295**

Table A.5. A listing of specialty prepware and serveware in Martínez Montiño's cookbook

Specialty prepware and serveware	Translation	Count
For storage/transporting		
banasta	woven basket (for transporting venison)	2
paja de centeno	rye straw (for packaging food)	2
taleguilla	small sack (for transporting dried flowers)	1
For preserving		
barril	barrel (for pickling tuna)	2
tablilla	small board (to test sugar stage)	2
barreñón	tub (for making mustard)	1
barreñoncillo vidriado	small glazed tub	1
berguera	fruit sieve (for candied fruit)	1
dornajo de barro	terracotta trough (for preserving venison)	1
For baked goods		
alorza	glazed terracotta jar (for preserved walnuts)	1
albornía	big glazed terracotta pot (for making meringue)	1
cestilla	small basket (for dough to rise)	1
librillo	terracotta bowl (for kneading dough)	1
For couscous		
almofía	basin (placed on top of simmering pot)	1
artesilla de palo	wooden trough	1
porcelana	porcelain dish (placed on top of simmering pot)	1
serilla redonda de las de Valencia	round woven basket from Valencia	1

(Continued)

Table A.5. *(Continued)*

Specialty prepware and serveware	Translation	Count
For other uses		
bacía	basin (for rinsing intestines)	2
angeo	coarse linen (to wrap boar head before boiling)	1
azucarero	sugar shaker	1
barquino de cuero	leather flask (for consommé for the ill)	1
flamenquilla	medium-sized serving plate	1
salserilla	gravy boat (for three different fish sauces)	1
trinchero	carving platter (for partridge)	1
Grand Total		**29**

Table A.6. A listing of utensils in Martínez Montiño's cookbook

To spread/stir			To cut/puncture			To separate		
Spoons			*For cutting*			*Sieves*		
cucharón	ladle; big spoon	43	cuchillo	knife	31	cedacillo	small sieve	22
cucharón de manjar blanco	blancmange spoon	6	cortadera	trimmer	11	cedazo	sieve	7
cucharita	small spoon	9	tijeras	scissors	1	colador	colander	17
cuchara	spoon	5	rallo	grater	1	espumadera	skimmer	10
cuchara cerrada	regular spoon	3	*For skewering*			harnero	sieve	2
cuchara de plata	silver spoon	2	asador	spit, skewer	23	harnerillos	smaller sieve	1
cuchara espumadera	skimmer	2	asadorcillo	small skewer	1	criba	wide-hole sieve	1
cucharilla	small spoon	1	broqueta	broquette	6	*Cloths*		
cucharoncito chiquito	very small spoon	1	broquetilla	small broquette	3	estameña	cheesecloth	25
remo de manjar blanco	paddle	1	filete	small skewer	1	paño	cloth	13
Spatulas			*For puncturing*			servilleta	napkin	11
paleta	spatula	20	tenedor	fork	7	mantel	tablecloth	5
paletilla	small spatula	1	tenedorcillo	small fork	1	manga	jelly bag	2
palillo, spatula	spatula	1	alfiler	pin	4	pañito	small cloth	2
For sprinkling			mechadera	larding needle	4	lienzo	linen	1
plumas	feathers	17	dedal	thimble	1	lino	linen	1
hisopillo	hyssop brush	3	punzón	awl	1	toalla	towel	1
			aguja	needle	3			
Total		115			99			121

(*Continued*)

Table A.6. (Continued)

To flatten			To seal/secure			Specialty utensils		
mortero	mortar	5	*Thread*			*For containing*		
prensa	press	3	hilo	thread	10	papel	paper	25
palo de masa	rolling pin	2	hilo de bala	twine	1	papelillo	paper	3
piedra (2)	stone	2	cordel	cord	1	pergamino	parchment	3
plato	plate	2	*Cloth*			cama (de lino)	couche	1
mazo	mallet	1	estopas	burlap	1	ropa	cloth (for rising dough)	1
palo	stick	1	sedeña	linen cloth	1	*For shaping*		
prensilla	small press	1	*Other*			buñolera	puff maker	3
			corcho	cork	6	caña	reed (for bollo de rodilla)	1
			piedra	rock	1	cañutos de cañas	reed tubes	1
						garabato	spoon hook (for puffs)	1
						hierro a manera de hongo	mushroom-shaped iron	1
						Other		
						cosa que pese dos arrobas	two-pound weight	1
						palillos para mondar los dientes	fennel sticks for toothpicks	1
						sello de la cortadera	seal on trimmer	1
Total		17			21			43
Grand total								416

Appendix 2
On Measurements

In terms of quantities of ingredients, more times than not, Martínez Montiño does not specify exactly how much is needed. However, where he does specify quantities of weight, volume, length, heat, or time, the following expressions are the ones that most commonly appear.

Weight

Arroba [arroba] This unit of weight (it could also measure mass or volume) was equivalent to 25 pounds (11.5 kilograms). Martínez Montiño uses it to measure *agraz* [sour grapes] and *amacenas* [damson plums]. He also uses it to designate the weight of an object used for applying pressure when making cheese. It is used in four recipes with the designations of half, two, and four.

Cuarterón [quarter pound] This measurement is used primarily to weigh sugar but is also used for *almendras* [almonds], *manteca* [fatback], *manteca de vacas* [butter], *farro* [farro], *harina de arroz* [rice flour], and *harina de trigo* [wheat flour]. He uses this term thirty-four times in his cookbook.

Maravedí [maravedi] This small monetary unit was the basis upon which other coins were measured and was minted in 1-, 2-, 4-, and 8-maravedi denominations and varied in size. Martínez Montiño uses this term six times to explain how much *pimienta* [black pepper] (4 mvs and 8 mvs), *miel* [honey] (8 mvs), *vino* [wine] (2 mvs), *anís* [anisette] (2 mvs), and *alcaravea* [caraway] (1/4 mvs) is needed in their respective recipes. This would be comparable today to a *penny* or a *quarter* of … The idea is how much quantity would equal the coin's weight on a scale.

Libra [pound] This standard unit actually varied according to region and to area of usage. Covarrubias explains that "es peso comúnmente de doze onzas, pero éstas se varían a más o a menos, conforme el uso de la tierra y la calidad de las cosas que se pesan" [It is commonly a weight of twelve ounces, but these varied more or less, according to its use in a given place and the type of thing being weighed] (764). He specifically states that "la libra carnizera pesa a

doble de la ordinaria" [the butcher pound weighs twice the ordinary] (764). Martínez Montiño uses this term 228 times, primarily for sugar, but also for meats, all sorts of fruits and nuts, other sweeteners, dairy products, flour, and dough. Common designations include half, one and a half, two, three, four, and six.

Onza [ounce] According to Covarrubias, the ounce was a sixteenth part of a pound, as it is today, although he also acknowledges that the pound was formerly divided into twelve ounces (837). Martínez Montiño uses the ounce thirty times to measure *azúcar* [sugar], five times more than some of the other ingredients measured in ounces like *almendras* [almonds], *canela* [cinnamon], *tocino* [fatback], *harina de trigo* [wheat flour], *clavo* [clove], and *agua de azahar* [orange blossom water].[1] He also uses the term to describe the weight of a finished product; for example, the two-ounce *mostachon* cookie or the four-ounce collation roll. Common designations include one and a half, two, four, six, eight, and up to ten.

Un poco de [a little] This is Martínez Montiño's most common measurement. It appears 849 times throughout the 506 recipes. It is primarily used with seasoning and also with heat.

Length

Cuarta [one quarter of a *vara castellana* (Castilian yard)] Used in the cookbook for the length of a cloth, it measures somewhere between 19 cm and 23 cm or 7.5 and 9 in.

Dedo [finger] Martínez Montiño uses this term fifty-one times to explain the length of pinwheels, meat, strips of dough, or the width of batter in its container. It is also used to indicate spacing between one item and another. Common designations are a half, one, one and a half, two, three, four, and six. 48 *dedos* make up a *vara*.

Legua [league] Used for distances when travelling with food, measures 4.83 km or 3 miles.

Ochava [one eighth of a *vara castellana* (Castilian yard)] Used in the cookbook for cuts of meat, marzipan roll, or dough. It measures somewhere between 9.5 and 11.4 cm or 3.75 and 4.5 in.

Pliego de papel [sheet of paper] According to documents at the Royal Palace, a *pliego de papel* at the seventeenth-century court measured approximately 43 by 21 cm or 17 by 8.25 in. In the cookbook, Martínez Montiño explains how to cut a single sheet to make up to sixteen individual sheets for baking. Common sizes are the *medio pliego* [half sheet] and the *cuartilla* [quarter sheet].

---

1 I suspect that sugar may be measured more often than other products because it was so closely tied to medical remedies. In recipes for medicinal use it is very common to have exact amounts of herbs, waters, and all ingredients used.

Pulgada [inch, 1/12 of a *pie* (foot) and 1/36 of a *vara* (yard)] Martínez Montiño uses *pulgada* or *pulgada y media* [an inch and a half] eight times in the cookbook for explaining how much batter to include, or the height of the edge of the dough. Note, although the same word is used today, the length in 1611 may have slightly varied. See *vara* below.

Sesma [one sixth of a *vara castellana* (Castilian yard)] Used in the cookbook for the length of a cloth. It measures between 12.7 and 15.24 cm or 5 and 6 in.

Vara [yard] A standard unit of measurement used in early modern Spain, though, according to the Real Academia Española, the length varied between 768 and 912 millimetres or between two and a half and three feet. José Castaño Álvarez notes the following comparisons: 1 vara = 2 codos o media = 3 pies o tercia = 4 palmos o cuarta = 5 quintos = 6 jemes o sesma = 7 sétimos = 8 cotos, media cuarta u octava = 9 novenos = 10 décimos = 12 dozavos = 36 pulgadas = 48 dedos [1 yard = 2 elbow lengths or a half = 3 feet or a third = 4 palm lengths or a quarter = 5 fifths = 6 lengths between the thumb and the index finger = 7 sevenths = 8 half a palm lengths, half of a quarter or an eighth = 9 ninths = 10 tenths = 12 twelfths = 36 inches = 48 fingers] (128).

Volume

Dry Measurement[2]

Celemín [celemin] A *celemín* is one twelfth of a *fanega* and measure 4.625 litres, approximately a gallon. It is used once to measure salt, and a "half celemin" is used twice to measure flour.

Cuartillo [quart, for dry ingredients] For dry measurements, a *cuartillo* is a quarter of a *celemín*, or one *quart*. However, dry measurements are normally expressed in *cups* instead of *quarts*. For this reason, I have translated dry measurements for *cuartillo* as cups. It should be noted that this same word differs for wet measurements, where a *cuartillo* is a quarter of an *azumbre*, which measures approximately two quarts. So, for wet measurements, a *cuartillo* is a *pint*. Although Martínez Montiño primarily uses the term for wet measurements, he does use it once to measure *trigo* [wheat], once ("medio cuartillo" [two cups]) for *cemite* [bran], and once ("tres cuartillos" [twelve cups]) for *sal* [salt].

Fanega [bushel] A *fanega* is the equivalent of twelve *celemines*. Bushels used to be equivalent to eight dry gallons, but today bushels define masses by the commodity and thus vary by product. Martínez Montiño uses this term just once for olives in brine.

---

2 For a comparative layout of dry measurements, see Castaño Álvarez 329.

Wet Measurement

Azumbre [two-quart measure] An *azumbre* is approximately equivalent to 2.05 litres or a little more than two quarts. Covarrubias explains the *azumbre* in the following way: "Se divide en cuatro medidas que llaman cuartillos" [It is divided into four measures called quarts] (40). Martínez Montiño uses the measurement for various liquids, including *agua* [water], *leche* [milk], *caldo* [broth/stock], *vino* [wine], *vinagre* [vinegar], and *miel* [honey]. He also uses the term to describe the size of pots or a glass flask; for example, "redomas de vidrio de a tres azumbres" [six-quart glass flasks] (514; 515). The denominations he uses are half, one, one and a half, two, three, and seven.

Cuartillo [pint, for wet ingredients] For wet measurements, a *cuartillo* is a quarter of an *azumbre*, which is approximately equivalent to 2.05 litres or a little more than two quarts. So this in turn means that a *cuartillo* is approximately a half a quart or a *pint*. As with the measurement *azumbre*, Martínez Montiño uses *cuartillo* for various liquids like *agua* [water], *leche* [milk], *caldo* [broth/stock], *vino* [wine], *vinagre* [vinegar], and *miel* [honey]. He also uses it to measure *zumo* [juice], *sustancia* [sustaining broth], *natas* [cream], and *aceite* [oil]. *Cuartillo* [pint] is a popular measurement, as noted by the many designations it has in the cookbook, half of a half, half, one, one and a half, three and five. In total, he uses the term forty-three times for wet ingredients.

While volume is sometimes provided with these traditional units, other times it is specified proportionately with common food, as is the case in the following examples: "Has le de echar tanto vinagre como quepa en una cáscara de avellana" [Pour in as much vinegar as fits in the shell of a hazelnut] (472; 473); "échale tanto vinagre como quepa en una cáscara de media naranja, y otra tanta agua" [add as much vinegar as fits in the rind of a half orange and the same amount of water] (168; 169).

Temperature

Often modern readers feel at a loss for how to cook early modern recipes, because the temperatures are not explicitly stated in numbers as they are today. But careful readers can begin to understand temperatures by comparing instructions for heat application among the different recipes. In fact, Martínez Montiño uses over a hundred variations in applying heat.

Most times the heat source is below the cooking instrument, and at times *trébedes* [trivets] are used to take extra care to not burn the ingredients (see Figure A2.1, letter I). But many times, for example in the case of the portable oven (what we think of today as a Dutch oven), the heat comes from both below and above. In fact, these portable ovens like the *tortera* are designed with lids with lips so that they can easily hold embers, which are also described in varying degrees from cooler, grey embers to red-hot embers (see Figure A2.1, letter O).

Figure A2.1. *Trébedes* (marked I, in the middle) and *tortera* (marked O), detail reproduced from a diagram of kitchen equipment and legend found in the front material of the 1760 edition of Martínez Montiño's *Arte de cocina*. Photo by author, courtesy of Museo Massó, Bueu, Spain. N.p., 2017.

Open Flame

From low to high:
  poquito [very little]
  poco o manso [little or gentle]
  la lumbre que ha de asar ... no ha de estar debajo, sino adelante, y ha de haber buena lumbre clara de tizos de carbón [the heat for roasting should not be directly below but rather in front of it. It should be a good, clean flame of charcoal coals]
  al fuego, poco lumbre abajo y poco encima [put it on low heat both above and below]
  moderado [moderate]
  no más de medio hervor [no more than a moderate boil]

buena [good]

al amor de la lumbre de manera que no se caliente, ni esté frío [near the heat so that it doesn't get too hot or too cold]

caliéntese bien [well heated]

al fuego a poca lumbre abajo, y mucha encima [with low flame below and high flame above]

a mucha furia [rapidly boiling]

In the Oven

Low heat
   A fuego manso [on low flame]
   a poca lumbre [on low flame]
   lumbre mansa [low heat]

Moderate heat
   Muy bien templado [thoroughly warmed]
   lumbre moderada abajo y arriba [moderate heat above and below], used for smaller ovens

High heat
   mucha lumbre [on high]

For specific activities
   métela en el horno a cuajar [put it in the oven to set]
   ponlo a perdigar en el horno [put it in the oven to parbake]

Time

It is well documented that the Spanish Hapsburgs were interested in the mechanization of time. Philip II owned several clocks, mostly imported from the Low Countries or Germany. Coinciding with Martínez Montiño in the palace was the official clock caretaker, Claudio Gribelín. Together with other clock conservationists, Jennin Cocquart, Gaspar Enríquez, Antonio Matheo, and Lorenzo de Evalo, he was paid a handsome salary and ate daily food from the royal kitchens.[3]

For the most part, time is inferred through the desired stage of the cooking process, as seen in the examples provided below. In about 10 per cent of the 506

---

3 Most of Philip II's clocks were destroyed when the Alcázar burned down, but one, made in 1583 by Hans de Evalo, still survives today and is the oldest of the royal collection in Spain. For more information, see "Relojes."

recipes, time is stated in terms of hours or fractions of hours; for example, half hour or a quarter of an hour. In one instance, time is highlighted in the very title of the recipe: "Cómo se manen las aves en dos horas" [How to tenderize poultry in two hours] (600–2; 601–3). And in the recipe "Cazuela de arroz sin dulce" [Unsweetened rice casserole], Martínez Montiño states an actual time of day "Y déjalo allí hasta la mañana, o desde la mañana hasta las once del día" [and let sit until morning, or from early morning until eleven a.m.] (350; 351). This specific hour implies that some clock was available to the kitchen staff and that cooks were not just aware of time but of the actual hour as well. However, in no instance are minutes or seconds acknowledged.

Inferred Time

hasta que esté en punto [until it is just right]
hasta que estén bien cocidos [until they are completely done]
hasta que esté la carne perdigada [until the meat is singed]
hasta que esté la masa bien cocida [until the dough is completely cooked]
cuezan hasta que se apure el caldo [boil until the stock has been reduced]
ándalo a una mano, hasta que venga a hacerse una crema un poco espesa [stir until it takes on a creamy consistency]

Appendix 3
Images from Recipes Recreated

Figure A3.1. "Pollos rellenos" [Chicken with stuffing]. This recipe was recreated because of the unusual description of using the claws as antlers. Image courtesy of Donna Green, 2016.

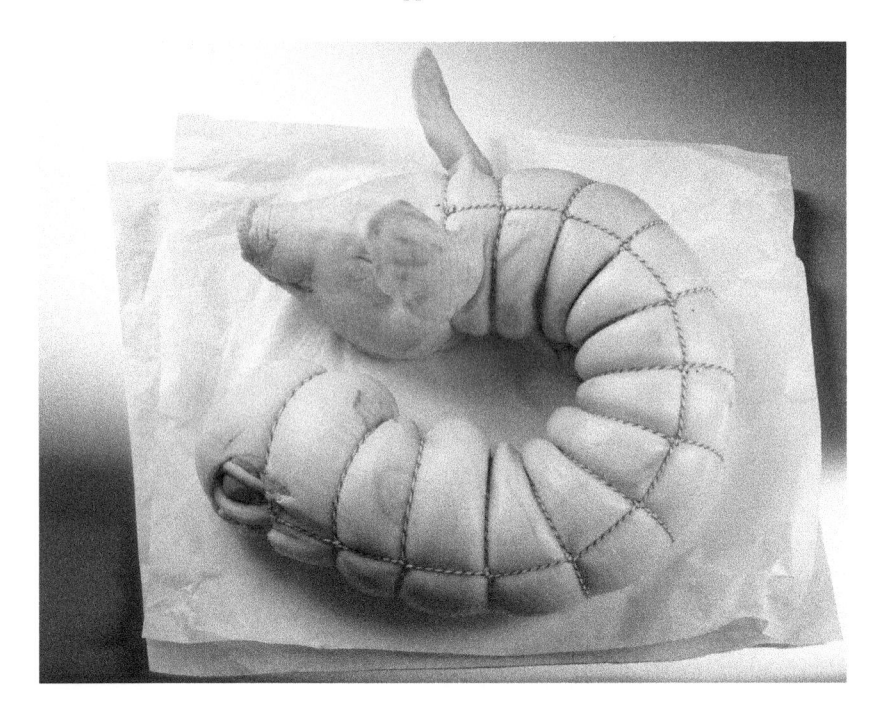

Figure A3.2. "Un lechón en salchichón" [Suckling pig served sausage style]. Image from "How to Cook Boned and Rolled Suckling Pig," courtesy of Jeff Baker, Farmison and Co, North Yorkshire, England, 24 April 2015. https://www.farmison.com/community/recipe/how-to-cook-boned-and-rolled-suckling-pig. Accessed 22 July 2022.

Images from Recipes Recreated 637

A3.3.A

A3.3.B

Figure A3.3.A–B. "Un platillo de pichones" [A squab dish]. This dish has several stages beginning with browning the birds, then braising them (first image), removing the flor, reducing the stock and enriching it with an egg yolk and vinegar mix, and finally serving it on slices of bread (second image). Note the wilted lettuce, the golden sauce, and the flor sprinkled on top in the final product. Image by author, July 2019.

Figure A3.4. *La flor* [flor]. The coagulated protein (middle layer) that separates from both the fat (top layer) and the juices (bottom layer) during the cooking process. In several recipes, Martínez Montiño separates out the flor before thickening the fatty juices in the pot. He later reserves the flor and sprinkles it over the top of the dish before serving. Image by author, July 2019.

Images from Recipes Recreated 639

A3.5.A

A3.5.B

A3.5.C

A3.5.D

Figure A3.5.A–D. "Artaletes de ave" [Poultry pinwheels] and "Otros artaletes de aves" [Other poultry pinwheels]. The first image shows the primary ingredients of chicken, goat, egg yolk, and mint, along with seasonings, that are necessary for these pinwheels. The second shows the filling process after pounding out the chicken but before rolling it up. The third is the meat loaf made with the left-over goat meat. And the fourth shows the final products served over plain sops (background) and golden sops with slices of goat meat (foreground). Images by author, December 2015.

Figure A3.6. "Carnero verde" [Green mutton stew], served on a bed of couscous. Prepared for the Cervantes Society of America, Austin, TX, October 2015. Image by author.

642　　　　　　　　　　Appendix 3

A3.7.A

A3.7.B

Figure A3.7.A–B. "Empanada de liebre" [Hare empanada]. This recipe follows Martínez Montiño's second suggested way of preparing the empanada, with no bones. We used rabbit meat instead of hare because that is what was available. Images by author, October 2015, Bloomington, IL.

Figure A3.8. "Plato de albondiguillas fritas" [Dish of fried meatballs]. This recipe includes instructions not only for meatballs but also for grilling thin slices of meat and fried slices of bread. Images by author, October 2015.

Figure A3.9. "Torta de orejones" [Dried apricot pie]. These pies were recreated for the banquet of the International Food Symposium held at Illinois Wesleyan University and Illinois State University, 28 and 29 March 2019. Image by author, March 2019.

A3.10.A

Images from Recipes Recreated 645

A3.10.B

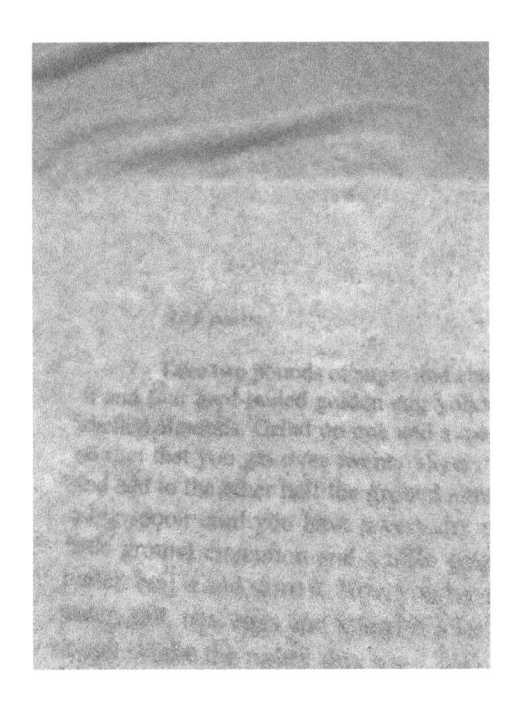

A3.10.C

A3.10.D

A3.10.E

Images from Recipes Recreated

A3.10.F

A3.10.G

Figure A3.10.A–G. "Bollo maimón" [Maimon layered pastry]. This pastry was made using hard red spring wheat from Janie's Mill (Ashkum, IL). It is stone milled and sifted, a milling technique that would better approximate the production process of early modern Spain than that of commodity wheat, which is roller milled with the bran and germ removed. In the first image, note the folds in the dough after ten minutes of hand kneading. The second and third show the results of the stretching process; as Martínez Montiño notes, it should be thin enough to see through. Here you can see the recipe through the dough. The fourth and fifth show the almond-cinnamon-yolk filling that is spooned between the layers with butter and simple syrup drizzled on top. The final two show the delicious finished product. Note the wavy edges and layers of dough inside. Images by author, August 2019.

648 Appendix 3

A3.11.A

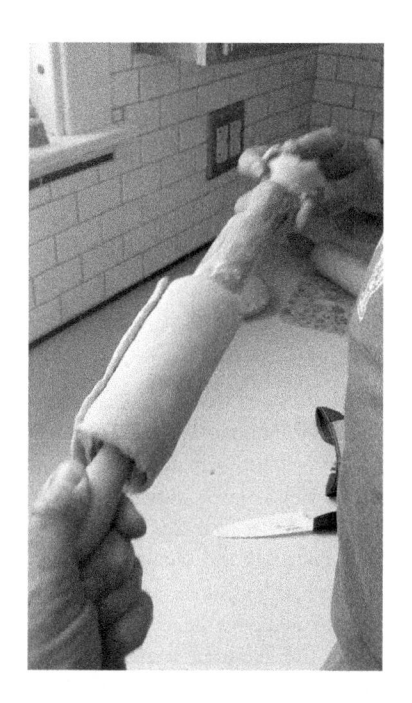

A3.11.B

Images from Recipes Recreated

A3.11.C

A3.11.D

Figure A3.11.A–D "Bollo de rodilla" [Spiral sweet roll]. This pastry layers fat within the dough by rolling the dough on a caña [reed] instead of the traditional folding technique (first image) and cut the rolls off in segments (second). We then fried it in butter and spooned the egg yolk over both sides (third). The final product tasted like French toast (fourth)! Image by author, June 2022.

A3.12.A

A3.12.B

Images from Recipes Recreated

A3.12.C

A3.12.D

A3.12.E

A3.12.F

Figure A3.12.A–F. "Buñuelos de viento" [Puffs]. Martínez Montiño includes six different *buñuelo* recipes in his cookbook. The first four images show the stages for making the second one, "Otros buñuelos de viento" [Other puffs]. The first two show how he cooks the batter like a crepe first, then the middle two show how he adds eggs to the cooked batter and then mixes the dough. The fifth shows the consistency of the dough for the first three *buñuelo* recipes, while the last shows the resultant puffs for "Buñuelos de viento" [Puffs], "Otros buñuelos de viento" [Other puffs], and a third one with the same name, "Otros buñuelos de viento" [Other puffs]. Images by author, May 2016.

Images from Recipes Recreated 653

A3.13.A

A3.13.B

A3.13.C

A3.13.D

Images from Recipes Recreated 655

A3.13.E

A3.13.F

Figure A.13.A–F. "Quesadillas fritas de cuajada" [Fried cheese curd tarts]. The exciting discovery when making these curd tarts was the shape of the *candilejas* [oil lamp]. The first two show the separation of curds and whey; the third, the dough rolled out with filling on top; the fourth and fifth show the oil lamp shape with the multiple points; and the sixth shows the final product. All images are by the author, January 2016, except the oil lamp, courtesy of "Lámpara o candil de aceite judío," *Todocolección,* accessed 22 July 2022. https://www.todocoleccion.net/antiguedades/lampara-o-candil-aceite-judio-completamente-original-siglo-xvi-xvii-7-luces-bronce~x32951017

Figure A3.14. "Quesadillas de horno" [Baked cheese tart]. Image by author, February 2016.

Images from Recipes Recreated 657

A3.15.A

A3.15.B

658   Appendix 3

A3.15.C

Figure A3.15.A–C. "Platillo de alcachofas" [An artichoke dish]. Martínez Montiño does not specify how many artichokes are used. For this recreation we chose five (first image, already parboiled), sautéed them with the suggested seasonings (second), and reduced the number of eggs to a third of the suggested amount (six eggs instead of eighteen). The dish was then served on slices of cinnamon and sugar toast. Image by author, May 2019.

Images from Recipes Recreated 659

Figure A3.16. "Berenjenas rellenas" [Stuffed eggplant]. The strong spice flavour perfectly complements the fried eggplant. I've recreated this dish several times and it is always very popular. Image by author, September 2015.

Figure A3.17. "Calabaza rellena en el día de pescado" [Stuffed squash for fish days]. For this recipe, acorn squash was used. Photo courtesy of Jen Small, who recreated the dish for the "Culinary Tour through the History of Spain" banquet in Schaumberg, IL, January 2020.

660 Appendix 3

Figure A3.18. "Espinacas a la Portuguesa" [Spinach, Portuguese style]. Image by author, January 2016.

Figure A3.19.A

A3.19.B

Figures A3.19.A–B. "Sardinas rellenas de escabeche" [Pickle stuffed sardines]. The first image shows the stages of dipping stuffed fish in egg, frying them, and resting in heated brine. We used his recommended Portuguese brine with orange juice. B is the final result. Image by Carmela Ferradáns, July 2023.

Figure A3.20. "Tortilla blanca" [White omelette]. Spooning the butter over the top of the whipped whites and embedded yolks. Image by author, April 2016.

662   Appendix 3

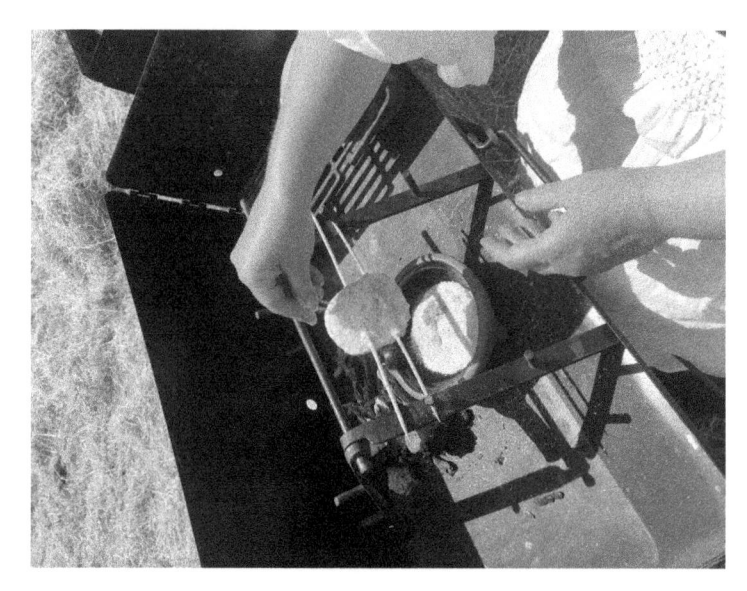

Figure A3.21. "Cómo se puede asar una pella de manteca de vacas en el asador" [How to roast a butterball on a spit]. In the image above, Donna Green roasts a butterball, continually adding the breadcrumb-sugar mixture. Note some of the fat drippings, of which Martinez Montiño warns his readers. Image courtesy of Donna Green, July 2018.

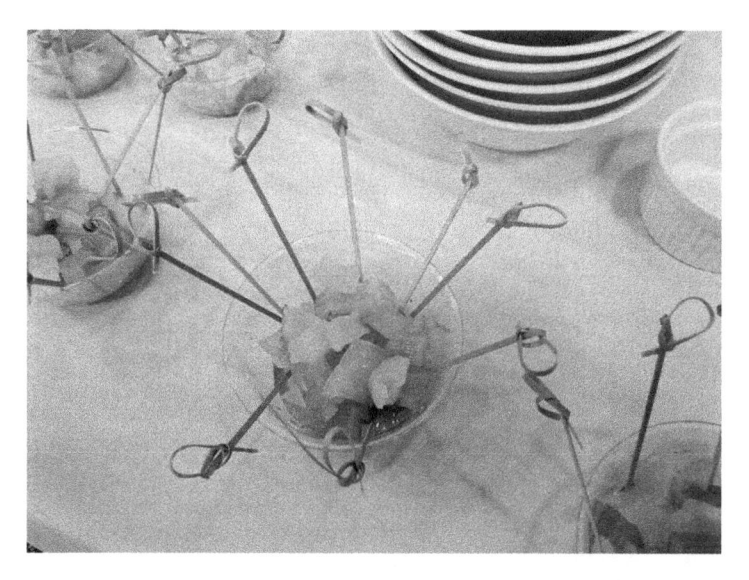

Figure A3.22. "Hinojo conservado" [Preserved fennel]. Diners at the "Culinary Tour through the History of Spain" banquet (Schaumberg, IL, January 2020) described it as "sweet with a vegetable texture" and compared it to a freshener, something similar to candied fennel seeds. Photo courtesy of Jen Small, who recreated the dish.

Glossary

Abadejo codfish. This fish appears once in the cookbook to provide reference for the less familiar *estocafíx* [stockfish], imported from Flanders.

Abstinencia abstinence. A full abstinence day refers to those days when no meat is consumed. For example, *manteca de vacas* [butter] and *aceite* [oil] are substituted for *tocino* [fatback]. Other substitutes include vegetables for meat, cheese for bone marrow, and garbanzo broth for meat stock. A full abstinence day is commonly referred to as a "día de pescado" [fish day], though once Martínez Montiño refers to it as "viernes" [Friday].

Acedera sorrel. Martínez Montiño uses sorrel in one poultry dish.

Acedo an acidic juice from a fruit or vegetable, perhaps from *acedera* [sorrel]. Covarrubias uses vinegar as an example. In the cookbook I have translated it as *sorrel juice*, used in fourteen recipes, to distinguish it from the more generic term *agrio* [sour, sour juice], which Martínez Montiño uses a hundred times.

Aceituna olive. Although primarily used as oil, olives are included in the banquet menus and Martínez Montiño has a detailed recipe for brining them.

Acemite (*cemite*, in Martínez Montiño) Bran. Martínez Montiño uses flour with this flaky husk of the wheat intact to make a heavier crust for a savoury pie.

Acenoria (today *zanahoria*) carrot. This popular vegetable is served as a salad, in stew, or with salted fish. Martínez Montiño notes different colours, in particular the black (today, purple) ones.

Achicoria chicory. Used only twice in the cookbook, chicory appears as an option for recipes with green-leaf vegetables.

Aderezar to prepare. This verb is used over seventy times in the cookbook.

Adornar to garnish. Martínez Montiño suggests garnishes for dozens of recipes.

Adobo marinade. Martínez Montiño uses several different *adobos*. For example, for veal he insists that it be garlic, oregano, vinegar, and salt (146–7).

Agraz sour grape. It was often used as a sour element to a dish, sometimes in place of vinegar. Martínez Montiño also incorporates *agraz en grano* [whole berries] and *agraz sacado* [mashed berries (an early stage of processing but still in solid form)].

Agrazón gooseberry. Martínez Montiño references this fruit and its different names in suggesting a seasonal alternative to sour grapes. It appears only once in the cookbook, in "Platillos sin verduras" [Dishes without green-leaf vegetables] (178–80; 179–81).

Agrio sour, acidic, pungent [adj.], or sour juice [noun]. This word is very commonly associated with juice from lemons and oranges or vinegar from grapes.

Aguja paladar swordfish. Martínez Montiño dedicates one recipe to this saltwater fish. He considers it a secondary choice to *sollo* (sturgeon) (388–9).

Ahogar to sauté. Martínez Montiño mostly uses this verb in recipes where ingredients are sautéed with fatback and minced onion.

Ajedrea summer savory. It is used in three different meat dishes. See *hierbas* for more information.

Ajo garlic. This vegetable appears in thirty-two different savoury recipes, raw, fried, in stuffings, and in marinades.

Ajopollo ajopollo. This sauce is made with oil, garlic, fried bread soaked in vinegar, and toasted almonds and is referenced in two recipes. For more on sauces, see the Introduction, "Sauces," 48, 49–50t.

Albañal large earthenware vat or basin. In Martínez Montiño's kitchen, this appliance was used for washing pots and pans and other kitchen utensils. Today it refers to a sewer drain.

Albérchigo apricot. At the time of the publication of Martínez Montiño's cookbook, *albérchigo* was understood as a type of apricot, even though today it is known as a type of peach. For more on Martínez Montiño's preparation of this fruit, see the Introduction, "Fruit, Vegetables, Nuts, and Seeds," 41.

Albericoque apricot. For more on Martínez Montiño's preparation of this fruit, see the Introduction, "Fruit, Vegetables, Nuts, and Seeds," 41.

Albornía glazed terracotta pitcher. The RAE defines it as a "vasija grande de barro vidriado de forma de taza" [big glazed earthenware pot in the shape of a cup].

Alcachofa artichoke. For more on Martínez Montiño's preparation of this vegetable, see the Introduction, "Fruit, Vegetables, Nuts, and Seeds," 43.

Alcaparra capers. For more on Martínez Montiño's preparation of this vegetable, see the Introduction, "Fruit, Vegetables, Nuts, and Seeds," 43.

Alcaraván stone curlew, a wading bird.

Alcaravea caraway. For more on spices and seasonings, see the Introduction, "Herbs, Spices, and Flowers," 47.

Alcorza candy coating. It is a sugar-starch mixture used as a hard sugar coating: for example, the outside of a Jordan almond, or a hard-coated sweet in its own right. Martínez Montiño uses it once as a topping for "Pastelón de cidra verde" [Big green citron pie] (586; 587).

Alcuzcucero couscoussier. Martínez Montiño describes in detail this specialty piece of cookware in his recipe for making couscous (463–7).

Alfitete fried pastry sheet. As Martínez Montiño explains in the recipe "Una gallina rellena en alfitete" [Stuffed hen served on fried pastry sheets], *alfitetes* are made with just flour, egg, salt, and lard and are deep fried (182; 183). In the anonymous *Um tratado da cozinha portuguesa do século XV* [translated as *A Treatise of Portuguese Cuisine from the 15th Century*], a similar recipe appears that explains both how to make the pastry sheet and how to serve poultry on top.

Almeja clam. For more on Martínez Montiño's preparation of this shellfish, see the Introduction, "Fish and Shellfish," 39.

Almendra almond. Martínez Montiño uses this nut frequently both in savoury and sweet dishes. They appear on his banquet menus, toasted, in sauces, broths, as butter and oil, and in a wide variety of baked goods, often in the form of marzipan.

Almendruco green almond. This nut appears in one recipe. The nuts are seasoned with spices, herbs, and cinnamon and sugar, and served on bread (360–1).

Almíbar simple syrup. This is a common ingredient in many pies and pastries.

Almirez metal mortar. Martínez Montiño uses this piece of kitchen equipment in dozens of recipes.

Almizcle musk or civet. Martínez Montiño uses it in two pastry recipes and in one for preserving fennel.

Almofía basin, another word for *jofaina*. It is used in one of the couscous recipes and in "Sopas a la Portuguesa" [Sops, Portuguese style] (472; 473).

Almojábana fried cheese pastry. These are made with soft cheese, flour, and egg yolk, kneaded until soft, then fried and dipped in whey and simple syrup. Martínez Montiño includes two recipes and offers several variations of them.

Ámbar ambergris. This substance comes from the intestines of the sperm whale. In her translation of Ibn-Razín's thirteenth-century Hispano-Muslim cookbook, *Best of Delectable Foods and Dishes from al-Andalus and al-Maghrib: A Cookbook by Thirteenth-Century Andalusi Scholar Ibn Razīn al-Tujībī (1227–1293)*, Nawal Nasrallah explains: "Based on al-Himyarī, *al-Rawḍ al miʽṭār* 339, the best of ambergris from the western zone … came from the coasts of Shadhūna (Medina-Sidonia) in southern Spain … It was generally believed to benefit the entire nervous system" (653).

Ánade duck. For more on Martínez Montiño's preparation of this aquatic fowl, see the Introduction, "Fowl," 35.

Aparejar to prepare or to have ready.

Apurar to finish off or reduce, as in a stock reduction.

Armar to assemble or arrange.

Arroba arroba. This is a unit of weight equivalent to approximately 11.34 kilograms or 25 pounds. See Appendix 2 for measurements.

Artalete pinwheel. Also known by its French name *roulade*. Although usually made by rolling up a thin fillet with an egg yolk filling and then baking it, Martínez Montiño also allows minced meat, particularly from poultry or veal, as a filling. Pinwheels are often held together with a brochette or small skewer. Generally, they accompany a whole bird or fillets of poultry, beef, or other meat. Elena Varela Merino documents that Martínez Montiño is the first to record recipes for *artaletes* (517–20). For more on the origin of the word, see Torres Martínez, "Léxico culinario en el libro."

Arveja pea. This vegetable appears in one recipe, "Potaje de arvejas" [Pea stew] (374; 375).

Asador spit, roaster, or roasting oven. For more on kitchen equipment, see Appendix 1, "Kitchen Furnishings and Equipment."

Asadura or *asadurilla* pluck. This term encompasses the internal upper organs of an animal, specifically the heart, liver, and lungs. Today this term is sometimes mistakenly used to mean all organ meats and sometimes all variety meats.

Asentar to set (food on a plate).

Atún tuna. For more on Martínez Montiño's preparation of this fish, see the Introduction, "Fish and Shellfish," 37.

Avellana hazelnut. While this nut is referenced once as a possible ingredient (494–5), it appears four times as a measurement, that is, to indicate the quantity of another ingredient.

Aventar to winnow. Martínez Montiño uses the verb just once in the recipe "Como se va de hacer el arroz" [How to make rice] (346–8; 347–9).

Avutarda great bustard. This bird is related to the crane; both are from the order of gruiformes. Both have long legs and are approximately the size of the turkey. It appears in two different recipes.

Azafrán saffron. This spice is one of the five ingredients that make up Martínez Montiño's *todas especias* [all spices] mix. The others are black pepper, clove, nutmeg, and ginger. For more on spices and seasonings, see the Introduction, "Herbs, Spices, and Flowers," 47.

Azahar orange blossom. Martínez Montiño uses this ingredient in aromatic water. It appears in over a dozen recipes, mostly for pies, puff pastries, and cookies.

Azúcar sugar. Sugar is one of the central ingredients in this cookbook. Some of the ways Martínez Montiño indicates different stages for boiling sugar are as follows.

He uses the following phrases for the early thread stage, where the temperature is only slightly above boiling point (100ºC, 212ºF):

> *azúcar en punto* sugar at the early thread stage
> *almíbar en punto* gently boiling simple syrup
> *azúcar clarificado en punto* clarified sugar, at thread stage
> *azúcar en buen punto* sugar syrup at boiling point
> *ponerlo en punto* the soft-ball stage

He uses the following phrases for thread stages at higher temperatures, although they would not exceed 112ºC, 234ºF, which would put the sugar stage into another category.

> *en punto subida* sugar at the late thread stage
> *en punto bien subida* a rolling boil

For more on the different types of sugar that Martínez Montiño uses, particularly the different boiling stages, see the Introduction, "Sweeteners," 45–6.

Azúcar clarificado clarified sugar. This involves a process of transforming raw sugar into loaf sugar by beating egg white in water, adding it to the sugar, boiling it, and then skimming off the impurities. What is left is simple syrup that crystallizes once again. Martínez Montiño explains this process in his recipe "Azúcar rosado blanco" [White rose sugar] (568–70; 569–71) and uses it in many of his preserved fruit recipes.

Azúcar molido y cernido sifted, ground sugar.

Azumbre two-quart measure. See Appendix 2 for measurements.

Bálago straw. Along with *heno* [hay], this material is used to buffer a glass container that is placed within a larger pot for making a sustaining broth. The straw helps protect the glass from banging against the pot it is in (488–9).

Baño blanco meringue. Martínez Montiño includes a recipe for making meringue and also uses it as a topping in a handful of pastries and one dessert.

Barbo barbel. This fish appears in two separate recipes.

Barquilla barquette mould (boat-shaped). This specialty piece of cookware is used once in the recipe "Cómo se puede asar una pella de manteca de vacas en el asador" [How to roast a butterball on a spit] (524–6; 525–7).

Barquillo a boat-shaped container. This container was often made from silver and used to store and serve wine at festivals or salt for baptisms. Here, Martínez Montiño suggests it as one of two options, along with a cauldron, in which to prepare a large quantity of brine.

Batido batter. It could also be translated as *mixture*, as used in "Cazuela mojí de berenjenas" [Moxi eggplant casserole]. The word appears in over a hundred recipes.

Beneficiar to dress a recently killed animal or to prepare a dish. It is used in eight different recipes.

Berenjena eggplant. This foodstuff is a leading vegetable in the cookbook and is prepared in a variety of ways.

Berguera berguera fruit sieve. This specialty piece of equipment was designed specifically for candied fruit. It consisted of a rectangular frame with esparto fabric or wire screen in the middle and a metal plate on the bottom. For more on kitchen equipment, see Appendix 1, "Kitchen Furnishings and Equipment."

Berro watercress. For more on Martínez Montiño's preparation of this vegetable, see the Introduction, "Fruit, Vegetables, Nuts, and Seeds," 43.

Berza collard green. This vegetable appears in seven recipes, among them sops and fish dishes.

Besugo sea bream. For more on Martínez Montiño's preparation of this fish, see the Introduction, "Fish and Shellfish," 38.

Bizcocho sweet biscuit. See *vizcochería*.

Bollo pastry. Martínez Montiño includes nine different pastries with the name *bollo*.

Borujón lump.

Borraja borage. For more on Martínez Montiño's preparation of this vegetable, see the Introduction, "Fruit, Vegetables, Nuts, and Seeds," 43.

Brasas red-hot embers. Martínez Montiño uses this level of heat in over a dozen recipes to cook a wide variety of dishes from stews, to rice, to fish and meat dishes, to sweeter dishes like clotted milk tarts or custard pie. It is more common than the less intense *rescoldo* [grey embers], a term that appears in seven recipes.

Brenca brenca. A term used to describe one of Martínez Montiño's signature sauces made with white wine, spices, salt, and lemon juice and served with poultry. For more on sauces, see the Introduction, "Sauces," 48, 49–50t.

Brodete egg yolk and vinegar infused broth. Martínez Montiño uses it in three poultry dishes and two egg dishes.

Broqueta brochette or small skewer. This kitchen appliance can be made out of wood or metal and is used for roasting poultry, fish, and small game and to hold pieces of food in place while baking.

Bruguete bruguete sauce. This white sauce is made from butter, watered-down vinegar, pepper, ginger, and nutmeg. It is served with carp. For more on sauces, see the Introduction, "Sauces," 48, 49–50t.

Buñolera kitchen instrument designed for making *buñuelos* [puffs]. The batter is placed in the scoop and dropped into the heated oil to form uniform puff balls.

Buñuelo puff (as in cream puff). The recipe for this dough is an early documentation of cream puff dough, also known as *pâte a choux*, centuries before Antonin Carême popularized it in France. With savoury dishes, when the *buñuelo* turns out slightly heavier, I sometimes translate the word as *fritter*.

Caballos cob irons. This piece of kitchen furnishing is a vertical structure whose primary purpose is to support a crossbar or rotisserie skewer. It usually has a variety of hooks that provide flexibility for how far the skewer is placed from the heat source. Unlike andirons, they are not designed to contain the heat. As andirons developed, they often included vertical rods, thus eliminating the need for a separate instrument, but *caballos* were still commonly used in rural Spain up to the twentieth century. My thanks to Carmen Abad Zardoya for clarifying its usage. For further information, see her article, "Herramientas," 86n5. For more on kitchen equipment, see Appendix 1, "Kitchen Furnishings and Equipment."

Cabra goat. For more on Martínez Montiño's preparation of this animal, see the Introduction, 32–3.

Cabrito kid. For more on Martínez Montiño's preparation of this animal, see the Introduction, 32–3.

Cacito, cacillo saucepan, usually with one handle. This is a common piece of cookware in Martínez Montiño's kitchen.

Cagalar caecum or blind gut. This part of the large intestine is attached to the appendix and is located where the small intestine meets the large. Martínez Montiño references this part of a deer when describing how to dress it.

Calabaza squash or gourd. *Calabaza* [squash and gourd] are members of the *Cucurbitaceae* family of plants. They are fruit-bearing, flowering vines that grow close to the ground. Gourds were cultivated in Africa, Asia, Europe, and the Americas for thousands of years before Columbus' arrival in the Americas. Squashes originated in the Americas and by the mid-sixteenth century were cultivated throughout Europe and Africa. This is Martínez Montiño's favourite vegetable. Throughout the cookbook, I've translated *calabaza* as *squash*, given their popularity across continents, though it is possible that Martínez Montiño also used gourds for any of his *calabaza* recipes. For more on Martínez Montiño's preparation of this vegetable, see the Introduction, "Fruit, Vegetables, Nuts, and Seeds," 42.

Calamares squid. For more on Martínez Montiño's preparation of this shellfish, see the Introduction, "Fish and Shellfish," 39.

Calda boiling water bath. Martínez Montiño refers to this cooking technique in two recipes for preserving citrus fruit.

Caldera cauldron. Martínez Montiño uses this piece of cookware in just one recipe, "Cómo se ha de salar el venado, y se pueda comer fresco" [How to salt venison and eat it fresh] (302–4; 303–5).

Caldo broth or stock. Technically, these terms are not interchangeable, since the latter always involves a simmering of bones to extract their flavour and gelatin. *Broth* refers to the simmering of the actual meat or fish, vegetables, or any food product, and doesn't necessarily include bones. Thus, when Martínez Montiño refers to *caldo de garbanzos*, the translation is always *garbanzo broth*. *Stock*, on the other hand is made from bones. In the recipe "Platillo de artaletes de ternera" [Dish of veal pinwheels], he explains how to prepare stock and says it is very rich: "mas con echar a cocer los huesos de la carne que picaste con agua y sal, y cueza una hora, y es mejor caldo para platillos que el de la olla" [Moreover, if you cooked the meat bones that you sprinkled with salted water, and boiled that for an hour, you will have a richer stock for the dishes than what you'll get out of the pot] (230; 231).

Candeal candeal. This is a highly esteemed wheat that produced white bread. The bread is known for its characteristic dense, white crumb, light crust, and round shape. *Candeal* appears in the cookbook six times to describe wheat, rolls, and bread. Specifically, Martínez Montiño suggests using leaven dough from candeal bread to make certain pastries and rolls.

Candilejas oil lamp. Martínez Montiño mentions this object in two pastry recipes to provide a visual on the shape of the final product.

Canela cinnamon. For more on spices and seasonings, see the Introduction, "Herbs, Spices, and Flowers," 47–8.

Cangrejo crab. For more on Martínez Montiño's preparation of this shellfish, see the Introduction, "Fish and Shellfish," 39.

Canilla shinbone or little spout. As a bone, this term appears in two recipes. As a piece of equipment, it describes a necessary part of the containers used to make verjuice in the recipe "Agraz para todo el año" [Verjuice for the whole year] (516; 517).

Caña de vaca Beef marrow. Martínez Montiño includes one recipe for preparing marrow and uses this ingredient in many for additional flavouring and to enhance the texture.

Cañuto (today, *canuto*) deep-fried pastry shells in the form of a tube. Martínez Montiño fills them with candied egg yolk threads.

Capirotada capirotada. This is a rich, layered meat and poultry dish. The term refers to the layering of the dish. Covarrubias explains, "se echa encima de

otro guisado, que va debaxo; y porque lo cubre a modo de capirote se dixo capirotada" [it is layered over another casserole which is below; and because it covers it like a *capirote* hat it is called *capirotada*] (297). The dish is still prepared in Mexico today but without the meat, something akin to bread pudding. It is generally consumed during Lent.

Capón capon. For more on Martínez Montiño's preparation of this farm-raised bird, see the Introduction, "Fowl," 33–6.

Caracol snail. For more on Martínez Montiño's preparation of this shellfish, see the Introduction, "Fish and Shellfish," 36–9.

Carbonadilla grilled meat or the cooked meat that will be grilled. Covarrubias writes of *carbonada*: "la carne que después de cocida se echa a tostar sobre las ascuas o el carbón encendido" [the meat that after cooking is roasted over embers or burning coal] (302). Also, the *Diccionario de autoridades* cites Martínez Montiño's recipe to define the term (2.1729).

Cardillo golden thistle. For more on Martínez Montiño's preparation of this vegetable, see the Introduction, "Fruit, Vegetables, Nuts, and Seeds," 43.

Cardo cardoon. For more on Martínez Montiño's preparation of this vegetable, see the Introduction, "Fruit, Vegetables, Nuts, and Seeds," 43.

Carnero mutton. For more on Martínez Montiño's preparation of this animal, see the Introduction, 31–2.

Carpa carp. For more on Martínez Montiño's preparation of this fish, see the Introduction, "Fish and Shellfish," 38–9.

Castaña chestnut. Martínez Montiño finishes the cookbook with a chestnut soup recipe (602–5).

Cazo large saucepan, usually with one handle. This is a common piece of cookware in Martínez Montiño's kitchen. For more on kitchen equipment, see Appendix 1, "Kitchen Furnishings and Equipment".

Cazolilla small saucepan or tartlet pan. Martínez Montiño uses this piece of cookware in a half dozen recipes. For more on kitchen equipment, see Appendix 1, "Kitchen Furnishings and Equipment."

Cazón dogfish. This fish appears in two recipes.

Cazuela casserole or stew. As a cooking utensil, the *cazuela* is a terracotta casserole that is wider than it is tall. It often has two handles, though it can also have none. As a dish to be consumed, *cazuela* can be translated as either *stew* or *casserole*, depending on the consistency. In contrast, the *olla*, a two-handled pot, is generally taller and used for making soups. The *cazuela* is a common piece of cookware in Martínez Montiño's kitchen. For more on kitchen equipment, see Appendix 1, "Kitchen Furnishings and Equipment."

Cebar to enrich. Over a dozen times Martínez Montiño explains how to enrich a dish, usually with garbanzo broth or an egg yolk and vinegar mixture.

Cebolla onion. For more on Martínez Montiño's preparation of this vegetable, see the Introduction, "Fruit, Vegetables, Nuts, and Seeds," 43.

Cecial salted hake. Martínez Montiño uses this fish in two recipes.

Cecina cured. This type of food preservation and flavouring process is mentioned in a handful of recipes, most notably in "Una olla podrida en Pastel" [A pie of hodgepodge stew] (284–6; 285–7) and "Lamprea en cecina" [Cured lamprey] (400–2; 401–3).

Cedazo or cedacillo sieve or strainer. The former is big while the latter is smaller. For more on kitchen equipment, see Appendix 1, "Kitchen Furnishings and Equipment."

Cedacillo de cerdas horsehair sieve. This utensil is a fine mesh sieve. Martínez Montiño uses it in three recipes.

Celemín celemin. This term measures one twelfth of a *fanega* or 4.625 litres. See Appendix 2 for measurements.

Cemite bran flour. See *Harina de cemite*.

Cercenaduras trimmed edges of dough. Martínez Montiño uses this word only once to describe the edges in the recipe "Quesadillas fritas de cuajada" [Fried cheese curd tarts] (320–2; 321–3).

Chorcha woodcock. For more on Martínez Montiño's preparation of this game bird, see the Introduction, "Fowl," 33–6.

Chorizo chorizo. Martínez Montiño includes one recipe for chorizo pork sausage, which is seasoned with the same spices as for *salchichón*: all spices (black pepper, clove, nutmeg, ginger, and saffron) and salt. It does not have paprika, like today's chorizo, and, unlike *salchichón*, which must be eaten fresh, chorizo can be stored for up to a year.

Cilantro cilantro. This herb is part of Martínez Montiño's most popular herb mix, *verduras* [herbs] or *todas verduras* [all herbs], which consists of parsley, spearmint, and cilantro and is used in close to one hundred recipes. For more on spices and seasonings, see the Introduction, "Herbs, Spices, and Flowers," 47–8.

Cilantro seco coriander. For more on spices and seasonings, see the Introduction, "Herbs, Spices, and Flowers," 47–8.

Ciruela plum. For more on Martínez Montiño's preparation of this fruit, see the Introduction, "Fruit, Vegetables, Nuts, and Seeds," 41.

Ciruela pasa prune. For more on Martínez Montiño's preparation of this fruit, see the Introduction, "Fruit, Vegetables, Nuts, and Seeds," 41.

Citrón citron. For more on Martínez Montiño's preparation of this fruit, see the Introduction, "Fruit, Vegetables, Nuts, and Seeds," 41.

Clavo clove. This spice is one of the five ingredients that make up Martínez Montiño's *todas especias* [all spices] mix. The others are black pepper, nutmeg, ginger, and saffron. For more on spices and seasonings, see the Introduction, "Herbs, Spices, and Flowers," 47–8.

Cobertera lid. For more on kitchen equipment, see Appendix 1, "Kitchen Furnishings and Equipment."

Cobre copper. This material is the base for a specific oven in eight recipes, a baking sheet, and other specialty items in the kitchen like a *gubilete* [shell kitchen mould] or the *alcuzcucero* [couscoussier]. The copper oven is specified for making certain pastries, rolls, and cookies, and even for finishing off a roasted butterball. Copper appears eighteen times in the cookbook.

Cocer to boil, cook, or bake. The translation of this verb depends on the context and method of cooking.

Cocer en seco to cook without any liquid in the cooking recipient. It is sometimes translated as *to bake*, though the process can take place either in an oven or over open flame. For examples, see "Calabaza rellena en el día de pescado" [Stuffed squash for fish days], "Calabaza en día de carne" [Squash for meat days] (364–6; 365–7).

Cocimiento boil. This noun is used to refer to a lobster boil, fish boil, or trout boil.

Cocina de boca king's kitchen. For more on the kitchen and the various positions within it, see the Introduction, 10–13.

Cocinero de la servilleta king's cook. For more on the kitchen and the various positions within it, see the Introduction, 10–13.

Cocinero mayor head cook. For more on the kitchen and the various positions within it, see the Introduction, 10–13.

Colación collation. This is a light meal allowed on days of fasting. It is usually eaten once a day and in the evening. In the early seventeenth century, it was also a term used for a light afternoon or early evening meal.

Colador colander. This is one of the items for separating ingredients. For more on kitchen equipment, see Appendix 1, "Kitchen Furnishings and Equipment."

Colapege isinglass. This is a gelatin-like substance that comes from sturgeon bladder. Martínez Montiño uses it in a recipe to create food art, "Otro plato de huevos hilados" [Another dish of candied egg yolk threads] (434–6; 435–7), and in "Gilea de vino" [Wine jelly] (532–4; 533–5).

Color colour. Martínez Montiño often uses colours to describe his food. Of the primary colours, blue describes a fish colour when cooked in vinegar and yellow describes the result of saffron or of hard-boiled egg yolks, a type of

almond butter, a sauce, and a poultry dish. However, the word *rojo* [red] does not appear; rather, Martínez Montiño uses red foods to describe the colour. For example, he discusses the resulting colour from pomegranate seeds, red wine, and roses. Of the secondary colours, green is certainly the most popular and is used often to describe fruits and vegetables and their related dishes; purple appears twice to describe grapes and mustard sauce; and finally, orange appears numerous times in the cookbook, but only as the fruit, not as a colour. The other prominent colours are *pardo* [brown], which appears four times in pastries made with cinnamon; *negro* [black, or sometimes translated as *dark*], which appears dozens of times; and *blanco* [white], which appears hundreds of times in the cookbook. He also uses the terms *tener color* [to have colour] or *buena color* [good colouring] to describe the desired colour of the top of a baked good; the colour of meat; and the colour or desired colour of fried dough, a roasted butterball, or custard.

Comino cumin. This spice shows up in thirteen recipes for game, sausages, and vegetables. It is used infrequently but effectively. For more on spices and seasonings, see the Introduction, "Herbs, Spices, and Flowers," 47–8.

Conejo rabbit. For more on Martínez Montiño's preparation of this animal, see the Introduction, 33.

Confite candied nuts or seeds. This sweet treat is added to salad or as part of the fruit course in banquets.

Congrio Conger eel. While no recipe uses conger eel as its main ingredient, it appears in two recipes as a fish option.

Conservas preserves. These primarily fruit-based spreads contain chunks of fruit surrounded by jelly. They are used in pastries, pies, and fried dough recipes and, on three occasions, are suggested as garnishes. They also appear in two or three poultry recipes, primarily as a garnish.

Cortadera trimmer. Apart from the kitchen knife, this is the instrument most cited in the cookbook for cutting. It is used in recipes for pies, pastries, and fried dough. For more on kitchen equipment, see Appendix 1, "Kitchen Furnishings and Equipment."

Costrada puff pastry pie. It is made with fine layers of dough (usually several on the bottom and about half as many on top) and finished with a sugar crust on top. These pies can be sweet or savoury.

Criadilla de carnero o de pollo sheep or chicken testicles. For more information, see *turmas*.

Criadilla de tierra truffle. Martínez Montiño includes six recipes for truffles and another six in which he suggests adding them to the dish. For more on Martínez Montiño's preparation of this vegetable, see the Introduction, "Fruit, Vegetables, Nuts, and Seeds," 43.

Criba wide-hole sieve. Similar to the *cedazo*, the *criba* is used for sifting. However, its holes are generally bigger, and in the seventeenth century, it was used for cleaning grains and legumes, while the *cedazo* was finer and used for removing impurities from flour (Morala Rodríguez 312). For more on kitchen equipment, see Appendix 1, "Kitchen Furnishings and Equipment."

Cuajada clotted milk (as a noun) and set (as an adjective). As a noun, it is the basis for a handful of pastry recipes.

Cuarta one quarter of a *vara castellana* [Castilian yard]. See Appendix 2 for measurements.

Cuarterón quarter pound. See Appendix 2 for measurements.

Cuartillo pint, for wet ingredients; and quart, for dry ingredients. See Appendix 2 for measurements.

Contrahecho faux. Martínez Montiño prepares *faux* recipes five times, often for abstinence or partial abstinence meals. One example is "Sopa de vaca a la Portuguesa, contrahecho en día de pescado" [Beef sops, Portuguese style, faux for fish days] (472; 473).

Datil date. For more on Martínez Montiño's preparation of this fruit, see the Introduction, "Fruit, Vegetables, Nuts, and Seeds," 41.

Desangrar to bleed. Martínez Montiño uses this technique in recipes for game, suckling pig, and poultry.

Desatar to thin. Martínez Montiño uses this technique in dozens of recipes, primarily by adding broth, water, or vinegar to a recipe; less frequently by adding milk or wine.

Descarnar to separate meat from bones. Martínez Montiño uses this technique in over a dozen recipes.

Desganado lacking appetite. Martínez Montiño uses this adjective to describe a typical person who might benefit from his "Pistos para enfermos" [Pisto soup for the ill] (498; 499).

Deshacer to melt or to dissolve (liquid); to tear apart or to crumble (solids). Martínez Montiño uses this technique in more than two dozen recipes.

Desollar to skin. Martínez Montiño uses this technique for removing the skin from many different animals: pig, sheep, squab, turkey, hare, deer, kid, carp, and eel.

Desparramarse to break up, to break apart. This verb appears in a few fried dough recipes to warn cooks what may happen and how to avoid the situation or fix it once it occurs.

Despojos extremities. These are variety meats that do not include organs; for example, head, ears, tongue, blood, trotters. Martínez Montiño refers to them once in "Cómo se ha de beneficiar un jabalí" [How to dress boar] (286–8; 287–9).

Día de carne meat day. Martínez Montiño often distinguishes between meat and fish days. On meat days one is permitted to use meat and all by-products like bone marrow, pork lard, and fatback. In several recipes he states that poultry dishes made on a meat day can contain meat instead of offal as part of the ingredients.

Día de pescado fish day. This term is another way to reference a full abstinence day. Fish and shellfish were consumed and certain meat products were avoided. *Manteca de vacas* [butter] and *aceite* [oil] were substituted for *tocino* [fatback]. Other substitutes include vegetables or some by-products for meat, cheese for bone marrow, and garbanzo broth for meat stock. Martínez Montiño uses this term in fifteen different recipes; once he uses "viernes" [Friday].

Dornajo small, round earthenware trough. Generally, it was used to feed pigs, wash dishes, and do other chores. This piece of kitchenware is used in the process of salting venison in the récipe "Cómo se ha de salar el venado, y se pueda comer fresco" [How to salt venison and eat it fresh] (302–4; 303–5). For more on kitchen equipment, see Appendix 1, "Kitchen Furnishings and Equipment."

Durazno clingstone peach. For more on Martínez Montiño's preparation of this fruit, see the Introduction, "Fruit, Vegetables, Nuts, and Seeds," 41.

Embeber to absorb or to incorporate. This verb is used over a dozen times, often to describe liquid or flour being added to a mixture and also eggs being incorporated into a mixture.

Embroquetar to skewer on a brochette. This verb is used in three recipes. All have to do with securing a bird and searing it before putting it on the spit to roast.

Empanizar to crystallize. This verb is used in the recipe "Unas rebanadas de pan conservadas" [Preserved bread slices] (550–2; 551–3) to explain what happens if the sugar gets overcooked when it's heating up for the bread slices.

Empapelar To wrap in paper. Martínez Montiño uses this technique to hold in the flavours of roasted poultry.

Empollar (today *ampollar*) to blister or to bubble up. Martínez Montiño uses this verb several times when describing pie or pastry dough or when making roux to thicken a stew.

Empollita (today *ampollita*) little blister or little bubble. *Empollita* is the diminutive of *empolla*, which was once an alternative to *ampolla* or *blister*. This term is used in several recipes that deal with pies and pastries or with thickening a stew with flour.

Encerada elastic or soft-boiled. This adjective is primarily used in the phrase "masa encerada" to describe a soft, elastic dough. However, in the recipe

"Huevos dorados" [Golden eggs], Martínez Montiño also uses the adjective to describe a boiled egg at the perfect soft-boil stage (450; 451).

Eneldo dill. It appears in two recipes: "Potaje de habas" [Fava bean stew] (352–4; 353–5) and "Sopas a la Portuguesa" [Sops, Portuguese style] (472; 473). See *hierbas* for more information.

Engrudo paste. Martínez Montiño uses this term in the recipe "Potaje de arvejas" [Pea stew] (374; 375), to describe what happens if you add too much flour when making roux.

Enguila (today *anguila*) eel. For more on Martínez Montiño's preparation of this fish, see the Introduction, "Fish and Shellfish," 37–8.

Enjugarse to dry. Martínez Montiño uses this verb in different ways in eight recipes. First, he describes what happens to the simple syrup or honey on top of pastries as they are finished. Sometimes he suggests putting the finished product in the warm oven so that the syrup dries on top. Second, the term is used when describing the final stage of making certain sausages like *longaniza* and *salchicha*. Finally, he uses the term for making rice, which he suggests be rinsed and then let dry before cooking.

Enjundia fat tissue. Martínez Montiño uses this part of the animal in six recipes. Mostly it refers to the fat or fatty tissue that surrounds a bird's ovaries, but it can also mean any kind of animal fat. This fat is not rendered. For more on Martínez Montiño's use of different fats, see the Introduction, "Fats," 46–7.

Enjuto dry. Martínez Montiño uses this adjective in eight recipes (as opposed to *seco* [dry], which appears over a hundred times). Often it simply describes a desired outcome, but at times it is used to suggest that a recipe might need adjusting. This is the case in "Potaje de arvejas" [Pea stew] (374; 375) when he suggests adding a plain omelette on top if the peas are *enjutas*.

Entresijo mesentery. See *redaño*.

Escabeche brine. Martínez Montiño uses the phrase *en escabeche* or *de escabeche* for pickling tuna, sea bream, sardines, and eggplant.

Escarola escarole. For more on Martínez Montiño's preparation of this vegetable, see the Introduction, "Fruit, Vegetables, Nuts, and Seeds," 43.

Escorzonera black salsify or Spanish salsify. This is a root vegetable native to southern Europe. As its name in English suggests, it is generally thought to have spread through Europe from Spain. It appears in just one recipe, "Raíces de escorzonera" [Black salsify root] (572; 573). For more on Martínez Montiño's preparation of this vegetable, see the Introduction, "Fruit, Vegetables, Nuts, and Seeds," 43.

Espaldilla shoulder. Martínez Montiño refers to this part of the animal when discussing how to cut up or serve smaller animals like rabbit, hare, kid, or suckling pig.

Espárragos asparagus. For more on Martínez Montiño's preparation of this vegetable, see the Introduction, "Fruit, Vegetables, Nuts, and Seeds," 43.

Espetar to skewer on a spit. This verb is used over a dozen times for meat, fish and shellfish, poultry, and even for roasting empanadas, pinwheels, and butterballs.

Espinaca spinach. For more on Martínez Montiño's preparation of this vegetable, see the Introduction, "Fruit, Vegetables, Nuts, and Seeds," 43.

Esponjar to fluff. This verb and its noun, *esponja*, and adjective, *esponjado*, forms are used two dozen times in the cookbook. They primarily reference the consistency of eggs and egg batter but are also used to describe fried dough and rice.

Espuma foam. This word is used to describe egg whites when they reach a certain stage while being whipped, or the bubbly layer that rises to the top, for example, when boiling fruit or melting butter.

Espumadera skimmer. This kitchen utensil is used to add or remove items from hot liquid; for example, when making candied fruit. It is also used to press beaten egg yolks through to make "Huevos hilados" [Candied egg yolk threads] (432–4; 433–5) or batter when making certain types of fried dough. For more on kitchen equipment, see Appendix 1, "Kitchen Furnishings and Equipment."

Espumado foamy or defoamed. The use of this adjective depends on the context. At times Martínez Montiño is describing the resultant foam; for example, when water is added to honey and then boiled, "échale un poco de agua y cueza hasta que esté bien espumado" [add a little water and boil until it is very foamy] (518–19). Other times he focuses on the result of removing the foam, "tendrás dos libras de manteca fresca derretida y espumada, y bien clara" [Have two pounds of melted, skimmed, very clear, fresh butter] (500–1).

Espumar to skim. This verb is used for recipes that indicate skimming foam off the top of a substance, usually something coming to a boil like butter or fruit.

Estameña cheesecloth. This kitchen cloth is the most commonly used cloth in the cookbook and appears in twenty-five recipes. Generally, it is a wool cloth used for straining liquid and could be attached to a wire mesh. For more on kitchen equipment, see Appendix 1, "Kitchen Furnishings and Equipment."

Estocafix stockfish. Martínez Montiño includes one recipe for this fish, which is brought in from Flanders. It requires pounding and soaking before it is boiled, sautéed, and braised.

Estofar to stew. This common cooking technique appears dozens of times.

Estregar to rub, to scrub. This verb is used in eight different recipes and describes how to prepare certain vegetables, nuts, meat, fish, and even grains for cooking.

Faisán pheasant. For more on Martínez Montiño's preparation of this game bird, see the Introduction, "Fowl," 33–6.

Fanega bushel. See Appendix 2 for measurements.

Farro farro. Today, farro refers to three ancient wheat species: einkorn, emmer, and spelt. However, for Martínez Montiño and, more generally, in early modern Spain, farro refers to the cooking process, the boiling of the grain. It is a generic porridge-like dish, and, for Martínez Montiño, made from barley. He suggests cooking it in almond milk and says that it is beneficial for the ill. Covarrubias also associates it with barley: "Ordinariamente en España se haze del grano de la cevada limpio y quebrantado y descortezado, del qual se haze escudilla para los enfermos" [In Spain it is usually made from the grain barley that has been cleaned, cracked, and hulled, and made into a dish for the sick] (585).

Fartes Fartes. This was a popular fried dough recipe throughout Europe, as evidenced by its appearance in other early modern cookbooks. Martínez Montiño combines honey and crumbled puff pastry to make the filling. For more information, see the Introduction, "International References," 61.

Filete a small thin spike. This kitchen utensil is used for grilling or roasting meat or vegetables. For example, see "Artaletes asados" [Roasted pinwheels] (478; 479). For more on kitchen equipment, see Appendix 1, "Kitchen Furnishings and Equipment."

Flamenquilla flamenquilla. The RAE defines the *flamenquilla* in the following way: "Plato mediano, de forma redonda u oblonga, mayor que el trinchero y menor que la fuente" [a medium-sized dish, either round or oblong, bigger than a trencher but smaller than a platter]. It is used just once in the cookbook for a suggested serving dish for "Otra sopa borracha" [Other drunken sops] (456; 457).

Flaón custard. Martínez Montiño combines egg yolks, sugar, milk, and a little flour. In once recipe it is baked as a pie; in another, it is cooked without a crust.

Flor flor. This culinary term refers to the coagulated protein that separates from both the fat and the juices when meat cooks. Martínez Montiño often separates out the flor and reserves it before thickening a dish with an egg-vinegar mixture. He then spoons it on top of the dish as a finishing touch. The flor appears in twelve different recipes.

Flor de la malva mallow blossom. For more on Martínez Montiño's preparation of this vegetable, see the Introduction, "Fruit, Vegetables, Nuts, and Seeds," 43.

Floreado finely sifted. This adjective is used with both *trigo* [wheat] and *harina* [flour] and refers to the result of removing most of the bran during the sifting process. This term appears in two dozen recipes.

Frasia frasia. The part of the small intestines attached to the mesentery. Martínez Montiño describes veal *frasia* as "el mejor plato de la ternera" [the best veal dish] (306–7).

Fricasea fricassee. The recipe "Fricasea de cosas fiambres" [Cold meat fricassees] (332; 333) is specified as road trip food; that is, something easy to prepare when there is not a lot of time. As the title suggests, Martínez Montiño uses leftovers or meat already cooked and turned cold. He explains that fricassees can be made with many different meats, including poultry, kid head, beef tripe, or mutton stomach. The meat is added to fried fatback and onion, and finished in broth seasoned with vinegar, green herbs, all spices, and salt. He expressly indicates that the dish needs to come to a boil twice. The *fricasea* should be served immediately over slices of bread.

Frisuelo funnel cakes. See *frutas de sarten*.

Fruta fruit. For the variety of fruit included in the cookbook, see the Introduction, 39–42.

Fruta de sartén fried dough. Martínez Montiño includes a wide variety of recipes for dough fried in oil.

> *Fruta de almendras* fried almond pastry
> *Frutas de cañas* fried dough with marrow filling
> *Fruta de chicharrones* crackling fried dough
> *Fruta de Fartes* Fartes fried dough
> *Fruta de fillos* fried dough with spongy edges
> *Fruta de frisuelos* funnel cakes
> *Fruta de natas* fried cream
> *Fruta de piñas* pine nut fried dough
> *Fruta de prestiños* prestiño fried dough
> *Fruta rellena* stuffed fried dough

Galanga galangal. This spice is similar to ginger. For more on spices and seasonings, see the Introduction, "Herbs, Spices, and Flowers," 47–8.

Galladura red dot of egg. Martínez Montiño references this part of the egg once as something that will be left behind in preparing "Huevos hilados" [Candied egg yolk threads] (432–4; 433–5).

Gallina hen. For more on Martínez Montiño's preparation of this farm-raised bird, see the Introduction, "Fowl," 33–6.

Galopín galopin. For more on the kitchen and the various positions within, see the Introduction, 10–13.

Gámbaro prawn. For more on Martínez Montiño's preparation of this shellfish, see the Introduction, "Fish and Shellfish," 39.

Ganga pin-tailed sand grouse. This ground-dwelling bird is mentioned twice in the cookbook, along with *pluvias* [plovers] and *sisones* [little bustards]; first,

as a bird that would taste good with quince sauce, and second, in the instructions on how to carve a small bird at the table.

Ganso goose. For more on Martínez Montiño's preparation of this aquatic fowl, see the Introduction, "Fowl," 33–6.

Garabato de cuchara semicircular spoon hook. It is usually made of iron and hangs on the wall in order to hang kitchen equipment; in this case, a spoon hook. Martínez Montiño uses it for the purpose of making puffs in the form of a loop, as opposed to a *buñolera*, which makes round puffs. For more on kitchen equipment, see Appendix 1, "Kitchen Furnishings and Equipment."

Garbanzo garbanzo. For more on Martínez Montiño's preparation of this vegetable, see the Introduction, "Fruit, Vegetables, Nuts, and Seeds," 43.

Gigote minced. Martínez Montiño includes this word in eight different recipes, for preparing minced capon, crane, mutton, hare and rabbit, and sturgeon. He often serves part of the meat minced and the other part whole.

Ginebrada clotted milk tart. This pastry is on the menu both for a Christmas banquet and a late afternoon supper. Martínez Montiño includes two different recipes for making it.

Gragea sprinkle (noun). Martínez Montiño uses this decorative candy in just one recipe, "Fruta de piñas" [Pine cone fried dough] (328–30; 329–31).

Granada pomegranate. For more on Martínez Montiño's preparation of this fruit, see the Introduction, "Fruit, Vegetables, Nuts, and Seeds," 41.

Granado intact. Martínez Montiño uses the adjective to describe the finished quality of rice. At one point he clarifies that it means "que no se pegue un grano con otro" [the grains ... won't stick to one another] (350–1).

Grano de paraíso grains of Paradise. For more on spices and seasonings, see the Introduction, "Herbs, Spices, and Flowers," 47–8.

Granujado shredded or granular. Martínez Montiño describes fish and meat with this adjective (shredded) in preparation for a savoury pie. He also uses the word to describe a desired consistency for couscous and almond butter (granular).

Grulla crane. For more on Martínez Montiño's preparation of this aquatic fowl, see the Introduction, "Fowl," 33–6.

Grusela gooseberry. For more information, see *agrazón*.

Gubilete (today *cubilete*) shell. This kitchen mould is a specialty item generally made of copper or tin with a round or curved (abarquillado) shape. The top is wider than the bottom. Martínez Montiño references this mould in "Huevos en puchero" [Eggs in a stew pot] (452; 453) but also in a handful of recipes to signify the shape and size of the crust being formed. For more on kitchen equipment, see Appendix 1, "Kitchen Furnishings and Equipment."

Guinda cherry/sour cherry. For more on Martínez Montiño's preparation of this fruit, see the Introduction, "Fruit, Vegetables, Nuts, and Seeds," 41.

Haba fava bean. For more on Martínez Montiño's preparation of this vegetable, see the Introduction, "Fruit, Vegetables, Nuts, and Seeds," 44.

Harina de cemite flour with bran, or whole-grain wheat flour. Martínez Montiño uses this heavier flour when making crusts for heavy meat dishes such as boar empanadas or a hodgepodge stew pie.

Harina de tahona mill flour. This type of flour, which was processed in a mill powered by draft animals, was highly valued, as it produced a finer flour. Martínez Montiño references it in six different recipes.

Harina floreada finely sifted flour. Martínez Montiño uses this term (or *trigo floreado* [finely sifted wheat]) in two dozen recipes.

Hebra grain (as in meat fibre) or string. When describing how to cut veal, pork, or boar, Martínez Montiño explains to cut "al través de la hebra" [against the grain] some half dozen times. As a kitchen utensil, *hebra* [string] is used in a couple of recipes to tie up a piece of meat before it goes into the stew pot. He also uses the term to describe strands of eggs when making "Huevos hilados" [Candied egg yolk threads] (432–4; 433–5).

Hender to slit. Martínez Montiño uses this verb in ten different recipes for meat, fish, and vegetables. Sometimes he describes opening up the prepared food for its visual effect when served at the table. As example of this is in "Cómo se adereza una cabeza de ternera" [How to prepare veal head] when he describes three different ways to present the dish (308; 309).

Heno hay. Along with *bálago* [straw], this material is used to buffer a glass carafe that is placed within a larger pot for making a sustaining broth. The hay helps protect the glass from banging again the pot it is in (488–9).

Heñir to knead. This verb appears in the recipe "Panecillos de colaciones" [Collation rolls] to describe how to treat the dough (504–6; 505–7).

Hierbabuena spearmint. This green herb is part of Martínez Montiño's most popular herb mix, *verduras* [herbs] or *todas verduras* [all herbs], which consists of parsley, spearmint, and cilantro and is used in close to one hundred recipes. For more on spices and seasonings, see the Introduction, "Herbs, Spices, and Flowers," 47–8.

Hierba de cuajar herbal rennet. Martínez Montiño specifies *cardoons* whose dried flowers have enzymes that are often used to *curdle* milk. It appears in two recipes.

Hierbas herbs or leafy greens. Martínez Montiño primarily uses this term to refer to herbs. The ones he cites most are *mejorana* [marjoram], *salvia* [sage], *hisopillo* [winter savory], and *ajedrea* [summer savory], but sometimes he also

includes *hinojo* [fennel], *oregáno* [oregano], and *eneldo* [dill]. However, in five different recipes, he uses *hierbas* to refer to *leafy green vegetables* and includes *lechugas* [lettuce], *escarolas* [escarole], *riponces* [rampion bellflower], and *chicorias dulces* or *amargas* [sweet or bitter chicory] as examples. In about a half dozen recipes, *hierbas* are referred to as *verduras* with this same meaning of green leafy vegetables. However, by far the most common meaning of *verduras* or *todas verduras* is the combination of *perejil*, *hierbabuena*, and *cilantro verde* [parsley, spearmint, and cilantro], as indicated in his recipe "Cazuela de truchas" [Trout stew] (392; 393).

Hierbas del jardín garden herbs. When adding garden herbs to the eighteen different recipes that include this term, Martínez Montiño generally specifies which ones. See *hierbas* for more information.

Higadillo liver (of a bird). In the fifteen recipes that use *higadillo* as one of the ingredients, thirteen refer to hen liver. Martínez Montiño suggests that it be roasted or fried instead of boiled.

Hilo de bala twine. This is used to secure suckling pig or mutton once it has been opened and stuffed and is ready to be closed back up again. For more on kitchen equipment, see Appendix 1, "Kitchen Furnishings and Equipment."

Hinojo fennel. Martínez Montiño uses it in ten different recipes. For more on his preparation of this herb and vegetable, see the Introduction, "Fruit, Vegetables, Nuts, and Seeds," 43.

Hisopillo winter savory or hyssop brush. As a herb, this term is used in seventeen different recipes. See *hierbas* for more information. Though the technical term may be unfamiliar to many, the *hisopillo* was used in the Church as an instrument for sprinkling holy water. Its name derives from *hisopo* [hyssop], a plant well known for its antiseptic properties. In the kitchen, it either takes the form of a brush, most likely first made with sprigs from the hyssop plant, to which Martínez Montiño probably refers, or of a perforated ball on the end of a stick. This specialty kitchen utensil appears in four recipes. In each case, it is used for sprinkling water on top of a dish.

Hojas verdes leafy greens. Martínez Montiño uses this phrase only once. The more common phrase is *hierbas*. See *hierbas* for more information.

Hojaldrado puff pastry dough. Martínez Montiño uses this dough in two dozen recipes. Most recipes are sweet, but there are several savoury ones as well. At times, he stretches the dough so thin that he insists that one can see through it.

Hojaldre puff pastry. This dough is made from flour, sugar, butter, and water. It is versatile, and while Martínez Montiño has seven recipes with the name in the title, there are many more pastries that use this dough as well.

Hojuela pastry sheet. Often this sheet, which is from sweet dough that is rolled out, is then fried and used as a base on which to serve savoury dishes, mostly poultry. It is also used to make a wide variety of pastries. *Hojuelas* appear in twenty different recipes.

Hongo wild mushroom. For more on Martínez Montiño's preparation of this vegetable, see the Introduction, "Fruit, Vegetables, Nuts, and Seeds," 43.

Hormigos hormigos. This is a sweet dish made with breadcrumbs, almonds, and honey. In Delicado's *La lozana andaluza*, the character Aldonza includes *hormigos* in the catalogue of great foods that came from her grandmother's kitchen (177–9), thus providing an example of tastes that cross social boundaries. However, Martínez Montiño only references this dish; he does not include a recipe for it.

Hornillo small oven. Martínez Montiño references this oven in just two recipes, for lobster and for artichokes. For more on kitchen equipment, see Appendix 1, "Kitchen Furnishings and Equipment."

Horno de cobre copper oven. Martínez Montiño recommends using a copper oven in eight recipes. See *cobre* for more information, and for more on kitchen equipment, see Appendix 1, "Kitchen Furnishings and Equipment."

Horno de pan bread oven. Martínez Montiño recommends using a bread oven in seven recipes. All are for bread, rolls, savoury pies, rolls, pastries, or a certain type of cookie. For more on kitchen equipment, see Appendix 1, "Kitchen Furnishings and Equipment."

Huevo egg. This is one of the most widely used foodstuffs in the entire cookbook, appearing close to eight hundred times, far more than sugar, butter, salt, or even water. Below are some of the ways eggs appear in the cookbook. For more information, see the Introduction, 44.

Arrollado rollup
Con vino with wine
Crecido expanded
Dorado golden
Dulce sweet
Duro hard
Encerado (today *pasado por agua*) soft-boiled
Encañutado sweet canuto
En puchero in a stew pot
Escalfado poached
Esponjado fluffy
Estrellado fried
Hilado candied (only the yolk)
Mejido sweet scrambled (only the yolk)

> *Relleno* stuffed
> *Revuelto* scrambled
> *Seco* dry or well done
> *Telilla* membrane (of the yolk)

Humo smoke or odour. Martínez Montiño uses this word in two different ways. First, it is used in the context of smoking a foodstuff or the smoke that results when burning something. For example, in one recipe he explains, "luego quemarás pan ... y pásalo por un poco de agua fría, porque se le quite el humo, que esto tiene el pan que al punto se le quita" [Next, burn some bread ... dip them [the pieces of bread] in a little cold water to get rid of the smoke; whatever is coming off the bread will instantly stop] (294–5). Second, he uses the word to describe a distinguishing feature of a foodstuff: its odour. In particular, he cites certain fish – *congrio* [conger eel], *merluza* [hake], or *cazón* [dogfish] – and dill.

Jabalí boar. For more on Martínez Montiño's preparation of this animal, see the Introduction, 33.

Jadeo jadeo. This signature sauce is made with stock, wine, vinegar, egg yolk, butter, and seasoning. It is found in the recipe "Un platillo de jadeo de manos de Ternera" [A dish of calves' feet with *jadeo* sauce] (330; 331). For more on sauces, see the Introduction, "Sauces," 48, 49–50t.

Jadrea summer savory. See *hierbas* for more information.

Jalea jelly. This sweetener is made from sugar, pectin, acid, and fruit juice. Its consistency is firm and it is a clear spread. Martínez Montiño includes five different recipes for it.

> *Gilea de vino* wine jelly
> *Jalea de membrillo* quince jelly
> *Memoria de Jalea de granadas* memoir of pomegranate jelly
> *Memoria de Jalea de amacenas* memoir of damson plum jelly
> *Memoria de la Jalea de agraz* memoir of sour grape jelly

Jarrete shank. Martínez Montiño uses this part of the animal in seven veal, ham, and mutton dishes.

Jengibre ginger. This aromatic root is one of the five ingredients that make up Martínez Montiño's *todas especias* [all spices] mix. The others are black pepper, clove, nutmeg, and saffron. For more on spices and seasonings, see the Introduction, "Herbs, Spices, and Flowers," 47–8.

Jibia cuttlefish. For more on Martínez Montiño's preparation of this shellfish, see the Introduction, "Fish and Shellfish," 39.

Lamprea lamprey. For more on Martínez Montiño's preparation of this fish, see the Introduction, "Fish and Shellfish," 37–8.

Lampreado lamprea style. Based on Martínez Montiño's recipes, *lampreado* refers to a dish with a sweet and sour brown sauce with cinnamon. For more on this method of preparation found in the cookbook, see the Introduction, "Fish and Shellfish," 37–8.

Langosta lobster. For more on Martínez Montiño's preparation of this shellfish, see the Introduction, "Fish and Shellfish," 39.

Laurel bay leaf. For more on herbs, see the Introduction, "Herbs, Spices, and Flowers," 47–8.

Lebrada lebrada. For this sauce that accompanies a stewed hare dish, Martínez Montiño adds wine, seasons with all spices, cinnamon, and salt, and adds water if necessary. He then adds sugar and some honey. He also offers a series of alternative ways to prepare the sauce. For more on sauces, see the Introduction, "Sauces," 48, 49–50t.

Leche milk. Cow milk is used in some sixty recipes. Alternatives include *leche de cabra* [goat milk], *leche de almendras* [almond milk], and *leche de piñones* [pine nut milk]. Each of these appears in a handful of recipes. For more on Martínez Montiño's use of milk and milk alternatives, see the Introduction, "Dairy Products," 44–5.

Lechón suckling pig. For more on Martínez Montiño's preparation of this animal, see the Introduction, 32.

Lechuga lettuce. For more on Martínez Montiño's preparation of this vegetable, see the Introduction, "Fruit, Vegetables, Nuts, and Seeds," 43.

Lenteja lentil. For more on Martínez Montiño's preparation of this vegetable, see the Introduction, "Fruit, Vegetables, Nuts, and Seeds," 44.

Leudar to leaven or to rise. This verb appears in three recipes for rolls.

Libra pound. See Appendix 2 for measurements.

Librillo (today *lebrillo*) terracotta bowl. This kitchen appliance, whose top is wider than its bottom, was used for kitchen chores like kneading dough, cleaning the insides of a pig, or washing dishes. The term appears once in the cookbook for a bowl used for kneading dough.

Liebre hare. For more on Martínez Montiño's preparation of this animal, see the Introduction, 33.

Limón lemon. For more on Martínez Montiño's preparation of this fruit, see the Introduction, "Fruit, Vegetables, Nuts, and Seeds," 41.

Limoncillo lime. For more on Martínez Montiño's preparation of this fruit, see the Introduction, "Fruit, Vegetables, Nuts, and Seeds," 41.

Lino rastradillo See *sedeña*.

Liviano lung. Martínez Montiño uses this part of the calf, kid, or sheep in eight different recipes.

Longaniza longaniza sausage. The name comes from Lucania in southern Italy. This type of sausage dates back to ancient Rome. Martínez Montiño includes one recipe for *longaniza* pork sausage. It is made with pork tenderloin, while *chorizo* is made with lean pork. *Chorizo* is marinated in wine, vinegar, and salt, while *longaniza* contains all of that and is seasoned with pepper, clove, ginger, and cumin. Martínez Montiño notes that His Majesty often eats this type of sausage.

Maná manna. This term refers to food God provided the Israelites in the desert for forty days and nights (Ex. 16:11–36), but, according to Valles Rojo, in the seventeenth century it was "una especialidad de confiteros, más pequeña que la gragea" [a specialty of candy makers, smaller than sprinkles] (423).

Manido dry-aged. This adjective is used to describe the condition of boar meat, mutton, and beef, and once for poultry. It refers to the process of tenderizing meat in which the meat is left to hang, thereby allowing enzymes to break down tissues and making the meat more tender, and allowing water to evaporate and making the flavour more concentrated. Martínez Montiño uses it in a half dozen recipes.

Manjar blanco blancmange. This was a very popular dish throughout early modern Europe. Martínez Montiño's recipe uses shredded hen breast, milk, rice flour, and a lot of sugar. In addition to his recipe for making it, Martínez Montiño includes eight other blancmange recipes and references it in twenty others.

Manteca lard. This fat appears in almost 150 recipes. For more on Martínez Montiño's use of different fats, see the Introduction, "Fats," 46–7.

Manteca de vaca butter. This fat appears in some 150 recipes. For more on Martínez Montiño's use of different fats, see the Introduction, "Fats," 46–7.

Maravedí maravedí. See Appendix 2 for measurements.

Marisco shellfish. For more on Martínez Montiño's preparation of this shellfish, see the Introduction, "Fish and Shellfish," 39.

Masa encerada elastic dough. Martínez Montiño uses this term to describe dough for pastries, empanadas and turnovers, puffs and fried dough, tarts, wafers, cookies, and rolls in about fifteen different recipes. In "Empanadas de perdices" [Partridge empanadas] (160; 161), he explains how to laminate dough, a key process for making puff pastry and other flaky pastry doughs.

Masa de levadura leaven dough. Martínez Montiño uses this type of dough for pastry, bread, and rolls in eight different recipes.

Mastresala (today *maestresala*) steward. For more on the kitchen and the various positions within, see the Introduction, 10–13.

Mayordomo major domo. For more on the kitchen and the various positions within, see the Introduction, 10–13.

Mazapán marzipan. This almond paste adds sweetness to dozens of recipes for pastries, puff pastries, pies, rolls, tarts, and cookies, as well as egg, stuffed fruit, and poultry dishes.

Mechar to lard. This technique adds fat to a meat dish and thereby gives it additional flavour and juice. Martínez Montiño uses it in over two dozen recipes.

Mejillón mussel. For more on Martínez Montiño's preparation of this shellfish, see the Introduction, "Fish and Shellfish," 39.

Mejorana marjoram. See *hierbas* for more information.

Melocotón firm peach. For more on Martínez Montiño's preparation of this fruit, see the Introduction, "Fruit, Vegetables, Nuts, and Seeds," 41.

Membrillo quince. For more on Martínez Montiño's preparation of this fruit, see the Introduction, "Fruit, Vegetables, Nuts, and Seeds," 39–41.

Menear to shake or to stir. This verb means *to shake* when used in context of the frying pan and *to stir* when used in the context of a spoon.

Menudo or *menudillo* giblets. The offal from fowl, which includes gizzard, liver, heart, and neck. Martínez Montiño uses them in stews and pies and even has a recipe for "Empanada de menudos de pavos" [Turkey giblet empanada] (458–60; 459–61).

Menudo small. When used to refer to chopping sizes, *diced*, and when the phrase is *muy menudo*, *minced*.

Merienda late afternoon supper. Although today *merienda* is thought of as a snack, for Martínez Montiño it constitutes an early supper, something akin to an English high tea.

Mermelada marmalade or jam. If this word is translated as *marmalade*, it refers to a citrus spread made from the peel and pulp of the fruit, which is cooked for a long time and has no pectin. In his recipe "Una torta de cidra verde" [Green citron pie] (244–6; 245–7), Martínez Montiño's description of how citron is prepared resembles a marmalade, though he does not use that term. As *jam*, it refers to a thick mixture of fruit, pectin, and sugar that has been boiled until the fruit is soft and fairly thick. Martínez Montiño has one recipe for quince jam and references it in another recipe for a marzipan pie.

Mero grouper. This fish appears only once, as a fish option that goes well with green mutton sauce.

Migaja pinch. Martínez Montiño uses this measurement eighteen times, primarily for spices and salt.

Migajón crumb. This centre part of the bread is referenced seven times. Usually it is removed and mashed together with other ingredients to act as a thickener of sorts.

Molido ground. This adjective is overwhelmingly used to describe the desired consistency of sugar. Occasionally it is used for anise, clove, coriander, and oregano as well.

Molleja gizzards and sweetbreads. Gizzards are found in three poultry recipes and sweetbreads in five recipes for kid and two for veal.

Mollete mollete. This type of bread describes a soft, white bread roll. It appears in eight recipes, primarily in sweet dishes.

Mollo mollo broth. This appears once in the cookbook in a rabbit recipe where the meat is first roasted, then covered in broth and seasoned with black pepper, nutmeg, ginger, saffron, and vinegar. *Mollo* is related to the Portuguese *molho* [sauce]. Given Martínez Montiño's deep connections to Portugal, his recipe "Conejos en mollo" [Rabbit in mollo broth] (154; 155) could be another recipe with Portuguese origins.

Mondar to peel, to shell, to shuck, to clean. This verb overwhelmingly refers to removing the rind from fruits and vegetables. It is used this way in over thirty recipes. It is also used ten times to mean shelling nuts, twice to mean shucking beans, once to mean cleaning rice, and one other time to mean cleaning one's teeth.

Mosqueteado speckled. This adjective probably comes from *mosquete* [musket] to describe an effect similar to the spray of pellets that dotted the surface of the target. It is used to described the appearance of batter that contains cinnamon and clove.

Mostachón mostachon cookie. Today *mostachón* is a spongy finger cake, something similar to a madeleine. Martínez Montiño's recipe is for a long cookie flavoured with cinnamon and rosewater but with no butter or eggs. It was more familiar than other cookies, as he references its size and shape in other pastry recipes. Martínez Montiño also notes that these cookies are the king's favourite because they are moderately spiced.

Mostaza mustard. In the seventeenth century, *mostaza* had a dark purple or brown colour, nothing like the popular yellow mustard or even Dijon mustard of today. Martínez Montiño explains that it is made by mixing mustard powder with vinegar and adding it to grape must. He provides several varieties based on his main recipe. He also recommends serving mustard in five very different recipes: eggs, fricassee, kid head, boar, and stockfish. Finally, he uses mustard as a point of comparison for texture when describing how to make two other sauces.

Moyuelo moyuelo. As Martínez Montiño describes it, *moyuelo* is a rough bran. He sprinkles some on the baking sheet to bake mostachon cookies so they won't stick.

Mozo de cocina kitchen boy. For more on the kitchen and the various positions within, see the Introduction, 10–13.

Nabo turnip. For more on Martínez Montiño's preparation of this vegetable, see the Introduction, "Fruit, Vegetables, Nuts, and Seeds," 43.

Naranja orange. For more on Martínez Montiño's preparation of this fruit, see the Introduction, "Fruit, Vegetables, Nuts, and Seeds," 41, and, for orange blossom water, 48.

Nata cream. For more on Martínez Montiño's use of cream, see the Introduction, "Dairy Products," 44–5.

Názula Nazula curd cheese. According to Covarrubias, this type of cheese was commonly used in and around Toledo and is a regionalism for *requesón*. Martínez Montiño uses the term in three different recipes.

Nuez nutmeg or walnut. As a spice (nutmeg), this is one of the five ingredients that make up Martínez Montiño's *todas especias* [all spices] mix. The others are black pepper, clove, ginger, and saffron. For more on spices and seasonings, see the Introduction, "Herbs, Spices, and Flowers," 47–8. As a nut (walnut), it appears in one recipe on preserving walnuts. It is also the preferred wood for cutting boards.

Oblea wafer. Martínez Montiño uses this food item exclusively as a kitchen utensil. In almost twenty different recipes he recommends placing wafers as protection between a baked good and the bottom of a sheet pan or portable oven so that the food item will not stick.

Ochava one eighth of a *vara castellana* [Castilian yard]. See Appendix 2 for measurements.

Oficial cook. For more on the kitchen and the various positions within, see the Introduction, 10–13.

Olla pot. More specifically, the *olla* is a two-handled pot, usually tall and usually for making soups. This is a common piece of cookware in Martínez Montiño's kitchen. For more on kitchen equipment, see Appendix 1, "Kitchen Furnishings and Equipment."

Onza ounce. See Appendix 2 for measurements.

Oregáno oregano. See *hierbas* for more information.

Orejón dried apricot. This fruit is used just once in a dried apricot pie.

Oruga arugula. The *eruca vesicaria* variety is native to the Mediterranean and was commonly grown in seventeenth-century Spain. Today's *arugula* (*eruca sativa*) is a sub-variety from this plant, and generally has a less bitter flavour. Martínez Montiño uses it in eight recipes. For his two arugula sauce recipes, he uses a type of dried paste made from arugula and stored in blocks shaped from bread rolls moulds. For more on Martínez Montiño's preparation of this vegetable, see the Introduction, "Fruit, Vegetables, Nuts, and Seeds," 43.

Ostión oyster. For more on Martínez Montiño's preparation of this shellfish, see the Introduction, "Fish and Shellfish," 39.

Paje page. For more on the kitchen and the various positions within, see the Introduction, 10–13.

Paloma dove or pigeon. For more on Martínez Montiño's preparation of this game bird, see the Introduction, "Fowl," 33–6.

Palomino wild squab. For more on Martínez Montiño's preparation of this game bird, see the Introduction, "Fowl," 33–6.

Pan bread. This is one of the most used ingredients in the cookbook. Martínez Montiño includes specialty breads like *candeal* [candeal], *mollete* [mollete], or *de leche* [milk] and uses bread as a main ingredient for *torrijas* [torrijas] and *migas* [breadcrumbs]. However, it is most often used as a thickener, for which he often toasts and soaks the bread; or as a bed on which to serve a dish, as he does for sops. He also grates, shreds, and slices it.

Panecillo roll or bread roll amount. As bread, Martínez Montiño includes three recipes for rolls and uses or references them in twenty recipes. As a measurement, he uses it in four recipes to describe the quantity of salt or arugula one needed that was equivalent to a roll. Although the quantity for this measurement is unknown, based on his calculations in the "Oruga de azúcar" [Arugula and sugar sauce] (518; 519) and "Oruga con miel" [Arugula and honey sauce] (518; 519), I surmise it may be about one ounce, because in the former he uses one *panecillo* for six ounces of sugar and in the latter a 1:8 ratio of arugula to honey. Since, generally, honey is sweeter than sugar, I am surmising that the *panecillo* to sugar ratio is 1:6. Ruperto de Nola also includes this type of measurement in his recipe "Oruga buena" [Good arugula (sauce)]. He states, "Tomar una libra de los panes de la oruga" [take a pound from the arugula loaves] (331). Finally, Martínez Montiño uses this same measurement for salt in the recipes "Migas de leche" [Breadcrumbs with milk] (238–40; 239–41), "Fruta de chicharrones" [Crackling fried dough] (326; 327), and "Manjar blanco" [Blancmange] (342; 343).

Paño, pañito dish cloth or towel. For more on kitchen equipment, see Appendix 1, "Kitchen Furnishings and Equipment."

Papín sweet cream sauce. Recipes for making it are found in "Un plato de papín tostado, con cañas, huevos mejidos, y hojuelas" [Toasted sweet cream with marrow, sweet scrambled egg yolks, and pastry sheets] (552; 553) and "Papín de harina de trigo" [Sweet cream sauce made with wheat flour] (584–6; 585–7).

Pasa raisin. This dried fruit appears once in the banquet menus and in a spinach recipe accompanied with pine nuts.

Pasa de Corinto currant, dried. For more on Martínez Montiño's preparation of this fruit, see the Introduction, "Fruit, Vegetables, Nuts, and Seeds," 42.

Pastel pie. Martínez Montiño includes a wide variety of sweet and savoury *pasteles* [pies]. These are in addition to the *pastelones* [big pies] and *tortas* [pies], of which there are many as well.

Pastel en bote crustless pie. Martínez Montiño uses this phrase to refer to minced meat or fish served over slices of bread in the shape of a pie.

Pastelón big pie. Martínez Montiño includes eight different sweet and savoury *pastelones* [big pies]. These are in addition to the *pasteles* [pies] and *tortas* [pies], of which there are many more.

Pavo turkey. This New World foodstuff is the opening recipe for the cookbook. Martínez Montiño later includes a recipe for turkey giblet empanadas and another on how to carve turkey at the table. For more on his preparation of this farm-raised bird, see the Introduction, "Fowl," 33–6.

Pebrada black pepper sauce. Martínez Montiño recommends this sauce for certain fowl, hare, veal head, boar udder, kid trotters, and trout dishes. In addition to the black pepper, he adds ginger, cinnamon, and clove to his *pebrada*. For more on sauces, see the Introduction, "Sauces," 48, 49–50t.

Pepino cucumber. This vegetable is highlighted in the recipe for pickling cucumbers. For more on Martínez Montiño's preparation of this vegetable, see the Introduction, "Fruit, Vegetables, Nuts, and Seeds," 43.

Pepitas, de calabaza, de melón seeds, of squash, of melon. These seeds are used in just a handful of recipes. In one, their health benefits are noted (494–5).

Pepitoria pepitoria. In the seventeenth century, *pepitoria* was a stew made from poultry offal. In Martínez Montiño's recipe, possibly the first recorded version, the dish is made from the head, neck, wings, and feet of the bird, includes a roux-based sauce finished with saffron, and uses other organ meat – the liver and oviduct – and hard-boiled egg yolks as garnish. Today *pepitoria* refers to a poultry dish made with egg, either added in raw or already cooked.

Pera pear. There are three main pear recipes in the cookbook and a smattering of references. For more on Martínez Montiño's preparation of this fruit, see the Introduction, "Fruit, Vegetables, Nuts, and Seeds," 41.

Percebe gooseneck barnacle. For more on Martínez Montiño's preparation of this shellfish, see the Introduction, "Fish and Shellfish," 39.

Perdigar to sear (on a grill); to wilt (in a little fat); to parboil (in water); to parbake (in the oven); and to parcook (when method is not specified). This fascinating verb covers various cooking methods, all of which indicate a partial cooking process, albeit with different mediums. *Perdigar* is typically the first stage of a multi-stage cooking process and is used in sixty different recipes.

Perdigón partridge chick. Martínez Montiño references this bird only twice; once for a broth for the ill and once to accompany a mutton dish. For more on Martínez Montiño's preparation of this farm-raised bird, see the Introduction, "Fowl," 33–6.

Perdiz partridge. In eleven recipes, partridge is the primary ingredient, and in another four, it appears as a secondary ingredient or a suggested

accompaniment. For more on Martínez Montiño's preparation of this game bird, see the Introduction, "Fowl," 33–6.

Perejil parsley. This green herb is part of Martínez Montiño's most popular herb mix, *verduras* [herbs] or *todas verduras* [all herbs], which consists of parsley, spearmint, and cilantro and is used in close to one hundred recipes. For more on spices and seasonings, see the Introduction, "Herbs, Spices, and Flowers," 47–8.

Pernil leg. Martínez Montiño has one recipe in which he explains how to cook the leg: "Un pernil cocido sin remojar" [Leg boiled without soaking] (462; 463). More often he references "tocino de pernil" [ham fat], which he highlights in two savoury pastries and references in a handful of others.

Perol round-bottom pot. The *perol* is round on the bottom, generally made of copper, and often used interchangeably with a *caldero* [cauldron], *olla* [pot], or *cazuela* [casserole]. For more on kitchen equipment, see Appendix 1, "Kitchen Furnishings and Equipment."

Pescado o pescada cecial salted hake. Martínez Montiño uses this fish in two recipes.

Pezón base of the stem or top of certain vegetable or fruit. When referring to artichoke, cabbage, borage, lettuce, spinach, and cherries, *pezón* is the base of the stem. When referring to carrot, onion, and eggplant, it is the top of the vegetable.

Picante pungent or with spices. Martínez Montiño uses *picante* [pungent] to describe sauces for roasted fowl and mustard. Three times in the cookbook, when describing boar empanadas, veal brain, and even the mostachon cookie that has spice in it, *picante* [with spice] does not mean spicy hot as it does today; rather it means with a spice flavour.

Picatoste fried bread slice. Martínez Montiño includes four picatoste recipes, three with chopped offal on top of bread baked in a greased portable oven and one with blancmange. In addition, he includes another seven recipes that suggest serving the dish on top of, with, or under these slices of bread. For more on the origin of the word, see Torres Martínez, "Léxico culinario en el libro."

Pichón farm-raised squab. This is a popular choice among poultry and is often included with chicken and hen as one of the poultry options in a given recipe. For more on Martínez Montiño's preparation of this game bird, see the Introduction, "Fowl," 33–6.

Pieza piece or generic piece of cookware. When referring, for example, to a piece of meat or fish, *pieza* means *piece*. But, more generally, it has no corresponding parallel in English in the way Martínez Montiño often uses it to refer to *a generic piece of cookware*. Here and in the majority of cases, I have translated it as *bowl*, but throughout the cookbook the context often dictates

other translations, including *pot* and *dish*. Martínez Montiño uses it fifty-nine times in his cookbook.

Pimienta black pepper. This spice is one of the five ingredients that make up Martínez Montiño's *todas especias* [all spices] mix. The others are clove, nutmeg, ginger, and saffron. For more on spices and seasonings, see the Introduction, "Herbs, Spices, and Flowers," 47–8.

Piñón pine nut. This versatile nut is found in banquet menus and used in casseroles, stuffing, egg dishes, a spinach dish, a fish dish, and as a garnish. As milk it serves as a substitute for dairy.

Pisto pisto soup. Although Martínez Montiño explains that *pistos* are incredibly common, they have nothing to do with the now famous *pisto manchego*. As deduced from his recipe, seventeenth-century pisto was a strained soup that included ground poultry as the main ingredient.

Platillo small plate. Depending on the context, *platillo* can refer to a figurative, individual dish, as in a single serving or a smaller serving. It can also refer to a literal small plate. In the cookbook the term appears 123 times, of which over 80 per cent refer to a figurative, individual dish.

Plato plate. As in English, this term is both literal and figurative. It appears over three hundred times and is used to designate a physical plate over 80 per cent of the time. The *plato* is used both for serving food and for preparing it. It can refer to a plate, like a dinner plate, a serving platter, or a plate used as cookware and placed in the oven.

Pliego de papel sheet of paper. See Appendix 2 for measurements.

Pluvia plover. This wading bird is mentioned twice in the cookbook, along with *gangas* [pin-tailed sand grouses] and *sisones* [little bustards]: first, as a bird that would taste good with quince sauce, and second, in the instructions on how to carve a small bird at the table.

Pollo chicken. For more on Martínez Montiño's preparation of this farm-raised bird, see the Introduction, "Fowl," 33–6.

Portador food runner. For more on the kitchen and the various positions within, see the Introduction, 10–13.

Poso dregs (leaves or grounds, depending on the liquid). Martínez Montiño uses this term to explain its absence, that is, what should not appear when making "Agraz para todo el año" [Verjuice for the whole year] (516; 517).

Puchero tall stew pot or cooking pot. In the cookbook, this cookware is used in "Sustancias para enfermos" [Sustaining broth for the ill] (488–90; 489–91) to explain one of the ways to prepare broth. It is also used in the recipe for preparing *farro* [farro]. For more on kitchen equipment, see Appendix 1, "Kitchen Furnishings and Equipment."

Puches porridge. While Martínez Montiño does not include a recipe for *puches*, he uses it several times as a point of comparison when describing the consistency of another recipe like "Papín de harina de trigo" [Sweet cream sauce made with wheat flour] (584–6; 585–7) or "Potaje de calabaza redonda" [Round squash stew] (370; 371).

Puerco pork. For more on Martínez Montiño's preparation of this animal, see the Introduction, "Meat, Fowl, Fish, and Shellfish," 32.

Puerro leek. For more on Martínez Montiño's preparation of this vegetable, see the Introduction, "Fruit, Vegetables, Nuts, and Seeds," 43.

Pulgada inch. This measurement also corresponds to 1/12 of a *pie* (foot) and 1/36 of a *vara* (yard). See Appendix 2 for measurements.

Pulpo octopus. For more on Martínez Montiño's preparation of this shellfish, see the Introduction, "Fish and Shellfish," 39.

Punzar to prick. Martínez Montiño uses this verb only a handful of times but in a wide variety of situations, from opening up meat to release juices to creating holes in a pie crust so that the steam escapes and bubbles in the crust don't form.

Quesadilla cheese tart. Unlike the Mexican quesadilla that is made with corn (or wheat) tortillas folded over and filled with cheese and/or other ingredients, the *quesadilla* in Martínez Montiño's recipe is a sweet pastry that is either baked or fried.

Queso asadero Asadero cheese. This is a mild, chewy cheese that is both creamy and sliceable. It is used in two recipes.

Queso fresco farmer cheese. I have selected this translation because the curd cheese has some or most of the liquid pressed out and seems to be consistent with what Martínez Montiño is describing. Other common translations today are *cottage cheese* (fresh curd cheese) and *ricotta cheese* (whey cheese). It appears in nine different recipes.

Ralo thin. Martínez Montiño uses this adjective about two dozen times to describe the consistency of batter or sauce.

Rana frog. Martínez Montiño includes two recipes for frog. For more on his preparation of this amphibian, see the Introduction, "Fish and Shellfish," 36–9.

Rebozar to coat. This verb primarily refers to coating or dipping a food item in whipped eggs, sometime whole, other times just the whites or just the yolks, before frying. Two times Martínez Montiño uses fat instead of eggs to coat something.

Recado mixture. In the *Diccionario de autoridades* the definition of *recado* is "Se toma tambien por la diária provisión … que se trahe de la Plaza o tiendas, para comer" [It can also mean the daily provision … that is brought from the

Plaza or shops, to eat] (5.1737). The RAE explains that *recado* has several different meanings today, including *daily shopping, dressing, seasoning,* and *filling*. Three times Martínez Montiño's usage is similar to the last one, and I have translated it as *mixture* (of ingredients).

Recaudo mixture. Although in a culinary context *recaudo* often refers to seasoning, the seven different times Martínez Montiño uses the word, it means the same as *recado*.

Recio strong, vigorous. Martínez Montiño uses this word both as an adjective and an adverb in many different contexts. When tying up a piece of meat, it means *tightly*; when boiling, it means a *rolling* boil; when scrubbing vegetables, it means *firmly*; and when beating batter, it means *vigorously*. As an adjective he uses it to describe a *strong* or a *tough* skin. Although used only eight times, its translation changes with almost every use.

Receta recipe. This word actually is not in the cookbook and its absence is worth noting. Historically, *receta* was used for medical prescriptions, while cooking manuals used *suerte* [kind, type], or *orden* [instruction]. *Procedimiento* [procedure] is found in other cookbooks but is not a term Martínez Montiño uses. The first appearance of *receta* in a cookbook with instructions only for food that doesn't include medical recipes is later in the eighteenth century.

Redaño caul fat or mesentery. This membranous tissue joins part of the small intestine to the back wall of the abdomen. It also holds the stomach and small intestines within the abdominal cavity. Martínez Montiño has one recipe that provides detail on how to prepare it and he uses it in some dozen recipes. I translate it as *caul fat* when used as a cooking ingredient and *mesentery* when discussing an animal part.

Redoma carafe. Martínez Montiño uses this specialty cookware item in three recipes, to make sustaining broth, elderberry vinegar, and verjuice. For the broth, he specifies that it should be made of glass. *Redomas* were also often made of clay.

Regalado exquisite or delicate. Several times Martínez Montiño uses this adjective to describe the excellence of a dish. On one occasion, in the recipe "Una escudilla de caldo" [A bowl of (hen) broth], he uses it to describe the delicate state of a person: "para hacer una escudilla de caldo para una persona enferma, o regalada" [To make a bowl of broth for a sick or delicate person] (492–3).

Repollo cabbage. Martínez Montiño includes one recipe for cabbage. For more on Martínez Montiño's preparation of this vegetable, see the Introduction, "Fruit, Vegetables, Nuts, and Seeds," 43.

Repulgo crimped edge. Martínez Montiño describes this type of pastry crust in eleven recipes.

Requesón curd cheese. This ingredient is central to the recipe "Manteca de názulas" [Nazulas butter] (520–2; 521–3) and also appears in a handful of recipes as an optional ingredient.

Rescoldo grey embers. Martínez Montiño includes this heat source in seven recipes for very different dishes: broths, pastries, meat, fish, and vegetables. The charcoal is not as hot as *brasas* [red-hot coals], which appears in seventeen equally diverse recipes.

Rezumar to ooze. This verb appears in just one recipe: "Cómo se puede asar una pella de manteca de vacas en el asador" [How to roast a butterball on a spit] (524–6; 525–7).

Riñon kidney. Martínez Montiño includes two recipes for veal and two for rabbit.

Riñonada loin. This cut of meat appears in a half dozen recipes. It always refers to mutton or veal.

Riponces rampion bellflower. This leafy green vegetable appears in six recipes as an optional vegetable. Its shoots are highlighted in "Pastel de criadillas de tierra" [Truffle pie] (406–8; 407–9). For more on Martínez Montiño's preparation of this vegetable, see the Introduction, "Fruit, Vegetables, Nuts, and Seeds," 43.

Rociar to sprinkle (scented water) or to dot (butter or lard). Martínez Montiño uses this verb in twenty pie and pastry recipes.

Rosa rose. This flower is used in scented water, to enhance elderberry vinegar, and for colouring sugar.

Rosquilla ring-shaped pastry. *Rosquillas* are one of the long-standing traditional sweet pastries in Spain. They are ring shaped and generally finished with sugar that is either sprinkled on, ladled over, or used for dipping. There exist many varieties. Some resemble doughnuts, while other are harder, like a cookie, and others somewhere in between. Martínez Montiño has two *rosquilla* recipes, "Memoria de las rosquillas" [Memoir of ring-shaped pastries] (530; 531) and "Otra suerte de rosquillas" [Another kind of ring-shaped pastries] (530; 531), that both resemble more the consistency of a cookie. He also includes a recipe for icing them. For more on pastries, see the Introduction, "Grains," 27t, 28–9.

Sábado Saturday. This day refers to the day when Christians practised partial abstinence, during which only limited animal products like offal could be consumed. On Saturdays one could also eat *tocino* [fatback], as Martínez Montiño points out at the end of the recipe "Torta de ternera, o de cabrito" [Veal or kid pie] (248; 249). He references Saturday dishes six times in the cookbook (in comparison to "día de pescado" [fish day] or "viernes" [Friday], which he mentions sixteen times).

Sábalo shad. While there are no recipes dedicated to this fish, it does appear as a suggested fish to pair with fava beans.

Salchicha sausage. Martínez Montiño includes one recipe for *salchicha* pork sausage, which, different from *chorizo* and *salchichón*, is seasoned with pepper, ginger, fennel, and salt. It is eaten fresh.

Salchichón sausage. Martínez Montiño includes one recipe for *salchichón* pork sausage, which is seasoned with the same spices as *chorizo*: all spices (black pepper, clove, nutmeg, ginger, and saffron) and salt. Unlike *chorizo*, which can last up to a year, Martínez Montiño notes that *salchichón* is meant to be eaten fresh, either fried or grilled.

Salmuera brine. This saline liquid is made for preserving venison.

Salpicón salpicon. Martínez Montiño includes two salpicon recipes, one for beef and one for fish. This popular dish used up leftovers by adding diced onion, vinegar, and salt and pepper to taste.

Salpimentar to salt and pepper or to sprinkle with spices. Most times this verb means to season with salt and pepper, but on three different occasions, Martínez Montiño specifies sprinkling spices when using this verb.

Salsa sauce. Martínez Montiño includes twenty-six different sauces ranging from those made from poultry, pig liver, or boar, to herb or wine and vinegar-based sauces, to fruit-, nut-, or vegetable-based sauces, including a popular quince sauce, lemon, almond, caper, and barberry sauces; as well as various egg-based sauces. For more on sauces, see the Introduction, "Sauces," 48, 49–50t.

Salserilla small dish for sauce. This specialty item for serving sauces is used in just one recipe: "Cómo se puede freír, y asar, y cocer un pescado todo en un tiempo, sin partirlo" [How to fry, roast, and boil a fish at the same time without cutting it up] (414–16; 415–17).

Salvia sage. This herb is used in a dozen different recipes for meat and poultry. For more on Martínez Montiño's use of herbs and spices, see the Introduction, "Herbs, Spices, and Flowers," 47–8.

Sándalo sandalwood. This aroma appears only twice in the cookbook: once, in a recipe to create food art, "Otro plato de huevos hilados" [Another dish of candied egg yolk threads] (434–6; 435–7), and then in "Sopa de vaca a la portuguesa, contrahecho en día de pescado" [Beef sops, Portuguese style, faux for fish days] (472; 473), where its woody fragrance and reddish-brown colour help to provide the faux beef sops with a "meaty" flavour and look.

Sardina sardine. Martínez Montiño includes two sardine recipes, one for turnovers and another for pickling. For more on Martínez Montiño's preparation of this fish, see the Introduction, "Fish and Shellfish," 36–9.

- **Saúco** elderberry. Martínez Montiño uses this fruit to make a flavoured vinegar. For more on Martínez Montiño's preparation of this fruit, see the Introduction, "Fruit, Vegetables, Nuts, and Seeds," 42.
- **Sazonar** to season. This verb appears over three hundred times in the cookbook and is used both when adding and adjusting spices and when flavouring with sweeteners.
- **Sedeña** fine tow. Less coarse fibres from flax that come from the second raking. In one recipe, "Cómo se puede freír, y asar, y cocer un pescado todo en un tiempo, sin partirlo" [How to fry, roast, and boil a fish at the same time without cutting it up] (414–16; 415–17), he uses tow to wrap fish before cooking on a spit.
- **Sesma** length measuring between 12.7 and 15.24 cm or 5 and 6 in. The term also corresponds to one sixth of a *vara castellana* (Castilian yard). See Appendix 2 for measurements.
- **Seso** brain. Martínez Montiño provides one recipe for veal brain and also includes brain from hen, kid, sheep, sucking pig, and lobster in eight other recipes.
- **Sisón** little bustard. This game bird is mentioned twice in the cookbook, along with *gangas* [pin-tailed sand grouse] and *pluvias* [plovers]: first, as a bird that would taste good with quince sauce, and second, in the instructions on how to carve a small bird at the table.
- **Solomo** (today *solomillo*) tenderloin. This cut of meat can be either beef or pork. It appears twice in the suggested banquet menus.
- **Sollo** sturgeon. If we assess taste by sheer number of recipes that appear in his cookbook, then it is clear that Martínez Montiño's favourite fish, big or small, freshwater or saltwater, is *sollo*. He states that it is the fish that most resembles meat and he repeatedly uses methods of sturgeon preparation as a base for other recipes. For more on Martínez Montiño's preparation of this fish, see the Introduction, "Fish and Shellfish," 36–9.
- **Sopa** sop. While we commonly think of *sopa* as *soup*, in this cookbook and more generally in seventeenth-century Spain and beforehand, *sopa* [sop] is a piece of bread placed on the bottom of a dish that soaks up the juices of the dish or a piece of bread that has some type of liquid – usually, stock, broth, wine, or cream – poured on top of it. Sops, which appear in over forty different recipes, are described and consumed in a variety of ways. Among those prepared in the royal kitchens, Martínez Montiño discusses white sops, milk sops, golden sops, and cream sops. For more on Martínez Montiño's preparation and use of sops, see the Introduction, "Grains," 26.
- **Suero** whey. This is the liquid that separates from the curd in milk when it is clotted. Martínez Montiño uses this ingredient in six different recipes for pastries, tarts, and butter.

Sustancia essence or sustaining broth. This liquid mostly refers to the juice that is released when cooking meat. In two recipes that explain how to make soup for the ill, I translate the term as *sustaining broth*.

Tahona animal-powered flour mill. This type of mill was powered by a draft animal. It contrasts with other types of milling; for example, by hand. In Martínez Montiño it is clearly the most valued process, since it produces a finer flour. Martínez Montiño references it in six different recipes, and in the recipe "Panecillos de colaciones" [Collation rolls] directly compares "de tahona" [animal-powered mill] to "de molino" [grinder] (504–6; 505–7).

Tallarín strip. Although today we think of *tallarines* as noodles, for Martínez Montiño the word means a strip of fried pastry dough. In a half dozen recipes, Martínez Montiño offers the option of using strips of dough that are fried instead of a full sheet of pastry dough. In the recipe "Hojaldrillas fritas" [Little fried puff pastries], he explains, "De la masa de las empanadas Inglesas podrás hacer unos tallarines, o unos cuadrillos, y fríelos. Son muy buenos para componer platos, como son platos de pastelillos de conservas" [With English empanada dough you can make strips or little squares and fry them. They are great for arranging plates, like a plate of little pastries with preserves] (506–7).

Tarazón piece. Nuria Polo Cano points out that *tarazón* is one of the few culinary terms that comes from Leonese (240). It means *a piece of something*, especially of meat or fish. Martínez Montiño uses this term in three fish dishes. It could very well be related to *tranche* (from the French *trancher*), which means "a cutting, a cut; a piece cut off, a slice." Thanks to Ken Albala for pointing this connection out.

Tenca tench. This fish appears as an option in one recipe. For more on Martínez Montiño's preparation of this fish, see the Introduction, "Fish and Shellfish," 36–9.

Tender to roll out or to spread. Martínez Montiño uses this verb in twenty-six recipes to signify rolling out a piece of dough. Two times it means to spread, as in batter across a baking sheet or fatback across a piece of poultry.

Teniente underdone. Martínez Montiño uses this adjective once to describe the state of ham after its first stage of cooking.

Ternera veal. This type of meat appears frequently in the cookbook. It is one of the most popular meat products. For more on Martínez Montiño's preparation of this animal, see the Introduction, "Meat, Fowl, Fish, and Shellfish," 29–31.

Tieso firm. Martínez Montiño uses this adjective a half dozen times, primarily to describe the crust for pies or pastries.

Tijelada Portuguese custard. This type of custard is a regional dessert from Abrantes. Martínez Montiño compares his blancmange tartlet recipe to it.

Tinaja large terracotta jar. This specialty piece is used for storing verjuice.

Tinelo kitchen dining room.

Tocino fatback. This type of fat is taken off the back of the pig under the skin. It is the most common form of fat from the pig and is typically salt cured. It appears in 135 recipes. For more on Martínez Montiño's use of different fats, see the Introduction, "Fats," 46–7.

Tocino de pernil ham fat. This fat is acquired from the leg and is full of fat and collagen. It appears in eight recipes and is twice used to make *torreznos*. For more on Martínez Montiño's use of different fats, see the Introduction, "Fats," 46–7.

Tocino de redaño caul lard. This fat is taken from the mesentery around the digestive organs. It is the lowest grade of lard and is generally used for wrapping meat. For more on Martínez Montiño's use of different fats, see the Introduction, "Fats," 46–7.

Tocino gordo extra fatty fatback. This fat appears in dozens of recipes. For more on Martínez Montiño's use of different fats, see the Introduction, "Fats," 46–7.

Tocino magro meaty fatback. This fat, laden with ham, appears in six recipes. For more on Martínez Montiño's use of different fats, see the Introduction, "Fats," 46–7.

Todas especias all spices. This is the most common spice mixture used in the cookbook and not to be confused with Jamaican *allspice*. Martínez Montiño specifies that this combination is made up of black pepper, clove, nutmeg, ginger, and saffron.

Todas hierbas all leafy greens. Martínez Montiño uses *lechugas* [lettuce], *escarolas* [escarole], *riponces* [rampion bellflower], and *chicorias dulces* or *amargas* [sweet or bitter chicory] as examples (176–9; 594–7). He also uses the expression *hojas verdes* for *leafy greens*. See *hierbas* for more information.

Todas verduras green herbs. Most often it refers to the specific mixture of *perejil*, *hierbabuena*, and *cilantro verde* [parsley, spearmint, and cilantro]. See *hierbas* for more information.

Toronja toronja. For more on Martínez Montiño's preparation of this fruit, see the Introduction, "Fruit, Vegetables, Nuts, and Seeds," 41–2.

Torrezno roasted pork belly. This type of meat preparation is highlighted in seven recipes and referenced in another six. Twice Martínez Montiño insists on making *torreznos* from good-quality pork fat from Garrovillas, a town in Extremadura known for its excellent pork products.

Torrijas torrijas. This is a classic Spanish sweet dish made by saturating bread with milk (or sometimes another liquid like wine or animal fat), dipping it in beaten eggs, and frying it. It is then rolled in sugar and has cinnamon sprinkled on top.

There are four recipes that feature torrijas and another two dozen that use torrijas as a bed on which to place a dish, as part of assembling a dish, or as a garnish.

Torta pie. Martínez Montiño includes a wide variety of sweet and savoury *tortas* [pies]. These are in addition to the close to two dozen *pasteles* [pies] and eight *pastelones* [big pies] as well. For more on pastries, see the Introduction, "Grains," 28–9.

Tortera covered tart pan. This piece of cookware is deeper than the common tart pan today and also has a lipped lid designed for holding coals or other forms of heat. It is used to bake pastries, both sweet and savoury, and also other dishes. It is the fourth most common piece of cookware in Martínez Montiño's kitchen after the *sartén* [frying pan], *cazuela* [casserole], and *olla* [pot]. For more on kitchen equipment, see Appendix 1, "Kitchen Furnishings and Equipment."

Tortilla omelette or tortilla or cookie. This term has its origin in its round, small shape. Some fifteen times, it does refer to an egg omelette, but five times it references a batter made with flour, water, and salt that results in a flat, small, round tortilla. Once Martínez Montiño uses the term to refer to a frosted cookie made with sugar, eggs, and flour (528–9).

Tortolilla ground dove. This small bird is referenced once to explain how to roast small birds. They are best eaten with a sweet and sour sauce. For more on Martínez Montiño's preparation of this game bird, see the Introduction, "Fowl," 33–6.

Tostar to toast or to brown. Martínez Montiño most often uses this verb for toasting bread. However, on occasion he uses it to finish off a foodstuff and give it a little colour. In those instances, I translate the verb as "to brown."

Trabado thick. Martínez Montiño uses this adjective four times to address the consistency of a dish.

Traer a una mano to stir with one hand. Martínez Montiño uses this phrase a couple of dozen times to draw attention to the importance of the stirring process.

Trébedes trivet. Martínez Montiño uses this cookware item five times. For more on kitchen equipment, see Appendix 1, "Kitchen Furnishings and Equipment."

Trigo floreado finely sifted flour. There would be very little bran left in the flour. Martínez Montiño uses this term (or *harina floreada* [finely sifted flour]) in two dozen recipes.

Trinchero carving platter. Martínez Montiño uses this serveware once in his recipe for roast partridge. For more on kitchen equipment, see Appendix 1, "Kitchen Furnishings and Equipment."

Tripa intestine. As is to be expected, Martínez Montiño uses pig large intestines for making sausages. For fish and snails and certain birds, he discards it. For other birds and for venison, he washes it thoroughly before using. The main recipe for *tripas* is "Cómo se adereza una frasia de ternera" [How to prepare veal *frasia*], in which he sautés the small intestine and the mesentery with fatback, onion, and seasoning and thickens with egg yolk and vinegar (306–8; 307–9).

Trucha trout. More than a half dozen recipes feature trout. For more on Martínez Montiño's preparation of this fish, see the Introduction, "Fish and Shellfish," 37.

Turmas testicles. Martínez Montiño primarily uses this animal part from sheep and chicken as a garnish. It appears in four different recipes. He also uses the term *criadillas*.

Untar to grease. In dozens of recipes, Martínez Montiño greases a sheet, pot, pan, or portable oven primarily with lard before using it. At times he also applies fat directly to the foodstuff, for example when roasting.

Uspot uspot. Varela Merino notes that it is an example of a hapax legomenon, a word used only once in the language, though it most likely stems from the medieval French *hochepot* (2.2095), which is a traditional stew dating back to the earliest French cooking source, *The manuscript of Sion*.

Uva grape. This fruit is used exclusively in the mustard recipe.

Uva pin gooseberry. The term *uvas pin* most likely derives from the Italian name for gooseberries, *uva spina*. For more information, see *agrazón*.

Vasija pot or container. This all-purpose cookware item translates as "pot" for cooking and "container" for preparing or storing foods or liquids. It is cited in over a dozen recipes.

Vaso crust. In the majority of the dozen recipes in which Martínez Montiño cites the *vaso*, it refers to a large pie. However, the size may vary, as noted in "Cazolillas de manjar blanco" [Blancmange tartlets] (346; 347).

Veedor inspector or supervisor. For more on the kitchen and the various positions within, see the Introduction, 10–13.

Venado venison. There are ten recipes for venison, each focusing on either a specific part of the animal (for example, antler tips, intestines, liver, tenderloin) or mode of preparation (for example, how to make jerky). Martínez Montiño also has a recipe for packing venison to travel with it. For more on his preparation of this animal, see the Introduction, "Meat, Fowl, Fish, and Shellfish," 33.

Vencejo swift. This small bird is referenced once to explain how to roast small birds. They are best eaten with a sweet and sour sauce. For more on Martínez Montiño's preparation of this game bird, see the Introduction, "Fowl," 33–6.

Verduras herbs or green-leaf vegetables. Martínez Montiño's most popular herb mix, *verduras* or *todas verduras*, is a combination of parsley, spearmint, and cilantro and is used in close to one hundred recipes. In about a half dozen recipes, *verduras* refers to *green-leaf vegetables*. See *hierbas* for more information.

Vidriado glazed. This adjective refers to dishware and cookware as it is used in over a half dozen recipes. It also refers to a sugar topping for various pastries, where it appears again in over a half dozen recipes.

Vinagre vinegar. Added to stocks and sauces, essential to marinades, used in conjunction with sugar or honey for the perfect sweet and sour taste, or mixed with wine or oil, vinegar appears in a wide range of meat, poultry, fish, and vegetable dishes. The combination of four egg yolks and a dash of vinegar is also used dozens of time in the cookbook and brings a rich texture and a zesty lift to dishes.

Vino wine. This liquid appears over a hundred times and is most often used in small quantities. In over a dozen recipes, Martínez Montiño specifies *vino tinto* [red wine], and in two dozen recipes, *vino blanco* [white wine].

Vizcochería pastry making. This word is part of the title and has maintained the "v" throughout the many editions, even when *vizcocho* has changed to *bizcocho* in the recipes. The cookbook contains a wide range of pastries, including the following. For more on pastries, see the Introduction, "Grains," 27t, 28–9.

Bizcochelos ladyfingers
Bizcochos sweet biscuits
Bollitos pardos cinnamon rolls
Bollo round pastry
Bollo de rodilla spiral sweet roll
Bollo roscón ring-shaped pastry
Buñuelos de viento puffs
Cazolilla tartlet
Costrada puff pastry pie
Empanadillas turnovers
Frutas de … fried dough
Ginebradas clotted milk tart
Hojaldrilla puff pastry pie
Hojaldre puff pastry
Melindres de azúcar sugar ring cookies
Mostachones mostachon cookies
Pasteles pies
Pastel hojaldrado puff pastry pie
Quesadilla cheese tart
Rosquillas ring-shaped pastries
Tabletas bars

Tabletas de masa twists
Torta cake and pie
Tortillas delgadas de aceite thin, frosted cookies

Zanahoria carrot. Although this is the known word for *carrot* today and is also in the cookbook, the other word Martínez Montiño uses is *acenoria*.

Zarceta teal. In the one recipe in which this waterfowl appears, Martínez Montiño recommends roasting the bird and serving it with quince sauce. For more on his preparation of this aquatic fowl, see the Introduction, "Fowl," 33–6.

Zorzal thrush. This small bird is referenced once to explain how to roast small birds. They are best eaten with a sweet and sour sauce. For more on Martínez Montiño's preparation of this game bird, see the Introduction, "Fowl," 33–6.

Zumo juice. This liquid is in almost one hundred recipes, and the overwhelming references are for lemon juice. Orange juice is also popular, and on a handful of occasions Martínez Montiño specifies citron, pomegranate, and sour grape juices or the juice from a roast.

Zurciga zurciga sauce. This egg-cheese sauce is flavoured with garlic, all spices, and, at times, nuts. It is unique to Martínez Montiño and in the recipes "Capirotada de huevos" [Eggs, capirotada style] (440; 441) and "Otra capirotada de huevos rellenos" [Another stuffed egg recipe, capirotada style] (440; 441), he explains how to make it.

Works Cited

Abad Zardoya, Carmen. "Herramientas curiosas para cosas particulares y extraordinarias: tecnología, espacios y utillaje en la cocina histórica española." *La cocina en su tinta*. Madrid: Servicio de Publicaciones de la Biblioteca Nacional de España, 2010. 85–117.

— "Ratas, cenizas y perlas: El vocabulario del color en los interiores del siglo XVIII." *Res Mobilis. Revista Internacional de investigación en mobiliario y objetos decorativos* vol. 5, no. 5, 2016, 21–46.

Albala, Ken. *The Banquet: Dining in the Great Courts of Late Renaissance Europe*. Urbana and Chicago: University of Illinois Press, 2007.

— *The Great Gelatin Revival: Savory Aspics, Jiggle Shots and Outrageous Desserts*. Urbana and Chicago: University of Illinois Press, 2023.

"Alfitete." *Medieval Cookery*. http://medievalcookery.com/search/display.html?treat:6. Accessed 28 July 2018.

Altamiras, Juan de. *Nuevo arte de cocina*. Madrid: Magalia Ediciones, [2000].

Alvar-Ezquerra, Alfredo. "Comer y 'ser' en la Corte del Rey Católico. Mecanismos de diferenciación social en el cambio de siglo." *Materia crítica. Formas de ocio y de consumo en la cultura áurea*. Ed. Enrique García Santo-Tomás. Madrid: Iberoamericana, 2009. 295–320.

Anderson, Lara. *Cooking Up the Nation: Spanish Culinary Texts and Culinary Nationalization in the Late Nineteenth and Early Twentieth Century*. Woodbridge: Tamesis, 2013.

Andrés Ucendo, José Ignacio, and Ramón Lanza García. "El abasto de pan en el Madrid del siglo XVII." *Studia histórica: Historia moderna* vol. 34, 2012, 61–97.

"Antiguas pesas y medidas." OpenCourse Ware. Universidad Politécnica de Madrid. E.T.S. De Ingenieros agrónomos. Pdf. Accessed 10 Oct. 2021.

Archivo de Palacio. Fondo Personal. Caja 634 Expediente 56. "Martínez, Francisco, Cocinero mayor de S. M." Accessed 6 June 2016.

Arjona, Prudente. "Harina, pan, tahonas y molinos." *Rota al día. Periódico digital independiente de Rota*. 26 Jan. 2019. https://rotaaldia.com/art/24882/harina-pan-tahonas-y-molinos. Accessed 21 Nov. 2021.

Arteaga, Angel. "Sobrehúsa." *Palabraría*. 16 Nov. 2015. http://palabraria.blogspot.com/2015/11/sobrehusa.html. Accessed 10 Dec. 2015.

Ayala Simón, Eduardo. "Italianismos en DRAE 1992 (versión electrónica), heterogeneidad en las marcas del sector de las comidas." Atti del XX Convegno [Associazione Ispanisti Italiani]. Ed. Domenico Antonio Cusato, Loretta Frattale, vol. 2, 2002, 37–50.

"Azotes." Armas y armaduras de España. 26 Feb. 2012. http://armasyarmadurasenespaa.blogspot.com/2012/02/azotes.html. Accessed 29 Apr. 2016.

"Azúcar." *Larousse gastronomique en español*. Trans. Josep María Pinto. Barcelona: Éditions Larousse, 2004. 79–86.

"Barquillo." *Gran encyclopedia de Navarra*. Fundación Cajanavarra, http://www.enciclopedianavarra.com/?page_id=5072. Accessed 21 Nov. 2021.

Bernabé, Luis. "Identity, Mixed Unions and Endogamy of the Moriscos: The Assimilation of the New Converts Revisited." *Mediterranean Historical Review* vol. 35, no. 1, June 2020, 79–99.

Bernis, Carmen. *El traje y los tipos sociales en El Quijote*. Madrid: Ediciones El Viso, 2001.

A Book of Cookrye. 1584. A.W., London, 1591. STC 24897 – Early English Text microfilms reel 1613:9. Trans. Mark and Jane Waks. http://jducoeur.org/Cookbook/Cookrye.html. Accessed 16 Apr. 2016.

Bourdieu, Pierre. *Distinction: A Social Critique of the Judgement of Taste*. 1979. Intro. Tony Bennett. Trans. Richard Nice. New York: Routledge, 1984, 2010.

Boy, Jaime. *Diccionario teórico, práctico, histórico y geográfico de comercio*. Barcelona: Valentín Torras, 1840.

Bravo Lozano, Jesús. "Puentes para el estudio del trabajo femenino en la edad moderna. El caso de Madrid a fines del s. XVII." *VI Jornadas de investigación interdisciplinaria sobre la mujer. El trabajo de las mujeres: siglos XVI–XX*. Ed. María Jesús Matilla and Margarita Ortega. Madrid: Universidad Autónoma de Madrid, 1987. 143–60.

Brears, Peter. *Cooking and Dining in Tudor and Early Stuart England*. London: Prospect Books, 2015.

Bró, Joseph, printer and editor. *Nuevo arte de cocina, añadido en esta última impressión. Sacado de la escuela de la experiencia económica*. By Juan Altamiras. Gerona, Spain, 1770. http://bdh-rd.bne.es/viewer.vm?id=0000094336&page=1. Accessed 1 Nov. 2021.

Cambra, R. "Denominaciones del melocotón." *Estación experimental de aula dei Zaragoza* vol. 13, Oct. 1984, 1–122. http://digital.csic.es/bitstream/10261/11638/1/DENOMINACIONES%20DEL%20MELOCOTON.PDF. Pdf. Accessed 23 Dec. 2015.

Campbell, Jodi. *At the First Table: Food and Social Identity in Early Modern Spain*. Lincoln: University of Nebraska Press, 2017.

Cardaillac, Louis. *Moriscos y cristianos: un enfrentamiento polémico. 1492–1640*. Madrid: Fondo de Cultura Económica, 1979.

Cascardi, Anthony. "Gracián and the Authority of Taste." *Rhetoric and Politics: Baltasar Gracián and the New World Order*. Ed. Nicholas Spadaccini and Jenaro Talens. Minneapolis: University of Minnesota Press, 1997. 255–86.

Casey, James. *Early Modern Spain: A Social History.* New York: Routledge, 1999.
Castaño Álvarez, José. *El libro de los pesos y medidas.* Madrid: La esfera de los libros, 2015.
Castella, Krystina. *A World of Cake: 150 Recipes for Sweet Traditions from Cultures Near and Far.* North Adams, MA: Storey Publishing, 2010.
Ciérbide, Ricardo, and Javier Corcín, eds. *Libro de confitura para el uso de Elias Gómez maestro cicero y confiero de la ciudad de Olite. Año de 1818.* Olite: Ayuntamiento de Olite, 2006.
Corbacho, Nacho S. "Molletes antequeranos que saben a pura tradición." *Eldiario.es.* 16 Mar. 2017. https://www.eldiario.es/andalucia/pasaporte/Molletes-Antequera-Pan-sabe-tradicion_0_622937778.html. Accessed 5 Feb. 2019.
Corominas, Joan. *Breve diccionario etimológico de la lengua castellana.* Madrid: Editorial Gredos, [1967].
Corral, José del. *Ayer y hoy de la gastronomía madrileña.* Madrid: Ediciones La Librería, 2000.
Covarrubias, Sebastián de. *Tesoro de la lengua castellana o española.* 1611. https://iedra.es/static/img/dics/covarrubias.jpg. Accessed 10 Oct. 2021.
Cruz Cruz, Juan. *La cocina mediterránea en el inicio del Renacimiento. Martino da Como "Libro de arte culinaria," Ruperto de Nola "Libro de guisados."* Huesca: La Val de Onsera, 1997.
"Los cuchillos en la historia de Albacete." *Recuerdo El blog.* 3 Oct. 2013. https://recuerdoelblog.wordpress.com/2013/10/03/los-cuchillos-en-la-historia/#jp-carousel-82.
Delicado, Francisco. *La lozana andaluza.* Ed. Claude Allaigre. 6th ed. Madrid: Cátedra, 2011.
"Denominaciones de origen." Asoliva. 2016. Accessed 19 July 2018. http://www.asoliva.com/denominaciones_origen.
Diccionario de autoridades (1726–1739). Diccionario histórico de la lengua española. Real Academia Española. https://apps2.rae.es/DA.html. Accessed 30 Dec. 2022.
Eberenz, Rolf. "De lo crudo a lo cocinado: sobre el léxico fundamental de lavculinaria en la historia del español (siglos xiii a xvii)." *Revista de filología española* vol. 96, no. 1, 2016, 81–112.
Eléxpuru, Inés. *La cocina de al-Andalus.* Madrid: Alianza Editorial, 1994.
Escolar Sobrino, Hipólito. "Introducción." *De los incunables al siglo XVII.* Ed. Hipólito Escolar Sobrino. Madrid: Fundación Germán Sánchez Ruipérez, 1994. 11–33.
Espinel, Vicente. *Vida del escudero Marcos de Obregón I.* Ed. María Soledad Carrasco Urgoiti. Madrid: Clásicos Castalia, 1980.
Establés Susán, Sandra. *Diccionario de mujeres impresoras y libreras de España e Iberoamérica entre los siglos XV y XVIII.* Zaragoza: Prensas de la Universidad de Zaragoza, 2018.
European Commission. "Meat Market Observatory – Beef and Veal." Apr. 2016. https://ec.europa.eu/agriculture/sites/agriculture/files/market-observatory/meat/beef/doc/methodology-cxarcase-remainders_en.pdf. Accessed 18 July 2018.
Feros, Antonio. *Kingship and Favoritism in the Spain of Philip III, 1598–1621.* Cambridge: Cambridge University Press, 2000.
Gallego Burín, Antonio, and Alfonso Gámir Sandoval. *Los moriscos del reino de Granada según el sínodo de Guadix de 1554.* Granada: Universidad de Granada, 1996.

García, L. Jacinto. *Carlos V a la mesa. Cocina y alimentación en la España renacentista*. Bremen, 2000.

Gimeno Betí, Lluís. *De lexicografia valenciana. Estudi del vocabulari del Maestrat Joaquim García Girona*. Valencia: l'Institut Interuniversitari de filología valenciana, 1998.

Gispert Cruells, Montserrat. "Las plantas americanas que revolucionaron los guisos, aderezos y repostería de la comida occidental." *Los sabores de España y América*. Ed. Antonio Garrido Aranda. Huesca: La Val de Onsera, 2006. 213–30.

Gloning, Thomas. "Re: [Kochbuchforschung] A 1611 Spanish fish recipe with a German reference." E-mail message to Carolyn Nadeau, 23 July 2019.

Gómez Laguna, Santiago. "Aclaraciones sobre la olla podrida." *Cuadernos de Gastronomía* vol. 3, June 1993, 9–14.

Gorrotxategi Pikasarri, José Mari. *Historia de la confitería y repostería vasca*. [San Sebastián]: Sendoa, 1987.

Granada, Fray Luis de. *Introducción del símbolo de la fé*. Ed. José María Balcells. Madrid: Cátedra, 1989.

Granado, Diego. *Libro del arte de cozina*. Ed. Xavier Benet i Pinós. Lleida: Pagès, 1991.

Green, Donna. "Butter." E-mail correspondence, 13 July 2018.

Guillot Ortiz, Daniel. "Iconografía de variedades de Daucus carota comercializadas en España (primera mitad del siglo XX)." *Bouteloua* vol. 12, no. 11–19, 2012, 20–31.

Guitián, Jorge. "Buceando en la historia de la gastronomía: El incierto señor Francisco Martínez Montiño (o Motiño)." *Diario del Gourmet de Provincias y del Perro Gastrónomo*, 24 Mar. 2010. http://gourmetymerlin.blogspot.com/2010/03/buceando-en-la-historia-de-la.html. Accessed 12 June 2018.

Gutiérrez Cuadro, Juan, and Francesc Rodríguez. "El campo léxico de 'grasa' en el español del siglo XIX." *Revista de Investigación Lingüística* vol. 11, 2008, 137–63.

Gutiérrez Flores, Daniela. "Kitchen Selves: Cooks and the Literary Culture of the Early Modern Spanish Atlantic (1520–1750)." PhD dissertation, University of Chicago, 2022.

Hayward, Vicky. *New Art of Cookery by Juan Altamiras: A Spanish Friar's Kitchen Notebook*. New York: Rowman and Littlefield, 2017.

– "Spanish Dried Agraz: Sparks of Acidity." *New Art of Cookery by Juan Altamiras: A Spanish Friar's Kitchen Notebook*. https://newartofcookery.com/news/recipes/spanish-dried-agraz-sparks-of-acidity/. Accessed 23 Jan. 2020.

Hernández de Maceras, Domingo. *Libro del arte de Cocina* [Book on the Art of Cooking]. 1607. *La alimentación en la España del Siglo de Oro*. Ed. María de los Ángeles Pérez Samper. Huesca: La Val de Onsera, 1998.

Herrera, Gabriel Alonso de. *Obra de agricultura*. 1513. Ed. José Urbano Martínez Carreras. Biblioteca de autores españoles 235. Madrid: Ediciones Atlas, 1970.

Herrero, David. "Los caracoles de San Marcos." *El español*. elespanol.com/castilla-y-leon/region/palencia/20220424/caracoles-san-marcos/667433295_0.html. Accessed 24 Apr. 2022.

Herrero-García, Miguel. *La vida española del siglo XVII. I. Las bebidas*. Madrid: Gráfica Universal, 1933.

Hidalgo, Dionosio. *Diccionario general de bibliografía española*. Vol 1. Madrid: Las Escuelas Pias, 1862–81.

Hieatt, Constance, ed. *An Ordinance of Pottage*. London: Prospect Books, 1988.

Hoey, Michael. *Textual Interaction: An Introduction to Written Discourse Analysis*. New York: Routledge, 2001.

Huarte de San Juan, Juan. *Examen de ingenios para las ciencias*. Ed. Guillermo Serés. Madrid: Cátedra, 1989.

Huici Miranda, Ambrosio, ed. and trans. *La cocina hispano-magrebí durante la época almohade: Segun un manuscrito anónimo del siglo XIII*. Gijón: Trea, 2005.

Ibn Razīn al-Tujībī. *Best of Delectable Foods and Dishes from al-Andalus and al-Maghrib: A Cookbook by Thirteenth-Century Andalusi Scholar Ibn Razīn al-Tujībī (1227–1293)*. Ed. and trans. Nawal Nasrallah. Brill, 2021.

— *Fidālat al-khiwān fī ṭayyibāt al-ṭaʿām wa-al-alwān: ṣūrah min fann al-ṭabkh fī al-Andalus wa-al-Maghrib fī bidāyat ʿaṣr Banī Marīn*. Beirut: Dār al-Gharb al-Islāmī, 1984. http://www.library.yale.edu/neareast/exhibitions/cuisine.html. Accessed 17 May 2020.

"Impresoras en Madrid s. SVII." *Mujeres impresoras. Guía de recursos bibliográficos*. Compiled by Lourdes Gutiérrez. National Library of Spain. Accessed 21 Nov. 2021.

"Información sectorial." Asoliva. 2016. http://www.asoliva.com/informacion_sectorial. Accessed 19 July 2018.

Ingram, Rebecca. *Women's Work: How Culinary Cultures Shaped Modern Spain*. Nashville: Vanderbilt Univeristy Press, 2022.

Kamen, Henry. *Philip of Spain*. New Haven: Yale University Press, 1997.

Ketcham Wheaton, Barbara. "Cookbooks as Resources for Social History." *Food in Time and Place: The American Historical Association Companion to Food History*. Ed. Paul Freedman, Joyce E. Chaplin, and Ken Albala. Berkeley: University of California Press, 2014.

— "Reading Historic Cookbooks: A Structured Approach." Radcliffe Institute for Advanced Study, Harvard University. Seminar Lecture, June 2015.

Klumpp, Andreas. "Re: [Kochbuchforschung] A 1611 Spanish fish recipe with a German reference." E-mail message to Carolyn Nadeau, 12–23 July 2019.

Krohn, Deborah. *Food and Knowledge in Renaissance Italy*. Farnham: Ashgate, 2015.

Laguna, Andrés. *Pedacio Dioscorides Anazarbeo, annotado por el doctor Andrés Laguna, medico dignissmio de Julio III, pontífice máximo nuevamente ilustrado, y añadido, demonstrando las figuras de plantas, y animales en estampas finas, y dividido en dos tomos*. 6 vols. 1555. Madrid: Alonso Balbas, 1733.

Laudan, Rachel. "From Moorish Chicken to Mestizo Chicken." *Rachel Laudan: A Historian's Take on Food and Food Politics*. 30 Apr. 2017. https://www.rachellaudan.com/2017/04/from-moorish-chicken-to-mestizo-chicken.html. Accessed 15 May 2017.

León Tello, Francisco José, and María Virginia Sanz Sanz. *Estética y teoría de la arquitectura en los tratados españoles del siglo XVIII*. Madrid: Consejo Superior de Investigaciones científicas, 1994.

Libro de cocina de la Gesta de Independencia: Nueva España, 1817. Ed. José Luis Curiel Monteagudo. México: Consejo Nacional para la Cultura y las Artes, Dirección General de Culturas Populares e Indígenas, 2002.

Libro de Sent soví [first half of fourteenth century]. *The Book of Sent Soví: Medieval Recipes from Catalonia*. Ed. Joan Santanach, trans. Robin Vogelzang. London and Barcelona: Woodbridge and Barcino-Tamesis, 2008.

Manual de mugeres en el qual se contienen muchas y diversas reçeutas muy buenas. 1475–1525. Ed. Alicia Martínez Crespo. Salamanca: Ediciones Universidad Salamanca, 1995.

Martínez Llopís, Manuel. *La dulcería española. Recetarios histórico y popular*. Madrid: Alianza Editorial, 1999.

Martínez Millán, José, and José Eloy Hortal Muñóz. "El funcionamiento diario de palacio: los oficios de la casa." *La corte de Felipe IV (1621–1665): reconfiguración de la Monarquía católica*. Tomo 1, vol. 1. Ed. José Martínez Millán and José Eloy Hortal Muñoz. Madrid: Polifemo, 2015. 440–73.

Martínez Montiño, Francisco. *Arte de cocina, pastelería, vizcochería y conservería*. Madrid: Luis Sánchez, 1611. Biblioteca nacional de España, Ms. R1472. http://bdh.bne.es/bnesearch/detalle/bdh0000010713. Accessed 26 Oct. 2013.

Massiolot, François. *Le cuisinier roial et bourgeois, qui apprend à ordonner toute sorte de repas, & la meilleure maniere des ragoûts les plus à la mode & les plus exquis: ouvrage tres-utile dans les familles, & singulierement necessaire à tous maîtres d'hôtels, & ecuiers de cuisine*. Paris: Rene Dessagne, 1691.

Mata, Juan de la. *Arte de repostería*. 1747. Valladolid: Editorial Maxtor, 2003.

Mayntz, Melissa. "Crop Milk for Baby Birds: Specialized Feeding for Young Chicks." *The Spruce*. https://www.thespruce.com/glossary-definition-of-crop-milk-385209. Accessed 31 Jan. 2019.

"Memoir." *Oxford English Dictionary*. Oxford: Oxford University Press, 2016. 18 May 2016.

"Minor Fruits: Gooseberries and Currants." Department of Horticulture, Cornell University, 2015. http://www.hort.cornell.edu/fruit/mfruit/gooseberries.html. Accessed 2 Dec. 2022.

Moll, Jaime. *Problemas bibliográficos del libro del siglo de oro*. Biblioteca Virtual Miguel de Cervantes, 2009. http://www.cervantesvirtual.com/obra/problemas-bibliograficos-del-libro-del-siglo-de-oro--0/. Accessed 26 June 2019.

Monardes, Nicolás. *Libro que trata de la nieve y de sus propiedades, y del modo que se ha de tener en bever enfriado con ella y de los otros modos que ay de enfriar*. Seville: Alonso Escriuano, impressor, 1571.

— *Segunda parte del libro, de las cosas que se traen de nuestras Indias Occidentales, que siruen al uso de medicina: do se trata del tabaco, y de la sassafras, y del carlo sancto, y de otras muchas yeruas y plantas, simientes, y licores: que agora nuevamente han venido de aquellas partes, de grandes virtudes, y maravillosos effectos*. Seville: Alonso Escriuano, impressor, 1574.

Morala Rodríguez, José R. "Léxico histórico: sobre cribas, cedazos y harneros." Ministerio de Economía y Competitividad. jrmorala.unileon.es/biblioteca/HRCano.pdf. Accessed 27 Jan. 2108.

Mordechai, Karen. *Sunday Suppers*. New York: Clarkson Potter, 2014.

Moreno, María Paz. "Beyond the Recipes: Authorship, Text, and Context in Canonical Spanish Cookbooks." *Food, Texts and Cultures in Latin America and Spain*. Ed Rafael Climent-Espino and Ana María Gómez Bravo. Nashville: Vanderbilt University Press, 2020. 201–19.
– *De la página al plato: El libro de cocina en España*. Gijón: Trea, 2012.
Morii, Mayako. "How Do Lampreys Avoid Cholestasis after Bile Duct Degeneration?" *Cholestasis*. Ed. Valeria Tripodi. Rijeka, Croatia: Intech, 2012. 81–98. http://cdn.intechopen.com/pdfs-wm/28191.pdf.
Müllers, Fabian. *Le manuscrit de Sion. Cuisine médiévale*. Bayeux: Heimbal. 2015.
Muro, Ángel. *Diccionario general de cocina*. Vol 2. Madrid, 1892.
– *El practicón: tratado complete de cocina. Al alcance de todos y aprovechamiento de sobras*. 1894. Madrid: Edimat Libros, 2014.
Nabhan, Gary Paul. *Cumin, Camels, and Caravans: A Spice Odyssey*. Berkeley: University of California Press, 2014.
Nadeau, Carolyn. *Food Matters: Alonso Quijano's Diet and the Discourse of Food in Early Modern Spain*. Toronto: University of Toronto Press, 2016.
– "Furniture and Equipment in the Royal Kitchens of Early Modern Spain." *Food, Texts and Cultures in Latin America and Spain*. Ed. Rafael Climent-Espino and Ana María Gómez Bravo. Nashville: Vanderbilt University Press, 2020. 115–49.
Nasrallah, Nawal, trans. *Best of Delectable Foods and Dishes from al-Andalus and al-Maghrib: A Cookbook by Thirteenth-Century Andalusi Scholar Ibn Razīn al-Tujībī (1227–1293)*. Leiden: Brill, 2021.
– "Mediaeval Arabs Ate Sandwiches, Too: *Bazmāward* and *Awsāt* for the Record." *Studia Orientalia* vol. 4, no. 22, 2013, 175–94.
Nelson, Bradley. "A Ritual Practice for Modernity: Baltasar Gracián's Organized Body of Taste." *Reason and Its Others: Italy, Spain, and the New World*. Ed. David Castillo and Massimo Lollini. Nashville: Vanderbilt University Press, 2006. 79–100.
Nocheseda, Elena. "Panecillos de San Nicolas." *Tagalog Dictionary*. https://www.tagalog-dictionary.com/filipino-food/panecillos-de-san-nicolas. Accessed 20 Nov. 2021.
Nola, Ruperto de. *Libro de guisados*. In *La cocina mediterránea en el inicio del Renacimiento*. Ed. Juan Cruz Cruz. Huesca: La Val de Onsera, 1997. 227–375.
Notaker, Henry. *Printed Cookbooks in Europe 1470–1700*. New Castle, DE, and Houten, Netherlands: Oak Knoll Press and Hes & De Graaf Publishers, 2010.
Ong, Walter. *Orality and Literacy: The Technologizing of the Word*. London and New York: Methuen, 1982.
Pardo Bazán, Emilia. *La cocina española antigua*. Madrid: Sociedad anónima Renacimiento, 1913. Republished Valladolid: Maxtor, 2012.
Parkhurst Ferguson, Priscilla. *Accounting for Taste: The Triumph of French Cuisine*. Chicago: University of Chicago Press, 2004.
Pennell, Elizabeth. *My Cookery Books*. New York: Houghton Mifflin, 1903.
Pérez de Herrera, Christóbal. *Proverbios morales, y consejos christianos, muy provechosos*. [1576]. Madrid: Los herederos de F. del Hierro, 1733.

Pérez Samper, María de los Ángeles. *La alimentación en la España del Siglo de Oro, Domingo Hernández de Maceras, "Libro del arte de Cocina."* Huesca: La Val de Onsera, 1998.

– *Mesas y cocinas en la España del siglo XVIII*. Somonte-Cenero: Trea, 2011.

Pérez San Vicente, Guadalupe, ed. *Manuscrito Ávila Blancas. Gastronomía mexicana del siglo XVIII*. Mexico City: Restaurante El Cardenal, 1999.

– *Recetario de doña Dominga de Guzmán, siglo XVIII*. Mexico City: Sanborns, 1996.

Petroski, Henry. *The Toothpick: Technology and Culture*. New York: Vintage Books, 2008.

Pinheiro da Veiga, Thomé. *Fastiginia; o fastos geniales*. Trans. Narciso Alonso Cortés. Valladolid: Colegio de Santiago, 1916. HathiTrust Digital Library. Accessed 14 Mar. 2013.

Polo Cano, Nuria. "Introducción al léxico de un recetario de cocina del siglo XVII." *Comida y bebida en la lengua española, cultura y literaturas hispánicas*. Ed. Andjelka Pejovic, Vladimir Karanovic, and Mirjana Sekulic. Kragujevac: FILUM, 2012. 231–48.

The Prince of Transylvania's Court Cookbook from the 16th Century. The Science of Cooking. Ed. Glen Gorsuch, trans. Bence Kovacs. Medieval Cookery. http://www.medievalcookery.com/etexts/transylvania-v2.pdf. Accessed 23 Feb. 2018.

Quevedo, Francisco de. *La vida del Buscón llamado Don Pablos*. Ed. Domingo Ynduráin. Madrid: Cátedra, 1992.

RAE. Real Academia Española. *Diccionario de la lengua española*. https://dle.rae.es. Accessed 10 Oct. 2021.

"Relojes." *Centro Virtual Cervantes*. Spain: Instituto Cervantes, 1998–2015. http://cvc.cervantes.es/actcult/patrimonio/relojes/introduccion.htm. Accessed 20 May 2015.

Robert, Mestre. *Llibre del coc*. Ed. Joan Santanach. Barcelona: Editorial Barcino, 2018.

Rodríguez Marín, Francisco. "El yantar de Alonso Quijano el Bueno." *Estudios cervantistas*. Madrid: Ediciones Atlas, 1947. 421–39.

Ruan, Felipe. "A Taste for Symbolic Wealth: *Gusto* and Cultural Capital in Baltasar Gracián." *Revista Canadiense de Estudios Hispánicos* vol. 32, no. 2, Winter 2008, 315–31.

Salsete, Antonio. *El cocinero religioso*. Intro. Victor Manuel Sarobe Pueyo. Pamplona: Gobierno de Navarra, 1990.

Sarría Rueda, Amalia. "La imprenta en el siglo XVII." *De los incunables al siglo XVII*. Ed. Hipólito Escolar Sobrino. Madrid: Fundación Germán Sánchez Ruipérez, 1994. 141–200.

Scappi, Bartolomeo. *The Opera of Bartolomeo Scappi (1570): l'arte et prudenza d'un maestro cuoco. The Art and Craft of a Master Cook*. Trans. Terence Scully. Toronto and Buffalo: University of Toronto Press, 2008.

Serrano Larráyoz, Fernando. "Confitería y cocina conventual navarra del siglo XVIII. Notas y precisiones sobre el 'Recetario de Marcilla' y el 'Cocinero religioso' de Antonio Salsete." *Príncipe de Viana* no. 243, 2008, 141–85.

Shaw, Hank. "On Plucking Birds." *Hunter Angler Garden Cook*. https://honest-food.net/on-plucking-birds/. Accessed 6 Aug. 2018.

Simón Palmer, María del Carmen. *La alimentación y sus circunstancias en el Real Alcázar de Madrid*. Madrid: Instituto de Estudios Madrileños, 1982.

– *La cocina de palacio. 1561–1931*. Editorial Castalia, 1997.

– "El estatuto del cocinero: su evolución en el tiempo." *Food and History* vol 4., no. 1, 2006, 255–76.

Soto García, Ángel. "El Arte de cocina de Francisco Martínez Montiño: una introducción a su terminología culinaria." *Estudios interlingüísticos* vol. 8, 2020, 257–68.

– "*El Arte de cozina [...]* de Montiño (1611): dos ediciones valencianas de 1705 y dos ediciones fantasma." *Janus* vol. 10, 2021, 489–500.

– "Los términos culinarios en el *Arte de cocina, pastelería, vizcochería, y conservería (1611) de* Francisco Martínez Montiño." Dissertation, Universidad Nacional de Educación a Distancia (UNED), 2023.

Spiller, Elizabeth. "Recipes for Knowledge: Makers' Knowledge Traditions, Paracelsian Recipes and the Invention of the Cookbook, 1600–1660." *Renaissance Food from Rabelais to Shakespeare: Culinary Readings and Culinary Histories.* Ed. Joan Fitzpatrick. Ashgate, 2010. 55–72.

Spraker, Wendi. "Old Fashioned Sugar Cream Pie." *Loaves and Dishes: The Unapologic Love of Comfort Food.* https://www.loavesanddishes.net/old-fashion-sugar-cream-pie/. Accessed 12 Feb. 2019.

"Sugar." *Larousse Gastronomique.* Trans. Rosetta International. Clarkson Potter, 2001. 1155–62.

"Tablillas de difunto." *El Heraldo del Henares*, 30 Oct. 2017. https://www.elheraldodelhenares.com/cult/exposicion-de-tablillas-de-difunto-en-la-posada-del-cordon-de-atienza/. Accessed 10 May 2019.

Terreros y Pando, Esteban de. *Diccionario castellano con las voces de ciencias y artes y sus correspondientes de las tres lenguas francesa, latina e italiana.* Madrid: La viuda de Ibarra, hijos y compañía, 1786–93.

Torres Martínez, Marta. "Léxico culinario autorizado en el primer diccionario académico." *Cuadernos del Instituto Historia de la Lengua*, vol. 9, 2014, 295–321.

– "Léxico culinario en el *Libro de cuentas de cocina y repostería* de la casa de Arcos (1750)." *Cuadernos Associazione Ispanisti Italiani AISPI Estudios de lenguas y literaturas hispánicas* vol. 20, 2022, 117–40. DOI 10.14672/2.2022.2043.

Tovar, Rosa. "Mesa redonda 'La tradición repostería en las Tres Culturas.'" Fundación Tres Culturas del Mediterráneo. 22 March 2023. YouTube. https://www.youtube.com/watch?v=1sR6PA6-6sY&t=3073s. Accessed 5 May 2023.

"Tranche n.1." *OED Online.* Oxford University Press, June 2022, www.oed.com/view/Entry/204544. Accessed 11 July 2022.

Um tratado da cozinha portuguesa do século XV [A treatise of Portuguese cooking from the 15th century]. Biblioteca virtual Miguel de Cervantes. Accessed 23 Feb. 2018.

A Treatise of Portuguese Cuisine from the 15th Century. Trans. Fernanda Gomes. *Medieval Cookery.* http://www.medievalcookery.com/notes/tratado.html. Accessed 28 July 2018.

Usero Torrente, Antonio. *Principales falsificaciones de la manteca de vaca: discurso presentado para aspirar al grado de doctor en la Facultad de Farmacia por el Dr. Antonio*

Usero Torrente. [N.p.: n.p., 1899]. Biblioteca Digital Hispánica, Biblioteca Nacional de España. Accessed 10 June 2016.

Usunáriz, Jesús M., and Magalí Ortiz Martín, eds. *Francisco Martínez Montiño, Arte de cocina*. New York: IDEA, 2021.

Valles Rojo, Julio. *Cocina y alimentación en los siglos XVI y XVII*. Valladolid: Junta de Castilla y León, 2007.

Varela Merino, Elena. *Los galicismos en el español de los siglos XVI y XVII*. 2 vols. Madrid: Consejo Superior de Investigaciones, 2009.

West, Elizabeth, ed. *Santa Fe: 400 Years, 400 Questions: Commemorating the 400th Anniversary of the Founding of Santa Fe, New Mexico, in 1610*. Santa Fe: Sunstone Press, 2012.

Williams, Patrick. *The Great Favourite: The Duke of Lerma and the Court and Government of Philip III of Spain, 1598–1621*. Manchester: Manchester University Press, 2006.

Wright, Lawrence. *Home Fires Burning: The History of Domestic Heating and Cooking*. London: Routledge and Kegan Paul, 1964.

Yarza, Ibán. *Pan de pueblo. Recetas e historias de los panes y panaderías de España*. Barcelona: Grijalbo, 2017.

Yelgo de Vázquez, Miguel. *Estilo de servir a príncipes con ejemplos morales para servir a Dios*. Ed Cosme Delgado, 1614. Sala Cervantes. Biblioteca nacional de España.

Index

Abad Zardoya, Carmen, 95n14, 124n34, 164n43, 184n69, 464n364, 524n407, 534n418, 572n454, 590n454
abadejo [codfish], 599
abstinence and partial abstinence, 8, 16, 24, 29–31, 41, 44, 95n11, 192n78, 218n114, 218n116, 248n336, 360n272
acedera. See sorrel
aceituna. See olive
acelgas. See swiss chard
acemite [cemite]. See bran
acenoria. See carrot
achicoria. See chicory
adobo. See marinade
agraz. See grape, sour; verjuice
agrazón. See gooseberry
aguja paladar. See swordfish
ajedrea, See savory, summer
ajo. See garlic
Albala, Ken, 47, 97n32, 98n44, 170n50, 434n340
albérchigo. See apricot
albericoque. See apricot
albóndiga/albondiguilla. See meatball
alcachofa. See artichoke
alcaparra. See caper
alcaraván [stone curlew], 35, 153
alcaravea. See caraway

alcorza [candy coating], 586
alfitete. See pastry, sheet
all spices, 39, 47, 149, 151, 161, 165–7, 171, 175, 179–81, 185, 195–205, 209–19, 221, 225–9, 253, 257, 283, 287, 291, 295–7, 305, 309, 315, 331–5, 339–41, 353–77, 383–9, 393–401, 405–7, 411, 415, 419–31, 439, 441, 449, 453, 459–61, 469–71, 475, 479, 505, 555, 589–95, 599, 603
almeja. See clam
almendra. See almond
almíbar. See under syrup, simple
almizcle. See musk
almojábana [fried cheese pastry], 318–21
almond, 149, 183–5, 211, 225, 257–61, 479–83, 489, 493–9, 503–5, 525, 529, 535, 547, 587, 595, 599; broth, 381, 435–7, 493–5; butter, 90, 495–7; green, 360n274, 361; oil, 525; pie, 249; sweet, 269, 545; toasted, 143, 167–9, 399, 555. *See also under* milk; sauce
Altamiras, Juan de, 5, 34, 71–2, 73, 98n43, 202n90, 224n128, 386n301, 396n308, 562n440
Alvar-Ezquerra, Alfredo, 234n134
Amador de la Aya, 123
ambergris, 480n375, 483, 581
Americas, the, 42, 74. *See also* New World

ánade. See duck
anise, 28, 54–5, 281, 339, 341, 449, 507, 509, 541, 543, 601; cracked, 531, 553; ground, 529, 537, 549
antler, 33, 299
Apicius, 234n135
apple, sour, 153, 169, 253, 269, 301, 363, 555
apricot, 41, 73, 257, 267, 563, 578n459; dried, 133, 247; pie, 247–53, 277
aroma, 48
artalete. See pinwheel
artichoke, 43, 283, 351–3, 359, 451
arugula, 147, 519. *See also under* sauce
arveja. See pea
asadura/asadurilla. See offal
asparagus, 39, 43, 405, 415; parboiled, 197
ave. See fowl
avutarda. See bustard
azafrán. See saffron
azúcar. See sugar
azumbre, 343

Baeza, Miguel de, 5, 94, 570n451
baked good, 44
bálago. See straw
banquet, 73, 109, 115, 130–41, 519, 605; of the senses, 77, 100n2; service of, 124–9
baño blanco. See meringue
barbel, 65, 135, 415, 419–21
barbo. See barbel
barley, 497
barnacle, gooseneck, 426n332
Bartolomé, Javier, 402n314
basin, 116n20, 307, 463, 466n367, 473
batter, 163, 237, 243, 315–17, 327–9, 377–9, 433, 487, 481, 503, 541–5, 549, 553, 599
bay leaf, 48, 53, 291, 376n290, 377, 459, 463, 535, 539, 555
bean, fava, 44, 353–5

beef, 29, 74, 147n1, 285, 294n206, 303, 467, 473; broth, 473; cured, 285, 371–3, 603; shank, 475; tenderloin, 139, 341; udder, 555
Berber, 59
berenjena. See eggplant
berguera. See under sieve
Bernabé, Luis, 97n30
Bernís, Carmen, 254n167
berros. See watercress
berza. See collard green
Best of Delectable Foods and Dishes from al-Andalus and al-Maghrib: A Cookbook by Thirteenth-Century Andalusi Scholar Ibn Razin al-Tujibi (1227–1293), 284n200, 480n375
besugo. See sea bream
bile, 151
bird, game, 35, 36, 149, 151, 153, 491, 561; small, 34, 35, 72, 134, 226, 312, 473, 559, 582. *See also* fowl
biscuit, sweet, 28–9, 47, 55, 145, 537–49. *See also* ladyfinger
bizcocho. See biscuits
blancmange, 44, 245, 261–7, 337, 343–7, 429, 483; fish, 585; paddle, 579; pie, 347; preserve, 503–5; spoon, 303, 317, 329, 429, 585, 587
blood, 211; pork, 339
boar, 33, 74, 126n38, 294n206; dressing, 287–9; empanada, 291–3, 297, 592n470; pie, 33, 293–7, 397, 593; tenderloin, 291, 303; udder, 475. *See also under* head cheese
boil: boar, 288, 290, 294; fish, 63, 382, 390, 414–16; ham, 272, 458, 462; lobster, 422, 424; toronja, 224; venison, 298, 304
bollo. See pastry
Book of Cookrye, 61
bone marrow. *See* marrow
bookseller, 8, 75–6t, 77, 82, 98n46

borage, 43, 221, 379–81, 597; blossom, 46, 569; fried, 327, 377; pie, 251; root, 564n443, 567; soup, 495
borraja. See borage
Bourdieu, Pierre, 54
brain: beef, 29, 31; hen, 34, 203; kid, 333; mutton, 439; veal, 65–6, 308–9, 338n250, 381, 439
bran, 28, 59, 258n173, 286n202, 510n394, 511; sifted, 268n183, 290n204, 463
brasas. See ember, red-hot
Bravo Lozano, Jesús, 240n146
bread, 27–8, 163, 169, 175, 179–81, 197, 201, 207, 221, 225, 229–31, 257, 283, 291–7, 331–3, 349, 365, 375, 385, 393, 405–7, 415, 433, 437–9, 443, 447, 451–3, 459, 471, 475, 519, 559, 583, 589, 603; candeal, 28, 262n177, 273, 275, 505; crumb (centre), 28, 262n177, 279, 311, 431, 495, 499, 599; fried, 309, 337, 345, 383, 395, 449; milk, 47, 485; mollete, 27–8, 239, 455, 551; preserve, 551; sweet, 189, 311, 483; toast, 145–53, 159, 165–73, 177, 187, 211–13, 233, 299, 351–3, 363, 381, 393, 397–9, 403, 415, 421, 435, 453, 475, 519–21, 551, 555, 595, 603; white, 155–7, 199, 205, 215, 233–5, 301, 311, 335, 361, 455, 469, 587
breadcrumb, 51, 215–17, 227, 237–45, 253, 257, 299–301, 309, 335–9, 349, 353, 357–61, 365, 369–71, 381, 385, 407–11, 415, 425, 429, 437, 441–3, 449, 461, 471, 499–501, 509, 525–7, 551, 589, 593; cat, 241
Brears, 95n10
brine, 41, 48, 303–5, 399, 423
brisket, 305–7
brochette, 143, 186n71, 187, 195, 227, 389, 477–9, 555

brodete, 51, 178n58, 178–9, 182–3, 442–3
broqueta. See brochette
broth, 142n4, 143, 147–57, 165, 175–83, 185, 189, 199–201, 209, 213, 223, 227–33, 281–5, 295, 299–301, 305–7, 315, 333, 349–53, 361–5, 369, 373, 381, 405–7, 411, 429, 443, 461, 471, 475, 489, 493, 521, 535, 555, 583, 595–7; pickling, 539; sustaining, 489–91, 499
bruguete, 415
brush: feather, 163, 323–5, 543, 547, 555; hyssop, 315, 465, 481, 531
b'stilla, Moroccan, 31
buñolera [scoop for puffs], 206, 318
buñuelo. See puff
bushel, 538n422, 539
bustard: great, 152n26, 153, 561; little, 35, 151–5
butter, 46–7, 149, 161, 169, 173, 185, 219, 229, 233–5, 239–41, 249–65, 269–71, 275–81, 299–301, 313, 323–7, 331, 335, 349–57, 361–7, 371–5, 381–401, 405, 409–15, 421, 425–31, 437–57, 467, 473, 481–3, 487, 501–9, 523–31, 537, 553, 585–7, 593–5, 599, 603; almond, 90; ball, 523–5; nazula, 521; sculpted, 126

cabbage, 373; prepare, 375
cabrito. See kid
cake, 329–31; funnel, 68, 379; Genoise, 538n423, 544n430; sponge, 281
calabaza. See squash
calamar. See squid
caldo. See broth; stock
calf, 147n1; feet, 331, 535, 593; head, 309. *See also under* veal
candle, 11, 47, 119
canela. See cinnamon
cangrejo. See crab

canilla [shinbone], 144–5, 592–3; [little spout], 516–17
cannoli, 597n10
canuto, sweet egg, 137, 216n112, 217, 449, 597
caña de vaca. See marrow
caper, 23, 33, 43, 48, 133, 155
capirotada. See under egg; sops
capon, 31, 33–4, 68, 143–5, 181, 205, 229, 427, 481, 505, 535, 557–9, 587, 601; stuffed, 187–9
caracol. See snail
caraway, 47, 213, 241, 287, 359–61, 371, 375, 399, 537
Cardaillac, Louis, 97n30
cardillo. See thistle, golden
cardo. See cardoon
cardoon, 43, 65, 409–11, 451; flower, 236n138, 255, 474n373
Carême, Antonin, 64
carnation, 514n397, 515
carnero. See mutton
carp, 38–9, 413–15
carrot, 111, 311, 533; black, 220n120, 533; colour, 25, 43, 220n120, 533; salad, 221; and salted hake, 57, 221; stew 219
carving, the art of, 124n33
Cascardi, Anthony, 53
Casey, James, 7–8
casserole, 151–3, 169, 173–7, 181, 185, 197–201, 205, 219–21, 231; cream, 235, 337; eggplant, 236n138, 359; rice, 349
castaña. See chestnut
Castaño Álvarez, José, 146n9, 228n131, 238n140, 462n363, 522n403, 538n422
Castella, Krystina, 544n430
cazón. See dogfish
cebolla. See onion
cecial. See hake

cecina. See under beef, cured
cemite [*acemite*]. *See* bran; *see under* flour, with/without bran
cercenadura [trimmed edge of dough], 320–1
Cervantes, Miguel de, 6, 58
chapter, references to, 16, 17–22, 111, 117, 144n7, 145, 153, 165, 199, 223, 255, 275, 553
cheese, 45, 167, 253, 319–23, 357–61, 365–71, 375, 411–13, 441, 475, 521; asadero, 484n377, 485, 507; cottage, 27, 45, 238n142, 268n187; curd, 45, 56, 238–9, 255, 269–71, 283–5, 319–21, 337, 349, 520–3; farmer, 233–7, 255, 319, 337, 449, 485; ricotta, 27, 45, 238n142, 268n187, 318n230
cheesecloth, 143, 149, 167, 211, 253, 289, 293–5, 311, 339, 375, 397, 433, 479–83, 489, 495–9, 513, 533
cherry, sour, 251, 257, 475; syrup, 251; pie, 251; preserve, 435
chestnut, 55, 111, 199, 205, 287, 537, 603; soup, 603
chicken, 33, 34, 41, 42, 159, 173, 179–81, 191, 197, 231, 331–3, 363–5, 375, 427, 457, 505, 589, 601; pie, 283; stuffed, 133, 137, 159, 171, 175–7, 187, 191, 203, 209, 218n115, 235, 344–5
chicory, 177, 597
chorcha. See woodcock
chorizo. See sausage
Ciébide, Ricardo, and Javier Corcín, 73, 432n337, 450n351, 562n440
cilantro, 48, 159, 173, 185, 199–201, 221, 227, 283, 351–5, 361, 377, 393, 467, 473, 583, 593, 603
cilantro, seco. See coriander
cinnamon, 27, 47, 58, 70, 71, 147, 150n23, 153–5, 169, 177, 204n91, 204n92, 205, 211–13, 225, 237, 247, 251, 259, 273, 279, 289,

293–5, 309, 327, 331, 345, 361–3, 381, 409, 457, 463, 469, 475, 481, 507–9, 510n392, 513, 534n419, 537–9, 555, 581, 589, 595; all spices and, 38, 149, 153, 167, 211, 217, 221, 253, 309, 339, 355–63, 369–73, 387, 398, 397–9, 411, 431, 441, 449, 459, 555, 591, 603; and clove, 41, 249, 273, 513, 581; ground, 143, 165, 245, 257, 261, 269, 273, 279, 289, 317–23, 329, 349, 479, 483, 511, 519, 529, 533, 551–3, 557; rolls, 529; and sugar, 27, 34, 41, 44, 61, 65, 159, 175–9, 183–5, 193, 197, 215–17, 233–7, 263, 273–5, 309, 323, 335, 349, 355–9, 365–71, 386n301, 409, 421, 431, 437, 441–9, 453, 457–9, 467–9, 473, 507, 508n390, 535, 551, 591–3, 597; stick, 143, 461, 475
ciruela. See plum
ciruela pasa. See prune
citron, 41; candied, 157, 181, 251, 261, 485, 517, 571, 575; juice, 517; pie, 45, 133, 245–7, 587; preserve, 587
clam, 39, 427
class, and food, 56
clavo. See clove
clove, 47, 143, 155, 167, 187, 205, 213, 243, 249, 273, 289, 297, 341, 351, 383, 421, 461–3, 469, 475, 481–3, 509, 513, 514n397, 534n419, 537–9, 557, 581
cobre. See copper
cocimiento. See boil
La cocina española antigua (Pardo Bazán), 73–4, 97n29
cocinero. See cook
codfish, 599
colación. See collation
colapege. See gelatin

collard greens, 287, 373, 393–5, 399, 473; shoots, 473
collation, 458n361, 459, 462n363, 505, 507, 511
comino. See cumin
conejo. See rabbit
confite. See under nuts, and seeds, sugar-coated
conserva. See preserve
cook, 12, 108–9, 120–5; authority, 55, 73, 87, 236n139; discretion of, 55–6; master, 10–11, 116n18
cookbook: critique of other, 70, 205; history of, 3–5; as cultural artefact, 3–5; German, 39; importance of, 108–11, 123; organization, 15–22; price of, 102n5; production of, 102n3; Spanish, 56–7, 61–3
cookie, sugar, 535
cooking, evolution of, 63–6
copper: baking sheet, 287; bowl, 463–5; lid, 487; mould, 368n280, 453; oven, 263, 287, 507, 527, 543, 547, 548n432, 553; pot, 59, 409, 453, 465, 513
Corbacho, Nacho, 238n141
coriander, 47, 205, 423; ground, 587
Corral, José del, 95n6
Corriente Córdoba, Federico, 97n28
costrada. See pie, puff pastry
court, Hapsburg, 5–8
couscous, 59–60, 74, 463–7
Covarrubias, Sebastián de, 41, 56, 153n2, 208n97, 220n119, 222n126
crab, 39, 425
crane, 69, 151–3, 214n108
cream, 44–5, 233–5, 238–43, 249, 255, 261, 267, 347, 481–3, 487, 551; fried, 551; heavy, 237; pastry, 584n465; sweet, 553, 585–7
crème anglaise. See under sauce, cream, sweet
criadilla. See testicle; truffle
croqueta, 66, 344n257

cuajada. See under milk, clotted
cucharón. See spoon, big
cucumber, 519
Le cuisinier roïal et bourgeois, 584n465
culantro, 61, 228n130, 472
cumin, 39, 47, 199, 211–13, 341, 358n270, 359, 405–7, 423, 439, 599
curlew, 153
currant, dried, 31, 37, 39, 42, 170n50, 191, 197, 225, 385, 393, 397, 425, 471
cuttlefish, 403

dairy product, 44–5
date, 41, 485
datil. See date
decoration, food as, 126n38, 137
despojos [extremities], 286–9
Diccionario de autoridades, 41, 52–3, 122n32, 162n40, 192n78, 226n129, 252n163
Diccionario general de bibliografía española, 112n14
Diccionario general de cocina, 73, 298n211
dill, 48, 55–6, 355, 473
dining room, 146n11
discourse colony, 69, 98n42
dish, fantastic, 125, 415, 434n338, 605
dogfish, 603
dornajo [small trough], 302–3
dough, 153, 161–5, 169, 217, 225, 243–59, 279, 307, 313, 317, 353, 395, 419–21, 425, 433, 445, 465, 469, 481, 489–91, 507–11, 527–9, 547, 553, 557; cream puff, 314n224, 316n225; dark, 213–15, 287, 291–7, 401, 459; elastic, 160n36, 161, 269, 273–5, 279, 317, 329, 503, 509, 527–31, 535, 553; fine, 265, 321–5, 387, 483, 503, 537, 545, 597; fried, 16, 48, 61, 64, 68–9, 135–9, 217, 222n123, 222n126, 223, 241, 263, 269–71, 318n228, 319, 322n236, 323, 327–9, 345–7, 376n290, 377–9, 469, 509, 537, 553; hard, 545; light, 215; leaven, 28, 131, 133, 139, 263, 273, 275, 279, 469; mollete, 485; sweet, 287, 315, 325, 461, 479, 503, 597; twists, 553; white, 291, 387, 397, 461
doughnut, 277
dove, 33, 35, 234n136, 559; collared, 137, 161; ground, 227
duck, 14, 28, 33, 41, 131, 149, 153–5, 165, 285
durazno. See peach

Easter, 603
eczema, 523
edition, of Martínez Montiño, 75–92
editor, 3, 8, 13, 72, 77, 79, 105. *See also* bookseller; printer
eel, 38, 68, 265–7, 389, 419, 603; conger, 603
egg, 44, 73, 153, 159–61, 171–5, 179, 185–93, 197, 207–9, 215–17, 223–31, 235–7, 249–55, 261, 269–71, 275–81, 285, 303, 311, 315–41, 349, 353–61, 365–71, 375–7, 381, 385–9, 397, 407–13, 423–39, 445–9, 453, 457–61, 469–71, 477, 485, 503, 509, 527–9, 531, 539, 543–5, 553, 575, 579, 585–91, 595, 603; *capirotada* style, 65, 282n199, 440–1; *capirote*, 449; expanded, 443; fried, 219–21, 241, 337, 455; golden, 258, 451; hard boiled, 173, 175, 179–81, 185–9, 195, 201, 209, 217, 225, 229, 257–9, 279, 283, 323, 367, 375, 385, 423, 457, 467–71, 479, 553, 583, 589; poached, 241, 355, 377, 381, 407, 453–5; scrambled, 183, 243, 251–7, 265, 279, 347, 355, 407, 431, 437, 443, 461, 485, 553, 575; shell, 433, 437, 531; soft boiled, 451; *tolosa*, 56, 442–3; wash, 271; whites, 223, 253, 447, 487,

507, 529–31, 535, 569. *See also* egg yolk
egg yolk, 51, 159–63, 179–81, 193–207, 215, 225–7, 233, 237, 243–9, 257, 261, 267–71, 279–83, 287, 299, 307–11, 315, 319–21, 325–7, 331, 335–7, 343–51, 359, 365–9, 373, 381, 385–7, 405–15, 429, 437, 441, 461, 475, 481, 487, 493, 501, 507–9, 523, 529, 537, 547–9, 551–3, 555, 589, 593, 597–9; candied threads, 44, 45, 60, 180n61, 181, 216n112, 223, 257–63, 432n337, 433–9, 461, 483, 587, 597; sweet scrambled, 41, 131–9, 182n65, 183, 203, 243, 247, 251, 253–5, 257, 265, 279, 347, 431, 437, 461, 485, 553, 573, 575, 577
eggplant, 25, 43, 58, 342n254, 358n266–7, 361, 365; moxi, 57, 137, 236n138, 359; pickled, 537; stuffed, 361
El practicón: tratado completo de cocina (Muro), 73, 116n18, 556n438
elderberry, 42; flower, 515–17; vinegar, 515–17
Eléxpuru, Inés, 150n19
ember: grey, 165, 169, 221, 331, 421, 491, 543; red-hot, 217, 231, 239, 317, 353, 415, 487, 489, 503
empanada: beef, 305; boar, 291–3, 297; cold, 135, 136, 291–3, 295, 311; dough, 271; English, 29, 32, 39, 53, 62, 130–3, 136–7, 162–3, 213–15, 286–7, 306–7, 310–11, 314–15, 324–5, 386–7, 408–9, 426–9, 460–1, 506–7, 596–7; partridge, 161; seamless, 160n38; 161; turkey, 459–61; venison, 301, 311
empanadailla, 74. *See also* turnover, mini
eneldo. *See* dill
England, 6, 7, 98n41. *See also* empanada, English
enguila (anguila). *See* eel

enjundía. *See* tissue, fatty
entresijo. *See* mesentery
equipment, kitchen, 117–25
escabeche. *See* brine
escarola. *See* escarole
escarole, 43, 177, 355, 597; stuffed, 131, 177, 589
escorzonera. *See* salsify
espaldilla. *See* shoulder
espárragos. *See* asparagus
esparto, 289, 575
espinaca. *See* spinach
espuma. *See* foam
espumadera. *See* skimmer
essence, 145–7, 151, 169–73, 229, 409, 493, 559, 601
estameña. *See* cheesecloth
estocafix. *See* stockfish
European Union, 147n1

faisán. *See* pheasant
fanega. *See* bushel
farro, 496–9, 594–5
fartes, 61, 508–11
fat, 46–7, 143, 147, 153, 157, 339, 349–51, 357, 369, 373–5, 457, 459, 475, 491–3, 521; caul, 46, 156n33, 170n49, 171, 197, 207, 225, 300n213, 301, 307, 337, 589–91, 595, 601; ham, 46, 126, 156n33, 157, 273, 373, 459, 467, 473, 479, 555, 597; pork, 27, 32, 56, 131, 133, 139, 270n189, 271, 275, 279, 301, 339, 435, 555. *See also* butter; fatback; lard; oil
fatback, 46, 143, 149, 156n33, 159, 165–81, 187–91, 197–9, 200n87, 209–15, 223, 227, 281–3, 297–9, 303, 309–11, 331–9, 341, 351, 355, 361, 365–73, 387, 393–5, 411, 431, 457–61, 471, 477–9, 483, 505, 553–5, 587, 593, 603; extra fatty, 161, 193–7, 201–9, 213–15, 289–93, 307, 315,

337, 371–3, 393, 429, 469, 477–9, 583, 589–91, 595; meaty, 161; minced, 153, 181–5, 229–31, 293–5, 307
feather, 14, 259–61, 335, 417, 477, 503, 509; hen, 493, 601
fennel, 39, 48, 383, 387, 399, 405, 519, 539, 599–601; preserved, 480n375, 562n441, 581–3
Feros, Antonio, 7
filete [thin spike], 478–9
fish, 36–9, 415–17, 423, 603; prepare, 381. *See also* barbel; carp; eel; freshwater; hake; lamprey; sea bream; sturgeon; trout; tuna
fish day, 24, 44, 47, 61, 218n116, 219, 235, 263, 275, 353, 355, 357, 361, 365, 367, 375, 395, 451, 473, 501. *See also* abstinence
Fitch, Richard, 524n407
flamenquilla, 456–7
Flanders, 7, 37, 126, 597; recipes with connection to, 392–3
flaón [custard pie], 486–7
flor, 65, 175–9, 197–9, 201–3, 209, 217, 307, 331, 369, 593. *See also* flower
flor de la malva. *See* mallow blossom
flour, 149, 161, 203, 211, 215, 219–23, 237, 253, 293, 309, 319–29, 369, 373–9, 383, 387, 399, 405, 409, 415, 435, 439, 465, 487, 505–7, 527–9, 545, 587, 599; with/without bran, 27, 28, 59, 258n173, 168n183, 286n202, 290n204, 463, 510n394, 511; finely sifted, 59, 307, 315, 455, 463, 485, 501–5, 509–11, 531, 541, 553, 585; mill, 462–3, 484–5, 502–3, 504–5, 540–1; pastry, 557; quality of, 290n204; rice, 343–5, 349; toasted, 169, 173, 399–401, 421, 555; rice, 163, 237, 549, 553, 585; wheat, 237, 243, 269–71, 277, 281, 287, 291, 311, 503, 539, 547–9, 553, 585

flower: cardoon, 255; eggplant, 537; elderberry, 515; rosemary, 569
foam, egg white, 447; fruit, 253, 562n442, 563, 573; honey, 519, 537; mustard, 515; sugar, 253, 569, 570n451
foodstuffs: international, 60–3; regional, 56–7; Muslim/Morisco, 57–60, 150n19
foreigner, 63, 150n21, 151
fowl, 33–6, 42, 60, 363–5; plucking, 140n45, 141, 161, 184n67. *See also* bird, small; capon; chicken; crane; curlew; dove; duck; grouse; hen; partridge; pheasant; pigeon; plover; squab; thrush; turkey; woodcock
France, recipes with connection to, 170–3
frasia. *See under* intestine
fricassee, 333; egg, 451–3
frisuelo [funnel cake], 68, 378–9
frog, 36, 39, 201, 429, 585, 603
frosting, 275
fruit, 39–42; firm, 139, 253, 378n294, 379. *See also* apricot; cherry, sour; citron; currant, dried; date; elderberry; gooseberry; grape; lemon; lime; orange; peach; pear; plum; pomegranate; prune; quince; raisin; toronja
fruta. *See* fruit
fruta de sartén. *See under* dough, fried
Fuḍalat-al-Hiwan (Ibn Razin al-Tujibi), 59

galangal, 47, 533, 534n416
galladura [red spot on egg], 432
Gallego Burín, Antonio, and Alfonso Gámir Sandoval, 462n362
gallina. *See* hen
galopín [kitchen boy], 8, 11–12, 120–3
gámbaro. *See* prawn
ganga. *See* grouse
ganso. *See* goose

garbanzo, 44, 211, 335, 363, 377, 473, 491–3; broth, 44, 218n116, 257, 355, 365–7, 385–7, 399, 405–13, 429, 441–3, 453, 467, 599; dark, 491

García, L. Jacinto, 142n2

garlic, 43, 53, 68, 147, 167–71, 191, 199, 211–13, 241, 285–7, 291, 295–7, 301, 341, 383, 405–7, 417, 419, 439–41, 599; green, 603

garnish, 41

Garrovillas, 57, 126n37, 454–5, 478–9

gatafura, 252n163, 253

gazpacho, *manchego*, 65, 162–3

gelatin, 16, 434n340

Genoa, recipes with connection to, 578–9

Germany, 39, 632; recipes with connection to, 62, 63, 130–1, 180–1, 390–1, 412n319

giblet, 32, 227, 483, 489; chicken, 71, 202n90; goose, 35; turkey, 34, 140n45, 459–61

gigote. See under specific animal

Gimeno Betí, Lluis, 57, 190n75

ginebrada. See under tart, clotted milk

ginger, 47, 149, 155, 167–9, 173, 177, 187, 193, 199, 203–7, 213, 251, 257, 283, 289, 299–301, 305–7, 311–13, 331, 341, 351, 383–5, 391, 409, 415, 421, 441, 461, 475, 483, 533–5, 583, 599–601

Gispert Cruells, Montserrat, 362n276

gizzard, 153, 181, 459–61

glass: as description, 329, 491, 569; container, 489, 491, 497, 499, 505, 517; carafe, 515

glaze, 267, 531, 543–7; golden, 269; lard, 163

goat. *See* kid; *see under* milk

gold, 491

goose, 35, 371, 561

gooseberry, 181

gourd, 42

Gracián, Baltasar, 53

gragea [sugar sprinkle], 222n124, 330

grain (meat fibre), boar, 291, 297; ham, 273; mutton, 167; pork fat, 555; veal, 229, 583

grain of paradise, 47, 204n91, 533, 534n417

granada. See pomegranate

Granada, Fray Luis de, 100n2

Granado, Diego de, 5, 34, 94n1, 96n27, 110n11, 204n92

grano de paraíso. See grain of paradise

grape, black, 513; must, 512n395; pie, 245; sour, 42, 48, 159, 181, 191, 333–5, 365–9, 477, 516n398, 517, 576n458, 583, 595; syrup, 513

Green, Donna, 524n406, 635, 662

greens, leafy, 43, 157, 167, 176n56, 177–9, 211–13, 297, 373, 595–7

grill, 143–7, 153, 161, 165, 169, 195

grouper, 603

grouse, pin-tailed sand, 35, 153, 559

grulla. See crane

grusela. See gooseberry

guardamangier [food distributor], 10, 11

gubilete. See under mould

guinda. See cherry, sour

Guitián, Jorge, 8

gusto. See taste

Gutiérrez Cuadro, Juan, and Francesc Rodríguez, 96n21, 118n24

Gutiérrez Flores, Daniela, 95n6

Gúzman, Dominga de, 74, 154n31, 182n66

haba. See bean, fava

hake, 6, 389; salted, 57, 221, 584n464, 585

ham: fatty, 57, 479; fresh, 133, 204n92; leg of, 459; shank, 133, 373, 459, 463, 601

hand washing, 122–5

hare, 33, 48, 153, 210n100, 211, 285; carving, 561; empanada, 72, 131,

137, 139, 150n23, 213; minced, 150n23, 155, 212n105, 213, 592n470; presenting, 561; stew, 211–15
harina. See flour
hawthorn, 181
hay, 489
Hayward, Vicky, 34, 97n39, 98n43, 112n14, 144n8, 208n97, 224n128, 386n301, 516n398
hazelnut, 495
head, 29. See also sheep, veal
head cheese, 33, 48; boar, 126n38, 289–91
hebra. See grain (meat fibre); thread
hen, 33, 34, 175–7, 231, 285, 343, 467, 489, 493, 499–505, 535; bones, 491; broth, 493; liver, 34, 35–6, 131, 137, 143, 159, 219, 227, 283, 483, 593; Morisco style, 57, 74, 505; pie, 281; stuffed, 183–5, 219
heno. See hay
herb, 39, 47–8, 151, 153, 167, 173–5, 181, 203, 209, 229–31, 295–9, 391, 421, 467; all herbs, 48, 355, 360n273, 393, 473; curdling, 318n230, 319; garden, 65, 153, 291, 293, 305, 383, 421, 463; green, 39, 68, 173–7, 185, 195, 199, 217, 221, 227, 307, 311, 315, 331, 335, 351–5, 361–71, 375, 383–5, 393, 397, 399, 403–11, 415, 419, 427–9, 439–43, 449, 469–73, 479, 505, 583, 599, 603. See also cilantro; fennel; marjoram; parsley; sage; spearmint; thyme
heritage, culinary: Jewish influence in, 58; Muslim/Morisco influence in, 57–60, 182n66
Hernández de Maceras, Domingo, 5, 34, 57, 94n1, 95–6n14, 142n2, 142n3, 198n84
Herrera, Alonso de, 41
Herrero, David, 402n314
Herrero-García, Miguel, 492n381

hierba de cuajar. See rennet, herbal
hierba del jardín. See herb, garden
hierbabuena. See spearmint
hierbas. See greens, leafy
hilo de bala. See twine
hinojo. See fennel
hippocras, 534n419, 535
hisopillo. See savory, winter
Hochepot, 73
hoja verde. See greens, leafy
hojaldrado. See puff pastry, dough
hojaldre. See puff pastry
hojuela. See pastry, sheet
honey, 46, 147, 165, 211, 217–21, 237, 255, 269–75, 279–81, 317, 321–3, 331, 349, 359, 363, 371–3, 377–9, 393, 423, 437, 445, 453–5, 467–9, 507, 511, 519, 537, 555, 581, 591, 603; whipped, 323, 329, 509
hongo. See mushrooms, wild
hormigos, 258–9, 259–60
Huarte de San Juan, Juan, 324n238
huevo. See egg
huevo mejido. See egg yolk, sweet scrambled

Ibn Razin al-Tujibi, 59, 284n200, 480n375
Infantado, duque de, 8–9
infirm, recipes for, 35, 51–2, 227, 489–93, 500n386, 499–501, 547, 601. See also sick, recipes for
Ingram, Rebecca, 98n45
ingredients, 22–51. See also foodstuffs; *and individual foodstuffs*
inspector, food, 11–13, 95n8, 127, 129
intestine, 29, 31, 151–3, 170n49, 331, 337–41, 601; bird, 63, 151, 153; frasia, 30–1, 74, 306n217, 307, 331; kid, 51, 331; pig, 339, 601; snail, 405; sperm whale, 480n375; veal, 307–9, 339; venison, 299, 306n217
isinglass, 15, 434n340, 435, 533–5

jabalí. See boar
jalea. See jelly
jam, 16, 41, 267, 575, 576n456
jar: glass (*vidrio*), 14, 565, 577; glazed terracotta (*alorza/alhorza*), 580n461, 581; large terracotta (*tinaja*), 517
jarrete [shank]. *See under* beef; ham; mutton; veal
jelly: bag, 533–5; grape, sour, 577; plum, damson, 577; pomegranate, 577; quince, 203, 575–7; wine, 60, 533–5
jengibre. See ginger
jibia. See cuttlefish
Juana, princess of Portugal, 8, 60, 123
jug, 118n25, 119
juice: acidic, 48; sour, 145, 169, 173, 185, 193, 197–9, 203, 257, 279–83, 335, 351, 355, 365, 373, 377, 387, 395, 409, 419, 427–9, 443, 471, 483, 517, 555, 589–91, 597. *See also* lemon; orange; grape; sorrel

Kamen, Henry, 97n31
Ketcham Wheaton, Barbara, 94, 142n2
kid, 32–3, 171–3, 181, 185, 189, 193–7, 315, 457, 471–3, 583, 603; bread, 451, 589; feet, 331, 535; head, 33, 51, 331–7; lung, 333–5, 591; pie, 249; pluck, 225, 333–7; stuffed, 469–71; trotter, 331, 593
kidney, 29; veal, 215, 337
king, taste preferences of, 53–5, 192n77, 206n95, 207, 538n423. *See also* Philip III
Kitab al-tabij fi l-Magrib wa-l-Andalus fi 'asr al-muwahhudin li-mu'allif mayhul [Tratado sobre cocina en el Magrib y al-Andalus en época almohade, de autor desconocido], 59, 480n375
kitchen: cleanliness of, 11, 116–25; equipment and utensils in, 13–15, 79, 116–25; finances of, 68, 109, 380n297; personnel in, 10–12, 67–9; the king's vs the state, 11, 123; space of 95n10; storage, 125
Klumpp, Andreas, 390n304, 412n319
knife, sharpening of, 125
knuckle, 29
Krohn, 95n10

La cocina española antigua (Pardo Bazán), 73–4, 97n29
La lozana andaluza, 58, 258n174, 356n264
ladyfinger, 28, 47, 54, 64, 480n375, 526n408, 527–9, 548n433
Laguna, Andrés, 41, 220n120, 256n168, 514n397
lamb, 41
lamination, 28
lamprea. See lamprey
lamprey, 37–8, 187, 264n180, 401–3, 419
langosta. See lobster
lard, 32, 46, 149–53, 159, 163, 167, 183, 187, 193–7, 203, 215–17, 223–33, 237, 243, 249–51, 255, 265, 271–9, 283–7, 291–7, 303, 307–11, 315–19, 323–31, 335–7, 341–9, 357, 363–5, 369, 375, 379, 385–9, 397, 405, 411, 421, 429–33, 443–7, 453–5, 467–73, 475, 477, 483–5, 507–9, 555, 589, 591, 597–9, 603; caul, 46; leaf, 597; meaty, 285
larding needle, 171–3, 291, 341
Laudan, Rachel, 74, 182n66
laurel. See bay leaf
Le cuisinier roîal et bourgeois, 584n465
Le manuscript de Sion, 98n44
leavening agent, 485
lebrada. See under sauce
leche. See milk
lechón. See pig, suckling
lechuga. See lettuce

leek, 43; white, 585
legumes, 44
lemon, 41, 151, 217, 505; Ceutí, 73, 562n440, 567; juice, 48–51, 143, 147–53, 159, 167, 171, 175–81, 185–99, 207, 215, 225–33, 281–3, 289, 315, 331, 339–41, 353–7, 369, 373, 381, 385–9, 397, 401, 405–9, 415, 419–21, 425–9, 441, 447–9, 457, 461, 469–71, 475, 501, 531–5, 555, 569, 583, 589, 599; ponci, 247; pie, 247; rind, 150n19; wheel, 157, 167, 189, 227, 341, 423, 451, 469–71, 479, 539, 555
Lent, 44, 434n338, 603
lentil, 44
Lerma, Duke of, 7, 23
lettuce, 157, 173–7, 197, 353–9, 471, 589, 595–7; stalk, 571
librillo [bowl], 316
Libro de cocina de la gesta de independencia (anonymous), 74
Libro de confitura para el uso de Elias Gómez Maestro cerero y confitero de la ciudad de Olite, 73, 432n337, 450n351, 562n440
Libro de guisados (Nola), 4, 57, 66, 94n1, 150n23
Libro de Sent soví [The book of Sent soví] (anonymous), 4, 57
Libro del arte de cocina [Book on the art of cooking] (Hernández de Maceras), 5, 52, 57, 94n1, 95–6n14, 142n2, 198n84
liebre. See hare
lime: candied, 250n160, 251; pie, 251; preserve, 261; sweet, 257
limón. See lemon
limoncello. See lime
linen: 62, 122n32, 254n167, 255, 289, 416n320, 465, 513, 523, 567; *sedeña*, 416–17
linguistics, cookbook as a case study, 79–93

lino. See linen
liver, 29, 459; hen, 34, 35–6, 131, 137, 143, 159, 219, 227, 283, 483, 593; kid, 333, 469, 591; pig, 167; poultry, 189, 215, 219; prepare, 591–3; turkey, 143; veal, 521; woodcock, 151
liviano. See lung
Llibre del coc [Book on cookery] (Maestre Robert), 5, 57, 66, 94n1, 150n23, 520n401
lobster, 39, 42, 56, 423–5; tail, 585
loin, 157; beef, 305, 337; boar, 295–7; mutton, 191, 207; pork, 283–5, 341; veal, 305, 337
longaniza. See under sausage
lord, service for, 95n7, 117, 124–5, 207, 333, 493; taste of, 23, 55, 147, 185, 343, 367, 419, 547
Los quatro libros del arte de confitería, 5, 570n451
La lozana andaluza, 58, 258n174, 356n264
lye, solution, 225

madrecillas. See oviduct
maestresala. See steward
major domo, 10, 11–13, 127
mallow blossom, 569
malva, flor de. See mallow blossom
manjar blanco. See blancmange
manna, 222n124, 223
manteca. See lard
manteca de vaca. See butter
Manual de mugeres [Manual for women] (anonymous), 57, 336n249
Manuscrito Ávila Blancas, Gastronomía mexicana del s XVIII, 74, 234n137, 294n206, 356n265, 428n334, 566n446, 566n447
Le manuscrit de Sion, 98n44
marinade, 37, 41, 48, 147, 153, 163, 291, 295–7, 303, 307, 341, 383, 387,

395, 417–21, 475, 555; olive, 539; saltwater, 539
marisco. See shellfish
marjoram, 48, 150n20, 151–3, 159, 167, 171–3, 185, 195–7, 213, 273, 289–91, 295, 299, 305, 335, 383, 391, 399, 449, 457, 463, 475, 555
Markham, Gervase, 524n406
marrow, beef, 29, 31, 173, 175, 179–81, 185, 187–91, 195, 209, 217, 225, 229, 243, 247–9, 279–83, 323, 347–9, 357–9, 365, 367–9, 373–5, 433, 461, 469–71, 475, 481–3, 553, 587–9
Martínez Llopís, 570n451
Martínez Millán, José, and José Eloy Hortal Muñóz, 95n6
Martínez Montiño, Francisco, 3–5, 167n3, 191n5; attentiveness of, 66–9; biography, 8–15; in the Americas, 74; editions of, 75–92; legacy, 71–4; or Motiño, 8, 82, 100n1, 104n8; price of cookbook of, 82, 83, 102n3, 102n5, 103, 105; voice of, 69–71; years in service for, 5, 8–10, 82, 83, 122–3
marzipan, 28, 47, 137, 139, 238n140, 276n193, 525, 544n431, 547; in artalete, 193; in cookies, 537; in egg dishes, 435–7, 445; in pastries, 257–9, 269, 545; in pies, 251, 267, 347, 483, 587; in poultry dishes, 185, 193, 589; in puff pastry, 273, 275, 277, 469; in rolls, 485, 529; in stuffed toronja, 225; in tarts, 347, 485
masa. See dough
Massialot, François, 584n465
mastresala (maestresala). See steward
Mata, Juan de la, 46
mayordomo. See major domo
mazapán. See marzipan
measurement, 627–33
meat, 29–33
meatball, 29, 32, 39, 175, 179–81, 189, 197, 206n94, 207, 208n98, 215, 229–31, 283, 357, 369, 429, 471; Castilian, 209; big, 229–31, 471; borage, 257; fried, 215; frog, 429; hen liver, 137; poultry, 54, 118n24, 205–7; royal, 24, 31, 209; small, 181, 195, 231, 283, 471
meat day, 597, 603
mejillón. See mussel
mejorana. See marjoram
melocotón. See peach
melon, seed, 495
membrillo. See quince
menudo/menudillo. See giblet
merienda [late afternoon supper], 70, 114n17, 136–41, 156, 202, 324, 432
meringue, 279, 439, 529–31
mermelada. See jam
mero [grouper], 603
mesentery, 31, 33, 156n33, 170n49, 298n209, 299, 306n217, 307
Mesones, Juan de, 123
Mesta, 7
migajón. See under bread, crumb (centre)
migas. See breadcrumb
milk, 44–5, 195, 207, 223, 233–5, 239, 255, 319–21, 325–7, 335, 339, 343, 347–51, 365, 371, 377–9, 409–11, 429–31, 449, 453–5, 463, 481–7, 495–505, 521–3, 533–5, 551–3, 585, 595, 599, 603; almond, 351, 381, 435, 494n382, 495, 499, 585; clotted, 253–5, 503; goat, 32, 324n238, 325, 351, 431, 523; pastry, 277; pine nut, 431
mint, 201
minute, 488n380
Moll, Jaime, 77
molleja. See gizzard; sweetbread
mollete. See under bread; dough; roll
mollo, 56, 154–5
Monardes, Nicolás, 492n381, 532n415
Morala Rodríguez, José R., 572n452

morcilla. *See under* sausage, blood
Mordechai, Karen, 48
Morii, Mayako, 400n312
Morisco, expulsion of, 7. *See under* foodstuffs; heritage
mostachon (cookie), 269, 511, 529
mostaza. *See* mustard
mould, 116n19, 135, 452n355; barquette, 117, 527, 535; copper, 453; *gubilete* 368–9, 432–3, 452–3
moyuelo [bran], 510–11
mozo [kitchen boy], 11–12, 95n6, 118–19, 120–5, 240–1
Müllers, Fabian, 98n44
Muro, Ángel, 73, 116n18, 298n211, 556n438
mushrooms, wild, 599
musk, 28, 54, 480n375, 481, 527, 581
mussel, 39, 427
must, 513, 527
mustard, 297, 333, 453, 512n395, 519, 531, 599; black, 204n92, 296n207, 513–15; powder, 513
mutton, 31–2, 36, 42, 144n8, 153, 170n50, 179, 357, 463, 467, 471, 493, 501, 555, 583, 603; caul fat, 307, 589; chop, 457; empanada, 293; essence and sustaining broth, 229, 491, 493, 601; in pastries and pies, 57, 227, 279, 283, 285, 479; leg, 62, 72, 133, 145–7, 167–73, 209, 229, 473, 479, 491–3, 589, 601; loin, 31, 191, 207, 457, 471, 479; in stuffing, 42, 191, 223, 357, 361; marinated, 555; meatballs, 207, 209, 231; offal, 133, 333, 439, 591, minced, 133, 137, 145–7, 169–73, 178n60, 209, 283, 361; shank, 170, 473, 493; stew, 167–71, 227, 373; stew, green, 23, 37, 39, 51, 65, 200n86, 201–3, 227, 383, 405, 407, 429, 603; stuffed, 171; tail, 467, 589, 595

nabo. *See* turnip
Nadeau, Carolyn, 57, 94n3, 95n10, 124n34, 452n355
naranja. *See* orange
Nasrallah, Nawal, 98n40, 284n200, 308n220, 480n375
nata. *See* cream
názula. *See* cheese, curd
nettle, 603
New World, 6–7, 34, 42, 110n11, 142n2, 250n160, 462n362
Nocheseda, Elena, 536n421
Nola, Ruperto de, 5, 57, 66, 94n1, 150n23, 178n60, 210n100
Notaker, Henry, 4, 77, 79, 82, 98n46, 604n479, 606n480
Nuevo arte de cocina (Altamiras), 5, 71–2
nuez. *See* nutmeg; walnut
nut, 40; and seeds, sugar-coated, 70, 135, 137, 157
nutmeg, 47, 149, 155, 167–9, 173, 177, 187, 193, 199, 203–7, 251, 273, 283, 289, 299–301, 305–7, 311–13, 331, 351, 385, 391, 401, 409, 415, 421, 425, 441, 461, 469, 475, 509, 583, 587, 599
ñoclo. *See under* wafer, bite-sized

oblea. *See* wafer
octopus, 39, 403, 603
offal, 29–31, 32–3, 42, 210n101; hen, 34
oficial [cook]. *See* cook
oil, 46, 155–7, 163–5, 213, 219–23, 241, 253, 279–81, 313, 319, 329, 351–5, 359–65, 371, 377, 383, 393–5, 399–403, 411, 417–23, 439, 443–7, 467, 477, 507–11, 517, 529, 597–9, 603; egg, 523; valencia, 155
olive, 43, 71, 133–7, 157, 204n92, 404n315; fried, 287; leaf, 539; marinade, 539; oil, 46, 54, 97n39, 154n31, 377

olla podrida. See stew, hodgepodge
omelette: Carthusian, 445–7; folded, 447; (*tortilla*), 51, 73, 138–9, 234–5, 240–1, 290–1, 300–1, 316–17, 374–5, 444–9, 540–3; water, 445; white, 447
onion, 43, 165, 193, 199–203, 209–13, 219, 229, 287, 293, 307, 311–13, 331, 351, 355–7, 361–73, 377, 383–5, 389, 393–5, 399, 403–9, 415–21, 425–31, 453, 459, 469, 583, 593, 599, 603; boiled; chopped, 159, 169; diced, 153, 157, 333, 595; fried, 155, 175, 181, 191, 197, 257, 293, 401, 505; green, 603; minced, 149, 155, 173, 177, 181–3, 197–9, 221, 227, 231, 309, 333, 337, 355, 415, 483, 591; raw, 169–73; ring, 157, 399; roasted; sautéd, 185; stuffed, 236n138, 411–13
orange, 41, 169, 407, 421, 425–9, 599; juice, 48, 147, 153, 159, 171, 175–81, 187–9, 195, 199, 215, 353–5, 369–73, 383, 395, 401, 407, 419–23, 427, 473, 479, 555, 589–93, 597
orange blossom. *See under* water
oregano, 48, 147, 169, 291, 295–7, 383, 417–19, 445, 475
orejón. See under apricot, dried
organ meat. *See* offal
oruga. See arugula; *see under* sauce, arugula
ostión. See oyster
oviduct, 32, 34, 219
oyster, 39, 187, 409; pie, 427; prepare, 427

page [page], 11, 13
pajarillo. See under bird, small; fowl
palace positions, 10–11
paloma. See pigeon
palomino. See squab
pan. See bread
panecillo. See roll
panetela, 501

paper, 10, 14, 113, 161, 260n175, 273, 467, 533, 541–9; greased, 14, 163, 261, 269, 279, 307; half sheet, 271, 547–51, 555–7, parchment, 515; quarter sheet, 275, 469, 543; with flour, 435, 439, 507, 509, 553; with *moyuelo*, 511; wrapped in, 34, 142n3, 143, 555, 557
papín. See under sauce, cream, sweet
Papin, Denis, 28
Pardo Bazán, Emilia, 3, 16, 73–4, 97n29, 98n45, 178n58, 448n349, 600n473
Parkhurst Ferguson, Priscilla, 23
parsley, 48, 173, 179, 185, 195–201, 213, 221, 227, 283, 287, 297, 305–9, 335, 351, 391–3, 413, 417, 439, 467, 491, 583, 593, 603. *See also under* sauce
partial abstinence. *See* abstinence
partridge, 33, 35, 36, 131, 149–51, 283–5, 477, 457, 493, 499, 559, 601; carving, 559; chick, 135, 147, 499; empanada, 72, 139, 161; essence of; 493, 690–1; roast, 72, 131, 137, 149–51, 163–5, 212n104, 283–5, 457, 477; sops, 65; stuffed, 553–5
pasa. See raisin
pasa de Corinto. See currant, dried
pastel. See pie
pastel en bote. See under pie, crustless
pastry, 28, 47, 64; airy, 257; dough, 161, 261–3, 269, 597; fried, 271, 599; fried cheese, 319–21; hat, 261–3; Maimon, 259; Muslim, 47; ring-shaped, 47, 64, 144n7, 219, 265–7, 275, 445, 523, 527–31, 535–7, 543, 553; savoury, 461; sheet, 159, 181–5, 203, 217, 223, 257, 261. *See also individual pastries*
pâte à choux. See under dough, cream puff
pavo. See turkey
pea, 44; stew, 375
peach, 41, 253; clingstone, 253, 563–5, 578n459

pear, 41, 253, 257, 393, 565; candied, 573; Cermeña, 180n62, 181, 277, 435, 553; purée, 565
pebrada. See under sauce, pepper, black
Pennell, Elizabeth, 87
pennyroyal, shoot, 473
Pentecost, 603
pepino. See cucumber
pepita. See seed
pepitoria, 70, 71, 140n45, 148n14, 202–5, 374–5
pepper, black, 47, 143, 149, 151–9, 163, 167–9, 173, 177, 181–3, 187, 193–5, 199, 203–7, 213, 227, 241, 251, 253, 283, 289, 297–301, 307–13, 331, 337, 341, 351, 353, 373, 381–7, 391, 395, 401, 407–9, 413–29, 441, 457, 461–3, 475–7, 483, 509, 521, 533–9, 561, 583, 587–9, 593, 599–601; long, 60, 97n32, 532n415, 533
pera. See pear
perdigón. See under partridge, chick
perdiz. See partridge
perejil. See parsley
Pérez de Herrera, Christóbal, 100n2
Pérez Samper, María de los Ángeles, 8, 46, 148n18
Pérez San Vicente, Guadalupe, 74, 182n66, 234n137, 294n206, 356n265, 428n334, 566n446, 566n447
pernil [leg of ham], 462–3
pernil, tocino de. See fat, ham
pero, agrio. See apple, sour
pescado cecial. See hake, salted
pesebre (percebe). See barnacle
pestle, 167
pheasant, 33, 35, 561
Philip II, 5–7, 121
Philip III, 7, 53, 97n31
pícaro. See scullion
picatoste. See under bread, fried
pichón. See under squab, farm-raised

pickle, 48
pie, 149, 153, 161, 179, 249, 293–7, 283–7, 313; brown, 269; cream, 243–5; crustless, 230, 385, 386n301, 415, 425, 471, 587–9, 591; custard, 487; Lady, 479–83; puff pastry (*costrada*), 71, 131, 139, 224–7, 236n138, 247, 250–1, 253, 369, 386–7, 395, 396–7, 407, 482–3; puff pastry (*hojaldrado*), 133, 135, 236n138, 251, 258n170, 280–1; quantities, 253–5; teat, 137, 224n127, 225, 279; white, 483
pig, suckling, 32, 41, 131, 135, 165, 533–5; carving, 561; feet, 149, 287, 313, 429–31; prepare like, 413, 471, 533; sauce for, 167; sausages, 137, 139, 167. See also under pork
pigeon, 36, 285; wood, 133, 141, 147–9, 151, 155, 234n136
pimienta. See pepper, black
pine nut, 31, 139, 173, 189, 225, 377, 385, 431–3, 441, 471, 535. See also under milk
pinwheel, 23, 29, 31–2, 54, 64, 68, 131, 133, 137, 188n74, 189, 193–9, 229–31, 235, 283, 389, 479
piñón. See pine nut
pisto. See under soup
Pius V, 95n11
Platina, 52
plato/platillo 172n51
platter, carving, 164–5, 456n359
plover, 35, 153, 559
pluck, 24, 45, 48, 71, 141, 185, 210n101, 211, 219, 225–7, 333, 335, 337, 461, 489, 590n468
plum, 41, 96n19, 149; damson, 576n456; Genoese, 579; monk, 256n168, 257
pluma. See feather
pluvia. See plover
pollo. See chicken

Polo Cano, Nuria, 57, 142n2
pomegranate, 41, 143–5, 157
pork, 32, 58, 533–5, 601; carving, 561; ear, 287; ham, 339; tenderloin, 285, 291, 313, 341
pork belly, roasted, 57, 131–9, 243, 270n189, 271, 277, 279, 311–13, 325, 385, 454–7, 463, 479, 554n435, 555
porridge, 371, 521, 547, 585; wheat, 593–5
portador [food runner], 11–12
portero [doorman/kitchen security], 11–12
Portugal, 6, 8, 10, 60–2, 97n31, 123, 254n167; recipes with connection to, 27, 60–2, 81, 86, 154n30, 347, 349, 377, 388n302, 420n327, 421–3, 472n370, 473, 488n378
poso [dregs], 516–17
potato, 110n11
poultry, 42, 43, 193, 203, 229, 285, 493, 547, 587, 601; presenting, 557–9. *See also* fowl
El practicón: tratado completo de cocina (Muro), 73, 116n18, 556n438
prawn, 427
preserve, 48, 51, 154n29, 263–5, 269, 277–9, 347, 435–7
prestiño, 329
printer, 77, 79, 83, 84, 87, 102n3, 105 606n480. *See also* bookseller. *See also under* women
prune, 41, 165, 397, 555
puche. See porridge
puchero [stew pot], 14, 452, 490, 496
puerco. See pork
puerro. See leek
puff, 206n94, 207, 243, 309, 315–19, 320n231, 320n232, 338n250, 339, 376n290; blancmange, 343–5; borage, 381; cheese, 321, 507; rice, 349
puff pastry, 47, 191, 243, 271–7, 369, 467, 555; dough, 131, 161, 167, 191, 217, 243, 253, 257–9, 263–5, 273, 277, 281, 347, 369, 461–3, 467–9, 479, 591; fried, 217, 507; stuffed, 469. *See also under* pie
puff scoop, 207
pulpo. See octopus

Los quatro libros del arte de confitería, 5, 570n451
queen, taste preferences of, 53, 55, 123, 549
quesadilla. See tart, cheese
queso. See cheese
Quevedo, Francisco de, 57, 586n467
quince, 39–41, 153, 165, 169, 177, 203, 209, 253, 257, 363, 393, 513, 555–7, 579; paste, 575, 579; pie, 461; rind, 267, 277
Quiñones, María de, 83, 98n48

rabbit, 33, 155–7, 163; empanada, 477; stuffed, 477
raisin, 126n37, 133–7, 170n50, 191n5, 377
rampion bellflower, 176n56, 177, 283; leaves, 597; shoot, 39, 43, 197, 405, 409
rana. See frog
rebollo, 68, 264–5
redaño. See fat, caul; mesentery
redoma [carafe], 488–9, 51–5, 516–17
relleno. See stuffing
rennet, animal, 237, 255, 441; herbal, 236n138, 237, 359, 411, 475
repollo. See cabbage
repulgo [crimped edge]: with, 212, 264, 290, 314; without, 160, 216, 270
requesón. See cheese, curd
rescoldo. See embers, grey
rice, 347–51, 585, 595
riñón. See kidney
riñonada [loin], mutton, 31, 191, 207, 471, 479; veal, 305, 337, 471, 479
riponce. See rampion bellflower

roast, 143–65, 171, 185–7, 227–9
roll, 47; butter, 485; candeal, 263, 279, 507; cinnamon, 529; collation, 505–7; fitete, 56, 64, 268–71; *mollete*, 239, 278n195, 279, 459, 473; round, 277; Saint Augustine, 537; Saint Nicolas, 536n421; studded, 279; sweet, 189, 263
rolling pin, 265, 403, 529, 553, 599
rosa. See rose
rose, 567–71; bud, 515
rosemary, 223
rosquilla. See pastry, ring-shaped
roux, 65, 202n89, 202n90

sábalo. See shad
saffron, 47, 155, 159, 179, 203–5, 217, 241, 285, 313, 351–3, 359, 363–5, 407–9, 421–3, 437, 441, 449, 461, 469, 475, 539, 555, 583, 595, 599
sage, 48, 151–3, 167, 173, 289–91, 295, 305, 399, 459, 463
salad, 71, 138n42, 156n32, 157, 221, 602n476
salchicha. See sausage
salchichón. See under sausage
salmuera. See brine
salpicon, 157; beef, 157
salsa. See sauce
Salsete, Antonio, 210n102
salsify, root, 572n453, 573
salvia. See sage
San Juan, 580
Sánchez, Luis, 77, 98n46, 100n2
sandalwood, powder, 435; shoots, 472n372, 473
sandwich, 65–6, 308n220
sardine, 313, 423
Sarriá Rueda, Amalia, 77
sauce, 48, 49–50t, 64–5; ajopollo, 416n322, 419; almond, 143, 149, 437; arugula, 29, 37, 131, 147, 297, 311, 383, 399, 519; black, 33, 149, 153, 215, 293–5, 373, 395, 413, 419, 519, 593; boar, 291–3; brenca, 229; butter, 351; caper, 33, 43, 48, 155; cherry, 475; chicken, roast, 159; cream, sweet, 138n44, 325, 475, 553, 585–8; egg yolk-vinegar, 44, 51; flour, 149; garlic, 417; grape, 159, 477; jadeo, 331; lamprea, 555; lebrada, 48, 210–11; lemon, 149; liver, 521; moreta, 65, 420–1; mutton, green, 603; parsley, 68, 198n84, 199, 392n309, 393, 431, 599; partridge, 163, 165; pepper, black 151, 155, 213, 309, 393–5, 475, 593; plum, 149; pomegranate, 143–5, 477; prune, 397; quince, 33, 35, 41, 153; suckling pig, 167; sweet and sour, 227; verjuice, 595; zurciga, 64–5, 441
saúco. See elderberry
sausage 29, 135, 220n119, 285, 336, 461, 601; black pepper (*salchichón*), 32, 126n37, 134–9, 166–7, 286–7, 338–9, 370–1, 374–5, 600–1, 602–3; blood, 32, 44, 133, 235, 285, 309, 336n249; 337–9, 423; *chorizo*, 32, 284n201, 341; *longaniza*, 32, 284n201, 285, 340–1; neck skin, 461; pork, 32, 167, 339–41; *salchicha*, 73, 283, 285, 341, 601
savory, summer, 48, 171, 293, 298n210, 299, 449, 473, 555; winter, 48, 151, 171–3, 213, 273, 289–91, 298n210, 299, 305, 383, 459, 463, 475, 555
Scappi, Bartolomeo, 5, 47, 95n10, 96n27, 204n91, 204n92
scullion, 120–3
sea bream, 38, 60–1, 133, 421–3
seasoning, 47–8
sebo. See tallow
sedeña. See linen
seed, 24, 70–1, 135, 137, 157, 593; grain of paradise, 534n417; grape, 245,

595; melon, 495; mustard, 512n395; pepper, 532n415; pomegranate, 143, 157, 577; quince, 363, 557; squash, 52, 491, 495. *See also under* nuts

semolina, 595

senses, humanist debate on the, 52, 77, 100n2

Serrano Larráyoz, Fernando, 210n102

service, 11–12, 66, 124–9

seso. See brain

shad, 355

Shaw, Hank, 140n45

sheep, feet, 331; head, 287; testicles, 133, 195–7, 219, 283

shellfish, 39, 42; prepare, 427; *see also* barnacle; clam; crab; lobster; mussel; octopus; oyster; prawn; snail

shoulder, boar, 297; hare, 561; kid, 469, 471; pig, 561; rabbit, 157; venison, 303

sick, recipes for, 51–2

sieve, 143, 149, 165, 211, 245, 295, 311, 315, 465–7, 481–3, 495, 517–19, 541, 555, 565, 573, 581, 595; *berguera*, 572–5; horsehair, 577–9

Simón Palmer, María del Carmen, 10–12, 95n6

sisón. See bustard, little

skewer, 195, 389, 477–9, 555; reed, 143, 193, 479, 543; wooden, 227, 231, 525–7

skimmer, 251, 255, 289, 345, 379, 411, 429, 433–5, 455, 573, 575, 577, 597

skin: chicken, 175; mutton, 171; pork, 167

Small, Jen, 364n278, 580n462, 659

snail, 39; pie, 405; prepare, 403–5; stuffed, 405

snow, 10, 492n381, 493, 601

sobrehusa, 221

sollo. See sturgeon

solomo (solomillo). See tenderloin

sopa. *See* sops

sops, 26–7, 95n12, 144n6, 159, 163, 173–5, 187–9, 195–7, 233–5, 309, 335–41, 363, 367, 383, 389–91, 399, 411–15, 425, 441–3, 455, 471–3, 479, 561, 591–3; aragonese, 521; beef, 236n138; 473; borage, 381; *capirotada*, 283–5; cheese, 165; cream, 145, 185–7, 233, 505; drunken, 74, 454–9; golden, 187, 193, 219, 233, 299, 505, 589; lettuce, 355–7, 589; milk, 453–5; squash, 371; trout, 393; turnip, 373; white, 213, 297, 305

sorrel, 43, 70, 181, 603; juice, 209, 215, 231–3, 299, 355, 369, 391, 583, 591–5, 603

Soto García, Ángel, 97n38, 98n49

soup: borage, 495, chestnut, 603, *panatela*, 500n386, 501; *pisto*, 498n385, 499; Portuguese, 61

Spain, sixteenth and seventeenth century, 5–8. *See also under* cookbook, Spanish

spatula, 159, 185–7, 193, 217, 229, 237, 345, 365, 379, 389, 447–9, 455, 523, 527, 551

spearmint, 48, 159, 171–3, 179, 185, 193–9, 213, 221, 227, 257, 283, 287, 293, 319–23, 335, 351, 361, 389, 391–3, 417, 425, 439, 449, 459, 467, 473, 583, 593, 603

spice, 125

Spiller, Elizabeth, 98n41

spinach, prepare, 377

spit, 143, 151–3, 159–63, 171, 187, 227, 295, 337, 401, 415, 475–9, 493, 525–7, 555–7, 591, 601

spoon, big, 143, 239–41, 257, 289, 359, 541; for two hands, 112n14, 541; illustrations of, 113

squab, 31, 33–5, 41–2, 68, 137, 140n45, 141, 161, 172n51, 173–9, 197–9,

201, 229, 231, 331–3, 345, 353, 357, 363–5, 375, 385, 457, 479, 589, 601; empanada, 191, 597; farm-raised, 35, 161, 172n51, 173; minced, 383, 479; pie, 242n19, 249, 283, 355, 479; skin, 185; stuffed, 185–7; wild, 23, 35, 133–7, 161, 172n51, 173, 199, 227
squash, 42–3, 362n276, 367–9, 485, 491, 495, 562n440, 573; dried, 571; fried, 369; prepare, 363–5; round, 27, 369–71; seeds, 491; stew, 365, 371; stuffed, 365, 369
squid, 39, 403
suero. See whey
starch, 543–7, 595
stew, 153–7, 165–7; bean, 353–5; carrot, 221; hare, 211; hodgepodge, 32, 35, 53, 55, 131, 135, 141, 283, 285–7, 399; mutton, 167–71, 201–3; poultry, 197, 227; small bird, 32, 72, 200n86, 227
steward, 11–13, 95n7, 103, 107, 121, 124–7, 556n437
stock, 163, 169–73, 177, 183, 193, 197–9, 205–7, 211, 217, 230n133, 231, 287–93, 311, 331–3, 411, 467, 479, 491, 499, 505, 517, 521, 583, 593; poultry, 497; hen, 501; meat, 379, 391
stockfish, 597–9
stone fruit, 255
strainer, 167
straw, 489
stuffing, 31, 159, 171, 183–91, 203, 207, 219, 223, 357, 367, 369, 423, 427, 441, 469–71, 477
sturgeon, 36–7, 41, 382n299, 389; balls, 385; empanada; 387; grilled, 383–5; pie, 385–7; prepare, 383
sugar: as main ingredient, 519, 535–7, 567, 569–71; clarifying, 257, 562n441, 565, 569, 573–5; rose coloured, 562n440, 567, 569; thread stage of, 45–6, 96n20, 183, 244n154, 245, 254n166, 255, 261, 433, 437, 475, 483, 543, 563, 568n448, 567–73, 577–9, 597. *See also* syrup, simple
sustancia. See broth, sustaining
sweetbreads: veal, 29–30, 32, 131, 137, 227, 483; kid, 189, 195, 219, 283, 451
sweetener, 45–6
swift, 35, 227
Swiss chard, pie, 253
swordfish, 37, 388n303, 389
syrup: rosemary flower, 569; simple, 183–5, 217, 225, 237, 243, 244n154, 247, 251, 255–63, 267, 275–9, 313, 317–21, 325–7, 345–7, 363, 433, 437–9, 451, 455–7, 461, 467–9, 479, 485, 505–9, 515, 534n419, 547, 551, 557, 562n441, 563–5, 568n449, 573–7, 578n459, 581, 597–9

table, in the kitchen, 116–19
tahona [mill]. *See under* flour
tallarín [strip], 242, 262, 264, 346, 362, 506
tallow, 47
tart, 47; cheese, 321–3, 485–7; clotted milk, 64, 130–1, 138–9, 252–3, 500–3
tartlets, 347
taste, 51–63
teal, 152n28, 153
tenca [tench], 414–15
tenderloin, 131, 283, 340n253; beef, 139, 341; boar, 291, 303; pork, 285, 291, 313, 341; venison, 303
ternera. See veal
Tesoro de la cocina mexicana, 74
testicles: chicken, 283, 589; sheep, 32, 133, 195, 197, 219, 283
thistle, golden, 43, 602n476, 603
thread, 185, 191; egg, 433, 435; twine, 172
thrush, 33, 227, 285

thyme, 39, 404n315, 405
tigelada [Portuguese custard tart], 61, 346n259, 488–9
tinaja. See under jar
tinelo [kitchen dining room], 146
tissue, fat, 31, 46, 118n24, 119, 131, 146n10, 170n49, 204n93, 205, 275, 281, 301, 339, 587
tocino. See fatback; fat, ham; lard, caul
todas especias. See all spices
todas hierbas. See greens, leafy
todas verduras. See under herb, all
tongue, 371; beef, 29, 31, 149, 177, 307, 555; pork, 287, 307; sheep, 287
Toledo, 56, 690
Tolosa. *See under* egg
toronja, 31, 41–2, 72, 567; stuffed, 222–5
Torres Martínez, Marta, 97n38, 188n74
torrezno. See pork belly, roasted
torrija, 44, 177, 181, 215–17, 235–7, 283, 331, 335, 357–9, 365–7, 375, 381, 385, 409, 441–3, 449, 457, 473; recipe, 455
torta. See pie
tortilla [small pie], 289, 316–17, 326–7, 380–1, 548–9. *See also* omelette
tórtola. See dove, collared
Tovar, Rosa, 97n35
tow, fine, 417
Treatise of Portuguese Cuisine from the 15th Century, 182n63
trébedes. See trivet
trimmer, 216n133, 217, 243, 251, 261, 529, 537, 553, 597
trinchero. See platter, carving
tripa. See intestine
trivet, 342, 435, 513, 585, 587
trout, 37, 41; casserole, 393; pie, 395; prepare, 389–91; stew, 391–3
trucha. See trout
trufa. See truffle

truffle, 197, 283, 313, 383, 405–9, 427; pie, 407; stew; 407
tuna, 41, 42, 387, 399; fat, 387, 397–9; lamprea style, 398; pickled, 399; pie, 397; prepare, 395; stew, 399
turd, 239
turkey, 33, 34–5, 142n2, 143, 601; giblet, 34–5, 140n45, 459–61; presenting, 559
turmas. See testicles
turnip, 43, 213, 287, 297, 370n284, 373; lamprea style, 373; prepare, 371–3
turnover, 28, 44, 47, 55–6, 65–6, 72, 133, 139, 163, 242n152, 271, 308n220, 310n222, 311–15, 323–7, 389, 409; mini, 217, 243, 325, 347
turtle, 491
twine, 166, 170, 172
twist, 47

Ucendo, Andrés, and Lanza García, 504n389
udder, 29, 33, 337; roasted, 177. *See also* beef; boar
Usero Torrente, Antonio, 96n21
uspot, 73, 311
Usunáriz, Jesús, and Magalí Ortiz Martín, 94n1, 95n11, 126n37
uva. See grape
uva pin. See gooseberry

Valencia, 56, 87, 154–5, 464n364
Valles Rojo, Julio, 36, 38, 95n11, 222n124, 306n217, 372n285
Varela Marino, Elena, 120–2n31, 188n74
Varenne, La, 65
vaso [crust], 45, 214, 282, 286, 292, 346, 400, 410, 428, 486, 492, 586, 600
veal, 29, 31, 147, 153, 171, 179–81, 185–9, 195, 207, 223, 229–31, 279, 283, 315, 339, 357, 461–3, 471, 589, 603; bread, 483; chop, 479; leg, 209, 213, 583; loin, 305, 471, 479; lung,

339, 361; pie, 249; shank, 163, 181, 249, 311; stew, 583
veedor. See inspector, food
vegetable, 42–3, 192n78. *See also individual vegetables*
venado. See venison
vencejo. See swift
venison, 33, 51, 74, 294n206, 298n212; 301; dressing, 287–9; empanada, 214n108; jerky, 305; minced, 155; prepare, 299; salted, 303; tenderloin, 303
verdura. See herb; greens, leafy; vegetable
verjuice, 42, 191, 201, 369, 427, 517, 577, 595
Vida del escudero Marcos de Obregón (Vicente Espinel), 464n364
vidrio. See under jar
vinegar, 48–51, 147, 151–9, 163–81, 185, 197–203, 213, 219–21, 227, 233, 289–97, 301, 305–11, 315, 331–3, 341, 351, 355, 363, 377, 383–7, 391–3, 399–401, 405–7, 413–23, 431, 453, 459, 463, 473–7, 505, 513–15, 519, 537, 555, 589, 593, 599–603; elderberry, 515–17; white, 515, 519; wine, 519

wafer, 261, 269, 275–81, 509–11, 529, 537, 543–7, 587; bite-sized, 139, 509; white, 267, 547
walnut: preserved, 581; press, 229; size of, 201, 239, 361, 473, 487, 547; wood, 119, 121, 289
walnut press, 229
water, 119; alkaline, 37, 567, 581, 599; orange blossom, 36, 48, 247, 273, 439, 469, 479–83, 505, 537, 543–7, 557; rose, 28, 36–8, 54, 243–7, 251, 481–5, 511, 527, 547, 553
watercress, 43, 355
West, Elizabeth, 74
wheat. *See* flour; porridge
whey, 319–21, 503, 523
Williams, Patrick, 7
wine, 147–9, 151, 161–3, 167, 173, 177, 185, 211, 227, 247, 251, 271–3, 277, 289–301, 305, 309–11, 339–41, 383, 387, 391, 397–9, 409, 421, 425, 429, 435, 443, 449, 461–3, 475, 507–9, 535, 553–7, 599; red, 143, 153–5, 169, 213, 289, 393, 401, 413, 421, 455–7, 475, 533, 555; white, 151, 165, 169, 217, 229, 289–91, 297, 313, 329–31, 351–3, 379, 383, 457–9, 509, 529–33, 551
women, 62, 98n46, 255, 378n292, 523; in the kitchen, 67, 98n46, 240n146, 343; domestic manuals for, 77; and printing, 82, 98n48
wood, for kitchen furniture and equipment, 118–21
woodcock, 33, 151

Yarza, Ibán, 238n141
yeast, 505
Yelgo de Vázquez, Miguel, 12–13, 126n37, 556n437–8

zanahoria. See carrot
zarceta. See teal
zorzal. See thrush
zurciga. See under sauce

Milton Keynes UK
Ingram Content Group UK Ltd.
UKHW052319181223
434589UK00017BA/82/J